The Complete Birds of the World
ILLUSTRATED EDITION

COVERS

1. BOMBYCILLIDAE: *Bombycilla garrulus,* Bohemian Waxwing. **2.** MELIPHAGIDAE: *Manorina melanotis,* Black-eared or Dusky Miner. **3.** COLUMBIDAE: *Streptopelia risoria,* Barbary Dove. **4.** SULIDAE: *Sula dactylatra,* Masked or Blue-faced Booby. **5.** PSITTACIDAE: *Lorius domicellus,* Purple-naped Lory. **6.** GRUIDAE: *Balearica pavonina,* Crowned Crane. **7.** SYLVIIDAE: *Locustella naevia,* Grasshopper Warbler; CUCULIDAE: *Cuculus canorus,* Common Cuckoo. **8.** TYTONIDAE: *Tyto alba,* Common Barn or White Owl.

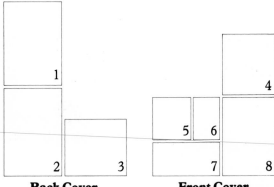

Back Cover   **Front Cover**

The Complete Birds
of the World
ILLUSTRATED EDITION

Michael Walters

DAVID & CHARLES
Newton Abbot   London

To the memory of Reg Moreau, who gave me my first help and encouragement in my green time but died before I could thank him. I hope he would have approved of this book.

The author is responsible for the text only; identifications of birds illustrated in this book have been provided entirely by the publisher.

ISBN 0-7153-8170-9

Printed in the United States of America.

ILLUSTRATIONS

Dr. Herbert R. Axelrod: 67 (top), 71, 118, 127 (bottom), 131, 137 (top), 146, 179, 180, 213 (top), 216

Henry J. Bates and Robert Busenbark: 319 (bottom)

D. R. Baylis: 61 (bottom), 63 (bottom), 64 (top), 64 (bottom), 65 (bottom), 66 (top), 66 (bottom), 69, 70 (top), 70 (bottom), 72 (top), 74 (top left), 74 (bottom), 76, 80 (bottom)

I. Bennett: 102 (bottom)

H. and J. Beste: 111

H. Bielfeld: 166, 249 (top), 256 (top), 306 (top left, right)

M. Bonnin: 48 (bottom), 98 (bottom), 99 (bottom), 149 (bottom), 198 (bottom), 245 (bottom)

E. Bound: 19 (bottom right), 27, 45 (bottom), 56 (top), 103 (top), 108 (top right), 220 (bottom), 243 (top), 313 (bottom), 316 (bottom)

Th. Brosset: 115 (bottom), 143 (top)

M. Carter: 10 (bottom), 103 (bottom)

N. H. P. Cayley: 91 (bottom)

N. Chaffer: 94 (top), 95 (bottom), 97 (bottom), 98 (top), 198 (top), 199 (bottom), 215 (bottom), 227 (bottom right), 236 (bottom), 242 (bottom), 316 (top)

G. Churchett: 32 (bottom), 315 (top)

A. Clements: 14 (bottom), 169 (top)

R. Dorin: 52

Sam Fehrenz: 182 (top, bottom)

R. Fletcher: 168 (bottom)

Foreign Bird League: 164 (bottom)

T. & P. Gardner: 22 (top), 129 (bottom), 197 (bottom left), 213 (bottom), 237 (top, bottom), 242 (top), 270 (top), 275 (top)

R. Garstone: 214 (top)

K. Gillett: 15 (top), 103 (bottom)

R. Good: 15 (bottom), 44 (bottom), 89 (top), 238 (top), 315 (bottom)

J. Gould: 17 (top right), 22 (bottom), 31 (top), 33 (bottom), 59 (top), 87 (bottom), 88 (top, bottom), 102 (top), 127 (top left), 162 (top), 192, 193 (top, bottom), 194 (bottom), 229 (left, right), 236 (top left)

R. H. Green: 220 (top), 228 (top)

Hanseaten-Verlag: 267 (top)

Keith Hindwood: 172 (top), 225 (bottom), 271, 274 (top)

Eric Hosking: 117 (top)

Paul Kwast: 108 (bottom), 199 (top), 212, 247 (bottom), 248 (bottom), 249 (bottom), 251 (bottom), 252, 253 (bottom), 254 (top), 255, 256 (bottom), 264 (top), 268 (bottom), 272 (bottom), 279, 284 (bottom), 285 (bottom), 294 (top, bottom), 295 (bottom), 297 (top), 300 (top, bottom), 303 (bottom right), 304

W. Labbett: 18 (bottom), 230 (right)

Harry V. Lacey: 61 (top), 115 (top), 118 (top), 135, 138, 145, 296, 305, 306 (bottom), 310

E. Laslett: 97 (top)

P. Leysen: 60, 79, 112, 167, 184, 201, 290, 299, 301, 302, 303 (bottom left)

G. Mathews: 14 (top), 83 (top), 194 (top), 241 (top right)

A. J. Mobbs: 129 (top)

Irene & Michael Morcombe: 116, 275 (bottom), 318

W. Moreland: 320 (bottom)

P. Munchenberg: 108 (top left)

Nederlandse Bond van Vogelliefhebbers: 253 (top)

Paradise Park Hawaii: 133 (top)

F. Park: 34 (bottom), 45 (top right), 92 (bottom), 243 (bottom left)

T. Pescott: 9 (top), 11 (bottom), 12 (top), 58 (top left), 65 (top), 85 (top), 86 (bottom), 208 (bottom), 227 (bottom left)

Robert Prange: 133 (bottom)

Fritz Prenzel: 114

Hans Reinhard: 205 (bottom), 309

M. F. Roberts: 287

L. Robinson: 140 (top right, bottom right), 141, 142 (top right), (bottom)

San Diego Zoo: 29 (top), 82 (top), 89 (bottom), 101, 124 (bottom), 136, 140 (top left), 144, 161 (top), 190, 191 (bottom), 314 (top)

H. Schrempp: 58 (top right), 157 (bottom), 158 (top), 205 (top), 206 (top), 258 (top), 263 (top), 297 (bottom), 303 (top)

L. Sourry: 85 (bottom)

South African Tourist Corp.: 1 (top right, left), 178 (bottom)

K. Stepnell: 11 (top), 13 (top), 84 (bottom left, right), 196 (top), 222 (top), 226 (left)

E. & N. Taylor: 243 (bottom right)

G. Taylor: 163 (bottom), 221 (bottom), 222 (bottom), 228 (bottom), 234 (bottom), 238 (bottom)

W. Taylor: 48 (top), 95 (top)

Dale Thompson: 188 (bottom)

Three Lions, Inc.: 202

Tierfreunde: 183, 200, 224, 232 (bottom left), 260, 298

Simon Trevor: 178 (top)

P. Trusler: 87 (top)

Louise Van der Meid: 89 (centre), 166 (right), 177 (bottom), 288 (bottom), 319 (top)

Vogelpark Walsrode: 18 (top left), 19 (top), 25 (top), 35 (bottom left, right), 40 (top), 58 (bottom), 62 (bottom), 63 (top), 67 (bottom), 68 (bottom), 72 (bottom left, right), 75 (top), 90 (bottom), 92 (top), 96 (top), 100 (bottom), 118 (bottom left, right), 119 (top, bottom), 123 (bottom), 128 (bottom), 137 (bottom), 142 (top left), 143 (bottom), 152 (top), 172 (bottom), 174 (top), 177 (top), 185 (top, bottom), 188 (top), 191 (top), 207 (bottom), 217 (top right), 235 (top), 236 (top right), 247 (top), 248, 250, 258 (bottom), 262 (top), 268 (top, bottom), 269, 270 (bottom), 272 (top), 276 (top), 278 (top, bottom), 280 (top, bottom), 282 (top), 284 (top), 285 (top), 286 (top), 288 (top) 291 (top), 295 (top)

Dr. Matthew M. Vriends: 120 (top, bottom), 124 (top), 134, 187, 262 (bottom), 263 (bottom), 264 (bottom), 266 (top, bottom), 267 (bottom), 286 (bottom), 307, 308

T. Waite: 148 (top), 223, 245 (top)

G. Weatherstone: 147 (top)

J. Wessels: 19 (bottom left), 100 (top)

E. Whitbourn: 13 (bottom), 99 (top), 197 (bottom right)

A. Whittenbury: 225 (top)

K. Woodcock: 162 (bottom)

H. Wright: 139 (top), 204 (bottom), 230 (left)

A. Young: 173 (top), 314 (bottom)

E. Zillman: 110 (top right), 148 (top), 157 (top)

Covers: FRONT COVER: centre row courtesy of Vogelpark Walsrode; bottom left by W. Möller. BACK COVER: upper photo courtesy of Vogelpark Walsrode, lower by Irene and Michael Morcombe.

Contents

Introduction

This book attempts to list every bird species known to exist or to have existed in recent (ie post-Pleistocene) times. This includes species known only from skeletal remains (but not fossil birds), and a number whose status remains doubtful for a variety of reasons. These may be species based on a single specimen which is believed to be a hybrid (or in exceptional cases, an artifact); or those known only from paintings in books and/or descriptions in travelogues. Such species are usually placed in square brackets, and in the case of species based on travellers' accounts, the name of the traveller-author is also given in square brackets.

The sequence of families follows that of J. L. Peters' *Check List of the Birds of the World* which has been appearing since 1930. Of its fifteen volumes, volumes 8 and 11 have still to appear at the time of writing. Sometimes particular families or groups have subsequently been the subject of monographs and taxonomic revisions by other authors, and in such cases their arrangement has been followed. Peters' *Check List* quotes the original reference in literature to each taxon concerned; for species which have been first described subsequent to the relevant volume of Peters', I have quoted the original reference.

A species entry consists of first the scientific name, followed by the name of the authority who first used that name, and then by the English name. Some books use standard abbreviations for the names of authorities, and tend to be inconsistent in giving or not giving their initials. I have chosen to make only one abbreviation here, Linnaeus is abbreviated to L. All other names are written in full, and initials are omitted, except in the case of the Gmelins, where 'Gmelin' means J. F. Gmelin, and the others, who appear but rarely, have their initials appended. In selecting English names for species from the various alternatives available, I have generally tried to use the shortest, most convenient and most euphonic name. This has meant in a good many cases abbreviating the rather long, cumbersome names which appear in recent textbooks, and I deplore the modern practice among American authors of changing established names to others which are both ugly and cumbersome. The remainder of the entry lists the data in the following order: distribution, habitat, food, nest site, clutch size, incubation - share of sexes and period, fledging period. Under nest site, 'hole' means a hole in a tree unless otherwise stated. Figures for incubation and fledging periods are in days except where otherwise stated. A number of abbreviations have been used:

N, S, E, W	North, South, East, West, respectively
n	nest
e	eggs (ie clutch size)
I	incubation
F	fledging period
♂	male
♀	female
n/k	not known
n/s	not stated. This is used in reference to eggs and means that the eggs have been described but there is no information on clutch size
c	circa, ie approximately
b	breeding (range)
w	wintering, winter
P	parasitic (in reference to nest parasites)

Normally these abbreviations are used whenever possible, but in a few cases they have been departed from. For example 'Northern Borneo' to indicate the northern portion of Borneo is written out in full, as N Borneo could create confusion with the state of North Borneo, ie Sabah. Similarly 'Southern Australia' is normally given in full. The full word-form has also been used before the initials USA. I have not been too concerned with the niceties of political nomenclature, provided the meaning is clear. I have used Ceylon instead of Sri Lanka, but Thailand instead of Siam. Tanganyika in this book means the mainland portion of Tanzania (ie *not* including Zanzibar). Congo refers to the basin of the Congo river (the territory of the former Belgian Congo). Gold Coast means the coastal portion of Ghana.

Where data on a particular species is incomplete, as it is in a great many species, I have tended to say 'no data' or 'not known' when I have found a source which states that this information is unknown, and to leave a blank when sources have been silent on the subject. At the beginning of each family there is a brief account of its general characteristics and, where a piece of data is identical for all species of that family, this information is included in the family account, and not repeated under each species. In some families this results in the species entries being no more than a list of species and distribution.

It will be found that in a good many cases in the text no information is given under a species where information is in fact known. This is inevitable where much ornithological data is to be found only in the vast accumulation of papers in (often) obscure journals. A good many of these have been consulted but it would be the work of a lifetime or longer to personally check every paper ever written. A general book such as this one will, therefore, of necessity be found to be incomplete. Areas such as South America and Australasia are particularly deficient in this respect.

Technical terms are kept to a minimum, however, the terms 'type' and 'type-locality' probably need some explanation. The 'type' specimen of a species is the specimen on which the original description of that species is based, and the 'type-locality' is the locality from which the specimen came. This is only relevent to this book in cases where the validity of a species based on one specimen, or on a very small series of specimens is in doubt.

Note: The manuscript for this book was completed in 1977. Since then a number of monographs and taxonomic reviews of various groups have appeared, including volume 8 and a revised edition of volume 1 of Peters' *Check List of the Birds of the World*. It has unfortunately not been possible to incorporate this new information in this book.

ACKNOWLEDGEMENTS

I am grateful to I. C. J. Galbraith, Dr D. W. Snow and Derek Goodwin for reading the manuscript and making helpful comments; to Colin Harrison for his constant encouragement during the period of writing; and to the late David Higham, whose idea it was, and whom I wish with all my heart could have seen the final result.

STRUTHIORNIDAE Ostriches The largest of living birds. Flightless, with strong, powerful legs adapted for running. Inhabit open arid country, usually in bands of 10–50 individuals. Omnivorous. The family once extended from S Europe to Mongolia as well as the present range.

Struthio camelus *L* OSTRICH Grasslands and semi-desert over the greater part of Africa. An extinct dwarf race once inhabited the deserts of Syria and Arabia / n hollow in ground / e up to 30 in a nest but laid by several ♀♀, estimate 15–20 per hen (maximum) / I ♂♀ (mainly ♂) 35–42 [A number of sub-fossil species based on bones and/or eggshell fragments have been described]

[**Struthio bidactylus** (*Gray*) LE VAILLANT'S OSTRICH Unidentifiable/based on Le Vaillant's description / may have been another extinct dwarf race]

RHEIDAE Rheas Large flightless birds superficially resembling Ostriches, but smaller. Inhabit treeless open country, travelling in flocks. Omnivorous. Polygamous, the ♂ collecting a harem of 5–6 ♀♀ which lay in a communal nest, the resultant clutch of up to 50 eggs being incubated by the ♂. Incubation c42.

Rhea americana (*L*) COMMON RHEA Widely distributed over S America E of Andes

[**Rhea nana** *Lydekker* DWARF RHEA based on a single egg, possibly the dwarf egg of Common or Darwin's Rhea. The 'small rheas' seen around at the time may have been Tinamous]

Pterocnemia pennata (*d'Orbigny*) DARWIN'S RHEA Highlands from Peru S to Straits of Magellan

CASUARIIDAE Cassowaries Large powerful flightless birds inhabiting forest. A casque on the head is used to fend off obstructions when running through forest. Skin of head and neck is naked and brightly coloured, and there are wattles hanging from the throat. A large number of species and races have been described on the basis of variations in colour of these wattles, these are now generally combined in three species. For a detailed discussion see Warren *Annals and Magazine of Natural History* ser 12, vol ix (1956), pp 753–63. Feed on berries and fruit; nest a shallow platform of leaves on forest floor; eggs 3–6 dark green, incubation by ♂.

Casuarius casuarius (*L*) COMMON CASSOWARY N Australia, New Guinea and E Indonesia/rain forest / seeds and fruit /n ground / e 3–4

Casuarius bennetti *Gould* DWARF CASSOWARY New Guinea and New Britain

Casuarius unappendiculatus *Blyth* SINGLE-WATTLED CASSOWARY New Guinea and adjacent islands

DROMAIIDAE Emus The surviving species is the second largest living bird (after Ostrich). Flightless, inhabiting arid plains, woodland and desert; running and swimming well. Feeds on fruit, berries and insects. Nests on ground at base of trees; eggs 7–10 sometimes up to 16, incubation by ♂, 59–61.

Dromaius novaehollandiae (*Latham*) EMU Much of interior of Australia, extinct in Tasmania

Dromaius diemenianus (*Jennings*) DWARF EMU Kangaroo Is /extinct /unique

Dromaius ater *Vieillot* (=**Dromaeus minor** *Spencer*) BLACK EMU King Is /extinct /bones only

DINORNITHIDAE Moas Extinct family of flightless birds formerly occurring in New Zealand. Known to science only from bones and a few eggs and feathers. Available evidence suggests they were hunted by the Maoris and survived till the mid-nineteenth century; it has even been claimed that a few may still survive in remote places. A number of genera and species have been described, but any list or discussion of these is outside the scope of this book.

AEPYORNITHIDAE Elephant Birds Extinct family of birds formerly inhabiting Madagascar. Known only from bones and eggs and not known when they became extinct. About 8 species have been described, varying greatly in size.

APTERYGIDAE Kiwis Fowl-sized flightless birds inhabiting thick, swampy forests. Plumage long and coarse, the rudimentary wings completely hidden. Feed on grubs and worms. Nest in a burrow. Eggs usually 1, rarely 2, enormous chalky white, almost a fourth of the female's body size. Incubation by ♂ 75–80.

Apteryx australis *Shaw* COMMON KIWI New Zealand: N Island, S Island and Stewart Island (3 races)

Apteryx owenii *Gould* OWEN'S or LITTLE GREY KIWI S Island, New Zealand (? formerly N Island)

Apteryx hastii *Potts* ROAROA KIWI W coast of

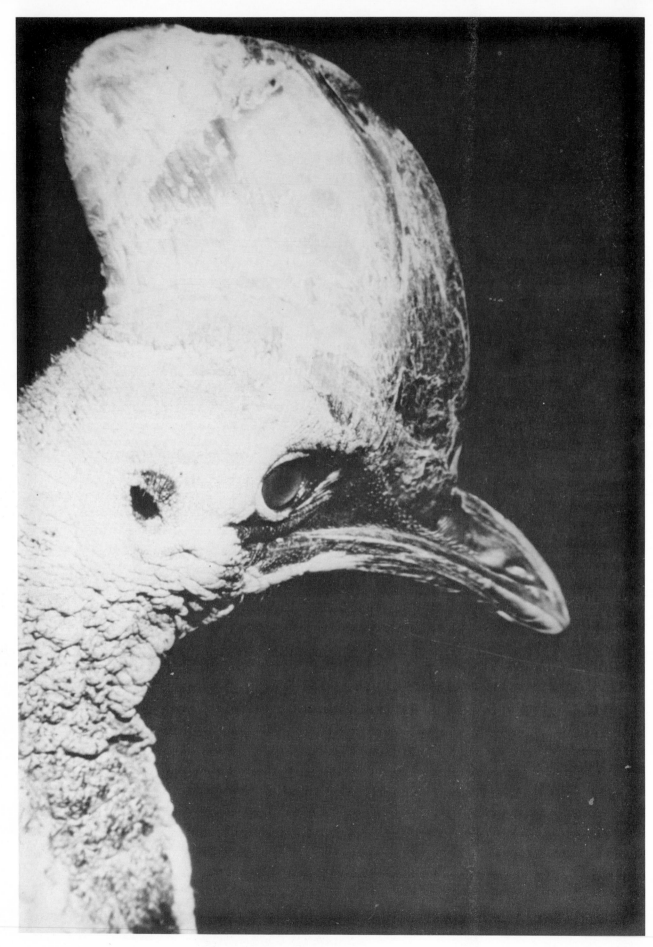

CASUARIIDAE: *Casuarius casuarius*, Common Cassowary.

STRUTHIORNIDAE:
Struthio camelus,
Ostrich

Ostrich derby in South Africa

RHEIDAE:
Rhea americana,
Common Rhea,
Greater Rhea

Plate 1

S Island, New Zealand

TINAMIDAE Tinamous Primitive ground birds superficially resembling quails and inhabiting a wide range of habitats. Feed on seeds, berries and insects. Nest on the ground. Eggs 1–12 in vivid clear colours with a hard porcelain-like gloss. Incubation by ♂ c21. Young highly precocious. Range from S Mexico to Patagonia.

Tinamus tao *Temminck* GREAT GREY TINAMOU Guyana and Venezuela S to Bolivia and E to S Brazil

Tinamus solitarius (*Vieillot*) SOLITARY TINAMOU E Brazil, Paraguay and N Argentina

Tinamus osgoodi *Conover* BLACK TINAMOU S Huila in Colombia and Cusco, Peru

Tinamus major (*Gmelin*) GREAT TINAMOU S Mexico S to Bolivia and S Brazil

Tinamus guttatus *Pelzeln* WHITE-THROATED TINAMOU Amazon basin

Nothocercus bonapartei (*Gray*) HIGHLAND or BONAPARTE'S TINAMOU Highlands of Costa Rica and Panama, Andes from Venezuela to Peru

Nothocercus julius (*Bonaparte*) VERREAUX'S or TAWNY-BREASTED TINAMOU Andes from Venezuela to Ecuador

Nothocercus nigrocapillus (*Gray*) HOODED TINAMOU Mts of Peru and Bolivia

Crypturellus cinereus (*Gmelin*) CINEREOUS TINAMOU Amazon and Orinoco basins, the Guianas, W Colombia and W Ecuador (*C. berlepschi* is occasionally treated as a distinct species)

Crypturellus soui (*Hermann*) LITTLE or PILEATED TINAMOU Mexico S to Bolivia and S Brazil

Crypturellus ptaritepui *Zimmer and Phelps* (in *Amer Mus Novit*, no 1,274 (1945), p 1) TEPUI TINAMOU Mts of S Venezuela

Crypturellus obsoletus (*Temminck*) BROWN TINAMOU Andes from Venezuela to Argentina, S Brazil and Paraguay

Crypturellus undulatus (*Temminck*) UNDULATED TINAMOU Much of S America E of Andes and S to Argentina

Crypturellus brevirostris (*Pelzeln*) SHORT-BILLED or RUSTY TINAMOU Upper Amazon basin, N Brazil and Cayenne

Crypturellus bartletti (*Sclater and Salvin*) BARTLETT'S TINAMOU SW Amazon basin

Crypturellus variegatus (*Gmelin*) VARIEGATED TINAMOU Amazon and Upper Orinoco basins, Guyana and Cayenne

Crypturellus atrocapillus (*Tschudi*) RED-LEGGED TINAMOU Upper and N Amazon basins, Guyana, Surinam and N Venezuela

Crypturellus noctivagus (*Wied*) YELLOW-LEGGED TINAMOU E Brazil (several forms, formerly included here, are now regarded as races of *atrocapillus*)

Crypturellus duidae *Zimmer* GREY-LEGGED or DUIDA TINAMOU Parts of Colombia and Venezuela

Crypturellus cinnamomeus (*Lesson*) RUFESCENT or CINNAMON TINAMOU Mexico to Costa Rica; NE Colombia and W Venezuela [*C. idoneus* (Todd) is now considered conspecific]

Crypturellus transfasciatus (*Sclater and Salvin*) STEERE'S or PALE-BROWED TINAMOU W Ecuador and NW Peru [*C. rubripes* (Taczanowski) is a synonym]

Crypturellus strigulosus (*Temminck*) BRAZILIAN TINAMOU S Amazon basin

Crypturellus casiquiare (*Chapman*) CASIQUIARE or BARRED TINAMOU Junction of rivers Casiquiare and Guainía Venezuela and river Vaupés on Colombia–Brazil boundary

Crypturellus boucardi (*Sclater*) BOUCARD'S TINAMOU Mexico to N Costa Rica

[**Crypturellus columbianus** (*Salvadori*) COLOMBIAN TINAMOU NW Colombia. Status apparently uncertain. R. M. de Schaunsee has regarded it as a race of *boucardi* and of *noctivagus*. See *The Species of birds of South America* (1966), p 7; 'The Birds of the Republic of Colombia', pt 3, p 1,140 (in *Caldasia*, vol 5, no 26) and *Proc Acad Nat Sci Phil* (1950), pp 113–14]

Crypturellus saltuarius *Wetmore* (in *Proc Biol Soc Washington*, vol 63 (1951), p 171) MAGDALENA TINAMOU Magdalena Valley, C Colombia / unique

Crypturellus kerriae *Chapman* CHOCO or KERR'S TINAMOU Baudo Mts, Colombia / 2 specimens

Crypturellus parvirostris (*Wagler*) SMALL-BILLED TINAMOU Amazon basin and S to NW Argentina

Crypturellus tataupa (*Temminck*) TATAUPA TINAMOU NE Brazil S to Argentina and E to Peru, Bolivia and Paraguay

Rhynchotus rufescens (*Temminck*) RUFOUS or

RED-WINGED TINAMOU Brazil from S of Amazon to Bolivia, Paraguay and N Argentina

Nothoprocta taczanowskii (*Sclater and Salvin*) TACZANOWSKI'S TINAMOU C and SE Peru [NB: I have not been able to determine if the status of *N. godmani* Taczanowski, known from an immature type, and generally identified with *N. taczanowskii* has ever been proved]

Nothoprocta kalinowskii *Berlepsch and Stolzmann* KALINOWSKI'S TINAMOU C and SE Peru

Nothoprocta ornata (*Gray*) ORNATE TINAMOU Andes from Peru to Chile and W Argentina [NB: The name *Nothoprocta ornata* is credited to Taczanowski in *Birds of South America* (1966), p 8, apparently in error]

Nothoprocta perdicaria (*Kittlitz*) CHILEAN TINAMOU Mts of Chile, introduced on Easter Is

Nothoprocta cinerascens (*Burmeister*) BRUSHLAND TINAMOU S Bolivia, W Paraguay and W Argentina

Nothoprocta pentlandii (*Gray*) ANDEAN TINAMOU Andes from Ecuador to N Chile and W Argentina

Nothoprocta curvirostris *Sclater and Salvin* CURVE-BILLED TINAMOU Andes of Ecuador and Peru

Nothura boraquira (*Spix*) WHITE-BELLIED or MARBLED NOTHURA NE Brazil to Paraguay and Bolivia

Nothura minor (*Spix*) LEAST NOTHURA E and C Brazil

[**Nothura schreineri** *Mirando-Ribero* from Minas Geraes, unique, and tentatively synonomised with *N. boraquira*, does not appear to have ever been definitely identified]

Nothura darwinii *Gray* DARWIN'S NOTHURA Andes from Peru to NW Argentina

Nothura maculosa (*Temminck*) SPOTTED NOTHURA E Brazil S through Paraguay and Uruguay to E Argentina

Nothura chacoensis *Conover* CHACO NOTHURA Arid parts of Paraguayan chaco and N Argentina

Taoniscus nanus (*Temminck*) DWARF TINAMOU SE Brazil (? Paraguay and N Argentina), range very imperfectly known

Eudromia elegans *d'Orbigny and Geoffroy* ELEGANT TINAMOU Chile and Argentina

Eudromia formosa (*Lillo*) (= **E. mira** *Brodkorb*) QUEBRACHO or LILLO'S TINAMOU Quebracho woodland in W Paraguay and parts of Argentina

Tinamotis pentlandii *Vigors* PUNA or PENTLAND'S TINAMOU Puna zone of Andes from S Peru to Chile and Argentina

Tinamotis ingoufi *Oustalet* PATAGONIAN or INGOUF'S TINAMOU Patagonia

SPHENISCIDAE Penguins Large to medium-sized, flightless birds, wings modified into flippers for underwater swimming. Feathers stiff, close-packed, forming insulating mat. About 18 species, all in Southern Hemisphere. Feed on marine life. Breed on shores, often in colonies. Pelagic outside breeding season.

Aptenodytes forsteri *Gray* EMPEROR PENGUIN Antarctica/e 1 balanced on feet protected by flap of skin and feathers

Aptenodytes patagonica *Miller* KING PENGUIN Sub-antarctic seas b on various islands/e 1 incubated as in *forsteri*

Pygoscelis papua (*Forster*) GENTOO PENGUIN Circumpolar b antarctic islands on high areas of exposed rock/e 2

Pygoscelis adeliae (*Hombron and Jacquinot*) ADELIE PENGUIN Antarctica, S Orkneys and S Shetlands/sometimes nest, sometimes incubate as *forsteri*

Pygoscelis antarctica (*Forster*) CHINSTRAP PENGUIN S Orkneys, S Shetlands etc

Eudyptes pachyrhynchus *Gray* CRESTED PENGUIN New Zealand/n a few sticks in caves or under stones/e 1–3/I ♂♀ 35

Eudyptes atratus *Finsch* (= **E. robustus** *Oliver*) SNARES PENGUIN Snares Is/n on ground in scrub/e 2

Eudyptes (sp) Chatham Is / extinct /? no specimens / ? = *E. pachyrhynchus* or *atratus*

Eudyptes sclateri *Buller* ERECT-CRESTED PENGUIN Islands round New Zealand / e 1 on bare rock (e ? 2, accounts differ)

Eudyptes crestatus (*Miller*) ROCKHOPPER PENGUIN Islands in S Atlantic and Indian Oceans/n a hollow/e 2–3/I 35

Eudyptes schlegeli *Finsch* ROYAL PENGUIN Macquarie Is/n ground/e 1

Eudyptes chrysolophus (*Brandt*) MACARONI PENGUIN Islands in S Atlantic and S Indian Oceans

Megadyptes antipodes (*Hombron and Jacquinot*) YELLOW-CROWNED PENGUIN New Zealand and offshore islands/n ground or hole/ e 2

Eudyptula minor (*Forster*) FAIRY or LITTLE

CASUARIIDAE:
Casuarius casuarius,
Common Cassowary,
Australian Cassowary

DROMAIIDAE:
Dromaius novaehollandiae,
Emu

Plate 2

APTERYGIDAE:
Apteryx australis,
Common Kiwi,
Brown Kiwi

TINAMIDAE:
Eudromia elegans,
Elegant Tinamou,
Elegant Crested-Tinamou

Plate 3

BLUE PENGUIN Australia, Tasmania and New Zealand / n burrow / e 2 / I 38

Eudyptula albosignata *Finsch* WHITE-FLIPPERED PENGUIN Banks Peninsula, New Zealand / n burrow / e 2 / I 38

Spheniscus demersus (*L*) BLACKFOOT, CAPE or JACKASS PENGUIN South Africa / n hollow in ground / e 2 / I 35

Spheniscus humboldti *Meyen* HUMBOLDT PENGUIN Peru to S Chile / n tunnel or crevice / e 2–3 / I 28

Spheniscus magellanicus (*Forster*) MAGELLAN PENGUIN Chile, Argentina and Falklands / n burrow / e 2 / I ? 22–4

Spheniscus mendiculus *Sundevall* GALAPAGOS PENGUIN Galapagos / n in caves (shores rocky, unsuitable for burrowing) / e 2

GAVIIDAE Divers or Loons Foot-propelled diving birds occurring in North Holarctic seas, sometimes coming up rivers to breed. Sexes alike. Food chiefly fish. Breed on ground near water, eggs olive-brown spotted darker. One genus with 4 species.

Gavia stellata (*Pontoppidan*) RED-THROATED DIVER or LOON N Holarctic w further S / e 2, rarely 1–3 / I ♂♀ 24–9

Gavia arctica (*L*) BLACK-THROATED DIVER or LOON N Holarctic w further S / n a scrape / e 2, rarely 1–3 / I ♂♀ 29. N.B. If as Vaurie indicates, there is an overlap in the breeding ranges of *arctica* and *G. a. pacifica* then the latter must be considered a species.

Gavia immer (*Brünnich*) GREAT NORTHERN DIVER or COMMON LOON Nearctic and NW Atlantic / e 2, rarely 1–3 / I ♂♀ 29–30

Gavia adamsii (*Gray*) WHITE-BILLED DIVER or YELLOW-BILLED LOON N Siberia and NW Nearctic / e 2

PODICIPEDIDAE Grebes Small to medium water birds with sleek plumage and lobate webbed feet set very far back. Weak fliers, several of the isolated relict species being almost or completely flightless. Feed on small fish and other aquatic life, diving with agility. Nests are in water among reeds, or floating. Eggs, white and chalky, but soon stained with the rotting vegetation of the nest. Incubation by both sexes, 20–30 days. Some species breed in fresh water and move to seacoasts and estuaries in winter.

Podiceps ruficollis (*Pallas*) LITTLE GREBE or DABCHICK Europe, much of Africa and Madagascar, across Asia to Japan, Indonesia, N New Guinea and the Solomons / lakes, rivers and small ponds / n in water / e 2–10 / I ♂♀ 23–5

Podiceps novaehollandiae *Stephens* BLACK-THROATED GREBE or AUSTRALIAN DABCHICK S New Guinea, Australia, Tasmania, Rennell Is, New Hebrides and New Caledonia / n floating / e 4–6

Podiceps pelzelnii *Hartlaub* MADAGASCAR GREBE Madagascar, formerly widespread, now very rare

Podiceps rufolavatus *Delacour* ALAOTRA GREBE Lake Alaotra, Madagascar

Podiceps dominicus (*L*) LEAST GREBE Tropical C and S America and Greater Antilles / n in water / e 2–7 / I ♂♀ 21

Podiceps rufopectus *Gray* NEW ZEALAND DABCHICK New Zealand / lakes and swamps / n in deep vegetation (very few found) / e 1–3

Podiceps poliocephalus *Jardine and Selby* HOARY-HEADED GREBE Australia and Tasmania / lakes, streams and estuaries / n floating / e 4

Podiceps rolland *Quoy and Gaimard* WHITE-TUFTED GREBE Falklands and S America from Peru southward / lakes / n floating / e 4–6

Podiceps occipitalis *Garnot* SILVER GREBE Andes from Peru S, and Falklands / lakes / n floating / e 4–6

Podiceps taczanowskii *Berlepsch and Stolzmann* PUNA GREBE Lake Junin, Peru

Podiceps auritus (*L*) HORNED or SLAVONIAN GREBE Breeds N Europe and Asia to the Amur, northern N America w S to Mediterranean, Caribbean and China / ponds, streams and rivers / n in water / e 3–10 / I ♂♀ 20–5 (accounts vary)

Podiceps nigricollis *Brehm* BLACK-NECKED or EARED GREBE Europe from Denmark E across temperate Asia to the Amur, Asia Minor, E and S Africa, western N America / lakes and ponds / n in water / e 2–8 / I ♂♀ 20–1

Podiceps cristatus (*L*) GREAT CRESTED GREBE Europe, much of Asia, Africa S of Sahara, Australia, Tasmania and New Zealand / lakes and ponds / n in reed beds / e 1–9 / I ♂♀ 27–9

Podiceps griseigena (*Boddaert*) RED-NECKED GREBE E Europe, across much of temperate Asia and western N America, spreading to parts of the E in winter / lakes, ponds and estuaries / n in water / e 2–7 / I ♂♀ 23

Podiceps major (*Boddaert*) GREAT GREBE Much of S America / lakes and rivers / n floating / e 3–5

Podiceps gadowi *Hachisuka* GADOW'S GREBE Mauritius / extinct, 1 bone only

Aechmophorus occidentalis (*Lawrence*) WESTERN GREBE b S Canada and northern USA w S to Mexico / fresh, brackish and salt water / n in water or floating / e 3–4 / I ♂♀ c23

Podilymbus podiceps (*L*) PIED-BILLED GREBE Breeds locally over the greater part of the Americas and W Indies / ponds, marshes and coastal lagoons / n floating / e 2–10 / I ♂♀ 23

Podilymbus gigas *Griscom* ATITLAN GREBE Lake Atitlan, Guatemala

Centropelma micropterum (*Gould*) SHORT-WINGED GREBE Lake Titicaca, Andes

DIOMEDEIDAE Albatrosses Very large, long-winged pelagic birds, coming to land only to breed, and feeding on marine life of various kinds. Colonial nesting (except the Sooty Albatrosses). Nest usually on ground, sometimes on cliffs. Eggs 1, white, some species lightly spotted. Sexes alike.

Diomedea exulans *L* WANDERING ALBATROSS Southern oceans 30°–60°S

Diomedea epomophora *Lesson* ROYAL ALBATROSS Southern oceans b Auckland Islands

Diomedea irrorata *Salvin* WAVED ALBATROSS Galapagos

Diomedea albatrus *Pallas* STELLER'S ALBATROSS or SHORT-TAILED ALBATROSS N Pacific b Wake and Bonin Is

Diomedea nigripes *Audubon* BLACK-FOOTED ALBATROSS N Pacific b NW of Hawaii

Diomedea immutabilis *Rothschild* LAYSAN ALBATROSS N Pacific

Diomedea melanophris *Temminck* BLACK-BROWED ALBATROSS Southern oceans

Diomedea bulleri *Rothschild* BULLER'S ALBATROSS S Pacific b Snares Is and the Chathams

Diomedea cauta *Gould* SHY ALBATROSS S Pacific and Indian Oceans

Diomedea desolationis (*Salvadori*) DESOLATE ALBATROSS Desolation Is / 1 specimen

Diomedea chlororhynchos *Gmelin* YELLOW-NOSED ALBATROSS S Atlantic and Indian Oceans, b Tristan, Gough, the Crozets and St Paul

Diomedea chrysostoma *Forster* GREY-HEADED ALBATROSS Southern oceans

Diomedea eremita (*Murphy*) CHATHAM ALBATROSS Pyramid Rock, Chatham Is (breeding), sedentary

Phoebetria fusca (*Hilsenberg*) SOOTY ALBATROSS Breeds Tristan and Gough, wandering S Atlantic and Indian Oceans

Phoebetria palpebrata (*Forster*) LIGHT-MANTLED SOOTY ALBATROSS Southern oceans b S Georgia, Kerguelen and islands S of New Zealand

PROCELLARIIDAE Fulmars, Prions, Shearwaters and Gadfly Petrels Medium to large, long-winged, pelagic birds, coming to land only to breed and often nocturnal at breeding places. Nesting often colonial, on coasts or islands, usually in burrows, sometimes on cliffs (*Fulmarus, Daption*) or on open ground (*Macronectes*). Eggs 1, white. Sexes alike, but some species have 2 or more colour phases.

Macronectes giganteus (*Gmelin*) NORTHERN GIANT PETREL Southern oceans b Heard Is, Falklands, S Georgia, S Orkneys, S Shetlands, islands off Antarctica, Macquarie, Marion and the Crozets / dimorphic / fish and whale offal / n ground

Macronectes halli (*Mathews*) SOUTHERN GIANT PETREL or HALL'S PETREL Southern oceans b Chatham, Auckland, Campbell, Stewart, Antipodes Is, Gough, Kerguelen, Macquarie, Marion and Crozets / non-dimorphic, and more southerly than above / n ground

Daption capense (*L*) CAPE PETREL, CAPE PIGEON or PINTADO Southern oceans b S Georgia, S Orkneys, S Shetlands, Grahamland and Kerguelen / fish, oil and blubber / n ground or cliff

Fulmaris glacialis (*L*) FULMAR N Atlantic and N Pacific oceans / fish and oil / n cliff ledge / I ♂♀ 40–60 (sic) / F 48–57

Fulmarus glacialoides (*Smith*) SILVER PETREL, SILVER-GREY PETREL or SOUTHERN FULMAR Southern oceans / fish and offal / n cliff ledge

Halobaena caerulea (*Gmelin*) BLUE PETREL Southern oceans b Kerguelen and Falklands / habits little known

Pachyptila vittata (*Gmelin*) BROAD-BILLED PRION Southern oceans / crustaceans

Pachyptila desolata (*Gmelin*) DOVE PRION Southern oceans / crustaceans

Pachyptila belcheri (*Mathews*) SLENDER-BILLED PRION Southern oceans

Pachyptila turtur (*Kuhl*) FAIRY PRION

Opposite:
SPHENISCIDAE:
Aptenodytes patagonica,
King Penguin

SPHENISCIDAE:
Eudyptes crestatus,
Rockhopper Penguin

SPHENISCIDAE:
Pygoscelis adeliae,
Adelie Penguin

Plate 4

Plate 5

Southern oceans
Pachyptila crassirostris (*Mathews*) FULMAR PRION Southern oceans b islands round New Zealand
Pachyptila salvini (*Mathews*) MEDIUM-BILLED PRION Southern oceans b Marion and Crozets

[NB: All the Prions are very similar and it is a matter of opinion as to how many species are involved]

Thalassoica antarctica (*Gmelin*) ANTARCTIC PETREL Antarctica and islands close by fish and medusae/n ground on steep slopes
Adamastor cinereus (*Gmelin*) GREAT GREY SHEARWATER or PEDIUNKER Southern oceans b Tristan, Gough, Kerguelen, Macquarie and the Antipodes
Procellaria aequinoctialis *L* SHOEMAKER or WHITE-CHINNED PETREL Southern oceans/fish and offal [*Procellaria conspicillata* (Spectacled Shearwater) is a colour phase of this species]
Procellaria westlandica *Falla* WESTLAND PETREL Westland, New Zealand b hilly forested country inland from Barrytown
Procellaria parkinsoni *Gray* PARKINSON'S PETREL S Pacific b New Zealand/fish and offal
Calonectris leucomelas (*Temminck*) STREAKED SHEARWATER W Pacific Ocean b Bonins and Pescadores
Calonectris diomedea (*Scopoli*) CORY'S SHEARWATER Mediterranean, N Atlantic and W Indian Oceans/mollusca and offal/n burrow or among stones
Calonectris edwardsii (*Oustalet*) CAGARRA SHEARWATER Cape Verde Is
Puffinus creatopus *Coues* PINK-FOOTED SHEARWATER E Pacific/small fish
Puffinus carneipes *Gould* FLESH-FOOTED SHEARWATER C and S Pacific b Australia and New Zealand/fish, molluscs etc
Puffinus gravis (*O'Reilly*) GREAT SHEARWATER Atlantic b Tristan da Cunha/squid etc
Puffinus pacificus (*Gmelin*) WEDGE-TAILED SHEARWATER Indian and Pacific Oceans/squid etc
Puffinus bulleri *Salvin* BULLER'S SHEARWATER S Pacific b New Zealand/squid etc
Puffinus griseus (*Gmelin*) SOOTY SHEARWATER Breeds S Pacific wandering to N Pacific and Atlantic/squid, fish etc
Puffinus tenuirostris (*Temminck*) SHORT-TAILED SHEARWATER or MUTTON BIRD

W Pacific b Tasmania and S Australia
Puffinus heinrothi *Reichenow* HEINROTH'S SHEARWATER New Britain/no data
Puffinus nativitatis *Streets* CHRISTMAS SHEARWATER Tropical Pacific b Laysan, Christmas and other islands
Puffinus puffinus (*Brünnich*) MANX SHEARWATER E North Atlantic/fish, mollusca
[**Puffinus yelkouan** (*Acerbi*) LEVANTINE SHEARWATER E Mediterranean, and **Puffinus mauretanicus** *Lowe* BALEARIC SHEARWATER W Mediterranean, are probably races of **Puffinus puffinus**]

NB: opinions differ as to the status of the following three species, which may also be races of *P. puffinus*:
Puffinus opisthomelas *Coues* BLACK-VENTED SHEARWATER Pacific coast of N America/fish
Puffinus gavia (*Forster*) FLUTTERING SHEARWATER Australia and New Zealand
Puffinus huttoni *Mathews* HUTTON'S SHEARWATER Snares Is ?

Puffinus auricularis *Townsend* TOWNSEND'S SHEARWATER E Pacific b Revilla Gigedo Is
Puffinus newelli *Henshaw* HAWAIIAN SHEARWATER Hawaii, formerly believed extinct
Puffinus assimilis *Gould* LITTLE SHEARWATER Atlantic, Pacific and Indian Oceans (various races)
Puffinus l'herminieri *Lesson* AUDUBON'S SHEARWATER Atlantic, Indian and Pacific oceans/fish
[**Puffinus persicus** *Hume* PERSIAN SHEARWATER Arabian Sea, probably a race of *P. l'herminieri*]
Pterodroma macroptera (*Smith*) GREAT-WINGED PETREL Southern oceans b Tristan, the Crozets, Kerguelen, Australia and New Zealand/plankton/I ?♂
Pterodroma aterrima (*Bonaparte*) MASCARINE PETREL Mascarine Is, formerly/4 specimens only, believed extinct. Rediscovered b Reunion ?
Pterodroma lessonii (*Garnot*) WHITE-HEADED PETREL Southern oceans b Kerguelen, Bounty, Auckland and Antipodes/plankton ?
Pterodroma hasitata (*Kuhl*) CAPPED PETREL Mid-Atlantic b Hispaniola (formerly Guadeloupe) also Dominica and Martinique/fish
Pterodroma caribbaea *Carte* JAMAICAN PETREL Jamaica, probably extinct. Believed by

some authorities to be a dark phase of *P. hasitata*

Pterodroma cahow (*Nichols and Mowbray*) BERMUDA PETREL or CAHOW Bermuda/formerly believed extinct

Pterodroma incerta (*Schlegel*) SCHLEGEL'S PETREL b Tristan da Cunha, wandering S Atlantic and Indian Ocean

Pterodroma rostrata (*Peale*) PEALE'S PETREL b Society, Marquesas and New Caledonia

Pterodroma rupinarum Olsen ('Palaeornithology of St Helena', *Smithsonian Cont to Palaeobiology*, no 23 (1975) CHASM PETREL St Helena/extinct post 1502/bones only

Pterodroma becki *Murphy* BECK'S PETREL Solomon Is/2 specimens

Pterodroma alba (*Gmelin*) PHOENIX PETREL Pacific Ocean b Christmas Is, Phoenix, Marquesas, Tonga and Tuamotu/n on ground under bushes

Pterodroma inexpectata (*Forster*) MOTTLED PETREL Pacific Ocean b New Zealand region

Pterodroma fisheri *Ridgway* FISHER'S PETREL N Pacific/unique and possibly an aberrant specimen of *inexpectata*

Pterodroma scalaris (*Brewster*) SCALED PETREL New York/unique, and possibly a wandering aberrant specimen of *inexpectata*

Pterodroma solandri (*Gould*) SOLANDER'S PETREL or BIRD OF PROVIDENCE S Pacific b Lord Howe, Tuamotu and Austral Is

Pterodroma ultima *Murphy* MURPHY'S PETREL C Pacific b Tuamotu Archipelago, Austral, Oeno and Dulcie Is

Pterodroma brevirostris (*Lesson*) (= **P. lugens** *Kuhl*) KERGUELEN PETREL Southern oceans b Kerguelen

Pterodroma heraldica (*Salvin*) SALVIN'S PETREL Islands in S Pacific

Pterodroma neglecta (*Schlegel*) KERMADEC PETREL Islands in S Pacific

Pterodroma arminjoniana (*Giglioli and Salvadori*) TRINIDAD PETREL S Atlantic b S Trinidad and Round Is (Mauritius) [**Pterodroma trinitatis**, *Giglioli and Salvadori* is the dark phase of *P. arminjoniana*]

Pterodroma wortheni (*Rothschild*) ROTHSCHILD'S PETREL Galapagos/unique, believed to be a hybrid

Pterodroma magentae (*Giglioli and Salvadori*) MAGENTA PETREL Chatham Is/1 specimen, mid-Pacific, proved similar to bones found in Chatham Is (Bourne), believed extinct, but sightings suggest some may still breed in Chathams

Pterodroma oliveri (*Mathews and Iredale*) OLIVER'S PETREL Kermadec Is/probably extinct/ 1 specimen (probably a race of *alba*)

Pterodroma mollis (*Gould*) SOFT-PLUMAGED PETREL Atlantic and Indian Oceans

Pterodroma phaeopygia (*Salvin*) DARK-RUMPED PETREL Galapagos and Hawaii (2 races), generally non-pelagic

Pterodroma externa (*Salvin*) JUAN FERNANDEZ PETREL Juan Fernandez and Tristan (2 races)

Pterodroma cervicalis (*Salvin*) SUNDAY ISLAND PETREL Sunday Is in Kermadecs, possibly conspecific with *externa*

Pterodroma cookii (*Gray*) COOK'S PETREL New Zealand (Hen and Chicken Is) and Juan Fernandez, wandering over S Pacific (NB: one of the races of this species said to nest on surface, very unusual)

Pterodroma leucoptera (*Gould*) COLLARED PETREL S Pacific

Pterodroma hypoleuca (*Salvin*) BONIN PETREL Pacific Ocean b Bonin, Chatham and Hawaiian Is

Pterodroma longirostris (*Stejneger*) STEJNEGER'S PETREL N Pacific b Mas Afuera (*P. pycrofti* Falla, b New Zealand, is now usually treated as a race)

Pterodroma nigripennis (*Rothschild*) BLACK-WINGED PETREL Kermadec and Austral Is

Pterodroma baraui *Jouanin* (*Bulletin Museum Natural History*, Paris 35, 393–7) BARAU'S PETREL Indian Ocean b Reunion

[The following 4 species are known only from short descriptions in the m/s notes of the explorer Solander. No specimens obtained and the descriptions do not agree with any other known species:

Pterodroma atrata MOURNING PETREL (? = dark phase of *P. heraldica*)

Pterodroma sordida SORDID PETREL (? = pale phase of *P. neglecta*)

Pterodroma agilis AGILE PETREL (? = *P. cervicalis*)

Pterodroma velificans SAILING PETREL (? = *P. externa*)

These suggested identifications are from Dr W. R. P. Bourne]

SPHENISCIDAE:
Pygoscelis adeliae,
Adelie Penguin

Opposite:
SPHENISCIDAE:
Pygoscelis antarctica,
Chinstrap Penguin

Plate 6

Plate 7

Pagodroma nivea (*Forster*) SNOWY PETREL Antarctic waters / n ground surface, under a rock

Bulweria bulweri (*Jardine and Selby*) BULWER'S PETREL Atlantic and Pacific Oceans b various island groups

Bulweria macgillivrayi (*Gray*) MACGILLIVRAY'S PETREL Fiji / unique

Bulweria fallax *Jouanin* JOUANIN'S PETREL Arabian Sea and Gulf of Aden b not known

Bulweria bifax *Olsen* (*Smithsonian Cont to Palaeobiology*, no 23, 1975) TWO-FACED PETREL St Helena / extinct / bones only

HYDROBATIDAE Storm Petrels Small petrels with a rapid fluttering flight, often seen following ships and feeding on planktonic organisms which they snatch from the surface of the water. Pelagic outside breeding season. Nest in colonies usually on offshore or oceanic islands; nest a burrow in soft soil or turf. Egg 1, white. Nocturnal at breeding colony. Occur throughout the oceans of the world.

Oceanites oceanicus (*Kuhl*) WILSON'S PETREL Atlantic and Indian Oceans b S Shetlands, S Orkneys and S Georgia / I ♂♀ 39–48 / F 52

Oceanites gracilis (*Elliot*) ELLIOT'S PETREL S Pacific b probably west coast of S America but n not found [*O. g. galapagoensis*, Lowe's Petrel, breeds Galapagos Is]

Pelagodroma marina (*Latham*) FRIGATE PETREL Atlantic and Australian seas b many islands / I ♂♀

Fregetta grallaria (*Vieillot*) WHITE-BELLIED PETREL b Juan Fernandez, Rapa Is, Lord Howe Is (3 races)

Fregetta tropica (*Gould*) BLACK-BELLIED PETREL Circumpolar b islands in South Seas

[Several other species of this genus have been described, but it is now generally accepted that they are colour phases of the two above species or aberrant individuals. See Murphy and Snyder: *Am Mus Novit*, no 1596 (1952) for discussion of the 'Pealea' phenomenon. The specimens formerly assigned to *Pealea lineata* (Peale) are now referred to individuals of both species of Fregetta and to *Oceanites oceanicus*, though Oliver *New Zealand Birds* 2nd ed (1955) retains the name *Oceanites maorianus* (Mathews) for the 3 known specimens of this form]

Nesofregetta albigularis (*Finsch*) WHITE-THROATED PETREL Pacific Ocean b Christmas Is,

Phoenix, Marquesas, Fiji and New Hebrides (per Bourne, *Bull BOC* (1957), p 40. *N. fuliginosa* (Gmelin) should be used)

Nesofregetta moestissima (*Salvin*) SAMOAN PETREL Samoa, unique. Believed by some to be a dark phase of *albigularis*

Garrodia nereis (*Gould*) GREY-BACKED PETREL b New Zealand and nearby islands, S Georgia, Falklands and Kerguelen

Hydrobates pelagicus (*L*) STORM PETREL E North Atlantic and Mediterranean / I ♂♀ c38 / F 56–61

Oceanodroma tethys (*Bonaparte*) GALAPAGOS PETREL Galapagos and islands off Peru / n rock chinks or holes in guano

Oceanodroma castro (*Harcourt*) MADEIRAN or HARCOURT'S PETREL b islands in tropical Atlantic and Pacific Oceans

Oceanodroma leucorhoa (*Vieillot*) LEACH'S PETREL N Atlantic and N Pacific / I ♂♀ 50 ? / F 50 ?

Oceanodroma macrodactyla *Bryant* GUADELOUPE PETREL Guadeloupe, probably extinct

Oceanodroma markhami (*Salvin*) MARKHAM'S PETREL Coast of Peru and Chile b ground unknown

Oceanodroma tristrami *Salvin* TRISTRAM'S PETREL b Japan and possibly Laysan (*Cymochorea owstoni*, Mathews and Iredale, is a synonym)

Oceanodroma melania (*Bonaparte*) BLACK FORK-TAILED PETREL b islands off Lower California (sometimes placed in monotypic genus *Loomelania*)

Oceanodroma matsudariae *Kuroda* MATSUDAIRA'S PETREL b Japan wandering south

Oceanodroma monorhis (*Swinhoe*) SWINHOE'S PETREL b islands off Japan and Taiwan, believed now to be a dark race of Leach's Petrel [*Oceanodroma monorhis socorroensis* Townsend, breeds islands off Mexico and Lower California]

Oceanodroma homochroa (*Coues*) ASHY PETREL b islands off California

Oceanodroma hornbyi (*Gray*) HORNBY'S PETREL Pacific coast of S America

Oceanodroma furcata (*Gmelin*) GREY FORK-TAILED PETREL N Pacific b various island groups

Halocyptena microsoma *Coues* LEAST PETREL

Pacific coast of America b San Benito Is / n rock crevices or under slabs of rock

PELECANOIDIDAE Diving Petrels Small petrels superficially resembling Auks (convergence) and diving for food (fish) in a similar way. Breeding habits as Storm Petrels. Confined to the colder waters of the Southern Hemisphere. Four or five species are generally recognised, so similar that they can only be distinguished in the hand. For detailed treatment see Murphy and Harper 'A Review of the Diving Petrels', *Bull Amer Mus Nat Hist* (1921) and Bourne, *Bull BOC* (1968), 88, p 77

Pelecanoides garnotii (*Lesson*) PERUVIAN DIVING PETREL W coast of S America

Pelacanoides magellani (*Mathews*) MAGELLAN DIVING PETREL Cape Horn

Pelecanoides georgicus *Murphy and Harper* GEORGIAN DIVING PETREL S Georgia and Macquarie Island

Pelecanoides urinatrix (*Gmelin*) COMMON DIVING PETREL S Atlantic and Indian Oceans

[**Pelecanoides exsul** *Salvin* KERGUELEN DIVING PETREL Crozet, Kerguelen and Auckland Is]

PHAETHONTIDAE Tropic Birds Graceful white birds with black markings on head and wings; long wings and 2 extremely long central tail feathers. Throughout tropical oceans, breeding on islands. No nest, the single egg laid on a ledge or under a shrub; food, fish and squid. Poor swimmers, seldom resting on surface of water. Four species, not differing much in habits, various races.

Phaethon aethereus *L* RED-BILLED TROPIC BIRD Tropical oceans

Phaethon indicus *Hume* LESSER RED-BILLED TROPIC BIRD N Indian Ocean b Dahlak Is and Persian Gulf (?)

Phaethon lepturus *Daudin* YELLOW-BILLED or WHITE-TAILED TROPIC BIRD Tropical oceans

Phaethon rubricauda *Boddaert* RED-TAILED TROPIC BIRD Indian and Pacific Oceans

PELECANIDAE Pelicans Large clumsy-looking birds with short stout legs. Bill long with a pouch below for scooping up fish; and in hot weather acting as a cooling device for evaporating body moisture. Capable of strong sustained flight. Feed on fish, Brown Pelicans dive, others fish communally on surface. Nest in large colonies on ground or in trees. Eggs 1–4, chalky white. One genus and about 8 species.

Pelecanus onocrotalus *L* GREAT WHITE PELICAN SE Europe, Asia and Africa / n tree / e 2–4 [*Pelecanus roseus* (Gmelin) Rosy Pelican, was used for an eastern race of this species, but present information does not enable them to be separated, and the type of *roseus* is a specimen of *P. philippensis*]

Pelecanus rufescens *Gmelin* PINK-BACKED PELICAN Africa, S Arabia and Madagascar

Pelecanus philippensis *Gmelin* SPOT-BILLED PELICAN Coasts of India, Ceylon, SE Asia and Indonesia / n tree / e 3–4 / I ♂♀ 30

Pelecanus crispus *Bruch* DALMATIAN PELICAN SE Europe across Asia to China / n tree or reed bed

Pelecanus conspicillatus *Temminck* AUSTRALIAN PELICAN Australia and New Guinea, accidentally in New Zealand / n ground / e 2–3

Pelecanus erythrorhynchos *Gmelin* AMERICAN WHITE PELICAN Canada and USA wintering in Caribbean and C America / n ground / e 1–6 / I ♂♀ ? 29

Pelecanus occidentalis *L* BROWN PELICAN Coasts of USA, the Caribbean and Galapagos / n in trees or on ground where no trees / e 2–3 / I ♂♀ ? 28

Pelecanus thagus *Molina* PERUVIAN PELICAN Coasts of Peru and Chile

SULIDAE Gannets and Boobies Goose-sized seabirds with streamlined bodies, long pointed wings and straight, stout, sharp bills. Feed on fish caught by plummeting down vertically from a height and pursuing the fish underwater. Air sacs under the facial skin cushion impact with water. Breed on coasts and islands, often in enormous colonies. Eggs blue, completely covered with a chalky white layer. The generic division seems principally to be one of convenience.

Morus bassanus (*L*) NORTHERN GANNET N Atlantic / n cliff or cliff top / e 1 (rarely 2) / I ♂♀ 43–5 / F ? 60

Morus capensis (*Lichtenstein*) CAPE GANNET S Africa / n cliff or cliff top

Morus serrator (*Gray*) AUSTRALIAN GANNET Australian seas b Tasmania, Bass Strait and New Zealand / n ground / e 1

Sula nebouxii *Milne-Edwards* BLUE-FOOTED BOOBY Galapagos and islands off Peru and Mexico / n ground / e 1–3 / I ♂♀

Sula variegata (*Tschudi*) PERUVIAN or VARIEGATED BOOBY Islands off Peru and

Plate 8

Opposite:
SPHENISCIDAE:
Spheniscus demersus,
Blackfoot, Cape or
Jackass Penguin

PODICIPEDIDAE:
Podiceps poliocephalus,
Hoary-Headed Grebe

GAVIIDAE:
Gavia arctica,
Black-throated Diver or Loon,
Arctic Loon

Plate 9

Chile / n cliff ledges

Sula abbotti *Ridgway* ABBOTT'S BOOBY Assumption and Christmas Is (Indian Ocean) n in tree

Sula dactylatra *Lesson* MASKED or BLUE-FACED BOOBY Tropical oceans (several races) / n rock ledge / e 1–2

Sula sula (*L*) RED-FOOTED BOOBY Tropical oceans / n tree or ground / e 1 / I ♂♀ 42–6

Sula leucogaster (*Boddaert*) BROWN BOOBY Tropical Atlantic and Pacific Oceans / n ground / e 2–3 / I ♂♀ 40–3

PHALACROCORACIDAE **Cormorants and Shags** Medium to large birds from small duck to goose sized, generally dark in colour and with patches of bright coloured skin. Inhabit coastal waters, lakes and rivers, seldom seen far from land. Catch fish by diving from the surface. Nest usually in colonies. Eggs blue, covered with a white chalky layer.

Phalacrocorax auritus (*Lesson*) DOUBLE-CRESTED CORMORANT Coasts of N America / n ground or tree / e 2–9 / I ♂♀ 24–9 (accounts vary) / F 70

Phalacrocorax olivaceus (*Humboldt*) OLIVACEOUS or BIGUA CORMORANT Coasts of tropical and S America / remarkable for diversity of habitat, breeding on arid islets, trees of tropical swamps and banks of mountain lakes / n tree / e 2–6

Phalacrocorax sulcirostris (*Brandt*) LITTLE BLACK CORMORANT or SHAG Australia and New Zealand / lakes streams and coasts / n tree / e 3–5

Phalacrocorax carbo (*L*) COMMON or GREAT CORMORANT Widely distributed over Old World and the Atlantic coast of N America / n ground or tree, coast or inland / e 3–4 rarely more / I ♂♀ 28 / F c60 [*Phalacrocorax lucidus* (Lichtenstein), usually treated as a race of *carbo*, was reported breeding sympatrically with it by Williams, *Bull Brit Orn Cl*, 86, 48–50]

Phalacrocorax fuscicollis *Stephens* INDIAN SHAG India, Ceylon and Burma / fresh water / n tree / e 3–6 / I ♂♀

Phalacrocorax capensis (*Sparrman*) CAPE CORMORANT Coasts of S Africa

Phalacrocorax nigrogularis *Ogilvie-Grant and Forbes* SOCOTRAN CORMORANT Socotra, Aden and Persian Gulf

Phalacrocorax neglectus (*Wahlberg*) WAHLBERG'S CORMORANT Coasts of S Africa

Phalacrocorax capillatus (*Temminck and Schlegel*) TEMMINCK'S CORMORANT Japan, Korea (? and E Siberia) salt, sometimes fresh, water

Phalacrocorax pencillatus (*Brandt*) BRANDT'S CORMORANT Pacific coast of N America estuaries and islands / n ground / e 3–6 / I ♂♀

Phalacrocorax aristotelis (*L*) COMMON SHAG Coasts of Europe, N Africa and Mediterranean / marine / n on ground / e 3 / I ♂♀ 24–8 / F period unknown

Phalacrocorax pelagicus *Pallas* PELAGIC CORMORANT N Pacific coasts / n cliff / e 3–7 / I ♂♀ 26

Phalacrocorax perspicillatus *Pallas* SPECTACLED CORMORANT Bering Is / extinct 1852 / 5 specimens

Phalacrocorax urile (*Gmelin*) RED-FACED CORMORANT Kamchatka, and coasts and islands of Bering Sea / marine / n cliff / e 3–4

Phalacrocorax magellanicus (*Gmelin*) ROCK SHAG Falklands and coasts of southern S America / marine / n tops of stacks

Phalacrocorax bougainvillii (*Lesson*) GUANAY CORMORANT Peru and Chile / marine / n tops of islands

Phalacrocorax featherstoni *Buller* FEATHERSTON'S SHAG Chatham Is / decreasing / n cliffs

Phalacrocorax varius (*Gmelin*) YELLOW-FACED CORMORANT or PIED SHAG S Australia, Tasmania and New Zealand / marine and fresh water b islands or swamps / n ground, bush or tree / e 2–3

Phalacrocorax fuscescens (*Vieillot*) BLACK-FACED CORMORANT S Australia and Tasmania coasts / n rocks / e 2–4

Phalacrocorax carunculatus (*Gmelin*) KING SHAG, BRONZE SHAG etc New Zealand and islands to east / n rock stacks / e 2–3, 1–2 (variable in different races)

[NB: This assemblage of forms is very sedentary and has given rise to a number of types now generally regarded as races, but all have been considered as species]

    P. carunculatus (*Gmelin*) KING SHAG Marlborough Sounds district

    P. chalconotus (*Gray*) BRONZE SHAG Stewart Is and southern S Island

    P. onslowi *Forbes* Chatham Is

    P. ranfurlyi *Ogilvie-Grant* Bounty Is

    P. colensoi *Buller* Auckland Is

    P. campbelli (*Filhol*) Campbell Is

P. huttoni *Buller* Stewart Is. and southern S Island (the validity of this form has been queried)

Phalacrocorax verrucosus (*Cabanis*) KERGUELEN CORMORANT Kerguelen Is

Phalacrocorax gaimardi (*Lesson*) RED-FOOTED SHAG Coasts of Peru, Chile and Patagonia

Phalacrocorax punctatus (*Sparrman*) SPOTTED SHAG, BLUE SHAG (2 races) New Zealand / sea cliffs and rocky islands / e 2–4

Phalacrocorax atriceps *King* IMPERIAL, or MAGELLAN BLUE-EYED SHAG Southern S America and S Shetlands

Phalacrocorax purpurascens (*Brandt*) (= **Phalacrocorax traversi** *Rothschild*) ROTHSCHILD'S SHAG Macquarie Is / e 3 (this form has been placed as a race of both *atriceps* and *albiventer*)

Phalacrocorax albiventer (*Lesson*) WHITE-NECKED SHAG Southern S America and Falklands [*P. vanhoeffeni*, Crozet Is, is usually regarded as race of above]

Phalacrocorax georgianus *Lönnberg* SOUTH GEORGIAN BLUE-EYED SHAG South Georgia / n broken rocks and grass tussocks / e 2–3

Phalacrocorax melanoleucos (*Vieillot*) LITTLE PIED CORMORANT Australasia and New Zealand / marine and fresh water / n tree / e 3–5 (*P. brevirostris* Gould, is sometimes separated)

Phalacrocorax africanus (*Gmelin*) LONG-TAILED CORMORANT or REED DUIKER Africa and Madagascar / marine and fresh water / n ground or tree / e 2–4

Phalacrocorax niger (*Vieillot*) LITTLE CORMORANT India, Ceylon, Burma, Malaya, Sumatra, Java and Borneo / estuaries and fresh water / n tree or in long grass / e 3–5 / I ♂♀

Phalacrocorax pygmaeus (*Pallas*) PYGMY CORMORANT E Europe, W Asia and Algeria

Morony, Bock and Farrand, *Reference List of the Birds of the World* (1975), retain *Halietor* for these last 4 species

Nannopterum harrisi (*Rothschild*) FLIGHTLESS CORMORANT Galapagos – Narborough and Albemarle Is / n ground

ANHINGIDAE Anhingas The Anhinga is a cormorant-like bird with an exceptionally long slender neck and stiletto-like bill, which it uses to spear fish. Nests usually in mixed colonies with herons and cormorants. A number of species have been named but they are now usually regarded as forms of a single species. Occurs almost throughout the tropical and subtropical parts of world.

Anhinga anhinga (*L*) ANHINGA, DARTER or SNAKE BIRD Tropical regions / fresh waters / n tree / e 3–6 / I ♂♀

Anhinga nanus *Newton and Gadow* MAURITIAN DARTER Mauritius / extinct / bones only

FREGATIDAE Frigate Birds The Frigate Birds are large black or black and white pelagic birds with long pointed wings, deeply forked tails and raptor-like flight. The males have brightly coloured pouches on the throat which are inflated in display. Feed chiefly on fish pirated from other birds. Capable of long sustained flight, but cannot take off from a flat surface. Nest of sticks in trees or on rocks. Eggs 1–2, chalky white. Five species throughout the tropical seas. Incubation is by both sexes for approximately 6 weeks. Species differ little in habits.

Fregata aquila (*L*) ASCENSION ISLAND FRIGATE BIRD Ascension Is

Fregata andrewsi *Mathews* CHRISTMAS ISLAND FRIGATE BIRD Christmas Is, Indian Ocean

Fregata magnificens *Mathews* MAN O'WAR BIRD or MAGNIFICENT FRIGATE BIRD Tropical waters of Atlantic and Pacific / n tree / e 1

Fregata minor (*Gmelin*) GREAT FRIGATE BIRD Islands of Indian and Pacific Oceans and S Trinidad

Fregata ariel (*Gray*) LESSER FRIGATE BIRD Islands of Indian and Pacific Oceans and S Trinidad / n bush / e 1–2

[A Frigate Bird, now extinct, formerly inhabited St Helena. It is not known what species it represented, or if it was an otherwise unknown species (Murphy)]

ARDEIDAE Herons, Egrets and Bitterns Large birds of marsh and water feeding largely on fish and other aquatic creatures. Renowned for 'powder-downs' – specialised feathers which fray at tip producing powder used in dressing feathers. Many species have decorative courtship plumes. Nests untidy, of sticks, often in trees over water. Eggs usually pale blue or bluish-green.

Ardea sumatrana *Raffles* DUSKY HERON Burma, Malay Peninsula through Indonesia to

DIOMEDEIDAE:
Phoebetria palpebrata,
Light-mantled
Sooty Albatross

DIOMEDEIDAE:
Diomedea cauta,
Shy Albatross,
White-Capped Albatross

Plate 10

PROCELLARIIDAE:
Puffinus tenuirostris,
Short-tailed Shearwater or
Mutton Bird

PROCELLARIIDAE:
Macronectes giganteus,
Northern Giant Petrel,
Giant Fulmar

Plate 11

Australia/coasts and estuaries/aquatic animals/ n tree/e 2

Ardea insignis *Hume* ex *Hodgson* (= **Ardea imperialis** *Baker*) GREAT WHITE-BELLIED HERON Sikkim and Bhutan through Assam to N Burma/swampy forest/n tree/e 3–4 (3 nests known)

Ardea goliath *Cretzschmar* GOLIATH HERON Egypt and Africa S of the Sahara, wanders to India/shores and swamps b singly in colonies of other species

Ardea humbloti *Milne-Edwards and Grandidier* MADAGASCAR HERON Madagascar and ? Aldabra/mangroves

Ardea melanocephala *Vigors and Children* BLACK-HEADED HERON Africa S of Sahara and Madagascar/n tree/e 2–4

Ardea cinerea *L* GREY HERON Europe, Asia, parts of Africa/n tree or reed bed/e 3–5/I ♂♀ 25–8/F 50–5

Ardea herodias *L* GREAT BLUE HERON N America/lakes, coastal marshes and rivers/ n tree, bush or ground/e 3–7/I ♂♀ 28

Ardea occidentalis *Audubon* GREAT WHITE HERON Florida, Cuba, Isle of Pines, Jamaica (sometimes regarded as conspecific with *A. herodias*) [*A. wurdemanni* is a hybrid between *A. herodias* and *A. occidentalis*]

Ardea cocoi *L* COCOI HERON S America/ swamps/fish and insects/n tree/e n/s

Ardea pacifica *Latham* WHITE-NECKED HERON Australia and Tasmania / swamps and lakes/ insects and small vertebrates/n tree/e 4

Ardea purpurea *L* PURPLE HERON S Europe across Asia to China; Africa and Madagascar/ marshes/n ground or bush rarely tree/e 3–6/ I ♂♀ 24–8/F c42

Ardea novaehollandiae *Latham* WHITE-FACED HERON E Indonesia, Australia, Tasmania, and New Zealand/swamps and lakes/crustacea, frogs and insects/n tree/e 3–5

Ardea picata *Gould* PIED HERON Celebes, New Guinea, N Australia and adjacent islands/ swamps/insects and vertebrates/n tree/e 3–4

Megaphoyx megacephala *Milne-Edwards* FLIGHTLESS HERON Rodriguez/bones [*Leguat*]

Megaphoyx duboisi *Rothschild* DUBOIS' HERON Réunion [*Du Bois*]

Pilherodius pileatus (*Boddaert*) CAPPED HERON Panama to Peru and Brazil / swampy forests/fish and frogs

Butorides virescens (*L*) GREEN HERON

S Canada, USA and C America/n tree/e 3–9/ I 17

Butorides sundevalli *Reichenow* GALAPAGOS HERON Galapagos

Butorides striatus (*L*) STRIATED or GREEN-BACKED HERON Almost cosmopolitan through tropical parts of world, north to Japan and Amurland/fish, frogs and insects / n tree or mangrove/e 3–5/I ♂♀

Butorides rufiventris (*Sundevall*) RUFOUS-BELLIED HERON South Africa / n low tree (Jackson) or tree/e 2

Butorides mauritanicus *Newton and Gadow* MAURITIAN HERON Mauritius/bones only

Ardeola ralloides (*Scopoli*) SQUACCO HERON Africa, S Europe and Middle East/insects and fish/n tree or reeds/e 2–4

Ardeola idae (*Hartlaub*) MADAGASCAR SQUACCO HERON Madagascar

Ardeola grayii (*Sykes*) INDIAN POND HERON Persian Gulf across India to Malaya and islands in Indian Ocean/fish, frogs, insects / n tree/ e 3–5/I ♂♀ 24

Ardeola bacchus (*Bonaparte*) CHINESE POND HERON S China, Borneo and Malay Peninsula/ n tree/e 3–5

Ardeola speciosa (*Horsfield*) JAVAN POND HERON Borneo, Celebes, Sumatra, Java and Sumbawa

Bubulcus ibis (*L*) CATTLE EGRET or BUFF-BACKED HERON Iberia and most of tropical Africa and Asia to Japan and Indonesia/insects disturbed by cattle/n tree/e 1–3 or 3–6 (varies in different areas)/I ♂♀

Egretta caerulea (*L*) LITTLE BLUE HERON b Caribbean and tropical S America wandering north/n tree or bush/e 3–6/I ♂♀ 22–4

Egretta ardesiaca (*Wagler*) BLACK HERON Tropical Africa/coastal/n tree/e 3–4

Egretta vinaceigula (*Sharpe*) SLATY EGRET Transvaal and Caprivi [*Benson* etc *Bull BOC* 1971]

Egretta rufescens (*Gmelin*) REDDISH EGRET C America and Caribbean (dimorphic)/swamps/ n tree or bush/e 3–7/I ♂♀

Egretta alba (*L*) GREAT WHITE HERON, GREAT WHITE EGRET or LARGE EGRET Almost cosmopolitan but absent from much of Europe/ fish, frogs, insects / n tree /e 3–4/I ♂♀ ? 25–6

Egretta garzetta (*L*) LITTLE EGRET S Europe, Africa, S and C Asia, Indonesia and Australia/ fish, frogs, insects/n tree/e 3–5/I ♂♀ 21–5

Egretta dimorpha *Hartert* DIMORPHIC EGRET or MASCARENE REEF HERON Madagascar and Aldabra

Egretta eulophotes (*Swinhoe*) SWINHOE'S EGRET S and C China, Taiwan and Celebes/ little data

Egretta gularis (*Bosc*) WESTERN REEF HERON W Africa/n tree/e 3–4

Egretta schistacea (*Hemprich and Ehrenberg*) RED SEA REEF HERON Red Sea coasts and (?) Socotra/n tree/e 2–3

Egretta asha (*Sykes*) INDIAN REEF HERON Persian Gulf to Ceylon/n tree/e 3–4

Egretta sacra (*Gmelin*) EASTERN REEF HERON E and SE Asia, Indonesia, Australasia, New Zealand and Pacific islands/rocky shores and reefs/marine life/n tree or rocks/e 2–4 (Oliver, *New Zealand Birds*, 2nd ed (1955) retains *Egretta* (*Demigretta*) *matook* (*Vieillot*) for the New Zealand bird (Blue Reef Heron) in which only the dark phase occurs)

Egretta intermedia (*Wagler*) MEDIAN EGRET E Africa, India to China and Japan, Indonesia and Australia/n tree/c 2–5 (clutch size varies in different parts of range)/I ♂♀ ? 21

Egretta thula (*Molina*) SNOWY EGRET USA, C and S America/n tree/e 3–6/I ♂♀ 18

Egretta tricolour (*Müller*) LOUISIANA HERON Caribbean/n tree/e 3–7/I ♂♀ 21

Agamia agami (*Gmelin*) CHESTNUT-BELLIED HERON or AGAMI HERON C America to Peru and Brazil/swamps/fish/n tree over water/e ? 2

Syrigma sibilatrix (*Temminck*) WHISTLING HERON Southern S America

Nycticorax nycticorax (*L*) BLACK-CROWNED NIGHT HERON Europe, Asia, Africa and the Americas, except extreme north/fish, frogs, insects/n reeds, bushes or trees/e 3–8/I ♂♀ 24–6 (? 21)

Nycticorax caledonicus (*Gmelin*) RUFOUS NIGHT HERON Indonesia, Australia, New Caledonia and the Solomon Is/sea inlets and margins of swamps and rivers/aquatic animals/ n tree/e 2–5

Nycticorax leuconotus (*Wagler*) WHITE-BACKED NIGHT HERON Africa S of Sahara/n reeds or bush/e 2–5

Nycticorax magnificus *Ogilvie Grant* HAINAN NIGHT HERON Mountains of Hainan/no data

Nycticorax violaceus (*L*) YELLOW-CROWNED NIGHT HERON USA to S Brazil/mangroves/ n tree/e 3–5/I ♂♀

Gorsachius goisagi (*Temminck*) JAPANESE BITTERN E China, Japan, Riu Kius, Taiwan and Philippines/e 3 ?

Gorsachius melanolophus (*Raffles*) TIGER BITTERN India, SE Asia and Indonesia/fish, frogs, lizards, molluscs, insects etc/n tree/e 3–5

Zonerodius heliosylus (*Lesson*) FOREST BITTERN Salawatti, New Guinea and Aru Is

Tigriornis leucolophus (*Jardine*) AFRICAN TIGER HERON W and C Africa/streams/n tree/ e n/k

Tigrisoma lineatum (*Boddaert*) RUFESCENT TIGER HERON C and S America/wet forests and plantations/fish and insects/n tree/e 1 or 3 (accounts differ)

Tigrisoma fasciatum (*Such*) FASCIATED TIGER HERON Venezuela to Argentina

Tigrisoma salmoni *Sclater and Salvin* SALMON'S TIGER HERON Ecuador and Colombia/ n and e n/k

Tigrisoma mexicanum *Swainson* (= **Heterocnus cabanisi** (*Heine*)) BARE-THROATED TIGER HERON Mexico to Panama/n tree/e 2–3 NB: For name change of this species see Monroe, 'Birds of Honduras' and Van Rossem in *Auk*, 59 (1942), p 572 'The name of the Mexican Tiger Bittern'

Zebrilus undulatus (*Gmelin*) ZIGZAG HERON The Guianas to C Brazil

Ixobrychus minutus (*L*) LITTLE BITTERN Eurasia and Africa except north and Orient/fish, frogs, insects etc/n floating mat or tree/e 4–10/ I ♂♀ 16–19/F 30

Ixobrychus sinensis (*Gmelin*) YELLOW BITTERN Japan, China, India, Ceylon, SE Asia, Indonesia, Caroline Is/fish, frogs, insects etc/ n reed beds/e 4–6

Ixobrychus involucris (*Vieillot*) STRIPE-BACKED BITTERN S America/n tree/e 2–3

Ixobrychus exilis (*Gmelin*) LEAST BITTERN C and eastern North America S to Paraguay/ n in reeds/e 4–6/I ♂♀ 16–17/F 10–14

Ixobrychus eurhythmus (*Swinhoe*) SCHRENCK'S BITTERN Transbaikalia, N China and Japan, migrating to Indonesia/no data

Ixobrychus cinnamomeus (*Gmelin*) CINNAMON BITTERN or CHESTNUT BITTERN China, India, Ceylon, Indonesia/fish, frogs, insects/n in reeds/e 4–6/I ♂♀

Ixobrychus sturmii (*Wagler*) DWARF BITTERN Africa S of Sahara/insects/n in bush over water/ e 2–4

PROCELLARIIDAE:
Pachyptila salvini,
Medium-billed Prion

PROCELLARIIDAE:
Daption capense,
Cape Petrel, Cape Pigeon or
Pintado

Plate 12

HYDROBATIDAE:
Pelagodroma marina,
Frigate Petrel,
White-faced Storm Petrel

PELECANOIDIDAE:
Pelecanoides urinatrix,
Common Diving Petrel,
Subantarctic Diving-Petrel

Plate 13

Ixobrychus flavicollis (*Latham*) BLACK BITTERN India and China to Australia and Solomon Is / fish, frogs, insects / n in reeds or trees / e 3–5 / I ♂♀

Botaurus stellaris (*L*) EURASIAN BITTERN Africa and the temperate Palaearctic / n in reeds / e 3–7 / I ♀ 25–6 / F c56

Botaurus poiciloptilus (*Wagler*) BROWN BITTERN Australia, Tasmania and New Zealand / n in reeds / e 3–7 / I ♀? 28 / F? 14

Botaurus lentiginosus (*Montagu*) AMERICAN BITTERN N America wintering in C America n in reeds / e 3–7 / I ? ♀ 28 / F? 14

Botaurus pinnatus (*Wagler*) PINNATED BITTERN C and S America

COCHLEARIIDAE An aberrant heron-like bird with a broad, scoop-like bill, but its feeding habits are imperfectly known and reports as to how this bill is used, conflict. Nocturnal, hiding in mangroves during the day.

Cochlearius cochlearius (*L*) BOATBILL Mexico to Peru and Brazil / swamps / n tree / e 2–4 / I ♂♀

BALAENICIPITIDAE A huge stork-like bird with a massive bill which it uses to probe in muddy waters for lungfish and gars

Balaeniceps rex *Gould* SHOEBILL or WHALEHEAD Africa from White Nile S to Katanga and Uganda / n ground / e 2

SCOPIDAE A medium-sized, heron-like bird with a trailing crest. It builds an extremely elaborate domed nest which can be 6ft (1.8m) or so across.

Scopus umbretta *Gmelin* HAMMERHEAD or HAMMERKOP Africa S of Sahara, Madagascar, SW Arabia / n tree / e 3–6

CICONIIDAE Storks Long legged, long but stout billed and generally long necked birds, occurring throughout the warmer parts of the world except New Zealand, Oceania and northern N America. They tend to live in drier habitats than other members of the Order and lack the powder downs. Many species are migratory. Feed on frogs, fishes, small birds and animals.

Mycteria americana *L* WOOD STORK Caribbean and much of S America / n tree / e 3–5 / I ♂♀ 28–32

Mycteria ibis (*L*) WOOD IBIS Africa, S of Sahara, Madagascar / insects and vertebrates / n tree / e 2–3

Mycteria leucocephala (*Pennant*) PAINTED STORK India to SE Asia / fish / n tree / e 2–5 / I ♂♀

Mycteria cinerea (*Raffles*) SOUTHERN PAINTED STORK or MILKY STORK Malaya to Cambodia, Sumatra and Java / n tree / e 3 [*Tantalus* (ie *Mycteria*) *lacteus Temminck*. There seems to be no ground for Delacour's reinstatement of this name, *Ibis* (1929), pp 208–9. The two names, *cinereus* and *lacteus* appear to refer to the adult and juvenile plumages of the same species]

Anastomus oscitans (*Boddaert*) OPEN-BILLED STORK India to SE Asia / inland waters / molluscs / n tree / e 2–6 / I ♂♀ 24–5

Anastomus lamelligerus *Temminck* AFRICAN OPEN-BILLED STORK Africa and Madagascar / molluscs / n reed beds or trees / e 2–3

Ciconia abdimii (*Lichtenstein*) ABDIM'S STORK Africa S of Sahara / n on huts or trees / e 2–4

Ciconia episcopus (*Boddaert*) WOOLLY-NECKED or BISHOP STORK Africa and India to Indonesia / forest marshes / frogs, reptiles, crabs, insects etc / n tree / e 2–5 / I ♂♀

Ciconia ciconia (*L*) WHITE STORK E Europe and W Asia, wintering in Africa / forest and habitation / frogs, reptiles, insects etc / n ground, roofs of buildings, trees / e 1–7 / I ♂♀ 29–30 / F 53–5 [*Ciconia boyciana* Swinhoe, of Amurland, Korea and Japan, is sometimes separated]

Ciconia nigra (*L*) BLACK STORK E Europe across temperate Asia to China and Sakhalin wintering further S / forest / frogs, fish, insects etc / n tree or cliff / e 3–5 / I ♂♀ 32–46 / F 63–71

Ciconia maguari (*Gmelin*) (= **Euxenura galeata** (*Molina*)) MAGUARI STORK S America / n ground

Ephippiorhynchus asiaticus (*Latham*) BLACK-NECKED STORK India to SE Asia: New Guinea, and N and E Australia (discontinuous) / marshes, rivers and mangrove / fish etc / n tree / e 3–5 / I ♂♀

Ephippiorhynchus senegalensis (*Shaw*) SADDLE-BILL STORK (or JABIRU) Africa S of Sahara to Orange River / vertebrates / n tree / e 1

Jabiru mycteria (*Lichtenstein*) JABIRU C and S America / lagoons and marshes / n tree / e 2–3

Leptoptilos dubius (*Gmelin*) ADJUTANT STORK India to Borneo / n tree / e 2–4 / I ♂♀

Leptoptilos javanicus (*Horsfield*) LESSER or HAIRCRESTED ADJUTANT India to Java and S China / n tree / no other data

Leptoptilos crumeniferus (*Lesson*) MARABOU

STORK Africa S of Sahara / carrion and vertebrates / n tree / e 2–3

THRESKIORNITHIDAE Ibises and Spoonbills Medium sized wading birds with naked faces and sometimes naked heads and necks. Ibises have slender downcurved bills, and Spoonbills flat broad ones. Lack powder downs. Occur through the warm temperate and tropical regions except Oceania.

Threskiornis aethiopicus (*Latham*) SACRED IBIS Africa S of Sahara, S Arabia, Aldabra, Madagascar (formerly Egypt) / fish and insects / n tree or ground / e 2–3

Threskiornis melanocephalus (*Latham*) (ASIATIC) WHITE IBIS India to China and Japan / n tree / e 2–4 / I ♂♀ 23–5

Threskiornis molucca (*Cuvier*) AUSTRALIAN WHITE IBIS Australasia / lakes and pools / small vertebrates, crustacea and insects / n bush / e 3–4

Carphibis spinicollis (*Jameson*) STRAW-NECKED IBIS Australia and Tasmania / lakes and rivers / small vertebrates, crustacea and insects / n reed bed / e 3–4

Pseudibis papillosa (*Temminck*) BLACK IBIS India / n tree / e 2–4 / no other data

Pseudibis davisoni (*Hume*) DAVISON'S IBIS Burma and SE Asia / n tree / e ? 2

Pseudibis gigantea (*Oustalet*) GIANT IBIS Cochin China, Cambodia and Peninsular Siam / virtually no data [Red Data Book]

Comatibis eremita (*L*) WALDRAPP Locally in N Africa E to Mesopotamia, formerly in S and C Europe / insects / n among rocks / e 2–3

Geronticus calvus (*Boddaert*) BALD IBIS S Africa mountains / n among rocks / e 2–3 / I 21

Nipponia nippon (*Temminck*) CRESTED IBIS [Ussuriland, Japan, Korea and N China, formerly] probably restricted to Japan / very rare and endangered (probably less than 20–30 birds) / n tree / e 2 [Red Data Book]

Lampribis olivacea (*DuBus*) GREEN IBIS W and C Africa and islands in Gulf of Guinea / n tree / e 3

Lampribis rara *Rothschild, Hartert and Kleinschmidt* SPOTTED-BREASTED IBIS C Africa / worms and insects / n and e n/k

Hagedashia hagedash (*Latham*) HADADA Africa S of Sahara / worms and insects / n tree / e 3

Bostrychia carunculata (*Rüppell*) WATTLED IBIS Mountains of Ethiopia / small animals / n tree or bush on cliff / e 2

Harpiprion caerulescens (*Vieillot*) PLUMBEOUS IBIS C Brazil, Paraguay, Uruguay and N Argentina

Theristicus caudatus (*Boddaert*) WHITE-THROATED BLACK-FACED or BUFF-NECKED IBIS Much of S America / frogs, worms etc / n cliff ledges / e 2–3 [*T. branickii* Berlepsch and Stolzmann and *T. melanopis* (Gmelin) are now regarded as races of the above]

Cercibis oxycerca (*Spix*) SHARP-TAILED IBIS Basin of the Orinoco

Mesembrinibis cayennensis (*Gmelin*) CAYENNE IBIS Tropical S America / swampy forest / worms and insects / n tree / e 2

Phimosus infuscatus (*Lichtenstein*) WHISPERING IBIS S America S to Uruguay

Eudocimus albus (*L*) AMERICAN WHITE IBIS Southern USA and the Caribbean / crabs, crayfish etc / n tree or bush over water / e 2–5 / I 21

Eudocimus ruber (*L*) SCARLET IBIS Tropical S America / lagoons / crustaceans etc / n tree / e 2–4 / I ♂♀ 24

Plegadis falcinellus (*L*) GLOSSY IBIS Temperate and tropical Eurasia to Indonesia and Australia, Africa, Madagascar, West Indies and the Caribbean / insects etc / n trees, bushes or reed beds / e 3–4 / I ♂♀ 21 / F c14

Plegadis chihi (*Vieillot*) (= **P. guarauna** (*L*) now used for the Limpkin p 42) WHITE-FACED IBIS America from Oregon to Argentina / n marshes / e 3 / I ?♂♀ 21–2

Plegadis ridgwayi (*Allen*) PUNA IBIS Highlands of Peru and Bolivia

Lophotibis cristata (*Boddaert*) MADAGASCAR IBIS Madagascar

Platalea leucorodia *L* COMMON SPOONBILL NE Africa and Europe across Asia to Japan / marsh life – animal and vegetable / n tree or reed beds / e 3–5 usually 4 / I ♂♀ 21 / F c28

Platalea minor *Temminck and Schlegel* BLACK-FACED SPOONBILL China, Korea and Japan

Platalea alba *Scopoli* AFRICAN SPOONBILL Africa and Madagascar / insects / n tree, rocks or reed beds / e 2–4

Platalea regia *Gould* BLACK-BILLED SPOONBILL or ROYAL SPOONBILL Australasia and New Zealand / coastal and inland swamps and marshes / aquatic life / n in swamp vegetaton, bushes or trees / e 3–5

Platalea flavipes *Gould* YELLOW-BILLED or YELLOW-LEGGED SPOONBILL Australia / coastal

PHAETHONTIDAE:
Phaethon lepturus,
Yellow-billed or
White-tailed Tropic Bird

PELECANIDAE:
Pelecanus conspicillatus,
Australian Pelican

Plate 14

SULIDAE:
Sula dactylatra,
Masked or Blue-faced Booby

PHALACROCORACIDAE:
Phalacrocorax fuscescens,
Black-faced Cormorant

Plate 15

and inland swamps and marshes / aquatic life/ n marsh / e 3–5

Ajaia ajaja (*L*) ROSEATE SPOONBILL Caribbean, S America to Chile and Argentina / aquatic life/ n mangrove tree / e 2–5

PHOENICOPTERIDAE Flamingoes Tall pinkish-white aquatic birds with very long legs and necks and squat triangular bills furnished with a sieve which they sweep through the water to extract microscopic life, their food. Gregarious. Nest in huge colonies round borders of lakes. Nest made of mud, tall and pedestal-like. Eggs 1, chalky white. Incubation 30–2 days, by both sexes. Six species, but the three species of genus *Phoenicopterus* often treated as races of 1 species.

Phoenicopterus ruber *L* ROSY or SCARLET FLAMINGO Caribbean and Galapagos Is

Phoenicopterus roseus *Pallas* ROSY or GREATER FLAMINGO Mediterranean, W Asia and Africa, formerly more extensive/ e 1–2

Phoenicopterus chilensis *Molina* CHILEAN FLAMINGO or GUAICHETE (native) Temperate S America

Phoeniconaias minor (*Geoffroy*) LESSER FLAMINGO Rift valleys of Africa, Persian Gulf, NW India

Phoenicoparrus andinus (*Philippi*) ANDEAN FLAMINGO or TOCOCO (native) Chilean Andes

Phoenicoparrus jamesi (*Sclater*) JAMES'S FLAMINGO or CHURURO (native) Andes of S Peru and N Chile

[There is a possibility that another flamingo, unknown to science and called by the natives, JETETE, also exists in the Chilean Andes]

ANHIMIDAE Screamers Fairly long-legged wading and swimming South American birds, allied to geese, swans and ducks but very unlike them in appearance with bills resembling game birds. Feathers on head downy, wings armed with two sharp spurs, feet only slightly webbed. Feed on water plants. Nest in grassy marshes. Eggs 2–6 white, I ♂♀ 42–4 days. Young precocial, leaving nest soon after hatching.

Anhima cornuta (*L*) HORNED SCREAMER Tropical S America

Chauna torquata (*Oken*) CRESTED SCREAMER Paraguay, S Brazil, Uruguay, N and E Argentina

Chauna chavaria (*L*) BLACK-NECKED SCREAMER N Colombia and N Venezuela

ANATIDAE Geese, Swans and Ducks Swimming birds with short legs and webbed feet. Necks long (geese) very long (swans) or moderate (ducks). Nest is usually on the ground, and frequently lined with down. Eggs pale blue-green, creamy or white, unspotted. The relationships of the various tribes and subfamilies is complicated, readers requiring further information should consult Delacour *Waterfowl of the World* 4 vols, whose arrangement is followed here.

Anseranas semipalmata (*Latham*) MAGPIE GOOSE Australia, Tasmania, S New Guinea/ swamps / n reeds / e 5–14 / I 35

Dendrocygna guttata *Schlegel* SPOTTED WHISTLING DUCK Indonesia, New Guinea, Bismarck Archipelago / n hollow trees / e n/k

Dendrocygna eytoni (*Eyton*) PLUMED WHISTLING DUCK or EYTON'S TREE DUCK Australia and Tasmania / n ground / e 10–12/ I ♂♀ 28

Dendrocygna arcuata (*Horsfield*) WANDERING WHISTLING DUCK Indonesia, Australia, New Caledonia and Fiji / n reeds / e 6–15 / I ♂♀ 30

Dendrocygna bicolor (*Vieillot*) FULVOUS WHISTLING DUCK Discontinuous / Mexico and southern USA, S America: E Africa, Madagascar: India and Ceylon to Pegu, no geographical variation / n reeds / e 20+(?) 6–8(?) / I ♂♀ 30–2

Dendrocygna arborea (*L*) BLACK-BILLED WHISTLING DUCK West Indies / n reeds / e 10–12/ I ♂♀ 30

Dendrocygna javanica (*Horsfield*) INDIAN WHISTLING DUCK India to S China, Borneo, Taiwan and the Riu Kiu Is / n reeds or trees/ e 6–12 / I ♂♀ ? 30 ? 22–4

Dendrocygna viduata (*L*) WHITE-FACED WHISTLING DUCK S America S to Uruguay, Africa S of Sahara, Madagascar and Comoros/ n hollow tree / e 8–12 / I ♂♀ 28–30

Dendrocygna autumnalis (*L*) RED-BILLED WHISTLING DUCK C and S America to N Argentina / n hollow trees / e 8–12 / I ♂♀ 27

Coscoroba coscoroba (*Molina*) COSCOROBA SWAN S Brazil to Tierra del Fuego and Falklands / n ground or floating / e 4–9 / I ♀ 35

[**Coscoroba davidi** (*Swinhoe*) DAVID'S SWAN China / unique, specimen lost / is now generally ignored, but Swinhoe's description matches no other known species]

Cygnus atratus (*Latham*) BLACK SWAN

Australia, Tasmania, introduced New Zealand/ n reed beds/e 4–8/I ♂♀ 34–7

Cygnus chathamicus *Oliver* CHATHAM SWAN Chatham Is/bones only (*C. sumnerensis* Forbes, may be the same but is not now identifiable)

Cygnus olor (*Gmelin*) MUTE SWAN Europe and temperate Asia, south in winter, feral in other places/water weeds/n banks or islets in swamps/ e 4–7 rarely 12/I ♀ 35–8

Cygnus melanocoryphus (*Molina*) BLACK-NECKED SWAN S Brazil to Tierra del Fuego and Falklands/water weeds/n rushes/e 4–7/I ♀ 34–6

Cygnus cygnus (*L*) WHOOPER SWAN Palaearctic b N and E Asia/n banks/e 4–7/I ♀ 35–42

Cygnus buccinator *Richardson* TRUMPETER SWAN Parts of N America, formerly more extensive/n ground/e 5–8/I ♀ 36–40

Cygnus columbianus (*Ord*) WHISTLING SWAN N America/weeds, small snails/n ground/ e 4–7/I ♀ 35–40

Cygnus bewickii *Yarrell* BEWICK'S SWAN b Siberian tundra temperate Eurasia / n estuaries/e 5–7/I ♀ 34–8

Anser cygnoides (*L*) SWAN GOOSE (origin of Chinese Domestic Goose) E Asia/e 5–10/I ♀ 28–30

Anser anser (*L*) GREYLAG GOOSE (origin of other Domestic Geese) Europe, temperate and sub-tropical Asia/vegetarian/n ground / e 4–7 rarely 12/I ♀ 27–8

Anser albifrons (*Scopoli*) WHITE-FRONTED GOOSE Holarctic, discontinuous, various races/ n ground in tundra/e 4–7/I ♀ 28

Anser erythropus (*L*) LESSER WHITE-FRONTED GOOSE b Siberian tundra w Asia and E. Europe / n ground / e 4–5 rarely –7 / I ♀ 25

Anser fabalis (*Latham*) BEAN GOOSE Eurasia except the S, and SW Europe/n ground/e 4–8/ I ♀ 25–9 [NB: The various races of this species are very complicated. *A. brachyrhynchus* Baillon, Pink-footed Goose, is regarded as a race of the Bean. *A. neglectus* Sushkin, is a synonym of *A. fabalis*]

Anser coerulescens (*L*) SNOW GOOSE (including BLUE GOOSE) N America, E Greenland and extreme E Siberia to Japan/n ground/e 4–7/ I ♀ 22–5 [NB: there are 2 races, the Greater Snow Goose (monomorphic) and the Lesser (dimorphic), the Blue Goose being the dark phase Lesser. In some literature these are listed as 3 species]

Anser rossi (*Cassin*) ROSS'S GOOSE b Perry River, Canada w S to California/n ground/e 5–9/ I ♀ 24

Anser canagicus (*Sewastianov*) EMPEROR GOOSE Bering Sea area and Kamchatka / n ground/e 3–8/I ♀ 24

Anser indicus (*Latham*) BAR-HEADED GOOSE Central Asia w India/n beside lakes, ground/ e 3–8/I ♀ 28–30

Branta sandvicensis (*Vigors*) HAWAIIAN GOOSE or NÉNÉ Hawaii (rare)/uplands/fruits and herbs/n ground/e 5–8/I ♀ 30

Branta canadensis (*L*) CANADA GOOSE N America, Kamchatka to Japan, feral in Europe and New Zealand; about 12 races, varying enormously in size/n ground/e 4–10/I ♀ 25–30

Branta leucopsis (*Bechstein*) BARNACLE GOOSE b E Greenland, Spitzbergen and S Novaya Zemlya w NW Europe/grass, leaves and moss/ n outcrops and cliff ledges/e 3–6 /I ♀(?) 24–5

Branta ruficollis (*Pallas*) RED-BREASTED GOOSE W Siberia w Caspian and Aral Sea areas/ n cliffs and bluffs/e 5–9/I 25

Branta bernicla (*L*) BRENT GOOSE or BRANT Circumpolar and marine arctic, S in winter along coasts/grasses etc/n among rocks/e 3–8/ I ♀(?), 30(?), 24–5(?) reports differ

Cereopsis novaehollandiae *Latham* CAPE BARREN GOOSE Islands off coast of S Australia/ grass/n ground/e n/s/I ♀ 35

Cereopsis novaezeelandiae *Forbes* NEW ZEALAND CAPE BARREN GOOSE New Zealand/ bones only

Pachyanas chathamica *Oliver* CHATHAM DUCK Chatham Is/extinct/bones only

Euryanas finschi *Van Beneden* NEW ZEALAND DUCK S Island, New Zealand/bones only

Cnemionis calcitrans *Owen* SOUTH ISLAND GOOSE S Island, New Zealand/bones only

Cnemiornis septentrionalis *Oliver* NORTH ISLAND GOOSE N Island, New Zealand/bones only

Chloephaga melanoptera (*Eyton*) ANDEAN GOOSE Andes of Peru and Chile / grass / n ground on moors/e 6–10/I ♀ 30

Chloephaga poliocephala *Sclater* ASHY-HEADED GOOSE Southern S America/n ground/ e 4–6/I ♀ 30

Chloephaga rubidiceps *Sclater* RUDDY-HEADED GOOSE Falklands and Tierra del Fuego/ grass/n among tussocks/e 4–11/I ♀ 30

Chloephaga picta (*Gmelin*) (= **C. leucoptera**

Plate 16

FREGATIDAE:
Fregata magnificens,
Man-o'war Bird or
Magnificent Frigate Bird

ARDEIDAE:
Ixobrychus minutus,
Little Bittern

ARDEIDAE: *Botaurus stellaris,* Eurasian Bittern

Opposite:
ANHINGIDAE:
Anhinga anhinga,
Anhinga, Darter or
Snake Bird

Plate 17

(*Gmelin*)) MAGELLAN or UPLAND GOOSE S Chile, S Argentina, Tierra del Fuego and Falklands/ n among bushes on ground / e 5–7 / I ♀ 30–2 [*Chloephaga dispar* Phillipi and Landbeck, is a colour morph of this species]

Chloephaga hybrida (*Molina*) KELP GOOSE Coasts of S Chile, Tierra del Fuego and Falklands / seaweeds / n shores / e 5–6 / I ♀ about 30

Cyanochen cyanopterus (*Rüppell*) BLUE-WINGED GOOSE Mts of Ethiopia / invertebrates / n n/s/e 6–7/I ♀ 30

Neochen jubata (*Spix*) ORINOCO GOOSE Amazon and Orinoco basins / grass and weeds / n hollow trees / e 6–10 / I 28–30

Alopochen aegyptiacus (*L*) EGYPTIAN GOOSE Africa (except deserts and deep forest) and N to Syria / grass and leaves / n ground, ledges or trees / e 5–8 / I 28–30

Tadorna tadornoides (*Jardine and Selby*) AUSTRALIAN SHELDUCK or MOUNTAIN DUCK S Australia and Tasmania / grass and water weeds / n holes / e 8–15 / I ♀ 30–3

Tadorna variegata (*Gmelin*) PARADISE SHELDUCK New Zealand / weeds etc / n holes in trees or burrows / e 5–11 / I 30

Tadorna cana (*Gmelin*) SOUTH AFRICAN SHELDUCK S Africa / n burrow / e 6–15 / I 30

Tadorna ferruginea (*Pallas*) RUDDY SHELDUCK N Africa and temperate Asia w S Asia and Nile basin / vagrant elsewhere / grass and invertebrates / n rock holes, burrows or hollow trees / e 6–16 / I ♀ 28–30

Tadorna radjah (*Lesson*) RADJAH SHELDUCK N and NE Australia, New Guinea, Moluccas and adjacent islands / invertebrates / n tree holes / e 6–12 / I 30

Tadorna tadorna (*L*) COMMON SHELDUCK Temperate and sub-tropical Eurasia, salt-water / invertebrates / n burrow / e 8–16 / I ♀ 28–30

Tadorna cristata (*Kuroda*) KOREAN CRESTED SHELDUCK Korea and Ussuriland, probably extinct

Lophonetta specularoides (*King*) CRESTED DUCK Andes and Patagonia / invertebrates / n burrow / e 5–8 / I 30

Tachyeres pteneres (*Forster*) MAGELLANIC FLIGHTLESS STEAMER DUCK S Chile to Staten Is / e 6–12

Tachyeres brachypterus (*Latham*) FALKLAND FLIGHTLESS STEAMER DUCK Falklands / n sandy hummocks / e 6–12

Tachyeres patachonicus (*King*) FLYING STEAMER DUCK S Chile to Tierra del Fuego, Falklands / invertebrates / n ground / e 7–9

Anas sparsa *Eyton* AFRICAN BLACK DUCK Central and S Africa / seeds and water weeds / n reeds and holes / e 5–11 / I ♀ 25

Anas specularis *King* BRONZE-WINGED DUCK S Andes / weeds and invertebrates / n ? / e ?

Anas platyrhynchos *L* MALLARD N Hemisphere, temperate and sub-tropical areas / n ground or holes / e 7–16 / I ♀ 22–8 [*A. laysanensis* (Laysan Duck), extinct, was a race]

Anas rubripes *Brewster* AMERICAN BLACK DUCK Eastern N America (as Mallard)

Anas poecilorhyncha *Forster* SPOT-BILLED DUCK India, Ceylon, N Burma, N Vietnam, China, Ussuriland, Korea, Japan (discontinuous) / e 8–14 / I ♀ (?♂) 24

Anas superciliosa *Gmelin* GREY DUCK Indonesia to Tahiti, Australia, Tasmania, New Zealand and the Chathams / e 5–13 / I ♀ 28

Anas luzonica *Fraser* PHILIPPINE DUCK Philippines / n long grass / e 10 / I ♀ 25–6

Anas melleri *Sclater* MELLER'S DUCK Madagascar, introduced Mauritius / I 28

Anas undulata *DuBois* YELLOW-BILLED DUCK E and S Africa / e 6–12 / I ♀ 26–7

Anas gibberifrons *Müller* GREY TEAL Australasia and Andamans / n hole / e 8–12 / I ♀ 24

Anas bernieri (*Hartlaub*) MADAGASCAR TEAL W Madagascar / no data

Anas castanea (*Eyton*) CHESTNUT TEAL Australia and Tasmania / n ground, bushes or tree holes / e 7–13 / I ♀ 23

Anas aucklandica (*Gray*) BROWN TEAL New Zealand and adjacent islands / n ground / e 5–8 / I n/k [Birds from Auckland Is are a distinct, flightless race, e 3–4, I 18+ ♀ (see Weller, *Auk* (1975), pp 280–297)]

Anas flavirostris *Vieillot* CHILEAN TEAL Parts of S America / n ground or hole / e 5–6 / I ♀ 26

Anas crecca *L* COMMON TEAL and AMERICAN GREEN-WINGED TEAL Temperate Holarctic w N Africa and S Asia / weeds and invertebrates / n ground / e 8–16 / I ♀ 21–2

Anas formosa *Georgi* BAIKAL TEAL E Asia / n in grass or willows / e 8–10 / I ♀ 28

Anas falcata *Georgi* FALCATED TEAL E Asia / n ground / e 6–10 / I ♀ 24–5

Anas strepera *L* GADWALL N Hemisphere S of

60° (and Fanning Is, probably extinct)/weeds and invertebrates/n ground/e 7–16/I ♀ 27–8

Anas penelope L EUROPEAN WIGEON Eurasia and N Africa/weeds/n ground/e 6–10/I ♀ 24–5

Anas americana *Gmelin* AMERICAN WIGEON N America/weeds/n ground/e 6–13/I ♀ 24–5

Anas sibilatrix *Poeppig* CHILOË WIGEON Southern S America/e 6–9/I ♀ 24–5

Anas bahamensis L BAHAMA PINTAIL Parts of S America, W Indies and Galapagos (discontinuous)/e 6–10/I ♀ 25–6

Anas georgica *Gmelin* YELLOW-BILLED PINTAIL Andes and southern S America, Falklands and S Georgia/e 5–12/I 24–5

Anas acuta L NORTHERN PINTAIL Holarctic/weeds/n ground/e 6–12/I ♀ 23 [*A. eatoni* Sharpe, Kerguelen Is, and *A. drygalskii* Reichenow, Crozets, are dull races]

Anas erythrorhyncha *Gmelin* RED-BILLED TEAL E and S Africa/n reed beds/e 6–12/I ♀ 23–5 (?)

Anas angustirostris *Ménétriès* MARBLED TEAL Mediterranean E to Persia and N India/n reeds/e 9–13/I ♀ 25

Anas capensis *Gmelin* CAPE TEAL C and S Africa/n ground/e 6–9/I ♀ 21

Anas punctata *Burchell* HOTTENTOT TEAL S and E Africa, Madagascar/n papyrus beds/e 6–8/I 18–20

Anas versicolor *Vieillot* SILVER TEAL Southern S America and Falklands/n reeds/e 5–10/I ♀ 24–5

Anas querquedula L GARGANEY Eurasia (except N), NE and W Africa, Indonesia/weeds and invertebrates/n ground/e 7–14/I ♀ 21–3

Anas discors L BLUE-WINGED TEAL East N America w through C and northern S America/weeds and invertebrates/n in long grass/e 6–15/I ♀ 23–4

Anas cyanoptera *Vieillot* CINNAMON TEAL W America, N and S (discontinuous)/n reeds/e 6–14/I ♀ 24–5

Anas platalea *Vieillot* RED SHOVELER Southern S America/e 6–8/I ♀ 25

Anas smithi *Hartert* CAPE SHOVELER S Africa/n reeds/e n/k

Anas rhynchotis *Latham* AUSTRALIAN SHOVELER Australia, Tasmania, New Zealand/e 7–10/I ♀ 24

Anas clypeata L NORTHERN SHOVELER, SPOONBILL (America) Much of Holarctic/n reed beds/e 7–14/I ♀ 23–5

Anas waigiuensis (*Rothschild and Hartert*) SALVADORI'S TEAL Waigeu Is and mts of New Guinea/mountain streams

Anas leucophrys *Vieillot* RINGED TEAL S Bolivia to Uruguay and N Argentina/e 5–8/I 23

Anas theodori *Newton and Gadow* THEODORE'S DUCK Mauritius/extinct/bones only

Rhodonessa caryophyllacea (*Latham*) PINK-HEADED DUCK India-Oudh and Nepal to Manipur and Assam/very rare, believed extinct/n ground/e 5–10

Malacorhynchus membranaceus (*Latham*) PINK-EARED DUCK Australia and Tasmania/n tree limb or tree hole/e 3–6/I ♂♀

Hymenolaimus malacorhynchos (*Gmelin*) BLUE MOUNTAIN DUCK New Zealand/mountain torrents/e 4–5

Merganetta armata *Gould* TORRENT DUCK Andes/n ground/e 2–5

Stictonetta naevosa (*Gould*) FRECKLED DUCK Tasmania and parts of Australia/rare/n bushes/e 6–10

Polysticta stelleri (*Pallas*) STELLER'S EIDER E Siberia and Alaska w in N Pacific/marine/mollusca etc/n ground/e 6–10/I ♀

Somateria mollissima (L) COMMON EIDER Almost circumpolar/marine/mollusca etc/n ground/e 4–6 rarely 3–10/I ♀ 27–8

Somateria fischeri (*Brandt*) SPECTACLED EIDER E Siberia and Alaska w Aleutians/marine/n ground/e 5–9/I ♀

Somateria spectabilis (L) KING EIDER Circumpolar/marine but b fresh water/mollusca etc/n ground/e 4–7/I ♀

Netta rufina (*Pallas*) RED-CRESTED POCHARD Parts of Europe, S and C Asia/mainly vegetable/n ground/e 6–13/I ♀ 26–8

Netta peposaca (*Vieillot*) ROSYBILL Southern central S America/mainly vegetable/n ground/e –14/I ♀ 23–5

Netta erythropthalma (*Wied*) SOUTHERN POCHARD Northern S America, S and E Africa (2 races)/mainly vegetable/n ground/e 5–9/I ♀ 23–5

Aythya valisineria (*Wilson*) CANVASBACK N America/weeds and seeds/n ground/e 7–10/I ♀ 23–8

Aythya ferina (L) EUROPEAN POCHARD N Europe, W and C Asia w S Europe and S Asia/mainly vegetable/n ground/e 6–16/I ♀ 24–6

Aythya americana (*Eyton*) REDHEAD

ARDEIDAE:
Egretta ardesiaca,
Black Heron

ARDEIDAE:
Egretta thula,
Snowy Egret

ARDEIDAE:
Egretta intermedia,
Median Egret,
Intermediate Egret

Plate 18

ARDEIDAE:
Ardea pacifica,
White-necked Heron

ARDEIDAE:
Bulbulcus ibis,
Cattle Egret or
Buff-backed Heron

ARDEIDAE:
Tigrisoma lineatum,
Rufescent Tiger Heron

Plate 19

SC Canada and USA/water weeds/n ground/ e 10–16/I ♀ 24

Aythya innotata (*Salvadori*) MADAGASCAN WHITE-EYED POCHARD E Madagascar/n ground/ e 6–8/I ♀ 26–8

Aythya australis (*Eyton*) AUSTRALASIAN WHITE-EYED POCHARD Australasia, New Zealand and Solomons / n ground / e –16 / I ♀

Aythya nyroca (*Güldenstädt*) FERRUGINOUS DUCK or WHITE-EYED POCHARD S and E Europe, N Africa, S and W Asia/ varied diet/ n ground/e 7–14/I ♀ 25–7

Aythya baeri (*Radde*) BAER'S POCHARD Amurland w Japan, China, SE Asia/n ground

Aythya collaris (*Donovan*) RING-NECKED DUCK S Canada and USA/'four fifths vegetable' (Delacour)/n ground/e 8–12/I ♀

Aythya fuligula (*L*) TUFTED DUCK Palaearctic and Oriental (except extreme S) / omnivorous / n ground / e 6–14/I ♀ 23–5

Aythya novaeseelandiae (*Gmelin*) NEW ZEALAND SCAUP New Zealand, Auckland and Chatham Is/fresh water/n ground/e 5–8

Aythya affinis (*Eyton*) LESSER SCAUP or LITTLE BLUEBILL N and C America/inland and marine/ omnivorous/n ground/e 9–15/I ♀ 23–6

Aythya marila (*L*) GREATER SCAUP or BLUEBILL N Palaearctic and NW Nearctic w further S / marine and inland / mollusca etc/ n ground/e 7–12/I ♀ 23–7

Amazonetta brasiliensis (*Gmelin*) BRAZILIAN TEAL Eastern S America / forest waters omnivorous / n ground or tree / e 6–8 / I 25

Chenonetta jubata (*Latham*) MANED DUCK Australia and Tasmania / grain etc / n holes/ e 8–10/I 28

Aix sponsa (*L*) CAROLINA or WOOD DUCK N America / inland / vegetable / n tree-holes/ e 10–14/I ♀ 28–32

Aix galericulata (*L*) MANDARIN DUCK Amurland to N China and Japan w further S feral in England/inland/vegetable/n tree-holes/ e 9–12/I ♀ 28–30

Nettapus auritus (*Boddaert*) AFRICAN PYGMY GOOSE Africa, S of Sahara, Madagascar/inland/ water-lily seeds/n hole/e 8–13

Nettapus pulchellus *Gould* GREEN PYGMY GOOSE N Australia and parts of New Guinea and Indonesia/inland/n holes and reeds/e 8–13

Nettapus coromandelianus (*Gmelin*) COTTON PYGMY GOOSE or COTTON TEAL Indian sub-continent, S China, SE Asia, Indonesia to

parts of New Guinea and NE Australia/inland/ seeds and leaves/n holes/e 8–15/I ♀ 15–16

Sarkidiornis melanotus (*Pennant*) COMB DUCK Northern S America, Africa S of Sahara, Indian sub-continent and SE Asia / inland/ aquatic vegetation/n holes/e 7–15/I 30 (♀?)

Sarkidiornis mauritiana *Newton and Gadow* BLACK AND WHITE WINGED COMB DUCK Mauritius and (?)Réunion/bones and travellers' accounts

Cairina moschata (*L*) MUSCOVY DUCK C and tropical S America / inland / vegetable / n 'hollows'/e 8–15/I 35

Cairina scutulata (*Müller*) WHITE-WINGED DUCK SE Asia, Sumatra and Java / inland/ grain, fish etc/n holes/e 7–10/I 30

Cairina hartlaubii (*Cassin*) HARTLAUB'S DUCK W Africa/inland/n and e n/k

Plectropus gambensis (*L*) SPUR-WINGED GOOSE Africa S of Sahara except the SW/inland/ n ground/e 7–12/I n/k

Melanitta nigra (*L*) COMMON or BLACK SCOTER N Palaearctic and Bering Sea w further S and coasts of N America / marine / mollusca/ n ground inland/e 5–7 rarely 13/I ♀ 27–8

Melanitta fusca (*L*) VELVET SCOTER N Holarctic, but absent from some parts/marine and inland / mollusca / n ground inland / e 5–8 rarely –14 / I ♀ 27–8

Melanitta perspicillata (*L*) SURF SCOTER Parts of N America/marine, b inland/mollusca/ n ground inland/e 5–9/I ♀

Camptorhynchus labradorius (*Gmelin*) LABRADOR DUCK Atlantic coast of N America/ extinct 1875

Histrionicus histrionicus (*L*) HARLEQUIN DUCK N Pacific and W Atlantic /marine, b inland / mollusca etc / n ground inland / e 5–8/ I ♀ 31–2

Clangula hyemalis (*L*) LONG-TAILED DUCK Circumpolar w further S / marine, b inland/ mollusca/n ground/e 5–11/I ♀ 23–4

Bucephala clangula (*L*) GOLDENEYE Holarctic/marine and brackish, b inland/mollusca/ n ground and holes/e 6–15/I ♀ 26

Bucephala islandica (*Gmelin*) BARROW'S GOLDENEYE Iceland, S Greenland, Labrador and Pacific N America / marine, b inland / n holes/e 8–15/I 30

Bucephala albeola (*L*) BUFFLE-HEAD N America/ inland and marine / animal and vegetable/n hole/e 7–16/I ♀ 21–2

Mergus albellus *L* Smew Parts of Palaearctic/ inland and marine/fish etc/n hole/e 5–14/I ♀

Mergus cucullatus *L* Hooded Merganser S Canada and USA / inland / insects and mollusca/n hole/e 5–12/I ♀ 31(?)

Mergus octosetaceus *Vieillot* Brazilian Merganser SE Brazil/n hole

Mergus australis *Hombron and Jacquinot* Auckland Islands Merganser Auckland Is/ believed extinct

Mergus serrator *L* Red-breasted Merganser Holarctic except boreal and continental areas/ inland and marine / fish / n ground / e 7–19/ I ♀ 29

Mergus squamatus *Gould* Chinese Merganser Amur and Manchuria w Korea and China/inland and brackish/fish

Mergus merganser *L* Goosander Holarctic except boreal and continental areas/inland and brackish/fish/n ground/e 7–16/I ♀ 34–5

Oxyura jamaicensis *(Gmelin)* Ruddy Duck Central and southern N America, C America and the Andes / inland / vegetable / n ground/ e 6–20/I 20–1

Oxyura vittata *(Philippi)* Argentine Ruddy Duck Southern S America

Oxyura maccoa *(Eyton)* Maccoa Duck E and S Africa/inland/n reed beds/e 3–7

Oxyura australis *Gould* Blue-billed Duck S Australia and Tasmania /lakes/ e 5–6

Oxyura leucocephala *(Scopoli)* White-headed Duck Locally in parts of S Europe and WC Asia/inland /n ground/e 6–13

Oxyura dominica *(L)* Masked Duck Caribbean and tropical S America / inland/ vegetable/ n rushes/e 3–4

Thalassornis leuconotus *Eyton* White-backed Duck E and S Africa and Madagascar/ inland /seeds / n floating /e 3–7 8–14 (accounts differ)

Biziura lobata *(Shaw)* Musk Duck Southern Australia and Tasmania / inland / animal / n tree or rushes/e 2–3

Heteronetta atricapilla *(Merrem)* Black-headed Duck S America from S Brazil to N Argentina/inland/P

CATHARTIDAE New World Vultures (Condors and Turkey Vultures) Large birds of prey of ancient lineage, dating from the Oligocene, and differing structurally from Old World vultures which they superficially resemble. Largely carrion-eating. Strong fliers, voiceless, and with weaker bills than most other birds of prey.

Cathartes aura *(L)* Turkey Vulture Temerate and tropical America/plains, desert and forest/n hole/e 2/I ♂♀ 38–41/ F 70–80

Cathartes burrovianus *Cassin* (= **C. urubitinga,** *Pelzeln*) Yellow-headed Vulture Mexico, C and S America / data uncertain, but similar to *C. aura*

Cathartes melambrotus *Wetmore* Greater Yellow-headed Vulture Northern S America/ no data

Coragyps atratus *(Bechstein)* Black Vulture USA, C and S America/plains, forests, habitation/n ground or hole/e 2/I ♂♀ 32–9/ F 39

Sarcorhamphus papa *(L)* King Vulture Mexico to Argentina/ forest and savannah/ n hollow stump (1 known)/e 1 (captivity)/I ♂♀ 56–8

Sarcorhamphus sacra *(Bartram)* Painted Vulture Florida and (?) Carolina / extinct/ probably a race of *S. papa* (See Harper, *Auk* (1936), pp 381–92 and *Auk* (1942), p 104)

Gymnogyps californianus *(Shaw)* Californian Condor California (decreasing and endangered) formerly from Washington to Lower California / mountains / n usually cave floors/e 1/I ♂♀ 42–50 ?/ F n/s but young bird tended for over a year, parents breed only every other year

Vultur gryphus *L* Andean Condor Andes/ mountains / n ledge / e 1 / I ♂♀ 54–8/ young capable of flight at 6 months but cared for, for over a year. Parents breed every other year

PANDIONIDAE Osprey Large hawk, size of a small eagle. Wings long and narrow. Lower surface of toes has sharp spikes which help in holding the fish on which it feeds. One species

Pandion haliaetus *L* Osprey Almost cosmopolitan/ lakes, rivers and coasts/ n tree / e 2–4/ I ♂♀ 32–8/ F c42

ACCIPITRIDAE Hawks, Eagles, Buzzards, Kites and Old World Vultures Diurnal, raptorial birds with sharply hooked bills and fleshy ceres. Feet and claws strong and powerful. In size variable, from sparrow sized to some of the largest flying birds. Almost entirely carnivorous. Reproductive rate slow, clutch size small, and life span usually comparatively long. The arrangement and data for the Birds of Prey follows Brown and Amadon *Eagles, Hawks and Falcons of the World* (2 vols), 1968

ARDEIDAE:
Egretta alba,
Great White Heron,
Great White Egret or
Large Egret, Great Egret

ARDEIDAE:
Bubulcus ibis,
Cattle Egret or
Buff-backed Heron

Plate 20

ARDEIDAE:
Ardea
cinerea,
Grey
Heron

Plate 21

Aviceda cuculoides *Swainson* AFRICAN BAZA
S half of Africa / woodland / insects and lizards /
n tree / e 2–3 / I 33 ?

Aviceda madagascariensis (*Smith*)
MADAGASCAR BAZA Madagascar / woodland and
scrub / reptiles / n and e no data

Aviceda jerdoni (*Blyth*) JERDON'S BAZA
India (discontinuous); Ceylon and SE Asia to
Indonesia / forests / insects and small verte-
brates / n tree / e 2–3

Aviceda subcristata (*Gould*) CRESTED BAZA
Lombok to Solomons and Australia / forests /
insects and small animals / n tree / e 2–3 rarely
4 / I ♂♀

Aviceda leuphotes (*Dumont*) BLACK BAZA
Nepal to Szechwan and S China w in India
and SE Asia / mountains / insects and small
animals / n tree / e 2–3 / I ♂♀

Leptodon cayennensis (*Gmelin*) (=
Odontriorchis (**Falco**) **palliatus**
Temminck) CAYENNE KITE Mexico and trop-
ical S America / forests / invertebrates / e ?3 / no
other data [*Odontriorchis* (= *Leptodon*) *forbesi*
Swann has been described, but considered by
Brown to be an immature variant. The form is
known only from one skin]

Chondrohierax uncinatus (*Temminck*)
HOOK-BILLED KITE Tropical America / forests /
largely snails / n tree / e ?2 [Several species
formerly recognised, now combined in 1]

Henicopernis longicauda (*Garnot*) LONG-
TAILED HONEY BUZZARD New Guinea and
adjacent islands / forests / insects

Henicopernis infuscata *Gurney* BLACK
HONEY BUZZARD New Britain / no data

Pernis apivorus (*L*) COMMON HONEY
BUZZARD Eurasia and Indonesia / woodlands /
chiefly wasps and bees / n tree / e 1–3 / I ♂♀ 30–5 /
F 40–4 but return to nest for feeding till 55 days
old

Pernis celebensis *Walden* BARRED HONEY
BUZZARD Celebes and Philippines / data probably as for common species but poorly docu-
mented

Elanoides forficatus (*L*) SWALLOW-TAILED
KITE Eastern USA, C and much of S America /
forest and swamps / insects / n tree / e 2–4

Machaerhamphus alcinus *Westerman* BAT
HAWK SE Asia to New Guinea and Africa S of
Sahara / forest and bushveld / bats and birds /
n tree / e 1–2 / I ♀ c30 / F 35–40

Gampsonyx swainsonii *Vigors* PEARL KITE

S America / savannah / birds and insects / n tree /
e ?3 / I ♀ (1 nest known)

Elanus leucurus (*Vieillot*) WHITE-TAILED KITE
USA, C and S America / open country / mice /
n tree / e 4–5 / I ♀ c30 / F 35–40

Elanus caeruleus (*Desfontaines*) BLACK-
SHOULDERED KITE Africa, S Asia and Indonesia /
savannah / insects and small vertebrates / n tree /
e 3–5 / I ♂♀ 25–8 / F 30–5

Elanus notatus *Gould* AUSTRALIAN BLACK-
SHOULDERED KITE Australia / open country / mice /
n tree / e 3–4

Elanus scriptus *Gould* LETTER-WINGED KITE
Interior of Australia / dry country / mammals /
n tree / e 3–6 / I ♀ 21+ / F c35

Chelictinia riocourii (*Vieillot*) AFRICAN
SWALLOW-TAILED KITE Africa / desert / insects /
n tree / e 4

Rostrhamus sociabilis (*Vieillot*) EVERGLADE
KITE Caribbean and S America / near fresh
water / snails / n grass or bush / e 3–4 /
I ♂♀

Rostrhamus hamatus (*Temminck*) SLENDER-
BILLED KITE Northern S America / woods /
snails / n tree (1 nest known)

Harpagus bidentatus (*Latham*) DOUBLE-
TOOTHED KITE Central and northern S America
rain forest / lizards and insects / n tree / e ?1–2

Harpagus diodon (*Temminck*) RUFOUS-
THIGHED KITE North and east S America / n tree /
e ?2 (1 set known)

Ictinia plumbea (*Gmelin*) PLUMBEOUS KITE
Tropical zone of New World / forest / insects /
n tree / e 1–2 / F c30

Ictinia misisippiensis (*Wilson*) MISSISSIPPI
KITE USA and C America / woods or open
country / insects / n tree / e 1–3 (usually 2) /
I ♂♀ 30 / F 34

Lophoictinia isura (*Gould*) SQUARE-TAILED
KITE Australia / open country / varied diet / n
tree / e 2–3 / I ♀

Hamirostra melanosternon (*Gould*) BLACK-
BREASTED BUZZARD KITE Australia / open country /
varied diet including eggs / n tree / e 2 / I ♀

Milvus migrans (*Boddaert*) BLACK KITE
Europe, Africa, S Asia to S China, New Guinea
and Australia / habitat variable / omnivorous
(scavenger) / n tree, building or crag / e 1–5 /
I ♂♀ 38 / F 42

Milvus milvus (*L*) RED KITE Europe, W Asia
and N Africa / woods / mammals and birds /
n tree / e 1–5 / I ♀ 28–30 / F45–50

[*Milvus lineatus* (Gray) formerly considered distinct, is now included in *Milvus migrans*, and *M. fasciicauda* (Hartert) from the Cape Verde Is, though generally included in *M. milvus*, may perhaps be a race of *M. migrans*, or a distinct species]

Haliastur sphenurus (*Vieillot*) WHISTLING EAGLE Australia, New Guinea, New Caledonia, Solomon Is (?Tasmania)/ near water/animals and insects/n tree/e 2–3/ F 40+
Haliastur indus (*Boddaert*) BRAHMINY KITE India to S China, Australasia and Solomons/ near water/scavenger/n tree/e 1–4/I ♀ 26–7 ?/ F 50–5
Haliaeetus leucogaster (*Gmelin*) WHITE-BELLIED SEA EAGLE India to S China, Australasia and the Bismarck Archipelago/ coasts and rivers/fish and carrion/n tree or rock/ e 2–3/I ♂♀ (mostly ♀) 51 ?/F 65–70
Haliaeetus sanfordi *Mayr, Am Mus Novit* no 820 (1935) p 1, SANFORD'S EAGLE Solomon Islands/coast and forest/fish, birds etc
Haliaeetus vocifer (*Daudin*) AFRICAN FISH EAGLE Africa S of Sahara/lakes and rivers/fish/ n tree/e 1–3/I ♀ (sometimes also ♂) 44–5/ F 65–70
Haliaeetus vociferoides *Des Murs* MADAGASCAR FISH EAGLE Madagascar / coast/ fish/n tree/no other data
Haliaeetus leucoryphus (*Pallas*) PALLAS' EAGLE Interior of Asia / lakes and rivers/ fish/ n tree or ground/e 2–4/I ♀ ?♂ 30–40 (accounts differ)/F 70–105
Haliaeetus leucocephalus (*L*) BALD EAGLE N America, decreasing/coasts, lakes and rivers/ fish, birds and mammals/n tree, rock or ground/ e 1–3/I ♂♀ 31–46/F 70–7
Haliaeetus albicilla (*L*) WHITE-TAILED EAGLE Greenland and much of the N Palaearctic/ coasts, rivers and lakes/fish, birds and mammals/ n tree or crag/e 1–3/I ♂♀ 35–45/ F 70
Haliaeetus pelagicus (*Pallas*) STELLER'S EAGLE E Asia from Kamchatka to Japan/coasts/ fish and birds/n tree or crag/e 1–3/I ? 38–45/ F 70 [*H. niger* Heude from Korea has been variously described as a species, a race of *H. pelagicus*, or a colour phase of same. Accounts conflict]
Harpagornis moorei *Haast* MOORE'S EAGLE New Zealand/bones only
Harpagornis assimilis *Haast* HAAST'S EAGLE

New Zealand/bones only
Icthyophaga nana (*Blyth*) LESSER FISHING EAGLE Himalayas to SE Asia, Borneo and Celebes/forest rivers/fish/n tree/e 2–3
Icthyophaga icthyaetus (*Horsfield*) GREY-HEADED or GREATER FISHING EAGLE India to SE Asia and Philippines / forest rivers / fish/ n tree/e 2–4/I ♂♀ 28–30
Gypohierax angolensis (*Gmelin*) PALM NUT VULTURE Africa S of Sahara / forest and savannah/ husk of oil-palm nuts / n tree / e 1/ I 44/F 90+ ?
Neophron percnopterus (*L*) EGYPTIAN VULTURE S Europe, Africa, Middle East, India/ open country / refuse and carrion / n crags or buildings/e 1–3/I ♂♀ 42/F c90
Gypaetus barbatus (*L*) LAMMERGEIER or BEARDED VULTURE S Europe to Africa, India and Tibet/ mountains / bones and carrion / n crags/ e 1–2/I ?♀ 53/F 110 (details from captive birds)
Necrosyrtes monachus (*Temminck*) HOODED VULTURE W, E and SE Africa / forest and habitation / carrion / n tree or crag / e 1 / I ♀ (sometimes also ♂) 46/F 120
Gyps bengalensis (*Gmelin*) INDIAN WHITE-BACKED VULTURE India and SE Asia/woods and cultivation / carrion / n tree / e 1 / I ♂♀ 45–52/ F c90
Gyps africanus *Salvadori* AFRICAN WHITE-BACKED VULTURE W and E Africa / savannah/ carrion/n tree/e 1/I ♀
Gyps indicus (*Scopoli*) INDIAN VULTURE India and SE Asia / savannah and cultivation/ carrion/n tree or crag/e 1/I ♂♀ c50
Gyps rueppellii (*Brehm*) RÜPPELL'S VULTURE Drier parts of Africa / carrion / n crag / e 1–2/ I n/k/F c90
Gyps himalayensis *Hume* HIMALAYAN VULTURE Mountains from Turkestan to Tibet and Koko Nor/carrion/n cliff/e 1
Gyps fulvus (*Hablizl*) GRYPHON VULTURE S Europe, N Africa and Asia to Himalayas/ mountains/carrion/n crags/e 1/I ♂♀ c52/F c70
Gyps coprotheres (*Forster*) CAPE VULTURE S Africa/mountains and plains/carrion/n cliffs/ e 1/I ♂♀ 52+/ F c80–90
Torgos tracheliotus (*Forster*) LAPPET-FACED VULTURE Africa/bush and desert/carrion, eggs and insects/n tree/e 1/I n/k/F c110–20
Sarcogyps calvus (*Scopoli*) INDIAN BLACK or KING VULTURE India, SE Asia and Yunnan/ jungle/carrion/n tree/e 1/I ♂♀ 45

ARDEIDAE:
Egretta garzetta,
Little Egret

ARDEIDAE:
Botaurus poiciloptilus, Brown
Bittern, Australian Bittern

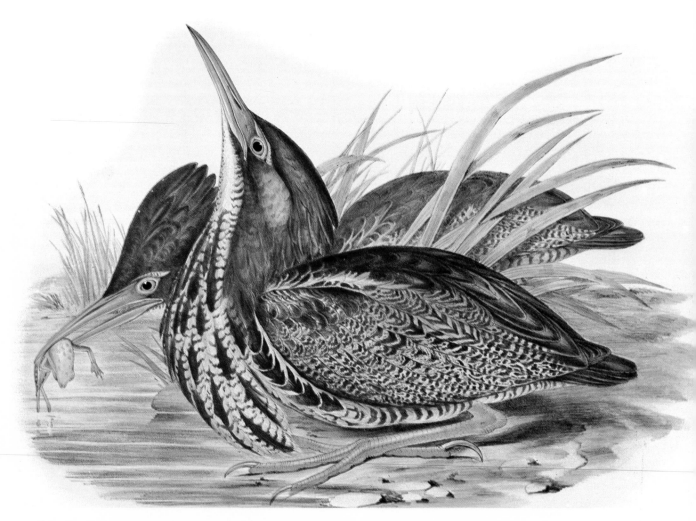

Plate 22

BALAENICIPITIDAE:
Balaeniceps rex,
Shoebill or Whalehead,
Whale-headed Stork

The Cattle Egret,
Bubulcus ibis, catches more insects by following large animals than by hunting alone.

Plate 23

Aegypius monachus (*L*) CINEREOUS VULTURE Mediterranean across Asia to Urals, Himalayas, China and Japan / mountains / carrion / n tree or rock ledge / e 1 / I ♂♀ 52–5 / F 90–150 (accounts vary)

Trigonoceps occipitalis (*Burchell*) WHITE-HEADED VULTURE Africa S of Sahara / bush and desert / carrion / n tree / e 1 / I ♀ 43

Circaetus gallicus (*Gmelin*) SHORT-TOED EAGLE Africa and S Europe E to India and Mongolia, and in winter to Indonesia / desert and savannah / mainly reptiles / n tree / e 1 / I ♀ (rarely also ♂) 47 / F 70–5

Circaetus cinereus *Vieillot* BROWN HARRIER EAGLE Africa S of Sahara / wooded country / reptiles / n tree / e 1 / I ♀ 40–52 / F 85

Circaetus fasciolatus *Gurney* BANDED SNAKE EAGLE E Africa / forested valleys / reptiles / n tree / no other data

Circaetus cinerascens *Müller* SMALL SNAKE EAGLE Tropical Africa / wet savannahs / snakes / n tree / e 1

Terathopius ecaudatus (*Daudin*) BATELEUR Africa S of Sahara / open country / carrion and small animals / n tree / e 1 I ♀ 42–3 / F 90–125

Spilornis holospilus (*Vigors*) PHILIPPINE SERPENT EAGLE Philippines / wooded valleys / virtually no data

Spilornis rufipectus *Gould* CELEBES SERPENT EAGLE Celebes and Sula Is / savannah / reptiles / n and e n/k

Spilornis cheela (*Latham*) CRESTED SERPENT EAGLE India to S China, SE Asia and Indonesia / forests / reptiles / n tree / e 1 / I ♀ 35 / F c60

Amadon lists the following forms, hitherto regarded as races, as possible species, but requiring further study:

S. minimus C Nicobar Is
S. abbotti Simeulue, W Sumatran Is
S. asturinus (=*salvadorii*) Nias, Sumatran Is
S. sipora Mentawai group, Sumatran Is
S. kinabaluensis Borneo
S. spilonotus (?=*holospilus*) Philippines

but see Amadon, *Bull BOC*, 94 (1974), p 159 for a recent discussion of this genus

Spilornis klossi *Richmond* NICOBAR SERPENT EAGLE Great Nicobar Is / no data

Spilornis elgini (*Blyth*) ANDAMAN SERPENT EAGLE Andaman Is / forests of interior / n n/k

Dryotriorchis spectabilis (*Schlegel*) CONGO SERPENT EAGLE W and C Africa / forests / reptiles / n n/k

Eutriorchis astur *Sharpe* MADAGASCAR SERPENT EAGLE Madagascar / humid forests of NE / no data

Polyboroides typus *Smith* (not *typicus*, Smith) GYMNOGENE Africa S of Sahara / forests / omnivorous / n tree / e 1–3 / I ♂♀ 40 ? / F c60

Polyboroides radiatus (*Scopoli*) MADAGASCAR HARRIER HAWK Madagascar / woods / varied / n tree / e n/k

Geranospiza caerulescens (*Vieillot*) CRANE HAWK Mexico to Paraguay / woodland near water / reptiles, insects, birds / n tree

Circus assimilis *Jardine and Selby* SPOTTED HARRIER Australia, Tasmania, Celebes and nearby islands / dry places / lizards and insects / n tree / e 2–4 / I ?♀

Circus aeruginosus (*L*) MARSH HARRIER, SWAMP HAWK Almost the whole of the Old World / marshes / frogs etc / n ground / e 3–8 / I ♀ 33–8 / F 40

Circus ranivorus (*Daudin*) AFRICAN HARRIER E and S Africa / marshes / mammals and birds / n ground / e 3–5 / I ♂♀ 30 / F 38–41

Circus maurus (*Temminck*) BLACK HARRIER Natal and Cape Province / marshes / frogs etc

Circus cyaneus (*L*) HEN HARRIER or MARSH HAWK Holarctic, widely distributed / moors / mammals etc / n ground / e 4–12 / I ♀ 29–39 / F 35

Circus cinereus *Vieillot* CINEREOUS HARRIER Southern S America and Falklands / open country / n ground / e 3–4

Circus macrourus (*S. G. Gmelin*) PALLID HARRIER E Europe to Tianshan w S to Africa and India / plain and steppe / vertebrates and insects / n ground / e 3–6 / I ♀ 30 / F 35–45

Circus pygargus (*L*) MONTAGU'S HARRIER Europe and W Asia w S to Africa and India / moors and marshes / varied / n ground / e 3–10 / I ♀ 27–30 / F 32–42

Circus melanoleucus (*Pennant*) PIED HARRIER E Asia / marshes / frogs etc / n ground / e 4–5 / I ♀ 30 / F c70 ?

Circus buffoni (*Gmelin*) LONG-WINGED HARRIER Eastern S America / marshes / vertebrates / n ground

NB: *Circus spilonotus*, Kaup and *C. approximans*, Peale, formerly considered distinct, are now

...

regarded as sub-species of *aeruginosus*

Circus eylesi *Scarlett* EYLES'S HARRIER New Zealand / bones only

Melierax metabates *Heuglin* DARK CHANTING GOSHAWK W and C Africa and SW Arabia / bush and scrub / vertebrates / n tree/ e 1–2/ I ♀

Melierax canorus *Rislach* (= **M. musicus** (*Daudin*)) PALE CHANTING GOSHAWK E and S Africa / bush and desert / lizards and insects/ n tree/e 1–2/I ♀

Melierax gabar (*Daudin*) GABAR GOSHAWK Africa S of Sahara and SW Arabia / savannah and bush/birds/n tree/e 1–3/ I ♀ 33/ F 30+

Megatriorchis doriae *Salvadori and D'Albertis* DORIA'S GOSHAWK New Guinea / forest / birds, including birds of paradise/no other data

Erythrotriorchis radiatus (*Latham*) RED GOSHAWK Interior of N and E Australia/ brushwood along rivers / birds, lizards and fish/ n tree/e 1–2 (?3)

Accipiter gentilis (*L*) NORTHERN GOSHAWK Much of Holarctic, N to timber line/forest and woodland / birds and small mammals / n tree/ e 1–5/I ♂♀ but mainly ♀ 36–8/F 45

Accipiter henstii (*Schlegel*) HENST'S GOSHAWK Madagascar / forest and savannah / birds and small mammals/n tree/e 2 (1 nest known)

Accipiter melanoleucus *Smith* BLACK or GREAT SPARROWHAWK Forested areas of Africa S of Sahara/birds and small mammals/n tree/ e 2–4/I ♀ ? 30/ F 35

Accipiter meyerianus (*Sharpe*) MEYER'S GOSHAWK Moluccas, Solomons, New Britain, Japen (? New Guinea)/virtually no data

Accipiter buergersi (*Reichenow*) BÜRGER'S SPARROWHAWK Lower mts of E New Guinea/ forest/no data

Accipiter ovampensis *Gurney* OVAMPO SPARROWHAWK Ghana to Ethiopia and S to SW Africa and Transvaal/savannah and thornbush veld/birds, small mammals and insects/n tree/ e 2–3

Accipiter madagascariensis *Smith* MADAGASCAR SPARROWHAWK Madagascar/scrub and savannah/n tree/e 3 (1 nest known)

Accipiter gularis (*Temminck and Schlegel*) JAPANESE LESSER SPARROWHAWK Sayan, Kentei, Manchuria, Korea, S Kuriles, Hondo, Ryukyus and E China w SE Asia and Indonesia/forest and woodland/birds/n tree/e 3

Accipiter virgatus (*Temminck*) BESRA SPARROWHAWK Indian sub-continent to mts of S China; Philippines, Java, Sumatra and Borneo/ forest / small birds, lizards and insects/ n tree/e 2–5

Accipiter nanus *Stresemann* (in *Orn Monatsber*, 40 (1932), pp 113–15) CELEBES LITTLE SPARROWHAWK Mts of Celebes/mountain forest/ birds and insects/n tree

Accipiter rhodogaster (*Schlegel*) VINOUS-BREASTED SPARROWHAWK Celebes, Muna, Buton, Peling, Banggai, Sula Is/forest/birds, mammals, lizards and insects/n and e n/k

Accipiter erythrauchen *Gray* MOLUCCAN SPARROWHAWK Moluccas/no data

Accipiter cirrocephalus (*Vieillot*) COLLARED SPARROWHAWK Australia, Tasmania, New Guinea, Louisiades, islands W of New Guinea/ scrub and woodland/birds/n tree/e 2–4/I ♀ 19

Accipiter brachyurus (*Ramsay*) NEW BRITAIN SPARROWHAWK New Britain no data

Accipiter nisus (*L*) EUROPEAN SPARROWHAWK b Europe, Middle East, N Africa and Asia to N India, W China and S Kamchatka w Africa, India and Burma/forest, woodland and cultivation/mainly birds, some other small vertebrates and insects/n tree/e 2–7/I ♀ (rarely ♂) 39–42 (total) 32–5 per egg/F 24–30

Accipiter rufiventris *Smith* RUFOUS-BREASTED SPARROWHAWK E and S Africa from Ethiopia to Cape / forest and woodland / birds, small mammals and insects/n tree/e 2–4/I n/k/F 25

Accipiter striatus *Vieillot* SHARP-SHINNED HAWK Widely but irregularly through the Americas, but not breeding in the whole of its range / forest and brush / birds, occasionally small mammals, lizards, insects/n tree/e 4–5/ I ♂♀ 34–5/F 23

Accipiter erythropus (*Hartlaub*) RED-THIGHED SPARROWHAWK Forests of W Africa from Gambia to W Uganda and Angola/birds and insects/n and e no data

Accipiter minullus (*Daudin*) AFRICAN LITTLE SPARROWHAWK E and S Africa from Ethiopia to Cape/ woodland, veld and cultivation / birds, mammals, insects/n tree/e 2–3/I ♂♀ 31–2/ F 25–6

Accipiter castanilius *Bonaparte* CHESTNUT-BELLIED SPARROWHAWK Nigeria and Cameroon E to E Congo / deep forest / birds, lizards and mammals/n and e n/k

Accipiter tachiro (*Daudin*) AFRICAN

Plate 24

Opposite:
CICONIIDAE:
Ciconia ciconia,
White Stork

CICONIIDAE:
Ephippiorhynchus senegalensis,
Saddle-bill Stork

CICONIIDAE:
Leptoptilos crumeniferus,
Marabou Stork

L. crumeniferus is often considered rather ugly because of its naked, pink throat sac and its pointed, massive bill.

Plate 25

GOSHAWK Africa S of Sahara/forest and woodland/birds, mammals, lizards, frogs and insects/ n tree/e 2-3/I ♀ 28-30/F 32

Accipiter trivirgatus (*Temminck*) CRESTED GOSHAWK Indian sub-continent, SE Asia, Yunnan, S China, Taiwan, Sumatra, Java, Borneo, Philippines / forest and cultivation/ birds, mammals and lizards/n tree/e 2-3/I and F no definite data

Accipiter griseiceps (*Schlegel*) CELEBES CRESTED GOSHAWK Celebes, Muna, Buton and Togian / forest / birds, mammals, lizards and insects/n tree

Accipiter trinotatus *Bonaparte* SPOT-TAILED ACCIPITER Celebes, Muna and Buton / forest/ chiefly reptiles

Accipiter luteoschistaceus *Rothschild and Hartert* BLUE AND GREY SPARROWHAWK New Britain/no data

Accipiter fasciatus (*Vigors and Horsfield*) AUSTRALIAN GOSHAWK Australia, Tasmania, New Guinea, Rennell Is and islands N and W to Flores, Timor and Christmas Is (Indian Ocean) and E to New Caledonia and Loyalty Is/ forest clearings, savannah and open grassland/ mammals, birds, reptiles, insects and centipedes/ n tree/e 2-4/I ♀ (?♂) 30/F c30

Accipiter henicogrammus (*Gray*) GRAY'S GOSHAWK Batjan, Halmahera and Morotai / no data

Accipiter novaehollandiae (*Gmelin*) WHITE, GREY and VINOUS-CHESTED GOSHAWKS (various races) Australia, Tasmania, New Guinea and islands W to Sumbawa and E to Solomons / forest, woodland and cultivation/birds, mammals, reptiles, insects/n tree/e 2-4/I ♂♀

Accipiter griseogularis (*Gray*) GREY-THROATED GOSHAWK Moluccas / forest / rats, lizards

Accipiter melanochlamys (*Salvadori*) BLACK-MANTLED ACCIPITER Mountain forests of New Guinea/birds, frogs, insects/n and e n/k

Accipiter imitator *Hartert* IMITATOR SPARROWHAWK Choiseul and Ysabel in Solomons/no data

Accipiter albogularis *Gray* PIED GOSHAWK Solomon Is, Santa Cruz Is, Feni Is/ no data [*Accipiter eichorni* Hartert, formerly considered distinct, in now treated as a race of *albogularis*]

Accipiter haplochrous *Sclater* NEW CALEDONIA SPARROWHAWK New Caledonia/ forest/ birds, lizards, insects

Accipiter rufitorques (*Peale*) FIJI GOSHAWK Fiji and (? Rotuma) / lizards, insects, birds / n tree/e 1-3

Accipiter poliocephalus *Gray* NEW GUINEA GREY-HEADED GOSHAWK New Guinea and adjacent islands / ? forest / reptiles and insects/ no other data

Accipiter princeps *Mayr* (in *Am Mus Novit*, no 709 (1932), p 3) NEW BRITAIN GREY-HEADED GOSHAWK New Britain/3 specimens/no data

Accipiter soloensis (*Horsfield*) GREY FROG HAWK b Korea, China and Taiwan w Indonesia / woodlands, swamps and ricefields/ chiefly frogs/n tree/e 2-5/I ♀ c30

Accipiter brevipes (*Severtzov*) LEVANT SPARROWHAWK b Balkans to S Russia and Asia Minor w SW Persia to Egypt/forest and woodland / birds and mammals / n tree / e 3-5 / I ♀ (?21-35) F ?40-5

Accipiter badius (*Gmelin*) SHIKRA S Asia N to Transcaucasia and S China; Africa S of Sahara savannah and cultivation / mainly lizards, also birds, mammals and insects/n tree/ e 2-7/I ♀ 30-5, 18-21 (accounts differ)/F c30

Accipiter butleri (*Gurney*) NICOBAR SHIKRA Nicobar Is/in trees/lizards/n tree

Accipiter francesii *Smith* FRANCE'S SPARROWHAWK Madagascar and Comoros/ forest and savannah/reptiles, insects and birds/ n tree/e 3-4/I ♀

Accipiter collaris *Sclater* AMERICAN COLLARED SPARROWHAWK Mts from Merida (Venezuela) to Santa Marta (Colombia)/forest/ known only from a few specimens

Accipiter superciliosis (*L*) TINY SPARROWHAWK Nicaragua to Peru and N Argentina / forest borders / n tree / e 3 (1 nest known)/no other data

Accipiter gundlachi *Lawrence* GUNDLACH'S HAWK Cuba/rare and possibly extinct/no data

Accipiter cooperii (*Bonaparte*) COOPER'S HAWK S Canada, USA and N Mexico / forest/ mainly birds/n tree/e 4-6/I ♀(♂) 34-6/F 30-4

Accipiter bicolor (*Vieillot*) BI-COLOURED HAWK S Mexico to Tierra del Fuego and Staten Is / forest / birds / n tree / e 4 / I ♀ 20-1 (*A. guttifer* and *A. chilensis* are sometimes considered distinct species)

Accipiter poliogaster (*Temminck*) GREY-BELLIED GOSHAWK Lowland forests of S America / no data [*A. pectoralis* (Bonaparte) is the immature plumage]

Accipiter alphonsi *Newton and Gadow* ALPHONSE'S SPARROWHAWK Mauritius / bones only

Urotriorchis macrourus (*Hartlaub*) AFRICAN LONG-TAILED HAWK Rain forests of W and C Africa from Ghana to Congo / small mammals and birds / n and e n/k

Butastur rufipennis (*Sundevall*) GRASSHOPPER BUZZARD EAGLE Africa in the savannah belt just S of Sahara / insects / n tree / e 1–3

Butastur liventer (*Temminck*) RUFOUS-WINGED BUZZARD EAGLE SE Asia, Borneo, Java, Celebes, Banggai and Sula Archipelago / savannah and cultivation / n tree / e 2–3

Butastur teesa (*Franklin*) WHITE-EYED BUZZARD EAGLE India and Burma / thin woodland, open country and cultivation / insects, lizards etc / n tree / e 2–3 / I ♀ c19

Butastur indicus (*Gmelin*) GREY-FACED BUZZARD EAGLE b Ussuriland, S Manchuria, Japan and E China w SE Asia and Indonesia / wooded country / reptiles, insects, frogs, small mammals / n tree / e 2–3 / I ♀ / F 35

Kaupifalco monogrammicus (*Temminck*) LIZARD BUZZARD Africa S of Sahara / savannah / reptiles, small mammals, birds and insects / n tree / e 1–3 / I ♀ / F ?30

Leucopternis schistacea (*Sundevall*) SLATE-COLOURED HAWK Amazon basin / forest / no data

Leucopternis plumbea *Salvin* PLUMBEOUS HAWK E Panama, W Colombia, W Ecuador and NW Peru / forest / no data

Leucopternis princeps *Sclater* BARRED or PRINCE'S HAWK Costa Rica to Ecuador / forest / reptiles ? / no other data

Leucopternis melanops (*Latham*) BLACK-FACED HAWK Amazon basin N of Amazon forest / reptiles ? / no other data

Leucopternis kuhli *Bonaparte* WHITE-BROWED HAWK Amazon basin S of Amazon / forest / no data

Leucopternis lacernulata (*Temminck*) WHITE-NECKED HAWK E and S Brazil / forest / insects / no other data

Leucopternis semiplumbea *Lawrence* SEMIPLUMBEOUS HAWK Nicaragua to NW Ecuador / forest / reptiles and (?) birds / n tree

Leucopternis albicollis (*Latham*) WHITE HAWK Mexico S to Bolivia and Mato Grosso / forest edges / reptiles / n tree / e ?1

Leucopternis occidentalis *Salvin* GREY-BACKED HAWK W Ecuador / no data

Leucopternis polionota *Kaup* MANTLED HAWK E and S Brazil, Paraguay and N Argentina / small snakes and birds

Buteogallus anthracinus (*Lichtenstein*) COMMON BLACK HAWK Southern USA, C America, W Indies and N coast of S America, pacific S America S to Peru (*B. subtilis* and *B. gundlachii* are sometimes separated) / savannah, mangrove, wooded streams / small vertebrates, crabs, insects / n tree / e 1–3

Buteogallus aequinoctialis (*Gmelin*) RUFOUS CRAB HAWK or AEQUINOCTIAL HAWK Swampy forests of Atlantic coast of S America from Orinoco Delta to Paraná / crabs / n tree / e 1–2

Buteogallus urubitinga (*Gmelin*) GREAT BLACK HAWK Mexico, C America and much of tropical S America S to N Argentina / forest and scrub, usually near water / small vertebrates, crabs, insects / n tree / e ?1

Harpyhaliaetus solitarius (*Tschudi*) BLACK SOLITARY EAGLE C America and Pacific slope of S America to Peru / forest / snakes / n tree / e ?1

Harpyhaliaetus coronatus (*Vieillot*) CROWNED SOLITARY EAGLE Bolivia, Paraguay, S Brazil, S to N Patagonia / chaco and savannah / ? mammals and birds / n and e n/k

Heterospizias meridionalis (*Latham*) SAVANNAH HAWK E Panama through much of tropical S America to C Argentina / savannah and marsh / vertebrates and invertebrates / n tree / e 1–2

Busarellus nigricollis (*Latham*) FISHING BUZZARD or BLACK-COLLARED HAWK Tropical lowlands from Mexico to Paraguay and north central Argentina / open country near water / chiefly fish / n tree / e n/s

Geranoaetus melanoleucos (*Vieillot*) (= **Buteo fuscescens** (*Vieillot*)) GREY or BLACK-CHESTED EAGLE-BUZZARD Andes from Venezuela to Tierra del Fuego / thin woodland and steppe / small mammals and birds / n tree or cliff ledge / e 2

Parabuteo unicinctus (*Temminck*) BAY-WINGED or HARRIS'S HAWK Lowlands from south-western USA to S Chile and C Argentina / sparse woodland and semi-desert / birds and mammals / n tree / e 2–4 / I 28 / F c37

Buteo nitidus (*Latham*) GREY HAWK, MEXICAN GOSHAWK or SHINING BUZZARD South-western USA to E Bolivia, S Brazil and north central Argentina / thin wood and riverine

CICONIIDAE:
Mycteria ibis,
Wood Ibis,
Yellow-billed Stork

THRESKIORNITHIDAE:
Eudocimus albus,
American White Ibis

Plate 26

THRESKIORNITHIDAE:
Ajaia ajaja,
Roseate Spoonbill

THRESKIORNITHIDAE:
Threskiornis molucca,
Australian White Ibis

Plate 27

forest / chiefly reptiles / n tree / e 1–3 / I ♂♀

Buteo magnirostris (*Gmelin*) ROADSIDE, INSECT or LARGE-BILLED HAWK Mexico to C Argentina / varied habitat / vertebrates and invertebrates, particularly insects / n tree / e 2 (?1)

Buteo leucorrhous (*Quoy and Gaimard*) RUFOUS-THIGHED HAWK Mts from Venezuela to NW Argentina / broken forest / beetles ?

Buteo ridgwayi (*Cory*) RIDGWAY'S HAWK Hispaniola and offshore islets / forest / birds, lizards and mammals / n tree (2 known) / e n/k

Buteo lineatus (*Gmelin*) RED-SHOULDERED HAWK S Canada, USA and N Mexico / woodland and open country / omnivorous / n tree / e 2–5 / I ♂♀ 28 / F 35–40

Buteo platypterus (*Vieillot*) BROAD-WINGED HAWK Eastern N America and parts of W Indies / forest / invertebrates, reptiles, batracians and mammals / n tree / e 2–4 / I ♂♀ 21–5 / F 41

Buteo brachyurus *Vieillot* SHORT-TAILED HAWK S Florida, C Mexico S to N Argentina / local / mangrove (Florida), broken country and hill-forest / rodents, birds and insects / n tree / e n/s (all known nests from Florida)

Buteo swainsonii *Bonaparte* SWAINSON'S HAWK b western N America from Alaska to Mexico w pampas of Argentina but range and movements imperfectly understood / plains and open country / largely insects, also small vertebrates / n tree, cactus, cliff, bank or ground / e 2–4 / I ♂♀ 28 / F c28

Buteo galapagoensis (*Gould*) GALAPAGOS HAWK Galapagos / ? ubiquitous / varied diet / n tree or ground / e 1–2

Buteo albicaudatus *Vieillot* WHITE-TAILED HAWK S Texas to northern fringe of Patagonia / open country and thin forest / vertebrates / n tree / e 1–3

Buteo polyosoma (*Quoy and Gaimard*) RED-BACKED or VARIABLE HAWK Andes from Colombia to Tierra del Fuego, Falklands and Mas Afuera / open country / vertebrates and insects / n tree, cactus or grass tussock / e 1–3 / I ♂♀ 40–50

Buteo poecilochrous *Gurney* GURNEY'S BUZZARD High Andes from Colombia to N Chile and NW Argentina / n ?cliff

Buteo albonotatus *Kaup* ZONE-TAILED HAWK Locally distributed from southern USA to Bolivia and Paraguay / dry deciduous forest / vertebrates / n tree / e 1–3

Buteo solitarius *Peale* HAWAIIAN HAWK Island of Hawaii / almost ubiquitous between 2,000 and 5,000ft (600–1,500m) / mainly rats / n tree / e n/k

Buteo ventralis *Gould* RUFOUS-TAILED HAWK Forests of Patagonia / n tree / e ?1–3

Buteo jamaicensis (*Gmelin*) RED-TAILED HAWK N and C America from timber-line S to Panama, W Indies / varied habitat / vertebrates and landcrabs / n tree or cactus / e 1–4 / I ♂♀ 28–32 / F 45

Buteo buteo (*L*) COMMON BUZZARD b much of Palaearctic w Africa and S Asia / forest and moor / rodents, birds, reptiles and large insects / n tree or crag / e 1–6 / I ♂♀ 33–5 / F 30+

Buteo oreophilus *Hartert and Neumann* AFRICAN MOUNTAIN BUZZARD S Ethiopia to the Cape / mountain forest / reptiles, frogs, mammals and insects / n tree / e 2 / I ♀ 30 / F ?40

Buteo brachypterus *Hartlaub* MADAGASCAR BUZZARD Madagascar / woodland and savannah up to 6,000ft (1,800m) / insects and vertebrates / n tree or crag / e 2 / I ♀

Buteo lagopus (*Pontoppidan*) ROUGH-LEGGED BUZZARD Holarctic, but not breeding throughout its range / tundra and moor / birds and mammals / n rock ledge / e 3–4 (up to 7 in lemming-years) / I ♀ (sometimes ♂) 28–31 / F 41

Buteo rufinus (*Cretzschmar*) LONG-LEGGED BUZZARD Dry, open plains of SE Europe; N Africa, and Asia to Afghanistan / mammals, lizards and carrion / n tree, crag or ground / e 2–5

Buteo hemilasius *Temminck and Schlegel* UPLAND BUZZARD b C Asia from Altai to Transbaikalia and Tibet w N India, Burma, China and Korea / steppe / mammals and birds / n crag / e 2–5 / I c30 / F 45

Buteo regalis (*Gray*) FERRUGINOUS HAWK SW Canada and western USA w southwestern USA and N Mexico / open dry country / mainly small mammals / n tree or bluff / e 3–5 / I ?28

Buteo auguralis *Salvadori* AFRICAN RED-TAILED BUZZARD Sierra Leone to Ethiopia and Angola / forest and savannah / reptiles, mammals, frogs and insects / n tree or crag / e 2–3 / I ♂♀

Buteo rufofuscus (*Forster*) JACKAL or AUGUR BUZZARD Ethiopia and Somaliland to the Cape / savannah / vertebrates and insects / n tree or crag / e 1–3 / I ♀ ? 35–40 / F 70

Morphnus guianensis (*Daudin*) GUIANA CRESTED EAGLE Honduras to N Paraguay and

Argentina / lowland rain forest / no data [*M. taeniatus* Gurney, is a colour phase]

Harpia harpyja (*L*) HARPY EAGLE S Mexico to N Argentina / lowland forest / mammals and birds / n tree / e ?2

Harpyopsis novaeguineae *Salvadori* HARPY-LIKE EAGLE New Guinea / lowland forest / n tree / e ?1

Pithecophaga jefferyi *Ogilvie-Grant* MONKEY-EATING EAGLE Philippines: Leyte, Samar (extinct on both), Luzon (possibly extinct), Mindanao (believed about 50 pairs remain)/forest 500–4,000ft (150–1,200m)/mammals / n tree / e 1/ I ♂♀ 60/ F c105

Ictinaetus malayensis (*Temminck*) INDIAN BLACK EAGLE Indian sub-continent and SE Asia to Moluccas / hill forest / mammals, birds and eggs/ n tree / e 1–2/ I ?♀

Aquila pomarina *Brehm* LESSER SPOTTED EAGLE Discontinuous, b C and E Europe, Caucasus and Transcaucasia w Africa: India and N Burma (resident)/forest and woodland/ small mammals, birds, insects etc/n tree/e 1–3/ I ♀ (rarely ♂) 42–5/ F 50–5

Aquila clanga *Pallas* GREATER SPOTTED EAGLE b N Europe across Asia to Amurland and S to Persia and NW India w S Europe, NE Africa and S Asia / forest and savannah / small mammals, birds, insects etc/n tree or ground/e 1–3/ I ♀ 42–4/F 60–5

Aquila rapax (*Temminck*) TAWNY EAGLE Rumania to Transbaikalia, Mongolia and India, much of Africa / savannah, steppe and desert / carrion, small animals and insects/n tree, crag or ground / e 1–3 / I ♂♀ 45/ F 55 [*A. nipalensis* (Hodgson) 'Steppe Eagle', formerly separated, is now regarded as conspecific]

Aquila heliaca *Savigny* IMPERIAL EAGLE S Europe, Morocco and E across Asia to Lake Baikal, N India and China w N Africa and S Asia / lowland plains / mammals, reptiles, birds and carrion/ n tree / e 2–3/ I ♂♀ 43/ F 60

Aquila wahlbergi *Sundevall* WAHLBERG'S EAGLE Savannahs of Africa S of Sahara, except the extreme S / reptiles, small mammals and birds / n tree / e 1–2/ I ♀ (rarely ♂) 46/ F 62–80

Aquila gurneyi *Gray* GURNEY'S EAGLE W New Guinea, W Papuan Is and Moluccas/ apparently no data (formerly placed in *Spizaetus*)

Aquila chrysaetos (*L*) GOLDEN EAGLE Holarctic/moor and mountain forest/mammals and

birds/n crag, ledge or tree/e 1–3/I ♀ or ♂♀ 43–5 ?35/ F 65–80

Aquila audax (*Latham*) WEDGE-TAILED EAGLE Australia, Tasmania and ? New Guinea/forest, savannah and desert / mammals, birds and carrion /n tree or ground / e 1–3/ I ♀/ F 63–70

Aquila verreauxii *Lesson* VERREAUX'S EAGLE Africa S of Sahara / mountains, desert, scrub and savannah / mammals and sometimes birds/ n crag or tree/e 1–3/ I ♂♀ 43–6/ F 95–9

Hieraaetus fasciatus (*Vieillot*) BONELLI'S EAGLE S Europe, S Asia, Lesser Sunda Is, Africa S of Sahara / mountain forest, bush and savannah / mammals and birds / n tree or crag/ e 1–3/ I ♂♀ 42–3/ F 55–80

Hieraaetus pennatus (*Gmelin*) BOOTED EAGLE S Europe, N Africa and Asia E to Transbaikalia w Africa and S Asia / forest and woodland/ mammals, birds and reptiles / n tree or crag/ e 1–2/ I ?♀ ?30

Hieraaetus morphnoides (*Gould*) LITTLE EAGLE Australia and New Guinea / forest/ mainly mammals / n tree / e 1–2/ I ♀/F 45–50

Hieraaetus dubius (*Smith*) (= *H. ayresii* (*Gurney*)) AYRES' HAWK EAGLE Africa S of Sahara / forest and well-wooded savannah/ mainly birds/ n tree / e 1–2/ I ♀ 45/ F 75

Hieraaetus kienerii (*Geoffroy*) CHESTNUT-BELLIED HAWK EAGLE Ceylon and SW India: Himalayas to Malay Peninsula and through Indonesia to Celebes and Philippines (discontinuous) / forest / birds and small mammals/ n tree/e 1/ I ♂♀

Spizastur melanoleucus (*Vieillot*) BLACK AND WHITE HAWK EAGLE Mexico, C America, S America E of Andes and S to N Argentina/ forest and open forest / ? birds

Lophaetus occipitalis (*Daudin*) LONG-CRESTED EAGLE Africa S of Sahara / cultivation and well-wooded savannah / chiefly mammals/ n tree /e 1–2/ I ♀/ F 55

Spizaetus africanus (*Cassin*) CASSIN'S HAWK EAGLE Rain forests of W Africa from Togoland to Gabon and Congo / birds and squirrels / no other data

Spizaetus cirrhatus (*Gmelin*) CHANGEABLE HAWK EAGLE, CRESTED HAWK EAGLE (the insular forms are uncrested) India, Ceylon, SE Asia, through Indonesia to Philippines / savannah and cultivation (continental forms) forest (insular forms) / mammals, birds and reptiles/ n tree /e 1/ I ♀

Plate 28

Opposite:
A young *P. ruber* among adult birds.

ANHIMIDAE:
Anhima cornuta,
Horned Screamer

PHOENICOPTERIDAE:
Phoenicopterus ruber,
Rosy or Scarlet Flamingo,
Greater Flamingo

Plate 29

Spizaetus nipalensis (*Hodgson*) HODGSON'S, MOUNTAIN or FEATHER-TOED HAWK EAGLE Continental Asia S of Himalayas and E to S China; Ceylon, Hainan, Taiwan, Japan / mountain forest / mammals, birds and reptiles / n tree / e 1 (? 3 in Japan) / I ♀ / I + F = 80

Spizaetus bartelsi *Stresemann* JAVA HAWK EAGLE Wooded hills of W Java / rare / no data

Spizaetus lanceolatus *Temminck and Schlegel* CELEBES HAWK EAGLE Celebes and Sula Is / forest / n tree (1 known)

Spizaetus philippensis *Gould* PHILIPPINE HAWK EAGLE Philippines and Palawan / rare / no data

Spizaetus alboniger (*Blyth*) BLYTH'S HAWK EAGLE Mountain forests of S Burma, Malay Peninsula, Sumatra, N Pagi and Borneo / mammals and birds

Spizaetus nanus *Wallace* WALLACE'S HAWK EAGLE Lowland forests of Malaya, Borneo, Sumatra and Nias / no data (this species for long was confused with immature plumages of *S. alboniger*. Synonymised with same by Sharpe in Catalogue of Birds of the British Museum. Omitted from Peters' *Check List*, vol 1)

Spizaetus tyrannus (*Wied*) BLACK HAWK EAGLE Lowland forests from Mexico to N Argentina / no data

[**Spizaetus devillei** *Dubois* is the immature of *Oroaetus isidori*]

Spizaetus ornatus (*Daudin*) ORNATE HAWK EAGLE Rain forested lowlands from Mexico to N Argentina / birds and mammals / n tree (1 known)

Stephanoaetus coronatus (*L*) CROWNED EAGLE Africa S of Sahara / forest and rocky hill / mainly mammals / n tree / e 1–2 / I ♂♀ 49 / F 270–350

Oroaetus isidori (*Des Murs*) ISIDOR'S EAGLE Slopes of Andes from Venezuela to NW Argentina / hill forest / mammals and birds / n tree / e 1 (?) / I ?♀

Polemaetus bellicosus (*Daudin*) MARTIAL EAGLE Africa S of Sahara / savannah and thornbush / mammals, birds and reptiles / n tree / I ♀ (?♂) c45 (33+ 48—) / F 99

SAGITTARIIDAE Secretary Bird Large, terrestrial eagle-like bird with rounded wings and very long legs. A crest of long spatulate feathers on head. Taxonomic position uncertain; usually placed with the birds of prey but has resemblances also to the Cariamidae and the fossil family Phororhacidae. One species

Sagittarius serpentarius (*Miller*) SECRETARY BIRD Africa S of Sahara / open grassy country / small mammals, insects, birds, eggs and snakes / n tree / e 2–3 / I ♀ (?♂) c45 / F c40

FALCONIDAE Falcons and Caracaras Long-winged, streamlined raptors with bare tarsi and feet. True falcons are generally swift-flying predatory species, Caracaras sluggish and scavenging.

Daptrius ater *Vieillot* BLACK, or YELLOW-THROATED CARACARA Amazon basin and the Guianas / forest and savannah / carrion, insects and fruit / n and e no reliable data; said to nest in a tree and lay 2–3 eggs

Daptrius americanus (*Boddaert*) RED-THROATED CARACARA S Mexico S to C Peru and Mato Grosso / humid forest / wasp larvae, fruit and seeds / n ? tree / e ? 2–3

Phalcoboenus carunculatus *Des Murs* CARUNCULATED CARACARA Andes of Ecuador and SW Colombia / virtually no data

Phalcoboenus megalopterus (*Meyen*) MOUNTAIN CARACARA Andes from Peru to N Chile and NW Argentina / mountains above timber-line / carrion, insects, birds etc / n cliff / e 2–3

Phalcoboenus albogularis *Gould* WHITE-THROATED or DARWIN'S CARACARA Andes of Chile and Argentina; Patagonia and Tierra del Fuego / forest / no other reliable data

Phalcoboenus australis (*Gmelin*) FORSTER'S or STRIATED CARACARA Falklands, and islands off Tierra del Fuego / scavenger / n grass tussock / e 1–3

Polyborus lutosus *Ridgway* GUADALUPE CARACARA Guadalupe Is (California) / extinct c1900

Polyborus plancus (*Miller*) COMMON CARACARA Extreme south of USA, S to Tierra del Fuego / open country / omnivorous / n tree or ground / e 2–4 / I ?♀ 28 [*P. cheriway* (Jacquin) 'Cheriway Caracara' is now regarded as conspecific]

Milvago chimango (*Vieillot*) CHIMANGO Tierra del Fuego N to S Brazil / open country / omnivorous / n tree or ground / e 2–3

Milvago chimachima (*Vieillot*) YELLOW-HEADED CARACARA Panama and much of S America S to N Argentina / scrub and savannah / omnivorous / n tree / e ?2

Herpetotheres cachinnans (*L*) LAUGHING

FALCON Tropical lowlands from Mexico to N Argentina / open forest / reptiles / n tree-cavity / e 1

Micrastur ruficollis (*Vieillot*) BARRED FOREST FALCON S Mexico S to N Argentina / forest / no data

Micrastur plumbeus *Sclater* SCLATER'S FOREST FALCON Lowlands of W Colombia and NW Ecuador / rare / no data

Micrastur mirandollei (*Schlegel*) SLATY FOREST FALCON Lowland forests from Costa Rica to Peru and E to Guianas and Para / no data

Micrastur semitorquatus (*Vieillot*) COLLARED FOREST FALCON Tropical forests from Mexico to N Argentina / birds, mammals, reptiles and insects / n and e n/k

Micrastur buckleyi *Swann* BUCKLEY'S FOREST FALCON Amazonian Ecuador and Peru / known from about 10 specimens / no data

Spiziapteryx circumcinctus (*Kaup*) SPOT-WINGED FALCONET Deserts and semi-deserts of W and N Argentina / no data

Polihierax semitorquatus (*Smith*) AFRICAN PYGMY FALCON E and S Africa from S Sudan to R Orange / desert and thornbush / insects and small animals / n in nests of other species (eg weavers) / e 2–3 / I ♀

Polihierax insignis *Walden* FIELDEN'S FALCONET SE Asia / open woodland / insects and small birds / n and e no reliable data

Microhierax caerulescens (*L*) RED-LEGGED FALCONET Himalayas and N India, through SE Asia (except Malay Peninsula) / forest / insects / n hole / e 4–5 / I ?♀

Microhierax fringillarius (*Drapiez*) BLACK-LEGGED FALCONET Malay Peninsula, Sumatra, Java, Bali, Borneo / forest / insects / n hole / e 2–5 / I ♂♀

Microhierax latifrons *Sharpe* BORNEAN FALCONET NW Borneo / forest / insects / n and e n/k

Microhierax erythrogonys (*Vigors*) PHILIPPINE FALCONET Philippines / forest / insects / n hole

Microhierax melanoleucus (*Blyth*) PIED FALCONET Assam, SE China, Laos and N Annam / forest / insects and small vertebrates / n hole / e 3–4

Falco naumanni *Fleischer* LESSER KESTREL Mediterranean region E across southern central Asia to China w S to Africa and India / desert, steppe and cultivation / insects, also small vertebrates / n building, cliff or hole in tree / e 3–6 / I ♂♀ mainly ♀ 28 / F 26–8

Falco rupicoloides *Smith* GREATER or WHITE-EYED KESTREL E and S Africa from Somalia to Cape / scrubby plains / insects and small vertebrates / n tree / e 3–5

Falco alopex (*Heuglin*) FOX KESTREL Dry belt from Ghana to Sudan, Ethiopia and Kenya / rocky hills and gorges / insects and small mammals / n hole in cliff / e n/s

Falco sparverius *L* AMERICAN KESTREL or SPARROW HAWK The Americas N and S to treeline, West Indies and Juan Fernandez / open country, scrub and desert / large insects and small vertebrates / n hole / e 3–7 / I ♀ (rarely ♂) 29–30 / F 30

Falco tinnunculus *L* COMMON KESTREL Much of Europe, Asia and Africa / plains, heaths and cultivation / mainly small mammals and birds, also insects, small reptiles, frogs etc / n hole or ledge / e 4–9 / I ♀ (sometimes ♂) 27–9 / F 27–34

Falco newtoni (*Gurney*) MADAGASCAR KESTREL and ALDABRA KESTREL Madagascar: Aldabra (2 races) open country and cultivation / insects and small vertebrates / n hole in tree, rock or building / e n/s / I ?♀

Falco punctatus *Temminck* MAURITIUS KESTREL Mauritius, now confined to a few forested localities, and almost extinct / birds and insects

Falco araea (*Oberholzer*) SEYCHELLES KESTREL Seychelles / forest and cultivation / lizards / n hole in rock or building / e 1–2

Falco moluccensis (*Bonaparte*) MOLUCCAN KESTREL Java through Lesser Sundas to Celebes and Moluccas / open country / insects and small vertebrates / n not described / e 4

Falco cenchroides *Vigors and Horsfield* NANKEEN KESTREL Australia (? Tasmania) and mts of New Guinea, wandering in winter to Java / open country and habitation / insects, small birds and mammals / n hole in tree or rock / e 4–5 / I ♀ 26 / F 21

Falco ardosiaceus *Vieillot* GREY KESTREL Moist savannah regions of Africa S of Sahara / mainly insects and lizards / n hole or old nest of other species / e 3–5 / I ♀

Falco dickinsoni *Sclater* DICKINSON'S KESTREL Africa from Tanzania to Portuguese E Africa and W to Angola / savannah / insects

ANATIDAE: *Anser anser,* Greylag Goose

ANATIDAE: *Anser cygnoides,* Swan Goose

Plate 30

ANATIDAE:
Nettapus coromandelianus
Cotton Pygmy Goose or
Cotton Teal

ANATIDAE: *Cygnus buc-
cinator*, Trumpeter Swan

Plate 31

and small vertebrates / n site uncertain / e 2–3
Falco zoniventris *Peters* BANDED KESTREL
Madagascar / savannah / insects and small
reptiles
Falco vespertinus *L* RED-FOOTED FALCON
C Europe across Asia to N China, Lake Baikal
and Amurland w in Africa (includes *F.
amurensis* Radde, formerly considered a distinct
species) / open country / insects and small
vertebrates / n tree (old nest of Rook) / e 2–5
(?6) / I ♂♀ 21–7 / F 26–7
Falco chicquera *Daudin* TURUMTI or RED-
HEADED FALCON India S of Himalayas and
Africa S of Sahara / open country, savannah and
desert / birds and lizards / n in old corvid nests /
e 3–5 / I ?♀
Falco columbarius *L* MERLIN or PIGEON
HAWK b much of Holarctic w S to Ecuador,
N Africa and Arabia / marsh, moor and desert /
mainly birds but insects and other small vertebrates also / n ground or old tree-nest of other
species / e 2–7 / I ♂♀ 28–32 / F 25–30
Falco berigora (*Vigors and Horsfield*) BROWN
HAWK Australia, Tasmania, New Guinea,
Dampier and adjacent islands / almost ubiqui-
tous / insects, small mammals and birds / n old
nest of other species / e 2–5 / I ♂♀
Falco novaezeelandiae *Gmelin* NEW
ZEALAND FALCON New Zealand / forest and rocky
islands / large insects and small vertebrates / n
tree or rock ledge / e 2–3
Falco subbuteo *L* HOBBY Palaearctic w to
Africa, India and S China / bush, savannah and
cultivation / insects and small vertebrates / n in
old tree-nest of other bird / e 2–4 / I ♂♀ 28
Falco cuvieri *Smith* AFRICAN HOBBY Africa
S of Sahara / savannah / insects and birds / n tree
(usually old nest of other bird) / e 3 / I ♀
Falco severus *Horsfield* ORIENTAL HOBBY
Himalayas through SE Asia (not Malaya) and
Indonesia to New Guinea, New Britain and
Solomons / forest / insects, small birds and bats /
n old nest of other bird / e 3–4 / I ♂♀ 25
Falco longipennis *Swainson* LITTLE FALCON
or AUSTRALIAN HOBBY Australia and Tasmania
w to New Guinea, New Britain, and Moluccas
forest and semi-desert / insects and birds / n tree
nest of other species / e 2–3 (I cannot find any
comment in Brown and Amadon on the status
of *Falco longipennis hanieli* Hellmayr, apparently
an endemic form in the Lesser Sunda Is)
Falco eleanorae *Géné* ELEANORA'S FALCON

b Canary Is and islands in Mediterranean w
Madagascar / woodland, scrub and cliffs / insects
and small vertebrates / n cliff ledge near sea /
e 1–4 / I ♀ 28 / F 28–35
Falco concolor *Temminck* SOOTY FALCON
b Libyan Desert and Red Sea Coast in w S to
Madagascar / scrub, rock and desert / mainly
birds / n hole in ground or ledge / e 1–4
Falco rufigularis *Daudin* (= *F. albigularis
Daudin*) BAT FALCON Mexico, C America and
much of tropical S America S to N Argentina /
open forest and clearings / bats, birds and
insects / n hole / e ? 2–3 / F c35–40
Falco femoralis *Temminck* (= *F. fusco-
caerulescens Vieillot*) APLOMADO FALCON
S Mexico S to Tierra del Fuego / light forest /
chiefly birds and large insects / n in old nest of
other bird / e 2–4 / I ?♂♀
Falco hypoleucos *Gould* GREY FALCON
Australia / arid open country / birds, also insects,
lizards and mammals / n tree / e 2–4 / I ?♀
Falco subniger *Gray* BLACK FALCON Australia
and Tasmania / ubiquitous except dense forest /
chiefly birds / n old nest of other bird / e 3–4
Falco biarmicus *Temminck* LANNER FALCON
Africa and S Europe / open country, savannah
and desert / chiefly birds / n crag or tree / e 3–4 /
I ♂♀
Falco mexicanus *Schlegel* PRAIRIE FALCON
Arid plains and steppes of interior of N
America / birds and mammals / n cliff / e 3–6 /
I ♂♀ 29–31 / F 40
Falco jugger *Gray* LAGGAR FALCON
Afghanistan, Baluchistan and India / open
country / insects and small vertebrates / n crag or
building / e 2–5 / I ♂♀
Falco cherrug *Gray* SAKER FALCON C Europe
across Asia to Tibet and Manchuria w S to
Ethiopia, Arabia, N India and S China / plains
and steppes / large insects and small vertebrates /
n ground or old tree-nest of other bird / e 3–6 /
I ♂♀ 28 / F 40–5
[**Falco altaicus** (*Menzbier*) ALTAI FALCON
Mts of C Asia / n high crag / status uncertain,
but now generally treated as a race of *cherrug*]
Falco rusticolus *L* GYRFALCON Circumpolar
on Arctic coasts and islands, including Iceland
some migrate S in winter / tundra, mountain and
arctic woodland / birds and some mammals / n
cliff / e 2–7 / I ♀ (rarely ♂) 28–9 / F 46–9
Falco deiroleucus *Temminck* ORANGE-
BREASTED FALCON Locally distributed from

Mexico S to N Argentina and S Brazil / rare/ scrub and forest / birds / n ? hole in building/ e ?3

Falco fasciinucha *Reichenow and Neumann* TAITA FALCON E and C Africa / rare and local/ mountains / birds / n rock ledge / e 3 (1 nest known)

Falco kreyenborgi *Kleinschmidt* PALLID or KLEINSCHMIDT'S FALCON Known from 5 specimens collected at Magellan Straits / status uncertain

Falco peregrinus *Tunstall* PEREGRINE FALCON or DUCK HAWK Almost cosmopolitan / varied habitat, but commonest on mountain and sea cliffs / varied but chiefly birds /n cliff, ground or tree/ e 2–6 / I ♂♀ 28–9 / F 35–42

[**Falco pelegrinoides** *Temminck* BARBARY FALCON E Canary Is and coasts of N Africa often treated as conspecific with *F. peregrinus*]

MEGAPODIIDAE Megapodes Gallinaceous birds ranging from bantam to Turkey-sized, with large powerful feet. Feed on seeds and fruits. Nest, a mound of rotting vegetation where the eggs hatch from the heat of the decaying. Incubation 8–9 weeks. Young precocial, able to fly at birth. Twelve species in the Australasian region. Clutch size seems unrecorded for most species.

Megapodius freycinet *Gaimard* COMMON SCRUB FOWL Nicobars, E Indonesia to Australia and New Hebrides / forest and thickets/ berries, seeds, roots and insects/ e 15 ? e 6–8 ? (*Megapodius burnabyi*, *M. stairi* and *M. andamanensis* appear to be based on eggs collected on islands where megapodes are not now known to occur. These names are *nomen nuda*)

Megapodius laperouse *Gaimard* MARIANA SCRUB FOWL Marianas and Palau Is

Megapodius pritchardii *Gray* PRITCHARD'S SCRUB FOWL or MALAU FOWL Niuafou, C Polynesia / n burrow / e 1–12 ?/ I 26 at least

Megapodius wallacei *Gray* MOLUCCA SCRUB FOWL Moluccas and Misol / e ?

Leipoa ocellata *Gould* MALLEE FOWL Australia / dense arid woodland / buds, flowers, fruit and insects/ n attended by ♂

Alectura lathami *Gray* BRUSH TURKEY Queensland and New South Wales/ forest/ fruit, berries and insects/ n attended by ♂

Talegalla cuvieri *Lesson* RED-BILLED BRUSH TURKEY Salawatti, Misol and NW New Guinea

Talegalla fuscirostris *Salvadori* BLACK-BILLED BRUSH TURKEY S New Guinea and Aru Is

Talegalla jobiensis *Meyer* BROWN-COLLARED BRUSH TURKEY N and E New Guinea and Japen

Aepypodius arfakianus (*Salvadori*) WATTLED BRUSH TURKEY Misol and New Guinea/ mountains

Aepypodius bruijnii (*Oustalet*) BRUIJN'S BRUSH TURKEY Waigeu / a few specimens only

Macrocephalon maleo *Müller* MALEO FOWL Celebes / lays eggs in sand, no mound

CRACIDAE Chachalacas Guans and Curassows Fairly large to large, turkey-like arboreal birds, generally dull-coloured, but in the higher evolved species (Curassows, some Guans) brightly coloured knobs and wattles on the face and cere. Feed on vegetation, fruits, insects and worms. Nest in trees. Eggs 2–3, dull white, large for the size of bird. Tropical and sub-tropical America. I ♀.

Ortalis vetula (*Wagler*) PLAIN CHACHALACA S Texas to Costa Rica / e 3 / I 22–5 ?

Ortalis cinereiceps *Gray* GREY-HEADED CHACHALACA Honduras to N Colombia / e 3/ I 22 at least

Ortalis garrula (*Humboldt*) CHESTNUT-WINGED CHACHALACA N Colombia / open woodland / c 3 / I 26 approx

Ortalis ruficauda *Jardine* RUFOUS-VENTED CHACHALACA N Colombia to Orinoco and some Lesser Antilles / forest-edge and scrub / e 2–4

Ortalis erythroptera *Sclater and Salvin* ECUADORIAN or RUFOUS-HEADED CHACHALACA Ecuador / arid scrub

Ortalis poliocephala (*Wagler*) WEST MEXICAN CHACHALACA W Mexico / e 3

Ortalis canicollis (*Wagler*) CHACO CHACHALACA Chaco of Bolivia, Paraguay and N Argentina/ e 3

Ortalis leucogastra *Gould* WHITE-BELLIED CHACHALACA S Mexico to Nicaragua / e 2–3

Ortalis motmot (*L*) VARIABLE CHACHALACA Basins of Amazon and Orinoco, and other parts of Brazil / discontinuous / scrub / e 2–3 [Note: *Ortalis superciliaris*, *O. guttata*, *O. araucuan*, *O. squamata* and *O. columbiana*, formerly considered distinct, are now combined in this species]

Penelope argyrotis (*Bonaparte*) BANDED GUAN N Colombia and N Venezuela / forest

Penelope barbata *Chapman* BEARDED GUAN

ANATIDAE:
*Anas
castanea,*
Chestnut
Teal

ANATIDAE:
Anas superciliosa,
Grey Duck, Australian
Gray Duck

Plate 32

ANATIDAE:
Anas clypeata,
Northern Shoveler, Spoonbill

ANATIDAE:
Stictonetta naevosa,
Freckled Duck

Plate 33

Andes from S Ecuador to N Peru/forest

Penelope montagnii (*Bonaparte*) ANDEAN GUAN Andes from N Venezuela to Bolivia/forest

Penelope ortoni *Salvin* ORTON'S or BAUDO GUAN Colombia to Ecuador, W of Andes/forest

Penelope marail (*Müller*) MARAIL GUAN Guianas and area between Amazon and Orinoco/forest/e 3/I 29

Penelope superciliaris *Temminck* RUSTY-MARGINED or SUPERCILIATED GUAN Brazil and E Paraguay/e 3/I 26

Penelope dabbenei *Hellmayer and Conover* (= **P. nigrifrons** *Dabbene*) DABBENE'S or RED-FACED GUAN Andes of Bolivia and N Argentina/forest

Penelope obscura *Temminck* DUSKY GUAN Discontinuous/parts of Bolivia, S Brazil to N Argentina and Uruguay/forest

Penelope jacquacu *Spix* SPIX'S GUAN Amazon and Orinoco basins/forest/e 2

Penelope albipennis *Taczanowski* WHITE-WINGED GUAN NW Peru/believed extinct/3 specimens

Penelope perspicax *Bangs* CAUCA GUAN Central Andes of Colombia/rare

Penelope purpurascens *Wagler* CRESTED GUAN Mexico to Ecuador and Venezuela/forest/e 2–3

Penelope jacucaca *Spix* BROWN GUAN E Brazil

Penelope ochrogaster *Pelzeln* CHESTNUT-BELLIED GUAN Mato Grosso/forest

Penelope pileata *Wagler* WHITE-CRESTED GUAN Obidos, Brazil/forest

Aburria pipile (*Jacquin*) PIPING GUAN Tropical S America/forest/e 3?

Aburria jacutinga (*Spix*) BLACK-FRONTED GUAN SE Brazil, Paraguay and N Argentina/forest/e 3/I 28 (possibly race of Piping Guan)

Aburria aburri (*Lesson*) WATTLED GUAN Andes from Venezuela to Peru/forest

Chamaepetes unicolor *Salvin* BLACK GUAN C America/n and e unknown

Chamaepetes goudotii (*Lesson*) SICKLE-WINGED or GOUDOT'S GUAN Andes from Colombia to Peru/forest

Penelopina nigra (*Fraser*) HIGHLAND GUAN or BLACK CHACHALACA C America/e 2

Oreophasis derbianus *Gray* HORNED GUAN S Mexico and Guatemala

Nothocrax urumutum (*Spix*) NOCTURNAL CURASSOW Upper Amazon basin/forest/e 4/I 28 (in incubator)

Crax tomentosa *Spix* CRESTLESS CURASSOW Venezuela and Orinoco basin/forest/e 2/I 20 (under domestic hen)

Crax salvini (*Reinhardt*) SALVIN'S CURASSOW E Ecuador/forest/e 2?

Crax mitu *L* RAZOR-BILLED CURASSOW S Amazon basin [and E Brazil, probably extinct]/forest/e 2?/I 30

Crax pauxi *L* HELMETED CURASSOW NW Venezuela and N Colombia/forest/e 2

Crax unicornis *Bond and de Schaunsee* HORNED CURASSOW Peru and Bolivia (2 restricted spots)

Crax rubra *L* GLOBOSE, MEXICAN or GREAT CURASSOW Mexico to Ecuador/forest/e 2

Crax alberti *Fraser* ALBERT'S or BLUE-BILLED CURASSOW E Colombia/forest

Crax daubentoni *Gray* DAUBENTON'S or YELLOW-BILLED CURASSOW N Venezuela/forest/e 2?

Crax alector (= **nigra**) *L* CRESTED CURASSOW Guianas, N Brazil and S Venezuela/forest/e 2 (?3)

Crax globulosa *Spix* WATTLED CURASSOW Upper Amazon basin/forest/e 2

Crax fasciolata *Spix* SCLATER'S or BARE-FACED CURASSOW Brazil to N Argentina/forest/e 2/I ♂♀ (probably error, it would be unique for ♂ Cracid to incubate)

Crax blumenbachii *Spix* BLUMENBACH'S or RED-BILLED CURASSOW SE Brazil/rare/forest/e 4 (sic, probably 2 ♀♀ involved)

TETRAONIDAE Grouse Heavily built gallinaceous birds inhabiting the temperate regions of the Northern Hemisphere. Some species are highly polygamous, with elaborate social and courtship behaviour. Legs feathered to the toes; sometimes toes are also feathered Mainly vegetarian feeders, but some insects are taken. Young often precocial. F here indicates period before young fly.

Tetrao urogallus *L* CAPERCAILLIE Europe, W and C Asia/forest/n ground/e 4–15 usually 5–8/I ♀ 26–9/F 2–3 weeks

Tetrao urogalloides *Middendorf* (= **T. parvirostris**, *Bonaparte*) ROCK CAPERCAILLIE E Siberia, Kamchatka and Sakhalin/n and e n/k

Lyrurus tetrix (*L*) BLACK GROUSE N Europe and N Asia/moor and forest/n ground/e 5–13/I ♀ 24–9/F 2–3 weeks

Lyrurus mlokosiewiczi (*Taczanowski*)

CAUCASIAN GROUSE Caucasus / forest and moor / n ground / e 2–10 / I 20–5?

Dendragapus obscurus (*Say*) DUSKY GROUSE, BLUE GROUSE, GREY GROUSE Rocky Mountains / forest / fruit, buds, seeds and insects / n ground / e 7–10

Dendragapus fuliginosus (*Ridgway*) SOOTY GROUSE Coastal ranges of N America (W of Rockies) / forest / insects, seeds, fruit and leaves / n ground / e 6–10 / I ♀ 18–24

Lagopus scoticus (*Latham*) RED GROUSE Scotland and Ireland / moors / n ground / e 4–17 usually 6–11 / I ♀ 21–6 / F 12–13 (sometimes regarded as race of Willow Grouse)

Lagopus lagopus (*L*) WILLOW GROUSE N Holarctic, almost circumpolar / forest and tundra / leaves, buds, berries and insects / n ground / e 5–20 / I 22–6

Lagopus mutus (*Montin*) ROCK PTARMIGAN Holarctic, tundra and alpine zone / leaves, buds, berries and insects / n ground / e 3–12 / I ♀ 24–6 / F 10

Lagopus leucurus (*Richardson*) WHITE-TAILED PTARMIGAN Rockies from Alaska to New Mexico / alpine zone / insects, buds and leaves / n ground / e 4–15

Canachites canadensis (*L*) SPRUCE GROUSE Nearctic spruce forest / spruce needles, berries and insects / n ground / e 8–16 / I ♀ 17

Canachites franklinii (*Douglas*) FRANKLIN'S GROUSE Alaska to Montana / forest / spruce needles, berries and insects / n ground / e ?6

Falcipennis falcipennis (*Hartlaub*) SICKLE-WINGED GROUSE E Siberia and Sakhalin / forest / n ground / e c8

Tetrastes bonasia (*L*) HAZEL GROUSE N, C and E Europe, N and E Asia / forest / n ground / e 6–15 / I ♀ c21 / F c21

Tetrastes sewerzowi *Przewalski* SEWERZOW'S GROUSE Koko Nor, Kansu and W Szechwan

Bonasa umbellus (*L*) RUFFED GROUSE N America / forest / nuts, seeds, buds and fruit / n just off ground / e 9–12 / I ♀ 21–8

Pedioecetes phasianellus (*L*) SHARPTAIL GROUSE Western N America / prairie / insects, fruit, leaves, seeds / n ground / e 10–15 / I ♀ 21

Tympanuchus cupido (*L*) PRAIRIE CHICKEN Central N America / prairie / insects, seeds, berries etc / n ground / e 7–17 / I 21–8 (the Greater and Lesser Prairie Chickens are now generally regarded as conspecific)

Centrocercus urophasianus (*Bonaparte*) SAGE GROUSE Western N America / sagebrush plains / largely sagebrush leaves / n ground / e 7–17 / I ♀ 22

PHASIANIDAE Partridges, Pheasants and Quails Generally brightly or very brightly coloured gallinaceous birds, very variable in size from very small quails to large pheasants. Often with spurs on the back of the naked tarsus, males of the larger species usually very brightly coloured and the females comparatively dull. Generally seed eating, but also feed on insects, fruits etc. Nest on the ground. Eggs very variable, white or richly mottled.

Dendrortyx barbatus *Gould* BEARDED PARTRIDGE Vera Cruz, Mexico / mountain forest

Dendrortyx macroura (*Jardine and Selby*) MEXICAN LONG-TAILED PARTRIDGE Mexico

Dendrortyx leucophrys (*Gould*) GUATEMALAN LONG-TAILED PARTRIDGE Guatemala, El Salvador, Honduras, Nicaragua and Costa Rica

Oreortyx picta (*Douglas*) PLUMED QUAIL, MOUNTAIN QUAIL Pacific USA from Washington to Lower California / seeds, leaves, shoots, berries and insects / e 10–12 / I ?♀♂ 21

Callipepla squamata (*Vigors*) SCALED QUAIL Mexico and south-western USA / scrub / insects and some seeds / e 9–16 / I ♀ 21

Lophortyx californica (*Shaw*) CALIFORNIA QUAIL Western USA / scrub and grass / seeds and some insects / e 12–16 / I 18

Lophortyx gambelii *Gambel* GAMBEL'S QUAIL Mid-west USA and Lower California / desert / seeds, buds and berries / e 10–12 (?18–20) / I ♀ 21–4

[**Lophortyx leucoprosopon** *Reichenow* REICHENOW'S QUAIL Unknown / known only from aviary pair, possibly hybrid]

Lophortyx douglasii (*Vigors*) DOUGLAS'S QUAIL W Mexico

Philortyx fasciatus (*Gould*) BARRED QUAIL SW Mexico

Colinus virginianus (*L*) BOB WHITE USA, Mexico, C America and W Indies / grass and cultivation / seeds, grain and insects / e 7–20 / I ♂♀ 23–4

Colinus nigrogularis (*Gould*) BLACK-THROATED QUAIL C America

Colinus cristatus (*L*) (including **C. leucopogon**) CRESTED QUAIL C America, Venezuela, Colombia, the Guianas

Odontophorus gujanensis (*Gmelin*) MARBLED

ANATIDAE:
Anser coerulescens,
Snow Goose

ANATIDAE:
Cereopsis novaehollandiae,
Cape Barren Goose

Plate 34

ANATIDAE:
*Anser
cygnoides,*
Swan
Goose

ANATIDAE:
Netta peposaca,
Rosybill, Rosy-billed Pochard

ANATIDAE:
Dendrocygna viduata,
White-faced Whistling Duck,
White-faced Tree Duck

Plate 35

QUAIL C America to Amazon basin and E Peru/
forest/insects and berries/n ground/e ?2
Odontophorus erythrops *Gould* PARAMBA
QUAIL C America to Ecuador
Odontophorus capueira (*Spix*) CAPUEIRA
QUAIL E Brazil
Odontophorus atrifrons *Allen* BLACK-
FRONTED QUAIL Colombia
Odontophorus melanonotus *Gould* BLACK-
BACKED QUAIL W Ecuador
Odontophorus hyperythrus *Gould*
CHESTNUT-THROATED QUAIL Colombia
Odontophorus speciosus *Tschudi* RUFOUS-
BREASTED QUAIL Ecuador, Peru and Bolivia
Odontophorus strophium (*Gould*) GORGETED
QUAIL Bogota, Colombia
Odontophorus dialeucos *Wetmore* (in
Smithsonian Misc Coll, 145, 6 (Dec 1963), p 5
and *Birds of Panama*, vol 1, p 327) TACARCUNA
QUAIL Darien, Panama/no data
Odontophorus columbianus (*Gould*)
VENEZUELAN QUAIL N Venezuela
Odontophorus leucolaemus *Salvin* BLACK-
BREASTED QUAIL Costa Rica and W Panama
Odontophorus balliviani *Gould* BALLIVIAN'S
or STRIPE-FACED QUAIL Peru and Bolivia
Odontophorus stellatus (*Gould*) STARRED
QUAIL E Ecuador and E Peru
Odontophorus guttatus (*Gould*) SPOTTED
QUAIL Mexico and C America
Dactylortyx thoracicus (*Gambel*) LONG-TOED
PARTRIDGE or SINGING QUAIL Mexico and C
America
Cyrtonyx montezumae (*Vigors*)
MONTEZUMA'S QUAIL South-western USA and
Mexico/semi-desert/bulbs, acorns, seeds etc/
e 8–14/I ♂♀ period n/k
Cyrtonyx sallei *Verreaux* SALLE'S QUAIL
W Mexico
Cyrtonyx ocellatus (*Gould*) OCELLATED QUAIL
SW Mexico to N Nicaragua
Rhynchortyx cinctus (*Salvin*) LONG-LEGGED
COLIN or BANDED QUAIL Honduras to
Colombia and Ecuador/e ?3
Lerwa lerwa (*Hodgson*) SNOW PARTRIDGE
Himalayas from Afghanistan to Szechwan/
alpine pastures/e 3–6
Ammoperdix griseogularis (*Brandt*) SEESEE
PARTRIDGE Iraq to Sind/scrub/e 8–16
Ammoperdix heyi (*Temminck*) SAND
PARTRIDGE Egypt, Palestine and S Arabia/
semi-desert/e 5–7

Tetraogallus caucasicus (*Pallas*) CAUCASIAN
SNOWCOCK Caucasus/alpine meadows/e up to
10/I ♀
Tetraogallus caspius (*S. G. Gmelin*) CASPIAN
SNOWCOCK Asia Minor and Persia/mountains/
alpine scrub/e 6–9/I ?
Tetraogallus tibetanus *Gould* TIBETAN
SNOWCOCK Tibet, Sikkim and W China/alpine
pasture/e 4–7
Tetraogallus altaicus (*Gebler*) ALTAI
SNOWCOCK Altai and Mongolia/alpine scrub/
e known, clutch-size undetermined
Tetraogallus himalayensis *Gray*
HIMALAYAN SNOWCOCK Tian Shan, Pamirs and
W Himalayas/mountain/e 5–8/I ♀ 31
Tetraophasis obscurus (*Verreaux*)
VERREAUX'S PHEASANT GROUSE Koko Nor,
Kansu and Szechwan
Tetraophasis szechenyii *Madarász*
SZÉCHENY'S PHEASANT GROUSE E Tibet,
Szechwan and Yunnan
Alectoris graeca (*Meisner*) ROCK PARTRIDGE
S Europe/hillside, scrub and semi-desert/
e 6–21/I ♀ 24–6
Alectoris chukar (*Gray*) CHUKOR PARTRIDGE
Asia Minor to Mongolia/e 7–12/I ? ♀
Alectoris rufa (*L*) RED-LEGGED PARTRIDGE
W Europe, Corsica, Madeira, Canary Is/scrub/
e 7–20/I ♂♀ 23–4
Alectoris barbata (*Bonnaterre*) BARBARY
PARTRIDGE N Africa and Canaries/e 10–18
Alectoris melanocephala (*Rüppell*)
RÜPPELL'S PARTRIDGE Arabia/rocky hillsides/
seeds/n under bush/e 1–11
Alectoris magna *Przewalski* PRZEWALSKI'S
ROCK PARTRIDGE E Tibet and Kansu
Alectoris philbyi *Bates* (in *Ibis* (1937), p 829
(form upheld by Vaurie)) PHILBY'S ROCK
PARTRIDGE W Arabia
Anurophasis monorthonyx *van Oort* SNOW
MOUNTAIN QUAIL New Guinea (Mt Wilhelmina
and Mt Carstenz in Snow Mts)/e 3

NB: The arrangement of species in the Genus
Francolinus follows B. P. Hall, *Bull Brit Mus
(Nat Hist)*, vol 10, no 3 (1963)
Francolinus francolinus (*L*) BLACK
FRANCOLIN Asia Minor to E Himalayas/forest/
e 6–9/I ♀ 18–19
Francolinus pictus (*Jardine and Selby*)
PAINTED FRANCOLIN India and Ceylon/scrub/
e 4–8/I ♀

Francolinus pintadeanus (*Scopoli*) BURMESE FRANCOLIN SE Asia, S China and Hainan/ scrub/e 3–7

Francolinus leucoscepus *Gray* YELLOW-NECKED FRANCOLIN Ethiopia, Kenya and Uganda/bush and cultivation/e 3–7

Francolinus rufopictus (*Reichenow*) GREY-BREASTED FRANCOLIN Ukerewe Is and borders of Lake Victoria/thorn scrub/e 4

Francolinus swainsonii (*Smith*) SWAINSON'S FRANCOLIN Damaraland to Transvaal

Francolinus afer (*Müller*) RED-NECKED FRANCOLIN C and S Africa/discontinuous/scrub and cultivation/e 5–9

Francolinus erckelii (*Rüppell*) ERCKEL'S FRANCOLIN Ethiopia and Egyptian Sudan/ plateaux

Francolinus ochropectus *Dorst and Jouanin* DORST'S FRANCOLIN Somaliland

Francolinus castaneicollis *Salvadori* CHESTNUT-NAPED FRANCOLIN Ethiopia and British Somaliland/hills/e 5–7

Francolinus jacksoni *Grant* JACKSON'S FRANCOLIN Kenya/mountain grassland/e 3+

Francolinus nobilis *Reichenow* HANDSOME FRANCOLIN Uganda/forest/n and e n/k

Francolinus camerunensis *Alexander* CAMEROON FRANCOLIN Cameroon mountain/ high forest slopes

Francolinus swierstrai (*Roberts*) SWIERSTRA'S FRANCOLIN S Angola

Francolinus ahantensis *Temminck* AHANTA FRANCOLIN Gambia to Togoland

Francolinus squamatus *Cassin* SCALY FRANCOLIN WC, C and EC Africa/forest and bush/e 4–8

Francolinus griseostriatus *Ogilvie-Grant* GREY-STRIPED FRANCOLIN Angola

Francolinus bicalcaratus (*L*) DOUBLE-SPURRED FRANCOLIN W Africa

Francolinus clappertoni *Children* CLAPPERTON'S FRANCOLIN Savannah belt S of Sahara

Francolinus icterorhynchus *Heuglin* HEUGLIN'S FRANCOLIN C Africa/savannah/e 6–8

Francolinus hildebrandti *Cabanis* HILDEBRANDT'S FRANCOLIN E Africa / hill woods and scrub/e 4–8

Francolinus hartlaubi *Bocage* HARTLAUB'S FRANCOLIN Angola/e n/k

Francolinus capensis (*Gmelin*) CAPE FRANCOLIN Cape of Good Hope/e 5–7

Francolinus adspersus *Waterhouse* RED-BILLED FRANCOLIN SW Africa/e 5–6

Francolinus harwoodi *Blundell and Lovatt* HARWOOD'S FRANCOLIN Ethiopia / cliffs of gorges / n and e n/k (known from 7 specimens)

Francolinus streptophorus *Ogilvie-Grant* RING-NECKED FRANCOLIN Uganda and W Tanganyika/stony hills/e 4–5

Francolinus sephaena (*Smith*) CRESTED FRANCOLIN E Africa/bush/e 4–8

Francolinus psilolaemus *Gray* RELICT FRANCOLIN E Africa (4 isolated localities, see Hall for map)/no data

Francolinus shelleyi *Ogilvie-Grant* SHELLEY'S FRANCOLIN E Africa/woods and grass/e 3–8

Francolinus africanus *Stephens* (= **F. afer** *Latham*) GREY WING S Africa

Francolinus levaillantoides *Smith* (= **F. gariepensis**, *Smith*) ORANGE RIVER FRANCOLIN S and E Africa/e 5–8

Francolinus levaillantii (*Valenciennes*) REDWING FRANCOLIN E and S Africa (scattered localities)/hills/e 4–8

Francolinus finschi *Bocage* FINSCH'S FRANCOLIN S Angola

Francolinus coqui (*Smith*) COQUI FRANCOLIN S and E Africa / grass and bush/ e 3–8

Francolinus schlegelii *Heuglin* SCHLEGEL'S FRANCOLIN C Africa/grass and scrub/e ? 2

Francolinus albogularis *Hartlaub* WHITE-THROATED FRANCOLIN W Africa

Francolinus nahani *Dubois* NAHAN'S FRANCOLIN C Africa / forest / n tree hollow (1 known)/e n/s

Francolinus lathami *Hartlaub* FOREST FRANCOLIN W and C Africa/forest/seeds and insects (?)/n ground/e 2–3

Francolinus pondicerianus (*Gmelin*) GREY FRANCOLIN S Persian Gulf, Muscat, India and Ceylon/plains and scrub/e 4–9/I ♀ 18–19

Francolinus gularis (*Temminck*) SWAMP FRANCOLIN Ganges Plain and Assam / swamps/ e 4–6/I ♀

Perdix perdix (*L*) GREY PARTRIDGE Europe and W Asia / moor and cultivation / e 8–23/ I ♀ 23–5

Perdix dauuricae (*Pallas*) (= **P. barbata** (*Verreaux and Des Murs*)) DAURIAN PARTRIDGE C and E Asia

Perdix hodgsoniae (*Hodgson*) TIBETAN

ANATIDAE: *Aix sponsa*, Carolina or Wood Duck

ANATIDAE: *Aix galericulata*, Mandarin Duck

Plate 36

ANATIDAE: *Anas platyrhynchos,* Mallard

Plate 37

PARTRIDGE Himalayas, Tibet and mts of W China / plateaux / e 8–10

Rhizothera longirostris (*Temminck*) LONG-BILLED PARTRIDGE SE Asia, Sumatra, Borneo

Margaroperdix madagarensis (*Scopoli*) MADAGASCAR PARTRIDGE Madagascar

Melanoperdix nigra (*Vigors*) BLACK PARTRIDGE Malay Peninsula, Sumatra, Borneo

Coturnix coturnix (*L*) COMMON QUAIL Palaearctic, Africa / grass / e 6–18 / I ♀ 16–21

Coturnix japonica *Temminck and Schlegel* JAPANESE QUAIL Japan and Sakhalin, w to China and SE Asia

Coturnix coromandelica (*Gmelin*) RAIN QUAIL India, Burma, Ceylon / grass / e 6–11 / I ♀ 18–19

Coturnix delegorguei *Delegorgue* HARLEQUIN QUAIL Africa and S Arabia / grass / e 5–10

Coturnix pectoralis *Gould* STUBBLE QUAIL Australia and Tasmania / grassland and cultivation / seeds and insects / e 7–10

Coturnix novaezelandiae *Quoy and Gaimard* NEW ZEALAND QUAIL New Zealand / extinct 1870 / e 10–12

Synoicus ypsilophorus (*Bosc*) (= S. *australis* *Latham*) BROWN QUAIL Australia, Tasmania, New Guinea, Lesser Sunda Is [Introduced New Zealand] / grassland / seeds and insects / e up to 12

Excalfactoria adansonii (*Verreaux*) BLUE QUAIL Africa S of Sahara / plains / e 6–9

Excalfactoria chinensis (*L*) PAINTED QUAIL S and E Asia through Indonesia to Australia / swamp and grassland / seeds and insects / e 4–8 / I ♀ c16

Perdicula asiatica (*Latham*) JUNGLE QUAIL Kashmir, N and W India / scrub jungle / e 4–8 / I ♀ 16–18

Perdicula argoondah (*Sykes*) ROCK QUAIL SE India / scrub and desert / e 4–8 / I ♀ 16–18

Perdicula erythrorhyncha (*Sykes*) BUSH QUAIL Peninsular India / scrub and forest / e 4–7 (rarely 10) / I ♀ 16–18

Perdicula manipurensis *Hume* MANIPUR QUAIL Assam and Manipur / scrub jungle / e 4 (only 1 nest known)

Arborophila torqueola (*Valenciennes*) COMMON HILL PARTRIDGE Himalayas through hills of N Burma and Yunnan to Tonkin / forested hillsides and ravines / n ground / e 3–5 (?9)

Arborophila rufogularis (*Blyth*) RUFOUS-THROATED HILL PARTRIDGE Himalayas E across Burma and Thailand to Annam / forest and secondary scrub / n ground / e 4–5 (?8)

Arborophila atrogularis (*Blyth*) WHITE-CHEEKED HILL PARTRIDGE Assam and Upper Burma / forest / n ground / e 3–7

Arborophila crudigularis (*Swinhoe*) SWINHOE'S HILL PARTRIDGE Mountains of Taiwan

Arborophila mandellii *Hume* MANDELL'S HILL PARTRIDGE Hills N of Brahamaputra from Sikkim and Bhutan to E Assam / forest / n ground / e 4 (1 nest known)

Arborophila brunneopectus (*Blyth*) BAR-BACKED HILL PARTRIDGE E Assam across Burma to Annam

Arborophila rufipectus *Boulton* BOULTON'S HILL PARTRIDGE W Szechwan / unique

Arborophila gingica (*Gmelin*) RICKETT'S HILL PARTRIDGE Mountains of SE China / woodland and scrub / n and e ? n/k

Arborophila davidi *Delacour* DAVID'S HILL PARTRIDGE Near Saigon, Cochin-China / unique

Arborophila cambodiana *Delacour and Jabouille* CAMBODIAN HILL PARTRIDGE Cambodia and Siam / ? no data

Arborophila orientalis (*Horsfield*) HORSFIELD'S HILL PARTRIDGE Mts of Malaya, Sumatra and Java

Arborophila javanica (*Gmelin*) JAVAN HILL PARTRIDGE Mts of Java

Arborophila rubrirostris (*Salvadori*) RED-BILLED HILL PARTRIDGE Mts of Sumatra

Arborophila hyperythra (*Sharpe*) RED-BREASTED HILL PARTRIDGE Mts of NW Borneo

Arborophila ardens (*Styan*) HAINAN HILL PARTRIDGE Mts of Hainan

Arborophila charltonii (*Eyton*) EYTON'S or SCALY-BREASTED HILL PARTRIDGE Much of SE Asia and Borneo

Arborophila merlini *Delacour and Jabouille* ANNAM HILL PARTRIDGE Annam

Caloperdix oculea (*Temminck*) FERRUGINEOUS WOOD PARTRIDGE Malay Peninsula, Sumatra and Borneo

Haematortyx sanguiniceps *Sharpe* CRIMSON-HEADED PARTRIDGE Northern Borneo

Rollulus rouloul (*Scopoli*) ROULROUL PARTRIDGE Tenasserim S through Malay Peninsula; Sumatra and Borneo

Ptilopachus petrosus (*Gmelin*) STONE PARTRIDGE Tropical belt of Africa / rocky hills and cliffs / n ground / e 4–6

Bambusicola fytchii *Anderson* ANDERSON'S BAMBOO PARTRIDGE W Szechwan S through Yunnan to N Burma, Shan States and Tonkin / scrub and bamboo jungle / n ground / e 4–6 / I ♀ 18–19

Bambusicola thoracica (*Temminck*) CHINESE BAMBOO PARTRIDGE China and Taiwan / bamboo scrub / n ground / e 2–6

Galloperdix spadicea (*Gmelin*) RED SPURFOWL India / dry scrub-jungle and cultivation / n ground / e 3–5 / I ♀

Galloperdix lunulata (*Valenciennes*) PAINTED SPURFOWL Much of India / dry scrub-jungle / n ground / e 3–5 / I ♀

Galloperdix bicalcarata (*Forster*) CEYLON SPURFOWL Ceylon / forest / n ground / e 2–5

Ophrysia superciliosa (*Gray*) MOUNTAIN QUAIL NW Himalayas / long grass on hillsides / n and e n/k / extinct

Pheasants are species of the Phasianidae which are strikingly sexually dimorphic, and have been the subject of several specialised studies. This arrangement of the genera to which the term 'Pheasant' is applied follows Delacour's *Pheasants of the World*. I ♀.

Ithaginis cruentus (*Hardwicke*) BLOOD PHEASANT Himalayas and mts of W China / mountain forest / e 5–12 / I 29

Tragopan melanocephalus (*Gray*) WESTERN TRAGOPAN W Himalayas / forest / n tree / e 3–6 / I ♀ 28

Tragopan satyra (*L*) SATYR TRAGOPAN C and E Himalayas / forest / n tree / e 3–6

Tragopan blythi (*Jerdon*) BLYTH'S TRAGOPAN Assam and N Burma [E Bhutan (*T. b. molesworthi*)] / forest / n tree / e 3–6

Tragopan temminckii (*Gray*) TEMMINCK'S TRAGOPAN Mts of W China, N Burma and SE Tibet / forest / n tree / e 3–6

Tragopan caboti (*Gould*) CABOT'S TRAGOPAN Fokien and Kwangtung / mountain forest / n tree / e 3–6

Pucrasia macrolopha (*Lesson*) KOKLASS PHEASANT W Himalayas and mts of China / discontinuous / forest / e 20–30 ? / I 21–2

Lophophorus impejanus (*Latham*) IMPEYAN PHEASANT or HIMALAYAN MONAL Himalayas / open forest / e 4–8 / I 27–30 ?

Lophophorus sclateri *Jerdon* SCLATER'S MONAL SE Tibet to Yunnan / n and e n/k

Lophophorus lhuysii *St Hilaire and Verreaux* CHINESE MONAL Mts of Koko Nor and Szechwan / n and e n/k

Gallus gallus (*L*) RED JUNGLEFOWL (origin of Domestic Fowl) E India, SE Asia, Sumatra and Java, feral elsewhere / forest / e ? 6–8 / I 19–21

Gallus sonneratii *Temminck* GREY JUNGLEFOWL W Peninsular India / forest / e 3–10 / I 20–1

Gallus lafayettei *Lesson* CEYLON JUNGLEFOWL Ceylon / forest and scrub / e 2–4 / I 20–1

Gallus varius (*Shaw and Nodder*) GREEN JUNGLEFOWL Java and Lesser Sunda Is / scrub / e 6–10 / I 21

Lophura leucomelana (*Latham*) KALIJ PHEASANT Himalayas through Burma to W Siam / forest / e 5–15 / I 24–5

Lophura nycthemera (*L*) SILVER PHEASANT SE Asia and S China / forest / e 4–8 / I 23–5

Lophura imperialis (*Delacour and Jabouille*) IMPERIAL PHEASANT C Annam / forest / e 5–7 / I 25

Lophura edwardsi (*Oustalet*) EDWARDS' PHEASANT C Annam / mountain forest / e 4–7 / I 21–3

Lophura swinhoei (*Gould*) SWINHOE'S PHEASANT Taiwan / forest / e 6–12 / I 25

Lophura inornata (*Salvadori*) SALVADORI'S PHEASANT S Sumatra / no data

Lophura (?inornata) hoogerwerfi *Chasen* ATJEH PHEASANT W Sumatra / 2 ♀♀ / no data

Lophura erythrophthalma (*Raffles*) CRESTLESS FIREBACK Malaya, Sumatra, Borneo / lowland forest / e 3–6 / I 24

Lophura ignita (*Shaw and Nodder*) CRESTED FIREBACK Malaya, Sumatra, Borneo / lowland forest / e 4–8 / I 24–5

Lophura diardi (*Bonaparte*) SIAMESE FIREBACK Siam and Indo China / forest / e 5–8 / I 24–5

Lophura bulweri (*Sharpe*) WATTLED PHEASANT or BULWER'S PHEASANT Borneo / forest / e ?2 ?5 / I n/k

Crossoptilon crossoptilon (*Hodgson*) WHITE EARED-PHEASANT Tibet, Szechwan, Yunnan and Koko Nor / forest / bulbs and roots / e 4–7 / I 24

Crossoptilon mantchuricum *Swinhoe* BROWN EARED-PHEASANT Shansi and Chihli / forest / bulbs and roots / e 5–8 / I 26–7

Crossoptilon auritum (*Pallas*) BLUE EARED-PHEASANT Kansu and NW Koko Nor / forest / bulbs and roots / e 5–8 / I 26–8

Catreus wallichi (*Hardwicke*) CHEER

Plate 38

Opposite:
ANATIDAE:
*Cygnus
olor,*
Mute
Swan

ANATIDAE;
Cygnus atratus,
Black Swan

ANATIDAE:
*Cygnus
cygnus,*
Whooper Swan

Plate 39

PHEASANT Himalayas / brush and cliffs / e 9–14 / I 26

Syrmaticus ellioti (*Swinhoe*) ELLIOT'S PHEASANT SE China / forest / e 6–8 / I 25

Syrmaticus humiae (*Hume*) HUME'S PHEASANT Mts of N Burma and adjacent regions / open forest / e 6–11

Syrmaticus mikado (*Ogilvie-Grant*) MIKADO PHEASANT Taiwan / mountain forest / e 5–10 / I 26–8

Syrmaticus soemmerringi (*Temminck*) COPPER PHEASANT Japan / woods / e 6–13 / I 24–5

Syrmaticus reevesi (*Gray*) REEVES' PHEASANT N and W China / wooded hills / e 7–15 / I 24–5

Phasianus colchicus *L* COMMON PHEASANT Temperate Asia, feral and semi-domestic elsewhere / e 8–15 / I 22–7 ♀, exceptionally ♂ (the Common Pheasant occurs in a vast array of races and forms, many of which have in the past been given specific status)

Phasianus versicolor *Vieillot* GREEN PHEASANT Japan / forest and plain / biology similar to Common Pheasant

Chrysolophus pictus (*L*) GOLDEN PHEASANT W China / scrub / e ? / I 22 (nest unknown in wild)

Chrysolophus amherstiae (*Leadbeater*) LADY AMHERST'S PHEASANT SE Tibet, Szechwan and Yunnan / forest and scrub / e 6–12 / I 23

Polyplectron chalcurum *Lesson* BRONZE-TAILED PEACOCK PHEASANT Sumatra / mountain forest / e 2 / I 22

Polyplectron inopinatum (*Rothschild*) ROTHSCHILD'S PEACOCK PHEASANT Malaya / mountains / no data

Polyplectron germaini *Elliot* GERMAIN'S PEACOCK PHEASANT S Vietnam / forest / e 2 / I 22

Polyplectron bicalcaratum (*L*) GREY PEACOCK PHEASANT Sikkim to Hainan and Siam / e 2–6 / I 21

Polyplectron malacense (*Scopoli*) MALAY PEACOCK PHEASANT Malaya, Sumatra, E Borneo / lowland forest

Polyplectron emphanum (*Temminck*) PALAWAN PEACOCK PHEASANT Palawan / forest / e 2 / I 18

Rheinartia ocellata (*Elliot*) CRESTED ARGUS Annam and Malaya / discontinuous / mountain forest / e 2 / I 25

Argusianus argus (*L*) GREAT ARGUS Malaya, Sumatra and Borneo / e 2 / I 24–5

Argusianus bipunctatus (*Wood*) DOUBLE-BANDED ARGUS Known only from a portion of a single feather of unknown origin

Pavo cristatus *L* INDIAN PEAFOWL India and Ceylon / forest and domestication / e 4–8 / I 27–30

Pavo muticus *L* GREEN PEAFOWL Burma, SE Asia and Java / forest / e 4–8 / I 27–30 [fertile hybrids occur between these two species of Pavo, and different coloured strains are known]

Afropavo congensis *Chapin* CONGO PEACOCK EC Congo basin / rain forest / e 3–4 / I 26

NUMIDIDAE Guineafowl Medium sized fowl-like birds with grey-spangled plumage and bare heads. Seven species in Africa; nesting on the ground.

Phasidus niger *Cassin* BLACK GUINEAFOWL African equatorial forest region

Agelastes meleagrides *Bonaparte* WHITE-BREASTED GUINEAFOWL Liberia and Ghana

Numida meleagris (*L*) HELMETED GUINEAFOWL Africa and adjacent islands [introduced West Indies] / e 6–10 (*mitrata*) 10–20 (*meleagris*). Praed and Grant give the clutch sizes of these two races as consistently different

Guttera plumifera (*Cassin*) PLUMED GUINEAFOWL WC Africa

Guttera edouardi (*Hartlaub*) CRESTED GUINEAFOWL W and E Africa / e 8–10

Guttera pucherani (*Hartlaub*) KENYA GUINEAFOWL E Africa and Zanzibar / e 3–4 (? 5–10)

Acryllium vulturinum (*Hardwicke*) VULTURINE GUINEAFOWL E Africa / e ? 14

MELEAGRIDIDAE Turkeys Large, heavy pheasant-like birds with naked heads. Inhabit open mixed forests. Domestication of Common Turkey dates from sixteenth century; n ground. Feed on seeds, leaves and insects.

Meleagris gallopavo *L* COMMON TURKEY Mexico and South USA / e 8–15 / I ♀ 28

Agriocharis ocellata (*Cuvier*) OCELLATED TURKEY Yucatan

OPISTHOCOMIDAE Hoatzin A bird of doubtful affinities, but usually placed with the game birds. Others have placed it with the Cuckoos. Feeds on tough leathery leaves and inhabits shrubby trees bordering streams. The young are remarkable in having claws on the wings with which they creep along branches.

Opisthocomus hoazin (*Müller*) HOATZIN Basins of Amazon and Orinoco / n tree / e 2–3 / I n/k

MESITORNITHIDAE Mesites Medium-small birds probably most closely related to rails, and almost flightless. Inhabit forest and brush in Madagascar, feeding on insects and seeds; n in tree or bush; e 1 (rarely 2–3).

Mesitornis variegata (*Geoffroy*) WHITE-BREASTED MESITE E Madagascar

Mesitornis unicolor (*Des Murs*) BROWN MESITE or ROATELO E Madagascar

Monias benschi *Oustalet and Grandidier* BENSCH'S RAIL SW Madagascar

TURNICIDAE Buttonquails and Hemipodes Small, dull-coloured running birds, superficially resembling Quails. They are weak fliers, inhabiting grasslands and rarely flying unless pressed. The female is the more brightly coloured, takes the active role in courtship and builds the nest, which is on the ground. The male incubates and cares for the young. Incubation lasts about 13 days. The young are precocial and run almost as soon as they hatch. The eggs are 3–5 (usually 4) in number are greyish and thickly speckled. Feed on insects and grass-seeds. Native to warmer parts of Old World.

Turnix sylvatica (*Desfontaines*) ANDALUCIAN HEMIPODE S Spain, Africa and S Asia through Indonesia / grassland and scrub jungle / e 4

Turnix maculosa (*Temminck*) AUSTRALIAN HEMIPODE Papuan area, Australia and Solomon Is / grassland / e 4

Turnix worcesteri *McGregor* PHILIPPINE BUTTONQUAIL Luzon / 4 specimens / status uncertain

Turnix nana (*Sundevall*) NATAL BUTTONQUAIL Parts of Africa / grass and scrub / e 3–4

Turnix hottentotta *Temminck* HOTTENTOT BUTTONQUAIL SW Cape Province / e 4–6

Turnix tanki *Blyth* YELLOWLEGGED BUTTONQUAIL Indian sub-continent, SE and E Asia / grassland and semi-desert / e 4

Turnix suscitator (*Gmelin*) BARRED BUTTONQUAIL Indian sub-continent to S China, Japan, Indonesia and Philippines / e 4

Turnix nigricollis (*Gmelin*) MADAGASCAR BUTTONQUAIL Madagascar

Turnix ocellata (*Scopoli*) SPOTTED BUTTONQUAIL Luzon

Turnix melanogaster (*Gould*) BLACK-BREASTED BUTTONQUAIL Queensland and New South Wales / wet forest / e 3–4

Turnix varia (*Latham*) PAINTED BUTTONQUAIL

Australia and New Caledonia / grassy woodlands and scrubby hillsides / e 4

Turnix castanota (*Gould*) CHESTNUT-BACKED BUTTONQUAIL N Australia / dry savannah / e 4 (*T. olivii*, Robinson, is sometimes separated)

Turnix pyrrhothorax (*Gould*) RED-CHESTED BUTTONQUAIL Australia / grassland / e 4

Turnix velox (*Gould*) LITTLE BUTTONQUAIL S and E Australia / grassland / e 4

Ortyxelos meiffrenii (*Vieillot*) LARK QUAIL or QUAIL PLOVER W and E Africa / dry scrub / e 2

PEDIONOMIDAE Plains Wanderer A bird related to the Hemipodes and often included in the same family. It differs mainly in retaining the hind toe (absent in the Turnicidae), in having paired instead of single carotid arteries, and having pointed rather than oval eggs.

Pedionomus torquatus *Gould* PLAINS WANDERER or COLLARED HEMIPODE Central deserts of Australia / e 4–5

GRUIDAE Cranes Large, long-legged, long-necked birds, usually with the head partly bare of feathers in the adult, feathered in the immature. Inhabit open marshlands, wet plains and prairies. Gregarious. Feed on vegetable matter, grain, worms, small animals etc. Nest bulky, on the ground. Eggs usually 2, very occasionally 1 or 3. Fourteen species. Cosmopolitan except S America, New Zealand and Pacific.

Grus grus (*L*) GREY CRANE Much of Europe and Asia w S to Africa / marshes and cultivation / e 1–3 / I ♂♀ 28–30 / F 70

Grus nigricollis *Przewalski* BLACK-NECKED CRANE C Asian plateaux / swampy ground / e 2

Grus monacha *Temminck* HOODED CRANE E Siberia to Japan and China / rare

Grus canadensis (*L*) SANDHILL CRANE N America, extreme E Siberia and Cuba / e 1–2

Grus japonensis (*Müller*) MANCHURIAN CRANE or JAPANESE CRANE Manchuria, Japan and China / very rare and decreasing / e 1–2

Grus americana (*L*) WHOOPING CRANE N America / reduced and very rare (18 birds in 1969)

Grus vipio *Pallas* WHITE-NAPED CRANE E Asia / e 2

Grus antigone (*L*) SARUS CRANE India and SE Asia, also Queensland in Australia / plains and marshes / e 2 / I ♂♀ 28–34

Grus rubicunda (*Perry*) BROLGA Australia

ANATIDAE:
Mergus merganser,
Goosander,
Common Merganser

ANATIDAE:
Chloephaga rubidiceps,
Ruddy-headed Goose

Plate 40

ANATIDAE:
Aix sponsa,
Carolina or Wood Duck

ANATIDAE:
Branta canadensis,
Canada Goose

Plate 41

and S New Guinea / grassland, cultivation and swamp / e 2

Grus leucogeranus *Pallas* SIBERIAN or GREAT WHITE CRANE Siberia w N India and China / rare and decreasing (1,000 pairs in 1965) / e 2

Bugeranus carunculatus (*Gmelin*) WATTLED CRANE E and S Africa from Somaliland to Cape / marsh / e 1–2

Anthropoides virgo (*L*) DEMOISELLE CRANE S Europe, Asia and N Africa w further S / e 1–3 / I ♂♀ 28–30

Anthropoides paradisea (*Lichtenstein*) BLUE, PARADISE or STANLEY CRANE High veld of S Africa / grassland and swamp / e 2

Balearica pavonina (*L*) CROWNED CRANE Africa S of Sahara / swamps / e 2–3

ARAMIDAE Limpkin A largish marsh bird forming a link between Cranes and Rails having the skeletal structure of the former and the outward appearance of the latter. Feed on molluscs and other aquatic life. Nest, bulky, on ground or in bushes.

Aramus guarauna (*L*) (= **A. scolopaceus** (*Gmelin*) LIMPKIN Caribbean and S America / n ground or bush / e 4–8 (usually 6) / I ♂♀

PSOPHIIDAE Trumpeters Squat dumpy birds with long legs and necks and short fowl-like bills. Males have a loud trumpet-like call. Plumage soft and velvety, wings weak. Gregarious. Inhabit forests; n ground, e 6–10 white or green.

Psophia crepitans *L* COMMON TRUMPETER Amazon basin, N of river / forest / fruit and insects / n hole (sic)

Psophia leucoptera *Spix* WHITE-WINGED TRUMPETER Upper Amazon basin and Rio Negro

Psophia viridis *Spix* GREEN-WINGED TRUMPETER Amazon basin S of river

RALLIDAE Rails, Crakes, Coots and Gallinules Small to medium sized running, wading or swimming birds typically inhabiting marsh and water but some are terrestrial. Weak fliers, island forms showing a strong tendency to become completely flightless. Omnivorous. Legs long and stout with long toes, partially webbed in some swimming species.

The classification of this family has posed many problems. I have chosen to follow the recent revision by Olsen *Wilson Bull* (1973) pp 381–416.

Himantornis haematopus *Hartlaub*

NKULENGA RAIL W Africa / forest / seeds, frogs and invertebrates / n ? tree / e 3–6

Canirallus oculeus (*Hartlaub*) GREY-THROATED RAIL W Africa / forest / n ground / e 2–3

Canirallus kioloides (*Pucheran*) KIOLOIDES RAIL Madagascar / seeds and insects / n in lianas / e 2

Canirallus rubra (*Schlegel*) CHESTNUT RAIL W New Guinea / mountain forest / no other data

Canirallus leucospila (*Salvadori*) WHITE-STRIPED RAIL New Guinea / mountain forest / no other data

Canirallus mayri (*Hartert*) MAYR'S RAIL Cyclops Mts, New Guinea / mountain forest / no other data

Canirallus forbesi (*Sharpe*) FORBES' RAIL Owen Stanley Range, New Guinea / mountain forest / no other data

Sarothura rufa (*Vieillot*) RED-CHESTED CRAKE Africa S of Sahara / marsh / insects and vegetable matter / n ground / e 3–5

Sarothura lugens (*Böhm*) CHESTNUT-HEADED CRAKE C Africa / marsh / n and e n/k

Sarothura pulchra (*Gray*) WHITE-SPOTTED CRAKE C and W Africa / swampy forest / insects etc / n ground / e 4 or 2 (accounts differ)

Sarothura elegans (*Smith*) BUFF-SPOTTED CRAKE C, E and SE Africa / grassland and secondary forest / n ground / e 3–5

Sarothura boehmi *Reichenow* BÖHM'S CRAKE W and C Africa / swamps / seeds / n ground / e 4

Sarothura affinis (*Smith*) (= **S. lineata** *Swainson*) JARDINE'S CRAKE or CHESTNUT-TAILED CRAKE SE Africa / marsh and moor / n ground / e 3–4 [*S. antonii* is a race of this species]

Sarothura insularis (*Sharpe*) MADAGASCAR CRAKE Madagascar / forest clearings and secondary bush / n ground / e up to 4

Sarothura watersi (*Bartlett*) WATERS' CRAKE Betsileo and massif of Tsaratanana, Madagascar / wet grassland / no other data

Sarothura ayresi (*Gurney*) AYRES' CRAKE Ethiopia, rarely in S Africa / no data

Sarothura lynesi *Grant and Mackworth Praed* (in *Bull BOC*, vol 55 (1934), p 17) LYNES' CRAKE SW Africa / swamps / no data

Coturnicops exquisita (*Swinhoe*) SWINHOE'S CRAKE Transbaikalia and Ussuriland w China and Japan / no reliable data

Coturnicops noveboracensis (*Gmelin*)

YELLOW RAIL N America / meadows and ravines / n ground / e 8–10

Coturnicops notata *Gould* MARKED RAIL or DARWIN'S RAIL Parts of S America / little data (see de Schaunsee 'Noctulae Naturae', no 357 (1962) for a summary of what is known about this species)

Micropygia schomburgkii (*Schomburgk*) OCELLATED CRAKE S Venezuela, Guianas, Mato Grosso / grassland / no data

Rallina fasciata (*Raffles*) RED-LEGGED CRAKE SE Asia, Indonesia, Palaus and Moluccas / swamps / n ground / e 4–8 / I ♂♀

Rallina eurizonoides (*Lafresnaye*) BANDED CRAKE Philippines, Celebes, Taiwan, Riu Kius, India and SE Asia / damp woods / n ground or off ground / e 4–8 / I ♂♀

Rallina canningi (*Blyth*) ANDAMAN CRAKE Andamans / marshy jungle / n ground / no other data

Rallina tricolor *Gray* RED-NECKED RAIL N Queensland, New Guinea, Bismarck Archipelago and adjacent islands / swamps, wet forests near water / small animals and insects / n ground / e 4–5 (?3) accounts differ

Anurolimnas castaneiceps (*Sclater and Salvin*) CHESTNUT-HEADED CRAKE SE Colombia and E Ecuador / forest / no other data

Anurolimnas fasciatus (*Sclater and Salvin*) (= **Porzana hauxvelli** *Sclater and Salvin*) HAUXWELL'S CRAKE SE Colombia and NE Peru / no data

Anurolimnas viridis (*Müller*) CAYENNE CRAKE Tropical S America / grassland / n off ground in bushes / e n/s

Laterallus jamaicensis (*Gmelin*) BLACK RAIL or CRAKE Parts of USA, Cuba, Jamaica, parts of S America / discontinuous / marshes / n ground / e 4–10

Laterallus spilopterus (*Durnford*) SPOT-WINGED CRAKE Argentina and Uruguay / no data

Laterallus spilonotus *Gould* GALAPAGOS CRAKE Galapagos / almost ubiquitous / n ground e up to 5 / I 23–5 / F 80–5

Laterallus exilis (*Temminck*) TEMMINCK'S or GREY-BREASTED CRAKE E Nicaragua and tropical S America / n ground / e 3 (1 clutch known)

Laterallus xenopterus *Conover* HORQUETA or RUFOUS-FACED CRAKE Paraguay / unique

Laterallus melanophaius (*Vieillot*) RUFOUS-SIDED CRAKE Tropical S America / discontinuous / n off ground / e 2–3

Laterallus albigularis (*Lawrence*) WHITE-THROATED CRAKE Central and tropical S America / n ground / e 3–5

Laterallus ruber (*Sclater and Salvin*) RED RAIL or RUDDY CRAKE Mexico and C America / swamp / n ground / e 4–6

Laterallus levraudi (*Sclater and Salvin*) LEVRAUD'S or RUSTY-FLANKED CRAKE N Venezuela / no data

Laterallus leucopyrrhus (*Vieillot*) RED AND WHITE CRAKE Paraguay and S Brazil to Buenos Aires and Uruguay / n ground / e 3

Nesoclopeus poeciloptera (*Hartlaub*) FIJI RAIL Fiji / probably extinct / n ground / e 6

Nesoclopeus woodfordi (*Ogilvie Grant*) WOODFORD'S RAIL Solomon Is / no data

Gallirallus australis (*Sparrman*) WEKA RAIL New Zealand / forest and swamp / n ground / e 4 (?3) / I ♂♀ 27

Gallirallus insignis (*Sclater*) INSIGNIA RAIL New Britain / mountain forests / n n/k / e – eggs attributed to the species exist

Gallirallus torquatus (*L*) BARRED RAIL Philippines, Celebes, Sulus, Tukang, Besi, Salawatti and NW New Guinea / marshes / n ground / e 3–4

Gallirallus owstoni (*Rothschild*) GUAM RAIL Guam, Marianne Is / forest and grassland / snails and insects / n ground / e 3 (1 nest known)

Gallirallus wakensis *Rothschild* WAKE ISLAND RAIL Wake Is / probably extinct

Gallirallus dieffenbachii *Gray* DIFFENBACH'S RAIL Chatham Is in the Chatham Group / extinct

Gallirallus modestus (*Hutton*) MODEST RAIL Mangare Is in the Chatham Group / extinct / n hole in ground / 1 egg known

Gallirallus striatus (*L*) SLATY-BREASTED RAIL India, SE Asia, Indonesia, S China and Taiwan / swamps / n ground / e 5–9 / I ♂♀ 19–22

Gallirallus philippensis (*L*) BANDED LAND RAIL Philippines, Australasia, New Zealand and Melanesia / aquatic vegetation / insects and seeds / n ground / e 4–6, 5–9 (accounts differ) / I ♂♀ 18–19

Gallirallus ecaudata (*Miller*) (= **Rallus pacificus** *Gmelin*) TAHITI RAIL Tahiti / extinct / no data / known only from paintings

Gallirallus sylvestris (*Sclater*) WOODHEN Lord Howe Is / n ground / e 1–4

Gallirallus minor (*Hamilton*) LITTLE WOODHEN Castle Rocks, New Zealand / extinct / bones only

ANATIDAE:
Cairina moshata,
Muscovy Duck

ANATIDAE:
Denorocygna eytoni,
Plumed Whistling Duck or
Eyton's Tree Duck

Plate 42

ANATIDAE:
Anas platyrhynchos,
Domestic Mallard (domestic
white-crested drake (left) and
wild individual)

CATHARTIDAE:
Sarcorhamphus papa,
King Vulture

Plate 43

Gallirallus hartreei *Scarlett* ('A small wood-hen from New Zealand', *Notornis*, 17 (1970) pp 68–74) SCARLETT'S EXTINCT RAIL New Zealand / extinct / bones only (now thought to be a synonym of *Gallinula hodgeni*)

(?) Gallirallus (Diaphorapteryx) hawkinsi (*Forbes*) GIANT CHATHAM RAIL Chatham Is/ extinct / bones only

Tricholimnas lafresnayanus (*Verreaux and Des Murs*) LAFRESNAYE'S RAIL New Caledonia/ forests / possibly extinct

[**Tricholimnas conditicius** *Peters and Griscom* GILBERT RAIL Apiang Is, Gilbert group/ 1 specimen / (? extinct). This specimen is now believed to be a mislabelled immature of *G. sylvestris* (Greenaway, J.C., *Breviora Mus Comp Zool*, no 5 (1952), pp 1–4)]

Gallirallus insignis (*Forbes*) NOTABLE RAIL New Zealand / extinct / bones only (this species probably requires renaming)

Capellirallus karamu *Falla* CAVE RAIL Karama, New Zealand / bones only

Crecopsis egregia (*Peters*) AFRICAN CRAKE Tropical Africa / grass and marsh / n ground or floating / e 5–7

Crex crex (*L*) CORNCRAKE or LANDRAIL Europe and W Asia w into tropical Africa/ grassland and cultivation / n ground / e 6–14 / I ♀ 14–15 / F 30–4

Rougetius rougetii (*Guérin-Méneville*) ROUGET'S RAIL Ethiopia / marshes and moor/ n ground / e 4–8

Aramidopsis plateni (*Blasius*) PLATEN'S RAIL Celebes / known only from 10 specimens

Dryolimnas cuvieri (*Pucheran*) MASCARENE RAIL Madagascar, Mauritius and Aldabra (formerly Assumption, extinct race) / n ground/ e 3–4

Dryolimnas pectoralis (*Temminck*) LEWIN RAIL Australia, Tasmania, New Guinea [Flores, race known from unique type] / reed beds/ insects, snails and worms / n ground / e 4–6

Dryolimnas muelleri (*Rothschild*) MÜLLER'S RAIL Auckland Islands / believed extinct, but rediscovered 1966, on Adam's Is in the group/ status unknown (possibly conspecific with *pectoralis*)

Atlantisia rogersi *Lowe* INACESSIBLE RAIL Inacessible Is, Tristan group / ubiquitous / n ground / e 2

Atlantisia elpenor *Olsen* ELPENOR RAIL Ascension Is / extinct / bones only

Atlantisia podarces (*Wetmore*) GREAT ST HELENA RAIL St Helena / extinct / bones only

Rallus longirostris *Boddaert* CLAPPER RAIL Caribbean, northern S America and southern N America / marshes / n ground / e 6–14 / I ♂♀ 14

Rallus wetmorei *Zimmer and Phelps* (*Am Mus Novit*, 127 (1944), p 3) WETMORE'S RAIL Coastal swamps of Venezuela / no data

Rallus elegans *Audubon* KING RAIL Southern USA, Mexico, Cuba / marshes / seeds etc / n ground / e 6–15

Rallus limicola *Vieillot* VIRGINIA RAIL N and C America S to Ecuador / lakes and marshes/ n ground / e 7–12 / I ♀ 15

Rallus antarcticus *King* AUSTRAL RAIL C Chile and Argentine S to Magellan Strait/ probably no data (sometimes treated as a race of *limicola*)

Rallus aquaticus *L* WATER RAIL Palaearctic/ marshes and reed beds / n ground / e 5–16/ I ♂♀ 19–20 / F 7–8 weeks

Rallus semiplumbeus *Sclater* BOGOTA RAIL Colombia and Ecuador / marshy edges of inland lakes

Rallus caerulescens *Gmelin* KAFFIR RAIL E and S Africa Isolated populations in Sierra Leone and São Thomé / swamps / n ground/ e 4–6

Rallus madagascariensis *Verreaux* MADAGASCAR RAIL Madagascar / marshes

Aramides mangle (*Spix*) SPIX'S WOOD RAIL, LITTLE WOOD RAIL E Brazil / mangrove

Aramides axillaris *Lawrence* RUFOUS-CROWNED RAIL C America to Guianas and Ecuador / n tree / e 5

Aramides cajanea (*Müller*) CAYENNE or GREY-NECKED RAIL Tropical America / bogs/ n ground or bush (accounts differ) / e 3–5 (rarely 6–7)

Aramides wolfi *Berlepsch and Taczanowski* WOLF'S WOOD RAIL Ecuador / forest and secondary growth

Aramides gutteralis *Sharpe* RED-THROATED WOOD RAIL ? Peru / 1 specimen of doubtful origin

Aramides ypecaha (*Vieillot*) YPECAHA RAIL E South America / n shrub or herbage / e 5

Aramides saracura (*Spix*) SARACURA or SLATY-BREASTED RAIL SE Brazil and Paraguay/ forest

Aramides calopterus *Sclater and Salvin* RED-WINGED WOOD RAIL E Ecuador / no data

Aramides concolor (*Gosse*) UNIFORM RAIL Jamaica (extinct race) and Tropical America/ n n/k/e ?2, 1 clutch known

Aphanapteryx bonasia (*Sélys-Longchamps*) (= **A. broeckii** *Schlegel*) VAN DEN BROECKE'S RED RAIL or PETER MUNDY'S HEN Mauritius/ extinct c1675/ bones only and paintings

Aphanapteryx leguati (*Milne-Edwards*) LEGUAT'S BLUE RAIL Rodriguez/extinct/bones [and Leguat]

[**Aphanapteryx herberti** (*Schlegel*) HERBERT'S HEN Mauritius [Sir Thomas Herbert]]

[**Kuina mundyi** *Hachisuka* MUNDY'S YELLOW RAIL Mauritius [Mundy]]

[**Leguatia gigantea** *Schlegel* GIANT WATERHEN Mauritius Rodriguez and (?) Réunion [Leguat]. There is no proof that this bird was a rail, it might have been a ratite]

Cyanornis coerulescens (*Sélys-Longchamps*) FLIGHTLESS GREAT GALLINULE Réunion/bones [and Du Bois]

Gymnocrex rosenbergii (*Schlegel*) ROSENBERG'S RAIL N and C Celebes/no data

Gymnocrex plumbiventris (*Gray*) BARE-EYED RAIL N Moluccas, Misol, New Guinea, Aru Is and New Ireland/marshy forests/n ground/e n/s

Amaurornis akool (*Sykes*) BROWN CRAKE India, NE Indo-China and SE China/swamps and woods/n ground or off ground/e 5–6/I ♂♀

Amaurornis olivacea (*Meyen*) BUSH-HEN E Indonesia to N Australia forest and long grass near water/small animals, insects and seeds/n ground/e 4–6

Amaurornis isabellina (*Schlegel*) ISABELLINE WATERHEN Celebes/no data

Amaurornis phoenicurus (*Pennant*) WHITE-BREASTED WATERHEN Indian sub-continent, SE Asia, S China, Indonesia, Hainan and Taiwan / marshes / n ground or off ground/ e 6–7/I ♂♀

Amaurornis olivieri (*Grandidier and Berlioz*) OLIVER'S RAIL Madagascar / no data, known only from few specimens

Amaurornis flavirostra (*Swainson*) BLACK CRAKE Africa S of Sahara/swamps/n ground/ e 3–6

Porzana parva (*Scopoli*) LITTLE CRAKE S Europe, SW Asia and Mediterranean/marsh/ n ground/e 4–7/I ♂♀ 'less than 23 days'

Porzana pusilla (*Pallas*) BAILLON'S CRAKE Europe, temperate and tropical Asia, Africa/ streams/n ground/e 4–8/I ♂♀ 20–1

Porzana porzana (*L*) SPOTTED CRAKE Europe and W Asia/w Africa and India/swamps/n ground or off ground/e 6–15/I ♂♀ 18–21

Porzana fluminea *Gould* AUSTRALIAN SPOTTED CRAKE Australia and Tasmania/margins of water-bodies/aquatic life and vegetation/ e 4–6

Porzana carolina (*L*) SORA or CAROLINA CRAKE N and C America to Peru, Venezuela and W Indies/swamps/n ground or floating/ e 5–18/I ♂♀ 14 or 16–18 (accounts differ)

Porzana albicollis (*Vieillot*) ASH- or WHITE-THROATED CRAKE Tropical eastern South America/grassland/n ground/e 2–3 (?6)

Porzana fusca (*L*) RUDDY CRAKE Indian sub-continent, SE Asia, Indonesia, China and Japan / swamps / n ground / e 6–9 / I ♂♀

Porzana paykullii (*Ljungh*) CHESTNUT-BREASTED CRAKE E Siberia, Korea and NE China w to Borneo and Java/n ground/e 7–9

Porzana bicolor *Walden* ELWES'S CRAKE Himalayas, mts of W China and N Burma/ jungle/n ground or off ground/e 5–8/I ♂♀

Porzana tabuensis (*Gmelin*) SPOTLESS CRAKE or SOOTY RAIL Australasia, New Zealand, New Caledonia and Polynesia (various races)/reeds and thickets / aquatic life / n ground or over water/e 4–6

Porzana astrictocarpus *Olsen* LITTLE ST HELENA RAIL St Helena/extinct sometime after 1502/bones only

Porzana palmeri (*Frohawk*) LAYSAN RAIL Laysan Is/probably extinct/n ground/e 2–5

[**Porzana millsi** (*Dole*) MILLS' RAIL Hawaii extinct (possibly a colour variation of *sandwichensis*)]

Porzana sandwichensis *Gmelin* SANDWICH RAIL Hawaii/extinct (*P. wilsoni*, Finsch, is a synonym)

Porzana atra *North* HENDERSON ISLAND RAIL Henderson Is [The status of *Rallusnigra*, Miller, has never been cleared up. It is known only from a coloured plate (J. F. Miller, *Icon Anim* (1784), pl 50 f.B.). No locality. Miller confused the issue by later identifying the bird as a form of *Porzana tabuensis*. The plate represents a bird closely allied to *P. atra*, but see also Lysaght, *Bull Brit Orn Cl* 76 (1956), pp 97–8.]

Porzana monasa (*Kittlitz*) KITTLITZ'S RAIL Kusai Is, Carolines/2 specimens

Poliolimnas cinereus (*Vieillot*) ASHY CRAKE

PANDIONIDAE:
Pandion haliaetus,
Osprey

ACCIPITRIDAE:
Haliaeetus leucogaster,
White-bellied Sea Eagle

Plate 44

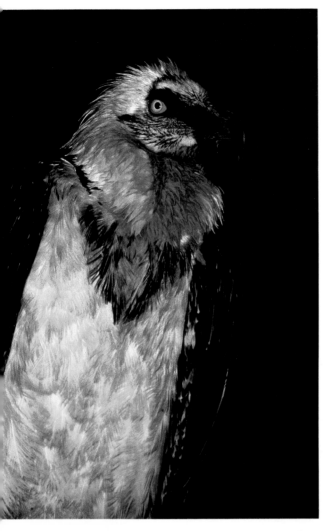

ACCIPITRIDAE: *Haliastur indus,* Brahminy Kite

ACCIPITRIDAE:
Gypaetus barbatus,
Lammergeier or Bearded
Vulture

ACCIPITRIDAE:
Hieraaetus morphnoides,
Little Eagle

Plate 45

Malaya, Indonesia, Australasia, Melanesia, Micronesia and Polynesia / swamps and mangrove / insects and aquatic life / n ground or over water / e 3–6

Poliolimnas flaviventris (*Boddaert*) YELLOW-BREASTED RAIL Greater Antilles and S America / swamps / n among water plants / e 3–5

Aenigmatolimnas marginalis (*Hartlaub*) STRIPED CRAKE Africa / swamps and woods / n ground / e 4–5

Cyanolimnas cerverai *Barbour and Peters* ZAPATA RAIL Zapata in S Cuba / bushy swamp

Neocrex erythrops (*Sclater*) RED-FACED or PAINT-BILLED CRAKE Northern S America / n ground / e 7 (1 nest known) (*N. columbianus*, Bangs, is sometimes separated)

Pardirallus maculatus (*Boddaert*) SPOTTED RAIL Tropical eastern S America, Cuba, Belise (1 specimen) [A spotted rail also occurred in Jamaica but became extinct before any specimens were preserved] / river banks and rice fields / fish and insects / n ground or rushes over water / e 3–7

Pardirallus sanguinolentus (*Swainson*) (= **Rallus rytirhynchos** *Vieillot*) PLUMBEOUS RAIL S America from Peru southward / riverbanks / n ground / e 4–6 (?3)

Pardirallus nigricans (*Vieillot*) BLACKISH RAIL Tropical S America / e 2 (1 clutch in captivity)

Eulabeornis castaneoventris *Gould* CHESTNUT-BELLIED RAIL N Australia and Aru Is / mangrove swamps / aquatic animals / n tree / e 4

Habroptila wallacii *Gray* WALLACE'S RAIL Halmahera / swampy thickets / shoots and beetles / n and e n/k

Habroptila inepta (*D'Albertis and Salvadori*) INEPT RAIL New Guinea / very local / mangrove swamps

Gallicrex cinerea (*Gmelin*) WATERCOCK or KORA Indian sub-continent to S China, Japan, SE Asia and Indonesia / swamps / n ground / e 3–6 / I ♀ (?♂)

[The Purple Gallinules of the Old World are now generally considered to constitute a single species. It seems useful, however, to indicate the main groupings of 'super' sub-species, formerly considered species, which themselves consisted of a number of different races or sub-species]:

Porphyrio porphyrio (*L*) BLUE GALLINULE

W Mediterranean / n floating / e 3–5

Porphyrio madagascariensis (*Latham*) GREEN-BACKED GALLINULE Africa and Madagascar / swamps / n over water / e 2–6

Porphyrio poliocephalus (*Latham*) EASTERN PURPLE GALLINULE Tropical Asia, through Indonesia and Australia to New Zealand and Fiji / swamps / n floating / e 3–7

Porphyrio pulverulentus *Temminck* PHILIPPINE GALLINULE Philippines (Bohol, Luzon, Mindanao and Mindoro)

Porphyrio alleni *Thomson* (quoted erroneously as 'Thompson' by Ripley, *Rails of the World*, 1977) ALLEN'S GALLINULE Africa S of Sahara / swamps and lakes / n floating / e 2–5

Porphyrio martinica (*L*) AMERICAN PURPLE GALLINULE Tropical America / lakes and swamps / n floating / e 4–10

Porphyrio flavirostris (*Gmelin*) (= **P. parva** (*Boddaert*)) LITTLE or AZURE GALLINULE The Guianas, N and C Brazil, Paraguay / grassland and ricefields / n ground / e 4–5 / I ♂♀

Porphyrio mantelli (*Owen*) TAKAHE New Zealand / typical race, N Island, extinct: *P. m. hochstetteri* (Meyer), S Island, now confined to valleys in extreme S / n ground / e 1–4

Porphyrio albus (*White*) WHITE GALLINULE Lord Howe Is / extinct. The validity of this white form was for long unproved (see Greenway, *Extinct and Vanishing Birds of the World*, 2nd ed, pp 250–3). Two other forms, *P. stanleyi* and *P. raperi*, also described from Lord Howe Is, are probably synonyms of *P. albus*, although Rothschild was of the opinion that 2 forms occurred, one on Lord Howe Is and the other on Norfolk Is. Recently bones excavated on Lord Howe Is proved that *P. albus* is a species related to *P. mantelli* and if the genus *Notornis* be recognised would be placed therein.

Pareudiastes pacificus *Hartlaub and Finsch* SAMOAN GALLINULE Samoa / possibly extinct / n ground / e 2

Pareudiastes silvestris *Mayr* (Birds collected during the Whitney South Sea Expedition *xxii* 'Three New Genera from Polynesia and Melanesia', *Amer Mus Novit*, 590 (1933) pp 1–6) EDITH'S GALLINULE San Cristobal Is / no data / unique

Gallinula (= **Porphyriops**) **melanops** (*Vieillot*) SPOT-FLANKED GALLINULE Eastern and southern S America / n ground / e 4–8

Gallinula tenebrosa *Gould* DUSKY GALLINULE

Australia and Indonesia / coastal and inland swamps / vegetation / n ground or bush / e 5–9

Gallinula chloropus *L* Moorhen or Florida Gallinule Almost cosmopolitan except Australasia and Oceania / swamps / n ground / e 4–8 / I ♂♀ 19–22

Gallinula nesiotis *Sclater* Tristan Gallinule Tristan da Cunha Is / extinct

Gallinula comeri (*Allen*) Gough Gallinule Gough Is / n ground / e 2 / I 21

Gallinula angulata *Sundevall* Lesser or Little Moorhen Africa S of Sahara / swamps / n ground / e 4–8

Gallinula ventralis *Gould* Native Hen Australia plains and lake margins / vegetation / n ground or over water / e 5–7

Gallinula mortierii (*DuBus*) Tasmanian Hen Tasmania / fresh water / vegetation / n ground / e 7–9

Gallinula hodgeni (*Scarlett*) New Zealand Gallinule New Zealand / bones only

Fulica atra *L* Common or Black Coot Greater part of the Old World / lakes / n floating / e 7–10 / I ♂♀ 21–4 / F c56

Fulica cristata *Gmelin* Crested Coot Tropical Africa / swamps / n in water, floating, or on low bough over water / e 4–8 or more

Fulica americana *Gmelin* American Coot Tropical America, temperate N America, Hawaiian Is / lakes and swamps / n floating / e 8–12, ?16–22 / I ♂♀ 21–2

[**Fulica ardesiaca** *Tschudi* Slate-coloured Coot Andes from Ecuador to N Chile / lakes / n reedbeds / e ? (this bird is now considered a race of *americana*, see Morrison, *Bull BOC* vol 59 (1939) p 55)]

Fulica armillata *Vieillot* Red-gartered Coot Southern S America / lakes / n floating / e 4–8

Fulica caribaea *Ridgway* Caribbean Coot W Indies / rare and of uncertain status

Fulica leucoptera *Vieillot* White-winged Coot Southern S America / lakes and rivers / n floating / e 4–9

Fulica rufifrons *Philippi and Landbeck* Red-fronted Coot Southern S America and Falklands / lakes / n floating / e 4–8

Fulica gigantea *Eydoux and Souleyet* Giant Coot Puna zone of Andes / lakes / n floating / e 6–7

Fulica cornuta *Bonaparte* Horned Coot High Andes, scattered localities / lakes / n on artificial islands of stones built by the bird in lakes / e 3–5

Fulica newtonii *Milne-Edwards* Du Bois' Coot Mauritius and Rodriguez / extinct / bones only [and Du Bois]

Fulica chathamensis *Forbes* New Zealand Coot New Zealand / bones only

Aptornis defossor *Owen* Great Aptornis S Island, New Zealand / bones only

Aptornis otidiformis (*Owen*) Lesser Aptornis N Island, New Zealand / bones only

(Ripley believes that the *Aptornis* are not rails and should be placed near the Kagu)

Nesotrochis debooyi *Wetmore* Debooy's Rail Puerto Rico and adjacent islands / extinct / bones only

Nesotrochis picapicensis (*Fischer and Stephan*) Picapica Rail Cuba / extinct / bones only

Nesotrochis steganinos *Olson* Sinewed Rail Haiti / extinct / bones only

Hovacrex roberti (*Andrews*) Hova Rail Madagascar / extinct / bones only

Capellirallus karamu *Falla* Karamu Rail N Island, New Zealand / extinct / bones only

HELIORNITHIDAE Finfoots and Sungrebes Rail-like birds with elongated bodies, long necks and bills, and long stiff tails. The feet have lobed webs similar to those of grebes and coots. They inhabit marsh and waters feeding on fish and aquatic vegetation. Three species of relict distribution.

Podica senegalensis (*Vieillot*) African Finfoot Africa / wooded streams / n over water / e 2

Heliopais personata (*Gray*) Masked Finfoot Bengal to Sumatra / forest clearings / n tree over water / e 5–6 / I ♂♀

Heliornis fulica (*Boddaert*) Sun Grebe From Vera Cruz S to N Argentina / stagnant creeks / n bush / e 4

RHYNOCHETIDAE Kagu A long-legged greyish bird of uncertain affinities. Little is known if its habits. It inhabits dense mountain forest and is almost flightless. In captivity a stick nest is made on the ground, a single egg being laid. Owing to introduction of rats, cats and other predators to its native island it is now in serious danger of extinction.

Rhynochetos jubatus *Verreaux and Des Murs* Kagu New Caledonia / mountain forest / invertebrates / n ? ground / e 1

ACCIPITRIDAE:
Accipiter nisus, European Sparrowhawk

Plate 46

ACCIPITRIDAE:
Aquila chrysaetos,
Golden Eagle

ACCIPITRIDAE:
Terathopius ecaudatus,
Bateleur

Plate 47

EURYPIGIDAE Sunbittern A bittern-like bird of forest streams along which it stalks hunting fish heron-fashion. The wings are delicately patterned in blacks, greys and browns, and are opened in courtship and threat display. The nest is a domed structure in a tree with a side entrance. The 2 eggs are grey, spotted with red. The young grow rapidly and are full-grown at two months.

Eurypyga helias (*Pallas*) SUNBITTERN Tropical America/forests and creeks/n tree/e 2

CARIAMIDAE Seriamas Greyish-brown, long-legged, running, ground birds with erect posture, erectile crests, short broad down-curved bills, longish necks, short wings and long tails. They seldom fly. Feed primarily on insects, snakes, lizards and berries. Two eggs are laid, incubated by both sexes. They are considered to be the only living descendants of a group of large carnivorous ground birds which flourished in the early Tertiary period.

Cariama cristata (*L*) RED-LEGGED or CRESTED SERIAMA Mato Grosso to Paraguay and NW Argentina/n ground

Chunga burmeisteri (*Hartlaub*) BLACK-LEGGED or BURMEISTER'S SERIAMA NW Argentina/n tree

OTIDAE Bustards Large ground birds inhabiting open grassy plains and savannahs. They can fly strongly but prefer to run in escaping from predators. Several species are crested, others are moustached. They are omnivorous, but feed largely on grain and insects. Eggs are laid on the ground with little attempt at a nest; and are handsomely marbled in greens, browns and reds. Incubation is by the female and lasts from 20–30 days. The young fledge at 5–6 weeks. About 25 species in the temperate and tropical Old World.

Otis tetrax (*L*) LITTLE BUSTARD Europe, C and W Asia/plains/n ground/e 3–5/I ♀ 20–1

Otis tarda *L* GREAT BUSTARD C and S Europe across temperate Asia to Japan and Amurland/plains/n ground/e 2–4/I ♀ 25–8/F 35

Neotis cafra (*Lichtenstein*) STANLEY BUSTARD S Africa/grass veld/n ground/e 2

Neotis ludwigii (*Rüppell*) LUDWIG'S BUSTARD S Africa/plains/n ground/e 1–2

Neotis denhami (*Children*) DENHAM'S BUSTARD Tropical Africa/plains/n ground/e 2

Neotis nuba (*Cretzschmar*) NUBIAN BUSTARD Niger to Lake Chad and N Sudan/desert/n ground/e 2

Neotis burchellii (*Heuglin*) BURCHELL'S BUSTARD Jebel Dul, S of Sennar/unique

Neotis heuglinii (*Hartlaub*) HEUGLIN'S BUSTARD Somaliland / scrub and semi-desert/ n ground/e 2

Ardeotis arabs (*L*) GREAT ARABIAN BUSTARD S Arabia and N Africa / plains and bush / n ground/e 2

Ardeotis kori (*Burchell*) KORI BUSTARD E Africa/plains/n ground/e 2

Ardeotis nigriceps (*Vigors*) GREAT INDIAN BUSTARD India/scrub and grassland/n ground/ e 1–2/I ♀

Chlamydotis undulata (*Jacquin*) HOUBARA BUSTARD E Canary Is, N Africa and SW Asia / semi-desert/n ground/e 2–4/I ♀

Lophotis savilei *Lynes* SAVILE'S PYGMY BUSTARD W Africa from Senegambia to Darfur and Nigeria / thick bush / n and e n/k (now generally treated as a race of *ruficrista*)

Lophotis ruficrista (*Smith*) CRESTED BUSTARD E and S Africa/bush/n ground/e 2

Afrotis atra *L* LITTLE BLACK BUSTARD S Africa/bush/n ground/e 1

Eupodotis vigorsii (*Smith*) BLACK-THROATED BUSTARD or VAAC KORHAAN S Africa / plains/ n ground/e 2

Eupodotis australis (*Gray*) AUSTRALIAN BUSTARD Australia and New Guinea / open country with scattered trees/n ground/e 1–2

Eupodotis rueppellii (*Wahlberg*) RÜPPELL'S BUSTARD SW Africa/plains/n n/s/e 1

Eupodotis humilis (*Blyth*) LITTLE BROWN BUSTARD N Somaliland/bush and thick thorn scrub/n ground/e 2

Eupodotis senegalensis (*Vieillot*) SENEGAL BUSTARD Africa S of Sahara / desert and scrub/ n ground/e 2

Eupodotis caerulescens (*Vieillot*) BLUE BUSTARD S Africa/grass veld/n ground/e 2

Eupodotis bengalensis (*Gmelin*) BENGAL FLORICAN India and Cambodia / discontinuous/ savannah/n ground/e 2/I ♀ 30

Lissotis melanogaster (*Rüppell*) BLACK-BELLIED BUSTARD Africa S of Sahara/grassland/ n ground/e 1–2

Lissotis hartlaubii (*Heuglin*) HARTLAUB'S BUSTARD Egyptian Sudan S to Tanganyika/ grassland/n and e n/k

Sypheotides indica (*Miller*) LESSER FLORICAN India/savannah/n ground/e 3–5/I ♀

JACANIDAE Jacanas or Lily Trotters
Birds of tropical lakes and pools with long legs and exceedingly long toes which enable them to walk over floating vegetation. They have frontal shields like coots and gallinules and horny spurs on the bend of the wing. They feed on insects, small fish and seeds of water plants. The nest is floating, and the eggs, 4 in number, are glossy brown, heavily pencilled with black. Incubation lasts 22-4 days. Eight species distributed through the tropics.

Microparra capensis (*Smith*) LESSER JACANA E Africa from White Nile to the Cape / lakes / n floating / e 2-4

Actophilornis africana (*Gmelin*) AFRICAN JACANA Africa S of Sahara / lakes / n floating / e 4

Actophilornis albinucha (*Geoffroy St Hilaire*) MADAGASCAR JACANA Madagascar / lakes / n floating / e 4

Irediparra gallinacea (*Temminck*) COMB-CRESTED JACANA or LOTOSBIRD Indonesia, New Guinea, N and E Australia / still, fresh waters / n floating / e 4

Hydrophasianus chirurgus (*Scopoli*) PHEASANT-TAILED JACANA or WATER PHEASANT Kashmir to S China and Philippines / lotos ponds / n floating / e 4 / I ♂ 26

Metopidius indicus (*Latham*) BRONZE-WINGED JACANA India, SE Asia, Java and Sumatra / ponds / n floating / e 4 / I ♂ (? 16; Baker's estimate was 14–16, but Ali says that although the period is unknown it must be longer)

Jacana spinosa (*L*) NORTHERN JACANA C America and Greater Antilles

Jacana jacana (*L*) WATTLED JACANA Equatorial S America

ROSTRATULIDAE Painted Snipe Birds superficially resembling Snipe but very much more brightly coloured, the female being larger and more brightly coloured than the male, and being responsible for courtship. They inhabit reedy marshes feeding on worms, molluscs etc. The nest is either on the ground or floating, the eggs are 2–6 (usually 4) in number; and are incubated by the male for 19 days. Two species.

Rostratula benghalensis (*L*) GREATER PAINTED SNIPE Africa, S Asia and E and S to Australia / marshes / n ground or floating / e 3–4 / I ♂

Nycticryptes semicollaris (*Vieillot*) LESSER PAINTED SNIPE Southern S America (except extreme S) / grassy marshland

HAEMATOPODIDAE Oystercatchers
Large conspicuous, noisy, plover-like birds with long, blunt, vertically flattened bills used for prizing shellfish off rocks. They occur in small numbers on open beaches and rocky coasts throughout the world, except the polar regions and oceanic islands. They are black, black and white or brown and white in colour. The nest is a depression on open shingle, 2 to 4 eggs are laid. Both sexes incubate for a period of 24–7 days. Fledging lasts about 5 weeks.

Haematopus bachmani *Audubon* WESTERN BLACK OYSTERCATCHER Aleutians and western N America

Haematopus palliatus *Temminck* AMERICAN PIED OYSTERCATCHER Coasts of the Americas

Haematopus ostralegus *L* COMMON PIED OYSTERCATCHER Most of the Old World

Haematopus meadewaldoi *Bannerman* MEADE-WALDO'S BLACK OYSTERCATCHER Canary Is / extinct ?

Haematopus moquini *Bonaparte* AFRICAN BLACK OYSTERCATCHER S Africa

Haematopus unicolor *Forster* NEW ZEALAND BLACK OYSTERCATCHER New Zealand (hybridises with *ostralegus* in N Island)

Haematopus leucopodus *Garnot* MAGELLANIC OYSTERCATCHER Falklands and southern S America from Chiloë and Chubút S

Haematopus fuliginosus *Gould* SOOTY OYSTERCATCHER Australia

Haematopus ater *Vieillot and Oudart* BLACKISH OYSTERCATCHER Falklands and coasts of southern S America

CHARADRIIDAE Plovers Small to medium-sized plumpish wading birds, with pigeon-like bills which are shorter than the head, and swollen at the tip. Mostly gregarious. The nest is a depression on the ground, the eggs usually 4 in number, but 3–5 occur. Both sexes incubate, the period lasting 20–30 days. The young fledge in 3–5 weeks. They feed largely on marine or terrestrial invertebrates. About 63 species throughout the world except the polar regions.

Vanellus leucurus (*Lichtenstein*) WHITE-TAILED PLOVER b C and SW Asia w S to Egypt and N India / marshes / e 4

Vanellus gregarius (*Pallas*) SOCIABLE PLOVER b C Asia w S to Egyptian Sudan and N India / plateaux and cultivation / e 3–5

Vanellus vanellus (*L*) COMMON LAPWING

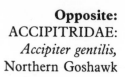

ACCIPITRIDAE:
Circus aeruginosus,
Marsh Harrier

ACCIPITRIDAE:
Elanus scriptus,
Letter-winged Kite

Plate 48

Plate 49

Much of Europe and Asia and S to N Africa in winter/cultivation/e 3–5/I 24–31/F 33
Vanellus chilensis (*Molina*) SOUTHERN LAPWING Tropical S America/grasslands
Vanellus crassirostris (*Hartlaub*) LONG-TOED LAPWING E Africa from White Nile to Zululand/swamps/n in water/e 2–3
Vanellus melanocephalus (*Rüppell*) SPOT-BREASTED PLOVER Highlands of N Ethiopia
Vanellus cinereus (*Blyth*) GREY-HEADED LAPWING b Mongolia to Japan w S to India/marshes/e 4
Vanellus indicus (*Boddaert*) RED-WATTLED LAPWING SW, S and SE Asia/plains near water/e 4
Vanellus albiceps *Gould* WHITE-HEADED PLOVER Tropical Africa / swamps and river-banks/e 2–3
Vanellus macropterus (*Wagler*) (= **Vanellus** (**Rogibix**) **tricolor** *Horsfield*) JAVANESE WATTLED LAPWING Sumatra, Java and Timor
Vanellus novaehollandiae *Stephens* SOUTHERN MASKED PLOVER Tasmania and E Australia, colonised New Zealand in twentieth century/open grasslands, swamps and estuaries/e 4
Vanellus miles (*Boddaert*) NORTHERN MASKED PLOVER N Australia, New Guinea and adjacent islands/beaches and cultivation/e 3–5
Vanellus senegallus (*L*) SENEGAL WATTLED PLOVER Much of Africa S of Sahara/grassland and swamp/e 3–4
Vanellus lugubris (*Lesson*) SENEGAL PLOVER W, C and E Africa/grass and cultivation/e 3
Vanellus melanopterus (*Cretzschmar*) BLACK-WINGED PLOVER E Africa and S Arabia/plains/e 3
Vanellus coronatus (*Boddaert*) CROWNED LAPWING E and S Africa/grassland/e 2–4
Vanellus spinosus (*L*) SPUR-WINGED PLOVER From larger islands of E Mediterranean S to the southern limit of the central savannah belt of Africa/cultivation and alluvial plains/e 3–4
Vanellus armatus (*Burchell*) BLACKSMITH PLOVER E and S Africa from Kenya and Angola to the Cape/grassland/e 2–4
Vanellus duvaucellii (*Lesson*) RIVER LAPWING N and E India, Yunnan and SE Asia/river-banks/e 3–4
Vanellus cayanus (*Latham*) PIED PLOVER S Venezuela to Peru and Paraguay
Vanellus resplendens (*Tschudi*) ANDEAN

LAPWING Andes from Ecuador to N Chile
Vanellus tricolor (*Vieillot*) BANDED PLOVER Australia and Tasmania/dry grassland/e 4
Vanellus superciliosus (*Reichenow*) BROWN-CHESTED WATTLED PLOVER Northern belt of tropical Africa/open grassland/n and e n/k
Vanellus malarbaricus (*Boddaert*) YELLOW-WATTLED LAPWING India and Ceylon/cultivation and grassland/e 4
Vanellus tectus (*Boddaert*) BLACKHEAD PLOVER Tropical belt of Africa/dry plains or open bush/e 2–3
Pluvialis squatarola (*L*) GREY, SILVER or BLACK-BELLIED PLOVER Widely distributed b Holarctic w tropics and S Hemisphere/e 3–4/I 23
Pluvialis apricaria (*L*) GOLDEN PLOVER Europe and W Asia/e 3–4/I 27–8/F c28
Pluvialis dominica (*Müller*) PACIFIC GOLDEN PLOVER b East Asia and N America w S America, Oceania, Australasia and S Asia/e 3–5
Pluvialis obscurus (*Gmelin*) NEW ZEALAND DOTTEREL New Zealand / estuaries and sand flats/e 3
Charadrius rubricollis *Gmelin* RED-CAPPED DOTTEREL Southern Australia and Tasmania/water margins/e 2
Charadrius hiaticula *L* RINGED PLOVER Europe, W Asia and N America, W Africa and S America/e 3–5/I 23–5/F 25
Charadrius melodus *Ord* PIPING PLOVER N America/beaches/e 4
Charadrius dubius *Scopoli* LITTLE RINGED PLOVER Temperate and tropical Eurasia and Africa/e 3–5/I 24–6/F 21–4
Charadrius alexandrinus *L* KENTISH or SNOWY PLOVER Widely distributed, absent from N Asia, New Zealand and Oceania/e 2–5/I 24
Charadrius venustus *Fischer and Reichenow* CHESTNUT-BANDED PLOVER SW and E Africa / shores/e 2
Charadrius alticola (*Berlepsch and Stolzmann*) PUNA PLOVER Puna zone from Peru to Chile and Argentina
Charadrius falklandicus *Latham* TWO-BANDED PLOVER b Falklands and southern S America N to Chiloë and Rio Negro w N to N Chile and E Argentina
Charadrius bicinctus *Jardine and Selby* DOUBLE-BANDED DOTTEREL Australia, Tasmania and New Zealand/coastal waters/e 2–3

Charadrius peronii *Schlegel* MALAY. PLOVER Indonesia

Charadrius collaris *Vieillot* COLLARED PLOVER Tropical America

Charadrius pecuarius *Temminck* KITTLITZ' SAND PLOVER Nile basin and Africa S of Sahara / riverbanks / e 2

Charadrius sanctaehelenae (*Harting*) WIREBIRD St Helena

Charadrius thoracicus (*Richmond*) BLACK-BANDED SAND PLOVER Madagascar

Charadrius placidus *Gray and Gray* LONG-BILLED RINGED PLOVER b from Ussuriland to N China and Japan w S to N India, Burma and Annam / margins of rivers and lakes / e 3–4

Charadrius vociferus *L* KILLDEER N America and Caribbean: Peru / e 3–5 / I ♂ (?♀) ?24–9

Charadrius tricollaris *Vieillot* THREE-BANDED PLOVER Africa S of Sahara and Madagascar / riverbanks and lake shores / e 2–3

Charadrius mongolus *Pallas* LESSER SAND PLOVER b C, E and NE Asia w to S Asia, E Africa and Australia / b plains and plateaux / e 3

Charadrius wilsonia *Ord* WILSON'S PLOVER Caribbean and from Lower California to Peru

Charadrius leschenaultii *Lesson* GREATER SAND PLOVER b C Asia, w S Asia, E Africa to Australia and Solomons

Peltohyas australis (*Gould*) AUSTRALIAN DOTTEREL Southern Australia scrub and semi-desert / e 3 [This genus was formerly placed in the Glareolidae]

Elseyornis melanops (*Vieillot*) BLACK-FRONTED DOTTEREL Australia and Tasmania / margins of fresh waters / e 4

Eupoda asiatica (*Pallas*) CASPIAN PLOVER SW Asia w S to S Africa / e 3

Eupoda veredus (*Gould*) ORIENTAL PLOVER b Mongolia and N China w S to Australia / open ground / n and e n/k (eggs attributed to this species are doubtful)

Eupoda montana (*Townsend*) MOUNTAIN PLOVER USA and Mexico

Erythrogonys cinctus *Gould* RED-KNEED DOTTEREL Australia / margins of coastal and inland waters / e 4

Eudromias ruficollis (*Wagler*) TAWNY-THROATED DOTTEREL b Chilean Andes w E to Uruguay

Eudromias morinellus (*L*) COMMON DOTTEREL Europe and Asia, chiefly mountains / e 2–4 / I ♂ 21–5 / F c30

Zonibyx modestus (*Lichtenstein*) RUFOUS-CHESTED DOTTEREL b Falklands, Tierra del Fuego and extreme S Patagonia w Chile, Argentina and Uruguay

Thinornis novaeseelandiae (*Gmelin*) SHORE PLOVER Formerly New Zealand, Chathams and Great Barrier Is, now confined to a few islets in the Chathams / n under boulder / e 3

Anarhynchus frontalis *Quoy and Gaimard* WRYBILL New Zealand / sand flats and river beds / e 2–3

Phegornis mitchellii (*Fraser*) DIADEMED PLOVER Local, recorded from scattered localities in the Andes

Pluvianellus socialis *Gray* MAGELLANIC PLOVER Straits of Magellan / e 2 / F 35–40. Jehl, P.S. 'Biology, Ecology and Relationship of an endemic Patagonian shorebird', *Trans of the San Diego Soc of NH*, 78, no 3 (1975), proposes that this bird should be placed in a monotypic family, the Pluvianellidae.

SCOLOPACIDAE Wading Birds Medium to small birds with thin, straight or down-curved bills for probing in mud and sand; and often longish to long legs. Mainly aquatic, frequenting swamps and seashores. Nest mainly on the ground (some species in trees), eggs generally dark in colour and tapered at one end. Most species breed in the Northern Hemisphere and winter in the Southern. About 82 species.

Aechmorhynchus cancellatus (*Gmelin*) 'BARRED SANDPIPER' OF LATHAM Christmas Is, Pacific Ocean / extinct / unique specimen lost, believed by some to be identical with *A. parvirostris*

Aechmorhynchus parvirostris (*Peale*) TUAMOTU SANDPIPER Tuamotu Is / rare / n ground / e 2

Prosobonia leucoptera (*Gmelin*) 'WHITE-WINGED SANDPIPER' OF LATHAM Tahiti / extinct / unique (Latham saw 3 other specimens, now lost)

Prosobonia ellisi *Sharpe* ELLIS'S SANDPIPER Eimeo / extinct, based on Ellis's painting in British Museum, generally considered to be synonymous with *P. leucoptera*

Bartramia longicauda (*Bechstein*) BARTRAM'S SANDPIPER or UPLAND PLOVER b N America w southern S America / n ground / e 3–5 / I ♂♀ 21 / F 30

Numenius minutus *Gould* LITTLE CURLEW

ACCIPITRIDAE:
Aquila verreauxii,
Verreaux's Eagle

ACCIPITRIDAE:
Gyps bengalensis,
Indian White-backed Vulture

Plate 50

ACCIPITRIDAE:
Torgos tracheliotus,
Lappet-faced Vulture

ACCIPITRIDAE:
Gypaetus barbatus,
Lammergeier or Bearded
Vulture

Plate 51

b C and E Asia (mountains?) w S to Australia

Numenius borealis (*Forster*) ESKIMO CURLEW b Alaska w Chile / now very rare / b tundras w pampas / n ground / e 3–4

Numenius phaeopus (*L*) WHIMBREL b N Holarctic w S to S America, Africa and Indo-Australasian region / b moors w shores / n ground / e 3–5 / I ♂♀ 24 / F ?28

Numenius tahitiensis (*Gmelin*) BRISTLE-THIGHED or OTAHEITE CURLEW b ? Alaska w Pacific Is

Numenius tenuirostris *Vieillot* SLENDER-BILLED CURLEW b W Siberia w Mediterranean / n ground / e 4 / I ♀

Numenius arquata (*L*) COMMON CURLEW b Europe, W and C Asia w S to Africa, S and SE Asia / b moors w shores / n ground / e 3–6 / I ♂♀ 28–30 / F 35–40

Numenius madagascariensis (*L*) EASTERN CURLEW b NE Siberia w through E Asia to Australia

Numenius americanus *Bechstein* LONG-BILLED CURLEW b scattered localities in N America w in Gulf of Mexico / n ground (prairies) / e 4–5 / I ♂♀

Limosa limosa (*L*) BLACK-TAILED GODWIT N Palaearctic w S to C Africa and S Asia / b tundra w shores / n ground / e 3–7 / I ♂♀ 24

Limosa haemastica (*L*) HUDSONIAN GODWIT b Arctic America w southern S America / n ground / e ?3–4

Limosa lapponica (*L*) BAR-TAILED GODWIT b N Europe, N Asia and NW America w S to tropical Africa, Australasia and Oceania / b tundra w shores / n ground / e 4 / I ♂♀ c21

Limosa fedoa (*L*) MARBLED GODWIT N America w S to Peru / b meadows w shores / n ground / e 3–5

Tringa erythropus (*Pallas*) SPOTTED REDSHANK b Scandinavia and N Asia w S to Mediterranean and S Asia / n ground / e 4 / I ♂ (?♀)

Tringa totanus (*L*) COMMON REDSHANK Europe and N Asia w S to Mediterranean and S Asia / n ground / e 3–5 / I ♂♀ 23–4 / F c30

Tringa flavipes (*Gmelin*) LESSER YELLOWLEGS b Canada w Chile and Argentina / n ground / e 3–4 / I ♂♀. *Note:* Reluctantly, I bow to what appears to be current practice in using the American vernacular for this species, whereas I would personally have preferred the old English 'Yellowshank'.

Tringa stagnatilis (*Bechstein*) MARSH SANDPIPER b SE Europe across mid-Asia w S to S Asia and Australia / n ground / e 4 / I ♂♀

Tringa nebularia (*Gunnerus*) GREENSHANK b Scotland, N Europe and N Asia w S to Africa, S Asia, Australia and New Zealand / n ground / e 3–5 / I ♂♀ 24–5 / F c30

Tringa melanoleuca (*Gmelin*) GREATER YELLOWLEGS b Canada w C and S America / n ground / e 3–5 / I ♀ (?♂) c21. See note to *Tringa flavipes* above.

Tringa ochropus *L* GREEN SANDPIPER b N Europe, W and C Asia w S to Africa and S Asia / n tree (old nest of other species) / e 2–4 / I ♀ (?♂) 20–3

Tringa solitaria *Wilson* SOLITARY SANDPIPER b N America w through S America / n tree (old nest of other species) / e 3–5

Tringa glareola *L* WOOD SANDPIPER b N Palaearctic w S to Africa, S Asia and Australasia / n ground / e 3–4 / I ♂♀

Tringa guttifer (*Nordmann*) NORDMANN'S GREENSHANK or ARMSTRONG'S SANDPIPER b Kamchatka, Sakhalin etc (? also Tibet) w SE Asia / n ground / e ?3

Tringa terek (*Latham*) (= **Xenus cinereus** (*Guldenstadt*)) TEREK SANDPIPER b N Asia w E Africa, S Asia and Australia / n ground / e 3–4 / I ♂

Actitis hypoleucos (*L*) COMMON SANDPIPER Europe and Asia w S to Africa and Australia / n ground / e 3–5 / I ♂♀ 21–3

Actitis macularia (*L*) SPOTTED SANDPIPER N America w S to Brazil / n ground / e 3–5 / I ♂ (?♀) 21

Catoptrophorus semipalmatus (*Gmelin*) WILLET N America w S to Peru / coasts / n ground / e 4

Heteroscelus brevipes (*Vieillot*) GREY-TAILED TATTLER or GREY-RUMPED SANDPIPER b E Siberia w through E Asia to Australia

Heteroscelus incanus (*Gmelin*) WANDERING TATTLER b Alaska and W Canada w Pacific America and Oceania / n ground / e 4 / I ♀

Aphriza virgata (*Gmelin*) SURFBIRD b Alaska w Pacific America / coasts / n ground / e 4

Arenaria interpres (*L*) RUDDY TURNSTONE Almost cosmopolitan on coasts / n ground / e 3–5 / I ♂♀

Arenaria melanocephala (*Vigors*) BLACK TURNSTONE b Alaska w S to California / coasts / n ground / e 4

Limnodromus griseus (*Gmelin*) SHORT-BILLED DOWITCHER C and E Canada w S to Brazil and Peru / swamps / n ground / e 4 / I ♀ (?♂) ?21

Limnodromus scolopaceus (*Say*) LONG-BILLED DOWITCHER Alaska and W Canada w S to Ecuador, rarely in E Asia

Limnodromus semipalmatus (*Blyth*) ASIATIC DOWITCHER b W Siberia w to China and SE Asia

Coenocorypha aucklandica (*Gray*) AUCKLAND SNIPE Islands adjacent to New Zealand / scrub and tussock / n ground / e 2, statements of clutches of 3 eggs being apparently erroneous

Gallinago solitaria *Hodgson* SOLITARY SNIPE C and E Asia (scattered localities) mountains and plateaux near water / n ground / e 4

Gallinago hardwickii (*Gray*) JAPANESE SNIPE b Japan and Kuriles w Australia, Tasmania and (once) New Zealand / mountain meadows / n ground / e 4

Gallinago nemoricola *Hodgson* WOOD SNIPE b Himalayas w S Asia, hill swamps / n n/k/1 egg collected (Baker) – but doubtful. I have examined this egg, and believe it to be the egg of a Common Snipe.

Gallinago stenura (*Bonaparte*) PINTAIL SNIPE b E Siberia w S and E Asia and Indonesia / alpine tundra near water / apparently no *authentic* description of nest or eggs, but some alleged eggs in collections

Gallinago megala *Swinhoe* SWINHOE'S SNIPE b E C Asia and (?) Sakhalin and Manchuria w S to Australia / meadow and forest / n ground / e 2–5

Gallinago nigripennis *Bonaparte* ETHIOPIAN SNIPE E and S Africa / moorland and marsh / n ground / e 2–3

Gallinago macrodactyla *Bonaparte* MADAGASCAR SNIPE Madagascar and Mauritius

Gallinago media (*Latham*) GREAT SNIPE b N Europe and W Asia w Africa / marshes / n ground / e 3–4 / I ♀ 22–4 / F ? 21–8

Gallinago gallinago (*L*) COMMON SNIPE b Europe and N Asia w Africa, S Asia and Indonesia / marshes / n ground / e 3–6 / I ♀ 19–20 / F ?14

Gallinago delicata (*Ord*) AMERICAN SNIPE b N America w S to Brazil / marshes / n ground / e 3–4 / I ♀ (?♂) 20 (*G. gallinago* and *G. delicata* are now generally regarded as conspecific)

Gallinago paraguaiae (*Vieillot*) MAGELLAN SNIPE S America

Gallinago nobilis *Sclater* NOBLE SNIPE Andes of Colombia and Ecuador

Gallinago undulata (*Boddaert*) GIANT SNIPE The Guianas, and a few scattered localities further south

Gallinago imperialis *Sclater and Salvin* IMPERIAL SNIPE Bogotá, Colombia / known from few specimens

Gallinago jamesoni (*Bonaparte*) ANDEAN SNIPE Andes of Colombia to Bolivia

Gallinago stricklandii (*Gray*) CORDILLERAN or STRICKLAND'S SNIPE S Chile and Falklands

Gallinago minima (*Brünnich*) JACK SNIPE b N Europe, N Asia (except extreme E) w S to Africa and India / bogs / n ground / e 3–4 / I ♀ 24

Scolopax rusticola *L* COMMON WOODCOCK Eurasia / woodlands / n ground / e 3–6 / I ♀ 20–2

Scolopax mira *Hartert* AMAMI WOODCOCK Amami-Oshima in the Ryu Kyu Is / little information (The status of this form is still not proven. Taka-Tsukasa and Hachisuka, *Ibis* 1925, p 903 claim that the Common Woodcock and the endemic form both breed on the island. However, Austin and Kuroda, *Birds of Japan* (1953) deny this. It would seem odd, however, for the Woodcock to produce such a well-defined race on Amami-Oshima while apparently showing no sign of sub-speciation in the rest of its range, and it seems convenient, therefore, to regard *S. mira* as a species)

Scolopax saturata *Horsfield* HORSFIELD'S WOODCOCK Mts of Sumatra and Java

Scolopax rosenbergii *Schlegel* ROSENBERG'S WOODCOCK Mts of New Guinea / mountain forest (usually treated as conspecific with *saturata*)

Scolopax celebensis *Riley* CELEBES WOODCOCK Celebes

Scolopax rochussenii *Schlegel* OBI WOODCOCK Obi, Moluccas

Scolopax minor *Gmelin* AMERICAN WOODCOCK Eastern N America / forest streams / n ground / e 4 / I ♂♀ 20–1

Calidris canutus (*L*) KNOT b N Canada, Greenland; Spitzbergen; New Siberian Is w S America; Africa; Australia and New Zealand (3 populations) / n ground / e 2–5 / I ♂♀ 20–5? / F 21 ?

Calidris tenuirostris (*Horsfield*) EASTERN or GREAT KNOT b NE Siberia (exact range un-

ACCIPITRIDAE:
Aquila audax,
Wedge-tailed Eagle

Opposite:
ACCIPITRIDAE:
Aquila chrysaetos,
Golden Eagle

Plate 52

Plate 53

certain) w S to Australia b alpine belt w shores/n ground/e 4 (1 nest known)

Calidris alba (*Pallas*) SANDERLING b Arctic America and Siberia w S to S America, Africa and Australia/n ground/e 3–4/I ♂♀ 23–4/F 14

Calidris pusilla (*L*) SEMIPALMATED SANDPIPER b Arctic America and extreme NE Siberia w S to Peru/n ground/e 3–4/I 17–19/F c28

Calidris mauri (*Cabanis*) WESTERN SANDPIPER b Alaska w S to Caribbean/tundra/n ground/e 4–5/I ♂♀ 21

Calidris ruficollis (*Pallas*) RED-NECKED STINT b N Asia and W Alaska w through E Asia to Australia/tundra in summer/n ground/eggs described but apparently no data on clutch size

Calidris minuta (*Leisler*) LITTLE STINT b N Europe and NW Asia w S to Africa and Ceylon/n ground/e 3–4/I ♂♀

Calidris temminckii (*Leisler*) TEMMINCK'S STINT b N Europe and NW Asia w Mediterranean to S Asia and Japan/n ground/e 3–4/I ♂ / F 21

Calidris subminuta (*Middendorff*) LONG-TOED STINT b E Siberia w S to India and Philippines/n ground/e ?2 ?4

Calidris minutilla (*Vieillot*) LEAST SANDPIPER or AMERICAN STINT b Arctic America w S to Peru/n ground/e 4/I ♂ (sometimes ♀)

Calidris fuscicollis (*Vieillot*) BONAPARTE'S or WHITE-RUMPED SANDPIPER b Arctic America w S America/n ground/e 4/I ♀

Calidris bairdii (*Coues*) BAIRD'S SANDPIPER b E Siberia and Arctic America w Argentina and Chile/n ground/e 3–4/I ♂♀

Calidris melanotos (*Vieillot*) PECTORAL SANDPIPER b E Siberia and Arctic America w Peru to C Chile/n ground/e 4/I ♀ 21–3/F 21

Calidris acuminata (*Horsfield*) SHARP-TAILED SANDPIPER b N Siberia (exact range uncertain) w through E Asia to Australia and Oceania/n and e n/k, though eggs exist which have been ascribed to this species

Calidris maritima (*Brünnich*) PURPLE SANDPIPER b Ellesmere Land to Franz Josef Land w North Atlantic / rocky shores / n ground/e 3–4/I ♂ (?♀) 21–2/F 21

Calidris ptilocnemis (*Coues*) ROCK SANDPIPER Coasts and islands of N Pacific from Kuriles to Alaska w S to Washington/rocky coasts/n ground/e 4/I ♂♀ 20 (sometimes

treated as a race of *C. maritima*)

Calidris alpina (*L*) DUNLIN Holarctic w S to Caribbean, Africa and S Asia/n ground/e 2–6/I ♂♀ 21–2/F 25

Calidris testacea (*Pallas*) (= **C. ferruginea** (*Brünnich*)) CURLEW SANDPIPER b in a few places in N Siberia w Africa, S Asia and Australia/n ground/e 3–4/I ♂♀

Eurynorhynchus pygmaeus (*L*) SPOON-BILLED SANDPIPER b Chukchi Peninsula w SE Asia/b tundra w pebbly shores/n ground/e 4/I ?♂

Limicola falcinellus (*Pontoppidan*) BROAD-BILLED SANDPIPER b N Europe and N Asia w to Mediterranean, S Asia and Australia/n ground/e 4/I ♂♀

Micropalma himantopus (*Bonaparte*) STILT SANDPIPER b Arctic America w S to Paraguay and Uruguay/n ground/e 3–4

Tryngites subruficollis (*Vieillot*) BUFF-BREASTED SANDPIPER b NW Canada and Alaska w S Argentina/n ground/e 4/I ♀

Philomachus pugnax (*L*) RUFF (female = 'Reeve' b N Europe and Asia w Africa and S Asia/n ground/e 3–4/I ♀ 21

Phalaropus fulicarius (*L*) GREY or RED PHALAROPE b Arctic coasts and islands w W Africa and Chile/n ground/e 3–6/I ♂ 14–19?/F 16–20?

Phalaropus lobatus (*L*) RED-NECKED or NORTHERN PHALAROPE b N Holarctic w in the tropical seas of the S Hemisphere/n ground/e 3–7/I ♂ 20/F 18–20

Phalaropus tricolor (*Vieillot*) WILSON'S PHALAROPE b Pacific N America w western S America/n ground/e 3–4/I ♂

[The three phalaropes are often placed in monotypic genera, and the group elevated into a separate family]

Ibidorhyncha struthersii *Vigors* IBISBILL High plateaux of C Asia and Himalayas/banks of mountain streams/n ground/e 4/I ♂♀

Himantopus himantopus (*L*) BLACK-WINGED STILT Almost cosmopolitan through the warmer parts of the world/swamps/n ground/e 3–5/I ♂♀ ?25–6

Himantopus novaezelandiae *Gould* BLACK STILT New Zealand / the status of this form is apparently unconfirmed, and it may be a melanistic phase occurring in New Zealand

Cladorhynchus leucocephala (*Vieillot*)

Banded Stilt Australia and New Zealand Salt marshes and salt lakes / crustacea and insects / n ground / e 3–4

Recurvirostra avosetta *L* Pied Avocet b Europe, W and C Asia w Africa and S Asia / n ground / e 3–5 / I ♂♀ 22–4 / F c42

Recurvirostra americana *Gmelin* American Avocet b western USA and S Canada w S to Guatemala / n ground / e 3–5

Recurvirostra novaehollandiae *Vieillot* Red-necked Avocet Australia and Tasmania / inland waters and coastal estuaries / aquatic animals and insects / n ground / e 4

Recurvirostra andina *Philippi and Landbeck* Andean Avocet Salt lagoons from Peru to Argentina

DROMADIDAE Crab Plover A plover-like bird with long legs, partially webbed front toes and a long, strong, pointed tern-like bill. Feeds on crabs, crustacea and mollusca. Nest in a hole in a sand bank, a single white egg being laid. One species.

Dromas ardeola *Paykull* Crab Plover N and W shores and islands of Indian Ocean / estuaries and reefs / n hole / e 1 (?2)

BURHINIDAE Thick-knees, Dikkops and Stone Curlews Plover-like birds with swollen knee-joints (hence their name) and fairly long legs. In habits and external appearance they resemble bustards. Occur on shores, riverbanks or dry pebbly areas. Food largely animal. No nest, the 1–3 eggs are laid on bare ground. Incubation 26–7 days, mostly by ♀ assisted occasionally by ♂.

Burhinus oedicnemus *(L)* Stone Curlew S Europe, N Africa, W and S Asia / e 2–3

Burhinus senegalensis *(Swainson)* Senegal Thick-knee W and NE Africa / e 2

Burhinus vermiculatus *(Cabanis)* Water Dikkop W, E and SE Africa / near rivers / e 2

Burhinus capensis *(Lichtenstein)* Cape Dikkop Africa S of Sahara and S Arabia / dry bush / e 2

Burhinus bistriatus *(Wagler)* Mexican Thick-knee Mexico, C America, northern S America and Hispaniola

Burhinus superciliaris *(Tschudi)* Peruvian Thick-knee Pacific coast of S America from Ecuador to S Peru

Burhinus magnirostris *(Latham)* Bush Curlew Australia plains and open woodland / insects / n ground / e 2

Esacus recurvirostris *(Cuvier)* Oriental Thick-knee Coasts and rivers of India, Ceylon, Burma

Esacus magnirostris *(Vieillot)* Beach Curlew Much of the Indonesian and Australasian regions / sandy beaches / crustacea and other shore life / n on beach, no nest / e 1

GLAREOLIDAE Coursers and Pratincoles These 2 groups form 2 well defined sub-families within the family. Coursers are long-legged, short-winged running birds inhabiting deserts. Have long, pointed, down-curved bills. Cryptically coloured, they crouch when danger threatens, fly reluctantly, but swiftly. Pratincoles have short legs, long, pointed wings and long, forked tails. Bills are short and they fly freely taking insects on wing. Both groups nest on ground, eggs 2–3. Sixteen species in the warmer parts of Old World.

Pluvianus aegyptius *(L)* Egyptian Plover W, WC and NE Africa / shores of lakes and rivers / e 2–3

Cursorius cursor *(Latham)* Cream-coloured Courser Much of Africa, SW Asia E to W India, Canaries and Cape Verde Is / e 2 / I ♀

Cursorius temminckii *Swainson* Temminck's Courser Africa S of Sahara / short grass and bush / e 2

Cursorius coromandelicus *(Gmelin)* Indian Courser India and Ceylon / stony plains and cultivation / e 2–3

Rhinoptilus africanus *(Temminck)* Two-banded Courser Africa S of Sahara but apparently discontinuous / thorn scrub / e 1

Rhinoptilus cinctus *(Heuglin)* Heuglin's Courser E and SW Africa / stony and sandy desert / e 2 / I ?♂

Rhinoptilus chalcopterus *(Temminck)* Violet-tipped or Bronze-winged Courser Africa S of Sahara / forest and thick bush / e 2–3

Rhinoptilus bitorquatus *(Blyth)* Jerdon's Courser Central part of peninsular India, last seen 1900, very rare and possibly extinct

Stiltia isabella *(Vieillot)* Australian Pratincole Australia, migrating to Indonesia / dry plains / insects / n ground / e 2

Glareola pratincola *(L)* Collared Pratincole S Europe, SW Asia and Africa / open ground / insects / n ground / e 2–4 / I ♂♀ 17–18 / F 22–30 ?

Glareola maldivarum *Forster* Oriental Pratincole E and S Asia from Manchuria to

ACCIPITRIDAE:
Gypohierax angolensis, Palm Nut Vulture

ACCIPITRIDAE:
Buteo buteo,
Common Buzzard

FALCONIDAE:
Polyborus plancus, Common
Caracara, Crested Caracara

Plate 54

P. plancus on nest

SAGITTARIIDAE:
Sagittarius serpentarius,
Secretary Bird

Plate 55

India w S to Indonesia and Australia/e 2–3
Glareola nordmanni *Fischer* BLACK-WINGED
PRATINCOLE SE Europe and SW Asia w through
Africa/e 2–4
Glareola ocularis *Verreaux* MADAGASCAR
PRATINCOLE E Africa and Madagascar / very
little data
Glareola nuchalis *Gray* WHITE-COLLARED
PRATINCOLE Africa S of Sahara, but not the
extreme S/rocky riverbeds/e 2
Glareola cinerea *Fraser* GREY PRATINCOLE
Sand-banks of large rivers from Ghana to Congo
Glareola lactea *Temminck* LITTLE PRATINCOLE
India, Ceylon, Burma, Thailand and S Laos/
sandbanks in rivers/e 2–4/I ♂♀
THINOCORIDAE Seedsnipe Small relatives
of waders adapted to a vegetarian diet and
superficially resembling sparrows in shape of
body and bill. Legs short, wings long and
tapering. A thin opercular flap covers the
nostrils. Gregarious. Nest a scantily lined
scrape in ground. Eggs 3–4. Young precocious,
leaving nest almost at once, little data on
breeding biology. Four species.
Attagis gayi *St Hilaire and Lesson* RUFOUS-
BELLIED SEEDSNIPE Andes from Ecuador S
Attagis malouinus (*Boddaert*) WHITE-
BELLIED SEEDSNIPE Tierra del Fuego and
Magellan Straits
Thinocorus orbignyianus *St Hilaire and
Lesson* GREY-BREASTED SEEDSNIPE Andes from
Peru to Tierra del Fuego
Thinocorus rumicivorous *Eschscholtz*
PATAGONIAN SEEDSNIPE Andes from Ecuador to
Tierra del Fuego, spreading E over Patagonia
and Uruguay in winter
CHIONIDIDAE Sheathbills Plump dove-
like birds with stout sharp bills, the upper
mandible saddled with a horny sheath which
partly shields the nostrils. Sheathbills are
believed to be relict forms descended from the
ancestral line of waders and gulls. Scavengers,
feeding on offal and also on eggs and chicks.
Nest on ground. Eggs 2–3 white, heavily
marked with black and brown blotches. Both
sexes incubate. Two species confined to
Antarctic regions.
Chionis alba (*Gmelin*) SNOWY SHEATHBILL
Grahamland, southern S America and adjacent
islands
Chionis minor *Hartlaub* BLACK-FACED
SHEATHBILL Price Edward, Marion, Crozet,

Possession, Kerguelen and Heard Is
STERCORARIIDAE Skuas and Jaegers
Gull-like birds, differing chiefly in having a
fleshy cere across the base of the upper mandible. Partial scavengers, also feeding by
chasing gulls and other birds and forcing them
to disgorge food. Nest on ground in temperate
and cold latitudes, some species wintering in
tropics.
The genus *Catharacta* is often merged in
Stercorarius, and the various forms are frequently considered to be conspecific. While
C. maccormicki is now treated by most authorities as a separate species, opinion is divided as
to the status of the other forms.
Catharacta skua *Brünnich* GREAT SKUA
b Iceland, Faeroes, Shetlands and Orkneys
w N Atlantic S to Gibraltar/e 1–3 (usually 2)/
I ♂♀ 28/F 6–7 weeks
Catharacta antarctica (*Lesson*) FALKLAND
SKUA b southern S America and Falklands w
up Pacific Coast to British Columbia and E to S
Africa
Catharacta lonnbergi *Mathews* LÖNNBERG'S
SKUA b sub-antarctic islands w southern oceans/
n ground/e 2–3/I ♂♀
Catharacta maccormicki (*Saunders*)
MACCORMICK'S SKUA b shores of Ross and
Weddell Seas w Antarctic oceans/e 2
Stercorarius pomarinus (*Temminck*)
POMARINE JAEGER b shores and islands of
Arctic Ocean w tropical oceans/e 2–3/I ♂♀
Stercorarius parasiticus (*L*) PARASITIC
JAEGER or ARCTIC SKUA b N Holarctic w trop-
ical seas and southern oceans/e 1–4 (usually 2)/
I ♂♀ 24/F 21–40 (opinions vary)
Stercorarius longicaudus *Vieillot* LONG-
TAILED JAEGER or BUFFON'S SKUA b N Holarctic
w W Africa, Mediterranean and Japan/e 1–3
(usually 2)/I ♂♀ 23/F c21
LARIDAE Gulls and Terns Gulls are fairly
large heavy-bodied birds with longish, stout
bills hooked at the tip and with webbed feet.
Generally omnivorous scavengers. Nest on
ground, cliffs or trees (rarely), frequently in
colonies. Inshore birds, seldom venturing far
out to sea. More or less cosmopolitan except in
desert and permanently frozen areas, often
travel far inland, and some species are completely inland inhabiting. Terns are lighter-
bodied, more streamlined birds, with thinner,
pointed bills.

Pagophila eburnea (*Phipps*) Ivory Gull b Spitzbergen, Franz Josef Land, N Greenland and Arctic American Archipelago w N coasts of Europe, Asia and America / pack-ice / n ground or cliff / e 1–3 / I ♂♀

Larus pacificus *Latham* Pacific Gull S Australia and Tasmania / coastal / waters omnivorous / n ground / e 2–3

Larus scoresbii *Traill* Dolphin Gull Southern S America / n grass tussock / e 3

Larus fuliginosus *Gould* Lava or Dusky Gull Galapagos / coasts / scavenger / n ground / e 2

Larus modestus *Tschudi* Grey Gull b coast of Peru w along Pacific coast of S America / sandy beaches and salt deserts / n ground / e 2

Larus heermanni *Cassin* Heermann's Gull b W coast of Mexico w from British Columbia to Guatemala / n ground / e 2–3

Larus leucophthalmus *Temminck* White-eyed Gull Red Sea and Gulf of Aden / n ground / e 3

Larus hemprichii *Bruch* Hemprich's Gull Red Sea and NW Indian Ocean / n ground, usually under shelter / e 3

Larus belcheri *Vigors* Belcher's Gull Coast of Peru / n ground / e 3

Larus crassirostris *Vieillot* Black-tailed Gull Coasts and islands of Sea of Japan / n ground / e 2–3 (?4–5) / I ♂♀ 24–7 / F 45–50

Larus audouinii *Payraudeau* Audouin's Gull Small islands in Mediterranean / n ground / e 2–3 / I ♂♀ 21–5

Larus delwarensis *Ord* Ring-billed Gull b much of N America w S to Caribbean b low islands / n ground / e 2–4 / I ♂♀ 21

Larus canus *L* Common Gull Discontinuous through much of Holarctic, b to the north w further south / n ground / e 2–5 / I ♂♀ 22–8 (various records) / F c5 weeks (*Larus kamtschatschensis* (Bonaparte) is sometimes separated)

Larus thayeri *Brooks* Thayer's Gull Banks Is and Ellesmere Land w British Columbia to California / n ground or cliff / e 2

Larus argentatus *Pontoppidan* Herring Gull Most of the Northern Hemisphere / n ground or cliff / e 2–6 (usually 3) / I ♂♀ 25–7 / F c42 NB: The type of *Larus affinis* Reinhardt, was shown by Jourdain, *Nov Zool* 35 (1925) pp 82–4 to be a synonym of *L. argentatus*. In terms of application, however, the name has been applied at various times to several different forms of *L. argentatus* and *L. fuscus*, so that care should be taken with references to the name in older literature.

Larus fuscus *L* Lesser Black-backed Gull Europe w S to W Africa / n ground or cliff / e 1–5 (usually 3) / I ♂♀ 26–8 / F 32

Larus californicus *Lawrence* Californian Gull b interior of N America w Pacific Coast / n ground beside lakes / e 2–5

Larus occidentalis *Audubon* Western Gull Pacific coast of N America from Washington to Gulf of California / coasts and islands / n ground / e 2–4 / I ♂♀ 24

Larus dominicanus *Lichtenstein* Kelp Gull Coasts and islands of the southern oceans / n ground / e 2–3

Larus schistisagus *Stejneger* Slaty-backed Gull b Kamchatka and Commander Is w to Alaska and Japan / n island cliffs / e 3

Larus marinus *L* Great Black-backed Gull Coasts and islands of N Atlantic w to Azores, Great Lakes and Caspian Sea rocky coasts and inland marshes / n ground on tops of stacks / e 2–5 / I ♂♀ 26–8 / F 56

Larus glaucescens *Naumann* Glaucous-winged Gull b N Pacific and Bering Sea w S to China and Baja California / n cliff ledge, broken cliffs and flat ground / e 2–4

Larus hyperboreus *Gunnerus* Glaucous Gull b Arctic Ocean (circumpolar) w into N Atlantic and N Pacific / n ground or cliff / e 2–4 / I probably ♂♀ 27–8

Larus glaucoides *Meyer* (= *L. leucopterus Vieillot*) Iceland Gull b Arctic Archipelago (?), Greenland and Jan Mayen w N Atlantic / n ground or cliff / e 2–3 / I and F n/k

[**Larus kumlieni** *Brewster* Kumlien's Gull Baffin Is; probably a race of *L. glaucoides*, formerly considered to be a hybrid]

[**Larus nelsoni** *Henshaw* Nelson's Gull Generally considered to be a hybrid between *L. hyperboreus* and *L. argentatus*. Few specimens exist]

Larus icthyaetus *Pallas* Great Black-headed Gull b S Russia to Mongolia w to E Mediterranean, Red Sea and India / n ground / e 2–4 / I and F n/k

Larus atricilla *L* Laughing Gull b Atlantic coast of USA, Caribbean and S California w S to Brazil and Peru / n ground / e 3–4 / I ♂♀ 20

Larus brunnicephalus *Jerdon* Brown-headed

FALCONIDAE:
Falco berigora, Brown Hawk,
Brown Falcon

FALCONIDAE:
Falco subbuteo,
Hobby

Plate 56

FALCONIDAE:
Falco peregrinus,
Peregrine Falcon or Duck
Hawk

FALCONIDAE;
Falco tinnunculus,
Common Kestrel

Plate 57

GULL b inland lakes of high plateaux of C Asia from Turkestan to Tibet and Mongolia w coasts of S Asia/n ground/e 3

Larus cirrocephalus *Vieillot* GREY-HEADED GULL Southern S America and E Africa, from Ethiopia to Lake Nyasa, also Lake Chad and Gambia/marshes and rocky coasts/n ground or floating/e 2–3

Larus serranus *Tschudi* ANDEAN GULL b High Andean lakes from Ecuador to N Chile w coasts/e 2

Larus pipixcan *Wagler* FRANKLIN'S GULL b N America w Caribbean and coasts of Peru and Chile/n ground or floating, on or beside prairie lakes/e 2–3/I ♂♀ 18–20

Larus novaehollandiae *Stephens* SILVER GULL Australia, New Zealand, adjacent islands and New Caledonia/coastal and inland waters/ n ground/e 2–3

Larus hartlaubii *Bruch* HARTLAUB'S GULL Coasts of SW Africa/coastal islands/n ground/ e 2–3 (often regarded as a race of *novaehollandiae*)

Larus melanocephalus *Temminck* MEDITERRANEAN GULL Mediterranean and Black Sea / swamps, lagoons and coasts / n ground/e 2–3

Larus relictus *Lönnberg* RELICT GULL C Asia/ no data

Larus bulleri *Hutton* BULLER'S or BLACK-BILLED GULL New Zealand/coasts and rivers/ n ground/e 2–3

Larus maculipennis *Lichtenstein* BROWN-HOODED GULL Southern S America/n ground in marshes/e 2–3

Larus ridibundus *L* BLACK-HEADED GULL Much of Eurasia w S to N Africa/coasts and inland marshes/n ground/e 2–6/I ♂♀ 20–6 (accounts vary)/F c42

Larus genei *Brème* SLENDER-BILLED GULL Mediterranean and N Indian Ocean / offshore islands and coastal lagoons/n ground/e 1–3/I ?♂♀

Larus philadelphia (*Ord*) BONAPARTE'S GULL N America and Caribbean / b near lakes and rivers in spruce forest w coasts and lagoons/ n tree/e 2–4/I ♀ (?♂)

Larus minutus *Pallas* LITTLE GULL Europe and Asia E to Lake Baikal/coasts and marshes/ n ground/e 2–7/I ♂♀

Larus saundersi (*Swinhoe*) SAUNDERS' GULL Mongolia and N China w on China coast and Japan

Larus tridactylus *L* BLACK-LEGGED KITTIWAKE N Pacific, N Atlantic and adjacent portions of the Arctic Ocean / n cliff / e 1–3/ I ♂♀ 21–4/F 28–35

Larus brevirostris *Bruch* RED-LEGGED KITTIWAKE Pribilov, Near and Commander Is/ n cliff/e 1–3/I ♂♀ 24–6

Larus sabini *Sabine* SABINE'S GULL b Arctic coasts and islands w N Pacific, vagrant elsewhere/ coasts and tundras / n ground / e 2–3/ I ♂♀ 23–6

Creagrus furcatus (*Neboux*) SWALLOW-TAILED GULL Galapagos Is/n ground/e 1

Rhodosthethia rosea (*Macgillivray*) ROSS'S GULL Arctic Ocean b NE Siberia and (once) Greenland/ n ground in swampy tundra in deltas of arctic rivers/e 2–3/I ♂♀ c21

Chlidonias hybrida (*Pallas*) WHISKERED TERN Warmer parts of the Old World/swamps and lagoons/n ground/e 2–4/I ♂♀

Chlidonias leucopterus (*Temminck*) WHITE-WINGED TERN b SE Europe across C Asia to Amurland w Africa, S Asia and Australia/ swamps and lagoons / n ground / e 2–4/ I ♂♀

Chlidonias niger (*L*) BLACK TERN b N America w S America; b Europe and W Asia w Africa/marshes, swamps and rivers/n ground/ e 2–4/I ♂♀ 14–16/F 28

Phaetusa simplex (*Gmelin*) LARGE-BILLED TERN S America/n ground/e 2–3

Sterna nilotica *Gmelin* GULL-BILLED TERN Almost cosmopolitan through the warmer parts of the world/ salt marshes, sandy coasts and lakes/n ground/e 2–5/I ♂♀ 22–3/F 28–35

Sterna caspia *Pallas* (= **Hydroprogne tschegrava** (*Lepechin*)) CASPIAN TERN Almost cosmopolitan through the warmer parts of the world, but local / lakes and sandy coasts / n ground/e 1–4/I ♂♀ 20–2/F 28–35

Sterna aurantia *Gray* RIVER TERN India to SE Asia/estuaries and rivers/n ground/e 3–4/ I ♂♀ 18–19

Sterna hirundinacea *Lesson* CASSIN'S TERN Southern S America/n ground/e 1–2

Sterna hirundo *L* COMMON TERN b Palaearctic and N Nearctic w S to tropical seas/ rivers, lakes and coastal islands / n ground/ e 2–4/I ♂♀ 22–6/F c30

Sterna paradisaea *Pontoppidan* (= **S. macrura** *Naumann*) ARCTIC TERN b Arctic regions and N Atlantic w Antarctic regions/

coasts and marshes/n ground/e 1–4/I ♂♀ 21–2/
F 21–8

Sterna vittata *Gmelin* ANTARCTIC TERN
Southern oceans/n ground/e 1–2

Sterna virgata *Cabanis* KERGUELEN TERN
b Marion, Heard, Kerguelen and Crozets

Sterna forsteri *Nuttall* FORSTER'S TERN
b interior of N America w Caribbean/marshes/
n ground/e 2–6/I ♂♀ 23

Sterna trudeaui *Audubon* TRUDEAU'S TERN
Coasts of southern S America (discontinuous)/
n ground/e 3–4

Sterna dougallii *Montagu* ROSEATE TERN
Widely, but irregularly distributed, from N
Atlantic and Caribbean through the Old World
tropics, the Far East and Australasia/rocky and
grassy coasts/n ground/e 1–3/I ♂♀ 21–6

Sterna striata *Gmelin* WHITE-FRONTED TERN
SE Australia, Tasmania, New Zealand and
adjacent islands/coastal waters and river beds/
n ground/e 1–2

Sterna repressa *Hartert* WHITE-CHEEKED
TERN S Red Sea, Arabian Sea and Persian Gulf/
n ground/e 1–3

Sterna sumatrana *Raffles* BLACK-NAPED TERN
Islands of Indian and W Pacific Oceans/coral
pools and lagoons/n ground/e 2

Sterna acuticauda *Gray* (= **S.
melanogaster** *Temminck*) BLACK-BELLIED
TERN Rivers of India, Burma and W Indo-
China/n ground/e 2–4/I ♂♀ 15–16

Sterna aleutica *Baird* ALEUTIAN TERN
N Pacific b on Sakhalin and 2 small islands in
Norton Sound, Alaska / n ground / e 2–3/
I ♂♀ 17

Sterna lunata *Peale* SPECTACLED TERN
Oceania/n ground/e 1

Sterna anaetheta *Scopoli* BRIDLED TERN
Tropical waters of the world/pelagic, breeding
on rocky islets / n ground, cave or hole / e 1/
I ?♂♀

Sterna fuscata *L* SOOTY TERN Tropical waters
of the world / pelagic, breeding on rocky and
coral islands/n ground/e 1–3/I ♂♀ 26/F 30

Sterna nereis *(Gould)* NEREIS TERN W and S
Australia, New Zealand and New Caledonia/
coasts / n ground/e 2

Sterna albistriata *(Gray)* BLACK-FRONTED
TERN New Zealand/coasts and rivers/n ground/
e 2

Sterna superciliaris *Vieillot* YELLOW-BILLED
TERN Rivers of S America E of Andes/e n/s

Sterna balaenarum *(Strickland)* DAMARA
TERN Coasts of W Africa/n ground or rocky
outcrop/e 1

Sterna lorata *Philippi and Landbeck* PERUVIAN
TERN Pacific coast of S America b Peru/n
ground/e 2

Sterna albifrons *Pallas* LITTLE TERN Almost
cosmopolitan through the temperate and
tropical seas/coasts and rivers/n ground/e 2–4/
I ♂♀ 19–22/F c30

Sterna saundersi *Hume* SAUNDERS' TERN
Red Sea, C Africa and Persian Gulf/n ground/
e 2

Sterna bergii *Lichtenstein* SWIFT TERN Tropical Old World waters/coasts/n ground/e 1–3

Sterna maxima *Boddaert* ROYAL TERN
W Africa and tropical waters of New World/
n ground/e 1–2

Sterna bengalensis *Lesson* CRESTED TERN
Mediterranean, Indian Ocean and Australasia/
n ground/e 1–2

Sterna zimmermanni *Reichenow* CHINESE
TERN Coast of E China from Shantung to
Fokien /? no data, known from few specimens

Sterna eurygnatha *Saunders* CAYENNE TERN
Coast of eastern S America /n ground /e ? 1–2

Sterna elegans *Gambel* ELEGANT TERN Pacific
coast of tropical America b Baja California/
n ground/e 1–2

Sterna sandvicensis *Latham* SANDWICH TERN
b North Atlantic w S to tropics of Atlantic and
Indian Oceans and the Pacific coast of tropical
America / inland lakes and low-lying coasts/
n ground/e 1–3/I ♂♀ 20–3/F 35

Larosterna inca *(Lesson)* INCA TERN Coast of
Peru and Chile/n niche, hollow or burrow/e 1–2

Procelsterna cerulea *(Bennett)* GREY
TERNLET Islands of Pacific Ocean/n cliff ledge/
e 1 (*P. albivitta*, Bonaparte, is sometimes
separated)

Anous stolidus *(L)* BROWN NODDY Tropical
waters of the world / offshore waters and islands/
n ground or shrub/e 1

Anous tenuirostris *(Temminck)* BLACK NODDY
b Seychelles and SW Australia / offshore
islands/n tree /e 1

Anous minutus *Boie* LESSER NODDY Islands of
S Atlantic and Pacific Oceans / coasts and
islands/n tree/e 1

Gygis alba *(Sparrman)* FAIRY TERN Tropical
waters of the world/ n none /e 1, laid on branch
of tree or bare rock

FALCONIDAE: *Falco longipennis,*
Little Falcon or Australian Hobby

FALCONIDAE:
Falco peregrinus, Peregrine
Falcon or Duck Hawk

FALCONIDAE:
Microhierax caerulescens,
Red-legged Falconet,
Red-thighed Falconet

Plate 58

MEGAPODIIDAE:
Megapodius freycinet,
Common Scrub Fowl,
Common Scrub Hen

MEGAPODIIDAE:
Leipoa ocellata,
Mallee Fowl

Plate 59

RHYNCHOPIDAE Skimmers Tern-like birds with the lower mandible larger than the upper. They feed by dragging the lower jaw in the water while flying just above the surface. Nest on sandy beaches, laying 2–7 eggs, which are incubated almost entirely by the female. Three species.

Rhynchops niger *L* BLACK SKIMMER Tropical America/inshore waters/n ground/e 3–7/I ♀

Rhynchops flavirostris *Vieillot* AFRICAN SKIMMER Coasts and rivers of tropical Africa/ n ground/e 2–5

Rhynchops albicollis *Swainson* INDIAN SKIMMER Larger rivers of India, Burma and Indo-China/n ground/e 3–4/I ♀ (?♂)

ALCIDAE Auks Small, stocky, short-winged seabirds [*Pinguinus* was large, with tiny useless wings] superficially resembling penguins, and confined to the cool and cold waters of the Northern Hemisphere. Feed on small fish, crustaceans etc obtained by diving. Flight fast and direct. Breed either singly or in colonies, in rock cracks, burrows in soft soil or on open ledges. Eggs of species nesting in concealed places white or pale, exposed eggs are brightly coloured and boldly marked.

Alle alle (*L*) LITTLE AUK Arctic Ocean (Greenland to Franz Josef Land) w in Atlantic/ n in colonies in cracks and crevices in cliffs/ e 1 (rarely 2)/I ♂♀ 24/F 20

Pinguinus impennis (*L*) GREAT AUK North Atlantic/extinct/n in colonies on bare low rocks/ e 1/I and F no information

Alca torda *L* RAZORBILL North Atlantic/n in colonies on cliff ledges/e 1 (rarely 2)/I ♂♀ 25/ F 12–15 (accounts differ)

Uria lomvia (*L*) THICK-BILLED MURRE or BRÜNNICH'S GUILLEMOT Coasts and islands of Arctic and Pacific Oceans/n in colonies on cliff ledges/e 1/I ♂♀ c28/F 3–4 weeks on ledge but fed by parents on sea

Uria aalge (*Pontoppidan*) COMMON MURRE or GUILLEMOT N Atlantic and N Pacific Oceans (S of *lomvia*)/n in colonies on cliff ledges or flat tops of stacks/e 1/I ♂♀ 28–30/F 14

Cepphus grylle (*L*) BLACK GUILLEMOT or TYSTIE Arctic and N Atlantic Oceans/n in rock crevices/e 2/I ♂♀ 21/F c28

Cepphus columba *Pallas* PIGEON GUILLEMOT N Pacific (Kamchatka to California)/ n in rock cracks or in burrows in soft soil/e 2/ I ♂♀ 21

Cepphus snowi *Stejneger* SNOW'S GUILLEMOT Kurile Is, very little information (may be race of *C. columba*)

Cepphus carbo *Pallas* SPECTACLED GUILLEMOT Siberia from Sea of Okhotsk to Korea and N Japan/n in rock crevices/e 1/I ♂♀

Brachyramphus marmoratus (*Gmelin*) MARBLED MURRELET N Pacific coasts and islands/n branch of forest tree

Brachyramphus brevirostris (*Vigors*) KITTLITZ'S MURRELET E Siberia and Aleutians [Alaska (?)] w to Japan/n on bare rock on mountain cliffs

Endomychura hypoleuca (*Xantus*) XANTUS' MURRELET Coasts and islands of California/n hollows in rocks or under bushes/ e 1–2/I ♂♀

Endomychura craveri (*Salvadori*) CRAVERI'S MURRELET Gulf of California/n hollows among rocks/e 2

Synthliboramphus antiquus (*Gmelin*) ANCIENT AUKLET N Pacific S to Japan and California/n rock cracks or burrows in small colonies/e 1–2/I ♂♀

Synthliboramphus wumizusume (*Temminck*) JAPANESE AUKLET Japan / habits probably similar to above

Ptychoramphus aleuticus (*Pallas*) CASSIN'S AUKLET Pacific coast of N America/n rock cracks or burrows/e 1/I ♂♀

Cyclorrhynchus psittacula (*Pallas*) PARRAKEET AUK Coasts of N Pacific/n in rock crevices or under stones or driftwood

Aethia cristatella (*Pallas*) CRESTED AUKLET E Siberia from Wrangell Is to Japan (winter)/ n rock cracks and stones/e I/I ♂♀

Aethia pusilla (*Pallas*) LEAST AUKLET Alaska and Siberian Pacific coast/n in rock crevices/e 1

Aethia pygmaea (*Gmelin*) WHISKERED AUKLET Kamchatka, Commander and Kurile Is, Aleutians (?)/n in small colonies in crevices in cliffs/e 1/I ♂♀

Cerorhinca monocerata (*Pallas*) RHINOCEROS AUK Coasts of N Pacific / n in burrow in soil/e 1/I ♂♀ ?21

Fratercula arctica (*L*) ATLANTIC PUFFIN Arctic and N Atlantic Oceans/n in burrow in colonies/e 1 (rarely 2)/I ♀ or ♂♀ (sic) 40–43/F 40

Fratercula corniculata (*Naumann*) HORNED PUFFIN Bering Sea and adjacent parts of Arctic and Pacific Oceans/n rock cracks or burrows/ e 1–2/I ♂♀

Lunda cirrhata (*Pallas*) TUFTED PUFFIN N Pacific/n in burrow/e 1/I ♂♀ 30

PTEROCLIDAE Sandgrouse Birds of open treeless country, superficially resembling grouse with pigeon heads. Long pointed wings and tails, with legs feathered down to toes. Toes also feathered in *Syrrhaptes*. Nest on ground, chicks being precocial, and eggs coloured buff or greenish, cryptically marked with brown or violet.

Syrrhaptes tibetanus *Gould* TIBETAN SANDGROUSE Pamirs to Koko Nor/e 3?/I ♂♀

Syrrhaptes paradoxus (*Pallas*) PALLAS' SANDGROUSE C Asiatic steppes from Russia to Transbaikalia / semi-desert / n scrape / e 2–4/ I ♂♀ 22–7 (NB: Unique and mysterious sporadic invasions take this species west to Europe and Britain)

Pterocles alchata (*L*) PIN-TAILED SANDGROUSE Mediterranean and W Asia/e 2–3/I ♂♀ 21–3

Pterocles namaqua (*Gmelin*) NAMAQUA SANDGROUSE SW and S Africa/e 3/I 16

Pterocles exustus *Temminck* CHESTNUT-BELLIED SANDGROUSE NE Africa, SW Arabia, Baluchistan and India/e 2–3/I ♂♀ 20?

Pterocles senegallus (*L*) SPOTTED SANDGROUSE N Africa across Asia to Sind/n ground/e 3

Pterocles orientalis (*L*) BLACK-BELLIED SANDGROUSE or IMPERIAL SANDGROUSE Canary Is and Mediterranean, S Russia to Afghanistan/ n ground/e 2–3

Pterocles coronatus *Lichtenstein* CROWNED SANDGROUSE NE Africa to Sind/e 3

Pterocles gutturalis *Smith* YELLOW-THROATED SANDGROUSE E Africa/e 2–3

Pterocles burchelli *Sclater* BURCHELL'S SANDGROUSE SW Africa/e 2–3

Pterocles personatus *Gould* GOULD'S or MASKED SANDGROUSE W Madagascar

Pterocles decoratus *Cabanis* BLACK-FACED SANDGROUSE Kenya and Tanganyika/e 2–3

Pterocles lichtensteinii *Temminck* LICHTENSTEIN'S SANDGROUSE NE Africa [S Arabia to Sind] / e 2–3. The Close-banded Sandgrouse, *P. arabicus*, has been considered both as a race of Lichtenstein's and of the Painted: depending on which it is considered to be, this will affect the ranges of the two species

Pterocles bicinctus *Temminck* DOUBLE-BANDED SANDGROUSE SW Africa/e 3 (2?)

Pterocles indicus (*Gmelin*) PAINTED SANDGROUSE India/e 2–3/I ♂♀

Pterocles quadricinctus *Temminck* FOUR-BANDED SANDGROUSE W and E Africa/ e 2–3

RAPHIDAE Dodos and Solitaires Large, flightless, pigeon-like birds with fat bodies and bulbous hooked beaks. Some authorities believe them to be nearer to rails than pigeons. Ate fruit and seeds. Eggs 1, laid on ground, incubated by both sexes. Three species, all extinct. Turkey-size.

Raphus cucullatus (*L*) DODO Mauritius/ extinct c1680

Raphus solitarius (*Sélys-Longchamps*) RÉUNION SOLITAIRE Réunion/extinct c1750

Pezophaps solitaria (*Gmelin*) RODRIGUEZ SOLITAIRE Rodriguez/extinct c1800

[**Victoriornis imperialis** *Hachisuka* WHITE DODO Réunion/the existence of 2 species on Réunion is unproven]

COLUMBIDAE Pigeons and Doves Stout-bodied birds with short necks and short, slender, rounded bills, with a fleshy cere. Feed on seeds and fruits. Nest of sticks, a flimsy platform. Eggs 1–2, white. Throughout the temperate and tropical regions but most species in Oriental and Australasian countries. The arrangement of this family follows Goodwin. Incubation usually by both sexes.

Columba livia *Gmelin* ROCK DOVE and FERAL and DOMESTIC PIGEONS Europe, N Africa, across Asia (? to China) [Feral Pigeon is cosmopolitan, and eastern limits of wild birds undetermined]/cliffs and buildings/n ledge or hole/e 2/I ♂♀ 17–18/F c30

Columba rupestris *Pallas* EASTERN ROCK PIGEON C and E Asia/cliffs and buildings/n ledges or holes

Columba leuconota *Vigors* SNOW PIGEON Himalayas, Tibet and W China/n caves/e 2/ I 17–19

Columba guinea *L* SPECKLED PIGEON Africa (discontinuous)/ open country / n holes / e 2/ I 15–16/F 20–3

Columba albitorques *Rüppell* WHITE-COLLARED PIGEON Ethiopia / rocky mountains/ n holes/e 2/I 16/F 27–8

Columba oenas *L* STOCK DOVE Europe, Mediterranean and W Asia / park and wood/ n holes/e 2/I ♂♀ 16/F 20–8

Columba eversmanni *Bonaparte* YELLOW-

CRACIDAE:
Penelope supercilliaris,
Rusty-margined or
Superciliated Guan

Plate 60

PHASIANIDAE:
Excalfactoria chinensis,
Painted Quail,
Blue Quail

PHASIANIDAE:
Pucrasia macrolopha,
Koklass Pheasant

Plate 61

EYED DOVE Turkestan and Afghanistan / open country / n holes

Columba oliviae *Stephenson Clarke* SOMALI ROCK PIGEON Coastal hills of Somaliland / n holes / e 1 (?)

Columba palumbus *L* WOOD PIGEON or RINGDOVE Europe, Mediterranean and W Asia / forests and cultivation / n tree / e 2 / I ♂♀ 17 / F 20–35

Columba trocaz *Heineken* TROCAZ PIGEON Madeira / laurel forests / n ledge or tree / e 1

Columba bollii *Godman* BOLL'S PIGEON Canary Is / laurel forests / n tree / e 1

Columba unicincta *Cassin* AFRICAN GREY PIGEON C and W Africa / forest / n tree

Columba junoniae *Hartert* LAUREL PIGEON Palma and Gomera, Canary Is / laurel forest / n holes / e 1

Columba arquatrix *Temminck* OLIVE PIGEON E and S Africa / forest / n tree / e 1 / I 17

Columba sjoestedti *Reichenow* CAMEROON PIGEON Highlands of Cameroon (? Fernando Po) / no data

Columba thomensis *Bocage* MAROON PIGEON São Thomé / forest

Columba pollenii *Schlegel* COMORO PIGEON Comoro Is / forest / n tree / e 1

Columba hodgsonii *Vigors* HODGSON'S PIGEON Himalayas to Burma and W China / forest / n tree / e 1

Columba albinucha *Sassi* WHITE-NAPED PIGEON E Congo and W Uganda / forest

Columba pulchricollis *Blyth* ASHY PIGEON Himalayas from Nepal to Siam, Taiwan / forest / n tree / e 1–2

Columba elphinstonii *Sykes* NILGIRI PIGEON SW India / hill-forest / n tree / e 1

Columba torringtoni *Bonaparte* CEYLON PIGEON Ceylon / hill-forest / n tree / e 1

Columba punicea *Blyth* PURPLE PIGEON SE Asia / forest / n tree / e 1 (?2)

Columba argentina *Bonaparte* SILVER PIGEON Small islands of W Indonesia / n tree / e 1

Colomba palumboides (*Hume*) ANDAMAN PIGEON Andamans and Nicobars / forest

Columba janthina *Temminck* BLACK PIGEON Riu-Kius, Bonins and Volcano Is / forest / n ? tree, ? holes, ? rocks (accounts vary) / e 1

Columba vitiensis *Quoy and Gaimard* WHITE-THROATED PIGEON Islands from Philippines to Samoa / forest / n tree / e 1 / I 17–19

Columba leucomela *Temminck* (= **C.**

norfolciensis, *Latham*, of Peters' Check List, now identified as *Gallicolumba norfolciensis*) WHITE-HEADED PIGEON E Australia / forest / n tree / e 1

Columba versicolor *Kittlitz* BONIN BLACK or SHINING PIGEON Bonin Is / extinct c1889

Columba jouyi (*Stejneger*) SILVER-CRESCENTED PIGEON Riu-Kius and Borodino Is / ? extinct

Columba pallidiceps (*Ramsay*) YELLOW-LEGGED PIGEON Bismarck Archipelago and Solomon Is / forest

Columba leucocephala *L* WHITE-CROWNED PIGEON Caribbean islands and Florida / forest / n tree / e 1–2

Columba squamosa *Bonnaterre* RED-NECKED PIGEON Caribbean islands / woods / n tree / e 1–2

Columba speciosa *Gmelin* SCALED PIGEON Tropical C and S America / forest / n tree / e 1–2

Columba picazuro *Temminck* PICAZURO PIGEON NE Brazil to N Argentina / wood and savannah / n tree / e 1–2

Columba corensis *Jacquin* BARE-EYED PIGEON Coasts of Colombia and Venezuela and adjacent islands / semi-desert / n tree / e 1

Columba maculosa *Temminck* SPOTTED PIGEON S Peru to N Argentina / semi-arid / n tree (?) / e 1 (?)

Columba fasciata *Say* BAND-TAILED PIGEON W America from British Columbia to N Argentina / mountain forest / n tree / e 1 / I 18–20

Columba arucana *Lesson* CHILEAN PIGEON Chile / forest / n tree / e 1

Columba caribaea *Jacquin* JAMAICAN BAND-TAILED PIGEON Jamaica / forest

Columba cayennensis *Bonnaterre* RUFOUS PIGEON C America, eastern and northern S America / open forest / n tree / e 1

Columba flavirostris *Wagler* RED-BILLED PIGEON Mexico and C America / semi-arid / n tree / e 1

Columba oenops *Salvin* SALVIN'S PIGEON Upper Marañon Valley in Peru / no data

Columba inornata *Vigors* PLAIN PIGEON Greater Antilles / open country and cultivation / n tree / e 1–2

Columba plumbea *Vieillot* PLUMBEOUS PIGEON Northern and eastern S America / woodland

Columba subvinacea (*Lawrence*) RUDDY PIGEON Costa Rica, Panama and tropical S America / woodland

Columba nigrirostris *Sclater* SHORT-BILLED

PIGEON C America /rain forest

Columba goodsoni *Hartert* GOODSON'S PIGEON W Colombia and W Ecuador /forest

Columba delegorguei *Delegorgue* DELEGORGUE'S PIGEON E Africa /forest /n tree /e 2

Columba iriditorques *Cassin* BRONZE-NAPED PIGEON C and W Africa /forest /n tree (1 nest known)

Columba malherbii *Verreaux* SÃO THOMÉ BRONZE-NAPED PIGEON São Thomé, Principe and Annobon /rare /forest

Columba mayeri *Prevost* MAURITIUS PINK PIGEON Mauritius /rare /forests of SW plateau / n tree /e 2 (1 nest known)

Columba duboisi (*Rothschild*) BOURBON PINK PIGEON Réunion [Dubois] / extinct

Streptopelia turtur (*L*) TURTLE DOVE Europe, W Asia and N Africa /woods /n tree / e 2 /I ♂♀ 13–14 /F 18

Streptopelia lugens (*Rüppell*) DUSKY DOVE E Africa and Yemen / mountain forest /n tree / e 2 /I ♀ (sic)

Streptopelia hypopyrrha (*Reichenow*) PINK-BELLIED DOVE Mountains near source of R Benui, Cameroon and Bauchi and Pankshin plateaux, Nigeria /no other data

Streptopelia orientalis (*Latham*) RUFOUS DOVE C and E Asia to Japan, India and Indo-China /forest /n tree /e 2 /I ♂♀

Streptopelia bitorquata (*Temminck*) JAVANESE COLLARED DOVE Java to Timor: Philippines and Sulu Archipelago, introduced N Borneo and Mariannes /n tree /e 2

Streptopelia decaocto (*Frivaldsky*) COLLARED DOVE Japan to India and British Isles in a narrow band, expansion across Europe fairly recent and may be still expanding /arid country or cultivation / n tree or ledge / e 2 / I 14–16/ F 15–17

Streptopelia risoria (*L*) BARBARY DOVE Domestic form of next species, feral in some places, and usually given specific status

Streptopelia roseogrisea (*Sundevall*) ROSE-GREY DOVE N Africa S of Sahara, and S Arabia/ semi-desert /n tree /e 2

Streptopelia reichenowi (*Erlanger*) REICHENOW'S DOVE Ethiopia and Somaliland

Streptopelia decipiens (*Hartlaub and Finsch*) ANGOLA DOVE Africa S of Sahara, except the extreme S /dry areas /n tree /e 1–2 /I 13–14

Streptopelia semitorquata (*Rüppell*) RED-EYED DOVE Africa S of Sahara, except the S African desert /forest and savannah /n tree / e 2/ I 12–13

Streptopelia capicola (*Sundevall*) RING-NECKED DOVE E and S Africa /savannah /n tree/ e 2 /I 12 /F 16–17

Streptopelia vinacea (*Gmelin*) VINACEOUS DOVE Africa, belt just S of Sahara /scrub and savannah /n tree /e 2

Streptopelia tranquebarica (*Hermann*) RED COLLARED DOVE India to S China and Indo-China /woods /n tree /e 2

Streptopelia picturata (*Temminck*) PAINTED DOVE Madagascar, Comoros, Seychelles, Aldabra /forest /n tree /e 2

Streptopelia chinensis (*Scopoli*) SPOTTED DOVE India, Ceylon, Indo-Malayan region and S China /woods /n tree /e 2

Streptopelia senegalensis (*L*) LAUGHING DOVE Africa, Arabia and Asia Minor to India/ scrub /n tree /e 2

Aplopelia larvata (*Temminck*) LEMON DOVE EC and S Africa /forest /n tree /e 2 /F 20–1

Macropygia unchall (*Wagler*) BAR-TAILED CUCKOO DOVE Himalayas, S China, SE Asia, Sumatra, Java and Lombok / mountain forest/ n tree /e 1

Macropygia amboinensis (*L*) PINK-BREASTED CUCKOO DOVE E Indonesia, New Guinea, Bismarck Archipelago /forest /n tree /e 1

Macropygia phasianella (*Temminck*) BROWN CUCKOO DOVE Parts of Indonesia and E Australia /forest /n tree /e 1 (?2)

Macropygia magna *Wallace* LARGE CUCKOO DOVE S Celebes and some of the Lesser Sunda Is /no data

Macropygia rufipennis *Blyth* ANDAMANS CUCKOO DOVE Andamans and Nicobars /secondary forest

Macropygia nigrirostris *Salvadori* LESSER BAR-TAILED CUCKOO DOVE New Guinea, Bismarck Archipelago and adjacent islands/ no data

Macropygia mackinlayi *Ramsay* MACKINLAY'S CUCKOO DOVE New Britain to Solomon Is /woodland /n tree /e 1

Macropygia ruficeps (*Temminck*) LITTLE CUCKOO DOVE SE Asia and W Indonesia /forest/ n tree /e 1

Reinwardtoena reinwardtsi (*Temminck*) REINWARDT'S LONG-TAILED PIGEON New Guinea and Moluccas / mountain forest / n ledges in caves and gorges

PHASIANIDAE:
Phasianus colchicus,
Common Pheasant,
Ring-necked Pheasant

PHASIANIDAE:
Syrmaticus reevesi,
Reeve's Pheasant

Plate 62

PHASIANIDAE:
Syrmaticus soemmerringi,
Copper Pheasant

PHASIANIDAE:
Syrmaticus ellioti,
Elliot's Pheasant

Plate 63

Reinwardtoena browni (*Sclater*) BROWN'S LONG-TAILED PIGEON New Britain and Duke of York's Is/no data

Reinwardtoena crassirostris (*Gould*) CRESTED LONG-TAILED PIGEON Solomon Is/hill forest/e 1 (?)

Turacoena manadensis (*Quoy and Gaimard*) WHITE-FACED PIGEON Celebes and adjacent islands/woodland

Turacoena modesta (*Temminck*) TIMOR BLACK PIGEON Timor/no data

Turtur chalcospilos (*Wagler*) EMERALD-SPOTTED DOVE E and S Africa/veldt and scrub/n tree/e 2

Turtir abyssinicus (*Sharpe*) BLACK-BILLED WOOD DOVE N Africa S of Sahara belt/dry scrub/n tree/e 2

Turtur afer (*L*) SAPPHIRE-SPOTTED DOVE Africa S of Sahara and S to Transvaal/woodland/n tree/e 2

Turtur tympanistria (*Temminck*) TAMBOURINE DOVE Forested parts of Africa/n tree/e 2/I ♂♀

Turtur brehmeri (*Hartlaub*) BLUE-HEADED WOOD DOVE or MAIDEN DOVE W Africa/forest/n tree (very few found)

Oena capensis (*L*) MASKED DOVE or NAMAQUA DOVE Africa S of Sahara, Madagascar, Socotra, SW Arabia/scrub/n bush/e 2/F 16

Chalcophaps indica (*L*) EMERALD DOVE India through SE Asia and Indonesia to N and E Australia/woodland/n tree/e 2/I 14/F 12–13

Chalcophaps stephani *Pucheran* BROWN-BACKED EMERALD DOVE Celebes to Solomon Is/e 2

Henicophaps albifrons *Gray* BLACK BRONZEWING New Guinea and adjacent islands/woodland

Henicophaps foersteri *Rothschild and Hartert* NEW BRITAIN BRONZEWING New Britain/no data

Phaps chalcoptera (*Latham*) COMMON BRONZEWING Australia and Tasmania/woodland/n tree or ledge/e 2

Phaps elegans (*Temminck*) BRUSH BRONZEWING SW, SE Australia and Tasmania/scrub/n shrub/e 2/I 16/F 22

Phaps histrionica (*Gould*) FLOCK PIGEON Interior of Australia/scrub and plains/n ground/e 2

Ocyphaps lophotes (*Temminck*) CRESTED PIGEON Australia/dry areas/n tree/e 2

Petrophassa plumifera (*Gould*) WHITE-BELLIED PLUMED PIGEON Interior of Australia/spinifex scrub/n ground/e 2

Petrophassa ferruginea (*Gould*) RED PLUMED PIGEON W Australia/spinifex scrub/n ground/e 2

Petrophassa scripta (*Temminck*) BLUE-EYED PARTRIDGE BRONZEWING E Australia/open country/n ground/e 2

Petrophassa smithii (*Jardine and Selby*) BARE-EYED PARTRIDGE BRONZEWING N Australia/savannah/n ground/e 2

Petrophassa rufipennis *Collett* CHESTNUT-QUILLED PIGEON Extreme N Australia/rocks

Petrophassa albipennis *Gould* WHITE-QUILLED PIGEON Extreme N Australia/rocks

Geopelia cuneata (*Latham*) DIAMOND DOVE Australia/woodland and mulga/n tree/e 2/I 12–13/F 11–12

Geopelia striata (*L*) ZEBRA DOVE Malaya through Indonesia to Australia, introduced elsewhere/cultivation/n tree/e 2

Geopelia humeralis (*Temminck*) BAR-SHOULDERED DOVE N and E Australia and S New Guinea/lowland forest/n tree/e 2

Leucosarcia melanoleuca (*Latham*) WONGA PIGEON E Australia/rain forest/n tree/e 2

Ectopistes migratoria (*L*) PASSENGER PIGEON Eastern N America/forest/extinct/n tree (colonial)/e 1/I 13/F 14

Zenaida macroura (*L*) MOURNING DOVE S Canada, USA, C America and Caribbean/woodland/n tree/e 2/I 14–15/F 13–15

Zenaida auriculata (*Des Murs*) EARED DOVE S America and Lesser Antilles/open country/n tree or ground/e 2/I 14

Zenaida aurita (*Temminck*) ZENAIDA DOVE West Indies and Yucatan/open woodland/n tree or in hole in rocks/e 2

Zenaida galapagoensis *Gould* GALAPAGOS DOVE Galapagos/rocks/n hole in rock/e 2/I 13/F 17

Zenaida asiatica (*L*) WHITE-WINGED DOVE Discontinuous: Caribbean and C America, S America from Ecuador to N Chile/scrub and mangrove (!)/n tree/e 2

Columbina passerina (*L*) ROSY DOVE Tropical America/open country/n tree/e 2/I 13–14/F 11

Columbina minuta (*L*) GREY GROUND DOVE Discontinuous: C and parts of northern S America/savannah/n ground or tree/e 2/I 14

Columbina buckleyi (*Sclater and Salvin*) BUCKLEY'S DOVE W Ecuador and NW Peru/ no data

Columbina talpacoti (*Temminck*) RUDDY DOVE, STONE DOVE, CINNAMON DOVE Central and north eastern S America/savannah/n tree/ e 2/I 11–13/F 12

Columbina picui (*Temminck*) PICUI DOVE NE Brazil to C Chile and Uruguay/savannah/ n tree/e 2

Columbina cruziana (*Prevost*) GOLD-BILLED DOVE Ecuador to Chile, arid regions of coast/ n ledge or tree/e 2/I 14/F 10–11

Columbina cyanopis (*Pelzeln*) BLUE-EYED GROUND DOVE Mato Grosso, Brazil / no data

Claravis pretiosa (*Ferrari-Perez*) BLUE DOVE Central and northern S America/woodlands/ n tree/e 2/I 14

Claravis godefrida (*Temminck*) PURPLE-BARRED DOVE SE Brazil and Paraguay/woods

Claravis mondetoura (*Bonaparte*) PURPLE-BREASTED or MONDETOURA DOVE Mexico to Peru/forest

Metriopelia ceciliae (*Lesson*) SPECTACLED DOVE Peru, Bolivia and N Chile

Metriopelia morenoi (*Sharpe*) MORENO'S DOVE NW Argentina/n holes?

Metriopelia melanoptera (*Molina*) BLACK-WINGED GROUND DOVE Andes/wooded hillsides and cactus scrub/n tree?/e 2?

Metriopelia aymara (*Prevost*) BRONZE-WINGED GROUND DOVE C Andes

Scardafella inca (*Lesson*) INCA DOVE Arizona to Costa Rica/open country/n tree/e 2/F 14–16

Scardafella squammata (*Lesson*) SCALY DOVE Brazilian tableland and arid region of north-eastern S America

Uropelia campestris (*Spix*) MAUVE-SPOTTED DOVE Campos of Brazil/grassland

Leptotila verreauxi *Bonaparte* WHITE-FRONTED DOVE Tropical and subtropical America/arid regions/n tree/e 2/I 14

Leptotila megalura *Sclater and Salvin* WHITE-FACED DOVE Bolivia and N Argentina/ no data

Leptotila rufaxilla (*Richard and Bernard*) GREY-FRONTED DOVE Eastern S America/ humid forest/n tree/e 2

Leptotila plumbiceps *Sclater and Salvin* GREY-HEADED DOVE Mexico to Colombia/ humid forest

Leptotila pallida *Berlepsch and Taczanowski* PALLID DOVE W Colombia and W Ecuador/ no data

Leptotila wellsi (*Lawrence*) WELLS'S DOVE or GRENADA DOVE Grenada Is/e 2

Leptotila jamaicensis (*L*) WHITE-BELLIED or VIOLET DOVE Yucatan, Jamaica and intervening islands/semi-arid/n tree/e 2

Leptotila cassinii *Lawrence* CASSIN'S DOVE C America to Colombia/lowland forest/n tree/ e 2

Leptotila ochraceiventris *Chapman* BUFF-BELLIED DOVE SW Ecuador/no data

Leptotila conoveri *Bard and de Schaunsee* CONOVER'S DOVE Colombia/no data

Geotrygon lawrencii *Salvin* LAWRENCE'S QUAIL DOVE Costa Rica and Panama, also Vera Cruz/mountain forest/n tree/e 1

Geotrygon costaricensis *Lawrence* COSTA RICAN QUAIL DOVE Costa Rica and Panama/ n tree/e 1 ?

Geotrygon goldmani *Nelson* GOLDMAN'S DOVE East Darien (Panama)

Geotrygon saphirina *Bonaparte* SAPPHIRE DOVE Colombia, Ecuador, Peru (discontinuous)

Geotrygon caniceps (*Gundlach*) GREY-HEADED QUAIL DOVE Cuba and Hispaniola / lowland forest/n undergrowth/e 1

Geotrygon versicolor (*Lafresnaye*) CRESTED QUAIL DOVE Jamaica/forest/n tree/e 2

Geotrygon veraguensis *Lawrence* VERAGUA DOVE Costa Rica to NW Ecuador/forest

Geotrygon linearis (*Prevost*) WHITE-FACED QUAIL DOVE S Mexico to E Colombia and Venezuela/mountain forest

Geotrygon frenata (*Tschudi*) PINK-FACED QUAIL DOVE W Colombia to N Bolivia/forest

Geotrygon chrysia *Bonaparte* KEY WEST QUAIL DOVE Bahamas, Cuba, Isle of Pines and Hispaniola/forest/n tree/e 1–2

Geotrygon mystacea (*Temminck*) BRIDLED QUAIL DOVE Lesser Antilles/forest /n undergrowth/e 1–2

Geotrygon violacea (*Temminck*) VIOLET QUAIL DOVE Nicaragua S through northern and eastern S America/no data

Geotrygon montana (*L*) RUDDY QUAIL DOVE Mexico and Caribbean to Paraguay/ forest/n tree/e 2

Starnoenas cyanocephala (*L*) BLUE-HEADED DOVE Cuba/forest/n tree/e 1–2

Caloenas nicobarica *L* NICOBAR or VULTURINE PIGEON Indonesia/woods/n tree/e 1

PHASIANIDAE: *Lophura ignita,* Crested Fireback

PHASIANIDAE: *Lophophorus impejanus,* Impeyan Pheasant or
Himalayan Monal, Himalayan Monal Pheasant

Plate 64

PHASIANIDAE;
Lophortyx californica,
California Quail

PHASIANIDAE;
Lophura leucomelana,
Kalij Pheasant

Plate 65

Gallicolumba luzonica (*Scopoli*) BLEEDING HEART PIGEON Luzon and Polillo/n bush ?/e 2 ?

[The next four species of 'Bleeding Heart Pigeons' from various Philippine Islands are evidently very closely related to each other, and may be conspecific]

Gallicolumba criniger (*Pucheran*) BARTLETT'S PIGEON Mindanao, Leyte, Samar and Basilan/e 1

Gallicolumba platenae (*Salvadori*) MINDORO PIGEON Mindoro/n tree/e 2

Gallicolumba keayi (*Eagle Clarke*) NEGROS PIGEON Negros

Gallicolumba menagei (*Bourns and Worcester*) TAWI-TAWI BLEEDING HEART Tawi-Tawi

Gallicolumba rufigula (*Pucheran*) GOLDEN-HEART PIGEON New Guinea and W Papua/ forest/n tree/e 1

Gallicolumba tristigmata (*Bonaparte*) CELEBES QUAIL DOVE Celebes/forest

Gallicolumba jobiensis (*Meyer*) WHITE-BREASTED GROUND PIGEON New Guinea to Solomon Is/forest/n ? tree/e 2

Gallicolumba kubaryi (*Finsch*) TRUK DOVE E Caroline Is/forest and open country/n tree-ferns ?/e 1 ?

Gallicolumba erythroptera (*Gmelin*) SOCIETY DOVE Society and Tuamotu Is/forest

Gallicolumba xanthonura (*Temminck*) WHITE-throated DOVE Marianas and Yap Is/ forest/n tree

Gallicolumba norfolciensis (*Latham*) NORFOLK ISLAND DOVE Norfolk Is/extinct/no specimens (this name was formerly used for *Columba leucomela*)

Gallicolumba stairi (*Gray*) FRIENDLY DOVE Fiji, Tonga and Samoa Is/e 2

Gallicolumba sanctaecrucis *Mayr* SANTA CRUZ GROUND DOVE Santa Cruz Archipelago and Espiritu Santu

Gallicolumba ferruginea (*Wagler*) TANNA DOVE Tanna Is/extinct/no specimens/known only from Forster's drawing

Gallicolumba salamonis (*Ramsay*) THICK-BILLED GROUND DOVE Ramos and San Christobal (Solomons)

Gallicolumba rubescens (*Vieillot*) MARQUESAS GROUND DOVE Marquesas/forest/ n tree?/e 2

Gallicolumba beccarii (*Salvadori*) GREY-

BREASTED QUAIL DOVE New Guinea to the Solomons/mountain forest/n near ground/e 1 ?

Gallicolumba canifrons (*Hartlaub and Finsch*) PELEW GROUND DOVE Palau Is/woodland on ridges

Gallicolumba hoedtii (*Schlegel*) WETAR DOVE Wetar Is/no data

Trugon terrestris *Gray* THICK-BILLED GROUND PIGEON New Guinea and Salawati/ lowland forest/n ground/e 1

Microgoura meeki *Rothschild* MEEK'S PIGEON Choiseul, Solomons/last seen 1904, presumed extinct/e 1, on ground, no nest

Otidiphaps nobilis *Gould* PHEASANT PIGEON New Guinea and adjacent islands/mountain forest/n n/k/e (captivity) 1/I 23–6

Goura cristata (*Pallas*) BLUE CROWNED PIGEON NW New Guinea and adjacent islands/forest/ n tree/e 1/I 28–9/F 30–6

Goura scheepmakeri *Finsch* MAROON-BREASTED CROWNED PIGEON S New Guinea/ forest/n tree/e 1

Goura victoria (*Fraser*) VICTORIA CROWNED PIGEON N New Guinea and Japen/forest/e 1

Didunculus strigirostris (*Jardine*) TOOTH-BILLED PIGEON Upolu and Savaii, Samoa/ wooded mountain sides/n tree ?

Phapitreron leucotis (*Temminck*) LESSER BROWN FRUIT DOVE Philippines/forest/ n tree

Phapitreron amethystina *Bonaparte* GREATER BROWN FRUIT DOVE Philippines/ forest

Treron fulvicollis (*Wagler*) CINNAMON-HEADED GREEN PIGEON Malaysian region/ mangrove etc/n tree/e 2

Treron olax (*Temminck*) LITTLE GREEN PIGEON Malaysian region/forest

Treron vernans (*L*) PINK-NECKED GREEN PIGEON Malaya to Celebes and Philippines/ forest/n tree/e 2

Treron bicincta (*Jerdon*) ORANGE-BREASTED GREEN PIGEON India, SE Asia, Ceylon, Hainan, Java/woods/n tree/e 2

Treron pompadora (*Gmelin*) POMPADOUR PIGEON Discontinuous: W India and Ceylon; Burma and SE Asia; Philippines/forest/n tree/ e 2

Treron curvirostra (*Gmelin*) THICK-BILLED GREEN PIGEON Nepal to Sumatra, Borneo and S Philippines/forest and open country/n tree/ e 2

Treron griseicauda *Bonaparte* GREY-FACED

GREEN PIGEON S Sumatra, Java, Bali, Celebes and adjacent small islands/no data

Treron teysmannii *Schlegel* SUMBA GREEN PIGEON Sumba/no data

Treron floris *Wallace* FLORES GREEN PIGEON Lombok, Sumbawa, Flores, Solor, Lomblen, Pantar and Alor/no data

Treron psittacea (*Temminck*) TIMOR GREEN PIGEON Timor and Samau/no data

Treron capellei (*Temminck*) GREAT GREEN PIGEON Malaysian region/no data

Treron phoenicoptera (*Latham*) YELLOW-LEGGED GREEN PIGEON India, Ceylon and SE Asia/forest and scrub/n tree/e 2/I 14?

Treron waalia (*Meyer*) YELLOW-BELLIED GREEN PIGEON Africa, belt S of Sahara and SW Arabia/savannah and scrub/n tree/e 2

Treron australis (*L*) MADAGASCAR GREEN PIGEON Madagascar and Moheli / forest and savannah

Treron calva (*Temminck*) AFRICAN GREEN PIGEON Africa S of Sahara/forest and savannah/n tree/e 1–2

Treron pembaensis *Pakenham* PEMBA PIGEON Pemba Is/forest and garden/n tree/e 2

Treron sanctithomae (*Gmelin*) SÃO THOMÉ GREEN PIGEON São Thomé and Rollas/forest/n tree/e 1 (1 nest known)

Treron apicauda *Blyth* PIN-TAILED GREEN PIGEON Himalayas to Laos and Annam/forest and plain/n tree/e 2

Treron oxyura (*Temminck*) YELLOW-BELLIED PIN-TAILED GREEN PIGEON Sumatra and W Java/mountains

Treron seimundi (*Robinson*) WHITE-BELLIED PIN-TAILED GREEN PIGEON Malaya and Annam/mountain forest

Treron sphenura (*Vigors*) WEDGE-TAILED GREEN PIGEON Himalayas to SE Asia, Sumatra, Java and Lombok/mountain forest/n tree/e 2/I 14/F 12

Treron sieboldii (*Temminck*) SIEBOLD'S PIGEON Japan, Taiwan and S China to Annam/wooded mountain slopes/n tree/e 2

Treron formosae *Swinhoe* FORMOSAN GREEN PIGEON Riu-Kius, Taiwan, Batan, Calayan and Camiguin

Ptilinopus cincta (*Temminck*) BLACK-BACKED FRUIT DOVE Lesser Sunda Is/forest

Ptilinopus alligator *Collet* BLACK-BANDED PIGEON South Alligator River, N Australia/rocky ridges

Ptilinopus dohertyi *Rothschild* RED-NAPED FRUIT DOVE Sumba/no data

Ptilinopus porphyrea (*Temminck*) PINK-NECKED FRUIT DOVE Sumatra, Java and Bali/forest

Ptilinopus marchei *Oustalet* MARCHE'S DOVE Luzon and Polillo, 'rare and found among stunted trees near the tops of mountains' (Goodwin)

Ptilinopus merrilli (*McGregor*) MERRILL'S FRUIT DOVE Luzon and Polillo / mountain forest

Ptilinopus occipitalis *Gray* YELLOW-BREASTED FRUIT DOVE Philippines/forest/no other data

Ptilinopus fischeri *Brüggemann* FISCHER'S FRUIT DOVE Celebes/mountain forest/n 'under root of old tree'/e 1 (1 nest known)

Ptilinopus jambu (*Gmelin*) JAMBU DOVE Malaysian region/forests/n tree/e 1

Ptilinopus subgularis *Meyer and Wiglesworth* DARK-CHINNED FRUIT DOVE Celebes and nearby islands/forest

Ptilinopus leclancheri (*Bonaparte*) LECLANCHER'S PIGEON Philippines/forest/n tree/e 1

Ptilinopus formosus (*Gray*) SCARLET-BREASTED FRUIT DOVE N Moluccas/hill forest

Ptilinopus magnificus (*Temminck*) MAGNIFICENT DOVE New Guinea to E Australia/forest/n tree/e 1

Ptilinopus perlatus (*Temminck*) PINK-SPOTTED FRUIT DOVE New Guinea and adjacent islands/forest and park

Ptilinopus ornatus *Schlegel* ORNATE DOVE New Guinea/forest

Ptilinopus tannensis (*Latham*) SILVER-SHOULDERED FRUIT DOVE New Hebrides and Banks Is

Ptilinopus aurantiifrons *Gray* ORANGE-FRONTED FRUIT DOVE New Guinea and adjacent islands/forest/n tree/e 1

Ptilinopus wallacii *Gray* WALLACE'S FRUIT DOVE SW New Guinea and islands to SW/lowland forest

Ptilinopus superbus (*Temminck*) SUPERB DOVE Celebes to Solomons and E Australia/forest / n tree/e 1

Ptilinopus perousii *Peale* RAINBOW DOVE Samoa, Fiji and Tonga/forest

Ptilinopus porphyraceus *Temminck* PONAPÉ DOVE Fiji, Tonga, Samoa and Caroline Is/forest/n tree/e 1

PHASIANIDAE:
Lophura edwardsi,
Edwards' Pheasant

PHASIANIDAE:
Lophura imperialis,
Imperial Pheasant

Plate 66

PHASIANIDAE:
Chrysolophus amherstiae,
Lady Amherst's Pheasant

PHASIANIDAE:
Tragopan temminckii,
Temminck's Tragopan

Plate 67

Ptilinopus pelewensis *Hartlaub and Finsch* PALAU DOVE Palau Is / woods / n tree / e 1

Ptilinopus rarotongensis *Hartlaub and Finsch* RAROTONGAN DOVE Rarotonga Is / no data

Ptilinopus roseicapilla (*Lesson*) ROSE-CAPPED DOVE Marianas / woodland

Ptilinopus regina *Swainson* PINK-CAPPED DOVE N and E Australia and Lesser Sunda Is / woods / n tree / e 1

Ptilinopus richardsii *Ramsay* SILVER-CAPPED DOVE E Solomons and Rennell Is / forest / n tree / e 1

Ptilinopus purpuratus (*Gmelin*) GREY-GREEN FRUIT DOVE Society and Tuamotu Is / no data

Ptilinopus greyii *Bonaparte* GREY'S FRUIT DOVE Gower Is to New Caledonia / no data

Ptilinopus huttoni *Finsch* HUTTON'S DOVE Rapa Is / no data

Ptilinopus dupetithouarsii (*Neboux*) WHITE-CAPPED FRUIT DOVE Marquesas / no data

Ptilinopus mercierii (*Des Murs and Prevost*) MOUSTACHED DOVE Marquesas / no data

Ptilinopus insularis *North* HENDERSON ISLAND FRUIT DOVE Henderson Is / no data

Ptilinopus coronulatus *Gray* LILAC-CAPPED DOVE New Guinea and adjacent islands / forest / n tree / e 1 / I 18 / F 12

Ptilinopus pulchellus (*Temminck*) CRIMSON-CAPPED DOVE New Guinea and adjacent islands / forest / n tree / e 1

Ptilinopus monacha (*Temminck*) BLUE-CAPPED DOVE N Moluccas / ? forest

Ptilinopus rivoli (*Prevost*) WHITE-BIBBED DOVE or MOON DOVE Moluccas through New Guinea to Bismarck Archipelago / mountain forest in New Guinea, the island races inhabiting lowland forest

Ptilinopus solomonensis *Gray* YELLOW-BIBBED DOVE Solomon Is, Bismarck Archipelago and islands in Geelvink Bay / lowland forest / n tree / e 1

Ptilinopus viridis (*L*) RED-BIBBED DOVE S Moluccas to N New Guinea: Solomons and islands off SE New Guinea / forest

Ptilinopus eugeniae (*Gould*) EUGENE'S DOVE San Cristobal and Ugi / forest (sometimes considered conspecific with *P. viridis*)

Ptilinopus iozonus *Gray* ORANGE-BELLIED FRUIT DOVE New Guinea and adjacent islands / forest

Ptilinopus insolitus *Schlegel* KNOB-BILLED DOVE Bismarck Archipelago / woodland / n tree / e 1 / I 19 / F 14 (1 nest known)

Ptilinopus hyogastra (*Temminck*) GREY-HEADED FRUIT DOVE Halmahera and Batjan / ? woodland

Ptilinopus granulifrons *Hartert* CARUNCULATED DOVE Obi Major / forest

Ptilinopus melanospila (*Salvadori*) BLACK-NAPED FRUIT DOVE E Indonesia / woodland

Ptilinopus naina (*Temminck*) DWARF FRUIT DOVE S New Guinea and adjacent islands / lowland forest

Ptilinopus arcanus *Ripley and Rabor* RIPLEY'S DOVE Mount Canalon, Negros Is / 1 specimen ♀

Ptilinopus victor (*Gould*) ORANGE DOVE E Fiji / forest / n tree / e 2

Ptilinopus luteovirens (*Hombron and Jacquinot*) GOLDEN or LEMON DOVE W Fiji / forest

Ptilinopus layardi (*Elliot*) YELLOW HEADED DOVE S Fiji / ? woodland

Drepanoptila holosericea (*Temminck*) CLOVEN-FEATHERED DOVE New Caledonia and Isle of Pines / forest / n tree / e 2

Alectroenas madagascariensis (*L*) MADAGASCAR BLUE PIGEON Madagascar / forest

Alectroenas sganzini (*Bonaparte*) COMORO BLUE PIGEON Comoros and Aldabra / forest

Alectroenas nitidissima (*Scopoli*) MAURITIUS BLUE PIGEON Mauritius / extinct c1830

Alectroenas rodericana *Milne-Edwards* RODRIGUEZ BLUE PIGEON Rodriguez / bones [Leguat]

Alectroenas pulcherrima (*Scopoli*) SEYCHELLES BLUE PIGEON Seychelles / forest / n tree / e 1

Ducula poliocephala (*Gray*) ZONE-TAILED PIGEON Philippines / trees

Ducula forsteni (*Temminck*) GREEN AND WHITE PIGEON Celebes / forest

Duculu mindorensis (*Whitehead*) MINDORO PIGEON Mindoro / woods

Ducula radiata (*Quoy and Gaimard*) GREY-HEADED ZONE-TAILED PIGEON Celebes / mountain forest / n rock ledges / e 1

Ducula carola (*Bonaparte*) SPOTTED IMPERIAL PIGEON Philippines / forest / n cliffs / e 1

Ducula aenea (*L*) GREEN IMPERIAL PIGEON India to SE Asia and Indonesia / forest / n tree / e 1

Ducula perspicillata (*Temminck*) SPECTACLED IMPERIAL PIGEON Moluccas / forest

Ducula concinna (*Wallace*) GOLD-EYED PIGEON E Indonesia / no data

Ducula pacifica (*Gmelin*) PACIFIC PIGEON Small islands of W Pacific

Ducula oceanica (*Lesson and Garnot*) MICRONESIAN PIGEON Micronesia / woodland

Ducula aurorae (*Peale*) AURORA PIGEON Tahiti and Aurora / woods / may be extinct on Tahiti

Ducula galeata (*Bonaparte*) MARQUESAS PIGEON Nukuhiva / no data

Ducula rubricera (*Bonaparte*) RED-KNOBBED PIGEON Bismarck Archipelago and Solomons / forest / n shrubs / e 1 ?

Ducula myristicivora (*Scopoli*) BLACK-KNOBBED PIGEON West Papuan Is and islands in Geelvink Bay / no data

Ducula rufigaster (*Quoy and Gaimard*) RUFOUS-BELLIED IMPERIAL PIGEON New Guinea, W Papuan Is and Japen / forest

Ducula basilica *Bonaparte* BASILICA PIGEON N Moluccas / ? forest

Ducula finschii (*Ramsay*) FINSCH'S IMPERIAL PIGEON Bismarck Archipelago / forest

Ducula chalconota (*Salvadori*) SHINING FRUIT PIGEON New Guinea / mountain forest

Ducula pistrinaria *Bonaparte* ISLAND IMPERIAL PIGEON Islands to N and E of New Guinea / forest

Ducula rosacea (*Temminck*) PINK-HEADED IMPERIAL PIGEON Lesser Sundas and nearby small islands / forest

Ducula whartoni (*Sharpe*) CHRISTMAS PIGEON or BLACK IMPERIAL PIGEON Christmas Is (Indian Ocean) / plateau forest / n tree / e 1–2 ?

Ducula pickeringii (*Cassin*) GREY IMPERIAL PIGEON Islands between Borneo and Philippines (small wooded islands)

Ducula latrans (*Peale*) PEALE'S PIGEON Fiji / forest

Ducula brenchleyi (*Gray*) CHESTNUT-BELLIED PIGEON Solomon Is / forest

Ducula bakeri (*Kinnear*) BAKER'S PIGEON N New Hebrides / mountain forest

Ducula goliath (*Gray*) GOLIATH PIGEON New Caledonia and Isle of Pines / mountain forest

Ducula pinon (*Quoy and Gaimard*) PINON PIGEON New Guinea and adjacent islands / forest / n tree / e 1

Ducula melanochroa (*Sclater*) SILVER-LACED PIGEON Bismarck Archipelago / no data

Ducula mullerii (*Temminck*) MÜLLER'S PIGEON New Guinea and Aru Is / woods / n tree / e 1

Ducula zoeae (*Lesson*) ZOE'S PIGEON New Guinea and adjacent islands / forest

Ducula badia (*Raffles*) MOUNTAIN IMPERIAL PIGEON India to Sumatra and Borneo / hill forest / n tree / e 1

Ducula lacernulata (*Temminck*) DARK-BACKED IMPERIAL PIGEON Java, Lombok, Bali and Flores / mountain forest

Ducula cineracea (*Temminck*) ASHY IMPERIAL PIGEON Timor and Wetar / mountain forest

Ducula bicolor (*Scopoli*) PIED IMPERIAL PIGEON Islands from Andamans to Moluccas / woods and mangroves / n tree / e 1

Ducula luctuosa (*Temminck*) WHITE FRUIT PIGEON Celebes and islands to E / woods

Ducula spilorrhoa (*Gray*) NUTMEG PIGEON New Guinea to N and E Australia / woodland and mangrove / n tree / e 1 / I ♂♀ 26–8 / F 24–8

Lopholaimus antarcticus (*Shaw*) TOPKNOT PIGEON E Australia / forest / n tree / e 1

Hemiphaga novaeseelandiae (*Gmelin*) NEW ZEALAND PIGEON New Zealand, Chatham Is (formerly Norfolk Is) / forest / n tree / e 1 / I 28 / F 36 (1 nest)

Cryptophaps poecilorrhoa (*Brüggemann*) CELEBES DUSKY PIGEON Celebes / forest

Gymnophaps albertisii *Salvadori* D'ALBERTIS' MOUNTAIN PIGEON New Guinea, New Britain, New Ireland and Batjan / mountain forest

Gymnophaps mada (*Hartert*) LONG-TAILED MOUNTAIN PIGEON Ceram and Buru / mountain forest

Gymnophaps solomonensis *Mayr* PALE MOUNTAIN PIGEON Solomon Is / hill forest

PSITTACIDAE Parrots and Allies Small to medium sized birds, usually brightly coloured, inhabiting tropical regions. Frequently arboreal with powerful bills for feeding on kernels and fruits, some (eg lories) with brush-like tongues for sweeping nectar and pollen from flowers. Some species also feed on grubs and larvae. Nest usually in a hole in a tree (except where stated), eggs white and glossy. Sexes similar, except in a few cases.

Strigops habroptilus *Gray* OWL PARROT or KAKAPO New Zealand, N and S Island /

PHASIANIDAE:
Ithaginis cruentus,
Blood Pheasant

PHASIANIDAE:
Excalfactoria chinensis,
Painted Quail, Blue Quail

Plate 68

PHASIANIDAE: *Ithaginis cruentus,*
Blood Pheasant

Plate 69

declining / nocturnal / forests / e 1–3 / I ♀

Nestor meridionalis (*Gmelin*) KAKA New Zealand / forests / e 4 / I ♀ 21 / F c70

Nestor notabilis *Gould* KEA New Zealand, S Island / mountain forests / e 2–4 / I ♀ 21–8 / F c90

Nestor productus (*Gould*) NORFOLK ISLAND PARROT Norfolk and Philip Is / extinct 1851 [*Nestor norfolcensis* Pelzeln (type in Liverpool Museum) is probably an aberrant specimen]

Chalcopsitta atra (*Scopoli*) BLACK LORY W New Guinea and adjacent islands / grassland and forest edges / gregarious / e 2

[**Chalcopsitta insignis** *Oustalet* RAJAH LORY Vogelkop, New Guinea, usually regarded as a race of above]

Chalcopsitta sintillata (*Temmick*) YELLOW-STREAKED LORY S New Guinea and Aru islands / lowland savannahs / flocks

Chalcopsitta duivenbodei (*Dubois*) BROWN LORY N New Guinea / lowlands

Chalcopsitta cardinalis (*Gray*) CARDINAL LORY C Melanesia / forest and mangroves

Eos cyanogenia *Bonaparte* BLACK-WINGED LORY Islands in Geelvink Bay, New Guinea / coconut palms near coast

Eos squamata (*Boddaert*) VIOLET-NECKED LORY W Papuan Is / coconut palms

Eros reticulata (*Müller*) BLUE-STREAKED LORY Tanimbar Islands / no data

Eos histrio (*Müller*) RED AND BLUE LORY Sangir, Talaud and Nenusa Is / forests / e 2 ?

Eos bornea (*L*) RED LORY Ceram, Amboina and adjacent islands / forests / gregarious / e 2 / F 50–60

[**Eos goodfellowi** *Ogilvie-Grant* GOODFELLOW'S LORY Obi, Moluccas; based on 2 aviary specimens, not preserved. Thought by Holyoak to be the juvenile of *E. bornea*, but this cannot be conclusive, particularly since *bornea* does not appear to occur on Obi]

Eos semilarvata *Bonaparte* BLUE-EARED LORY Ceram mountains

Pseudeos fuscata (*Blyth*) DUSKY LORY New Guinea / forest and habitation / gregarious

Trichoglossus ornatus (*L*) ORNATE LORIKEET Celebes / mountain woods / e 2 / I ♀ 27 / F 80

Trichoglossus haematodus (*L*) RAINBOW LORIKEET E Australia, New Guinea, Indonesia, Melanesia and Micronesia / forests and coconut plantations / gregarious / e 2–3 / I ♀ 25 / F c50

Trichoglossus rubiginosus (*Bonaparte*)

PONAPÉ LORY Ponapé, Caroline Is / coconut palms / e 1

Trichoglossus johnstoniae *Hartert* JOHNSTONE'S LORIKEET Mindanao, Philippines / mountain forests / e 2 / I ♀ 21 / F 28

Trichoglossus flavoviridis *Wallace* YELLOW AND GREEN LORIKEET Celebes and the Sula Is / mountain forests

Trichoglossus chlorolepidotus (*Kuhl*) SCALY-BREASTED LORIKEET Queensland and New South Wales / lowland woods / e 2–3 / I ♀ 25 / F c45

Trichoglossus euteles (*Temminck*) PERFECT LORIKEET Lesser Sunda Is / e 3 / I ♀ 23

Trichoglossus versicolor *Lear* VARIED LORIKEET Tropical North Australia / lowland woods / e 2–4 / I ♀ 20 / F 40

Trichoglossus iris (*Temminck*) IRIS LORIKEET Timor and Wetar / no data

Trichoglossus goldiei *Sharpe* GOLDIE'S LORIKEET Mountains of New Guinea / forest / e 2 ?

Lorius hypoinochrous *Gray* PURPLE-BELLIED LORY SE New Guinea and Melanesia / rain forests

Lorius lory (*L*) BLACK-CAPPED LORY New Guinea and Papuan Is / forests / e 2 / I ♀ 24 / F c60

Lorius albidinuchus (*Rothschild and Hartert*) WHITE-NAPED LORY New Ireland / no data

Lorius amabilis *Stresemann* STRESEMANN'S LORY New Britain / unique

Lorius chlorocercus *Gould* YELLOW-BIBBED LORY Eastern Solomon Is / forests

Lorius domicellus (*L*) PURPLE-NAPED LORY Ceram and Amboina / mountain forests / e 2 / I ♀ 24–6 / F c90 (?)

Lorius tibialis *Sclater* JAMRACH'S LORY unique, origin uncertain [type in British Museum (Natural History)]

Lorius garrulus (*L*) CHATTERING LORY Moluccas / palm groves / e 2 / I ♀ / F 26

Phigys solitarius (*Suckow*) COLLARED LORY Fiji Is / groves and city trees / e 2 / I 30 / F c60

Vini australis (*Gmelin*) BLUE-CROWNED LORY Samoa and Tonga / coconut plantations

Vini kuhlii (*Vigors*) KUHL'S LORY Rimatara and the Austral Is, introduced elsewhere / e 2 / F c50

Vini stepheni (*North*) STEPHEN'S LORY Henderson Is / no data

Vini peruviana (*Müller*) BLUE LORY Society, Tuamotu and Cook Is, formerly Tahiti /

coconut palms / e 2 / I ♂♀ 21 / F 8 weeks (?)

Vini ultamarina (*Kuhl*) ULTAMARINE LORY Nukuhiva and Huapu, Marquesas Is / e 2 / I ♂♀ / F c56

Glossopsitta concinna (*Shaw*) MUSK LORIKEET Tasmania and SE Australia / trees / gregarious / e 2

Glossopsitta pusilla (*Shaw*) LITTLE LORIKEET Tasmania and E Australia / trees / e 3–5 / I ♀ / F 30

Glossopsitta porphyrocephala (*Dietrichsen*) PURPLE CROWNED LORIKEET S Australia / dry areas with trees / e 4 / I ♀ 17 / F c56

Charmosyna palmarum (*Gmelin*) PALM LORIKEET Duff Group, Santa Cruz Is, Banks Is and New Hebrides / no data

Charmosyna rubrigularis (*Sclater*) RED-CHINNED LORIKEET New Britain, New Ireland and Dampier Is / mountain forests

Charmosyna meeki (*Rothschild and Hartert*) MEEK'S LORIKEET Solomon Is / mountain forest

Charmosyna toxopei (*Siebers*) BLUE-FRONTED LORIKEET Buru / only known from the original specimens

Charmosyna multistriata (*Rothschild*) STRIATED LORIKEET, GREENISH or YELLOW-STREAKED LORIKEET Southern slopes of the Snow Mountains, New Guinea / no data

Charmosyna wilhelminae (*Meyer*) WILHELMINA'S LORIKEET New Guinea / mountain forests

Charmosyna rubronotata (*Wallace*) RED-FRONTED LORIKEET N New Guinea and islands in Geelvink Bay / lowland forests / gregarious

Charmosyna placentis (*Temminck*) YELLOW-FRONTED or RED-FLANKED LORIKEET Papuan Is, New Guinea and Melanesia / lowland forests and savannah / e 2

Charmosyna diadema (*Verreaux and Des Murs*) DIADEMED LORIKEET New Caledonia / 2 specimens

Charmosyna amabilis (*Ramsay*) (= **C. aureicincta** (*Layard*)) GOLDEN-BANDED LORIKEET Fiji Is / mountain forests

Charmosyna margarethae *Tristram* DUCHESS LORIKEET Solomon Is / mountain and lowland forests

Charmosyna pulchella *Gray* FAIRY LORIKEET New Guinea / mountain forests

Charmosyna josefinae (*Finsch*) JOSEPHINE'S LORIKEET New Guinea / mountain forests

Charmosyna papou (*Scopoli*) FAIRY LORIKEET

or PAPUAN LORY New Guinea / mountain forest / I 3 weeks / F c60

Oreopsittacus arfaki (*Meyer*) WHISKERED LORIKEET New Guinea / mountain mist forests

Neopsittacus musschenbroekii (*Schlegel*) YELLOW-BILLED LORY Mts of New · Guinea / mountain forest / e 2

Neopsittacus pullicauda *Hartert* ORANGE-BILLED LORY Mts of New Guinea / high mountain forest

Psittaculirostris desmarestii (*Desmarest*) LARGE FIG PARROT New Guinea and W Papuan Is / lowland forest

Psittaculirostris edwardsi (*Oustalet*) EDWARDS' FIG PARROT Coast of N New Guinea from Humboldt Bay to Huon Gulf / lowland forest

Psittaculirostris salvadorii (*Oustalet*) SALVADORI'S FIG PARROT N Coast of New Guinea from Geelvink Bay to Humboldt Bay / no data

Opopsitta gulielmiterti (*Schlegel*) WILLIAM'S or ORANGE-BELLIED FIG PARROT New Guinea, Salawati, and Aru Is / lowland forest and swamp

Opopsitta diophthalma (*Hombron and Jacquinot*) DOUBLE-EYED FIG PARROT NE Australia, New Guinea, W Papuan Is / rain-forest / e 2

Micropsitta pusio (*Sclater*) BUFF-FACED PIGMY PARROT N New Guinea and Bismarck Archipelago / forests / n in termite nest in tree / e 2–3 ?

Micropsitta keiensis (*Salvadori*) YELLOW-CAPPED PYGMY PARROT W Papuan, Aru and Kei Is, W and S New Guinea / forests / n termitarium / I ♀ ?

Micropsitta geelvinkiana (*Schlegel*) GEELVINK PYGMY PARROT Numfor and Biak in Geelvink Bay / forest / n termitarium

Micropsitta meeki *Rothschild and Hartert* MEEK'S PYGMY PARROT Admiralty, St Matthias and Squally Is / n termitarium / no other data

Micropsitta finschii (*Ramsay*) RAMSAY'S PYGMY PARROT Solomons and Bismarck Archipelago / forest / n termitarium

Micropsitta bruijnii (*Salvadori*) ROSE-BREASTED PYGMY PARROT Ceram, Buru, New Guinea, Bismarck Archipelago, Solomons / forests / n stump

Probosciger aterrimus (*Gmelin*) PALM COCKATOO Papuan Is, New Guinea and Cape

PHASIANIDAE: *Crossoptilon mantchuricum*, Brown Eared-pheasant

PHASIANIDAE: *Crossoptilon crossoptilon*, White Eared-pheasant

Plate 70

PHASIANIDAE: *Lophura nycthemera,* Silver Pheasant

Plate 71

York Peninsula/forest/e 1/F 60 ?

Calyptorhynchus funereus (*Shaw*) BLACK COCKATOO SE and SW Australia, Tasmania/ scrub and forest/e 1–2/I ♀/F 76 ?

Calyptorhynchus magnificus (*Shaw*) BANKSIAN COCKATOO Australia/savannah and scrub / e 1–2 / I ♀ 30 / F c90

Calyptorhynchus lathami (*Temminck*) GLOSSY COCKATOO E Australia and Kangaroo Is/ forest/e 1/ I ♀

Callocephalon fimbriatum (*Grant*) GANG-GANG COCKATOO SE Australia, vagrant to King Is and Tasmania / mountain forests and valleys/ gregarious / e 2/I ♂♀ 30 F c50

Eolophus roseicapillus (*Vieillot*) GALAH or ROSEATE COCKATOO Australia, except the coast/grassland and scrub/e 2–5/I ♂♀ c28/F c40

Cacatua galerita (*Latham*) GREATER SULPHUR CRESTED COCKATOO Australia, New Guinea, Melanesia, introduced to New Zealand / forest and savannah / gregarious / e 2–3 / I ♂♀ 30/ F c40–60

Cacatua sulphurea (*Gmelin*) LESSER SULPHUR CRESTED COCKATOO Indonesia / forest / e 1–3/ I ♂♀ 24/F approx 10 weeks

Cacatua leadbeateri (*Vigors*) LEADBEATER'S or MAJOR MITCHELL'S COCKATOO Australia/ dry woodland/e 2–4/I ♂♀ 30/F 6–8 weeks

Cacatua ophthalmica *Sclater* BLUE-EYED COCKATOO New Britain and New Ireland/ forests/e 2/F 'more than 4 months'

Cacatua alba (*Müller*) GREAT WHITE COCKATOO N and C Moluccas/e 2/I ♂♀ 4 weeks/ F 2 months

Cacatua moluccensis (*Gmelin*) ROSE CRESTED COCKATOO S Moluccas/I ♂♀/little other data

Cacatua haematuropygia (*Müller*) RED-VENTED COCKATOO Philippine Is /cultivation

Cacatua goffini (*Finsch*) GOFFIN'S COCKATOO Tanimbar Is/no data

Cacatua sanguinea *Gould* LITTLE CORELLA or BARE-EYED COCKATOO Australia and S New Guinea /mangroves and open country / e 3–4

Cacatua tenuirostris (*Kuhl*) LONG-BILLED CORELLA SE and SW Australia / damp forest, declining /e 2–3/I ♂♀ 24/F 7 weeks

Cacatua ducorps (*Bonaparte*) DUCORP'S COCKATOO Solomon Is/forest and cultivation

Nymphicus hollandicus (*Kerr*) COCKATIEL Australia (interior)/ open country /I ♂♀ 21–3/ F 4–5 weeks

Anodorhynchus hyacinthinus (*Latham*)

HYACINTHINE MACAW Interior of Brazil/forests/ n burrow in bank

Anodorhynchus glaucus (*Vieillot*) GLAUCOUS MACAW Paraguay, Uruguay and NE Argentina/ very rare and little data

Anodorhynchus leari *Bonaparte* INDIGO MACAW Brazil/known only from specimens in captivity

[**Anodorhynchus purpurascens** *Rothschild* VIOLET MACAW Guadeloupe [Don de Navaret]/ no specimens]

[**Anodorhynchus martinicus** *Rothschild* ORANGE-BELLIED MACAW Martinique [Père Bouton (1640)]/no specimens]

[**Anodorhynchus ater** (*Gmelin*) BLACK MACAW Mts of Guiana [Buffon]]

Ara gossei *Robinson* YELLOW-HEADED MACAW Jamaica/extinct 1765/ unique/specimen lost

[**Ara erythrocephala** *Gosse* GREEN AND YELLOW MACAW Jamaica/ extinct early nineteenth century [Mr Hill]]

[**Ara guadeloupensis** *Rothschild* GUADELOUPE RED MACAW Guadeloupe / extinct early eighteenth century [DuTertre (1667)]]

[**Ara atwoodi** *Clark* DOMINICAN MACAW Dominica/extinct [Atwood (1791)]]

[**Ara erythrura** *Rothschild* MYSTERIOUS MACAW 'One of the West Indian Islands' [De Rochefort (1658)]]

Ara autocthones *Wetmore* ST CROIX MACAW St Croix Is/known only from a single bone

Ara ararauna (*L*) BLUE AND YELLOW MACAW Tropical S America/forests/e 2/I ♀ or ♂♀ 24–6/ F 13 weeks

Ara caninde (*Wagler*) CANINDE MACAW May be a race of above

Ara militaris (*L*) MILITARY MACAW Mexico and tropical S America/open woodland/e 2

Ara ambigua (*Bechstein*) GREAT GREEN MACAW C America, Ecuador and SW Colombia/ forests

Ara macao (*L*) RED AND YELLOW, or SCARLET MACAW C and tropical S America / forest and savannah

Ara chloroptera *Gray* RED AND BLUE, GREEN-WINGED or CRIMSON MACAW Tropical S America/forests /n holes in cliffs /e 2

Ara tricolor *Bechstein* CUBAN MACAW Cuba and Isle of Pines /extinct c1885

Ara rubrogenys *Lafresnaye* RED-FRONTED MACAW Cochabamba, Bolivia/forests /no other data

Ara auricollis *Cassin* GOLDEN-COLLARED MACAW Bolivia to Argentina/forests

Ara severa (*L*) CHESTNUT-FRONTED MACAW Tropical S America/forests/e 2/I 28

Ara manilata (*Boddaert*) RED-BELLIED MACAW Trinidad and tropical S America/savannah/e 2

Ara maracana (*Vieillot*) ILLIGER'S MACAW East Brazil and Paraguay/forests

Ara couloni *Sclater* BLUE-HEADED MACAW E Peru/no data

Ara nobilis (*L*) NOBLE MACAW or HAHN'S MACAW Tropical S America/savannahs/e 4 (sic)

Cyanopsitta spixii (*Wagler*) LITTLE BLUE MACAW Brazil/palm groves/no other data

Aratinga acuticaudata (*Vieillot*) BLUE-CROWNED CONURE or BLUE-FRONTED CONURE Eastern S America/forests/e 2?

Aratinga guarouba (*Gmelin*) GOLDEN CONURE NE Brazil/rainforest/e up to 6/I ♀

Aratinga holochlora (*Sclater*) GREEN CONURE or SALVIN'S CONURE C America and Socorro Is

Aratinga strenua (*Ridgway*) NICARAGUAN GREEN CONURE Pacific coast of Mexico to Nicaragua, probably a race of *holochlora*

Aratinga finschi (*Salvin*) FINSCH'S CONURE C America/woodland and cultivation

Aratinga wagleri (*Gray*) SCARLET-FRONTED CONURE Venezuela to Peru/forest

Aratinga mitrata (*Tschudi*) MITRED CONURE Peru to Argentina/temperate and subtropical forest and cultivation

Aratinga erythrogenys (*Lesson*) RED-MASKED CONURE Ecuador to Peru/e 4/I 4 weeks/F 6 weeks approx

Aratinga leucophthalmus (*Müller*) WHITE-EYED CONURE Tropical S America/open forest/e 3–4

Aratinga chloroptera (*Souancé*) HISPANIOLAN CONURE Hispaniola, formerly Mona Is, and Puerto Rica/forest and cultivation

Aratinga euops (*Wagler*) CUBAN CONURE Cuba, formerly Isle of Pines/forest/e 2–5

Aratinga auricapilla (*Kuhl*) GOLDEN-CAPPED CONURE E Brazil/forest and open woodland

Aratinga jendaya (*Gmelin*) JENDAYA CONURE NE Brazil/forest/e 3/I ♀ c26/F approx 8 weeks

Aratinga solstitialis (*L*) SUN CONURE The Guianas and NE Brazil/open forest/e 4/I ♀ 4 weeks/F approx 8 weeks

Aratinga weddellii (*Deville*) DUSKY-HEADED or WEDDELL'S CONURE Amazon headwaters/forest patches in savannah

Aratinga nana (*Vigors*) OLIVE-THROATED CONURE Jamaica

Aratinga astec (*Souancé*) ASTEC CONURE Mexico and C America/forest and scrub/n in termitaria

Aratinga canicularis (*L*) PETZ'S CONURE WC America/forests/n termitaria/e 3–5/I ♀ 30/F 6 weeks

Aratinga pertinax (*L*) BROWN-THROATED CONURE Panama, northern S America and off-shore islands/savannah and scrub/n termitarium/e 5/I ♀ (?♂) 23/F 6 weeks

Aratinga cactorum (*Kuhl*) CACTUS CONURE E Brazil/open forest and scrub/e 4/I ♀/F 6 weeks

Aratinga aurea (*Gmelin*) PEACH FRONTED CONURE Brazil to S Bolivia, N Paraguay and NW Argentina/open country/e 2–3

[Aratinga labati (*Rothschild*) LABAT'S CONURE Guadeloupe [Labat]/no specimens]

Nandayus nenday (*Vieillot*) NANDAY CONURE SE Bolivia to Chile and Argentina / savannah e 4

Leptosittaca branickii *Berlepsch and Stolzmann* GOLDEN-PLUMED PARROT Andes, range uncertain/forests

Ognorhynchus icterotis (*Massena and Souancé*) YELLOW-EARED CONURE Andes of Columbia and Ecuador/wax palms (!)

Rhynchopsitta pachyrhyncha (*Swainson*) THICK-BILLED PARROT Mexican plateau / pine forests, feeds on cones of Mexican stone pine/I 28 ♀/F 59 (?)

Rhynchopsitta terrisi *Moore* MAROON-FRONTED PARROT Sierra Madre in Mexico/probably a race of *pachyrhyncha*

Conuropsis carolinensis (*L*) CAROLINA PEROQUET Eastern USA/extinct

Cyanoliseus patagonus (*Vieillot*) BURROWING PARROT Chile, Argentine and possibly Uruguay/plains/n in holes in sandstone cliffs, colonial/e 3/I ♀ approx 24–5/F 8 weeks

Cyanoliseus whitleyi (*Kinnear*) WHITLEY'S CONURE Described 1926 from an aviary specimen/unique/subsequently said by some to be a hybrid

Pyrrhura cruentata (*Wied*) BLUE-THROATED CONURE E Brazil/forest

Pyrrhura devillei (*Massena and Souancé*) BLAZE-WINGED CONURE E Bolivia, N Paraguay and SW Mato Grosso/no data

Pyrrhura frontalis (*Vieillot*) MAROON-

PHASIANIDAE:
Polyplectron emphanum,
Palawan Peacock Pheasant

PHASIANIDAE:
Polyplectron bicalcaratum,
Grey Peacock Pheasant

PHASIANIDAE:
Colinus virginianus,
Bob White

Plate 72

Plate 73

BELLIED CONURE SE Brazil, Paraguay, Uruguay/
forest/I ♀ approx 30/F 45

Pyrrhura perlata (*Spix*) PEARLY CONURE
NE Brazil/humid forests/e 3–4/I ♀ 23/F
approx 7 weeks

Pyrrhura rhodogaster (*Sclater*) CRIMSON-
BELLIED CONURE C Brazil, S of Amazon/no data

Pyrrhura molinae (*Massena and Souancé*)
GREEN-CHEEKED CONURE Mato Grosso, Bolivia
and NW Argentine/forests/e 3

Pyrrhura hypoxantha *Salvadori* YELLOW-
SIDED CONURE Mato Grosso/3 specimens

Pyrrhura leucotis (*Kuhl*) WHITE-EARED or
MAROON-FACED CONURE N Venezuela and
E Brazil/forest/e 5–9/I ♀ 27

Pyrrhura picta (*Müller*) PAINTED CONURE
Colombia, and the Amazon and Orinoco
basins/forests/e 3–4

Pyrrhura viridicata *Todd* SANTA MARTA
CONURE Santa Marta Mts, Colombia/forests

Pyrrhura egregia (*Sclater*) DEMERARA
CONURE SE Venezuela to W Guyana and NE
Brazil/forests

Pyrrhura melanura (*Spix*) MAROON-TAILED
CONURE Amazon headwaters/tropical forests/
e 4/I approx 25/F 7–8 weeks

Pyrrhura berlepschi (*Salvadori*)
BERLEPSCH'S CONURE Huallaga Valley, Peru/
doubtful validity, possibly a form of *melanura*

Pyrrhura rupicola (*Tschudi*) ROCK CONURE
S Peru and N Bolivia/no data

Pyrrhura albipectus *Chapman* WHITE-
NECKED CONURE SE Ecuador/forests

Pyrrhura calliptera (*Massena and Souancé*)
BROWN-BREASTED CONURE Colombia/mountain
forests

Pyrrhura hoematotis *Souancé* RED-EARED
CONURE N Venezuela/subtropical and montane
forests

Pyrrhura rhodocephala (*Sclater and Salvin*)
ROSE-CROWNED CONURE W Venezuela/moun-
tain forests

Pyrrhura hoffmanni (*Cabanis*) HOFFMAN'S
CONURE Costa Rica and W Panama/mountains

Enicognathus ferrugineus (*Müller*)
AUSTRAL PARRAKEET Chile and Andes S to
Tierra del Fuego/'Nothofagus' forests/e 4–8

Enicognathus leptorhynchus(*King*) SLENDER-
BILLED PARRAKEET WC Chile / forest and
farmland/n hollow in tree, but where no trees
will build in hole in rock, or where neither, a
constructed nest of twigs/e 2–6/I ♂♀

Myopsitta monachus (*Boddaert*) QUAKER or
MONK PARRAKEET Bolivia and S Brazil to
Argentina/open woods and palm groves/n
colonial communal structure of sticks, unique
among parrots/e 5–8/F approx 6 weeks

Bolborhynchus aymara (*d'Orbigny*) SIERRA
PARRAKEET Andes from Bolivia to Chile and
Argentina/barren hillsides/n hole in bank/e 7/
I ♀ 28 F/6 weeks

Bolborhynchus aurifrons (*Lesson*)
MOUNTAIN or GOLD-FRONTED PARRAKEET Coast
and Andes from Peru to Santiago/scrub and
cultivation/n hole in bank

Bolborhynchus lineola (*Cassin*) BARRED
PARRAKEET Mexico to Peru/mountain forest

Bolborhynchus orbygnesius (*Souancé*)
ANDEAN PARRAKEET Peruvian Andes / bushy
mountain slopes

Bolborhynchus ferrugineifrons (*Lawrence*)
RUFOUS-FRONTED PARRAKEET C Andes of
Columbia/6 specimens

Forpus cyanopygius (*Souancé*) TURQUOISE-
RUMPED PARROTLET Mexico / open / woodland/
e 3/F 5 weeks

Forpus passerinus (*L*) GREEN-RUMPED
PARROTLET Tropical S America, Jamaica (introduced)/scrub and open forest/n in termitarium/
e 5–7/I ♀ (?♂) c18/F approx 5 weeks

Forpus xanthopterygius (*Spix*) BLUE-WINGED
PARROTLET Tropical S America S of the
Amazon/open forest/e 3–8/I ♀ c18/F 4 weeks

Forpus conspicillatus (*Lafresnaye*)
SPECTACLED PARROTLET E Panama, Colombia
and Venezuela/savannah/e 4

Forpus sclateri (*Gray*) SCLATER'S PARROTLET
Amazon basin/forest

Forpus coelestis (*Lesson*) PACIFIC PARROTLET
or CELESTIAL PARROTLET S Ecuador and N Peru/
coasts /dry scrublands / n often in old nest of
other species/e 4–6/I ♀ 17/F approx 30

Forpus xanthops (*Salvin*) YELLOW-FACED
PARROTLET Marañón Valley, NW Peru/open
dry scrub

Brotogeris tirica (*Gmelin*) PLAIN PARRAKEET
E and S Brazil/open country and cultivation/
e 4/I ♀ 26/F 7 weeks

Brotogeris versicolorus (*Müller*) CANARY-
WINGED PARRAKEET Tropical S America/forest
and park/e 5/I ♀ 26/F 8 weeks

Brotogeris pyrrhopterus (*Latham*) GREY-
CHEEKED PARRAKEET W Ecuador and Peru/
arid scrub/e 5/I 4 weeks/F 5 weeks

Brotogeris jugularis (*Müller*) TOVI PARRAKEET Mexico to Venezuela and Colombia / arid scrub / e 4 / I ♀ 3 weeks

Brotogeris cyanoptera (*Pelzeln*) (credited to Salvadori by Peters) COBALT-WINGED PARRAKEET Amazon headwaters / open country

Brotogeris gustavi Berlepsch GUSTAVE'S PARRAKEET N Peru / probably a race of *cyanoptera*

Brotogeris chrysopteris (*L*) GOLDEN-WINGED PARRAKEET The Guianas, parts of Brazil and Venezuela / forest / e 3–4

Brotogeris sanctithomae (*Müller*) TUI PARRAKEET Amazon basin / forest

Nannopsittaca panychlora (*Salvin and Godman*) TEPUI PARRAKEET High mountain peaks of Venezuela and Guyana / no data

Touit batavica (*Boddaert*) LILAC-TAILED PARROTLET Venezuela, Guyana, Surinam, Tobago and Trinidad / lowland forests / n in termitarium / e 6

Touit huetii (*Temminck*) SCARLET-SHOULDERED PARROTLET North-western S America / tropical forest

Touit dilectissima (*Sclater and Salvin*) RED-WINGED PARROTLET NW corner of S America / forest

Touit purpurata (*Gmelin*) SAPPHIRE-RUMPED PARROTLET The Guianas, Venezuela and N Brazil / savannah forests / e 3–5

Touit melanota (*Wied*) BROWN-BACKED PARROTLET SE Brazil / forest

Touit surda (*Kuhl*) GOLDEN-TAILED PARROTLET E Brazil / coastal and mountain forest

Touit stictoptera (*Sclater*) SPOT-WINGED PARROTLET Columbia and Ecuador / forest [*Touit emmae* (Salvadori) is the ♀ of *stictoptera*]

Pionites melanocephala (*L*) BLACK-HEADED CAIQUE Amazon basin, N of river and Orinoco basin / forest and savannah / e 3 / I ♀ 27 / F 73

Pionites leucogaster (*Kuhl*) WHITE-BELLIED CAIQUE Amazon basin, S of river / forest / e 4 / I ♀ 4 weeks / F 10 weeks

Pionopsitta pileata (*Scopoli*) PILEATED PARROT SE Brazil, Paraguay and NE Argentine / forest / e 2

Pionopsitta haematotis (*Sclater and Salvin*) BROWN-HOODED PARROT C America / forest

Pionopsitta pulchra Berlepsch ROSE-FACED PARROT W Colombia and W Ecuador / forest / no data

Pionopsitta barrabandi (*Kuhl*) BARRABAND'S PARROT Upper Amazon basin / forest

Pionopsitta pyrilia (*Bonaparte*) SAFFRON-HEADED PARROT NW Corner of S America / forest

Pionopsitta caica (*Latham*) CAICA PARROT Guianas, Venezuela and NW Brazil / forest

Gypopsitta vulturina (*Kuhl*) VULTURINE PARROT Lower Amazon / forest

Hapalopsitta melanotis (*Lafresnaye*) BLACK-WINGED PARROT Peru and Bolivia / forest / no data

Hapalopsitta amazonina (*Des Murs*) RUSTY-FACED PARROT Venezuela, Colombia and Ecuador / mountain forests / no data

Graydidascalus brachyurus (*Kuhl*) SHORT-TAILED PARROT Amazon basin / forest

Pionus menstruus (*L*) BLUE-HEADED PARROT Tropical S America, Panama and Trinidad / forest and cultivation / e 3

Pionus sordidus (*L*) RED-BILLED PARROT Mts from Venezuela to Bolivia / forest

Pionus maximiliani (*Kuhl*) MAXIMILIAN'S PARROT Brazil to Argentina

Pionus tumultuosus (*Tschudi*) PLUM-CROWNED PARROT Peru and Bolivia / mountain forests / no data

Pionus seniloides (*Massena and Souancé*) GREY-HEADED PARROT Andes of Ecuador and Colombia / forest and cultivation

Pionus senilis (*Spix*) WHITE-CAPPED PARROT S Mexico and C America / rainforest / e 3 / I ♀

Pionus chalcopterus (*Fraser*) BRONZE-WINGED PARROT Mts of Venezuela, Colombia, Ecuador and Peru / forest

Pionus fuscus (*Müller*) DUSKY or VIOLET PARROT Venezuela, the Guianas and N Brazil / forest

Amazona violacea (*Gmelin*) VIOLET GUADELOUPE PARROT Guadeloupe [DuTertre (1667) and Labat (1742)] / no specimens

Amazona martinica Clark MARTINIQUE PARROT Martinique [Labat] / no specimens

Amazona collaria (*L*) YELLOW-BILLED JAMAICAN PARROT Jamaica / mid-level forests / e 2–4

Amazona leucocephala (*L*) WHITE-HEADED AMAZON PARROT Bahamas, Cuba, Isle of Pines and Caymen Is / forest / e 3–4 / I ♀

Amazona ventralis (*Müller*) HISPANIOLAN PARROT Hispaniola and Gonave, introduced to Puerto Rico / forest / e 2–4 / I ♀ approx 25 / F approx 2 months

PHASIANIDAE:
Lophura swinhoei,
Swinhoe's Pheasant

PHASIANIDAE:
Ithaginis cruentus,
Blood Pheasant-female

PHASIANIDAE:
Tragopan satyra,
Satyr Tragopan

Plate 74

PHASIANIDAE:
Chrysolophus pictus,
Golden Pheasant

Two
C. pictus
fighting.

Plate 75

Amazona albifrons (*Sparrman*) SPECTACLED PARROT Mexico and C America / dry forest and scrub

Amazona xantholora (*Gray*) YELLOW-LORED AMAZON PARROT Yucatan Peninsula, Cozumel Is and British Honduras / forest

Amazona agilis (*L*) BLACK-BILLED JAMAICAN PARROT Jamaica / mid-level forests / e 2–4

Amazona vittata (*Boddaert*) PUERTO RICAN PARROT Puerto Rico / an extinct race inhabited Culebra Is / the native race is rare and decreasing / e 1–3 usually 2

Amazona tucumana (*Cabanis*) ALDER PARROT S Bolivia and NW Argentina / alder forests / e 4

Amazona pretrei (*Temminck*) PRETREI'S PARROT SE Brazil and NE Argentina / forests

Amazona viridigenialis (*Cassin*) GREEN-CHEEKED AMAZON PARROT NW Mexico / forest

Amazona finschi (*Sclater*) LILAC CROWNED AMAZON PARROT W Mexico / forests / e 1–2 / I 28

Amazona autumnalis (*L*) RED-FRONTED AMAZON PARROT Mexico, C America, Colombia, Ecuador and NW Brazil / wet forest and mangrove / e 2

Amazona braziliensis (*L*) RED-TAILED PARROT SE Brazil / forest / rare and threatened

Amazona dufresniana (*Shaw*) BLUE-CHEEKED PARROT Guianas and E Brazil / forest and mangrove

Amazona festiva (*L*) FESTIVE PARROT Orinoco basin, Upper Amazon basin / forests

Amazona xanthops (*Spix*) YELLOW-FACED PARROT E and C Brazil / arid cerrado

Amazona barbadensis (*Gmelin*) YELLOW-SHOULDERED AMAZON PARROT Venezuela and offshore islands / arid coasts

Amazona aestiva (*L*) BLUE-FRONTED AMAZON PARROT E Brazil, Paraguay, Bolivia and N Argentina / forest / I ♀ 29

Amazona ochrocephala (*Gmelin*) LEVAILLANT'S PARROT Mexico, C America and tropical S America / forest / e 3–4 / I 29

Amazona amazonica (*L*) ORANGE-WINGED AMAZON PARROT Tropical S America / swamp and forest / e 2–5 / I ♀ 3 weeks / F 2 months

Amazona mercenaria (*Tschudi*) SCALY-NAPED AMAZON PARROT Mts from Venezuela to Bolivia / forest

Amazona farinosa (*Boddaert*) MEALY AMAZON PARROT S Mexico, C America and tropical S America / humid forest / e ?3

Amazona vinacea (*Kuhl*) VINACEOUS AMAZON PARROT S Brazil, Paraguay and S Argentina

Amazona versicolor (*Müller*) ST LUCIA PARROT Island of St Lucia / mountain forest / rare and decreasing

Amazona arausiaca (*Müller*) RED-NECKED AMAZON PARROT Dominica / mountain forest

Amazona guildingii (*Vigors*) ST VINCENT PARROT St Vincent / mountain forest / e 2 / I ♀

Amazona imperialis Richmond IMPERIAL PARROT Dominica / high mountain forest

Deroptyus accipitrinus (*L*) HAWK-HEADED PARROT Tropical S America / forest and savannah

Triclaria malachitacea (*Spix*) VIOLET-BELLIED PARROT SE Brazil / forest / I ♀ 3 weeks

Poicephalus robustus (*Gmelin*) CAPE PARROT W, C and SE Africa / forest / e 2–4 / I 26 / F 9–11 weeks

Poicephalus gulielmi (*Jardine*) JARDINE'S PARROT C Africa / forest

Poicephalus cryptoxanthus (*Peters*) BROWN-HEADED PARROT SE Africa / forest

Poicephalus crassus (*Sharpe*) NIAM-NIAM PARROT Cameroons / forest and savannah

Poicephalus senegalus (*L*) SENEGAL PARROT W Africa / open forest and savannah / e 2–3 / I ♂♀ 25 / F 9 weeks

Poicephalus rufiventris (*Rüppell*) ORANGE-BELLIED PARROT Kenya and Ethiopia / dry thornbush and scrub

Poicephalus meyeri (*Cretzschmar*) MEYER'S PARROT E and S Africa, except the extreme south / forest, savannah and scrub / e 2–4 / I 30 / F 8 weeks

Poicephalus rueppellii (*Gray*) RÜPPELL'S PARROT Angola / dry woodland

Poicephalus flavifrons (*Rüppell*) YELLOW-FACED PARROT Mountain forests of Ethiopia

Psittacus erithacus L AFRICAN GREY PARROT Central belt of Africa / forest / e 3–4 / I ♀ 21 or 30 / (not determined) / F 10 weeks

Coracopsis vasa (*Shaw*) VASA PARROT Madagascar and the Comoros / forest and savannah / e 3 ?

Coracopsis nigra (*L*) BLACK PARROT Madagascar and the Comoros / forest (e 2–3 in *C. n. barklyi*, Newton, rare and endangered race, confined to Praslin Is in Seychelles)

Eclectus roratus (*Müller*) ECLECTUS PARROT N Queensland, New Guinea and islands from Sumba to the Solomons / lowland forest / e 2 /

I ♀ 26 / F 12 weeks

Psittrichas fulgidus (*Lesson*) PESQUETS' PARROT New Guinea / mountain forest

Geoffroyus geoffroyi (*Bechstein*) RED-CHEEKED PARROT or GEOFFROY'S PARROT Lesser Sunda Is, Moluccas, N Queensland, New Guinea and the Papuan Is / lowland forest and savannah / e 3

Geoffroyus simplex (*Meyer*) LILAC-COLLARED PARROT New Guinea mts / e 3

Geoffroyus heteroclinus (*Hombron and Jacquinot*) SONG PARROT Bismarck Archipelago and Solomons / lowland forest

Prioniturus luconensis *Steere* GREEN RACQUET-TAILED PARROT Luzon and Marinduque / cornfields (!)

Prioniturus discurus (*Vieillot*) BLUE-CROWNED RACQUET-TAILED PARROT Philippines and Sulu Archipelago / forest and cultivation / e 3

Prioniturus montanus *Ogilvie Grant* MOUNTAIN RACQUET-TAILED PARROT Luzon, Mindanao and the Sulu Archipelago / forest

Prioniturus flavicans *Cassin* CRIMSON-SPOTTED RACQUET-TAILED PARROT N Celebes / forest

Prioniturus platurus (*Vieillot*) GOLDEN-MANTLED RACQUET-TAILED PARROT Celebes and adjacent islands / forest and round villages

Prioniturus mada *Hartert* BURU RACQUET-TAILED PARROT Buru / forest / e 5 ?

Tanygnathus megalorynchos (*Boddaert*) GREAT-BILLED PARROT Indonesia / small islands and coasts of larger islands

Tanygnathus lucionensis (*L*) BLUE-CROWNED PARROT Philippines and Sulu Archipelago / forest and open country

Tanygnathus sumatranus (*Raffles*) (= **T. mulleri** (*Müller*)) MÜLLER'S PARROT, EVERETT'S PARROT, BURBIDGE'S PARROT (various races have different English names) Philippines, Celebes and adjacent islands / forest / e 2

Tanygnathus heterurus *Salvadori* RUFOUS-TAILED PARROT Unique / origin uncertain Celebes (?)

Tanygnathus gramineus (*Gmelin*) BLACK-LORED PARROT Buru / 3 specimens

Lophopsittacus mauritanicus *Owen* BROAD-BILLED PARROT Mauritius / extinct / bones only [and Harmanzoon m/s 1601–2]

Lophopsittacus bensoni *Holyoak* HOLYOAK'S PARROT Mauritius / bones only

Necropsittacus rodericanus *Milne-Edwards*

RODRIGUEZ PARROT Rodriguez / extinct / bones and contemporary accounts

Necropsittacus francicus *Rothschild* DUBOIS' MAURITIUS PARROT Mauritius [Dubois] / doubtful

Necropsittacus borbonicus *Rothschild* DUBOIS' RÉUNION PARROT Réunion [Dubois] / doubtful

Mascarinus mascarinus (*L*) MASCARENE PARROT Réunion (? Mauritius) / extinct 1834 / 2 specimens

Psittacula eupatria (*L*) ALEXANDRINE PARRAKEET Indian sub-continent and SE Asia / forest and cultivation / e 2–4 / I ♂♀ 28 / F 6 weeks

Psittacula wardi (*Newton*) SEYCHELLES PARRAKEET Seychelles / extinct

Psittacula krameri (*Scopoli*) ROSE-RINGED PARRAKEET From the Cape Verdes across N and C Africa to India, Ceylon, Burma and SE China / woodland and cultivation / e 2–6 / I ♂♀ 22–4 / F 6–7 weeks

Psittacula echo (*Newton and Newton*) MAURITIUS PARRAKEET Mauritius / rare / forest / e 2

Psittacula exsul (*Newton*) NEWTON'S PARRAKEET Rodriguez / extinct / 2 specimens

Psittacula eques (*Boddaert*) DAUBENTON'S PARRAKEET Réunion / extinct [DuBois] / no specimens

Psittacula himalayana (*Lesson*) SLATY-HEADED PARRAKEET Himalayas from Afghanistan to Assam / forest / e 4–5

Psittacula finschii (*Hume*) HUME'S PARRAKEET SE Asia and Yunnan, may be a race of above

Psittacula cyanocephala (*L*) PLUM-HEADED PARRAKEET India and Ceylon / forest and cultivation / e 4–6 / I ?♀ ?♂♀ (accounts differ)

Psittacula roseata *Biswas* ROSE-HEADED or BLOSSOM-HEADED PARRAKEET Bengal, Burma and SE Asia / forest and cultivation

Psittacula intermedia (*Rothschild*) INTERMEDIATE PARRAKEET Unknown / 7 specimens

Psittacula columboides (*Vigors*) BLUE-WINGED or MALABAR PARRAKEET Western Ghats of India / forest / e 3–4 / I ♀ / F 8 weeks

Psittacula calthorpae (*Blyth*) LAYARD'S PARRAKEET Ceylon / hill forests / e 3–4 / I 3 weeks / F 7 weeks

Psittacula derbiana (*Fraser*) LORD DERBY'S PARRAKEET SE Tibet, Szechwan and Yunnan / mountain forests / rare / e ? 2 / I ? 31 ? 18–20 / F 50

PHASIANIDAE: *Pavo cristatus*, Indian Peafowl

Opposite:
PHASIANIDAE:
Pavo cristatus,
Indian Peafowl

Plate 76

Plate 77

Psittacula alexandri (*L*) MOUSTACHED PARRAKEET Himalayas, Burma, SE Asia, Andamans, S China, Hainan, Java, Bali, S Borneo (? Hong Kong) / forest / e 3–4 / I ♀ 28 / F 51

Psittacula longicauda (*Boddaert*) LONG-TAILED PARRAKEET Malay Peninsula, Borneo, Sumatra, Andamans, Nicobars and some other islands / forest / e 2–3

Psittacula caniceps (*Blyth*) BLYTH'S PARRAKEET Nicobar Is

Polytelis swainsoni (*Desmarest*) BARRABAND'S PARRAKEET or SUPERB PARROT Inland parts of New South Wales, Victoria and S Australia / open forest / e 4–6 / I ♀ 22 / F 30

Polytelis anthopleptis (*Lear*) REGENT PARROT S Australia / woodland and scrub / e 4–6

Polytelis alexandrae *Gould* QUEEN ALEXANDRA'S PARRAKEET or PRINCESS PARROT Interior of Australia / arid scrub / e 4–6 / I ♀ 23 / F 5 weeks

Aprosmictus erythropterus (*Gmelin*) RED-WINGED PARROT N and E Australia and S New Guinea / scrub and forest / e 3–5 rarely 6 / I ♀ 3 weeks / F 5 weeks

Aprosmictus jonquillaceus (*Vieillot*) TIMOR RED-WINGED PARROT Timor and Wetar / no data

Alisterus scapularis (*Lichtenstein*) KING PARROT E Australia / mountain forest / e 3–6/ I ♀ 20 / F 5 weeks

Alisterus chloropterus (*Ramsay*) GREEN-WINGED PARROT New Guinea / lowland and mid-mountain forest

Alisterus amboinensis (*L*) AMBOINA PARROT E Indonesia, Moluccas and W New Guinea / forest

Prosopeia tabuensis (*Gmelin*) SHINING PARRAKEET Fiji Is (introduced on Tonga) / forest / e 3 / I 3 weeks

Prosopeia personata (*Gray*) MASKED PARROT Fiji Is / forest

Psittacella brehmii *Schlegel* BREHM'S PARROT New Guinea mountains / forest or grassland (!)

Psittacella picta *Rothschild* PAINTED or TIMBER-LINE PARROT New Guinea mountains / forest or grassland

Psittacella modesta *Schlegel* MODEST PARROT W New Guinea mountains / forest

Psittacella madaraszi *Meyer* MADARASZ'S PARROT E New Guinea / rainforest

Bolbopsittacus lunulatus (*Scopoli*) GUIABERO Philippines

Psittinus cyanurus (*Forster*) BLUE-RUMPED PARRAKEET Malayan Peninsula and W Indonesia / forest and cultivation / e 2–3 / I ♀ ?

Agapornis cana (*Gmelin*) MADAGASCAR LOVEBIRD Madagascar (introduced Mascarenes, Seychelles etc) / brush and open forest / e 3–6 / I ♀ 23 / F 43 days

Agapornis pullaria (*L*) RED-FACED LOVEBIRD WC and EC Africa / savannah / e 3–6 ?/ I ♀ 22 / F 42

Agapornis taranta (*Stanley*) BLACK-WINGED LOVEBIRD Ethiopia / mountain forests / F 55

Agapornis swinderniana (*Kuhl*) BLACK-COLLARED LOVEBIRD W and C Africa / lowland forest

Agapornis roseicollis (*Vieillot*) PEACH-FACED LOVEBIRD SW Africa / dry country / e 3–6 ?/ I 23/ F 43

Agapornis fischeri *Reichenow* FISCHER'S LOVEBIRD NW Tanganyika / savannah / I 23 / F 38

Agapornis personata *Reichenow* MASKED LOVEBIRD NE Tanganyika / savannah / I 23 / F 44

Agapornis lilianae *Shelley* NYASA LOVEBIRD Zambia and Malawi / open woodland and farmland / I 22 / F 44

Agapornis nigrigenis *Sclater* BLACK-CHEEKED LOVEBIRD Zambia / wooded river valleys / I 24/ F 40

Loriculus vernalis (*Sparrman*) VERNAL HANGING PARROT India to SE Asia and the Andamans / dry jungle and cultivation / e 2–4 / I ♂♀

Loriculus beryllinus (*Forster*) SINHALESE HANGING PARROT Ceylon / open forest / e 2–3/ I ♀ 19 / F 5 weeks

Loriculus philippensis (*Müller*) PHILIPPINE HANGING PARROT or COLASISI Philippine Is / forests / e 3 ?

[**Loriculus salvadorii** *Hachisuka* SALVADORI'S HANGING PARROT Mindanao, Philippines / possibly a variant of above / 2 specimens]

Loriculus galgulus (*L*) BLUE-CROWNED HANGING PARROT Malaya, Sumatra, Borneo and adjacent islands / open forest / e 3 ?/ F 5 weeks

Loriculus stigmatus *Müller* CELEBES HANGING PARROT Celebes and Togian Is / open forest / e 2 ?/ stated to be double brooded!

Loriculus amabilis *Wallace* MOLUCCAN HANGING PARROT Moluccas, Great Sangi, Sula

Is, Peling and Banggai / open forest and cultivation / e 3

Loriculus exilis *Schlegel* GREEN HANGING PARROT Celebes / double brooded ?

Loriculus flosculus *Wallace* WALLACE'S HANGING PARROT Flores / no data

Loriculus pusillus *Gray* YELLOW-THROATED HANGING PARROT Java and Bali / e 2 / I ♀

Loriculus aurantifrons *Schlegel* BAT LORIKEET or ORANGE-FRONTED HANGING PARROT New Guinea and adjacent islands / lowland forest / e 4

Loriculus tener *Sclater* SCLATER'S HANGING PARROT Bismarck Archipelago / may be conspecific with above

Platycercus caledonicus (*Gmelin*) GREEN ROSELLA Tasmania and islands in Bass Strait / all habitats / e 4–6 / I ♀ 3 weeks / F 5 weeks

Platycercus elegans (*Gmelin*) CRIMSON ROSELLA or PENNANT'S PARRAKEET E and SE Australia, introduced New Zealand and Norfolk Is / mountain forest and gardens / e 5–8 / I ♀ 3 weeks / F 5 weeks

Platycercus flaveolus *Gould* YELLOW ROSELLA Interior of SE Australia / eucalypts on riverbanks / e 4–5 / I ♀ 3 weeks / F 5 weeks

Platycercus adelaidae *Gould* ADELAIDE ROSELLA SE corner of S Australia / believed to be the result of a hybrid between the Crimson and Yellow Rosellas

Platycercus eximius (*Shaw*) EASTERN or COMMON ROSELLA SE Australia and Tasmania, introduced New Zealand / lightly timbered country / e 4–9 / I ♀ 3 weeks / F 5 weeks

Platycercus adscitus (*Latham*) MEALY or PALE HEADED ROSELLA NE Australia / lowland forest and savannah / e 3–5 / I ♀ 3 weeks / F 5 weeks

Platycercus venustus (*Kuhl*) NORTHERN ROSELLA NW Australia / savannah / e ·2–4 / I ♀ 3 weeks / F 5 weeks

Platycercus icterotis (*Kuhl*) WESTERN ROSELLA or STANLEY PARRAKEET SW Australia / open forest and cultivation / e 3–7 / I ♀ 25 / F 30

Platycercus masterianus *Ramsay* MASTERS' PARRAKEET Interior of New South Wales / believed to be a persistent hybrid between the Crimson and Mealy Rosellas

Barnardius barnardi (*Vigors and Horsfield*) BARNARD'S PARROT E Australia / open woodland / e 4–6 / I ♀ 20 / F 5 weeks

Barnardius zonarius (*Shaw*) BAUER'S PARROT or PORT LINCOLN PARROT W Australia / ubiquitous / e 4–7 / I ♀ 20 / F 5 weeks

Purpuricephalus spurius (*Kuhl*) RED-CAPPED PARROT SW Australia / forest and cultivation / e 4–7 / I ♀ 20 / F 5 weeks

Psephotus haematonotus (*Gould*) REDRUMP PARROT SE Australia / plains and cultivation / e 4–7 / I ♀ 3 weeks / F 30

Psephotus varius *Clark* MULGA PARROT Interior of Australia / scrub and mulga / e 4–6

Psephotus haematogaster *Gould* BLUEBONNET SE and S Australia / plains and scrub / e 4–7 / I ♀ 22 / F 30

Psephotus chrysopterygius *Gould* GOLDEN-SHOULDERED PARROT N Australia / savannah / I ♀ 23 / F 5 weeks

Psephotus pulcherrimus (*Gould*) PARADISE PARROT SE Queensland / always rare and now probably extinct / e 4–5 / I ♀ 3 weeks

Neophema bourki (*Gould*) BOURKE'S PARROT C and S Australia / acacia scrub / e 3–6 / I ♀ 18 / F 4 weeks

Neophema chrysostoma (*Kuhl*) BLUE-WINGED PARROT SE Australia and Tasmania / forest, grass and scrub / e 4–6 / I ♀ 18 / F 4 weeks

Neophema elegans (*Gould*) ELEGANT PARROT Parts of S Australia / grassland and scrub / e 4–5 / I ♀ 18 / F 4 weeks

Neophema petrophila (*Gould*) ROCK PARROT Coasts and islands of S Australia / sand dunes and rocky islets / n in a crevice under a slab of rock / e 4–5 / I ♀ 18 / F c30

Neophema chrysogaster (*Latham*) ORANGE-BELLIED PARROT Tasmania and coasts of W Victoria, formerly more widespread / grassland and dunes / e 4–6

Neophema pulchella (*Shaw*) TURQUOISE PARROT SE Australia / rare / forest and grass / e 4–5 / I ♀ 20 / F 4 weeks

Neophema splendida (*Gould*) SCARLET-CHESTED PARROT S Australia / scrub / e 3–6 / I ♀ 20 / F 4 weeks

Lathamus discolor (*White*) SWIFT PARROT SE Australia and Tasmania / wood and parkland / migratory / e 3–5 / I ♀ 20 / F 10 weeks

Eunymphicus cornutus (*Gmelin*) HORNED PARRAKEET Ouvea and New Caledonia / forest / e 2–4

Cyanoramphus unicolor (*Lear*) ANTIPODES GREEN PARROT Antipodes / tall grass

Cyanoramphus novaezelandiae (*Sparrman*) RED-FRONTED PARROT New Zealand, New

PHASIANIDAE:
Pavo cristatus,
Indian Peafowl (albino)

PHASIANIDAE:
Gallus sonneratii,
Grey Junglefowl

Plate 78

PHASIANIDAE: *Gallus gallus*, Red Junglefowl

Plate 79

Caledonia, Kermadecs, Chatham Is, Antipodes, Auckland Is, extinct on Macquarie and Lord Howe Is/ in forests on larger islands, terrestrial on smaller islands/ e 5–9/ I ♀ 20/ F 5–6 weeks

[Cyanoramphus capitatus (*Shaw*) RED-HOODED PARROT From one of the southern islands/ no specimens/ other extinct species of this group may also have occurred]

Cyanoramphus auriceps (*Kuhl*) YELLOW-FRONTED PARROT New Zealand and Chatham Is/ forest/ e 5–9/ I ♀ 20/ F 5–6 weeks

Cyanoramphus malherbi *Souancé* ORANGE-FRONTED PARROT S Island New Zealand/ forests/ rare

Cyanoramphus zealandicus (*Latham*) BLACK-FRONTED PARROT Tahiti/ extinct mid-nineteenth century

Cyanoramphus ulietanus (*Gmelin*) SOCIETY PARROT Raiatea, Society Is / 2 specimens, collected by Cook, 1773

Melopsittacus undulatus (*Shaw*) BUDGERIGAR Australia / scrub / e 4–6 rarely 8/ I ♀ 18/ F 30

Pezoporus wallicus (*Kerr*) GROUND PARROT Tasmania and coasts of S Australia/ rare/ local/ e 3–4

Geopsittacus occidentalis *Gould* NIGHT PARROT Interior of Australia/ believed extinct/e 4

MUSOPHAGIDAE Turacos Fairly large arboreal birds with weak flight, but able to run fast through tree foliage. Mostly brightly coloured in blues and greens (except for the Go-away birds which are grey and white) and with red markings on the wings produced by a pigment, turacin, unique to this family. They feed largely on fruit and a few insects. Nests are fragile but bulky platforms of twigs. Eggs 2–3, white or greenish white. Confined to Africa. (Moreau *Ibis* (1958) vol 100 pp 27–112 recognises fewer genera and species.)

Tauraco persa (*L*) GUINEA TURACO W Africa/ forest/ seeds and fruit/ n tree/ e 2

Tauraco livingstonii *Gray* LIVINGSTONE'S TURACO C and E Africa/ forest and open wood-land/ fruit/ n tree/ e 2–3

Tauraco reichenowi (*Fischer*) REICHENOW'S TURACO Coasts of SE Africa/ rare/ virtually no data

Tauraco schalowi (*Reichenow*) SCHALOW'S TURACO C and E Africa / highland forest and savannah, also riverside forest and open wood-land/ fruit/ n tree/ e 2

Tauraco corythaix (*Wagler*) KYNSNA TURACO S Africa/ evergreen forest/ fruit/ n tree/ e 2 ('up to 5' recorded!)

Tauraco schuttii (*Cabanis*) BLACK-BILLED TURACO C Africa/ forest/ fruit/ n tree/ e 2

Tauraco fischeri (*Reichenow*) FISCHER'S TURACO E Africa and Zanzibar/ open country/ n and e n/k

Tauraco erythrolophus (*Vieillot*) RED-CRESTED TURACO Lower Congo and Angola/ light wood and savannah/ no other data

Tauraco bannermanni (*Bates*) BANNERMANN'S TURACO High mountain valleys of N Cameroon highlands/ fruit/ no other data

Tauraco ruspolii (*Salvadori*) PRINCE RUSPOLI'S TURACO S Ethiopia / woods at 6,000ft (1,800m) / rare / n and e n/k

Tauraco leucotis (*Rüppell*) WHITE-CHEEKED TURACO Ethiopia and Eritrea/ bush veld/ fruit/ n tree/ e 2/ I ♂♀ 23

Tauraco macrorhynchus (*Fraser*) BLACK-TIPPED CRESTED TURACO and RED-TIPPED CRESTED TURACO W Africa and Fernando Po / forest and bush / fruit and insects / n tree, or ground (Fernando Po) (2 races)/ e 1–2

Tauraco hartlaubi (*Fischer and Reichenow*) BLUE-CRESTED TURACO Kenya and Tanganyika/ highland forest/ fruit and insects/ n bush or tree/ e 2

Tauraco leucolophus (*Heuglin*) WHITE-CRESTED TURACO C Africa/ tall forest and scrub near forests/ fruit/ n tree/ e 2

Gallirex porphyreolophus (*Vigors*) VIOLET-CRESTED TURACO E and SE Africa/ open wood-land and dense bush/ fruit/ n tree/ e 2–3

Ruwenzorornis johnstoni (*Sharpe*) JOHNSTON'S TURACO Mts of Ruanda and the Ruwenzori range/ bamboo-clumps/ insects and fruit/ n tree/ e n/k

Musophaga violacea *Isert* VIOLET TURACO W Africa / tall galley forest / fruit and seeds/ n tree/ e 2

Musophaga rossae *Gould* LADY ROSS'S TURACO C and EC Africa/ forest /fruit/ n tree/ e 2

Corythaeola cristata (*Vieillot*) GREAT BLUE TURACO WC and EC Africa / forest / fruit / n tree/ e 1–2

Crinifer leucogaster (*Rüppell*) WHITE-BELLIED GO-AWAY BIRD Ethiopia, Somaliland, Kenya and E Tanganyika / dry thorn bush/ fruit/ n tree/ e 2–3

Crinifer zonurus (*Rüppell*) EASTERN GREY PLANTAIN EATER E Africa / open bush and parkland / fruit / n tree / e 2–3

Crinifer africanus (*Latham*) WESTERN GREY PLANTAIN EATER W Africa / trees in open country / fruit / n tree / e 2–3. Mackworth Praed and Grant use *Crinifer piscator* (Boddaert) for this species, presumably following Mathews and Iredale (*Aust Avian Record*, 3 (1915) p 44), but see note by Peters (*Birds of the World*, vol 4, p 10).

Crinifer concolor (*Smith*) COMMON GO-AWAY BIRD E and S Africa / open bush / fruit / n tree / e 2–3

Crinifer personata (*Rüppell*) BARE-FACED GO-AWAY BIRD E Africa / acacia country at edges of forests / seeds / n tree / e 2–3

CUCULIDAE Cuckoos, Anis, Coucals and Roadrunners Variable sized birds with slender bodies, long tails and stout legs. Generally inhabitants of forests, feeding on insects (particularly hairy caterpillars); some inhabit savannah. Nesting habits variable, some genera being parasitic, others nest-building.

Clamator glandarius (*L*) GREAT SPOTTED CUCKOO Mediterranean, W Asia, parts of Africa / migrates through Africa (breeding distribution curiously discontinuous) / insects / P on corvids and starlings

Clamator coromandus (*L*) CHESTNUT-WINGED CUCKOO Indian sub-continent, SE Asia, S China and Indonesia / forest and scrub-jungle / caterpillars / P on laughing thrushes

Clamator jacobinus (*Boddaert*) BLACK AND WHITE CUCKOO Africa, S of Sahara through Asia to India, Burma and Ceylon / scrub and cultivation / insects / P on babblers, shrikes, bulbuls etc. (The nomenclature of the various forms here included seems confused. *Clamator serratus* is often considered distinct and *C. pica* as either synonymous with *C. serratus* or as a race of *C. jacobinus*. It seems best, at least for the time to treat them as conspecific, following Ali and Ripley)

Clamator levaillantii (*Swainson*) LE VAILLANT'S CUCKOO Africa S of Sahara / bush / insects / P on bulbuls and babblers (= *C. cafer* (Lichtenstein) of some authors, see note under *Cuculus cafer*)

Pachycoccyx audeberti (*Schlegel*) THICK-BILLED CUCKOO Tropical Africa and Madagascar / light woodland / insects / P on helmet shrikes and violet-backed starlings

Cuculus crassirostris (*Walden*) CELEBES CUCKOO N and C Celebes

Cuculus sparverioides *Vigors* LARGE HAWK CUCKOO India, SE Asia and Indonesia / wooded hillsides and valleys / insects and spiders / P on laughing thrushes and other small birds

Cuculus varius *Vahl* COMMON HAWK CUCKOO India and Ceylon / deciduous forest and cultivation / insects etc / P on babblers and laughing thrushes

Cuculus vagans *Müller* MOUSTACHED HAWK CUCKOO SE Asia, Java and Borneo / e n/k

Cuculus fugax *Horsfield* HODGSON'S HAWK CUCKOO S, SE and E Asia and Indonesia / undergrowth in hill forest / insects and fruit / P on flycatchers and shortwings

Cuculus solitarius *Stephens* RED-CHESTED CUCKOO Africa S of Sahara / woodland streams / caterpillars / P

Cuculus cafer *Lichtenstein* BLACK CUCKOO Africa S of Sahara / trees near water / insects / P on bulbuls, chats, prinias etc (= *C. clamosus* Latham. It appears that Lichtenstein's name has been found to refer to the Black Cuckoo, not to *Clamator levaillantii* for which species the name was formerly used)

Cuculus gabonensis *Lafresnaye* GABON CUCKOO WC Africa / forest / ex-oviduct eggs only known (generally treated as a race of *C. cafer* but Mackworth Praed and Grant treat as species)

Cuculus micropterus *Gould* INDIAN CUCKOO India, SE Asia, China, Sumatra, Java, Borneo / open woodland up to 12,000ft (3,600m) / insects / P chiefly on drongos

Cuculus canorus *L* COMMON CUCKOO The greater part of the Palaearctic, Oriental and Ethiopian regions / forest and open country / insects and other invertebrates / P on various passerines

Culculus saturatus *Blyth* BLYTH'S, HIMALAYAN or ORIENTAL CUCKOO E Asia, S to India and Australia / hill forest and orchard insects / P chiefly on warblers

Cuculus poliocephalus *Latham* LITTLE CUCKOO Afghanistan to Japan and Indonesia (*C. p. rochii* of Madagascar, wintering in Africa, is a separate race) / well-wooded country / insects / P on warblers

Cuculus pallidus (*Latham*) PALLID CUCKOO Australia and Tasmania / variable woodland / insects / P

Cercococcyx mechowi *Cabanis* MECHOW'S

PHASIANIDAE:
Gallus gallus,
Red Junglefowl

PHASIANIDAE:
Gallus lafayettei,
Ceylon Junglefowl

Plate 80

PHASIANIDAE:
Gallus gallus,
Red Junglefowl (Domestic fowl
Rhode Island Red)

PHASIANIDAE:
Gallus gallus,
Red Junglefowl (Silkies,
domestic fowl)

Plate 81

CUCKOO W and C Africa/dense forest/e n/k

Cercococcyx olivinus *Sassi* OLIVE CUCKOO W and C Africa/forest/oviduct egg only known

Cercococcyx montanus *Chapin* BARRED CUCKOO EC Africa/forest/P ? on broadbills

Cacomantis sonneratii (*Latham*) BAYBANDED CUCKOO India, Ceylon, SE Asia and Indonesia/forest and light woods round cultivation/insects/P on ioras, bulbuls and small babblers

Cacomantis merulinus (*Scopoli*) PLAINTIVE CUCKOO India, Ceylon, SE Asia, S China, Java, Philippines, Celebes / light open forest and cultivation/insects/P on warblers

Cacomantis variolosus (*Vigors and Horsfield*) BRUSH CUCKOO Malaya, Indonesia New Guinea, Australia, Bismarck Archipelago, Solomon Is (many insular forms) / forest, savannah and mangroves/insects

Cacomantis castaneiventris (*Gould*) CHESTNUT-BREASTED CUCKOO New Guinea, Papuan Is, Cape York Peninsula / forest and bush/insects

Cacomantis heinrichi *Streseman* HEINRICH'S CUCKOO Batjan and Halmahera

Cacomantis pyrrophanus (*Vieillot*) FAN-TAILED CUCKOO Australia, Tasmania, New Guinea and islands to Fiji / forests (locally distributed)/insects/P on warblers

Rhamphomantis megarhynchus (*Gray*) LONG-BILLED CUCKOO N New Guinea, Waigeu and Aru Is/lowland forest/known only from a few specimens

Chrysococcyx osculans (*Gould*) BLACK-EARED CUCKOO b Australia on migration to Papuan area/dry scrub and woodland/insects/P mainly on warblers

Chrysococcyx cupreus (*Shaw*) AFRICAN EMERALD CUCKOO Equatorial Africa / forest glades and clearings / insects / P on various species including bulbuls and puffbacks

Chrysococcyx flavigularis *Shelley* YELLOW-THROATED CUCKOO W Africa / forest / rare, virtually no data

Chrysococcyx klaas (*Stephens*) KLAAS'S CUCKOO C and S Africa: S Arabia (discontinuous, 2 races) / forest and open country/caterpillars/P on various species

Chrysococcyx caprius (*Boddaert*) DIDRIC CUCKOO Africa S of Sahara / open country/insects/P on various species

Chrysococcyx maculatus (*Gmelin*) ASIATIC EMERALD CUCKOO Himalayas to SE Asia and

W China / evergreen jungle / insects / P on sunbirds and spiderhunters

Chrysococcyx xanthorhynchus (*Horsfield*) VIOLET CUCKOO SE Asia, Indonesia / evergreen forest / no reliable data (supposed eggs in sunbird and spiderhunter nests could be *C. maculatus*)

Chrysococcyx basalis (*Horsfield*) HORSFIELD'S CUCKOO b Australia and Tasmania w Indonesia / savannah / insects and berries / P on Malurus, Acanthiza, Petroica and others

Chrysococcyx lucidus (*Gmelin*) GOLDEN CUCKOO Australasia, New Zealand and Melanesia/forest/insects/P mainly on *Gerygone* and *Rhipidura*

Chrysococcyx malayanus (*Raffles*) BRONZE CUCKOO Malaya, Indonesia and N Australia/forest / insects / P on *Gerygone*

Chrysococcyx crassirostris (*Salvadori*) ISLAND CUCKOO Moluccas

Chrysococcyx ruficollis (*Salvadori*) REDDISH-THROATED CUCKOO New Guinea mountain forest /no data

Chrysococcyx meyeri *Salvadori* MEYER'S CUCKOO New Guinea / forest to 5,000ft (1,500m) / hairy caterpillars / no other data

Nannococcyx psix *Olsen* (*Smithsonian Cont to Paleobiology*, no 23, 1975) CRUMBY CUCKOO St Helena / extinct post 1502/bones only

Caliechthrus leucolophus (*Müller*) WHITE-CROWNED KOEL New Guinea and Salawati/forest/insects

Surniculus lugubris (*Horsfield*) DRONGO CUCKOO India, SE Asia, S China and Indonesia/open forest and cultivation / insects and occasionally fruit/P on drongos and other birds

Microdynamis parva (*Salvadori*) BLACK-CAPPED CUCKOO New Guinea / ? forest / ? fruit/no other data

Eudynamis scolopacea (*L*) COMMON KOEL India, Ceylon, SE Asia, S China, Australasia and Solomons / light woods and cultivation/insects, fruits and eggs/P on crows, friarbirds and honeyeaters (varying in different parts of its range)

Eudynamis taitensis (*Sparrman*) LONG-TAILED CUCKOO New Zealand and Polynesia/forest/insects, lizards, birds and eggs/P

Scythrops novaehollandiae *Latham* CHANNEL-BILLED CUCKOO Flores to Australia/forest and woodland / insects and fruit / P on crows and currawongs

Coccyzus pumilus *Strickland* DWARF CUCKOO
Colombian Andes and Upper Orinoco Valley
Coccyzus cinereus *Vieillot* ASH-COLOURED
CUCKOO Paraguay southwards
Coccyzus erythropthalmus (*Wilson*) BLACK-
BILLED CUCKOO b Central N America w north-
western S America / woods and orchards / insects /
n tree / e 2–7 / I ♂♀ / tendency to be Parasitic
Coccyzus americanus (*L*) YELLOW-BILLED
CUCKOO b USA w C America / woods and
orchards / insects (largely caterpillars) / n tree /
e 2–7 (usually 3–4) / I chiefly ♀ 14
Coccyzus euleri (*Cabanis*) PEARLY-BREASTED
CUCKOO Orinoco and Lower Amazon basins
Coccyzus minor (*Gmelin*) MANGROVE CUCKOO
Coasts and islands of Caribbean; Cocos Is /
mangrove / insects
Coccyzus melacoryphus *Vieillot* DARK-
BILLED CUCKOO S America, Galapagos and
Trinidad / mangrove and plantation / insects
Coccyzus lansbergi *Bonaparte* GRAY-CAPPED
CUCKOO Colombia, Venezuela, W Ecuador
Piaya rufigularis (*Hartlaub*) RUFOUS-
BREASTED CUCKOO Hispaniola and Gonave /
forest / n and e n/k
Piaya pluvialis (*Gmelin*) JAMAICAN CUCKOO
Jamaica / hill scrub / n tree or bush / e 2–4
Piaya cayana (*L*) SQUIRREL CUCKOO C and S
America / light forest and savannah / insects /
n tree / e n/s
Piaya melanogaster (*Vieillot*) BLACK-BELLIED
CUCKOO Northern S America / forest / insects /
n and e n/k
Piaya minuta (*Vieillot*) MINUTE CUCKOO
E Panama and northern S America / mangrove
and shrubbery / insects / n tree / e n/s
Saurothura merlini *d'Orbigny* CUBAN
LIZARD CUCKOO Bahamas, Cuba, Isle of Pines /
woodland and thickets / n tree / e 2–3
Saurothura vetula (*L*) JAMAICAN LIZARD
CUCKOO Jamaica / hill, woodland and scrub /
n tree / e 2–3
Saurothura vieilloti *Bonaparte* VIEILLOT'S
LIZARD CUCKOO Puerto Rico / woodland / n tree /
e 2–3
Saurothura longirostris (*Hermann*)
HISPANIOLAN LIZARD CUCKOO Hispaniola,
Gonave, Tortuga, Saona / woodland / n tree /
e 2–3
Ceuthmochares aereus (*Vieillot*) YELLOW-
BILLED COUCAL Equatorial Africa / thickets and
creepers / grasshoppers and tree-frogs / n in

herbage 8–12ft (2.5–4m) from ground / e 2–3
Rhopodytes diardi (*Lesson*) BLACK-BILLED
MALKOHA Malaya, Sumatra and Borneo / forest /
insects
Rhopodytes sumatranus (*Raffles*) CHESTNUT-
BELLIED MALKOHA Malay Peninsula, Borneo
and adjacent small islands / forest / insects
Rhopodytes tristis (*Lesson*) GREEN-BILLED
MALKOHA SE Asia, S China, Hainan, Sumatra,
Kangean Is / dense jungle / insects / n tree or
creeper clump / e 2–4
Rhopodytes viridirostris (*Jerdon*) BLUE-
FACED MALKOHA S India and Ceylon / open
jungle and scrub jungle / insects, lizards etc /
n thorn bush / e 2 (sometimes 3)
Taccocua leschenaultii *Lesson* SIRKEER India /
thorn-jungle and semi-desert / insects, lizards
and fruit / n in euphorbia / e 2–3 / I ♂♀
Rhinorthia chlorophaea (*Raffles*) RAFFLES'S
MALKOHA Malay Peninsula, Sumatra, Borneo
and Banka / forest / insects
Zanclostomus javanicus (*Horsfield*) RED-
BILLED MALKOHA Malay Peninsula, Sumatra,
Java, Borneo, Natuna Is / forest / insects
Rhamphococcyx calyorhynchus (*Temminck*)
CELEBES MALKOHA Celebes, Togian and Buton
Rhamphococcyx curvirostris (*Shaw*)
CHESTNUT-BREASTED MALKOHA W Indonesia,
Philippines and Malay Peninsula / forest / insects /
n tree / e 2
Phaenicophaeus pyrrhocephalus (*Pennant*)
RED-FACED MALKOHA S India and Ceylon /
heavy forest / berries / n shrub / e 2–3
Dasylophus superciliosus (*Dumont*) ROUGH-
CRESTED CUCKOO N Philippines
Lepidogrammus cumingi (*Fraser*) SCALY
CUCKOO Luzon and Marinduque (Philippines)
Crotophaga major *Gmelin* GREATER ANI
Tropical S America / mangrove / insects / n tree /
e 2–3
Crotophaga ani *L* SMOOTH-BILLED ANI
Northern S America and W Indies / savannah,
bushy fields and plantations / n tree or bush,
several ♀♀ lay in a nest, up to 29 eggs per nest /
I ♂♀ 15
Crotophaga sulcirostris *Swainson* GROOVE-
BILLED ANI Mexico, C and Northern S America /
? insects / n ? bush / e ? 7
Guira guira (*Gmelin*) GUIRA CUCKOO Eastern
S America
Tapera naevia (*L*) STRIPED CUCKOO C and
S America S to Uruguay / savannah / insects /

NUMIDIDAE;
Agelastes meleagrides,
White-breasted Guineafowl

MELEAGRIDIDAE;
Meleagris gallopavo,
Common Turkey

Plate 82

TURNICIDAE:
Turnix castanota,
Chestnut-backed Buttonquail

GRUIDAE:
Grus canadensis,
Sandhill Crane

Plate 83

P on spinetails/ I 15

Morococcyx erythropygus (*Lesson*) LESSER GROUND CUCKOO Mexico and C America

Dromococcyx phasianellus (*Spix*) PHEASANT CUCKOO C and S America, S to Paraguay

Dromococcyx pavoninus *Pelzeln* PEACOCK CUCKOO Northern and eastern S America

Geococcyx californiana (*Lesson*) GREATER ROADRUNNER South-western USA and Mexico/ scrub, semi-desert and open plains / invertebrates, small reptiles, birds, eggs etc / n tree or cactus / e 2–6 (? up to 12)

Geococcyx velox (*Wagner*) LESSER ROADRUNNER Mexico and C America

Neomorphus geoffroyi (*Temminck*) RUFOUS-VENTED GROUND CUCKOO C and tropical S America

Neomorphus squamiger *Todd* SCALED GROUND CUCKOO Rio Tajóz, C Brazil (Peters believed it might be a race of *geoffroyi*)

Neomorphus radiolosus *Sclater and Salvin* BANDED GROUND CUCKOO NW Ecuador

Neomorphus rufipennis (*Gray*) RUFOUS-WINGED GROUND CUCKOO Orinoco basin

Neomorphus pucheranii (*Deville*) RED-BILLED GROUND CUCKOO Upper Amazon basin

Carpococcyx radiceus (*Temminck*) 'MALAYAN GROUND CUCKOO' (sic) Sumatra and Borneo

Carpococcyx renauldi *Oustalet* RENAULD'S GROUND CUCKOO S and E Siam, Indo-China/ e 4 (1 authentic captive clutch known)

Coua delalandei (*Temminck*) DELALAND'S CUCKOO E Madagascar and Sainte Marie/ probably extinct (about 7 specimens exist)

Coua gigas (*Boddaert*) GIANT COUA W and S Madagascar / dry forest / insects

Coua coquereli *Grandidier* COQUEREL'S COUA W Madagascar / humid forest and dry bush/ insects and fruit

Coua serriana *Pucheran* RED-BREASTED or PUCHERAN'S COUA NE Madagascar / forests/ insects and fruit

Coua reynaudii *Pucheran* RED-FRONTED or REYNAUD'S COUA NW and E Madagascar/ humid forests / insects and fruit

Coua cursor *Grandidier* RUNNING COUA SW Madagascar / arid regions

Coua ruficeps *Gray* RED-CAPPED COUA, OLIVE-CAPPED COUA (races) W Madagascar/ forest and savannah / insects

Coua cristata (*L*) CRESTED COUA N, E and W Madagascar / forest and bush / insects and

fruit / n tree

Coua verreauxi *Grandidier* VERREAUX'S COUA SW Madagascar / sandy deserts and dry forests

Coua caerulea (*L*) BLUE COUA E and NW Madagascar / forests / insects and fruit

Centropus milo *Gould* BUFF-HEADED COUCAL Solomon Is

Centropus goliath *Bonaparte* GOLIATH COUCAL N Moluccas

Centropus violaceus *Quoy and Gaimard* VIOLET COUCAL New Britain and New Ireland

Centropus menbeki *Lesson and Garnot* GREATER COUCAL Papuan Is / lowland forest/ insects and vertebrates

Centropus ateralbus *Lesson* PIED COUCAL New Britain, New Ireland and (?) Rook Is

Centropus chalybeus (*Salvadori*) BIAK COUCAL Biak and (?) Numfor / 'thick secondary growth'/ no other data

Centropus phasianinus (*Latham*) PHEASANT COUCAL Australia and New Guinea / 'various kinds of thick vegetation in damp localities' (Macdonald) / insects and small animals / n in grass off ground / e 4

Centropus spilopterus *Gray* KEI COUCAL Kei Is

Centropus bernsteini *Schlegel* BERNSTEIN'S COUCAL New Guinea, Vulcan Is and (?) Salawati / grass and bush / n grass off ground / e 2 ['Le coucal negre' of LeVaillant has never been satisfactorily identified: *Poliphilus maurus*, Stephens; *Centropus aethiops*, Cuvier; and *Corydonix nigerrimus*, Vieillot, were based on it. Shelley in Sharpe's *Catalogue of the Birds of the Brit Mus* (*Nat Hist*) says that the figure of LeVaillant's bird resembles *C. bernsteini* but 'the account of its habits is fabulous'.]

Centropus chlororhynchus *Blyth* CEYLON COUCAL SW Ceylon / hill forests / omnivorous but largely animal / n bush / e 2–3

Centropus rectunguis *Strickland* SHORT-TOED COUCAL Malaya, Sumatra and Borneo

Centropus steerii *Bourns and Worcester* STEERE'S COUCAL Mindoro

Centropus sinensis (*Stephens*) COMMON COUCAL or CROW PHEASANT India and Ceylon to S China, SE Asia and Indonesia / varied: jungle to orchards and paddyfields / omnivorous but largely animal / n bush / e 3–5 / I ♂♀ / F ? 28

Centropus andamanensis *Beavan* BROWN COUCAL Andamans and Coco Is / chiefly cultivation / little data but believed similar to

Common Coucal
Centropus nigrorufus (*Cuvier*) SUNDA COUCAL Sumatra and Java
Centropus viridis (*Scopoli*) GREEN COUCAL Philippines
Centropus toulou (*Müller*) BLACK COUCAL Madagascar, Aldabra and Assumption
Centropus bengalensis (*Gmelin*) LESSER COUCAL India to S China, SE Asia and Indonesia / 'confined to a specialised habitat – stretches of tall grassland and dense scrub jungle bordering forest, and reedbeds and "seas" of elephant grass on the edge of swamps and jhells, and in flood plains' (Ali and Ripley)/ grasshoppers / n bush / e 3–4 / I ♂♀ [treated by Ali and Ripley as conspecific with *C. toulou*]
Centropus grillii *Hartlaub* BLACK-BELLIED COUCAL E Africa/swamps and marshes/insects/ n bush or grass tuft/e 4 (treated by Mackworth Praed and Grant as a race of *C. toulou*)
Centropus leucogaster (*Leach*) GREAT BLACK-THROATED COUCAL W Africa / secondary forest, swampy bush and grass / insects, snails and frogs / n bush / e n/s
Centropus anselli *Sharpe* GABOON COUCAL WC Africa/damp forest clearings/omnivorous/ n bush / e 3
Centropus monachus *Rüppell* BLUE-HEADED COUCAL W and E Africa / swamps and forest clearings / varied animal matter / n bush / e 3
[**Centropus epomidis** *Bonaparte* RUFOUS-BELLIED COUCAL Gold Coast and S Nigeria/ possibly a colour variety of *senegalensis*]
Centropus senegalensis (*L*) SENEGAL COUCAL Africa (except the NW), S Arabia and Socotra / bush and grassy woodland / insects, reptiles and rodents / n off ground in herbage/ e 2–4 (*C. superciliosis* Hemprich and Ehrenberg, is sometimes treated as a separate species)
Centropus melanops *Lesson* BLACK-FACED COUCAL Philippines
Centropus celebensis *Quoy and Gaimard* CELEBES COUCAL Celebes
Centropus unirufus (*Cabanis and Heine*) RUFOUS COUCAL Luzon and Polillo
TYTONIDAE Barn and Grass Owls Differ from typical owls in their heart-shaped facial disc, long legs and serrated comb on the claw of the middle toe (qv STRIGIDAE Owls)
Tyto soumagnei (*Milne-Edwards*) MADAGASCAR GRASS OWL Madagascar
Tyto alba (*Scopoli*) COMMON BARN OWL or WHITE OWL Almost cosmopolitan, except temperate Asia / cliffs, woods and habitation/ rodents and birds / n hole or ledge / e 3–11 (usually 4–7)/I ♀ 32–4 / F 64–86
Tyto rosenbergii (*Schlegel*) ROSENBERG'S OWL Celebes
Tyto inexpectata (*Schlegel*) UNEXPECTED or MINAHASSA OWL Northern peninsula of Celebes
Tyto nigrobrunnea *Neumann* (*Bull Brit Orn Cl, 59, 89 (1939)*) BLACK-BROWN OWL Sula Is/ status uncertain / unique ♀
Tyto novaehollandiae (*Stephens*) MASKED OWL Australia, Tasmania, New Guinea, Manus, Baru and Tenimber / forest / mammals / n hole / e 2–4
Tyto aurantia (*Salvadori*) NEW BRITAIN BARN OWL New Britain
Tyto tenebricosa (*Gould*) SOOTY OWL Australia, New Guinea, Japen / forests / n hole/ e 2 (only 1 hatches)
Tyto capensis (*Smith*) CAPE GRASS OWL S Africa / grassland / small mammals / n none/ e 4–6 on ground (other accounts say n on ground in a hollow lined with soft grass!)
Tyto longimembris (*Jerdon*) EASTERN GRASS OWL Australia, New Guinea, India, S China, Taiwan, Luzon and Fiji (discontinuous) / grassland / small mammals [often considered as a race of *T. capensis*]
Tyto cavatica *Wetmore* PUERTO RICAN BARN OWL Puerto Rico /extinct/ bones only
Tyto sauzieri *Newton and Gadow* SAUZIER'S GRASS OWL Mauritius /extinct/ bones only
Tyto newtoni *Rothschild* NEWTON'S BARN OWL Mauritius/ bones only
Phodilus badius *Horsfield* ORIENTAL BAY OWL Himalayas, SE Asia, Ceylon, Indonesia / forest/ insects and vertebrates / n hole / e 3–5
Phodilus prigoginei *Schouteden* CONGO BAY OWL Muusi, E Congo / unique
STRIGIDAE Owls Carnivorous birds with hooked beaks, strong grasping feet with razor-sharp talons, and soft fluffy plumage which stands out from the body giving Owls a fat dumpy appearance. Largely nocturnal in habits, but some species hunt by day. Their superficial resemblance to the Birds of Prey is a result of parallel evolution. The eyes are set very far forward in a facial disc giving the birds a larger field of binocular vision than in other groups.

Nest generally in a hole or hollow. Eggs pure

GRUIDAE:
Balearica pavonina
Crowned Crane

GRUIDAE: *Grus rubicunda*, Brolga

Close-up of head of *G. rubicunda*

Plate 84

RALLIDAE: *Porzana tabuensis*, Spotless Crane, Sooty Rail

RALLIDAE: *Fulica atra*, Common or Black Coot, Coot

Plate 85

white, almost spherical. Usually both sexes incubate and both sexes feed the young. Most of the arrangement and data for this section comes from *Owls of the World* (ed John Burton). About 140 species throughout the world except Antarctica and some oceanic islands. [NB: The large number of races and species in the genus *Otus* is very complicated, particularly in the Indonesian region, where many islands have one or more endemic forms. Opinions vary much as to the arrangement. I have attempted to sort these to some extent and to indicate the debatable forms where it seemed useful to do so. This arrangement should, however, be considered as no more than provisional until this group has been examined in more detail. See also Addenda, p 239.]

Otus sagittatus (*Cassin*) WHITE-FRONTED SCOPS OWL Tenasserim, W Thailand and Malaya (? Sumatra)

Otus rufescens (*Horsfield*) REDDISH SCOPS OWL Malaya, Sumatra, Banka, Java, Borneo, Jolo

Otus icterorhynchus (*Shelley*) SANDY or CINNAMON SCOPS OWL Gold Coast and Cameroon

Otus irenaea *Ripley* SOKOKE SCOPS OWL or MRS MORDEN'S OWLET Sokoke forest, Kenya/ endangered [See Ripley *Ibis* 108 (1966), pp 136–7 and plate 1; also Red Data Book]

Otus spilocephalus (*Blyth*) SPOTTED SCOPS OWL Mountains from India to S China, Taiwan, Java, Sumatra and Borneo / forest/ insects / n hole / e 2–5 [The following 'species' are sometimes considered distinct, but are considered by Hekstra (in *Owls of the World*) to be forms of *O. spilocephalus*]:

    O. vandewateri (*Robinson and Kloss*) Sumatra

    O. angelinae (*Finsch*) Java

    O. hambroecki (*Swinhoe*) Taiwan

    [*Otus longicornis* Ogilvie-Grant, Luzon in the Philippines, is considered by Hekstra to be a race of *O. spilocephalus*; other authorities place it with the *Otus scops* complex]

    [*Otus bakkamoena nigrorum* Rand (1950) is generally considered to be a race of *O. bakkamoena*, but is placed by Hekstra as a race of *O. spilocephalus*]

Otus balli (*Hume*) ANDAMAN SCOPS OWL Andamans / habitation / caterpillars / n hole / e 2–3

Otus alfredi (*Hartert*) EVERETT'S OWL Flores/ mountain forests

Otus brucei (*Hume*) STRIATED SCOPS OWL Middle East / semi-desert / insects and small birds / n hole / no other data (the validity of this species has been questioned. It may be a form or race of the *Otus scops* group)

Otus scops (*L*) COMMON SCOPS OWL S Europe, W and C Asia / forest, park and habitation/ insects / n hole / e 3–6 / I ♀ 24–5 / F c21

Otus sunia (*Hodgson*) ORIENTAL SCOPS OWL W, S and E Asia, Philippines and parts of rest of Indonesia (considered by Hekstra to be distinct, but by most other authorities to be conspecific with *Otus scops*)

Otus umbra (*Richmond*) MENTAUR SCOPS OWL Simalur and Engano

Otus senegalensis (*Swainson*) (= *Scops capensis* Smith. *Otus capensis* Smith = *Asio capensis*, p 90) CAPE SCOPS OWL Africa S of Sahara / savannah

Otus flammeolus (*Kaup*) FLAMMULATED OWL Western N America and Guatemala / n hole/ e 3–4

Otus brookii (*Sharpe*) RAJAH BROOKE'S SCOPS OWL Sumatra, Java and Borneo

Otus rutilus (*Pucheran*) MADAGASCAR SCOPS OWL Madagascar and Anjuan

Otus pembaensis *Pakenham* RUSSET SCOPS OWL Pemba / n ground

Otus insularis (*Tristram*) SEYCHELLES OWL Mahé in Seychelles (sometimes considered a race of *O. rutilus*)

Otus manadensis (*Quoy and Gaimard*) CELEBES SCOPS OWL SE Asian Is (discontinuous)

Otus beccarii (*Salvadori*) MISORI OWL Biak (probably conspecific with *O. manadensis*)

Otus silvicola (*Wallace*) FLORES SCOPS OWL Flores and Sumbawa / coastal forests

Otus bakkamoena *Pennant* COLLARED SCOPS OWL S and E Asia and Indonesia / forest/ insects etc / n hole / e 3–5

Otus whiteheadi (*Ogilvie-Grant*) WHITEHEAD'S SCOPS OWL Luzon (often regarded as a race of either *bakkamoena* or *spilocephalus*). [*Otus megalotis* Walden, is known only from the unique type collected at Manilla on Luzon in the Philippines (specimen now in British Museum). This has been claimed to be probably a juvenile of one of the colour phases of *O. whiteheadi*, and if this is so, the name, which antidates *whiteheadi* must replace it.]

Otus asio (*L*) COMMON SCREECH OWL N America / forest and scrub / insects / e 3–7 / I ♀ 26

Otus trichopsis (*Wagler*) SPOTTED SCREECH OWL or WHISKERED OWL SE Arizona to El Salvador / mountain forest

Otus barbarus (*Sclater and Salvin*) BEARDED SCREECH OWL Guatemala highlands / mountain forest

Otus guatemalae (*Sharpe*) VERMICULATED SCREECH OWL Mexico to Ecuador and Venezuela / sub-montane forest [*Otus cassini* (Ridgway) Vera Cruz / mountain forests, and *Otus hastatus* (Ridgway) W Mexico / semi-desert, are sometimes treated as species, sometimes as races of the foregoing]

Otus nudipes (*Daudin*) PUERTO RICAN SCREECH OWL Puerto Rico, St Thomas, St John and St Croix / forests / insects

Otus roboratus *Bangs and Noble* ROBORATE SCREECH OWL NW Peru

Otus cooperi (*Ridgway*) PACIFIC SCREECH OWL C America / scrub

Otus choliba (*Vieillot*) SPIX SCOPS OWL or CHOLIBA SCREECH OWL Costa Rica to Argentine / savannah

Otus atricapillus (*Temminck*) BLACK-CAPPED or LONG-TUFTED SCREECH OWL C and SE Brazil

Otus sanctaecatharinae (*Salvin*) ST CATHERINE'S SCREECH OWL S Brazil / dry forests / no data (may be a race of *O. atricapillus*)

Otus ingens (*Salvin*) RUFESCENT SCREECH OWL Andes from Colombia to Bolivia / scrub

Otus watsonii (*Cassin*) TAWNY-BELLIED SCREECH OWL Amazon and Orinoco basins

Otus clarkii *Kelso and Kelso* BARE-SHANKED SCREECH OWL Costa Rica and Panama

Otus albogularis (*Cassin*) WHITE-THROATED SCREECH OWL Andes from Venezuela to Ecuador

Otus ·minimus (*Carriker*) CARRIKER'S OWL Bolivia / unique

Otus leucotis (*Temminck*) WHITE-FACED SCREECH OWL Africa S of Sahara / woodland, bush and long grass / mice and insects / n tree often in old raptor nest / e 2–4

Otus hartlaubi (*Giebel*) SÃO THOMÉ SCOPS OWL São Thomé

Otus lawrencii (*Sclater and Salvin*) BARE-LEGGED OWL or CUBAN SCREECH OWL Cuba / forest (otherwise placed in the monotypic genus *Gymnoglaux*)

Otus podarginus (*Hartlaub and Finsch*) PALAU SCOPS OWL Palau Is

Otus gurneyi (*Tweeddale*) GIANT SCOPS OWL Marinduque and Mindanao

Otus commersoni *Oustalet* COMMERSON'S SCOPS OWL Mauritius [Commerson and Desjardins] / no remains

Lophostrix letti (*Büttikofer*) MANED OWL W and C Africa / forests / insects

Lophostrix cristata (*Daudin*) CRESTED OWL S Mexico to Ecuador and the Guianas / forests / insects

Bubo virginianus (*Gmelin*) GREAT HORNED OWL Throughout the Americas / ubiquitous / varied diet / n as *B. bubo* / e 1–6 or more

Bubo bubo (*L*) GREAT EAGLE OWL Europe, Asia and N Africa / n ledge, cave or old eagle's nest / e 3–6 / I ♀ 35

Bubo capensis *Smith* CAPE EAGLE OWL E and S Africa / rodents etc / n ground or old abandoned nest of crow (accounts differ) / e 2–3

Bubo africanus (*Temminck*) SPOTTED EAGLE OWL W and E Africa and S Arabia / savannah / vertebrates / n hole, ground or abandoned nest / e 2–3

Bubo poensis *Fraser* FRASER'S EAGLE OWL Equatorial Africa and Fernando Po

Bubo vosseleri *Reichenow* NDUK EAGLE OWL Usambaru Mts, Tanganyika (usually regarded as a race of *B. poensis*)

Bubo nipalensis *Hodgson* FOREST EAGLE OWL Indian sub-continent and SE Asia / mountain rain-forest / vertebrates / n hole, floor of cave or old eagle nest / e 1

Bubo sumatrana (*Raffles*) BARRED EAGLE OWL SE Asia, Java, Bali and Borneo / mountain rain forest

Bubo shelleyi (*Sharpe and Ussher*) SHELLEY'S EAGLE OWL Liberia, Gold Coast and S Cameroon / 4 specimens

Bubo lacteus (*Temminck*) MILKY EAGLE OWL Africa S of Sahara / open forest / varied diet / n abandoned nest (eg of Hammerkop) / e 1–2 (usually 2)

Bubo coromandus (*Latham*) DUSKY EAGLE OWL Indian sub-continent and SE Asia / groves and habitation / varied diet / n tree / e 2

Bubo leucostictus *Hartlaub* AKUN EAGLE OWL W and C Africa / insects (?)

Bubo leguati *Rothschild* LEGUAT'S EAGLE OWL Rodriguez / extinct / bones [Leguat]

Bubo philippensis (*Kaup*) PHILIPPINE EAGLE OWL Philippines / mountain rain forest

Nyctea scandiaca (*L*) SNOWY OWL Holarctic tundras and Arctic islands / variable diet / n ground / e 3–13 / I ♀ 32–4 / F 51–7

Ketupa blakistoni (*Seebohm*) BLAKISTON'S

RALLIDAE:
Gallinula chloropus,
Moorhen or Florida Gallinule,
Gray Moorhen

RALLIDAE:
Dryolimnas pectorallis,
Lewin Rail, Lewin's Water
Rail

Plate 86

RALLIDAE:
Eulabeornis castaneoventris,
Chestnut-bellied Rail

RALLIDAE:
Amaurornis olivacea,
Bush-hen

Plate 87

Fish Owl Manchuria, Sakhalin, Kuriles and Hokkaido/crayfish/n ground

Ketupa zeylonensis (*Gmelin*) Brown Fish Owl Middle East to SE Asia, Ceylon and S China/near water/fish and frogs/n tree/e 1–2 (Ali) 3 (Fogden)/I ? 30

Ketupa flavipes (*Hodgson*) Tawny Fish Owl Kashmir to S China, SE Asia and Taiwan/forest streams/fish etc/n tree or hole/e 2

Ketupa ketupu (*Horsfield*) Buffy Fish Owl SE Asia and islands E to Borneo/forest streams/fish/n hole or tree/e 1

Scotopelia peli (*Bonaparte*) Pel's Fishing Owl Africa S of Sahara/near water/fish etc/n old eagle's, or hole; some accounts say it *builds* a nest like an eagle's/e 2–4

Scotopelia ussheri *Sharpe* Ussher's or Rufous Fishing Owl Sierra Leone, Liberia and Gold Coast / near water / fish etc / n and e n/k

Scotopelia bouvieri *Sharpe* Vermiculated Fishing Owl W and C Africa/near water/fish etc/n and e n/k

Pulsatrix perspicillata (*Latham*) Spectacled Owl S Mexico to N Argentina/forest/varied/n hole/e 2

Pulsatrix koeniswaldiana (*Bertoni and Bertoni*) White-chinned or Tawny-browed Owl S Brazil, E Paraguay and NE Argentina/no data

Pulsatrix melanota (*Tschudi*) Rusty-barred Owl E Ecuador and E Peru/no data

Surnia ulula (*L*) (Northern) Hawk Owl N Holarctic/coniferous forest/mammals and birds/n tree or hole/e 3–13/I ♀ (?♂)

Glaucidium passerinum (*L*) Eurasian Pygmy Owl Europe, W, C and E Asia/open forest/varied/n hole/e 3–8/I ♀ 28

Glaucidium gnoma *Wagler* American Pygmy Owl Western N America from Alaska to Guatemala/forest/n hole/e 2–7

Glaucidium siju (*d'Orbigny*) Cuban Pygmy Owl Cuba and Isle of Pines/'woodland'/n hole/e 3–4

Glaucidium minutissimum (*Wied*) Least Pygmy Owl C and eastern S America/forest and bush

Glaucidium jardinii (*Bonaparte*) Andean Pygmy Owl Mountains from Costa Rica to Peru and Venezuela

Glaucidium brasilianum (*Gmelin*) Ferrugineous Pygmy Owl C and S America/

woodland/n hole/e 3–4

Glaucidium perlatum (*Vieillot*) Pearl-spotted Owlet Africa S of Sahara to Orange River/savannah/varied/n hole in tree/e 2–4

Glaucidium castaneum *Reichenow* Chestnut Owlet Ituri, Congo/lowland rain forest/very few specimens/no other data [NB: In Peters' *Check List* this name is attributed to Neumann, which appears to be an error]

Glaucidium tephronotum *Sharpe* Red-chested Owlet Africa S of Sahara to Orange River/savannah/varied/n hole in tree/e 2–4

Glaucidium capense (*Smith*) Barred Owlet E and S Africa / thick bush / insects and some rodents/n 'hollow tree or bough'/e 3

Glaucidium brodiei (*Burton*) Collared Owlet Himalayas, SE Asia, S China, Hainan, Taiwan, Sumatra, Borneo/hill forest/birds and insects/n hole/e 3–5

Glaucidium radiatum (*Tickell*) Barred Jungle Owlet India and Ceylon / forest insects and small vertebrates/n hole/e 3–4

Glaucidium castanonotum (*Blyth*) Chestnut-backed Owlet Ceylon / forest/ insects/n hole/e 2

Glaucidium cuculoides (*Vigors*) Cuckoo Owlet Himalayas to SE Asia, S China and Hainan: Java and Bali (not Sumatra)/forest/insects and small vertebrates / n hole / e 3–5/ I ? ♂♀

Xenoglaux loweryi *O'Neill and Graves* (*Auk*, 94 (1977), pp 409–16) Long-whiskered Owlet San Martin, N Peru/3 specimens

Micrathene whitneyi (*Cooper*) Elf Owl South-eastern USA and Mexico/forest and cactus/insects/n hole/e 2–5/I ♂♀ 14

Uroglaux dimorpha (*Salvadori*) Papuan Hawk Owl New Guinea and Japen/very rare/? forest/insects and rodents

Ninox rufa (*Gould*) Rufous Owl N Australia, New Guinea, Waigeu, Aru Is/forest/opossums/n hole/e 2

Ninox strenua (*Gould*) Powerful Owl New South Wales and Victoria / forest/opossums/n hole/e 2–3/I ♀ 35–6/F 35

Ninox connivens (*Latham*) Barking Owl or Winking Owl Australia, E New Guinea and Moluccas/ forest and savannah / n hole / e 3/ I ♀ 37/F 35

Ninox novaeseelandiae (*Gmelin*) MOREPORK OWL or BOOBOOK OWL Australasia, New Zealand and Lesser Sunda Is / forest and scrub / insects etc / n hole / e 3–4 / I ♀ 33 / F 40

Ninox scutulata (*Raffles*) BROWN HAWK OWL S and E Asia and Indonesia / forest / insects and small vertebrates / n hole / e 3–5 / I ♂♀ 24

Ninox affinis *Beavan* ANDAMAN HAWK OWL Andaman and Nicobar Is / no data

Ninox superciliaris (*Vieillot*) MADAGASCAR HAWK OWL W Madagascar / forests

Ninox philippensis *Bonaparte* PHILIPPINE HAWK OWL Philippines [The Philippine Hawk or Boobook Owls are now considered to be conspecific (see Dupont *Philippine Birds*) and the ranges of the various forms have been corrected from those given in Peters' *Check List*]

Ninox perversa *Stresemann* OCHRE-BELLIED HAWK OWL Celebes / rain forest

Ninox squamipila (*Bonaparte*) MOLUCCAN HAWK OWL Moluccas and Christmas Is (Indian Ocean)

Ninox theomacha (*Bonaparte*) SOOTY-BACKED OWL New Guinea, W Papuan Is, D'Entecasteau and Louisade Is / forest / insects

Ninox punctulata (*Quoy and Gaimard*) SPECKLED HAWK OWL Celebes / open forest

Ninox meeki *Rothschild and Hartert* MEEK'S HAWK OWL Admiralty Is

Ninox solomonis *Sharpe* CARTERET'S HAWK OWL (NEW IRELAND HAWK OWL) New Britain, New Ireland, New Hanover

Ninox odiosa *Sclater* NEW BRITAIN HAWK OWL New Britain

Ninox jacquinoti (*Bonaparte*) SOLOMON HAWK OWL Solomon Is

Sceloglaux albifacies (*Gray*) LAUGHING OWL New Zealand / probably extinct / open country / n under boulders / e 2 / I ♀ 25

Athene noctua (*Scopoli*) LITTLE OWL Europe, N Africa, W and C Asia E to Korea / forest, open country and habitation / varied / n hole, rarely old dove nest etc / e 2–8, usually 3–5 / I ♀ 28–9 / F 26

Athene brahma (*Temminck*) SPOTTED OWLET India and SE Asia / ravines and habitation / insects and small vertebrates / n hole / e 3–5 / I ♂♀

Athene blewitti (*Hume*) FOREST OWLET or BLEWITT'S OWL Forests of C India / no data / probably extinct / last seen 1914 / Ali and Ripley searched unsuccessfully for it in 1975. See also Ripley 'Reconsideration of *Athene blewitti*

(Hume)', *Journal Bombay Nat Hist Soc*, 73, pp 1–4

Athene murivora *Milne-Edwards* RODRIGUEZ LITTLE OWL Rodriguez / extinct / bones only and one anonymous early account, which stated that they lived in trees and ate little birds and lizards.

Speotyto cunicularia (*Molina*) BURROWING OWL The Americas from British Columbia to Tierra del Fuego / semi-desert / insects etc / n hole in ground / e 2–11 / I ♂♀ 28

Ciccaba virgata (*Cassin*) MOTTLED OWL C and S America / n hole or old raptor nest / e 2

Ciccaba nigrolineata *Sclater* BLACK AND WHITE OWL S Mexico to W Ecuador / forest edges / insects

Ciccaba huhula (*Daudin*) BLACK-BANDED OWL Eastern S America / no data

Ciccaba albitarsus (*Bonaparte*) RUFOUS-BANDED OWL Colombia, Ecuador and Venezuela / mountain forest

Ciccaba woodfordii (*Smith*) AFRICAN WOOD OWL or WOODFORD'S OWL Africa S of Sahara / forest and bush / varied / n hole or old raptor nest / e 1

Strix butleri (*Hume*) HUME'S WOOD OWL SW Asia / 3 specimens / no data

Strix seloputo *Horsfield* SPOTTED WOOD OWL SE Asia, Java, Bawean and Palawan / forest / beetles / e 1–2

Strix ocellata (*Lesson*) MOTTLED WOOD OWL India / cultivation / vertebrates / n hole / e 1–3

Strix leptogrammica *Temminck* BROWN WOOD OWL Indian sub-continent to SE Asia, S China and W Indonesia / forest / vertebrates / n tree or ground / e 2

Strix aluco (*L*) TAWNY OWL Europe, N Africa and across W and C Asia to Korea / woods, gardens, habitation, rarely open country / insects and vertebrates / n hole or old nests of crows, raptors etc / e 1–8, usually 2–4 / I ♀ 28–30 / F 29–37 (accounts differ)

Strix occidentalis (*Xantus*) SPOTTED OWL Western N America / forests / varied / n hole, old raptor nest or rock crevice / e 2–4

Strix varia *Barton* BARRED OWL Eastern N America and C America / forest / vertebrates / n hole / e 2–3 (rarely 4–5) / I ♀ 28 / F c42

Strix hylophila *Temminck* RUSTY-BARRED OWL S Brazil

Strix rufipes *King* RUFOUS-LEGGED OWL Southern S America

Strix uralensis *Pallas* URAL OWL N Europe,

RALLIDAE:
Gallicrex cinerea,
Watercock or Kora

RALLIDAE:
Rallina tricolor,
Red-necked Rail

Plate 88

RALLIDAE:
Gallinula mortierii,
Tasmanian Hen,
Tasmanian Waterhen

EURYPIGIDAE:
Eurypyga helias,
Sunbittern

CARAIAMIDAE:
Chunga burmeisteri,
Black-legged or
Burmeister's Seriama

Plate 89

Siberia, Manchuria, Japan and Korea / forest / varied / n hole or old raptor nest / e 2–6 / I ♀ 27–8

Strix davidi (*Sharpe*) PÈRE DÁVID'S OWL Mts of W Szechwan (considered by some authorities to be a race of *S. uralensis*)

Strix nebulosa *Forster* GREAT GREY OWL Coniferous forests of N Holarctic / varied / n old raptor nest / e 4 / I ♀ 30

Rhinoptynx clamator (*Vieillot*) STRIPED OWL C and S America / forest / mammals / n ground / e ?2 (1 nest with 2 young known) [*Otus macrurus* Kaup, from Mexico is known only from 1 specimen (lost) and is usually placed in this genus (Rhinoptynx). Peters regarded the species as unidentifiable.]

Asio otus (*L*) COMMON LONG-EARED OWL Holarctic / forest / mammals, birds and insects / n old domed or open nests of other birds, rarely ground / e 3–8, usually 4–5 / I ♀ (?♂) 27–8 / F 23–4

Asio abyssinicus (*Guérin-Méneville*) AFRICAN LONG-EARED OWL Ethiopia and Congo / open grassland and ravines / n and e n/k (sometimes treated as conspecific with *A. otus*)

Asio stygius (*Wagler*) STYGIAN OWL C and S America, Cuba, Hispaniola and Isle of Pines / n tree or ground / e 2

Asio madagascariensis *Smith* MADAGASCAR LONG-EARED OWL E Madagascar

Asio flammeus (*Pontoppidan*) SHORT-EARED OWL Much of Holarctic, S America, W Indies, Galapagos, Hawaii and Ponapé (discontinuous) / open country / small mammals and birds / n ground / e 3–8 (up to 14 during vole plagues) / I ♀ 24–8 / F 24–7

Asio capensis *Smith* AFRICAN MARSH OWL Africa and Madagascar / swamps and damp places / insects etc / n ground / e 2–4

Pseudoscops grammicus (*Gosse*) JAMAICAN OWL Jamaica / woodland and open country / n holes / e 2

Nesasio solomonensis (*Hartert*) FEARFUL OWL Solomon Is (Bougainville, Choiseul and Santa Isabel) / forest

Aegolius funereus (*L*) BOREAL or TENGMALM'S OWL Holarctic coniferous forest belt / small mammals and birds / n hole / e 3–6, rarely 7–10 / I ♀ 25+ / F 30–6 (estimated)

Aegolius acadicus (*Gmelin*) SAW-WHET OWL N America / n hole / e 4–7 / I 21–8 / F 28

Aegolius ridgwayi (*Alfaro*) ALFARO'S or UNSPOTTED SAWWHET OWL Guatemala / unique

Aegolius harrisii (*Cassin*) BUFF-FRONTED OWL S America, in the NW and SE (discontinuous)

STEATORNITHIDAE   Oilbird Lean-bodied, long-winged birds related to the nightjars and allies. Feet small, almost useless, the birds feeding while on the wing, on fruit of oil-palms, and spending the day in caves, generally on ledges. Nest, a truncated cone of droppings on cave ledge, eggs 2–4 white. One species.

Steatornis caripensis *Humboldt* OILBIRD Northern S America (local) / seaside and mountain caves / palm nuts / n cave ledge / e 2–4 / I ♂♀

PODARGIDAE   Frogmouths Weak-flying birds with large, flat, horny hooked bills and a tremendous gape. They spend the day sitting lengthwise on branches which they are camouflaged to resemble. Nest in the fork of a horizontal branch. Eggs 1–3, white, incubated by both sexes, generally the female by night, the male by day; 12–13 species.

Podargus strigoides (*Latham*) TAWNY FROGMOUTH Australia and Tasmania / open woodland / insects and small vertebrates / e 2–3

Podargus papuensis *Quoy and Gaimard* PAPUAN FROGMOUTH Cape York Peninsula, New Guinea and Papuan Is / forest and savannah / insects / e 1

Podargus ocellatus *Quoy and Gaimard* MARBLED FROGMOUTH Cape York Peninsula, New Guinea and islands from Waigeu to Solomons / forest / insects / e 1

Batrachostomus auritus (*Gray*) LARGE FROGMOUTH Malaya, Sumatra, Borneo and Bunguran / forest / orthoptera / e 1

Batrachostomus harterti *Sharpe* DULIT FROGMOUTH Mts of C Borneo / 7 specimens / no data (a specimen in Sarawak Museum resembles *harterti* in colour, but *auritus* in size)

Batrachostomus septimus *Tweeddale* PHILIPPINE FROGMOUTH Philippines / forest / insects / e 1

Batrachostomus stellatus (*Gould*) GOULD'S FROGMOUTH Malaya, Sumatra, Banka, Borneo and Gt Natuna / forest / locusts / e ?1

Batrachostomus moniliger *Blyth* SINHALESE FROGMOUTH Ceylon and SW India / jungle / insects / e 1

Batrachostomus hodgsoni (*Gray*) HODGSON'S FROGMOUTH Mts from Sikkim to SE Asia / jungle / insects / e 1–2

Batrachostomus poliolophus *Hartert* PALE-
HEADED FROGMOUTH Sumatra mts
Batrachostomus mixtus *Sharpe* SHARPE'S
FROGMOUTH Mts of Borneo/very few specimens
known/no data (often treated as a race of
poliolophus)
Batrachostomus javensis (*Horsfield*)
JAVAN FROGMOUTH Malaya, Java, Sumatra,
Borneo, Palawan, Banguey, Banka and Billiton/
secondary forest / e 1
Batrachostomus affinis *Blyth* BLYTH'S
FROGMOUTH Malay Peninsula, Sumatra and
Borneo/forest/e 1–2
NYCTIBIIDAE Potoos Large nightjar-like
birds lacking rictal bristles. They spend the day
sitting bolt upright on broken stumps or
branches and look like a continuation of the
branch. Feed on insects caught flycatcher-
fashion by darting from perch. No nest, the
single spotted egg is laid in a depression on top
of a broken stump, incubated by both sexes.
Five species.
Nyctibius grandis (*Gmelin*) GREAT POTOO
Panama to Rio de Janeiro
Nyctibius aethereus (*Wied*) LONG-TAILED
POTOO Tropical S America
Nyctibius griseus (*Gmelin*) LESSER POTOO
Jamaica, C and tropical S America
Nyctibius leucopterus (*Wied*) WHITE-WINGED
POTOO E Colombia and E Ecuador; coastal
region of E Brazil (discontinuous)
Nyctibius bracteatus *Gould* RUFOUS POTOO
Amazonian Colombia, Ecuador and Peru;
British Guiana
AEGOTHELIDAE Owlet Nightjars (some-
times called **Moth Owls** or **Owlet Frog-
mouths**) Small dumpy birds, superficially
resembling tiny, long-tailed owls. Feed on
ground insects, and on night-flying insects,
hawked on the wing. Shy and solitary. Nest in a
hollow tree, eggs 3–4, white or spotted.
Aegotheles crinifrons (*Bonaparte*)
MOLUCCAN OWLET NIGHTJAR Halmahera and
Batjan
Aegotheles insignis *Salvadori* LARGE or
RUFOUS OWLET NIGHTJAR Mts of New Guinea/
forest edge and open forest
Aegotheles cristatus (*White*) CRESTED OWLET
NIGHTJAR Australia, Tasmania and S New
Guinea
Aegotheles savesi *Layard and Layard*
NEW CALEDONIAN OWLET NIGHTJAR New

Caledonia/unique
Aegotheles bennettii *Salvadori and D'Albertis*
BARRED OWLET NIGHTJAR New Guinea, Aru Is,
Ferguson and Goodenough Is
Aegotheles wallacii *Gray* WALLACE'S OWLET
NIGHTJAR W New Guinea
Aegotheles albertisi *Sclater* D'ALBERTIS'S
OWLET NIGHTJAR Mountain forests of New
Guinea (sometimes misspelled *albertisii*)
Aegotheles archboldi *Rand* (*Amer Mus Novit
no 1102 (1941) p 10*) ARCHBOLD'S OWLET
NIGHTJAR Oranje Mts, New Guinea [NB:
Morony, Bock and Farrand state that *archboldi*
is given as a race of *albertisi*, by Peters' *Check
List*, vol 4. As this volume was published in
1940, before *archboldi* was described, this
would be impossible]
CAPRIMULGIDAE Nightjars Medium-
sized nocturnal or crepuscular birds with long,
pointed wings, and small feet of little use for
walking. Plumage soft and fluffy, generally
mottled greys and browns criptically resembling
bark and dead leaves. Feed on insects captured
in flight. Most species make no nest, but lay the
1 or 2 beautifully marbled eggs on the bare
ground.
Lurocalis semitorquatus (*Gmelin*) SHORT-
TAILED NIGHTHAWK Tropical C and S America/
forests
Chordeiles pusillus *Gould* LEAST NIGHTHAWK
Interior of Brazil and Guyana
Chordeiles rupestris (*Spix*) SAND-COLOURED
NIGHTHAWK Upper Amazon
Chordeiles acutipennis (*Hermann*) LESSER
NIGHTHAWK South-western USA, C and
tropical S America / mangrove swamps and
damp woodland
Chordeiles minor (*Forster*) COMMON
NIGHTHAWK The greater part of N America
w through C and much of S America
Chordeiles gundlachii *Lawrence* ANTILLEAN
NIGHTHAWK W Indies (Greater Antilles)
Nyctiprogne leucopyga (*Spix*) BAND-TAILED
NIGHTHAWK Tropical S America
Podager nacunda (*Vieillot*) NACUNDA
NIGHTHAWK S America S to Patagonia
Eurostopodus guttatus (*Vigors and Horsfield*)
SPOTTED NIGHTJAR N and E Australia, migra-
ting to Aru Is—supposed to occur in New
Ireland (sic)/dry woodland/e 1
Eurostopodus mysticalis (*Temminck*)
(= **E. albogularis** (*Vigors and Horsfield*))

OTIDIDAE:
Eupodotis australis,
Australian Bustard

OTIDIDAE:
Otis tarda, Great Bustard

Plate 90

JACANIDAE:
Actophilornis africana,
African Jacana

JACANIDAE:
Irediparra gallinacea,
Comb-crested Jacana or
Lotosbird

Plate 91

WHITE-THROATED NIGHTJAR E Australia and
Solomon Is/forests/e 1
Eurostopodus   diabolicus   *Stresemann*
KALABAT NIGHTJAR Mt Kalabat, N Celebes
Eurostopodus papuensis (*Schlegel*) PAPUAN
NIGHTJAR New Guinea and Salawati/n ground/
e 1/I ♂♀ (1 nest known)
Eurostopodus archboldi (*Mayr and Rand*)
ARCHBOLD'S NIGHTJAR New Guinea/mountain
forest/no data
Eurostopodus temminckii (*Gould*) LESSER
EARED NIGHTJAR Malay Peninsula, Sumatra,
Banka and Borneo/forest rivers/e ?1
Eurostopodus macrotis (*Vigors*) GREATER
EARED NIGHTJAR Travancore: Assam to SE Asia:
Philippines, Simalur and Celebes/wooded plains
and hills / e 1 / I and F n/k
Veles binotatus (*Bonaparte*) DUSKY NIGHTJAR
Ghana and S Cameroon/forest/little known
Nyctidromus albicollis (*Gmelin*) COMMON
PAURAQUE or WHITE-NECKED NIGHTJAR C and
tropical S America / river-borders and forest
clearings/n none/e 2/I ♂♀
Phaenoptilus nuttallii (*Audubon*) COMMON
POORWILL Western N America / forest, bush
and arid areas/e 2/I ♂♀
Siphonorhis brewsteri (*Chapman*) LEAST
PAURAQUE Hispaniola and Gonave / rare and
endangered/e 2
Siphonorhis americanus (*L*) JAMAICAN
PAURAQUE Jamaica/extinct/3 specimens
Otophanes   mcleodii   *Brewster*   EARED
POORWILL W Mexico
Otophanes yucatanicus (*Hartert*) YUCATAN
POORWILL SE Mexico and N Guatemala
Nyctiphrynus ocellatus (*Tschudi*) OCELLATED
POORWILL Parts of S America [also Nicaragua,
unique specimen of separate race]
Caprimulgus carolinensis *Gmelin* CHUCK-
WILLS WIDOW South-eastern USA and
Caribbean/forest/e 2
Caprimulgus   rufus   *Boddaert*   RUFOUS
NIGHTJAR Panama, tropical S America and St
Lucia/lowland woodland/e 2
Caprimulgus   cubanensis   (*Lawrence*)
GREATER ANTILLEAN NIGHTJAR Cuba, Isle of
Pines and Hispaniola/woodland/e 2
Caprimulgus salvini *Hartert* CHIP WILLOW
E Mexico
Caprimulgus   sericocaudatus   (*Cassin*)
SILKY-TAILED NIGHTJAR C America (*C. badius*
(Bangs and Peck) is sometimes separated)

Caprimulgus ridgwayi (*Nelson*) TUCUCHILLO
W Mexico, Honduras and Guatemala
Caprimulgus vociferus *Wilson* WHIP-POOR-
WILL C America and south-western USA/open
forest and clearings/e 2/I 20-1
Caprimulgus   noctitherus   (*Wetmore*)
PUERTO-RICAN NIGHTJAR Puerto Rico/believed
extinct till re-discovered in 1961/rare/no data
Caprimulgus saturatus (*Salvin*) SOOTY
NIGHTJAR Mts of Costa Rica and Panama
Caprimulgus longirostris *Bonaparte* BAND-
WINGED NIGHTJAR Temperate S America,
including the Andes from Colombia to Chile/
forest/n scrape/e 2
Caprimulgus cayennensis *Gmelin* CAYENNE
NIGHTHAWK   C   America   and   northern
S America
Caprimulgus candicans (*Pelzeln*) WHITE-
WINGED NIGHTJAR C Brazil and Paraguay
Caprimulgus   maculicaudus   (*Lawrence*)
PIT SWEET Scattered localities in tropical
S America
Caprimulgus parvulus *Gould* LITTLE
NIGHTJAR Scattered localities in tropical S
America
Caprimulgus maculosus (*Todd*) CAYENNE
NIGHTJAR Cayenne/unique (?)
Caprimulgus nigrescens *Cabanis* BLACKISH
NIGHTJAR or DARK NIGHTHAWK Amazon basin/
'rocks near rivers' (Chubb)/n shallow hollow/e 2
Caprimulgus whiteleyi (*Salvin*) RORAIMA
NIGHTJAR Mt Roraima, Guyana / ? no data
Caprimulgus hirundinaceus *Spix* PYGMY
NIGHTJAR E Brazil
Caprimulgus ruficollis *Temminck* RED-
NECKED NIGHTJAR Iberia and N Africa/forested
ridges and semi-desert/e 2/I and F n/k
Caprimulgus   indicus   *Latham*   JUNGLE
NIGHTJAR S and E Asia from India and Ceylon
to Amurland and S to Indonesia and Palau Is
not breeding in all of range/forest glades and
hillsides/insects/e 2/I ♂♀ 16-17
Caprimulgus   europaeus   *L*   EUROPEAN
NIGHTJAR Europe, W and C Asia w Africa/
open country/e 2/I ♂♀ 18/F 16-18
Caprimulgus   aegyptius   *Lichtenstein*
EGYPTIAN NIGHTJAR SW Asia and Sahara/
desert/e 2/I ♂♀ 17-18/F c30
Caprimulgus   mahrattensis   *Sykes*   SYKES'
NIGHTJAR Afghanistan, Baluchistan, Sind and
NW India/semi-desert/e 2/I ♂♀
Caprimulgus centralasicus *Vaurie* (*Amer*

Mus Novit, no 1,985 (1960) p 1) VAURIE'S NIGHTJAR Guma, W Sinkiang / unique

Caprimulgus nubicus *Lichtenstein* NUBIAN NIGHTJAR Socotra and deserts bordering Red Sea / scrub / e 2 / I and F n/k

Caprimulgus eximius *Temminck* GOLDEN NIGHTJAR Parts of Sahara region / reddish-yellow gravelly patches / e 2

Caprimulgus madagascariensis *Sganzin* MADAGASCAR NIGHTJAR Madagascar and Aldabra / e ?2 (1 Madagascar nest with 1 egg and an oviduct egg about to be laid)

Caprimulgus macrurus *Horsfield* LARGE-TAILED or LONG-TAILED NIGHTJAR From India and Ceylon through SE Asia to Indonesia, Hainan, Philippines, N Australia and Papuan Is / forest, gardens and open country / e 2 / I ♂♀

Caprimulgus pectoralis *Cuvier* CUVIER'S NIGHTJAR S Africa / woodland / e 2

Caprimulgus fervidus *Sharpe* FIERY-NECKED NIGHTJAR C and S Africa / forest / e 2

Caprimulgus guttifer *Grote* USAMBARA NIGHTJAR Tanganyika / mountain savannah / e 2

Caprimulgus rufigena *Smith* RUFOUS-CHEEKED NIGHTJAR SC and S Africa, wandering N (movements little understood) / e 2

Caprimulgus fraenatus *Salvadori* DARK NIGHTJAR E Africa / steppes and mountain slopes / e 2 [*Caprimulgus keniensis*, Van Someren (unique) is variously treated as a race or as a synonym of *C. fraenatus*]

Caprimulgus donaldsoni *Sharpe* DONALDSON-SMITH'S NIGHTJAR Somaliland to Kenya / dry bush / no data

Caprimulgus poliocephalus *Rüppell* RÜPPELL'S or ABYSSINIAN NIGHTJAR E Africa from Ethiopia to Tanganyika / light bush / e 2

Caprimulgus asiaticus *Latham* LITTLE INDIAN NIGHTJAR India, Ceylon and SE Asia / scrub and cultivation / e 2 / I ♂♀

Caprimulgus natalensis *Smith* WHITE-TAILED NIGHTJAR Parts of Africa, S of Sahara / swamps and damp grass / e 2

Caprimulgus ruwenzorii *Ogilvie-Grant* RUWENZORI NIGHTJAR Ruwenzori Mts / ridges / no data

[**Caprimulgus koesteri** *Neumann* BENGUELLA NIGHTJAR Benguella / highlands / no data / this form, described by Neumann as a species was treated as a race of *C. poliocephalus* by Peters, and by Mackworth Praed and Grant as a race of *C. ruwenzorii* (itself treated by Peters as a race of *poliocephalus*)]

Caprimulgus inornatus *Heuglin* PLAIN NIGHTJAR W Africa and Sahara, to Somaliland, Uganda and SW Arabia / e 2

Caprimulgus stellatus *Blundell and Lovat* STAR-SPOTTED NIGHTJAR Ethiopia to Kenya / no data

[**Caprimulgus ludovicianus** *Stephenson Clarke* SW Ethiopia / unique (possibly a synonym of *C. inornatus*)]

Caprimulgus affinis *Horsfield* (includes *C. monticolus Franklin*) FRANKLIN'S, SAVANNAH or ALLIED NIGHTJAR India through SE Asia to Taiwan, S China and Indonesia / scrub and forest / e 2 (among stones) / I ♂♀

Caprimulgus tristigma *Rüppell* FRECKLED NIGHTJAR Tropical belt of Africa S of Sahara / rocky hillsides / e 2 on ground in rocky areas

Caprimulgus concretus *Bonaparte* BONAPARTE'S NIGHTJAR Sumatra, Biliton and Borneo / no data

Caprimulgus pulchellus *Salvadori* SALVADORI'S NIGHTJAR Sumatra and Java

Caprimulgus enarratus *Gray* COLLARED NIGHTJAR NW and E Madagascar / forest

Caprimulgus batesi *Sharpe* BATES'S FOREST NIGHTJAR Equatorial forest zone from Cameroon to Congo / e 1

Caprimulgus fossii *Hartlaub* GABON NIGHTJAR C and E Africa / grassland / e 2 in short grass or bare ground

[**Caprimulgus clarus** *Reichenow* Parts of E Africa. The systematic status of this form appears to be in doubt. It is sometimes treated as a species, sometimes as a race of *C. fossii* and sometimes as a race of *C. climacurus*]

Caprimulgus climacurus *Vieillot* LONG-TAILED NIGHTJAR Semi-arid regions of Equatorial Africa, N and S of the forest belt / trees and scrub / e 2

Macrodipteryx longipennis (*Shaw*) STANDARD-WINGED NIGHTJAR Africa from Senegal to Ethiopia / savannah / e 2

Semeiophorus vexillarius *Gould* PENNANT-WINGED NIGHTJAR Africa S of equatorial forest belt to Transvaal / varied habitat / e 2

Hydropsalis climacocerca (*Tschudi*) LADDER-TAILED NIGHTJAR Amazon basin and N to the Guianas

Hydropsalis braziliana (*Gmelin*) SCISSOR-TAILED NIGHTJAR S America from S bank of Amazon to Uruguay

Plate 92

Plate 93

Uropsalis segmentata (*Cassin*) SWALLOW-TAILED NIGHTJAR Colombia, Ecuador, Peru and Bolivia

Uropsalis lyra (*Bonaparte*) LYRE-TAILED NIGHTJAR Colombia, Ecuador, Venezuela and Peru

Macropsalis creagra (*Bonaparte*) LONG-TRAINED NIGHTJAR SE Brazil

Eleothreptus anomalus (*Gould*) SICKLE-WINGED NIGHTJAR Paraguay, SE Brazil and N Argentina

APODIDAE Swifts Medium to small birds with small weak legs, useless for walking, and long, pointed wings. Capable of rapid and sustained flight, only occasionally resting by clinging to vertical surfaces, some species are believed to be capable of sleeping on the wing. Food, small insects caught on the wing. Nest usually glued with saliva to a vertical surface, some of the Swiftlets, *Collocalia*, using no other material than saliva (the source of 'birds' nest soup').

Genus *Collocalia* (**Swiftlets**) This genus is so complicated in its taxonomy as to seem to warrant a different approach to the rest of the book. Therefore, I have attempted to give a complete list of forms, the arrangement of species follows that of Medway, 'Field characters as a guide to the specific relations of Swiftlets' *Proceedings of the Linnean Society of London*, vol 177, pt 2 (1966), pp 151–72, and the treatment of the *whiteheadi* group that of Somadikarta ('A recharacterization of *Collocalia papuensis*'), in *Proc US Nat Mus* (1967), vol 124, no 3,620, pp 1–8).

Collocalia brevirostris (*Horsfield*) HIMALAYAN SWIFTLET Himalayas to mountains of Tonkin and W China and Java/hills with caves/n cliff walls or caves/e 2

- *C. b. brevirostris* (Horsfield): Himalayas to N Burma
- *C. b. vulcanorum* Stresemann: Java in the high craters
- *C. b. rogersi* Deignan: S Shan States, W Thailand and Laos
- *C. b. inopina* Thayer and Bangs: Mts of Hupeh
- *C. b. pellos* Thayer and Bangs: Mts of Szechwan

[**Collocalia innominata** *Hume*, the status of this form is doubtful, the name is based on a single specimen from the Andaman Is where it has never been seen since. It has been identified at various times with *C. maxima*, with *C. (vanikorensis) capnitis* or as a race of *C. brevirostris*]

Collocalia whiteheadi *Ogilvie-Grant* WHITEHEAD'S SWIFTLET Philippines and Palawan

- *C. w. whiteheadi* Ogilvie-Grant: Philippines, except Mindanao
- *C. w. origensis* Oberholzer: Mindanao, except the peak of Mt Apo
- *C. w. apoensis* Hachisuka: Peak of Mt Apo
- *C. w. palawanensis* Stresemann (= *C. w. tsubame* Hachisuka): Palawan

Collocalia papuensis *Rand* THREE-TOED SWIFTLET Lowlands of New Guinea

Collocalia nuditarsus *Salomonsen* NAKED-LEGGED SWIFTLET Highlands of New Guinea

Collocalia orientalis *Mayr* GUADALCANAL SWIFTLET Guadalcanal/unique

- *C. o. leletensis* (Salomonsen), New Ireland Swiftlet, New Ireland, unique

Collocalia gigas *Hartert and Butler* GIANT SWIFTLET Malay Peninsula, Sumatra, Java and (?) Borneo/n of vegetation

Collocalia fuciphaga (*Thunberg*) THUNBERG'S SWIFTLET, EDIBLE-NEST SWIFTLET Cochinchina, Malay Peninsula and Sunda Is/caves

- *C. f. fuciphaga* (Thunberg): Java and Kangean Is [*javensis* and *bartelsi* are synonyms]
- *C. f. dammermani* Rensch: Flores
- *C. f. vestita* (Lesson): Sumatra and Billiton
- *C. f. amechana* Oberholzer: Anamba Is and Malaya
- *C. f. germani* Oustalet: Cochinchina, Borneo and Palawan
- *C. f. micans* Stresemann: Sumba, Savu and Timor
- *C. f. perplexa* Riley: Small islands off E coast of Borneo
- *C. f. inexpectata* Hume: Andaman and Nicobar Is

Collocalia maxima *Hartert ex Hume* (= **C. lowi** *Sharpe*) LOW'S SWIFTLET, BLACK-NEST SWIFTLET Coasts of Tenasserim and Malay Peninsula, Anamba Is, Sumatra, Nias, W and northern Borneo, Labuan / limestone caves/ n cave-wall/e 1

- *C. maxima* Hartert: range as above [*C. l. robinsoni* Stresemann is a synonym]

C. m. tichelmani Stresemann: SE Borneo
Collocalia esculenta (*L*) WHITE-BELLIED
SWIFTLET, GLOSSY SWIFTLET Malaya,
Andamans and Nicobars, Christmas Is (Indian
Ocean) through Indonesia to New Guinea,
Bismarck Archipelago, Solomon Is, New
Caledonia and New Hebrides/n cliff or wall of
building/e 2/I ♂♀

    C. e. esculenta (L): Celebes, Moluccas, New
        Guinea and adjacent islands

    C. e. stresemanni Rothschild and Hartert:
        Bismarck Archipelago and Admiralty Is

    C. e. makirensis Mayr: San Cristobal

    C. e. uropygialis Gray: New Caledonia and
        New Hebrides

    C. e. erwini Collin and Hartert: High mts of
        S New Guinea

    C. e. becki Mayr: N and C Solomon Is

    C. e. perneglecta Mayr: Southwest Is

    C. e. neglecta Gray: Alor, Savu, Timor,
        Wetar, Kisar, Damar

    C. e. sumbawae Stresemann: Sumbawa, Flores
        and Sumba

    C. e. linchi Horsfield and Moore: SE Sumatra,
        Java, Bali, Lombok, Kangean and Bawean
        Is

    C. e. dodgei Richmond: Mts of N Borneo and
        Sumatra

    C. e. cyanoptila Oberholser: Malaya, E
        Sumatra, Billiton and lowlands of Borneo

    C. e. natalis Lister: Christmas Is (Indian
        Ocean)

    C. e. elachyptera Oberholser: Merguei
        Archipelago and (?) peninsular Thailand

    C. e. affinis Beavan: Andaman and Nicobar Is

    C. e. isonota Oberholser: Luzon, Mindoro,
        Mindanao, Bongao (Philippines)

    C. e. bagobo Hachisuka: Summit of Mt Apo
        (Mindanao)

    C. e. oberholsei Stresemann: W Sumatra,
        Nias and Mentawi

    C. e. desiderata Mayr: Rennell Is

    C. e. minuta Stresemann: Islands of Djampea
        and Kalao in the Flores Sea

Collocalia marginata *Salvadori*
PHILIPPINE SWIFTLET Philippines and Palawan
Collocalia troglodytes *Gray* PYGMY
SWIFTLET Philippines and Palawan
Collocalia francica (*Gmelin*) GREY-RUMPED
SWIFTLET Mauritius and Réunion/n on cave
walls/e 2
Collocalia elaphra *Oberholser* SEYCHELLES

SWIFTLET Seychelles/n in cave/e 1
Collocalia spodiopyga (*Peale*) PACIFIC
WHITE-RUMPED SWIFTLET N Queensland and
islands from Celebes to Tonga (not New Guinea)

    C. s. spodiopyga (Peale): Samoa

    C. s. assimilis Stresemann: Fiji

    C. s. townsendi Oberholser: Tonga

    C. s. eichorni Hartert: New Britain, New
        Ireland and St Matthias

    C. s. ceramensis Van Oort: Ceram and Buru

    C. s. infuscata Salvadori: Halmahera, Ternate
        and Morotai

    C. s. sororum Stresemann: Celebes

    C. s. reichenowi Stresemann: Guadalcanal
        (Solomons)

    C. s. leucopygia Wallace: New Hebrides,
        Loyalty Is, New Caledonia

    C. s. terrareginae (Ramsay): N Queensland

Collocalia unicolor (*Jerdon*) INDIAN EDIBLE
NEST SWIFTLET Ceylon and coasts and hills of
S India/e 2
Collocalia vanikorensis (*Quoy and Gaimard*)
UNIFORM or LOWLAND SWIFTLET Islands from
Celebes through New Guinea to New Caledonia
and Cape York Peninsula

    C. v. vanikorensis (*Quoy and Gaimard*):
        Solomon Is, to New Hebrides and New
        Caledonia

    C. v. granti Mayr: S and E New Guinea and
        Fergusson Is

    C. v. tagulae Mayr: Louisiade Archipelago

    C. v. moluccarum Stresemann: Moluccas

    C. v. yorki Mathews: Cape York Peninsula

    C. v. steini Stresemann and Paludan: Numfor

    C. v. waigeuensis Stresemann and Paludan:
        Waigeu

    C. v. lihirensis Mayr: St Matthias, Tabar and
        Lihir

    C. v. coultasi Mayr: Manus Is

    C. v. aenigma Riley: C and SE Celebes

    C. v. heinrichi Stresemann: S Celebes

    C. v. capnitis Thayer and Bangs: Hupeh,
        China

    C. v. bartschi Mearns: Guam

    C. v. pelewensis Mayr: Palau Is

    C. v. amelis Oberholzer: Luzon, Marinduque,
        Cebu and Mindanao (Philippines)

    C. v. mearnsi Oberholzer: Luzon, Mindoro,
        Panay, Negros, Cebu, Mindanao

(these last two forms are presumed to be
sympatric but reproductively isolated on
the islands where they both occur)

CHARACRIIDAE;
Charadrius mongolus,
Lesser Sand Plover,
Mongolian Plover

CHARADRIIDAE:
Vanellus miles,
Northern Masked Plover

Plate 94

CHARADRIIDAE:
Vanellus tricolor,
Banded Plover

CHARADRIIDAE:
Pluvialis squatarola,
Silver or Black-bellied Plover

Plate 95

Collocalia inquieta (*Kittlitz*) CAROLINE SWIFTLET Caroline Is / n on cave walls and ceilings / e 2

   C. i. inquieta (Kittlitz): Kusaie

   C. i. ponapensis Mayr: Ponapé

   C. i. rukensis Kuroda: Ruk and (?) Yap

Collocalia salangana *Streubel* (*C. fuciphaga* was for long used for this bird) 'THUNBERG'S SWIFTLET' n generally in caves

   C. s. salangana Streubel: Java

   C. s. natunae Stresemann: Natuna Is and northern Borneo

   C. s. aerophila Oberholzer: Islands off W coast of Sumatra

   C. s. maratua Riley: Borneo and small islands off NE coast

Collocalia hirundinacea *Stresemann* MOUNTAIN SWIFTLET New Guinea, Dampier Is and Goodenough Is, several races from different mountains have been described / forest and open country / n, 3 have been found on ledges in vertical sinkhole in forest, each containing a single chick

Collocalia leucophaea (*Peale*) TAHITI SWIFTLET Society and Marquesas Is

   C. l. leucophaea (Peale): Society Is

   C. l. ocista Oberholzer: Marquesas Is

Collocalia sawtelli *Holyoak* (*Bull BOC*, 94 (1974), pp 146–7) SAWTELL'S SWIFTLET Atiu, Cook Is

Streptoprocne zonaris (*Shaw*) WHITE-COLLARED SWIFT C and tropical S America, Greater Antilles

Streptoprocne biscutata (*Sclater*) BISCUTUTATE SWIFT E Brazil

Streptoprocne semicollaris (*De Saussure*) WHITE-NAPED SWIFT C Mexico

[The arrangement of the genera *Cypseloides* and *Chaetura* is complicated. Some of the Asiatic species were separated as *Hirundapus*, and the species *Cypseloides senex* and *Streptoprocne semicollaris* were placed in a duotypic genus *Aerornis*]

Chaetura caudacuta (*Latham*) WHITE-THROATED NEEDLETAIL S and E Asia / rocky hills / insects / n rock-clefts and hollow trees (*Chaetura cochinchinensis* Oustalet, SE Asia, Java and Sumatra, is almost certainly a race)

Chaetura gigantea (*Temminck*) BROWN NEEDLETAIL India, through SE Asia and Indonesia to Philippines / forest / n ground / e 3–5

Chaetura celebensis *Sclater* SPINE-TAILED SWIFT Celebes and Philippines

[**Chaetura ernesti** *Bartels* ERNEST'S NEEDLETAIL Halimoen Mts, Java / unique / status uncertain, but possibly a race of *C. celebensis*]

Chaetura chapmani *Hellmayr* CHAPMAN'S SWIFT Cayenne and Trinidad: Mato Grosso (unique type of separate race)

Chaetura pelagica (*L*) CHIMNEY SWIFT b N America w probably S America / habitation / n hollow trees and chimneys / e 3–6

Chaetura vauxi (*Townsend*) (includes *C. richmondi*) VAUX'S SWIFT Western N America and C America / n hollow tree / e 3–6

Chaetura gaumeri *Lawrence* YUCATAN SWIFT Yucatan Peninsula and Cozumel Is (possibly a race of *C. vauxi*)

Chaetura leucopygialis *Blyth* SILVER-RUMPED SWIFT S Tenasserim over Malay Peninsula, Sumatra, Java, Borneo and N Natuna Is / open country / n and e n/k

Chaetura sabini *Gray* SABINE'S SWIFT W Africa and Fernando Po / n tree hollows / e 2–3

Chaetura thomensis *Hartert* SÃO THOMÉ SPINE-TAILED SWIFT São Thomé / very little data / e 2–4 (Abbé de Naurois, personal communication)

Chaetura sylvatica (*Tickell*) WHITE-RUMPED NEEDLETAIL India and Burma (local) / forest / n hollow tree / e 3–5

Chaetura nubicola *Brodkorb* BRODKORB'S SWIFT Mt Ovando, Chiapas / unique

Chaetura cinereiventris *Sclater* GREY-RUMPED SWIFT Tropical S America, Panama, Nicaragua, Granada, Trinidad and Tobago

Chaetura egregia *Todd* PALE-RUMPED SWIFT Bolivia, SE Peru and NE Mato Grosso

Chaetura spinicauda (*Temminck*) BAND-RUMPED SWIFT Costa Rica S through north-east and northern S America

Chaetura martinica (*Hermann*) LESSER ANTILLEAN SWIFT Guadaloupe, Dominica, Martinique, St Lucia and St Vincent / mountain forest / n hollow tree or cave (?) / e 3

Chaetura ussheri *Sharpe* MOTTLED-THROATED SWIFT Africa from Senegal to Angola and Tanganyika / forest / n hole in tree / e n/k

Chaetura melanopygia *Chapin* CHAPIN'S SWIFT Ituri Forest

Chaetura andrei *Berlepsch and Hartert* ANDRE'S SWIFT Orinoco Valley (Venezuela) and eastern S America from Brazil to Argentine

Chaetura brachyura (*Jardine*) SHORT-TAILED SWIFT North-eastern S America, Trinidad and Tobago, St Vincent and (?) Grenada / n chimney or cave / e 3–6

Cypseloides senex (*Temminck*) GREAT DUSKY SWIFT S Brazil, Paraguay and NE Argentina

Cypseloides cherriei *Ridgway* SPOT-FRONTED SWIFT Costa Rica and Colombia

Cypseloides fumigatus (*Streubel*) SOOTY SWIFT E Panama and parts of S America (exact distribution uncertain)

[*Cypseloides major* Rothschild, of Peters' *Check List* is now regarded as a race of *C. fumigatus* and renamed *C. fumigatus rothschildi* owing to the preoccupation of the name by *Chaetura major* Bertoni (1900) a synonym of *Cypseloides senex*]

Cypseolides rutila (*Vieillot*) CHESTNUT-COLLARED SWIFT Mexico S to Peru, the Guianas and Trinidad

Cypseloides niger (*Gmelin*) BLACK SWIFT Western N America, C America, West Indies / sea cliffs and mountains / n cliff wall or hole / e 1

Cypseloides cryptus *Zimmer* (*Auk*, vol 62, pp 586–92) ZIMMER'S SWIFT Known from scattered localities in C and S America

Cypseloides phelpsi *Collins* (*Contrib Sci*, no 229 (1972)) PHELPS' SWIFT S Venezuela and adjacent parts of Guyana and Brazil

Cypseloides lemosi *Eisenmann and Lehmann* (*Amer Mus Novit*, no 2117 (1962)) WHITE-CHESTED SWIFT Cauca River basin, SW Colombia / open country

Zoonavena grandidieri (*Verreaux*) GRANDIDIER'S SWIFT Madagascar / forest / n and e apparently n/k

Mearnsia picina (*Tweeddale*) PHILIPPINE SPINE-TAILED SWIFT Philippines

Mearnsia novaeguinae (*D'Albertis and Salvadori*) NEW GUINEA SPINE-TAILED SWIFT New Guinea / lowland forest and garden / no other data

Mearnsia cassini (*Sclater*) CASSIN'S SWIFT W Africa and Fernando Po / ? no data

Mearnsia boehmi (*Schalow*) BÖHM'S SWIFT Angola to Tanganyika / woodland clearings

Apus melba (*L*) ALPINE SWIFT Mountains from SE Europe to Himalayas and through Africa and Madagascar / cliffs and crags / n hole, eave or cliff / e 2–3 / I ♂♀ 18–23 / F c6 weeks

Apus aequatorialis (*Müller*) MOTTLED SWIFT Mts of Africa S of Sahara / rocky cliffs / n cliff / e n/k

Apus reichenowi *Neumann* REICHENOW'S SWIFT Kenya / no data

Apus apus (*L*) COMMON SWIFT Europe and much of Asia w through Africa to S Asia / ubiquitous / n eave, hole or cliff / e 2–4 (usually 3) / I ♀ (?♂) 18–19 / F 35–56 (accounts differ, generally said to be 42–5)

Apus niansae (*Reichenow*) NYANZA SWIFT Ethiopia, Kenya, Tanganyika and Malawi / rocky places / n crevices in cliffs / e 1–2

Apus barbatus (*Sclater*) AFRICAN or BEARDED SWIFT S Africa, N to Malawi, Madagascar and Mayotte (often treated as conspecific with *A. apus*)

Apus sladeniae (*Ogilvie-Grant*) FERNANDO PO SWIFT Fernando Po and Cameroon

Apus toulsoni (*Barboza du Bocage*) LOANDA SWIFT Cabinda and NW Angola / no data

Apus pallidus (*Shelley*) PALLID SWIFT Mediterranean, Madeira, Canary Is, S to British Somaliland and E through S Arabia and Persia to Sind / n cliff or eave / e 2

Apus acuticaudus (*Blyth*) DARK-BACKED SWIFT Khasia Hills (Assam) and (?) Nepal / gorges and rocky places / n cliff / e 2–4 / I ♂♀

Apus pacificus (*Latham*) FORK-TAILED or WHITE-RUMPED SWIFT C, E, NE, S and SE Asia w S to Australia / varied habitat / n rock face / e 2–3

Apus schoutedeni *Prigogine* (*Rev Zool Bot Afr*, 62 (1960), p 103) SCHOUTEDEN'S SWIFT Mt Nyombe in E Congo / 2 specimens / no other data

Apus unicolor (*Jardine*) PLAIN SWIFT Madeira, W Canary Is, Cape Verde Is and Fernando Po / varied habitat / n caves and rock holes / e 2 (*A. alexandri*, Hartert, Cape Verde Is, is sometimes separated)

Apus myoptilus (*Salvadori*) SCARCE SWIFT C Ethiopia, Nanyuki (Kenya), Mt Kilimanjaro and Malawi / known from 4 specimens

Apus batesi (*Sharpe*) BATES'S BLACK SWIFT Cameroon and E Congo / forest / n cave or under rock / e 2

Apus caffer (*Lichtenstein*) CAFFER SWIFT Parts of E and S Africa / cliffs and habitation / n in old swallow nest / e 2–3

Apus horus (*Heuglin*) HORUS SWIFT E and S Africa, except extreme S / n tunnel in sandbank / e 2

Apus affinis (*Gray*) HOUSE SWIFT Widely

SCOLOPACIDAE:
Himantopus himantopus,
Black-winged Stilt

CHARADRIIDAE:
Pluvialis apricaria,
Golden Plover, Eurasian
Golden Plover (nestlings)

Plate 96

SCOLOPACIDAE:
Recurvirostra novaehollandiae,
Red-necked Avocet

SCOLOPACIDAE:
Calidris testacea
(= *C. ferruginea*),
Curlew Sandpiper

Plate 97

distributed from Africa through S Asia to W Indonesia / cliffs and habitation / n on buildings / e 1–4 / I ♂♀ 18–26

Aeronautes andecolus (*d'Orbigny and Lafresnaye*) ANDEAN SWIFT S Andes from Peru to N Chile and Argentina

Aeronautes saxatilis (*Woodhouse*) WHITE-THROATED SWIFT Western N America and C Mexico S to El Salvador / mountain cliffs / n crevice in cliff / e 3–6

Aeronautes montivagus (*d'Orbigny and Lafresnaye*) WHITE-TIPPED SWIFT N Andes from Peru to Venezuela

Panyptila sanctihieronymi *Salvin* GERONIMO SWIFT Mts of W Guatemala / variable habitat / n rock crevices in inaccessible ravines / e apparently n/k

Panyptila cayennensis (*Gmelin*) CAYENNE SWIFT Nicaragua S to northern S America / n tree or wall

Tachornis phoenicobia *Gosse* ANTILLEAN PALM SWIFT Cuba, Isle of Pines, Jamaica and Hispaniola

Micropanyptila furcata *Sutton* PYGMY SWIFT NW Venezuela / types only

Reinarda squamata (*Cassin*) NEOTROPICAL PALM SWIFT The Guianas, Upper Orinoco and E Peru

Cypsiurus parvus (*Lichtenstein*) PALM SWIFT Old World tropics from W Africa to Philippines / open country / n on underside of palm frond / e 2–3

HEMIPROCNIDAE Crested or Tree Swifts Swifts with crests and long, forked tails; plumage softer than typical swifts and brighter in males, the feathers of the back are irridescent. Inhabit open woodlands, feeding on insects caught on wing and resting on high bare branches. Nest a tiny structure glued to an exposed tree limb. Egg 1, bluish-grey glued to the centre of the nest. Three species, S Asia and Australasia. Incubation by both sexes.

Hemiprocne longipennis (*Rafinesque*) CRESTED SWIFT Indian sub-continent through SE Asia to parts of Indonesia (*H. l. coronata* (Tickell) from India, Ceylon and parts of SE Asia is sometimes considered a separate species)

Hemiprocne mystacea (*Lesson*) MOUSTACHED or WHISKERED SWIFT New Guinea and islands from Moluccas to Bismarck Archipelago and Solomons

Hemiprocne comata (*Temminck*) LESSER TREE SWIFT Malay Peninsula and much of Indonesia

TROCHILIDAE Hummingbirds A very large family containing the smallest birds known, sizes vary from $2\frac{1}{2}$–$8\frac{1}{2}$ in (6–22 cm). Males usually brilliantly coloured, the females usually duller. Feed largely on small insects and nectar, the latter collected by hovering in front of flowers, insect-fashion and sucking up the juices. Males take no part in nesting, the work being done entirely by female. Nest a neat cup usually on branch of a tree, or sometimes attached to a rock or palm-frond. Eggs 2, white, very large for the size of the bird. Incubation 14–19 days. Fledging 19–25 days. Some doubtful species are known only from trade-skins, received from Bogotá, and of unknown origin.

Doryfera johannae (*Bourcier*) BLUE-FRONTED LANCEBILL Andes from Venezuela to N Peru and mountains of Guyana

Doryfera ludovicae (*Bourcier and Mulsant*) GREEN-FRONTED LANCEBILL Costa Rica, Panama and Andes from Venezuela to N Bolivia

Androdon aequatorialis *Gould* TOOTH-BILLED HUMMING BIRD E Panama and Pacific slope of Colombia and Ecuador

Rhamphodon naevius (*Dumont*) SAW-BILLED HERMIT SE Brazil

Rhamphodon dohrnii (*Bourcier and Mulsant*) HOOK-BILLED HERMIT E Brazil

Glaucis hirsuta (*Gmelin*) HAIRY HERMIT Grenada, Trinidad, Tobago, E Panama and northern S America E of Andes and S to São Paulo

Glaucis aenea *Lawrence* BRONZY HERMIT Nicaragua and Costa Rica, Pacific coast of Colombia, NW Ecuador

Threnetes niger (*L*) SOOTY BARBTHROAT Cayenne

Threnetes leucurus (*L*) WHITE-TAILED BARBTHROAT Amazon basin

Threnetes ruckeri (*Bourcier*) RUCKER'S or BAND-TAILED BARBTHROAT Nicaragua to Panama and W Venezuela, W Colombia and W Ecuador

Threnetes loehkeni *Grantsau* (*Pap Avuls Zool*, 22, art 23 (Aug 1969), p 246) BRONZE-TAILED BARBTHROAT Amapá, Brazil 6 specimens

Phaethornis yaruqui (*Bourcier*) WHITE-WHISKERED HERMIT W Colombia and W Ecuador

Phaethornis guy (*Lesson*) GREEN HERMIT or GUY'S HERMIT Costa Rica, Panama, Colombia, E Ecuador, E Peru, NE Venezuela and Trinidad

Phaethornis syrmatophorus *Gould* TAWNY-BELLIED or TRAIN-BEARING HERMIT Colombia, Ecuador and NE Peru

Phaethornis superciliosus (*L*) LONG-TAILED HERMIT SW Mexico through C America and northern S America to Amazon basin

[*P. fumosus Schlüter* 1915 = **P. fuliginosus** *Schlüter* 1913 not *P. fuliginosus* Simon 1901, is identified (with a query) by Peters as a synonym of *P. guy*]

Phaethornis malaris (*Nordmann*) GREAT-BILLED or NORDMANN'S HERMIT Cayenne and adjacent Brazil

Phaethornis eurynone (*Lesson*) SCALE-THROATED HERMIT SE Brazil, E Paraguay, NE Argentina

Phaethornis hispidus (*Gould*) WHITE-BEARDED HERMIT Tropical zone from Venezuela to Bolivia

Phaethornis anthophilus (*Bourcier*) PALE-BELLIED or BLACK-CHEEKED HERMIT N Colombia, W Venezuela and Pearl Is (Bay of Panama) [*P. fuliginosus* Simon, now generally identified as a race of *P. anthophilus* is apparently known only from Bogotá trade-skins; range not known]

Phaethornis bourcieri (*Lesson*) STRAIGHT-BILLED or BOURCIER'S HERMIT Amazon basin

Phaethornis philippii (*Bourcier*) NEEDLE-BILLED or DE PHILIPPI'S HERMIT SE Amazonian Brazil and E Peru (? Bolivia)

Phaethornis squalidus (*Temminck*) (includes **P. rupurumii** *Boucard*) MEDIUM or DUSKY-THROATED HERMIT Guyana, Amazon basin and Venezuela S of Orinoco

Phaethornis augusti (*Bourcier*) SOOTY-CAPPED or SALLE'S HERMIT Mountains from Colombia to Guyana

Phaethornis pretrei (*Lesson and DeLattre*) PLANALTO or PRETRE'S HERMIT Planalto campo region of C and S Brazil, E Bolivia and Argentina

Phaethornis subochraceus *Todd* BUFF-BELLIED HERMIT NE Bolivia and Mato Grosso

Phaethornis nattereri *Berlepsch* CINNAMON-THROATED or NATTERER'S HERMIT C and E Brazil/scattered records only

Phaethornis maranhaoensis *Grantsau* (*Pap Avuls Zool*, 22, art 7 (Sept 1968), p 57) MARANHÃO HERMIT Imperatriz, Maranhão, Brazil

Phaethornis gounellei *Boucard* BROAD-TIPPED or GOUNELL'S HERMIT C and E Brazil

Phaethornis ruber (*L*) REDDISH HERMIT Guianas and Amazon and Orinoco basins

Phaethornis stuarti *Hartert* WHITE-BROWED or STUART'S HERMIT S Peru and N Bolivia

Phaethornis griseogularis *Gould* GREY-THROATED HERMIT Tropical zone of Colombia, Ecuador and Peru E of Andes (? Guyana)

[**Phaethornis porcullae** *Carriker* PORCULLA HERMIT Porculla Pass, Peru. Known only from 2 females. De Schaunsee, *Birds of South America* (1966), p 161 identifies this with *P. griseogularis* but Peters' *Check List*, vol 5, p 14 footnote states it is most like *P. nattereri*]

[**Phaethornis zonura** *Gould* GOULD'S HERMIT N Peru/probably a synonym of *P. griseogularis*]

[**Phaethornis apheles** *Heine* HEINE'S HERMIT N Peru. I can find no comment on this form other than the statement by Peters, vol 5, p 16, that it is '*perhaps* (italics mine) the same as *P. zonura*']

Phaethornis longuemareus (*Lesson*) LITTLE HERMIT Mexico to Panama, and S America from E Peru through Ecuador, Colombia, Venezuela and the Guianas to Trinidad

Phaethornis idaliae (*Bourcier and Mulsant*) MINUTE HERMIT SE Brazil (*P. viridicaudatus* Gould, is apparently the ♀)

Phaethornis margarettae *Ruschi* 1972, *Bol Mus Biol Mello Leitao*, 35:1 and **Phaethornis nigrirostris** *Ruschi* 1973, *op cit*, 36:2 (I have not seen these references)

Eutoxeres aquila (*Bourcier*) COMMON or WHITE-TIPPED SICKLEBILL Costa Rica, Panama, Colombia, Ecuador and NE Peru

Eutoxeres condamini (*Bourcier*) CONDAMINES' or BUFF-TAILED SICKLEBILL SE Colombia, E Ecuador and E Peru

Phaeochroa cuvierii (*DeLattre and Bourcier*) SCALY-BREASTED or CUVIER'S HUMMINGBIRD C America and N Colombia

Campylopterus curvipennis (*Lichtenstein*) WEDGE-TAILED SABREWING Mexico and E Guatemala

Campylopterus largipennis (*Boddaert*) GREY-BREASTED SABREWING The Guianas, Orinoco and Amazon basins

Campylopterus rufus *Lesson* RUFOUS SABREWING Highlands of Chiapas, W

SCOLOPACIDAE: *Numenius phaeopus*, Whimbrel

SCOLOPACIDAE: *Cladorhynchus leucocephala*, Banded Stilt

Plate 98

SCOLOPACIDAE:
Heteroscelus incanus,
Wandering Tattler

SCOLOPACIDAE:
Limosa lapponica,
Bar-tailed Godwit

Plate 99

Guatemala and El Salvador

Campylopterus hyperythrus *Cabanis* RUFOUS-BREASTED SABREWING Isolated mountains in Venezuela

Campylopterus duidae *Chapman* BUFF-BREASTED or DUIDA SABREWING Isolated mountains in S Venezuela and adjacent N Brazil

Campylopterus hemileucurus (*Lichtenstein*) VIOLET SABREWING S Mexico to Panama

Campylopterus ensipennis (*Swainson*) BLUE-THROATED or WHITE-TAILED SABREWING N Venezuela, Trinidad and Tobago

Campylopterus falcatus (*Swainson*) LAZULINE SABREWING Andes from Venezuela to Ecuador

Campylopterus phainopeplus *Salvin and Godman* SANTA MARTA SABREWING Santa Marta Mts of Colombia

Campylopterus villaviscensio (*Bourcier*) NAPO SABREWING Ecuador

Eupetomena macroura (*Gmelin*) SWALLOW-TAILED HUMMINGBIRD Guianas, much of Brazil, Paraguay, E Bolivia and E Peru

Florisuga mellivora (*L*) WHITE-NECKED JACOBIN S Mexico, C America and S over much of northern S America to N Bolivia and Mato Grosso, also Trinidad and Tobago

Melanotrochilus fuscus (*Vieillot*) BLACK JACOBIN E and SE Brazil

Colibri delphinae (*Lesson*) BROWN VIOLET-EAR Guatemala to Panama, and S America to Peru, Bolivia, Guyana and Trinidad / forest border and savannah

Colibri thalassinus (*Swainson*) GREEN VIOLET-EAR Mexico to Panama, and Andes from Venezuela to Bolivia/open mountain slopes

Colibri coruscans (*Gould*) GOULD'S or SPARKLING VIOLET-EAR Mountains from Venezuela to N Argentina and isolated peaks in Bolivar and Amazonas/open mountain slopes

[**Pinarolaema buckleyi** *Gould* (*Ann and Mag Nat Hist* V (1880) p 489) may be a colour phase]

Colibri serrirostris (*Vieillot*) WHITE-VENTED VIOLET-EAR E Bolivia, S Brazil and N Argentina/ scrub and savannah

Anthracothorax viridigula (*Boddaert*) GREEN-THROATED MANGO NE Venezuela, the Guianas and NE Brazil

Anthracothorax prevostii (*Lesson*) GREEN-BREASTED or PREVOST'S MANGO Mexico to Panama, Old Providence, St Andrews, and Venezuela through Colombia and W Ecuador to extreme NW Peru (*Lamprornis iridescens* Gould, formerly placed as a race of *A. nigricollis* is now considered a race of *prevostii*)

Anthracothorax veraguensis *Reichenbach* VERAGUAN MANGO Pacific slope of W Panama (treated by some authors as a race of *prevostii*)

Anthracothorax nigricollis (*Vieillot*) BLACK-THROATED MANGO E Panama and much of S America E of Andes S to N Argentina, also in N Colombia

Anthracothorax dominicus (*L*) DOMINICAN MANGO Hispaniola, Puerto Rico and adjacent small islands

Anthracorax viridis (*Audebert and Vieillot*) GREEN MANGO Interior of Puerto Rico (? St Thomas)

Anthracorax mango (*L*) JAMAICAN MANGO Jamaica

[**Crinis chlorolaemus** (*Elliot*) ELLIOT'S TOPAZ E Colombia and (?) SE Brazil/ generally considered to be a hybrid: *Anthrocothorax nigricollis* × *Chrysolampis mosquitus*]

Avocettula recurvirostris (*Swainson*) SWAINSON'S HUMMINGBIRD or FIERY-TAILED AWLBILL Guianas, SE Venezuela, NE Brazil and E Ecuador

Eulampis jugularis (*L*) PURPLE CARIB Lesser Antilles

Sericotis holosericeus (*L*) GREEN CARIB E Puerto Rico, Virgin Is and Lesser Antilles

Chrysolampis mosquitus (*L*) RUBY-TOPAZ HUMMINGBIRD Colombia, Venezuela, Guianas, Brazil and NE Bolivia

[**Chrysolampis gigliolii** *Oustalet* is an artifact]

Orthorhynchus cristatus (*L*) ANTILLEAN CRESTED HUMMINGBIRD Lesser Antilles and Virgin Is

Klais guimeti (*Bourcier*) VIOLET-CROWNED HUMMINGBIRD Sub-tropical zone from Nicaragua to W Venezuela and Bolivia

Abeillia abeillei (*Lesson and DeLattre*) ABEILLE'S HUMMINGBIRD SE Mexico to Nicaragua

Stephanoxis lalandi (*Vieillot*) PLOVERCREST S Brazil and NE Argentina

Lophornis ornata (*Boddaert*) TUFTED COQUETTE E Venezuela, Trinidad, Guianas, N Brazil

Lophornis gouldii (*Lesson*) GOULD'S or DOT-EARED COQUETTE N and C Brazil (Para to Mato Grosso)

Lophornis magnifica (*Vieillot*) FRILLED

COQUETTE C and S Brazil

Lophornis delattrei (*Lesson*) DE LATTRE'S or RUFOUS-CRESTED COQUETTE SW Mexico to Panama, and mts from Colombia to Bolivia

Lophornis stictolopha *Salvin and Elliot* SPANGLED COQUETTE Andes from W Venezuela to Peru

[**Lophornis melaniae** *Floericke* DUSKY COQUETTE Status doubtful, 1 specimen of uncertain origin; ? melanistic specimen of some known species]

Lophornis chalybea (*Vieillot*) FESTIVE COQUETTE Parts of Venezuela, Colombia, Ecuador, Peru, Bolivia: (SE Brazil = typical race; the other populations are sometimes considered specifically distinct as *L. verreauxii* 'Butterfly Coquette')/forest and scrub

Lophornis pavonina (*Salvin and Godman*) PEACOCK COQUETTE Isolated mountains in Guyana and Venezuela/forest

[**Lophornis insignibarbis** *Simon* BEARDED COQUETTE Known only from a Bogotá trade-skin, possibly a hybrid]

Paphosia helenae (*DeLattre*) PRINCESS HELENA'S COQUETTE Mexico to Costa Rica

Paphosia adorabilis (*Salvin*) ADORABLE COQUETTE SW Costa Rica and Chiriquí

Popelairia popelairii (*DuBus*) POPELAIRE'S or WIRE-CRESTED THORNTAIL E Colombia, E Ecuador and NE Peru/thickets

Popelairia langsdorffi (*Temminck*) BLACK-BREASTED or LANGSDORFF'S THORNTAIL Amazon basin and S Brazil/forest

Popelairia letitiae (*Bourcier and Mulsant*) COPPERY or LETITIA'S THORNTAIL Bolivia/ 2 ♂ specimens

Popelairia conversii (*Bourcier and Mulsant*) GREEN THORNTAIL Costa Rica, Panama, Colombia and W Ecuador/forest

Discosura longicauda (*Gmelin*) RACQUET TAIL Guianas, S Venezuela, N and E Brazil/ forest, scrub and savannah

Chlorestes notatus (*Reichenbach*) BLUE-CHINNED SAPPHIRE Trinidad, Tobago, N and E Venezuela, Guianas, Amazonian Colombia and Ecuador, and much of Brazil/forest and scrub

Chlorestes hypocyaneus (*Gould*) BLUE-BREASTED SAPPHIRE Brazil / unique / status doutbful, possibly a hybrid

Chlorestes subcaeruleus (*Elliot*) ELLIOT'S SAPPHIRE Brazil/? status (qv Elliot, *Ibis* (1874),

p 87 and Cory, *Catalogue of Birds of the Americas*, vol XIII, p 201)

Chlorostilbon mellisugus (*L*) BLUE-TAILED EMERALD (= **C. prasinus** (*Lesson*) of Peters' *Check List*, vol 5, and several other forms there listed. See de Schaunsee, *Birds of S America*, 1966, p 168 for remarks on this group) Much of northern S America/scrub and savannah

Chlorostilbon aureoventris (*d'Orbigny and Lafresnaye*) GLITTERING EMERALD E and S Brazil, Paraguay, Uruguay, Bolivia and N Argentina/scrub and savannah

Chlorostilbon assimilis *Lawrence* ALLIED EMERALD SW Costa Rica, Pearl Is and arid Pacific coast of Panama

Chlorostilbon canivetii (*Lesson*) CANIVET'S EMERALD Mexico, C America and offshore islands

Chlorostilbon ricordii (*Gervais*) CUBAN EMERALD Cuba, Isle of Pines and Bahamas

Chlorostilbon swainsonii (*Lesson*) HISPANIOLAN EMERALD Hispaniola and Gonave

Chlorostilbon maugaeus (*Audebert and Vieillot*) PUERTO RICAN EMERALD Puerto Rico

Chlorostilbon russatus (*Salvin and Godman*) COPPERY EMERALD Mts of Colombia and W Venezuela/forest edge and scrub

Chlorostilbon gibsoni (*Fraser*) RED-BELLIED EMERALD N Colombia and NW Venezuela scrub

Chlorostilbon inexpectatus (*Berlepsch*) BERLEPSCH'S EMERALD Bogotá (Colombia)/ unique/status uncertain

Chlorostilbon stenura (*Cabanis and Heine*) NARROW-TAILED EMERALD Mts of Colombia and Venezuela/scrub

Chlorostilbon alice (*Bourcier and Mulsant*) ALICE'S or GREEN-TAILED EMERALD Coast mts of Venezuela/scrub

[**Chlorostilbon micans** (*Salvin*) BRILLIANT EMERALD Unique, based on an old taken-down mount in the Gould Collection. This specimen is now generally ignored, but as it is so striking it seems best to retain it with a query, at least for the time being/no locality]

Chlorostilbon poortmani (*Bourcier*) SHORT-TAILED or POORTMAN'S EMERALD Venezuela and Colombia/scrub (there is a disagreement as to whether *poortmani* should be spelled with one n or two)

Chlorostilbon auratus (*Cabanis and Heine*) CABANIS' EMERALD Peru/unique/status doubtful

BURHINIDAE:
Esacus magnirostris,
Beach Curlew,
Beach Stone Curlew

BURHINIDAE:
Burhinus magnirostrus,
Bush Curlew,
Southern Stone-Curlew

Plate 100

GLAREOLIDAE: *Glareola maldivarum*, Oriental Pratincole, Eastern Collared Pratincole

Plate 101

Smaragdochrysis iridescens (*Gould*) IRIDESCENT EMERALD S Brazil/unique/believed to be a hybrid

Cynanthus sordidus (*Gould*) DUSKY HUMMINGBIRD W and S Mexico

Cynanthus latirostris *Swainson* BROAD-BILLED HUMMINGBIRD South-western USA and Mexico

Ptochoptera iolaema (*Reichenbach*) NATTERER'S EMERALD Ypanema, Brazil/unique/collected by Natterer/believed by Berlioz to be a hybrid, and by de Schaunsee as 'perhaps an artifact', though to accept the latter would presumably imply criticism of Natterer's honesty.

Cyanophaia bicolor (*Gmelin*) BLUE-HEADED HUMMINGBIRD Dominica, Martinique and (?) Guadeloupe [*Thalurania belli* Verrill (Dominica) placed in the synonomy, is believed to be a variety]

Thalurania furcata (*Gmelin*) FORK-TAILED WOODNYMPH Mexico to Panama, and most of the tropical lowlands of S America, S to N Argentina/forest, stream-banks and clearings [The following 4 forms are sometimes regarded as conspecific with *T. furcata* and sometimes given specific rank]:

> **Thalurania ridgwayi** *Nelson* MEXICAN WOODNYMPH W Jalisco, Mexico / ? unique
>
> **Thalurania fannyi** (*DeLattre and Bourcier*) GREEN-CROWNED WOODNYMPH Darien and Pacific slope of Colombia
>
> **Thalurania colombica** (*Bourcier*) BLUE-CROWNED WOODNYMPH N Colombia and NW Venezuela
>
> **Thalurania hypochlora** *Gould* EMERALD-BELLIED WOODNYMPH W Ecuador

Thalurania watertonii (*Bourcier*) WATERTON'S or LONG-TAILED WOODNYMPH Coastal Brazil (Para to Bahia)/forest and scrub

Thalurania glaucopis (*Gmelin*) VIOLET-CAPPED WOODNYMPH E and S Brazil, Paraguay, Uruguay and Missiones/forest

Thalurania lerchi *Mulsant and Verreaux* LERCH'S WOODNYMPH Known only from Bogotá trade-skins/possibly a hybrid

The following 7 species are probably referable to the genus *Thalurania*:

> **Eucephala scapulata** *Gould* BLACK-BELLIED WOODNYMPH Cayenne/unique/probably a hybrid

Eucephala caeruleolavata *Gould* REEVE'S WOODNYMPH Brazil/unique/status uncertain, possibly a hybrid

Augasma cyaneoberillina *Berlioz* (*L'Oiseau*, 35 (1965), p 7) BERLIOZ'S WOODNYMPH Bahia, Brazil/2 specimens, of uncertain status

Augasma smaragdinea *Gould* EMERALD WOODNYMPH Brazil/5 ♂♂/believed to be possibly hybrids

Augasma chlorophana *Simon* SOUTHERN WOODNYMPH SE Brazil/possibly the ♀ of *A. smaragdinea*

'Eucephela smaragdocaerulea' *Gould* Bahia/possibly a hybrid [This 'species' is omitted from Peters' *Check List* and from the Catalogue of Type Specimens of Birds in the British Museum (Natural History). Salvin in *Catalogue of Birds in British Museum* places it as a synonym of *Augasma smaragdinea*; de Schaunsee (1966) resurrected this name, following Berlioz, but apparently overlooking the fact that the type of *smaragdocaerulea* is the same specimen as the type of *smaragdinea*. A new name is therefore necessary for the specimen (in the British Museum) to which this is intended to apply]

Hylocharis chlorocephalus *Bourcier* GREEN-HEADED HUMMINGBIRD Known only from 1 specimen of uncertain origin

Neolesbia nehrkorni (*Berlepsch*) NEHRKORN'S HUMMINGBIRD Bogotá/2 specimens/possibly a hybrid

Panterbe insignis *Cabanis and Heine* IRAZU HUMMINGBIRD Highlands of Costa Rica and Panama, chiefly above 6,000ft (1,800m)

Damophila julie (*Bourcier*) JULIE'S or VIOLET-BELLIED HUMMINGBIRD Panama, N Colombia and W Ecuador

Lepidopyga coeruleogularis (*Gould*) SAPPHIRE-THROATED HUMMINGBIRD W Panama and N Colombia

Lepidopyga lilliae *Stone* SAPPHIRE-BELLIED HUMMINGBIRD Caribbean coast of Colombia/status uncertain

Lepidopyga goudoti (*Bourcier*) (includes **L. luminosa**) SHINING GREEN HUMMINGBIRD N Colombia and N Venezuela

Hylocharis xantusii (*Lawrence*) XANTUS'S HUMMINGBIRD S Baja California

Hylocharis leucotis (*Vieillot*) WHITE-EARED HUMMINGBIRD Mexico to Guatemala

Hylocharis eliciae (*Bourcier and Mulsant*) ELICIA'S SAPPHIRE S Mexico to Panama

Hylocharis sapphirina (*Gmelin*) RUFOUS-THROATED SAPPHIRE Much of S America E of Andes and S to N Argentina

Hylocharis cyanus (*Vieillot*) WHITE-CHINNED SAPPHIRE Amazon basin, N Colombia, Venezuela and the Guianas

Hylocharis chrysura (*Shaw*) GILDED HUMMINGBIRD E Bolivia, S Brazil, Paraguay, Uruguay and N Argentina

Hylocharis pyropygia (*Salvin and Godman*) FLAME-RUMPED SAPPHIRE Bahia/5 specimens

Hylocharis grayi (*DeLattre and Bourcier*) BLUE-HEADED SAPPHIRE E Panama and Pacific slope of Colombia to NW Ecuador

Chrysuronia oenone (*Lesson*) LESSON'S or GOLDEN-TAILED SAPPHIRE Trinidad (? extinct), Colombia, Venezuela, Upper Amazon basin and adjacent Andean slopes

Goldmania violiceps *Nelson* VIOLET-CAPPED or GOLDMAN'S HUMMINGBIRD E Panama and NW Colombia

Goethalsia bella *Nelson* PIRRE HUMMINGBIRD E Panama and NW Colombia

Trochilus polytmus *L* STREAMERTAIL Jamaica

Leucochloris albicollis (*Vieillot*) WHITE-THROATED HUMMINGBIRD SE Brazil, Paraguay and N Argentina

Leucochloris malvina (*Reichenbach*) REICHENBACH'S WHITE-THROATED HUMMINGBIRD SE Brazil / unique / possibly a hybrid

Polytmus guainumbi (*Pallas*) WHITE-TAILED GOLDENTHROAT Colombia, Venezuela, Trinidad, Guianas, E and C Brazil, Bolivia and Paraguay

Polytmus milleri (*Chapman*) TEPUI GOLDENTHROAT Upper slopes of mts of S Venezuela

Polytmus theresiae (*Da Silva Maia*) GREEN-TAILED GOLDENTHROAT Guianas, Venezuela, SE Colombia, Upper Amazon basin

Leucippus fallax (*Bourcier*) BUFFY HUMMINGBIRD Arid Caribbean coast of Colombia, Venezuela and adjacent islands

Leucippus baeri *Simon* TUMBES HUMMINGBIRD Arid coast of Peru

Leucippus taczanowskii (*Sclater*) SPOT-THROATED HUMMINGBIRD N and C Peru

Leucippus chlorocercus *Gould* OLIVE-SPOTTED HUMMINGBIRD E Peru, SE Ecuador and W Brazil

Taphrospilus hypostictus (*Gould*) MANY-SPOTTED HUMMINGBIRD E Ecuador, Peru, E Bolivia, SW Brazil and NW Argentina

Amazilia viridicauda (*Berlepsch*) GREEN AND WHITE HUMMINGBIRD Peru

Amazilia chionogaster (*Tschudi*) WHITE-BELLIED HUMMINGBIRD N Peru to Mato Grosso and N Argentina

Amazilia candida (*Bourcier and Mulsant*) WHITE-BELLIED EMERALD Mexico to Costa Rica

Amazilia chionopectus (*Gould*) WHITE-CHESTED EMERALD E Venezuela, Trinidad and the Guianas

Amazilia versicolor (*Vieillot*) VERSICOLOURED EMERALD Irregularly distributed through S America E of Andes and S to N Argentina [*A. hollandi* (*Todd*) is now regarded as a race]

Amazilia luciae (*Lawrence*) LUCY'S EMERALD Honduras / only a few specimens

Amazilia fimbriata (*Gmelin*) GLITTERING-THROATED EMERALD S America E of Andes and S to Paraguay

Amazilia distans *Wetmore and Phelps* (*Proc Bio Soc Wash*, 69 (1956), p 4) TACHIRA EMERALD Tachira, Venezuela

Amazilia lactea (*Lesson*) SAPPHIRE-SPANGLED EMERALD Bolivar, E and S Peru, N Bolivia, E Brazil

Amazilia amabilis (*Gould*) BLUE-CHESTED or LOVELY HUMMINGBIRD Pacific Colombia and W Ecuador, Darien

Amazilia decora (*Salvin*) CHARMING HUMMINGBIRD Nicaragua to Panama (often treated as conspecific with the preceding)

Amazilia cyaneotincta (*Gounelle*) BLUE-SPOTTED HUMMINGBIRD Known from 2 Bogotá trade-skins

Amazilia rosenbergi (*Boucard*) PURPLE-CHESTED or ROSENBERG'S HUMMINGBIRD W Colombia and W Ecuador

Amazilia boucardi (*Mulsant*) MANGROVE HUMMINGBIRD Pacific slope of Costa Rica

Amazilia franciae (*Bourcier and Mulsant*) ANDEAN EMERALD Andes from Colombia to N Peru

[**Amazilia veneta** (*Simon*) based on a single Bogotá trade-skin is believed to be a melanistic ♀ of *A. franciae*]

Amazilia leucogaster (*Gmelin*) PLAIN-BELLIED EMERALD The Guianas, N and E Brazil, Venezuela

Amazilia cyanocephala (*Lesson*) AZURE-

STERCORARIIDAE:
Stercorarius pomarinus,
Pomarine Jaeger

STERCORARIIDAE:
Catharcta lonnbergi,
Lönnberg's Skua

Plate 102

LARIDAE:
Chlidonias hybrida,
Whiskered Tern

LARIDAE:
Larus novaehollandiae,
Silver Gull

Plate 103

CROWNED HUMMINGBIRD S Mexico to N Nicaragua

Amazilia microrhyncha (*Elliot*) SMALL-BILLED AZURECROWN ? Honduras / ? unique

Amazilia cyanifrons (*Bourcier*) INDIGO-CAPPED HUMMINGBIRD N Colombia

Amazilia alfaroana *Underwood* ALFARO'S or UNDERWOOD'S HUMMINGBIRD Costa Rica / unique / often placed as race of *cyanifrons*

Amazilia beryllina (*Lichtenstein*) BERYLLINE HUMMINGBIRD Mexico, Guatemala, W Honduras and El Salvador

Amazilia cyanura *Gould* BLUE-TAILED HUMMINGBIRD Pacific C America from Guatemala to Costa Rica

Amazilia saucerrottei (*DeLattre and Bourcier*) BLUE-VENTED HUMMINGBIRD Nicaragua, Costa Rica, Colombia and W Venezuela

Amazilia tobaci (*Gmelin*) COPPER-RUMPED HUMMINGBIRD Venezuela, Trinidad, Tobago, (? Grenada)

Amazilia viridigaster (*Bourcier*) GREEN-BELLIED HUMMINGBIRD Andes of W Colombia, mts of Venezuela and Guyana

[**Amazilia inculta** (*Elliot*) Bogotá / believed to be a melanistic variety of *viridigaster*]

Amazilia edward (*DeLattre and Bourcier*) WHITE-BELLIED HUMMINGBIRD Panama, SW Costa Rica and Pearl Is

[**Amazilia ocai** *Gould* DE OCA'S HUMMINGBIRD Vera Cruz / stated to be a hybrid

[**Amazilia lerdi** (*d'Oca*) 'The true identity of this form is a mystery' (Peters' *Check List*, 5, p 72 footnote)]

[**Amazilia florenceae** (*van Rossem and Hachisuka*) Santa Barbara, Sonora / unique / ? hybrid

Amazilia rutila (*DeLattre*) CINNAMON HUMMINGBIRD Mexico to Costa Rica

Amazilia yucatanensis (*Cabot*) BUFF-BELLIED HUMMINGBIRD Mexico, Lower Rio Grande Valley in Texas, Belise and parts of Guatemala

Amazilia tzacatl (*De la Llave*) RUFOUS-TAILED HUMMINGBIRD Mexico through C America, Colombia, W Ecuador and mts of Merida (Venezuela)

Amazilia handleyi *Wetmore* (*Smithsonian Misc Coll*, vol 145, p 3) HANDLEY'S HUMMINGBIRD Isla Escudo de Veraguas, Bocas del Toro, Panama / no data / de Schaunsee

in *Birds of S America* (1966) says that *handleyi* is probably a race of *tzacatl*

Amazilia castaneiventris (*Gould*) CHESTNUT-BELLIED HUMMINGBIRD E Andes of Colombia

Amazilia amazilia (*Lesson*) AMAZILIA HUMMINGBIRD Ecuador and Peru

Amazilia violiceps (*Gould*) VIOLET-CROWNED HUMMINGBIRD Mexico

[Edwards resuscitates *Cyanomyia viridifrons* Elliot from the synonomy of the typical race of *A. violiceps* and gives it specific rank as 'Green-fronted Hummingbird' (qv Griscom and Moore 1950, *Pacific Coast, Avifauna*, vol 29, pt 1, p 173)]

The following species of *Amazilia* are placed by Peters in a note, and considered to be questionable:

Amazilia elegans (*Gould*) Unique, no locality

Amazilia neglectus (*Elliot*) Bolivia / unique / stated to be an artifact, also considered a hybrid

Amazilia aenobrunnea *Chapman* Bogotá trade-skin / unique / stated to be an artifact

Amazilia lucida *Elliot* Colombia / unique

Amazilia salvini (*Brewster*) Sonora / stated to be a hybrid

Amazilia bangsi (*Ridgway*) Costa Rica / stated to be a hybrid

[**Amazilia caeruleiceps** (*Gould*) Colombia / stated to be a hybrid (see Cory, *Catalogue of Birds of the Americas*, pt 2, no 1, p 175 footnote)]

Eupherusa eximia (*DeLattre*) STRIPE-TAILED HUMMINGBIRD S Mexico to W Panama

Eupherusa cyanophrys *Rowley and Orr* (*Condor* (1964) vol 66, p 82) OAXACA HUMMINGBIRD SW Oaxaca, Mexico. Mayr treats this as a race of *E. poliocerea* which is itself here regarded (following Peters and Edwards) as a race of *eximia* (Mayr, *Journal für Ornithologie* (1971), p 311)

Eupherusa nigriventris *Lawrence* BLACK-BELLIED HUMMINGBIRD Caribbean slope of Costa Rica, Chiriqui and Veraguas

Elvira chionura (*Gould*) WHITE-TAILED EMERALD SW Costa Rica, Chiriqui and Veraguas

Elvira cupreiceps (*Lawrence*) COPPERY-HEADED EMERALD Caribbean slope of Costa Rica 1,500–3,000ft (450–900m)

Microchera albocoronata (*Lawrence*)

SNOWCAP Caribbean slope of Nicaragua, Costa Rica and Panama

Chalybura buffonii (*Lesson*) WHITE-VENTED or BUFFON'S PLUMETEER E Panama, Colombia, N Venezuela and SW Ecuador (the last population, *C. intermedia*, may possibly be a separate species as may *C. caeruleogaster* of E Andes of Colombia)

Chalybura urochrysia (*Gould*) BRONZE-TAILED or GOULD'S PLUMETEER Nicaragua to Panama, W Colombia and NW Ecuador

Aphantochroa cirrochloris (*Vieillot*) SOMBRE HUMMINGBIRD C and E Brazil

Lamprornis clemenciae (*Lesson*) BLUE-THROATED HUMMINGBIRD Mexico and southwestern USA

Lamprornis amethystinus *Swainson* AMETHYST-THROATED HUMMINGBIRD Mexico and mts of Guatemala, El Salvador and Honduras

Lamprornis viridipallens (*Bourcier and Mulsant*) GREEN-THROATED MOUNTAIN GEM Mts of Chiapas, Guatemala, Honduras, El Salvador and Nicaragua

Lamprornis hemileucus (*Salvin*) WHITE-BELLIED MOUNTAIN GEM Caribbean slope of Costa Rica and W Panama 2,000–4,000ft (600–1,200m)

Lamprornis calolaema (*Salvin*) PURPLE-THROATED MOUNTAIN GEM Mts of N and C Costa Rica, W Nicaragua and W Panama

Lamprornis castaneoventris (*Gould*) WHITE-THROATED MOUNTAIN GEM Mts of SW Costa Rica and W Panama [for a discussion on the *calolaema-castaneoventris* group see Slud, 'Birds of Costa Rica' in *Bull Amer Mus Nat Hist*, vol 128 (1964), pp 159–60 and Blake, *Fieldiana Zool* (1958), pp 519–21]

Lamprolaima rhami (*Lesson*) GARNET-THROATED HUMMINGBIRD Mts of S Mexico, Guatemala, Honduras and N El Salvador

Adelomyia melanogenys (*Fraser*) SPECKLED HUMMINGBIRD Andes from Venezuela to Bolivia and NW Argentina

Anthocephala floriceps (*Gould*) BLOSSOMCROWN Mts of Colombia

Urosticte benjamini (*Bourcier*) WHITETIP W Colombia, Ecuador and NE Peru (*U. ruficrissa* Lawrence, is sometimes considered distinct)

Phlogophilus hemileucurus *Gould* ECUADOREAN PIEDTAIL E Ecuador

Phlogophilus harterti *Berlepsch and Stolzmann* PERUVIAN PIEDTAIL SE Peru

Clytolaema rubricauda (*Boddaert*) BRAZILIAN RUBY SE Brazil

Polyplancta aurescens (*Gould*) GOULD'S JEWELFRONT E Ecuador, E Peru, S Venezuela and Amazonian Brazil

Heliodoxa rubinoides (*Bourcier and Mulsant*) LILACTHROAT and ROSYTHROAT Andes of Colombia and W Ecuador

Heliodoxa leadbeateri (*Bourcier*) LEADBEATER'S or VIOLET-FRONTED BRILLIANT Mts from Venezuela to Bolivia

Heliodoxa jacula *Gould* GREEN-CROWNED BRILLIANT Costa Rica, Panama, Colombia and W Ecuador

Heliodoxa xanthogonys *Salvin and Godman* YELLOW-CHEEKED or VELVET-BROWED BRILLIANT Mts of S Venezuela, Guyana and Venezuelan border of N Brazil

Heliodoxa schreibersii (*Bourcier*) BLACK-THROATED or SCHREIBER'S HUMMINGBIRD E Ecuador, E Peru and W Brazil

Heliodoxa gularis (*Gould*) PUCE-THROATED HUMMINGBIRD E Ecuador and NE Peru

Heliodoxa branickii (*Taczanowski*) RUFOUS-WEBBED BRILLIANT Peru (also 2 specimens supposedly from N Bolivia)

Heliodoxa imperatrix (*Gould*) EMPRESS HUMMINGBIRD W Colombia to NW Ecuador

Eugenes fulgens (*Swainson*) RIVOLI'S HUMMINGBIRD Mts from S Arizona and New Mexico through Mexico and C America to Panama

Hylonympha macrocerca *Gould* SCISSOR-TAILED HUMMINGBIRD Paria Peninsula, Venezuela [for a summary of all that is known of this species see Phelps and Phelps jr, *Auk* 65 (1948), pp 62–5]

Sternoclyta cyanopectus (*Gould*) VIOLET-CHESTED HUMMINGBIRD Andes of N and W Venezuela

Topaza pella (*L*) CRIMSON TOPAZ The Guianas, S Venezuela, E Ecuador, Brazil round mouth of Amazon

Topaza pyra (*Gould*) FIERY TOPAZ E Ecuador, Rio Negro region of Brazil, Venezuela, Colombia, NE Peru

Oreotrochilus estella (*d'Orbigny and Lafresnaye*) ESTELLA'S or ANDEAN HILLSTAR Andes from Ecuador to Chile and Argentina (3 other species, formerly considered distinct: *O. chimborazo*, *O. stolzmanni* and *O. bolivianus*,

LARIDAE: *Sterna striata*, White-fronted Tern

Opposite:
Larus novaehollandiae,
Silver Gull

Plate 104

Plate 105

are now considered to be conspecific with this species)

Oreotrochilus leucopleurus *Gould* WHITE-SIDED HILLSTAR Andes of SE Bolivia, Chile and Argentina

Oreotrochilus melanogaster *Gould* BLACK-BREASTED HILLSTAR Andes of Peru

Oreotrochilus adela (*d'Orbigny and Lafresnaye*) ADELA'S or WEDGE-TAILED HILLSTAR Mts of C Bolivia

Urochroa bougueri (*Bourcier*) WHITE-TAILED HILLSTAR Colombia and Ecuador

Patagona gigas (*Vieillot*) GIANT HUMMINGBIRD Andes from Ecuador to Chile and W Argentina

Aglaeactis cupripennis (*Bourcier*) SHINING SUNBEAM Andes of Colombia, Ecuador and Peru

Aglaeactis aliciae *Salvin* ALICE'S or PURPLE-BACKED SUNBEAM N Peru

Aglaeactis castelnaudii (*Bourcier and Mulsant*) CASTELNAU'S or WHITE-TUFTED SUNBEAM C Peru

Aglaeactis pamela (*d'Orbigny*) PAMELA'S or BLACK-HOODED SUNBEAM Andes of Bolivia

Lafresnaya lafresnayi (*Boissoneau*) VELVET BREAST Andes from Venezuela to Peru (*Trochilus gayi* Bourcier and Mulsant, ascribed to this genus, is generally regarded as un-identifiable)

Pterophanes cyanopterus (*Fraser*) SAPPHIREWING Andes from Colombia to Bolivia

Coeligena coeligena (*Lesson*) BRONZE INCA Andes from Venezuela to Bolivia

Coeligena wilsoni (*DeLattre and Bourcier*) BROWN INCA Andes of SW Colombia and NW Ecuador

Coeligena prunellei (*Bourcier*) BLACK INCA E Andes of Colombia

Coeligena torquata (*Boissoneau*) COLLARED INCA Andes from Venezuela to Bolivia

Coeligena phalerata (*Bangs*) WHITE-TAILED STAR-FRONTLET Santa Marta Mts, Colombia

Coeligena bonapartei (*Boissoneau*) GOLDEN STAR-FRONTLET Andes of NW Venezuela and E Colombia

Coeligena orina *Wetmore* (*Smithsonian Misc Coll*, 122, no 8 (1953), p 4) DUSKY STAR-FRONTLET W Colombia / known only from ♂ specimens

Coeligena helianthea (*Lesson*) BLUE-THROATED STAR-FRONTLET Andes of E Colombia

and W Venezuela

Coeligena lutetiae (*DeLattre and Bourcier*) COMTE DE PARIS'S BUFF-WINGED STAR-FRONTLET Andes of Colombia and Ecuador

Coeligena violifer (*Gould*) VIOLET-FRONTED STAR-FRONTLET Andes of Peru and Bolivia

Coeligena iris (*Gould*) RAINBOW STAR-FRONTLET Andes of Ecuador and Peru

[**Coeligena traviesi** *Mulsant and Verreaux* TRAVIE'S INCA or LILAC-SPOTTED STAR-FRONTLET Several Bogotá trade-skins / stated to be possibly a hybrid]

[**Coeligena purpurea** *Gould* PURPLE INCA Popayan, Colombia / 2 specimens / possibly a hybrid]

[**Apatelosia lawrencei** (*Boucard*) LAWRENCE'S INCA Bogotá trade skin / unique / probably a hybrid]

Ensifera ensifera (*Boissoneau*) SWORD-BILLED HUMMINGBIRD Andes from Venezuela to Bolivia

Sephanoides sephanoides (*Lesson*) GREEN-BACKED FIRECROWN Chile and W Argentina, S to Tierra del Fuego, Chiloe and Mas Atierra

Sephanoides fernandensis (*King*) FERNANDEZ FIRECROWN Juan Fernandez Is of Mas Atierra and Mas Afuerra

Boissonneaua flavescens (*Loddiges*) BUFF-TAILED CORONET Andes of Venezuela, Colombia and Ecuador

Boissonneaua matthewsii (*Bourcier*) CHESTNUT-BREASTED or MATTHEWS CORONET Ecuador, Peru and SW Colombia

Boissonneaua jardini (*Bourcier*) JARDINE'S or VELVET-PURPLE CORONET Andes of W Colombia and W Ecuador

Heliangelus mavors *Gould* MAVORS or ORANGE-THROATED SUNANGEL Andes of NW Venezuela and E Colombia

Heliangelus spencei (*Bourcier*) MERIDA or SPENCER'S SUNANGEL Andes of Merida, Venezuela

Heliangelus amethysticollis (*d'Orbigny and Lafresnaye*) AMETHYSTINE SUNANGEL Andes from Venezuela to Bolivia [included in *amethysticollis* are *H. clarisse* (Longuemare) and *H. claudia* Hartert, the latter being apparently an aberration of *clarisse*]

Heliangelus strophianus (*Gould*) GORGETED SUNANGEL SW Colombia and NW Ecuador

[**Heliangelus violicollis** *Salvin* SARAYACU SUNANGEL Known from 2 specimens of uncertain origin (? Ecuador)/status dubious, but usually dismissed as an aberration of *H. strophianus*]

Heliangelus exortis (*Fraser*) PARZUDAKI'S or TOURMALINE SUNANGEL Andes from Colombia to Peru

Heliangelus viola (*Gould*) PURPLE-THROATED or VIOLA SUNANGEL W Ecuador and Peru

Heliangelus micrastur *Gould* GOULD'S SUNANGEL S Ecuador and Peru

The following species of *Heliangelus* are listed as species by Peters in *Check List*, vol 5, pp 107–8, but regarded as hybrids by de Schaunsee *Birds of South America*, 1966:

Heliangelus squamigularis *Gould* OLIVE-THROATED SUNANGEL Colombia

Heliangelus speciosus (*Salvin*) GREEN-THROATED SUNANGEL Bogotá trade-skins

Heliangelus rothschildi *Boucard* ROTHSCHILD'S SUNANGEL 2 Bogotá trade-skins. *Aeronympha prosantis* Oberholzer is usually synonymised with this form, but pencil m/s note in British Museum (Natural History) copy of Cory, *Catalogue of Birds of the Americas*, p 267, says that the two are quite different

Heliangelus luminosus (*Elliot*) GLISTENING SUNANGEL Bogotá trade-skins

[**Heliangelus dubius** *Hartert* HARTERT'S SUNANGEL Colombia / unique / Bogotá trade-skin / stated by Simon, *Hist Nat des Trochilidae* (1921) to be a melanistic form of *H. clarissae*]

Eriocnemis nigrivestis (*Bourcier and Mulsant*) BLACK-BREASTED PUFFLEG N Ecuador

Eriocnemis vestitus (*Lesson*) GLOWING PUFFLEG NW Venezuela, Colombia and W Ecuador

Eriocnemis godini (*Bourcier*) TURQUOISE-THROATED or GODIN'S PUFFLEG NW Ecuador and Bogotá trade-skins

[**Eriocnemis soderstromi** *Butler* SÖDERSTRÖM'S PUFFLEG Mt Pinchcha, Ecuador/unique/status doubtful, possibly an aberration of *H. godini*]

Eriocnemis cupreoventris (*Fraser*) COPPER-VENTED PUFFLEG NW Venezuela and E Colombia

Eriocnemis luciani (*Bourcier*) SAPPHIRE-VENTED PUFFLEG Ecuador and Peru

[**Eriocnemis isaacsonii** (*Parzudaki*) ISAACSON'S PUFFLEG 3 Bogotá trade specimens,

differing slightly/believed to be a hybrid]

Eriocnemis mosquera (*DeLattre and Bourcier*) GOLDEN-BREASTED or MOSQUERA'S PUFFLEG Andes of Colombia and N Ecuador

Eriocnemis glaucopoides (*d'Orbigny and Lafresnaye*) D'ORBIGNY'S or BLUE-CAPPED PUFFLEG Andes of Bolivia and NW Argentina

Eriocnemis mirabilis *de Schaunsee* (*Not Natural*, no 402 (1967), p 1) COLOURFUL PUFFLEG W Andes of Cauca, Colombia/forest

Eriocnemis alinae (*Bourcier*) EMERALD-BELLIED PUFFLEG Andes of Colombia, Ecuador and Peru

Eriocnemis derbyi (*DeLattre and Bourcier*) BLACK-THIGHED or DERBY'S PUFFLEG Andes of Colombia and N Ecuador

Haplophaedia aureliae (*Bourcier and Mulsant*) GREENISH PUFFLEG Darien, and Andes from Colombia to Peru

Haplophaedia lugens (*Gould*) HOARY PUFFLEG Andes of W Colombia and NW Ecuador

Ocreatus underwoodii (*Lesson*) BOOTED RACQUETTAIL Andes from Venezuela to Bolivia

Lesbia victoriae (*Bourcier and Mulsant*) BLACK-TAILED TRAINBEARER Colombia, Ecuador and Peru

Lesbia nuna (*Lesson*) GREEN-TAILED TRAINBEARER Andes from Venezuela to Bolivia

Sappho sparganura (*Shaw*) SAPPHO COMET Andes of Bolivia, N Chile and NW Argentina

Polyonymus caroli (*Bourcier*) BRONZE-TAILED COMET Andes of Peru

[**Zodalia glyceria** (*Gould*) and **Zodalia ortoni** (*Lawrence*) PURPLE-TAILED COMET Colombia and Ecuador/believed to represent respectively the immature ♂ and adult ♂ of a hybrid]

Ramphomicron microrhynchum (*Boissoneau*) PURPLE-BACKED THORNBILL Andes of Venezuela, Colombia, Ecuador and Peru

Ramphomicron dorsale *Salvin and Godman* BLACK-BACKED THORNBILL Santa Marta Mountains of Colombia

Metallura phoebe (*Lesson and DeLattre*) BLACK METALTAIL Andes of Peru and Bolivia

Metallura theresiae *Simon* COPPER METALTAIL N Peru

Metallura aenocauda (*Gould*) BRASSY or SCALED METALTAIL S Peru and Bolivia

Metallura eupogon (*Cabanis*) FIRE-THROATED METALTAIL Andes of Peru

Metallura malagae *Berlepsch* BOLIVIAN

Plate 106

Opposite:
LARIDAE:
Larus fuscus,
Lesser Black-backed Gull

ALCIDAE:
Alca torda,
Razorbill

ALCIDAE:
Fratercula arctica,
Atlantic Puffin

Plate 107

METALTAIL Bolivia known only from a few specimens / ? race of *aenocauda*

Metallura baroni *Salvin* VIOLET-THROATED METALTAIL Andes of Ecuador

Metallura williami (*DeLattre and Bourcier*) VIRIDIAN METALTAIL Andes of Colombia and Ecuador

Metallura tyrianthina (*Loddiges*) TYRIAN METALTAIL Mts from Venezuela to Bolivia

Metallura iracunda *Wetmore* (*Smithsonian Misc Coll*, no 106 (1947), p 3) PERIJÁ METALTAIL Perijá Mts of Colombia and Venezuela

Chalcostigma ruficeps (*Gould*) RUFOUS-CAPPED THORNBILL Andes from SE Ecuador to Bolivia

[**Chalcostigma purpureicauda** *Hartert* PURPLE-TAILED THORNBILL 2 specimens, Ecuador and Bogotá trade-skin / believed to be a hybrid]

Chalcostgima olivaceum (*Lawrence*) OLIVACEOUS THORNBILL Mts of Peru and Bolivia

Chalcostigma stanleyi (*Bourcier*) BLUE-MANTLED or STANLEY'S THORNBILL Mts of Ecuador, Peru and Bolivia

Chalcostigma heteropogon (*Boissoneau*) BRONZE-TAILED THORNBILL Andes of E Colombia and W Venezuela

Chalcostigma herrani (*DeLattre and Bourcier*) RAINBOW-BEARDED or HERRAN'S THORNBILL Andes of Colombia and W Ecuador

Oxypogon guerinii (*Boissoneau*) BEARDED HELMETCREST Mts of Colombia and NW Venezuela

Opisthoprora euryptera (*Loddiges*) LODDIGES' THORNBILL or MOUNTAIN AVOCETBILL Andes of Colombia and NE Ecuador

Taphrolesbia griseiventris (*Taczanowski*) GREY-BELLIED COMET Mts of Peru

Aglaiocercus kingi (*Lesson*) LONG-TAILED SYLPH (BLUE-TAILED and GREEN-TAILED SYLPHS) Mts from Venezuela to Bolivia

Aglaiocercus coelestis (*Gould*) HEAVENLY or VIOLET-TAILED SYLPH Colombia and Ecuador [NB: The arrangement of the genus *Aglaiocercus* is debatable, a number of species have been described, but are sometimes considered to be conspecific. I am following de Schaunsee *Birds of S America*, 1966, and see p 189 of that work for his comments]

Oreonympha nobilis *Gould* BEARDED MOUNTAINEER Andes of Peru

Augastes scutatus (*Temminck*) HYACINTH VISORBEARER Brazilian plateau

Augastes lumachellus (*Lesson*) HOODED VISORBEARER Brazilian plateau

Schistes geoffroyi (*Bourcier*) WEDGE-BILLED HUMMINGBIRD Mts from Venezuela to Bolivia

Heliothryx barroti (*Bourcier*) PURPLE-CROWNED FAIRY Mexico to Panama, Colombia and Ecuador

Heliothryx aurita (*Gmelin*) BLACK-EARED FAIRY Amazon and Upper Orinoco basins, the Guianas

Heliactin cornuta (*Wied*) SUNGEM C and E Brazil

Loddigesia mirabilis (*Bourcier*) LODDIGES' SPATULETAIL Andes of N Peru

Heliomaster constantii (*DeLattre*) CONSTANT or PLAIN-CAPPED STARTHROAT Mexico to Costa Rica

Heliomaster longirostris (*Audebert and Vieillot*) LONG-BILLED STARTHROAT Mexico to Panama, and much of tropical S America E of Andes and S to Bolivia and Mato Grosso

Heliomaster squamosus (*Temminck*) STRIPE-BREASTED STARTHROAT E Brazil

Heliomaster furcifer (*Shaw*) ANGELA or BLUE-TUFTED STARTHROAT Colombia in Amazonas, S Brazil, Bolivia, Paraguay, Uruguay and N Argentina

Rhodopis vesper (*Lesson*) EVENING or OASIS HUMMINGBIRD Peru and N Chile

Thaumastura cora (*Lesson*) CORA or PERUVIAN SHEARTAIL W Peru

Philodice bryante (*Lawrence*) COSTA RICAN WOODSTAR Highlands of Costa Rica and W Panama

Philodice mitchellii (*Bourcier*) MITCHELL'S or PURPLE-THROATED WOODSTAR Colombia and W Ecuador

Doricha enicura (*Vieillot*) SLENDER SHEARTAIL Highlands of Chiapas, Guatemala and El Salvador

Doricha eliza (*Lesson and DeLattre*) MEXICAN SHEARTAIL S Mexico

Tilmatura dupontii (*Lesson*) DUPONT'S HUMMINGBIRD S Mexico to Nicaragua

Microstilbon burmeisteri (*Sclater*) BURMEISTER'S or SLENDER-TAILED WOODSTAR Bolivia and N Argentina

Calothorax lucifer (*Swainson*) LUCIFER HUMMINGBIRD S Arizona, W Texas and Mexico

Calothorax pulcher *Gould* BEAUTIFUL HUMMINGBIRD S Mexico

Archilochus colubris (*L*) RUBY-THROATED HUMMINGBIRD- Eastern N America w Caribbean area

Archilochus alexandri (*Bourcier and Mulsant*) BLACK-CHINNED HUMMINGBIRD Western N America w Mexico

[**Trochilus violajugulum** *Jeffries* VIOLET-THROATED HUMMINGBIRD Santa Barbara, California / generally considered to be a hybrid *Calypte* × *Archilochus*]

Caliphlox amethystina (*Boddaert*) AMETHYST WOODSTAR Locally in S America E of Andes and S to N Argentina (Cory in *Catalogue of Birds of the Americas*, p 293 (footnote) suggests that *Ornismya othura* Lesson, which he places in the synonomy of *C. amethystina* with a query, may possibly be a distinct form)

Caliphlox evelynae (*Bourcier*) BAHAMA WOODSTAR Bahama Is

Mellisuga helenae (*Lembeye*) BEE HUMMINGBIRD Cuba and Isle of Pines

Mellisuga minima (*L*) VERVAIN HUMMINGBIRD Jamaica, Hispaniola, Gonave and Tortue

Calypte costae (*Bourcier*) COSTA'S HUMMINGBIRD South-western USA w into Mexico

Calypte anna (*Lesson*) ANNA'S HUMMINGBIRD California and N Baja California

Stellula calliope (*Gould*) CALLIOPE HUMMINGBIRD Western N America from S British Columbia to N Baja California

Atthis heloisa (*Lesson and DeLattre*) BUMBLEBEE HUMMINGBIRD Mexico, Guatemala and Honduras (*A. elliotti* Ridgway is sometimes separated)

Myrtis fanny (*Lesson*) FANNY'S or PURPLE-COLLARED WOODSTAR S Ecuador and Peru/ woodland and semi-arid land

Eulidia yarrellii (*Bourcier*) YARRELL'S or CHILEAN WOODSTAR Coasts of N Chile/arid country and gardens

Myrmia micrura (*Gould*) SHORT-TAILED WOODSTAR Arid portions of W Ecuador and W Peru

Acestrura mulsant (*Bourcier*) MULSANT'S or WHITE-BELLIED WOODSTAR Andes from Colombia to Bolivia/forest and scrub

[**Acestrura decorata** (*Gould*) DECORATED WOODSTAR Colombia / unique / possibly a hybrid]

Acestrura bombus (*Gould*) LITTLE WOODSTAR W Ecuador and N Peru/forest and scrub

Acestrura heliodor (*Bourcier*) HELIODOR'S or GORGETED WOODSTAR Mts of Venezuela, Colombia and Ecuador, E Panama / forest and scrub

Acestrura berlepschi (*Simon*) ESMERALDAS or BERLEPSCH'S WOODSTAR W Ecuador

[**Acestrura harterti** (*Simon*) HARTERT'S WOODSTAR C Andes of Colombia / unique/ possibly a hybrid]

Chaetocercus jourdanii (*Bourcier*) JOURDAN'S or RUFOUS-SHAFTED WOODSTAR Mts of Venezuela and E Colombia, Trinidad/ forest and scrub

Selasphorus platycercus (*Swainson*) BROAD-TAILED HUMMINGBIRD Mts of central USA w Mexico, sedentary race in mts of W Guatemala

Selasphorus rufus (*Gmelin*) RUFOUS HUMMINGBIRD Alaska to California w Mexico

Selasphorus sasin (*Lesson*) ALLEN'S HUMMINGBIRD Coasts of California and Santa Barbara Islands w Mexico

Selasphorus flammula *Salvin* VOLCANO HUMMINGBIRD High volcanoes of Costa Rica

Selasphorus torridus (*Salvin*) TORRID or HELIOTROPE-THROATED HUMMINGBIRD High volcanoes of Costa Rica and W Panama

Selasphorus simoni *Carriker* SIMON'S or CERISE-THROATED HUMMINGBIRD Volcanoes of Costa Rica

Selasphorus ardens *Salvin* GLOW-THROATED HUMMINGBIRD Highlands of W Panama

Selasphorus scintilla (*Gould*) SCINTILLANT HUMMINGBIRD Highlands of Costa Rica and W Panama. Peters, in *Birds of the World*, vol 5, p 142 (footnote) comments that he has given these last 4 specific rank mainly for lack of knowledge, their relationships are not clear, and some of them may well prove to be merely aberrations. Slud in 'Birds of Costa Rica' *Bull Am Mus Nat Hist*, 128 (1964), pp 163–4 considers *torridus* to be a colour morph of *flammula*, but no further definite information seems to be available on the others.

[**Selasphorus floresii** *Gould* FLORESI'S HUMMINGBIRD California and Mexico/ now considered to be a hybrid]

COLIIDAE Colies or Mousebirds Slender greyish birds with long, thin tails, not obviously related to any other group. Arboreal, they

COLUMBIDAE: *Phaps chalcoptera,*
Common Bronzewing

COLUMBIDAE:
Petrophassa plumifera,
White-bellied Plumed Pigeon

COLUMBIDAE:
Turtur tympanistria,
Tambourine Dove

Opposite:
COLUMBIDAE:
Ptilinopus superbus,
Superb Dove,
Superb Fruit Dove

Plate 108

Plate 109

scuttle, rodent-like, among the foliage, feeding on insects, buds, leaves and fruit. Outer toes reversible. Gregarious. Nest a platform of twigs in trees, surmounted by a lined cup of grasses, leaves etc. Eggs 2–4, rarely up to 7, white. Incubation, by both sexes, 12–14 days. Young leave the nest after a few days and can fly at 17–21 days. Six species, confined to Africa.

Colius striatus *Gmelin* SPECKLED MOUSEBIRD Africa S of Sahara / n tree or creeper / e 3/ I 11–13/ F 16–18

Colius castanotus *Verreaux and Verreaux* RED-BACKED MOUSEBIRD Angola

Colius colius (*L*) WHITE-BACKED MOUSEBIRD S Africa/n tree or creeper/e 3/I 11–13/F 16–18

Colius leucocephalus *Reichenow* WHITE-HEADED MOUSEBIRD Kenya, Tanganyika and S Somaliland

Colius indicus *Latham* RED-FACED MOUSEBIRD Parts of S and SE Africa/n tree or creeper/e 3

Colius macrourus (*L*) BLUE-NAPED MOUSEBIRD WC and E Africa/n tree/e 2–4

TROGONIDAE Trogons Brightly-coloured sedentary forest birds with broad, flat bills and weak feet. The feathers are soft and fluffy and the skin very thin and tender. Mostly sexually dimorphic. Feed on insects and fruit. They have a fast, twisting flight, but seldom fly for any distance. Nest in a hole in a tree, eggs 2–4, white, buff, or greenish-blue. Incubation about 19 days. Fledging period 15–23 days. Forests of the tropics.

Pharomachrus mocinno *de la Llave* QUETZAL C America / mountain forests / insects, fruits, frogs etc/n hole/e 2/I ♂♀ 17–18

Pharomachrus antisianus (*d'Orbigny*) D'ORBIGNY'S TROGON Venezuela to Bolivia/ forest

Pharomachrus fulgidus (*Gould*) WHITE-TIPPED TROGON Mts of Colombia, Venezuela and Ecuador (? Guyana)/forest and plantations

Pharomachrus auriceps (*Gould*) GOLDEN-HEADED TROGON Andes from Venezuela to Bolivia and Panama/mountain forest / 1 egg known, otherwise no data

Pharomachrus pavoninus (*Spix*) PAVONINE TROGON Upper Amazon basin and Rio Tapajóz / forest

Euptilotis neoxenus (*Gould*) EARED TROGON Mts of Mexico

Priotelus temnurus (*Temminck*) CUBAN TROGON Cuba and Isle of Pines

Temnotrogon roseigaster (*Vieillot*) HISPANIOLAN TROGON Hispaniola

Trogon massena *Gould* MASSENA TROGON S Mexico, C America and Pacific coast of Colombia / forest, mangroves and plantations/ fruit and insects/ n hole in termite nest/ e 2–3/ I ♂♀

Trogon clathratus *Salvin* LATTICE-TAILED TROGON Caribbean slope of Costa Rica and W Panama /forest /no other data

Trogon melanurus *Swainson* BLACK-TAILED TROGON Panama and much of S America E of Andes and S to Mato Grosso/forest/ ? no data

Trogon bairdii *Lawrence* BAIRD'S TROGON SW Costa Rica and W Panama/forest/no other data

Trogon comptus *Zimmer* (*Amer Mus Novit*, no 1, 380 (1948), p 42) BLUE-TAILED TROGON Colombia and (?) Ecuador/forest/no data

Trogon viridis *L* (= **T. strigilatus** *L*) WHITE-TAILED TROGON Panama and much of S America E of Andes and S to Mato Grosso/ forest, scrub and savannah / fruit and insects/ n hole in palm tree/e 2

Trogon citreolus *Gould* CITREOLINE TROGON Mexico to W Costa Rica/forest/no data (Slud considers the Black-headed Trogon, *T. melanocephala* to be specifically distinct, but apparently most other authorities disagree)

Trogon mexicanus *Swainson* MEXICAN TROGON Mexico, W Guatemala and Honduras

Trogon elegans *Gould* ELEGANT TROGON South-western USA to N Costa Rica

Trogon collaris *Vieillot* COLLARED TROGON Mexico, C America, and much of S America S to Peru and Amazonian Brazil /forest and open forest/fruit and insects/n hole/e 2

Trogon aurantiiventris *Gould* ORANGE-BELLIED TROGON Costa Rica and Panama mountain forest/n hole/e 1 (1 nest known)

Trogon personatus *Gould* MASKED TROGON Andes from Venezuela to Bolivia: Guyana/ forest

Trogon rufus *Gmelin* GRACEFUL or BLACK-THROATED TROGON C America and much of S America S to N Argentina / forest /fruit and insects/n hole/e 2 (see note to *T. curucui*)

Trogon surrucura *Vieillot* SURUCUA TROGON Brazil, Paraguay, Uruguay and N Argentina /forest

Trogon curucui *L* PURPLE-BREASTED or BLUE-

CROWNED TROGON S America E of the Andes and S to Bolivia and N Argentina / forest
NB: The species now known as *T. rufus* was formerly known as *T. curucui*, and the species now known as *T. curucui* was formerly known as *T. variegatus*

Trogon violaceus *Gmelin* VIOLACEOUS TROGON Mexico, C America, Colombia, Venezuela, the Guianas and Amazon basin/ forest edge and open woodland/fruit and insects/ n hole or hole in termite nest / e – apparently only 1 egg collected, clutch size n/k, possibly 3/ I ? 17

[**Trogon rossi** *Lowe* Unique type in Exeter Museum. Peters synonymises this with the typical race of *T. violaceus*. I am not entirely happy that the descriptions agree exactly, but it does appear to be related to or synonymous with one of the forms now included in the species]

Apaloderma narina (*Stephens*) NARINA TROGON Much of E and S Africa / forest and riverine scrub/insects and berries/n hole /e 2–4

Apaloderma aequatoriale *Sharpe* YELLOW-CHEEKED TROGON S Cameroon to N Angola and Congo /forest /insects /n hole /e 2

Heterotrogon vittatus (*Shelley*) BAR-TAILED TROGON Forested mountains of equatorial E Africa /insects /n and e n/k

Harpactes reinwardtii (*Temminck*) BLUE-BILLED TROGON Java and Sumatra

Harpactes fasciatus (*Pennant*) MALABAR TROGON Ceylon and W India /moist deciduous and evergreen forest / insects and berries / n hollow in top of tree stump / e 2–4 / I ♂♀

Harpactes kasumba (*Raffles*) RED-NAPED TROGON Malay Peninsula, Sumatra and Borneo/ forest /n and e n/k

Harpactes diardii (*Temminck*) DIARD'S TROGON Malay Peninsula, Sumatra, Borneo and Banka/forest/ insects and fruit /n hole /e n/s

Harpactes ardens (*Temminck*) PHILIPPINE TROGON Philippines

Harpactes whiteheadi *Sharpe* WHITEHEAD'S TROGON Kina Balu, N Borneo /forest /insects/ n and e n/k

Harpactes orrhophaeus (*Cabanis and Heine*) CINNAMON-RUMPED TROGON Malaya, Sumatra and Borneo/ forest /n and e n/k

Harpactes duvaucelii (*Temminck*) SCARLET-RUMPED TROGON Malay Peninsula, Sumatra, Borneo and adjacent small islands / forest/ insects /n hole /e n/s

Harpactes oreskios (*Temminck*) ORANGE-BREASTED TROGON SE Asia, Sumatra, Java, NW Borneo, Nias / forest / insects and fruit / n hole / e 3–4

Harpactes erthyrocephalus (*Gould*) RED-HEADED TROGON Himalayas from Nepal to mts of S China, SE Asia, Hainan and Sumatra/ secondary jungle / insects, leaves and berries/ n hollow in rotten tree-trunk/e 3–4/I ♂♀

Harpactes wardi (*Kinnear*) WARD'S TROGON Mts of N Burma and E Tonkin (also per Ali and Ripley in E Himalayas of Bhutan and North East Frontier Area) / hill forest / insects and berries / n and e n/k

ALCEDINIDAE Kingfishers Thick-set birds with short necks, short tails, large heads and long, strong pointed bills. They are usually brightly coloured, but some are dull. The sexes are usually alike or fairly similar, but in some species the females are slightly duller than the males. Some species are aquatic, feeding on fish, but others have adopted a terrestrial life and live in forests or savannahs, feeding on large insects and small vertebrates. They nest in holes, usually in banks, but some in hollow trees. The eggs are white. Both sexes incubate for a period of 18–24 days, the young remaining in the nest for 3 or 4 weeks after hatching. About 84 species, cosmopolitan in distribution except for the polar regions and some oceanic islands.

Ceryle lugubris (*Temminck*) CRESTED KINGFISHER Himalayas E to mts of S China and Japan / rocky torrential streams /fish/n hole in bank/ e 4–5/no other data

Ceryle maxima (*Pallas*) AFRICAN GIANT KINGFISHER Africa S of Sahara / forest and grassland (2 races, 1 in forest, 1 in grassland)/ fish and crabs /n hole in bank/e 3

Ceryle torquata (*L*) RINGED KINGFISHER Mexico, C America, Guadeloupe, Dominica and most of S America to Tierra del Fuego/ large rivers / fish / n hole in bank / e 3–6 / I ♂♀/ F 33–8

Ceryle alcyon (*L*) BELTED KINGFISHER N America w S to Caribbean / coasts, estuaries and rivers/fish/ n hole in bank/e 5–14/I ♂♀ 16 ? 23–4?/F c28

Ceryle rudis (*L*) PIED KINGFISHER Africa S of Sahara, Egypt and S Asia from Turkey through Indian region to S China, Hainan and SE Asia /stagnant fresh water/fish and aquatic

COLUMBIDAE:
Columba palumbus,
Wood Pigeon or Ringdove

COLUMBIDAE;
Ptilinopus alligator,
Black-banded Pigeon

COLUMBIDAE:
Geopelia cuneata,
Diamond Dove

Opposite:
COLUMBIDAE:
Columba livia,
Rock Dove, Feral and
Domestic Pigeons

Plate 110

Plate 111

insects/n hole in bank/e 3–6/I ?♂♀

Chloroceryle amazona (*Latham*) AMAZON KINGFISHER Mexico, C America and most of S America

Chloroceryle americana (*Gmelin*) GREEN KINGFISHER SE Texas through C and much of S America to Buenos Aires/rivers/fish/n hole in bank/e 3–6/I ♂♀

Chloroceryle inda (*L*) GREEN AND RUFOUS KINGFISHER Tropical C and S America S to Mato Grosso

Chloroceryle aenea (*Pallas*) AMERICAN PYGMY KINGFISHER S Mexico, C America and S America S to Mato Grosso

Alcedo hercules *Laubmann* BLYTH'S or GREAT BLUE KINGFISHER Sikkim through hills of SE Asia; Hainan / shady jungle streams / fish and aquatic insects/n hole in bank or ravine/e 4–6/ I ♂♀

Alcedo atthis (*L*) COMMON or LITTLE BLUE KINGFISHER Widely distributed over the Palaearctic and Oriental regions and S to Solomon Is / fresh water of all kinds / fish and other aquatic life/n hole in bank/e 4–10/I ♂♀ 19–21/ F 23–7

Alcedo semitorquata *Swainson* HALF-COLLARED KINGFISHER E and S Africa/streams and rivers/fish and crabs/n hole in bank/e 4

Alcedo meninting *Horsfield* DEEP-BLUE KINGFISHER or BLUE-EARED KINGFISHER Indian sub-continent through SE Asia and Indonesia to Philippines / hill forest streams / fish and aquatic insects/n hole in bank/e 5–8

Alcedo quadribrachys *Bonaparte* SHINING BLUE KINGFISHER WC and E Africa / forest streams/fish and crabs/n hole in bank or pit/ e 4–6

Alcedo euryzona *Temminck* BLUE-BANDED KINGFISHER Malay Peninsula, Sumatra, Java and Borneo / streams in primary forest / fish, crustaceans, lizards and insects/n and e ? n/k

Alcedo coerulescens *Vieillot* SMALL BLUE KINGFISHER Java, Bali, Kangean Is, Lombok and Sumbawa

Alcedo cristata *Pallas* MALACHITE KINGFISHER Africa S of Sahara, Madagascar, Comoros, São Thomé and Principé/lakes and wide rivers/fish and aquatic insects/n hole in bank/e 4–6

Alcedo leucogaster (*Fraser*) WHITE-BELLIED KINGFISHER W and C Africa and Fernando Po / forest streams and mangrove swamps/insects,

fish and frogs/n hole/e n/s

Myioceyx lecontei (*Cassin*) AFRICAN DWARF KINGFISHER Equatorial forest of Africa from Fautee to Gabon and Kasai: Uganda / forest streams / insects / n hole in bank or pit / e 3

Ispidina picta (*Boddaert*) AFRICAN PYGMY KINGFISHER Africa from S of Sahara to Zambia/ bush and woodland/insects/n hole in bank or anthill/e 3–5

Ispidina madagascariensis (*L*) MADAGASCAR PYGMY KINGFISHER Madagascar/ humid forest and savannah / insects and batracians (? reptiles)/n tunnel in bank/e ? n/k

[Genus *Alcyone*, consisting of *Ceyx azureus*, *C. websteri* and *C. pusillus* is placed here by some authorities]

Ceyx cyanopectus *Lafresnaye* DWARF RIVER KINGFISHER Philippines

Ceyx argentatus *Tweeddale* SILVERY KINGFISHER Philippines

[**Ceyx goodfellowi** *Ogilvie-Grant* GOODFELLOW'S KINGFISHER Tawi-Tawi and Mindanao / now treated as synonymous with *C. lepidus margarethae*]

Ceyx lepidus *Temminck* DWARF FOREST KINGFISHER Philippines, S through Moluccas, New Guinea and Bismarck Archipelago to Solomon Is/forest rivers and mountain streams/ insects and spiders/n and e ? n/k

Ceyx azureus (*Latham*) AZURE KINGFISHER Moluccas to New Guinea, Australia and Tasmania/ inland waters, coastal creeks, estuaries and mangroves/fish and insects/n hole in bank/e 5

Ceyx websteri (*Hartert*) BISMARCK KINGFISHER Bismarck Archipelago

Ceyx pusillus *Temminck* LITTLE KINGFISHER Halmahera through Papuan islands to New Guinea, Bismarck Archipelago, N Australia and Solomon Is/lakes and rivers/fish and insects/ n hole in bank/e 5

Ceyx erithacus (*L*) THREE-TOED FOREST KINGFISHER or BLACK-BACKED KINGFISHER Indian region and Ceylon through SE Asia to S China, Hainan, Sumatra, Andamans, Nicobars, Borneo and Nias, also Mindoro in Philippines / small jungle streams / fish, insects, crustaceans/n hole in bank/e 4–7/no other data

Ceyx rufidorsum *Strickland* RUFOUS-BACKED KINGFISHER Malay Peninsula and much of Indonesia to Philippines/forest streams/crabs and insects/n in termite mound/e 3

Ceyx melanurus (*Kaup*) PHILIPPINE FOREST KINGFISHER Philippines

Ceyx fallax (*Schlegel*) CELEBES FOREST KINGFISHER Celebes and Sanghir Is

Pelargopsis amauroptera (*Pearson*) BROWN-WINGED KINGFISHER E Bengal through Burma to Malaya and Langkawi Is/tidal creeks and mangrove/fish and crustaceans/n hole in bank/ e ?4

Pelargopsis capensis (*L*) STORK-BILLED KINGFISHER India and Ceylon through SE Asia and Indonesia/forest rivers/fish, frogs, lizards, mice and young birds/n hole in bank/ e 4–5/no other data

Pelargopsis melanorhyncha (*Temminck*) BLACK-BILLED KINGFISHER Celebes, Peling, Banggai and Sula Is

Lacedo pulchella (*Horsfield*) BANDED KINGFISHER SE Asia, Sumatra, Java, Borneo and adjacent small islands/forest/insects

Dacelo novaeguineae (*Hermann*) (= **Dacelo gigas** (*Boddaert*) LAUGHING KOOKABURRA E Australia, introduced to W Australia and Tasmania/dry forest and savannah/insects and small vertebrates/n hole in tree, bank or termite colony/e 3 [NB: There seems to have been considerable confusion over the correct name of this species. It has been corrected to *novaeguineae* in the latest Australian Check List, but some modern books use *gigas*]

Dacelo leachii *Vigors and Horsfield* BLUE-WINGED KOOKABURRA S New Guinea and N Australia / savannah trees and open forest/ insects and vertebrates / n hole in tree or termite mound/e 3–4

Dacelo tyro *Gray* TYRO KINGFISHER S New Guinea and Aru Is/savannah/insects/n and e n/k

Dacelo gaudichaud *Quoy and Gaimard* RUFOUS-BELLIED GIANT KINGFISHER New Guinea, W Papuan islands, Aru Is/forest and savannah/insects/n termite mound/e 2

Clytoceyx rex *Sharpe* SHOVEL-BILLED or EMPEROR KINGFISHER New Guinea / forest/ insects and snails/n and e n/k

Melidora macrorrhina (*Lesson*) HOOK-BILLED KINGFISHER New Guinea and islands to the west / forest / insects / n hole in arboreal termitary/e 2/I ♂ (?♀)

Cittura cyanotis (*Temminck*) BLUE-EARED KINGFISHER Celebes and Sangi Is

Halcyon coromanda (*Latham*) RUDDY KINGFISHER E and S Asia from Japan and India S and E to Indonesia and Philippines/jungle pools and mangrove / fish, crabs and insects/ n hole in bank/e 5–6/I ♂♀

Halcyon badia *Verreaux and Verreaux* CHOCOLATE-BACKED KINGFISHER WC and C Africa and Fernando Po/forest/insects/n hole in arboreal termitary/e 2

Halcyon smyrnensis (*L*) SMYRNA KINGFISHER S and SE Asia from Turkey to S China and Taiwan, Philippines, but not the rest of Indonesia/dry forest, paddyfields, rivers, seashore etc/small animals and insects /n hole in bank/e 4–7/I ♂♀

Halcyon pileata (*Boddaert*) BLACK-CAPPED KINGFISHER S and E Asia from India, China and Korea S and E through parts of Indonesia and Philippines (apparently absent from Taiwan) / mangrove and estuaries, sometimes rivers / fish, frogs, crabs and insects / n hole in bank/e 4–5

Halcyon cyanoventris *Vieillot* JAVA KINGFISHER Java and Bali

Halcyon leucocephala (*Müller*) GREY-HEADED KINGFISHER Cape Verde Is and across equatorial Africa to Yemen/bush country/insects, frogs and small reptiles/n hole in bank/e 3–4

Halcyon senegalensis (*L*) WOODLAND KINGFISHER Equatorial Africa / forest, not always near water / insects, lizards and young birds/n hole in tree/e 3–4

[**Halcyon cyanoleuca** (*Vieillot*) is sometimes separated, but more usually treated as a race of *senegalensis*]

Halcyon senegaloides *Smith* MANGROVE KINGFISHER Coasts of E and SE Africa/mangrove/crabs etc/n hole in bank or tree/e 3

Halcyon malimbica (*Shaw*) BLUE-BREASTED KINGFISHER W and C Africa and islands in Gulf of Guinea/high trees in forests/insects/ n hole in tree/e 3–4 (Grant and Mackworth Praed erroneously quote Shaw as spelling this name *malimbicus*)

Halcyon albiventris (*Scopoli*) BROWN-HOODED KINGFISHER E and SE Africa/bush and open forest / crabs, worms, insects / n hole in bank/e 4–5

Halcyon chelicuti (*Stanley*) STRIPED KINGFISHER E and S Africa, except the extreme S/open forest, cultivation and desert/insects/ n hole/e 3–5

PSITTACIDAE:
Strigops habroptilus,
Owl Parrot or Kakapo

Plate 112

PSITTACIDAE:
Nestor notabilis,
Kea

Plate 113

Halcyon nigrocyanea *Wallace* BLUE-BLACK KINGFISHER New Guinea, Salawatti, Batanta and Japen / forest / crabs, fish and lizards

Halcyon winchelli *Sharpe* WINCHELL'S KINGFISHER Philippines

Halcyon diops (*Temminck*) MOLUCCAN KINGFISHER Moluccas

Halcyon macleayii *Jardine and Selby* AUSTRALIAN FOREST KINGFISHER E New Guinea Aru Is, northern and eastern Australia, occurring on migration on islands round New Guinea / forest edge and savannah / invertebrates / n hole in termite mound / e 5

Halcyon albonotata *Ramsay* NEW BRITAIN KINGFISHER New Britain

Halcyon leucopygia (*Verreaux*) ULTAMARINE KINGFISHER Solomon Is / forest / no other data

Halcyon farquhari *Sharpe* CHESTNUT-BELLIED KINGFISHER Central New Hebrides

Halcyon pyrrhopygia *Gould* RED-BACKED KINGFISHER Northern and eastern Australia / dry woodland and savannah / insects and small vertebrates / n hole in bank or termite mound / e 3–5

Halcyon torotoro (*Lesson*) LESSER YELLOW-BILLED KINGFISHER New Guinea, adjacent small islands and Cape York Peninsula / forest / insects and earthworms / n termite mound / e 1–3

Halcyon megarhyncha (*Salvadori*) MOUNTAIN or GREATER YELLOW-BILLED KINGFISHER Mts of New Guinea / mountain forest / insects and lizards

Halcyon australasia (*Vieillot*) AUSTRALASIAN KINGFISHER Lombok, Sumba, Timor, Wetar, Roma, Damar, Babar, Leti, Moa and Timorlaut

Halcyon sancta *Vigors and Horsfield* SACRED KINGFISHER b Australia, New Zealand and adjacent islands, Norfolk Is, Lord Howe Is, New Caledonia and Loyalty Is, occurring on migration in S Indonesia, New Guinea, Bismarck Archipelago and Solomon Is / forest edge, savannah and habitation / insects and crabs / n hole in tree, bank or termite mound / e 5

Halcyon cinnamomina *Swainson* MICRONESIAN KINGFISHER Palau Is, Ponapé and Guam / forest, rarely open country / insects and lizards / n hole / e 2

Halcyon funebris (*Bonaparte*) FUNEREAL KINGFISHER Halmahera and Ternate

Halcyon chloris (*Boddaert*) MANGROVE or WHITE-COLLARED KINGFISHER Widely distributed from Red Sea coast across S Asia to Australasia, Micronesia, Melanesia and E to Tonga / mangroves, estuaries and rivers / crabs and insects / n hole in tree or termite mound / e 3–4 / I ?♂♀

Halcyon saurophaga *Gould* WHITE-HEADED KINGFISHER New Guinea region from Moluccas to Bismarck Archipelago, and Solomons, Hermit Is, Admiralty Is and Ninigo Group coral cliffs and mangrove / crabs, lizards, fish and insects / n hole / e ?2 (1 nest with 2 young)

Halcyon recurvirostris (*Lafresnaye*) FLAT-BILLED KINGFISHER Upolu and Savaii (Samoa) / bush and clearings / insects / n hole / e ? n/k

Halcyon venerata (*Gmelin*) VENERATED KINGFISHER Tahiti and Moorea

Halcyon tuta (*Gmelin*) RESPECTED KINGFISHER Borabora (Society Is)

Halcyon ruficollaris *Holyoak* (*Bull Brit Orn Cl*, 94 (1974), p 147) RED-COLLARED KINGFISHER Mangaia, Cook Is

Halcyon gambieri *Oustalet* MANGAREVA KINGFISHER Mangareva (extinct) and Niau in Tuamotu Archipelago

Halcyon godeffroyi *Finsch* MARQUESAN KINGFISHER Marquesas

Halcyon miyakoensis *Kuroda* MIYAKO KINGFISHER Miyakoshima in the Ryukyu Is / unique and presumed extinct (Kuroda (1919) *Dobuts, Zasshi* 31, p 231)

Halcyon bougainvillei *Rothschild* MOUSTACHED KINGFISHER Solomon Is / no data

Halcyon concreta *Temminck* RUFOUS-COLLARED KINGFISHER Malay Peninsula, Sumatra, Borneo, Banka and Billiton / forest / insects / n hole / e 2

Halcyon lindsayi (*Vigors*) SPOTTED WOOD KINGFISHER Philippines: Luzon, Negros and Mindanao

Halcyon fulgida *Gould* BLUE AND WHITE KINGFISHER Lombok, Sumbawa and Flores

Halcyon monacha *Bonaparte* HOODED KINGFISHER Celebes / lowland forest

Halcyon princeps (*Reichenbach*) MOUNTAIN KINGFISHER Mountains of Celebes

Tanysiptera hydrocharis *Gray* ARU PARADISE KINGFISHER S New Guinea and Aru Is / ? no data

Tanysiptera galeata *Gray* COMMON or BEAUTIFUL PARADISE KINGFISHER Moluccas, Papuan islands, New Guinea, Karkar, Tarawai, Rossel and Vulcan Is / forest / insects / n hole in tree or termite mound / e 5

Tanysiptera riedelii *Verreaux* BIAK PARADISE KINGFISHER Biak Is / no data

Tanysiptera carolinae *Schlegel* NUMFOR PARADISE KINGFISHER Numfor Is / no data

Tanysiptera ellioti *Sharpe* ELLIOT'S KOFIAU PARADISE KINGFISHER Kofiau Is (near Misol)/ no data

Tanysiptera nympha *Gray* PINK-BREASTED PARADISE KINGFISHER New Guinea / local and rare / forest and mangrove / no other data

Tanysiptera danae *Sharpe* BROWN-BACKED PARADISE KINGFISHER SE New Guinea / no data

Tanysiptera sylvia *Gould* WHITE-TAILED PARADISE KINGFISHER N Queensland, S New Guinea, New Britain, Rook Is and Duke of York Is / lowland rain forest / insects and small vertebrates / n hole in termite mound / e 3–4

TODIDAE Todies Small kingfisher-like birds with peculiarly flattened bills, serrated along the edge. They are brightly coloured with a buzzing flight. Feed on insects and small lizards. The nest is a tunnel in the ground, eggs 2–5 in number, white. Both sexes incubate. Five species, confined to the Caribbean.

Todus multicolor *Gould* CUBAN TODY Cuba and Isle of Pines / forest and woodland

Todus angustirostris *Lafresnaye* NARROW-BILLED TODY Hispaniola / mountain forest

Todus todus (*L*) JAMAICAN TODY Jamaica/ wooded hills and mountains

Todus mexicanus *Lesson* PUERTO RICAN or HYPOCHONDRIAC TODY Puerto Rico / semi-arid scrub and damp hill forest

Todus subulatus *Gray* BROAD-BILLED TODY Hispaniola and Gonave / semi-arid scrub

MOMOTIDAE Motmots Medium-sized birds with soft plumage and long, racquet-shaped tails. Usually found singly or in pairs in deep forest, feeding on insects, lizards and some fruit. Nest usually in an excavated tunnel in bank, sometimes a rock-crevice. Eggs 3–4, white. Incubation by both sexes, 17–21 days. Fledging from 4–5 weeks, but information scanty for some species. About 8 species in Central and South America.

Hylomanes momotula *Lichtenstein* TODY MOTMOT Mexico, C America and extreme NW Colombia / humid forest / n and e n/k

Aspatha gularis (*Lafresnaye*) BLUE-THROATED MOTMOT Mexico to El Salvador / forest

Electron platyrhynchum (*Leadbeater*) BROAD-BILLED MOTMOT C and tropical S America, S to Mato Grosso / forest / n and e no data

Electron carinatum (*Du Bus*) KEEL-BILLED MOTMOT S Mexico to Costa Rica / humid forest

Eumomota superciliosa (*Sandbach*) TURQUOISE-BROWED MOTMOT S Mexico to Costa Rica / humid forest

Baryphthengus ruficapillus (*Vieillot*) RUFOUS MOTMOT Nicaragua to N Argentine (absent from some parts) / forest / e n/k (*Baryphthengus martii* (Spix) is sometimes separated)

Momotus mexicanus *Swainson* RUSSET-CROWNED MOTMOT Arid regions of Mexico and Guatemala / scrub and thicket

Momotus momota (*L*) BLUE-CROWNED MOTMOT Mexico, C and much of S America/ rain forest / e 3 / I ♂♀ c21

[(? **Baryphthengus**) **dombeyi** (*Lesson*, ex Levaillant) LEVAILLANT'S MOTMOT Peru / not identified with any known species / extinct or mythical ? qv Sclater, *Proc Zool Soc London* (1867), p 258 and Sharpe, *Cat Birds Brit Mus*, vol 17, p 330 footnote]

MEROPIDAE Bee-Eaters Brightly coloured birds with sleek, streamlined bodies and small weak legs. All except 2 species have tails with the 2 central feathers elongated. Food, insects (with bees and wasps the most important) mostly caught on the wing. Nest in tunnels in sandy banks or sometimes holes in the ground. Eggs 2–8, white. Incubation about 22 days, by both sexes. Fledging about 4 weeks. Gregarious birds, feeding, roosting and breeding in flocks and colonies. Tropical and warm temperate parts of the Old World. [The treatment here used follows that of C. H. Fry, *Ibis* (1969)].

Merops hirundinaeus *Lichtenstein* SWALLOW-TAILED BEE-EATER Much of Africa S of Sahara (except SW) / savannah / n hole in bank / e 3–4

Merops revoilii *Oustalet* SOMALI BEE-EATER Somaliland / 1 nest (with young) known, tunnel in wall of well / e n/k

Merops pusillus *Müller* LITTLE BEE-EATER Africa S of Sahara / n hole in bank / e 2–5

Merops variegatus *Vieillot* BLUE-BREASTED BEE-EATER Equatorial Africa / n hole in bank / e 2

Merops lafresnayii *Guérin* LAFRESNAYE'S BEE-EATER Ethiopia and Eritrea

Merops oreobates (*Sharpe*) CRIMSON-CHESTED BEE-EATER E Africa / n hole in bank/ e 2–3

PSITTACIDAE: *Trichoglossus haematodus*, Rainbow Lorikeet, Rainbow Lory

Plate 114

PSITTACIDAE:
Lorius garrulus,
Chattering Lory

Close-up of the head
of *T. haematodus.*

Plate 115

Merops bullockoides *Smith* White-
fronted Bee-eater Parts of E and S Africa/
n hole in bank or pit/e 2–4

Merops bulocki *Vieillot* Yellow-throated
and Red-throated Bee-eaters Africa from
Senegal to Blue Nile/n hole in bank/e 2–5

Merops gularis *Shaw* Black Bee-eater
W and C Africa/n hole in bank or cliff/e 2

Merops muelleri (*Cassin*) Blue-headed Bee-
eater Equatorial Africa/n hole in bank/e 2

[**Merops badius** L var β **Merops Adansonii**
'Vaill. 13' *Kuhl, Buffoni and Daubenton* (based
on Daubenton and Levaillant) is generally
regarded as an unidentifiable description,
though it has been claimed to be a variant of
M. muelleri, or as an artifact (see note Peters'
Check List, vol 5, pp 232–3). However, an
examination of the sources suggests to me that
it is a bad description, or an aberrant specimen,
of *Merops vividis* (*M. badius* = *M. viridis*)]

Merops albicollis *Vieillot* White-throated
Bee-eater b S Sahara from Senegal to SW
Arabia w S to Tanganyika/n hole in bank/e 6

Merops boehmi *Reichenow* Böhm's Bee-
eater C Africa/n hole in bank or flat ground/
e 2–3

Merops leschenaulti *Vieillot* Bay-headed
Bee-eater Indian region, SE Asia, Andamans,
Java and Bali/n hole in bank/e 5–6/I ♂♀

[**Merops erythrocephalus** *Gmelin* is probably
a synonym of *M. leschenaulti*, and has sometimes
been used for it, but the matter is open to
doubt. Gmelin's is the older name]

Merops apiaster L European Bee-eater
Mediterranean and SW Asia w through Africa
and to India (casual in C and N Europe)/plains
and open woodland / n hole in bank / e 4–8
(? 9–10)/I ?♂♀

Merops superciliosus L Brown-breasted
Bee-eater Much of Africa/n hole in bank/e 3–4

Merops philippinus L Blue-tailed Bee-
eater b Indian Region, SE Asia, S China w
through Indonesia and may breed in places
there; a race occurring in New Britain and
parts of New Guinea appears to be sedentary/
n hole in bank/e 5–7

Merops ornatus *Latham* Rainbow Bee-eater
b Australia w Lesser Sunda Is, Papuan region
and Solomons/open timbered country/n tunnel
and ground /e 4–5

Merops orientalis *Latham* Little Green
Bee-eater Arid belt of Africa from Senegal to

Ethiopia and Egypt; S Asia from Arabia to
Vietnam (not Malaya)/n hole in bank/e 4–7/
I ♂♀

Merops viridis L (= **M. bicolor** *Boddaert*)
Blue-throated Bee-eater S China S through
SE Asia to parts of Indonesia

Merops malimbicus *Shaw* Rosy Bee-eater
C and WC Africa/local/n hole in bank/e 2

Merops nubicus *Gmelin* Northern Carmine
Bee-eater Thorn scrub belt from Senegal to
Ethiopia and Tanganyika/n hole in river bank/
e 3–5

Merops nubicoides *Des Murs and Pucheran*
Southern Carmine Bee-eater Africa from
Malawi S to Natal/n hole in bank/e 2–4

[**Merops persicus** *Pallas* Blue-cheeked Bee-
eater Egypt and SW Asia from Palestine to NW
India w through Arabia to S Africa /n hole in
ground or mound/e 4–5/I ?♂♀ (treated by a
number of authors as a race of *M. superciliosus*)]

Merops breweri (*Cassin*) Black-headed Bee-
eater C Africa /n n/k – 1 oviduct egg known

Nyctiornis amicta (*Temminck*) Red-breasted
Bee-eater Tenasserim, Malay Peninsula,
Sumatra, Banka and Borneo

Nyctiornis athertoni (*Jardine and Selby*)
Blue-bearded Bee-eater India through SE
Asia; Hainan/n hole in bank/e 4–6/I ♂♀?

Meropogon forsteni *Bonaparte* Celebes Bee-
eater Celebes/n hole in bank/e ?2

LEPTOSOMATIDAE   **Cuckoo-Roller**
Differs from the Rollers and Ground Rollers
in being sexually dimorphic and in having
powder-down. One species.

Leptosomus discolor (*Hermann*) Cuckoo-
roller or Courol Madagascar and the
Comoros/forest and brush/insects/n and e
apparently n/k

BRACHYPTERACIIDAE Ground Rollers
(this family is often given only sub-family
status) Mainly similar to true Rollers but less
arboreal and duller and more protectively
coloured. They have longer legs and shorter
wings. Confined to Madagascar, and almost
nothing appears to be known of their nesting
habits.

Brachypteracias leptosomus (*Lesson*)
Short-legged Ground Roller E Madagascar/
heavy forest/insects and reptiles

Brachypteracias squamigera *Lafresnaye*
Scaled Ground Roller E Madagascar/heavy
forest/insects

Atelornis pittoides (*Lafresnaye*) PITTA-LIKE GROUND ROLLER E Madagascar / heavy forest/ insects
Atelornis crossleyi *Sharpe* CROSSLEY'S GROUND ROLLER E Madagascar / heavy forest/ insects
Uratelornis chimaera *Rothschild* LONG-TAILED GROUND ROLLER SW Madagascar /dry bush / insects / 'the natives say that the nest is placed in a hole in the ground' (Rand)
CORACIIDAE Rollers Predominantly blue-and-brown birds superficially resembling crows, but sometimes with forked or racquet tails. The two inner front toes are connected but the outer one is free. Feed on insects, generally caught in the air, but small animals also taken on ground. Nest is an unlined tree-hole, the eggs, 2 to 4 in number, are white. Incubation is believed to be by both species and takes 18–23 days. Fledging period about 3 to 4 weeks.
Coracias garrulus L COMMON ROLLER b Europe, W and C Asia and Morocco w S through Africa / light wood and cultivation/ insects, lizards and frogs etc/n hole in tree or cliff/e 4–5 (?6–7)/I ♂♀ 18–19/F 26–8
Coracias abyssinica *Herrmann* ABYSSINIAN ROLLER Drier parts of tropical Africa from Senegal to SW Arabia / insects and small animals/n hole / e 4–6
Coracias caudata L LILAC-BREASTED ROLLER E and S Africa (except the extreme S)/ insects and small animals/n hole/e 2–3
Coracias spatulata *Trimen* RACQUET-TAILED ROLLER N Angola to Tanganyika, S Rhodesia and Mozambique / insects and small animals/ n hole/e 2–3
Coracias noevia *Daudin* RUFOUS-CROWNED ROLLER Africa S of Sahara / open woodland/ insects and small reptiles/n hole/e 2
Coracias benghalensis (L) INDIAN ROLLER Indian region, SE Asia and W to E Arabia/ light forest and cultivation / insects and small animals/n hole in tree/e 3–5/I ♂♀ 18
Coracias temminckii (*Vieillot*) TEMMINCK'S ROLLER Celebes, Buton and Muna
Coracias cyanogaster *Cuvier* BLUE-BELLIED ROLLER Senegal to Sudan/ savannah /virtually no data
Eurystomus glaucurus (*Müller*) BROAD-BILLED ROLLER Much of tropical Africa and Madagascar/large insects/n hole/e 2–3
Eurystomus gularis *Vieillot* BLUE-THROATED ROLLER Africa from Senegal to Uganda and S to Angola/forest/insects/n hole/e 3
Eurystomus orientalis (L) DOLLAR BIRD Indian region through SE Asia and Indonesia to Australia, New Guinea, Bismarck Archipelago and Solomons / secondary jungle and forest clearings / insects and small animals / n hole/ e 3–4/I ♂♀
UPUPIDAE Hoopoes Cinnamon-pink birds with conspicuous black and white wings, striking crests and long, delicately pointed bills. Feed on insects caught on wing and also scavenge round garbage tips. Nest in a hole, the site becoming filthy and smelly with excreta and food remains. Flight erratic, delicate and undulating. Several species were formerly recognised, but these are now generally combined as races of one species, though the recent discovery of a giant, almost flightless, extinct species raises the question of relationships within the family.
Upupa epops L HOOPOE Widely distributed through Europe, Asia and Africa / wood-borders, park and cultivation / n hole or tree, wall etc/e 5–8 (rarely 9–12)/I ♀ 18/F 20–7
Upupa antaios *Olsen* ('Palaeornithology of St Helena' *Smithsonian Cont to Paleobiology*, no 23 (1975)) GIANT HOOPOE St Helena / extinct post-1502/bones only
PHOENICULIDAE Wood Hoopoes Differ from true hoopoes in having metallic plumage, largely blues, greens and purples, and in lacking a crest. More gregarious.
Phoeniculus purpureus (*Miller*) GREEN WOOD HOOPOE Africa S of Sahara/forest and woodland/insects/n hole/e 3–5
Phoeniculus damarensis (*Ogilvie-Grant*) VIOLET WOOD HOOPOE Damaraland, Kenya and S Ethiopia/forest and woodland/insects/n and e ? n/k
[There has been considerable confusion regarding these 2 species, which are merged by Peters, who actually gives *damarensis* as a synonym of the typical race of *purpureus*, presumably on the grounds that the type locality of the former is Damaraland, to which area he confines *P. p. purpureus*. However, the type locality of *P. p. purpureus*, which was given by Miller as 'Africa and India' has been amended by Sclater in *Syst Av Aethiop* (1924) to Knysna, Southern Cape Province]
Phoeniculus somaliensis (*Ogilvie-Grant*)

PSITTACIDAE:
Trichoglossus chlorolepidotus,
Scaly-breasted Lorikeet

Plate 116

PSITTACIDAE:
Trichoglossus versicolor,
Varied Lorikeet

PSITTACIDAE:
Calyptorhynchus funereus,
Black Cockatoo

PSITTACIDAE:
Calyptorhynchus magnificus,
Banksian Cockatoo, Red-tailed

Plate 117

BLACK-BILLED WOOD HOOPOE British Somaliland, S Ethiopia and NE Kenya / forest/ insects / n hole / e 3

Phoeniculus bollei (*Hartlaub*) WHITE-HEADED WOOD HOOPOE Equatorial Africa from Ghana to Kenya / highland forest / insects/ n hole / e 2

Phoeniculus castaneiceps (*Sharpe*) FOREST WOOD HOOPOE Equatorial Africa from Ghana to Uganda / forest / fruit and insects / n and e n/k

Phoeniculus aterrimus (*Stephens*) BLACK WOOD HOOPOE Africa from Senegal, Lake Chad and Ethiopia, S to Benguella and Lake Albert / bush country / insects / n hole / e n/k

Phoeniculus cavei *Macdonald* (*Bull Br Orn Club*, vol 67 (1946) p 5) CAVE'S WOOD HOOPOE SE Sudan / unique

Rhinopomastus minor (*Rüppell*) ABYSSINIAN SCIMITAR-BILL E Africa from Somaliland to C Tanganyika / bush and forest / insects and seeds / n hole / e 3

Rhinopomastus cyanomelas (*Vieillot*) COMMON SCIMITAR-BILL E Africa from Kenya to Natal / open woodland / insects and seeds/ n hole / e 2–3

BUCEROTIDAE Hornbills Large birds with enormous down-curved bills, usually with a horny casque. Many, but not all inhabit heavy forests and they are generally omnivorous, feeding on fruits, insects and small animals. Nest in holes, the female incubating and being walled in during the period of incubation, fed by male. Eggs 1–6, white. Incubation period about 28–40 days, the young mature after another 4 to 8 weeks. About 45 species spread through the Old World tropics.

Tockus birostris (*Scopoli*) COMMON GREY HORNBILL India / open country and cultivation/ fruit, insects and small animals / n hole / e 2–4

Tockus griseus (*Latham*) MALABAR GREY HORNBILL Ceylon and SW India / open forest/ fruit, insects and small animals / n hole / e 2–4

Tockus fasciatus (*Shaw*) AFRICAN PIED HORNBILL Equatorial Africa from Gambia to W Uganda and N Angola / secondary forest / insects and fruit / n hole / e 'up to 4'

Tockus alboterminatus (*Büttikofer*) CROWNED HORNBILL E and S Africa / light forest / insects and fruit / n hole / e 2–3 (*T. melanoleucus* was formerly used for this species)

Tockus bradfieldi (*Roberts*) BRADFIELD'S HORNBILL Ovamboland, Rhodesia and N Bechuanaland / n hole / e 'up to 5'

Tockus pallidirostris (*Hartlaub and Finsch*) PALE-BILLED HORNBILL Angola to Malawi and Tanganyika / dry woodland

Tockus nasutus (*L*) AFRICAN GREY HORNBILL W and S Arabia, much of Africa S of Sahara except extreme S / bush-country / fruit, insects and small reptiles / n hole / e 2–4

Tockus hemprichii (*Ehrenberg*) HEMPRICH'S HORNBILL Eritrea, Ethiopia and Somaliland/ insects / little other data

Tockus montieri *Hartlaub* MONTIERE'S HORNBILL Ovamboland and Benguella / ? no data

Tockus hartlaubi *Gould* DWARF BLACK HORNBILL W Africa from French Guinea to Congo / high trees of forest / insects / n hole/ e n/k

Tockus camurus *Cassin* RED-BILLED DWARF HORNBILL W and WC Africa / wet forest/ insects ? / n hole / e n/k

Tockus erythrorhynchus (*Temminck*) RED-BILLED HORNBILL W, E and SE Africa / bush and open woodland / areas fruit and insects/ n hole / e 3–6

Tockus flavirostris (*Rüppell*) YELLOW-BILLED HORNBILL E and S Africa from Ethiopia to Natal and Angola (not extreme S) / bush and open woodland / fruit and insects / n hole / e 2–3

Tockus deckeni (*Cabanis*) VON DER DECKEN'S HORNBILL E Africa from Ethiopia to C Tanganyika / arid thorn bush / fruit and berries/ n hole / e 2–3

Tockus jacksoni (*Ogilvie-Grant*) JACKSON'S HORNBILL E Africa / dry country / insects and fruit / n and e n/k

Berenicornis comatus (*Raffles*) WHITE-CROWNED HORNBILL Malay Peninsula, C Annam, Sumatra and Borneo / forest / n and e ? n/k

Berenicornis albocristatus (*Cassin*) WHITE-CRESTED HORNBILL WC Africa / forest/ insects / n hole / e ? n/k

Ptilolaemus tickelli (*Blyth*) BROWN HORNBILL Hills of Assam, Tenasserim and Vietnam/ evergreen forest / fruit and insects / n hole/ e 3–4 / I ♀ ?24

Anorrhinus galeritus (*Temminck*) BUSHY-CRESTED HORNBILL Malay Peninsula, Sumatra, Borneo and Natuna Is / forest / n hole / e ? n/k

Penelopides panini (*Boddaert*) TARICTIC HORNBILL Philippines / forest / fruit / n hole / e 3

Penelopides exharatus (*Temminck*) CELEBES HORNBILL Celebes

Aceros nipalensis (*Hodgson*) RUFOUS-NECKED HORNBILL Himalayas and hills of SE Asia/ evergreen forest/fruit/n hole/e 1–2

Rhyticeros corrugatus (*Temminck*) WRINKLED HORNBILL Malay Peninsula, Borneo, Sumatra and Batu Is/forest/n and e ? n/k

Rhyticeros leucocephalus (*Vieillot*) WRITHE-BILLED HORNBILL Philippines/forest/fruit

Rhyticeros cassidex (*Temminck*) BUTON HORNBILL Celebes, Buton and Muna

Rhyticeros undulatus (*Shaw*) WREATHED HORNBILL Assam through SE Asia, Sumatra, Java, Bali, Borneo and adjacent small islands/ forest/fruit and small animals/n hole/e 2

Rhyticeros plicatus (*Forster*) PAPUAN HORNBILL S Burma, Malay Peninsula, Sumatra, Borneo, Moluccas, New Guinea, Bismarck Archipelago, Solomon Is / forest / fruit and small animals/n hole/e 2–3

Rhyticeros everetti (*Rothschild*) EVERETT'S HORNBILL Sumba

Rhyticeros narcondami *Hume* NARCONDAMI HORNBILL Narcondami Is, Bay of Bengal/ forest/fruit/n and e ? n/k

Anthracoceros malayanus (*Raffles*) MALAYSIAN BLACK HORNBILL Malay Peninsula, Sumatra, Banka, Billiton, Borneo/e 3

Anthracoceros coronatus (*Boddaert*) MALABAR PIED HORNBILL India and Ceylon, Malay Peninsula, Sumatra and small islands to Borneo/open forest and habitation/fruit, fish and small animals/n hole/e 2–3

Anthracoceros albirostris (*Shaw*) [= **A. malabaricus** (*Gmelin*)] INDIAN PIED HORNBILL E Indian region, SE Asia and S China / open forest and habitation / fruit, fish and small animals/n hole/e 2–3

Anthracoceros montani (*Oustalet*) SULU HORNBILL Sulu Archipelago / hill forest / fruit/ n and e n/k

Anthracoceros marchei *Oustalet* PALAWAN HORNBILL Palawan and adjacent islands/forest/ fruit/n and e n/k

Bycanistes fistulator (*Cassin*) PIPING HORNBILL Sierra Leone to Niger Delta/forest/ fruit

Bycanistes sharpii (*Elliot*) LAUGHING HORNBILL Ghana to Congo and Sudan/forest/ fruit/n hole/e 2

Bycanistes buccinator (*Temminck*) TRUMPETER HORNBILL Africa from Kenya to Angola and the Cape/forest and thorn bush/ fruit and insects/n hole/e 2

Bycanistes cylindricus (*Temminck*) BROWN-CHEEKED HORNBILL Sierra Leone to Dahomey/ forest/n and e n/k

Bycanistes albotibialis (*Cabanis and Reichenow*) WHITE-THIGHED HORNBILL WC Africa from Nigeria to Congo/forest/fruit, insects, and young birds/n hole/e n/k

Bycanistes subcylindricus (*Sclater*) GREY-CHEEKED HORNBILL Ashanti to Tanganyika/ forest/fruit, insects and young birds/n hole or rock cleft/e 1

Bycanistes brevis *Friedmann* SILVER-CHEEKED HORNBILL E Africa from Ethiopia to Malawi/forest strips/fruit and insects/n hole/ e 2

Ceratogymna atrata (*Temminck*) BLACK-CASQUED HORNBILL W and C Africa and Fernando Po/forest/fruit and insects/n hole/ e ? 1

Ceratogymna elata (*Temminck*) YELLOW-CASQUED HORNBILL Portuguese Guinea to W Cameroon/forest/fruit/n and e n/k

Buceros rhinoceros *L* RHINOCEROS HORNBILL Malay Peninsula, Sumatra, Java, Borneo/ forest/fruit/n and e no reliable information

Buceros bicornis *L* GREAT INDIAN HORNBILL Locally in India, SE Asia and Sumatra/ever-green and deciduous forest / fruit and small animals/n hole/e 1–3/I ? 31

Buceros hydrocorax *L* RUFOUS HORNBILL Philippines/forest/fruit/n and e n/k

Rhinoplax vigil (*Forster*) HELMETED HORNBILL Malay Peninsula, Sumatra and Borneo / forest / fruit, lizards, small birds and eggs

Bucorvus abyssinicus (*Boddaert*) ABYSSINIAN GROUND HORNBILL Africa from Gambia to Kenya and Ethiopia/open country/insects and small animals/n hole/e 2

Bucorvus leadbeateri (*Vigors*) (= **B. cafer** (*Schlegel*)) AFRICAN GROUND HORNBILL Africa from Lake Tanganyika S to Cape / open country/insects and small animals/n hole/e 1–3

GALBULIDAE Jacamars Graceful, iri-descent-plumaged birds with long bills and tails. Feed on insects caught in the air. The nest is in a burrow in the ground, the 3–4 eggs are white, and both sexes incubate, the ♀ generally at night, incubation lasting 19–21 days. The

PSITTACIDAE:
Myopsitta monachus,
Quaker or Monk Parrakeet

PSITTACIDAE:
Pyrrhura leucotis,
White-eared or Maroon-faced
Conure, Maroon-faced
Parrakeet

PSITTACIDAE:
Pyrrhura rhodogaster,
Crimson-bellied Conure,
Crimson-bellied Parakeet

Plate 118

PSITTACIDAE:
Pionites leucogaster,
White-bellied Caique,
White-bellied Parrot

PSITTACIDAE:
Brotogeris jugularis,
Tovi Parrakeet,
Orange-chinned Parakeet

Plate 119

young fledge in 3 weeks.

Galbalcyrhynchus leucotis *Des Murs* CHESTNUT JACAMAR Upper Amazon basin/ forest clearings (*G. purusianus* is sometimes separated)

Brachygalba lugubris (*Swainson*) BROWN JACAMAR Parts of Orinoco and Amazon basins/ open forest and bush

[**Brachygalba phaeonota** *Todd* Tonantins, Brazil/unique/now generally regarded as a race of *B. lugubris*]

Brachygalba goeringi *Sclater and Salvin* PALE-HEADED JACAMAR E Colombia and N Venezuela/open woods and thickets

Brachygalba salmoni *Sclater and Salvin* DUSKY-BACKED JACAMAR E Panama and NW Colombia

Brachygalba albogularis (*Spix*) WHITE-THROATED JACAMAR Rio Javary, Peru–Brazil border/forest

Jacamaralcyon tridactyla (*Vieillot*) THREE-TOED JACAMAR SE Brazil

Galbula albirostris *Latham* YELLOW-BILLED JAMACAR Amazon and Orinoco basins/forest (*G. cyanicollis*, Cassin, is sometimes separated)

Galbula galbula (*L*) GREEN-TAILED JACAMAR Amazon and Orinoco basins/forest

Galbula tombacea *Spix* WHITE-CHINNED JACAMAR Amazon basin/forest near streams and ponds

Galbula cyanescens *Deville* BLUE-FRONTED JACAMAR Upper Amazon basin, S of the river/ forest

Galbula pastazae *Taczanowski and Berlepsch* COPPER-CHESTED JACAMAR E Ecuador and W Brazil

Galbula ruficauda *Cuvier* RUFOUS-TAILED JACAMAR Mexico to Panama and the greater part of tropical S America/forest clearings and secondary growth

Galbula leucogastra *Vieillot* BRONZE JACAMAR Orinoco and Upper Amazon basins/forest

Galbula dea (*L*) PARADISE JACAMAR Upper Amazon basin/forest edge and savannah

Jacamerops aurea (*Müller*) GREAT JACAMAR Tropical S America, Panama and Costa Rica/ forest

BUCCONIDAE Puffbirds Birds related to the Jacamars, but generally dressed in brown plumage, with large heads, short necks and flattened, hook-tipped bills. They are largely insectivorous. The nest is a burrow in the

ground or in a termitary, and 2–3 white eggs are laid. Nothing is known of incubation or fledging periods. About 30 species in tropical America.

Notharchus macrorhynchus (*Gmelin*) WHITE-NECKED PUFFBIRD C and S America from S Mexico to NE Argentina/treetops in open forest, savannah and cerradão

Notharchus pectoralis (*Gray*) BLACK-BREASTED PUFFBIRD E Panama; C Colombia to NW Ecuador/forest

Notharchus ordii (*Cassin*) BROWN-BANDED PUFFBIRD S Venezuela and NW Brazil/forest

Notharchus tectus (*Boddaert*) PIED PUFFBIRD E Panama and parts of north-western S America and Amazon basin/forest, mangroves and savannah

Bucco macrodactylus (*Spix*) CHESTNUT-CAPPED PUFFBIRD Parts of north-western S America and Orinoco Valley/forest

Bucco tamatia (*Gmelin*) SPOTTED PUFFBIRD Parts of Amazon and Orinoco basins/forest edge, shrubbery and savannah

Bucco noanamae *Hellmayr* SOOTY-CAPPED PUFFBIRD W Colombia/forest and scrub

Bucco capensis *L* COLLARED PUFFBIRD Amazon basin/forest

Nystalus radiatus (*Sclater*) BARRED PUFFBIRD W Panama to Ecuador/open forest bordering streams

Nystalus chacuru (*Vieillot*) WHITE-EARED PUFFBIRD E Peru, E Bolivia, S Brazil, Paraguay and NE Argentina/open woodland, campos and cerradão

Nystalus striolatus (*Pelzeln*) STRIOLATED PUFFBIRD E Ecuador S to N Bolivia, parts of Brazil

Nystalus maculatus (*Gmelin*) SPOT-BACKED PUFFBIRD E and S Brazil, Bolivia and N Argentina/forest, shrubbery and campos

Hypnelus ruficollis (*Wagler*) RUSSET-THROATED PUFFBIRD Local in parts of Colombia and Venezuela/dry scrub and open woodland (*Hypnelus bicinctus*, Gould, is treated as a race)

Malacoptila striata (*Spix*) CRESCENT-CHESTED PUFFBIRD E and SE Brazil/forest

Malacoptila fusca (*Gmelin*) WHITE-CHESTED PUFFBIRD North-eastern S America N of Amazon/forest

Malacoptila semicincta *Todd* SEMI-COLLARED PUFFBIRD Recorded from S Peru, W Brazil and N Bolivia

Malacoptila fulvogularis *Sclater* BLACK-

STREAKED PUFFBIRD Andes from Colombia to Bolivia / savannah and open woodland

Malacoptila rufa (*Spix*) RUFOUS-NECKED PUFFBIRD Upper and Middle Amazon basin, S of Amazon

Malacoptila panamensis (*Lafresnaye*) BROWN PUFFBIRD Guatemala to Colombia / forest undergrowth and shrubbery

Malacoptila mystacalis (*Lafresnaye*) MOUSTACHED PUFFBIRD Andes of Colombia and Venezuela / forest (Peters believed this to be a zonal representative of *M. panamensis*)

Micromonacha lanceolata (*Deville*) LANCEOLATED MONKLET Parts of Costa Rica, Panama, Colombia, E Ecuador, E Peru and extreme W Brazil / forest

Nonnula rubecula (*Spix*) RUSTY-BREASTED NUNLET S America E of the Andes and S of the Orinoco / forest

Nonnula sclateri *Hellmayr* FULVOUS-CHINNED or SCLATER'S NUNLET W Brazil

Nonnula brunnea *Sclater* BROWN NUNLET Tropical zone of E Colombia, E Ecuador and E Peru

Nonnula frontalis *Sclater* GREY-CHEEKED NUNLET Panama and N Colombia (see note to *N. ruficapilla*)

Nonnula ruficapilla (*Tschudi*) RUFOUS-CAPPED NUNLET E Peru to Mato Grosso / open forest and savannah [This species and *N. frontalis* may be conspecific]

Nonnula amaurocephala *Chapman* CHESTNUT-HEADED NUNLET W Brazil

[**Microtrogon galbuloides** *Bertoni* has never been identified with any known Puffbird, the other species in this 2-species genus was **Microtrogon fulvescens** *Bertoni* which is synonymous with *Nonnula rubecula*]

Hapaloptila castanea (*Verreaux*) WHITE-FACED NUNBIRD Subtropical zone of W Colombia and W Ecuador / forest

Monasa atra (*Boddaert*) BLACK NUNBIRD S Venezuela, Guianas and N Brazil / forest

Monasa nigrifrons (*Spix*) BLACK-FRONTED NUNBIRD Colombia E of Andes to N Bolivia, parts of Brazil / forest

Monasa morphoeus (*Hahn and Küster*) WHITE-FRONTED NUNBIRD From Nicaragua to Amazonia and Rio de Janeiro / forest / insects, spiders etc / n burrow in ground / e ?3 / F 30

Monasa flavirostris *Strickland* YELLOW-BILLED NUNBIRD E Colombia, E Ecuador, E Peru and W Brazil / forest

Chelidoptera tenebrosa (*Pallas*) SWALLOW-WINGED PUFFBIRD S America, E of Andes and S to São Paulo / forest edge, savannah, dead trees and clearings

CAPITONIDAE Barbets Plump, brightly coloured birds with short necks, big heads, and large, heavy bills fringed with conspicuous bristles. They are arboreal and feed on fruit, flowers and insects. The nest is a hole in a tree or arboreal termitary; the eggs, usually 2–4 in number, are incubated for 13–15 days. Over 70 species throughout the world's tropics, but particularly in Africa.

Capito aurovirens (*Cuvier*) SCARLET-CROWNED BARBET Headwaters of Amazon / forest

Capito maculicoronatus *Lawrence* SPOT-CROWNED BARBET W Colombia and Panama / forest treetops and vine-covered trees

Capito squamatus *Salvin* ORANGE-FRONTED BARBET SW Colombia and W Ecuador / secondary growth

Capito hypoleucus *Salvin* WHITE-MANTLED BARBET Magdalena region of Colombia / forest

Capito dayi *Cherrie* BLACK-GIRDLED BARBET W Brazil / forest

Capito quinticolor *Elliot* FIVE-COLOURED BARBET Tropical zone of Pacific coast of Colombia / 5 specimens / forest

Capito niger (*Müller*) BLACK-SPOTTED BARBET Amazon and Orinoco basins / forest, swampy woods and secondary growth

Eubucco richardsoni (*Gray*) LEMON-THROATED BARBET Headwaters of Amazon / forest and scrub

Eubucco bourcierii (*Lafresnaye*) RED-HEADED BARBET Costa Rica to Panama and Andes of Colombia and Ecuador / forest undergrowth and clearings

Eubucco tucinkae (*Seilern*) SCARLET-HOODED BARBET Andes of SE Peru / secondary growth

Eubucco versicolor (*Müller*) VERSICOLOURED BARBET Peru and NW Bolivia / forest

Semnornis frantzii (*Sclater*) PRONG-BILLED BARBET Costa Rica and W Panama

Semnornis ramphastinus (*Jardine*) TOUCAN BARBET Andes of Colombia and Ecuador / forest

Psilopogon pyrolophus *Müller* FIRE-TUFTED BARBET Malay Peninsula and Sumatra / mountain forest above 3,000ft (900m) / fruit / n and e n/k

PSITTACIDAE:
Amazona ventralis,
Hispaniolan Parrot

PSITTACIDAE:
Amazona albifrons,
Spectacled Parrot, White
fronted Parrot

Opposite
PSITTACIDAE
Amazona
ochrocephala
Le Vaillant's
Parrot
Yellow-headed
Parrot

Plate 120

Plate 121

Megalaima virens (*Boddaert*) GREAT BARBET Himalayas to mts of SE Asia and S China/ hill forest/fruit and insects/n hole/e 3–4

Megalaima lagrandieri *Verreaux* LAGRANDIER'S BARBET Laos and Vietnam

Megalaima zeylanica (*Gmelin*) GREAT GREEN BARBET India, Ceylon/gardens and well-wooded country/fruit and insects/n hole/e 2–4 (NB: some of the races formerly included in this species are now considered to be races of *M. lineata*)

Megalaima lineata (*Vieillot*) LINEATED BARBET Himalayas, Assam, SE Asia, Java and Bali/gardens and light forest/fruit, insects and lizards/n hole/e 2–4/I ♂♀ c14–15

Megalaima viridis (*Boddaert*) LITTLE GREEN BARBET S India/gardens and wooded country/ fruit, nectar and insects/n hole/e 2–4/I ♂♀

Megalaima faiostricta (*Temminck*) GREEN-EARED BARBET S China, Thailand and Indo-China

Megalaima corvina (*Temminck*) BROWN-THROATED BARBET Java/forest

Megalaima chrysopogon (*Temminck*) GOLD-WHISKERED BARBET Peninsular Siam, Malaya, Sumatra and Borneo/submontane forest and coastal swamp-jungle/fruit/n and e n/k

Megalaima rafflesii (*Lesson*) MANY-COLOURED BARBET Malay Peninsula, Sumatra, Banka, Billiton, Mendanan, Borneo/lowland forest/n and e n/k

Megalaima mystacophanos (*Temminck*) GAUDY BARBET Malay Peninsula, Sumatra, Borneo and Batu Is/lowland forest/fruit and insects/n hole/e 4 (1 nest known)

Megalaima javensis (*Horsfield*) KOTOREA BARBET Java/lowland forest

Megalaima flavifrons (*Cuvier*) YELLOW-FACED BARBET Ceylon/forest/fruit (rarely insects)/n hole/e 2–3

Megalaima franklinii (*Blyth*) GOLDEN-THROATED BARBET Mts from Nepal east through SE Asia/hill forest/fruit/n hole/e 3–4/I ♂♀

Megalaima oorti (*Müller*) EMBROIDERED BARBET Sumatra, Malay Peninsula, S Laos, S Annam, SE China, Taiwan and Hainan (discontinuous)/mountain forest/n and e n/k

Megalaima asiatica (*Latham*) BLUE-THROATED BARBET N India through SE Asia/ forest, light wood and garden/fruit and some-times insects/n hole/e 3–4/I ♂♀

Megalaima monticola (*Sharpe*) MOUNTAIN BARBET Mts of northern Borneo/mountain forest and cultivation/fruit and insects/n and e n/k

Megalaima incognita *Hume* MOUSTACHED BARBET Tenasserim, SE Thailand and Indo-China/n and e n/k

Megalaima henricii (*Temminck*) YELLOW-CROWNED BARBET Peninsular Thailand, Malaya, Sumatra, Borneo/lowland forest/fruit/n and e n/k

Megalaima armillaris (*Temminck*) BLUE-CROWNED BARBET Java and Bali

Megalaima pulcherrima (*Sharpe*) KINABALU or GOLDEN-RUMPED BARBET Mts of NW Borneo/ rare/forest/fruit/n and e n/k

[**Megalaima robustirostris** (*Baker*) LARGE-BILLED BARBET N Cachar hills/now regarded as synonymous with *M. australis cyanotis*]

Megalaima australis (*Horsfield*) BLUE-EARED BARBET Sikkim through SE Asia to Sumatra, Java, Bali, Borneo and adjacent small islands/ thick forest/fruit and insects/n hole/e 2–4/ I ♂♀

Megalaima eximia (*Sharpe*) BLACK-THROATED BARBET Mts of Borneo/no data

Megalaima rubricapilla (*Gmelin*) SMALL BARBET Ceylon/open forest/n hole/e 2–4

Megalaima malabarica (*Blyth*) CRIMSON-THROATED BARBET W coast of India from Goa to S Travancore/evergreen forest/fruit/n hole/ e 2–4

Megalaima haemacephala (*Müller*) COPPERSMITH Indian sub-continent, SE Asia, Sumatra, Java, Bali: Philippines/deciduous forest/fruit and insects/n hole/e 2–4/I ♂♀

Calorhamphus fuliginosus (*Temminck*) BROWN BARBET Malay Peninsula, Sumatra, Borneo/swamp-jungle and hill forest/insects and fruit/n hole/e n/s

Gymnobucco calvus (*Lafresnaye*) NAKED-FACED BARBET W and SW Africa from Sierra Leone to Benguella/mountains/fruit and insects/n hole of dead tree/e 3

Gymnobucco peli *Hartlaub* BRITTLE-NOSED BARBET Ghana to Gabon/mountain forest/ fruit/n and e – no reliable information

Gymnobucco sladeni *Ogilvie-Grant* SLADEN'S BARBET Upper Congo/forests/n and e n/k

Gymnobucco bonapartei *Hartlaub* GREY-THROATED BARBET WC and EC Africa/forest/ fruit and insects/n hole/e 3–5

Buccanodon leucotis (*Sundevall*) WHITE-EARED BARBET E Africa from Kenya to Natal; Angola/forest/fruit and insects/n hole/e 2–6

Buccanodon olivaceum (*Shelley*) GREEN BARBET E Africa from Kenya to N Mozambique/ mountain forest/fruit/n hole/e up to 6

Buccanodon anchietae *Bocage* YELLOW-HEADED BARBET Angola and S Congo / open woodland/fruit/n hole/e 4

Buccanodon whytii (*Shelley*) WHYTE'S BARBET E Africa from Lake Tanganyika to Ndola, Zambia / open woodland / fruit and insects/n hole/e 4–6

Buccanodon duchaillui (*Cassin*) YELLOW-SPOTTED BARBET W Africa from Sierra Leone to Congo/forest/fruit and insects/n hole/e n/k

[Genus *Pogoniulus*. In his discussion of this genus, Peters (*Check List of the Birds of the World*, vol V, p 44) implies that *Bucco nanus* Boddaert, and *Bucco parvus* Gmelin, are unidentifiable. Both were based on the 'Barbu de Sénégal' of Daubenton, Pl enlum no 746, f 2. This plate is quite identifiable as an immature Coppersmith (*Megalaima haemacephala*)]

Pogoniulus scolopaceus (*Bonaparte*) SPECKLED TINKERBIRD Tropical Africa and Fernando Po/forest/insects/n hole/e up to 4

Pogoniulus leucomystax (*Sharpe*) MOUSTACHED GREEN TINKERBIRD Kenya, Tanganyika and Malawi/mountain forest/fruit and insects/n hole/e 2

Pogoniulus simplex (*Fischer and Reichenow*) GREEN TINKERBIRD Kenya, Tanzania and Malawi/mountain forest/no data

Pogoniulus coryphaeus (*Reichenow*) WESTERN GREEN TINKERBIRD W Cameroons, E Congo, W Uganda and Benguella /clearings in mountain forest/insects and fruit/n hole/ e 3

Pogoniulus pusillus (*Dumont*) RED-FRONTED TINKERBIRD E Africa from Kenya to Swaziland/ scrub and juniper forest/fruit and insects/n hole/ e 2–3

Pogoniulus chrysoconus (*Temminck*) YELLOW-FRONTED TINKERBIRD Much of Africa from Air in Sahara southwards to Transvaal and Damaraland/forest and open woodland/insects and fruit/n hole/e 2–3

Pogoniulus bilineatus (*Sundevall*) GOLDEN-RUMPED TINKERBIRD E and EC Africa from Kenya to Natal/forest/fruit and insects/n hole/ e 2–4

Pogoniulus makawai *Benson and Irwin* (*Bull Brit Orn Cl*, 85, (1965), p 6) WHITE-CHESTED TINKERBIRD Zambia/unique

Pogoniulus leucolaima (*Verreaux and Verreaux*) LEMON-RUMPED TINKERBIRD W and C Africa and Fernando Po/forest and gardens/ insects and fruit/n hole/e 2–3

Pogoniulus subsulphureus (*Fraser*) YELLOW-THROATED TINKERBIRD W and C Africa and Fernando Po / forest / fruit and berries/n hole/e 1–3

Pogoniulus atroflavus (*Sparrman*) RED-RUMPED TINKERBIRD Guinea/forests / insects and fruit/n hole/e ?3

Tricholaema lacrymosum *Cabanis* SPOTTED-FLANKED BARBET Uganda, Kenya and Tanganyika / acacia woodland / insects and fruit/n hole/e 3

Tricholaema leucomelan (*Boddaert*) PIED BARBET S Africa N to Angola and Zambia/ bush and thornveldt/fruit/n hole/e 3–4

Tricholaema diadematum (*Heuglin*) RED-FRONTED BARBET Africa from Ethiopia to Malawi and Angola / scrub / insects, fruit and birds' eggs/n hole/e 2

Tricholaema melanocephalum (*Cretzschmar*) BROWN-THROATED BARBET Ethiopia, Somaliland, parts of Kenya and Tanganyika / desert scrub / fruit and insects/ n and e n/k

Tricholaema flavibuccale *Reichenow* YELLOW-CHEEKED BARBET Tanganyika/unique

Tricholaema hirsutum (*Swainson*) BLACK-THROATED BARBET W Africa from Sierra Leone to N Angola

Tricholaema flavipunctatum *Verreaux and Verreaux* HAIRY-BREASTED BARBET Uganda and NE Zaire/forest/fruit /n hole/e n/k

Lybius undatus (*Rüppell*) BANDED BARBET Ethiopia / trees and bushes at high altitudes/ no data

Lybius vieilloti (*Leach*) VIEILLOT'S BARBET Scrub-belt of S Sahara from Senegal to Ethiopia/scrub/insects/n hole/e 3

Lybius torquatus (*Dumont*) BLACK-COLLARED BARBET E and S Africa (except the dry SW)/ scrub and woodland/fruit and insects/n hole/e 3

Lybius guifsobalito *Herrmann* BLACK-BILLED BARBET E Africa from Ethiopia to Lake Victoria/ open woodland and bush/fruit/n and e n/k

Lybius rubrifacies (*Reichenow*) RED-FACED BARBET The region W and SW of Lake Victoria/

PSITTACIDAE:
Eclectus roratus,
Eclectus Parrot

PSITTACIDAE:
Melopsittacus undulatus,
Budgerigar

Plate 122

PSITTACIDAE:
Psittacus erithacus,
African Grey Parrot

PSITTACIDAE:
Psittacula krameri,
Rose-ringed Parrakeet

Plate 123

forest/no other data

Lybius chaplini *Stevenson Clarke* CHAPLIN'S BARBET Lower Kafue valley of Zambia / fig trees/figs/n hole/e 2 (1 nest known, parasitised by *Indicator minor*)

Lybius leucocephalus (*Defilippi*) WHITE-HEADED BARBET Equatorial belt of Africa/large trees in open country/fruit, seeds and insects/ n hole/e 3

Lybius minor (*Cuvier*) BLACK-BACKED BARBET Regions of Congo and Zambia/woodland and forest edges/fruit and insects/n in nest of tree-building ants/e n/k

Lybius melanopterus (*Peters*) BROWN-BREASTED BARBET E Africa from Somaliland to Mozambique / thin woodland or semi-desert/ fruit/n and e n/k

Lybius bidentatus (*Shaw*) DOUBLE-TOOTHED BARBET Portuguese Guinea to N Angola, Tanganyika and Ethiopia/forest, woodland and cultivation/fruit/n hole/e ?3–4

Lybius dubius (*Gmelin*) BEARDED BARBET Senegal to Logone River, semi-arid places/ forest and savannah/fruit/n hole/e ?2 ?3–4 (accounts differ)

Lybius rolleti (*Defilippi*) BLACK-BREASTED BARBET Savannah belt from Shari to Bahr el Ghazal / forest and cultivation / figs etc / n hole / e n/k

Trachyphonus purpuratus *Verreaux and Verreaux* YELLOW-BILLED BARBET W Africa from Sierra Leone to Angola/forest/fruit and insects/n hole/e up to 4

Trachyphonus vaillantii *Ranzani* LEVAILLANT'S BARBET S Africa N to Congo and Pangani/bush and woodland/termites/n hole/ e 3–5

Trachyphonus erythrocephalus *Cabanis* RED AND YELLOW BARBET Ethiopia and Tanganyika/desert bush/insects/n hole in bank/ e 2

Trachyphonus darnaudii (*Prévost and Des Murs*) D'ARNAUD'S BARBET Ethiopia and Tanganyika/thornbush/fruit/n vertical hole in ground / e 2–4 (*T. usambiro* is sometimes separated)

Trachyphonus margaritatus (*Cretzschmar*) YELLOW-BREASTED BARBET Ethiopia, Somaliland and the arid belt of Africa W to Air/desert bush/ insects/n hole in wall or earth bank/e 4–6

INDICATORIDAE Honeyguides Dull-coloured birds allied to the Barbets and remark-able for the habit of some species of leading men and animals to bees' nests. They feed largely on insects, particularly bees and wasps and their honey and wax. All species, so far as is known, are parasitic in their nesting habits. About a dozen species, mostly in Africa, but some in Asia.

Prodotiscus insignis (*Cassin*) CASSIN'S HONEYGUIDE Much of equatorial Africa/forest/ largely scale-insects and wax/P on White-Eyes, Rock Sparrows and Tinkerbirds

Prodotiscus regulus *Sundevall* WAHLBERG'S HONEYGUIDE E Africa from Sennar to Natal/ wattle-trees / insects, flowers, scale-insects and their wax / ? P on Yellow-throated Petronia

Melignomon zenkeri *Reichenow* ZENKER'S HONEYGUIDE S Cameroon to N Angola / forest/ wax/n and e n/k

Indicator exilis (*Cassin*) LEAST HONEYGUIDE Much of equatorial Africa/forest/insects and wax/no reliable data on n and e (*I. willcocksi* Alexander and *I. meliphilus* Oberholzer, are sometimes separated)

[**Indicator propinquus** *Friedmann* Cameroons/ unique / this is now regarded as synonymous with *I. willcocksi*]

Indicator minor *Stephens* LESSER HONEYGUIDE Much of Africa S of Sahara/forest/bees and other insects/P on small birds

Indicator conirostris (*Cassin*) THICK-BILLED HONEYGUIDE Gold Coast and Nigeria E to Ruwenzori / forest / insects and wax / P on Barbets

Indicator variegatus *Lesson* SCALY-THROATED HONEYGUIDE E and S Africa from Ethiopia to the Cape / varied habitat / beeswax, honey and grubs, also caterpillars / P on woodpeckers, sparrows etc

Indicator maculatus *Gray* SPOTTED HONEYGUIDE W Africa from Gambia to Cameroon/forest/insects and wax/n and e n/k

Indicator archipelagus *Temminck* MALAYSIAN HONEYGUIDE Malay Peninsula, Sumatra, Borneo/swamp-jungle and forest/n and e n/k

Indicator indicator (*Sparrman*) GREATER HONEYGUIDE Africa S of Sahara / variable habitat / beeswax, honey and grubs / P on barbets, woodpeckers etc

Indicator xanthonotus *Blyth* ORANGE-RUMPED HONEYGUIDE Himalayas / forest with cliffs and rock scarps/bees and beeswax /n and e n/k but probably P on barbets

Indicator pumilio *Chapin* (*Bull Brit Orn Cl*, 78 (1958), p 46) DWARF HONEYGUIDE W Kenya, Uganda and the Kivu area/mountain forest/insects and wax/n and e n/k

Melichneutes robustus (*Bates*) LYRE-TAILED HONEYGUIDE Cameroons to Upper Ituri/lowland forest/wax/n and e n/k

RAMPHASTIDAE Toucans Generally fairly strikingly marked birds with enormous brightly coloured bills, in some cases almost as big as the rest of the body. They are arboreal birds feeding on fruit, insects and sometimes fledgling birds. Nest is in a tree hole, the eggs are white and 2–4 in number. Incubation is by both sexes and lasts about 16 days. The fledging period is about 6 to 7 weeks. About 40 species in the forests of tropical America.

Aulacorhynchus sulcatus (*Swainson*) GROOVE-BILLED TOUCANET Venezuela/forest

Aulacorynchus calorhynchus (*Gould*) YELLOW-BILLED TOUCANET Santa Marta Mts, Colombia and Merida and Sierra de Perijá in Venezuela/forest (sometimes treated as a race of *A. sulcatus*)

Aulacorhynchus derbianus *Gould* CHESTNUT-TIPPED TOUCANET Mts from Ecuador to Guyana/forest

Aulacorhynchus prasinus (*Gould*) EMERALD TOUCANET Mexico, C America and Andes from Venezuela to Peru/forest

Aulacorhynchus caeruleogularis (*Gould*) BLUE-THROATED TOUCANET Costa Rica to Darien/n hole/e 3–4/I ♂♀

Aulacorhynchus haematopygus (*Gould*) CRIMSON-RUMPED TOUCANET Andes from Venezuela to Ecuador / forest

Aulacorhynchus coeruleicinctus *d'Orbigny* BLUE-BANDED TOUCANET Sub-tropical zone of Peru and Bolivia/forest

Aulacorhynchus huallagae *Carriker* YELLOW-BROWED TOUCANET Huallaga Valley, Peru/forest

Pteroglossus torquatus (*Gmelin*) COLLARED TOUCAN Mexico to Panama/forest

Pteroglossus frantzii *Cabanis* FIERY-BILLED TOUCAN Costa Rica to N Venezuela/may be conspecific with *P. torquatus*

Pteroglossus sanguineus *Gould* STRIPE-BILLED TOUCAN W coast of Colombia and NW Ecuador /forest / may be conspecific with *P. torquatus*

Pteroglossus erythropygius *Gould* PALE-MANDIBLED TOUCAN W Ecuador/forest/may be conspecific with *P. torquatus*

Pteroglossus castanotis *Gould* CHESTNUT-EARED TOUCAN E Colombia to NE Peru and W and S Brazil, and Bolivia to Paraguay and NE Argentina/forest

Pteroglossus aracari (*L*) ARACARI TOUCAN Brazil, Venezuela and the Guianas / forest, savannah and plantations

Pteroglossus pluricinctus *Gould* MANY-BANDED TOUCAN Tropical zone from E Peru to Upper Orinoco/forest

Pteroglossus viridis (*L*) GREEN TOUCAN Brazil N of Amazon extending N to the Guianas/forest and savannah

Pteroglossus inscriptus *Swainson* LETTERED TOUCAN Brazil S of the Amazon/forest and palm groves

[**Pteroglossus didymus** *Sclater* Upper Amazonia / unique / now generally regarded as synonymous with *P. viridis humboldti*]

Pteroglossus bitorquatus *Vigors* RED-NECKED TOUCAN Amazonian Brazil

Pteroglossus olallae *Gyldenstolpe* MAROON-BACKED TOUCAN Rio Juruá, Brazil / unique/ possibly a hybrid *P. torquatus × P. mariae* (Zimmer, *Auk*, vol 60 (1943), p 251)

Pteroglossus flavirostris *Fraser* IVORY-BILLED TOUCAN Amazonian Colombia, E Ecuador, S Venezuela and NW Brazil/forest

Pteroglossus azara (*Vieillot*) AZARA TOUCAN W Brazil

Pteroglossus mariae *Gould* MARIA'S TOUCAN E Peru, N Bolivia and Brazil S of Amazon to Rio Purús/forest [NB: The arrangement of these three forms, *flavirostris*, *azara* and *mariae* is complicated, and I cannot entirely reconcile the description given by de Schaunsee (1970) *Birds of S America* with the specimens in the British Museum (Natural History). In recent literature *azara* (to my eyes the most distinctive of the three and the oldest of the three names) is generally relegated to a race of *flavirostris*, while *mariae* is separated, following Todd, *Proc Biol Soc Washington*, 56 (1943), pp 161–2. I have felt it best to list all three forms until a revision of the group is carried out]

Pteroglossus beauharnaesii *Wagler* CURL-CRESTED TOUCAN Amazonian Peru, W Brazil, and N Bolivia/forest

Selenidera spectabilis *Cassin* YELLOW-EARED TOUCANET Honduras to NW Colombia/forest

PSITTACIDAE:
Eclectus roratus,
Eclectus Parrot

PSITTACIDAE:
Polytelis swainsoni,
Barraband's Parrakeet or
Superb Parrot

Opposite:
PSITTACIDAE:
Alisterus scapularis,
King Parrot,
Australian King Parrot

Plate 124

Plate 125

Selenidera culik (*Wagler*) GUIANA TOUCANET The Guianas and N Brazil / forest and savannah

Selenidera reinwardtii (*Wagler*) REINWARDT'S or GOLDEN-COLLARED TOUCANET Upper Amazonia from Colombia to Peru and extreme W Brazil / forest

[**Selenidera langsdorfii** (*Wagler*) is considered conspecific with *S. reinwardtii*]

Selenidera maculirostris (*Lichtenstein*) SPOT-BILLED TOUCANET E and S Amazonian Brazil S to N Argentina

Selenidera gouldii (*Natterer*) GOULD'S TOUCANET NE Brazil (qv de Schaunsee *Birds of S America* (1966), p 211)

Selenidera nattereri (*Gould*) TAWNY-TUFTED or NATTERER'S TOUCANET E Venezuela, NW Brazil and the Guianas / forest

Baillonius bailloni (*Vieillot*) SAFFRON or BAILLON'S TOUCAN SE Brazil / forest

Andigena laminirostris *Gould* LAMINATED TOUCAN SW Colombia and W Ecuador / forest

Andigena hypoglauca *Gould* GREY-BREASTED TOUCAN Andes of Colombia, E Ecuador and E Peru / humid temperate forest

Andigena cucullata (*Gould*) HOODED TOUCAN Andes of Peru and Bolivia / humid temperate forest

Andigena nigrirostris (*Waterhouse*) BLACK-BILLED TOUCAN Andes of Colombia and NE Ecuador / forest

Ramphastos vitellinus *Lichtenstein* CHANNEL-BILLED TOUCAN Much of tropical S America E of Andes and S to São Paulo / forest (*R. ariel* Vigors and *R. culminatus* Gould, are sometimes separated)

Ramphastos dicolorus *L* RED-BREASTED TOUCAN SE Brazil, Paraguay and NE Argentina / forest

Ramphastos citreolaemus *Gould* CITRON-THROATED TOUCAN Magdalena and Cauca valleys of Colombia / forest

Ramphastos sulfuratus *Lesson* KEEL-BILLED TOUCAN SE Mexico, C America across N Colombia to Perija in Venezuela / forest. *Ramphastos piscivorus* L 1766, based on plate 64, vol 2, of Edwards, *A Natural History of Birds* (1743), was formerly used for this species. Edwards' plate resembles *R. sulfuratus* except for the white throat, which may indicate an extinct race, an individual variant, or a bad painting. Peters (*Auk*, 48 (1930), pp 406–7) says that Edwards plate is unidentifiable.

Ramphastos swainsonii *Gould* SWAINSON'S TOUCAN SE Honduras to W Ecuador / forest / fruit, insects and small vertebrates / n hole / e n/k (possibly conspecific with *R. ambiguus*)

Ramphastos ambiguus *Swainson* BLACK-MANDIBLED TOUCAN E Andes from Peru to Venezuela / forest

Ramphastos brevis *de Schaunsee* CHOCO TOUCAN Pacific Darién, to W Ecuador / humid forest

Ramphastos aurantiirostris *Hartert* ORANGE-BILLED TOUCAN Venezuela and the Guianas / forest / probably conspecific with *R. tucanus*

Ramphastos tucanus *L* RED-BILLED TOUCAN SE Venezuela, the Guianas and N Brazil / forest, savannah and palm groves

Ramphastos cuvieri *Wagler* CUVIER'S TOUCAN Upper Amazon and Upper Orinoco basins / probably conspecific with *R. tucanus*

Ramphastos inca *Gould* INCA TOUCAN E Bolivia / the status of this form is doubtful, it is often treated as a race of *R. cuvieri*

Ramphastos toco *Müller* TOCO TOUCAN Eastern S America from the Guianas to N Argentina / woodland, secondary growth, coconut plantations and palm groves

[**Ramphastos picatus** *L* Believed to be an artifact]

[**Ramphastos osculans** *Gould* An unstable population occurring where the ranges of the three races of *R. vitellinus* meet]

PICIDAE Woodpeckers, Wrynecks and Piculets Variable-sized birds adapted to insectivorous diets, and generally arboreal in habit. Woodpeckers have straight, pointed bills, short feet and stiffened tail feathers. They hammer trees with their bills to find grubs, and the tongue is long, barbed and sticky to aid in the capture of these. Nest in holes in trees, excavated in the case of Woodpeckers, but Wrynecks and Piculets tend to use abandoned woodpecker holes. The eggs are white. About 210 species throughout the world except Australia, the oceanic islands and Madagascar.

Jynx torquilla *L* EURASIAN WRYNECK b temperate Palaearctic and Mediterranean w S to equatorial Africa and S Asia / forest, woodland and orchard / insects, chiefly ants / n hole / e 5–14 / I ♂♀ 12–14 / F 19–21

Jynx ruficollis *Wagner* RED-BREASTED WRYNECK Africa S of Sahara (but not W of

Cameroons) / savannah / insects (chiefly ants)/ n hole/ e 2–4

Picumnus cinnamomeus *Wagler* CHESTNUT PICULET Parts of Venezuela and N Colombia/ arid scrub, thickets and forest

Picumnus rufiventris (*Bonaparte*) RUFOUS-BREASTED PICULET E Ecuador to N Bolivia/ forest edge

Picumnus fulvescens *Stager* (in *Contrib in Science, Los Angeles Co Mus*, 46 (1961), p 1) TAWNY PICULET Brazil / known from 5 specimens

[**Picumnus fuscus** *Pelzeln* NATTERER'S PICULET Rio Guaporé, Brazil / unique / possibly juvenile of some other species]

Picumnus castelnau *Malherbe* PLAIN-BREASTED PICULET E Ecuador and NE Peru

Picumnus spilogaster *Sundevall* (=**P. leucogaster,** *Pelzeln*) WHITE-BELLIED PICULET Middle Orinoco in Venezuela and Rio Branco in Brazil / open woodlands and thickets

Picumnus limae *Snethlage* OCHRACEOUS PICULET E Brazil

Picumnus olivaceus *Lafresnaye* OLIVACEUS PICULET Honduras to W Venezuela and W Ecuador / forest edge, thicket and cultivation / n hole / e 2–3 / I ♂♀ 14 / F 24–5

Picumnus granadensis *Lafresnaye* GREYISH PICULET Andes of Colombia / forest and scrub

Picumnus nebulosus *Sundevall* MOTTLED PICULET S Brazil

Picumnus nigropunctatus *Zimmer and Phelps* (*Am Mus Novit*, no 1,455 (1950), p 6) BLACK-DOTTED PICULET Orinoco delta / forest

Picumnus exilis (*Lichtenstein*) GOLDEN-SPANGLED PICULET Venezuela, the Guianas and N Brazil / forest edge and savannah

Picumnus borbae *Pelzeln* BAR-BREASTED PICULET E Peru, W and S Brazil

Picumnus aurifrons *Pelzeln* GOLDEN-FRONTED PICULET Parts of Colombia, Ecuador and Peru; W Brazil and Brazil S of the Amazon/ forest and scrub

Picumnis temminckii *Lafresnaye* OCHRE-COLLARED PICULET SE Brazil, Paraguay and NE Argentina / forest

Picumnus cirrhatus *Temminck* WHITE-BARRED PICULET Eastern S America from Guyana to N Argentina / forest, patches of wood and parks

Picumnus dorbygnianus *Lafresnaye* OCELLATED PICULET Bolivia and (?) Peru / forest

Picumnus sclateri *Taczanowski* ECUADORIAN

or SCLATER'S PICULET Ecuador and N Peru /arid scrub

Picumnus steindachneri *Taczanowski* SPECKLE-CHESTED PICULET NE Peru

Picumnus subtilis *Stager* (*Contrib in Science, Los Angeles Co Mus*, 153 (1968), p 1) SUBTLE PICULET SE Peru (not in de Schaunsee 1970)

Picumnus squamulatus *Lafresnaye* SCALED PICULET Colombia and Venezuela / forest

Picumnus minutissimus (*Pallas*) ARROW-HEAD PICULET Surinam, Cayenne, E and S Brazil, Bolivia / plantations, savannah and mangroves (*P. pallidus* Snethlage, and *P. albosquamatus* d'Orbigny, and *P. guttifer* Sundevall, are now all regarded as races of *minutissimus*)

Picumnus varzeae *Snethlage* VARZEA PICULET Islands in the Amazon near Oleidos and on the lower Rio Jamundá / swampy forest

Picumnus pygmaeus (*Lichtenstein*) SPOTTED PICULET NE Brazil

Picumnus asterias *Sundevall* BLACKISH PICULET Brazil / unique / exact locality not known

Picumnus pumilus *Cabanis and Heine* ORINOCO PICULET Maipures on the upper Orinoco in Columbia (*synonym P. stellae*)/known only from the type of *P. pumilus*, without locality, and the original series of 11 specimens of *P. stellae* all from Maipures

Picumnus innominatus *Burton* SPECKLED PICULET India, SE Asia, S China, Sumatra, Borneo / low jungle and scrub / ants / n hole/ e 3–4 / I ♂♀ ?11

Nesoctites micromegas (*Sundevall*) ANTILLEAN PICULET Gonave and Hispaniola/ humid forest /n hole /e 3–6

Verreauxia africana (*Verreaux and Verreaux*) AFRICAN PICULET Nigeria, S Cameroon, Gabon and Congo / forest and secondary growth / insects/ n hole /e n/s

Sasia ochracea *Hodgson* WHITE-BROWED PICULET Himalayas through mts of SE Asia and SE China / scrub and jungle / ants /n hole /e 3–4

Sasia abnormis (*Temminck*) RUFOUS PICULET Malay Peninsula, Sumatra, Billiton, Java, Borneo and Nias / bamboo thickets and forest undergrowth / beetles, ants and spiders / n hole / e n/s

Geocolaptes olivaceus (*Gmelin*) GROUND WOODPECKER S Africa N to Natal and the Drakensberg / open country and broken rocky hills / ground insects / n hole in bank / e 3–5

Plate 126

PSITTACIDAE:
Calyptorhynchus lathami,
Glossy Cockatoo

PSITTACIDAE:
Calyptorhynchus funereus,
Black Cockatoo

PSITTACIDAE:
Eolophus roseicapillus,
Galah or Roseate Cockatoo

Opposite:
PSITTACIDAE:
Lorius domicellus,
Purple-naped Lory

Plate 127

Colaptes auratus (*L*) COMMON FLICKER Much of N America, C America, Cuba and the Cayman Is / open and burnt forest, orchard and cultivation insects and berries / n hole / e 3–12 / I ♂♀ 9–16 (*C. cafer* (Gmelin) and *C. chrysoides* (Malherbe) are often separated)

Colaptes rupicola *d'Orbigny* ANDEAN FLICKER Mts from Peru to N Chile / open country

Colaptes pitius (*Molina*) CHILEAN FLICKER Andes of Chile and Argentina / open woodland

Colaptes campestris (*Vieillot*) CAMPOS FLICKER E Brazil and E Bolivia / campos and palm groves

Colaptes campestroides (*Malherbe*) FIELD FLICKER S Brazil, Paraguay, Uruguay and Argentina S to La Pampa / savannah and woodland

Nesoceleus   fernandinae (*Vigors*) FERNANDINA's or CUBA FLICKER Cuba / palm groves in open country

Chrysoptilus melanochloros (*Gmelin*) GREEN-BARRED WOODPECKER E Brazil, E Paraguay, Uruguay and NE Argentina / palm groves and swampy woods

Chrysoptilus melanolaimus (*Malherbe*) GOLDEN-BREASTED WOODPECKER Bolivia and Paraguay S through Argentina to Buenos Aires / woodland, savannah, grassland and orchard

Chrysoptilus punctigula (*Boddaert*) SPOT-BREASTED WOODPECKER E Darién through N Venezuela, N Colombia, the Guianas to NE Brazil / open woodland, mangrove and cerrado

Chrysoptilus atricollis (*Malherbe*) BLACK-NECKED WOODPECKER Peru / columnar cacti and open woods

Piculus rivolii (*Boissonneau*) CRIMSON-MANTLED WOODPECKER Andes from Venezuela to Bolivia / forest

Piculus auricularis (*Salvin and Godman*) GREY-CROWNED WOODPECKER W Mexico

Piculus aeruginosus (*Malherbe*) BRONZE WOODPECKER NE Mexico

Piculus rubiginosus (*Swainson*) GOLDEN-OLIVE WOODPECKER C America, mts from Colombia S to Bolivia and E to Guyana, Trinidad and Tobago / forest, scrub and secondary growth / n hole / e 4 / I ♂♀ / F ?c24

Piculus simplex (*Salvin*) RUFOUS-WINGED WOODPECKER Honduras; and Nicaragua to W Panama

Piculus flavigula (*Boddaert*) YELLOW-THROATED WOODPECKER Much of S America E

of Andes and S to Rio de Janeiro / forest and savannah

Piculus callopterus (*Lawrence*) STRIPE-CHEEKED WOODPECKER Panama

Piculus leucolaemus (*Natterer and Malherbe*) WHITE-THROATED WOODPECKER Upper Amazon basin / forest

Piculus aurulentus (*Temminck*) WHITE-BROWED WOODPECKER SE Brazil, Paraguay and NE Argentina / forest

Piculus chrysochloros (*Vieillot*) GOLDEN-GREEN WOODPECKER Much of S America E of Andes and S to NE Argentina (the race *P. c. aurosus* (Nelson) from Marraganti, Panama, is known only from the unique type) / forest and savannah

Campethera punctuligera (*Wagler*) FINE-SPOTTED WOODPECKER Senegal to Lake Chad and Bahr el Ghazal / open woodland / termites / n hole / e 2–3

Campethera nubica (*Boddaert*) NUBIAN WOODPECKER E Africa from Sudan to Mozambique / open woodland and bush / insects / n hole / e 2–3 (*C. scriptoricauda* (Reichenow) is sometimes separated)

Campethera bennettii (*Smith*) BENNETT'S WOODPECKER SE Africa from Lake Victoria to Transvaal and S Angola / acacia and thorn scrub / insects / n hole / e 3

Campethera cailliautii (*Malherbe*) LITTLE SPOTTED WOODPECKER E Africa from Lake Victoria to Mozambique / palm groves / ants and termites / n hole / e 2–3

Campethera notata (*Lichtenstein*) KNYSNA WOODPECKER S Cape Province and Natal / coastal bush and open plantation / n hole / e 2

Campethera abingoni (*Smith*) GOLDEN-TAILED WOODPECKER Africa S of Sahara / all types of wooded country / insects / n hole / e 2–3

Campethera taeniolaema (*Reichenow and Neumann*) FINE-BANDED WOODPECKER Kenya / highland forest / insects / n and e n/k

Campethera tullbergi (*Sjöstedt*) TULLBERG's WOODPECKER Cameroon Highlands / forest / no other data

Campethera maculosa (*Valenciennes*) AFRICAN GOLDEN-BACKED WOODPECKER Portuguese Guinea, Sierra Leone, Liberia and Ghana / forest and secondary forest / ants / n hole / e n/k

Campethera permista (*Reichenow*) GREEN-BACKED WOODPECKER Ghana to N Angola and

SW Ethiopia / lowland forest and secondary growth / ants / n hole / e 3

Campethera caroli (*Malherbe*) BROWN-EARED WOODPECKER Liberia to N Angola and W Kenya / forest / ants and termites / n hole / e 3

Campethera nivosa (*Swainson*) BUFF-SPOTTED WOODPECKER Casamance to N Angola and Kenya; Fernando Po / forest / ants and larvae / n hole in nest of tree ants / e 2

Celeus flavescens (*Gmelin*) BLONDE-CRESTED WOODPECKER E Brazil, Bolivia, Paraguay and N Argentina / forest

Celeus lugubris (*Malherbe*) PALE-CRESTED WOODPECKER Bolivia, Mato Grosso, Paraguay and NW Argentina / scrub and swampy forest

Celeus spectabilis *Sclater and Salvin* RUFOUS-HEADED WOODPECKER Bolivia and E Ecuador

Celeus castaneus (*Wagler*) CHESTNUT WOODPECKER SE Mexico, C America

Celeus immaculatus (*Berlepsch*) IMMACULATE WOODPECKER Panama / unique

Celeus elegans (*Müller*) ELEGANT WOODPECKER Parts of Amazon and Orinoco basins / forest, savannah and mangrove (*C. jumana* (Spix) is now generally regarded as a race)

Celeus grammicus (*Natterer and Malherbe*) SCALE-BREASTED WOODPECKER Headwaters of the Amazon / forest

Celeus loricatus (*Reichenbach*) CINNAMON WOODPECKER Nicaragua S through lowlands of Colombia to Ecuador / forest and clearings

Celeus undatus (*L*) WAVED WOODPECKER The Guianas, N and NE Brazil / forest and savannah

Celeus flavus (*Müller*) CREAM-COLOURED WOODPECKER Amazon and Orinoco basins / forest, mangroves, savannah and plantations

Celeus torquatus (*Boddaert*) RINGED WOODPECKER Amazon and Orinoco basins

Micropternus brachyurus (*Vieillot*) RUFOUS WOODPECKER Indian region, SE Asia, S China, Hainan and W Indonesia / forest and bamboo jungle / insects and fruit / n hole / e 2–3

Picus viridis *L* GREEN WOODPECKER Europe, N Turkey, N Iran to Baluchistan / open woodland, parkland and heath / insects / n hole / e 4–11/ I ♂♀ 18–19 / F 18–21

Picus vaillantii (*Malherbe*) LEVAILLANT'S WOODPECKER Morocco to Tunisia / hill woods / n hole / e 4–8

Picus awokera *Temminck* JAPANESE WOODPECKER Japan / mixed forest / insects and fruit / n hole / e 7–8

Picus squamatus *Vigors* GREAT SCALY WOODPECKER Mts from Transcaspia to Sikkim / forest / insects / n hole / e 5–6

Picus viridanus *Blyth* STREAKED-BREASTED WOODPECKER SE Asia / forest, lowland coastal scrub and jungle / n hole / e 2–3

Picus xanthopygaeus (*Gray and Gray*) (=**P. myrmecophoneus**, *Stresemann*) LITTLE SCALY WOODPECKER India, Ceylon and SE Asia (except Laos and Malaya) / open forest and plantations / mainly ants and termites / n hole / e 3–5

Picus vittatus *Vieillot* LACED WOODPECKER Malaya, Sumatra, Java, Bali, Kangean and Langkavi Is / mangrove and bamboo / n hole / e 4

Picus canus *Gmelin* ASHY WOODPECKER C and E Europe, across C Asia to Himalayas, SE Asia, China, Manchuria, Korea, Hokkaido, Hainan, Taiwan and Sumatra / forest / ants and termites / n hole / e 4–5 / I ♂♀

Picus rabieri (*Oustalet*) RED-COLLARED WOODPECKER Tonkin, Laos and Annam

Picus erythropygius (*Elliot*) BLACK-HEADED WOODPECKER S Burma, S Thailand, S Vietnam, Cambodia / bamboo jungle and clearings / n hole / e 2

Picus flavinucha *Gould* GREATER YELLOW-NAPED WOODPECKER Himalayas, SE Asia, S China, Hainan, Sumatra / mountain forest / insects / n hole / e 3–4 / I ♂♀

Picus puniceus *Horsfield* CRIMSON-WINGED WOODPECKER Malay Peninsula, Sumatra, Bangka, Borneo, Nias, Java / lowland forest / n and e n/k

Picus chlorolophus *Vieillot* LESSER YELLOW-NAPED WOODPECKER Indian region, SE Asia, S China, Hainan, Sumatra / jungle / insects / n hole / e 2–4 / I ♂♀

Picus mentalis *Temminck* CHEQUERED-THROATED WOODPECKER Malay Peninsula, Sumatra, Java, Bangka, Borneo / lowland forest / insects and fruit / n hole / e 3

Picus miniaceus *Pennant* (=**P. miniatus** *Forster*) BANDED WOODPECKER Malay Peninsula, Sumatra, Java, Nias, Billiton, Bangka, Borneo / forest / insects and eggs / n and e n/k

Dinopium benghalense (*L*) LESSER GOLDEN-BACKED WOODPECKER Indian sub-continent / forest and cultivation / insects / n hole / e 3 / I ♂♀

Dinopium shorii (*Vigors*) HIMALAYAN GOLDEN-BACKED WOODPECKER Mts from Nepal

PSITTACIDAE:
Cacatua tenuirostris,
Long-billed Corella

PSITTACIDAE:
Cacatua moluccensis,
Rose Crested Cockatoo,
Salmon-Crested Cockatoo

Plate 128

PSITTACIDAE;
Cacatua sulphurea, Lesser
Sulphur Crested Cockatoo

PSITTACIDAE:
Cacatua sanguinea,
Little Corella or
Bare-eyed Cockatoo

Plate 129

to Burma / forest / presumably insects / n hole /
e 2–3

Dinopium javanense (*Ljungh*) GREATER
GOLDEN-BACKED WOODPECKER W India: SE
Asia, Greater Sundas and Philippines / open
forest and cultivation / insects / n hole / e 2–3

Dinopium rafflesii (*Vigors and Horsfield*)
RAFFLES' WOODPECKER Malay Peninsula,
Sumatra, Borneo, Bangka / hill forest / n and e n/k

Gecinulus grantia (*McClelland*) PALE-
HEADED WOODPECKER Nepal through Indo-
China to S China / forest and bamboo jungle /
insects / n hole / e 3

Gecinulus viridis *Blyth* BAMBOO WOODPECKER
C and S Burma, Thailand and Malay Peninsula /
bamboo forest / n and e n/k

Meiglyptes tristis (*Horsfield*) BUFF-RUMPED
WOODPECKER Malay Peninsula, Sumatra,
Borneo, Java and adjacent small islands / lowland
forest and orchards / n hole / e 2

Meiglyptes jugularis (*Blyth*) BLACK-AND-
BUFF WOODPECKER SE Asia / forest / n hole /
e–1 hard-set egg known

Meiglyptes tukki (*Lesson*) BUFF-NECKED
WOODPECKER Malay Peninsula, Sumatra,
Borneo and adjacent small islands / lowland
forest / n and e n/k

Mulleripicus pulverulentus (*Temminck*)
GREAT SLATY WOODPECKER N India, SE Asia,
Sumatra, Java, Borneo, Palawan and adjacent
small islands / lowland forest / insects / n hole /
e 3–4 / I ♂♀

Mulleripicus funebris (*Valenciennes*) SOOTY
WOODPECKER Philippines (*M. fuliginosus*,
Tweeddale, is now considered to be a race of
funebris)

Mulleripicus fulvus (*Quoy and Gaimard*)
FULVOUS WOODPECKER Celebes, Muna and
Togian Is

Dryocopus martius (*L*) GREAT BLACK
WOODPECKER Europe, coniferous forest belt of
Asia to China, Mongolia, Sakhalin, Hokkaido
and the Kurile Is / n hole / e 4–9 / I ♂♀ 12–14 /
F 24–8

Dryocopus javensis (*Horsfield*) WHITE-
BELLIED WOODPECKER Andamans, W India, S
Korea, E China and N Indonesia to Philippines,
Java and Bali / forest and plantations / insects /
n hole / e 2–4 / I ♂♀ (?)

Dryocopus pileatus (*L*) PILEATED
WOODPECKER Canada and USA / forest and
swamp forest / insects and berries / n hole / e 3–6

Dryocopus lineatus (*L*) LINEATED
WOODPECKER Mexico, C America and S America
S to N Argentina / forest, mangrove, savannah,
campos, orchard and cerradão / n hole / e 3–4 /
I ♂♀ (*D. erythrops* (Valenciennes) is regarded as
a race)

Dryocopus schulzi (*Cabanis*) BLACK-BODIED
WOODPECKER Argentina and (?) Paraguay /
woodland scrub

[**Dryocopus major** (*Dabbene*) from the Argen-
tinian chaco / status undetermined, but some
believe it may possibly prove to be a valid
species]

Dryocopus galeatus (*Temminck*) HELMETED
WOODPECKER S Brazil, Paraguay and NE
Argentina / forest

Asyndesmus lewis (*Gray*) LEWIS'S
WOODPECKER b Vancouver Is, S British
Columbia and western USA w S to Baja
California / open country / insects and berries /
n hole, usually in dead tree / e 5–9 / I ♂♀ c14

Melanerpes erythrocephalus (*L*) RED-
HEADED WOODPECKER E Canada and much of
USA / forest and habitation / insects and berries /
n hole / e 4–7 / I ♂♀ c14

Melanerpes portoricensis (*Daudin*) PUERTO
RICAN WOODPECKER Puerto Rico / woodland and
plantation / n hole / e ? 3–6

Melanerpes herminieri (*Lesson*) GUADELOUPE
WOODPECKER Guadeloupe / wooded hills

Melanerpes formicivorus (*Swainson*) ACORN
WOODPECKER Pacific coast of USA from Oregon
through Mexico and C America to Andes of
Colombia / forest / insects and acorns / n hole / e
4–6 (?10) / I by several individuals including the
breeding pair

[NB: the remaining species of Melanerpes are
sometimes separated as the genus *Centurus*]

Melanerpes hypopolius (*Wagler*) BALSAS
WOODPECKER Mexico

Melanerpes uropygialis (*Baird*) GILA
WOODPECKER Western USA S to Baja California /
scrub and semi-desert / n hole / e 3–5 / I ♂♀ c21

Melanerpes carolinus (*L*) RED-BELLIED
WOODPECKER Central and eastern USA / forest,
woodland and swamp / insects and berries / n
hole / e 3–8 / I ♂♀ 14

Melanerpes aurifrons (*Wagler*) GOLDEN-
FRONTED WOODPECKER Texas, Mexico and C
America to Costa Rica / open forest / insects and
berries / n hole / e 4–7 / I ♂♀ 12 / F 30

Melanerpes chrysogenys (*Vigors*) GOLDEN-CHEEKED WOODPECKER W Mexico

Melanerpes superciliaris (*Temminck*) EYEBROWED WOODPECKER Cuba, Isle of Pines, Bahamas / wooded areas and palm groves

Melanerpes caymanensis (*Cory*) CAYMAN WOODPECKER Grand Cayman (now usually treated as a race of *superciliaris*)

Melanerpes radiolatus (*Wagler*) JAMAICAN WOODPECKER Jamaica / forest and plantation

(*Chryserpes striatus* is sometimes placed here) NB: Bond places *superciliaris* (including *caymanensis*) *radiolatus* and *striatus* in the genus *Centurus*

Melanerpes rubricapillus (*Cabanis*) RED-CROWNED WOODPECKER C America, Colombia, Venezuela, Trinidad and Tobago / scrub, cactus and parks / n hole / e – more than 2, but only 2 young reared / I ♂♀ / F 31–3 (*M. pygmaeus* (Ridgway) is sometimes separated)

Melanerpes pucherani (*Malherbe*) PUCHERAN'S WOODPECKER Mexico to W Ecuador / forest / n hole / I ♂♀

Melanerpes chrysauchen *Salvin* GOLDEN-NAPED WOODPECKER SW Costa Rica, W Panama, N Colombia / forest and coffee plantations / n hole / e 3–4 / I ♂♀ 12 / F 33–7

Melanerpes flavifrons (*Vieillot*) YELLOW-FRONTED WOODPECKER S Brazil, Paraguay and NE Argentina

Melanerpes cruentatus (*Boddaert*) YELLOW-TUFTED WOODPECKER Tropical S America E of Andes / forest and burned clearings

Melanerpes rubrifrons (*Spix*) RED-FRONTED WOODPECKER E Venezuela, the Guianas and N Brazil / forest and burned clearings (believed to be a morph of *cruentatus*)

[**Melanerpes hargitti** *Du Bois* is believed to be a hybrid *M. cruentatus* × *M. rubrifrons*]

Leuconerpes candidus (*Otto*) WHITE WOODPECKER S Brazil, Paraguay, Uruguay and N Argentina / cerrado, palm groves and savannah

Sphyrapicus varius (*L*) YELLOW-BELLIED SAPSUCKER N America and Caribbean / forest and woodland / cambium sap, insects, berries and nuts / n hole / e 3–7 / I ♂♀ 14

Sphyrapicus thyroideus (*Cassin*) WILLIAMSON'S SAPSUCKER S British Columbia and western USA / mountain pine forest / sap, insects and berries / n hole / e 3–7 / I ♂♀

Trichopicus cactorum (*d'Orbigny*) WHITE-FRONTED WOODPECKER S Peru to Uruguay and N Argentina / groves, scrubby woods and cacti

Venilornis fumigatus (*d'Orbigny*) SMOKY WOODPECKER Mexico, C America and Andes from Venezuela to Bolivia / forest borders and plantations

Venilornis spilogaster (*Wagler*) WHITE-SPOTTED WOODPECKER S Brazil, Paraguay, Uruguay and N Argentina / dry, open forest

Venilornis passerinus (*L*) LITTLE WOODPECKER Much of S America E of the Andes / forest and cerrado

Venilornis frontalis (*Cabanis*) DOT-FRONTED WOODPECKER NW Argentina / forest

Venilornis maculifrons (*Spix*) YELLOW-EARED WOODPECKER SE Brazil

Venilornis cassini (*Malherbe*) GOLDEN-COLLARED WOODPECKER Venezuela, the Guianas and N Brazil / forest and scrub

[**Venilornis chocoensis** *Todd*, known only from 2 specimens from Colombia, is now considered to be a race of *V. cassini*]

Venilornis affinis (*Swainson*) STAINED WOODPECKER Amazon and upper Orinoco basins / forest and scrub

Venilornis kirkii (*Malherbe*) RED-RUMPED or KIRK'S WOODPECKER C America to W Ecuador; Venezuela, Trinidad and Tobago / forest, mangrove and shrubbery

Venilornis callonotus (*Waterhouse*) SCARLET-BACKED WOODPECKER Arid Pacific slope of Ecuador and Peru / arid scrub and dry forest

Venilornis sanguineus (*Lichtenstein*) BLOOD WOODPECKER The Guianas and (?) Venezuela / mangrove, swampy forest and plantation

Venilornis dignus (*Sclater and Salvin*) YELLOW-VENTED WOODPECKER Andes from Colombia to Peru / forest

Venilornis nigriceps (*d'Orbigny*) BAR-BELLIED WOODPECKER Andes from Colombia to Bolivia / forest

Dendropicos fuscescens (*Vieillot*) CARDINAL WOODPECKER Africa S of Sahara / scrub and open woodland / insects / n hole / e 2–3

Dendropicos stierlingi *Reichenow* STIERLING'S WOODPECKER Lake Nyasa and N Mozambique / open woodland / insects / n and e n/k

Dendropicos elachus *Oberholzer* LITTLE GREY WOODPECKER African semi-arid belt from Senegal to Aïr and Darfur / rare / arid areas / beetles and larvae / n and e n/k

Dendropicos abyssinicus (*Stanley*)

PSITTACIDAE: *Ara ararauna*, Blue and Yellow Macaw

Plate 130

PSITTACIDAE: *Ara militaris*, Military Macaw

Plate 131

ABYSSINIAN WOODPECKER Ethiopia / mountains/ rare / no data

Dendropicos poecilolaemus (*Reichenow*) UGANDA WOODPECKER N Cameroon to Uganda and Kenya / open country / insect larvae / n hole/ e n/k

Dendropicos gabonensis (*Verreaux and Verreaux*) GABOON WOODPECKER Gabon and Cameroons / lowland forest and secondary growth/ insects

Dendropicos lugubris (*Hartlaub*) MELANCHOLY WOODPECKER W Africa/woodland and bush /ants /n hole /e n/k

[NB: Salim Ali and Ripley in *Handbook of the birds of India and Pakistan* merge *Dendrocopos* in *Picoides*]

Dendrocopos major (*L*) GREAT SPOTTED WOODPECKER Palaearctic and Oriental regions/ forest and habitation / insects and berries / n hole/e 3–8/I ♂♀ 16/F 18–21

Dendrocopos leucopterus (*Salvadori*) WHITE-WINGED WOODPECKER C Asia from Transcaspia to Dzungaria / forest, scrub and habitation /n hole/e 4–7

Dendrocopos syriacus (*Ehrenberg*), sometimes credited to *Hemprich and Ehrenberg* SYRIAN WOODPECKER Balkan states and Asia Minor to Transcaucasia and Persia / forest and scrub/ insects and seeds/n hole/e up to 11

Dendrocopos assimilis (*Blyth*) SIND WOODPECKER SE Persia, Baluchistan, Sind and W Punjab / thorn forest and scrub jungle/ insects/n hole/e 3–4/I ♂♀

Dendrocopos himalayensis (*Jardine and Selby*) HIMALAYAN WOODPECKER Himalayas/ hill forest/beetle grubs, conifer seeds and nuts/ n hole/e 3–5/I ♂♀

Dendrocopos darjellensis (*Blyth*) DARJEELING WOODPECKER Nepal to Indo-China, Sikang and W Yunnan / forest / insect larvae/ n hole/e 2–4

Dendrocopos medius (*L*) MEDIUM SPOTTED WOODPECKER Europe and Asia Minor to Persia/ forest /insects /n hole /e 3–8

Dendrocopos leucotos (*Bechstein*) WHITE-BACKED WOODPECKER N and E Europe across C and N Asia to China and Japan /forest/ insects, berries, nuts/n hole/e 3–6/I ♂♀ 14–16/ F c27–8

Dendrocopos cathpharius (*Blyth*) CRIMSON-BREASTED WOODPECKER Mts from Nepal to Laos and W China/ forest/ insects and nectar/ n hole / e 2–4

Dendrocopos hyperythrus (*Vigors*) RUFOUS-BELLIED WOODPECKER Himalayas to SE Asia, mts of W China, Manchuria and Korea/ forest / insects / n hole / e 4–5/ I ♂♀ [Ali and Ripley retain the monotypic genus, *Hypopicus*, for this species]

Dendrocopos auriceps (*Vigors*) BROWN-FRONTED WOODPECKER NW Himalayas to SE Asia, mts of W China, Manchuria and Korea/ forest / insects / n hole / e 4–5/ I ♂♀

Dendrocopos atratus (*Blyth*) STRIPED-BREASTED WOODPECKER Hills of Burma, N Thailand and Laos / forest on ridges and hill slopes / insects / n hole / e 4–5/ I ♂♀ (Baker observed both sexes on nest at same time)

Dendrocopos macei (*Vieillot*) FULVOUS-BREASTED WOODPECKER E Himalayas to E Ghats, parts of SE Asia, Andamans, Java, Bali and (?) Sumatra/ open forest/insects, seeds and berries/n hole /e 3–5/I ♂♀

Dendrocopos mahrattensis (*Latham*) YELLOW-CROWNED WOODPECKER India, Ceylon and Burma/thorn-jungle and habitation/insects, flowers and fruit/n hole/e 3/I ♂♀

Dendrocopos minor (*L*) LESSER SPOTTED WOODPECKER Much of Palaearctic/ open woodland and habitation/insects and berries/n hole/ e 3–8/I ♂♀ 14/F 21

Dendrocopos canicapillus (*Blyth*) GREY-HEADED PYGMY WOODPECKER China and Korea, Taiwan, Hainan, SE Asia, Indian region, Sumatra and Borneo/forest and cultivation/insects, fruit and flowers/n hole/e 4–5/ I ♂♀ ?12–13

Dendrocopos wattersi (*Salvadori and Giglioli*) FORMOSAN WOODPECKER Taiwan/ this form may be the immature of *D. canicapillus kaleensis* (*Swinhoe*), the Taiwan race

Dendrocopos kizuki (*Temminck*) JAPANESE PYGMY WOODPECKER Hopeh, Korean region, Japan, S Kurile Is, Ryukyu Is and Izu Is/ forest /n hole / e 5–7

Dendrocopos nanus (*Vigors*) INDIAN PYGMY WOODPECKER India and Ceylon / light forest, bamboo and cultivation / insects, flowers and fruit/n hole/e 3–4/I ♂♀

Dendrocopos moluccensis (*Gmelin*) MALAYSIAN PYGMY WOODPECKER Malay states, W and S Indonesia/no data

Dendrocopos maculatus (*Scopoli*) PHILIPPINE

PYGMY WOODPECKER Philippines

Dendrocopos temminckii (*Malherbe*) CELEBES PYGMY WOODPECKER Celebes and Togian

Dendrocopos obsoletus (*Wagler*) BROWN-BACKED WOODPECKER W, C and E Africa/ bush/ insect larvae/ n hole/ e 2

Dendrocopos dorae (*Bates and Kinnear*) ARABIAN WOODPECKER W Arabia

Dendrocopos albolarvatus (*Cassin*) WHITE-HEADED WOODPECKER Western USA / forest/ insects/ n hole/ e 3–7/ I ♂♀ 14

Dendrocopos villosus (*L*) HAIRY WOODPECKER N and C America / forest, woodland and habitation / insects and fruit / n hole/ e 3–6/ I ♂♀ 15/ F 28

Dendrocopos pubescens (*L*) DOWNY WOODPECKER Much of N America / forest, woodland and habitation / insects and fruit/ n hole/ e 3–8/ I 12

Dendrocopos borealis (*Vieillot*) RED-COCKADED WOODPECKER Southern USA/ forest/ insects and fruit / n hole / e 3–5

Dendrocopos nuttalii (*Gambel*) NUTTALL'S WOODPECKER California/ open forest and woodland / insects and fruit / n hole / e 3–6/ I ♂♀ 14

Dendrocopos scalaris (*Wagler*) LADDER-BACKED WOODPECKER South-east USA, Mexico and Belize / forest, woodland and cactus scrub/ insects and fruit/ n hole/ e 2–6/ I ♂♀ 13

Dendrocopos arizonae (*Hargitt*) ARIZONA WOODPECKER Mexico, SW New Mexico and S Arizona / forest and wooded hillsides / insects and fruit/ n hole/ e 3–4/ I ♂♀ ?14

Dendrocopos stricklandi (*Malherbe*) BROWN-BARRED WOODPECKER Mexico

Dendrocopos mixtus (*Boddaert*) CHEQUERED WOODPECKER Southern S America/ open forest

Dendrocopos lignarius (*Molina*) STRIPED WOODPECKER Bolivia, Chile and Argentina/ forest edge, dense brush, pastures and orchards

Picoides tridactylus (*L*) THREE-TOED WOODPECKER Widely, but irregularly distributed through the Holarctic/ forest/ insects and fruit/ n hole/ e 4/ I ♂♀ 14

Picoides arcticus (*Swainson*) ARCTIC WOODPECKER Alaska, Canada and northern USA/ coniferous forest/ insects and fruit/ n hole/ e 2–6/ I ♂♀ 14

Sapheopipo noguchii (*Seebohm*) OKINAWA WOODPECKER Okinawa / forest / n hole / e ?2/ no other data

Xiphidopicus percussus (*Temminck*) CUBAN GREEN WOODPECKER Cuba and Isle of Pines/ woodland

Chryserpes striatus (*Müller*) STRIATED WOODPECKER Hispaniola / forest, swamp and semi-arid country

Polipicus elliotii (*Cassin*) ELLIOT'S WOODPECKER Cameroons to Uganda / forest/ insect larvae/ n and e n/k (*P. johnstoni* (Shelley) is now generally regarded as a race; *Polipicus* is sometimes merged in *Mesopicos*)

Mesopicos goertae (*Müller*) EASTERN GREY WOODPECKER Equatorial Africa/ forest and bush/ insects / n hole / e 2–4

Mesopicos griseocephalus (*Boddaert*) OLIVE WOODPECKER E and S Africa from SW Tanganyika to Angola and Cape / highland forest/ insect larvae / n hole / e 2–3

Thripias namaquus (*Lichtenstein*) BEARDED WOODPECKER C, E and SE Africa / bush and open woodland/ insect larvae / n hole / e 3–4

Thripias xantholophus (*Hargitt*) GOLDEN-CROWNED WOODPECKER Cameroons to Uganda and Angola/ forest / insect larvae / n hole / e n/k (sometimes placed in *Mesopicos*)

Thripias pyrrhogaster (*Malherbe*) FIRE-BELLIED WOODPECKER W Africa from Sierra Leone to Nigeria/ forest/ insect larvae / n and e n/k

Hemicircus concretus (*Temminck*) GREY-BREASTED WOODPECKER Malay Peninsula, Sumatra, Bangka, Borneo and Java/ lowland forest and secondary growth/ n hole/ e n/k

Hemicircus canente (*Lesson*) HEART-SPOTTED WOODPECKER W coast of India: Assam through SE Asia (discontinuous) / teak and bamboo jungle and coffee plantations / insects / n hole/ e 2–3

Blythipicus pyrrhotis (*Hodgson*) BAY WOODPECKER E Himalayas, SE Asia, S China and Hainan / mountain forest / insects / n hole/ e 2–4

Blythipicus rubiginosus (*Swainson*) MAROON WOODPECKER Malay Peninsula, Sumatra and Borneo /lowlands and mts up to 5,000ft (1,500 m) in forest undergrowth and gullies / n hole/ e 2

Chrysocolaptes validus (*Temminck*) ORANGE-BACKED WOODPECKER Malay Peninsula, Sumatra, Borneo and Java/ lowland forest/ n hole/ e 2

Chrysocolaptes festivus (*Boddaert*) WHITE-NAPED WOODPECKER India and Ceylon / forest/ insects/ n hole/ e 1–2/ I ♂♀

PSITTACIDAE:
Nymphicus hollandicus,
Cockatiel

PSITTACIDAE: *Ara nobilis,* Noble Macaw or Hahn's Macaw, Red-shouldered Macaw

Plate 132

PSITTACIDAE;
Aratinga guarouba,
Golden Conure,
Golden Parakeet

PSITTACIDAE:
Aratinga wagleri,
Scarlet-fronted Conure,
Scarlet-fronted Parakeet

Plate 133

Chrysocolaptes lucidus (*Scopoli*) CRIMSON-BACKED WOODPECKER Himalayas through SE Asia and Indonesia to Philippines / foothills forest / insects and nectar / n hole / e 1–2, 4–5 (accounts differ) / I ? 14–15 / F ? 24–6

Phloeoceastes guatemalensis (*Hartlaub*) FLINT-BILLED or PALE-BILLED WOODPECKER Mexico and C America / n hole / e 2 / I ♂♀

Phloeoceastes melanoleucos (*Gmelin*) CRIMSON-CRESTED WOODPECKER Tropical S America E of Andes / forest, campos, swampy woods and plantations

Phloeoceastes leucopogon (*Valenciennes*) CREAM-BACKED WOODPECKER S Brazil, Paraguay, Uruguay and N Argentina / forest and woodland

Phloeoceastes guayaquilensis (*Lesson*) GUAYAQUIL WOODPECKER W Ecuador and NW Peru

Phloeoceastes rubricollis (*Boddaert*) RED-NECKED WOODPECKER Amazon and Orinoco basins / forest

Phloeoceastes robustus (*Lichtenstein*) ROBUST WOODPECKER S Brazil, Paraguay and N Argentina / forest

Phloeoceastes pollens (*Bonaparte*) POWERFUL WOODPECKER Parts of Colombia, Ecuador and Peru / forest

Phloeoceastes haematogaster (*Tschudi*) CRIMSON-BELLIED WOODPECKER Pacific slope of Andes from Panama to Peru / forest

Campephilus principalis (*L*) IVORY-BILLED WOODPECKER Cuba: formerly forest swamps of south-eastern USA, now very rare and on the verge of extinction, confined to a very few localities / insects and fruit / n hole / e 1–4(?5)

Campephilus imperialis (*Gould*) IMPERIAL WOODPECKER Mexico / pine-oak mountain forests / rare and endangered / n hole / e 2

Campephilus magellanicus (*King*) MAGELLANIC WOODPECKER S Chile and S Argentina / forest / n hole / e 4

EURYLAIMIDAE Broadbills A distinctive group of brightly coloured tropical birds living in wet jungles and cloud forest, and feeding on insects and fruit. The nest is a purse-like structure built in trees, but little is known of their breeding habits.

Smithornis capensis (*Smith*) AFRICAN BROADBILL Africa from Liberia to Kenya and S to Natal and Angola / forest and scrub / insects / n tree / e 3

Smithornis rufolateralis *Gray* RED-SIDED BROADBILL Liberia to W Uganda / forest / insects / n tree / e 1–2

Smithornis sharpei *Boyd Alexander* GREY-HEADED or SHARPE'S BROADBILL Fernando Po, Cameroons and Congo / forest / insects / n tree / e 2

Pseudocalyptomena graueri *Rothschild* GRAUER'S BROADBILL E Belgian Congo / about 7 specimens / forest / insects / n and e n/k

Corydon sumatranus (*Raffles*) DUSKY BROADBILL SE Asia, Sumatra, Borneo and N Natuna Is / forest / n tree / e 3

Cymberhynchus macrorhynchos (*Gmelin*) BLACK AND RED BROADBILL Southern SE Asia, Sumatra, Bangka, Billiton and Borneo / forest and mangrove / insects / n tree / e 3

Eurylaimus javanicus *Horsfield* BANDED BROADBILL SE Asia, Sumatra, Java, Billiton, Borneo and N Natuna Is / forest / n tree / e 2–3

Eurylaimus ochromalus *Raffles* BLACK AND YELLOW BROADBILL Malay Peninsula, Sumatra, Billiton, Borneo, N Natuna Is and Pulo Tuangku / forest and cultivation / n tree / e 3

Eurylaimus steerii *Sharpe* WATTLED BROADBILL Philippines / forest / insects

Serilophus lunatus (*Gould*) COLLARED BROADBILL Himalayas, mts of SE Asia, Yunnan, Hainan and Sumatra / forest / insects / n tree / e 4–5 / I ♂♀

Psarisomus dalhousiae (*Jameson*) LONG-TAILED BROADBILL Himalayas, SE Asia, Sumatra and NW Borneo / forest / insects / n tree / e 5–6 / I ♂♀

Calyptomena viridis *Raffles* GREEN BROADBILL Malay Peninsula, Sumatra, Borneo and some adjacent small islands / forest / fruit / n tree / e 2

Calyptomena hosii *Sharpe* HOSE'S MAGNIFICENT BROADBILL Mts of Borneo / forest / fruit and insects / n and e n/k

Calyptomena whiteheadi *Sharpe* WHITEHEAD'S BROADBILL Mts of northern Borneo / forest / fruit / n tree / e 2

DENDROCOLAPTIDAE Woodcreepers Brownish arboreal birds, superficially resembling Treecreepers, but not considered to be related to them. They feed mainly on insects found among tree bark. The nest is in a crevice, eggs white and 2–3 in number. Incubation period averages about 15 days. Confined to Central and South America.

Dendrocincla tyrannina (*Lafresnaye*) TYRANNINE CREEPER Andes of W Venezuela, Colombia, Ecuador and N Peru/forest
[**Dendrocincla macrorhyncha** *Salvadori and Festa* Puna region of E Ecuador / unique, believed to be an abnormally large specimen of *tyrannina*]
Dendrocincla fuliginosa (*Vieillot*) PLAIN-BROWN CREEPER Honduras to Panama and S through much of S America to N Argentina/forest/n hollow palm/e 2
Dendrocincla anabatina *Sclater* TAWNY-WINGED CREEPER S Mexico to Costa Rica/forest/n hole/e 2/I by one parent, believed to be ♀ 20–1/F 19
Dendrocincla merula (*Lichtenstein*) WHITE-CHINNED CREEPER Amazon basin and the Guianas
Dendrocincla homochroa (*Sclater*) RUDDY CREEPER S Mexico through C America to Venezuela/forest/n hole/e 2
Sittasomus griseicapillus (*Vieillot*) OLIVACEOUS CREEPER S Mexico, C America and much of S America S to N Argentina/forest/n hole (1 nest known)/e n/k
Deconychura longicauda (*Pelzeln*) LONG-TAILED CREEPER Honduras to Panama, Amazon basin and the Guianas/forest/n hole/e 2
Deconychura stictolaema (*Pelzeln*) SPOT-THROATED CREEPER Amazon basin/forest
Glyphorhynchus spirurus (*Vieillot*) WEDGE-BILLED CREEPER S Mexico, C America, valleys of Colombia and Venezuela and Amazon basin/forest and woodland/n hole/e 2/I ♂♀
Drymornis bridgesii (*Eyton*) SCIMITAR-BILLED CREEPER Paraguay, Uruguay and Argentina/ground in open forest
Nasica longirostris (*Vieillot*) LONG-BILLED CREEPER E and S Colombia, Upper Orinoco and Upper Amazon basins, Cayenne/forest
Dendrexetastes rufigula (*Lesson*) CINNAMON-THROATED CREEPER Amazon basin/forest
Hylexetastes perrotii (*Lafresnaye*) RED-BILLED CREEPER E Venezuela, Guyana and Cayenne, N Brazil/forest, sometimes savannah
Hylexeyastes stresemanni *Snethlage* BAR-BELLIED CREEPER NW and W Brazil, E Peru/forest
Xiphocolaptes promeropirhynchus (*Lesson*) STRONG-BILLED or GIANT CREEPER S Mexico, C America, Andes from Venezuela to Peru,

Upper Orinoco and Upper Amazon basins/forest and open woodland (*X. orenocoensis* Berlepsch and Hartert, is sometimes separated)
Xiphocolaptes albicollis (*Vieillot*) WHITE-THROATED CREEPER S Brazil, E Paraguay and NE Argentina/forest
[**Xiphocolaptes villanovae** *Lima* VILA NOVA WOODCREEPER Vila Nova / status uncertain, possibly a race of *albicollis* or a distinct species/ no data, qv Pinto, *Arg Zool Est São Paulo*, XI (1961), p 238. Not recorded in Peters *Check List of the Birds of the World*, vol 7]
Xiphocolaptes falcirostris (*Spix*) MOUSTACHED CREEPER E Brazil
Xiphocolaptes franciscanus *Snethlage* SNETHLAGE'S CREEPER Minas Gerais / unique/ status uncertain (see *Bol Mus Nac Rio de Janeiro* (1927), pl 3)
Xiphocolaptes major (*Vieillot*) GREAT RUFOUS CREEPER S Brazil, E and S Bolivia, Paraguay, N Argentina/forest and open woodland
Dendrocolaptes certhia (*Boddaert*) BARRED CREEPER S Mexico, C America and much of S America S to Bolivia and W Brazil/forest
Dendrocolaptes concolor *Pelzeln* CONCOLOR CREEPER N Brazil S of Amazon from Rio Madeira to the Tocantins/forest
Dendrocolaptes hoffmannsi *Hellmayr* HOFFMANN'S CREEPER Rio Madeira to Rio Xingu/forest
Dendrocolaptes picumnus *Lichtenstein* BLACK-BANDED CREEPER Guatemala to Panama and much of S America E of Andes and S to N Argentina/forest/n hole/e 2
Dendrocolaptes platyrostris *Spix* PLENALTO CREEPER E and C Brazil, Paraguay and N Argentina/forest
Xiphorhynchus picus (*Gmelin*) STRAIGHT-BILLED CREEPER Pacific slope of Panama and much of equatorial S America E of Andes and S to Peru and C Brazil / savannah, swampy woods, mangroves / n hole in arboreal termite nest/e n/s
Xiphorhynchus necopinus (*Zimmer*) ZIMMER'S CREEPER Lower and middle Amazon valleys/forest
Xiphorhynchus obsoletus (*Lichtenstein*) STRIPED CREEPER Orinoco and N Amazon basins, the Guianas/swampy forest/n hole in arboreal termite nest/e 2
Xiphorhynchus ocellatus (*Spix*) OCELLATED

PSITTACIDAE:
Rhynchopsitta pachyrhyncha,
Thick-billed Parrot

Plate 134

PSITTACIDAE: *Pyrrhura rhodogaster,* Crimson-bellied Conure, Crimson-bellied Parakeet

Plate 135

CREEPER Amazon basin/forest
Xiphorhynchus spixii (*Lesson*) SPIX'S CREEPER Upper Amazon basin/forest
Xiphorhynchus elegans (*Pelzeln*) ELEGANT CREEPER Upper Amazon basin in Colombia, Ecuador and Peru; and Brazil S of Amazon/forest
Xiphorhynchus pardalotus (*Vieillot*) CHESTNUT-RUMPED CREEPER SE Venezuela, the Guianas and NE Brazil/forest and savannah
Xiphorhynchus guttatus (*Lichtenstein*) BUFF-THROATED CREEPER Guatemala to Panama and much of S America S to Bolivia and S Brazil/forest, mangrove and plantation/n hole/e n/s
Xiphorhynchus flavigaster *Swainson* LAUGHING CREEPER or IVORY-BILLED WOODHEWER Mexico to Costa Rica/forest
Xiphorhynchus stratigularis (*Richmond*) RICHMOND'S CREEPER Altamira, Tamaulipas/unique
Xiphorhynchus eytoni (*Sclater*) DUSKY-BILLED or EYTON'S CREEPER Brazil N of the Amazon from Rio Jamundá E and S from Rio Juruá E to Maranhâo and Ceará
Xiphorhynchus lachrymosus (*Lawrence*) BLACK-STRIPED CREEPER E Nicaragua, Costa Rica, Panama, Colombia and NW Ecuador/forest
Xiphorhynchus erythropygius (*Sclater*) SPOTTED CREEPER S Mexico, C America and Pacific slopes of Colombia and NW Ecuador/forest
Xiphorhynchus triangularis (*Lafresnaye*) OLIVE-BACKED CREEPER Andes from Venezuela to Bolivia/forest
Lepidocolaptes leucogaster (*Swainson*) WHITE-BELLIED CREEPER Mexico
Lepidocolaptes souleyetii (*Des Murs*) STREAK-HEADED or SOULEYET'S CREEPER Mexico to Panama, Colombia, Venezuela, the Guianas, and parts of the Upper and Northern Amazon basin/open woods, plantations and arid scrub/n hole/e 2/I ♂♀ 15/F 18–19
Lepidocolaptes angustirostris (*Vieillot*) NARROW-BILLED CREEPER S Amazon basin, Bolivia, and S to the pampas of Argentina/campos and cerrado
Lepidocolaptes affinis (*Lafresnaye*) SPOT-CROWNED or ALLIED CREEPER Mexico to Panama, and Andes from Venezuela to Bolivia/forest and open woodland/n hole/e 2/I ♂♀ 17/F 19
Lepidocolaptes squamatus (*Lichtenstein*)

SCALED CREEPER Brazil and parts of Paraguay and N Argentina/forest
Lepidocolaptes fuscus (*Vieillot*) LESSER CREEPER E and SE Brazil, E Paraguay and NE Argentina/forest
Lepidocolaptes albolineatus (*Lafresnaye*) LINEATED CREEPER Amazon and Orinoco basins (including E Venezuela and the Guianas)/forest
Campylorhamphus pucheranii (*Des Murs*) GREATER SCYTHEBILL W Andes of Colombia, E Ecuador and SE Peru
Campylorhamphus trochilirostris (*Lichtenstein*) RED-BILLED SCYTHEBILL E Panama and much of S America S to N Argentina/swampy forest and woodland
Campylorhamphus pusillus (*Sclater*) BROWN-BILLED SCYTHEBILL Costa Rica, Panama and Andes of Colombia (? W Ecuador)/forest
Campylorhamphus procurvoides (*Lafresnaye*) CURVE-BILLED SCYTHEBILL Guianas, Orinoco and Amazon basins/forest
Campylorhamphus falcularius (*Vieillot*) BLACK-BILLED SCYTHEBILL S Brazil, E Paraguay and N Argentina/forest
FURNARIIDAE Ovenbirds or Horneros
The Ovenbirds are a large family with rather diverse habits; traditionally named Ovenbirds after the intricate clay nests some species build, said to resemble an old-fashioned Dutch oven. To avoid confusion with the Parulid warbler called the Ovenbird, there has been a tendency among recent American writers to refer to the family as Horneros (the native South American name). Ovenbirds are predominantly forest birds, but some occur in open country, some build elaborate stick-structured nests and some nest in tunnels. Eggs are generally 2–6 in number, white or pale blue. So far as is known, both sexes incubate, for a period varying from 2–3 weeks and the young remain in the nest for 12–18 days. About 215 species in Central and South America.
Geobates poecilopterus (*Wied*) CAMPOS MINER Campos of C Brazil
Geosita maritima (*d'Orbigny and Lafresnaye*) GREYISH MINER Arid coastal regions of Peru and N Chile/semi-desert/n tunnel/e 2 (1 known nest)
Geosita peruviana *Lafresnaye* COASTAL MINER Arid coastal regions of Peru/sandy hillsides
Geosita saxicolina *Taczanowski* DARK-

WINGED MINER Mts of C Peru / stony slopes with sparse vegetation

Geositta isabellina (*Philippi and Landbeck*) CREAM-RUMPED MINER Mts of C Chile and W Argentina / open rocky slopes / n tunnel / e n/k

Geositta rufipennis (*Burmeister*) RUFOUS-BANDED MINER Andes of W Bolivia, Chile and Argentina / bushy, rocky slopes / n tunnel in earth / e 3

Geositta punensis *Dabbene* PUNA MINER Andes above 9,000ft (2,700m) (puna zone) in Bolivia, S Peru, N Chile and NW Argentina / semi-desert / n tunnel in earth / e ?2–3

Geositta cunicularia (*Vieillot*) COMMON MINER Highlands and lowlands of southern S America from Peru and S Brazil to Tierra del Fuego / sandy country and grassy puna / n tunnel in sand or earth / e 2–3

Geositta antarctica *Landbeck* SHORT-BILLED MINER Tierra del Fuego and islands in Magellan Strait w N to Chile and Argentina / open country / n tunnel in sand / e 3

Geositta tenuirostris (*Lafresnaye*) SLENDER-BILLED MINER Andes of Peru, Bolivia and NW Argentina / open hillsides and cultivation

Geositta crassirostris *Sclater* THICK-BILLED MINER W Peru to 8,000ft (2,400m) / rocks and crags

Upucerthia dumetaria *Geoffrey St-Hilaire* SCALE-THROATED EARTHCREEPER S Peru, W Bolivia S through Chile and Argentina to Tierra del Fuego / semi-arid slopes and thorny bush / n tunnel / e 2–3 [qv Estaban, *Acta Zool Lilloana*, 12 (1951), p 422 for reasons for considering *U. saturatior* a separate species]

Upucerthia albigula *Hellmayr* WHITE-THROATED EARTHCREEPER Puna zone of SW Peru and N Chile / desert scrub and wet meadows / n tunnel in bank / e 2 (1 nest known)

Upucerthia validirostris (*Burmeister*) BUFF-BREASTED EARTHCREEPER Puna zone of W Argentina / bushy hillsides and streambeds

Upucerthia jelskii (*Cabanis*) PLAIN-BREASTED EARTHCREEPER Andes of C Peru and W Bolivia S to N Chile / rocky and bushy slopes / n and e n/k

Upucerthia serrana *Taczanowski* STRIATED EARTHCREEPER Andes of Peru / stony hillsides with scattered vegetation

Upucerthia andaecola *d'Orbigny and Lafresnaye* ROCK EARTHCREEPER Andes of Bolivia and NW Argentina / rocky slopes / n and e ?n/k

Upucerthia ruficauda (*Meyen*) STRAIGHT-BILLED EARTHCREEPER Puna zone of Peru and Bolivia, Andes of N Chile and NW Argentina / rocky slopes / n tunnel / e 2–3

Upucerthia certhioides (*d'Orbigny and Lafresnaye*) CHACO EARTHCREEPER Argentina and Paraguayan chaco / thick scrub and dry flats

Upucerthia harterti *Berlepsch* BOLIVIAN EARTHCREEPER SC Bolivia

Eremobius phoenicurus *Gould* BAND-TAILED EARTHCREEPER W and S Argentina / hill scrub / n and e n/k

Chilia melanura (*Gray*) CRAG CHILIA N and C Chile / rock faces and outcrops / n rock cleft, tunnel in earth or hole in cactus / e 3–4

Cinclodes antarcticus (*Garnot*) BLACKISH CINCLODES Falklands and islands off the southern end of S America / clump of coarse vegetation near rocky beaches / n and e n/k

Cinclodes patagonicus (*Gmelin*) DARK-BELLIED CINCLODES C Chile and W Argentina S to Tierra del Fuego and islands S and E / rocky shores of sea and inland waters / n tunnel in bank or rock cleft / e 2–3

Cinclodes oustaleti *Scott* GREY-FLANKED CINCLODES Chile and Chilean islands to Tierra del Fuego, Juan Fernandez Is / rocky streams and seashores / n hole in stream bank / e 2–3

Cinclodes fuscus (*Vieillot*) BAR-WINGED CINCLODES Andes from Venezuela to Tierra del Fuego, and southern S America from Uruguay southwards / wet pampas, outcrops and streams / n rock cleft, hole in wall etc / e ?2–3

[**Cinclodes comechingonus** *Zotta and Gavio* COMECHINGONES CINCLODES Sierra de Comechingones and Pampa de Achala, Argentina / status not fully understood (possibly a race of *fuscus*)]

Cinclodes pabsti *Sick* (*Beitr Neotrop Fauna*, 6, no 2 (1969), p 64) LONG-TAILED CINCLODES Plateaux of SE Brazil

Cinclodes atacamensis (*Philippi*) WHITE-WINGED CINCLODES Mts of Peru, W Bolivia, N Chile and NW Argentina / rocky slopes near streams / n rock cleft, wall of building etc / e 2

Cinclodes palliatus (*Tschudi*) WHITE-BELLIED CINCLODES Andes of Peru / rocky slopes and streams

Cinclodes taczanowskii *Berlepsch and Stolzmann* SURF CINCLODES Coasts of W Peru

Plate 136

PSITTACIDAE:
Agapornis roseicollis,
Peach-faced Lovebird

PSITTACIDAE:
Agapornis nigrigenis,
Black-cheeked Lovebird

Opposite:
PSITTACIDAE:
Prosopeia
tabuensis,
Shining
Parrakeet,
Red Shining Parrot

Plate 137

and Isla San Martín (treated by some as a race of *nigrofumosus*)

Cinclodes nigrofumosus (*d'Orbigny and Lafresnaye*) SEASIDE CINCLODES Coast of N Chile and Mocha Is / rocky coasts / n rock cleft or tunnel in earth / e 3–4

Cinclodes excelsior *Sclater* STOUT-BILLED CINCLODES Scattered high mountains in Colombia, Ecuador and Peru / open slopes

Clibanornis dendrocolaptoides (*Pelzeln*) CANEBRAKE GROUNDCREEPER SE Brazil, E Paraguay and NE Argentina / bamboo thickets in sub-tropical woodland

Furnarius rufus (*Gmelin*) RUFOUS OVENBIRD (the species of this genus are alternatively called Horneros) C and S Brazil, Bolivia, Paraguay, Uruguay and N Argentina / groves, often near habitation / n domed mud structure in conspicuous positions, walls, gates, sides of treetrunks etc / e 4–5

Furnarius leucopus *Swainson* PALE-LEGGED OVENBIRD Amazon basin N to Guyana, Venezuela and Colombia / campos, clearings, arid coastal regions

Furnarius torridus *Sclater and Salvin* PALE-BILLED OVENBIRD N Peru and W Brazil / campos

Furnarius minor *Pelzeln* LESSER OVENBIRD Amazon valley of NE Peru, W Brazil and S Colombia

Furnarius figulus (*Lichtenstein*) BANDED OVENBIRD Amazon Valley of Brazil, and E Brazil / open scrub

Furnarius cristatus *Burmeister* CRESTED OVENBIRD Chaco of Paraguay and Argentina / bushy and scrubby plains

Limnornis curvirostris *Gould* CURVE-BILLED REEDHAUNTER S Brazil, NE Argentina and Uruguay / reedbeds

Limnoctites rectirostris (*Gould*) STRAIGHT-BILLED REEDHAUNTER Brazil, Uruguay and E Argentina / reedbeds and dry rocks

Sylviorthorhynchus desmursii *Des Murs* DES MURS' SPINETAIL Chile and W Argentina / humid forest in thick undergrowth and bamboo thickets / n in grass, just off ground / e 3–4

[**Sylviorthorhynchus fasciolatus** *Philippi* is an artifact]

Aphrastura spinicauda (*Gmelin*) THORN-TAILED RAYADITO Chile, W Argentina, Isla Mocha, Chiloé, Isla Melchior and Tierra del Fuego / forest and clearings / n hole / e 3

Aphrastura masafuerae (*Philippi and*

Landbeck) MASAFUERA RAYADITO Masafuera Is / apparently no data

Phleocryptes melanops (*Vieillot*) RUSHBIRD Much of southern S America from Peru and S Bolivia to Tierra del Fuego / reedbeds / n in reeds / e 2–4

Leptasthenura andicola *Sclater* ANDEAN TIT-SPINETAIL Andes from Venezuela to Bolivia / matted vegetation near streams

Leptasthenura striata (*Philippi and Landbeck*) STREAKED TIT-SPINETAIL Mts of Peru and N Chile / bushy slopes and cacti / n and e n/k

Leptasthenura pileata *Sclater* RUSTY-CROWNED TIT-SPINETAIL Mts of Peru / bushy and wooded places

Leptasthenura xenothorax *Chapman* WHITE-BROWED TIT-SPINETAIL Cusco, Peru / unique

Leptasthenura striolata (*Pelzeln*) STRIOLATED TIT-SPINETAIL SE Brazil

Leptasthenura aegithaloides (*Kittlitz*) PLAIN-MANTLED TIT-SPINETAIL Peru, Bolivia, Chile and Argentina / thick brush and deserts / n hole in cactus or old domed nest of another bird / e 2

Leptasthenura platensis *Reichenbach* TUFTED TIT-SPINETAIL Argentina, Uruguay and S Brazil / trees in dense foliage

Leptasthenura fulginiceps (*d'Orbigny and Lafresnaye*) BROWN-CAPPED TIT-SPINETAIL Andes of Bolivia and W Argentina / dense scrub

Leptasthenura yanacensis *Carriker* TAWNY TIT-SPINETAIL Parts of Peru and Bolivia / open brush

Leptasthenura setaria (*Temminck*) ARAUCARIA TIT-SPINETAIL Paraná and Santa Catarina in Brazil, N Argentina / araucaria woodland

Spartonoica maluroides (*d'Orbigny and Lafresnaye*) BAY-CAPPED WREN-SPINETAIL S Brazil, Uruguay and N Argentina / marshes and bushy pastures

Schizoeaca coryi (*Berlepsch*) OCHRE-BROWED THISTLETAIL Paramo zone of Andes of Venezuela

Schizoeaca fuliginosa *Lafresnaye* WHITE-CHINNED THISTLETAIL Paramo zone of Andes of W Venezuela, Colombia, N Ecuador and N Peru / tangled undergrowth

Schizoeaca griseomurina (*Sclater*) MOUSE-COLOURED THISTLETAIL Paramo zone of S Ecuador

Schizoeaca palpebralis *Cabanis* EYERINGED THISTLETAIL Paramo zone of Andes of Peru

Schizoeaca helleri *Chapman* PUNA THISTLE-
TAIL Puna zone of Andes of Cusco; see note to
S. harterti

Schizoeaca harterti *Berlepsch* BLACK-
THROATED THISTLETAIL Andes of N Bolivia; de
Schaunsee (1970) believes this species and *S.
helleri* may be conspecific with *S. palpebralis*

Schoeniophylax phryganophila (*Vieillot*)
CHOTOY SPINETAIL E Bolivia, C and E Brazil,
Paraguay, Uruguay and N Argentina / sawgrass
swamp and savannah

Oreophylax moreirae (*Ribeiro*) ITATIAIA
SPINETAIL Campos (6,500–8,500ft 2,000–2,600
m) on Sierra do Itatiaya, Brazil

Synallaxis ruficapilla *Vieillot* RUFOUS-CAPPED
SPINETAIL SE Brazil, Paraguay, Uruguay and
NE Argentina / forest undergrowth

Synallaxis superciliosa *Cabanis* BUFF-BROWED
SPINETAIL Mts of S Bolivia and NW Argentina /
forest undergrowth

Synallaxis poliophrys *Cabanis* GREY-BROWED
SPINETAIL Cayenne (systematic position uncertain)

Synallaxis azarae *d'Orbigny* AZARA'S
SPINETAIL Andes (and valleys) from Venezuela
to Bolivia / forest undergrowth

Synallaxis frontalis *Pelzeln* SOOTY-FRONTED
SPINETAIL Bolivia, S and E Brazil, Paraguay,
Uruguay and N Argentina / bushy pastures and
thorn scrub

Synallaxis moesta *Sclater* DUSKY SPINETAIL
Colombia, E Ecuador and NE Peru / scrub

Synallaxis cabanisi *Berlepsch and Leverkühn*
CABANIS' SPINETAIL Scattered localities in
Venezuela, Surinam, Cayenne, Colombia, Peru
and Bolivia / forest undergrowth

Synallaxis spixi *Sclater* CHICLI SPINETAIL
S Brazil, Paraguay, Uruguay and N Argentina /
thickets and fern brakes

Synallaxis hypospodia *Sclater* CINEREOUS-
BREASTED SPINETAIL E Peru, N Bolivia and
parts of Brazil

Synallaxis subpudica *Sclater* SILVERY-
THROATED SPINETAIL E Andes of Colombia and
Ecuador / forest undergrowth

Synallaxis albescens *Temminck* PALE-
BREASTED CASTLEBUILDER SW Costa Rica,
Panama and the greater part of S America E of
Andes and S to the pampas / savannah / n shrub
or low tree / e 2 (?3) / I ♂♀

Synallaxis courseni *Blake* (*Auk*, 88 (1971),
p 179) APURIMAC SPINETAIL Apurimac, Peru /

no data

Synallaxis brachyura *Lafresnaye* SLATY
CASTLEBUILDER C America from Honduras to
Panama, Colombia and the Pacific slope of
Ecuador: E Brazil / forest and savannah / n shrub /
e 2–3 / I ♂♀ 18–19 / F 17

Synallaxis albigularis *Sclater* DARK-
BREASTED SPINETAIL S Colombia, E Ecuador,
E Peru and W Brazil / scrub

Synallaxis propinqua *Pelzeln* WHITE-BELLIED
SPINETAIL Parts of Amazon basin and Cayenne

Synallaxis gujanensis (*Gmelin*) PLAIN-
CROWNED SPINETAIL Amazon and Orinoco
basins, and the Guianas / n shrub or low tree /
e 2–3 / I ♂♀ 18 (de Schaunsee (1966) believed
that *S. maranonica* and *S. albilora* may possibly
be distinct)

Synallaxis cinerascens *Temminck* GREY-
BELLIED SPINETAIL SE Brazil, Paraguay and
NE Argentina / forest undergrowth

Synallaxis tithys *Taczanowski* BLACKISH-
HEADED SPINETAIL SW Ecuador and NW Peru /
arid scrub

Synallaxis cinnamomea *Lafresnaye* STRIPED
SPINETAIL Trinidad, Tobago and mts of
Colombia and Venezuela / forest undergrowth
with campos

Synallaxis fuscorufa *Sclater* RUSTY-HEADED
SPINETAIL Santa Marta Mts, Colombia / bushes
and thickets

Synallaxis unirufa *Lafresnaye* RUFOUS SPINE-
TAIL Andes of Venezuela, Colombia, E Ecuador
and Peru / forest undergrowth

Synallaxis rutilans *Temminck* RUDDY SPINE-
TAIL Amazon and Orinoco basins, also Cayenne
and Surinam / n bush or low tree / e n/k

Synallaxis erythrothorax *Sclater* RUFOUS-
BREASTED CASTLEBUILDER S Mexico to El
Salvador / n tree / e 3–4 / I ♂♀ 17–18 / F c15

Synallaxis cherriei *Gyldenstolpe* CHESTNUT-
THROATED SPINETAIL N Peru, E Ecuador and
Mato Grosso / forest and savannah undergrowth

Synallaxis stictothorax *Sclater* NECKLACED
SPINETAIL SW Ecuador and N Peru / arid scrub

Synallaxis zimmeri *Koepcke* (*Publ Mus Hist
Nat Javier Prado* (1957), series A, no 18)
RUSSET-BELLIED SPINETAIL W slope of Peruvian
Andes 6,000–9,000ft (1,800–2,700m)

Synallaxis gularis *Lafresnaye* WHITE-BROWED
SPINETAIL Andes from Venezuela to Peru /
forest undergrowth

Gyalophylax hellmayri (*Reiser*) RED-

PSITTACIDAE: *Agapornis personata*, Masked Lovebird

Plate 138

PSITTACIDAE:
Platycercus adelaidae,
Adelaide Rosella

PSITTACIDAE:
Platycercus venustus,
Northern Rosella

Plate 139

SHOULDERED SPINETAIL NE Brazil

Certhiaxis cinnamomea (*Gmelin*) YELLOW-THROATED SPINETAIL Much of S America E of Andes and S to N Argentina / marshes and mangroves / n mangrove roots / e 2–3

Certhiaxis mustelina (*Sclater*) RED-AND-WHITE SPINETAIL Amazon Valley from NE Peru to Belém

Poecilurus candei (*d'Orbigny and Lafresnaye*) WHITE-WHISKERED SPINETAIL N Colombia and W Venezuela / pasture, scrub and cacti

Poecilurus kollari (*Pelzeln*) HOARY-THROATED SPINETAIL Rio Branco in N Brazil / campos

Poecilurus scutatus (*Sclater*) OCHRE-CHEEKED or OCHRE-THROATED SPINETAIL E Bolivia, Mato Grosso and NW Argentina / forest undergrowth

Cranioleuca sulphurifera (*Burmeister*) SULPHUR-BEARDED SPINETAIL Local in S Brazil, Uruguay and E Argentina / open woodland

Cranioleuca semicinerea (*Reichenbach*) GREY-HEADED SPINETAIL NE Brazil and Goiaz

Cranioleuca obsoleta (*Reichenbach*) OLIVE SPINETAIL SE Brazil, E Paraguay and NE Argentina / forest

Cranioleuca pyrrhophia (*Vieillot*) STRIPED-CROWNED SPINETAIL E and S Bolivia, W Paraguay, Uruguay and Argentina S to Rio Negro / forest clearings and thickets

Cranioleuca subcristata (*Sclater*) CRESTED SPINETAIL Mts of Venezuela and E Colombia / forest

Cranioleuca hellmayri (*Bangs*) STREAKED-CAPPED SPINETAIL Santa Marta Mts, Colombia / forest

Cranioleuca curtata (*Sclater*) ASH-BROWED SPINETAIL Andes from Colombia to Peru / forest

[**Cranioleuca furcata** (*Taczanowski*) FORK-TAILED SPINETAIL Chirimoto in N Peru / 2 specimens – ? immature of *C. curtata*]

Cranioleuca demissa (*Salvin and Godman*) TEPUI SPINETAIL Mts of S Venezuela and W Guyana / forest

Cranioleuca erythrops (*Sclater*) RED-FACED SPINETAIL Mts of Costa Rica; Colombia and W Ecuador / thickets bordering humid forest / n tree / e 2

Cranioleuca vulpina (*Pelzeln*) RUSTY-BACKED SPINETAIL Basins of Amazon and Orinoco / thickets near water / n bush / e 3

Cranioleuca pallida (*Wied*) PALLID SPINETAIL SE Brazil

Cranioleuca antisiensis (*Sclater*) LINE-CHEEKED SPINETAIL Andes of Ecuador and Peru / woods and thickets

[**Cranioleuca baroni** (*Salvin*) BARON'S SPINETAIL N and C Peru (now generally regarded as a race of *antisiensis*)]

Cranioleuca marcapatae *Zimmer* MARCAPATA SPINETAIL Marcapata in Peru, 10,000ft (3,000m)

Cranioleuca albiceps (*d'Orbigny and Lafresnaye*) LIGHT-CROWNED SPINETAIL Andes of Bolivia

Cranioleuca albicapilla (*Cabanis*) CREAMY-CRESTED SPINETAIL C and S Peru

Cranioleuca muelleri (*Hellmayr*) SCALED SPINETAIL N Brazil on both banks of Lower Amazon and Mexicana Is

Cranioleuca gutturata (*d'Orbigny and Lafresnaye*) SPECKLED SPINETAIL Amazon and Orinoco basins, Cayenne: E Colombia (Bogotá trade-skins) / forest

Siptornopsis hypochondriacus (*Salvin*) GREAT SPINETAIL N Peru

Asthenes pyrrholeuca (*Vieillot*) LESSER CANASTERO S Bolivia, Paraguay, Uruguay, and parts of Chile and Argentina / scrub and stony slopes / n wet meadows and near mountain streams in bush / e 3–4 ?2 (*Canastero*='Basket-maker', a reference to the stout, thorny, woven nest)

Asthenes dorbignyi (*Reichenbach*) CREAM-BREASTED or D'ORBIGNY'S CANASTERO Peru, Bolivia, N Chile and NW Argentina / ground among scattered bushes / n bush or cactus / e 2

Asthenes berlepschi (*Hellmayr*) BERLEPSCH'S CANASTERO N Bolivia, 2 localities only

Asthenes baeri (*Berlepsch*) SHORT-BILLED CANASTERO Paraguay, Uruguay, S Brazil and N Argentina / open scrubby forest

Asthenes patagonica (*d'Orbigny*) PATAGONIAN CANASTERO Patagonia / semi-arid scrub / n bush / e 3

Asthenes steinbachi (*Hartert*) CHESTNUT CANASTERO W Argentina / ground among scattered bushes

Asthenes humicola (*Kittlitz*) DUSKY-TAILED or KITTLITZ' CANASTERO Chile and W Argentina / thorn scrub / n bush / e 3–4

Asthenes modesta (*Eyton*) CORDILLERAN CANASTERO Mts of Peru and Bolivia S through Chile and W Argentina / semi-arid land and stony slopes / n bush / e 3–4 (but Johnson in *Birds of Chile* describes a nest under a stone – unique for this genus)

Asthenes cactorum *Koepcke* (*Beit Zur Neotrop Fauna*, bd 1, heft 3 (1959), p 243) CACTUS CANASTERO Arid pacific slope of Peru/ among tall cacti in rocky ravines / n in cacti/ e ? n/k

Asthenes pudibunda (*Sclater*) CANYON CANASTERO Western mts of Peru and Bolivia/ cactus hillsides and thorn scrub

Asthenes ottonis (*Berlepsch*) RUSTY-FRONTED CANASTERO SE Peru

[**Asthenes heterura** (*Berlepsch*) IQUITO CANASTERO Bolivia (now generally treated as a race of *pudibunda*)]

Asthenes wyatti (*Sclater and Salvin*) STREAK-BACKED or WYATT'S CANASTERO Andes from Venezuela to Peru/ shrubs, rocks and marshy areas

Asthenes humilis (*Cabanis*) STREAK-THROATED or HUMBLE CANASTERO Mts of Peru and Bolivia/ stony grassland

Asthenes anthoides (*King*) AUSTRAL CANASTERO Aconcagua S to Tierra del Fuego, puna zone of Peru to N Argentina / damp meadows and tussocks / n shrub / e n/s/ see de Schaunsee (1966), p 253 for comments on the transfer to this species of some forms formerly considered races of *A. wyatti*. Johnson (*Birds of Chile*) suggests that one of these, *A. lilloa* (Oustalet) 'Lillo's Canastero' might possibly be a separate species.

Asthenes sclateri (*Cabanis*) CORDOBA CANASTERO Sierra de Córdoba, Argentina/ bushy pastures (possibly a race of *A. anthoides*)

Asthenes hudsoni (*Sclater*) HUDSON'S CANASTERO Uruguay and Argentina S to Rio Negro / marshes and rough pasture

Asthenes virgata (*Sclater*) JUNIN CANASTERO Junin (Peru)

Asthenes maculicauda (*Berlepsch*) SCRIBBLE-TAILED CANASTERO Andes of Peru, Bolivia and NW Argentina / bushy pastures / ? no data

Asthenes flammulata (*Jardine*) MANY-STRIPED CANASTERO Andes from Colombia to Peru/ bushy slopes

Asthenes urubambensis (*Chapman*) LINE-FRONTED CANASTERO Andes of Peru and N Bolivia/ mossy trees and thickets

[**Siptornis leptasthenuroides** *Lillo*, from Tucuman, is placed here by Peters with the note that it has never been satisfactorily identified]

Thripophaga macroura (*Wied*) STRIATED SOFT-TAIL E Brazil / forest

Thripophaga cherriei *Berlepsch and Hartert* ORINOCO SOFT-TAIL Capuano on the Upper Orinoco / forest

Thripophaga fusciceps *Sclater* PLAIN SOFT-TAIL Scattered localities in Brazil, Bolivia, Ecuador and Peru

Thripophaga berlepschi *Hellmayr* RUSSET-MANTLED or BERLEPSCH'S SOFT-TAIL N Peru in Amazonas

Phacellodomus sibilatrix *Sclater* LITTLE THORNBIRD Paraguay and N Argentina / scrub

Phacellodomus rufifrons (*Wied*) RUFOUS-FRONTED THORNBIRD Apparently discontinuous through N Venezuela, NE Colombia, N Peru, Brazil, Paraguay, Bolivia and Argentina /grass-land / n in isolated tree / e 3 / I ♂♀ 21–2 / F c17 (the nest is a complicated many-chambered structure, the other chambers being occupied by non-breeding birds. See Skutch, *Wilson Bulletin*, 1969)

Phacellodomus straticeps (*d'Orbigny and Lafresnaye*) STREAK-FRONTED THORNBIRD Andes of Peru, Bolivia and N Argentina /open bushy slopes

Phacellodomus erythropthalmus (*Wied*) RED-EYED THORNBIRD E Brazil/ coastal forests

Phacellodomus ruber (*Vieillot*) GREATER THORNBIRD Bolivia, W and C Brazil, Paraguay and N Argentina / palm groves and wet cerrado

Phacellodomus straticollis (*d'Orbigny and Lafresnaye*) FRECKLED THORNBIRD E Bolivia, SE Brazil, Uruguay and N Argentina / bushy country

Phacellodomus dorsalis *Salvin* CHESTNUT-BACKED THORNBIRD N Peru / arid zone

Coryphistera alaudina *Burmeister* LARK-LIKE BUSHRUNNER S and E Bolivia, S Brazil, Uru-guay, N Argentina and Paraguayan chaco/scrub/ n tree

Anumbius anumbi (*Vieillot*) FIREWOOD GATHERER SE Brazil, Paraguay, Uruguay and N Argentina/ open scrub / n large stick structure in tree, telegraph pole etc

Siptornis straticollis (*Lafresnaye*) SPECTACLED PRICKLETAIL Colombia and E Ecuador / forest

Xenerpestes minlosi *Berlepsch* DOUBLE-BANDED SOFT-TAIL E Panama and Colombia/ undergrowth

Xenerpestes singularis (*Taczanowski and Berlepsch*) SINGULAR or EQUATORIAL SOFT-TAIL Ecuador / ? unique

PSITTACIDAE:
Platycercus adscitus,
Mealy or Pale Headed Rosella

PSITTACIDAE:
Platycercus caledonicus,
Green Rosella

PSITTACIDAE:
Platycercus flaveolus,
Yellow Rosella

Plate 140

PSITTACIDAE:
Platycercus elegans,
Crimson Rosella or
Pennant's Parrakeet

Plate 141

Metopothrix aurantiacus *Sclater and Salvin* PLUSHCROWN Upper Amazon basin / forest clearings

Roraimia adjusta (*Salvin and Godman*) RORAIMIAN BARBTAIL Mts of S Venezuela and W Guyana / forest

Margarornis squamiger (*d'Orbigny and Lafresnaye*) PEARLED TREERUNNER Andes from Venezuela to Bolivia / forest

Margarornis bellulus *Nelson* BEAUTIFUL TREERUNNER Cerro Pirrí in Darién

Margarornis rubiginosus *Lawrence* RUDDY TREERUNNER Costa Rica and Panama / open woodland and clearings

Margarornis stellatus *Sclater and Slavin* DOTTED TREERUNNER W Andes of Colombia and NW Ecuador / wet forest

Margarornis guttuligera (*Sclater*) RUSTY-WINGED BARBTAIL Andes of NW Venezuela, Colombia, Ecuador and Peru / wet forest

Margarornis brunnescens *Sclater* SPOTTED BARBTAIL Costa Rica, Panama, and mts from Venezuela to W Bolivia / humid forest / n attached to mossy log / e 2

Margarornis tatei (*Chapman*) WHITE-THROATED or TATE'S BARBTAIL Mts of NE Venezuela / forest undergrowth

Pseudocolaptes lawrencii *Ridgway* BUFFY or LAWRENCE'S TUFTEDCHEEK Costa Rica, Panama and Andes of Colombia and Ecuador / forest / n hole / e – 1 known, no data on clutch size / F ? 29

Pseudocolaptes boissonneautii (*Lafresnaye*) STREAKED TUFTEDCHEEK Coastal mts of N Venezuela, and Andes from Venezuela to Bolivia / forest

Berlepschia rikeri (*Ridgway*) PINTAILED PALMCREEPER Local in Guyana, S Venezuela and N Brazil / palm groves

Pseudoseisura cristata (*Spix*) RUFOUS CACHALOTE E Bolivia, C and E Brazil, Paraguay / open woodland

Pseudoseisura lophotes (*Reichenbach*) BROWN CACHALOTE S Brazil, Paraguay, W Uruguay and N Argentina / open groves of low trees

Pseudoseisura gutturalis (*d'Orbigny and Lafresnaye*) WHITE-THROATED CACHALOTE W and N Argentina / arid stony country

Hyloctistes subulatus (*Spix*) STRIPED WOODHAUNTER Nicaragua to Panama, W Colombia, W Ecuador, parts of upper Amazon basin / forest

Ancistrops strigulatus (*Spix*) CHESTNUT-WINGED HOOKBILL Upper Amazon basin / forest

Anabazenops fuscus (*Vieillot*) WHITE-COLLARED LEAFGLEANER Forests of SE Brazil

Syndactyla rufosuperciliata (*Lafresnaye*) BUFF-BROWED LEAFGLEANER Slopes of Andes of Peru and Bolivia, SE Bolivia, SE Brazil, Paraguay, Uruguay and N Argentina / dense bushes

Syndactyla subalaris (*Sclater*) LINEATED LEAFGLEANER Costa Rica, Panama, Andes from Venezuela to Peru / forest

Syndactyla guttulata (*Sclater*) GUTTULATED LEAFGLEANER Mts of N Venezuela / forest

[**Syndactyla mirandae** (*Snethlage*) Goiaz / the type of this 'species' has been declared to be a synonym of *Philydor dimidiatus*]

Simoxenops ucayalae (*Chapman*) PERUVIAN RECURVEBILL Peru / about 3 specimens

Simoxenops striatus (*Carriker*) BOLIVIAN RECURVEBILL N Bolivia

Anabacerthia variegaticeps (*Sclater*) SCALY-THROATED LEAFGLEANER S Mexico to Costa Rica / forest / n and e apparently n/k

[**Anabacerthia temporalis** (*Sclater*) SPOT-BREASTED LEAFLGEANER Pacific coasts of Colombia and Ecuador / often considered to be a race of *A. variegaticeps*]

Anabacerthia straticollis *Lafresnaye* MONTANE LEAFGLEANER Mts from Venezuela to NW Bolivia / forest

Anabacerthia amaurotis (*Temminck*) WHITE-BROWED LEAFGLEANER SE Brazil and NE Argentina

Philydor atricapillus (*Wied*) BLACK-CAPPED LEAFGLEANER SE Brazil, E Paraguay and NE Argentina / forest

Philydor erythrocercus (*Pelzeln*) RUFOUS-RUMPED LEAFGLEANER Panama, and parts (but not all) of S America S to Bolivia and Amazon basin / forest

Philydor hylobius *Wetmore and Phelps* (*Proc Zool Soc Washington*, 69 (1956), p 4) NEBLINA LEAFGLEANER Mts of Venezuela–Brazil border / forest

Philydor pyrrhodes (*Cabanis*) CINNAMON-RUMPED LEAFGLEANER The Guianas, Amazon and Orinoco basins / forest undergrowth

Philydor dimidiatus (*Pelzeln*) RUSSET-MANTLED LEAFGLEANER E Brazil, Mato Grosso and Paraguay / forest

[**Philydor baeri** *Hellmayr* BAER'S LEAFGLEANER

E Brazil and NE Paraguay / now generally considered to be a race of *P. dimidiatus*]

Philidor lichtensteini *Cabanis and Heine* OCHRE-BREASTED or LICHTENSTEIN'S LEAFGLEANER SE Brazil, E Paraguay and NE Argentina / forest undergrowth

Philidor rufus (*Vieillot*) BUFF-FRONTED LEAFGLEANER Costa Rica, Panama, Venezuela, Colombia, E Ecuador, E Peru, Bolivia, C and S Brazil, E Paraguay and NE Argentina / forest

Philidor erythropterus (*Sclater*) CHESTNUT-WINGED LEAFGLEANER Upper Amazon basin / forest

Philidor ruficaudatus (*d'Orbigny and Lafresnaye*) RUFOUS-TAILED LEAFGLEANER Upper Amazon basin / forest / e 2 – sets of eggs having been taken, the nest has evidently been seen, but no published description appears to exist.

Automolus leucopthalmus (*Wied*) WHITE-EYED LEAFGLEANER E and S Brazil, NE Paraguay and NE Argentina / bamboo thickets

Automolus infuscatus (*Sclater*) OLIVE-BACKED LEAFGLEANER Upper Amazon basin / forest undergrowth

Automolus dorsalis *Sclater and Salvin* CRESTED LEAFGLEANER SE Colombia, E Ecuador and E Peru / forest

Automolus rubiginosus (*Sclater*) RUDDY LEAFGLEANER SW Mexico, C America, Colombia, Venezuela, W Guyana, Ecuador, Peru and N Bolivia / forest and secondary forest

Automolus roraimae *Hellmayr* (=**A. albigularis** (*Salvin and Godman*) WHITE-THROATED LEAFGLEANER S Venezuela (?Guyana) / forest

Automolus ochrolaemus (*Tschudi*) BUFF-THROATED LEAFGLEANER S Mexico, C America and north-western S America to Bolivia, upper Amazon and Guianas / forest undergrowth / n tunnel in bank / e 2–3 / I ♂♀ 20–1 / F 18

Automolus rufipileatus (*Pelzeln*) CHESTNUT-CROWNED LEAFGLEANER Orinoco and Amazon basins / forest

Automolus ruficollis (*Taczanowski*) RUFOUS-NECKED LEAFGLEANER SW Ecuador and NW Peru / forest

Automolus melanopezus (*Sclater*) BROWN-RUMPED LEAFGLEANER SE Colombia, E Ecuador and W Brazil

Hylocryptes erythrocephalus *Chapman* HENNA-HOODED LEAFGLEANER SW Ecuador and

W Peru / forest

Hylocryptus rectirostris (*Wied*) CHESTNUT-CAPPED LEAFGLEANER Mato Grosso and adjacent states

Cichlocolaptes leucophrus (*Jardine and Selby*) PALE-BROWED TREEHUNTER Coast of SE Brazil (spelled *leucophrys* in some books)

Heliobletus contaminatus *Berlepsch* SHARP-BILLED TREEHUNTER SE Brazil, E Paraguay and NE Argentina / forest

Thripadectes flammulatus (*Eyton*) FLAMMULATED TREEHUNTER Andes of Venezuela, Colombia and Ecuador / forest

Thripadectes holostictus (*Sclater and Salvin*) STRIPED TREEHUNTER Andes from Venezuela to N Bolivia / forest

Thripadectes melanorhynchus (*Tschudi*) BLACK-BILLED TREEHUNTER Andes of E Colombia, E Ecuador and E Peru / forest

Thripadectes rufobrunneus (*Lawrence*) STREAKED-BREASTED TREEHUNTER Highlands of Costa Rica and W Panama / n tunnel in bank / e 2 (NB: Wetmore, in *Birds of Panama*, vol 3, p 103, mentions a c/3 in the British Museum (Natural History) which is, in fact a c/2+a single egg. There is thus no evidence of a clutch size greater than 2)

Thripadectes virgaticeps *Lawrence* STREAKED-CAPPED TREEHUNTER Mts of N Venezuela, Colombia and Ecuador / humid forest

Thripadectes scrutator *Taczanowski* BUFF-THROATED TREEHUNTER Andes of C Peru

Thripadectes ignobilis (*Sclater and Salvin*) UNIFORM TREEHUNTER W Andes of Colombia and NW Ecuador / forest

Xenops milleri (*Chapman*) RUFOUS-TAILED XENOPS Scattered localities in E Colombia (Peters); much of Amazon basin, Surinam and Cayenne (de Schaunsee) / forest

Xenops tenuirostris *Pelzeln* SLENDER-BILLED XENOPS Orinoco and Amazon basins, Surinam and Cayenne / forest

Xenops rutilans *Temminck* STREAKED XENOPS Costa Rica, Panama, Colombia, Venezuela, Upper Amazon basin, S Brazil and N Argentina / forest / n hole / e 2

Xenops minutus (*Sparrman*) PLAIN XENOPS S Mexico, C America and much of northern and western S America S to Bolivia and Paraguay / forest / n hole / e 2 / I ♂♀ 15–17 / F 13–14

Megaxenops parnaguae *Reiser* GREAT XENOPS NE Brazil / forest

PSITTACIDAE:
Deroptyus accipitrinus,
Hawk-headed Parrot

PSITTACIDAE:
Lathamus discolor,
Swift Parrot

PSITTACIDAE: *Psephotus chrysopterygius,* Golden-shouldered Parrot

Plate 142

PSITTACIDAE:
Callocephalon fimbriatum,
Gang-gang Cockatoo

PSITTACIDAE: *Myopsitta monachus,* Quaker or Monk Parrakeet—Blue Mutation

Plate 143

[**Megaxenops ferrugineus** *Berlioz* is a synonym of *Simoxenops ucayalae*]

Pygarrhichas albogularis (*King*) WHITE-THROATED TREERUNNER Andean forests of Chile and W Argentina S to Tierra del Fuego/n hole/e 2–3

Sclerurus scansor (*Ménétriés*) RUFOUS-BREASTED LEAFSCRAPER C and E Brazil (? Paraguay and NE Argentina)

Sclerurus albigularis *Sclater and Salvin* GREY-THROATED LEAFSCRAPER Costa Rica, Panama, Colombia, Venezuela, Trinidad and Tobago, SE Ecuador, N Peru and N Bolivia/humid forest/n tunnel in bank/e 2

Sclerurus mexicanus *Sclater* TAWNY-THROATED LEAFSCRAPER S Mexico, C America and parts of northern S America/forest

Sclerurus rufigularis *Pelzeln* SHORT-BILLED LEAFSCRAPER Amazon basin/forest

Sclerurus caudacutus (*Vieillot*) BLACK-TAILED LEAFSCRAPER Amazon basin/forest

Sclerurus guatemalensis (*Hartlaub*) SCALY-THROATED LEAFTOSSER S Mexico, C America, Pacific slope of Colombia (? W Ecuador)/forest/n tunnel in bank/e 2/I ♂♀ 21/F 15

Lochmias nematura (*Lichtenstein*) STREAMCREEPER Darién and widely, but apparently irregularly, distributed through S America S to N Argentina/mountain streams/n tunnel/e 2

FORMICARIIDAE Antbirds A large family of primitive passerines; largely small to medium-sized birds, variable in appearance but plumaged in browns, blacks and whites. They are forest dwellers, chiefly of the lower regions and the forest floor. Feed largely on insects, many species following moving columns of army ants to feed on the insects disturbed by them. The nesting habits are little known, but those of the few species which have been studied suggest they may be typical of the family as a whole. The nest is a simple cup in a tree, eggs 2–3 in number, and incubation is by both sexes, the female incubating by night, male and female taking turns by day. Incubation period is about 15–16 days, fledging period 8–11 days.

Cymbilaimus lineatus (*Leach*) FASCIATED ANTSHRIKE Nicaragua, to Panama, coastal lowlands of Colombia and Ecuador, the Guianas, Orinoco and Amazon basins/lower growth and forest borders/n tree/e 2/I ♂♀

Hypodaleus guttatus (*Vieillot*) SPOT-BACKED

ANTSHRIKE E and S Brazil, E Paraguay and NE Argentina/forest and bamboo thickets

Batara cinerea (*Vieillot*) GIANT ANTSHRIKE E and S Bolivia, Paraguay, SE Brazil and N Argentina/thick forest undergrowth

Mackenziaena leachii (*Such*) LARGE-TAILED or LEACH'S ANTSHRIKE SE Brazil, E Paraguay and NE Argentina/bamboo thickets and forest undergrowth

Mackenziaena severa (*Lichtenstein*) TUFTED ANTSHRIKE SE Brazil, E Paraguay and NE Argentina/thick forest undergrowth

Frederickena viridis (*Vieillot*) BLACK-THROATED ANTSHRIKE E Venezuela, the Guianas and Brazil N of Lower Amazon/forest, rarely savannah

Frederickena unduligera (*Pelzeln*) UNDULATED ANTSHRIKE Upper Amazon basin/forest

Taraba major (*Vieillot*) GREAT ANTSHRIKE S Mexico, C America and much of S America S to N Argentina/swampy forest/n shrub/e 2/I ♂♀ 17–18/F 12–13

Sakesphorus canadensis (*L*) BLACK-CRESTED ANTSHRIKE Colombia, Venezuela, the Guianas and Upper Amazon basin/mangroves and cultivation/n shrub/e 2/I ♂♀ 14/F 12

Sakesphorus cristatus (*Wied*) SILVER-CHEEKED ANTSHRIKE Campos of E Brazil

Sakesphorus bernardi (*Lesson*) COLLARED ANTSHRIKE Ecuador and Peru/arid scrub

Sakesphorus melanonotus (*Sclater*) BLACK-BACKED ANTSHRIKE Venezuela and NE Colombia/thick scrub

Sakesphorus melanothorax (*Sclater*) BAND-TAILED ANTSHRIKE Cayenne, Surinam and Brazil on W side of Rio Tapajós

Sakesphorus luctuosus (*Lichtenstein*) GLOSSY ANTSHRIKE Lower Amazon, Goiaz and Mato Grosso/river thickets

Biatas nigropectus (*Lafresnaye*) BEARDED ANTSHRIKE SE Brazil and N Argentina/thick forest undergrowth

Thamnophilus doliatus (*L*) BARRED ANTSHRIKE Mexico, C America and much of S America E of Andes and S to N Argentina; Trinidad and Tobago/thickets, savannah and riverbanks/n shrub/e 2/I ♂♀ 14/F 12–13

Thamnophilus multistriatus *Lafresnaye* BAR-CRESTED ANTSHRIKE Mts of Colombia/forest borders

Thamnophilus palliatus (*Lichtenstein*) LINED

ANTSHRIKE Upper Amazon basin and S Brazil/ forest and thickets

Thamnophilus bridgesi *Sclater* BRIDGE'S ANTSHRIKE SW Costa Rica and W Panama/ edges of rain forest/n tree/e 2/I ♂♀ 14–16/ F 9–11

Thamnophilus nigriceps *Sclater* BLACK ANTSHRIKE Darien and Colombia/thick forest undergrowth

Thamnophilus praecox *Zimmer* COCHA ANTSHRIKE Ecuador–Peru border/unique ♀

Thamnophilus nigrocinereus *Sclater* BLACKISH-GREY ANTSHRIKE Amazon and Orinoco basins, also Cayenne/forest

Thamnophilus cryptoleucus (*Menegaux and Hellmayr*) CASTLENAU'S ANTSHRIKE N Peru and NW Brazil

Thamnophilus aethiops *Sclater* WHITE-SHOULDERED ANTSHRIKE Amazon and Upper Orinoco basins/forest and clearings

Thamnophilus unicolor (*Sclater*) UNIFORM ANTSHRIKE Colombia, Ecuador and Peru/ forest and forest border

Thamnophilus schistaceus (*d'Orbigny*) BLACK-CAPPED ANTSHRIKE Upper Amazon basin/forest undergrowth

Thamnophilus murinus *Sclater and Salvin* MOUSE-COLOURED ANTSHRIKE Upper Amazon and Upper Orinoco basins, extending to the Guianas/forest and savannah

Thamnophilus aroyae (*Hellmayr*) UPLAND ANTSHRIKE SE Peru and NW Bolivia

Thamnophilus punctatus (*Shaw*) SLATY ANTSHRIKE Caribbean slope of C America, Darien, Colombia, Venezuela, the Guianas, much of Brazil, Ecuador and N Peru/forest undergrowth, savannah/n tree/e 2/I ♂♀ c14/ F c9

Thamnophilus amazonicus *Sclater* AMAZONIAN ANTSHRIKE (*T. ruficollis*, as used for this species, was suppressed by the International Committee for Zoological Nomenclature, see *Bulletin Zoological Nomenclature* (1975), p 177) Amazon Basin, S Colombia, Venezuela and the Guianas/forest

Thamnophilus insignis *Salvin and Godman* STREAK-BACKED ANTSHRIKE Mts of S Venezuela/ forest

Thamnophilus caerulescens *Vieillot* VARIABLE ANTSHRIKE Peru, Bolivia, N Argentina, Paraguay, Uruguay E and C Brazil / forest undergrowth, scrub and savannah

Thamnophilus torquatus *Swainson* RINGED ANTSHRIKE E and S Brazil (? Bolivia)/ cerrado

Thamnophilus ruficapillus *Vieillot* RUFOUS-CAPPED ANTSHRIKE Peru, Bolivia, S Brazil, Paraguay, Uruguay, N Argentina / forest undergrowth and brush near water

Pygiptila stellaris (*Spix*) SPOT-WINGED or STARRED ANTSHRIKE Orinoco and Amazon basins, Surinam and Cayenne/forest treetops

Megastictus margaritatus (*Sclater*) PEARLY ANTSHRIKE Upper Amazon basin/forest

Neoctantes niger (*Pelzeln*) BLACK BUSHBIRD Amazon headwaters

Clytoctantes alixii *Elliot* RECURVE-BILLED BUSHBIRD Colombia and NW Venezuela/local/ forest undergrowth

Xenornis setifrons *Chapman* SPECKLE-BREASTED or SPINY-FACED ANTSHRIKE E Panama and NW Colombia/forest

Thamnistes anabatinus *Sclater and Salvin* RUSSET ANTSHRIKE S Mexico to Panama, and Colombia to N Bolivia/forest and thickets/n tree/e n/k

Dysithamnus stictothorax (*Temminck*) SPOT-BREASTED ANTVIREO SE Brazil / forest / n tree/ e 2/I ♂♀ ?14/F 11 (1 nest known)

Dysithamnus mentalis (*Temminck*) PLAIN ANTVIREO S Mexico, C America and much of S America S to N Argentina/forest undergrowth/ n tree/e 2/I ♂♀ 15/F 9

Dysithamnus straticeps *Lawrence* STREAKED ANTVIREO E Nicaragua and Costa Rica/humid forest/n tree/e 2/I ♂♀ 14/F 11

Dysithamnus puncticeps *Salvin* SPOTTED ANTVIREO E Costa Rica to Colombia and W Ecuador/forest/n tree/e n/k

Dysithamnus xanthopterus (*Burmeister*) RUFOUS-BACKED ANTVIREO SE Brazil

Thamnomanes ardesiacus (*Sclater and Salvin*) DUSKY-THROATED ANTSHRIKE Amazon basin and the Guianas/forest undergrowth

Thamnomanes saturninus (*Pelzeln*) SATURNINE ANTSHRIKE E Peru and W Brazil

Thamnomanes occidentalis (*Chapman*) WESTERN ANTSHTIKE W Andes of Colombia and Ecuador/forest

Thamnomanes plumbeus (*Wied*) PLUMBEOUS ANTSHRIKE N Venezuela, E Colombia, E Ecuador, SE Brazil/forest

Thamnomanes caesius (*Temmick*) CINEREOUS ANTSHRIKE Amazon basin and the

Plate 144

PSITTACIDAE:
Melopsittacus undulatus,
Budgerigar

Opposite:
PSITTACIDAE:
Neophema pulchella,
Turquoise Parrot

Plate 145

Guianas, and S to Rio de Janeiro / forest and savannah

Thamnomanes schistogynus *Hellmayr* BLUISH-SLATE ANTSHRIKE E Peru, N Bolivia and SW Brazil

Myrmotherula brachyura (*Hermann*) PYGMY ANTWREN E Panama and Upper Amazon basin/ forest borders and secondary forest / n and e n/k

Myrmotherula obscura *Zimmer* SHORT-BILLED ANTWREN Upper Amazon basin / forest

Myrmotherula sclateri *Snethlage* SCLATER'S ANTWREN Brazil S of Amazon and SE Peru/ forest

[**Myrmotherula kermiti** *Cherrie*, known from 1 ♀ from the Rio Gi-Paraná, may be a race of *M. sclateri* or possibly a distinct species. Usually treated as a synonym of *sclateri*]

Myrmotherula klagesi *Todd* KLAGES'S ANT-WREN A few localities on lower Amazon / forest undergrowth

Myrmotherula surinamensis (*Gmelin*) STREAKED ANTWREN Panama and Pacific coasts of Colombia and Ecuador; Upper Orinoco basin, the Guianas and parts of the Amazon basin / forest borders / n tree / e 2

Myrmotherula ambigua *Zimmer* YELLOW-THROATED ANTWREN E Colombia, S Venezuela and NW Brazil / forest undergrowth

Myrmotherula cherriei *Berlepsch and Hartert* CHERRIE'S ANTWREN Upper Orinoco to Rio Negro in N Brazil / forest

Myrmotherula guttata (*Vieillot*) RUFOUS-BELLIED ANTWREN S Venezuela, the Guianas and Brazil N of Amazon / undergrowth in savannah

Myrmotherula longicauda *Berlepsch and Stolzmann* STRIPED-CHESTED ANTWREN Ecuador, Peru and N Bolivia

Myrmotherula hauxwelli (*Sclater*) PLAIN-THROATED or HAUXWELL'S ANTWREN Amazon basin / forest

Myrmotherula gularis (*Spix*) STAR-THROATED ANTWREN SE Brazil

Myrmotherula gutturalis *Sclater and Salvin* BROWN-BELLIED ANTWREN SE Venezuela, the Guianas and Brazil N of Amazon / forest undergrowth

Myrmotherula fulviventris (*Lawrence*) CHEQUERED or FULVOUS ANTWREN Honduras to Panama, Colombia and W Ecuador / forest / n tree / e 2 / I ♂♀

Myrmotherula leucopthalma (*Pelzeln*) WHITE-EYED ANTWREN Amazon basin S of the river

Myrmotherula haematonota (*Sclater*) STIPPLED ANTWREN Upper Amazon basin

Myrmotherula ornata (*Sclater*) ORNATE ANTWREN Edges of Amazon basin from Colombia to Mato Grosso / forest

Myrmotherula erythrura *Sclater* RUFOUS-TAILED ANTWREN Upper Amazon basin / forest

Myrmotherula erythronotos (*Hartlaub*) HOODED ANTWREN SE Brazil

Myrmotherula axillaris (*Vieillot*) WHITE-FLANKED or BLACK ANTWREN El Salvador to Panama and much of S America E of Andes and S to Bolivia and S Brazil / forest undergrowth / n tree / e 2 / I ♂♀ 16 / F 7–8

Myrmotherula schisticolor (*Lawrence*) SLATY ANTWREN S Mexico, C America and Andes from Venezuela to Peru / forest under-growth / n tree / e 2 / I ♂♀ 15

Myrmotherula sunensis *Chapman* RIO SUNO ANTWREN SE Colombia to Peru / forest

Myrmotherula longipennis *Pelzeln* LONG-WINGED ANTWREN Amazon basin / forest

Myrmotherula minor *Salvadori* SALVADORI'S ANTWREN NE Peru, W Brazil (Rio Purús) and SE Brazil

Myrmotherula iheringi *Snethlage* IHERING'S ANTWREN Brazil from S bank of Amazon to Mato Grosso

Myrmotherula grisea *Carriker* ASHY ANTWREN Sta Anna (2,200ft, 670m) Bolivia/ 7 specimens

Myrmotherula unicolor (*Ménétriés*) UNICOLOURED ANTWREN SE Brazil

Myrmotherula behni *Berlepsch and Leverkühn* PLAIN-WINGED ANTWREN Venezuela and E Colombia, Guyana and adjacent Brazil/ forest

Myrmotherula urosticta (*Sclater*) BAND-TAILED ANTWREN SE Brazil

Myrmotherula menetriesii (*d'Orbigny*) GREY ANTWREN Amazon basin, E Venezuela and the Guianas / forest treetops

Myrmotherula assimilis *Pelzeln* LEADEN ANTWREN Upper Amazon basin

Dichrozona cincta (*Pelzeln*) BANDED ANTWREN Amazon basin / forest

Myrmorchilus strigilatus (*Wied*) STRIPE-BACKED or WIED'S ANTBIRD E and S Brazil, S Bolivia, W Paraguay and N Argentina / dense undergrowth

Herpsilochmus pileatus (*Lichtenstein*) CAPPED ANTWREN E and S Brazil, Paraguay, N Argentina and C Peru/ scrub and forest

Herpsilochmus sticturus *Salvin* SPOT-TAILED ANTWREN Parts of Colombia, Venezuela, the Guianas and Brazil on N bank of middle Amazon/ wet savannah and forest near streams

[**Herpsilochmus dugandi** *de Schaunsee* from Ecuador and Colombia, known only from ♀♀ may be a race of *H. sticturus* or a distinct species]

Herpsilochmus stictocephalus *Todd* TODD'S ANTWREN E Venezuela, Guyana and Cayenne/ forest treetops

Herpsilochmus dorsimaculatus *Pelzeln* SPOT-BACKED ANTWREN S Venezuela, SE Colombia and adjacent NW Brazil/ forest

Herpsilochmus roraimae *Hellmayr* RORAIMA ANTWREN Mts of S and E Venezuela, Guyana and adjacent N Brazil/ forest

Herpsilochmus pectoralis *Sclater* PECTORAL ANTWREN Coasts of E Brazil/ dry caatinga

Herpsilochmus longirostris *Pelzeln* LARGE-BILLED ANTWREN Tableland of S Brazil (Mato Grosso etc)

Herpsilochmus axillaris (*Tschudi*) YELLOW-BREASTED ANTWREN SW Colombia, Ecuador and Peru/ forest

Herpsilochmus rufimarginatus (*Temminck*) RUFOUS-WINGED ANTWREN Pacific slope of E Darien, Venezuela, E Andes from Colombia to Bolivia, S and E Brazil, Paraguay and N Argentina/ forest

Microrhopias quixensis (*Cornalia*) DOT-WINGED or VELVETY ANTWREN S Mexico, C America, and much of tropical S America S to Peru and S parts of Amazonian Brazil/ forest/ n tree/ e 2/ I ♂♀

Formicivora iheringi *Hellmayr* NARROW-BILLED ANTWREN E Brazil

Formicivora grisea (*Boddaert*) WHITE-FRINGED, BLACK-BREASTED or BODDAERT'S ANTWREN Islands in Bay of Panama, Colombia, Venezuela, Tobago and adjacent islands (not Trinidad), the Guianas and much of Brazil/ savannah and campos

Formicivora serrana (*Hellmayr*) SERRA ANTWREN SE Brazil

Formicivora melanogaster *Pelzeln* BLACK-BELLIED ANTWREN E and S Brazil and E Bolivia/ brush near streams

Formicivora rufa (*Wied*) RUSTY-BACKED

ANTWREN E Peru, through E Bolivia, plateau of SC Brazil to E Brazil (banks of Lower Amazon) and N to Surinam/ savannah and campos

Drymophila ferruginea (*Temminck*) FERRUGINOUS ANTBIRD SE Brazil, NE Paraguay and NE Argentina / bushes

Drymophila genei (*de Filippi*) RUFOUS-TAILED ANTBIRD SE Brazil

Drymophila ochropyga (*Hellmayr*) OCHRE-RUMPED ANTBIRD SE Brazil

Drymophila devillei (*Menegaux and Hellmayr*) STRIATED ANTBIRD Fringes of Upper Amazon basin

Drymophila caudata (*Sclater*) LONG-TAILED ANTBIRD Mts from Venezuela to Bolivia/ secondary growth

Drymophila malura (*Temminck*) DUSKY-TAILED ANTBIRD SE Brazil, E Paraguay and NE Argentina/ forest undergrowth

Drymophila squamata (*Lichtenstein*) SCALED ANTBIRD S and E Brazil/ humid forest

Terenura maculata (*Wied*) STREAKED-CAPPED ANTWREN SE Brazil, E Paraguay and NE Argentina/ bushes

Terenura callinota (*Sclater*) RUFOUS-RUMPED ANTWREN Panama, Andes from Colombia to Peru: Guyana (unique type of separate race)/ forest

Terenura humeralis *Sclater and Salvin* CHESTNUT-SHOULDERED ANTWREN E Ecuador, NE Peru and parts of W Brazil

Terenura sharpei *Berlepsch* YELLOW-RUMPED ANTWREN Yungas of Cochabamba, Bolivia; SE Peru (*T. xanthonota*, synonym)/ known only from ♂♂

Terenura spodioptila *Sclater and Salvin* ASH-WINGED ANTWREN Upper Orinoco and Amazon basins, the Guianas/ forest

Cercomacra cinerascens (*Sclater*) GREY ANTBIRD Amazon basin, N and E Venezuela and the Guianas/ forest undergrowth

Cercomacra brasiliana *Hellmayr* RIO DE JANEIRO ANTBIRD SE Brazil

Cercomacra tyrannina (*Sclater*) DUSKY or TYRANNINE ANTBIRD SE Mexico, C America, Andes from Venezuela to Ecuador and parts of N Amazon basin / forest undergrowth / n tree/ e 2/ I ♂♀/ F 11

Cercomacra nigrescens (*Cabanis and Heine*) BLACKISH ANTBIRD Widely, but apparently irregularly distributed through S America E of

MUSOPHAGIDAE: *Tauraco hartlaubi*, Blue-crested Turaco, Hartlaub's Turaco

Plate 146

CUCULIDAE:
Cuculus pallidus,
Pallid Cuckoo

CUCULIDAE:
Geococcyx californiana,
Greater Roadrunner

Plate 147

Andes and S to Mato Grosso/swampy forest

Cercomacra serva (*Sclater*) BLACK ANTBIRD SE Colombia to N Bolivia and W Brazil on the upper Juruá/forest undergrowth

Cercomacra nigricans *Sclater* JET ANTBIRD Pacific slope of Panama through parts of Colombia and Venezuela (Orinoco etc) to N Brazil on Rio Branco/thick forest undergrowth/n bush/e 2 (1 nest known)

Cercomacra carbonaria *Sclater and Salvin* RIO BRANCO ANTBIRD Forte de São Joaquin on upper Rio Branco, Brazil

Cercomacra melanaria (*Ménétriés*) MATO GROSSO ANTBIRD N Bolivia and Mato Grosso

Cercomacra ferdinandi *Snethlage* BANANAL ANTBIRD Ilha do Bananal (W Goiaz, Brazil)

Sipia berlepschi (*Hartert*) STUB-TAILED or BERLEPSCH'S ANTBIRD Pacific coast of Colombia and NW Ecuador/forest

Sipia rosenbergi (*Hartert*) ESMERALDAS or ROSENBERG'S ANTBIRD Pacific coast of Colombia and NW Ecuador/forest

Pyriglena leuconota (*Spix*) WHITE-BACKED FIRE-EYE Colombia to Bolivia and across S Amazon basin to Pará and S to Mato Grosso

Pyriglena atra (*Swainson*) FRINGE-BACKED or BLACK FIRE-EYE Santo Amaro, E Brazil

Pyriglena leucoptera (*Vieillot*) WHITE-SHOULDERED FIRE-EYE S Brazil and E Paraguay/forest undergrowth

Rhopornis ardesiaca (*Wied*) SLENDER ANTBIRD Baia, Brazil/3 specimens

Myrmoborus leucophrys (*Tschudi*) WHITE-BROWED ANTBIRD Amazon basin and N to the Guianas and Orinoco delta/undergrowth in swampy forest

Myrmoborus lugubris (*Cabanis*) ASH-BREASTED ANTBIRD Amazon basin

Myrmoborus myotherinus (*Spix*) BLACK-FACED ANTBIRD Amazon and upper Orinoco basins/forest

Myrmoborus melanurus (*Sclater and Salvin*) BLACK-TAILED ANTBIRD NE Peru

Hypocnemis cantator (*Boddaert*) WARBLING ANTBIRD Amazon basin and N to the Guianas/wet forest and savannah/n bush/e n/s

Hypocnemis hypoxantha *Sclater* YELLOW-BROWED ANTBIRD SE Colombia, E Ecuador and NE Peru: E Brazil from Rio Tapajóz to Rio Xingú/forest

Hypocnemoides melanopogon (*Sclater*) BLACK-CHINNED ANTBIRD Upper Orinoco and

Amazon basins and N to the Guianas/undergrowth in swampy forest

Hypocnemoides maculicauda (*Pelzeln*) BAND-TAILED ANTBIRD S Amazon basin and S to Mato Grosso/river thickets

Myrmochanus hemileucus (*Sclater and Salvin*) BLACK-AND-WHITE ANTBIRD Upper Amazon basin

Gymnocichla nudiceps (*Cassin*) BARE-CROWNED ANTBIRD C America and N Colombia/forest and secondary growth/n and e n/k

Sclateria naevia (*Gmelin*) SILVERED ANTBIRD Orinoco and Amazon basins and N to the Guianas/coastal mangroves and swampy forest (the unique ♀ type of *Myrmeciza dubia* Snethlage, is synonymised by Peters with the ♀ of *Sclateria naevia toddi*, but Pinto in *Catálogo das Aves do Brazil* (1938) lists it as a species)

Percnostola rufifrons (*Gmelin*) BLACK-HEADED ANTBIRD N Amazon basin and the Guianas/forest and savannah

Percnostola macrolopha *Berlioz* (*L'Oiseau*, 36 no 1 (1966), p 2) WHITE-LINED ANTBIRD Peru/unique ♂

Percnostola schistacea (*Sclater*) SLATE-COLOURED ANTBIRD SE Colombia, NE Peru and W Brazil/forest

Percnostola leucostigma *Pelzeln* SPOT-WINGED ANTBIRD Amazon basin and adjacent mountains and N to the Guianas/undergrowth of forest and savannah

Percnostola caurensis (*Hellmayr*) CAURA ANTBIRD Upper Orinoco, upper tracts of other Venezuelan rivers, and adjacent Brazil/forest

Percnostola lophotes *Hellmayr and Seilern* RUFOUS-CRESTED ANTBIRD Peru

[NB: See Peters' *Check List*, vol 7, p 232 for a note on the unsatisfactory arrangement of the genus *Myrmeciza*. Some authorities merge *Myrmoderus* and *Myrmophylax* in *Myrmeciza*]

Myrmeciza longipes (*Swainson*) WHITE-BELLIED ANTBIRD Panama, Colombia, Venezuela, Guyana and Brazil N of Amazon, Trinidad/undergrowth and secondary growth/n undergrowth/e 2

Myrmeciza exsul *Sclater* CHESTNUT-BACKED ANTBIRD Nicaragua to Panama, N Colombia and Pacific slope of Colombia and Ecuador/forest and swampy undergrowth/n undergrowth/e 1–2/I ♂♀/F ?10

Myrmeciza ferruginea (*Müller*) FERRUGINOUS

ANTBIRD Lower Amazon and the Guianas / forest / n ground / e 2

Myrmeciza ruficauda (*Wied*) SCALLOPED ANTBIRD Coastal forests of SE Brazil

Myrmeciza laemosticta *Salvin* DULL-MANTLED or SALVIN'S ANTBIRD Parts of Costa Rica, Panama, Colombia, NW Ecuador and W Venezuela / forest / n and e n/k, but 1 clutch of eggs attributed to the species is known

Myrmeciza disjuncta *Friedmann* YAPACANA ANTBIRD Cerro Yapacana on the Upper Orinoco / forest

Myrmeciza pelzelni *Sclater* GREY-BELLIED ANTBIRD E Colombia and upper Rio Negro (Brazil and Venezuela) / forest

Myrmeciza hemimelaena *Sclater* CHESTNUT-TAILED ANTBIRD Upper and S Amazon basin / forest

Myrmeciza hyperythra (*Sclater*) PLUMBEOUS ANTBIRD Upper Amazon basin / forest

Myrmeciza goeldii (*Snethlage*) GOELDI'S ANTBIRD Rio Purús (W Brazil) and SE Peru / forest

Myrmeciza melanoceps (*Spix*) WHITE-SHOULDERED ANTBIRD Upper Amazon basin

Myrmeciza fortis (*Sclater and Salvin*) SOOTY ANTBIRD Upper Amazon basin / forest

Myrmeciza immaculata (*Lafresnaye*) IMMACULATE ANTBIRD Costa Rica, Panama, and Andes from Venezuela to Ecuador / forest / n and e n/k

Myrmeciza griseiceps (*Chapman*) GREY-HEADED ANTBIRD Andes of SW Ecuador and NW Peru / forest

Myrmoderus loricatus (*Lichtenstein*) WHITE-BIBBED ANTBIRD SE Brazil / humid forest

Myrmoderus squamosus (*Pelzeln*) SQUAMOUS ANTBIRD SE Brazil

Myrmophylax atrothorax (*Boddaert*) BLACK-THROATED ANTBIRD Upper and N Amazon basin and the Guianas / undergrowth of forest and savannah

Myrmophylax stictothorax *Todd* SPOT-BREASTED ANTBIRD Apacy, Rio Tapajóz, Brazil / 2 specimens

Formicarius colma *Boddaert* RUFOUS-CAPPED ANT-THRUSH E Colombia, Venezuela, the Guianas, E Ecuador, E Peru and much of Brazil / forest

Formicarius analis (*d'Orbigny and Lafresnaye*) BLACK-FACED ANT-THRUSH S Mexico, C America, Colombia, Venezuela, Trinidad and Amazon basin / lowland forest /

n cavity in hollow branch / e 2 / I ♂♀ / F 18

Formicarius rufifrons *Blake* (*Fieldiana Zool*, 39 no 7 (1957), p 51) RUFOUS-FRONTED ANT-THRUSH Madre di Dios, Peru / known from 2 ♀♀

Formicarius nigricapillus *Ridgway* BLACK-HEADED ANT-THRUSH Caribbean slope of Costa Rica and Panama, and Pacific slope of Colombia and W Ecuador / forest and scrub

Formicarius rufipectus *Salvin* RUFOUS-BREASTED ANT-THRUSH Caribbean slope of Costa Rica and Panama, Andes of Colombia, Ecuador and Peru / forest

Chamaeza campanisona (*Lichtenstein*) SHORT-TAILED ANT-THRUSH Mts from Venezuela to Bolivia, E Paraguay and SE Brazil; and E to mts of Guyana / forest and bamboo thicket

Chamaeza nobilis *Gould* STRIATED ANT-THRUSH Upper Amazon basin / forest floor

Chamaeza ruficauda (*Cabanis and Heine*) RUFOUS-TAILED ANT-THRUSH Mts of Colombia and N Venezuela, SE Brazil / forest

Chamaeza mollissima *Sclater* BARRED ANT-THRUSH Andes of Colombia and Ecuador, cloud forests of N Bolivia / forest

Pithys albifrons (*L*) WHITE-FACED ANTBIRD Amazon basin and N to the Guianas / forest and savannah

Pithys castanea *Berlioz* WHITE-MASKED ANT-BIRD Andoas, Ecuador / unique

Gymnopithys rufigula (*Boddaert*) RUFOUS-THROATED ANTBIRD Upper Orinoco valley, the Guianas and Brazil S to Amazon / undergrowth in forest and savannah

Gymnopithys salvini (*Berlepsch*) WHITE-THROATED ANTBIRD E Peru, Bolivia and adjacent W Brazil

Gymnopithys lunulata (*Sclater and Salvin*) LUNULATED ANTBIRD E Peru and SE Ecuador

Gymnopithys bicolor (*Lawrence*) BICOLOURED ANTBIRD Honduras, Nicaragua, Costa Rica, Panama, Pacific coast of Colombia and W Ecuador / lowland rain forest / n cavity in hollow stump / e 2 / I ♂♀ 15–16 / F 12–15

Gymnopithys leucaspis (*Sclater*) WHITE-CHEEKED ANTBIRD Colombia, E Ecuador, W Brazil and N Peru / forest undergrowth [*leucaspis* and *bicolor* are usually regarded as conspecific]

Rhegmatorhina gymnops *Ridgway* BARE-EYED ANTBIRD N Brazil S of Amazon from Tapajóz to Xingú

CUCULIDAE:
Cuculus saturatus,
Blyth's Himalayan or
Oriental Cuckoo

CUCULIDAE:
Cuculus canorus,
Common Cuckoo

Plate 148

TYTONIDAE:
Tyto novaehollandiae,
Masked Owl

CUCULIDAE:
Cacomantis pyrrophanus,
Fan-tailed Cuckoo

Plate 149

Rhegmatorhina berlepschi (*Snethlage*) HARLEQUIN ANTBIRD Left bank of Rio Tapajóz

Rhegmatorhina cristata (*Pelzeln*) CHESTNUT-CRESTED ANTBIRD Rio Uaupés, NW Brazil

Rhegmatorhina hoffmannsi (*Hellmayr*) WHITE-BREASTED or HOFFMANN'S ANTBIRD W. Brazil (Rio Madeira)

Rhegmatorhina melanosticta (*Sclater and Salvin*) HAIRY-CRESTED ANTBIRD E Ecuador, N Peru, N Bolivia and adjacent W Brazil

Hylophylax naevioides (*Lafresnaye*) SPOTTED ANTBIRD Nicaragua to Panama and Colombia/forest/n tree/e 2/I ♂♀/F 11

Hylophylax naevia (*Gmelin*) SPOT-BACKED ANTBIRD Amazon and upper Orinoco basins/forest

Hylophylax punctulata (*Des Murs*) DOT-BACKED ANTBIRD Amazon basin/forest

Hylophylax poecilonota (*Cabanis*) SCALY-BACKED ANTBIRD Amazon and upper Orinoco basins, and the Guianas / savannah undergrowth

Phlegopsis nigromaculata (*d'Orbigny and Lafresnaye*) BLACK-SPOTTED BARE-EYE Amazon basin / forest undergrowth

Phlegopsis erythroptera (*Gould*) REDDISH-WINGED BARE-EYE Amazon basin/forest undergrowth

Phlegopsis barringeri *de Schaunsee* (*Not Naturae*, no 241 (1951), p 1) ARGUS BARE-EYE Narino, Colombia/ unique ♂

Phlegopsis borbae *Hellmayr* PALE-FACED BARE-EYE Brazil 2 specimens / forest undergrowth (this species is sometimes placed in the monotypic genus *Skutchia*)

Phaenostictus mcleannani (*Lawrence*) OCELLATED ANTBIRD Nicaragua to Panama; S Colombia and NW Ecuador / forest undergrowth

Myrmornis torquata (*Boddaert*) WING-BANDED ANTBIRD Nicaragua, Darien and S America E of Andes and S to Mato Grosso/forest undergrowth

Pittasoma michleri *Cassin* BLACK-CROWNED ANTPITTA Costa Rica, Panama and NW Colombia/forest/n tree/e 2

Pittasoma rufopileatum *Hartert* RUFOUS-CROWNED ANTPITTA W Colombia and NW Ecuador/forest

Grallaricula flavirostris (*Sclater*) OCHRACEOUS ANTPITTA Costa Rica, Panama; Andes from Colombia to Bolivia / forest undergrowth

Grallaricula ferrugineipectus (*Sclater*) RUSTY ANTPITTA Mts of Venezuela, Colombia and N Peru/undergrowth in humid forest

Grallaricula nana (*Lafresnaye*) CROWNED ANTPITTA Mts of Venezuela and Colombia/forest undergrowth

Grallaricula loricata (*Sclater*) SCALLOPED ANTPITTA Coastal mts of N Venezuela / forest undergrowth

Grallaricula peruviana *Chapman* PERUVIAN ANTPITTA NW Peru

Grallaricula lineifrons (*Chapman*) CRESCENT-FACED or CRESCENTED ANTPITTA N Ecuador/ ? unique

Grallaricula cucullata (*Sclater*) HOODED ANTPITTA Andes of Colombia and W Venezuela/forest undergrowth

Myrmothera campanisona (*Hermann*) THRUSH ANTPITTA Amazon basin and some adjoining mts, and N to the Guianas/forest

Myrmothera simplex (*Salvin and Godman*) BROWN ANTPITTA Mts of Venezuela and adjacent Brazil/forest

Grallaria dignissima *Sclater and Salvin* STRIPED ANTPITTA SE Colombia, E Ecuador and NE Peru/forest

Grallaria squamigera *Prévost and Des Murs* UNDULATED ANTPITTA Andes from Venezuela to Bolivia/forest

Grallaria excelsa *Berlepsch* GREAT ANTPITTA Mts of Venezuela /forest

Grallaria gigantea *Lawrence* GIANT ANTPITTA Andes of Colombia and Ecuador / forest

Grallaria guatimalensis *Prévost and Des Murs* SCALED ANTPITTA S Mexico, C America, parts of Ecuador, Peru, Colombia, Venezuela and N Brazil; Trinidad/forest and undergrowth, often near streams/n on mossy log/e 2

Grallaria varia (*Boddaert*) VARIEGATED ANTPITTA Eastern S America from Venezuela and the Guianas to N Argentina / forest and bamboo thickets

Grallaria alleni *Chapman* MOUSTACHED ANTPITTA Cauca, Colombia / ? unique /forest

Grallaria haplonota *Sclater* PLAIN-BACKED or SCLATER'S ANTPITTA Mts of Venezuela and NW Ecuador/forest

Grallaria chthonia *Wetmore and Phelps* (*Proc Biol Soc Washington*, 69 (1956), p 6) TACHIRA ANTPITTA Venezuela /forest /3 specimens

Grallaria milleri *Chapman* BROWN-BANDED

or MILLER'S ANTPITTA C Andes of Colombia/ forest

Grallaria bangsi *Allen* SANTA-MARTA or BANGS'S ANTPITTA Santa Marta Mts, Colombia/ forest undergrowth

Grallaria quitensis *Lesson* TAWNY ANTPITTA Andes of Colombia, Ecuador and Peru/ forest

Grallaria eludens *Lowery and O'Neill* (*Auk*, 86 (1969), p 1 pl 1) ELUSIVE ANTPITTA Balta, Peru

Grallaria erythrotis *Sclater and Salvin* RUFOUS-FACED ANTPITTA Yungas of N Bolivia/ forest

Grallaria hypoleuca *Sclater* BAY-BACKED or WHITE-BELLIED ANTPITTA Andes of Colombia, Ecuador and Peru/forest, often near streams. The following 3 species are now generally considered to be races of *G. hypoleuca*:

   G. przewalskii *Taczanowski* PRZEWALSKI'S ANTPITTA N Peru

   G. erythroleuca *Sclater* RED AND WHITE ANTPITTA Andes of SE Peru

   G. capitalis *Chapman* BAY ANTPITTA E Peru

Grallaria nuchalis *Sclater* CHESTNUT-NAPED ANTPITTA Andes of Colombia and Ecuador/ forest

Grallaria albigula *Chapman* WHITE-THROATED ANTPITTA SE Peru and E Bolivia, NW Argentina

Grallaria ruficapilla *Lafresnaye* CHESTNUT-CROWNED ANTPITTA Mts from Venezuela to Peru/forest

Grallaria rufocinerea *Sclater and Salvin* BICOLOURED ANTPITTA Andes of Colombia

Grallaria griseonucha *Sclater and Salvin* GREY-NAPED ANTPITTA Mts of Venezuela/ forest

Grallaria rufula *Lafresnaye* RUFOUS ANTPITTA Venezuela to Bolivia/forest undergrowth

Grallaria andicola (*Cabanis*) STRIPE-HEADED ANTPITTA Peru and NW Bolivia/ fern brakes and bushes under stunted trees

The remaining species are sometimes separated as the genus *Hylopezus*:

Grallaria macularia (*Temminck*) SPOTTED ANTPITTA Upper Orinoco and parts of Amazon basin, the Guianas/forest

Grallaria fulviventris *Sclater* FULVOUS-BELLIED ANTPITTA Nicaragua to Panama, Colombia and E Ecuador/forest

Grallaria berlepschi *Hellmayr* AMAZONIAN or

BERLEPSCH'S ANTPITTA Amazon basin, S of Amazon

Grallaria perspicillata *Lawrence* STREAK-CHESTED or SPECTACLED ANTPITTA Nicaragua to Panama and Colombia, and W Ecuador/forest/ n tree/e 2/I ♂♀

Grallaria ochroleuca (*Wied*) SPECKLED ANTPITTA E and SE Brazil, E Paraguay and NE Argentina/forest and bamboo thickets

CONOPOPHAGIDAE Antpipits and Gnateaters This small, poorly known group of birds inhabit the Amazon basin and the adjoining foothills. Little is known of their relationships and almost nothing of their breeding habits. The genus *Corythopis*, the Antpipits, is retained in this family for convenience, though it has been suggested recently that it belongs in the Tyrannidae and has been placed there by de Schaunsee (1970), who also suggests that *Conopophaga* should probably belong with the Formicariidae.

Conopophaga lineata (*Wied*) RUFOUS GNATEATER S Brazil, E Paraguay and NE Argentina/bamboo thickets

[**Conopophaga cearae** *Gray* E Brazil/status not fully understood, but probably a race of *C. lineata*]

Conopophaga aurita (*Gmelin*) CHESTNUT-BELTED GNATEATER Amazon basin and N to the Guianas/forest undergrowth

Conopophaga roberti *Hellmayr* HOODED GNATEATER NE Brazil/forest undergrowth

Conopophaga peruviana *Des Murs* ASH-THROATED GNATEATER E Ecuador, E Peru and W Brazil

Conopophaga ardesiaca *d'Orbigny and Lafresnaye* SLATY GNATEATER SE Peru and Bolivia

Conopophaga castaneiceps *Sclater* CHESTNUT-CROWNED GNATEATER Andes of Colombia, Ecuador and Peru / forest undergrowth

Conopophaga melanops (*Vieillot*) BLACK-CHEEKED GNATEATER E and SE Brazil/forest

Conopophaga melanogaster (*Ménétriés*) BLACK-BELLIED GNATEATER Brazil S of Amazon and N Bolivia

Corythopis delalandi (*Lesson*) SOUTHERN ANTPIPIT E Bolivia, Mato Grosso and E Brazil S to Paraguay and NE Argentina / forest undergrowth

Corythopis torquata *Tschudi* RINGED

Plate 150

Opposite:
TYTONIDAE:
Tyto alba,
Common Barn Owl or
White Owl

STRIGIDAE:
Asio capensis,
African Marsh Owl

STRIGIDAE:
Nyctea scandiaca,
Snowy Owl

Plate 151

ANTPIPIT Amazon basin, Orinoco basin and the Guianas / wet forest

RHINOCRYPTIDAE Tapaculos Terrestrial birds of grassy plains or the undergrowth of forests. Their rounded wings are short and feeble and they fly poorly. They have strong legs. The tail is carried cocked, and pointing towards the head, hence the native name *tapacolo* = 'cover your bottom'. They feed on insects, buds and seeds, and scratch on the ground for food rather like game birds. Their breeding habits are varied, some species nesting in tree holes or rock crevices, others in tunnels, and some construct domed nests in trees. Eggs are 2–3 in number and white. Nothing is known of incubation or fledging periods.

Pteroptochos castaneus (*Philippi and Landbeck*) CHESTNUT-THROATED HUET-HUET C Chile / forest / n burrow in ground or hole in tree stump / e 2

Pteroptochos tarnii (*King*) BLACK-THROATED HUET-HUET S Chile and W Argentina / beach forest / n burrow in ground or hole in rotten stump / e 2–3

Pteroptochos megapodius *Kittlitz* MOUSTACHED TURKA N and C Chile / bush-covered hillsides on sea-coast / insects / n burrow in ground / e 2–3 / I ♂♀

Scelorchilus albicollis (*Kittlitz*) WHITE-THROATED TAPACULO N and C Chile / semi-arid hillsides on sea-coast / n burrow in ground / e 2–3 / I ♂♀

Scelorchilus rubecula (*Kittlitz*) CHUCAO Chile and W Argentina / beach forest and thickets / n hole in ground or tree roots / e 2–3

Rhinocrypta lanceolata (*St Hilaire*) CRESTED GALLITO Paraguay, N Argentina, E Bolivia / dry open brush / n bush / e ?2

Teledromas fuscus (*Sclater and Salvin*) BARRANCOLINO or SANDY GALLITO W Argentina / open bush and dry gravelly hillsides

Liosceles thoracicus (*Sclater*) RUSTY-BELTED TAPACULO Amazon basin / forest

Merulaxis ater *Lesson* SLATY BRISTLEFRONT SE Brazil / forest

Merulaxis stresemanni *Sick* (*Journal für Ornithologie*, 101 (1960), p 155) STRESEMANN'S BRISTLEFRONT E Brazil / forest / 2 specimens

Melanopareia torquata (*Wied*) COLLARED CRESCENTCHEST C and E Brazil, E Bolivia / open cerrado with anthills

Melanopareia maximiliani (*d'Orbigny*) OLIVE-CROWNED or MAXIMILIAN'S CRESCENT-CHEST Bolivia, Paraguayan chaco and N Argentina / bushes and sawgrass

Melanopareia maranonicus *Chapman* MARAÑON CRESCENTCHEST N Peru / arid country

Melanopareia elegans (*Lesson*) ELEGANT CRESCENTCHEST W Ecuador and NW Peru / arid scrub

Scytalopus unicolor *Salvin* UNICOLOURED TAPACULO Andes from Venezuela to Bolivia / mossy forest / n ground (1 known) / e ?2

Scytalopus speluncae (*Ménétriés*) MOUSE-COLOURED TAPACULO SE Brazil and N Argentina / forest undergrowth

Scytalopus macropus *Berlepsch and Stolzmann* LARGE-FOOTED TAPACULO Peru / moss-covered vegetation and rocks among mountain torrents

Scytalopus femoralis (*Tschudi*) RUFOUS-VENTED TAPACULO Colombia to N Bolivia [Peters] Panama to Colombia and W Ecuador [de Schaunsee] / mossy forest

Scytalopus argentifrons *Ridgway* SILVER-FRONTED TAPACULO Highlands of Costa Rica and Panama / mountain rain forest / n and e n/k

Scytalopus chiriquensis *Griscom* CHIRIQUI TAPACULO Mts of W Panama

Scytalopus panamensis *Chapman* PANAMA TAPACULO Colombia and E Panama / mossy forest

[Wetmore, in *Birds of Panama* includes *S. chiriquensis* as a race of *S. argentifrons*, but separates *S. vicinior* Zimmer from *S. panamensis* as a good species.]

Scytalopus latebricola *Bangs* BROWN-RUMPED TAPACULO Mts of Venezuela, Colombia and Ecuador / open woodland and dense thickets / n and e n/k

Scytalopus novaecapitalis *Sick* (*Bol Mus Nac Rio de Janeiro*, no 185 (1958) p 14) BRAZILIA TAPACULO Federal district of Brazilia / 3 specimens

Scytalopus indigoticus (*Wied*) WHITE-BREASTED or INDIGO TAPACULO SE Brazil

Scytalopus magellanicus (*Gmelin*) ANDEAN, CHURRIN or MAGELLANIC TAPACULO Andes from Venezuela to Tierra del Fuego and Falkland Is / dark forest ravines and thickets, often near streams / n tree or bank / e 2–3

Scytalopus superciliaris *Cabanis* WHITE-BROWED TAPACULO Bolivia and W Argentina / alder thickets

Myornis senilis (*Lafresnaye*) ASHY TAPACULO Andes of Colombia and Ecuador (? Venezuela)/ forest undergrowth

Eugralla paradoxa (*Kittlitz*) KITTLITZ'S or OCHRE-FLANKED TAPACULO Chile from Maule to Chiloé Is and W Argentina / forest undergrowth / n thorn bush / e 2–3

Acropternis orthonyx (*Lafresnaye*) OCELLATED TAPACULO Andes from Venezuela to Ecuador / forest

Psilorhamphus guttatus (*Ménétriés*) SPOTTED BAMBOO WREN SE Brazil and NE Argentina bamboo thickets (the position of this genus is apparently still uncertain, and some authorities consider it should be placed in the Formiariidae or in the Sylviidae)

COTINGIDAE Cotingas A large diverse family of tropical American primitive passerines. Males are generally brightly coloured, often with crests or wattles, females duller. Comparatively little is known of the habits of these forest birds. I have largely followed the arrangement given in de Schaunsee *Guide to the Birds of S. America* (1970), for convenience, but see also D. W. Snow; Breviora 1973 no 409 (who stresses that any arrangement of this family is provisional).

Rupicola rupicola (*L*) GUIANAN or ORANGE COCK-OF-THE-ROCK Guianas, Brazil N of Amazon, Venezuela S of Orinoco and extreme E Colombia / forest and secondary growth / n cave / e ?2

Rupicola peruviana (*Latham*) PERUVIAN or RED COCK-OF-THE-ROCK Andes from Venezuela to N Bolivia / rocky ravines above streams [NB: The Cocks-of-the-Rock are separated by some authorities into a family, the *Rupicolidae*]

Laniisoma elegans (*Thunberg*) SHRIKE COTINGA Scattered localities from Venezuela to Bolivia and SE Brazil / forest

Phibalura flavirostris (*Vieillot*) SWALLOW-TAILED COTINGA SE Brazil, N Paraguay, W Bolivia and NE Argentina / forest

Tijuca atra *Férussac* BLACK-AND-GOLD COTINGA SE Brazil

Carpornis cucullatus (*Swainson*) HOODED COTINGA or BERRYEATER SE Brazil

Carpornis melanocephalus (*Wied*) BLACK-HEADED COTINGA or BERRYEATER SE Brazil/ forest

Porphyrolaema porphyrolaema (*Deville and Sclater*) PURPLE-THROATED COTINGA SE Colombia, E Ecuador, NE Peru and W Brazil/ forest

Cotinga amabilis *Gould* LOVELY COTINGA SE Mexico to Costa Rica / n tree / I ♀

Cotinga ridgwayi *Ridgway* TURQUOISE or RIDGEWAY'S COTINGA Costa Rica and Panama/ n tree / e 2 / I ♀ (1 nest known)

Cotinga nattererii (*Boissoneau*) BLUE or NATTERER'S COTINGA Venezuela, Colombia, Ecuador and Panama / forest

Cotinga maynana (*L*) PLUM-THROATED or MAYNAS COTINGA Upper Amazon basin / forest

Cotinga cayana (*L*) SPANGLED COTINGA Amazon and Orinoco basins and the Guianas/ forest, savannah and open woodland / insects and berries

Cotinga cotinga (*L*) PURPLE-BREASTED COTINGA N Brazil, S Venezuela and the Guianas/ forest / berries

Cotinga maculata (*Müller*) BANDED COTINGA Coastal zone of SE Brazil / forest

Xipholena punicea (*Pallas*) POMPADOUR COTINGA Guianas, S Venezuela, E Colombia and NW Brazil / forest / berries

Xipholena lamellipennis (*Lafresnaye*) WHITE-TAILED or LAFRESNAYE'S COTINGA Brazil S of Amazon / forest and palms

Xipholena atropurpurea (*Wied*) WHITE-WINGED or WIED'S COTINGA Coastal Brazil/ forest

Carpodectes nitidus *Salvin* SNOWY COTINGA Honduras to N Panama

Carpodectes antoniae *Ridgway* ANTONIA'S COTINGA Costa Rica and W Panama

Carpodectes hopkei *Berlepsch* WHITE COTINGA Pacific coast of Colombia S to NW Ecuador / forest

Conioptilon mcilhennyi *Lowery and O'Neill* BLACK-FACED COTINGA Loreto, Amazonian Peru

Ampelion rubrocristatus (*Lafresnaye and d'Orbigny*) RED-CRESTED COTINGA Mts from Venezuela to N Bolivia / forest edge and open woodland

Ampelion rufaxilla (*Tschudi*) CHESTNUT-CRESTED COTINGA Colombia to Bolivia / forest

Ampelion stresemanni (*Koepcke*) WHITE-CHEEKED COTINGA Peru / mountain woodland

Ampelion sclateri (*Taczanowski*) BAY-VENTED or SCLATER'S COTINGA Peru (Junin)

Pipreola riefferii (*Boissonneau*) GREEN-AND-BLACK FRUITEATER Andes from Venezuela to Peru / forest

Opposite:
STRIGIDAE:
Otus scops,
Common Scops Owl

STRIGIDAE:
Strix varia,
Barred Owl

STRIGIDAE:
Asio otus,
Common Long-eared Owl

Plate 152

Plate 153

Pipreola intermedia *Taczanowski* BAND-TAILED FRUITEATER Peru and N Bolivia

Pipreola lubomirskii *Taczanowski* BLACK-CHESTED or LUBOMIRKSI'S FRUITEATER Colombia, E Ecuador and NE Peru / forest / now usually treated as a race of *P. aureopectus*

Pipreola jucunda *Sclater* ORANGE-BREASTED FRUITEATER Pacific slope of Colombia S to W Ecuador / forest / now usually treated as a race of *P. aureopectus*

Pipreola pulchra (*Hellmayr*) MASKED or BEAUTIFUL FRUITEATER Peru / now usually treated as a race of *P. aureopectus*

Pipreola aureopectus (*Lafresnaye*) GOLDEN-BREASTED FRUITEATER Mts from Venezuela to Colombia / heavy forest / 3 ♀♀ from W Colombia may represent an undescribed species

Pipreola frontalis (*Sclater*) SCARLET-BREASTED FRUITEATER SE Ecuador, E Peru and N Bolivia

Pipreola chlorolepidota (*Swainson*) (= **Euchlornis sclateri,** *Cornalia*) FIERY-THROATED FRUITEATER E Ecuador, E Peru, ? Colombia / forest

Pipreola formosa (*Hartlaub*) HANDSOME FRUITEATER N Venezuela / forest

Pipreola whitelyi *Salvin and Godman* RED-BANDED or WHITELY'S FRUITEATER Guyana and Venezuela

Pipreola arcuata (*Lafresnaye*) BARRED FRUITEATER Andes from Venezuela to N Bolivia / forest

Ampelioides tschudii (*Gray*) SCALED FRUITEATER Andes from Venezuela to Peru / forest

Iodopleura pipra (*Lesson*) BUFF-THROATED PURPLETUFT or LESSON'S COTINGA Guyana (2 specimens): SE Brazil / forest edge

Iodopleura fusca (*Vieillot*) DUSKY PURPLETUFT Guianas and Venezuela (Bolivar) / forest edge / fruit

Iodopleura isabellae *Parzudaki* WHITE-BROWED PURPLETUFT or ISABELLA'S COTINGA Amazon basin / forest and secondary growth

[**Iodopleura guttata** *Lesson* locality unknown (type lost) / does not seem to have been satisfactorily identified with any of the known species]

Calyptura cristata (*Vieillot*) KINGLET COTINGA SE Brazil

Chirocylla uropygialis (*Sclater and Salvin*) SCIMITAR-WINGED COTINGA N Bolivia

Xenopsaris albinucha (*Burmeister*) WHITE-NAPED XENOPSARIS Parts of Venezuela, E Brazil, Paraguay, N Bolivia and Argentina / thickets, river banks and treetops. This genus is sometimes placed in the Tyrannidae; its position is still in doubt

Pachyramphus viridis (*Vieillot*) GREEN-BACKED BECARD Much of tropical S America S to N Argentina / forest

Pachyramphus versicolor (*Hartlaub*) BARRED BECARD Costa Rica, Panama and Andes from Venezuela to N Bolivia / ravines and forest borders / n tree

Pachyramphus surinamus (*L*) GLOSSY-BACKED BECARD Surinam, Cayenne and NE Brazil / forests / insects

Pachyramphus spodiurus *Sclater* SLATY BECARD Ecuador and Peru / forest and open woods

Pachyramphus rufus (*Boddaert*) CINEREOUS BECARD Panama through much of tropical S America E of Andes S to Amazon / savannah, plantations, mangroves and swampy forest / insects and berries / n tree / e n/s

Pachyramphus castaneus (*Jardine and Selby*) CHESTNUT-CROWNED or RUFOUS BECARD Tropical S America from Andes eastward and S to N Argentina / forest

Pachyramphus cinnamomeus *Lawrence* CINNAMON BECARD S Mexico, C America, Colombia, NW Venezuela and NW Ecuador lowland rain forest / n tree / e n/k / I ♀ / F 20–2

Pachyramphus polychopterus (*Vieillot*) WHITE-WINGED or VIEILLOT'S BECARD Guatemala to Panama and tropical S America from Andes eastward; and S to N Argentina / mangrove, plantations and open woodland / insects and berries / n tree / e ?2 ?3–4 (accounts differ) / I ♀ 18–19 / F 21

Pachyramphus marginatus (*Lichtenstein*) BLACK-CAPPED BECARD Tropical S. America from Andes eastward and S to S Brazil / flooded forest, savannah and clearings / insects

Pachyramphus albogriseus *Sclater* BLACK-AND-WHITE BECARD Nicaragua to Panama and Venezuela to Peru / forest

Pachyramphus major (*Cabanis*) MEXICAN BECARD Mexico, Guatemala, Honduras and E Nicaragua

Platypsaris niger (*Cabanis*) JAMAICAN BECARD Jamaica / wooded hills / n tree / e 3

Platypsaris rufus (*Vieillot*) CRESTED BECARD Peru, Bolivia, Paraguay, E and S Brazil and N

Argentina / scrub and campos

Platypsaris homochrous (*Sclater*) ONE-COLOURED BECARD N Venezuela, N Colombia, W Ecuador and NW Peru / open woodland

Platypsaris aglaiae (*Lafresnaye*) ROSE-THROATED BECARD S Texas to Costa Rica / scrub and thin secondary growth / fruit / n tree / e 5–6 / I ♀ / F 18–19

Platypsaris minor (*Lesson*) PINK-THROATED BECARD Amazon basin and the Guianas / forest, shrubbery and savannah / fruit and insects / n tree

Tityra cayana (*L*) BLACK-TAILED or CAYENNE TITYRA Much of tropical S America E of Andes and S to N Argentina / forest, open woods, dead and burnt forest / fruit / n old woodpecker or other tree hole

Tityra semifasciata (*Spix*) MASKED TITYRA Mexico, C America and much of tropical S America E of Andes and S to S Brazil and Bolivia / open woods and dead forest / n hole / e 2 / I ♀ 21 / F 24+

Tityra inquisitor (*Lichtenstein*) INQUISITOR or BLACK-CROWNED TITYRA S Mexico, C America and much of tropical S America S to N Argentina / forest and dead forest / insects / n hole / e ?3 / I ♀ / F 25

Haematoderus militaris (*Shaw*) CRIMSON FRUITCROW Lower Amazon and the Guianas

Querula purpurata (*Müller*) PURPLE-THROATED FRUITCROW Costa Rica, Panama and much of tropical S America to Bolivia and S Brazil / forest / insects and fruit / n tree

Pyroderus scutatus (*Shaw*) RED-RUFFED FRUITCROW Uplands of S America S to N Argentina / forest

Cephalopterus glabricollis *Gould* BARE-NECKED UMBRELLABIRD Costa Rica and Panama

Cephalopterus ornatus *Geoffroy St Hilaire* ORNATE UMBRELLABIRD Amazon basin and the Guianas / forest, particularly on river islands

Cephalopterus penduliger *Sclater* LONG-WATTLED UMBRELLABIRD W Colombia and W Ecuador / forest

Perissocephalus tricolor (*Müller*) CAPUCHIN-BIRD or CALFBIRD Guianas, Venezuela and N Brazil / forest / fruit and insects / n tree / e 1 / I ♀ 26–7 / F 27

Gymnoderus foetidus (*L*) BARE-NECKED FRUITCROW Guianas and Amazon basin / forest and campos / fruit and insects

Procnias tricarunculata (*Verreaux*) THREE-WATTLED BELLBIRD Highlands of Nicaragua, Costa Rica and Panama / n and e n/k

Procnias alba (*Hermann*) WHITE BELLBIRD N Brazil, SE Venezuela and the Guianas / forest

Procnias nudicollis (*Vieillot*) BARE-THROATED BELLBIRD SE Brazil, SE Paraguay and NE Argentina / forest

Procnias averano (*Hermann*) BEARDED BELL-BIRD N Brazil, parts of Colombia, Venezuela and Guyana / forest

Phoenicircus carnifex (*L*) RED COTINGA N Brazil, Bolivar and the Guianas / forest / berries

Phoenicircus nigricollis (*Swainson*) BLACK-NECKED COTINGA Amazon basin / forest

PIPRIDAE Manakins Small, dumpy, brightly coloured birds of American tropical and sub-tropical forests; usually sexually dimorphic, the females being dull coloured. They feed on insects and berries. All the nesting duties are carried out by the female, the nest is usually in a tree, the eggs 2 in number and the incubation period from 19–21 days. About 60 species.

Pipra erythrocephala (*L*) GOLDEN-HEADED MANAKIN E Panama, parts of N Amazon basin, Colombia, Venezuela and the Guianas / forest undergrowth

Pipra rubrocapilla *Temminck* RED-HEADED MANAKIN NE Peru, Brazil S of Amazon and N Bolivia / forest

Pipra mentalis *Sclater* YELLOW-THIGHED or RED-CAPPED MANAKIN Mexico to Panama; Pacific Colombia and Ecuador / forest under-growth / n tree / e 2

Pipra chloromeros *Tschudi* ROUND-TAILED MANAKIN Peru and Bolivia / forest

Pipra cornuta *Spix* SCARLET-HORNED MANAKIN Guyana, mts of S Venezuela and adjacent Brazil / forest

Pipra pipra (*L*) WHITE-CROWNED MANAKIN Amazon basin, the Guianas and coast of Brazil / undergrowth in forest and savannah

Pipra isidorei *Sclater* BLUE-RUMPED or ISIDOR'S MANAKIN E Colombia, E Ecuador and N Peru / forest

Pipra caeruleocapilla *Tschudi* CERULEAN-CAPPED MANAKIN C and E Peru / forest

Pipra coronata *Spix* CROWNED MANAKIN Costa Rica, Panama and north-western S America / forest / n tree / e 2 / I 17–19 / F 13–16

Pipra exquisita *Hellmayr* EXQUISITE MANAKIN C Peru and Amazonian Brazil S of Amazon

Plate 154

STRIGIDAE:
Asio flammeus,
Short-eared Owl

Opposite:
STRIGIDAE:
Asio otus,
Common Long-eared Owl

Plate 155

(sometimes regarded as conspecific with *coronata*)

Pipra serena (*L*) WHITE-FRONTED MANAKIN Venezuela, Brazil N of the Amazon and the Guianas / forest

Pipra iris *Schinz* OPAL MANAKIN Lower Amazon / forest

Pipra vilasboasi *Sick* GOLDEN-CROWNED MANAKIN SW Pará, Brazil / 3 ♂♂ known / forest

Pipra nattereri *Sclater* SNOW-CAPPED or NATTERER'S MANAKIN C Amazonian Brazil / forest

Pipra obscura *Sick* SICK'S MANAKIN SW Pará, Brazil / known only from a ♀ and an immature ♂ (? conspecific with *P. vilasboasi*)

Pipra aureola (*L*) CRIMSON-HOODED MANAKIN Amazon basin and the Guianas / wet open forest / insects and berries / n shrub / e 2

[Pipra anomala *Todd* ANOMALOUS MANAKIN Pará, Brazil / unique / possibly a hybrid]

Pipra fasciicauda *Hellmayr* BAND-TAILED MANAKIN S Amazon basin to N Argentina / forest

Pipra filicauda (*Spix*) WIRE-TAILED MANAKIN N Venezuela, E Colombia, E Ecuador and NE Peru

[Teleonema heterocerca (*Sclater*) SHARP-TAILED MANAKIN Brazil / unique, type lost / believed to be a hybrid]

Antilophia galeata (*Lichtenstein*) HELMETED MANAKIN C and S Brazil tableland and NE Paraguay / swampy forest

Chiroxiphia linearis (*Bonaparte*) LONG-TAILED MANAKIN S Mexico to Costa Rica

Chiroxiphia lanceolata (*Wagler*) LANCE-TAILED MANAKIN Costa Rica to N Venezuela / open woodland and secondary forest

Chiroxiphia pareola (*L*) BLUE-BACKED MANAKIN The Guianas, Amazon basin, Tobago (not Trinidad) / forest undergrowth / berries

Chiroxiphia caudata (*Shaw and Nodder*) SWALLOW-TAILED MANAKIN SE Brazil, Paraguay and NE Argentina / forest

Masius chrysopterus (*Lafresnaye*) GOLDEN-WINGED MANAKIN Venezuela to NE Peru / forest

Ilicura militaris (*Shaw and Nodder*) PINTAILED or MILITARY MANAKIN SE Brazil / forest

[Pipra melanocephala *Vieillot*, related to *Ilicura militaris*, is alleged to have occurred on Trinidad. Type lost, and name preoccupied.

Existence doubtful. See Hellmayr *Catalogue of Birds of the Americas*, pt 6, p 60 footnote]

Corapipo gutturalis (*L*) WHITE-THROATED MANAKIN The Guianas, S Venezuela and adjacent Brazil / forest / see note to *C. altera*

Corapipo leucorrhoa (*Sclater*) WHITE-BIBBED MANAKIN E Colombia and NW Venezuela / forest / n tree / e 2 / see note to *C. altera*

Corapipo altera *Hellmayr* WHITE-RUFFED MANAKIN SE Honduras to NW Colombia / forest. NB: these last 3 species are sometimes considered conspecific

Manacus manacus (*L*) WHITE-BEARDED MANAKIN The Guianas, Trinidad, Venezuela, parts of Colombia, Amazon basin and S to N Argentina (in Colombia this hybridises with *M. vitellinus* with which it is sometimes regarded as conspecific) / forest and undergrowth / berries / n shrub / e 2

Manacus candei (*Parzudaki*) WHITE-COLLARED or CANDE'S MANAKIN SE Mexico to NE Costa Rica

Manacus vitellinus (*Gould*) GOLDEN-COLLARED or GOULD'S MANAKIN Colombia / forest

Manacus aurantiacus (*Salvin*) ORANGE-COLLARED or SALVIN'S MANAKIN SW Costa Rica and W Panama / n tree / e 2 / I 19 / F 13–18

Manacus cerritus *Peters* ALMIRANTE MANAKIN Panama (*M. vitellinus*, *M. aurantiacus* and *M. cerritus* are often considered to be conspecific)

[Manacus coronatus (*Boucard*) BOUCARD'S MANAKIN Known only from the unique type, a 'Bogotá skin' of unknown locality; is generally considered to be a hybrid]

Machaeropterus pyrocephalus (*Sclater*) FIERY-CAPPED MANAKIN Amazon basin / forest

Machaeropterus regulus (*Hahn*) STRIPED MANAKIN Amazon basin

Allocotopterus deliciosus (*Sclater*) CLUB-WINGED MANAKIN W Andes of Colombia and NW Ecuador

Xenopipo atronitens *Cabanis* BLACK MANAKIN Amazon basin, Guianas, S. Venezuela and S Colombia / thick bush in savannah / berries

Chloropipo unicolor *Taczanowski* JET MANAKIN N and C Peru

Chloropipo uniformis *Salvin and Godman* OLIVE or UNIFORM MANAKIN Mts of S Venezuela and (?) Guyana / forest

Chloropipo holochlora *Sclater* GREEN MANAKIN Andes from Colombia to Peru / forest

Chloropipo flavicapilla (*Sclater*) YELLOW-HEADED MANAKIN Andes of Colombia/forest

Neopipo cinnamomea (*Lawrence*) CINNAMON MANAKIN The Guianas, Upper Amazon basin/forest

Heterocercus linetatus (*Strickland*) FLAME-CROWNED MANAKIN NE Peru and W and C Amazon, Brazil

Heterocercus flavivertex *Pelzeln* YELLOW-CROWNED MANAKIN Brazil N of Amazon, Amazonian Venezuela and Colombia/forest

Heterocercus aurantiivertex *Sclater and Salvin* ORANGE-CROWNED MANAKIN Amazonian Ecuador and NE Peru

Heterocercus luteocephalus (*Lesson*) GOLDEN-CRESTED MANAKIN Unique, of unknown locality/possibly a hybrid

Neopelma aurifrons (*Wied*) WIED'S MANAKIN E Brazil

Neopelma chrysolophum *Pinto* (=**N. luteocephala** (*Lafresnaye*)) PINTO'S MANAKIN May represent a species or a southern race of *N. aurifrons*

Neopelma sulphureiventer (*Hellmayr*) SULPHUR-BELLIED MANAKIN E Peru, N Bolivia and adjacent Brazil

Neopelma chrysocephalum (*Pelzeln*) ORANGE or SAFFRON-CRESTED MANAKIN Guianas, S Venezuela, SE Colombia and NW Brazil/forest and open savannah/berries and insects

Neopelma pallescens (*Lafresnaye*) PALE-BELLIED or YELLOW-CRESTED MANAKIN NE and C Brazil/campos and cerradão

Tyranneutes virescens (*Pelzeln*) TINY MANAKIN Guyana, Surinam, E Bolivar and N Brazil/undergrowth in forest/insects and berries

Tyranneutes stolzmanni (*Hellmayr*) DWARF MANAKIN Amazon basin/forest

Piprites pileatus (*Temminck*) BLACK-CAPPED or PILEATED MANAKIN Wooded region of S Brazil and NE Argentina/forest

Piprites chloris (*Temminck*) WING-BARRED or TEMMINCK'S MANAKIN S America E of Andes and S to N Argentina/forest

Piprites griseiceps *Salvin* GREY-HEADED MANAKIN Costa Rica and Nicaragua

Sapayoa aenigma *Hartert* BROAD-BILLED or ENIGMA MANAKIN Tropical pacific coast from E Panama to NW Ecuador

Schiffornis major *Des Murs* GREATER MANAKIN Amazon basin/forest

Schiffornis virescens (*Lafresnaye*) GREENISH MANAKIN SE Brazil, SE Paraguay and N Argentina/forest

Schiffornis turdinus (*Wied*) THRUSH MANAKIN SE Mexico S to E Brazil and N Bolivia/forest undergrowth/insects and berries/n tree/e 1–2/I 20–2/F 15

TYRANNIDAE Tyrant Flycatchers Generally plain-coloured birds (though some are brightly coloured), superficially resembling the Old World Flycatchers, but more aggressive, often with fairly powerful bills, and usually with erectile feathers on the crown. Generally insectivorous, but some species also feed on fruit. Nesting habits vary. About 365 species throughout the Americas, but commonest in the tropics.

The arrangement here follows de Schaunsee *Birds of S America* (1966 and 1970), and Cory and Hellmayr, *Catalogue of Birds of the Americas.*

Agriornis livida (*Kittlitz*) GREAT or KITTLITZ'S SHRIKE TYRANT S Argentina and Chile to Tierra del Fuego/scrub and fields/insects and small animals/n bush/e 2–4

Agriornis microptera *Gould* GREY-BELLIED SHRIKE TYRANT SE Peru to Argentina and Chile (? Paraguay and Uruguay)/bush/n bush/e ?1

Agriornis montana (*Lafresnaye and d'Orbigny*) MOUNTAIN or BLACK-BILLED SHRIKE TYRANT Andes from Colombia to W Argentina/rocky slopes and habitation/n crevice/e 2–3

Agriornis albicauda (*Philippi and Landbeck*) WHITE-TAILED SHRIKE TYRANT Andes from Ecuador to Chile and Argentina/open scrub/n and e n/k

Neoxolmis rufiventris (*Vieillot*) CHOCOLATE TYRANT Patagonia and Tierra del Fuego w N to Uruguay/open scrub/n and e n/k

Xolmis cinerea (*Vieillot*) GREY MONJITA or PEPOAZA Eastern S America from Brazil S of Amazon to N Argentina/cerrado and habitation

Xolmis velata (*Lichtenstein*) VEILED or WHITE-RUMPED MONJITA C and E Brazil, Bolivia and Paraguay/scrub and campos

Xolmis dominicana (*Vieillot*) DOMINICAN or BLACK AND WHITE MONJITA SE Brazil, Uruguay, Paraguay and N Argentina/open scrub

Xolmis coronata (*Vieillot*) BLACK-CROWNED

STRIGIDAE:
Strix aluco,
Tawny Owl

STRIGIDAE:
Bubo bubo,
Great Eagle Owl

Plate 156

STRIGIDAE:
Ninox rufa,
Rufous Owl

STRIGIDAE:
Otus asio,
Common Screech Owl

Plate 157

MONJITA Pampas of Argentina w N to Bolivia and SE Brazil / open scrub

Xolmis irupero (*Vieillot*) WIDOW or WHITE MONJITA E Brazil, Uruguay, Paraguay, E Bolivia and N Argentina / open country and habitation

Xolmis murina (*d'Orbigny and Lafresnaye*) BROWN MONJITA S Argentina w N to E Bolivia and Paraguayan chaco / open scrub

Xolmis rubetra (*Burmeister*) CHAT-LIKE or RUSTY-BACKED MONJITA W Argentina / open scrub

Xolmis rufipennis (*Taczanowski*) RUFOUS-WEBBED TYRANT Andes of Peru and Bolivia / woodland, brush and grassland

Pyrope pyrope (*Kittlitz*) FIRE-EYED DIUCÓN Andes of Chile and Argentina S to Tierra del Fuego / open woodland / insects / n tree / e 2–3

Muscisaxicola rufivertex *d'Orbigny and Lafresnaye* RUFOUS-NAPED GROUND TYRANT Peru, Chile, W Bolivia and Argentina / stony hillsides / n crevice / e 2–4

Muscisaxicola albilora *Lafresnaye* WHITE-LORED GROUND TYRANT Andes of Chile and Argentina w N to S Ecuador / stony hillsides / n crevice / e 2–4

Muscisaxicola juninensis *Taczanowski* PUNA GROUND TYRANT Puna zone of Peru, W Bolivia, N Chile and NW Argentina / stony hillsides / n crevice / e 2

Muscisaxicola flavinucha *Lafresnaye* OCHRE-NAPED GROUND TYRANT Argentina and Chile S to Tierra del Fuego w N to Peru / stony hillsides / n crevice / e 2–4

Muscisaxicola capistrata (*Burmeister*) CINNAMON-BELLIED or BURMEISTER'S GROUND TYRANT Tierra del Fuego and adjacent islands w N to Peru / stony hillsides / n crevice / e 2–4

Muscisaxicola frontalis (*Burmeister*) BLACK-FRONTED GROUND TYRANT Andes from S Peru to Chile and Argentina / stony hillsides / n crevice / e ?2 (1 nest with 2 young)

Muscisaxicola albifrons (*Tschudi*) WHITE-FRONTED GROUND TYRANT Andes from C Peru to N Chile / stony hillsides / n crevice / e 2

Muscisaxicola alpina (*Jardine*) PLAIN-CAPPED or ALPINE GROUND TYRANT Paramo zone of Andes from Colombia to Chile and W Argentina / n crevice / e 2 (2 nests known)

Muscisaxicola macloviana (*Garnot*) DARK-FACED GROUND TYRANT Falklands and Andes from Tierra del Fuego to N Chile w N to Peru /

n ground / e 2–3

Muscisaxicola maculirostris *d'Orbigny and Lafresnaye* SPOT-BILLED GROUND TYRANT Andes from Colombia to Chile and Argentina

Muscisaxicola fluviatilis *Sclater and Salvin* LITTLE GROUND TYRANT Upper Amazon basin

Muscigralla brevicauda *Lafresnaye and d'Orbigny* SHORT-TAILED GROUND TYRANT Coasts of Ecuador and Peru / arid scrub and roadsides / n and e n/k

Lessonia rufa (*Gmelin*) NEGRITO FLYCATCHER Peru and S Brazil to Tierra del Fuego / damp open land near water / insects / n ground / e 2–3

Myiotheretes straticollis (*Sclater*) STREAK-THROATED BUSH-TYRANT Andes from Venezuela to NW Argentina / shrubby ravines and haciendas

Myiotheretes pernix (*Bangs*) SANTA MARTA BUSH TYRANT Santa Marta Mts, Colombia / shrubby ravines

Myiotheretes fumigatus (*Boissonneau*) SMOKY BUSH TYRANT Andes from Venezuela to Peru / shrubby hillsides

Myiotheretes fuscorufus (*Sclater and Salvin*) RUFOUS-BELLIED BUSH TYRANT SE Peru and N Bolivia / shrubby hillsides

Myiotheretes signatus *Taczanowski* JELSKI'S BUSH TYRANT C Peru / 2 specimens / shrubby hillsides

Myiotheretes erythropygius (*Sclater*) RED-RUMPED BUSH TYRANT Mts from Colombia to NW Bolivia / shrubby slopes and ravines

Ochthoeca oenanthoides (*Lafresnaye and d'Orbigny*) D'ORBIGNY'S CHAT TYRANT Andes from Peru to Chile and W Argentina / bushy hillsides and valleys / insects / n and e n/k

Ochthoeca fumicolor *Sclater* BROWN-BACKED CHAT TYRANT NW Venezuela to N Bolivia / thickets

Ochthoeca leucophrys (*Lafresnaye and d'Orbigny*) WHITE-BROWED CHAT TYRANT Andes from Peru to N Chile and Argentina / fields and hedgerows / insects / n and e n/k

Ochthoeca piurae *Chapman* PIURA CHAT TYRANT Andes of NW Peru / shrubby hillsides and arid regions

Ochthoeca rufipectoralis (*Lafresnaye and d'Orbigny*) RUFOUS-BREASTED CHAT TYRANT NW Venezuela to N Bolivia / forest and bushy hillsides

Ochthoeca cinnamomeiventris (*Lafresnaye*) SLATY-BACKED CHAT TYRANT Andes from

Venezuela to Bolivia / forest (*O. nigrita* and *O. thoracica* are now regarded as conspecific with *O. cinnamomeiventris*)

Ochthoeca frontalis (*Lafresnaye*) (=**O. albidiadema** (*Lafresnaye*)) CROWNED CHAT TYRANT Andes from Colombia to Peru / shrubby hillsides

Ochthoeca pulchella *Sclater and Salvin* GOLDEN-BROWED CHAT TYRANT Andes of SW Ecuador, Peru and N Bolivia / shrubby hillsides

Ochthoeca diadema (*Hartlaub*) YELLOW-BELLIED or HARTLAUB'S CHAT TYRANT Andes from Venezuela to Peru / shrubby hillsides

Sayornis phoebe (*Latham*) EASTERN PHOEBE N America E of Rockies w S to Mexico and Cuba / woodland and habitation / insects and berries / n crevice in rock or building / e 3–8/ I ♀ 15–16 / F 15–16

Sayornis nigricans (*Swainson*) BLACK PHOEBE Western USA, S through Mexico and C America, and S America from Venezuela to Bolivia and N Argentina / woodland and habitation, usually near water / insects and berries / n crevice in rock or building / e 4–5/ I ♀ 17 / F 21

Sayornis saya (*Bonaparte*) SAY'S PHOEBE Western N America from Alaska S, w S to Mexico / prairie and desert scrub / insects and berries / n crevice in rock or building / e 3–7/ I 12 / F c21

Colonia colonus (*Vieillot*) LONG-TAILED TYRANT Much of tropical S America S to N Argentina / forest and scrub / insects / n old woodpecker hole / e ? n/k / I ♀

Gubernetes yetapa (*Vieillot*) STREAMER-TAILED TYRANT Bolivia, S Brazil, Paraguay and N Argentina / open woodland

Alectrurus tricolor (*Vieillot*) COCK-TAILED TYRANT Bolivia, S Brazil, Paraguay and N Argentina / brush and woodland

Yetapa risoria (*Vieillot*) STRANGE-TAILED TYRANT S Brazil, Paraguay, Uruguay and E and C Argentina / grassland and marsh

Knipolegus lophotes *Hellmayr* CRESTED BLACK TYRANT S Brazil and Uruguay / forest borders and thickets

Knipolegus nigerrimus (*Vieillot*) VELVETY or VIEILLOT'S BLACK TYRANT SE Brazil / forest borders and thickets

Knipolegus aterrimus (*Kaup*) KAUP'S or WHITE-WINGED BLACK TYRANT E Peru, Bolivia, EC Brazil and Argentina / forest borders and thickets

Knipolegus orenocensis *Berlepsch* ORINOCO or RIVERSIDE TYRANT Orinoco valley and S Amazon basin / forest borders and thickets

Knipolegus poecilurus (*Sclater*) RUFOUS-TAILED TYRANT Andes from Venezuela to Bolivia; Trinidad and Tobago / forest borders and thickets

Knipolegus cyanirostris (*Vieillot*) BLUE-BILLED BLACK TYRANT SE Brazil, Paraguay, Uruguay and E Argentina / forest border and thickets

Knipolegus cabanisi *Schulz* CABANIS'S or PLUMBEOUS TYRANT SE Peru, E Bolivia and NW Argentina / forest border and thickets

[**Knipolegus subflammulatus** *Berlioz* BERLIOZ'S TYRANT Bolivia / 4 specimens thought to be possibly immatures of *K. cabanisi*]

Phaeotriccus poecilocercus (*Pelzeln*) PELZELN'S or AMAZONIAN BLACK TYRANT Guyana and N Amazon basin / forest

Phaeotriccus hudsoni (*Sclater*) HUDSON'S BLACK TYRANT b S Argentina w N to Bolivia and S Brazil / open scrub

Entotriccus straticeps (*Lafresnaye and d'Orbigny*) CINEREOUS TYRANT b W Argentina w N to Bolivia and S Brazil / open scrub

Hymenops perspicillata (*Gmelin*) SPECTACLED TYRANT b Argentina w N to Bolivia and S Brazil / reedbeds and swamps / insects / n ground / e 2–3

Muscipipra vetula (*Lichtenstein*) SHEAR-TAILED GREY TYRANT SE Brazil, Paraguay and N Argentina / scrub

Fluvicola pica (*Boddaert*) PIED WATER TYRANT Much of tropical S America S to Argentina / riverbanks and marshes / insects and seeds / n low vegetation / e 2–3

Fluvicola nengeta (*L*) (=**F. climazura** (*Vieillot*)) MASKED WATER TYRANT Arid zone of SW Ecuador and NW Peru: E Brazil / riverbanks, marshes and parks

Arundinicola leucocephala (*L*) WHITE-HEADED MARSH TYRANT Freshwater marshes of tropical S America / marshes and riverbanks / insects / n low vegetation / e 2–3

Pyrocephalus rubinus (*Boddaert*) VERMILION FLYCATCHER South-western USA, C America and much of tropical S America S to N Argentina; Galapagos / arid scrub / insects / n tree / e 2–3

Ochythornis littoralis (*Pelzeln*) DRAB WATER

STRIGIDAE:
Glaucidium perlatum,
Pearl-spotted Owlet

STRIGIDAE:
Otus leucotis,
White-faced Screech Owl,
White-faced Scops-Owl

Plate 158

STRIGIDAE:
Athene noctua,
Little Owl

STRIGIDAE:
Micrathene whitneyi,
Elf Owl

Plate 159

TYRANT Guianas and Upper and S Amazon basin / sandy riverbanks

Tumbezia salvini (*Taczanowski*) TUMBES or SALVIN'S TYRANT NW Peru / arid littoral zone

Satrapa icterophrys (*Vieillot*) YELLOW-BROWED SATRAP E and C Brazil to Argentina and Bolivia w N to Venezuela / woodland and cultivation

Machetornis rixosus (*Vieillot*) FIRE-CROWNED TYRANT or CATTLE FLYCATCHER Venezuela, Colombia, E and C Brazil, Uruguay, Paraguay, Bolivia and N Argentina / pasture

Muscivora forficata (*Gmelin*) SCISSOR-TAILED FLYCATCHER b south-central USA w S to Panama / prairie and habitation / insects and berries / n tree / e 4–6 / I ♀ 12–13 / F c14

Muscivora tyrannus (*L*) SWALLOW-TAILED or FORK-TAILED FLYCATCHER Widely distributed from S Mexico to Argentina, frequently wandering well outside its normal range / semi-arid savannah and habitation / insects and berries / n tree / e 4

Sirystes sibilator (*Vieillot*) SIRYSTES Amazon basin / forest and cerradão

Tyrannus tyrannus (*L*) EASTERN KINGBIRD Widely distributed from southern USA to Argentina / campos, savannah, prairie etc / insects and berries / n tree / e 3–5 / I ♂♀ / F 10–18

Tyrannus caudifasciatus (*d'Orbigny*) LOGGERHEAD KINGBIRD or PETCHARY Bahamas, Cuba, Isle of Pines, Caymans, Jamaica, Hispaniola, Puerto Rico, Vieques / open woodland / n tree or shrub / e 2–4

Tyrannus cubensis *Richmond* GIANT KINGBIRD Cuba, Isle of Pines, Great Inagua and Caicos / woodland / n tree or shrub / e 2–4

Tyrannus vociferans *Swainson* CASSIN'S KINGBIRD South-western USA and Mexico w S to Guatemala / sagebrush plains, ravines and rocky hillsides / insects and fruit / n tree / e 2–5 / I ♀ 12–14

Tyrannus crassirostris *Swainson* THICK-BILLED KINGBIRD Mexico

Tyrannus verticalis *Say* ARKANSAS or WESTERN KINGBIRD b SW Canada and western USA w S to Guatemala / wanders to eastern USA / prairie and habitation / insects and berries / n tree or bush / e 3–7 / I ♀ (?♂) 12–14

Tyrannus melancholicus *Vieillot* TROPICAL or AZARA'S KINGBIRD Arizona S through C and S America to Argentina / savannah parkland / insects and berries / n tree or shrub / e 2–3

(*T. couchii* Baird, may be a separate species)

Tyrannus dominicensis (*Gmelin*) GREY KINGBIRD b south-eastern USA and W Indies w Northern S America / savannah / insects / n tree or shrub / e 2–4

Tyrannus niveigularis *Sclater* SNOWY-THROATED KINGBIRD Colombia, Ecuador and Peru / arid scrub

Tyrannus albogularis *Burmeister* WHITE-THROATED KINGBIRD Amazon basin / savannah and forest edge

[**Tyrannus apolites** (*Cabanis and Heine*) HEINE'S KINGBIRD Rio de Janeiro, Brazil / unique / believed by some to be a hybrid]

Tyrannopsis sulphurea (*Spix*) SULPHURY FLYCATCHER Scattered localities in Trinidad, the Guianas, Venezuela to Peru and Brazil / open forest and sandy areas / insects and berries / n palm tree

Tyrannopsis luteiventris (*Sclater*) DUSKY-CHESTED FLYCATCHER Surinam, and upper Amazon basin / forest edge / insects

Empidonomus varius (*Vieillot*) (=**E. jelskii** *Sztolcman*) VARIED FLYCATCHER Tropical S America E of Andes and S to Argentina / open woodland / insects and berries / n tree / e 2

Empidonomus aurantioatrocristatus (*Lafresnaye and d'Orbigny*) BLACK AND YELLOW-CRESTED FLYCATCHER or CROWNED SLATY FLYCATCHER b E Brazil to C Argentina w N of range / open brush and forest edge

Legatus leucophaius (*Vieillot*) PIRATIC or STRIPED FLYCATCHER (*Empidonomus minor*, Sztolcman, is stated to be probably a synonym) S Mexico, C America and much of tropical S America / open woodland / berries and insects / n domed nest of other species / e ?1 (nest parasite)

Conopias trivirgata (*Wied*) THREE-STRIPED FLYCATCHER Amazon basin and S to N Argentina / open woodland

Conopias cinchoneti (*Tschudi*) LEMON-BROWED or CINCHON FLYCATCHER Andes from Venezuela to Peru / forest

Conopias parva (*Pelzeln*) WHITE-RINGED FLYCATCHER S America N of Amazon, Panama and Costa Rica / forest / insects and berries / n old woodpecker hole / e 2

Megarhynchus pitangua (*L*) BOAT-BILLED FLYCATCHER Mexico, C America and much of tropical S America / forest edge / insects / n tree

Myiodynastes luteiventris *Sclater* SULPHUR-

BELLIED FLYCATCHER S Arizona to Costa Rica w northern S America / open woodlands and clearings

Myiodynastes maculatus (*Müller*) STREAKED FLYCATCHER Mexico, C America and much of tropical S America / open woodland, plantations etc / insects and berries / n hole / e n/s (*M. solitatius* (Vieillot) is sometimes separated)

Myiodynastes bairdi (*Gambel*) BAIRD'S FLYCATCHER Arid coast of Ecuador and Peru

Myiodynastes chrysocephalus (*Tschudi*) GOLDEN-CROWNED FLYCATCHER Andes from Venezuela to Peru, E Panama / forest edge

Myiodynastes hemichrysus (*Cabanis*) GOLDEN-BELLIED FLYCATCHER Highlands of Costa Rica and W Panama

Myiozetetes cayanensis (*L*) RUSTY-MARGINED FLYCATCHER Panama and much of tropical S America S to Brazil and Bolivia / forest and open country / insects and berries / n shrubbery / e 2–3 / I 16 / F 19

Myiozetetes similis (*Spix*) VERMILION-CROWNED or SOCIAL FLYCATCHER Much of tropical S America / open woodland, often near water

Myiozetetes granadensis *Lawrence* GREY-CAPPED FLYCATCHER Nicaragua to Panama and much of tropical S America S to Brazil and Bolivia / clearings

Myiozetetes inornatus *Lawrence* WHITE-BEARDED FLYCATCHER Coast of Venezuela and Orinoco valley / savannah

Pitangus sulphuratus (*L*) GREAT KISKADEE S America from Colombia, Venezuela and the Guianas to Argentina / open woodland and parks / omnivorous / n tree or telegraph pole / e 2–3

Pitangus lictor (*Lichtenstein*) LESSER KISKADEE Panama, and S America E of Andes and S to Brazil / mangroves and plantations / insects / n tree / e 3

Myiarchus semirufus *Sclater and Salvin* RUFOUS or SEABOARD FLYCATCHER Arid coast of Peru / arid coast and foothills

Myiarchus ferox (*Gmelin*) SHORT-CRESTED FLYCATCHER SW Costa Rica, Panama and S America E of Andes, S to Argentina / savannah and mangroves / berries and insects / n hole / e 2

Myiarchus apicalis *Sclater and Salvin* APICAL FLYCATCHER Colombia / arid scrub

Myiarchus cephalotes *Taczanowski* PALE-EDGED or TACZANOWSKI'S FLYCATCHER Mts from Venezuela to Bolivia / forest

Myiarchus phaeocephalus *Sclater* SOOTY-CROWNED or ASHY-FRONTED FLYCATCHER Arid zone of W Ecuador and NW Peru / arid scrub (*M. toddi* Chapman, is now regarded as a race)

Myiarchus tyrannulus (*Müller*) BROWN-CRESTED or WIED'S FLYCATCHER Widely distributed through the Americas from southern USA to S Brazil and Paraguay / mangroves, forest etc / insects / n tree cavity / e 2–4 (This species is complicated. The *magister*, *brachyurus* and *oberi* groups, formerly considered distinct are now included)

Myiarchus swainsoni *Cabanis and Heine* SWAINSON'S FLYCATCHER Widely distributed through S America E of Andes / mangrove, savannah etc (includes *pelzelni*, *ferocior* and *phaenotus*)

[**Myiarchus sclateri** *Lawrence* SCLATER'S TYRANT Martinique / arid acacia hillsides / Bond treats this as a race of *stolidus*, formerly it was regarded as closely allied to *tyrannulus*]

Myiarchus stolidus (*Gosse*) STOLID FLYCATCHER Greater Antilles and Bahamas / woodland and mangrove / n tree cavity / e 2–4

Myiarchus antillarum (*Bryant*) PUERTO RICAN FLYCATCHER Puerto Rico and adjacent islands / possibly conspecific with *M. stolidus*

Myiarchus barbirostris (*Swainson*) SAD FLYCATCHER Jamaica / Bond regards this as a species in *Check List of the Birds of the West Indies* (1956) but in the *Field Guide to the Birds of the West Indies* as a race of *tuberculifer*.

Myiarchus crinitus (*L*) CRESTED FLYCATCHER b eastern N America w S Florida, Caribbean and N Colombia / open woodland / insects and berries / n hole / e 4–8 / I ♀ 13–15 / F 18

Myiarchus cinerascens (*Lawrence*) ASHY-THROATED FLYCATCHER b western USA w S to Guatemala / scrub and thickets / insects and berries / n hole / e 3–7 / I ♀ 15

Myiarchus nuttingi *Ridgway* NUTTING'S FLYCATCHER Mexico to Costa Rica

Myiarchus yucatanensis *Lawrence* YUCATAN FLYCATCHER Yucatan and Cosumel Is

Myiarchus tuberculifer (*d'Orbigny and Lafresnaye*) DUSKY-CAPPED or OLIVACEOUS FLYCATCHER S Arizona through C America and tropical S America to N Argentina / woodland and pasture / n tree cavity / e 3–5

Myiarchus validus *Cabanis* RUFOUS-TAILED FLYCATCHER Jamaica / wooded hills and moun-

Plate 160

Opposite:
STRIGIDAE:
Strix uralensis,
Ural Owl

PODARGIDAE:
Podargus strigoides,
Tawny Frogmouth

STRIGIDAE:
Bubo bubo,
Great Eagle Owl

Plate 161

tains / n tree cavity / e 3–5 / see note in Morony, Bock and Farrand, *Reference List of the Birds of the World* (1975), p 168 who recognise other species in genus *Myiarchus* following unpublished communication with Lanyon

NB: The genera *Attila*, *Pseudattila*, *Casiornis*, *Laniocera*, *Rhytipterna* and *Lipaugus* were formerly placed in the Cotingidae.

Attila spadiceus (*Gmelin*) STREAKED ATTILA S Mexico, C America and much of tropical S America S to Rio de Janeiro / forest and savannah / ? lizards / n tree / e 1

Attila bolivianus (*Lafresnaye*) RUFOUS ATTILA Upper Amazon basin / forest

Attila rufus (*Vieillot*) GREY-HOODED ATTILA SE Brazil

Attila citriniventris *Sclater* CITRON-BELLIED ATTILA Upper Amazon basin / forest

Attila cinnamomeum (*Gmelin*) CINNAMON ATTILA Amazon basin and N to the Guianas / mangroves and swampy forest / insects and amphibia / n tree / e 3

Attila torridus *Sclater* OCHRACEOUS ATTILA W Ecuador / forest

Pseudattila phoenicurus (*Pelzeln*) RUFOUS-TAILED ATTILA C and S Brazil, Paraguay and N Argentina, also Venezuela / forest

Casiornis rufa (*Vieillot*) RUFOUS CASIORNIS E and C Brazil, Paraguay, E Bolivia and N Argentina / scrub

Casiornis fusca *Sclater* DUSKY or ASH-THROATED CASIORNIS E Brazil / scrub

Laniocera hypopyrrha (*Vieillot*) CINEREOUS MOURNER Amazon basin and N to the Guianas / forest / insects

Laniocera rufescens (*Sclater*) SPECKLED MOURNER Guatemala to Colombia and W Ecuador / forest / insects and berries

Rhytipterna simplex (*Lichtenstein*) GREYISH MOURNER Amazon basin, Venezuela and the Guianas / open forest

Rhytipterna immunda (*Sclater and Salvin*) PALE-BELLIED or CAYENNE MOURNER The Guianas, SE Colombia and N Brazil / bushy savannah / fruit

Rhytipterna holoerythra (*Sclater and Salvin*) RUFOUS MOURNER Guatemala S to Colombia and NW Ecuador / forest

Lipaugus fuscocinereus (*Lafresnaye*) DUSKY PIHA Andes of Colombia and E Ecuador / forest

Lipaugus lanioides (*Lesson*) CINNAMON-VENTED PIHA SE Brazil

Lipaugus vociferans (*Wied*) SCREAMING PIHA Amazon basin and the Guianas / forest and savannah / fruit and insects

Lipaugus streptophorus (*Salvin and Godman*) ROSE-COLLARED PIHA Guyana, Venezuela and adjacent Brazil / forest

Lipaugus subalaris (*Sclater*) GREY-TAILED PIHA E Ecuador and Peru

Lipaugus cryptolophus (*Sclater and Salvin*) OLIVACEOUS PIHA Andes from Colombia to Peru / forest

Lipaugus unirufus *Sclater* RUFOUS PIHA S Mexico to Colombia and Ecuador / forest / n tree / e 1 / I ♀ 25–6 / F 28–9

Nesotriccus ridgwayi *Townsend* COCOS ISLAND FLYCATCHER Cocos Is

Deltarhynchus flammulatus (*Lawrence*) FLAMMULATED FLYCATCHER S Mexico

Nuttallornis borealis (*Swainson*) OLIVE-SIDED FLYCATCHER b western N America from Alaska to Baja California and Carolina w S to Peru / woods and pastures / insects / n tree / e 3–4 / I 14 / F c21

Contopus virens (*L*) WOOD PEEWEE b N America from Alaska and Canada S to Costa Rica w northern S America / forest and woodland / insects and some berries / n tree / e 2–4 / I ♀ 12–13 (*C. richardsonii* and *C. sordidulus*, are now generally regarded as conspecific with *C. virens*)

Contopus latirostris (*Verreaux*) LESSER ANTILLEAN PEEWEE Puerto Rico, Guadeloupe, Dominica, Martinique and St Lucia / mountain forest and cultivation / n tree / e 2–4

Contopus caribaeus (*d'Orbigny*) GREATER ANTILLEAN PEEWEE Cuba, Jamaica, Hispaniola, Bahamas and adjacent islets / forest, orchard and mangrove / n tree / e 2–4

Contopus cinereus (*Spix*) ASH-COLOURED PEEWEE S Mexico, C America and much of tropical S America S to Argentina / scrub and open woodland / insects

Contopus albogularis (*Berlioz*) WHITE-THROATED PEEWEE Cayenne / unique ♂ / forest

Contopus nigrescens (*Sclater and Salvin*) BLACKISH PEEWEE E Ecuador, NE Peru and Acary Mts of Guyana / forest

Contopus pertinax (*Cabanis and Heine*) COUES' FLYCATCHER South-western USA and C America to Nicaragua / mountain forest / insects / n tree / e 3–4 (*C. emleni* Stone, *Proc.*

A. N. Sci. Phil. 1931, 83 p 1 (from Honduras) may belong here)

Contopus lugubris (*Lawrence*) LUGUBRIOUS PEEWEE Highlands of Costa Rica and W Panama / n tree / e ? 1–2

Contopus fumigatus (*Lafresnaye and d'Orbigny*) GREATER or SMOKY PEEWEE Tropical S America S to Argentina / forest

Contopus ochraceus (*Sclater and Salvin*) OCHRACEOUS PEEWEE High mts of Costa Rica (Irazú and Turrialba)

Empidonax flaviventris (*Baird*) YELLOW-BELLIED FLYCATCHER b eastern N America w S to Panama / light woodland / insects and berries / n ground / e 3–5

Empidonax virescens (*Vieillot*) ACADIAN FLYCATCHER b eastern N America w S to Ecuador and Peru / swampy woodland / insects and berries / n tree / e 2–4 / I 13

Empidonax minimus (*Baird*) LEAST FLYCATCHER b eastern N America w S to Panama, Caribbean and Peru / open woodland and open country / insects and berries / n tree / e 3–6 / I♀ (?♂) 12

Empidonax hammondii (*Xantus*) HAMMOND'S FLYCATCHER b western N America w S to Guatemala / open coniferous forest / n tree / e 3–4 / I ♀ 12

Empidonax oberholseri *Phillips* (=**E. wrightii** not Baird) WRIGHT'S FLYCATCHER Western USA w S to Mexico / open forest and scrub / insects / n tree / e 2–4 / I 12–15 (?17)

Empidonax wrightii *Baird* (=**E. griseus** *Brewster*) GREY FLYCATCHER S California, S Arizona and Mexico / sagebush plains and desert scrub / insects / n bush / e 3–4 (NB: see Phillips, *Auk* (1939), pp 311–12, for comments on the renaming of the 2 above species)

Empidonax affinis (*Swainson*) (=**E. fulvipectus,** *Lawrence*) PINE FLYCATCHER Pine forests of Mexico

Empidonax difficilis *Baird* WESTERN FLYCATCHER Western N America S to Mexico / open woodland / insects and berries / n tree or bush / e 3–5 / I 12

Empidonax flavescens *Lawrence* YELLOWISH FLYCATCHER Highlands from S Mexico to Costa Rica / n cliff or hole / e 2–3 / I ♀ / F 17

Empidonax albigularis *Sclater and Salvin* WHITE-THROATED FLYCATCHER S Mexico to Panama

Empidonax alnorum *Brewster* (=**E. traillii** not *Audubon*) TRAILL'S or ALDER FLYCATCHER b north-eastern N America w Colombia, Ecuador, Peru and N Argentina / dense scrub and thickets / insects and berries / n tree or bush / e 3–4

Empidonax traillii (*Audubon*) (=**E. brewsteri** *Oberholzer*) WILLOW FLYCATCHER b western N America w S to Bolivia / swamps and riverine thickets / insects and berries / n bush / e 2–4 / I ♀ 12

Empidonax euleri (*Cabanis*) EULER'S FLYCATCHER S America E of Andes and S to Argentina: Grenada / open woods and clearings / n tree / e 2–3 / this is apparently a complex group of forms, including *E. lawrencei*, see note in de Schaunsee, *The Species of birds of South America* (1966), p 354

Empidonax griseipectus *Lawrence* GREY-BREASTED FLYCATCHER SW Ecuador and NW Peru / arid scrub

Empidonax atriceps *Salvin* BLACK-CAPPED FLYCATCHER Costa Rica and W Panama

Empidonax fulvifrons (*Giraud*) BUFF-BREASTED FLYCATCHER South-western USA to Guatemala / open forest and hill scrub / insects / n tree / e 2–4

Aechmolophus mexicanus *Zimmer* (*Auk* (1938), pp 663–5 and (1939), p 189) PILEATED FLYCATCHER Mexico / no data

Xenotriccus callizonus *Dwight and Griscom* (*American Museum Novitates*, 254, 2, 8 March 1927) BELTED FLYCATCHER Guatemala / no data

Cnemotriccus fuscatus (*Wied*) FUSCOUS FLYCATCHER S America E of Andes and S to Argentina / forest and plantation / insects

Mitrephanes phaeocercus (*Sclater*) TUFTED FLYCATCHER W Mexico to Panama and Andes from Colombia to Bolivia / open woodland / n tree / e 2 / I ♀

Terenotriccus erythrurus (*Cabanis*) RUDDY-TAILED FLYCATCHER S Mexico to Panama and Amazon basin / forest

Aphanotriccus capitalis (*Salvin*) SALVIN'S FLYCATCHER E Costa Rica and E Nicaragua

Aphanotriccus audax (*Nelson*) BLACK-BILLED or NELSON'S FLYCATCHER E Panama and NW Colombia / forest

Myiobius sulphureipygius (*Sclater*) SULPHUR-RUMPED FLYCATCHER Mexico, C America and Pacific Colombia

Myiobius villosus *Sclater* TAWNY-BREASTED FLYCATCHER Venezuela to Bolivia: Darien Mts /

APODIDAE:
Collocalia esculenta,
White-bellied Swiftlet,
Glossy Swiftlet

AEGOTHELIDAE: *Aegotheles cristatus,* Crested Owlet Nightjar

Plate 162

CAPRIMULGIDAE:
Caprimulgus europaeus
European Nightjar,
Eurasian Nightjar

CAPRIMULGIDAE:
Eurostopodus guttatus,
Spotted Nightjar

Plate 163

forest and open woodland

Myiobius barbatus (*Gmelin*) WHISKERED FLYCATCHER S America E of Andes S to Brazil/forest

Myiobius atricaudus *Lawrence* BLACK-TAILED FLYCATCHER SW Costa Rica, Panama and S America E of Andes and S to S Brazil/forest

Myiotriccus ornatus (*Lafresnaye*) ORNATE FLYCATCHER Andes from Colombia to Peru

Pyrrhomyias cinnamomea (*Lafresnaye and d'Orbigny*) CINNAMON FLYCATCHER Venezuela to Peru, Bolivia and N Argentina/clearings in thick forest

Myiophobus flavicans (*Sclater*) FLAVESCENT FLYCATCHER Mts from Venezuela to Peru/forest

Myiophobus phoenicomitra (*Taczanowski and Berlepsch*) ORANGE-CHESTED FLYCATCHER Andes of Colombia and Ecuador/forest

Myiophobus cryptoxanthus (*Sclater*) OLIVE-CHESTED FLYCATCHER E Ecuador and NE Peru

Myiophobus inornatus *Carriker* UNADORNED FLYCATCHER SE Peru and N Bolivia

Myiophobus pulcher (*Sclater*) HANDSOME FLYCATCHER Andes from Colombia to Peru/forest

Myiophobus lintoni *de Schaunsee* ORANGE-BANDED FLYCATCHER SW Ecuador/3 specimens

Myiophobus ochraceiventris (*Cabanis*) OCHRACEOUS-breasted FLYCATCHER Peru and NW Bolivia

Myiophobus fasciatus (*Müller*) BRAN-COLOURED FLYCATCHER Costa Rica, Panama, and much of tropical S America/forest and savannah/insects/n tree/e ?2

Myiophobus roraimae (*Salvin and Godman*) RORAIMAN FLYCATCHER Guyana, Venezuela and Colombia/forest

[**Myiophobus rufipennis** *Carriker* PUNO FLYCATCHER La Oroya, Peru/more usually treated as a race of *roraimae*]

Hirundinea ferruginea (*Gmelin*) SWALLOW FLYCATCHER or CLIFF FLYCATCHER Much of tropical S America/ravines, arid hillsides and open woodland

Onychorhynchus coronatus (*Müller*) ROYAL FLYCATCHER S Mexico, C America and S America E of Andes and S to Argentina/savannah and forest/insects/n tree/e 2/this genus is, by some authorities, divided into several species

Platyrinchus platyrhynchos (*Gmelin*) (=**P.**

senex *Sclater and Salvin*) WHITE-CRESTED SPADEBILL Amazon basin and N to Guianas/forest edge/insects

Platyrinchus leucoryphus *Wied* (=**P. platyrhynchos**, not *Gmelin*) RUSSET-WINGED SPADEBILL SE Brazil and E Paraguay/forest

Platyrinchus mystaceus (*Vieillot*) WHITE-THROATED SPADEBILL S Mexico, C America and much of tropical S America/forest

Platyrinchus coronatus *Sclater* GOLDEN-CROWNED SPADEBILL Orinoco and Amazon basins, Pacific Colombia and Ecuador/forest

Platyrinchus saturatus *Salvin and Godman* CINNAMON-CRESTED SPADEBILL Amazon basin, S Orinoco and the Guianas/forest

Platyrinchus flavigularis *Sclater* YELLOW-THROATED SPADEBILL Parts of Venezuela, Colombia, Ecuador and Peru/forest

Cnipodectes subbrunneus (*Sclater*) BROWNISH FLYCATCHER Panama, Colombia, W. Ecuador, NE Peru and W Brazil/forest

Tolmomyias sulphurescens (*Spix*) WHITE-EYED or YELLOW-OLIVE FLYCATCHER S Mexico, C America and much of tropical S America/forest/beetles/n tree/e 2

Tolmomyias assimilis (*Pelzeln*) SIMILAR FLYCATCHER Costa Rica, Panama, the Guianas, Orinoco and Amazon basins/forest

Tolmomyias poliocephalus (*Taczanowski*) GREY-CROWNED FLYCATCHER Guianas, S Orinoco, Amazon basin and E Brazil/forest, savannah and plantations/insects/n tree/e 2

Tolmomyias flaviventris (*Wied*) YELLOW-BREASTED FLYCATCHER S America, S Orinoco, Amazon basin and E Brazil/forest, savannah, swampy woodland and plantation/insects/n tree/e 2-3/I ?♀ 17

Rhynchocyclus olivaceus (*Temminck*) OLIVACEOUS FLATBILL Panama and much of tropical S America E of Andes/swampy woodland and savannah/insects

Rhynchocyclus brevirostris (*Cabanis*) SHORT-BILLED or EYE-RINGED FLATBILL S Mexico, C America, Pacific Colombia and Ecuador/forest

Rhynchocyclus fulvipectus (*Sclater*) FULVOUS-BREASTED FLATBILL Parts of Columbia, Ecuador, Peru and N Bolivia/forest

Rhamphotrigon ruficauda (*Spix*) RUFOUS-TAILED FLATBILL Amazon basin and the Guianas/savannah and forest/insects and berries

Rhamphotrigon fuscicauda *Chapman*

DUSKY-TAILED FLATBILL NE Ecuador, E Peru and N Bolivia/forest

Rhamphotrigon megacephala (*Swainson*) LARGE-HEADED FLATBILL NW and S Venezuela, S Colombia, W Brazil, N Bolivia, E Paraguay and N Argentina/forest and bamboo

Todirostrum nigriceps *Sclater* BLACK-HEADED TODY-TYRANT Costa Rica, Panama, Venezuela, Colombia and W Ecuador/forest and scrub/insects/n tree/e 1/I ♀

Todirostrum chrysocrotaphum *Strickland* PAINTED TODY-TYRANT Amazon basin and the Guianas/insects/n tree/e ? n/k (*T. pictum* Salvin, is sometimes separated)

Todirostrum calopterum *Sclater* JARDINE'S GOLDEN-WINGED TODY-TYRANT SE Colombia, E Ecuador and E Peru

Todirostrum poliocephalum (*Wied*) GREY-HEADED TODY-TYRANT SE Brazil/forest edge and habitation

Todirostrum cinereum (*L*) COMMON TODY-TYRANT S Mexico, C America and much of tropical S America/savannah and parkland/insects/n tree/e 2/I ♀ 18/F 18

Todirostrum maculatum (*Desmarest*) SPOTTED TODY-TYRANT Amazon basin, Orinoco delta, the Guianas and Trinidad/mangrove, scrub and habitation/insects/n tree/e 2/I ♀ 17/F 17–18

Todirostrum fumifrons *Hartlaub* SMOKE-FRONTED TODY-TYRANT Surinam, Cayenne and E Brazil/bush and savannah/insects

Todirostrum senex (*Pelzeln*) ANCIENT TODY-TYRANT Borba, Rio Madeira, Brazil/known only from the type in Vienna Museum

Todirostrum capitale *Sclater* BLACK AND WHITE TODY-TYRANT SE Colombia, E Ecuador, NE Peru and W Brazil/forest

Todirostrum albifacies *Blake* WHITE-CHEEKED or BLAKE'S TODY-TYRANT SE Peru/unique ♀

Todirostrum russatum *Salvin and Godman* RUDDY TODY-TYRANT Mts of SE Venezuela and N Brazil/forest

Todirostrum plumbiceps (*Lafresnaye*) OCHRE-FACED or LEAD-CROWNED TODY-TYRANT SE Peru to S Brazil and N Argentina

Todirostrum latirostre (*Pelzeln*) RUSTY-FACED TODY-TYRANT Amazon basin/scrub (*Euscarthmornis nattereri* (Hellmayr) is a synonym)

Todirostrum sylvia (*Desmarest*) SLATE-HEADED or DESMAREST'S TODY-TYRANT Amazon and Orinoco basins, and the Guianas/thickets

[**Todirostrum hypospodium** *Berlepsch* BERLEPSCH'S TODY-TYRANT Known only from a 'Bogotá' trade-skin/no locality/doubtful, believed to be an aberrant specimen of *T. sylvia*]

Ceratotriccus furcatus (*Lafresnaye*) FORK-TAILED PYGMY TYRANT SE Brazil

Oncostoma cinereigulare (*Sclater*) NORTHERN BENTBILL Mexico to W Panama

Oncostoma olivaceum (*Lawrence*) SOUTHERN BENTBILL Panama and Colombia/open woodland and plantations

Idioptilon nidipendulum (*Wied*) HANGNEST TODY-TYRANT E Brazil/forest

Idioptilon straticolle (*Lafresnaye*) STRIPED-NECKED TODY-TYRANT N Peru and C Brazil/forest

Idioptilon rufigulare (*Cabanis*) BUFF-THROATED TODY-TYRANT E Peru and N Bolivia/5 specimens

Idioptilon spodiops (*Berlepsch*) YUNGAS TODY-TYRANT N Bolivia/forest

Idioptilon aenigma (*Zimmer*) ZIMMER'S TODY-TYRANT Amazonian Brazil/forest

Idioptilon mirandae (*Snethlage*) BUFF-BREASTED or MIRANDA'S TODY-TYRANT E Brazil/forest

[**Idioptilon kaempferi** *Zimmer* KAEMPFER'S TODY-TYRANT Salto Pirai, Santa Catharina, Brazil/unique/possibly a race of *I. mirandae*]

[**Idioptilon inornatum** (*Pelzeln*) PELZELN'S TODY-TYRANT Rio Içana, NW Brazil/unique/possibly a race of *I. margaritaceiventer*]

Idioptilon margaritaceiventer (*d'Orbigny and Lafresnaye*) PEARLY-VENTED TODY-TYRANT Much of tropical S America/forest

Idioptilon granadense (*Hartlaub*) BLACK-THROATED TODY-TYRANT Mts from Venezuela to Peru/forest

Idioptilon zosterops (*Pelzeln*) WHITE-EYED TODY-TYRANT Amazon basin and the Guianas/forest/insects

Idioptilon orbitatum (*Wied*) EYE-RINGED TODY-TYRANT SE Brazil/forest

Microcochlearius josephinae (*Chubb*) BOAT-BILLED or JOSEPHINE'S TODY-TYRANT Essequibo River, Guyana/unique

Snethlagea minor (*Snethlage*) SNETHLAGE'S TODY-TYRANT Amazonian Brazil and Surinam/forest

Poecilotriccus ruficeps (*Kaup*) RUFOUS-

TROCHILIDAE:
Clytolaema rubricauda,
Brazilian Ruby

TROCHILIDAE;
Ensifera ensifera,
Sword-billed Hummingbird

Plate 164

Plate 165

CROWNED TODY-TYRANT Andes from Venezuela to Peru / forest

Taeniotriccus andrei *Berlepsch and Hartert* BLACK-CHESTED or ANDRE'S TYRANT S Venezuela and N Brazil / forest

[**Taenotriccus klagesi** *Todd* KLAGES'S TYRANT Rio Tapajós, Brazil / unique / status unsettled but believed to be the female of *T. andrei*]

Lophotriccus pileatus (*Tschudi*) SCALE-CRESTED TYRANT Costa Rica, Panama and Andes from Venezuela to Peru and SW Brazil / forest / n tree / e ?2

Lophotriccus vitiosus (*Bangs and Penard*) DOUBLE-BANDED TYRANT Amazon Basin and the Guianas / forest

Lophotriccus eulophotes *Todd* LONG-CRESTED or TODD'S TYRANT Rio Purus, Brazil / known from 5 specimens / bamboo thickets

Coleopteryx galeatus (*Boddaert*) HELMETED PYGMY TYRANT Amazon basin and the Guianas / forests and plantations

Atalotriccus pilaris (*Cabanis*) PALE-EYED PYGMY TYRANT Pacific Panama, N Colombia, Venezuela and Guyana / forest and thickets

Myiornis auricularis (*Vieillot*) EARED PYGMY TYRANT C Peru, N Bolivia, E Paraguay, E Brazil and N Argentina / forest

Myiornis atricapillus (*Lawrence*) BLACK-CAPPED PYGMY TYRANT Costa Rica and Panama, W Colombia and W Ecuador / now generally treated as a race of *M. ecaudatus*

Myiornis ecaudatus (*Lafresnaye and d'Orbigny*) SHORT-TAILED PYGMY TYRANT Amazon basin, Orinoco basin, Trinidad and the Guianas / open forest and shrubbery / insects

Pseudotriccus pelzelni *Taczanowski and Berlepsch* BRONZE or PELZELN'S PYGMY TYRANT E Panama and pacific slope from Colombia to Peru / open forest

Pseudotriccus simplex (*Berlepsch*) BOLIVIAN PYGMY TYRANT SE Peru and Bolivia

Pseudotriccus ruficeps (*Lafresnaye*) RUFOUS-HEADED PYGMY TYRANT Andes from Colombia to Bolivia / forest

Hemitriccus diops (*Temminck*) DRAB or TEMMINCK'S PYGMY TYRANT SE Brazil and E Paraguay / forest

Hemitriccus obsoletus (*Ribeiro*) BROWN-BREASTED or ITATIAYA PYGMY TYRANT SE Brazil

Hemitriccus flammulatus *Berlepsch* FLAMMULATED PYGMY TYRANT SE Peru, N Bolivia and Mato Grosso

Pogonotriccus eximius (*Temminck*) NATTERER'S or SOUTHERN BRISTLE TYRANT SE Brazil, E Paraguay and NE Argentina / forest

Pogonotriccus opthalmicus *Taczanowski* PERUVIAN or MARBLE-FACED BRISTLE TYRANT Andes from Venezuela to Bolivia / forest

Pogonotriccus gualaquizae *Sclater* ECUADOREAN or GUALAQUIZA BRISTLE TYRANT E Ecuador and N Peru

Pogonotriccus poecilotis (*Sclater*) VARIEGATED BRISTLE TYRANT Andes from Venezuela to N Peru / forest

Pogonotriccus orbitalis *Cabanis* SPECTACLED BRISTLE TYRANT E Ecuador, C Peru and N Bolivia

Pogonotriccus venezuelanus *Berlepsch* VENEZUELAN BRISTLE TYRANT Coastal mountains of Venezuela / forest

Pogonotriccus flaviventris (*Hartert*) YELLOW-BELLIED BRISTLE TYRANT Mts of Venezuela: SE Peru / forest. The extension of the range to SE Peru is apparently based on 1 specimen in the Berlepsch collection, which Hellmayr (*Catalogue of the Birds of the Americas*, part 5, p 349 footnote) says may prove to be a separate form

Leptotriccus sylviolus *Cabanis and Heine* BAY-RINGED or WOOD TYRANT SE Brazil, SE Paraguay and NE Argentina

Phylloscartes flavovirens (*Lawrence*) YELLOW-GREEN TYRANNULET Panama / forest

Phylloscartes virescens *Todd* GREEN TYRANNULET The Guianas / forest / insects and berries

Phylloscartes ventralis (*Temminck*) YELLOW-BELLIED or MOTTLED-CHEEKED TYRANNULET C Peru, Bolivia, Uruguay, Paraguay, E Brazil and N Argentina / forest

Phylloscartes chapmani *Gilliard* CHAPMAN'S TYRANNULET Venezuela / forest

Phylloscartes nigrifrons (*Salvin and Godman*) BLACK-FACED TYRANNULET Venezuela / forest

Phylloscartes oustaleti (*Sclater*) OUSTALET'S TYRANNULET SE Brazil / forest

Phylloscartes difficilis (*Ihering and Ihering*) DIFFICULT TYRANNULET Coastal mountains of SE Brazil

Phylloscartes paulistus *Ihering and Ihering* SÃO PAULO TYRANNULET SE Brazil and E Paraguay

Phylloscartes superciliaris (*Sclater and Salvin*) RUFOUS-BROWED TYRANNULET Costa

Rica, Panama, N Venezuela and Bogotá trade-skins/forest

Phylloscartes roquettei *Snethlage* MINAS GERAIS or SNETHLAGE'S TYRANNULET Minas Gerais, Brazil / unique

Capsiempis flaveola (*Lichtenstein*) YELLOW TYRANNULET From Nicaragua S over much of tropical S America / shrubbery and campos/ insects

Euscarthmus meloryphus *Wied* TAWNY-CROWNED PYGMY TYRANT Much of tropical S America / scrub and cerrado

Euscarthmus rufomarginatus (*Pelzeln*) RUFOUS-EDGED PYGMY TYRANT E Brazil and Surinam/savannah (NB: This species is omitted from de Schaunsee *The species of the Birds of South America*, 1966. It is present in his later work *A Guide to the Birds of South America*, 1970)

Pseudocolopteryx dinellianus *Lillo* DINELLI'S DORADITO NW Argentina, wandering N / open scrub

Pseudocolopteryx sclateri (*Oustalet*) CRESTED or SCLATER'S DORADITO E Brazil, N Paraguay, N Argentina / bogs and mangrove swamps

Pseudocolopteryx acutipennis (*Sclater and Salvin*) SHARP-WINGED or SUBTROPICAL DORADITO Andes from Colombia to N Argentina / shrubbery

Pseudocolopteryx flaviventris (*Lafresnaye and d'Orbigny*) WARBLING DORADITO C Chile and Argentina N to Paraguay and S Brazil/ scrub and swamps / insects / n reeds / e 3–4

Polystictus pectoralis (*Vieillot*) NARROW-TAILED TYRANT or BEARDED TACHURI Much of tropical S America E of Andes and S to N Argentina / marshes and scrub

Polystictus superciliaris (*Wied*) GREY-BACKED or SUPERCILIATED TACHURI E Brazil/ campos

Culicivora caudacuta (*Vieillot*) WIRE-TAILED TYRANT S Brazil, E Bolivia, N Argentina and Paraguay / brush

Tachuris rubrigastra (*Vieillot*) MANY-COLOURED RUSH TYRANT Coastal and riverine marshes from S Peru and S Brazil S to N Argentina / marshes and reedbeds / insects / n reeds / e 2–3

Anairetes parulus (*Kittlitz*) TUFTED TIT-TYRANT Andes from Colombia to Tierra del Fuego / bushes and semi-arid hillsides / insects/ n shrub / e 2–3

Anairetes fernandezianus (*Philippi*) JUAN-FERNANDEZ TIT-TYRANT Mas Atierra (Juan Fernandez) / forest / last seen in 1917 / no other data

Anairetes flavirostris *Sclater and Salvin* YELLOW-BILLED TIT-TYRANT Andes from Peru to N Chile and Argentina / thickets near streams and cultivation

Anairetes reguloides (*Lafresnaye and d'Orbigny*) CRESTED TIT-TYRANT Peru to N Chile / cultivation and scrubby hillsides

Anairetes alpinus (*Carriker*) ASH-BREASTED TIT-TYRANT Peru to N Bolivia

Uromyias agilis (*Sclater*) AGILE TIT-TYRANT Colombia and N Ecuador / forest

Uromyias agraphia (*Chapman*) UNSTREAKED TIT-TYRANT SE Peru

Stigmatura napensis *Chapman* LESSER WAGTAIL-TYRANT Upper Amazon basin / scrub

Stigmatura budytoides (*Lafresnaye and d'Orbigny*) GREATER WAGTAIL-TYRANT NE Brazil, Bolivia, Paraguay and N / Argentina scrub

Serpophaga hypoleuca *Sclater and Salvin* RIVER TYRANNULET Orinoco basin, Cuzco region of Peru and S bank of lower Amazon/ open spaces along rivers

Serpophaga cinerea (*Tschudi*) TORRENT TYRANNULET Mts of Costa Rica and Panama; Andes from Venezuela to Bolivia / rocky streams

Serpophaga subcristata (*Vieillot*) WHITE-CRESTED TYRANNULET Parts of Bolivia, Paraguay, S Brazil and N Argentina / scrub and forest

Serpophaga munda *Berlepsch* WHITE-BELLIED or BERLEPSCH'S TYRANNULET Parts of Bolivia, Paraguay, S Brazil and N Argentina/ thickets

Serpophaga griseiceps *Berlioz* GREY-CROWNED TYRANNULET Cochabamba, Bolivia/ 4 specimens

Serpophaga nigricans (*Vieillot*) SOOTY TYRANNULET SE Bolivia, Paraguay, Uruguay, SE Brazil, N Argentina / scrub

Serpophaga araguayae *Snethlage* BANANAL TYRANNULET Bananal Is, Brazil / unique

[**Serpophaga berliozi** *Dorst* (*Bull Mus Nat Hist Nat Paris* vol 29, pt 2 (1957), p 208) BERLIOZ'S TYRANNULET E Peru / unique / stated by de Schaunsee, after examination of type, to be a synonym of *Myiopagis gaimardii*]

Inezia subflava (*Sclater and Salvin*) PALE-TIPPED TYRANNULET Amazon, Orinoco and

TROCHILIDAE:
Aglaiocercus kingi,
Long-tailed Sylph (Blue-tailed
and Green-tailed Sylphs)

TROGONIDAE:
Pharomachrus mocinno,
Quetzal, Resplendent Quetzal

Plate 166

ALCEDINIDAE: *Dacelo novaeguineae (= Dacelo gigas),* Laughing Kookaburra

Plate 167

Magdalena basins and the Guianas/ mangrove and savannah/ insects/ n tree/ e n/s

Inezia tenuirostris (*Cory*) SLENDER-BILLED TYRANNULET N Colombia and N Venezuela/ desert and humid woodland

Inezia inornata (*Salvadori*) PLAIN TYRANNULET Bolivia, S Brazil, Paraguay and NW Argentina/ scrub

Mecocerculus leucophrys (*Lafresnaye and d'Orbigny*) WHITE-THROATED TYRANNULET Andes from Venezuela to N Argentina/forest and scrub

Mecocerculus poecilocercus (*Sclater and Salvin*) WHITE-TAILED TYRANNULET Andes from Colombia to Peru/forest

Mecocerculus hellmayri *Berlepsch* BUFF-BANDED or HELLMAYR'S TYRANNULET SE Peru and Bolivia

Mecocerculus calopterus (*Sclater*) RUFOUS-WINGED TYRANNULET W Ecuador and W Peru/ forest

Mecocerculus minor (*Taczanowski*) SULPHUR-BELLIED TYRANNULET W Venezuela, Colombia E of Andes and NW Peru/forest

Mecocerculus stictopterus (*Sclater*) WHITE-BANDED TYRANNULET Andes from Venezuela to N Bolivia/forest

Colorhamphus parvirostris (*Darwin*) PATAGONIAN TYRANT b Andes from S Chile to Tierra del Fuego w C Chile and C Argentina/ forest/n shrub/e 2

Elaenia flavogaster (*Thunberg*) YELLOW-BELLIED ELAENIA S Mexico, C America, Lesser Antilles and much of tropical S America/ savannah and habitation / insects and berries/ n tree/e 2-3

Elaenia martinica (*L*) CARIBBEAN ELAENIA Islands of S Caribbean / scrub, mangrove and forest / n tree / e 2-3

Elaenia fallax *Sclater* GREATER ANTILLEAN ELAENIA Jamaica and Hispaniola/forest borders and thickets /n tree /e 2

Elaenia spectabilis (*Pelzeln*) LARGE ELAENIA Irregularly through tropical S America from Amazon basin to N Argentina / forest and riparian thickets

Elaenia albiceps (*Lafresnaye and d'Orbigny*) WHITE-CRESTED ELAENIA Colombia to Tierra del Fuego migrating eastwards / scrub and open mountain slopes / insects and berries/ n bush/ e 2-3

Elaenia parvirostris *Pelzeln* SMALL-BILLED ELAENIA b Bolivia and S Brazil to N Argentina w N to Surinam and Trinidad /forest edge and open woodland

[**Elaenia aenigma** *Stresemann* (*Orn Monatsber* 1937, vol 45, pt 3, p 75) ENIGMATIC ELAENIA Mt Illinitza, Ecuador / stated by de Schaunsee to be a synonym of *E. parvirostris*]

Elaenia mesoleuca *Cabanis and Heine* OLIVACEOUS ELAENIA SE Brazil, E Paraguay and N Argentina /forest

Elaenia strepera *Cabanis* SLATY ELAENIA b S Bolivia and N Argentina w N to Peru, Colombia and Venezuela /forest

Elaenia gigas *Sclater* MOTTLE-BACKED or GIANT ELAENIA E Andes from Colombia to Bolivia /forest

Elaenia pelzelni *Berlepsch* BROWNISH or PELZELN'S ELAENIA NE Peru, W and C Amazonian Brazil

Elaenia cristata *Pelzeln* CRESTED ELAENIA N Amazon basin, Venezuela and the Guianas/ savannah /berries /n tree/ e 2

Elaenia chiriquensis *Lawrence* LAWRENCE'S or LESSER ELAENIA SW Costa Rica, Panama and much of tropical S America / scattered localities in drier, open country/ berries

Elaenia ruficeps *Pelzeln* RUFOUS-CROWNED ELAENIA Brazil N of Amazon, E Colombia, Venezuela and Guianas / forest / berries and insects

Elaenia frantzii *Lawrence* MOUNTAIN or FRANTZIUS'S ELAENIA Mts from Guatemala to W Venezuela / forest clearings / insects, seeds and berries/n tree/e 2/I ♀ 15

Elaenia obscura (*Lafresnaye and d'Orbigny*) HIGHLAND or DUSKY ELAENIA Peru and S Brazil to N Argentina /forest

Elaenia dayi *Chapman* GREAT ELAENIA Mts of Venezuela / forest (*E. tyleri* Chapman, is conspecific)

Elaenia pallatangae *Sclater* SIERRA or PALLATANGA ELAENIA Mts from Venezuela to Bolivia /forest

Myiopagis gaimardii (*d'Orbigny*) GAIMARD'S or FOREST ELAENIA Panama, N Colombia, Venezuela, the Guianas and Amazon basin/ forest borders and humid woodland /berries and insects/n tree/e n/s

Myiopagis caniceps (*Swainson*) GREY ELAENIA Darien, S to Amazon and E to Cayenne /woodland

Myiopagis subplacens (*Sclater*) PACIFIC or FRASER'S ELAENIA W Ecuador and NW Peru/ dry scrub

Myiopagis flavivertex (*Sclater*) YELLOW-CROWNED ELAENIA Amazon basin, the Guianas and Amacuro delta / forest / insects

Myiopagis viridicata (*Vieillot*) AZARA'S or GREENISH ELAENIA Mexico, C America and much of tropical S America E of Andes and S to N Argentina / woodland streams

Myiopagis cotta *Gosse* COTTA'S ELAENIA Jamaica / forest and shrubbery / n tree / e 3

Suiriri suiriri (*Vieillot*) SUIRIRI FLYCATCHER Lower Amazon basin and S to N Argentina / open scrub and mangroves

Sublegatus modestus (*Wied*) SCRUB FLYCATCHER S America S to N Argentina / mangrove and scrub / insects and berries (the northern and southern forms are separated by some authorities)

Phaeomyias murina *Spix* MOUSE-COLOURED TYRANNULET Panama and much of tropical S America S to N Argentina / scrub and cultivation / berries and insects / n tree / e 2 / I ♀ 14 / F 17

Phaeomyias leucospodia (*Taczanowski*) STOLZMANN'S or GREY-AND-WHITE TYRANNULET Coasts of SW Ecuador and Peru / arid scrub

Camptostoma imberbe *Sclater* NORTHERN BEARDLESS FLYCATCHER SW USA to Costa Rica / scrub and open forest / insects and seeds / n tree / e 1–3

Camptostoma obsoletum (*Temminck*) SOUTHERN BEARDLESS FLYCATCHER Costa Rica S through tropical S America to N Argentina / arid scrub, woodland and cultivation / insects and berries / n tree / e 2 (it is possible that *imberbe* and *obsoletum* may be conspecific)

Xanthomyias virescens (*Temminck*) GREENISH TYRANNULET NE Venuezela, E and S Brazil, E Paraguay and N Argentina / forest

Xanthomyias reiseri (*Hellmayr*) REISER'S TYRANNULET E Brazil and NE Paraguay

Xanthomyias sclateri (*Berlepsch*) SCLATER'S TYRANNULET SE Peru, Bolivia and NW Argentina / forest

Phyllomyias fasciatus (*Thunberg*) PLANALTO TYRANNULET E, C and S Brazil, E Paraguay and N Argentina / forest

Phyllomyias griseiceps (*Sclater and Salvin*) SOOTY-HEADED or CRESTED TYRANNULET Darien and much of tropical S America S to the Amazon / shrubbery

Tyranniscus nigrocapillus (*Lafresnaye*) BLACK-CAPPED TYRANNULET Andes from Venezuela to Peru / forest

Tyranniscus uropygialis (*Lawrence*) TAWNY-RUMPED TYRANNULET Scattered localities from Venezuela to Peru / forest

Tyranniscus cinereiceps (*Sclater*) ASHY-HEADED TYRANNULET Scattered localities in Andes from Colombia to Peru

Tyranniscus australis *Olrog and Contino* (*Inst Mig Lillo y Facult Cienc Nat*, 12 no 39 (1 Dec 1966), p 113) OLROG'S TYRANNULET NW Argentina / ? no data

Tyranniscus vilissimus (*Sclater and Salvin*) PALTRY TYRANNULET S Mexico, C America and mts of Colombia and Venezuela / forest edge and open forest

Tyranniscus bolivianus (*d'Orbigny*) BOLIVIAN TYRANNULET SE Peru and N Bolivia

Tyranniscus cinereicapillus (*Cabanis*) RED-BILLED TYRANNULET NE Ecuador and C Peru

Tyranniscus gracilipes *Sclater and Salvin* SLENDER-FOOTED TYRANNULET Amazon basin and the Guianas / forest and savannah / berries

Tyranniscus viridiflavus (*Tschudi*) GOLDEN-FACED TYRANNULET N Venezuela, Colombia, W Ecuador and N Peru / forest and scrub

Oreotriccus plumbiceps (*Lawrence*) PLUMBEOUS-CROWNED TYRANNULET Andes from Colombia to Peru / forest

Oreotriccus griseocapillus (*Sclater*) GREY-CAPPED TYRANNULET SE Brazil

Tyrannulus elatus (*Latham*) YELLOW-CROWNED TYRANNULET Amazon (? and Orinoco) basins and the Guianas / forest and habitation / berries

Acrocordopus burmeisteri (*Cabanis and Heine*) ROUGH-LEGGED TYRANNULET Costa Rica S through scattered localities in tropical S America to N Argentina (*A. zeledoni* (Lawrence) and *A. leucogonys* (Sclater and Salvin) are sometimes separated)

Ornithion inerme *Hartlaub* WHITE-LORED or HARTLAUB'S TYRANNULET Amazon basin and N to the Guianas

[**Microtriccus fasciatus** *Carriker* (*Proceedings of the Academy of Natural Sciences of Philadelphia* 86, 1934, p 328) is stated by de Schaunsee to be a synonym of *O. inerme*]

Microtriccus semiflavus (*Sclater and Salvin*) YELLOW-BELLIED TYRANNULET S Mexico, C America, N Venezuela, Colombia and NW Ecuador / forest (*M. brunneicapillus* (Lawrence) is sometimes separated)

Leptopogon superciliaris *Tschudi* SLATY-CAPPED FLYCATCHER Mts of Costa Rica, Panama and Venezuela to Bolivia / forest / n tree

ALCEDINIDAE:
Alcedo atthis,
Common or Little Blue
Kingfisher

ALCEDINIDAE:
Dacelo leachii,
Blue-winged Kookaburra

Plate 168

ALCEDINIDAE:
Halcyon macleayii,
Australian Forest Kingfisher

ALCEDINIDAE:
Dacelo novaeguineae
(= Dacelo gigas),
Laughing Kookaburra

Plate 169

Leptopogon amaurocephalus *Tschudi* SEPIA-CAPPED FLYCATCHER Mexico, C America, much of tropical S America E of Andes and S to Argentina/forest and scrub

Leptopogon rufipectus (*Lafresnaye*) RUFOUS-BREASTED FLYCATCHER Andes from Venezuela to Ecuador/forest

Leptopogon taczanowskii *Hellmayr* INCA FLYCATCHER Andes of Peru

Mionectes straticollis (*Lafresnaye and d'Orbigny*) STREAKED-NECKED FLYCATCHER Andes from Colombia to N Bolivia/forest and shrubbery

Mionectes olivaceus *Lawrence* OLIVE-STRIPED FLYCATCHER Costa Rica, Panama and mts from Venezuela to Peru/forest and shrubbery

Pipromorpha oleaginea (*Lichtenstein*) OCHRE-BELLIED or OLEAGINEOUS FLYCATCHER S Mexico, C America and S America E of Andes and S to Amazon basin/forest and shrubbery/insects and berries

Pipromorpha mcconnelli *Chubb* McCONNELL'S FLYCATCHER Amazon basin, Venezuela and the Guianas/spiders

Pipromorpha rufiventris (*Cabanis*) GREY-HOODED or RUFOUS-BELLIED PIPROMORPHA SE Brazil, E Paraguay and NE Argentina

[**Pipromorpha turi**, *Sztolcman*, is stated by de Schaunsee to be a synonym of *P. oleaginea*] NB: The position of the genus *Corythopis* is in doubt, de Schaunsee (1970) places it at the end of the Tyrannidae, but I have left it in the Conopophagidae, where it has been traditionally placed and where most people are likely to look for it.

OXYRUNCIDAE Sharpbill Small, drab birds with orange crests, believed to be most closely related to the Tyrannidae. Almost nothing is known of their habits. Known to eat fruit, but nests and eggs are undescribed.

Oxyruncus cristatus (*Swainson*) SHARPBILL Mts of Costa Rica, Panama and tropical S America

PHYTOTOMIDAE Plantcutters Small, plump, finch-like birds related to the Cotingas. Inhabit open woodland, dry bush and cultivation, feeding on leaves, fruit and buds. The nest is in a tree or bush, the eggs, 2–4 in number, are bluish-green, spotted with brown, and incubation is by the female.

Phytotoma rutila *Vieillot* WHITE-TIPPED or REDDISH PLANTCUTTER Mts from Bolivia to Argentina

Phytotoma rara *Molina* CHILEAN PLANT-CUTTER Atacama and W Argentina; Falkland Is/orchard and cultivation

Phytotoma raimondii *Taczanowski* PERUVIAN PLANTCUTTER Coasts of NW Peru

PITTIDAE Pittas Medium-sized, plump birds with stout bills, strong legs and short stumpy tails. Many species are very brightly coloured, others are drabber. Most inhabit the floors of rain forests, and are very uniform in their habits. Feed on insects and other invertebrates. The nest is a large globular structure, either near the ground or high in a tree. The eggs are 2–7 (usually 4–6) in number, white to buffy, and speckled with dark brown. Both sexes incubate but the incubation period remains undetermined. They inhabit the Old World tropics. There is no reliable check list of the Pittas. The list below is the best summary I can manage of the various sources; I have not attempted to make any taxonomic decisions!

Pitta caerulea (*Raffles*) GREAT BLUE or GIANT PITTA Malaya, Sumatra and Borneo

Pitta schneideri *Hartert* SCHNEIDER'S PITTA Mts of N Sumatra

Pitta arcuata *Gould* BLUE-BANDED PITTA Borneo and Palawan

Pitta granatina *Temminck* GARNET PITTA Malaya, Sumatra and Borneo (*P. venusta*, Müller is sometimes separated)

Pitta baudi *Müller and Schlegel* BLUE-HEADED PITTA Borneo

Pitta guajana (*Müller*) IRENE PITTA Malaya and the Greater and Lesser Sundas (*P. elegans*, Temminck and Laugier, is sometimes separated)

Pitta brachyura (*L*) BLUE-WINGED and GREEN-WINGED PITTA (variable through range) Indian sub-continent E to Japan and S through Indonesia (*P. nympha*, Temminck and Schlegel, *P. megarhyncha*, Schlegel and *P. moluccensis* (Müller) are sometimes separated).

Pitta sordida (*Müller*) HOODED PITTA Himalayas, through SE Asia and Indonesia to New Guinea and the Philippines

Pitta reichenowi *Madarasz* GREEN-BREASTED PITTA Cameroons to Uganda

Pitta angolensis *Vieillot* AFRICAN PITTA Tropical Africa

Pitta nipalensis (*Hodgson*) BLUE-NAPED PITTA Himalayas and mts of northern SE Asia

Pitta erythrogaster (*Temminck*) RED-BREASTED and BLUE-BREASTED PITTAS (variable according to locality) NE Queensland N through the Papuan area to Celebes, New Britain and New Ireland. There are a considerable number of island forms of this species, many of which were listed as separate species in Mathews *Systema Avium Australasianarum*

Pitta kochi *Bruggemann* KOCH'S PITTA N Luzon (Philippines)

Pitta steerii (*Sharpe*) STEERE'S PITTA Mindanao, Bohol, Leyte and Samar

Pitta oatesi (*Hume*) FULVOUS PITTA Burma, Thailand and Indo-China

Pitta soror *Ramsay* BLUE-BACKED PITTA SE China, Hainan, Indo-China and SE Thailand

Pitta ellioti *Oustalet* ELLIOT'S PITTA Low elevations in Indo-China

Pitta cyanea *Blyth* BLUE PITTA Himalayas and northern SE Asia / dark ravines and undergrowth in forest

Pitta gurneyi *Hume* GURNEY'S PITTA S Burma and peninsular Thailand

Pitta phayrei *Blyth* PHAYRE'S PITTA SE Burma and Thailand

Pitta iris *Gould* RAINBOW PITTA NW Australia / mangrove, bamboo and rain forest

Pitta versicolor *Swainson* NOISY PITTA E Australia, the lesser Sundas and adjacent small groups

Pitta anerythra *Rothschild* BLACK-FACED PITTA Solomon Is / this species appears to be unique in laying a single egg

Pitta maxima *Müller and Schlegel* GREAT PITTA Halmahera and Batjan

Pitta superba *Rothschild and Hartert* SUPERB PITTA Admiralty Is

XENICIDAE (given as **ACANTHISITTIDAE** by some authorities) **New Zealand Wrens** Small wren-like birds believed to be descended from a Pitta-like ancestor. They have poor flight. The nest is a covered structure with a side entrance, the eggs are white, and both sexes share in incubation.

Acanthisitta chloris (*Sparrman*) RIFLEMAN New Zealand / forest / insects / n hole / e 4–5 / I ♂♀

Xenicus gilviventris *Pelzeln* ROCK WREN S Island, New Zealand / scrub above timberline / n rock crevice / e 5 (Edwards calls this 'South Island Wren' presumably to avoid confusion with *Salpinctes obsoletus* (Troglodytidae))

Xenicus longipes (*Gmelin*) BUSH WREN New Zealand / forest / insects / n hole / e 2

Traversia lyalli *Rothschild* TRAVERS' WREN Stephen Is, Cook St, New Zealand / extinct /

discovered and exterminated in 1894 by the lighthouseman's cat!

PHILEPITTIDAE Asities and False Sunbirds Plump, stout-legged, arboreal birds of uncertain affinities, but believed to be descended from a Pitta-like ancestor.

Philepitta castanea (*Müller*) VELVETY ASITY Madagascar / forests of the humid east / berries / n scrub / e 3

Philepitta schlegeli *Schlegel* SCHLEGEL'S ASITY Madagascar / forests of Sambirano / fruit and insects

Neodrepanis coruscans *Sharpe* FALSE SUNBIRD Madagascar / forests of the humid east / nectar and insects

Neodrepanis hypoxantha *Salomonsen* SMALL-BILLED NEODREPANIS Madagascar / forests of the humid east / 12 specimens known (Benson)

MENURIDAE Lyrebirds Comparatively large passerines of uncertain origin and relationships, remarkable for the large lyre-shaped tails of the males. Two species.

Menura novaehollandiae (*Latham*) SUPERB LYREBIRD E New South Wales, E Victoria and Tasmania / mountain forest and granite outcrops / worms, crustaceans and insects / n ground or cliff / e 1 / I ♀ 35–40

Menura alberti (*Bonaparte*) ALBERT'S LYREBIRD SE Queensland / mountain forest with crag and cliff / other data as *novaehollandiae*

ATRICHORNITHIDAE Scrub Birds Wren-like birds structurally resembling Lyrebirds.

Atrichornis rufescens (*Ramsay*) RUFOUS SCRUB BIRD NE New South Wales / mountain forest / insects and seeds / n ground / e 2 / I ♀

Atrichornis clamosus (*Gould*) NOISY SCRUB BIRD Extreme SW corner of W Australia / dense vegetation of coastal scrub and hill gullies / insects and seeds / n ground / e 1 / this species was long thought to be extinct, but was rediscovered in 1960

ALAUDIDAE Larks Small, dull-coloured terrestrial birds famed for their songs and song flights. Generally inhabit open country, nesting on the ground and laying from 2–6 speckled eggs. Feed on insects and seeds. Generally Old World, but one species also in N America.

Mirafra javanica *Horsfield* SINGING BUSH LARK C and E Africa, W Arabia, Indian subcontinent, SE Asia, Philippines, Borneo, Java, Bali, Lesser Sundas, New Guinea and Australia / open country / seeds and insects /

Plate 170

Opposite:
ALCEDINIDAE:
Alcedo atthis,
Common or Little Blue
Kingfisher

ALCEDINIDAE:
Alcedo cristata,
Malachite Kingfisher

ALCEDINIDAE:
Ispidina picta,
African Pygmy Kingfisher

Plate 171

n grass tuft / e 2–4

Mirafra sharpii *Elliot* RED SOMALI LARK British Somaliland / no data

Mirafra hova *Hartlaub* MADAGASCAR BUSH LARK Madagascar / grassland and savannah/ insects and seeds / n ground / e 2

Mirafra cordofanica *Strickland* KORDOFAN BUSH LARK Upper Niger to Darfur and Kordofan / rare / sandy soil where prairie grass 'Heskanit' grows / n and e n/k

Mirafra williamsi *Macdonald* WILLIAMS' BUSH LARK Kenya / about 4 specimens

Mirafra cheniana *Smith* LATAKOO LARK S Africa N to Angola and Rhodesia / grassy plains / n ground / e 3–4

Mirafra albicauda *Reichenow* WHITE-TAILED BUSH LARK C and E Africa / open country / n ground / e 2

Mirafra passerina *Gyldenstolpe* MONOTONOUS BUSH LARK Bushveld from Rhodesia to Damaraland / n ground / e 3

Mirafra candida *Friedmann* CANDIDA LARK Kenya / believed to be possibly a rufous phase of *M. javanica*

Mirafra pulpa *Friedmann* FRIEDMANN'S LARK Ethiopia / 3 specimens known / status in doubt

Mirafra hypermetra (*Reichenow*) RED-WINGED BUSH-LARK E Africa from S Sudan to N Tanganyika and the Somalilands / open country / n grass tuft / e ?2–4

Mirafra somalica (*Witherby*) SOMALI LONG-BILLED LARK British Somaliland / hardly any data / e 4 (1 clutch known)

Mirafra africana *Smith* RUFOUS-NAPED BUSH LARK Africa S of Sahara / grassland and cultivation / n tussock / e 2–3

Mirafra chuana (*Smith*) SHORT-CLAWED LARK High veld of the W Transvaal area and E Bechuanaland / thorn scrub / n and e n/k

Mirafra angolensis *Bocage* ANGOLAN LARK Angola, S Zaire and Zambia / open high grassland / n and e n/k

Mirafra rufocinnamomea (*Salvadori*) FLAPPET LARK Africa S of Sahara S to Barotseland / bush or open woodland / n tussock / e 2–4

Mirafra apiata (*Vieillot*) CLAPPER LARK S Africa N to Barotseland / local / bush and open country / n ground / e 2

Mirafra africanoides *Smith* FAWN-COLOURED LARK E and S Africa / steppe / n ground / e n/s

Mirafra collaris *Sharpe* COLLARED LARK British and Ethiopian Somaliland and NE Kenya / patches of brick-red soil / n grass tuft / e 3

Mirafra assamica *Horsfield* RUFOUS-WINGED BUSH LARK Indian sub-continent and SE Asia/ open grassland and cultivation / n ground/ e 3–4

Mirafra rufa *Lynes* RUSTY BUSH LARK Niger, Darfur and Kordofan / open bush / n and e n/k

Mirafra gilletti *Sharpe* GILLETT'S LARK Ethiopia and the Somalilands / well-watered hill country / n grass-tuft / e 3

Mirafra poecilosterna (*Reichenow*) PINK-BREASTED LARK E Africa from Sudan to Kilimanjaro / thorn scrub / n ground / e 2 (1 nest known)

Mirafra sabota *Smith* SABOTA LARK Parts of S Africa / bush country / n ground / e 3

Mirafra erythroptera *Blyth* RED-WINGED BUSH LARK India and Pakistan / open plains and plateaux / n ground / e 2–4

Mirafra nigricans (*Sundevall*) DUSKY BUSH LARK W, C, and SE Africa / open ground among trees / n ground / e 2

Heteromirafra ruddi (*Grant*) LONG-CLAWED LARK S Africa: British Somaliland (discontinuous, 2 races) / n tussock / e 3

Certhilauda curvirostris (*Hermann*) LONG-BILLED LARK S Africa N to Transvaal and SW Africa / sandy ground and bush / n under tussock/ e 2–3

Certhilauda albescens (*Lafresnaye*) KARROO LARK Cape Province and southern SW Africa/ desert and open bush / n ground / e 2–3

Certhilauda albofasciata *Lafresnaye* SPIKE-HEELED LARK S Africa N to Angola and the Zambezi / open country and desert / n tussock/ e 2–4

Eremopterix australis (*Smith*) BLACK-EARED FINCH LARK (birds of this genus are also called SPARROW LARKS) Damaraland to W Transvaal and Cape Province / short-grass plains / n under grass tuft / e 2

Eremopterix leucotis (*Stanley*) CHESTNUT-BACKED FINCH LARK Semi-arid parts of Africa S of Sahara / bare sandy or stony ground / n ground / e 1

Eremopterix signata (*Oustalet*) CHESTNUT-HEADED FINCH LARK E Africa from SE Sudan to Kenya / stony desert-scrub / n and e n/k

Eremopterix verticalis *Smith* GREY-BACKED FINCH LARK S Africa N to W Rhodesia and Angola / bare sandy and stony ground / n ground/ e 2

Eremopterix nigriceps (*Gould*) BLACK-CROWNED FINCH LARK Cape Verde Is across arid belt of Africa to Arabia, Iraq, Baluchistan and the NW Indian region / open country and sparse bush / n ground / e 2

Eremopterix grisea (*Scopoli*) ASHY-CROWNED FINCH LARK India, Pakistan and Ceylon / stony wastes and cultivation / n ground / e 2–3 / I ♂♀

Eremopterix leucopareia (*Fischer and Reichenow*) FISCHER'S FINCH LARK Parts of Uganda, Kenya and Malawi / short-grass plains / n ground / e 2–3

Ammomanes cincturus (*Gould*) BAR-TAILED or BLACK-TAILED SAND LARK Deserts of Sahara, Arabia, Afghanistan and Thar / n rock-crevice or under stones / e n/k

Ammomanes phoenicurus (*Franklin*) RUFOUS-TAILED LARK Drier parts of India / scrub plains and plateaux / seeds and insects / n ground or bank / e 2–4 / I ♂♀

Ammomanes deserti (*Lichtenstein*) SAND LARK or DESERT LARK Deserts of Sahara, Arabia, Middle East through Persia to Afghanistan and Thar / n rock crevice or among stones / e 3–4

Ammomanes dunni (*Shelley*) DUNN'S LARK S Sahara and SW Arabia / grass plains / n and e n/k

Ammomanes grayi (*Wahlberg*) GRAY'S LARK SW Africa / desert / n and e n/k

Ammomanes burrus *Bangs* FERRUGINOUS LARK or RED LARK Bushmanland to Klein Karas in SW Africa / apparently no data

Alaemon alaudipes (*Desfontaine*) GREATER HOOPOE LARK Cape Verde Is and deserts of Sahara, Arabia, Syria, Khorassan, Afghanistan and Thar / n ground / e 2 / I ♂♀

Alaemon hamertoni *Witherby* LESSER HOOPOE LARK British Somaliland and Somalia / no data

Ramphocoris clotbey (*Bonaparte*) CLOTBEY LARK North edge of Sahara from Morocco to Egypt, N Arabia and Syrian desert (local) / desert / n ground / e 2–6

Melanocorypha calandra (*L*) CALANDRA LARK Mediterranean region and Middle East to Transcaspia and Russian Turkestan / plains and cultivation / n ground / e 4–5 (?6–7)

Melanocorypha bimaculata (*Ménétriés*) BIMACULATED LARK b WC Asia from Kirghiz steppes to Turkey and Afghanistan w S to India, Sudan and Arabia / semi-desert / seeds and insects / n ground / e 3–4

Melanocorypha maxima *Blyth* LONG-BILLED CALANDRA LARK Tibet, Sikang, Koko Nor and N Sikkim / high marsh / seeds and insects / n ground / e 2–3

Melanocorypha mongolica (*Pallas*) MONGOLIAN LARK Transbaikalia, Manchuria, Mongolia w S to N China / grassland / virtually no data / Dementiev et alia, *Birds of the Soviet Union*, vol 5, gives no information on eggs of this species, however there are 2 eggs in the collection of the British Museum (Natural History) (? clutch) ascribed to this species, and the eggs were also known to Nehrkorn (1899)

Melanocorypha leucoptera (*Pallas*) WHITE-WINGED LARK Caucasus across C Asia to Omsk and Zaissan Nor w S to Turkey / grassy steppes / n ground / e 3–8 / I ♀ 12

Melanocorypha yeltonensis (*Forster*) BLACK LARK b SE Russia to Altai w to Black Sea and Turkestan / steppe / n ground / e 4–5 (?6–8) / I ♀ 15–16

Calandrella cinerea (*Gmelin*) SHORT-TOED LARK Mediterranean, S through much of Africa and E across Asia to Mongolia / plains, semi-desert, tidal mudflats etc / n grass / e 2–3 / I ?♀ 13 (*C. brachydactyla* (Leisler) is sometimes separated)

Calandrella blanfordi (*Shelley*) BLANFORD'S LARK Somaliland and adjacent parts of Ethiopia and Eritrea (? Arabia) / no data

Calandrella acutirostris *Hume* HUME'S SHORT-TOED LARK E Iran to Koko Nor w S to N India / semi-desert / seeds and insects / n ground / e 2–3 / I ♂♀

Calandrella raytal *Blyth* RAYTAL LARK Makran Coast across N India to Assam and Burma / sandy shores and riverbanks / seeds and insects / n ground / e 2–3 / I ♂♀

Calandrella rufescens (*Vieillot*) RUFOUS or LESSER SHORT-TOED LARK Canary Islands, S Spain, deserts from Sahara through NE and E Africa to Kenya and E to Transbaikalia / n ground / e 2–3 (*C. cheleensis* (Swinhoe) is sometimes separated, as is *C. somalica* (Sharpe))

Calandrella razae (*Alexander*) RAZO LARK Razo Is (Cape Verdes) / n ground or shrub / e 3 / I ♂♀ 13 [The taxonomic position of this species has always been controversial. It is sometimes placed in a monotypic genus, *Razocorys*, but B. P. Hall, *Bull Brit Orn Cl* (1963), p 133 places it in *Alauda*. I am here following Peters, *Check List of the Birds of the World*, vol 9, p 52, as this is where most people are likely to look for it]

ALCEDINIDAE:
Ceyx azureus,
Azure Kingfisher

ALCEDINIDAE:
Halcyon albiventris,
Brown-hooded Kingfisher

Plate 172

ALCEDINIDAE:
Halcyon sancta,
Sacred Kingfisher

ALCEDINIDAE:
Alcedo quadribrachys,
Shining Blue Kingfisher

Plate 173

Calandrella conirostris (*Sundevall*) PINK-BILLED LARK S Africa N to SW Africa and Transvaal/veldt and cultivation/n ground/e 2–3

Calandrella starki *Shelley* STARK'S LARK S Angola through Damaraland to E Transvaal/grassland/n ground/e 2

Calandrella sclateri *Shelley* SCLATER'S LARK Namaqualand and C Cape Province / ? no data

Calandrella fringillaris (*Sundevall*) BOTHA'S LARK Orange Free State/e 2–3/no other data

Calandrella obbiensis (*Witherby*) OBBIA LARK Obbia in Somaliland/no data

Calandrella personata (*Sharpe*) MASKED LARK Known only from scattered localities in Kenya and Ethiopia/bare ground/no data

Chersophilus duponti (*Vieillot*) DUPONT'S LARK Algeria to NW Egypt, occasional in Iberia and S France / scrub and semi-desert/n ground/e 3–4

Pseudalaemon fremantlii (*Lort Phillips*) SHORT-TAILED LARK Ethiopia to N Tanganyika/open plains/n ground/e 2

Galerida cristata (*L*) COMMON CRESTED LARK Widely distributed through the temperate parts of Europe, Asia and Africa S to the Niger/open country and cultivation / seeds and insects / n ground/e 2–3/I ♂♀, ♀ (accounts differ) 12–13/F 9–11

Galerida theklae (*Brehm*) THEKLA LARK Iberia, N Sahara from Morocco to Egypt: Ethiopia to Kenya (but Mackworth Praed and Grant treat the E African races of *theklae* as races of *malabarica*)/broken scrub, plains and plateaux/n ground/e 2–6

Galerida malabarica (*Scopoli*) MALABAR CRESTED LARK Western half of Indian Peninsula/scrub-jungle and cultivation/seeds and insects/n ground/e 2–3

Galerida deva (*Sykes*) DECCAN LARK India from Punjab to Madras/stony plateaux and dry cultivation/seeds and insects/n ground/e 2–3

Galerida modesta *Heuglin* SUN LARK Africa from Upper Volta to Upper White Nile and S to Congo and NW Uganda/short grass and bare ground/n ground or among stones/e 1–2

Galerida magnirostris (*Stephens*) THICK-BILLED LARK S Africa N to Transvaal/sandy soil and cultivation/n ground/e 2–3

Lullula arborea (*L*) WOOD LARK Europe, Mediterranean Africa, Near and Middle East to Transcaspia/open woodland, scrub, parkland etc/n ground/e 1–6/I ♀ 12–16/F 11–12

Alauda arvensis *L* SKYLARK Much of Palaearctic and mts of NW Africa / Asiatic birds w into N India/grassland, sand-dune and cultivation/n ground/e 3–7/I ♀ 11/F c20

Alauda gulgula *Franklin* LESSER SKYLARK C and E Asia S to Indian region, SE Asia and Philippines / grassland / seeds and insects / n ground/e 2–4/I ♂♀

Eremophila alpestris (*L*) HORNED LARK or SHORE LARK Widely distributed through the Holarctic and S to N Africa and Mexico/alpine pastures and stony ground (seashores in winter)/n ground/e 2–5/I 10–14/F 9–12

Eremophila bilopha (*Temminck*) TEMMINCK'S LARK Stony portions of Sahara through N Arabia to W Iraq/n ground/e 2–4

HIRUNDINIDAE Swallows and Martins Aerial birds superficially resembling Swifts, with streamlined bodies and long wings. Tails often forked. Feed on small insects and generally construct elaborate nests of mud pellets attached to vertical or horizontal surfaces: some, however, nest in holes. Almost cosmopolitan.

Pseudochelidon eurystomina *Hartlaub* AFRICAN RIVER MARTIN Gabon and on Lower Congo and Ubangi Rivers / n hole in flat sandbank/e 3

Pseudochelidon sirintarae *Kitti Thonglongya* (*Thai Nat Scien Papers*, Fauna Series, no 1, 1968) WHITE-EYED RIVER MARTIN b range unknown w C Thailand/reed beds

Tachycineta bicolor (*Vieillot*) TREE SWALLOW b Canada and northern USA w S to Caribbean and C America/forest and habitation/n hole/e 4–6 (?7–10)/I 13–16/F 16–24

Tachycineta albilinea (*Lawrence*) MANGROVE SWALLOW Mexico and C America: coast of Peru/mangroves, lakes and riverbanks/n hole/e 3

Tachycineta albiventer (*Boddaert*) WHITE-WINGED SWALLOW S America E of Andes and S to S Brazil

Tachycineta leucorrhoa (*Vieillot*) WHITE-RUMPED SWALLOW South-central S America

Tachycineta leucopyga (*Meyen*) CHILEAN SWALLOW Southern S America / forest and habitation/n hole or eaves/e 4–6

Tachycineta thalassina (*Swainson*) VIOLET-GREEN SWALLOW Western N America and C America/forest and habitation/n hole in tree or rock/e 4–7/I 13–14

Callichelidon cyaneoviridis (*Bryant*)

BAHAMA SWALLOW Bahamas, some birds w in E Cuba / pine forests / n hole or eaves / e 3

Kalochelidon euchrysea (*Gosse*) GOLDEN SWALLOW Jamaica and Hispaniola (local) / forest and open country in mountains / n hole or eaves / e 3

Progne tapera (*L*) BROWN-CHESTED MARTIN S America E of Andes and S to Uruguay / open woodland and dead trees / n in old Ovenbird nests or arboreal termitaries (sometimes placed in monotypic genus *Phaeoprogne*)

Progne subis (*L*) PURPLE MARTIN Much of N and C America / forest and habitation / n hole in tree, cliff or building / e 3–8 / I ♀ 12–15 (?20) / F 24–8

Progne dominicensis (*Gmelin*) WHITE-BELLIED MARTIN W Indies and a few localities in C America / seacliffs and habitation / n hole in rock, under eaves or old Woodpecker hole / e 3–6

Progne chalybea (*Gmelin*) GREY-BREASTED MARTIN Mexico, C America and northern S America S to Uruguay / forest and habitation / n hole in tree or building / e 3–5 / I ♀ 15–16

Progne modesta *Gould* SOUTHERN MARTIN Galapagos, Peru, Bolivia and Argentina w N to S Brazil / open country, seacliffs and rocky outcrops / n hole in tree or building / e ?

Notiochelidon murina (*Cassin*) BROWN-BELLIED SWALLOW Andes from Venezuela to Bolivia

Notiochelidon cyanoleuca (*Vieillot*) BLUE-AND-WHITE SWALLOW Much of C and S America / ubiquitous / n hole in bank / e 3–6

Notiochelidon flavipes (*Chapman*) PALE-FOOTED SWALLOW Peru, Colombia / 3 specimens known in 1959

Notiochelidon pileata (*Gould*) COBÁN SWALLOW Guatemala

Atticora fasciata (*Gmelin*) WHITE-BACKED SWALLOW S America E of Andes and S to Bolivia / forest rivers

Atticora melanoleuca (*Wied*) BLACK-COLLARED SWALLOW S America E of Andes and S to Brazil / forest rivers / n 'in tissues of rocks in the water' (Haverschmidt)

Neochelidon tibialis (*Cassin*) WHITE-THIGHED SWALLOW Panama, Upper Amazon basin and SE Brazil

Alpochelidon fucata (*Temminck*) TAWNY-HEADED SWALLOW Venezuela, S to Bolivia, Uruguay and N Argentina

Stelgidopteryx ruficollis (*Vieillot*) AMERICAN ROUGH-WINGED SWALLOW or GALLEY MARTIN Widely distributed through the Americas except the extreme N and S / variable habitat / n holes of various kinds / e 4–8 / I ♀ 12–16 / F 20–1

Cheramoeca leucosternum (*Gould*) BLACK AND WHITE SWALLOW or WHITE-BACKED SWALLOW W, S and C Australia / open country with sandy banks and riverbanks / n hole in bank / e 4–5

Pseudohirundo griseopyga (*Sundevall*) GREY-RUMPED SWALLOW W, C, and E Africa / open fields and forest clearings / n hole in bank or ground / e 2–4

Riparia paludicola (*Vieillot*) PLAIN SAND MARTIN Africa, Madagascar, parts of S and SE Asia and Philippines / n hole in bank / e 1–5

Riparia congica (*Reichenow*) CONGO SAND MARTIN Middle and Lower Congo River / n hole in bank / e n/k

Riparia riparia (*L*) SAND MARTIN or BANK SWALLOW Holarctic and Oriental w through Africa and S America / riverbanks etc / n hole in bank / e 3–4 / I ♂♀

Riparia cincta (*Boddaert*) BANDED MARTIN E and S Africa / high grassland / n hole in bank or cliff / e 3–5

Phedina borbonica (*Gmelin*) MASCARINE MARTIN Madagascar, Mauritius and Réunion, migrating to E Africa / n rocky ledge of cave or cliff / e n/s

Phedina brazzae *Oustalet* BRAZZA'S MARTIN S Congo basin and Angola / along rivers / n tunnel in bank / e 3

Ptyonoprogne rupestris (*Scopoli*) CRAG MARTIN Atlas Mts, mts from S Europe across C Asia to Himalayas and mts of W Szechwan / grassy hills with crags / n cliffs / e 3–4

Ptyonoprogne obsoleta (*Cabanis*) PALE CRAG MARTIN Mts of N Africa through Arabia to Baluchistan and Sind / cliffs, caves and ruined buildings / n roof of cave etc / e 3

Ptyonoprogne fuligula (*Lichtenstein*) AFRICAN ROCK MARTIN Irregularly distributed through much of Africa S of Sahara / cliffs / n wall or cliff / e 2–3

Ptyonoprogne concolor (*Sykes*) DUSKY CRAG MARTIN India and SE Asia / crags and tall buildings in cities / n cave or eave / e 2–4 / I ♂♀

Hirundo rustica *L* BARN SWALLOW Widely distributed in N Hemisphere w S through S Hemisphere / n wall or eave / e 4–6 / I ♀ 14–16

MOTMOTIDAE:
Baryphthengus ruficapillus,
Rufous Motmot

TODIDAE: *Todus todus,* Jamaican Tody

Plate 174

MEROPIDAE:
Merops orientalis,
Little Green Bee-eater

MEROPIDAE:
Merops albicollis,
White-throated Bee-eater

MEROPIDAE:
Merops nubicoides
Southern Carmine Bee-eater

Plate 175

Hirundo lucida *Hartlaub* RED-CHESTED SWALLOW Equatorial Africa from Senegal to N Congo / habitation / n beam or wall / e 3–4 (some authors credit *Hirundo lucida* to Verreaux. The full original reference as quoted by J. L. Peters is: *Hirundo lucida* 'J. Verreaux', Hartlaub, *Journ für Orn*, 6 (1858), p 42)

Hirundo angolensis *Bocage* ANGOLA SWALLOW E and EC Africa / n cliff, cave or building / e 3

Hirundo tahitica *Gmelin* HOUSE SWALLOW, WELCOME SWALLOW, COAST SWALLOW, PACIFIC SWALLOW [this species has various well-established English names in various parts of its range and is divided by some authors into several species, as *javanica* (House Swallow), *tahitica* (Pacific Swallow), *neoxena* (Welcome Swallow)] S India and Ceylon, through Malaya, Indonesia and Polynesia to the Society Is, Australia and Papuan areas, also Melanesia/ forest, plantations etc / n wall or cliff / e 2–4/ I ♂♀

Hirundo albigularis *Strickland* WHITE-THROATED SWALLOW Africa S of Zambezi/ habitation / n cliff, cave or building / e 3–4

Hirundo aethiopica *Blanford* ETHIOPIAN SWALLOW Nigeria to Ethiopia and Tanganyika/ habitation / n cave or building / e 3–4

Hirundo smithii *Leach* WIRE-TAILED SWALLOW Africa S of Sahara, S and SE Asia /open country and cultivation / n rock or building / e 3–5/ I ♀ 14–15/ F 15–16

Hirundo andrewi *Williams* (*Bull Br Orn Cl*, 86 (1966), p 40) ANDREW'S SWALLOW Known from the type collected on migration at Lake Naivasha, Kenya, believed to breed in Ethiopia

Hirundo atrocaerulea *Sundevall* BLUE SWALLOW Tanganyika to Natal / n bank, wall or roof of antbear burrow / e 2–3

Hirundo nigrita *Gray* WHITE-THROATED BLUE SWALLOW W and C Africa / forest streams / n rock or tree-trunk / e 3–4

Hirundo leucosoma *Swainson* PIED-WING SWALLOW W Africa from Senegal to Nigeria/ n wall / e 4

Hirundo megaensis *Benson* WHITE-TAILED SWALLOW S Ethiopia / open grass country/ n and e n/k – suspected of nesting in tall anthills

Hirundo nigrorufa *Bocage* BLACK-AND-RED SWALLOW Angola to Zambia / n on side of pit/ e n/k

Hirundo dimidiata *Sundevall* PEARL-BREASTED SWALLOW Africa S of Tanganyika / woodland and cultivation / n building / e 3

Hirundo cucullata *Boddaert* GREATER STRIPED SWALLOW S Africa w N to Tanganyika/n cave, building or under bridge / e 3–5

Hirundo abyssinica *Guérin-Méneville* LESSER STRIPED SWALLOW Africa S of Sahara / n cave or under roof / e 3

Hirundo semirufa *Sundevall* RUFOUS-CHESTED SWALLOW Africa S of Sahara / open country / n hollow tree, anthill or under roof/ e 2–4

Hirundo senegalensis *L* AFRICAN MOSQUE SWALLOW Africa S of Sahara (except the extreme S) / n hole in tree or building / e 3–4

Hirundo daurica *L* RED-RUMPED or DAURIAN SWALLOW C, S, and E Asia, Mediterranean region S through Africa to Congo and Tanganyika / light forest and cultivation / n cave or building / e 2–5 / I ♂♀

Hirundo striolata *Temminck and Schlegel* ORIENTAL MOSQUE SWALLOW Assam through SE Asia and Indonesia / n cave or building / e 3–5

Petrochelidon rufigula (*Bocage*) RED-THROATED ROCK MARTIN Angola to Zambia/ cliffs / n cliff / e 2

Petrochelidon preussi (*Reichenow*) PREUSS'S CLIFF SWALLOW W Africa from Timbuktu to Congo / n cliffs and buildings / e 2–3

Petrochelidon andecola (*d'Orbigny and Lafresnaye*) ANDEAN SWALLOW Puna zone from Peru to N Chile / n hole in cliff / e ? n/k

Petrochelidon nigricans (*Vieillot*) TREE MARTIN Australia, Timor, Flores, New Guinea, Bismarck Archipelago, Solomon Is / open woodland and habitation / n hole in tree, cliff or building / e 4

Petrochelidon spilodera (*Sundevall*) AFRICAN CLIFF SWALLOW S Africa N to Congo / open country / n rock or building / e 3–4

Petrochelidon pyrrhonota (*Vieillot*) (=**P. albifrons** (*Rafinesque*)) AMERICAN CLIFF SWALLOW b N and C America w southern S America / cliffs and habitation / n cliff or building/ e 3–6

Petrochelidon fulva (*Vieillot*) CAVE SWALLOW C America, Greater Antilles, SW Ecuador and W Peru (discontinuous) / ravines, caves, cliffs and habitation / n cave, hole in cliff or building/ e 3–5 (?2)

Petrochelidon fluvicola (*Blyth*) INDIAN CLIFF MARTIN Kabul and much of India / open

country near water / n under bridges, arches etc /
e 3–4 / I ♂♀

Petrochelidon ariel (*Gould*) FAIRY MARTIN
Australia and Tasmania / open country near
water / n cliff or building / e 4–5

Petrochelidon fuliginosa (*Chapin*) FOREST
CLIFF SWALLOW Forested areas of S Cameroon /
n cave or building / e 3

Delichon urbica (*L*) HOUSE MARTIN b Palaearctic w Africa and S and SE Asia / open
country, cliffs and habitation / n wall or cliff /
e 2–6 / I ♂♀ 14–15 / F 19–22

Delichon dasypus (*Bonaparte*) ASIATIC HOUSE
MARTIN S and E Asia from India to Kurile Is
w S to Indonesia / cliffs and mountain villages /
n cliff (? or building) / e 3–4 [often considered
conspecific with *urbica*]

Delichon nipalensis *Horsfield and Moore*
NEPAL MARTIN Himalayas to mts of Burma-
Yunnan border / cliffs and river valleys / n cliff /
e 3–5 / I ♂♀

Psalidoprocne nitens (*Cassin*) SQUARE-TAILED
ROUGH-WINGED SWALLOW W and C Africa /
forest and habitation / n hole in bank / e 2

Psalidoprocne fuliginosa *Shelley* CAMEROON
ROUGH-WINGED SWALLOW Mts of Cameroon
and Fernando Po / mountain forest (habitation
in Fernando Po) / n sometimes on buildings,
others n/k / e n/k

Psalidoprocne albiceps *Sclater* WHITE-
HEADED ROUGH-WINGED SWALLOW E Africa
from Upper White Nile to Malawi / hills and
forest glades / n hole in bank / e 2–4

Psalidoprocne pristoptera (*Rüppell*) BLUE
ROUGH-WINGED SWALLOW Eritrea and Ethiopia /
high plateaux / n hole in bank / e 3

[**Psalidoprocne oleaginea** *Neumann* SW
slopes of Ethiopian plateau / more often considered a race of *P. orientalis*]

Psalidoprocne antinorii *Salvadori* BROWN
ROUGH-WINGED SWALLOW Mts of Ethiopia S
to Lake Rudolph / edge of forest / n and e n/k

Psalidoprocne petiti *Sharpe and Bouvier*
PETIT'S SWALLOW British Cameroons to Congo /
forest glades and open spaces / n hole in bank / e 2

Psalidoprocne holomelaena (*Sundevall*)
BLACK ROUGH-WINGED SWALLOW C and S
Africa / forest glades / n hole in bank / e 2

Psalidoprocne orientalis *Reichenow* EASTERN
ROUGH-WINGED SWALLOW C, E, and S Africa
(except extreme S) / high plateaux and edges of
mt forests / n hole in bank / e 2

Psalidoprocne mangbettorum *Chapin*
MANGBETU SWALLOW Congo district / savannah /
n hole in bank / e 3 (treated by some as a race of
prisoptera)

Psalidoprocne chalybea *Reichenow* SHARI
SWALLOW SE Nigeria to River Ituri / forest
clearings / n and e n/k

Psalidoprocne obscura (*Hartlaub*) FANTI
SWALLOW Sierra Leone to Cameroon / forest
edge and grassland / n hole in bank / e 2

MOTACILLIDAE Wagtails and Pipits
Small slender-bodied ground birds with long
tails which they wag vertically. Generally fairly
strikingly coloured (Wagtails and Longclaws)
or brownish (Pipits). Inhabit open country.
Feed on insects. Nest on the ground, eggs 3–7,
white to buff, speckled with browns and greys.
Incubation period about 12–16 days and
fledging about 14.

Dendronanthus indicus (*Gmelin*) FOREST
WAGTAIL E Asia, b from Siberia to N China
w S to India and Java / forest / n tree / e 5

Motacilla flava *L* YELLOW WAGTAIL Widely
distributed through Eurasia to W Alaska and
S w to parts of Africa [NB: the name 'Yellow
Wagtail' is properly applied to only one race of
this complex of forms, most of which have
distinctive English names of their own: as
Blue-headed, Black-headed, Sykes' Wagtail,
etc] / fields and water meadows, etc / n ground /
e 4–8 / I ♀ (?♂) 13–16 / F 12–13

Motacilla citreola *Pallas* YELLOW-HEADED or
CITRINE WAGTAIL Much of NC Asia w S to
Himalayas and Burma / wet meadows and
tundra, alpine zone in S n ground / e 4–5

Motacilla cinerea *Tunstall* (some authors
persist in using *M. caspica* (S. G. Gmelin))
GREY WAGTAIL Palaearctic w S to Africa, S
Asia and New Guinea / mountain streams, in
winter lakeshores and seashores / n hole of cliff
or rock crevice / n 3–7 / I ♀ (?♂) 13–14 / F 12

Motacilla alba *L* WHITE and PIED WAGTAILS
Much of Eurasia and N Africa w S to C Africa /
open country / n hole in wall, bank, cliff etc /
e 3–7 (? 9–11) / I ♂♀ 13–14 / F 14–15

Motacilla grandis *Sharpe* JAPANESE WAGTAIL
Japan / lowlands near water / n ground / e 5–7

Motacilla madaraspatensis *Gmelin* WHITE-
BROWED WAGTAIL India / near water / n hole in
wall, bank etc / e 3–5

Motacilla aguimp *Dumont* AFRICAN PIED
WAGTAIL Africa S of Sahara / riverbanks and

Plate 176

Opposite:
MEROPIDAE:
Merops apiaster,
European Bee-eater,
Common Bee-eater

UPUPIDAE:
Upupa epops,
Hoopoe

CORACIIDAE:
Coracias benghalensis,
Indian Roller

Plate 177

habitation/insects/n bank or building/e 2–3

Motacilla clara *Sharpe* MOUNTAIN WAGTAIL Africa S of Sahara/rocky mountain streams/ n ledge or rock crevice/e 2–3

Motacilla capensis *L* CAPE WAGTAIL Africa from Kenya and Angola S to Cape/swamps and lakes/n ground/e 3 (*M. simplicissima* Neumann 'Angola Wagtail' is sometimes separated)

Motacilla flaviventris *Hartlaub* MADAGASCAR WAGTAIL Madagascar/open brush and clear-ings, often near water/n crevice/e 2–3

Tmetothylacus tenellus (*Cabanis*) GOLDEN PIPIT British Somaliland to Kenya and NE Tanganyika/dry scrub/insects and seeds/n in grass/e 2–4

Macronyx capensis (*L*) CAPE LONGCLAW SE Africa from Rhodesia to Cape / open country and cultivation/n grass tuft/e 3–4

Macronyx croceus (*Vieillot*) YELLOW-THROATED LONGCLAW Senegal to Sudan, and S to Natal and N Angola / open country and cultivation / insects and seeds / n under grass tuft/e 3–4

Macronyx fuellebornii *Reichenow* FULLEBORN'S LONGCLAW Tanganyika across Congo to Angola and Zambia/highland grass-land/n top of grass tuft/e 3

Macronyx sharpei *Jackson* SHARPE'S LONGCLAW Highlands of either side of the Kenya rift-valley/open grass downs/n ? ground/ e 2–3

Macronyx flavicollis *Rüppell* ABYSSINIAN LONGCLAW Mts of Ethiopia / high mountain plateaux/n in growing grass/e 2–3

Macronyx aurantiigula *Reichenow* PANGANI LONGCLAW Kenya and Somali Republic / open bush and thorn scrub/n under grass tuft/e 2

Macronyx ameliae *de Tarragon* ROSY-BREASTED LONGCLAW E Africa from W Kenya to Natal and Angola /open grassland near water/ n under tussock /e 3–4

Macronyx grimwoodi *Benson* GRIMWOOD'S LONGCLAW Zambia and EC Angola / open grassland near water/n and e n/k

Anthus novaeseelandiae (*Gmelin*) (includes **Anthus richardi,** *Vieillot*) RICHARD'S PIPIT Widely distributed through Africa, Asia except the N, and SE through Indonesia to the Australasian and New Zealand areas / open country of various types / insects / n ground/ e ? 3–6 (*Anthus latistriatus* Jackson, is a melanic aberration)

Anthus leucophrys *Vieillot* PLAIN-BACKED PIPIT Africa S of Sahara /open country and cultivation/insects and seeds/n ground ?/e 3

Anthus vaalensis *Shelley* SANDY PIPIT E Ethiopia, Somalia and Kenya: S Africa N to Angola and the Zambezi/open country/n grass tuft/e 3

Anthus pallidiventris *Sharpe* LONG-CLAWED PIPIT Angola, Gabon and Congo/grassland and forest clearings/n and e n/k

Anthus melindae *Shelley* MALINDI PIPIT Kenya to S Italian Somaliland/rare and local/ no data

Anthus campestris (*L*) TAWNY PIPIT b much of temperate Eurasia and NW Africa w S to Africa N of Equator and Indian region/sandy wastes, scrub, semi-desert and cultivation/ insects /n ground /e 4–6/I ♀ or ♂♀ (accounts differ) 13–14 /F 14

Anthus godlewskii (*Taczanowski*) BLYTH'S PIPIT b EC Asia from Transbaikalia to Man-churia and Tibet w India and Ceylon/rocky mountain slopes/n ground/e ? 3–5 (no reliable data)

Anthus berthelotii *Bolle* BERTHELOT'S PIPIT Madeira and Canary Is/all open country/n under bush or stone/e 2–5

Anthus similis *Jerdon* LONG-BILLED PIPIT Africa through Arabia and Middle East to Indian region and Burma / variable habitat/ insects and seeds/n ground or among herbage/ e 2–4

Anthus brachyurus *Sundevall* SHORT-TAILED PIPIT Angola and Congo to Uganda, Tangan-yika and Natal / uplands with short grass/ insects and seeds/n grass tufts/e 2–3

Anthus caffer *Sundevall* LITTLE PIPIT Ethiopia to Natal and W to Angola/bush and sandy patches/n base of grass tuft/e 2–3

Anthus trivialis (*L*) TREE PIPIT b Europe across C Asia to Lake Baikal and Yakutsk w Africa and S Asia/forest, scrub and meadow-land / insects and seeds / n ground / e 4–8/ I ♀ 13–14 /F 12–13

Anthus nilghiriensis *Sharpe* NILGIRI PIPIT Mts of SW Madras/open hilltops/insects and seeds/n ground /e 2–3

Anthus hodgsoni *Richmond* HODGSON'S PIPIT b Russia to Kamchatka and S to Himalayas w S Asia and Indonesia / forest glades and scrubby hillsides /seeds and insects /n ground/ e 3–5

Anthus gustavi *Swinhoe* PETCHORA PIPIT b tundra from Russia to the Kolyma and Chukotsk Peninsula w Indonesia; 2 other populations (? non-migratory) in Commander Is and S Ussuriland / swamps and marshes/ insects / n ground / e 4–5

Anthus pratensis (*L*) MEADOW PIPIT b W Palaearctic to Petchora w N Africa and Middle East / very variable in open country / seeds, insects and other invertebrates/n ground/e 3–7/ I ♀ 13–14/F 13–14

Anthus cervinus (*Pallas*) RED-THROATED PIPIT b N Palaearctic w Africa, E and S Asia/ marsh, tundra etc/insects and seeds/n ground on hummock in marsh/e 4–7/I ♀

Anthus roseatus *Blyth* ROSY PIPIT b Afghanistan to Sinkiang, Himalayas, Tibet and Szechwan w N India to S China / b alpine meadows and upland marshes, w marshes and ricefields/insects and seeds/n ground/e 3–4

Anthus spinoletta (*L*) WATER PIPIT, ROCK PIPIT and AMERICAN PIPIT Widely but irregularly distributed through Holarctic / alpine pastures, seacliffs, mountain streams and rocky shores / seeds and invertebrates / n hole in rock or bank / e 2–6 / I ♀ c14/F 16

Anthus sylvanus (*Blyth*) UPLAND PIPIT b Himalayas to Szechwan w India/steep grassy slopes with bushes/n under grass tuft or stone/ e 3–5

Anthus spragueii (*Audubon*) SPRAGUE'S PIPIT Western N America w S to Mexico/prairies, parkland etc/insects and seeds /n ground/e 4–6/ I ♀/F 10–11 ?

Anthus furcatus *Lafresnaye and d'Orbigny* SHORT-BILLED PIPIT S America from S Brazil and Peru S to Patagonia/open country/n ground/ e 2–5

Anthus hellmayri *Hartert* HELLMAYR'S PIPIT S America from Peru and S Brazil to N Argentina

Anthus lutescens *Pucheran* YELLOWISH PIPIT Savannah regions of S America E of Andes, and Pacific slope of Panama

Anthus chacoensis *Zimmer* CHACO PIPIT Occurs (non-breeding) in Argentine chaco and Paraguay/b n/k

Anthus correndera *Vieillot* CORRENDERA PIPIT Mts from Peru to S Patagonia, lowlands from S Brazil S, Falkland Is /grasslands and swamps / n ground / e ? 2–4, 3–5

Anthus nattereri *Sclater* OCHRE-BREASTED PIPIT Paraguay and SE Brazil

Anthus bogotensis *Sclater* PARAMO PIPIT Mts from Venezuela to Argentina

['*Anthus venturi*'. In 1899, Venturi collected an aberrant clutch of pipit eggs at Barracas al Sud, Buenos Aires, and dubbed them with this (m/s) name. It is not clear if he had a skin of the parent which he believed to be a new species. These eggs may be referable to those of one of the known South American pipits. They are in the British Museum (Natural History), reg no 1941.4.3.55]

Anthus antarcticus *Cabanis* SOUTH GEORGIA PIPIT Island of South Georgia / seashore, streams and inland pools / invertebrates / n ground or rock crevice / e n/s

Anthus gutturalis *De Vis* NEW GUINEA PIPIT Mts of New Guinea / alpine ridges / insects and seeds / n ? ground / e n/k

Anthus sokokensis *van Someren* SOKOKE PIPIT Sokoke Forest (Kenya) and NE Tanganyika / forest undergrowth / no data

Anthus crenatus *Finsch and Hartlaub* YELLOW-TUFTED PIPIT Mts from Cape Province to Transvaal / grassy hills and mountain slopes/ n under stone or tuft / e 3

Anthus lineiventris *Sundevall* STRIPED PIPIT Locally in S Africa, N to Angola and Tanganyika/ rocky wooded hillsides / seeds and insects / n ground / e 3

Anthus chloris *Lichtenstein* YELLOW-BREASTED PIPIT Cape Province to Transvaal / open grassland /n grass tuft / e 3

CAMPEPHAGIDAE Cuckoo Shrikes and Minivets Small to medium-sized, primitive insect eaters of uncertain affinities. Cuckoo Shrikes are generally dull greyish in colour, some species superficially resemble Shrikes or Cuckoos. Minivets are generally brightly coloured in blacks, reds, yellows and oranges. Breeding habits, where known, are fairly uniform; the nest is an open cup in a tree; the 2–5 eggs are white, green or blue, blotched and speckled. Incubation may be by both sexes or by the female alone, and lasts 13–14 days in the smaller species. About 70 species, distributed through the warmer parts of the Old World.

Pteropodocys maxima (*Rüppell*) GROUND CUCKOO SHRIKE Australia / wooded savannah/ insects /n tree / e 2–3

Coracina novaehollandiae (*Gmelin*) LARGE CUCKOO SHRIKE Indian sub-continent through

BUCEROTIDAE:
Buceros bicornis,
Great Indian Hornbill,
Great Pied Hornbill

BUCEROTIDAE:
Bucorvus leadbeateri
(*=B. cafer*),
African Ground Hornbill,
Southern Ground Hornbill

Plate 178

BUCEROTIDAE: *Rhyticeros* species

Plate 179

SE Asia to S China, Java, Lesser Sundas, Australia and Tasmania, Australian races winter in Papuan area and Solomons (the various forms placed in this species are so peculiar in their distribution that I suspect more than one species may prove to be involved)/open woodland and plantations/insects/n tree/e 2–3

Coracina fortis (*Salvadori*) BURU CUCKOO SHRIKE Buru

Coracina atriceps (*Müller*) CERAM CUCKOO SHRIKE Ternate, Halmahera, Batjan and Ceram

Coracina pollens (*Salvadori*) KEI CUCKOO SHRIKE Kei and Tanimber Is

Coracina schistacea (*Sharpe*) SLATY CUCKOO SHRIKE Peleng and Sula Is

Coracina caledonica (*Gmelin*) MELANESIAN GREYBIRD Solomon Is, New Hebrides, Lifu and New Caledonia

Coracina caeruleogrisea (*Gray*) STOUT-BILLED GREYBIRD W, C, S and SE New Guinea, Aru Is and Japen/forest and bush/insects

Coracina temminckii (*Müller*) TEMMINCK'S GREYBIRD Celebes/mountain forests

Coracina larvata (*Müller*) BLACK-FACED GREYBIRD Mts of Sumatra, Java and Borneo

Coracina striata (*Boddaert*) BARRED CUCKOO SHRIKE Andamans, Malay Peninsula, Sumatra and Borneo and adjacent small islands, Kangean Is, Philippines/forest/n tree

Coracina bicolor (*Temminck*) MUNA GREYBIRD Celebes and Muna

Coracina lineata (*Swainson*) LINEATED GREYBIRD New Guinea, Waigeu, Numfor, New Britain, New Ireland, Solomons, E Australia/rain forest/insects and fruit/n tree/e 2

Coracina boyeri (*Gray*) BOYER'S or RUFOUS-UNDERWING GREYBIRD Misol, Japen and parts of N and S New Guinea/forest/insects and fruit

Coracina leucopygia (*Bonaparte*) MUNA CUCKOO SHRIKE Celebes and Muna

Coracina papuensis (*Gmelin*) PAPUAN GREYBIRD Moluccas, Papuan region, Solomons and Admiralty Is, N Australia/savannah, mangrove and secondary growth/insects/n tree/e 2

Coracina robusta (*Latham*) LITTLE CUCKOO SHRIKE E Australia/savannah and mangrove/insects and fruit/n tree/e 2–3

Coracina longicauda (*De Vis*) BLACK-HOODED GREYBIRD C and SE New Guinea/

mountain forest/insects, small lizards and fruit/n tree/e 1

Coracina parvula (*Salvadori*) HALMAHERA GREYBIRD Halmahera

Coracina abbotti (*Riley*) MOUNTAIN GREYBIRD High mts of Celebes

Coracina analis (*Verreaux and Des Murs*) NEW CALEDONIAN GREYBIRD New Caledonia

Coracina caesia (*Lichtenstein*) GREY CUCKOO SHRIKE or AFRICAN GREYBIRD Occurs locally in parts of W, E and S Africa/forest/insects/n tree/e 1–2

Coracina pectoralis (*Jardine and Selby*) WHITE-BREASTED GREYBIRD or CUCKOO SHRIKE Greater part of tropical Africa/open woodland and bush/insects/n tree/e 1–2

Coracina graueri *Neumann* GRAUER'S CUCKOO SHRIKE Forests NW of Lake Tanganyika/n and e n/k

Coracina cinerea (*Müller*) MADAGASCAR CUCKOO SHRIKE Madagascar and Grand Comoro Is/dense scrub and mangrove/insects/n tree

Coracina azurea (*Cassin*) BLUE CUCKOO SHRIKE W and C Africa/forest/insects/n and e n/k

Coracina typica (*Hartlaub*) MAURITIUS CUCKOO SHRIKE Mauritius

Coracina newtoni (*Pollen*) NEWTON'S CUCKOO SHRIKE Réunion

Coracina caerulescens (*Blyth*) PHILIPPINE GREYBIRD Cebu and Luzón

Coracina dohertyi (*Hartert*) SUMBA GREYBIRD Sumba

Coracina tenuirostris (*Jardine*) CICADABIRD or LONG-BILLED GREYBIRD Widely distributed over the Australasian and E Indonesian regions in a great many insular forms, extending to the Solomons and Ponapé/forest and mangrove/insects/n tree/e 1

Coracina morio (*Müller*) MÜLLER'S GREYBIRD Celebes, Buton, Sula Is, Moluccas, New Guinea and Japen; Sulu Is and Mindanao, Basilan, Luzón and Mindoro/? no data

Coracina schisticeps (*Gray*) GRAY'S GREYBIRD New Guinea, Misol and D'Entrecasteaux Archipelago/forest/fruit

Coracina melaena (*Lesson*) BLACK GREYBIRD New Guinea, Aru Is, Japen and Waigeu/forest

Coracina montana (*Meyer*) BLACK-BELLIED GREYBIRD Mts of New Guinea/forest/fruit

Coracina holopolia (*Sharpe*) CICADA

GREYBIRD Solomon Is

Coracina mcgregori (*Mearns*) SHARP-TAILED GREYBIRD N Mindanao (Philippines)

Coracina panayensis (*Steere*) WHITE-WINGED GREYBIRD Guimaras, Negros and Panay (Philippines)

Coracina polioptera (*Sharpe*) LESSER CUCKOO SHRIKE SE Asia / open forest and cultivation / n tree / e 2–3

Coracina melaschistos (*Hodgson*) DARK-GREY or BLACK-WINGED CUCKOO SHRIKE Himalayas and W China S through SE Asia, Hainan and Taiwan / forest / insects / n tree / e 2–4

Coracina fimbriata (*Temminck*) LESSER GREYBIRD Malay Peninsula, Sumatra (and adjacent islands), Borneo, Java and Bali / forest and cultivation / n tree / e 2–3

Coracina melanoptera (*Rüppell*) BLACK-HEADED CUCKOO SHRIKE Himalayas, India, Bangladesh and Ceylon / open forest and scrub jungle / insects and berries / n tree / e 2–3 / I ♂♀

Campochaera sloetii (*Schlegel*) ORANGE CUCKOO SHRIKE W and S New Guinea / forest / insects and fruit

Chlamydochaera jefferyi *Sharpe* BLACK-BREASTED TRILLER Mts of northern Borneo

Lalage melanoleuca (*Blyth*) BLACK AND WHITE TRILLER Philippines

Lalage nigra (*Forster*) PIED TRILLER Nicobars, Malay Peninsula, Sumatra, W Java, Borneo, Celebes, Philippines and some adjacent small islands / forest edge and secondary growth / insects / n tree / e 2

Lalage sueurii (*Vieillot*) WHITE-WINGED TRILLER E Java, Lesser Sundas, S Celebes and islands in Celebes Sea: interior of Australia migrating to N Australia and SE New Guinea (discontinuous) / open forest and woodland / insects / n tree / e 2–3

Lalage aurea (*Temminck*) MOLUCCAN TRILLER N Moluccas

Lalage atrovirens (*Gray*) BLACK-BROWED TRILLER N New Guinea, W Papuan Islands, Biak, Tanimber Is / forest / fruit

Lalage leucomela (*Vigors and Horsfield*) WHITE-BROWED TRILLER E Australia, Kei Is, Aru Is, New Guinea, E Papuan Is, Bismarck Archipelago / open forest, savannah and mangrove / fruit and insects / n tree / e 1

Lalage maculosa (*Peale*) POLYNESIAN TRILLER New Hebrides, Fiji, Tonga, Samoa and adjacent islands / clearings in forest and bush, and cultivation / insects

Lalage sharpei *Rothschild* SAMOA TRILLER Upolu, Samoa / ? no data

Lalage leucopyga (*Gould*) LONG-TAILED TRILLER Solomons, New Hebrides, Loyalty Is, New Caledonia and Norfolk Is

Campephaga phoenicea (*Latham*) RED-SHOULDERED CUCKOO SHRIKE Africa S of Sahara / forest and woodland / insects / n tree / e 2

[**C. petiti** (*Oustalet*) parts of Equatorial Africa, may be a distinct species, but is generally treated as a race of *C. phoenicea* (see Chapin, *Bull Amer Mus Nat Hist*, 75A (1953), p 201 and Peters, *Check List of Birds of the World*, vol 9, p 205 footnote 2; Mackworth-Praed and Grant treat it as a species in *African Handbook of Birds*, Ser 2, vol 2, p 400]

Campephaga quiscalina *Finsch* PURPLE-THROATED CUCKOO SHRIKE Equatorial belt of Africa / deep forest / insects / n and e n/k

Campephaga lobata (*Temminck*) WATTLED CUCKOO SHRIKE Equatorial belt of Africa from Ghana to Lake Tanganyika / forest / insects / n and e n/k

Campephaga sulphurata *Lichtenstein* BLACK CUCKOO SHRIKE Africa S of the Equatorial belt / forest / caterpillars, fruit and tree seeds / n tree / e 2 (*C. hartlaubi* Salvadori, is a colour phase)

Pericrocotus roseus (*Vieillot*) ROSY MINIVET Himalayas from Afghanistan through N Burma and Thailand to Szechwan and China S of Yangtse w in plains of N India and SE Asia / forest / insects / n tree / e 3–4

Pericrocotus divaricatus (*Raffles*) ASHY MINIVET Amurland, Manchuria, Korea, Taiwan and Japan w S through China, SE Asia and Indonesia / forest / insects / n tree / e 4–7 / I ♀

Pericrocotus tegimae *Stejneger* RYUKYU MINIVET Ryukyu Islands and islands S of Kyushu

Pericrocotus cinnamomeus (*L*) SMALL MINIVET Indian sub-continent, SE Asia, Java, Bali, Paláwan, Sumatra, Simalur, Andamans, Billiton and Borneo / thorn-jungle and scrub / n tree / e 2–4 / I ♀

Pericrocotus lansbergei *Büttikofer* SUMBAWA MINIVET Sumbawa and Flores

Pericrocotus erythropygius (*Jerdon*) WHITE-BELLIED MINIVET Dry zone of Sind, Peninsular India and C Burma / dry forest and semi-desert / insects and spiders / n bush / e 3 / I ♀

BUCEROTIDAE: *Rhyticeros* species

Plate 180

CAPITONIDAE: *Megalaima asiatica*, Blue-throated Barbet

Plate 181

Pericrocotus solaris *Blyth* YELLOW-THROATED MINIVET Mountains from Himalayas through SE Asia to S China, W Sumatra and N Borneo/ open forest/insects/n tree/e 3

Pericrocotus ethologus *Bangs and Phillips* LONG-TAILED MINIVET E Afghanistan, Himalayas, SE Asia and parts of China to Manchuria/ open forest/insects/n tree/e 3–4

Pericrocotus brevirostris (*Vigors*) SHORT-BILLED MINIVET Himalayas, SE Asia and SE China/forest and cultivation/insects and buds/ n tree

Pericrocotus miniatus (*Temminck*) SUNDA MINIVET Mts of Java and W Sumatra

Pericrocotus flammeus (*Forster*) SCARLET MINIVET Indian sub-continent, SE Asia, SE China and Hainan, Greater Sundas to Philippines, Bali and Lombok/forest/insects/n tree/ e 2–3/I ♀ (?♂)/the eggs of this group of forms are so peculiarly variable as to suggest that more than one species may be involved

Hemipus picatus (*Sykes*) PIED FLYCATCHER SHRIKE India and Ceylon, SE Asia, W Sumatra and NE Borneo/scrub and forest/insects/n tree/ e 2–3/I ♂♀

Hemipus hirundinaceus (*Temminck*) BLACK-WINGED PYGMY TRILLER Malay Peninsula, Sumatra and adjacent islands, Billiton, Borneo, Java and Bali

Tephrodornis gularis (*Raffles*) LARGE WOOD SHRIKE India, SE Asia, Fukien, Sumatra, Java and Borneo/forest and open woodland/insects/ n tree/e 2–4/I ♂♀

Tephrodornis pondicerianus (*Gmelin*) COMMON WOOD SHRIKE Indian sub-continent and SE Asia/scrub jungle/insects and spiders/ n tree/e 3–4/I ♂♀

PYCNONOTIDAE Bulbuls Moderate-sized passerines, generally drab in colour, but many species are noted for their songs. They are noisy and gregarious, inhabiting woodland and cultivation. The nest is an open cup in a tree, eggs 2–5 in number, usually of a beautiful mottled purplish-pink colour. Incubation is usually by the female. About 120 species ranging through Africa and tropical Asia.

Spizixos canifrons *Blyth* CRESTED FINCHBILL Assam, N parts of SE Asia and W Yunnan/ forest and scrub/seeds, fruit and insects/n bush/ e 2–4

Spizixos semitorques *Swinhoe* COLLARED FINCHBILL S China and Taiwan/hill scrub/n tree or bush/e 3–4

Pycnonotus zeylanicus (*Gmelin*) STRAW-COLOURED BULBUL Malay Peninsula, Sumatra, Nias, Java and Borneo

Pycnonotus striatus (*Blyth*) STRIATED BULBUL Himalayas through hills of SE Asia to W and S Yunnan/forest/berries and insects/n bush/ e 3

Pycnonotus leucogrammicus (*Müller*) STREAKED BULBUL W Sumatra/mountains

Pycnonotus tympanistrigus (*Müller*) OLIVE-CROWNED BULBUL W Sumatra/mountains

Pycnonotus melanoleucos (*Eyton*) BLACK AND WHITE BULBUL Malay Peninsula, Sumatra, Siberut, Borneo

Pycnonotus priocephalus (*Jerdon*) GREY-HEADED BULBUL SW India (Bombay to Kerala) hills/swamp-jungle/fruit and insects/n bush/ e 1–2

Pycnonotus atriceps (*Temminck*) BLACK-HEADED BULBUL Andamans, Bangladesh through S part of SE Asia; Sumatra and W Sumatran islands, Bangka, Billiton, Java, Bali, Borneo, Paláwan, Bawean and Maratua/gardens and light forest/berries and insects/n tree/e 2–3

Pycnonotus melanicterus (*Gmelin*) YELLOW BULBUL Indian sub-continent, SE Asia, Sumatra, Java and northern Borneo/forest and scrub/fruit and insects/n bush/e 2–4/I ♂♀

Pycnonotus squamatus (*Temminck*) SCALY-BREASTED BULBUL Malay Peninsula, Sumatra, Java, Borneo

Pycnonotus cyaniventris *Blyth* GREY-BELLIED BULBUL Malay Peninsula, Sumatra and Borneo

Pycnonotus jocosus (*L*) RED-WHISKERED BULBUL India, SE Asia and S China, Andamans, introduced to New South Wales, Nicobar Is, and Mauritius/scrub and cultivation/fruit, nectar and insects/n bush/e 2–3/I 12–14

Pycnonotus xanthorrhous *Anderson* ANDERSON'S or BROWN-BREASTED BULBUL S China and the northern part of SE Asia/hill scrub/n bush/e 2–3

Pycnonotus sinensis (*Gmelin*) CHINESE BULBUL S China, N Vietnam, Hainan, Taiwan and S Ryukyu Is/scrub and cultivation/ n bush or tree/e 3–5

Pycnonotus taivanus *Styan* STYAN'S BULBUL Taiwan/n ground/e n/s

Pycnonotus leucogenys (*Gray*) WHITE-CHEEKED BULBUL Iraq, Persian Gulf area, S

Afghanistan, Pakistan and Himalayas to E Assam / scrub, cultivation and semi-desert/ fruit, nectar and insects / n bush / e 2–4 / I 24 (*P. leucotis* (Gould) 'White-eared Bulbul' is sometimes considered a separate species)

Pycnonotus cafer (*L*) RED-VENTED BULBUL Indian sub-continent, Burma and W Yunnan, introduced Fiji / hill scrub and cultivation/ fruit, nectar and insects / n tree or bush / e 2–3/ I ♂♀ 14 (see note under *P. aurigaster*)

Pycnonotus aurigaster (*Vieillot*) WHITE-EARED or YELLOW-VENTED BULBUL SE Asia, S China, Java, introduced Sumatra and Singapore/ hill scrub / fruit, nectar and insects / n tree or bush / e 2–3 [NB: *P. cafer* and *P. aurigaster* appear to be imperfectly separated, and where they overlap in range on the Burma-Thailand border, a number of persistent and fertile hybrids occur. These have been given such names as *P. burmanicus* and *P. nigropileus*]

Pycnonotus xanthopygos (*Ehrenberg*) BLACK-CAPPED BULBUL Turkey to W Arabia (see note under *P. barbatus*)

Pycnonotus nigricans (*Vieillot*) RED-EYED BULBUL Parts of S Africa N to Angola / hot dry areas / fruit / n tree / e 3–5

Pycnonotus capensis (*L*) CAPE BULBUL Extreme S Africa / scrub / fruit / n bush / e 2–3

Pycnonotus barbatus (*Desfontaine*) COMMON BULBUL Whole of Africa / ubiquitous / fruit and berries / n tree, bush or herbage / e 2–3 (NB: the relationships of the various forms here included in the *barbatus* assemblage are complicated. Some authorities separate *P. dodsoni* Sharpe, and *P. tricolor* (Hartlaub). Mackworth Praed and Grant place the races *layardi*, *micrus* and *spurius* in the species *P. xanthopygos*, thus extending its range into E Africa.)

Pycnonotus eutilotus (*Jardine and Selby*) PUFF-BACKED BULBUL Malay Peninsula, Sumatra, Bangka, Billiton and Borneo

Pycnonotus nieuwenhuisii (*Finsch*) BLUE-WATTLED BULBUL Sumatra: Borneo (2 races, each known only from a very restricted area)

Pycnonotus urostictus (*Salvadori*) YELLOW-WATTLED BULBUL Philippines

Pycnonotus bimaculatus (*Horsfield*) ORANGE-SPOTTED BULBUL Highlands of Sumatra, Java and Bali

Pycnonotus finlaysoni *Strickland* STREAK-THROATED BULBUL SE Asia / scrub-jungle and cultivation / n tree or bush / e ?3

Pycnonotus xantholaemus (*Jerdon*) YELLOW-THROATED BULBUL Kerala, Mysore and E Ghats of India / sparse thorn scrub jungle / berries and insects / n bush / e 2–3

Pycnonotus pencillatus *Blyth* YELLOW-TUFTED BULBUL Highlands of Ceylon. / ravine-jungle and cultivation / n bush or shrub / e 2

Pycnonotus flavescens *Blyth* BLYTH'S or FLAVESCENT BULBUL Assam through Burma, W Yunnan, N Thailand, Laos, Tonkin and Annam: highlands of northern Borneo / forest and secondary growth / berries and insects/ n bush / e 2–4 / I ♂♀

Pycnonotus goiavier (*Scopoli*) YELLOW-VENTED BULBUL Cochin-China, S Cambodia, S Thailand, Malay Peninsula, Sumatra, Bangka, Billiton, Java, Bali, Lombok, Borneo and Philippines

Pycnonotus luteolus (*Lesson*) WHITE-BROWED BULBUL Ceylon and coasts of Peninsular India/ dry scrub / fruit, nectar and insects / n bush / e 2

Pycnonotus plumosus *Blyth* OLIVE-WINGED BULBUL Malay Peninsula, Sumatra, Java, Borneo, Paláwan and intervening small islands

Pycnonotus blanfordi *Jerdon* BLANFORD'S BULBUL From S Burma, Thailand and C Indo-China S to N Malaya / thorn scrub / n tree or bush / e 2–3

Pycnonotus simplex *Lesson* WHITE-EYED BULBUL Malay Peninsula, Sumatra (and islands), Java, Bangka, Billiton, Borneo, Anamba and Natuna Is

Pycnonotus brunneus *Blyth* RED-EYED BULBUL Malay Peninsula, Sumatra, Borneo and adjacent islands

Pycnonotus erythropthalmos (*Hume*) SPECTACLED BULBUL Malay Peninsula, Borneo, Billiton, Sumatra and West Sumatran islands

Pycnonotus masukuensis (*Shelley*) SHELLEY'S GREENBUL Mts of Tanganyika, N Malawi, W Kenya and the Ituri Forest / forest near water/ insects and fruit / n tree / e 2

Pycnonotus montanus (*Reichenow*) CAMEROON MOUNTAIN BULBUL Mts of Cameroon / secondary growth and forest clearings/ fruit and insects / n and e n/k

Pycnonotus virens (*Cassin*) LITTLE GREENBUL Equatorial belt of Africa, including Zanzibar and Fernando Po / from mountain forest to lowland scrub / seeds and berries / n bush or herbage / e 2

Pycnonotus hallae (*Prigogine*) (*Bull Brit Orn*

Opposite:
RAMPHASTIDAE:
Ramphastos dicolorus,
Red-breasted Toucan

RAMPHASTIDAE:
Ramphastos cuvieri,
Cuvier's Toucan

RAMPHASTIDAE:
Ramphastos cuvieri,
Cuvier's Toucan

Plate 182

Plate 183

Cl, vol 92 (1972), p 138) MRS HALL'S BULBUL E Zaire / no data

Pycnonotus gracilis (*Cabanis*) LITTLE GREY GREENBUL Africa from Sierra Leone to Uganda / forest / insects and fruit / n n/s / e 2

Pycnonotus ansorgei (*Hartert*) ANSORGE'S BULBUL Sierra Leone to E Congo, parts of Kenya / forest / insects and fruit / n and e n/k

Pycnonotus curvirostris (*Cassin*) CASSIN'S BULBUL Sierra Leone to Kenya, Fernando Po / forest / berries / n and e n/k

Pycnonotus importunus (*Vieillot*) SOMBRE GREENBUL E and S Africa from Somaliland to Cape Province / bush and cultivation / berries and insects / n shrub / e 2

Pycnonotus latirostris (*Strickland*) YELLOW-WHISKERED GREENBUL Equatorial belt of Africa, including Fernando Po / forest / fruit and insects / n shrub or herbage / e 2

Pycnonotus gracilirostris (*Strickland*) SLENDER-BILLED GREENBUL Equatorial belt of Africa, including Fernando Po / thick forest / fruit, seeds and grasshoppers / n and e n/k

Pycnonotus tephrolaemus (*Gray*) GREY-THROATED GREENBUL or OLIVE-BREASTED MOUNTAIN GREENBUL Equatorial belt of Africa from Nigeria eastwards, including Fernando Po / mountain forest / fruit and insects / n shrub / e 1–2 (some authorities separate *nigriceps* (Shelley) 'Kilimanjaro Bulbul')

Pycnonotus milanjensis (*Shelley*) STRIPED-CHEEKED GREENBUL E Africa from SE Kenya to Mozambique / lower highland, forest and scrub / seeds, fruit and worms / n bush or tree / e 2

Calyptocichla serina (*Verreaux*) GOLDEN BULBUL or SERINE GREENBUL Forests from Sierra Leone to E Congo / forest and secondary forest / ? fruit / n and e n/k

Baeopogon indicator (*Verreaux*) HONEYGUIDE GREENBUL Equatorial belt of Africa from Sierra Leone to S Sudan and Angola / tree-tops in high forest / fruit / n ? tree / e ?2

Baeopogon clamans (*Sjöstedt*) SJÖSTEDT'S or WHITE-TAILED GREENBUL British Cameroons to NE Congo / forest / berries and wasps / n and e n/k

Ixonotus guttatus *Verreaux* SPOTTED GREENBUL Liberia to E Congo and Uganda / forest / fruit and insects / n shrub or large herb / e n/s

Chlorocichla falkensteini (*Reichenow*) YELLOW-THROATED BULBUL British Cameroons to N Angola and Lower Congo / secondary growth and forest clearings / berries / n shrub or tree / e 2

Chlorocichla simplex (*Hartlaub*) SIMPLE LEAFLOVE Forests from Portuguese Guinea to Angola, Congo and Kasai / forest clearings and undergrowth / fruit / n bush or tree / e 2

Chlorocichla flavicollis (*Swainson*) YELLOW-THROATED LEAFLOVE Equatorial belt of Africa / forest and open woodland / fruit and insects / n bush / e 2

Chlorocichla flaviventris (*Smith*) YELLOW-BELLIED GREENBUL E and S Africa from Kenya to Angola, SW Africa and Natal / lowland scrub / seeds, berries and insects / n shrub, tree or herbage / e 2

Chlorocichla laetissima (*Sharpe*) JOYFUL GREENBUL Congo, Uganda, S Sudan and W Kenya / forests above 4,000ft (1,200m) / berries / n and e n/k

Chlorocichla prigoginei de Roo (*Rev Zool Bot Afr*, 75 (1967), p 392) PRIGOGINE'S GREENBUL Maboya-Butemba, NW of Lake Edward / no data, discovered in a collection of museum skins, and otherwise unknown

Thescelocichla leucopleura (*Cassin*) WHITE-TAILED or SWAMP GREENBUL Equatorial belt of Africa from Sierra Leone to Congo and W Uganda / swamp palms / fruit and insects / n and e n/k

Phyllastrephus scandens *Swainson* COMMON LEAFLOVE Equatorial belt of Africa from Senegal to Tanganyika / thickets on river banks / insects / n in creepers / e 2

Phyllastrephus terrestris *Swainson* TERRESTRIAL BROWNBUL E and S Africa from Kenya to Angola and Cape Province / scrub and bush / insects / n bush / e 2

Phyllastrephus strepitans (*Reichenow*) NORTHERN BROWNBUL E Africa from S Sudan to Tanganyika / scrub and lowland forest / insects / n and e n/k

Phyllastrephus cerviniventris (*Shelley*) GREY-OLIVE GREENBUL E Africa from Kenya to Mozambique / forests / insects / n shrub / e 2

Phyllastrephus fulviventris (*Cabanis*) PALE OLIVE GREENBUL Lower Congo and W Angola / gallery forest and river scrub / n and e n/k

Phyllastrephus hypochloris (*Jackson*) TORO GREENBUL S Sudan to Uganda and E Congo / forests / insects / n and e n/k

Phyllastrephus poensis (*Alexander*) CAMEROON OLIVE GREENBUL Fernando Po, S Nigeria and Cameroons / forest / insects / n shrub / e 2

Phyllastrephus baumanni (*Reichenow*) BAUMANN'S GREENBUL Sierra Leone to S Nigeria / forest / ants and berries / n and e n/k

Phyllastrephus poliocephalus (*Reichenow*) YELLOW-BELLIED BULBUL SE Nigeria and British Cameroon / rain forest above 4,000ft (1,200m) / ? insects / n and e n/k

Phyllastrephus flavostriatus (*Sharpe*) YELLOW-STREAKED GREENBUL E Africa from Tanganyika to E Cape Province / scrub and forest / insects / n shrub / e 2 (some authorities separate *P. alfredi* (Shelley))

Phyllastrephus debilis (*Sclater*) SLENDER GREENBUL E Africa from Kenya to Mozambique / mountain forest / insects / n tree / e n/k

Phyllastrephus lorenzi *Sassi* SASSI'S GREENBUL E Congo forests / known only from very few specimens no data

Phyllastrephus albigularis (*Sharpe*) WHITE-THROATED GREENBUL Sierra Leone to Uganda and N Angola / forests / insects / n shrub / e 2

Phyllastrephus fischeri (*Reichenow*) FISCHER'S GREENBUL Coastal belt of E Africa from Tana River to Netia / lowland forest / insects and fruit / n undergrowth / e 2

Phyllastrephus placidus (*Shelley*) SHELLEY'S GREENBUL Highlands from Kenya to Mozambique / mountain forest / insects and fruit / n undergrowth / e 2 (see note to *P. cabanisi*)

Phyllastrephus cabanisi (*Sharpe*) CABANIS' GREENBUL S Sudan to Tanganyika, Congo and Angola / forest / insects and fruit / n undergrowth / e 2 [NB: *cabanisi* and *placidus* are usually treated as races of *fischeri*, but Dowsett in *Bull Brit Orn Cl* (1972), p 132, says they are best separated]

Phyllastrephus orostruthus *Vincent* DAPPLED BULBUL Amani Forest (Tanganyika) and Namuli Mt (Mozambique) – 2 races, each little known / mountain forests

Phyllastrephus icterinus (*Bonaparte*) ICTERINE GREENBUL Fernando Po and Sierra Leone to Uganda and mouth of River Congo / forest / insects / n shrub / e 2

Phyllastrephus xavieri (*Oustalet*) XAVIER'S GREENBUL Cameroon through Congo forests to W Uganda / forest / fruit and insects / n shrub / e 2

Phyllastrephus madagascariensis (*Gmelin*) COMMON TETRAKA Madagascar / forest / insects / n and e ? n/k

Phyllastrephus zosterops (*Sharpe*) SHORT-BILLED TETRAKA Madagascar / forest and scrub / insects / n and e ? n/k

Phyllastrephus tenebrosus (*Stresemann*) DUSKY TETRAKA EC Magadascar / no data

Phyllastrephus xanthrophrys (*Sharpe*) YELLOW-BROWED FODITANY EC Magadascar / forest

Phyllastrephus cinereiceps (*Sharpe*) GREY-CROWNED FODITANY E Madagascar / forest and scrub

Phyllastrephus apperti *Colston* COLSTON'S BULBUL SW Madagascar / 2 specimens / see Colston, *Ibis* (1972), pp 89–92 for all that is known of this species

Bleda syndactyla (*Swainson*) COMMON BRISTLEBILL Equatorial belt of Africa from Senegal to Kenya and Zambia / dense undergrowth / food n/k / n bush / e 2

Bleda eximia (*Hartlaub*) GREEN-TAILED BRISTLEBILL Fernando Po and Sierra Leone to Congo, Uganda and S Sudan / undergrowth / insects / n and e n/k

Bleda canicapilla (*Hartlaub*) GREY-HEADED BRISTLEBILL Sierra Leone to S Nigeria / forest undergrowth / ants / n among creepers / e 2

Nicator chloris (*Valenciennes*) YELLOW-SPOTTED NICATOR Equatorial belt of Africa from Senegal to Uganda / forest / n tree or bush / e 2

Nicator gularis *Hartlaub and Finsch* EASTERN NICATOR E Africa from Kenya to Natal / forest / n tree or bush / e ?2

Nicator vireo *Cabanis* YELLOW-THROATED NICATOR C Africa from Cameroons to Angola and W Uganda / forest / n and e n/k (the genus *Nicator* is placed in the Laniidae by some authors)

Criniger barbatus (*Temminck*) BEARDED BULBUL Equatorial Africa from Sierra Leone to Congo Basin / forest / insects and seeds / n and e n/k

Criniger calurus (*Cassin*) RED-TAILED GREENBUL Equatorial Africa from Sierra Leone to Congo and Uganda / forests / fruit and insects / n tree / e 2 (see note to *C. olivaceus*)

Criniger ndussumensis *Reichenow* WHITE-BEARDED BULBUL S Nigeria to Congo / forest / n and e no definite information (see note to *C. olivaceus*)

RAMPHASTIDAE: *Ramphastos swainsonii*, Swainson's Toucan, Chestnut-mandibled Toucan

Plate 184

RAMPHASTIDAE:
Ramphastos toco,
Toco Toucan

RAMPHASTIDAE:
Ramphastos vitellinus,
Channel-billed Toucan

Plate 185

Criniger olivaceus (*Swainson*) OLIVE BULBUL Senegal to Ghana, and S Nigeria to N Congo/forest / n and e no definite information [NB: *calurus*, *ndussumensis* and *olivaceus* intergrade in places and their relationship is not properly understood. They are treated as species here, though authorities are by no means agreed on this. See Hall, *An Atlas of Speciation in African Passerine Birds*, p 69 for comments]

Criniger finschii *Salvadori* FINSCH'S BULBUL Malaya, Sumatra and Borneo

Criniger flaveolus (*Gould*) WHITE-THROATED BULBUL Himalayas from Garwhal to mts of Burma and W Thailand/evergreen jungle/fruit and insects/n bush/e 3–4/I 13 ♂♀

Criniger pallidus *Swinhoe* PUFF-THROATED BULBUL SE Asia, S Yunnan and Hainan/forest/insects, seeds and fruit/n bush/e 2–4

Criniger ochraceus *Moore* (sometimes credited to *Horsfield and Moore*) OCHRACEOUS BULBUL Southern SE Asia, Sumatra and northern Borneo / forest / insects, seeds and fruit/n tree or bush/e 2–4

Criniger bres (*Lesson*) GREY-CHEEKED BEARDED BULBUL Malay Peninsula, E Sumatra, Java, Bali, Borneo and Pálawan

Criniger phaeocephalus (*Hartlaub*) CRESTLESS BULBUL Malay Peninsula, Sumatra, Borneo and the intervening islands

Setornis criniger *Lesson* LONG-BILLED BULBUL E Sumatra, Bangka and Borneo

Hypsipetes viridescens (*Blyth*) VIRIDESCENT BULBUL Assam, Burma and SW Thailand/forest and secondary growth/berries and (?) insects/n bush/e 3

Hypsipetes propinquus (*Oustalet*) GREY-EYED BULBUL SE Asia

Hypsipetes charlottae (*Finsch*) CHARLOTTE'S, FINSCH'S OLIVE BULBUL or DULL-BROWN BULBUL Malay Peninsula, Sumatra, Borneo and intervening islands

Hypsipites palawanensis (*Tweeddale*) GOLDEN-EYED BULBUL Pálawan

Hypsipetes criniger (*Blyth*) HAIRY-BACKED BULBUL Malay Peninsula, Sumatra, N Natuna Is, Mansalar, Borneo

Hypsipetes philippinus (*Forster*) RUFOUS-BREASTED BULBUL Philippines

Hypsipetes rufigularis *Sharpe* ZAMBOANGA BULBUL Mindanao and Basilan

Hypsipetes siquijorensis (*Steere*) SIQUIJOR BULBUL Tablas, Romblón, Cebú and Siquijor

Hypsipetes everetti (*Tweeddale*) EVERETT'S or YELLOW-WASHED BULBUL Philippines and Sulu Archipelago

Hypsipetes affinis (*Hombron and Jacquinot*) MOLUCCAN BULBUL Moluccas, Sangi, Togian, Sula and Banggai Is

Hypsipetes indicus (*Jerdon*) YELLOW-BROWED BULBUL S India and Ceylon / secondary jungle and cultivation/fruit and insects/n tree/e 2–3

Hypsipetes mcclellandii *Horsfield* MCCLELLAND'S BULBUL Himalayas, SE Asia and S China/open forest and secondary growth/fruit/n tree/e 2–4

Hypsipetes malaccensis *Blyth* STREAKED or GREEN-BACKED BULBUL Cochin China, Malay Peninsula, Lingga, Sumatra, Bangka and Borneo

Hypsipetes virescens (*Temminck*) GREEN-WINGED or SUMATRAN BULBUL Mts of Java and W Sumatra

Hypsipetes flavala (*Blyth*) ASHY or BROWN-EARED BULBUL Himalayas, SE Asia, S China and Hainan, Sumatra, northern Borneo/forest/berries, nectar and insects/n bush/e 2–4/I ♂♀ 13–14 [Edwards separates *H. castanotus* 'Chestnut Bulbul' and gives the distribution as Oriental mainland, but this is misleading as the type-locality of *Hemixus castanonotus* Swinhoe (which I assume is the form referred to, and which is usually treated as a race of *H. flavala*), is the island of Hainan]

Hypsipetes amaurotis (*Temminck*) BROWN-EARED BULBUL Japan, Bonin, Volcano and Ryukyu Is, Taiwan, Philippines / Japanese races winter in Korea and China/forest and habitation / insects and fruit / n tree or shrub/e 3–5

Hypsipetes crassirostris *Newton* SEYCHELLES or THICK-BILLED BULBUL Seychelles / forest/n tree/e 2

Hypsipetes borbonicus (*Forster*) OLIVACEOUS BULBUL Réunion and Mauritius / forest

Hypsipetes madagascariensis (*Müller*) BLACK BULBUL From Madagascar through islands of Indian Ocean, S and SE Asia to Taiwan, S China and Hainan / forest and cultivation/fruit, nectar and insects / n tree or bush/e 2–4

Hypsipetes nicobariensis *Moore* NICOBAR BULBUL Nicobars/forest and gardens/no other data

Hypsipetes thompsoni (*Bingham*) BINGHAM'S

BULBUL S Burma and NW Thailand/hill forest/
n hole in bank or low herbage on bankside,
almost on the ground/e 2–4

Neolestes torquatus *Cabanis* BLACK-COLLARED
BULBUL Gabon, N Angola and Congo / grassy
woodland /fruit/n bush/e 2

Tylas eduardi *Hartlaub* KINKIMAVO Madagas-
car/forest and bush/insects/n and e ?n/k

**IRENIDAE Ioras, Leafbirds and Fairy
Bluebirds** Bulbul-like birds, but sexually
dimorphic, the males being comparatively
brightly coloured. Feed mainly on fruit and
nectar, but some seeds and insects are taken.
They are forest birds, building tree nests and
laying 2–4 eggs.

Aegithina tiphia (*L*) COMMON IORA Indian
sub-continent, SE Asia, Indonesia (part)/open
forest and scrub-jungle / insects and spiders/
n tree / e 2–4/ I ♂♀

Aegithina nigrolutea (*Marshall*) MARSHALL'S
IORA NC India/thorn and scrub-jungle/insects
and spiders/n tree/e 2–3

Aegithina viridissima (*Bonaparte*) GREEN
IORA Malaya and peninsular Thailand, Sumatra,
Borneo and adjacent islands

Aegithina lafresnayei (*Hartlaub*) GREAT IORA
Thailand, Indo-China and S Burma

Chloropsis flavipennis (*Tweeddale*) YELLOW-
QUILLED LEAFBIRD Cebu and Mindanao

Chloropsis palawanensis (*Sharpe*) PALAWAN
LEAFBIRD Paláwan

Chloropsis sonnerati *Jardine and Selby*
GREAT GREEN LEAFBIRD Malay Peninsula,
Sumatra, Java, Borneo and adjacent islands

Chloropsis cyanopogon (*Temminck*) LESSER
GREEN LEAFBIRD Thailand and Malaya,
Sumatra, Borneo and Banguey

Chloropsis cochinchinensis (*Gmelin*)
JERDON'S, GOLDMANTLED or BLUE-WINGED
LEAFBIRD Ceylon and S India: Assam and SE
Asia, Sumatra, Java, Borneo, Billiton and
Natuna Is/scrub-jungle and cultivation/insects,
fruit and nectar/n tree/e 2–3

Chloropsis aurifrons (*Temminck*) GOLDEN-
FRONTED LEAFBIRD India and Ceylon, southern
SE Asia (not Malaya), Sumatra / forest and
scrub/insects and berries/n tree/e 2–3

Chloropsis hardwickei *Jardine and Selby*
ORANGE-BELLIED LEAFBIRD Himalayas, northern
SE Asia, S China, Hainan, Malaya/forest and
scrub/insects, fruit and nectar/n tree/e 3

Chloropsis venusta (*Bonaparte*) MASKED

LEAFBIRD Sumatra

Irena puella (*Latham*) FAIRY BLUEBIRD India,
SE Asia, Sumatra, Java, Borneo and adjacent
islands, Paláwan, Balábec and Calamianes/
forest and coffee plantations / fruit and nectar/
n tree / e 2–3/I ♀

Irena cyanogaster *Vigors* PHILIPPINE
BLUEBIRD Philippines

LANIIDAE Shrikes Small to medium-sized
birds with large, broad heads; stout, hooked
bills and predatory habits. They feed mainly
on large insects, but also on small birds,
mammals and reptiles, and have a habit of
keeping a larder of corpses impaled on thorns.
The nest is in a bush or tree, eggs 3–6 in number,
and incubation, which lasts 14–16 days as a
rule, is generally by the female. About 73
species, all but one confined to the Old World.

Eurocephalus rueppelli *Bonaparte* RÜPPELL'S
WHITE-CROWNED SHRIKE E Africa from S
Sudan to Tanganyika / open woodland / n tree
or shrub/e 2–3

Eurocephalus anguitimens *Smith* SMITH'S
WHITE-CROWNED SHRIKE Rhodesia to Bechuanaland and SW Africa / open woodland and
bush/n tree/e 2–3

Prionops plumata (*Shaw*) STRAIGHT-CRESTED
HELMET SHRIKE Africa S of Sahara (except
extreme S)/open bush and woodland/insects/
n tree or shrub/e 3–4

Prionops poliolopha *Fischer and Reichenow*
GREY-CRESTED HELMET SHRIKE Kenya and W
Tanganyika / open woodland and bush / n tree/
e n/s

Prionops cristata *Rüppell* CURLY-CRESTED
HELMET SHRIKE Cameroon to Sudan and
Uganda / open woodland and bush / insects/
n shrub or tree/e 4

Prionops caniceps (*Bonaparte*) RED-BILLED
HELMET SHRIKE Sierra Leone to Congo and
Uganda/forest /n and e n/k

Prionops alberti *Schouteden* YELLOW-CRESTED
HELMET SHRIKE Mts above 4,500ft (1,350m)
from W of Lake Edward to W of Lake Tan-
ganyika/n tree/e n/k

Prionops retzii *Wahlberg* RETZ'S HELMET
SHRIKE E Africa from Somaliland to Bechuanaland and SW Africa / forest / insects / n tree or
bush/e 3–4

Prionops gabela *Rand* ANGOLA HELMET
SHRIKE Angola/woodland and forest clearings/
n and e n/k

RAMPHASTIDAE:
Pteroglossus aracari,
Aracari Toucan,
Black-necked Aracari

RAMPHASTIDAE:
Ramphastos sulfuratus,
Keel-billed Toucan

Plate 186

RAMPHASTIDAE: *Andigena cucullata,* Hooded Toucan, Hooded Mountain-Toucan

Plate 187

Prionops scopifrons (*Peters*) CHESTNUT-FRONTED SHRIKE Kenya to Mozambique / open woodland and bush / n tree / e n/k

Lanioturdus torquatus *Waterhouse* CHAT SHRIKE Damaraland N to S Angola / thorn bush / n tree / e n/s

Nilaus afer (*Latham*) BRUBRU SHRIKE Much of Africa S of Sahara / woodland and open bush / n tree / e 2–4 (some authorities separate *N. nigritemporalis* Reichenow)

Dryoscopus pringlii *Jackson* PRINGLE'S PUFFBACK SHRIKE Somaliland to NE Tanganyika / dry thorn scrub / n tree / e n/k

Dryoscopus gambensis (*Lichtenstein*) GAMBIAN PUFFBACK SHRIKE Equatorial belt of Africa from Senegal to Sudan and Tanganyika / bush and habitation / n bush or tree / e 2

Dryoscopus cubla (*Shaw*) BLACK-BACKED PUFFBACK SHRIKE E and S Africa from Kenya to Cape and S Angola / light bush and open woodland / n tree / e 2–3

Dryoscopus senegalensis (*Hartlaub*) RED-EYED PUFFBACK SHRIKE Nigeria to Congo, Tanganyika and Uganda / forest clearings and secondary growth / n tree / e n/k

Dryoscopus angolensis *Hartlaub* PINKFOOTED PUFFBACK SHRIKE C Africa from Cameroon to Lake Tanganyika / forest and dense woodland / n and e n/k

Dryoscopus sabini (*Gray*) SABINE'S PUFFBACK SHRIKE Sierra Leone to Lower Congo / forest and secondary growth / n and e n/k

Tchagra minuta (*Hartlaub*) BLACK-CAPPED BUSH SHRIKE Equatorial belt of Africa S to Angola and Zambia / savannah / n bush / e 2–3

Tchagra senegala (*L*) BLACK-HEADED BUSH SHRIKE S Arabia and almost the whole of Africa / desert scrub, bush and habitation / n tree or bush / e 2–3

Tchagra tchagra (*Vieillot*) TCHAGRA BUSH SHRIKE Cape Province to E Transvaal / thorn bush / n bush / e 2–5

Tchagra australis (*Smith*) BROWN-HEADED BUSH SHRIKE Africa S of Sahara, except extreme S / scrub and savannah / n bush / e 2–3

Tchagra jamesi (*Shelley*) THREE-STREAKED BUSH SHRIKE S Sudan to Kenya and Uganda / thorn scrub / n bush / e 2–3

Tchagra cruenta (*Ehrenberg*) ROSY-PATCHED SHRIKE NE Africa from S Egypt to NE Tanganyika / thorn scrub and aloe desert / n bush / e 2–3

Laniarius ruficeps (*Shelley*) RED-NAPED BUSH SHRIKE Ethiopia to Kenya / scrub / n bush / e 2–3

Laniarius luehderi *Reichenow* LÜHDER'S SHRIKE C Africa from Mt Cameroon to Uganda and Angola / forest clearings / n tree or bush / e 2

Laniarius ferrugineus (*Gmelin*) BOUBOU SHRIKE Africa S of Sahara / forest and scrub / n bush / e 2 (some authorities separate *L. aethiopicus* (Gmelin) 'Tropical Boubou')

Laniarius barbarus (*L*) GONOLEK Equatorial Africa from Senegal to Congo and Ethiopia / thick bush near water / n tree / e 2

Laniarius mufumbiri *Ogilvie-Grant* MUFUMBIRI SHRIKE Papyrus swamps of Lake Edward and N Lake Victoria / ? no data

Laniarius atrococcineus (*Burchell*) CRIMSON-BREASTED BOUBOU SE Africa from Rhodesia to Angola and the Orange River / thorn-jungle / n tree / e 2–3

Laniarius atroflavus *Shelley* YELLOW-BREASTED BOUBOU C Africa / forest / n tree / e n/s

Laniarius funebris (*Hartlaub*) SLATE-COLOURED BOUBOU Ethiopia to Kenya / scrub / n bush / e 2–3

Laniarius leucorhynchus (*Hartlaub*) SOOTY BOUBOU Equatorial Africa from Sierra Leone to Congo and Uganda / forest / n tree / e 2

Laniarius fuelleborni (*Reichenow*) BLACK BOUBOU Fernando Po and E Nigeria to Congo, Uganda and Tanganyika / forest / n tree / e 2

[NB: Some authorities recognise extra species in *Laniarius*, which are here treated as races following Rand in Peters' *Check List*, vol 9]

Telophorus bocagei (*Reichenow*) GREY BUSH SHRIKE C Africa from Cameroon to W Kenya and Angola / forest and secondary growth / n tree / e 2

Telophorus sulphureopectus (*Lesson*) SULPHUR-BREASTED BUSH SHRIKE Much of Africa S of Sahara, except extreme S / scrub and riverine trees / n tree / e 2–3

Telophorus olivaceus (*Shaw*) OLIVE BUSH SHRIKE E Africa from Malawi to Cape Province / forest / n tree or bush / e 2

Telophorus nigrifrons (*Reichenow*) BLACK-FRONTED BUSH SHRIKE E Africa from Kenya to Transvaal / forest / n tree / e 2

Telophorus multicolor (*Gray*) MANY-COLOURED BUSH SHRIKE Equatorial Africa from Sierra Leone to Angola and Lake Tanganyika / forest / n and e n/k

Telophorus kupeensis (*Serle*) SERLE'S BUSH SHRIKE Kupe Mts, British Cameroon / mountain forest / n and e n/k

Telophorus zeylonus (*L*) BOKMAKIERIE S Africa N to Angola and Transvaal / bush and cultivation / n bush / e 3–4

Telophorus viridis (*Vieillot*) PERRIN'S SHRIKE C Angola to S Congo and Zambia / forest / n and e n/k

Telophorus quadricolor (*Cassin*) FOUR-COLOURED BUSH SHRIKE E Africa from Kenya to Natal / thickets and coastal bush / n bush / e 2–3

Telophorus dohertyi (*Rothschild*) DOHERTY'S SHRIKE Mts above 5,000ft (1,500m) in W Kenya, W Uganda and E Congo / dense mountain scrub / n and e n/k

Malaconotus cruentus (*Lesson*) FIERY-BREASTED SHRIKE Equatorial Africa from Sierra Leone to Congo and Uganda / thickets and forest undergrowth / n tree / e 2–3

Malaconotus lagdeni (*Sharpe*) LAGDEN'S SHRIKE Liberia to Ghana: Mts of E Congo basin mountain forest n tree e 2 (1 nest of eastern race known)

Malaconotus gladiator (*Reichenow*) GREEN-BREASTED SHRIKE Forest strips of Cameroon Mt and neighbouring highlands / 4 specimens / no other data

Malaconotus blanchoti (*Stephens*) (=**M. hypopyrrhus** *Hartlaub*, of some authors) GREY-HEADED BUSH SHRIKE Much of Africa S of Sahara, except extreme S / forest and bush / n tree / e 2–3

Malaconotus alius *Friedmann* ULUGURU SHRIKE Uluguru Mts, Tanganyika / forest / n and e n/k

Corvinella corvina (*Shaw*) YELLOW-BILLED or LONG-TAILED SHRIKE Senegal to Sudan and Uganda / woodland and bush / fruit, insects and reptiles / n tree or bush / e 4–5

Corvinella melanoleuca (*Jardine*) MAGPIE SHRIKE E Africa from S Kenya to Angola and Natal / scrub / n thorn bush / e 3–4

Lanius tigrinus *Drapiez* TIGER SHRIKE E Asia from Ussuriland to N China and Japan w S to Indonesia / open forest / insects / n tree / e 3–6

Lanius souzae *Bocage* SOUZA'S SHRIKE Congo basin, Malawi, Zambia, W Tanganyika / woodland / n tree or bush / e 2–3

Lanius bucephalus *Temminck and Schlegel* BULL-HEADED SHRIKE E Asia from Ussuriland to Japan and China / forest clearings and habitation / insects and small birds / n tree or bamboo / e 3–6 / I ♀ 14–15 / F c14

Lanius cristatus *L* BROWN SHRIKE C and E Asia w S to India, SE Asia and Indonesia / scrub and hill forest / insects and small vertebrates / n tree or bush / e 2–6

Lanius collurio *L* RED-BACKED SHRIKE Much of the temperate Palaearctic w S to E Africa / scrub and bush / insects, small birds and mammals / n bush / e 5–7 / I ♀ (?♂) 14–16 / F 12–15 [NB: *Lanius c. collurio* hybridises freely with *L. c. phoenicuroides*; the following names refer to such hybrids: *L. raddei*, *L. darwini*, *L. salina*, *L. bogdanowi*, *L. loudoni*, *L. velizhanini*, *L. zarudnyi*, *L. pseudocollurio*]

Lanius collurioides *Lesson* CHESTNUT-RUMPED or BURMESE SHRIKE Assam, Burma, Thailand and Indo-China / secondary jungle and cultivation / insects and small mammals / n tree / e 3–6

Lanius gubernator *Hartlaub* EMIN'S SHRIKE Portuguese Guinea to Cameroon, NE Congo and Sudan / scrub / n and e n/k

Lanius vittatus *Valenciennes* BAY-BACKED SHRIKE Afghanistan, Baluchistan and NW Indian region / scrub and cultivation / insects and small vertebrates / n bush / e 3–5

Lanius schach *L* RUFOUS-BACKED and BLACK-HEADED SHRIKES (races) C and E Asia from Russian Turkestan and China S to Indian sub-continent, SE Asia and Indonesia as far as New Guinea / open woodland and cultivation / insects and small vertebrates / n tree or bush / e 3–6 / I ♂♀

Lanius tephronotus (*Vigors*) TIBETAN SHRIKE Himalayas, Tibet, Szechwan and Koko Nor w S to N India, northern SE Asia and Yunnan / hill scrub / insects and small vertebrates / n bush / e 4–6

Lanius validirostris *Ogilvie-Grant* STRONG-BILLED SHRIKE Mts of Luzon, Mindoro and Mindanao

Lanius mackinnoni *Sharpe* MACKINNON'S SHRIKE C Africa from Angola to W Kenya and Tanganyika / forest and open woodland / n bush / e 2–3

Lanius minor *Gmelin* LESSER GREY SHRIKE S Europe, W and C Asia w S through Arabia and E Africa / thorn scrub, semi-desert and cultivation / insects / n tree / e 5–7 / I ♂♀ 15 / F c14

Lanius ludovicianus *L* LOGGERHEAD SHRIKE Temperate and tropical N America and Mexico /

PICIDAE:
Dendrocopos major,
Great Spotted Woodpecker

RAMPHASTIDAE:
Aulacorhynchus haematopygus,
Crimson-rumped Toucanet

Plate 188

scrub, orchard and cultivation / insects, invertebrates and small vertebrates / n tree or bush / e 4–6 / I ♂♀ 14

Lanius excubitor *L* GREAT GREY SHRIKE Holarctic, Africa N of Sahara and Indian region w S through Nile Valley to E Africa / semi-desert and dry forest / insects and small vertebrates / n bush or tree / e 5–9 / I ♀ (?♂) 15 / F 19–20

Lanius elegans *Swainson* GREY SHRIKE Arid belt S of Sahara / n bush or tree / e 2–3

Lanius excubitoroides *Prévost and Des Murs* (sometimes quoted as **L. excubitorius**) GREY-BACKED FISCAL SHRIKE Cameroon to Ethiopia, Tanganyika and Congo / bush / n tree or thorn bush / e 2–4

Lanius sphenocercus *Cabanis* WEDGE-TAILED or CHINESE SHRIKE E Asia from Ussuriland and Mongolia S to S China / scrub and meadow / insects and small vertebrates / n tree / e 6 (1 nest known)

Lanius cabanisi *Hartert* LONG-TAILED FISCAL SHRIKE SE Italian Somaliland S to E Tanganyika / scrub / n tree or bush / e 3–4

Lanius dorsalis *Cabanis* TEITA FISCAL SHRIKE Ethiopia to NE Tanganyika / desert bush / n thorn bush / e 3–4

Lanius somalicus *Hartlaub* SOMALI FISCAL SHRIKE E and S Ethiopia and British Somaliland to N Kenya / dry bush / n tree or bush / e 4

Lanius collaris *L* COMMON FISCAL SHRIKE Africa S of Sahara / scrub and open country / n tree or bush / e 2–4

Lanius marwitzi *Reichenow* UHEHE FISCAL SHRIKE SW Tanganyika / bush / n and e n/k

Lanius newtoni *Bocage* NEWTON'S FISCAL SHRIKE São Thomé / no data

Lanius senator *L* WOODCHAT SHRIKE C and S Europe, W Asia to Iran, and the Mediterranean w S to tropical Africa and Arabia / scrub, pasture and woodland / insects and small birds / n tree or bush / e 5–7 / I ♀(♂) 16 / F 19–20

Lanius nubicus *Lichtenstein* MASKED SHRIKE SE Europe, NE Africa and W Asia to Iran / woodland and scrub / insects / n tree or bush / e 4–7

Pityriasis gymnocephala (*Temminck*) BRISTLED SHRIKE Borneo

VANGIDAE Vangas Arboreal birds related to Shrikes, living in forests and confined to Madagascar. Their ancestry is uncertain. They feed on reptiles, insects and batracians. Information on nesting is very scanty, those for which there is information build stick nests in trees.

Calicalicus madagascariensis (*L*) RED-TAILED VANGA or TIT SHRIKE E, N and W Madagascar

Schetba rufa (*L*) RUFOUS VANGA E and W Madagascar

Vanga curvirostris *L* HOOK-BILLED VANGA Madagascar

Xenopirostris xenopirostris (*Lafresnaye*) LAFRESNAYE'S VANGA SW Madagascar / arid brush

Xenopirostris damii *Schlegel* VAN DAM'S VANGA NW Madagascar

Xenopirostris polleni (*Schlegel*) POLLEN'S VANGA NW Madagascar coast and E forests

Falculea palliata *Geoffroy St Hilaire* SICKLEBILLED VANGA or FALCULEA N, W and S Madagascar / forest and dense savannah / n tree

Leptopterus viridis (*Müller*) WHITE-HEADED VANGA E and W Madagascar

Leptopterus chabert (*Müller*) CHABERT VANGA Madagascar / forest and dense savannah

Leptopterus madagascarinus (*L*) BLUE VANGA Madagascar and Grand Comoro

Oriolia bernieri *Geoffroy St. Hilaire* BERNIER'S VANGA E Madagascar

Euryceros prevostii *Lesson* HELMETBIRD E Madagascar

BOMBYCILLIDAE Waxwings, Silky Flycatchers and the Hypocolius This family consists of three groups of birds of uncertain affinities. They are fruit-eating arboreal birds with soft silky plumage. Waxwings are remarkable for the waxy tips to the secondaries. Some authorities consider that the three groups here placed together merit separate family rank. (*Phainopepla* and *Phainoptila* belong with the Silky Flycatchers)

Bombycilla garrulus (*L*) BOHEMIAN WAXWING Coniferous forest belt of Holarctic, spreading further S in winter / berries / n tree / e 4–7 / I ♀ 14

Bombycilla japonica (*Siebold*) JAPANESE WAXWING b E Siberia from Aldan to Amur w Japan / coniferous forest / insects and berries / n and e n/k

Bombycilla cedrorum (*Vieillot*) CEDAR WAXWING b N America from Alaska to Georgia w S to Caribbean / coniferous forest / flowers, fruit and insects / n tree / e 3–6 / I 12–13

Ptilogonys cinereus *Swainson* GREY SILKY FLYCATCHER Mexico and W Guatemala

Ptilogonys caudatus *Cabanis* LONG-TAILED SILKY FLYCATCHER Costa Rica and W Panama/ open woodland and parkland/n and e ? n/k

Phainopepla nitens (*Swainson*) PHAINOPEPLA SW USA and Mexico/scrub and semi-desert/ n tree/e 2–4/I 14–16/F 19

Phainoptila melanoxantha *Salvin* PHAINOPTILA Highlands of Costa Rica and W Panama/forest/berries

Hypocolius ampelinus *Bonaparte* HYPOCOLIUS Locally distributed in the Tigris-Euphrates Valley and SW Arabia wandering to Oman, Baluchistan and India/semi-desert and scrub-jungle/berries (? insects)/n bush/e 4–5 (the affinities of this curious bird are very uncertain)

DULIDAE Palm Chat An isolate of uncertain affinities, but usually placed next to, or sometimes in, the Bombycillidae. It differs in having harder, harsher plumage. Palm chats nest communally in trees, building great stick nests.

Dulus dominicus (*L*) PALM CHAT Forests of Hispaniola and Gonave/flowers and berries/ n tree/e 2–4

CINCLIDAE Dippers Aquatic birds adapted to life in fast-flowing mountain streams, and believed to have been descended from wrens. They feed mainly on water insects and other aquatic life, and walk and fly under water to capture these. Four to five species, widely distributed over Eurasia and the Americas.

Cinclus cinclus (*L*) COMMON DIPPER Widely distributed through the Palaearctic and S to Himalayas and N Yunnan/mountain streams, descending to sea level where streams still flow rapidly/n cliff-faces, rock-crevices by streams, rarely branch of tree/e 3–7/I ♀ 15–17/F 19–25

Cinclus pallasii *Temminck* BROWN or PALLAS' DIPPER Asia from Kirghiz to Himalayas, northern SE Asia and N and E to Sakhalin and the Kuriles/mountain streams/n rock-crevice or bank near stream/e 3–6

Cinclus mexicanus *Swainson* AMERICAN or MEXICAN DIPPER Western N America S to Panama/mountain streams/n rock-ledge near stream/e 3–6/I ♀ 13/F 18

Cinclus leucocephalus *Tschudi* WHITE-CAPPED DIPPER Mts from Venezuela to Bolivia/ n rock crevice/e ? n/k

Cinclus schulzii *Cabanis* RUFOUS-THROATED DIPPER Mts of NW Argentina (sometimes treated as conspecific with *C. leucocephalus*)

TROGLODYTIDAE Wrens Small brown birds with skulking habits and very loud melodious songs. The wings are short and rounded, the legs comparatively stout, and the bill is slender and long-pointed. The flight is described as 'buzzing', and the tail is characteristically carried cocked over the back. About 60 species, throughout the Americas, with one species widely distributed over the northern hemisphere.

Campylorhynchus jocosus *Sclater* BOUCARD'S WREN Mts of SC Mexico

Campylorhynchus gularis *Sclater* SPOTTED WREN Pacific slope of Mexico

Campylorhynchus yucatanicus (*Hellmayr*) YUCATAN WREN Coastal Yucatán, Mexico

Campylorhynchus brunneicapillus (*Lafresnaye*) CACTUS WREN Mexico and southwestern USA/thorn scrub and semi-desert/ insects and fruit/n bush/e 3–7/I ♂♀

Camphylorhynchus griseus (*Swainson*) BICOLOURED WREN Colombia, Venezuela, Guyana and N Amazon basin/forest edge and clearings, semi-arid scrub and savannah

Campylorhynchus chiapensis *Salvin and Godman* GIANT WREN Pacific slope of Chiapas, Mexico

Campylorhynchus rufinucha (*Lesson*) RUFOUS-NAPED WREN Mexico to Costa Rica/ scrub and cultivation/n tree

Campylorhynchus albobrunneus (*Lawrence*) WHITE-HEADED WREN Panama and Pacific Colombia/forest edge and clearings

Campylorhynchus turdinus (*Wied*) THRUSH WREN Colombia and Amazon basin S to Mato Grosso/forest

Campylorhynchus nuchalis *Cabanis* STRIPE-BACKED WREN Valleys of Colombia and Venezuela/dry woodland and forest edge, often near streams

Campylorhynchus fasciatus (*Swainson*) FASCIATED WREN Peru and SW Ecuador/thorn scrub

Campylorhynchus zonatus (*Lesson*) BARRED WREN Mexico to Panama and parts of Colombia and NW Ecuador/dry forest and clearings

Campylorhynchus megalopterus *Lafresnaye* GREAT-WINGED WREN (or GREY WREN) Mts of Mexico

Odontorchilus cinereus (*Pelzeln*) TOOTH-

EURYLAIMIDAE: *Calyptomena viridus*, Green Broadbill, Lesser Green Broadbill

Plate 190

COTINGIDAE:
Rupicola peruviana,
Peruvian or Red Cock-of-the-
Rock, Andean Cock of the
Rock

PIPRIDAE: *Manacus manacus,*
White-bearded Manakin

Plate 191

BILLED WREN Brazil from R Xingu to Upper Madeira

Odontorchilus branickii (*Taczanowski and Berlepsch*) GREY-MANTLED WREN Ecuador and Peru

Salpinctes obsoletus (*Say*) ROCK WREN Western N America from S British Columbia to Costa Rica/cliffs, canyons and rocks/n hole in rock or bank/e 4–10/I ♀

Salpinctes mexicanus (*Swainson*) CANYON WREN Western N America from S British Columbia to Mexico / stony valleys and canyons/ n hole in rock or building / e 4–6

Hylorchilus sumichrasti (*Lawrence*) SUMICHRAST'S WREN Veracruz and N Oaxaca

Cinnycerthia unirufa (*Lafresnaye*) RUFOUS WREN Andes from Venezuela to Ecuador/forest

Cinnycerthia peruana (*Cabanis*) SEPIA WREN Andes from Colombia to Bolivia

Cistothorus platensis (*Latham*) GRASS WREN, SEDGE WREN, or SHORT-BILLED MARSH WREN Widely but irregularly distributed through the Americas / bogs and marshes, also grassland (some races)/insects/n sedges or grass/e 4–8/ I ♀ 12–14 (de Schaunsee, *The Species of Birds of South America* (1966), p 403 note, suggests that there may be more than 1 species involved in this complex)

Cistothorus meridae *Hellmayr* PÁRAMO WREN Páramo zone of Trujillo and Mérida, Venezuela/ grassland

Cistothorus apolinari *Chapman* APOLINAR'S WREN Marshes near Suba, Bogotá, Colombia / marshy meadows

Cistothorus palustris (*Wilson*) LONG-BILLED MARSH WREN N America and Mexico/marsh/ n tree, bush or herbage/e 3–10/I ♀ 13/F 13–14

Thryomanes bewickii (*Audubon*) BEWICK'S WREN SW British Columbia, USA and Mexico/ open woodland and habitation/insects/n any sort of hole/e 5–7/I ♀ 10–14/F 14

Thryomanes sissonii (*Grayson*) SOCORRO WREN Isla Socorro off Mexico

Ferminia cerverai *Barbour* ZAPATA WREN Cuba, in the dense shrubbery of the Zapata swamp/n bush/e 6

Thryothorus atrogularis *Salvin* BLACK-THROATED WREN Caribbean / lowlands of Nicaragua, Costa Rica and W Panama/forest and scrub

Thryothorus spadix (*Bangs*) SOOTY-HEADED WREN Pacific slope of E Panama and W

Colombia/forest undergrowth

Thryothorus fasciatoventris *Lafresnaye* BLACK-BELLIED WREN Costa Rica to parts of Colombia/forest undergrowth

Thryothorus euophrys *Sclater* PLAIN-TAILED WREN Andes of Ecuador and (?) Peru (*Pheugopedius atriceps* Chapman, known only from the type taken at Piura, Peru, is placed as a race of this species)/forest

Thryothorus genibarbis *Swainson* MOUSTACHED WREN Amazon basin and Andes from Venezuela to Ecuador/forest edge and cerrada

Thryothorus coraya (*Gmelin*) CORAYA WREN Much of northern S America S to Peru and the Amazon/savannah and forest undergrowth

Thryothorus felix *Sclater* HAPPY WREN Mexico

Thryothorus maculipectus *Lafresnaye* SPOT-BREASTED WREN Mexico to Nicaragua: Andes from Venezuela to Peru

Thryothorus rutilus *Vieillot* RUFOUS-BREASTED WREN Costa Rica, Panama, Venezuela and Colombia, Trinidad and Tobago/woodland undergrowth / for comments on the *rutilus-maculipectus* complex, see de Schaunsee (1966), p 404 note

Thryothorus nigricapillus *Sclater* BLACK-CAPPED WREN, BAY WREN E Nicaragua to Colombia and Ecuador / undergrowth of forest borders and gallery woodland

Thryothorus semibadius *Salvin* SALVIN'S or RIVERSIDE WREN SW Costa Rica and adjacent Panama / woodland edges and shrubbery near streams

Thryothorus thoracicus *Salvin* STRIPE-THROATED WREN E Nicaragua to Colombia and Ecuador / shrubbery and undergrowth of tall forest/insects, spiders etc/n tree / e 2–3/ I ♀/ F 16

Thryothorus pleurostictus *Sclater* BANDED WREN Mexico and Costa Rica/scrubby woodland, stream borders and thickety ravines

Thryothorus ludovicianus (*Latham*) CAROLINA WREN Eastern and southern USA and S to Mexico/forest and habitation/insects and seeds / n hole in tree or building/e 4–8/ I ♀ 12–14

Thryothorus albinucha (*Cabot*) WHITE-BROWED WREN Mexico, Guatemala and Nicaragua

Thryothorus rufalbus *Lafresnaye* RUFOUS

AND WHITE WREN S Mexico to Panama and Colombia / tangled growth, usually near streams
Thryothorus nicefori *de Schaunsee* NICEFORO'S WREN Andes of Santander in Colombia / woodland and coffee plantations
Thryothorus sinaloa (*Baird*) SINALOA WREN Mexico
Thryothorus modestus *Cabanis* PLAIN WREN Mexico to Panama / open country and scrub
Thryothorus leucotis *Lafresnaye* BUFF-BREASTED WREN Panama and much of S America S to Peru / and Mato Grosso / shrubbery and undergrowth
Thryothorus superciliaris *Lawrence* SUPERCILIATED WREN Arid coasts of Ecuador and Peru / arid scrub
Thryothorus guarayanus (*Lafresnaye and d'Orbigny*) FAWN-BREASTED WREN Bolivia and Mato Grosso
Thryothorus longirostris *Vieillot* LONG-BILLED WREN NE and C Brazil / forest edge and caatinga
Thryothorus griseus (*Todd*) GREY or AMAZON WREN South of the Amazon in extreme W Amazonas (Brazil)
Troglodytes troglodytes (*L*) COMMON or WINTER WREN Holarctic and S to Himalayas and N Burma / ubiquitous in thick undergrowth / insects / n tree, hedge or bush / e 3–16 / I ♀ 13–16 / F 16–17
Troglodytes aedon *Vieillot* HOUSE WREN Much of the Americas except N Canada / forest, scrub and habitation / insects and spiders / n hole in tree, building or elsewhere / e 5–12 / I 13 / F 12–18 (Some authorities consider *T. tanneri*, Townsend, of Clarion Is, *T. beani*, Ridgway, of Cozumel Is and *T. musculus*, Naumann, 'Southern House Wren', to be separate species)
Troglodytes solstitialis *Sclater* SUN WREN or MOUNTAIN WREN Mts from Mexico to Argentina / bush and scrub (*T. rufociliatus* Sharpe and *T. ochraceus* Ridgway are sometimes separated)
Troglodytes rufulus *Cabanis* TEPUI WREN Mts of Venezuela / woodland undergrowth and campos
Troglodytes browni *Bangs* TIMBERLINE WREN or IRAZÚ WREN High mts of Costa Rica and Panama / scrub and bamboo above timberline
Uropsila leucogastra (*Gould*) WHITE-BELLIED WREN Lowlands of Mexico, Belize and Guatemala
Henicorhina leucosticta (*Cabanis*) WHITE-BREASTED or LOWLAND WOOD WREN Lowlands of Mexico, C America, Colombia, Ecuador, Peru, Venezuela, the Guianas and N Brazil / forest and savannah
Henicorhina leucophrys (*Tschudi*) GREY-BREASTED WOOD WREN Highlands from Mexico to Panama and Venezuela to Bolivia / forest undergrowth
Henicorhina leucoptera *Fitzpatrick, Terborgh and Willard* (*Auk*, 94 (1977), pp 195–201) BAR-WINGED WOOD WREN Cordillera del Condor, N Peru / mountain forest / ? insects / n and e n/k (type series, 16 specimens, only)
Microcerculus marginatus (*Sclater*) NIGHTINGALE WREN Highland from Mexico to Colombia and Upper Amazon basin / forest undergrowth
Microcerculus ustulatus *Salvin and Godman* FLAUTIST WREN Mts of Venezuela and Guyana / forest undergrowth
Microcerculus bambla (*Boddaert*) WING-BANDED WREN Upper and N Amazon basin / forest undergrowth
Cyphorhinus thoracicus *Tschudi* CHESTNUT-BREASTED WREN Andes from Colombia to Peru / forest
Cyphorhinus arada (*Hermann*) ORGAN WREN, SONG WREN, MUSICIAN WREN Lowlands from Honduras to Panama, Pacific slopes of Colombia and Ecuador, Amazon basin, Venezuela and the Guianas / thick forest undergrowth and riverbanks [NB: There are 3 groups of races here, some authorities separate either or both of *C. phaeocephalus* Sclater, 'Song Wren' and *C. modulator* (d'Orbigny) 'Musician Wren' from *C. arada*. *C. arada* is called *C. aradus* in Peters' *Check List of Birds of the World*, vol 9, but de Schaunsee (1966) points out that Hermann's name is not an adjective, but a noun based on 'L'Arada' of Buffon, and therefore does not change gender to agree with the generic name]
MIMIDAE Mockingbirds, Catbirds and Thrashers Birds allied to wrens and thrushes, very variable in colour and pattern and with excellent powers of vocal mimicry. They build open cup nests. About 30 species in the warmer parts of the Americas.
Dumetella carolinensis (*L*) GREY or COMMON CATBIRD S Canada and USA w S to C America

PITTIDAE:
Pitta erythrogaster,
Red-breasted and Blue-breasted
Pittas

Plate 192

MENURIDAE:
Menura alberti,
Albert's Lyrebird

ATRICHORNITHIDAE:
Atrichornis clamosus,
Noisy Scrub Bird

Plate 193

and W Indies / forest and habitation / fruit and insects / n tree or bush / e 2–5 / I ♀ 12–13
Melanoptila glabrirostris *Sclater* BLACK CATBIRD Yucatan, Belize and N Guatemala
Melanotis caerulescens (*Swainson*) BLUE MOCKINGBIRD Mexico
Melanotis hypoleucus *Hartlaub* BLUE AND WHITE MOCKINGBIRD SE Mexico, Guatemala, N Honduras and El Salvador
Mimus polyglottos (*L*) NORTHERN MOCKINGBIRD USA, Bahamas, Caymans and Greater Antilles / forest and habitation / insects and fruit / n tree / e 3–6 / I ♂♀ 9–12
Mimus gilvus (*Vieillot*) TROPICAL MOCKINGBIRD S Mexico to the Guianas, N Brazil, Lesser Antilles and islands off the N coast of S America / campos, arid scrub and habitation
Mimus magnirostris *Cory* ST ANDREWS MOCKINGBIRD St Andrews (Caribbean Sea) / copses and orchards / n and e n/k
Mimus gundlachii *Cabanis* GUNDLACH'S MOCKINGBIRD Jamaica, Bahamas and cays off S Cuba / semi-arid scrub and habitation / n tree or bush / e ? 2
Mimus thenca (*Molina*) CHILEAN MOCKINGBIRD Chile from Atacama to Valdiva / bushy hillsides / n tree or cactus / e 2–4
Mimus longicaudatus *Tschudi* LONG-TAILED MOCKINGBIRD W Ecuador and N and W Peru / arid scrub, often near streams
Mimus saturninus (*Lichtenstein*) SATURNINE or CHALK-BROWED MOCKINGBIRD Lower Amazon basin S to Bolivia, Uruguay and N Argentina / campos and cerrado
Mimus patagonicus (*Lafresnaye and d'Orbigny*) PATAGONIAN MOCKINGBIRD W and S Argentina and S Chile / bushy hillsides and pasture / n tree or bush / e n/k
Mimus triurus (*Vieillot*) WHITE-BANDED MOCKINGBIRD C and E Bolivia, and Mato Grosso S to Río Negro in Argentina / bushy pasture
Mimus dorsalis (*Lafresnaye and d'Orbigny*) BROWN-BACKED MOCKINGBIRD Puna zone of Bolivia and NW Argentina / bushy hillsides
Nesomimus trifasciatus (*Gould*) GALAPAGOS MOCKINGBIRD Galapagos / ubiquitous / omnivorous / n tree or cactus/e 2–4 (some authorities recognise several species in the islands, others lump all the forms as races of one species)
Mimodes graysoni (*Lawrence*) SOCORRO

THRASHER Socorro Is, off Mexico
Oreoscoptes montanus (*Townsend*) SAGE THRASHER Western N America from S Canada to Mexico / sagebrush plains / insects and fruit / n sagebush / e 4–7 / I ♂♀
Toxostoma rufum (*L*) BROWN THRASHER S Canada and USA / forest and habitation / insects and fruit / n tree, shrub or ground / e 4–5 (?6) / I ♂♀ 11–14 / F 9–12
Toxostoma longirostre (*Lafresnaye*) LONG-BILLED THRASHER S Texas and Mexico / forest and scrub / insects and fruit / n bush / e 2–5
Toxostoma guttatum (*Ridgway*) COZUMEL THRASHER Cozumel Is, Mexico
Toxostoma cinereum (*Xantus*) GREY THRASHER Baja California / dry country and scrub / n tree or shrub / e 2–4
Toxostoma bendirei (*Coues*) BENDIRE THRASHER South-western USA and Mexico / open country / insects / n tree or shrub / e 3–5
Toxostoma ocellatum (*Sclater*) OCELLATED THRASHER Mexico
Toxostoma curvirostre (*Swainson*) CURVE-BILLED THRASHER South-western USA and Mexico / dry scrub and semi-desert / insects / n shrub and cactus / e 1–4 / I ♂♀ 13 / F 14–18
Toxostoma lecontei *Lawrence* LE CONTE'S THRASHER South-western USA, Baja, California and NW Sonora / hot desert plains / insects / n cactus / e 2–4 / I ♂♀
Toxostoma redivivum (*Gambel*) CALIFORNIA THRASHER California and NW Baja California / scrub / insects and fruit / n tree or shrub / e 2–4 / I ♂♀ 14 / F 12–14
Toxostoma dorsale *Henry* CRISSAL THRASHER South-western USA and Mexico / scrub / fruit and insects / n tree or bush / e 2–4 / I ♂♀ 14 / F 11–12
Cinclocerthia ruficauda (*Gould*) BROWN TREMBLER Lesser Antilles / rain forest and dry woodland / n cavity in tree or tree-fern / e 2–3
Ramphocinclus brachyurus (*Vieillot*) WHITE-BREASTED TREMBLER Martinique and St Lucia / semi-arid woodland / n bush / e 2
Donacobius atricapillus (*L*) BLACK-CAPPED MOCKINGTHRUSH E Panama and much of S America E of Andes and S to Bolivia and NE Argentina / marsh and riparian swampy scrub
Allenia fusca (*Müller*) SCALY-BREASTED THRASHER Lesser Antilles / forest and habitation / n tree / e 2–3
Margarops fuscatus (*Vieillot*) PEARLY-EYED

THRASHER West Indies and La Horquilla (Venezuela) / scrub woodland and mountain forest / n cavity in tree, or side of cave or cliff / e 2–3

PRUNELLIDAE Accentors Small, inconspicuously coloured sparrow-like birds with thin, sharp-pointed thrush-like bills; all except *P. modularis* are inhabitants of the high plateaux and mountains of Eurasia. They feed largely on insects in summer and on seeds and berries in winter. They build neat cup-nests and lay 3–5 immaculate greenish-blue eggs. Incubation period is about 15 days, both sexes incubating.

Prunella collaris (*Scopoli*) ALPINE ACCENTOR b mts from S Europe across C Asia to Japan and Sea of Okhotsk w more widespread over lower latitudes / mountain scrub and rocky ground / insects, berries and seeds / n tree or rock crevice / e 3–5 (?6) / I ♂♀ 15

Prunella himalayana (*Blyth*) ALTAI ACCENTOR Himalayas and C Asian ranges from Tian Shan to Lake Baikal / rocky hills / insects and seeds / n ground / e 4–5

Prunella rubeculoides (*Moore*) ROBIN ACCENTOR Himalayas and mts of E Tibet to W China and Koko Nor / alpine tundra and swamps / insects and seeds / n ground / e 3–4

Prunella strophiata (*Blyth*) RUFOUS-BREASTED ACCENTOR Mts from Afghanistan along Himalayas to S Tibet, N Burma and W China to Koko Nor / scrub-jungle and habitation / insects and seeds / n tree or bush / e 3–5 / I ♂♀

Prunella montanella (*Pallas*) SIBERIAN ACCENTOR Siberia from Urals to Wrangel Is and S to Korea / forest and scrub / n tree / e 3–5

Prunella fulvescens (*Severtzov*) BROWN ACCENTOR Widely over the mountain ranges of C Asia / alpine tundra / food n/k / n shrub / e 3–4

Prunella ocularis (*Radde*) RADDE'S ACCENTOR Mts of Armenia to Khurasan: Yemen / mountain scrub / no other data

Prunella atrogularis (*Brandt*) BLACK-THROATED ACCENTOR Urals to Altai and Tadzhikistan w S to Indian region / (w) scrub-jungle and cultivation (b) upper levels of cedar-spruce woods / n tree / e 4–5

Prunella koslowi (*Przewalski*) KOSLOW'S ACCENTOR Mts of Mongolia and Ningsia; Khobdo, Gobi and Ala Shan

Prunella modularis (*L*) DUNNOCK or HEDGE

SPARROW Europe, Asia E to Urals, W Iran and S to Lebanon / forest, woodland, scrub and moor / insects and seeds / n ground or bush / e 3–6 / I ♀ 11–15 / F 11–15

Prunella rubida (*Temminck and Schlegel*) JAPANESE ACCENTOR Japan and S Kuriles / dwarf mountain forest / n in dwarf conifer / e 3–4

Prunella immaculata (*Hodgson*) MAROON-BACKED ACCENTOR C Himalayas to SE Tibet, Yunnan and Szechwan / damp forest and cultivation / insects and seeds / n ? bush / e ? 3–4 (no reliable data)

TURDIDAE Thrushes and Chats A large diverse family of plumpish, soft-plumaged birds. They are closely allied to the Flycatchers and Old World Warblers, but have stronger flight, and generally 'booted' (unscaled) tarsi. They are largely insectivorous. A little over 300 species throughout most of the world except the very cold regions.

Brachypteryx stellata *Gould* GOULD'S SHORTWING Mts from Nepal to N Burma and Tonkin / rhododendron scrub and alpine zone / insects and seeds / n and e n/k

Brachypteryx hyperythra *Jerdon and Blyth* RUSTY-BREASTED SHORTWING Mts from E Nepal to Assam / forest undergrowth and bamboo scrub / no other data

Brachypteryx major (*Jerdon*) RUFOUS-BELLIED and WHITE-BELLIED SHORTWINGS Peninsular India / jungle / insects / n hole in bank or tree / e 2

Brachypteryx calligyna (*Stresemann*) CELEBES SHORTWING Celebes mts

Brachypteryx leucophrys (*Temminck*) LESSER SHORTWING Himalayas, mts of SE Asia and S China, Sumatra, Java, Bali, Lombok, Sumbawa and Timor / dense undergrowth / insects / n bush or among moss on rocks or tree trunks / e 3–4 / I ♂♀

Brachypteryx montana *Horsfield* BLUE SHORTWING Mts from E Nepal through N Burma to W and S China; Taiwan, Palawan, Philippines, northern Borneo, Sumatra, Java and Flores / oak and rhododendron forest / insects / n among moss on rocks or tree trunks / e 3

[**Brachypteryx joannae** *La Touche* LA TOUCHE'S SHORTWING Yunnan (Mengtse) / unique ♀ / this 'species' does not appear in current lists, but neither have I been able to find it in synonymy. For description see La

Opposite:
ALAUDIDAE:
Alauda arvensis,
Skylark

ALAUDIDAE:
Mirafra javanica,
Singing Bush Lark

ALAUDIDAE:
Alauda arvensis,
Skylark

Plate 194

Plate 195

Touche, *Bull Brit Orn Cl*, 43, p 21 and *Ibis* (1923), p 375. La Touche's skins went to Harvard, and the type was accepted as a valid species by Bangs (1930), 'Types of Birds now in Museum of Comparative Zoology', in *Bull Mus Comp Zool*, Harvard]

Zeledonia coronata *Ridgway* WREN THRUSH Mts of Costa Rica and W Panama / mountain forest / this species is often placed in a monotypic family

Erythropygia coryphaeus (*Lesson*) KARROO SCRUB ROBIN S Africa from SW Africa and Orange River S to Cape / dry scrub / insects and berries / n ground / e 2–4 / I 14–15

Erythropygia leucophrys (*Rüppell*) WHITE-BROWED or RED-BACKED SCRUB ROBIN E Africa from Sudan to S Angola and the Cape / bush and cultivation / insects / n herbage near ground / e 2–3

Erythropygia hartlaubi *Reichenow* BROWN-BACKED SCRUB ROBIN W Cameroon to Mt Kenya and N Angola / savannah and cultivation / insects / n herbage near ground / e 2–4

Erythropygia paena *Smith* KALAHARI SCRUB ROBIN Benguella and Transvaal S to Cape / scrub / n grass or bush / e 2–3

Erythropygia leucosticta (*Sharpe*) GOLD COAST SCRUB ROBIN Sierra Leone to Ghana: Congo region and N Angola / dense forest / n hollow stump / e n/k

Erythropygia quadrivirgata (*Reichenow*) EASTERN BEARDED SCRUB ROBIN E Africa from Somalia to Natal / scrub / insects / n hole or in undergrowth / e 2–3

Erythropygia barbata (*Hartlaub and Finsch*) WESTERN BEARDED SCRUB ROBIN Angola, Zambia, N and C Malawi / scrub / insects / n hollow stump / e 2–3

Erythropygia signata (*Sundevall*) BROWN SCRUB ROBIN Transvaal to E Cape Province / coastal forests / insects / n tree stump / e 2

Namibornis herero (*de Schaunsee*) HERERO CHAT W Damaraland / rocky bush / no other data

Cercotrichas podobe (*Müller*) BLACK SCRUB ROBIN Senegal across the thorn savannah belt to SW Arabia / arid scrub / insects / n ground or stump / e 2–3

Cercotrichas galactotes (*Temminck*) RUFOUS WARBLER or BUSH-CHAT Mediterranean region, across SW Asia to Afghanistan and Pakistan and S to Somaliland w S to Kenya and India /

scrub and stony country / insects / n bush / e 3–5 / I ♀ (the position of this species has been confused. It was formerly regarded as a sylvid warbler and is sometimes placed in *Erythropygia* or in the monotypic genus *Agrobates*)

Pinarornis plumosus *Sharpe* BOULDER CHAT or SOOTY BABBLER Rhodesia and adjacent Bechuanaland / boulder-strewn hillsides / insects and lizards / n rock crevice / e 2–3

Chaetops frenatus (*Temminck*) SOUTH AFRICAN ROCK-JUMPER Cape Province and Natal / boulder-strewn mountain slopes / insects / n ground / e 2–3

[**Achaetops pycnopygius** (*Sclater*) DAMARALAND ROCK-JUMPER, is now placed in the genus *Sphenoeacus* (Sylvidae)]

Drymodes brunneopygia *Gould* SOUTHERN SCRUB ROBIN South Australia, New South Wales and Victoria / mallee and scrubby sand-plain / insects / n on or near ground / e 1

Drymodes superciliaris *Gould* NORTHERN SCRUB ROBIN New Guinea, Aru Is, N Territory and Cape York Peninsula / open forest and forest edge / snails and ground invertebrates / n ground / e 2

Pogonocichla stellata (*Vieillot*) STARRED ROBIN E and C Africa from Sudan to the Cape / forest / insects / n ground or stump / e 2–3

Pogonocichla swynnertoni (*Shelley*) SWYNNERTON'S ROBIN E Rhodesia / mountain forest / n tree / e 2–3

(NB: the genera from *Sheppardia* to *Tarsiger* are frequently merged in *Erithacus*)

Sheppardia gabela (*Rand*) GABELA ROBIN Gabela (Angola) known only from a strip of rain forest along a mountain ridge / no data

Sheppardia cyornithopsis (*Sharpe*) AKALAT or WHISKERED REDSTART Sierra Leone and Liberia: S Cameroons: Congo: S Sudan (apparently discontinuous) / forest / insects / n and e n/k

Sheppardia aequatorialis (*Jackson*) EQUATORIAL REDSTART Congo, Uganda and W Kenya / forest undergrowth / n and e n/k

Sheppardia erythrothorax (*Hartlaub*) FOREST ROBIN Fernando Po and Sierra Leone to Congo and Uganda / swampy forest / insects / n ground / e n/k

Sheppardia sharpei (*Shelley*) SHARPE'S ROBIN Tanganyika and N Malawi / forest and bamboo / insects / n bush / e 2

Sheppardia gunningi *Haagner* GUNNING'S ROBIN E Africa from Kenya to Mozambique/ forest/insects/n and e n/k

Erithacus rubecula (*L*) ROBIN or REDBREAST Europe, Mediterranean islands and N Africa (including Canary Is) across C Asia, N to Urals and E to Mongolia/thick woodland and forest (near habitation in British Isles only)/n hole/ e 3–9/I ♀ 12–15/F 12–15

Pseudaeon sibilans (*Swinhoe*) SWINHOE'S PSEUDOROBIN or RUFOUS-TAILED ROBIN b E Siberia from Altai to Kamchatka w S to China, N Laos and Korea/taiga/n tree/e 5–6 (3 nests known)

Luscinia akahige (*Temminck*) JAPANESE ROBIN Japan, Seven Is of Izu and S Kuriles w to Formosa and S China/mountain forest/ n ground (on Izu Is will also nest in tree hole)/ e 4–5/may be closer to the *Erithacus* than the *Luscinia* group

Luscinia komadori (*Temminck*) RYUKYU ROBIN Ryu Kyu Is/apparently no available data/may be closer to the *Erithacus* than the *Luscinia* group

Luscinia luscinia (*L*) THRUSH NIGHTINGALE b E Europe and Asia E to Altai w S to Rhodesia/ forest/n ground/e 4–6/I ♀ 13/F 9–12

Luscinia megarhynchos *Brehm* NIGHTINGALE b C and E Europe through Asia to Tian Shan w S to Congo, Kenya and Arabia/forest/n ground/e 3–7/I ♀ 13–14/F 11–12

Luscinia calliope (*Pallas*) SIBERIAN RUBYTHROAT b Siberia from Urals to Kamchatka and Commander Is and S to Altai and N China w S to Indian region and Indonesia/ scrub and cultivation, usually near water/ insects/n ground/e 4–6/I ♀ 14/F 12

Luscinia svecica (*L*) BLUETHROAT Widely distributed over the Palaearctic and extreme W Alaska w S to Sudan and the Indian region/ scrub and swamp/n ground/e 5–9/I ♀ 14–15/ F 14

Luscinia pectoralis (*Gould*) WHITE-TAILED RUBYTHROAT b SC Asia from Tadzhikistan to Himalayas and W China w S to N Indian region/scrub and cultivation/insects etc/n under shrubs/e 3–4/I ♀

Larvivora ruficeps *Hartert* RED-HEADED ROBIN Known only from the 3 co-types taken in the Tsinling Mts, W China, and 1 migrant bird on Mt Brinchang, Malaya

Larvivora obscura *Berezowsky and Bianchi* BLACK-THROATED ROBIN SE Kansu and SW Shensi, China / no data / Goodwin believes *obscura* to be the adult ♂ of *pectardens* in non-breeding plumage

Larvivora pectardens (*David*) FIRETHROAT Mts of SE Tibet and Yunnan/dense bushes/ insects/n and e n/k /several authorities consider that *obscura* and *pectardens* are colour-phases of the same species

Larvivora brunnea *Hodgson* INDIAN BLUE CHAT Indian sub-continent and Chin Hills (Burma) / forest and cultivation / insects / n 'on a bank'/e 3–4/I ♀

[**Larvivora wickhami** *Baker*, which is synonymised by Ali and Ripley, following Stresemann, is regarded by Vaurie and others as a recognisable (Chin Hills) race of *brunnea*]

Larvivora cyane (*Pallas*) SIBERIAN BLUE CHAT b E Asia from Altai to River Lena, Ussuria and Japan w S to SE Asia and Indonesia/insects

Tarsiger cyanurus (*Pallas*) RED-FLANKED BLUETAIL or BLUESTART Lapland across N Asia to Kamchatka and Commander Is and S to Himalayas and W China/undergrowth in open forest/insects/n hole/e 3–5/I ♀

Tarsiger chrysaeus *Hodgson* GOLDEN ROBIN Pakistan and N India to SE Tibet and W China w S to Tonkin / rhododendron scrub and cultivation/insects/n hole in bank/e 3–4

Tarsiger indicus (*Vieillot*) WHITE-BROWED ROBIN Himalayas, SE Tibet and Yunnan (? Szechwan) w S to N Burma and Tonkin: mts of Taiwan above 6,000ft (1,800m) (endemic and sedentary) / sub-alpine forest/ insects/n hole in bank/e 3–4

Tarsiger hyperythrus (*Blyth*) RUFOUS-BREASTED ROBIN Nepal to SE Tibet and N Burma/rhododendron scrub/insects/n and e n/k

Tarsiger johnstoniae (*Ogilvie-Grant*) COLLARED ROBIN Mts of Taiwan above 6,000ft (1,800m)

Cossypha roberti (*Alexander*) ROBERTS' or WHITE-BELLIED CHAT Fernando Po, Cameroons and E Congo/forest/n and e n/k

Cossypha bocagei *Finsch and Hartlaub* BOCAGE'S CHAT Fernando Po, Cameroons, Congo and Zambia/forest outskirts/n hole/e 2

Cossypha polioptera *Reichenow* GREY-WINGED CHAT Locally distributed from Sierra Leone to Sudan and Zambia / forest / insects/

HIRUNDINIDAE:
Hirundo tahitica,
House Swallow, Welcome
Swallow, Coast Swallow,
Pacific Swallow

HIRUNDINIDAE:
Hirundo rustica,
Barn Swallow

Plate 196

MOTACILLIDAE:
Motacilla cinerea,
Grey Wagtail

CAMPEPHAGIDAE:
Coracina papuensis,
Papuan Greybird

CAMPEPHAGIDAE:
Coracina lineata,
Lineated Greybird

Plate 197

n n/k /e described, but no data on clutch size

Cossypha archeri *Sharpe* ARCHER'S CHAT Ruwenzori Mts to NW Lake Tanganyika/ forest undergrowth and scrub / insects / n and e n/k

Cossypha isabellae *Gray* CAMEROON MOUNTAIN CHAT E Nigeria and Mt Cameroon/ mountain forest / n in cleft of tree / e 2 (1 nest known)

Cossypha natalensis *Smith* NATAL CHAT E, C and S Africa from S Sudan to French Cameroons and the Cape / forest / insects and fruit / n ground or stump / e 2–3

Cossypha dichroa (*Gmelin*) CHORISTER CHAT S Cape Province to E Transvaal / forest / insects and fruit / n hole / e 2–3

Cossypha semirufa (*Rüppell*) RÜPPELL'S CHAT SE Sudan, Eritrea, Ethiopia and parts of Kenya / woodland and habitation / insects / n shrub or tree / e 3

Cossypha heuglini *Hartlaub* HEUGLIN'S CHAT Widely distributed in Africa S of Sahara except the W and extreme S / woodland and habitation / insects and seeds / n ground or stump / e 2–3

Cossypha cyanocampter (*Bonaparte*) BLUE-SHOULDERED CHAT Forests from Sierra Leone to Kenya / insects / n ? tree / e 2

Cossypha caffra (*L*) ROBIN CHAT E and S Africa from S Sudan to Cape / woodland and bush / insects and berries / n ground or stump / e 2–3

Cossypha anomela (*Shelley*) OLIVE-FLANKED CHAT Tanganyika to N Mozambique / dense woodland / n ? ground / e 2

Cossypha humeralis (*Smith*) WHITE-THROATED ROBIN CHAT Rhodesia to Natal/ thorn bush / n ground / e 2–3

Cossypha ansorgei (*Hartert*) CAVE CHAT W Angola, near limestone caves

Cossypha niveicapilla (*Lafresnaye*) SNOWY-HEADED CHAT Senegal to N Angola, W Kenya and Sennar / forest, bush and habitation / insects/ n top of stump / e 2–3

Cossypha heinrichi *Rand* ANGOLAN CHAT Gallery forest of Duque de Braganza in N Angola

Cossypha albicapilla (*Vieillot*) WHITE-CROWNED ROBIN CHAT Senegal to N Cameroon: SE Sudan and SW Ethiopia / dense bush and swamps / insects / n top of stump / e 2

Modulatrix stictigula (*Reichenow*) SPOT-THROAT Tanganyika and N Malawi / forest

undergrowth / insects and berries / n tree / e 2

Cichladusa guttata (*Heuglin*) SPOTTED MORNING WARBLER S Sudan to E Tanganyika/ scrub and palm trees / insects / n tree / e 2

Cichladusa arquata *Peters* SCRUB MORNING WARBLER S Kenya to Mozambique / scrub and cultivation / insects / n in palms or buildings / e 2

Cichladusa ruficauda (*Hartlaub*) RED-TAILED MORNING WARBLER Gabon S to Angola / scrub and cultivation / insects / n in palms or buildings/ e 2

Alethe diademata (*Bonaparte*) FIRE-CRESTED ALETHE Portuguese Guinea to Uganda and N Angola / forest / insects / n ground / e 2–3

Alethe poliophrys *Sharpe* RED-THROATED ALETHE Ruwenzori Mts to mts NW of Lake Victoria: Mt Kabobo (Congo) / mountain forest / ants / n and e n/k

Alethe fuelleborni *Reichenow* WHITE-CRESTED ALETHE E and S Tanganyika and N Malawi/ forest / insects and berries / n and e n/k

Alethe montana *Reichenow* USAMBARA ALETHE Usambara Mts (NE Tanganyika)/forest/insects/ n and e n/k

Alethe lowei *Grant and Mackworth-Praed* IRINGA ALETHE S Tanganyika and N Malawi/ forest / insects / n and e n/k

Alethe poliocephala (*Bonaparte*) BROWN-CHESTED ALETHE Locally distributed from Sierra Leone to Angola, Tanganyika and Sudan/ forest / insects and frogs / n and e n/k

Alethe choloensis *Sclater* CHOLO ALETHE E and S Malawi, and Namuli Mts (Mozambique)/forest / insects / n tree / e 3

Copsychus saularis (*L*) MAGPIE-ROBIN Indian sub-continent, SE Asia, S China and much of Indonesia E to Philippines / cultivation and habitation / insects / n hole, house eave etc/ e 3–6 / I ♂♀ 12–13

Copsychus sechellarum *Newton* SEYCHELLES MAGPIE-ROBIN Seychelles, now restricted to Frigate Is / *very rare and endangered*, 12 birds in 1965! / n in coconut palms / e 2 (NB: Penney in *Birds of Seychelles* describes the eggs as blue, but the 4 eggs in Cambridge Museum (Newton Coll) are heavily marked with brown)

Copsychus albospecularis (*Eydoux and Gervais*) MADAGASCAR MAGPIE-ROBIN Madagascar / forest and dense bush / n ? bush / e ? 2

Copsychus malabaricus (*Scopoli*) COMMON SHAMA Indian sub-continent, SE Asia, Hainan and W Indonesia (E to Borneo) / deciduous forest / insects / n hole / e 3–5 / I ♀ / F 12–13

Copsychus stricklandii *Motley and Dillwyn* WHITE-CROWNED SHAMA N and E Borneo and adjacent islands / forest / n and e n/k

Copsychus luzoniensis (*Kittlitz*) WHITE-BROWED SHAMA Philippines

Copsychus niger (*Sharpe*) PALAWAN SHAMA Balabac, Calamianes and Palawan

Copsychus cebuensis (*Steere*) BLACK SHAMA Cebu

Copsychus pyrropygus (*Lesson*) ORANGE-TAILED SHAMA Malaya, Sumatra and Borneo / swamp and forest / n and e n/k

Irania gutteralis (*Guérin-Méneville*) PERSIAN WHITE-THROATED ROBIN b Turkey to Afghanistan w S through Arabia to E Africa / stony slopes etc / n shrub / e 4–5

Phoenicurus alaschanicus (*Przewalski*) ALASHAN REDSTART Mts of W China

Phoenicurus erythronotus (*Eversmann*) EVERSMANN'S REDSTART Mts of C Asia from Tadzikistan to Altai and NW Mongolia w to Iran and Himalayan region / arid country / insects / n ground / e 6

Phoenicurus caeruleocephalus *Vigors* BLUE-CAPPED REDSTART b Tadzhikistan to Afghanistan and Altai / open forest and rocky ground / insects / n hollow under log or boulder / e 3–4

Phoenicurus ochruros (*S. G. Gmelin*) BLACK REDSTART Mediterranean Africa, Europe and W Asia (south of taiga belt) E to W China w S to India and NE Africa / rocky areas and habitation / n hole in rock or building / e 4–6 / I ♀ 12–16 / F 12–19

Phoenicurus phoenicurus (*L*) COMMON REDSTART Mediterranean region, Europe and Asia E to Lake Baikal w S to Tanganyika and NW Indian region / woodland, orchard and heath / n hole in stump, rock or building / e 4–10 / I ♀ 11–14 / F 14–20

Phoenicurus hodgsoni (*Moore*) HODGSON'S REDSTART Mts of SE Tibet and W China w into E Himalayas and N Burma / dry river beds and parkland / insects and berries / n hole in wall or bank / e 4–6

Phoenicurus frontalis *Vigors* BLUE-FRONTED REDSTART Himalayas and mts of SE Tibet and W China w to N Burma and Tonkin / alpine scrub and cultivation / insects, seeds and berries / n hole in tree, wall or bank / e 3–4

Phoenicurus schisticeps (*Gray*) WHITE-THROATED REDSTART Himalayas and mts of SE Tibet and W China w to N Burma and Tonkin / open forest, scrub and cultivation / insects, seeds and berries / n hole in bank, tree or rock cleft / e 3

Phoenicurus auroreus (*Pallas*) DAURIAN REDSTART b China, SE Tibet, Manchuria, Korea, N Mongolia and Amurland w S to N India, northern SE Asia, Hainan, Ryukyu Is and (rarely) Japan / open forest and cultivation / insects and berries / n hole in wall or bank / e 3–4

Phoenicurus moussieri (*Olphe-Galliard*) MOUSSIER'S REDSTART Atlas Mts / rocky ground / n ground or bush / e 3–6

Phoenicurus erythrogaster (*Güldenstädt*) GÜLDENSTÄDT'S REDSTART Caucasus: mts from Ferghana to Altai, Himalayas and W China / meadows and riverbeds / insects and berries / n hole in wall / e ?4 (the few known clutches are of questionable authenticity)

Rhyacornis bicolor (*Ogilvie-Grant*) WATER REDSTART Mts of N Luzon (Philippines)

Rhyacornis fuliginosus (*Vigors*) PLUMBEOUS REDSTART Himalayas, mts of northern SE Asia, SE Tibet, W China, Hainan and Taiwan / mountain streams / insects / n hole in stream bank / e 3–6 / I ♀

Hodgsonius phaenicuroides (*Gray*) HODGSON'S SHORTWING Himalayas to mts of W China w in SE Asia / bush-jungle and dense thickets / insects and berries / n bush / e 2–4 / I ♀

Cinclidium leucurum (*Hodgson*) BLUE ROBIN E Himalayas and mts of SE Asia / streams in evergreen forest / insects and berries / n hole in bank or rock / e 3–4 / I ♂♀

Cinclidium diana (*Lesson*) INDIGO ROBIN Mts of Java and Sumatra

Cinclidium frontale *Blyth* BLUE-FRONTED ROBIN Nepal and Sikkim: Tonkin and Laos / wet forest / no other data

Grandala coelicolor *Hodgson* GRANDALA Himalayas, mts of SE Tibet and W China / ridges and alpine meadows / insects and berries / n ledge of rock / e 2

Sialia sialis (*L*) EASTERN BLUEBIRD Eastern N America and Mexico S to Nicaragua / open country, orchard and cultivation / insects and fruit / n hole / e 3–7 / I ♂♀ 12 / F 15

Sialia mexicana *Swainson* WESTERN BLUEBIRD Western N America and Mexico / forest clearings and cultivation / insects and fruit / n hole / e 3–8 / I ♀

Sialia currucoides (*Bechstein*) ROCKY

CAMPEPHAGIDAE:
Lalage leucomela,
White-browed Triller

CAMPEPHAGIDAE:
Pteropodocys maxima,
Ground Cuckoo Shrike

Plate 198

PYCNONOTIDAE:
Pycnonotus leucogenys,
White-cheeked Bulbul

PYCNONOTIDAE:
Pycnonotus jocosus,
Red-whiskered Bulbul

Plate 199

MOUNTAIN BLUEBIRD Mts of western N America/ forest and alpine meadows / insects and fruit/ n hole / e 4–8 / I ♂♀ 14

Enicurus scouleri *Vigors* LITTLE FORKTAIL Mts of S Russia, Afghanistan, Himalayas, W China and Taiwan / rocky streams / insects / n cleft in rock / e 2–4

Enicurus velatus *Temminck* LESSER FORKTAIL Sumatra and Java

Enicurus ruficapillus *Temminck* CHESTNUT-NAPED FORKTAIL Malay Peninsula, Sumatra and Borneo / mountain and forest streams / insects/ n under ledge of rock / e 2 (1 nest known)

Enicurus immaculatus (*Hodgson*) BLACK-BACKED FORKTAIL Himalayas, Bangladesh, Burma and Thailand / rivers and rocky streams/ insects / n rock crevice / e 3 / I ♂♀

Enicurus schistaceus (*Hodgson*) SLATY-BACKED FORKTAIL Himalayas, Bangladesh, northern SE Asia and S China / forest streams and rivers / insects / n rock crevice / e 3–4 / I ♂♀

Enicurus leschenaulti (*Vieillot*) WHITE-CROWNED or LESCHENAULT'S FORKTAIL Himalayas, SE Asia, China, Hainan, Sumatra, Java, Bali, Borneo and adjacent small islands / forest streams and rivers / insects / n crevices in steep banks etc / e 3–4

Enicurus maculatus *Vigors* SPOTTED FORKTAIL Himalayas, parts of SE Asia and S China / forest streams / insects and molluscs/ n rock ledge or crevice / e 3–4 / I ♂♀

Cochoa purpurea *Hodgson* PURPLE COCHOA Himalayas, mts of Yunnan and northern SE Asia / dense humid forest and ravines / insects, molluscs and berries / n tree / e 3–4 / I ♂♀

Cochoa viridis *Hodgson* GREEN COCHOA Himalayas and mts of northern SE Asia / dense forest, often near streams / insects, molluscs and berries / n tree / e 2–4 / I ♂♀

Cochoa azurea (*Temminck*) BLUE COCHOA W Sumatra, W and C Java

Myadestes townsendi (*Audubon*) TOWNSEND'S SOLITAIRE Western N America from Alaska to Mexico / mountain forest and alpine meadow/ insects and berries / n on or near ground / e 3–5

Myadestes obscurus *Lafresnaye* BROWN-BACKED SOLITAIRE Mexico n and e n/k

Myadestes elizabeth (*Lembeye*) CUBAN SOLITAIRE Cuba and Isle of Pines / mountain forest / n side of bank / e 3

Myadestes genibarbis *Swainson* RUFOUS-THROATED SOLITAIRE Jamaica, Hispaniola, Dominica, Martinique, St Lucia, St Vincent/ mountain forest (also lowland forest in Jamaica and Hispaniola) / n side of bank / e 2

Myadestes ralloides (*d'Orbigny*) ANDEAN SOLITAIRE Mts from Costa Rica to Venezuela and W Bolivia / forest / fruit and insects / n tree/ e 3 / I 12–13 [Edwards separates *M. coloratus* Nelson, from E Panama]

Myadestes unicolor *Sclater* SLATY SOLITAIRE S Mexico to Nicaragua

Myadestes leucogenys (*Cabanis*) RUFOUS-FRONTED SOLITAIRE Guyana: W Ecuador, C Peru: SE Brazil / forest

Entomodestes leucotis (*Tschudi*) WHITE-EARED SOLITAIRE Sub-tropical zone of Peru and Bolivia / forest

Entomodestes coracinus (*Berlepsch*) BLACK SOLITAIRE W Colombia and W Ecuador / forest

Stizorhina fraseri (*Strickland*) FRASER'S FLYCATCHER-THRUSH Fernando Po and Cameroon to Angola and W Uganda / forest/ insects / n ? hole / e n/k

Stizorhina finschii (*Sharpe*) FINSCH'S FLYCATCHER-THRUSH Sierra Leone to Nigeria/ lowland forest / n hole / e n/k

[*Stizorhina* is regarded as a Flycatcher (Muscicapidae) by some authorities]

Neocossyphus rufus (*Fischer and Reichenow*) RED-TAILED THRUSH Cameroon to N Congo, Kenya and Tanzania / lowland forest and coastal scrub / ants / n hole / e n/s

Neocossyphus poensis (*Strickland*) WHITE-TAILED THRUSH Sierra Leone to N Angola and W Uganda / forest / n and e n/k

Cercomela sinuata (*Sundevall*) COMMON SICKLE-WINGED CHAT S Africa N to Transvaal/ bare scrub and cultivation / n ground / e 2–3

Cercomela familiaris (*Stephens*) RED-TAILED or FAMILIAR CHAT Africa S of Sahara / rocky highlands, woodland and cultivation / n rock hole / e 2–4

Cercomela tractrac (*Wilkes*) LAYARD'S CHAT SW Africa and Namaqualand / semi-desert/ insects / n ground / e 2–3

Cercomela schlegelii (*Wahlberg*) GREY-RUMPED SICKLE-WINGED CHAT S Africa N to S Angola and Orange Free State / ? ubiquitous/ insects and seeds / n ground / e 2–3

Cercomela fusca (*Blyth*) BROWN ROCK CHAT Pakistan and NE India / crags, quarries and old buildings / insects / n ground / e 2–3

Cercomela dubia (*Blundell and Lovat*) SOMBRE ROCK CHAT C Ethiopia / no data

Cercomela melanura (*Temminck*) BLACKSTART Locally distributed from W Arabia across Sahara / dry and rocky country / n rock hole / e 3–5

Cercomela scotocerca (*Heuglin*) BROWN-TAILED ROCK CHAT Parts of Ethiopia, Sudan and Somaliland / dry bush / n rock hole / e n/k

Cercomela sordida (*Rüppell*) HILL CHAT Mts of Ethiopia, Kenya and Tanganyika / rocky moorlands / n rock hole / e 3

Saxicola rubetra (*L*) WHINCHAT Europe, N Africa and Asia E to Altai and Iran w S to Equatorial Africa / grassland and moor / n ground / e 4–7 / I ♀ 13–14 / F 13–17

Saxicola macrorhyncha (*Stoliczka*) STOLICZKA'S CHAT S Afghanistan, Pakistan and NW India / desert scrub / insects / n and e n/k

Saxicola insignis *Gray* HODGSON'S CHAT b Kazakhstan to Altai and Mongolia w S to N India / grassland and reedbeds / insects / n cliff crevice / e 5

Saxicola dacotiae (*Meade-Waldo*) MEADE-WALDO'S CHAT Fuerteventura, Montana Clara and Allegranza (Canary Is) / scrub, cultivation and habitation / n hole in rock or wall / e 2–5

Saxicola torquata (*L*) STONECHAT Widespread through most of the Old World (except the Australasian region) / moors, fields and hill scrub / insects and berries / n ground / e 3–8 / I ♀ 13–15 / F 12–13

Saxicola leucura (*Blyth*) WHITE-TAILED BUSHCHAT Pakistan and N India / tall grass subject to flooding / insects / n among grass roots / e 3

Saxicola caprata (*L*) PIED CHAT S Asia from Transcaspia to India, SE Asia, Indonesia and New Guinea / scrub, coarse grassland and cultivation / insects / n holes in walls etc / e 2–5 / I ♀ 12–13

Saxicola jerdoni (*Blyth*) JERDON'S CHAT E India, Bangladesh, Burma, NE Laos and N Vietnam / grassland / insects / n ground / e 3–4 / I ♀

Saxicola ferrea *Gray* DARK-GREY BUSHCHAT Kashmir and Himalayas to Szechwan, S China and northern SE Asia / hill scrub and (in winter) cultivation / insects and seeds / e 4–5 (no evidence for 6, as stated by Stuart Baker) / I ♀

Saxicola gutteralis (*Vieillot*) TIMOR BUSHCHAT Timor and Semau

Myrmecocichla tholloni (*Oustalet*) CONGO MOORCHAT Gabon and Congo / grassland / n and e n/k

Myrmecocichla aethiops *Cabanis* ANT CHAT Senegal to Sudan and N Tanganyika / open woodland / insects / n hole in bank or termitary / e 3–5

Myrmecocichla formicivora (*Vieillot*) ANT-EATING CHAT S Africa N to S Rhodesia / open ground with termitaries / termites / n burrow in bank or roof of antbear burrow / e 3–4

Myrmecocichla nigra (*Vieillot*) SOOTY CHAT C Africa from Nigeria to Zambia and Sudan / light bush and grassland / n hole in ground or termite hill / e 4–5

Mymecocichla arnotti (*Tristram*) ARNOTT'S CHAT Africa from S Congo and Tanganyika to SW Africa and N Transvaal / open woodland / ants / n hole / e 3–4

Myrmecocichla albifrons (*Rüppell*) WHITE-FRONTED BLACK CHAT Senegal to N Congo and S Sudan / light bushland / n crevice under boulder / e 3

Myrmecocichla melaena (*Rüppell*) RÜPPELL'S BLACK CHAT Mts of Ethiopia / mountain streams and waterfalls / no other data

Thamnolaea cinnamomeiventris (*Lafresnaye*) MOCKING CLIFF CHAT Locally distributed through Africa S of Sahara / cliffs / n rock hole / e 3

Thamnolaea coronata *Reichenow* CROWNED CLIFF CHAT Togo to N Cameroons: Sudan (discontinuous) / rocky gorges and cliffs / n and e n/k

Thamnolaea semirufa (*Rüppell*) WHITE-WINGED CLIFF CHAT Highlands of Eritrea and Ethiopia / open plateaux / n rock crevice / e 3

Oenanthe bifasciata (*Temminck*) BUFF-STREAKED WHEATEAR E Cape Province to Transvaal / rocky hills / insects / n hole in rock or wall / e 3–4

Oenanthe isabellina (*Temminck*) ISABELLINE WHEATEAR b Middle East to Mongolia w S to N India and E Africa / sandy plains / insects and seeds / n burrow in ground / e 4–7 / I ♀ 15

Oenanthe bottae (*Bonaparte*) RED-BREASTED WHEATEAR Mts of Yemen, Ethiopia, Sudan and parts of W Africa (discontinuous) / mountain meadows / n and e n/k

Oenanthe xanthroprymna (*Hemprich and Ehrenberg*) RUFOUS-TAILED WHEATEAR W Asia from Turkey to W India w S to Sudan and

IRENIDAE:
*Chloropsis
aurifrons,* Golden-fronted
Leafbird

Plate 200

LANIIDAE:
Lanius excubitor,
Great Grey Shrike,
Northern Shrike

Plate 201

Arabia / semi-desert / insects / n rock crevices/ e 4–5

Oenanthe oenanthe (*L*) COMMON WHEATEAR Holarctic, b in the North, w in the South/ grassland, moor and marsh / n hole in ground or rock / e 3–8 / I ♂♀ 14 / F 15

Oenanthe seebohmi (*Dixon*) SEEBOHM'S WHEATEAR Morocco and Algeria (the status of this form is unsettled)

Oenanthe phillipsi (*Shelley*) PHILLIPS' WHEATEAR Somali Republic / grassland / insects/ n ground / e 3–4

Oenanthe deserti (*Temminck*) DESERT WHEATEAR Desert belt from Spanish Sahara across Africa and C Asia to Mongolia, moving S in w / rocky or sandy plateaux / insects / n ground or holes in rocks / e 3–6 / I ?♀

Oenanthe hispanica (*L*) BLACK-EARED and BLACK-THROATED WHEATEARS Mediterranean area E to Turkestan (the black-eared and black-throated forms are colour phases) / heath and cultivation / n ground or hole under stone / e 4–5/ I ♀

Oenanthe finschii (*Heuglin*) FINSCH'S WHEATEAR Middle East from Turkey to Caucasus, N Arabia and Afghanistan, spreading in w to Egypt and Baluchistan / semi-desert and stony foothills / insects / n hole in bank / e 4–5

Oenanthe picata (*Blyth*) PIED WHEATEAR (*O. opistholeuca* (Strickland) and *O. capistrata* (Gould) are colour phases) b Iran to Pamirs and Afghanistan w S to Pakistan and parts of India / semi-desert and cultivation / insects and berries / n hole in rock or wall / e 4–7

Oenanthe lugens (*Lichtenstein*) MOURNING WHEATEAR N Sahara belt, SW Arabia, Israel to Iraq and E Africa from Ethiopia to N Tanganyika / rocky outcrops / n hole in rock / e 1–6

Oenanthe monacha (*Temminck*) HOODED WHEATEAR E Egypt through Arabia to Iran and Pakistan / 'the most desolate desert ravines'/ n apparently undescribed in literature / e 3–6 (eggs in British Museum (Natural History) ascribed to this species)

Oenanthe alboniger (*Hume*) HUME'S WHEATEAR S Iran, Afghanistan, Pakistan and Kashmir / 'boulder-strewn sides of mullahs'/ insects / n hole in rock / e 4–5

Oenanthe pleschanka (*Lepechin*) PLESCHANKA'S WHEATEAR Cyprus and Romania across Asia to Urals, NE China and S to Pakistan w to E Africa and Arabia / stony

wasteland / insects and berries / n hole in rock/ e 4–6

Oenanthe leucopyga (*Brehm*) WHITE-RUMPED or WHITE-CROWNED WHEATEAR Sahara desert and through Arabia to Iraq / stony ground / n hole in rock or wall / e 2–5

Oenanthe leucura (*Gmelin*) BLACK WHEATEAR N and S coasts of W Mediterranean / cliffs and rocky slopes / n hole in rock / e 3–6 / I ♀ 16 / F c15

Oenanthe monticola *Vieillot* MOUNTAIN WHEATEAR S Africa N to Benguella and Transvaal / dry hill scrub and habitation / insects/ n under stones and in buildings / e 2–3 / I ♀ 13–14 / F 16–17

Oenanthe moesta (*Lichtenstein*) RED-RUMPED WHEATEAR N Saharan belt E to Arabia and W Iraq / semi-desert / n hole in ground / e 4–5

Oenanthe pileata (*Gmelin*) CAPPED WHEATEAR Locally distributed through the southern third of Africa / grassland and open sandy country/ n hole in ground / e 3

Chaimarrornis leucocephalus (*Vigors*) RIVER CHAT Mts from Pamirs through Himalayas to W China / swift-flowing streams and rivers / insects and berries / n hole in bank or tree / e 3–5 / I ♀

Saxicoloides fulicata (*L*) INDIAN CHAT Pakistan, WC and S India and Ceylon / scrub-jungle and habitation / insects / n hole in wall or bank / e 2–3 / I ♀ 11–12

Monticola imerinus (*Hartlaub*) MADAGASCAR ROBIN CHAT Madagascar / forest and scrub/ fruit and insects / n tree / e 3 / I ♀ / F c18 (for this species see Farkas, *Bull Brit Orn Cl* (1974), p 165) (formerly placed in the monotypic genus *Pseudocossyphus*)

Monticola bensoni *Farkas* (*Ostrich*, supplement 9 (1971), p 85) BENSON'S ROCK THRUSH W Madagascar / barren rocky areas / n rock crevice / e n/k

Monticola rupestris (*Vieillot*) CAPE ROCK THRUSH S Africa from Cape to Transvaal/ scrub / insects, small animals, seeds and berries / n rock crevice or ledge / e 3–5

Monticola explorator (*Vieillot*) SENTINEL ROCK THRUSH S Africa from Cape to Mozambique / open hillsides / insects, seeds and berries / n rock crevice or ledge / e 3–4

Monticola brevipes (*Waterhouse*) SHORT-TOED ROCK THRUSH S Africa (except extreme S) N to Angola and Transvaal / stony mountain scrub/ insects and seeds / n under a rock / e 3

Monticola rufocinereus (*Rüppell*) LITTLE ROCK THRUSH W Arabia and E Africa from Ethiopia to NE Tanganyika / forests and ravines / n and e n/k

Monticola angolensis *Sousa* ANGOLA ROCK THRUSH Africa from Congo and Tanganyika to Angola and Mozambique / open dry forest / ants and termites / n tree or hole / e 3–4

Monticola saxatilis (*L*) RUFOUS-TAILED ROCK THRUSH C and S Europe and N Africa across Asia to W China w Equatorial Africa N of forest belt / rocky hillsides / insects and berries / n rock crevice / e 4–5 / I ♀

Monticola gularis (*Swinhoe*) SWINHOE'S ROCK THRUSH Amur basin to N China w S China and northern SE Asia

Monticola cinclorhynchus (*Vigors*) BLUE-CAPPED ROCK THRUSH E Afghanistan to N India region w S India / forest and rocky slopes / insects, frogs etc, sometimes berries / n rock crevice, grass tuft, tree (once) / e 3–5 / I ♂♀ (*M. gularis* and *M. cinclorhynchus* are treated as conspecific by some authors)

Monticola rufiventris (*Jardine and Selby*) CHESTNUT-BELLIED ROCK THRUSH Pakistan and N India to W and S China w northern SE Asia / open forest near cliffs / insects and berries / n hole in cliff / e 3–4 / I ♀

Monticola solitarius (*L*) BLUE ROCK THRUSH Much of the Palaearctic (but not the N), N Africa and Oriental region w S to tropical Africa and Indonesia / rocky country near streams / insects, invertebrates, lizards, fruit etc / n hole in rock or wall / e 3–6 / I ♀ 12–13 / F 17

Myiophoneus blighi (*Holdsworth*) CEYLON WHISTLING THRUSH Hills of Ceylon / damp forest / insects, frogs etc / n ledge near stream / e 1–2 / I ♀?

Myiophoneus melanurus (*Salvadori*) SHINY WHISTLING THRUSH Mts of Sumatra

Myiophoneus glaucinus (*Temminck*) SUNDA WHISTLING THRUSH Sumatra, Java, Bali and Borneo / mountain forest and streams / frogs, insects, berries and woodlice / n mouth of cave / e 2

Myiophoneus robinsoni *Ogilvie-Grant* ROBINSON'S WHISTLING THRUSH Malaya mountains / gullies and mountain streams / n and e n/k

Myiophoneus horsfieldii *Vigors* MALABAR WHISTLING THRUSH Hills of peninsular India / streams in hill jungle / invertebrates, frogs, fruit

etc / n rock ledge near waterfall / e 2–4 / I ♂♀ 16–17

Myiophoneus insularis *Gould* TAIWAN WHISTLING THRUSH Taiwan / mid-mountain forest / n hole / e 2

Myiophoneus caeruleus (*Scopoli*) BLUE WHISTLING THRUSH From Bokhara through Indian region to W China and SE Asia: hills of Java / forest rivers and streams / omnivorous n rock ledge near stream / e 3–4 / I ♂♀

Geomalia heinrichi *Stresemann* HEINRICH'S THRUSH Mts of Celebes

Zoothera schistacea (*Meyer*) TENIMBER THRUSH Tenimber Is

Zoothera dumasi (*Rothschild*) BURU THRUSH and CERAM THRUSH Mts of Buru, Mts of Ceram

Zoothera interpres (*Temminck*) CHESTNUT-CAPPED THRUSH Scattered localities and islands in Indonesian region and Malay Peninsula

Zoothera erythronota (*Sclater*) LOMBOK THRUSH Lombok, Sumbawa, Sumba, Flores, Timor, Celebes and Peling

Zoothera wardii (*Blyth*) PIED THRUSH b Himalayas w Ceylon / forest and jungle ravines / insects and berries / n tree / e 3–4 / I ♂♀

Zoothera cinerea (*Bourns and Worcester*) ASHY THRUSH Mindoro and N Luzon

Zoothera peronii (*Vieillot*) TIMOR THRUSH Timor and Damar

Zoothera citrina (*Latham*) ORANGE-HEADED THRUSH Indian sub-continent, SE Asia, S China and Hainan, Sabah (Borneo), Java and Bali / damp forest near streams / insects, worms and fruit / n tree / e 3–5 / I ♂♀ 13–14 / F 12

Zoothera everetti (*Sharpe*) EVERETT'S THRUSH Mts of Sarawak and Sabah / apparently no data

Zoothera sibirica (*Pallas*) SIBERIAN THRUSH Siberia from Yenisei E to Transbaikalia and S to Mongolia and Japan w S to parts of Indonesia

Zoothera naevia (*Gmelin*) VARIED THRUSH Western N America S to California / forest, invertebrates, seeds and fruit / n tree / e 2–5 / I ♀ (see also *Z. pinicola*)

Zoothera pinicola (*Sclater*) AZTEC THRUSH Mts of Mexico [some authorities recognise the monotypic genera *Ixoreus* for *naevia*, and *Ridgwayia* for *pinicola*]

Zoothera piaggiae (*Bouvier*) ABYSSINIAN GROUND THRUSH E Africa from S Sudan to N Tanganyika / forest / insects and fruit / n tree or shrub / e 2

BOMBYCILLIDAE:
Bombycilla garrulus,
Bohemian Waxwing

Plate 202

TROGLODYTIDAE:
Troglodytes troglodytes,
Common or Winter Wren

MIMIDAE:
Nesomimus trifasciatus,
Galapagos Mockingbird

Plate 203

Zoothera tanganjicae (*Sassi*) ORANGE GROUND THRUSH Mts W of Lake Victoria / see Prigogine, *Bull Brit Orn Club* 97 (1977), 10–15 for comments on the status of this form

Zoothera oberlaenderi (*Sassi*) FOREST GROUND THRUSH NE Congo and Uganda lowland forest / rare / no data

Zoothera gurneyi (*Hartlaub*) GURNEY'S GROUND THRUSH E Africa from Kenya to E Cape Province / mountain forest / insects and fruit / n tree or shrub / e 3

Zoothera cameronensis (*Sharpe*) BLACK-EARED GROUND THRUSH Southern Cameroon / lowland forest / no other data

Zoothera princei (*Sharpe*) GREY GROUND THRUSH Sierra Leone to Uganda and NE Congo / forest / 1 nest in a tree with 3 eggs is *ascribed* to this species

Zoothera crossleyi (*Sharpe*) CROSSLEY'S GROUND THRUSH Cameroon and NE Congo / forest / no other data

Zoothera guttata (*Vigors*) (=**Z. fischeri** (*Hellmayr*)) SPOTTED GROUND THRUSH Scattered records from Kenya to Cape Province / forest and damp bush / insects / n tree or bush / e 2–3

Zoothera spiloptera (*Blyth*) SPOTTED-WINGED THRUSH Ceylon / forest and plantations / worms, insects and ? berries / n tree / e 2 / I ?♂♀

Zoothera andromedae (*Temminck*) ANDROMEDA THRUSH Discontinuously distributed through some islands in Indonesia

Zoothera mollissima (*Blyth*) PLAIN-BACKED THRUSH Himalayas to mts of SW China / mountain scrub and bare ground above tree-line / insects, molluscs and berries / n tree, ledge or ground (accounts differ) / e 4 (see note to *Z. dixoni*)

Zoothera dixoni (*Seebohm*) LONG-TAILED THRUSH Himalayas, Yunnan w northern SE Asia / forest and alpine flora (above tree-line) / insects, molluscs and berries / n tree / e 3 [NB: At one time *dixoni* and *mollissima* were regarded as synonymous, many clutches ascribed to these species are therefore suspect]

Zoothera dauma (*Latham*) WHITE'S THRUSH Widely but irregularly distributed through Asia and Australasia, wandering to Europe / dense forest with heavy undergrowth / insects and berries / n tree / e 3–5

Zoothera talaseae (*Rothschild and Hartert*) TALASEAE THRUSH New Britain

Zoothera margaretae (*Mayr*) SAN CRISTOBAL THRUSH Guadalcanal and San Cristobal (Solomons) / mountain forest / no other data

Zoothera monticola *Vigors* LARGE BROWN THRUSH Himalayas E to Tonkin / mountain streams in forest / insects, molluscs and berries / n tree / e 3–4

Zoothera marginata *Blyth* LESSER BROWN THRUSH Himalayas and SE Asia / damp forest near water / insects and molluscs / n tree / e 3–4 / I ♂♀

Zoothera terrestris (*Kittlitz*) BONIN THRUSH Bonin Is / extinct / 4 specimens

[**Turdus ulietensis** *Gmelin* BAY THRUSH Raitea Is (Society Islands) / extinct, no specimens; known only from J. G. A. Forster's drawing in the British Museum (Natural History). It is usually considered to be a *Zoothera*, but the taxonomic position cannot be determined accurately. See Greenway, *Extinct and Vanishing Birds of the World* and coloured plate in *Catalogue of the Birds of the British Museum* (1881), vol 5]

Amalocichla sclateriana *De Vis* SCLATER'S or GREATER NEW GUINEA THRUSH New Guinea mountains / forest / insects / n and e n/k

Amalocichla incerta (*Salvadori*) LESSER NEW GUINEA THRUSH New Guinea / mountains / forest / no data

Cataponera turdoides *Hartert* CELEBES MOUNTAIN THRUSH Celebes mts

Nesocichla eremita *Gould* STARCHY THRUSH Tristan da Cunha group / insects / n ground / e 2

Cichlherminia lherminieri (*Lafresnaye*) L'HERMINIER'S FOREST THRUSH Monserrat, Guadeloupe, Dominica and St Lucia / forest / n bush or tree / e 2–3

Phaeornis obscurus (*Gmelin*) HAWAIIAN THRUSH or OMAO Hawaiian Is / rare and endangered / forest / fruit and insects / n tree fern / e 1–2

Phaeornis palmeri *Rothschild* SMALL KAUAI THRUSH or PUAIOHI Kauai Is / rare and endangered, believed extinct till rediscovered in 1964 / forest / fruit and insects / n n/k / eggs have been laid by captive birds. (The LARGE KAUAI THRUSH is the Kauai race of the HAWAIIAN THRUSH)

Catharus gracilirostris *Salvin* BLACK-BILLED THRUSH Mts of Costa Rica and W Panama / forest / no other data

Catharus aurantiirostris (*Hartlaub*)

ORANGE-BILLED THRUSH Mexico to Venezuela and Trinidad/scrub and light woodland

Catharus fuscater (*Lafresnaye*) SLATY-BACKED THRUSH Costa Rica to Venezuela, Peru and N Bolivia/forest and woodland

Catharus occidentalis *Sclater* RUSSET THRUSH Mexico, Guatemala, El Salvador and Honduras

Catharus frantzii *Cabanis* HIGHLAND or FRANTZIUS'S THRUSH Mts of Costa Rica and Panama/forest

Catharus mexicanus (*Bonaparte*) BLACK-HEADED THRUSH Mexico to W Panama/forest and woodland

Catharus dryas (*Gould*) SPOTTED THRUSH Mts from Mexico to Bolivia

Catharus fuscescens (*Stephens*) VEERY N America (except extreme N) and C America w northern S America/forest/insects and fruit/ n ground/e 3–5/I 10–12/F 10

Catharus minimus (*Lafresnaye*) GREY-CHEEKED THRUSH NE Siberia, Canada and eastern USA w S to northern S America/ forest and tundra/fruit and seeds/n ground or bush/e 3–4/I 13–14

Catharus ustulatus (*Nuttall*) SWAINSON'S THRUSH N America w S to Argentina/forest, open woodland, orchards etc/fruit and insects/ n bush/e 3–5/I ♀ 14/F 10–12

Catharus guttatus (*Pallas*) HERMIT THRUSH N America w S to Mexico/open forest, tundra and alpine meadow/insects and fruit/n ground/ e 3–6/I ♀ 10–13/F 12

Catharus mustelinus (*Gmelin*) WOOD THRUSH Eastern N America w southern USA and C America/forest and habitation/insects and fruit/ n tree/e 2–5/I ♀ 13–14/F 12

Platycichla flavipes (*Vieillot*) YELLOW-LEGGED THRUSH Colombia, Venezuela, Guyana, Trinidad and Tobago, SE Brazil to N Argentina

Platycichla leucops (*Taczanowski*) PALE-EYED THRUSH Scattered localities on mountains in S America S to Bolivia

Turdus bewsheri *Newton* COMORO THRUSH Comoro Is

Turdus olivaceofuscus *Hartlaub* OLIVACEOUS THRUSH Principé and São Tomé/bush and cultivation/n ? tree/e n/s

Turdus olivaceus *L* OLIVE or CAPE THRUSH Fernando Po and Africa S of Sahara/open hillsides, forest and cultivation/insects and fruit/n tree/e 2–3/I 14/F 16

Turdus abyssinicus *Gmelin* AFRICAN MOUNTAIN THRUSH E Africa from Ethiopia to Mozambique/open hillsides, forest and cultivation/insects, worms, fruit etc/n tree or bush/ e 2

Turdus helleri (*Mearns*) TAITA THRUSH Taita Hills in SE Kenya/no data

Turdus libonyanus (*Smith*) KURRICHANE THRUSH S Africa from Congo and Tanganyika S (but not the extreme S)/light bush and cultivation/insects and fruit/n tree or bush/ e 2–3

Turdus tephronotus *Cabanis* AFRICAN BARE-EYED THRUSH E Africa from Congo and Tanganyika S (but not the extreme S)/light bush and cultivation/insects and fruit/n tree/ e 2–3

Turdus menachensis *Ogilvie-Grant* YEMEN THRUSH Yemen and S Saudi Arabia

Turdus ludoviciae (*Phillips*) SOMALI BLACK-BIRD N plateau of Somaliland/no data

Turdus litsipsirupa (*Smith*) GROUNDSCRAPER THRUSH Africa from Ethiopia to Cape of Good Hope and Angola/open woodland and cultivation/invertebrates/n tree or bush/e 3–4

Turdus dissimilis *Blyth* BLACK-BREASTED THRUSH Bangladesh, Assam and northern SE Asia; E Siberia from Yakutia to Manchuria and N Korea w S to meet the other race in northern SE Asia/forest and ravine/insects, molluscs and berries/n tree or bush/e 3–4/I ♂♀

Turdus unicolor *Tickell* TICKELL'S THRUSH Pakistan and N India w peninsular India/open forest and cultivation/insects, worms and fruit/ n tree/e 3–5

Turdus cardis *Temminck* GREY or JAPANESE THRUSH Japan and C China w S to SW Asia/ mountain forest/insects/n tree/e 3–5

Turdus albocinctus *Royle* WHITE-COLLARED BLACKBIRD Himalayas and SE Tibet/forest/ insects and fruit/n tree/e 3–4/I ?♀

Turdus torquatus *L* RING OUSEL Europe and SW Asia w to Sinai and Mediterranean Africa/ moor, scrub and mountain pasture/n ground or tree/e 3–6/I ♂♀ 13–14/F 13–14

Turdus boulboul (*Latham*) GREY-WINGED BLACKBIRD Himalayas and mts of Yunnan, Laos and Tonkin/forest and habitation/insects, worms and fruit/e 3–4/I ♀

Turdus merula *L* BLACKBIRD Europe, much of Asia (except NE) and N Africa, introduced New Zealand/forest, scrub and cultivation/ n tree/e 3–9/I ♀ 11–17/F 12–19

TURDIDAE:
Zoothera dauma,
White's Thrush

TURDIDAE:
Turdus merula,
Blackbird

Plate 204

TURDIDAE:
Erithacus rubecula,
Robin or Redbreast,
Eurasian Robin

E. rubecula feeding its young

Plate 205

Turdus poliocephalus *Latham* Island Thrush Islands from Christmas Is (Indian Ocean) and Indonesia through Melanesia to Fiji and Samoa; about 50 forms, mostly confined to single islands or small groups of islands/ clearings in mountain forest (New Guinea)/ insects and fruits/n rocky ledges above timberline (New Guinea)

Turdus chrysolaus *Temminck* Red-bellied or Brown-headed Thrush Japan and Kuriles w S to SE China and N Philippines/forest and bamboo scrub/n tree or shrub/e 3–4

Turdus celaenops *Stejneger* Seven Islands Thrush Yakushima and Seven Is of Izu/ woodland and cultivation / insects and fruit/ n tree / e 3–4

Turdus rubrocanus *Hodgson* Chestnut or Greyheaded Thrush Himalayas, SE Tibet and mts of W China/forest and cultivation/insects, berries and nectar/n tree/e 2–4

Turdus kessleri (*Przewalski*) Kessler's Thrush W China w S to SE Tibet/scrub and cultivation / ? berries

Turdus feae (*Salvadori*) Fea's Thrush Hopeh (N China) w ? India and Burma (winter range imperfectly known)/insects and berries

Turdus pallidus *Gmelin* Pale Thrush NE Siberia S to Amur w Chinese and Japanese areas/forest/insects and berries/n tree/e 4/I ♀

Turdus obscurus *Gmelin* Eyebrowed or Dark Thrush N Siberia from Yenisei to Kamchatka and S to Mongolia and Sakhalin w S to Indonesia and Himalayas/open forest/ insects, molluscs and berries/n tree/e 4–6

Turdus ruficollis *Pallas* Black-throated Thrush, Red-throated Thrush N and C Asia E to Lake Baikal w S to Himalayas, China and Iran/cultivation and grassland/insects, worms, molluscs and fruit/n tree or ground/e 4–7/I ♀

Turdus naumanni *Temminck* Naumann's Thrush, Dusky Thrush Much of Siberia E to Commander Is w S to Chinese region and Japan/ light forest and open woodland/worms, insects, seeds and berries / n tree or ground / e 4–7 (*Turdus eunomus* Temminck 'Dusky Thrush' is sometimes treated as a separate species)

Turdus pilaris *L* Fieldfare Europe, N and C Asia E to Lake Baikal w S to Iran and the Mediterranean; S Greenland (colonised 1937)/ woodland edge, scrub and cultivation/n tree or ground/e 3–8/I ♀ 11–14/F 12–16

Turdus iliacus *L* Redwing Europe, N and C Asia E to River Kolyma w S to Canary Is, N Africa and Iran/forest, tundra and (in winter) cultivation/n ground or shrub/e 2–8/I ♀ 11–15/ F 10–15

Turdus philomelos *Brehm* Song Thrush Europe, N and C Asia E to Lake Baikal w S to N Africa and Middle East/woodland, scrub and habitation/n tree or ground/e 3–9/I ♀ 11–15/ F 12–16

Turdus mupinensis *Laubmann* Laubmann's Thrush W China from Kansu to NW Yunnan

Turdus viscivorus *L* Mistle Thrush Europe and Asia E to Angara and S to N Indian region; occurring uncommonly S to N Africa in winter/ forest and cultivation/n tree/e 3–6/I ♀ 12–15/ F 12–16

Turdus aurantius *Gmelin* White-chinned Thrush Mts of Jamaica / forest and garden/ n tree / e 2–3

Turdus ravidus (*Cory*) Grand Cayman Thrush Grand Cayman Is/ low woodland / n and e n/k (see note to *T. plumbeus*)

Turdus plumbeus *L* Red-legged Thrush Bahamas, Cuba, Cayman Brac, Hispaniola, Gonave, Tortue, Puerto Rico and Dominica/ forest and garden / n tree or bush / e 3–5 [NB: *plumbeus* and *ravidus* are sometimes separated as the genus *Mimocichla*]

Turdus chiguanco *Lafresnaye and d'Orbigny* Chiguanco Thrush Ecuador to NE Chile/ orchards and shady woodland near streams

Turdus nigrescens *Cabanis* Sooty Robin Mts of Costa Rica and W Panama/forest

Turdus fuscater *Lafresnaye and d'Orbigny* Great Thrush Andes from Venezuela to Bolivia/grassland with stunted trees and bushes

Turdus serranus *Tschudi* Glossy Black Thrush Mts from Mexico to Venezuela and Bolivia/forest

Turdus nigriceps *Cabanis* Slaty Thrush or Black Robin SE Ecuador to Bolivia, S Brazil and Paraguay/forest

Turdus reevei *Lawrence* Plumbeous-backed Thrush W Ecuador and NW Peru/forest and scrub

Turdus olivater (*Lafresnaye*) Black-hooded Thrush Mts of Colombia and Venezuela/ forest, sometimes coffee plantations

Turdus maranonicus *Taczanowski* Marañon Thrush N Peru / dry woodland

Turdus fulviventris *Sclater* Chestnut-bellied Thrush Parts of Colombia, Venezuela,

E Ecuador and N Peru/forest
Turdus rufiventris *Vieillot* RUFOUS-BELLIED
THRUSH Parts of Brazil, Uruguay, Paraguay, N
Argentina and E Bolivia/park and woodland
Turdus falcklandii *Quoy and Gaimard*
AUSTRAL THRUSH S Chile, S Argentina,
Falklands, Juan Fernandez / pastures and
willow groves
Turdus leucomelas *Vieillot* PALE-BREASTED
THRUSH Irregularly distributed over northern
S America/savannah and open woodland
Turdus amaurochalinus *Cabanis* CREAM-
BELLIED THRUSH Brazil, and SE Peru to N and
C Argentina/thick woodland, park and orchard
Turdus plebejus (*Cabanis*) MOUNTAIN ROBIN
Mts from Mexico to W Panama/open woodland
and clearings/n tree/e ?2
Turdus ignobilis *Sclater* BLACK-BILLED ROBIN
Andes from Venezuela to Bolivia and mts of the
Guianas/forest edge and savannah
Turdus lawrencii *Coues* LAWRENCE'S THRUSH
Upper Amazon basin/forest
Turdus fumigatus *Lichtenstein* COCOA
THRUSH Parts of S America S to Rio de Janeiro
(but absent from much of the west), St Vincent
and Grenada / mountain forest and cocoa
plantations on St Vincent and Grenada, else-
where lowland forest / n tree/e 3
Turdus obsoletus *Lawrence* PALE-VENTED
THRUSH Costa Rica, Panama, Orinoco and
Upper Amazon basins/forest (NB: *T. obsoletus*
Lawrence takes priority over and includes *T.
hauxwelli* Lawrence of Ripley, in Peters' *Check
List*)
Turdus grayi *Bonaparte* GRAY'S ROBIN or
CLAY-COLOURED ROBIN Mexico, C America and
parts of Colombia/open woodland near streams
Turdus haplochrous *Todd* UNICOLOURED
THRUSH E Bolivia
Turdus nudigenis *Lafresnaye* AMERICAN
BARE-EYED THRUSH S Lesser Antilles, S
America S to the Amazon and part of S bank
of Lower Amazon; W of Andes S to W
Ecuador and NW Peru/lowland woodland and
cultivation/n tree/e 3
Turdus jamaicensis *Gmelin* WHITE-EYED
THRUSH Jamaica/mountain forest and wooded
hills/n tree/e 2-3
Turdus albicollis *Vieillot* WHITE-NECKED
THRUSH Mexico, C America and much of S
America S to N Argentina/forest, woodland
and garden (*T. assimilis* Cabanis is sometimes

separated)
Turdus rufopalliatus *Lafresnaye* RUFOUS-
BACKED ROBIN Mexico
Turdus swalesi (*Wetmore*) LA SALLE THRUSH
La Salle ridge on Haiti/dense shrubbery/n bush
or tree/e n/s
Turdus rufitorques *Hartlaub* RUFOUS-
COLLARED ROBIN SE Mexico, Guatemala and
W El Salvador
Turdus migratorius *L* AMERICAN ROBIN
N America and Mexico/forest and habitation/
insects, berries etc/n tree or building/e 3-5/
I 11-14/F 14-16
TIMALIIDAE Babblers A very diverse group
of passerines of variable size and colouration.
Babblers generally have soft, fluffy plumage and
strong legs and feet. Their wings are short and
rounded and their flight weak. The diversity of
the family has caused it to become a repository
for odd species of dubious affinities. About 280
species in warmer parts of the Old World.
Orthonyx temminckii *Ranzani* SOUTHERN
LOGRUNNER Mts of New Guinea: SE Queens-
land and New South Wales/mountain forest/
n ground/e 1-2
Orthonyx spaldingii *Ramsay* NORTHERN
LOGRUNNER Forests of coastal mts of N
Queensland/forest/insects/n ground or bush/
e 1
Androphobus viridis (*Rothschild and Hartert*)
GREEN-BACKED BABBLER Mts of W New Guinea
Psophodes olivaceus (*Latham*) EASTERN
WHIPBIRD Queensland to Victoria / forests/
insects/n undergrowth/e 2
Psophodes nigrogularis *Gould* BLACK-
THROATED WHIPBIRD Mallee scrub of southern
Australia / insects / n near ground in thick
vegetation/e 2
Sphenostoma cristatum *Gould* WEDGEBILL
Interior of Australia/mulga and arid savannah/
insects/n bush/e 2-3
Cinclosoma punctatum (*Shaw*) SPOTTED
QUAIL THRUSH Tasmania and SE Australia/dry
forest and woodland / seeds and insects / n
ground under log or tussock/e 2-3
Cinclosoma castanotum *Gould* CHESTNUT
QUAIL THRUSH Mallee scrub of interior of
Australia/seeds/n ground under cover/e 2-3
Cinclosoma cinnamomeum *Gould*
CINNAMON QUAIL THRUSH Widely distributed
over the drier parts of Australia / semi-desert
and scrub/seeds and insects/n ground/e 2-3

Opposite:
TURDIDAE:
Erithacus rubecula,
Robin or Redbreast,
Eurasian Robin

TURDIDAE:
Monticola rufiventris,
Chestnut-bellied Rock Thrush

TURDIDAE:
Luscinia luscinia,
Thrush Nightingale

Plate 206

Plate 207

(several races of *cinnamomeum* are considered by some authorities to be separate species)

Cinclosoma ajax (*Temminck*) AJAX SCRUB ROBIN Locally distributed in W, S and SE New Guinea / no data

Ptilorrhoa leucosticta (*Sclater*) HIGH-MOUNTAIN SCRUB ROBIN High mountains of New Guinea / forest / insects and (?) fruit / n hole near ground / e 2

Ptilorrhoa caerulescens (*Temminck*) LOWLAND SCRUB ROBIN Lowlands of New Guinea / forest / insects / n ground / e 2

Ptilorrhoa castanonota (*Salvadori*) MID-MOUNTAIN SCRUB ROBIN Mountain-slopes and lower mountains of New Guinea / forests / no data

Eupetes macrocerus *Temminck* RAIL BABBLER Malay Peninsula, Sumatra, Borneo and N Natunas / forest / insects (frequently mis-spelled *macrocercus*)

Melampitta lugubris *Schlegel* LESSER MELAMPITTA Mts of New Guinea / mountain forest / insects, snails and fruit / n and e n/k

Melampitta gigantea (*Rothschild*) GREATER MELAMPITTA Arfak and Nassau Mts, W New Guinea / no data

Ifrita kowaldi (*De Vis*) BLUE-CAPPED BABBLER Mts of New Guinea / forest / insects / n tree / e 1 (data states that 1 nest with 1 young only known, but 1 nest with 1 egg also in the Rothschild Collection at Tring)

Pellorneum ruficeps *Swainson* PUFF-THROATED or SPOTTED BABBLER Himalayas, India, SE Asia (except Malay Peninsula), S Yunnan / scrub and bamboo / insects / n ground / e 2–5 / I ♂♀ / F 12–13

Pellorneum palustre *Gould* MARSH BABBLER Assam / reeds, grass and bush / insects / n ground / e ?2–3

Pellorneum fuscocapillum (*Blyth*) BROWN-CAPPED BABBLER Ceylon / forest / insects / n ground or hole / e 2–3 / I ♂♀

Pellorneum capistratum (*Temminck*) BLACK-CAPPED BABBLER Malay Peninsula, N Natunas, Billiton, Bangka, Borneo, Banggai, Sumatra and Java / forest / insects

Pellorneum albiventre (*Godwin-Austen*) PLAIN BROWN BABBLER Hills from Assam through central SE Asia / scrub and bamboo / insects / n bush / e 3–5

Trichostoma tickelli (*Blyth*) TICKELL'S BABBLER Assam, SE Asia, Sumatra / forest and scrub / insects / n off ground / e 3–4

Trichostoma pyrrogenys (*Temminck*) TEMMINCK'S BABBLER Java, Sarawak and Sabah / forest / insects / n base of shrub / e n/s

Trichostoma malaccense (*Hartlaub*) SHORT-TAILED BABBLER Malay Peninsula, Sumatra, Borneo and adjacent small islands / forest / insects

[**Trichostoma feriatum** (*Chasen and Kloss*) SARAWAK BABBLER Gunong Mulu, Sarawak / unique / status uncertain, frequently treated as a race of *malaccense*]

Trichostoma cinericeps (*Tweeddale*) ASHY-HEADED BABBLER Palawan and Balabec

Trichostoma rostratum *Blyth* BLYTH'S JUNGLE BABBLER Malay Peninsula, Sumatra, Banggai, Biliton and Borneo / forest rivers / insects

Trichostoma bicolor (*Lesson*) FERRUGINEOUS JUNGLE BABBLER Malay Peninsula, E Sumatra, Bangka and Borneo / forest / ants / n ? near ground / e ? 2–3

Trichostoma sepiarium (*Horsfield*) HORSFIELD'S BABBLER Malay Peninsula, Sumatra, Java, Bali and Borneo / forest / insects / n ? bush

Trichostoma celebense (*Strickland*) CELEBES JUNGLE BABBLER Celebes, Pulau Buton and Togian Is

Trichostoma abbotti (*Blyth*) ABBOTT'S BABBLER E Himalayas, SE Asia, E Sumatra, Bawean, Billiton, Borneo and Pulau Mata Siri / forest / insects / n off ground / e 3–5

Trichostoma perspicillatum (*Bonaparte*) BÜTTIKOFER'S BABBLER Borneo / unique

Trichostoma vanderbilti (*de Schaunsee and Ripley*) VANDERBILT'S BABBLER Koengke, N Sumatra / unique

Trichastoma pyrrhopterum (*Reichenow and Neumann*) MOUNTAIN ILLADOPSIS Highlands from E Congo to Kenya and Malawi / forest / insects, snails and berries / n and e n/k

Trichastoma cleaveri (*Shelley*) BLACKCAP ILLADOPSIS Fernando Po and forests of W Africa from Sierra Leone to Moyen Congo / n tree / e 2

Trichostoma albipectus (*Reichenow*) SCALY-BREASTED ILLADOPSIS Forests from N Angola through Congo to Uganda, S Sudan and SW Kenya / insects / n and e n/k

Trichostoma rufescens (*Reichenow*) RUFOUS-WINGED ILLADOPSIS Forests of W Africa from

Sierra Leone to Ghana / insects and molluscs / n and e n/k

Trichostoma rufipenne *Sharpe* PALE-BREASTED ILLADOPSIS Fernando Po and forests from Sierra Leone to Congo, and thence to Uganda, SW Kenya, NE Tanganyika and Zanzibar / forest undergrowth / insects / n stump / e 2

Trichostoma fulvescens (*Cassin*) BROWN ILLADOPSIS Forests from Senegal to Congo, N Angola and Uganda / forest undergrowth / insects / n stump / e 2

Trichostoma puveli (*Salvadori*) PUVEL'S ILLADOPSIS Forests of W Africa from Portuguese Guinea to NE Congo / insects / n and e n/k

Trichostoma poliothorax (*Reichenow*) GREY-CHESTED ILLADOPSIS Fernando Po and highlands from Cameroons to Ruanda and SW Kenya (apparently discontinuous) / mountain forest / no other data

Leonardina woodi (*Mearns*) BAGOBO BABBLER Mindanao

Ptyrticus turdinus *Hartlaub* WHITE-BELLIED THRUSH BABBLER C Cameroons: E Congo and SW Sudan / dense bush near forest streams / insects / n and e n/k

Malacopteron magnirostre (*Moore*) MOUSTACHED BABBLER Malay Peninsula, Sumatra, Borneo and adjacent small islands / forest / insects

Malacopteron affine (*Blyth*) SOOTY-CAPPED BABBLER Malay Peninsula, Sumatra, Borneo and Pulau Bangkaru / forest / insects

Malacopteron cinereum *Eyton* SCALY-CAPPED BABBLER SE Asia, Java, Sumatra, Borneo and adjacent small islands / forest / insects and fruit

Malacopteron magnum *Eyton* RED-HEADED BABBLER Malay Peninsula, Sumatra, Pulau Bunguran and Borneo / forest / insects and seeds

Malacopteron palawanense *Büttikofer* PALAWAN BABBLER Palawan and Balabec

Malacopteron albogulare (*Blyth*) GREY-BREASTED BABBLER Malaya, NE Sumatra, Batu Is, NW Borneo / forest

Pomatorhinus hypoleucos (*Blyth*) LARGE SCIMITAR BABBLER Assam, northern SE Asia, Hainan / scrub and bamboo / insects and snails / n ground / e 2–3

Pomatorhinus erythrogenys *Vigors* RUSTY-CHEEKED SCIMITAR BABBLER Himalayas, mts of northern SE Asia, Taiwan, S and W China /

thick scrub / insects and berries / n ground / e 3 / I ♂♀ [*P. erythrocnemis* Gould, from Taiwan, is sometimes separated]

Pomatorhinus horsfieldii *Sykes* INDIAN SCIMITAR BABBLER Peninsular India and Ceylon / forest and scrub / insects and berries / n ground or bush / e 2–3 / I ♂♀ (sometimes regarded as a race of *P. schisticeps*)

Pomatorhinus schisticeps *Hodgson* SLATY-HEADED or WHITE-BROWED SCIMITAR BABBLER Himalayas and much of SE Asia / forest and scrub / insects and berries / n bush or herbage / e 3–4 / I ♂♀

Pomatorhinus montanus *Horsfield* YELLOW-BILLED SCIMITAR BABBLER Malay Peninsula, Sumatra, Java, Bali and Borneo / forest / n ground / e 2–3

Pomatorhinus ruficollis *Hodgson* RUFOUS-NECKED SCIMITAR BABBLER Himalayas, hills of northern SE Asia and S China, Hainan and Taiwan / forest / insects / n bush / e 3–5

Pomatorhinus ochraceiceps *Walden* RED-BILLED SCIMITAR BABBLER Northern SE Asia and NE Assam / forest undergrowth / insects and nectar / n ground / e 3–5

Pomatorhinus ferruginosus *Blyth* CORAL-BILLED SCIMITAR BABBLER Himalayas and northern SE Asia / dense scrub / insects / n bush / e 3–5

Garritornis isidorei (*Lesson*) RUFOUS BABBLER New Guinea and Misol / lowland forest / insects and small lizards / n tree / e n/k

Pomatostomus temporalis (*Vigors and Horsfield*) GREY-CROWNED BABBLER Australia and S New Guinea / savannah / insects and seeds / n tree / e 2–3

Pomatostomus superciliosus (*Vigors and Horsfield*) WHITE-BROWED BABBLER Interior of Australia / dry woodland and semi-desert / insects and seeds / n tree / e 4–5

Pomastostomus ruficeps (*Hartlaub*) CHESTNUT-CROWNED BABBLER SE Australia / mallee scrub / insects and seeds / n tree / e 4–5

Pomastostomus halli *Cowles* (*Emu*, vol 64, pp 1–5) MAJOR HALL'S BABBLER Interior of Queensland / woodland / insects and seeds

Xiphirhynchus superciliaris *Blyth* SLENDER-BILLED SCIMITAR BABBLER Himalayas from E Nepal to mts of N Burma and NW Yunnan / bush and bamboo / insects, berries and nectar / n ground / e 3–5

Jabouilleia danjoui (*Robinson and Kloss*)

TURDIDAE:
Turdus viscivorus,
Mistle Thrush

TURDIDAE: '
Zoothera dauma,
White's Thrush

Plate 208

TURDIDAE: *Copsychus malabaricus*, Common Shama, White-rumped Shama

Plate 209

SHORT-TAILED SCIMITAR BABBLER Col des Nuages and Lang Bian, Annam

Rimator malacoptilus *Blyth* LONG-BILLED SCIMITAR BABBLER Sikkim to NE Burma: Tonking: Highlands of W Sumatra/scrub and forest undergrowth/insects/n ground/e 4

Ptilocichla leucogrammica (*Bonaparte*) BORNEO WREN BABBLER Borneo/lowland forest

Ptilocichla mindanensis (*Blasius*) BLASIUS' WREN BABBLER Philippines

Ptilocichla falcata *Sharpe* FALCATED WREN BABBLER Palawan and Balabec

Kenopia striata (*Blyth*) STRIPED WREN BABBLER Malay Peninsula, E Sumatra and Borneo/forest/insects

Napothera rufipectus (*Salvadori*) SUMATRA WREN BABBLER Highlands of W Sumatra

Napothera atrigularis (*Bonaparte*) BLACK-THROATED WREN BABBLER Borneo/forest

Napothera macrodactyla (*Strickland*) LARGE WREN BABBLER Malay Peninsula, NE Sumatra and Java

Napothera marmorata (*Ramsay*) MARBLED WREN BABBLER Highlands of C Malaya and W Sumatra

Napothera crispifrons (*Blyth*) LIMESTONE BABBLER Calcareous formations of Thailand and N Indo-China

Napothera brevicaudata (*Blyth*) STREAKED or SHORT-TAILED WREN BABBLER Hills of Assam, W Yunnan and SE Asia/hill forest/insects/n ground/e 3–4

Napothera crassa (*Sharpe*) MOUNTAIN WREN BABBLER Mountains of Sabah and Sarawak/forest and ravine/insects and snails/n and e n/k

Napothera rabori *Rand* LUZON WREN BABBLER N Luzon/unique

Napothera epilepidota (*Temminck*) SMALL WREN BABBLER Hills of Assam, SE Asia, Hainan, Sumatra, Java and Borneo/dense dark forest/insects/n ground/e 3–5

Pnoepyga albiventer (*Hodgson*) SCALY-BREASTED WREN BABBLER Himalayas to N Burma, N Tonking and mts of Yunnan and Szechwan/forest and plantation/insects (? seeds)/n ground or tree/e 3–5/I ♂♀

Pnoepyga pusilla *Hodgson* PYGMY WREN BABBLER Himalayas, SE Asia, S China, Taiwan, Sumatra, Java, Flores and Timor/forest/insects/n tree/e 3–4

Spelaeornis caudatus (*Blyth*) RUFOUS-THROATED WREN BABBLER Sikkim, W Bengal,

E Bhutan/forest undergrowth/insects/n ? hole/e 3–4

Spelaeornis badeigularis *Ripley* MISHMI WREN BABBLER NE Assam/unique (see Ali and Ripley, *Handbook of Birds of India and Pakistan*, vol 6, p 161 footnote, for reasons for regarding this form as a species)

Spelaeornis troglodytoides (*Verreaux*) BAR-WINGED WREN BABBLER E Bhutan, NE Burma and NW Yunnan, Hsiking, NW Szechwan, Shensi/forest/insects/n and e n/k (this species also rejoices in the name 'Spotted Longtailed Wren Babbler')

Spelaeornis formosus (*Walden*) SPOTTED WREN BABBLER Sikkim, W Bengal, Bhutan, Assam, W Burma, SE Yunnan and NW Fukien/forest/insects/n ? ground/e ? 3–4 (no definite data)

Spelaeornis chocolatinus (*Godwin-Austen and Walden*) LONG-TAILED WREN BABBLER Assam, N Burma, SW Yunnan and NW Tonkin/forest/insects/n ground/e 3

Spelaeornis longicaudatus (*Moore*) TAWNY-BREASTED WREN BABBLER Assam and Manipur Hills/forest/insects/n ground/e 4

Sphenocichla humei (*Mandelli*) HUME'S or WEDGE BILLED WREN BABBLER Hills from Sikkim to N Burma/forest/insects/n tree/e 4 (1 nest known)

Neomixus tenella (*Hartlaub*) COMMON JERY Madagascar/dry woodland, scrub and mangrove/n tree/e 4

Neomixus viridis (*Sharpe*) GREEN JERY Humid east of Madagascar/forest and bush

Neomixus stratigula *Sharpe* STRIPE-THROATED JERY Madagascar/forest and bush/insects/n bush/e 3–5 (2 nests known)

Neomixus flavoviridis *Hartert* WEDGE-TAILED JERY C and S parts of humid east of Madagascar/forest

Stachyris rodolphei *Deignan* DEIGNAN'S BABBLER Thailand

Stachyris rufifrons *Hume* RED-FRONTED BABBLER Parts of S Burma and W Thailand, Malay Peninsula, Sumatra and Borneo/forest/insects and berries/n tree or ground/e 3–5/I ♂♀

Stachyris ambigua (*Harington*) HARINGTON'S BABBLER Himalayas from Sikkim E to NE Burma, N and W Thailand, Laos and NW Tonking/forest/n bush/e 4

Stachyris ruficeps *Blyth* RUFOUS-FRONTED BABBLER Sikkim E through northern SE Asia to China N to Yangtse Valley and S through Vietnam; Taiwan and Hainan / forest undergrowth / insects and berries / n bush or ground / e 3–4

Stachyris pyrrhops *Blyth* BLACK-CHINNED BABBLER Himalayas from N Pakistan to C Nepal / scrub and light forest / insects and berries / n bush / e 3–4

Stachyris chrysaea *Blyth* GOLDEN BABBLER Himalayas from Nepal eastward, SE Asia, W Yunnan, W Sumatra / scrub and secondary jungle / insects and berries / n in bamboo clumps / e 4

Stachyris plateni (*Blasius*) PLATEN'S BABBLER Samar, Leyte and Mindanao

Stachyris capitalis (*Tweeddale*) PHILIPPINE TREE BABBLER Philippines

Stachyris dennistouni (*Ogilvie-Grant*) GOLDEN-CROWNED TREE BABBLER NE Luzon

Stachyris speciosa (*Tweeddale*) TWEEDDALE'S BABBLER Negros

Stachyris whiteheadi (*Ogilvie-Grant*) WHITEHEAD'S TREE BABBLER Luzon

Stachyris striata (*Ogilvie-Grant*) STRIPED TREE BABBLER Highlands of N Luzon

Stachyris nigrorum *Rand and Rabor* NEGROS TREE BABBLER Highlands of Negros

Stachyris hypogrammica *Salomonsen* PALAWAN TREE BABBLER Palawan

Stachyris grammiceps (*Temminck*) WHITE-BREASTED BABBLER W Java

Stachyris herberti (*Baker*) HERBERT'S BABBLER Laos

Stachyris nigriceps *Blyth* BLACK-THROATED BABBLER Himalayas from C Nepal eastwards, SE Asia, Sumatra, Borneo, Pulau Tioman and N Natuna Is / forest and scrub / insects and berries / n ground or bush / e 3–5 / I ♂♀

Stachyris poliocephala (*Temminck*) GREY-HEADED BABBLER Malay Peninsula, Sumatra and Borneo / lowland forest / insects / n tree / e 1

Stachyris striolata (*Müller*) SPOT-NECKED BABBLER Hainan, SW China, western SE Asia and Malay Peninsula, Sumatra / forest / n and e n/k

Stachyris oglei (*Godwin-Austen*) OGLE'S, SNOWY-THROATED or AUSTEN'S SPOTTED BABBLER E Assam / moist scrub / insects / n ? ground / e 4

Stachyris maculata (*Temminck*) CHESTNUT-RUMPED BABBLER Malay Peninsula, Sumatra, Borneo and adjacent small islands / lowland forest / insects / n tree ? / e n/s (1 known)

Stachyris leucotis (*Strickland*) WHITE-NECKED BABBLER Malay Peninsula, Sumatra and Borneo / forest (lowland in Malaya, submontane in Borneo) / insects / n ? tree / e 3 (1 known)

Stachyris nigricollis (*Temminck*) BLACK-THROATED BABBLER Malay Peninsula, E Sumatra, Borneo / forest

Stachyris thoracica (*Temminck*) WHITE-COLLARED BABBLER S Sumatra and Java

Stachyris erythroptera (*Blyth*) CHESTNUT-WINGED BABBLER Malay Peninsula, Sumatra, Borneo and adjacent small islands / forest / insects

Stachyris melanothorax (*Temminck*) PEARL-CHEEKED BABBLER Mountains of Java and lowlands of Bali

Dumetia hyperythra (*Franklin*) WHITE-THROATED and TAWNY-BELLIED BABBLERS India, Ceylon and SW Nepal / scrub and grassland / insects and nectar / n bush / e 3–4

Rhopocichla atriceps (*Jerdon*) BLACK-HEADED BABBLER W Ghats, Kerala and Ceylon / reed beds and bamboo jungle / insects / n bush / e 2

Macronous flavicollis (*Bonaparte*) GREY-FACED TIT-BABBLER Java and Kangean Is

Macronous gularis (*Horsfield*) STRIPED or YELLOW-BREASTED TIT-BABBLER Lowlands of N India, SE Asia, S Yunnan, Sumatra, Borneo, Java, Palawan and a wide variety of islets and small islands (many coastal islets have their own separate races) / light and dense forest and grassland / insects / n bush / e 3–4

Macronous kelleyi (*Delacour*) KELLEY'S TIT-BABBLER Scattered localities in E Thailand, S Laos and Vietnam (see Deignan's note in Peters' *Check List*, vol 10, p 323 on this puzzling bird)

Macronous straticeps *Sharpe* BROWN TIT-BABBLER Philippines and Sulu Archipelago

Macronous ptilosus *Jardine and Selby* FLUFFY-BACKED TIT-BABBLER Malay Peninsula, Sumatra, Pulau Tanah Bula, Bangka, Billiton and Borneo / forest / insects / n near ground / e 3

Micromacronus leytensis *Amadon* LEYTE TIT-BABBLER Dagami, 1,500ft (450m), Barrio of Patok, eastern shoulder of Mt Lobu, Leyte (known only from type locality)

Timalia pileata *Horsfield* CHESTNUT-CAPPED BABBLER Himalayas from Nepal, SE Asia (except Malay Peninsula), isolated race in Java / reedbeds and scrub / insects / n bush or ground / e 3–5

TURDIDAE:
Turdus viscivorus,
Mistle Thrush

TURDIDAE:
Turdus migratorius,
American Robin

Plate 210

TURDIDAE: *Turdus merula*, Blackbird

Plate 211

Chrysomma sinense (*Gmelin*) YELLOW-EYED BABBLER E Pakistan across India through SE Asia (except Malay Peninsula) to S China/ scrub, bamboo and cultivation/insects, berries and nectar/n bush/e 3–4/I ♂♀/F 12–13

Moupina altirostris (*Jerdon*) JERDON'S BABBLER Bhutan and Assam, parts of Burma and Pakistan (discontinuous)/grassland/insects/ n bush/e 2–3?

Moupina poecilotis (*Verreaux*) CHESTNUT-TAILED BABBLER W China in parts of Szechwan, Yunnan and Hsikiang

Turdoides nipalensis (*Hodgson*) SPINY BABBLER W and C Nepal/dense scrub/insects/ n in grass/e 3–4

Turdoides altirostris (*Hartert*) IRAQ BABBLER Reed-beds of lower Tigris-Euphrates valley/ no reliable information relating to nests and eggs owing to confusion with *caudatus*

Turdoides caudatus (*Dumont*) COMMON BABBLER SE Iraq through Iran, S Afghanistan to Pakistan and peninsular India, Lacadive Is and Rameswaram Is/dry scrub and cultivation/ insects and nectar/n bush/e 3–5/I ♂♀ 13–15

Turdoides earlei (*Blyth*) EARLE'S BABBLER Pakistan, across N Indian plains to Burma/ reeds and tall grass/insects and snails/n bush or reeds/e 3–4

Turdoides gularis (*Blyth*) WHITE-THROATED BABBLER C and S Burma/scrub and habitation/ n bush/e 3–4

Turdoides longirostris (*Moore*) SLENDER-BILLED BABBLER Grasslands at foot of Himalayas from Nepal to Assam, and N Arakan/tall grass and reeds/insects/n bush/e 3–5

Turdoides malcolmi (*Sykes*) MALCOLM'S BABBLER (GREAT GREY BABBLER) Interior of peninsular India / dry scrub and cultivation/ insects, grain and berries / n shrub / e 3–4/ I – believed to be communal

Turdoides fulvus (*Desfontaines*) FULVOUS CHATTERER N Africa S to Aïr Massif and on E to Red Sea coasts of Sudan and Ethiopia/desert scrub / insects and seeds / n thorn bush / e 3–6

Turdoides squamiceps (*Cretzschmar*) ARABIAN BABBLER Arabia/desert scrub/n bush/ e 4–9

Turdoides aylmeri (*Shelley*) AYLMER'S BABBLER E Africa from Ethiopia to N Tanganyika/scrub/insects/n bush/e 2–3

Turdoides rubiginosus (*Rüppell*) RUFOUS CHATTERER E Africa from S Ethiopia to Uganda and N Tanganyika / thick bush near rivers/ insects/n bush/e 2–4

Turdoides subrufus (*Jerdon*) RUFOUS BABBLER W peninsular India/jungle and dense scrub/insects, berries and nectar/n tree/e 4

Turdoides striatus (*Dumont*) STRIATED BABBLER Ceylon and much of India and Pakistan/forest and cultivation/insects and nectar/ n tree/e 2–7/I ♂♀+? communal (*T. rufescens* (Blyth) of Ceylon, is sometimes treated as a species)

Turdoides affinis (*Jerdon*) WHITE-HEADED or YELLOW-BILLED BABBLER Ceylon and S India/ dry scrub and cultivation / insects, fruit etc/ n tree / e 3–4 (e 3–5 in *hills* of Ceylon)/I ♂♀ 14–17

Turdoides melanops (*Hartlaub*) BLACK-FACED BABBLER Parts of E and S Africa from Kenya to Angola (but not the extreme S)/bush/ n bush/e 2–3

Turdoides tenebrosus (*Hartlaub*) DUSKY BABBLER NE Congo, S Sudan and SW Ethiopia/ dense cover near water / n in creepers near ground/e 2–3

Turdoides reinwardtii (*Swainson*) BLACKCAP BABBLER W Africa from Senegal to Cameroon/ forest/n tree/e 2–3

Turdoides plebejus (*Cretzschmar*) BROWN BABBLER Africa from Senegal to Sudan, Ethiopia and W Kenya (*T. leucocephalus* (Cretzschmar) 'White-headed Babbler' is sometimes separated)

Turdoides jardineii (*Smith*) ARROW-MARKED BABBLER Much of E and S Africa (except extreme S)/bush/n bush/e 3

Turdoides squamulatus (*Shelley*) SCALY BABBLER Coasts of Kenya and Italian Somaliland/ dense bush/n n/k/e described but no data on clutch size

Turdoides leucopygius (*Rüppell*) WHITE-RUMPED BABBLER SE Sudan to Zambia and S Angola/bush, reed beds etc/n tree/e 3

Turdoides hindei (*Sharpe*) HINDE'S BABBLER E foothills of E Kenya highlands/scrub/n n/k/ e n/s

Turdoides hypoleucus (*Cabanis*) PIED BABBLER C Kenya and NE Tanganyika/scrub and forest edge/n thorn bush/e 3–4

Turdoides bicolor (*Jardine*) BICOLOURED BABBLER SW Africa, Bechuanaland and W Transvaal/dry bushveld/insects/n thorn bush/ e 2–5

Turdoides gymnogenys (*Hartlaub*) BARE-CHEEKED BABBLER SW Angola and northern SW Africa / dry plains / no other data

Babax lanceolatus (*Verreaux*) CHINESE or COMMON BABAX W and S China, N and W Burma and Assam / thin forest / n bush / e 2–4

Babax waddelli *Dresser* GIANT BABAX SE Tibet/arid scrub/insects and berries/n bush/e 3

Babax koslowi (*Bianchi*) KOSLOW'S BABAX Mekong Valley in S Tsinghai and N Hsikang

Garrulax cinereifrons *Blyth* ASHY-HEADED LAUGHING THRUSH SW Ceylon (wet zone)/ humid forest / insects / n bush / e 3–4

Garrulax palliatus (*Bonaparte*) GREY AND BROWN LAUGHING THRUSH Highlands of W Sumatra and northern Borneo / mountain forest/ fruit and insects / n and e 'Hose found a nest with young on Mt. Dulit' (Smithies)

Garrulax rufifrons *Lesson* RED-FRONTED LAUGHING THRUSH Mts of Java

Garrulax perspicillatus (*Gmelin*) SPECTACLED LAUGHING THRUSH China from Yangtse valley S to Tonkin / forest and cultivation / insects, fruit and seeds / n tree or bush / e 2–5

Garrulax albogularis (*Gould*) WHITE-THROATED LAUGHING THRUSH Himalayas and mts of SW China, Taiwan / forest and habitation/ insects and berries / n bush / e 3–4

Garrulax leucolophus (*Hardwicke*) WHITE-CRESTED LAUGHING THRUSH Himalayas, SE Asia and W Yunnan: W Sumatra / forest/ insects, berries and seeds / n shrub / e 3–6

Garrulax monileger (*Hodgson*) NECKLACED LAUGHING THRUSH Himalayas, SE Asia (except Malay Peninsula), S China and Hainan / forest/ insects, snails, berries etc / n tree / e 4–5

Garrulax pectoralis (*Gould*) GORGETED LAUGHING THRUSH Himalayas, SE Asia (except Malay Peninsula), SE China and Hainan/ forest and edges of cultivation / insects / n tree / e 3–7

Garrulax lugubris (*Müller*) BLACK LAUGHING THRUSH Mts of Malaya, W Sumatra and NE Borneo / forest / insects

Garrulax striatus (*Vigors*) STRIATED LAUGHING THRUSH Himalayas and hills of N and W Burma / forest / insects, berries and seeds / n in creepers / e 2

Garrulax strepitans *Blyth* TICKELL'S LAUGHING THRUSH S Burma and parts of Thailand / n and e n/k

Garrulax milleti *Robinson and Kloss* MILLET'S LAUGHING THRUSH S Annam

Garrulax maesi (*Oustalet*) GREY LAUGHING THRUSH Hainan, SW China and north-eastern SE Asia

Garrulax chinensis (*Scopoli*) CHINESE LAUGHING THRUSH Assam, SE Asia (except Malay Peninsula), Yunnan, S China and Hainan / scrub and tall grass / insects / n bush/ e 2–3/1 ♂♀ (*G. nuchalis* is sometimes separated)

Garrulax vassali (*Ogilvie-Grant*) WHITE-CHEEKED LAUGHING THRUSH S Laos and S Annam

Garrulax galbanus *Godwin-Austen* YELLOW-THROATED LAUGHING THRUSH SE Assam and W Burma / open forest and parkland / insects and seeds / n bush / e 2–4

Garrulax courtoisi *Menegaux* CURTOIS'S LAUGHING THRUSH Wuyuan (NE Kiangsi)/ formerly treated as a race of *galbanus*

Garrulax delesserti (*Jerdon*) WYNAAD LAUGHING THRUSH SW India: Bhutan, Assam, N Burma and N Laos / rain forest / insects, berries and seeds / n bush / e 2–4

Garrulax variegatus (*Vigors*) VARIEGATED LAUGHING THRUSH W Himalayas from Kashmir to Nepal / forest and garden / insects, berries and fruit / n tree / e 2–4 / 1 ♂♀

Garrulax davidi (*Swinhoe*) PÈRE DAVID'S LAUGHING THRUSH Manchuria and N China SW to Szechwan

Garrulax sukatschewi (*Berezowski and Bianchi*) SUKATSCHEV'S LAUGHING THRUSH S Kansu

Garrulax cineraceus (*Godwin-Austen*) MOUSTACHED LAUGHING THRUSH From hills of Assam across Burma to Yangtse Valley and S China provinces / scrub and secondary forest/ insects and berries / n bush / e 2–3

Garrulax rufogularis (*Gould*) RUFOUS-CHINNED LAUGHING THRUSH Himalayas from Pakistan to Assam, N Burma and Tonkin/ scrub and forest / insects, berries and seeds/ n bush or tree / e 2–4 / 1 ♂♀

Garrulax lunulatus (*Verreaux*) BARRED LAUGHING THRUSH W China from Kansu to Szechwan

Garrulax bieti (*Oustalet*) BIET'S LAUGHING THRUSH S Hsikiang and NW Yunnan

Garrulax maximus (*Verreaux*) GIANT LAUGHING THRUSH SE Tibet and W China/ subalpine forest / n in bamboo / e 2 (1 nest known)

TIMALIIDAE:
Leiothrix lutea,
Red-billed Leiothrix,
Peking Robin

Plate 212

TIMALIIDAE:
Garrulax albogularis,
White-throated Laughing
Thrush

TIMALIIDAE:
Pomatostomus temporalis,
Grey-crowned Babbler

Plate 213

Garrulax ocellatus (*Vigors*) SPOTTED LAUGH-ING THRUSH Himalayas to mts of SW Szechwan and NW Yunnan/light forest and scrub/insects and fruit/n bush or tree/e 2

Garrulax caerulatus (*Hodgson*) GREY-SIDED LAUGHING THRUSH Himalayas and hills of N Burma and W Yunnan / scrub and forest undergrowth / berries and seeds (? insects)/ n bush/e 2–3

Garrulax poecilorhynchus *Gould* SCALY-HEADED LAUGHING THRUSH Taiwan and mts of Fukien and Szechwan/n bush/e 3–5

Garrulax mitratus (*Müller*) CAPPED LAUGHING THRUSH Mts of Malaya, Sumatra and Borneo / forest / seeds, fruit, insects and snails/n in creepers/e 2

Garrulax ruficollis (*Jardine and Selby*) RUFOUS-NECKED LAUGHING THRUSH Himalayas from E Nepal to N Burma/forest, scrub and cultivation/n bush/e 3–4

Garrulax merulinus *Blyth* SPOT-BREASTED LAUGHING THRUSH Assam, W Yunnan and parts of northern and eastern SE Asia/forest and clearings/n shrub/e 2–3/I ♂♀

Garrulax canorus *L* HWAMEI LAUGHING THRUSH Taiwan, Hainan, Yangtse Valley and S China to north-eastern SE Asia/forest and scrub/n ground or bush/e 3–5

Garrulax sannio *Swinhoe* WHITE-CHEEKED LAUGHING THRUSH Assam, northern SE Asia and S China/forest and scrub /seeds, berries and snails/n bush/e 3–4

Garrulax cachinnans *Jerdon* NILGIRI LAUGHING THRUSH S India/forest undergrowth/ insects and berries/n bush or tree/e n/s

Garrulax jerdoni *Blyth* JERDON'S LAUGHING THRUSH S India / hill scrub and plantations/ insects and fruit/n bush/e 2–4/I ♂♀ [Ali and Ripley give *cachinnans* as a monotypic species, and place the taxa *fairbanki* and *meridionale* in *G. jerdoni*. All the populations are of local distribution, and may be conspecific]

Garrulax lineatus (*Vigors*) STREAKED LAUGHING THRUSH Mts from Tadzikistan along Himalayas to SE Tibet and Bhutan/ scrub and gardens/insects and berries/n bush/ e 2–4/I ♂♀

Garrulax virgatus (*Godwin-Austen*) STRIPED LAUGHING THRUSH Assam and Chin Hills / forest / insects / n bush / e 2–3

Garrulax austeni (*Godwin-Austen*) AUSTEN'S LAUGHING THRUSH Assam and Chin Hills/

forest/insects and seeds/n bush/e 2–4

Garrulax squamatus (*Gould*) BLUE-WINGED LAUGHING THRUSH Himalayas from Nepal to W Yunnan, Chin Hills and NW Tonkin/ streambanks and bush / insects, berries and seeds/n bush/e 2–4

Garrulax subunicolor (*Blyth*) SCALY or PLAIN-COLOURED LAUGHING THRUSH Himalayas from Nepal to W Yunnan, Chin Hills and NW Tonkin/forest and secondary growth/inverte-brates, berries and buds/n bush/e 3–4

Garrulax elliotii (*Verreaux*) ELLIOT'S LAUGHING THRUSH W China from Kansu to Yunnan/no reliable data/the 2 clutches of eggs in the British Museum (Natural History), 1 of each of the 2 races, are so different as to suggest that one of them is incorrectly identified, or that 2 species may be involved

Garrulax henrici (*Oustalet*) PRINCE HENRY'S LAUGHING THRUSH SE Tibet and SW Hsikiang/ scrub/n bush/e 2–3

Garrulax affinis *Blyth* BLACK-FACED LAUGH-ING THRUSH Himalayas from Nepal to mts of W China, N Burma and Tonkin; Taiwan / bush and forest/fruit and seeds

Garralax erythrocephalus (*Vigors*) CHESTNUT-CROWNED LAUGHING THRUSH Himalayas and mts of SE Asia / hill scrub and cultivation / invertebrates and vegetable matter/ n bush /e 2–3

Garrulax yersini (*Robinson and Kloss*) COLLARED LAUGHING THRUSH Lang Bian Plateau in S Annam

Garrulax formosus (*Verreaux*) RED-WINGED LAUGHING THRUSH SW Szechwan and NE Yunnan: Tonkin

Garrulax milnei (*David*) RED-TAILED LAUGHING THRUSH Burma, Yunnan, Laos, Tonkin, Kwangsi and Fukien / n in under-growth/e n/s

Liocichla phoenicea (*Gould*) CRIMSON-WINGED LIOCICHLA Nepal to Assam and W Burma /forest and secondary growth / insects, seeds and berries/n bush/e 2–4/I ♂♀

Liocichla ripponi (*Oates*) CRIMSON-HEADED LIOCICHLA E Burma to Tonkin and S Yunnan/ n bush or bamboo/e 2–3 (possibly conspecific with *phoenicea*)

Liocichla omeiensis *Riley* OMEI LIOCICHLA Mt Omei in Szechwan

Liocichla steerii *Swinhoe* STEERE'S LIOCICHLA Taiwan

Leiothrix argentauris (*Hodgson*) Silver-eared Mesia Himalayas, mts of SE Yunnan and SE Asia, W Sumatra / forest, scrub and cultivation / insects, seeds and berries / n bush / e 3–5 / I ♂♀ 14

Leiothrix lutea (*Scopoli*) Red-billed Leiothrix Himalayas, mts of northern SE Asia and S China / forest undergrowth / insects, seeds and berries / n bush / e 3–5 / I ♂♀

[**Leiothrix astleyi** *Delacour* Astley's Leiothrix Known only from aviary specimens; range and systematic status uncertain]

Cutia nipalensis *Hodgson* Cutia Himalayas from Nepal, and mountains of SE Asia / forest / insects, seeds and berries / n and e n/k

Pteruthius rufiventer *Blyth* Rufous-bellied Shrike Babbler Himalayas, mts of Yunnan and northern SE Asia / forest and scrub / insects / n and e n/k

Pteruthius flaviscapis (*Temminck*) Red-winged or Greater Shrike Babbler Himalayas, mts of SE Asia, Sumatra, Java and northern Borneo / forest / insects, seeds and berries / n tree / e 2–4

Pteruthius xanthochlorus *Gray* Green Shrike Babbler Himalayas, mts of northern SE Asia and SW China / forest / insects, berries and seeds / n tree / e 2–4

Pteruthius melanotis *Hodgson* Chestnut-throated or Black-eared Shrike Babbler Himalayas and mts of Yunnan and SE Asia / forest / insects / n tree / e 2–6 / I ♂♀

Pteruthius aenobarbus (*Temminck*) Chestnut-fronted Shrike Babbler Scattered localities in Assam, SE Asia and W Java / forest / insects / n and e n/k

Gampsorhynchus rufulus *Blyth* White-hooded Babbler E Himalayas from Sikkim; and SE Asia / secondary jungle and forest undergrowth

Actinodura egertoni *Gould* Rusty-fronted Barwing Himalayas from Nepal; and hills of Burma / forest and secondary growth / insects and fruit / n bush / e 3–4

Actinodura ramsayi (*Walden*) Spectacled Barwing SE Yunnan and northern SE Asia / forest / n bush or bamboo / e 2–3

Actinodura nipalansis (*Hodgson*) Hoary Barwing Nepal, Sikkim and Bhutan / forest / insects / n ? tree / e 2

Actinodura waldeni *Godwin-Austen* Walden's Barwing Assam, N Burma and NW Yunnan / forest / insects / n n/k

Actinodura souliei *Oustalet* Streaked Barwing NW Yunnan and NW Tonkin

Actinodura morrisoniana *Ogilvie-Grant* Taiwan Barwing Taiwan

Minla cyanouroptera (*Hodgson*), Blue-winged Siva Himalayas, mts of Szechwan, Yunnan and SE Asia / forest / insects / n bush / e 3–4

Minla strigula (*Hodgson*) Chestnut-tailed Minla or Bar-throated Siva Himalayas and hills of Yunnan and SE Asia / forest / insects, berries and seeds / n bush / e 3

Minla ignotincta *Hodgson* Red-tailed Minla Himalayas, northern SE Asia and SW China / forest / insects and seeds / n tree / e 2–4

Alcippe chrysotis (*Blyth*) Golden-breasted Fulvetta Himalayas from Nepal to northern SE Asia and SW China / hill forest / insects, berries and seeds / n bamboo clump / e 3–4

Alcippe variegaticeps *Yen* Yellow-fronted Fulvetta Yaoshan, Kwangsi

Alcippe cinerea (*Blyth*) Dusky Fulvetta Himalayas from Nepal to N Burma and N Laos / forest / n ground or bamboo clump / e 2–3

Alcippe castaneceps (*Hodgson*) Chestnut-headed Fulvetta Himalayas from Nepal to Yunnan and SE Asia / forest and bamboo / insects and tree sap / n in creepers / e 3–4 / I ♂♀

Alcippe vinipectus (*Hodgson*) White-browed Fulvetta Himalayas to mts of Burma, Yunnan and SE Hsikang / forest and bamboo / insects, seeds and berries / n bush / e 3

Alcippe straticollis (*Verreaux*) Striped Fulvetta SW Kansu, NW Szechwan and SE Hsikang / rhododendron and holly-oak forest / n bush or bamboo / e 4–5

Alcippe ruficapilla (*Verreaux*) Spectacled Fulvetta Yunnan and some adjacent areas

Alcippe cinereiceps (*Verreaux*) Brown-headed Fulvetta E Bhutan, SE Tibet, northern SE Asia, Taiwan and much of the southern half of China / forest and bamboo / insects / n and e n/k

Alcippe rufogularis (*Mandelli*) Rufous-throated Fulvetta Bhutan eastward through SE Asia (except Malay Peninsula) / forest and secondary growth / insects / n ground / e 3–4

Alcippe brunnea *Gould* Brown-capped Fulvetta S and W China, Taiwan and Hainan / ? no data

Alcippe dubia (*Hume*) Rufous-capped

TIMALIIDAE:
Sphenostoma cristatum,
Wedgebill

TIMALIIDAE:
Garrulax leucolophus,
White-crested Laughing
Thrush

Plate 214

TIMALIIDAE:
Orthonyx spaldingii,
Northern Logrunner

TIMALIIDAE:
Orthonyx temminckii,
Southern Logrunner

Plate 215

FULVETTA Assam, SE Asia and Yunnan/forest and scrub/insects/n ground/e 3–5/I ♂♀

Alcippe brunneicauda (*Salvadori*) BROWN FULVETTA Malay Peninsula, Sumatra, Borneo, Batu and N Natuna Is/forest/insects

Alcippe poiocephala (*Jerdon*) QUAKER BABBLER Peninsular India, Assam and SE Asia/ forest and scrub-jungle / insects and nectar/ n tree/e 2–3/I ♂♀

Alcippe pyrrhoptera (*Bonaparte*) JAVANESE FULVETTA W and C Java

Alcippe peracensis *Sharpe* MOUNTAIN FULVETTA Mts of Annam, Laos, SE Thailand and Malaya/forest/n and e n/k

Alcippe morrisonia *Swinhoe* GREY-EYED QUAKER BABBLER S China, northern SE Asia, Hainan and Taiwan/forest/n tree/e 4

Alcippe nipalensis (*Hodgson*) NEPAL QUAKER BABBLER Himalayas, Assam and Burma/forest/ insects, berries and nectar / n bush / e 3–5/ I ♂♀ 12

Alcippe abyssinica (*Rüppell*) ABYSSINIAN HILL BABBLER Cameroon, Fernando Po and mts from Angola to Malawi, Kenya and S Ethiopia/forest undergrowth/insects and berries/ n shrub/e 2–5

Alcippe atriceps (*Sharpe*) RUWENZORI HILL BABBLER British Cameroon, mts of NE Congo, W Uganda, Ruanda and Burundi / mountain forest/no other data

Lioptilus nigricapillus (*Vieillot*) BUSH BLACKCAP Forests of E Cape Province, Natal and N Transvaal/damp forest/fruit/n shrub/ e 2

Lioptilus gilberti (*Serle*) GILBERT'S BABBLER Kupé Mts, British Cameroon/mountain forest/ n and e n/k

Lioptilus rufocinctus *Rothschild* RED-COLLARED FLYCATCHER BABBLER Ruanda to Lake Tanganyika/forest/no other data

Lioptilus chapini (*Schouteden*) CHAPIN'S FLYCATCHER BABBLER Forests between Lake Albert and Lake Edward/mountain forest/no other data

Parophasma galinieri (*Guérin-Méneville*) ABYSSINIAN CATBIRD Mts of C and S Ethiopia/ forest/no other data/this species is sometimes considered to be a Flycatcher

Phyllanthus atripennis (*Swainson*) CAPUCHIN or BLACK-WINGED BABBLER Forests of W Africa from Senegal to Nigeria: NE Congo/forest/no other data

Crocias langbianis *Gyldenstolpe* GREY-CROWNED SIBIA Annam

Crocias albonotatus (*Lesson*) SPOTTED SIBIA Mts of W and C Java

Heterophasia annectens (*Blyth*) CHESTNUT-BACKED SIBIA Himalayas from Sikkim through hills of SE Asia (except Malay Peninsula) and W Yunnan/forest/insects and seeds/n tree/e 2–4/ I ♂♀

Heterophasia capistrata (*Vigors*) BLACK-HEADED, BLACK-CAPPED or RUFOUS SIBIA Himalayas from Pakistan to Assam / forest/ insects and berries/n tree/e 2–3/I ♀

Heterophasia gracilis (*McClelland*) GREY SIBIA Assam, W and N Burma and W Yunnan/ forest/insects, berries and seeds/n tree/e 2–4/ I ♂♀

Heterophasia melanoleuca (*Blyth*) TICKELL'S SIBIA Northern SE Asia and W China/forest/ fruit and insects/n tree/e 2–3

Heterophasia auricularis (*Swinhoe*) WHITE-EARED SIBIA Highlands of Taiwan

Heterophasia pulchella (*Godwin-Austen*) BEAUTIFUL SIBIA SE Tibet, Assam, NE Burma and W Yunnan/forest/insects/n tree/e ?1 (1 nest known)

Heterophasia picaoides (*Hodgson*) LONG-TAILED SIBIA Himalayas from Nepal, mts of SE Asia and W Sumatra / forest and scrub/ insects, buds and seeds/n tree/e n/s

Yuhina castaniceps (*Moore*) WHITE-BROWED YUHINA Himalayas from Sikkim, mts of northern SE Asia and S China: highlands of northern Borneo / secondary forest / insects, seeds and nectar/n nest-burrow of other species/e 3–4

Yuhina bakeri *Rothschild* BLYTH'S YUHINA Himalayas from Garwal to N Burma/forest and secondary growth/insects and berries/n bush/ e 3–4 / I ♂♀ (sic 'Baker's Yuhina'. Rothschild's name was a renaming of *Siva occipitalis* Blyth, preoccupied by *Yuhina occipitalis* Hodgson)

Yuhina flavicollis *Hodgson* YELLOW-NAPED YUHINA Himalayas from C Nepal through parts of northern SE Asia / forest and secondary growth / insects, nectar, berries and seeds / n ground or bush/e 3–4

Yuhina humilis (*Hume*) BURMESE YUHINA Mts of SE Burma / no data / often treated as a race of *Y. flavicollis*

Yuhina gularis *Hodgson* STRIPED YUHINA Himalayas from Garwhal to northern SE Asia and W China/forest/insects, berries and nectar/

n and e no authentic description

Yuhina diademata *Verreaux* DIADEMED YUHINA NE Burma, NW Tonkin and W China N to SW Szechwan/n undergrowth/e 2–3

Yuhina occipitalis *Hodgson* SLATY-HEADED or RUFOUS-VENTED YUHINA Himalayas from Nepal to NE Burma and NW Yunnan/forest/insects and berries/n tree/e ?2 (1 nest with 2 young known)

Yuhina brunneiceps *Ogilvie-Grant* FORMOSAN YUHINA Highlands of Taiwan

Yuhina nigrimenta *Blyth* BLACK-CHINNED YUHINA Himalayas from Garwhal to mts of northern SE Asia and S China/forest and secondary growth/insects, berries and nectar/ n tree/e 4

Yuhina zantholeuca (*Blyth*) (sometimes misquoted as 'xantholeuca') ERPORNIS or WHITE-BELLIED YUHINA E Himalayas, mts of SE Asia and S China, Taiwan, NW Sumatra and Borneo/forest/insects/n tree/e 2–3

Malia grata *Schlegel* CELEBES BABBLER Celebes

Myzornis pyrrhoura *Blyth* FIRE-TAILED MYZORNIS Himalayas from Nepal to NE Burma and NW Yunnan/bush and forest/insects, nectar and berries/n tree (1 known)/e n/k

Horizorhinus dohrni (*Hartlaub*) DOHRN'S THRUSH BABBLER Principé Is/ubiquitous/ insects/n bush/e 2

Oxylabes madagascariensis (*Gmelin*) OXYLABES Madagascar/forests of the humid east/no other data/this species was formerly placed in the Pycnonotidae

Mystacornis crossleyi (*Grandidier*) CROSSLEY'S BABBLER Madagascar/forests of the humid east/insects/n and e undescribed, but eggs believed to be of this species are in Cambridge Museum. The taxonomic position of this bird is doubtful

CHAMAEIDAE Wrentit A bird of uncertain affinities but believed to be related to the Paradoxornithidae.

Chamaea fasciata (*Gambel*) WRENTIT Western USA/scrub and chaparral/insects and fruit/ n bush/e 3–5/I ♂♀ 15–16/F 15–16

PARADOXORNITHIDAE Parrotbills Tit-like babblers with short heavy bills, laterally compressed like those of parrots. They inhabit generally open country and reedbeds feeding on insects, seeds and berries.

Panurus biarmicus (*L*) REEDLING or BEARDED TIT C and S Europe across SC Asia to Mon-golia and Manchuria/reedbeds/n low among reeds/e 5–12/I ♂♀ 12–13/F 9–12

Conostoma oenodium *Hodgson* GREAT PARROTBILL Himalayas from Garwhal to mts of SW Szechwan and NE Burma/bush and bamboo/insects, buds and fruit/n in bamboo clump/e 2–3

Paradoxornis paradoxus (*Verreaux*) THREE-TOED PARROTBILL W China

Paradoxornis unicolor (*Hodgson*) BROWN PARROTBILL Himalayas from Nepal to mts of SW Szechwan and NE Burma/bush and bamboo/buds and insects/n and e n/k

Paradoxornis flavirostris *Gould* GOULD'S PARROTBILL Himalayas from Nepal to Chin Hills in Burma/tall grass and reeds/insects and vegetable matter/n sapling/e 2–4

Paradoxornis guttaticollis *David* RUFOUS-HEADED PARROTBILL Assam and mts of W Szechwan, northern SE Asia and W China/ scrub, grass and bamboo/insects and seeds/n shrub or bamboo/e 2–3

Paradoxornis conspicillatus (*David*) SPECTACLED PARROTBILL W China

Paradoxornis ricketti *Rothschild* RICKETT'S PARROTBILL NW Yunnan

Paradoxornis webbianus (*Gould*) WEBB'S PARROTBILL E Manchuria, S Korea, China, Taiwan and extreme northern SE Asia/open forest and hill scrub/n bush/e 3–4 (?5)

[**Sutora styani** *Rippon*=**Paradoxornis styani** (*Rippon*) is stated to be a hybrid between *P. ricketti* and *P. webbianus* occurring in the Tali Valley, W Yunnan] (Rippon, *Bull BOC* (1903), p 54)

Paradoxornis alphonsianus (*Verreaux*) ASHY-THROATED PARROTBILL W China and NW Tonkin

Paradoxornis zappeyi (*Thayer and Bangs*) DUSKY PARROTBILL Wa-shan, in Hsikang

Paradoxornis przewalskii (*Berezowski and Bianchi*) PRZEWALSKI'S PARROTBILL S Kansu

Paradoxornis fulvifrons (*Hodgson*) FULVOUS PARROTBILL Himalayas from Nepal to SE Tibet and mts of W China/bamboo buds and insects/ n and e n/k

Paradoxornis nipalensis (*Hodgson*) NEPAL PARROTBILL C Nepal/forest and bamboo/buds and insects/n bush/e 2–4

Paradoxornis poliotis (*Blyth*) BLYTH'S PARROTBILL Yunnan, Burma and Himalayas to E Nepal and SE Tibet/forest/n bush/e n/s

TIMALIIDAE:
Garrulax monileger,
Necklaced Laughing Thrush,
Lesser Necklaced Laughing
Thrush

Plate 216

PICATHARTIDAE:
Picathartes oreas,
Grey-necked or Red-headed
Picathartes, Cameroon Bare-
headed Rockfowl

PICATHARTIDAE:
Picathartes gymnocephalus,
White-necked or Yellow-headed
Picathartes, Guinea Bare-
headed Rockfowl

SYLVIIDAE:
Sylvia atricapilla,
Blackcap

Plate 217

Paradoxornis verreauxi (*Sharpe*) GOLDEN PARROTBILL Shan States, Tonkin and mts of Szechwan, Hsikang and Fukien, Taiwan /forest/ n and e n/k

Paradoxornis davidianus (*Slater*) SHORT-TAILED PARROTBILL Northern SE Asia and Fukien/n bamboo/e n/k

Paradoxornis atrosuperciliaris (*Godwin-Austen*) BLACK-BROWED PARROTBILL Sikkim, Darjeeling, Assam, W Yunnan, N Burma and N Laos/scrub and bamboo/vegetable matter and insects/n bamboo/e 3

Paradoxornis ruficeps *Blyth* RED-HEADED PARROTBILL Himalayas from Nepal and northern SE Asia/reeds and grass/insects and seeds/n in reeds or bamboo/e 2–3

Paradoxornis gularis *Gray* GREY-HEADED PARROTBILL Himalayas from Sikkim, SE Asia (except Malay Peninsula), hills of S China, Hainan /bush and bamboo/ insects and vegetable matter/n sapling/e 2–4

Paradoxornis heudei *David* HEUDE'S PARROTBILL Reed beds bordering the Yangtse from a few miles above Nanking to a short distance below Chinkiang/n in reeds /e 5

PICATHARTIDAE Bald Crows or Picathartes Bald-headed passerines of uncertain affinities which have been placed with the Crows and the Starlings at various times, but are now generally considered to be near the Babblers.

Picathartes gymnocephalus (*Temminck*) WHITE-NECKED or YELLOW-HEADED PICATHARTES Forests of W Africa from Sierra Leone to Togoland / moss or creeper-covered rocks in forest at high altitudes / insects and molluscs/ n of mud attached to roof of cave or overhanging rock/e 2

Picathartes oreas *Reichenow* GREY-NECKED or RED-HEADED PICATHARTES Forests of S British Cameroon and SW French Cameroon / data similar to last species

[NB There have been reports of bald-headed birds resembling *Picathartes* from the Kazinga Channel in Uganda]

POLIOPTILIDAE Gnatcatchers Dainty, slender little birds resembling Old World warblers (Sylvidae) and sometimes included in that family. They are generally soft, bluish-grey in colour with long pointed bills.

Microbates collaris (*Pelzeln*) COLLARED GNATWREN SE Colombia, S Venezuela, Cayenne and parts of Brazil

Microbates cinereiventris (*Sclater*) HALF-COLLARED GNATWREN Caribbean lowlands of C America from Nicaragua southwards and parts of Colombia, Ecuador and Peru/forest

Ramphocaenus melanurus *Vieillot* LONG-BILLED GNATWREN Mexico, C America and much of tropical S America S to Peru and N and E Brazil/dry forest

Polioptila caerulea (*L*) BLUE-GREY GNATCATCHER S Canada, USA, Mexico, Cuba and the Bahamas / forest, swamp and habitation/ insects/n bush/e 4–5/I ♂♀ 13/F 10–12

Polioptila melanura *Lawrence* PLUMBEOUS GNATCATCHER SW California and Mexico/ scrub/insects and seeds /n tree or bush/e 3–5

Polioptila lembeyei (*Gundlach*) CUBAN GNATCATCHER E Cuba/semi-arid scrub/insects/ n bush/e 4–5

Polioptila nigriceps *Baird* BLACK-CAPPED GNATCATCHER Parts of Mexico

Polioptila albiloris *Sclater and Salvin* WHITE-LORED GNATCATCHER Parts of Mexico, Guatemala, Honduras, El Salvador, Nicaragua and Costa Rica

Polioptila plumbea (*Gmelin*) TROPICAL GNATCATCHER Mexico, C America and much of tropical S America S to Peru and N Brazil/ arid scrub, mangrove and plantations

Polioptila lactea *Sharpe* CREAM-BELLIED GNATCATCHER SE Brazil, E Paraguay and NE Argentina/shrubbery

Polioptila guianensis *Todd* GUIANAN GNATCATCHER Venezuela, the Guianas and parts of N Brazil/forest

Polioptila schistaceigula *Hartert* SLATE-THROATED GNATCATCHER E Panama through Colombia to W Ecuador/forest

Polioptila dumicola (*Vieillot*) MASKED GNATCATCHER C Brazil to Bolivia and N Argentina/cerrado and shrubbery

SYLVIIDAE Old World Warblers Small, dull-coloured, active birds with thin bills and rather weak legs. Insectivorous, and generally arboreal, though some species occur in swamps or grasses. Noted for their sweet warbling songs.

Megalurulus mariei *Verreaux* NEW CALEDONIAN GRASS WARBLER New Caledonia/ grassland and open heaths

Cichlornis whitneyi *Mayr* NEW HEBRIDES THICKET WARBLER New Hebrides in mts of Espiritu Santo

Cichlornis (? whitneyi) turipavae *Cain and Galbraith* SOLOMONS THICKET WARBLER Turipava, in mts of Guadalcanal, Solomon Is/ unique

Cichlornis grosvenori *Gilliard* NEW BRITAIN THICKET WARBLER Whiteman Mts, New Britain /forest /no other data

Ortygocichla rubiginosa *Sclater* NEW BRITAIN BABBLER-WARBLER (NB: given in Edwards *Coded List of the Birds of the World* as *O. fuliginosa*, apparently in error) New Britain/ n ? ground

Trichocichla rufa *Reichenow* LONG-LEGGED WARBLER Vanua Levu (formerly Viti Levu) Fiji / thought extinct, but re-discovered 1975/ forest

Buettikoferella bivittata (*Bonaparte*) BÜTTIKOFER'S WARBLER Timor (Edwards uses the original name for this genus, *Buettikoferia*, but this name has apparently been rejected on the grounds of preoccupation by the name *Büttikoferia*, Coleoptera)

Cettia subulata (*Sharpe*) TIMOR CETTIA Timor

Cettia fortipes (*Hodgson*) STRONG-FOOTED CETTIA Himalayas, SE Asia, Indonesia, S China and Taiwan /open forest, swamp-jungle and tea gardens / insects /n bush /e 3–5 / I ♂♀/ This species has been called *Cettia montanus* (Horsfield), but this name is pre-occupied by *Sylvia montana* Wilson (unidentifiable); for discussion see Phillips and Biswas, *Journal of the Bombay Natural History Society*, vol 65 (1968), pp 223–4.

Cettia brunnifrons (*Hodgson*) RUFOUS-FRONTED CETTIA Himalayas, S Tibet and N Yunnan/hill-scrub, forest clearings, tea gardens etc/insects/n bush/e 3–5

Cettia major (*Moore*) LARGE CETTIA E Himalayas, SE Tibet, Yunnan and Szechwan/ rhododendron forest/insects/n ? bush/e 2–3? (authenticity of known nests questioned by Ali and Ripley)

Cettia flavolivacea (*Hodgson*) ABERRANT CETTIA Himalayas, mts of northern SE Asia and S China /forest undergrowth, scrub and long grass/insects/n ground/e 3–4

Cettia acanthizoides (*Verreaux*) VERREAUX'S or YELLOW-BELLIED CETTIA Himalayas to S China and Taiwan/dense bamboo/insects /n bush/e 2–3

Cettia whiteheadi (*Sharpe*) WHITEHEAD'S CETTIA Mts of northern Borneo /forest undergrowth/insects /n and e n/k

Cettia squamiceps (*Swinhoe*) SHORT-TAILED CETTIA b Japan, S Sakhalin, Manchuria and Korea w S China, northern SE Asia and Luzon/ forest /insects /n ground/ e 5–7

Cettia pallidipes (*Blanford*) PALE-FOOTED CETTIA Himalayas, mts of northern SE Asia and S China: S Andaman Island/forest and grass-jungle/ insects /n bush / e 4

Cettia diphone (*Kittlitz*) CHINESE CETTIA b SE Siberia to Japan and N China w S to Indonesia and Philippines / brushwood and reeds/insects /n ground/e 4–5

Cettia cetti (*Temminck*) CETTI'S WARBLER Mediterranean region and E to Iran and Turkestan / swamps and streams in woods/ insects and worms / n bush over water / e 3–6/ I ♀ (?♂)

Psammathia annae *Hartlaub and Finsch* PALAU WARBLER Palau Is / forest undergrowth/ insects and seeds/n and e n/k (though Nehrkorn records the existence of 1 egg)

Bradypterus accentor (*Sharpe*) FRIENDLY or KINABALU WARBLER Mts Kinabalu and Trus Madi, Borneo /mountain forest /insects /n and e n/k

Bradypterus taczanowskius (*Swinhoe*) CHINESE BUSH WARBLER b Yenisei to Ussuriland: Tsinghai, Szechwan and Tibet: Yunnan (? populations) w SE Asia and S China/ grassland /insects /n ground/e 5/I ♀

Bradypterus caudatus (*Ogilvie-Grant*) LONG-TAILED GROUND WARBLER N Luzon: Mt Apo and Mt Malindang, Mindanao /mountain forest/ no other data

Bradypterus palliseri (*Blyth*) PALLISER'S WARBLER or CEYLON BUSH WARBLER Ceylon/ undergrowth in hill forest /insects and worms/ n shrub / e 2

Bradypterus thoracicus (*Blyth*) SPOTTED BUSH WARBLER Himalayas through Tibet and W China to Amurland, Lake Baikal and Altai/ scrub and grassland /insects /n shrub /e 3–4

Bradypterus major (*Brooks*) LARGE-BILLED BUSH WARBLER Astin Tagh and related ranges w W Himalayas: Mongolia/scrub and grassland/ insects /n near ground at base of shrub /e 3–4

Bradypterus luteoventris (*Hodgson*) BROWN BUSH WARBLER E Himalayas, northern SE Asia, C and S China / grassy downs and hill-scrub /insects /n bush or grass clump /e 3–5 /I ♂♀ 12–13

Bradypterus seebohmi *Ogilvie-Grant* RUSSET or MOUNTAIN BUSH WARBLER Mts of N Luzon;

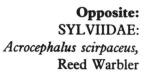

Opposite:
SYLVIIDAE:
Acrocephalus scirpaceus,
Reed Warbler

SYLVIIDAE:
Phylloscopus sibilatrix,
Wood Warbler

SYLVIIDAE:
Acrocephalus palustris,
Marsh Warbler

Plate 218

Plate 219

SE China, Taiwan, Java and Timor / clearings in mountain forest

Bradypterus baboecola (*Vieillot*) AFRICAN SEDGE WARBLER or SWAMP WARBLER C Africa from Nigeria to Angola and Botswana / reeds and swampy grass / n reeds / e 2–3

Bradypterus graueri *Neumann* GRAUER'S RUSH WARBLER Kivu and surrounding highlands / mountain swamps / known from 2 or 3 specimens

Bradypterus grandis *Ogilvie-Grant* GIANT SWAMP WARBLER or JA RIVER WARBLER Cameroon and Gabon / no data

Bradypterus carpalis *Chapin* WHITE-WINGED WARBLER Papyrus swamps of Uganda and E Congo / no data

Bradypterus alfredi *Hartlaub* BAMBOO WARBLER Mts of EC Africa / mountain forest / no other data

Bradypterus sylvaticus *Sundevall* KNYSNA SCRUB-WARBLER Scattered localities from S Natal to Table Mountain / bramble thickets / n and e n/k

Bradypterus barratti *Sharpe* BARRATT'S SCRUB-WARBLER Fernando Po and scattered mountains of C Africa / damp mountain undergrowth / n herbage / e 2–3 (NB: The following 2 'species', listed by Mackworth-Praed and Grant, are given by White's *Check List of African Birds* as races of *B. barratti*:

  B. camerunensis *Alexander* CAMEROON MOUNTAIN WARBLER Cameroon Mt / no data
  B. mariae *Madarasz* EVERGREEN FOREST WARBLER Parts of Kenya, Tanganyika, Malawi and Mozambique / undergrowth in rain forest / n undergrowth / e 2–3

Bradypterus victorini *Sundevall* VICTORIN'S BUSH-WARBLER Mts of S Cape Province / damp mountain scrub / n dense vegetation / e 2

Bradypterus castaneus (*Büttikofer*) CHESTNUT GRASS WARBLER Celebes, Ceram and Buru

Bradypterus cinnamomeus (*Rüppell*) CINNAMON BRACKEN WARBLER Ethiopia and Cameroon to Zambia / forest / n near ground / e 2–3

Bowdleria punctata (*Quoy and Gaimard*) FERNBIRD New Zealand, Snares Is / ferns in swamps, scrub and forest / insects / n near ground in tussock / e 2–4

Bowdleria rufescens (*Buller*) CHATHAM FERNBIRD Chatham Is / extinct, eggs apparently

collected, though no data on habits, nest or clutch size

Finschia novaeseelandiae (*Gmelin*) PIPIPI or BROWN CREEPER South Is, Stewart Is and adjacent islands, New Zealand / forest and scrub / insects / n tree / e 2–4

Schoenicola playtura (*Jerdon*) BROAD-TAILED GRASS WARBLER SW Ghats of India / hill scrub / insects / n grass tussock / e ?2–3

Schoenicola brevirostris (*Sundevall*) FAN-TAILED WARBLER Sierra Leone to Ethiopia, Angola and Malawi / grassland and bush / n near ground / e 2

Locustella luscinioides (*Savi*) SAVI'S WARBLER S Europe and Mediterranean region E to Turkestan / swamp and fens / insects / n reeds / e 3–6 / I ♀ 12 / F 12

Locustella certhiola (*Pallas*) PALLAS'S GRASSHOPPER WARBLER b Siberia and C Asia from Yenisei to Sea of Okhotsk and S to Tien Shan and Mongolia w S to India, SE Asia and Indonesia / n in grass / e 4–6

Locustella ochotensis (*Middendorff*) MIDDENDORFF'S WARBLER b Kamchatka, Sea of Okhotsk coast, Kuriles, Sakhalin, Korea (? Commander Is) w Indonesia / scrub and meadow / insects / n in grass / e 5–6

Locustella lanceolata (*Temminck*) LANCEOLATED WARBLER b Siberia from Perm to Sakhalin and Kamchatka w SE Asia and Indonesia / grassland and scrub / insects / n in tussock / e 5

Locustella fluviatilis (*Wolf*) RIVER WARBLER b E Europe and W Siberia to Irtysh w SE Africa / marshes and riversides / insects / n ground / e 5–7 / I 13

Locustella fasciolata (*Gray*) GRAY'S GRASSHOPPER WARBLER b S Siberia from upper Ob to Amur (? Sakhalin and N Japan) w E Indonesia / forest undergrowth, swamps and orchards / insects / n herbage / e 3–5

Locustella amnicola *Stepanyan* STEPANYAN'S WARBLER Sakhalin (? Kuriles and N Japan) / described from 2 adult ♂♂ collected June 1972. It is believed that all data on *L. fasciolata* (to which this species is most nearly allied) on Sakhalin, Hokkaido and the Kuriles, may refer to this species (Stepanyan, L. S. *Zoologicheskij Zh*, 51 (12), pp 1896–7: Russian with brief English summary). The status and validity of the 'species' is, however, as yet unsettled.

Locustella naevia (*Boddaert*) GRASSHOPPER

WARBLER Europe and W Asia E to Turkestan w NW Africa / marshes and open woodland/ insects / n ground or tussock / e 4–7 / I ♂♀ 13–15/ F 10–12

Acrocephalus melanopogon (*Temminck*) MOUSTACHED WARBLER b S Europe and N Africa E to Baluchistan / reed beds / insects / n bush or reeds / e 3–6 (NB: Parker and Harrison, *Bull Brit Orn Cl* (1963) have shown that the monotypic genus *Lusciniola*, retained by some for *melanopogon*, is not tenable)

Acrocephalus orinus *Oberholzer* HUME'S LARGE BILLED REED WARBLER Rampur/unique

Acrocephalus bistrigiceps *Swinhoe* VON SCHRENK'S REED WARBLER b Ussuriland and Japan w S China and SE Asia/long grass and reeds / insects / n reeds / e 4–6

Acrocephalus dumetorum *Blyth* BLYTH'S REED WARBLER b W Asia from Finland to Lake Baikal and S to Iran w S Asia / bushes and cultivation / insects / n shrub / e 4–6

Acrocephalus agricola (*Jerdon*) PADDYFIELD WARBLER b S Russia and WC Asia w S Asia long grass, reeds and rice/insects/n grass/e 4–5

Acrocephalus concinens (*Swinhoe*) BLUNT-WINGED WARBLER b Himalayas and China (apparently discontinuous) w S Asia/reeds and long grass/insects/n grass/e 4

Acrocephalus sorghophilus (*Swinhoe*) SPECTACLED REED WARBLER Recorded occasionally in various parts of China and Philippines b unknown

Acrocephalus schoenabaenus (*L*) SEDGE WARBLER b Europe, N Africa and across Asia to Tien Shan, Altai and N Iran w Africa/ reedbeds, woods and cultivation / insects, mollusca and berries / n bush or herbage / e 3–8/ I ♂♀ 13–14/F 13–14

Acrocephalus palustris (*Bechstein*) MARSH WARBLER b C and S Europe and Russia E to Kirghiz Steppes w Africa / osier beds and cultivation / insects and berries / n reeds or herbage / e 3–6 / I ♂♀ 12 / F 10–14

Acrocephalus scirpaceus (*Hermann*) REED WARBLER b Europe, N Africa and SW Asia E to Turkestan w Africa/reedbeds and parkland/ insects, molluscs and berries / n reeds or bush/ e 3–5/I ♂♀ 11–12/F 10–14

Acrocephalus paludicola (*Vieillot*) AQUATIC WARBLER b N and C Europe, Sicily and Sardinia, E to Perm and Ufa w Mediterranean and Africa / marshes / insects and mollusca/

n bush or herbage/e 4–6/I ♂♀/F 19

Acrocephalus arundinaceus (*L*) GREAT REED WARBLER b C and S Europe and Mediterranean E to Turkestan w Africa/reedbeds and marshes/insects and aquatic life/n reeds/e 3–6/ I ♂♀ 14–15/F 12

Acrocephalus stentoreus (*Hemprich and Ehrenberg*) CLAMOROUS REED WARBLER SW Asia (S of range of *arundinaceus*), parts of Indian region to S China: parts of Indonesia/ reeds and swamps/insects/n reeds/e 3–6 (NB: There appears to be doubt as to whether the Indonesian forms belong to *australis* or to *stentoreus* or indeed, if these two are conspecific)

Acrocephalus orientalis (*Temminck and Schlegel*) EASTERN GREAT REED WARBLER b SE Siberia and China/ w SE Asia / reed beds / n reeds/e 3–6

Acrocephalus australis *Gould* AUSTRALIAN REED WARBLER Australia, Solomon Is / reeds and mangroves / insects / n herbage / e 3–4 (see note to *A. stentoreus*)

Acrocephalus (? **australis**) **meyeri** *Stresemann* NEW BRITAIN REED WARBLER New Britain

Acrocephalus (? **australis**) **cervinus** *De Vis* NEW GUINEA REED WARBLER New Guinea (probably not different from *australis*)

? **Acrocephalus celebensis** *Heinroth* HEINROTH'S WARBLER S Celebes /possibly race of *stentoreus* (qv)

Acrocephalus griseldis (*Hartlaub*) BASRA REED WARBLER b S Iraq w E and SE Africa

Acrocephalus boeticatus (*Vieillot*) AFRICAN REED WARBLER S Sudan and Lake Chad to Angola, Malawi and Zambia / reed beds and dense herbage / insects / n reeds / e 2–4

Acrocephalus aedon (*Pallas*) THICK-BILLED WARBLER b E Asia from Ob to Amur, China and Japan w S India and SE Asia/marsh, swampy scrub and cultivation / insects / n tree / e 5–6/ *aedon* is often separated in the monotypic genus *Phragmaticola*, on the basis of certain structural differences. Its eggs also, are strikingly different from any other warbler

Acrocephalus brevipennis (*Keulemans*) DOHRN'S CANE WARBLER Cape Verde Is/ cane beds/n tree or among cane/e n/s

Acrocephalus aequinoctialis (*Latham*) CHRISTMAS WARBLER Christmas Is (Pacific Ocean) and Fanning Is

Acrocephalus atypha (*Wetmore*) TUAMOTUS

MALURIDAE:
Malurus elegans,
Red-winged Wren, Red-winged
Wren-Warbler

MALURIDAE:
Malurus leucopterus,
White-winged Wren,
Blue-and- White
Wren-Warbler

Plate 220

EPHTHIANURIDAE:
Ephthianura aurifrons,
Orange Chat

ACANTHIZIDAE:
Acanthiza nana,
Little Thornbill

Plate 221

REED WARBLER Tuamotus Is

Acrocephalus luscinia (*Quoy and Gaimard*) NIGHTINGALE WARBLER Marianas, Carolines and Nauru / marshes, cane-thickets etc / insects / n bush or reeds / e 1–2

Acrocephalus caffra (*Sparrman*) TAHITI WARBLER Society Is

Acrocephalus mendanae *Tristram* MARQUESAS WARBLER Marquesas Is

Acrocephalus familiaris (*Rothschild*) MILLERBIRD Laysan Is / extinct / ? ubiquitous / n herbage / e n/s

Acrocephalus kingi *Wetmore* NIHOA WARBLER Nihoa (Hawaii) / scrub / n herbage / e 1–2

Acrocephalus vaughanii *Sharpe* PITCAIRN WARBLER Henderson, Pitcairn and Rimitare Is

Acrocephalus rehsii (*Finsch*) PLEASANT WARBLER Pleasant Is

Orthotomus atrogularis *Temminck* DARK-NECKED TAILORBIRD Himalayas, SE Asia, Sumatra and Borneo / forest / insects / n tree / e 3–5 / I ♂♀

Orthotomus sericeus *Temminck* RUFOUS-HEADED or SILKY TAILORBIRD Malaya E to islands between Borneo and Philippines / forest and cultivation / insects / n tree / e ?5

Orthotomus sepium *Horsfield* ASHY TAILORBIRD Celebes, Java, Borneo, Bali, Lombok and Cagayan Sulu / forest and cultivation / insects / n tree / e ? n/k

Orthotomus cinereiceps *Sharpe* WHITE-EARED TAILORBIRD Philippines: Basilan and Mindanao / ? no data

Orthotomus samarensis *Steere* SAMAR TAILORBIRD Philippines: Bohol, Leyte, and Samar / deep forest

Orthotomus nigriceps *Tweeddale* BLACKHEADED TAILORBIRD Mindanao / deep forest

Orthotomus derbianus *Moore* LUZON TAILORBIRD S Luzon / ? no data

Orthotomus cucullatus *Temminck* GOLDEN-HEADED or MOUNTAIN TAILORBIRD E Himalayas, SE Asia, S China to Bali and Borneo, also Luzon and Mindanao / forest and scrub / insects / n tree / e 3–4

Orthotomus sutorius (*Pennant*) LONGTAILED TAILORBIRD Indian sub-continent, SE Asia to Java and S China / scrub and habitation / insects and nectar / n tree / e 3–5 / I ♂♀

(The genus *Chloropeta* is placed in the Muscicapidae by some authors)

Chloropeta natalensis *Smith* NATAL YELLOW WARBLER (YELLOW FLYCATCHER) S Tanganyika to Natal, Congo and Angola / reed beds / n plant or bush / e 2–4

Chloropeta similis *Richmond* MOUNTAIN YELLOW WARBLER (MOUNTAIN YELLOW FLYCATCHER) S Sudan to E Congo and Malawi / reed beds (presumably on high ground) / n shrub or herb / e 2

Chloropeta gracilirostris *Ogilvie-Grant* YELLOW SWAMP WARBLER or THIN-BILLED YELLOW WARBLER E Congo and W Uganda / reeds and papyrus / n and e n/k (placed by some authorities in *Calamonastides*)

Myopornis boehmi (*Reichenow*) BÖHM'S WARBLER Tanganyika to S Congo, Angola and Malawi / woodland and open bush / tree ants / n in old nests of weavers / e 'up to 4' (I follow Edwards in placing this genus here. Mackworth Praed and Grant, and Hall and Moreau, place it at the end of *Muscicapa*; Vaurie making it a sub-genus of *Muscicapa*)

Sphenoeacus afer (*Gmelin*) CAPE GRASSBIRD Cape Province to Natal and E Rhodesia / hill scrub and flat country near streams / n grass tuft / e 2–3 / I 14–17 / F 14–16

Sphenoeacus mentalis (*Fraser*) MOUSTACHE WARBLER W Africa to Ethiopia S from Angola to Lower Zambezi Valley / tall grass near open woodland / insects / n grass tussock / e 2

Sphenoeacus pycnopygius (*Sclater*) DAMARALAND ROCK JUMPER Mts of Damaraland and Kaokveld / scrub / insects / n ground / e 2–3 (formerly placed in the monotypic genus *Achaetops*, which genus has been variously treated as a babbler or a chat)

Mohoua albicilla (*Lesson and Garnot*) WHITEHEAD North Island, New Zealand, and offshore islands / forest / insects / n tree / e 2–4 / I ♂♀ 17 / F 14–18

Mohoua ochrocephala (*Gmelin*) YELLOWHEAD South Island, New Zealand (formerly also Stewart Is) / forest / insects / n tree / e 3–4 / I ?♀ 21 / F c14

Chaetornis striatus (*Jerdon*) BRISTLED GRASS WARBLER Locally distributed in the Indian sub-continent / coarse grass and thorn scrub / insects / n grass / e 4–5 / I ♀

Megalurus gramineus (*Gould*) LITTLE GRASSBIRD Much of Australia (except N) and Tasmania / swamps / invertebrates / n herbage / e 3–4

Megalurus albolimbatus (*D'Albertis and Salvadori*) FLY RIVER GRASS WARBLER Fly River area of New Guinea /lagoons and reed-beds/n in grass on marsh edge/e 3

Megalurus timorensis (*Wallace*) TAWNY GRASSBIRD N and E Australia, New Guinea area, to Philippines, Timor, Amboina and Celebes /swamp and scrub /insects / n herbage/ e 3

Megalurus palustris *Horsfield* STRIATED MARSH WARBLER N India, SE Asia, S China, Philippines, Java, Bali (? Sumatra) /grassland and cultivation/insects /n reeds/e 4

Megalurus pryeri *Seebohm* JAPANESE MARSH WARBLER Pacific coastal marshes of C Honshu/ reed beds/n in reeds/e 5–6/I ♀ 11/F 12–14

Graminicola bengalensis *Jerdon* LARGE GRASS WARBLER Himalaya foothills through northern SE Asia to Hainan / tall grass and reeds /insects /n grass or reeds in water/ e 4

Hippolais caligata (*Lichtenstein*) BOOTED WARBLER b W Asia to Afghanistan and Pakistan w Indian region/ scrub-jungle and cultivation/ insects /n bush or grass clump/e 3–4/I ♂♀

Hippolais icterina (*Vieillot*) ICTERINE WARBLER b N and E Europe and W Siberia to Altai w Africa/hedgerows and gardens /insects and fruit /e 4–6/I ♂♀ 13/F 13–14

Hippolais polyglotta (*Vieillot*) MELODIOUS WARBLER b S Europe and N Africa w Africa/ trees near water/insects and fruit /n bush /e 3–5/ I ♀ 12/F 12

Hippolais olivetorum (*Strickland*) OLIVE-TREE WARBLER b SE Europe to Iran w Egypt to Transvaal/n tree or bush/e 3–4

Hippolais languida (*Hemprich and Ehrenberg*) UPCHER'S WARBLER b SW Asia w SW Arabia, Baluchistan and Sudan to Kenya / hill scrub/ insects /n bush/e 4–5

Hippolais pallida (*Cabanis*) OLIVACEOUS WARBLER b S Europe, N Africa and E to Iran and Turkestan w Senegal to Yemen and Baluchistan / bush and cultivation / insects / n bush or undergrowth/e 2–3/I ♀ 13/F 15

Sylvia sarda *Temminck* MARMORA'S WARBLER Coasts and islands of W Mediterranean w S to N borders of Sahara/scrub/ n shrub/e 3–5

Sylvia undata (*Boddaert*) DARTFORD WARBLER W and SW Europe and NW Africa/heath and maquis-scrub/insects/n in long heather/e 3–6/ I ♂♀ 12–13/F 13

Sylvia conspicillata *Temminck* SPECTACLED WARBLER Mediterranean basin, Madeira, Canaries and Cape Verde Is /bush and scrub/ n bush/ e 3–6/I ♂♀ 12–14

Sylvia melanothorax *Tristram* CYPRUS WARBLER Cyprus /n scrub/e 3–5

Sylvia deserticola *Tristram* TRISTRAM'S WARBLER Mts of C Morocco, S Algeria and Tunisia / hill scrub and thickets in open mountain forest/n shrub/e 3–4/I 13

[**Sylvia ticehursti** *Meinertzhagen* TICEHURST'S WARBLER Tinghir, Moroccan Sahara/unique ♀/ this specimen has never been satisfactorily explained]

Sylvia nisoria (*Bechstein*) BARRED WARBLER b C and SE Europe and across Asia to Altai and NW Mongolia w S Arabia and E Africa/forest thickets and plantations / insects and berries/ n bush/e 3–6/I ♂♀ 14–15

Sylvia hortensis (*Gmelin*) ORPHEAN WARBLER b Mediterranean region and E to Turkestan w Africa in belt S of Sahara, Arabia and Indian region / open woodland, maquis-scrub etc/ insects and fruit/n tree/e 4–6/I ?♂♀

Sylvia borin (*Boddaert*) GARDEN WARBLER b Europe and E to Transcaucasia w C and S Africa/woodland bush and cultivation /insects and fruit/n bush or bramble/e 3–7/I ♂♀ 11–12/ F 9–10

Sylvia atricapilla (*L*) BLACKCAP b Europe and Mediterranean, Azores, Madeira, Canaries and Cape Verdes, and E to N Iran w in S of range/ open woodland and habitation / insects and berries /n bush/e 3–6/I ♂♀ 10–15/F 10–13

Sylvia communis *Latham* WHITETHROAT b Europe, W Asia, Turkey and N Africa and E to Afghanistan w Africa, Arabia and Indian region/open woodland and cultivation/insects and fruit /n bush /e 3–7/I ♂♀ 11–13/F 10–12

Sylvia curruca (*L*) LESSER WHITETHROAT b Europe and W Asia to Altai and Afghanistan w Africa to Lake Chad and Ethiopia, and W Arabia to India /forest and scrub /insects /n bush/e 3–7/I ♂♀ 10–11/F 11

[**Sylvia minula** *Hume* SMALL WHITETHROAT and **Sylvia althaea** *Hume* HUME'S WHITETHROAT, formerly regarded as species, are now usually treated as races of *S. curruca*]

Sylvia nana (*Hemprich and Ehrenberg*) DESERT WARBLER Deserts of N Africa, Middle East and C Asia /desert scrub /insects /n shrub/e 4–6/ I ♂♀

Sylvia rueppelli *Temminck* RÜPPELL'S

ACANTHIZIDAE:
Acanthiza lineata,
Striated Thornbill

ACANTHIZIDAE:
Cinclorhamphus mathewsi,
Rufous Songlark

Plate 222

ACANTHIZIDAE:
Acanthornis magnus,
Scrub Tit

Plate 223

WARBLER b Crete, Aegean Is and Turkey (? Greece) w NE Africa/scrub/insects/n bush/ e 4–6/I ♂♀ 13

Sylvia melanocephala (*Gmelin*) SARDINIAN WARBLER b Mediterranean region and E to Turkestan/open woodland, maquis-scrub and vineyards/insects and fruit/n bush/e 3–5 (?6)/ I ♂♀ 13–14/F 11

Sylvia mystacea *Ménétriés* MÉNÉTRIÉS' WARBLER b SW Asia from Palestine to Turkestan, Aral Sea and Caspian w NE Africa/ riverside scrub/n shrub/e 3–5/I 14

Sylvia cantillans (*Pallas*) SUBALPINE WARBLER b Mediterranean region some birds w S to Sudan/open woodland and bush/insects and seeds/n bush/e 3–5/I ♀ (?♂) 11–12/F 11–12

Sylvia leucomelana (*Hemprich and Ehrenberg*) RED SEA WARBLER Coast of Red Sea and Gulf of Aden/no data

Phylloscopus olivaceus (*Moseley*) PHILIPPINE LEAF WARBLER Philippines/lowland forest/no other data

Phylloscopus trochilus (*L*) WILLOW WARBLER b much of N Palaearctic w Africa and S Asia / open woodland and cultivation/ insects and fruit / n ground or bush / e 3–9/ I ♀ 11–14/F 12–15

Phylloscopus laurae (*Boulton*) MRS BOULTON'S WARBLER NE Zambia to S Congo/ mountain forest/no data/few specimens

Phylloscopus collybita (*Vieillot*) CHIFFCHAFF b much of Palaearctic w N Africa and S Asia/ forest and cultivation/insects/n herbage or bush/ e 4–7/I ♀ 13–14/F 14–15

Phylloscopus neglectus *Hume* PLAIN LEAF WARBLER b E Iran, Afghanistan and Pakistan w S to Baluchistan and Oman/scrub/insects/ n bush/e 3–5

Phylloscopus bonelli (*Vieillot*) BONELLI'S WARBLER b S Europe and N Africa E to Asia Minor w W and C Africa/forest and woodland/ n ground/e 4–6/I ♀

Phylloscopus tytleri *Brooks* TYTLER'S LEAF WARBLER b Upper Indus of Gilgit and Kashmir w W India (few records)/forest/insects/n tree/ e 4–5

Phylloscopus sibilatrix (*Bechstein*) WOOD WARBLER b Europe and W Asia w Africa/forest and parkland/insects/n ground/e 4–8/I ♀ 13/ F 11–12

Phylloscopus ruficapilla (*Sundevall*) YELLOW-THROATED WARBLER E and S Africa

from Kenya southwards / forest / insects/ n herbage/e 2–3

Phylloscopus umbrovirens (*Rüppell*) BROWN WARBLER SW Arabia and E Africa from Eritrea and Ethiopia to Uganda / tree-heath zone/ insects/n ground or tree/e 2–3

Phylloscopus laetus (*Sharpe*) RED-FACED LEAF WARBLER Mts of W Uganda, E Congo and Rwanda/mountain forest/n near ground/e 2 (1 nest known)

Phylloscopus herberti (*Alexander*) HERBERT'S LEAF WARBLER Fernando Po and mts of S Nigeria and Cameroon / mountain forest / no other data

Phylloscopus budongoensis (*Seth-Smith*) BUDONGO WARBLER Ituri Forest/forest/n and e n/k

Phylloscopus affinis (*Tickell*) TICKELL'S LEAF WARBLER b Himalayas and mts of W China w India / scrub and secondary jungle / insects/ n bush/e 3–5/I ♂♀ (see note to *P. arcanus*)

Phylloscopus subaffinis (*Ogilvie-Grant*) CHINESE YELLOW-BELLIED WARBLER b Mts of W and S China w SE Asia/mountain scrub and grassland/ ? no other data (see note to *P. arcanus*)

Phylloscopus (**subaffinis**) **arcanus** *Ripley* BUFF-BELLIED WARBLER Known only from a few winter visitors to Nepal b n/k [opinion appears to be still divided as to whether *affinis* and *subaffinis* are conspecific; *arcanus* is treated as a race of *subaffinis* (or of *affinis* if the two are treated as conspecific) but as so little is known of it, I have listed all three forms with a query]

Phylloscopus griseolus *Blyth* SULPHUR or OLIVACEOUS LEAF WARBLER b Mts from Altai to Afghanistan and Himalayas w India/forest and ravine/insects/n bush/e 4–5

Phylloscopus occipitalis (*Blyth*) GREAT CROWNED WARBLER b W Himalayas and Afghanistan w Peninsular India/forest/insects/ n hole in tree or wall etc/e 4

Phylloscopus coronatus (*Temminck and Schlegel*) CROWNED WARBLER b Szechwan: and Japan, Korea, Manchuria and Amurland w SE Asia, Sumatra and Java/forest/insects/n tree (but apparently on the ground in Japan)/e 3–7

Phylloscopus ijimae (*Stejneger*) IJIMA'S WARBLER b Seven Is of Izu w Ryukyu Is/ mixed woodlands/insects/n tree/e 3

Phylloscopus armandii (*Milne-Edwards*) MILNE-EDWARDS' WARBLER N and W China S to hills of northern SE Asia / dry forest and scrub-jungle

Phylloscopus schwarzi (*Radde*) RADDE'S WARBLER b C and E Siberia, Korea and Manchuria w SE Asia/forest and scrub/n bush/ e 5

Phylloscopus pulcher *Blyth* ORANGE-BARRED WARBLER Himalayas and mts of Tibet and W China / forest / insects and (?) sap of oak/ n tree/e 4

Phylloscopus subviridis (*Brooks*) BROOKS' LEAF WARBLER Turkestan, Afghanistan and NW Indian region/forest/insects/n ground/e 4

Phylloscopus proregulus (*Pallas*) PALLAS' WARBLER b Himalayas and mts of W China; S Siberia from Altai to Sakhalin/forest/insects/ n tree /e 3–6

Phylloscopus maculipennis (*Blyth*) GREY-FACED WARBLER Himalayas, Yunnan and mts of Szechwan/forest/insects/n tree/e n/k

Phylloscopus inornatus (*Blyth*) YELLOW-BROWED WARBLER Widely distributed through N and E Siberia and C Asia w S Asia/forest and cultivation /insects / n ground / e 4–7

Phylloscopus borealis (*Blasius*) EVERSMANN'S or ARCTIC WARBLER b N Eurasia and Alaska S in mts to Mongolia w S Asia and Indonesia/ forest/insects/n ground/e 4–7

Phylloscopus magnirostris *Blyth* LARGE-BILLED LEAF WARBLER b Himalayas and mts of W China w S India, Ceylon and SE Asia/ forest/insects/n hole or under log etc/e 3–5

Phylloscopus trochiloides (*Sundevall*) GREENISH WARBLER b Baltic to Ussuriland and S in mts to Iran and Himalayas w S Asia/forest and habitation/insects/n ground/e 3–6/I ♀

Phylloscopus tenellipes *Swinhoe* CONIFER WARBLER b Japan, Sakhalin and Ussuriland w SE Asia /forest and open woodland / insects/ n ground/e 5–6

Phylloscopus fulgiventer (*Hodgson*) SMOKY WARBLER Tibet and E Himalayas /scrub above timberline/insects/n and e n/k (possibly a race of *fuscatus*)

Phylloscopus fuscatus (*Blyth*) DUSKY WARBLER b from Szechwan to C, E and NE Siberia w S China and SE Asia / variable, scrub-jungle etc, probably breeds in scrub above timberline / insects / n ground or bush/ e 5–6

Phylloscopus reguloides (*Blyth*) BLYTH'S LEAF WARBLER Himalayas to northern SE Asia,

W and S China / forest / insects and berries / n hole in tree or wall/e 4–5

Phylloscopus davisoni (*Oates*) WHITE-TAILED WARBLER Northern SE Asia and W China/ forest / n ground / e 3–4

Phylloscopus cantator (*Tickell*) BLACK-BROWED WARBLER E Himalayas, northern SE Asia, S China and Hainan / forest / insects/ n ground/e 3–4 / I ♂♀

Phylloscopus trivirgatus (*Strickland*) MOUNTAIN LEAF WARBLER Sikang and S China, Indochina and Hainan E through Indonesia to Philippines, New Guinea and Solomons/ mountain forest/ insects / n ground / e ?2 ?4–6 (accounts differ)

Phylloscopus nitidus *Blyth* GREEN WARBLER b WC Asia from Caucasus to Transcaspia and Afghanistan w Indian region / mountain forest / n ground/e 4–6

Phylloscopus cebuensis (*Dubois*) CEBU WARBLER Cebu, Negros and Luzon / ? no data

Phylloscopus amoenus *Hartert* KULAMBANGRA WARBLER Kulambangra (Solomons)/mountain forest/no other data

Seicercus affinis (*Hodgson*) ALLIED FLYCATCHER-WARBLER E Himalayas, northern SE Asia and S China/forest/insects /n hole or bank hollow/e 4–5/I ♂♀

Seicercus burkii (*Burton*) BLACK-BROWED or YELLOW EYED FLYCATCHER WARBLER Himalayas, E India, northern SE Asia and S China /forest/ insects / n ground / e 4

Seicercus poliogenys (*Blyth*) GREY-CHEEKED FLYCATCHER-WARBLER E Himalayas, mts of Yunnan and northern SE Asia /forest/insects/ n ground / e 4 / I ♂♀

Seicercus albogularis (*Horsfield and Moore*) WHITE-THROATED FLYCATCHER-WARBLER E Himalayas, northern SE Asia, S China, Hainan and Taiwan / forest and scrub / insects / n in hollow of bamboo/e 3–5/I ♂♀

Seicercus grammiceps (*Strickland*) SUNDA FLYCATCHER-WARBLER Java, Bali and Sumatra/ ? no data

Seicercus schisticeps (*Gray*) BLACK-FACED FLYCATCHER-WARBLER E Himalayas, SE Tibet, Yunnan and northern SE Asia /forest /insects/ n in hollow of bamboo/e 4 (1 nest known)

Seicercus superciliaris (*Blyth*) YELLOW-BELLIED FLYCATCHER-WARBLER E Himalayas, SE Asia, Sumatra, Java, Borneo / forest and scrub/insects/n in hollow of bamboo stem/e 3–5

MUSCICAPIDAE: *Platysteira peltata*, Black-throated Wattle-eye

Plate 224

MUSCICAPIDAE:
Poecilodryas superciliosa,
White-browed Robin

MUSCICAPIDAE: *Rhipidura rufifrons,* Rufous Fantail, Rufous-fronted Fantail

Plate 225

Seicercus castaniceps (*Hodgson*) CHESTNUT-HEADED FLYCATCHER-WARBLER Himalayas, SE Asia, S China, Sumatra and Borneo / forest/ insects / n ground / e 4–5 / I ♂♀

Seicercus xanthoschistus (*Gray*) GREY-HEADED FLYCATCHER-WARBLER Himalayas and mts of Burma / forest and habitation / insects/ n ground / e 4–5

Seicercus hodgsoni (*Moore*) BROAD-BILLED FLYCATCHER-WARBLER E Himalayas, Yunnan and northern SE Asia / scrub and bamboo/ insects / n 1 known, site not recorded / e 3

Seicercus montis (*Sharpe*) YELLOW-BREASTED FLYCATCHER-WARBLER Mts of Malaya and Sumatra to Borneo, Palawan and Timor/ mountain forest / ? no other data

Cisticola exilis (*Vigors and Horsfield*) RED-HEADED CISTICOLA and YELLOW-HEADED CISTICOLA SW Ghats of India: Himalayas, SE Asia, Indonesia to Taiwan, New Guinea and N Australia / grassland / insects / n in grass / e 4–5/ I ♂♀ 11

Cisticola juncidis (*Rafinesque*) ZITTING CISTICOLA or FANTAIL WARBLER Africa S of Sahara, Indian sub-continent, SE Asia, Sumatra and W Java / grassland and paddyfields / insects and green seeds / n in grass / e 3–6 / I ♂♀ 10

Cisticola erythrops (*Hartlaub*) RED-FACED CISTICOLA Much of Africa S of Sahara except the SW / forest glades, scrub and swamp / n bush / e 2–3

Cisticola cantans (*Heuglin*) SINGING CISTICOLA W Africa and Sudan S to Mozambique / forest glades and scrub / n bush / e 2–3

Cisticola woosnami *Ogilvie-Grant* TRILLING CISTICOLA E Africa from Uganda to Tanganyika and Congo / woodland and bush / n in grass/ e 2–3

Cisticola lateralis (*Fraser*) WHISTLING CISTICOLA Gambia to S Sudan, N Angola and Congo / forest edge and soft vegetation in savannah woodland / n in grass / e 2

Cisticola bulliens *Lynes* BUBBLING CISTICOLA Lower Congo and N Angola / jungle, bush and saltings / n in grass / e 3

Cisticola anonyma (*Müller*) CHATTERING CISTICOLA Ghana to Ituri and Angola / grassy clearings in forest and edges of cultivation / n ? in grass / e 2

Cisticola hunteri *Shelley* HUNTER'S CISTICOLA Mts of Kenya and Tanganyika / bush near streams and swamps / n shrub or tussock / e 2–3

Cisticola discolor *Sjöstedt* BROWN-BACKED CISTICOLA Mts of Cameroon / grassy hollows and low bush / n in grass / e 2 (? conspecific with *C. hunteri*)

Cisticola nigriloris *Shelley* BLACK-LORED CISTICOLA S Tanganyika to N Malawi / bush and herbage / n grass / e 2–3 (? conspecific with *C. hunteri*)

Cisticola aberrans (*Smith*) LAZY CISTICOLA Malawi to E Cape Province / grassy hillsides and stream margins / n grass / e 3–4

Cisticola restricta *Traylor* (*Bull Brit Orn Cl* 86 (1967), pp 45–8) TANA RIVER CISTICOLA Known from 6(?) specimens from the Lower Tana River of Tanganyika

Cisticola emini *Reichenow* ROCK-LOVING CISTICOLA Sierra Leone to S Sudan, NE Congo and Kenya / bare rocks / n in grass patches on rock slabs / e 3 (? conspecific with *C. aberrans*)

Cisticola haesitata (*Sclater and Hartlaub*) SOCOTRA CISTICOLA Socotra / grass and bushes/ n and e n/k

Cisticola chiniana (*Smith*) RATTLING CISTICOLA Congo to Angola, S Sudan and Zambia / woodland and thorn bush / n herbage/ e 3

Cisticola cherina (*Smith*) MADAGASCAR CISTICOLA Madagascar / grassland, ricefields and swamps / n grass-tussock / e 3–5

Cisticola rufilata (*Hartlaub*) GREY CISTICOLA Africa from Congo southwards / dry woodland, scrub and sand veldt / n herbage / e 3 (see note to *C. tinniens*)

Cisticola subruficapillata (*Smith*) GREY-BACKED CISTICOLA SW Africa to W Cape Province / sand dune and scrub / n bush / e 3–4

Cisticola lais (*Finsch and Hartlaub*) WAILING CISTICOLA Kenya to Malawi and Mozambique/ dry mountain sides / n shrub / e 3–4

Cisticola njombe *Lynes* CHURRING CISTICOLA Tanganyika / wooded and grassy hillsides / n grass / e 3

Cisticola galactotes (*Temminck*) WINDING CISTICOLA Much of Africa S of Sahara except SW Africa / marshes and bush / insects / n sedge/ e 3–4

Cisticola pipiens *Lynes* CHIRPING CISTICOLA E Angola, S Congo and Zambia / swamps / n grass or sedges / e 3–4

Cisticola carruthersi *Ogilvie-Grant* CARRUTHERS' CISTICOLA N Congo and Kenya/ papyrus swamp / n ? grass / e 3–4

Cisticola tinniens (*Lichtenstein*) LEVAILLANT'S CISTICOLA E and S Africa from Kenya to Angola and the Cape /edges of rivers, ponds and lakes / n grass / e 3–5 (NB: The name 'Tinkling Cisticola' appears to be used commonly for both this species and *C. rufilata*, so I consider it best to abandon it altogether. If it *must* be used, however, it would seem more appropriate to apply it to *tinniens*)

Cisticola robusta (*Rüppell*) STOUT CISTICOLA E and S Africa from Ethiopia to Angola; apparently an isolate population in the Cameroon Highlands /forest glades and bush / n in grass /e 2–3

Cisticola natalensis (*Smith*) CROAKING CISTICOLA Africa S of Sahara / scrub and cultivation/ n grass /e 2–4

Cisticola cinereola *Salvadori* ASHY CISTICOLA E and S Ethiopia, Kenya and the Somalilands/ acacia and thornbush /n ? bush / e 2

Cisticola fulvicapilla (*Vieillot*) PIPING CISTICOLA, NEDDICKY, or TAWNY-HEADED GRASS WARBLER S and SE Africa from Angola, Congo and S Tanganyika southwards / open woodland and habitation/ n bush/ e 2–4

Cisticola angusticauda *Reichenow* TABORA CISTICOLA SW Kenya to SE Congo and Zambia / light woodland / n undergrowth / e 3 (probably conspecific with *fulvicapilla*)

Cisticola melanura (*Cabanis*) BLACK-TAILED CISTICOLA Angola and S Congo / trees and bushes / known from few specimens / no other data (Mackworth Praed and Grant place this species in *Apalis*)

Cisticola nana *Fischer and Reichenow* TINY CISTICOLA S Ethiopia to Tanganyika /acacia and thornbush/ n in grass /e 4

Cisticola ruficeps (*Cretzschmar*) RED-PATE CISTICOLA Gambia to Sudan, Ethiopia and N Uganda / bush and dry scrub/ n grass / e 3–4

Cisticola brachyptera (*Sharpe*) SHORT-WINGED or SIFFLING CISTICOLA Africa S of Sahara S to Angola and Mozambique/ savannah/ n grass or herbage / e 2–3, 4–5 (accounts differ)

Cisticola rufa (*Fraser*) RUFOUS CISTICOLA W Africa from Gambia to Cameroon/ savannah and semi-desert / n and e n/k

Cisticola chubbi *Sharpe* CHUBB'S CISTICOLA NE Congo to Kenya and Tanganyika/ mountain scrub/ n bush/ e 2–3

Cisticola troglodytes (*Antinori*) FOXY CISTICOLA Nigeria to Sudan, Ethiopia and Kenya / 'grass and trees' (sic) /n described but no data on nest site or eggs

Cisticola aridula *Witherby* DESERT CISTICOLA Senegal to Sudan and S to Angola and S Africa/ grassland belt/ n in grass/ e 3–5

Cisticola textrix (*Vieillot*) PINCPINC or CLOUD CISTICOLA SE Africa from Transvaal to Cape/ grassland and marsh/ n ground / e 4

Cisticola eximia (*Heuglin*) BLACK-BACKED CISTICOLA Portuguese Guinea to Eritrea and N Congo / grass plains / n in short grass / e 3

Cisticola dambo *Lynes* CLOUDSCRAPER CISTICOLA Congo and Angola / short grass dambos/ n in short grass / e 2–3

Cisticola brunnescens *Heuglin* PECTORAL-PATCH CISTICOLA Cameroon to Congo, Tanganyika and Rhodesia / grassy plains / n on ground or in grass/ e 3–5

Cisticola ayresii *Hartlaub* WING-SNAPPING CISTICOLA Gabon and Kenya southward/ grass plains/ n ground or in grass/ e 3–5

(I am very aware of the shortcomings of this list of the genus *Cisticola*, though I wonder if it is possible to provide a really satisfactory list. This one is based on Edwards, with extra species recognised by Mackworth Praed and Grant added, but see also Hall and Moreau, *Atlas of Speciation in African Passerine Birds* and Lynes (1930) Cisticola supplement to *The Ibis*)

Incana incana (*Sclater and Hartlaub*) SOCOTRA WARBLER Socotra/ bush and plains/ n bush/ e n/k

Scotocerca inquieta (*Cretzschmar*) STREAKED SCRUB-WARBLER Morocco across N Africa and Middle East to Pakistan/arid rocky hillsides and scrub / insects, small snails and seeds / n bush/ e 5–6

Rhopophilus pekinensis (*Swinhoe*) WHITE-BROWED CHINESE WARBLER, PEKING WARBLER Tian Shan to S Mongolia, Korea and N China/ bushy hills and mountains/ insects/ n bush/ e 5

Prinia flaviventris (*Delessert*) YELLOW-BELLIED PRINIA Indus basin: SE Asia and Sumatra / reed beds and riverine scrub etc/ insects/ n bush or grass/ e 4/I ♂♀

Prinia familiaris *Horsfield* BAR-WINGED PRINIA Sumatra, Java and Bali / forest and habitation/ n tree/ e ?2

Prinia buchanani *Blyth* RUFOUS FRONTED PRINIA Pakistan, N and C India/ scrub-jungle and semi-desert / insects / n grass tussock or thornbush/ e 4–5

MUSCICAPIDAE:
Petroica cucullata,
Hooded Robin, Hooded Robin-
Flycatcher

MUSCICAPIDAE:
Muscicapa striata,
Spotted Flycatcher

Plate 226

MUSCICAPIDAE:
Heteromyias cinereifrons,
Grey-headed Robin,
Gray-headed Thicket-
Flycatcher

MUSCICAPIDAE:
Monarcha trivirgatus,
Spectacled Monarch, Spectacl-
ed Monarch Flycatcher

MUSCICAPIDAE:
Petroica goodenovii,
Red-capped Robin,
Red-capped Robin-Flycatcher

Plate 227

Prinia hodgsoni *Blyth* ASHY-GREY PRINIA Himalayas, India, Ceylon, northern SE Asia and Yunnan/scrub and cultivation/insects and nectar/n in grass/e 3–4/I ♂♀ 10–11

Prinia socialis *Sykes* ASHY PRINIA Indian sub-continent and W Burma / scrub, grass and cultivation / insects and nectar / n bush / e 3–5/ I ♂♀ 12

Prinia rufescens *Blyth* RUFESCENT PRINIA SE Asia and E India / scrub, grassland and cultivation /insects/n in grass/e 3–4/I ♂♀

Prinia burnesii (*Blyth*) LONG-TAILED PRINIA Indus basin: Lower Ganges and Brahmaputra valley/long grass/insects/n grass/e 4

Prinia polychroa (*Temminck*) BROWN PRINIA Java: northern SE Asia and SE Yunnan/scrub and grassland

Prinia criniger *Hodgson* BROWN HILL PRINIA Mts from Afghanistan through Himalayas to S China and Taiwan /hill scrub and open forest/ insects/n grass/e 3–5/I ♂♀ 10–11

Prinia sylvatica *Jerdon* JUNGLE PRINIA Himalayas, India and Ceylon / bush-jungle/ insects and vegetable matter / n bush / e 3–5/ I ♂♀

Prinia atrogularis (*Moore*) BLACK-THROATED PRINIA E Himalayas, E Tibet, SE Asia, S China and Sumatra /hill scrub and open forest/ insects/n grass/e 3–5

Prinia cinereocapilla *Hodgson* GRAY-CROWNED or HODGSON'S PRINIA Himalayan foothills from Nepal to Bhutan / forest /insects and nectar/n and e no reliable data

Prinia gracilis (*Lichtenstein*) GRACEFUL PRINIA E Africa from Egypt to Somalia across S Asia to N India region/scrub-jungle and desert scrub/ insects and vegetable matter / n bush or grass/ e 3–5/I ♂♀ 12

Prinia maculosa (*Boddaert*) KARROO PRINIA S Africa, N to SW Africa and the Limpopo/ karroo veld, coastal scrub and mountain slopes/ n bush or grass/e 3–5

Prinia substriata (*Smith*) NAMAQUA PRINIA Karroo scrub of W Cape Province /n grass /e 2–4

Prinia flavicans (*Vieillot*) BLACK-CHEEKED PRINIA From Orange River to Transvaal, Kalahari, Damaraland and Benguella / scrub/ insects/n grass, shrub or tree/e 3–4/I 12–13

Prinia pectoralis (*Smith*) RUFOUS-EARED PRINIA S and SW Africa /semi-desert/n bush/ e 4

Prinia clamans (*Temminck*) CRICKET WARBLER or SCALY PRINIA The arid belt S of Sahara from Mali to Eritrea /n shrub/ e 3

Prinia erythroptera (*Jardine*) RED-WINGED PRINIA From W Africa to Sudan and Ethiopia and S to Zambia/grassy woodland/n shrub/e 2

Prinia subflava (*Gmelin*) TAWNY PRINIA Africa S of Sahara / secondary forest and grassland /insects /n herbage /e 2–4

Prinia inornata *Sykes* PLAIN PRINIA Indian sub-continent, SE Asia and S to Java /scrub and cultivation /insects and nectar /n bush or grass stem /e 3–6/I ♂♀ 11–12

Prinia somalica (*Elliot*) PALE PRINIA S Ethiopia; the Somalilands and Kenya/grassy steppe /n grass/ e 3–4

Prinia molleri *Bocage* SÃO THOMÉ PRINIA São Thomé /ubiquitous /n herbage /e n/s

Prinia epichlora (*Reichenow*) GREEN LONGTAIL Fernando Po and mts of Cameroon/ mountain woods and ravines /n and e n/k

Prinia leucopogon (*Cabanis*) WHITE-CHINNED PRINIA C Africa from Cameroons and S Sudan to N Angola, Zambia and W Kenya/forest edges and woodland / n bush / e 2 (*Prinia leontica* Bates, from Sierra Leone and Guinea is now considered to be a race of *P. leucopogon*)

Prinia robertsi *Benson* FOREST PRINIA E Rhodesia /forest scrub/ insects /n bush /e 3

Prinia bairdii (*Cassin*) BANDED PRINIA Kenya to E Congo/forest clearings /n ? herbage /e 3

(For the genus *Apalis* I have generally given Mackworth Praed and Grant's species but indicated where these have been merged by White):

Apalis thoracica (*Shaw and Nodder*) BAR-THROATED APALIS S and E Africa from Cape Province to Kilimanjaro /highland forest / n undergrowth/ e 2–3

[**Apalis** (**thoracica**) **flavigularis** *Shelley* YELLOW BAR-THROATED APALIS Mts from Tanganyika to Mozambique] (*A. murina* and *A. grisiceps*, once considered distinct, are now treated as conspecific with *A. thoracica*)

Apalis pulchra *Sharpe* BLACK-COLLARED APALIS Cameroon to Sudan, Kenya and Congo/ undergrowth of highland forest / insects/ n among upright stems and twigs/e 2–3

[**Apalis** (**pulchra**) **ruwenzorii** *Jackson* COLLARED APALIS Ruwenzori Mts and adjacent ranges /forest /no data]

Apalis ruddi *Grant* RUDD'S APALIS S Mozambique/lower-level inland forests/n tree/e 2

Apalis nigriceps (*Shelley*) BLACK-CAPPED APALIS Fernando Po and Sierra Leone to Uganda and N Congo/secondary forest/n and e n/k

Apalis jacksoni *Sharpe* BLACK-THROATED APALIS Cameroon to S Sudan, Kenya and Angola/forest glades/insects/n no data on site/e 2

Apalis chariessa *Reichenow* WHITE-WINGED APALIS Scattered localities from Kenya to Mozambique

Apalis binotata *Reichenow* MASKED APALIS Cameroon to Uganda and E Congo/lowland and highland forest/insects/n and e no reliable data

Apalis flavida (*Cassin*) BLACK-BREASTED APALIS, YELLOW-BREASTED APALIS Africa S of Sahara S to Angola and Transvaal/forest and bush/insects/n bush or herbage/e 3

Apalis porphyrolaema *Reichenow and Neumann* CHESTNUT-THROATED APALIS Mts from Kenya to NE Tanganyika and E Congo/ mountain forest/n and e n/k

[**Apalis (porphyrolaema) kaboboensis** *Prigogine* PRIGOGINE'S APALIS Mt Kabobo (Congo)/no data]

Apalis sharpii *Shelley* SHARPE'S APALIS Sierra Leone to Ghana/dense bush/no other data

[**Apalis (sharpii) bamendae** *Bannerman* BAMENDA APALIS Cameroon Mts: mts of Tanganyika/forest/n tree/e n/k]

[**Apalis (sharpii) goslingi** *Alexander* GOSLING'S APALIS Cameroon to N Congo/ lowland wooded river banks/no other data]

Apalis schoutedeni *Chapin* SCHOUTEDEN'S APALIS Tschikapa, S Kasai, Congo/unique

Apalis cinerea (*Sharpe*) GREY APALIS Fernando Po and Cameroon to Sudan/highland forest/n tree/e 3

Apalis (cinerea) alticola (*Shelley*) BROWN-HEADED APALIS Tanganyika to Zambia and Katanga/forest/n and e n/k

Apalis rufogularis (*Fraser*) BLACK-BACKED or BUFF-THROATED APALIS Fernando Po and Nigeria to S Sudan, Kenya and N Angola/ forest/n and e n/k

[**Apalis (rufogularis) nigrescens** (*Jackson*) BLACK-BACKED APALIS Uganda and W Kenya/ forest/n tree/e n/k]

[**Apalis (rufogularis) eidos** *Peters and Love-*

ridge PETERS' APALIS Idjwi Is, Lake Kivu, E Congo/mountain forests/no other data]

Apalis melanocephala (*Fischer and Reichenow*) BLACK-HEADED APALIS Mts of E Africa from Kenya to Rhodesia/forest/n tree/ e 2–3

Apalis rufifrons (*Rüppell*) RED-FACED APALIS Sudan and Ethiopia to Tanganyika/dry scrub/ insects/n bush/e 4–5

Apalis karamojae (*van Someren*) KARAMOJA APALIS E Uganda/no data

Apalis pulchella (*Cretzschmar*) BUFF-BELLIED or ACACIA WARBLER Lake Chad to Eritrea, Tanganyika and NE Congo/bush and open woodland/insects/n tree or bush/e 2–3

Apalis argentae *Moreau* KUNGWE APALIS W Tanganyika/no data

Apalis chirindensis *Shelley* SWYNNERTON'S APALIS Mts of E Rhodesia/forest/n tree/e 2–3

Nesillas typica (*Hartlaub*) COMMON TSIKIRITY Madagascar, Anjouan, Moheli and Gr Comoro/ bush and scrub/n grass/e 2

Nesillas mariae *Benson* MOHELI TSIKIRITY Moheli (for discussion of this form, and its relation to *N. typica* see Benson, *Ibis*, vol 103B (Centenary volume) (1960), pp 79–83)

Nesillas aldabranus *Benson and Penny* ALDABRA TSIKIRITY Aldabra/known only from ♂ and ♀ types and nest and eggs all in British Museum (Natural History) (see Benson and Penny, *Bull Brit Orn Cl*, vol 88 (1968), pp 102–8)

Thamnornis chloropetoides (*Grandidier*) KIRITIKA Madagascar/scrub and brush

Randia pseudozosterops *Delacour* RAND'S WARBLER Madagascar/forests of humid east/ rare/no other data

Artisornis moreaui *Sclater* LONG-BILLED FOREST WARBLER Forests of Usambara mts and Njesi Plateau (E Africa)/no data

Artisornis metopias (*Reichenow*) RED-CAPPED FOREST WARBLER Mts from Tanganyika to Mozambique/forest/n tree/e n/k

Scepomycter winifredae (*Moreau*) MRS MOREAU'S WARBLER Uluguru Mts, E Tanganyika/forest/n and e n/k

Drymocichla incana *Hartlaub* RED-WINGED GREY WARBLER Cameroon to Sudan and N Congo/swampy woods and near streams/insects/ n and e n/k

Eminia lepida *Hartlaub* GREY-CAPPED WARBLER Kenya to N Tanganyika and E Congo/

MUSCICAPIDAE:
Petroica vittata,
Dusky Robin

MUSCICAPIDAE:
Rhipidura leucophrys,
Willie Wagtail or Black
and White Fantail

Plate 228

PACHYCEPHALINAE:
Pachycephala lanioides,
White-breasted Whistler

PACHYCEPHALINAE:
Pachycephala simplex,
Brown Whistler

Plate 229

scrub and forest undergrowth / insects / n in creepers / e 2–3

Vitia parens *Mayr* SHADE WARBLER San Cristobal (Solomons) / mountain forest / no other data

Vitia ruficapilla *Ramsay* FIJI WARBLER Fiji / mountain forest / e described

Hypergerus atriceps (*Lesson*) ORIOLE WARBLER Senegal to Cameroon and N Congo / thickets and forest clearings / n suspended from palm leaves / e n/s (the position and status of this genus is still uncertain)

Bathmocercus cerviniventris (*Sharpe*) BLACK-FACED RUFOUS WARBLER Sierra Leone to Kenya and S to Congo / forest marshes and herbage along forest streams / n – no data on nest site / e n/k

Camaroptera superciliaris (*Fraser*) YELLOW-BROWED CAMAROPTERA Fernando Po and W and C Africa to Uganda / forest / n bush / e 3

Camaroptera chloronota *Reichenow* OLIVE-GREEN CAMAROPTERA E Congo to Kenya and Uganda / forest undergrowth / n tree / e 2

Camaroptera brachyura (*Vieillot*) BLEATING or GREEN-BACKED CAMAROPTERA Africa S of Sahara / forest, scrub and desert / n bush / e 2–3 (?4)

Camaroptera lopezi (*Alexander*) LOPEZ'S WARBLER or WHITE-TAILED CAMAROPTERA Mts of Fernando Po, Cameroon and Ruwenzori / mountain forest / n and e n/k

Camaroptera fasciolata (*Smith*) BARRED CAMAROPTERA Tanganyika to Angola and S Africa / grassy patches in woods / n tree / e 2–3 (*C. stierlingi* (Reichenow) is sometimes separated)

Camaroptera simplex (*Cabanis*) GREY CAMAROPTERA Angola and Congo to S Sudan and Ethiopia / scrub / n herbage / e 3

Euryptila subcinnamomea (*Smith*) CINNAMON-BREASTED GREY WARBLER Karroo scrub of SW Africa and W Cape Province / insects / n apparently in grass at foot of rock / e 2–4

Eremomela icteropygialis (*Lafresnaye*) YELLOW-BELLIED EREMOMELA Arid and desert scrub areas of Africa S of Sahara and S to Transvaal / open bush etc / n bush / e 2–3

Eremomela flavocrissalis *Sharpe* YELLOW-VENTED EREMOMELA Kenya and the Somalilands / open bush / insects / n bush / e 2

Eremomela pusilla *Hartlaub* GREEN-BACKED EREMOMELA Senegal to Congo and S Sudan / woodland and arid country / insects / n bush / e 2

Eremomela scotops *Sundevall* GREENCAP EREMOMELA Congo and Angola to Zambia and Malawi / savannah and open woodland / n tree / e 2–3

Eremomela atricollis *Bocage* BLACK-NECKED EREMOMELA Angola, Congo and Zambia / open woodland / n tree / e 2

Eremomela badiceps (*Fraser*) BROWN-CROWNED EREMOMELA Fernando Po and Sierra Leone to S Sudan, Uganda and Angola / secondary forest / n and e n/k

Eremomela turneri *van Someren* TURNER'S EREMOMELA E Congo and W Kenya / forest and cultivation

Eremomela usticollis *Sundevall* BURNT-NECK EREMOMELA Malawi and Mozambique / acacias / n tree or bush / e 1

Eremomela gregalis (*Smith*) KARROO EREMOMELA Karroo scrub of SW Africa and W Cape Province / insects / n grass tuft / e n/s

Bebrornis sechellensis (*Oustalet*) SEYCHELLES BRUSH WARBLER Seychelles, confined to Cousin, formerly also Marianne / dense scrub / insects / n bush / e 1–2 / I 15

Bebrornis rodericanus (*Newton*) RODRIGUEZ BRUSH WARBLER Rodriguez

Sylvietta leucophrys *Sharpe* WHITE-BROWED CROMBEC SW Uganda to Tanganyika and E Congo / mountain forest undergrowth / insects / n on twigs or plant stems / e 2

Sylvietta virens *Cassin* GREEN CROMBEC W Africa to Sudan, Uganda and Angola / forest and dense undergrowth / insects / n ? bush / e 2

Sylvietta denti *Ogilvie-Grant* LEMON-BELLIED CROMBEC Sierra Leone to ? Uganda / secondary forest / insects / n bush / e 1

Sylvietta ruficapilla *Bocage* RED-CAPPED CROMBEC Africa from S Congo to Zambia, Malawi and Mozambique / open woodland / insects / n bush / e 2

Sylvietta philippae *Williams* SHORT-TAILED CROMBEC Interior of the Somalilands / semi-desert

Sylvietta brachyura *Lafresnaye* COMMON CROMBEC Arid belt from Senegal to Red Sea, W Kenya and Cameroon / dry bush / insects / n bush / e 2

Sylvietta rufescens (*Vieillot*) LONG-BILLED CROMBEC Zambia and Malawi to Damaraland and Bechuanaland / bush and woodland / insects /

n thornbush/e 2

Sylvietta whytii *Shelley* RED-FACED CROMBEC Kenya to Rhodesia and Mozambique / open bush and woodland/n tree/e 2

Sylvietta isabellina *Elliott* SOMALI CROMBEC SE Ethiopia, Kenya and the Somalilands / dry scrub/n bush/e 2

Tesia cyaniventer *Hodgson* YELLOWBROWED TESIA Himalayas, SE Tibet, Yunnan and northern SE Asia /forest and bamboo/ insects/ n bush/e 3–5

Tesia olivea (*McClelland*) SLATYBELLIED TESIA Sikkim to Burma, Yunnan and Vietnam /forest/ insects /n n/k

Tesia castaneocoronata (*Burton*) CHESTNUT-HEADED TESIA Himalayas to mts of W China and northern SE Asia /open forest and brush/ insects /n bush/e 2/I ♂♀

Tesia superciliaris (*Bonaparte*) MALAYSIAN TESIA Java, Flores and Sumbawa / mountain forest

Hemitesia neumanni *Rothschild* NEUMANN'S WARBLER Mts of E Congo near Lake Tanganyika /mountain forests /no data

Macrosphenus concolor (*Hartlaub*) GREY LONGBILL Fernando Po and Sierra Leone to Gabon, Congo and Uganda /forest /n and e n/k

Macrosphenus pulitzeri *Boulton* PULITZER'S LONGBILL Known only from 2,000ft (600m) on the Angola escarpment

Macrosphenus flavicans *Cassin* YELLOW LONGBILL Fernando Po and Sierra Leone to Gabon, Congo and Uganda / forest / insects/ n and e n/k [*M. kempi* Sharpe is sometimes treated as a race of *flavicans*, sometimes as a good species. *M. leoninus* Neumann, known only from the unique type may be a form or juvenile of either *flavicans* or *kempi*]

Macrosphenus kretschmeri (*Reichenow and Neumann*) CRETZSCHMAR'S LONGBILL From Kilimanjaro S to N Mozambique/forest /insects/ n and e n/k (formerly placed in the monotypic genus *Suateliornis* and treated as a Bulbul)

Calamocichla newtoni (*Hartlaub*) MADAGASCAR SWAMP WARBLER Madagascar/ swamps /n bush /e 2–3 /I ?♀

Grauera vittata *Hartert* GRAUER'S WARBLER Mt forests of E Congo /no data

Amaurocichla bocagei *Sharpe* BOCAGE'S LONGBILL São Thomé/ no data

Parisoma subcaeruleum (*Vieillot*) CAPE TIT-WARBLER S Africa N to Angola and S

Zambia / thorn-bush and acacia / n thornbush/ e 2–3

Parisoma layardi *Hartlaub* LAYARD'S TIT-WARBLER S and SW Africa and Basutoland/ desert scrub/n bush/e 2

Parisoma bohmi *Reichenow* BANDED TIT-WARBLER Ethiopia S to Tanganyika / acacia scrub/n tree /e 2–3

Parisoma lugens (*Rüppell*) BROWN TIT-WARBLER Ethiopia and S Sudan to E Congo and Malawi /open forest and woodland /n tree /e 2

Parisoma buryi *Ogilvie-Grant* ARABIAN TIT-WARBLER Yemen and Asir Tihama/known only from a few specimens (the taxonomic position of this species is doubtful)

Stenostira scita (*Vieillot*) FAIRY WARBLER or FAIRY FLYCATCHER S Africa N to Transvaal/ trees and bushes along riverbanks/n tree/e 2–3. This species has been placed both in the Sylvidae and in the Muscicapidae by different authors

Calamornis rufescens (*Sharpe and Bouvier*) RUFOUS CANE WARBLER Fernando Po and Africa from Nigeria to S Sudan and Zambia/ reeds and papyrus /n reeds/e 2–3

Calamornis gracilirostris (*Hartlaub*) GREATER SWAMP WARBLER Lake Chad and S Sudan to Cape Province/swamps/n in rushes or grass in water/e 2–3 (*C. foxi* Sclater, is a race of *rufescens*. The genus is sometimes merged in *Acrocephalus*)

Hylia prasina (*Cassin*) GREEN HYLIA Fernando Po and Guinea to N Angola and W Kenya/ forest / scale insects and wax / n tree / e 1–2 [This species is often treated as a sunbird]

Dromaeocercus seebohmi *Sharpe* GREY EMU-TAIL Madagascar /grassy swamps of the mountains of the humid east /insects / n ? in sedges

Dromaeocercus brunneus *Sharpe* BROWN EMU-TAIL Madagascar /forests of the humid east /insects /n and e n/k

Genus INCERTA SEDIS

Lamprolia victoriae *Finsch* SILKTAIL Vanua Levu and Taveuni (Fiji) / mountain forest/ termites and beetles/n tree/e 1 (This bird is of very uncertain affinities, having been placed in the Paradisaeidae but now generally in the Sylvidae)

REGULIDAE Kinglets and Tit-Warblers This is a family of doubtful status, often considered to belong to the Sylvidae, but

PACHYCEPHALINAE:
Pachycephala pectoralis
Golden Whistler

PACHYCEPHALINAE:
Pachycephala inornata,
Gilbert Whistler

Plate 230

PARIDAE;
Parus major,
Great Tit

PARIDAE:
Parus caeruleus,
Blue Tit

Plate 231

separated by some authorities owing to some titmouse-like characteristics. The group was, in fact, originally placed with the Paridae. The genus *Leptopoecile* is generally placed next to *Regulus*, though Edwards *A Coded List of Birds of the World* retains *Regulus* in a monotypic family and puts *Leptopoecile* in the middle of the *Sylvidae*.

Leptopoecile elegans *Przewalski* CRESTED TIT-WARBLER Mts of E Tibet and W China/ fir forest and scrub above timber line / insects / n and e n/k

Leptopoecile sophiae *Severtzov* WHITE-BROWED TIT-WARBLER Mts from Tian Shan to Kansu and Szechwan / juniper scrub above timber line / insects / n bush / e 4–6

Regulus regulus (*L*) GOLDCREST Irregularly and discontinuously distributed through temperate Palaearctic S to Himalayas and Mediterranean / forest and woodland / insects / n tree / e 4–13 / I ♀ 14–17 / F 16–21

Regulus ignicapillus (*Temminck*) FIRECREST Europe, Asia Minor and N Africa, Madeira/ forest / insects / n tree or bush / e 7–12 / I 14–15

Regulus teneriffae *Seebohm* TENERIFFE KINGLET Teneriffe, Palma, Gomera and Hierro/ forest / n tree / e 3–6 (this bird has been variously treated as a race of *R. regulus* or of *R. ignicapillus* and since it has characteristics of both it seems more appropriate to give it specific rank)

Regulus goodfellowi *Ogilvie-Grant* FORMOSAN KINGLET Taiwan / mountain white fir forests/ no other data

[**Regulus cuvieri** *Audubon* CUVIER'S KINGLET Known only from Audubon's description and plate, *Birds of America* 1 (1829), p 155; believed to be a hybrid]

Regulus satrapa *Lichtenstein* GOLDEN-CROWNED KINGLET Much of N America moving S in winter / forest / insects / n tree/ e 5–10

Regulus calendula (*L*) RUBY-CROWNED KINGLET Much of N America w S to N Mexico / forest / insects and fruit / n tree / e 5–11/ I ♀

MALURIDAE Australian Wrens Aberrant, generally brightly-coloured relatives of the Sylvidae (often considered a sub-family of same) with long tails giving them a wren-like appearance. Generally inhabit scrub, feeding on insects and building domed nests. Eggs 2–5 in number.

Malurus cyaneus (*Latham*) SUPERB BLUE WREN SE Australia and Tasmania / woodland and savannah and habitation / insects / n bush / e 3–4

Malurus melanotus *Gould* BLACK-BACKED WREN Plains of EC Australia / woodland and savannah / insects / n bush or tussock / e 3–4

Malurus callainus *Gould* TURQUOISE WREN Parts of C and S Australia / arid scrub and grassland / insects / n bush / e 3–4

Malurus splendens (*Quoy and Gaimard*) SPLENDID BLUE WREN W Australia / forest and savannah / insects / n bush / e 3–4

Malurus lamberti *Vigors and Horsfield* VARIEGATED WREN E Australia / thickets, heaths and mangrove / insects / n ground or bush / e 3–4

Malurus assimilis *North* PURPLE-BACKED WREN Interior of Australia / mangrove and saltbush / n ground or bush / e 3–4

Malurus pulcherrimus *Gould* BLUE-BREASTED WREN SW Australia / n ground or bush / e 3–4

Malurus elegans *Gould* RED-WINGED WREN SW Australia / swampy thickets / n ground or bush / e 3–4

Malurus amabilis *Gould* LOVELY WREN Parts of N Australia / forest and woodland

Malurus leucopterus *Dumont* WHITE-WINGED WREN Interior of Australia / bushes and tussocks/ insects / n bush / e 3–4

Malurus melanocephalus (*Latham*) RED-BACKED WREN N and E Australia / coarse grassland with scattered bushes / insects / n bush/ e 3–4

Malurus coronatus *Gould* LILAC-CROWNED WREN N Australia / mangroves and vegetation along water margins / insects / n bush / e 3

Malurus alboscapularis (*Meyer*) BLACK AND WHITE WREN New Guinea / savannah / no other data

Stipiturus malachurus (*Shaw*) SOUTHERN EMU WREN Tasmania, SE and SW Australia/ swampy heaths and sandhill scrub / insects / n bush or tussock / e 3

Stipiturus mallee *Campbell* MALLEE EMU WREN Plains of SW New South Wales and N Victoria / mallee scrub / insects / n bush or tussock / e 3

Stipiturus ruficeps *Campbell* RUFOUS-CROWNED EMU WREN Interior of Australia/ dense grass / insects / n bush or grass / e 2

Todopsis cyanocephala (*Quoy and Gaimard*)

NEW GUINEA BLUE WREN New Guinea, Salawati, Biak and Aru Is/lowland swamp and bamboo thickets/n bush/e ?4 (1 nest with young)

Todopsis wallacii (*Gray*) WALLACE'S WREN New Guinea, Misol, Japen and Aru Is/lowland forest and swamp/no other data

Chenorhamphus grayi (*Wallace*) BROAD-BILLED WREN N and W New Guinea, Salawati and Amberpon/rain forest/no other data

Chenorhamphus insignis (*Sharpe*) RUFOUS WREN-WARBLER New Guinea/mountain forest/no other data

Amytornis textilis (*Dumont*) WESTERN GRASS WREN W Australia/scrub and saltbush/insects, seeds and fruits/n bush/e 2–3

Amytornis modestus (*North*) THICK-BILLED GRASS WREN S Australia and New South Wales/scrub and saltbush/insects, seeds and fruit/n bush/e 2–3

Amytornis purnelli (*Mathews*) DUSKY GRASS WREN C Northern Territory and W Queensland/rocky hillsides

Amytornis whitei *Mathews* RUFOUS GRASS WREN N part of interior of Australia/scrub and semi-desert/insects and seeds/n grass clump/e 3

Amytornis goyderi (*Gould*) EYREAN GRASS WREN Neighbourhood of Lake Eyre / cane grass on sandhills/n in cane clump/e ?2

Amytornis striatus (*Gould*) STRIATED GRASS WREN Plains of SE Australia/scrub and semi-desert/insects and seeds/n grass clump/e 3

Amytornis dorothea (*Mathews*) DOROTHY'S GRASS WREN Restricted to an area SW of Gulf of Carpentaria, Lower McArthur River/among rocks

Amytornis woodwardi *Hartert* WHITE-THROATED GRASS WREN Restricted area of N Australia/rocky outcrops

Amytornis housei (*Milligan*) BLACK GRASS WREN Restricted area of northern W Australia/rocky gorges/insects and seeds

Amytornis barbatus *Favaloro and McEvey* (1968) *Mem Nat Mus Victoria*, vol 28, p 1 GREY GRASS WREN NW New South Wales

EPHTHIANURIDAE Australian Chats A family of uncertain affinities, usually placed in or near the warblers.

Ephthianura albifrons (*Jardine and Selby*) WHITE-FACED CHAT Southern Australia / bush and scrub/insects and seeds/n bush/e 3–4

Ephthianura tricolor *Gould* CRIMSON CHAT Australia/ savannah /insects /n bush or tussock/e 3–4

Ephthianura aurifrons *Gould* ORANGE CHAT Interior of Australia / samphire and saltbush/insects/n bush or tussock/e 3–4

Ephthianura crocea *Cast and Ramsay* YELLOW CHAT Scattered localities on coasts on N and E Australia /river swamps

Ashbyia lovensis (*Ashby*) GIBBER CHAT EC Australia/arid plains/insects and seeds/n ground/e 2–4

ACANTHIZIDAE Australian Warblers This group of warblers is sometimes considered to be a separate family, sometimes merged with the Sylvidae, and sometimes with the Maluridae.

Cinclorhamphus mathewsi *Iredale* RUFOUS SONGLARK Australia / savannah /insects and seeds/n ground /e 3–4

Cinclorhamphus cruralis (*Vigors and Horsfield*) BROWN SONGLARK Australia/grassland and scrub/ insects and seeds/n ground/e 3–4

Eremiornis carteri *North* SPINIFEXBIRD W and C Australia/scrub/insects/n grass tussock/e 2

Dasyornis brachypterus (*Latham*) EASTERN BRISTLEBIRD Coast of New South Wales/heathland of coast and mountain /insects and seeds/ n herbage/e 2

Dasyornis longirostris (*Gould*) WESTERN BRISTLEBIRD Formerly SW Australia from Perth to Albany, now confined to a small area E of Albany/ rare /low scrub

Dasyornis broadbenti (*McCoy*) RUFOUS BRISTLEBIRD Restricted coastal areas of W Australia, eastern S Australia and W Victoria/scrub

Gerygone olivacea (*Gould*) WHITE-THROATED GERYGONE N and E Australia and SE New Guinea / open forest and woodland / insects/n tree /e 2–3

Gerygone palpebrosa *Wallace* BLACK-HEADED GERYGONE Cape York Peninsula /open forest and mangrove/ insects /n tree/e 2

Gerygone flavida *Ramsay* FAIRY GERYGONE Coast of Queensland/open forest and mangrove/insects and seeds (now generally accepted as a race of *palpebrosa*)

Gerygone chloronota *Gould* GREEN-BACKED GERYGONE Coasts of Arnhem and Kimberley regions/mangrove/insects/n tree/e 2–3

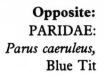
Opposite:
PARIDAE:
Parus caeruleus,
Blue Tit

PARIDAE:
Parus caeruleus,
Blue Tit

PARIDAE:
Parus major,
Great Tit

AEGITHALIDAE:
Aegithalos caudatus,
Long-tailed Tit

Plate 232

Plate 233

Gerygone magnirostris *Gould* LARGE-BILLED GERYGONE Coasts of N Australia / mangrove / insects / n tree / e 2–3 (*G. tenebrosa* (Hall) is sometimes separated)

Gerygone levigaster *Gould* BUFF-BREASTED GERYGONE Coasts of N and E Australia / mangrove and river margins / insects / n tree / e ?

Gerygone richmondi *Mathews* BROWN GERYGONE Coasts of E Australia / rain forest / insects / n tree

Gerygone fusca (*Gould*) FLYEATER or WHITE-TAILED GERYGONE S Indo-China through Indonesia to New Guinea and WC and E Australia / forest and parkland / insects / n tree e 2–3 (*G. sulphurea* Wallace, is often separated)

Gerygone inornata *Wallace* UNADORNED GERYGONE Timor, Savu, Kei, Dammer, Kisser and Roma

Gerygone chrysogaster (*Grau*) YELLOW-BELLIED GERYGONE New Guinea, Japen, W Papuan and Aru Is / lowland forest / n tree / e ?3

Gerygone albofrontata *Gray* CHATHAM ISLANDS WARBLER Chatham Is / bush and scrub / n bush / e 4

Gerygone ignata (*Quoy and Gaimard*) NEW ZEALAND GREY GERYGONE or RIRORIRO New Zealand / scrub and forest margin / insects / n tree / e 4–6 / I 17–19

Gerygone cinerea (*Salvadori*) PACIFIC GREY GERYGONE Mts of New Guinea / mountain forest / insects / n and e n/k

Gerygone flavolateralis *Gray* FAN-TAILED GERYGONE New Caledonia, New Hebrides and Banks Is / open country (New Caledonia), forest and plantation (New Hebrides and Banks Is) / n tree / e 8–15

Gerygone ruficollis (*Salvadori*) TREEFERN GERYGONE Mts of New Guinea / forest and treefern area above timberline / insects / n and e n/k

Gerygone rubra (*Sharpe*) RED-BACKED GERYGONE Mts of New Guinea / mountain forest / insects / n and e n/k

Smicrornis brevirostris *Gould* WEEBILL Australia and Tasmania / dry forest to semi-desert / insects / n tree / e 2–3 (sometimes divided into 2 species: *S. brevirostris* 'Brown Weebill' and *S. flavescens* 'Yellow Weebill')

Acanthiza murina (*De Vis*) BAR-TAILED THORNBILL Mts of New Guinea / forest / n tree / e ?2 (1 nest with 2 young known)

Acanthiza inornata *Gould* WESTERN THORNBILL SW Australia / dry forest / insects / n tree / e 3

Acanthiza nana *Vigors and Horsfield* LITTLE THORNBILL E Australia / dry forest and scrub / insects / n tree / e 2–4

Acanthiza lineata *Gould* STRIATED THORNBILL E Australia / dry forest / insects / n tree / e 3

Acanthiza pusilla *White* BROWN THORNBILL Tasmania and southern Australia / forest / insects and vegetable matter / n bush / e 3 (*A. apicalis* Gould is often treated as distinct)

Acanthiza ewingi *Gould* TASMANIAN THORNBILL Tasmania, King and Flinders Is / forest / n tree

Acanthiza robustirostris *Milligan* SLATE-BACKED THORNBILL Interior of Australia / mulga / insects / n tree / e 3

Acanthiza iredalei *Mathews* SAMPHIRE THORNBILL Interior of Southern Australia / saltbush and samphire semi-desert / insects / n bush / e 3

Acanthiza reguloides *Vigors and Horsfield* BUFF-TAILED THORNBILL E Australia / open forest / insects / n hole / e 3

Acanthiza chrysorrhoa (*Quoy and Gaimard*) YELLOW-TAILED THORNBILL Australia except N / open woodland and savannah / insects and seeds / n herbage / e 3

Acanthiza uropygialis *Gould* CHESTNUT-TAILED THORNBILL Southern Australia / dry savannah and woodland / insects and seeds / n hole / e 3

[**Acanthiza katherina** *De Vis* MOUNTAIN THORNBILL Restricted area of Queensland / mountain forest]

Sericornis frontalis (*Vigors and Horsfield*) WHITE-BROWED SCRUBWREN E and SE Australia and islands in Bass Strait / coastal bush / invertebrates and seeds / n herbage / e 3

Sericornis maculatus *Gould* SPOTTED SCRUBWREN SW and southern Australia / coastal bush

Sericornis humilis *Gould* BROWN SCRUBWREN Tasmania and islands in Bass Strait / bush

Sericornis beccarii *Salvadori* LITTLE SCRUBWREN N Cape York Peninsula and New Guinea / lowland forest and undergrowth / insects / n ground / e 3–4

Sericornis citreogularis *Gould* (=**S. lathami** (*Stephens*)) LEMON-THROATED SCRUBWREN E Australia / rain forest / insects and seeds / n tree / e 2–3

Sericornis spilodera (*Gray*) PALE-BILLED SCRUBWREN Mts of New Guinea, Japen, Waigeu and Aru Is / forest

[**Sericornis virgatus** (*Reichenow*) PERPLEXING SERICORNIS Japen and Arfak and Sepik Mts of New Guinea / no data / this complex of 5 mid-mountain races was separated out as a species by Rand and Gilliard *Birds of New Guinea*; formerly, and apparently still by other authorities, they are distributed between the species *beccarii* and *nouhuysi*]

Sericornis magnirostris *Gould* LARGE-BILLED SCRUBWREN E Australia / forest / insects / n tree or bush / e 3–4

Sericornis keri *Mathews* ATHERTON SCRUB-WREN Atherton Tableland, Queensland / no data / status uncertain

Sericornis nouhuysi (*van Oort*) MOUNTAIN SCRUBWREN Mts of C and E New Guinea / mountain forest / n pandanus / e 2

Sericornis nigroviridis (*Miller*) BLACK AND GREEN SERICORNIS 7,000ft (2,100m) in the Watut River area of NE New Guinea / unique

Sericornis perspicillatus (*Salvadori*) BUFF-FACED SCRUBWREN Mts of New Guinea / forest / insects / n shrub / e n/k

Sericornis rufescens (*Salvadori*) ARFAK SCRUBWREN Arfak Mts, New Guinea / no data

Sericornis papuensis (*De Vis*) PAPUAN SCRUBWREN Mts of New Guinea / mountain forest

Sericornis arfakianus (*Salvadori*) GREY-GREEN SCRUBWREN Mts of New Guinea / lower mountain forest

Oreoscopus gutteralis (*De Vis*) FERNBIRD or FERN WREN NE Queensland / rain forest / insects / n ground / e 2

(The genus Crateroscelis is of uncertain affinities, being sometimes placed here, and sometimes in the Timaliidae)

Crateroscelis murina (*Sclater*) LOWLAND MOUSE WARBLER New Guinea / lowland forest / no other data

Crateroscelis nigrorufa (*Salvadori*) MID-MOUNTAIN MOUSE WARBLER Lower mountains of New Guinea / no data

Crateroscelis robusta (*De Vis*) HIGH MOUNTAIN MOUSE WARBLER High mountains of New Guinea / mountain forest / insects / n and e n/k

Chthonicola sagittata (*Latham*) SPECKLED WARBLER E and SE Australia / woodland and scrub / insects and seeds / n ground / e 3

Calamanthus fuliginosus (*Vigors and Horsfield*) STRIATED FIELD WREN Southern Australia / moist heath, scrub and semi-desert / insects / n ground or tussock / e 3–4 (*C. campestris* (Gould) is sometimes separated)

Hylacola pyrrhopygia (*Vigors and Horsfield*) CHESTNUT-TAILED HEATH WREN SE Australia / woodland and scrub / insects / n ground / e 3–4

Hylacola cauta *Gould* SHY HEATH WREN SE and SW Australia / mallee scrub

[**Hylacola (?) tyrannulus** (*De Vis*) CHARLEVILLE HEATH WREN Based on a specimen collected near Charleville, now lost / status uncertain]

Aphelocephala leucopsis (*Gould*) SOUTHERN WHITEFACE Southern Australia / woodland and arid scrub / seeds and insects / n tree or hole / e 2–5

Aphelocephala pectoralis (*Gould*) CHESTNUT-BREASTED WHITEFACE Interior of S Australia / scrub and mulga / seeds and insects / n and e n/k

Aphelocephala nigricincta (*North*) BANDED WHITEFACE Interior of Australia / saltbush and mulga / seeds and insects / n bush / e 2–4

Pyrrholaemus brunneus *Gould* REDTHROAT WC and southern Australia / saltbush and arid scrub / insects and seeds / n herbage / e 3–4

Pycnoptilus floccosus *Gould* PILOTBIRD SE Australia / forest / insects / n ground or herbage / e 2

Origma solitaria (*Lewin*) (=**Origmella solitaria** or **rubricata**) ROCK WARBLER New South Wales / local / ravines and rocky gullies / insects / n rock or cave roof / e 3

Acanthornis magnus *Gould* SCRUB TIT Tasmania / forest / insects / n bush or fern / e 3–4

MUSCICAPIDAE Old World Flycatchers
A large family of generally small, insectivorous birds of very variable colour, some species being brightly coloured, others very dull. Generally arboreal in habits, some species with fine songs, but most have harsh call notes and the songs tend to be weak and monotonous. Nest, a neat cup in a tree or bush, or sometimes in a hole. Both sexes incubate but the female does more of the work. About 400 species throughout the Old World.

The arrangement of this family is complicated, and no authoritative list exists. I have followed the species list given by Edwards, *A coded List*

SITTIDAE:
Sitta europaea,
Eurasian Nuthatch

DAPHOENOSITTIDAE:
Neositta chryoptera,
Orange-winged Sitella or
Treerunner, Australian Sitella

Plate 234

PARIDAE:
Parus lugubris,
Sombre Tit

Plate 235

of the Birds of the World, 1974, amended where necessary. Following Edwards, I have left the genus *Myopornis* in the Sylvidae, though it is more usually regarded as a flycatcher.

Pomarea dimidiata *Hartlaub and Finsch* COOK ISLAND FLYCATCHER Rarotonga, Cook Is (Mathews' statement that it occurs in Samoa is probably erroneous)

Pomarea nigra (*Sparrman*) TAHITI FLY-CATCHER Society Is (Tahiti and Maupiti)

Pomarea mendozae (*Hartlaub*) MENDOZA FLYCATCHER Tahuata, Hivaoa, Motava, Huapu, and Nukuhiva (Marquesas)

Pomarea iphis *Murphy and Mathews* HUAHUNA FLYCATCHER Huahuna, Eiao (Marquesas)

Pomarea whitneyi *Murphy and Mathews* FATUHIVA FLYCATCHER Fatuhiva Is (Marquesas)

Peltops blainvillii (*Lesson and Garnot*) LOWLAND PELTOPS New Guinea lowlands, Misol, Salawati and Waigeu / forest

Peltops montanus *Stresemann* MOUNTAIN PELTOPS Mts of New Guinea / forest / n tree / e ? n/k

Rhipidura albicollis (*Vieillot*) WHITE-THROATED FANTAIL India, SE Asia, Szechwan, Sumatra, Borneo / forest, scrub and cultivation/ n tree / e 3 / I ♂♀ 12–13 / F 13–15

Rhipidura albogularis (*Lesson*) WHITE-SPOTTED FANTAIL Peninsular India. Rand and Fleming (*Fieldiana, Zoology*, 35: 539–40, recommended that this form should be treated as a race of *R. albicollis* and this is followed by Ali and Ripley in *Handbook of the Birds of India and Pakistan*)

Rhipidura aureola *Lesson* WHITE-BROWED FANTAIL Indian sub-continent E to Vietnam/ forest / n tree / e 3

Rhipidura javanica (*Sparrman*) PIED FANTAIL Java, Philippines, Palawan and Borneo / forest and cultivation / n palm tree / e n/s

Rhipidura superciliaris (*Sharpe*) BLUE FANTAIL Philippines

Rhipidura cyaniceps (*Cassin*) BLUE-HEADED FANTAIL Philippines

Rhipidura nigrocinnamomea *Hartert* BLACK AND CINNAMON FANTAIL Mindanao (Philippines)

Rhipidura threnothorax *Müller* SOOTY THICKET FANTAIL New Guinea, Japen, Salawati, Waigeu and Aru Is / forest
[For the *R. rufifrons* group (*rufifrons* to *malaitae*)

see Mayr and Moynihan, *Amer Mus Novit*, no 1,321, 1946]

Rhipidura rufifrons *Latham* RUFOUS FANTAIL Australia, Papuan area, Timor, Solomons, Marianas, Carolines and Santa Cruz Is / forest and mangrove / n tree / e 2–3

Rhipidura superflua *Hartert* BURU FANTAIL Buru

Rhipidura teijsmanni *Büttikofer* TEIJSMANN'S FANTAIL Celebes and adjacent islets

Rhipidura lepida *Hartlaub and Finsch* PALAU FANTAIL Palau Is

Rhipidura dedemi *van Oort* VAN OORT'S FANTAIL Ceram

Rhipidura opistherythra *Sclater* TENIMBER FANTAIL Tenimber Is

Rhipidura rufidorsa *Meyer* RED-BACKED FANTAIL New Guinea, Misol and Japen / forest undergrowth

Rhipidura dahli *Reichenow* BISMARCK FANTAIL New Britain and New Ireland

Rhipidura matthiae *Heinroth* HEINROTH'S FANTAIL St Matthias Is

Rhipidura malaitae *Mayr* MALAITA FANTAIL Malaita (Solomons)

Rhipidura maculipectus *Gray* BLACK THICKET FANTAIL New Guinea and Aru Is, W Papuan islands / swamps and cane grass

Rhipidura leucothorax *Salvadori* WHITE-BREASTED THICKET FANTAIL New Guinea/ lowland swamp and long grass

Rhipidura rennelliana *Mayr* RENNELL FANTAIL Rennell Is / no data

Rhipidura nebulosa *Peale* SAMOAN FANTAIL Samoa

Rhipidura tenebrosa *Ramsay* SOMBRE or DUSKY FANTAIL Solomon Is

Rhipidura hypoxantha *Blyth* YELLOW-BELLIED FANTAIL Himalayas to SE Tibet, Yunnan and Indo-China / forest / n tree / e 3

Rhipidura brachyrhyncha *Schlegel* DIMORPHIC FANTAIL New Guinea / high mountain forest

Rhipidura drownei *Mayr* MOUNTAIN FANTAIL Bougainville and Guadalcanal (Solomons)/ mountain forest

Rhipidura fuliginosa (*Sparrman*) GREY FANTAIL Solomons, S New Guinea, New Zealand and much of Australia and New Caledonia / forest, woodland, mangrove and cultivation / insects / n tree or bush / e 2–3

Rhipidura personata *Ramsay* KANDAVU

FANTAIL Kandavu (Fiji Is)

Rhipidura perlata *Müller* PERLATED FANTAIL Malaysia/lowland forest/n tree

Rhipidura euryura *Müller* WHITE-BELLIED FANTAIL Java

Rhipidura phoenicura *Müller* RED-TAILED FANTAIL Mts of Java

Rhipidura spilodera *Gray* SPOTTED FANTAIL New Caledonia, New Hebrides, Fiji (not Kandavu) and Banks group/forest and garden

Rhipidura atra *Salvadori* BLACK FANTAIL NW New Guinea and Waigeu/mountain forest

Rhipidura hyperythra *Gray* CHESTNUT-BELLIED FANTAIL New Guinea, Aru Is and Japen/forest

Rhipidura cockerelli *(Ramsay)* COCKERELL'S FANTAIL Solomon Is

Rhipidura albolimbata *Salvadori* FRIENDLY FANTAIL Mts of New Guinea/mountain forest/ n tree/e ? n/k

Rhipidura rufiventris *(Vieillot)* RED-VENTED FANTAIL Timor through Papuan area to Australia/forest and mangrove/n tree/e 2–3

Rhipidura leucophrys *(Latham)* WILLIE WAGTAIL or BLACK AND WHITE FANTAIL Australia, Papuan area and Solomons/forest to desert areas/n tree or bush/e 4

Seisura inquieta *(Latham)* RESTLESS FLYCATCHER Australia and S New Guinea/ vicinity of water/n tree/e 4

Chasiempis sandwicensis *(Gmelin)* ELEPAIO Hawaiian Is/forest and swamp/n tree/e 2–3/ I ♂♀ 18 (? 15–16)/F 16

Muscicapa hypoleuca *(Pallas)* WESTERN PIED FLYCATCHER Much of Europe, N Africa and W Asia w S to tropical Africa and SW Asia/ woodland and habitation / insects and berries/ n hole of tree, wall or building/e 4–10/I ♀ 12–13/ F 13–16

Muscicapa albicollis *Temminck* COLLARED FLYCATCHER E Europe to W Asia w S to tropical Africa/woodland and habitation/insects and berries/n hole in tree or wall/e 4–7/I ♀

Muscicapa strophiata *(Hodgson)* ORANGE-GORGETED FLYCATCHER Himalayas to S China and northern SE Asia./forest/n tree/e 3–4

Muscicapa henrici *(Hartert)* DAMAR FLYCATCHER Damar Is

Muscicapa parva *Bechstein* RED-BREASTED FLYCATCHER b from E Europe across C Asia to Sakhalin and Kamchatka w S Asia/forest and cultivation/n tree or hole/e 4–7/I ♀

Muscicapa subrufa *Hartert and Steinbacher* KASHMIR FLYCATCHER Kashmir to Ceylon/ forest/n hole/e 3–5 (often treated as a race of *M. parva*)

Muscicapa leucomelanura *(Hodgson)* (=*M. tricolor* (Hodgson) preoccupied by *M. tricolor* Hartlaub, and *M. tricolor* Vieillot) SLATY-BLUE FLYCATCHER Himalayas to SW Szechwan, SE Asia and Indonesia, moving S in winter/forest/ n hole or depression in bank/e 3–4

Muscicapa westermanni *(Sharpe)* LITTLE PIED FLYCATCHER Himalayas, through SE Asia to Indonesia and Philippines / forest and cultivation/n ground or under rock/e 3–4/I ♂♀

Muscicapa superciliaris *Jerdon* ULTAMARINE FLYCATCHER b Himalayas to SE Tibet and W China, moving S in winter/forest and cultivation/ n hole/e 3–5/I ♂♀

Muscicapa sapphira *(Blyth)* SAPPHIRE FLYCATCHER E Himalayas, mts of Burma, N Laos and Yunnan / forest / n hollow in tree-stump/e 4/I ♂♀

Muscicapa hyperythra *Blyth* DULL FLYCATCHER, SNOWY-BROWED FLYCATCHER or RUFOUS-BREASTED BLUE FLYCATCHER Indian region through SE Asia to Indonesia /forest/ n tree/e 4/I ♂♀

Muscicapa solitaria *(Müller)* SOLITARY or WHITE-THROATED FLYCATCHER Indo-China, Malaya and Sumatra

Muscicapa basilanica *(Hartert)* LITTLE SLATY FLYCATCHER Celebes to Philippines

Muscicapa rufigula *(Wallace)* CELEBES RED-THROATED FLYCATCHER Celebes

Muscicapa moniliger *(Hodgson)* GORGETTED FLYCATCHER Himalayas and mts of Burma and N Thailand/forest/n bank or bush/e 4

Muscicapa narcissina *(Temminck)* NARCISSUS FLYCATCHER E Asia and Japan, S to Philippines and northern Borneo in winter / forest / n tree/ e 5

Muscicapa zanthopygia *Hay* TRICOLOURED FLYCATCHER Korea/more usually treated as a race of *M. narcissina* [Called *M. xanthopygia* in *Cat Birds Brit Mus*]

Muscicapa platenae *(Blasius)* PALAWAN FLYCATCHER Palawan

Muscicapa buruensis *(Hartert)* BURU FLYCATCHER or MOLUCCAS SHRIKE-ROBIN Moluccas to Great Kei Is

Muscicapa dumetoria *Wallace* ORANGE-BREASTED FLYCATCHER Java, Lombok, Sum-

CLIMACTERIDAE:
Climacteris melanura,
Black-tailed Treecreeper

CERTHIIDAE:
Certhia familiaris,
Common Treecreeper

CLIMACTERIDAE:
Climacteris affinis,
White-browned Treecreeper

Plate 236

CLIMACTERIDAE:
Climacteris rufa,
Rufous Treecreeper

CLIMACTERIDAE:
Climacteris picumnus,
Brown Treecreeper

Plate 237

bawa, Sumatra, Borneo and Tenimber Is (apparently *not* in Bali)/forest

Muscicapa mugimaki *Temminck* MUGIMAKI FLYCATCHER b Siberia w Malay Peninsula, Celebes, Ternate and Moluccas

Muscicapa nigrorufa (*Jerdon*) BLACK-AND-ORANGE FLYCATCHER SW Ghats of India/forest and plantation/n bush/e 2

Muscicapa cyanomelana *Temminck* JAPANESE BLUE FLYCATCHER b Manchuria, N China and Japan w Malaysia/mountain forest/n rock crevice or tree-roots/e 4–5/I ♀

Muscicapa timorensis (*Hellmayr*) TIMOR BLUE FLYCATCHER Timor

Muscicapa harterti (*Siebers*) HARTERT'S FLYCATCHER Sumba

Muscicapa bonthaina (*Hartert*) CELEBES BLUE FLYCATCHER Celebes

Muscicapa herioti (*Ramsay*) BLUE-BREASTED FLYCATCHER Luzon (Philippines)

Muscicapa hodgsoni (*Moore*) (not *Muscicapa hodgsoni* (Verreaux) = *M. amabilis*) PYGMY BLUE FLYCATCHER E Himalayas through SE Asia to Sumatra and Borneo/forest/n among creepers (1 known)

Muscicapa hainana (*Ogilvie-Grant*) HAINAN BLUE FLYCATCHER Hainan and SE China

Muscicapa poliogenys (*Brooks*) BROOKS' FLYCATCHER E Himalayas from Nepal to mts of Burma; NE Ghats/forest/n hollow in bank/e 3–5/I ♂♀

Muscicapa turcosa *Brüggermann* MALAYSIAN BLUE FLYCATCHER Malaya, Sumatra and Borneo/lowland forest/n and e ? n/k

[Edwards lists *Muscicapa capensis* at this point. This name appears to refer to *Muscicapa capensis*, Linnaeus = *Batis capensis*]

Muscicapa crypta (*Vaurie*) VAURIE'S FLYCATCHER Luzon and Mindanao

Muscicapa sanfordi (*Stresemann*) SANFORD'S FLYCATCHER Celebes

Muscicapa caerulata (*Bonaparte*) LARGE-BILLED BLUE FLYCATCHER Sumatra and Borneo/lowland forest/n and e n/k

Muscicapa venusta *Deignan* BORNEAN BLUE FLYCATCHER Submontane forests of Borneo/no data

Muscicapa rufigastra (*Raffles*) MANGROVE BLUE FLYCATCHER and **Muscicapa tickelliae** (*Blyth*) TICKELL'S BLUE FLYCATCHER Indian sub-continent, SE Asia, Indonesia and Philippines/mangrove and dry forest/n hole in tree or

rock/e 3–5. These forms are variously treated as conspecific, or separated. I have not studied the problem. For a list of the races involved see Kuroda, *Birds of Java*.

Muscicapa concreta (*Müller*) WHITE-TAILED BLUE FLYCATCHER SE Asia, Sumatra and Borneo/forest/n rock-crevice/e 1 (1 nest known)

Muscicapa ruecki (*Oustalet*) RUECK'S BLUE FLYCATCHER Sumatra and (?) Malaya/no data

Muscicapa unicolor (*Blyth*) PALE BLUE FLYCATCHER Himalayas through SE Asia to Sumatra, Java and Borneo/forest/n crevice in boulder/e 4

Muscicapa pallipes *Jerdon* WHITE-BELLIED BLUE FLYCATCHER W Ghats of India/forest undergrowth and ravines/n rock ledge/e 4

Muscicapa banyumas (*Horsfield*) HILL BLUE FLYCATCHER SE Asia, Yunnan, Java, Borneo and Palawan/forest/n hollow in bank/e 4–5 (includes *M. lemprieri* (Sharpe))

Muscicapa rubeculoides (*Vigors*) BLUE-THROATED FLYCATCHER b Himalayas through northern SE Asia to Szechwan and Hupeh w S of range/forest and habitation/n hollow in bank/e 3–5/I ♂♀

Muscicapa hoevellii (*Meyer*) HOEVELL'S FLYCATCHER Central mts of Celebes

Muscicapa hyacinthina (*Temminck*) HYACINTHINE FLYCATCHER Timor and Wetar

Muscicapa vivida *Swinhoe* VIVID FLYCATCHER Szechwan through SE Asia to Sumatra, Assam and Taiwan/forest/n and e ? n/k

Muscicapa macgregoriae (*Burton*) SMALL NILTAVA Himalayas/bushes along streams/n rock-clefts by streams/e 3–5/I ♂♀ 12

Muscicapa sundara (*Hodgson*) BLUE-AND-ORANGE NILTAVA Himalayas to Yunnan, Burma and N Laos/forest/n hole in bank/e 4/I ♂♀ 12–13

Muscicapa davidi *La Touche* DAVID'S NILTAVA NW Fokien and Yunnan/no data

Muscicapa grandis (*Blyth*) GREAT NILTAVA Himalayas through SE Asia to Sumatra/forest, near streams/n among rocks beside streams/e 3–5

Muscicapa adusta (*Boie*) AFRICAN DUSKY FLYCATCHER Africa S of Sahara/forest and woodland/insects and berries/n tree, rock-ledge or building/e 2–3

Muscicapa aquatica *Heuglin* SWAMP FLYCATCHER Africa S of Sahara S to Zambia/swamps and grasslands/n old nest of weaver/e 2

Muscicapa sethsmithi (*van Someren*) YELLOW-FOOTED FLYCATCHER Fernando Po and Cameroon to Congo and Uganda / forest / n tree / e 2

Muscicapa cassini *Heine* CASSIN'S GREY FLYCATCHER Sierra Leone to Angola, Zambia and Uganda / forest / n tree / e 1–3

Muscicapa griseigularis (*Jackson*) GREY-THROATED FLYCATCHER Cameroon and Congo to Uganda / forest streams / n hole / e 2

Muscicapa caerulescens *Neave* (=**Muscicapa cinerea** (*Cassin*)) ASHY FLYCATCHER Africa S of Sahara / open woodland and thorn scrub / n tree / e 2–3

Muscicapa olivacens (*Cassin*) OLIVACEOUS FLYCATCHER Liberia and Gabon to Congo / forest / no other data

Muscicapa lendu (*Chapin*) CHAPIN'S FLYCATCHER NE Congo / unique

Muscicapa itombwensis (*Prigogine*) PRIGOGINE'S FLYCATCHER E Congo / mountain forest / no other data

Muscicapa epulata (*Cassin*) LITTLE GREY FLYCATCHER Liberia to Gabon and E Congo / forest / n tree / e n/k

Muscicapa tessmanni *Reichenow* TESSMAN'S FLYCATCHER Forests of W Africa from Ivory Coast to Muni and N Congo / n and e n/k [NB: originally described as a race of *Bradornis pallidus*, and treated as synonymous with *B. p. modestus* in some works]

Muscicapa comitata (*Cassin*) DUSKY BLUE FLYCATCHER Cameroon and Gabon to Angola / forest / n in old weaver nest / e 2–4

Muscicapa gambagae (*Alexander*) GAMBAGE DUSKY FLYCATCHER Ghana to Somalia and Arabia / light woodland and cultivation / n stump / e 2

Muscicapa sibirica *Gmelin* SIBERIAN SOOTY FLYCATCHER b Himalayas and W China: E Siberia from Lake Baikal to Japan, Kuriles and Kamchatka w SE Asia and W Indonesia / open forest / insects / n tree / e 3–4 / I ♀ (?♂)

Muscicapa griseisticta (*Swinhoe*) GREY-SPOTTED FLYCATCHER China to New Guinea through Philippines and Celebes / forest

Muscicapa ferruginea (*Hodgson*)) (=**M. cinereiceps** (*Sharpe*) FERRUGINOUS FLYCATCHER b mts from Himalayas to W China w SE Asia and Indonesia / forest / n tree / e 2–3 / I ♂♀

Muscicapa muttui (*Layard*) BROWN-BREASTED FLYCATCHER b mts of northern SE Asia and W China w S India and Ceylon / forest / n tree / e 4–5 / I ♂♀

Muscicapa latirostris *Raffles* BROWN FLYCATCHER or GREY-BREASTED FLYCATCHER b E Siberia and Japan: Himalayas: W Ghats w SE Asia, Indonesia and Moluccas / forest and cultivation / n tree / e 4 / I ♀

[**Muscicapa williamsoni** *Deignan* WILLIAMSON'S FLYCATCHER Thailand / status uncertain, but believed by Wells to be a race of *M. latirostris* (Wells, *Bull Brit Orn Cl*, 97 (1977), 83–7)]

Muscicapa ruficauda *Swainson* RUFOUS-TAILED FLYCATCHER b Russian Turkestan to Himalayas w SW India / forest / n tree or ground / e 3–4

Muscicapa striata (*Pallas*) SPOTTED FLYCATCHER b much of Europe and W Asia E to Baluchistan and Semipalatinsk w Africa and SW Asia / open woodland and scrub / insects and berries / n tree, beam or against wall / e 4–6 / I ♂♀ 12–14 / F 11–15

Muscicapa amabilis *Deignan* (=**M. hodgsoni** (*Verreaux*)) RUSTY-BREASTED BLUE FLYCATCHER E Himalayas to SW China and Thailand / forest and scrub / n bank among stones / e 4–5 / I ♂♀

Muscicapa thalassina *Swainson* VERDITER FLYCATCHER India to W China and Vietnam: Sumatra and Borneo / forest / n hole in wall, bank or rafter / e 3–5 / I ♂♀

Muscicapa albicaudata *Jerdon* NILGIRI FLYCATCHER SW Ghats and Nilgiri Hills of India / streams, plantations and habitation / n hole or eaves of building / e 2–3

Muscicapa sordida (*Walden*) SORDID FLYCATCHER Mountain forests of Ceylon / n rock-ledge / e 2–3

Muscicapa indigo (*Horsfield*) INDIGO FLYCATCHER Java, Sumatra and Borneo / mountain forest / n and e n/k

Muscicapa panayensis *Sharpe* PANAY FLYCATCHER Philippines, Celebes, Obi and Ceram

Artomyias fuliginosa *Verreaux* AFRICAN SOOTY FLYCATCHER S Nigeria to S Sudan, Uganda and Angola / forest clearings / n tree / e 2 (1 nest known)

Artomyias ussheri *Sharpe* USSHER'S FLYCATCHER Sierra Leone to Ghana / forest clearings / n and e n/k

DICAEIDAE:
Pardalotus striatus,
Yellow-tipped Diamondbird,
Yellow-tipped Pardalote

DICAEIDAE:
Pardalotus substriatus,
Striated Diamondbird,
Striated Pardalote

Plate 238

DICAEIDAE:
Pardalotus xanthopygus,
Yellow-tailed Diamondbird,
Yellow-tailed Pardalote

DICAEIDAE:
Dicaeum hirundinaceum,
Mistletoe Flowerpecker

Plate 239

Myioparus plumbeus (*Hartlaub*) GREY TIT-FLYCATCHER Africa S of Sahara / open bush and light woodland / n hole / e 2–3

Fraseria cinerascens *Hartlaub* WHITE-BROWED FOREST FLYCATCHER Guinea to N Congo / forest streams / n hole / e 2 (1 nest known)

Fraseria ocreata (*Strickland*) COMMON FOREST FLYCATCHER Fernando Po and Nigeria to Congo and Uganda / open woodland and cultivation / n hole / e 2–3

Melaenornis silens (*Shaw*) FISCAL FLYCATCHER S Africa N to Transvaal / scrub and habitation / n tree or bush / e 3

Melaenornis ardesiaca *Berlioz* YELLOW-EYED BLACK FLYCATCHER E Congo / forest / n tree / e 2

Melaenornis pammelaina (*Stanley*) SOUTHERN BLACK FLYCATCHER Congo and Zambia S to Natal and SW Africa / woodland and cultivation / n old nest of other species or in hole / e 2–3

Melaenornis edoloides (*Swainson*) NORTHERN BLACK (or EIDOLON) FLYCATCHER Senegal to Ethiopia and S to Tanganyika and Congo / woodland and cultivation / n tree / e 2–3

Melaenornis chocolatina (*Rüppell*) CHOCOLATE FLYCATCHER Mts of Angola and E Africa (discontinuous) / forest / n tree / e 2–3 [*M. fischeri* (Reichenow) and *M. brunneus* Cabanis, are now included]

Melaenornis annamarulae *Forbes-Watson* MRS FORBES-WATSON'S BLACK FLYCATCHER Mt Nimba, Liberia / forest / no other data [See Forbes-Watson, *Bull Brit Orn Cl*, 90 (1970), p 145]

Empidornis semipartitus (*Rüppell*) SILVERBIRD E Africa from Ethiopia to Tanganyika / open country / n bush / e 2

Bradornis mariquensis *Smith* MARIQUA FLYCATCHER SW Africa / open thornbush / insects / n tree or bush / e 2–4

Bradornis microrhynchus *Reichenow* LARGE FLYCATCHER E Africa from Ethiopia to Tanganyika (including *pumilus*) / woodland, scrub and cultivation / n tree / e 2

Bradornis pallidus (*Müller*) PALE FLYCATCHER Africa S of Sahara / woodland, thorn scrub and habitation / n tree / e 2–3

Bradornis infuscatus (*Smith*) CHAT FLYCATCHER Dry scrub areas on the western side of S Africa N to Benguella / n bush / e 2–3

Rhinomyias brunneata (*Slater*) CHINESE WHITE-GORGETED FLYCATCHER S China in summer, winter quarters unknown / wooded areas and bamboo thickets / n and e n/k

Rhinomyias olivacea (*Hume*) OLIVE-BACKED JUNGLE FLYCATCHER Malay Peninsula, Sumatra, Java, Bali and Borneo / n tree / e n/s

Rhinomyias umbratilis (*Strickland*) WHITE-THROATED JUNGLE FLYCATCHER Sumatra and Borneo / forest / n tree / e n/s

Rhinomyias ruficauda (*Sharpe*) RUFOUS-TAILED JUNGLE FLYCATCHER Philippines and Borneo / forest

Rhinomyias gularis *Sharpe* KINABALU JUNGLE FLYCATCHER Philippines and Borneo / forest / n tree / e n/s

Rhinomyias goodfellowi *Ogilvie-Grant* GOODFELLOW'S JUNGLE FLYCATCHER Mindanao

Rhinomyias insignis *Ogilvie-Grant* INSIGNIA JUNGLE FLYCATCHER N Luzon

Rhinomyias addita (*Hartert*) BURU JUNGLE FLYCATCHER Buru

Rhinomyias oscillans (*Hartert*) ACTIVE FLYCATCHER Flores

Rhinomyias colonus *Hartert* CELEBES JUNGLE FLYCATCHER Celebes and Sula islands

Humblotia flavirostris *Milne-Edwards and Oustalet* HUMBLOT'S FLYCATCHER Grand Comoro Is / known only from few specimens

Newtonia amphichroa *Reichenow* DARK NEWTONIA Madagascar / forests of the humid east

Newtonia brunneicauda (*Newton*) COMMON NEWTONIA Madagascar / forest, woodland and brush / insects / n and e ? n/k

Newtonia archboldi *Delacour and Berlioz* ARCHBOLD'S NEWTONIA Madagascar / brush and low forest of the sub-desert

Newtonia fanovanae *Gyldenstolpe* FANOVANA NEWTONIA Madagascar / unique / ? forests of humid east

Microeca leucophaea (*Latham*) JACKY WINTER, WHITE-TAILED MICROECA or BROWN FLYCATCHER Australia and Tasmania and parts of SE New Guinea / open woodland and cultivation / insects / n tree / e 2 [Rand and Gilliard credit this name to Vieillot, but according to Mathews, *Syst Av Aust*, pt II, p 547, *Sylvia leucophaea* Vieillot=*Lalage sueurii* (Campephagidae)]

Microeca flavovirescens *Gray* OLIVE MICROECA New Guinea, Aru Is, Misol, Batanta, Waigeu and Japen / forest / n tree / e 2

Microeca papuana *Meyer* PAPUAN MICROECA

New Guinea/mountain forest

Microeca flavigaster *Gould* LEMON-BREASTED MICROECA Australia and New Guinea/mangrove and woodland/n tree/e 1

Microeca griseoceps *De Vis* YELLOW MICROECA Tip of Cape York Peninsula and New Guinea/forest/no other data

[**Microeca brunneicauda** *Campbell* BROWN-TAILED MICROECA NW Australia and N Territory. This name is a synonym of *Pachycephala simplex*. See Parker, *Emu* 73, p 23, for a summary of all that is known about it.]

Microeca hemixantha *Sclater* TANIMBER MICROECA Tenimber Is

Culicicapa ceylonensis (*Swainson*) GREY-HEADED FLYCATCHER Indian sub-continent, SE Asia, Java, Borneo and Flores/forest/n rock or tree trunk/e 3–4

Culicicapa helianthea (*Wallace*) SUNFLOWER or CANARY FLYCATCHER Celebes, Banggai, Saleyer and Philippines

Monachella muelleriana (*Schlegel*) RIVER FLYCATCHER New Guinea/rivers/n tree/e ? n/k

Petroica australis (*Sparrman*) NEW ZEALAND ROBIN New Zealand/forest/insects and spiders/n tree/e 2–4/I ♀ 14–16/F 19

Petroica traversi (*Buller*) BLACK ROBIN Chatham Islands, but now very rare and confined to Little Mangere Islet/scrub/e 4

Petroica bivittata *De Vis* FOREST ROBIN High mts of New Guinea/mountain forest

Petroica vittata (*Quoy and Gaimard*) DUSKY ROBIN Tasmania, King Is and Barren Is

Petroica archboldi *Rand* ROCK ROBIN Mt Wilhelmina, New Guinea/rock above timber-line

Petroica macrocephala (*Gmelin*) TOMTIT New Zealand and adjacent islands/forest and scrub/n tree/e 3–4/I ♀ 17/F 17–18

Petroica cucullata (*Latham*) HOODED ROBIN Australia/open forest to arid tree savannah/n tree or bush/e 3

Petroica rhodinogaster (*Drapiez*) PINK ROBIN Tasmania and Victoria/forest/n low vegetation/e 3–4

Petroica phoenicea *Gould* FLAME ROBIN SE Australia and Tasmania/dry forest and woodland/insects/n tree/e 3

Petroica rosea *Gould* ROSE ROBIN E Australia/forest/insects/n tree/e 2–3

Petroica goodenovii (*Vigors and Horsfield*)

RED-CAPPED ROBIN Australia/open forest to semi-desert/n tree/e 2–3

Petroica multicolor (*Gmelin*) SCARLET ROBIN Australia and islands from Norfolk Is to Solomon Is, New Hebrides, Fiji and Samoa/dry forest and cultivation/n tree/e 3/I ♂♀

Tregellasia capito *Gould* PALE YELLOW ROBIN New Guinea and E Australia/rain forest/n tree/e 2

Tregellasia leucops (*Salvadori*) WHITE-FACED YELLOW ROBIN New Guinea and Cape York Peninsula/rain forest/n tree/e 2

Eopsaltria autralis (*White*) EASTERN YELLOW ROBIN E Australia/dry forest, woodland and cultivation/n tree/e 2–3

Eopsaltria griseogularis *Gould* WESTERN YELLOW ROBIN SW Australia/dry forest and cultivation/n tree/e 2

Eopsaltria georgiana (*Quoy and Gaimard*) WHITE-BREASTED YELLOW ROBIN Coast of SW Australia/dense coastal scrub/n bush or herbage/e 2

[**Eopsaltria sudestensis** *De Vis*, Sudest Is =*Pachycephala griseiceps sudestensis*]

Eopsaltria flaviventris *Sharpe* YELLOW-BELLIED ROBIN New Caledonia

Peneoenanthe pulverulenta (*Bonaparte*) MANGROVE ROBIN New Guinea, Aru Is and N coast of Australia from Exmouth Gulf to Rockingham Bay/mangrove/n tree/e 2

Poecilodryas placens (*Ramsay*) OLIVE-YELLOW ROBIN SE New Guinea/forest/n tree or sapling

Poecilodryas modesta (*De Vis*) BUFF-BREASTED ROBIN SE New Guinea

Poecilodryas superciliosa (*Gould*) WHITE-BROWED ROBIN N Australia and New Guinea/forest/n tree/e 2 (some authorities separate *P. cerviniventris*)

Poecilodryas hypoleuca (*Gray*) BLACK AND WHITE ROBIN New Guinea and W Papuan islands/forest

Poecilodryas albonotata (*Salvadori*) BLACK-THROATED ROBIN SW New Guinea/forest

Poecilodryas brachyura (*Sclater*) WHITE-BREASTED ROBIN New Guinea and Japen/forest

Peneothello sigillatus (*De Vis*) WHITE-WINGED ROBIN New Guinea/high mountain forest/n tree/e ?2 (1 nest with 2 young known)

Peneothello cryptoleucus *Hartert* GREY THICKET FLYCATCHER Arfak and Weyland Mts, New Guinea/forest undergrowth

ZOSTEROPIDAE: *Zosterops palpebrosa*, Oriental White-eye

Plate 240

ZOSTEROPIDAE:
Zosterops chloris,
Moluccan White-eye,
Mangrove White-eye

NECTARINIIDAE:
Nectarinia violacea,
Orange-breasted Sunbird

NECTARINIIDAE:
Nectarinia jugularis,
Olive-backed Sunbird,
Yellowbreasted Sunbird

Plate 241

Peneothello cyanus (*Salvadori*) SLATY or SALVADORI'S BLUE ROBIN Mts of New Guinea/forest undergrowth/n tree/e 1

Peneothello bimaculatus (*Salvadori*) WHITE-RUMPED THICKET FLYCATCHER New Guinea/mountain forest

Heteromyias albispecularis (*Salvadori*) GROUND THICKET FLYCATCHER Mts of New Guinea / forest undergrowth / n tree / e 1? (1 nest with 1 young)

Heteromyias cinereifrons (*Ramsay*) GREY-HEADED ROBIN N Queensland, forests of the Atherton tableland / rain forest / n bush or herbage / e 1 (closely resembles *albispecularis* with which it may be conspecific)

Pachycephalopsis hattamensis *Meyer* GREEN THICKET FLYCATCHER (or GREEN ROBIN?) Mts of W New Guinea/forest undergrowth

Pachycephalopsis poliosoma *Sharpe* WHITE-THROATED THICKET FLYCATCHER Mts of New Guinea/forest

Megabyas flammulatus *Verreaux* SHRIKE FLYCATCHER Fernando Po and Sierra Leone to Angola, Sudan and Uganda/forest/n and e n/k

Bias musicus (*Vieillot*) BLACK AND WHITE FLYCATCHER Sierra Leone to Congo and Uganda/forests and forest streams/n tree/e 2–3

Batis molitor (*Hahn and Küster*) WHITE-FLANKED PUFFBACK Much of E and S Africa except the eastern coast and the dry south-west/open woodland and forest edge/n tree/e 2

Batis minor *Erlanger* BLACK-HEADED PUFFBACK Cameroon and N Angola to Eritrea and N Somalia/bush and open woodland/n tree/e 2–3

Batis orientalis (*Heuglin*) SAVANNAH PUFF-BACK Nigeria and Lake Chad, Sudan and Eritrea/thorn scrub and open woodland/n tree/e 2

Batis pririt (*Vieillot*) PRIRIT PUFFBACK S Angola to Transvaal and N Cape Province/forest and tall bush/n tree/e 2

Batis capensis (*L*) CAPE PUFFBACK E and S Africa / forest, woodland and garden / n tree/e 2–3

Batis minulla (*Bocage*) ANGOLA PUFFBACK Cameroon to Angola and W Congo /n tree (1 known)/e n/k

Batis margaretae *Boulton* BOULTON'S PUFFBACK S Angola and NW Zambia /forest/n and e n/k

Batis soror *Reichenow* CHINSPOT PUFFBACK Coasts of E Africa from Kenya to Mozambique/

open woodland and savannah/n tree/e 2

Batis minima (*Verreaux*) VERREAUX'S PUFFBACK Gabon /♂ only known /no data

Batis poensis *Alexander* FERNANDO PO PUFFBACK Fernando Po and Cameroon to Liberia/forest/n and e n/k

Batis mixta (*Shelley*) EAST AFRICAN PUFFBACK E Africa/mountain forest/n tree/e 2–3

Batis diops *Jackson* RUWENZORI PUFFBACK Ruwenzori Mts/forest/no other data

Batis perkeo *Neumann* PYGMY PUFFBACK S Ethiopia to Kenya / thorn scrub and acacia/ n and e n/k

Batis senegalensis (*L*) SENEGAL PUFFBACK Senegal to Nigeria / semi-arid bush-country/ n tree/e 2

Batis fratrum (*Shelley*) ZULULAND PUFFBACK SE Africa from Rhodesia to Zululand/bush and coastal scrub/n tree or bush/e 2

Pseudobias wardi *Sharpe* WARD'S FLYCATCHER Madagascar / forests of the humid east /insects/ n and e n/k

Platysteira albifrons *Sharpe* WHITE-FRONTED WATTLE-EYE SW Congo and N Angola /no data

Platysteira cyanea (*Müller*) COMMON WATTLE-EYE W, C, and NE Africa /secondary forest and cultivation

Platysteira peltata *Sundevall* BLACK-THROATED WATTLE-EYE Coast of E Africa from Kenya to Natal / forest edge, gallery forest and riverine scrub, always near water/n tree/e 2

Platysteira castanea *Fraser* CHESTNUT WATTLE-EYE Fernando Po and S Nigeria to Angola and Kenya/forest/n scrub/e 2

Platysteira blissetti (*Reichenow*) BLISSETT'S WATTLE-EYE Fernando Po and Cameroon to Angola / dense scrub and secondary forest / n tree/e 2

Platysteira concreta *Hartlaub* YELLOW-BELLIED WATTLE-EYE Sierra Leone to Congo and Angola (discontinuous)/forest/n and e n/k

Platysteira tonsa *Bates* WHITE-SPOTTED WATTLE-EYE Fernando Po and S Nigeria to Congo /forest /n and e n/k

Erythrocercus livingstonei *Gray* LIVINGSTONE'S FLYCATCHER E Africa from Tanganyika to Mozambique / woodland and scrub /n bush /e 2

Erythrocercus mccalli (*Cassin*) CHESTNUT-CAPPED FLYCATCHER Guinea to Uganda and Cameroon /forest /n tree /e n/k

Erythrocercus holochlorus *Erlanger* LITTLE

YELLOW FLYCATCHER Kenya, Tanganyika and S Somaliland / forest / n and e n/k

Elminia longicauda (*Swainson*) BLUE ELMINIA Sierra Leone to S Sudan, Congo and N Angola / forest clearings and woodland / n tree / e 2

Elminia albicauda *Bocage* WHITE-TAILED ELMINIA Angola to Tanganyika, Congo and Zambia / forest clearings and woodland / n tree / e 2

Trochocercus cyanomelas (*Vieillot*) CRESTED FLYCATCHER E Africa from Somalia to Natal / forest and woodland / n tree or bush / e 2

Trochocercus nitens *Cassin* BLUE-HEADED CRESTED-FLYCATCHER S Nigeria to Angola and S Uganda / forest and bush / n tree / e 2

Trochocercus albonotatus *Sharpe* WHITE-TAILED CRESTED-FLYCATCHER Uganda, W Kenya, W Tanganyika, Zambia, Malawi and Rhodesia / highland forest / n tree or shrub / e 2

Trochocercus albiventris *Sjöstedt* WHITE-BELLIED CRESTED-FLYCATCHER Fernando Po and Cameroon to Uganda / forest / n tree / e 2

Trochocercus nigromitratus (*Reichenow*) DUSKY CRESTED or BLACK MITRED FLYCATCHER Liberia to Uganda / forest / n tree / e 2 (for comments on the identification of *albiventris* and *nigromitratus* see Mackworth Praed and Grant, Series 3, fol 2, p 147 footnote)

[NB: The genus *Terpsiphone* is complicated, some authorities recognising many more species than are here listed. See Hall and Moreau, *Atlas of African Passerine Birds*, pp 230–1 for distribution maps of this genus and discussion of hybrids among the African forms]

Terpsiphone cyanescens (*Sharpe*) BLUE PARADISE FLYCATCHER Calamines and Palawan

Terpsiphone talautensis (*Meyer and Wigglesworth*) TALAUT PARADISE FLYCATCHER Talaut Is

Terpsiphone atrocaudata (*Eyton*) BLACK PARADISE FLYCATCHER Japan south through China, Hainan and Taiwan to the Philippines / forested lowlands / n tree / e 3–5 / I ♂♀ 12–14

Terpsiphone paradisi (*L*) COMMON PARADISE FLYCATCHER Turkestan to Manchuria, SE Asia and Indonesia / open forest and cultivation / n tree / e 3–4 / I ♀ 15–16

Terpsiphone atrochalybea (*Thomson*) SÃO THOMÉ PARADISE FLYCATCHER São Thomé / forest and cultivation / n tree / e 2 [NB: The type

of this species was supposedly collected on Fernando Po, but this is now believed to be an error]

Terpsiphone mutata (*L*) MADAGASCAR PARADISE FLYCATCHER Madagascar / forest and brush / n tree / e 3

Terpsiphone rufocinerea (*Cabanis*) RUFOUS-VENTED PARADISE FLYCATCHER (*T. melampyra* (*Verreaux*), now regarded as unidentifiable, was formerly used for this species) Cameroon to Congo and Angola / forest, woodland and garden / n tree / e 2–3

Terpsiphone viridis (*Müller*) AFRICAN PARADISE FLYCATCHER Africa S of Sahara / forest, woodland and garden / n tree / e 2–3

Terpsiphone rufiventer (*Swainson*) RED-BELLIED or BLACK-HEADED PARADISE FLYCATCHER W Africa / forest / n tree / e 2

Terpsiphone corvina (*Newton*) SEYCHELLES PARADISE FLYCATCHER Seychelles, believed to survive only on La Digue / endangered / woodland / n tree / e 1–2 / I ♂♀

Terpsiphone bourbonensis (*Müller*) (=**T. desolata**, *Salomonsen*) MASCARENE PARADISE FLYCATCHER Mauritius and Réunion

Terpsiphone cinnamomea (*Sharpe*) (=**T. rufa** *Gray*) RUFOUS PARADISE FLYCATCHER Philippines

Philentoma pyrrhopterum (*Temminck*) CHESTNUT-WINGED MONARCH S Indo-China, Malaya, Sumatra and Borneo / lowland forest / n and e ? n/k

Philentoma velata (*Temminck*) MAROON-BREASTED MONARCH Malay Peninsula from Tenasserim S, Sumatra, Java and Borneo / forest / n tree

Hypothymis azurea (*Boddaert*) BLACK-NAPED BLUE MONARCH India, SE Asia to Lesser Sunda Is and Philippines / forest and cultivation / n tree / e 3 / I ♂♀ 12

Hypothymis puella (*Wallace*) SMALL BLUE MONARCH Celebes, Sula Is, Peling and Banggai

Hypothymis helenae (*Steere*) SHORT-CRESTED BLUE MONARCH Philippines

Hypothymis coelestis *Tweeddale* CELESTIAL MONARCH Philippines

Monarcha axillaris *Salvadori* BLACK MONARCH New Guinea Mts and Goodenough Is / forest

Monarcha rubiensis (*Meyer*) RUFOUS MONARCH N New Guinea / forest

Monarcha manadensis (*Quoy and Gaimard*)

MELIPHAGIDAE:
Manorina melanophrys,
Bell Miner

MELIPHAGIDAE:
Ramsayornis modestus,
Modest Honeyeater, Brown-
backed Honeyeater

Plate 242

MELIPHAGIDAE:
Anthochaera rufogularis,
Spiny-cheeked Wattlebird

MELIPHAGIDAE:
Anthochaera carunculata,
Red Wattlebird

MELIPHAGIDAE:
Myzomela sanguinolenta,
Scarlet Myzomela, Scarlet
Honeyeater

Plate 243

BLACK AND WHITE MONARCH New Guinea/ forest/n tree/e 2

Monarcha melanopsis (*Vieillot*) GREY-WINGED MONARCH S New Guinea and E Australia/forest and woodland/n tree/e 2

Monarcha leucotis *Gould* WHITE-EARED MONARCH Moluccas: coast of Queensland/wet forest and mangrove/n tree or bush/e 2

[**Monarcha divaga** *De Vis* = *Chaetorhynchus papuensis* (Dicruridae)]

[**Monarcha hebetior** *Hartert* HARTERT'S MONARCH St Mathias and New Hanover]

Monarcha frater *Sclater* BLACK-WINGED MONARCH New Guinea and Cape York Peninsula/forest and woodland

Monarcha cinerascens *Temminck* ASHY or ISLET MONARCH Timor, Moluccas and New Guinea to Solomons (chiefly confined to small islands)

Monarcha chrysomela (*Lesson and Garnot*) BLACK AND YELLOW MONARCH New Guinea, Aru Is, the Bismarck Archipelago, Biak etc/forest

Monarcha trivirgatus (*Temminck*) SPECTACLED MONARCH Flores, Timor, Moluccas, New Guinea, Louisiade Archipelago and NE Australia/wet forest and mangrove/n tree or bush/e 2

Monarcha sacerdotum *Mees* (*Zool Meded Leiden*, vol 46 (1973), no 12, p 179) PRIESTLY MONARCH Flores

Monarcha julianae *Ripley* KOFIAU MONARCH Kofiau Is/unique

Monarcha brehmii *Schlegel* BIAK MONARCH Biak Is/no data

Monarcha godeffroyi *Hartlaub* YAP MONARCH Yap Is/no data

Monarcha takatsukasae (*Yahmasina*) TINIAN MONARCH Tinian Is (Marianas)/n tree/e 2

Monarcha barbata *Ramsay* PIED MONARCH Soloman Is/mid-mountain forest/some of the forms in this group are sometimes regarded as species:

  Monarcha b. barbata Bougainville, Choiseul, Ysabel, Florida and Guadalcanal
  Monarcha malaitae *Mayr* Malaita
  Monarcha browni *Ramsay* Kulambangra, New Georgia, Vanguna and Gatukai
  Monarcha meeki *Rothschild and Hartert* Rendova and Tetipari
  Monarcha gangonae *Mayr* Ganonga
  Monarcha nigrotecta *Hartert* Vella Lavella and Bagga

Monarcha vidua (*Tristram*) San Cristobal
Monarcha squamulata (*Tristram*) Ugi
Monarcha alecto (*Temminck and Laugier*) SHINING MONARCH Moluccas, New Guinea and N coast of Australia/mangroves/n bush/e 2/the position of this species is uncertain, and it has been referred to various genera

Monarcha castaneiventris *Verreaux* CHESTNUT-BELLIED MONARCH Solomon Is/lowland and mountain forest/some of the following forms have been considered species:

  Monarcha c. castaneiventris Choiseul, Ysabel, Florida, Guadalcanal and Malaita
  Monarcha obscurior *Mayr* Russell Is
  Monarcha megarhyncha *Rothschild and Hartert* San Cristobal
  Monarcha ugiensis (*Ramsay*) Ugi
  Monarcha erythrosticta (*Sharpe*) Bougainville and Shortland Is
  Monarcha richardsii (*Ramsay*) central Solomon Is

Monarcha everetti *Hartert* EVERETT'S MONARCH Djampea Is

Monarcha loricatus *Wallace* BURU MONARCH Buru

Monarcha verticalis *Sclater* DUKE OF YORK MONARCH Duke of York Is (? rest of Bismarck Archipelago)

Monarcha castus *Sclater* LOETOE MONARCH Tenimber Is (probably a race of *M. pileatus*)

Monarcha mundus *Sclater* MUNDANE MONARCH Tenimber Is

Monarcha guttula *Garnot* SPOT-WINGED MONARCH N Guinea, W Papuan islands, Aru Is, Meos Num, Japen, D'Entrecasteaux and Louisiade Archipelago/forest/n tree/e 2

Monarcha leucurus *Gray* WHITE-TAILED MONARCH Kei Is

Monarcha menckei *Heinroth* MENCKE'S MONARCH St Mathias Is (Bismarck Archipelago)

Monarcha ateralba *Salomonsen* DYAUL MONARCH Dyaul Is, near New Ireland

Monarcha pileatus (*Salvadori*) PILEATED MONARCH Halmahera and Buru

Monarcha infelix *Sclater* UNHAPPY MONARCH Admiralty Is

[**Monarcha sericeus** (*Ramsay*) is a synonym of Neolalage]

Metabolus rugensis (*Hombron and Jacquinot*) TRUK MONARCH Truk (Caroline Is)/n tree/e 1

Arses kaupi *Gould* AUSTRALIAN PIED FLYCATCHER NE Queensland / rain forest and open forest / n tree or bush / e 2

Arses telescopthalmus *Garnot* FRILLED FLYCATCHER New Guinea, W Papuan islands, Aru Is, islands in Geelvink Bay lowland forest n tree / e 2

Arses lorealis *De Vis* FRILL-NECKED FLYCATCHER Cape York Peninsula / rain forest / n tree / e 2

Mayrornis lessoni (*Hombron and Jacquinot*) FIJI SLATY FLYCATCHER Fiji Is / forest

Mayrornis versicolor *Mayr* FIJI VERSI-COLOURED FLYCATCHER Ongea Levu (Fiji)

Mayrornis schistaceus *Mayr* VANIKORO FLYCATCHER Vanikoro (Santa Cruz Is)

Neolalage banksiana *Gray* SILKY, BUFF-BELLIED or BANKSIAN FLYCATCHER New Hebrides / plantations and habitation

Clytorhynchus vitiensis (*Hartlaub*) UNIFORM SHRIKEBILL Fiji, Tonga, Samoa and Fortuna Is

Clytorhynchus nigrogularis (*Layard*) BLACK-FACED SHRIKEBILL Fiji Is

Clytorhynchus pachycephaloides *Elliot* SOUTHERN SHRIKEBILL New Caledonia and New Hebrides

Clytorhynchus hamlini (*Mayr*) RENNELL SHRIKEBILL Rennell Is / no data

Myiagra caledonica *Bonaparte* MELANESIAN MYIAGRA New Caledonia, New Hebrides, Loyalty Is and Rennell Is

Myiagra vanikorensis (*Quoy and Gaimard*) VANIKORO MYIAGRA Samoa, Fiji and Santa Cruz Is

Myiagra albiventris (*Peale*) SAMOAN MYIAGRA Samoa

Myiagra cyanoleuca (*Vieillot*) SATIN MYIAGRA E Australia, Tasmania, New Britain, New Ireland, Louisiade Archipelago / mountain forest / n tree / e 3

Myiagra rubecula (*Latham*) LEADEN MYIAGRA E and N Australia, New Guinea and E Papuan islands / forest, savannah and man-grove / n tree / e 3

Myiagra ferrocyanea *Ramsay* STEEL-BLUE MYIAGRA Solomon Is

Myiagra oceanica *Pucheran* MICRONESIAN MYIAGRA Ruk Is, Ponapé, Palau Is and Marianas (including *P. erythrops*, *P. freycineti* and *P. pluto*) / n stump / e 1

Myiagra cervinicauda *Tristram* RED-TAILED MYIAGRA Solomon Is

Myiagra azureocapilla *Layard* BLUE-CROWNED MYIAGRA Fiji Is

Myiagra ruficollis (*Vieillot*) BROAD-BILLED MYIAGRA N Australia, New Guinea, Timor, Djampea, Kalao and Tenimber Is / mangrove / n tree / e 2

Myiagra atra *Meyer* BLACK MYIAGRA Numfor and Biak / open forest

Machaerirhynchus flaviventris *Gould* BOAT-BILLED FLYCATCHER or YELLOW-BREASTED FLATBILL NE Queensland and New Guinea, Aru and W Papuan Is / rain forest / n tree / e 2

Machaerirhynchus nigripectus *Schlegel* BLACK-BREASTED FLATBILL Mts of New Guinea / forest / n tree / e ?1 (1 nest with 1 young known)

Eutrichomyias rowleyi (*Meyer*) ROWLEY'S FLYCATCHER Great Sangai, Peling and Bonggai Is (see Meise, *Ornithologische Monatsberichte*, (1939), 134–6 for comments on this bird)

The following genus is sometimes placed in the Sylvidae.

Hyliota violacea *Verreaux* VIOLET-BACKED FLYCATCHER Liberia to S Cameroon and E Congo / no data

Hyliota flavigaster *Swainson* YELLOW-BELLIED FLYCATCHER Africa S of Sahara S to Angola and Mozambique / forest / n tree / e 2

Hyliota australis *Shelley* SOUTHERN YELLOW-BELLIED FLYCATCHER E Congo to Uganda, Angola and Mozambique / forest / n tree / e 2–3

[PACHYCEPHALINAE Whistlers or Thick-heads (This group is invariably treated as a sub-family of the Muscicapidae, and is separated here purely for convenience)]

Stocky-bodied flycatchers with large rounded heads, inhabiting scrub and forest undergrowth and feeding on insects. Nest large and sub-stantial in tree or shrub. Eggs 2–3. The group has been insufficiently studied and little information is available on individual species.

Eulacestoma nigropectus *De Vis* WATTLED SHRIKETIT Mts of New Guinea / forest

Falcunculus frontatus (*Latham*) AUSTRALIAN SHRIKETIT Australia (discontinuous) / dry forest and woodland / n tree / e 2–3 / some authorities divide this into 3 species

Oreoica gutturalis (*Vigors and Horsfield*) CRESTED BELLBIRD Interior of Australia / dry woodland and arid scrub / n bush / e 2–4

Pachycare flavogrisea (*Meyer*) GOLDEN-FACED PACHYCARE Mts of New Guinea / forest

MELIPHAGIDAE: *Meliphaga cassidix*, Helmeted Honeyeater

Plate 244

MELIPHAGIDAE:
Melithreptus validirostris,
Strong-billed Honeyeater

MELIPHAGIDAE:
Certhionyx variegatus,
Pied Honeyeater

Plate 245

Rhagologus leucostigma (*Salvadori*) MOTTLED WHISTLER Mts of New Guinea / forest / fruit

Hylocitrea bonensis (*Meyer and Wiglesworth*) HYLOCITREA Mts of Celebes

Pachycephala raveni (*Riley*) RANO RANO WHISTLER Mts of C Celebes

Pachycephala rufinucha *Sclater* RUFOUS-NAPED WHISTLER Mts of New Guinea / forest and undergrowth / fruit and insects / n bush / e 2

Pachycephala tenebrosa *Rothschild* SOOTY WHISTLER Mts of New Guinea / forest

Pachycephala olivacea *Vigors and Horsfield* OLIVE WHISTLER Tasmania and SE Australia / mountain forest / insects and berries / n bush / e 2–3

Pachycephala rufogularis *Gould* RED-LORED WHISTLER NW Victoria and SE corner of S Australia / mallee / insects and berries / n bush / e 2

Pachycephala inornata *Gould* GILBERT WHISTLER Southern Australia / dry woodland and mallee scrub / insects, seeds and berries / n tree or bush / e 2–3

Pachycephala hypoxantha (*Sharpe*) BORNEAN MOUNTAIN WHISTLER Mts of Borneo / forest / insects and seeds / n tree / e n/k

Pachycephala cinerea (*Blyth*) (= **Pachycephala grisola** (*Blyth*)) MANGROVE WHISTLER E Bengal through SE Asia to Indonesia and Philippines / coastal mangroves / n tree / e 2

Pachycephala phaionota (*Bonaparte*) ISLAND WHISTLER Moluccas, W Papuan islands, Aru Is and islands in Geelvink Bay / scrub on small wooded islands

Pachycephala hyperythra *Salvadori* RUFOUS-BREASTED WHISTLER New Guinea / forest

Pachycephala modesta (*De Vis*) BROWN-BACKED WHISTLER Mts of New Guinea / forest

Pachycephala philippensis (*Walden*) YELLOW-BELLIED WHISTLER Philippines

Pachycephala sulfuriventer (*Walden*) CELEBES MOUNTAIN WHISTLER Mts of Celebes

Pachycephala meyeri *Salvadori* VOGELKOP WHISTLER Vogelkop of New Guinea / mountain forest

Pachycephala soror *Sclater* SCLATER'S WHISTLER Goodenough Is and Mts of New Guinea / mid-mountain forest

Pachycephala simplex *Gould* BROWN WHISTLER New Guinea area and coast of northern Australia / forest and mangrove / insects / n tree / e 2

Pachycephala orpheus *Jardine* TIMOR WHISTLER Timor, Wetar and (?) S Celebes

Pachycephala pectoralis (*Latham*) GOLDEN WHISTLER Widely distributed from Java to Australia, Loyalty Is, Fiji and Tonga / forest and woodland / insects and berries / n tree / e 2–3 [The large assortment of forms now included in this species were formerly divided into about a dozen different species. See Galbraith, *Bulletin Brit Mus* (*Nat Hist*) (1956) vol 4, pt 4, for a detailed treatment of this group. *P. melanura* of Northern Australia is sometimes included and sometimes treated as a separate species]

[**Pachycephala melanops** (*Pucheran*) TONGA WHISTLER Tonga Is, and **Pachycephala caledonica** (*Gmelin*) GMELIN'S WHISTLER New Caledonia. These two species are merged in the *P. pectoralis* complex by Galbraith, but separated by Mayr]

Pachycephala flavifrons (*Peale*) SAMOAN WHISTLER Samoa

Pachycephala implicata *Hartert* SOLOMONS MOUNTAIN WHISTLER Bougainville and Guadalcanal (Solomons) / mountains

Pachycephala nudigula *Hartert* BARE-THROATED or SUNDA WHISTLER Sumbawa and Flores / mountains

Pachycephala lorentzi *Mayr* LORENTZ'S WHISTLER Snow and Telefomin Mts, New Guinea / high mountain forest

Pachycephala schlegelii *Schlegel* SCHLEGEL'S WHISTLER Mts of New Guinea / high mountain forest

Pachycephala aurea *Reichenow* YELLOW-BACKED WHISTLER Mts of SE New Guinea and S slopes of central ranges / secondary forest near rivers and secondary growth near ravines

Pachycephala rufiventris (*Latham*) RUFOUS WHISTLER Australia, SE New Guinea, Rossel Is, Moluccas and New Caledonia / forest, woodland, mangrove and habitation / insects and berries / n tree / e 2–3

Pachycephala monacha *Gray* BLACK-HEADED WHISTLER Aru Is and scattered localities in New Guinea / casuarina groves. This form and its race *dorsalis* are merged with *P. rufiventris* by Mayr (in *Peters Check List*) and others, but tentatively separated by Rand and Gilliard *Handbook of New Guinea Birds*.

Pachycephala lanioides *Gould* WHITE-BREASTED WHISTLER Australia coast from Carnarvon to east of Burketown / mangrove /

insects and aquatic life/n tree/e 2–3

Colluricincla megarhyncha (*Quoy and Gaimard*) RUFOUS THRUSH-FLYCATCHER Celebes to Papuan area and coast of Queensland/forest and mangrove/insects/n tree/e 2–3

Colluricincla parvula *Gould* LITTLE THRUSH-FLYCATCHER Coasts of NW Australia, N Territory and Melville Is/mangrove/insects/n tree or bush/e 2 (now generally considered conspecific with *megarhyncha*)

Colluricincla boweri (*Ramsay*) STRIPE-BREASTED THRUSH-FLYCATCHER NE Queensland/mountain rain forest/insects/n bush/e 2–3

Colluricincla harmonica (*Latham*) GREY THRUSH-FLYCATCHER Australia, Tasmania, islands in Bass Strait and SE New Guinea/savannah, forest and woodland/insects and small animals/n ground, tree or rock ledge/e 2–3 (*C. brunnea* Gould, and *C. rufiventris* Gould, are sometimes separated)

Colluricincla woodwardi *Hartert* SANDSTONE THRUSH-FLYCATCHER Coast of N Territory and northern W Australia/sandstone ridges/insects/n rock crevice/e 2–3

Pitohui kirhocephalus (*Lesson and Garnot*) VARIABLE PITOHUI Lowlands of New Guinea, W Papuan islands, Aru Is and islands in Geelvink Bay/forest/insects

Pitohui dichrous (*Bonaparte*) BLACK-HEADED PITOHUI Mid-mountain forests of New Guinea and Japen/n bush/e 1–2

Pitohui incertus *van Oort* MOTTLED-BREASTED PITOHUI S New Guinea from Noord to upper Fly River/lowland forest/rare, few specimens

Pitohui ferrugineus (*Bonaparte*) RUSTY PITOHUI Lowlands of New Guinea, W Papuan islands, Aru Is, and islands in Geelvink Bay/forest/n tree/e 1

Pitohui cristatus (*Salvadori*) CRESTED PITOHUI Mts of New Guinea/mid-mountain forest

Pitohui nigrescens (*Schlegel*) BLACK PITOHUI Mts of New Guinea/mid-mountain forest/n tree/e 1

Pitohui tenebrosus (*Hartlaub and Finsch*) MORNING BIRD Palau Is/forest/apparently no other data/there has been disagreement as to which genus this bird should belong to

Turnagra capensis (*Sparrman*) NEW ZEALAND THRUSH New Zealand, rare and now confined to parts of S Island/forest and scrub/seeds and fruit/n tree or shrub/e 2 (The position of this genus is uncertain, it is sometimes placed in the Turdidae)

NB: The various groups of Titmice, Nuthatches and Creepers have been variously treated as families, sub-families or merely genera by various systematists. I have placed them all as families here, but it should be noted that this is purely for convenience, and should not be taken to be taxonomically definitive.

AEGITHALIDAE Long-tailed Titmice Small Titmice with medium-long to long tails. Nest a woven bag nest, placed in a tree. Incubation generally by ♀, fed by ♂ on nest.

Aegithalos caudatus (*L*) LONG-TAILED TIT Palaearctic, S to Mediterranean/open woodland/insects and seeds/n tree/e 5–12/I ♀ (?♂) 14–18/F 15–16

Aegithalos leucogenys (*Horsfield and Moore*) WHITE-CHEEKED TIT E Afghanistan to Gilgit and Baluchistan/forest, scrub and bushes along rivers/insects/n bush/e 5–8

Aegithalos concinnus (*Gould*) RED-HEADED or BLACK-THROATED TIT Himalayas, mts of northern SE Asia, China and Taiwan/open forest and garden/insects, seeds and berries/n tree/e 3–8

Aegithalos iouschistos (*Blyth*) RUFOUS-FRONTED TIT Himalayas to N Burma and Szechwan/forest scrub/insects/n tree or bush/e described but clutch size not known (*A. niveogularis* (Gould) is a race)

Aegithalos fuliginosus (*Verreaux*) SOOTY TIT NW China

Psaltria exilis *Temminck* PYGMY TIT Mts of W and C Java/e 2–3

Psaltriparus minimus (*Townsend*) COAST BUSHTIT Western USA, S to Baja California/scrub and open wood/insects/n tree/e 5–12/I 12/F 14–15

Psaltriparus melanotis (*Hartlaub*) BLACK-EARED BUSHTIT Texas and New Mexico S to Guatemala/e 5–7

REMIZIDAE Penduline Tits Tits related to the true Tits, but remarkable for their felted bag-like nests which are usually suspended from a branch hanging over water. The Verdin, however, builds a large globular nest of thorny twigs.

Remiz pendulinus (*L*) COMMON PENDULINE TIT SE Europe across C Asia to China and Manchuria/forest near rivers/n penduline from

EMBERIZIDAE: *Emberiza bruniceps* (=*E. luteola*), Red-headed Bunting

Plate 246

CARDINALIDAE:
Passerina cyanea
(= *P. brissonii*),
Indigo Bunting

EMBERIZIDAE:
Lophospingus pusillus,
Black-crested Finch

Plate 247

branch over water / e 5–9

Anthoscopus punctifrons (*Sundevall*) SUDAN PENDULINE TIT Semi-desert belt S of Sahara from Timbucktu to N Eritrea / insects / n and e n/k

Anthoscopus parvulus (*Heuglin*) YELLOW PENDULINE TIT Arid belt W and S of range of *A. punctifrons*/insects /n penduline from branch/ e described but no clutch size available

Anthoscopus musculus (*Hartlaub*) MOUSE-COLOURED PENDULINE TIT (MOUSE TIT) Ethiopia to NE Tanganyika / rocky bush / n apparently not penduline / e 4

Anthoscopus flavifrons (*Cassin*) FOREST PENDULINE TIT Gold Coast, French Cameroons to NE Congo

Anthoscopus caroli (*Sharpe*) AFRICAN PENDULINE TIT Much of EC and S Africa/ forest and light woodland/insects /n penduline or in bush / e 4–8 (*A. sylviella* Reichenow, is sometimes treated as a separate species)

Anthoscopus minutus (*Shaw and Nodder*) CAPE PENDULINE TIT S Africa N to SW Africa and W Rhodesia

Auriparus flaviceps (*Sundevall*) VERDIN Southwest USA and N Mexico / semi-desert/ n tree or cactus / e 3–6 / 1 ?10

Pholidornis rushiae (*Cassin*) TINY TIT-WARBLER Fernando Po and forests from Sierra Leone to Congo and Uganda / little information/ n said to be like a weaver-bird / e 2 / *Pholidornis* has been placed at various times in the Dicaeidae, Sylviidae, Paridae, Nectariniidae, Hyliidae, Meliphagidae and Estrildidae. Traylor, in Peters' *Check List* places it at the end of the Estrildidae, but Vernon and Dean, *Bull Brit Orn Cl* (1975), p 20, recommend that it should be placed in the Remizidae.

Cephalopyrus flammiceps (*Burton*) FIRE-CAPPED TIT Himalayas from Kashmir to mts of W Szechwan and NW Yunnan / forest and orchard / buds and insects / n hole / e 4

PARIDAE Tits (Titmice) and Chickadees Small, dumpy birds with small strong legs and short, stout, pointed bills. Some species are crested. Generally inhabit wooded areas breeding in holes and crevices, eggs white, spotted with brown, generally the ♀ only incubates. Feed on insects and seeds, but many species live around habitation where they will learn to take various other foods, tear tops of milk bottles for cream etc. Distributed through the Northern Hemisphere and Africa.

Parus palustris *L* MARSH TIT Much of temperate Palaearctic / woodland, scrub and habitation / insects and seeds / n hole in tree or wall / e 5–11 / I ♀ 13–17 / F 16–21

Parus lugubris *Temminck* SOMBRE TIT SE Europe to Iran / mountain woodland and habitation / n hole / e 5–10

Parus montanus *Conrad* WILLOW TIT Much of Palaearctic N to tree-limit / forest scrub and swamp / insects / n hole in *dead* tree / e 5–13/ I ♀ 13–15 / F 17–19

Parus atricapillus *L* BLACK-CAPPED CHICKADEE Canada and Alaska from tree-line S to northern USA / forest / insects, buds and seeds / n hole / e 5–10 / I 12 / F 16

Parus carolinensis *Audubon* CAROLINA CHICKADEE Southern USA / forest and habitation / insects and seeds / n hole in *dead* tree/ e 5–8 / I 11 / F 17

Parus sclateri *Kleinschmidt* MEXICAN CHICKADEE Mexico and south-western USA/ conifer forest (?)/n hole in *dead* wood/e 6

Parus gambeli *Ridgway* MOUNTAIN CHICKADEE Western N America from S British Columbia to N Baja California / mountain forest / n hole / e 5–12

Parus superciliosus (*Przewalski*) WHITE-BROWED TIT Mts of W China from Sikang to W Szechwan

Parus davidi (*Berezowski and Bianchi*) PÈRE DAVID'S TIT Mts of W China from Sikang to W Szechwan

Parus cinctus *Boddaert* SIBERIAN TIT or GREY-HEADED CHICKADEE N Taiga belt of N Europe, Siberia, Alaska and NW Canada; montane woodlands of Altai and adjacent ranges in C Asia / forest / insects and seeds / n hole / e 6–10 / I ♀ 14–15 / F 19

Parus hudsonicus *Forster* BOREAL CHICKADEE Forests of Canada and extreme northern USA/ insects / n hole / e 4–9

Parus rufescens *Townsend* CHESTNUT-BACKED CHICKADEE W Coast of N America from Alaska to California / forest / insects and seeds / n hole/ e 5–9

Parus wollweberi (*Bonaparte*) BRIDLED TITMOUSE Parts of Mexico and south-eastern USA / forest / n hole / e 5–7

Parus rubidiventris *Blyth* RED-BELLIED TIT Mts of W and C Asia from Tian Shan through Himalayas to northern SE Asia and W China/

forest / insects and seeds / n hole in bank / e 4–6 (*P. rufonuchalis* Blyth, is sometimes regarded as distinct, but there does not appear to be consistency as to which of the various races are placed under which specific name)

Parus melanolophus *Vigors* BLACK-CRESTED TIT E Afghanistan to W Nepal / forest / insects and berries / n hole / e 4–10 (usually 5–6) / I ♂♀

Parus ater *L* COAL TIT Much of Palaearctic including mts of Algeria and Tunisia / forest and habitation / insects and seeds / n hole in tree, wall or bank / e 7–12 / I ♀ 14–18 / F 16–19

Parus venustulus *Swinhoe* YELLOW-BELLIED TIT China

Parus elegans *Lesson* ELEGANT TIT Philippines

Parus amabilis *Sharpe* PALAWAN TIT Palawan and Balabec

Parus cristatus *L* CRESTED TIT Locally in conifer forests of Europe, N Morocco and Asia E to Urals / insects and pine seeds / n hole / e 4–11 / I ♀ 13–18 / F 17–21

Parus dichrous *Blyth* BROWN-CRESTED TIT or GREY-CRESTED TIT Himalayas and mts of SE Tibet and W China N to Kansu / forest / insects / n hole / e 5 / I ♂♀

Parus afer *Gmelin* AFRICAN GREY TIT E and S Africa from Ethiopia to Angola and Cape / open woodland and bush / n hole in tree, bank or anthill / e 3

Parus griseiventris *Reichenow* NORTHERN GREY TIT C Africa from Angola to the Rhodesias and S Tanganyika / open woodland and bush / n hole in tree, bank or anthill / e 3

Parus niger *Vieillot* SOUTHERN BLACK TIT S Africa N to Angola and Zambia / open woodland and dry bush / n hole / e 3–4

Parus leucomelas *Rüppell* COMMON BLACK TIT Africa S of Sahara and N of the range of *P. niger* / forest and bush / n hole / e 1–5

Parus albiventris *Shelley* WHITE-BREASTED or WHITE-BELLIED TIT Mts from Nigeria to S Sudan and Tanganyika / forest, acacia and coastal scrub (sic, other statements give it as a mountain species) / n hole / e 3–5

Parus leuconotus *Guérin-Meneville* WHITE-BACKED TIT Highlands of Eritrea and Ethiopia / forested valleys / little known

Parus funereus (*Verreaux*) DUSKY TIT C Africa from Cameroons to Angola and Kenya / forest / n and e n/k

Parus fasciiventer *Reichenow* STRIPE-BREASTED TIT Ruwenzori Mts and nearby ranges / forest and tree-heath zone / n and e n/k

Parus fringillinus *Fischer and Reichenow* RED-THROATED TIT S Kenya and N and C Tanganyika / n hole / e 3

Parus rufiventris *Bocage* CINNAMON-BREASTED TIT Parts of WC and EC Africa from Congo to Rhodesia and C Tanganyika / open woodland / n hole / e 4

Parus major *L* GREAT TIT Widely distributed through Europe, NW Africa and Asia (except extreme NE) and Greater and Lesser Sunda Is / light forest and habitation / insects, buds and seeds / n hole in tree, wall or rock / e 7–15 / I ♂♀ 10–22 / F 16–22

Parus bokharensis *Lichtenstein* TURKESTAN TIT Russian Turkestan and Afghanistan / apparently no data

Parus monticolus *Vigors* GREEN-BACKED TIT Himalayas E through mts of northern SE Asia to S China and Taiwan and N through mts of W China to Kansu / light forest and cultivation / insects and berries / n hole in tree or wall / e 4–8

Parus nuchalis *Jerdon* WHITE-WINGED TIT NW India and locally in hills of S India / semi-desert / insects / n hole / e n/k

Parus xanthogenys *Vigors* YELLOWCHEEKED TIT W Himalayas and mts of northern SE Asia, S Annam and S China / forest and cultivation / insects and berries / n hole in tree or wall / e 4–7 (*P. spilonotus* Bonaparte is sometimes separated)

Parus holsti *Seebohm* YELLOW TIT Taiwan

Parus caeruleus *L* BLUE TIT Europe and SW Asia (to Iran), N Africa, Majorca, Canary Is / forest and habitation / insects, seeds and fruit / n hole in tree or wall / e 5–16 / I ♀ 12–16 / F 15–23

Parus cyaneus *Pallas* AZURE TIT Russia across C Asia to Amurland and S to Afghanistan and Koko Nor / woodland, scrub and marsh / insects and seeds / n hole / e 9–11 / I ♀ 13–14

Parus varius *Temminck and Schlegel* VARIED TIT Japan, S Kuriles, Korea, S Manchuria, Taiwan, Izu and Riu Kiu Is / forest / insects and seeds / n hole in tree or rock / e 7–8

Parus semilarvatus (*Salvadori*) WHITE-FRONTED TIT Luzon, Negros and Mindanao

Parus inornatus *Gambel* PLAIN TITMOUSE Baja California and southern-western USA / forest scrub / insects and fruit / n hole / e 3–9 / I ♀ 14

Parus bicolor *L* TUFTED TITMOUSE East-central and southern USA and N Mexico /

EMBERIZIDAE:
Paroaria coronata,
Red-crested Cardinal

EMBERIZIDAE:
Diuca diuca,
Common Diuca, Common
Diuca-Finch

Plate 248

EMBERIZIDAE:
*Tiaris
canora,*
Cuban
Grassquit,
Melodious
Grassquit

EMBERIZIDAE:
*Paroaria
capitata,*
Yellow-billed
Cardinal

Plate 249

forest and orchard / insects, seeds and fruit/ n hole / e 4–8 / I 12 / F 15–16 [*Parus alticristatus* Cassin (Black-crested Titmouse) is sometimes considered distinct, but Snow in *Peters' Check List* has pointed out that there is intergradation]
Melanochlorea sultanea (*Hodgson*) SULTAN TIT Himalayas, mts of SE Asia and S China, Sumatra / foothills forest and near cultivation/ n hole / e 6–7
Sylviparus modestus Burton YELLOW-BROWED TIT Himalayas, mts of northern SE Asia, W and S China and S Annam (discontinuous) / forest / insects / n hole / e 4–6
HYPOSITTIDAE Coral-billed Nuthatch A species with apparent affinities both with the Vanga-shrikes and the Sittidae, and it has been associated with both. Its systematic position is still uncertain. Forages on tree-trunks and large branches, never perching head-downwards as nuthatches do but working spirally upwards, like a treecreeper.
Hypositta corallirostris (*Newton*) CORAL-BILLED NUTHATCH Humid forests of E Madagascar / apparently no data
DAPHOENOSITTIDAE Sitellas or Treerunners Birds resembling Treecreepers, except for their soft tails, and building open cup nests in forked branches.
Neositta chryoptera (*Latham*) ORANGE-WINGED SITELLA or TREERUNNER Australia/ open forest / n tree / e 3 (the sub-species of this bird are sometimes treated as full species)
Neositta papuensis (*Schlegel*) PAPUAN SITELLA Mts of New Guinea / forest / no other data
Daphoenositta miranda De Vis PINK-FACED NUTHATCH or RED-FRONTED CREEPER Mts of New Guinea / forest / insects / no other data
TICHODROMADIDAE Wallcreeper A large member of the nuthatch-treecreeper group with broad, red wings (remarkable in this group) and a curious buoyant 'butterfly' flight.
Tichodroma muraria (*L*) WALLCREEPER Mts of C and S Europe across Asia to Mongolia and mts of W China / rock faces in mts / n hole in cliff or wall (especially mountain castles etc)/ e 3–5 / I ♀ 18–19 / F 21–6
SITTIDAE Nuthatches Small acrobatic arboreal birds with thin, straight, sharp-pointed bills and short stout legs. They feed largely on insects which they hunt among bark on tree-trunks, and some species also eat nuts. They are the only birds which habitually hunt by

walking down tree-trunks upside down. The two Rock Nuthatches are unusual in occurring on rocks not trees. The nest is in a hole in a tree-trunk, except for the Rock Nuthatches. The 4–10 eggs are speckled red-brown on a white ground. Only the ♀ incubates, fed on the nest by the ♂ for the 12–14 day incubation period. About 22 species in Eurasia and N America.
Sitta europaea L EURASIAN NUTHATCH Much of Palaearctic / forest, park and cultivation / n hole in tree or wall / e 4–13 / I 14–18 / F 23–5
Sitta nagaensis *Godwin-Austen* CHESTNUT-VENTED NUTHATCH Scattered localities from Tibet and Kansu to Burma, Fukien and Annam/ little data (sometimes treated as a race of *europaea*)
Sitta castanea *Lesson* CHESTNUT-BELLIED NUTHATCH Himalayas and India through SE Asia (except Malay Peninsula) / forest / insects, nuts etc / n in hole in tree or wall / e 5–7 / I ♂♀ (Baker) 11–12 ♀ (Gill)
[**Sitta cashmirensis** *Brooks* KASHMIR NUTHATCH Kashmir to N Baluchistan / e 5–7. The status of this form is uncertain. Sometimes treated as specifically distinct, sometimes as a race of *europaea* and sometimes as a race of *castanea*]
Sitta himalayensis *Jardine and Selby* WHITE-TAILED or HIMALAYAN NUTHATCH Himalayas to Yunnan and mts of SE Asia / forest / insects, nuts and seeds / n hole / e 4–7
Sitta victoriae *Rippon* WHITE-BROWED or VICTORIA NUTHATCH Mt Victoria (Burma) / no data
Sitta pygmaea *Vigors* PYGMY NUTHATCH Pine forested mountains of western N America from S British Columbia to Mexico / insects and seeds / n hole / e 4–9
Sitta pusilla *Latham* BROWN-HEADED NUTHATCH Pine forests of S and south-eastern USA, Grand Bahama Is / insects and seeds/ n hole / e 3–9 / I ♂♀ 14

The following 6 species constitute a super-species and are sometimes treated as conspecific:
Sitta whiteheadi *Sharpe* WHITEHEAD'S NUTHATCH Corsica / pine forests in mountains/ n hole / e 5–6
Sitta yunnanensis *Ogilvie-Grant* YUNNAN NUTHATCH Pine forests in mts of Yunnan and E Sikang

Sitta canadensis *L* RED-BREASTED NUTHATCH Pine forests of N America / seeds / and insects / n hole / e 4–7

Sitta villosa *Verreaux* CHINESE NUTHATCH N China, Korea and Manchuria

Sitta krueperi *Pelzeln* KRÜPER'S NUTHATCH Turkey E to Transcaucasia and S Caucasus/ coniferous forest / n hole / e 5–6

Sitta ledandi *Vielliard* (*Alauda*, vol 44, pt 3, supp spéc, pp 351–2) ALGERIAN or KALYBIAN NUTHATCH Djebel Babor, Algeria / mountain forest / n hole / e n/k

Sitta leucopsis *Gould* WHITE-CHEEKED NUTHATCH Himalayas and mts of W China/ forest / insects and seeds / n hole or crevice, apparently usually in a *dead* tree / e 4–8

Sitta carolinensis *Latham* WHITE-BREASTED NUTHATCH Much of N America and parts of Mexico / open forest / insects and nuts / n hole/ e 5–10 / I ♂♀ 12

Sitta neumayer *Michahelles* LESSER ROCK NUTHATCH SE Greece, Turkey and E to SE Iran / rocky areas / n clay structure in hollow in rock or tree / e 6–13

Sitta tephronota *Sharpe* GREATER ROCK NUTHATCH Iran to Kurdistan and Baluchistan/ rocky mountain areas / n (as *neumayer*) / e 4–7 [The relationships between the various races of *neumayer* and *tephronota* are still subject to debate. They are sometimes treated as conspecific, but Vaurie has shown that at least 2 races overlap in range in Iran without apparently interbreeding]

Sitta frontalis *Swainson* VELVET-FRONTED NUTHATCH Indian sub-continent, SE Asia, S Yunnan, Hainan, through Greater Sundas to Philippines / forest, mangrove and cultivation/ insects / n hole / e 3–5

Sitta solangiae (*Delacour and Jabouille*) YELLOW-BILLED NUTHATCH Vietnam / mountain forest

Sitta azurea *Lesson* BLUE NUTHATCH Malaya, Sumatra and Java / mountain forest / insects

Sitta magna *Ramsay* GIANT NUTHATCH Yunnan and Northern SE Asia / open forest/ n hole / e ?3 (1 nest with 3 young known)

Sitta formosa *Blyth* BEAUTIFUL NUTHATCH Himalayas and northern SE Asia / forest / n hole / e 4–6

CERTHIIDAE Treecreepers Small arboreal birds, generally brown and white in colouration with thin, pointed down-curved bills, for probing into holes in bark for insects on which they feed. They also have stiff tail feathers for clinging to bark.

Certhia familiaris *L* COMMON TREECREEPER Widely distributed through the Eurasian forests from British Isles to Japan and Amurland and S to Himalayas / forest, park and cultivation n crevice in tree / e 3–9 / I ♀ 14–15 / F 14–16

Certhia brachydactyla *Brehm* SHORT-TOED TREECREEPER C and S Europe, N Africa and SW Asia to Caucasus / light forest and cultivation / e 6–7 / I ♀ 15 / F 16–17 (There has been disagreement on the validity of *brachydactyla* as a separate species, and of the status of the many races which have been named of it and *familiaris*)

Certhia americana *Bonaparte* BROWN CREEPER Forests of N America, Mexico, Guatemala and Nicaragua / forest and cultivation / n crevice in tree / e 4–8 / F 13–14 (sometimes treated as conspecific with *familiaris*)

Certhia himalayana *Vigors* HIMALAYAN TREECREEPER Mts of C Asia from Transcaspia through Afghanistan and Himalayas to mts of Burma and W China / mountain forests, chiefly juniper / n crevice in tree / e 4–6 / I ♀ 13–14/ F c21

Certhia nipalensis *Blyth* NEPAL TREECREEPER Himalayas from C Nepal to S Tibet and NE Burma / forest / n and e n/k

Certhia discolor *Blyth* SIKKIM TREECREEPER Himalayas from Nepal E and mts of northern SE Asia / forest / n hole / e 3–4

SALPORNITHIDAE Spotted Creeper Small birds similar to treecreepers but with soft tails.

Salpornis spilonotus (*Franklin*) SPOTTED CREEPER Irregularly distributed through Africa S of Sahara, S to Angola and Rhodesia, reappearing in Himalayan foothills and plains of N India / open deciduous forest and mangrove/ insects / n tree / e 2–3 / I ♂♀

RHABDORNITHIDAE   Philippine Creepers These creepers have brush-like tongues, and feed both on insects and on nectar from flowers. They nest in holes.

Rhabdornis mysticalis (*Temminck*) STRIPE-HEADED CREEPER Philippines

Rhabdornis inornatus *Ogilvie-Grant* PLAIN-HEADED CREEPER Philippines

CLIMACTERIDAE Australian Treecreepers The members of this family differ from typical Treecreepers in feeding both on

EMBERIZIDAE: *Paroaria coronata,* Red-crested Cardinal

Plate 250

EMBERIZIDAE:
Emberiza citrinella,
Yellowhammer or
Yellow Bunting

EMBERIZIDAE:
*Emberiza
tahapisi,*
Cinnamon-breasted
Bunting

Plate 251

the ground and in the trees, and nesting in holes, like Nuthatches.

Climacteris erythrops *Gould* RED-BROWED TREECREEPER Mt forests of E Australia /insects/ n hole /e 2

Climacteris affinis *Blyth* WHITE-BROWED TREECREEPER Dry regions of Australia / scrub/ n hole /e 2–3

Climacteris picumnus *Temminck and Laugier* BROWN TREECREEPER E and SE Australia /forest /insects /n hole in tree or bank/ e 3–4

Climacteris rufa *Gould* RUFOUS TREECREEPER Parts of W Australia and the Gawler Range in S Australia /open woodland

Climacteris melanura *Gould* BLACK-TAILED TREECREEPER N and W Australia /open forest/ insects /n hole in tree or bank/ e 2–3

Climacteris leucophaea (*Latham*) WHITE-THROATED TREECREEPER Mts of New Guinea and E Australia /forest /insects /n hole /e 2–3

DICAEIDAE Flowerpeckers Small, dumpy birds with short, thick, down-curved bills and long tubular tongues. Many are brightly coloured and they feed on nectar, insects and small berries. Many species build purse-shaped nests hung from branches of trees. About 54 species in the Oriental and Australasian regions.

Melanocharis arfakiana (*Finsch*) OBSCURE BERRYPECKER Mts of New Guinea/known from 2 specimens

Melanocharis nigra (*Lesson*) BLACK BERRYPECKER New Guinea, Waigeu, Misol, Salawati, Aru Is, Japen and Meon Num/lowland forest /fruit, insects and spiders /n and e ?n/k

Melanocharis longicauda *Salvadori* MID-MOUNTAIN BERRYPECKER Mts of New Guinea 3,200–5,800ft (975–1,770m) /forest

Melanocharis versteri (*Finsch*) FAN-TAILED BERRYPECKER Mts of New Guinea / forest undergrowth /fruit and insects /n tree /e n/k

Melanocharis striativentris *Salvadori* STREAKED BERRYPECKER Mts of New Guinea/ no data

Rhamphocharis crassirostris *Salvadori* SPOTTED BERRYPECKER Mts of New Guinea/ forest

Prionochilus olivaceus *Tweeddale* OLIVE-BACKED FLOWERPECKER Philippines

Prionochilus maculatus (*Temminck and Laugier*) YELLOW-BREASTED FLOWERPECKER S Burma and Malay Peninsula, Sumatra, Billiton,

Nias, Borneo and Great Natuna /lowland forest

Prionochilus percussus (*Temminck and Laugier*) CRIMSON-BREASTED FLOWERPECKER S Burma and Malay Peninsula, Sumatra, Billiton, Banka, Tanahmasa, Borneo, Java and Great Natuna / lowland forest /n tree (1 nest with 1 egg described by Baker, but of slightly doubtful provenance)

Prionochilus plateni *Blasius* PLATEN'S FLOWERPECKER Palawan, Balabec and Culion Is

Prionochilus xanthopygius *Salvadori* YELLOW-RUMPED FLOWERPECKER Borneo and Great Natuna / forest / flowers, nectar, insects and spiders

Prionochilus thoracicus (*Temminck and Laugier*) SCARLET-BREASTED FLOWERPECKER Malaya, Billiton and Borneo /lowland forest

Dicaeum annae (*Büttikofer*) FLORES FLOWER-PECKER Sumbawa and Flores

Dicaeum agile (*Tickell*) THICK-BILLED FLOWERPECKER Indian sub-continent, SE Asia, N Sumatra, W Java, Sumba, Flores, Alor and Timor / forest and cultivation /fruit, nectar etc/ n tree /e 2–4

Dicaeum everetti (*Sharpe*) BROWN-BACKED FLOWERPECKER Borneo, Labuan, Gt Natuna, Malaya and Buitan Is /lowland forest /insects, flowers and spiders

Dicaeum aeruginosum (*Bourns and Worcester*) STRIPED FLOWERPECKER Philippines and Palawan

Dicaeum proprium *Ripley and Rabor* GREY-BREASTED FLOWERPECKER Mt Mayo, Mindanao, Philippines

Dicaeum chrysorrheum *Temminck and Laugier* YELLOW-VENTED FLOWERPECKER Himalayas from Sikkim E, S Yunnan, SE Asia, Sumatra, Borneo and Java / open jungle and orange orchards / berries, nectar and insects/ n tree /e 2–3 /I ♂♀

Dicaeum melanoxanthum (*Blyth*) YELLOW-BELLIED FLOWERPECKER Himalayas from Nepal to Assam, S Shan States, Yunnan and S Sikang w S to Tonkin and N Thailand /forest /n and e n/k

Dicaeum vincens (*Sclater*) LEGGE'S FLOWER-PECKER Ceylon / forest / berries, nectar and insects /n tree /e 2

Dicaeum aureolimbatum (*Wallace*) MINAHASSA FLOWERPECKER Celebes, Muna, Buton and Gt Sanghir

Dicaeum nigrilorae *Hartert* OLIVE-CAPPED

FLOWERPECKER Mts of Mindanao, Philippines
Dicaeum anthonyi (*McGregor*) ANTHONY'S FLOWERPECKER Mts of Mindanao and Luzon

Dicaeum bicolor (*Bourns and Worcester*) BICOLOURED FLOWERPECKER Philippines

Dicaeum quadricolor (*Tweeddale*) FOUR-COLOURED FLOWERPECKER Cebu / extinct, last seen 1906

Dicaeum australe (*Hermann*) AUSTRAL FLOWERPECKER Philippines

Dicaeum retrocinctum *Gould* MINDORO FLOWERPECKER Mindoro

Dicaeum trigonostigma (*Scopoli*) ORANGE-BELLIED FLOWERPECKER Assam, SE Asia and through Greater Sundas and adjacent small islands to Philippines / forest / n tree / e n/s

Dicaeum hypoleucum *Sharpe* WHITE-BELLIED FLOWERPECKER Philippines, Basilan and Sulu Is

Dicaeum erythrorhynchos (*Latham*) TICKELL'S FLOWERPECKER Ceylon and the greater part of India / forest, mangrove and cultivation / n tree / e 3 / I ♂♀

Dicaeum concolor *Jerdon* PLAIN FLOWERPECKER India, SE Asia, S China, Hainan, Taiwan, Sumatra, Java, Bali, Borneo, Gt Natuna, Andamans / isolated stands of trees in open country, forest edge and cultivation / berries, nectar and insects / n tree or bush / e 2–3 / I ♂♀

Dicaeum pygmaeum (*Kittlitz*) PYGMY FLOWERPECKER Philippines

Dicaeum nehrkorni *Blasius* NEHRKORN'S FLOWERPECKER Mts of Celebes

Dicaeum vulneratum *Wallace* CERAM FLOWERPECKER Ceram, Ambon, Saparua, Manawoka and Goram

Dicaeum erythrothorax *Lesson* BURU FLOWERPECKER Buru, Obi, Batjan, Halmahera and Morotai

Dicaeum pectorale *Müller* PAPUAN FLOWER-PECKER New Guinea and adjacent small islands / forest / berries and spiders / n tree / e 2 (*D. geelvinkianum* and *D. nitidum* are sometimes separated)

Dicaeum eximium *Sclater* BEAUTIFUL FLOWERPECKER Bismarck Archipelago

Dicaeum aeneum *Pucheran* MIDGET FLOWERPECKER Solomon Is (not San Christobal)

Dicaeum tristrami *Sharpe* TRISTRAM'S FLOWERPECKER San Christobal, Solomon Is

Dicaeum igniferum *Wallace* BLACK-BANDED FLOWERPECKER Sumbawa, Flores, Pantar and Alor

Dicaeum maugei *Lesson* BLUE-CHEEKED FLOWERPECKER Timor, Sawu, Seman, Roma, Damar, Babar, Moa, Saleyor, Djampea, Lombok and Nusa Penida Is

Dicaeum sanguinolentum *Temminck and Laugier* JAVAN FIRE-BREASTED FLOWERPECKER Java, Bali, Sumba, Flores and Timor

Dicaeum hirundinaceum (*Shaw and Nodder*) MISTLETOE FLOWERPECKER Australia, Aru, Kei, Tenimber and adjacent islands / forest / mistletoe berries / n tree / e 3

Dicaeum celebicum *Müller* BLACK-SIDED FLOWERPECKER Celebes, Tukangbesis, Banguey, Sula, Muton, Buton, Sangihe and Talaut

Dicaeum monticolom *Sharpe* BORNEAN FIRE-BREASTED FLOWERPECKER Mts of Borneo / forest / fruit and insects / n tree / e ?3

Dicaeum ignipectus (*Blyth*) BUFF-BELLIED FLOWERPECKER Himalayas, SE Asia, S China, Taiwan, Philippines and N Sumatra / forest, secondary growth and cultivation / berries, nectar and insects / n tree / e 2–3

Dicaeum cruentatum (*L*) SCARLET-BACKED FLOWERPECKER Himalayas, SE Asia, S China and Hainan, Sumatra and W Sumatran Is, Borneo and Karimata Is / open forest and orchards / berries, nectar and insects / n tree / e 2–3 / I ♀♂ 10–11

Dicaeum trochileum (*Sparrman*) SCARLET-HEADED FLOWERPECKER Java, Madura, Bali, Lombok, SE Borneo, Banka, Karimundjoroo, Bawean and Kangean Is

Oreocharis arfaki (*Meyer*) TIT BERRYPECKER, ARFAK FLOWERPECKER Mts of New Guinea / forest / berries

Paramythia montium *De Vis* CRESTED BERRYPECKER Mts of New Guinea / forest / berries / n tree / e 1 / I ♀ [Harrison and Parker, *Bull Brit Orn Club*, 86 (1966), pp 15–20, believe that *Oreocharis* and *Paramythia* are better placed with the Pycnonotidae]

The members of the following genus are called either Pardalotes or Diamondbirds in English:
Pardalotus quadrigintus *Gould* FORTY-SPOTTED DIAMONDBIRD or PARDALOTE Tasmania and King Is / forest / insects / n hole / e 3–4

Pardalotus punctatus (*Shaw and Nodder*) SPOTTED DIAMONDBIRD S and E Australia, Tasmania and Flinders Is / forest and woodland /

EMBERIZIDAE:
Tiaris olivacea,
Yellow-faced Grassquit

Opposite:
EMBERIZIDAE:
Poospiza garleppi,
Cochabamba Mountain-Finch

Plate 252

Plate 253

insects / n hole in bank / e 4

Pardalotus xanthopygus *McCoy* YELLOW-TAILED DIAMONDBIRD SW, S and SE Australia / dry woodland

Pardalotus rubricatus *Gould* RED-BROWED DIAMONDBIRD Australia / trees along watercourses / insects / n hole in bank / e 4

Pardalotus striatus (*Gmelin*) YELLOW-TIPPED DIAMONDBIRD Tasmania, islands in Bass Strait and SE Australia / dry forest and woodland / insects / n hole / e 4

Pardalotus ornatus *Temminck and Laugier* RED-TIPPED DIAMONDBIRD SE Australia / considered to have originated as a hybrid between *striatus* and *substriatus*

Pardalotus substriatus *Mathews* STRIATED DIAMONDBIRD Non-tropical parts Australia / dry forest and woodland / insects

Pardalotus melanocephalus *Gould* BLACK-HEADED DIAMONDBIRD Australia / n hole in bank

ZOSTEROPIDAE **White-eyes** Small yellowish-green and white birds with rings of white feathers round their eyes, rounded wings, and short, strong legs. They feed on insects, fruit and nectar. The nest is usually in the fork of a twig. Eggs are from 2–4 in number and are various shades of immaculate blue or bluish-white. An incubation period of 10 days has been quoted in captivity but this has been queried. White-eyes range largely through the tropical regions of the Old World. Much information used here is based on Mees' monograph 'A systematic review of the Indo-Australian Zosteropidae' in *Verh Rijksmus Nat Hist Leiden*, 3 pts, commencing 1957.

Zosterops erythropleura *Swinhoe* CHESTNUT-FLANKED WHITE-EYE b S Ussuriland, Amurland and Manchuria w S China, E Burma, Thailand and Indonesia / n and e n/k

Zosterops japonica *Temminck and Schlegel* JAPANESE WHITE-EYE Japan, Hokkaido, Volcano and Seven Is, Ryukyus, China, Hainan and small islands S to N Philippines, introduced on Bonin Is / c 3–5 (*meyeni* of Luzon is sometimes separated)

Zosterops palpebrosa (*Temminck*) ORIENTAL WHITE-EYE Indian sub-continent, W China, SE Asia, Sumatra, Java, Bali, Flores, W Borneo, S Natuna and Bangka / woods and gardens / e 2–5 / I ?10–11 / F 10

Zosterops ceylonensis *Holdsworth* CEYLON WHITE-EYE Ceylon / forests / e 3

Zosterops conspicillata (*Kittlitz*) BRIDLED WHITE-EYE Marianas, Caroline and Palau Is / forest edges and secondary growth / e 1–3

Zosterops salvadorii *Meyer and Wiglesworth* ENGANO WHITE-EYE Engano / no data

Zosterops atricapilla *Salvadori* BLACK-CAPPED WHITE-EYE Sumatra and Borneo / forest / e 2 ?

Zosterops everetti *Tweeddale* EVERETT'S WHITE-EYE Philippines, Sulu Is, Talut Is, Northern Borneo and Malay Peninsula / forest / e 3 (only 1 clutch definitely known)

Zosterops nigrorum *Tweeddale* PHILIPPINE WHITE-EYE Philippines / open and secondary forest / n and e n/k

Zosterops montana *Bonaparte* MOUNTAIN WHITE-EYE Scattered islands from Sumatra to Moluccas (for more detailed range see Peters' *Check List*, vol 12, pp 300–2 and Mees, op cit, no 35 (1957), p 172) / mountain scrub and woodland / e 2

Zosterops wallacei *Finsch* YELLOW-SPECTACLED WHITE-EYE Sumbawa, Komodo, Rintja, Flores, Lomblen and Sumba [Timor, erroneous] / open scrub and light monsoon forest / n and e n/k

Zosterops flava (*Horsfield*) YELLOW WHITE-EYE N coast of western Java and S coast of Borneo / coastal bushes and mangroves / n and e no reliable data

Zosterops chloris *Bonaparte* MOLUCCAN WHITE-EYE Parts of Celebes, Lesser Sundas and Moluccas, islands in the Java Sea and Bass Strait (discontinuous) / ubiquitous on small islands / e 2–4 (usually 3)

Zosterops consobrinorum *Meyer* LALOUMERA WHITE-EYE SE peninsula of Celebes / known only from 3 localities / no data

Zosterops grayi *Wallace* GREAT KEI WHITE-EYE Great Kei Is / no data

Zosterops uropygialis *Salvadori* LITTLE KEI WHITE-EYE Little Kei Is / no data

Zosterops anomala *Meyer and Wiglesworth* MAKASSAR WHITE-EYE S peninsula of Celebes / light secondary forest / n and e n/k

Zosterops atriceps *Gray* BATJAN WHITE-EYE Morotai, Halmahera and Batjan / lowlands / no other data

Zosterops atrifrons *Wallace* BLACK-FRONTED WHITE-EYE Celebes, Great Sanghir, Sula Is, Ceram, New Guinea, Japen / secondary forest / e 3

Zosterops hypoxantha *Salvadori* BISMARCK WHITE-EYE Bismarck Archipelago and Manus Is/forest edges/e 2–3

Zosterops mysorensis *Meyer* BIAK WHITE-EYE Biak/no data

Zosterops fuscicapilla *Salvadori* YELLOW-BELLIED MOUNTAIN WHITE-EYE Mts of W and C New Guinea, Goodenough Is/primary and secondary forest

Zosterops buruensis *Salvadori* BURU WHITE-EYE Buru/lower and middle mountain zone/no other data

Zosterops meeki *Hartert* MEEK'S WHITE-EYE Sudest Is in the Louisiade Archipelago/no data

Zosterops kuehni *Hartert* KÜHN'S WHITE-EYE Amboina and N coast of Ceram/no data

Zosterops novaeguinae *Salvadori* NEW GUINEA MOUNTAIN WHITE-EYE New Guinea and Aru Is/forest and secondary growth/n and e undescribed, but the existence of 1 egg recorded by Nehrkorn

Zosterops natalis *Lister* CHRISTMAS WHITE-EYE Christmas Is (Indian Ocean), introduced on Pulu Luar, Cocos Keeling group, ubiquitous on the island/e 2–4

Zosterops lutea *Gould* MANGROVE WHITE-EYE W and N Australia/mangroves/e 2–3

Zosterops griseotincta *Gray* LOUISIADE WHITE-EYE Louisiade Archipelago and various small islands in the vicinity/n and e collected but clutch size apparently not recorded

Zosterops rennelliana *Murphy* RENNELL WHITE-EYE Rennell Is/e ?2

Zosterops vellalavella *Hartert* VELLALAVELLA WHITE-EYE Vellalavella and Bragga (Solomons)

Zosterops luteirostris *Hartert* GIZO WHITE-EYE Gizo (Solomons)

Zosterops splendida *Hartert* GANONGA WHITE-EYE Ganonga (Solomons)

Zosterops kulambangrae *Rothschild and Hartert* (=**Z. ugiensis** (*Ramsay*)) KULAMBANGRA WHITE-EYE Kulambangra, New Georgia, Vanungu, Gatukai, Rendova and Tetipari (Solomons)/jungle and secondary growth/n and e n/k

Zosterops metcalfii *Tristram* METCALF'S WHITE-EYE Buku, Bougainville, Shortland, Choiseul, Bugotu and Florida Is/lowland forest/n and e n/k

Zosterops rendovae *Tristram* RENDOVA WHITE-EYE Bougainville, Guadalcanal and San Christobal/mist forest/n and e n/k

Zosterops murphyi *Hartert* MURPHY'S WHITE-EYE Kulambangra/no data

Zosterops stresemanni *Mayr* MALAITA WHITE-EYE Malaita Is (Solomons)

Zosterops sanctaecrucis *Tristram* SANTA CRUZ WHITE-EYE Santa Cruz/no data

Zosterops samoensis *Murphy and Mathews* SAMOA WHITE-EYE Savaii (Samoa)/seen by one observer in trees at 4,000ft (1,200m) above sea level/no other data

Zosterops explorator *Layard* LAYARD'S WHITE-EYE Fiji Is/forests and plantations/e 2

Zosterops flavifrons (*Gmelin*) YELLOW-FRONTED WHITE-EYE Banks group and New Hebrides/forest, scrub and garden/e 3

Zosterops minuta *Layard* SMALL LIFU WHITE-EYE Lifu (Loyalty Is)/forest, scrub and garden/e 2–4/I ?♂♀

Zosterops xanthochroa *Gray* GREEN-BACKED WHITE-EYE New Caledonia/forest and garden/e 2–4

Zosterops lateralis (*Latham*) GREY-BREASTED SILVER-EYE E and SE Australia, Tasmania, New Zealand (colonised 1855) and adjacent islands to Loyalty Is, New Hebrides and Fiji/habitat variable/e 2–4/I 10–11/F 12–14 [*Z. gouldi* Bonaparte (=*Z. australasiae* (*Vieillot*)) is sometimes considered to be a species, but is more usually treated as a race of *Z. lateralis*]

Zosterops strenua *Gould* LORD HOWE WHITE-EYE Lord Howe Is/extinct/e 2 (1 clutch known)

Zosterops tenuirostris *Gould* SLENDER-BILLED WHITE-EYE Norfolk Is/forest and secondary growth/e 2–4

Zosterops albogularis *Gould* NORFOLK WHITE-EYE Norfolk Is/confined to the main forest reserve/e 2

Zosterops inornata *Layard* LARGE LIFU WHITE-EYE Lifu (Loyalty Is)/scrub and forest/e ?2

Zosterops cinerea (*Kittlitz*) GREY-BROWN WHITE-EYE Palau Is, Ponape and Kusaie (Carolines)/secondary bush and grassland (at least on some islands)/apparently only 2 nests known, each containing 1 egg – possibly incomplete clutches

(The arrangement of the African species of the genus *Zosterops* follows Moreau (in *Peters' Check List*, vol 12), who stressed that the arrangement was tentative)

EMBERIZIDAE:
Sporophila albogularis,
White-throated
Seedeater

FRINGILLIDAE:
Coccothraustes vespertinus,
Evening
Grosbeak

Plate 254

EMBERIZIDAE:
Poospiza nigrorufa,
Black-and-Rufous
Warbling-Finch

Plate 255

Zosterops abyssinica *Guérin-Méneville* AFRICAN WHITE-BREASTED WHITE-EYE Yemen, and E Africa from Ethiopia to E Tanganyika / forested valleys / no other data

Zosterops pallida *Swainson* PALE WHITE-EYE Southern SW Africa, NW Cape Province, SW Transvaal and Orange Free State / trees and bushes / insects / n bush or tree / e 2

Zosterops senegalensis *Bonaparte* AFRICAN YELLOW WHITE-EYE Africa S of Sahara and S to Angola and Transvaal; Grand Comoro Is / open woodland and thornbush / insects and fruit / n tree / e 2–3 (some authorities separate *Z. eurycricotus* Fischer and Reichenow, and *Z. kikuyuensis* Sharpe)

Zosterops virens *Sundevall* GREEN WHITE-EYE Cape Province, Natal, Zululand, Transvaal, SE Bechuanaland and S Mozambique / forest-edge / insects and fruit / n bush or tree / e 2 (may be conspecific with *Z. pallida*)

Zosterops borbonica (*Gmelin*) GREY WHITE-EYE Mauritius and Réunion

Zosterops ficedulina *Hartlaub* PRINCIPÉ WHITE-EYE Principé and São Thomé / no data

Zosterops griseovirescens *Barboza du Bocage* ANNOBON WHITE-EYE Annobon Is (Gulf of Guinea) / bush and scrub / n bush / e 2

Zosterops maderaspatana (*L*) MADAGASCAR WHITE-EYE Madagascar, Gloriosa, Aldabra, Anjouan, Mohéle and Europa Is / forest and bush / insects / n tree / e 3 (1 nest known)

[**Zosterops hovarum** *Tristram* HOVA GREY-BACKED WHITE-EYE 'This white-eye is known only from the type, which was purchased with a parcel of apparently unlabelled Madagascar bird skins and assumed also to have come from there' (Rand, 'Distribution and Habits of Madagascar Birds', *Bull Amer Mus Nat Hist* (1936), p 475. Moreau synonymises this with *Z. maderaspatana*]

Zosterops semiflava *Newton* HALF-YELLOW WHITE-EYE Marianne Is (Seychelles) / extinct

Zosterops mayottensis *Schlegel* CHESTNUT-FLANKED WHITE-EYE Mayotte (Comoros)

Zosterops modesta *Newton* SEYCHELLES WHITE-EYE Mahé / mixed secondary forest, usually at high altitudes

Zosterops mouroniensis *Milne-Edwards and Oustalet* MT KARTHALA WHITE-EYE Gr Comoro, above 5,500ft (1,700m)

Zosterops olivacea (*L*) OLIVE WHITE-EYE Mauritius and Réunion (*Z. chloronothos*

(Vieillot) from Mauritius, is sometimes separated)

Zosterops vaughani *Bannerman* PEMBA WHITE-EYE Pemba Is / ubiquitous on the island / insects and fruit / n bush / e 2

Speirops brunnea *Salvadori* FERNANDO PO SPEIROPS Fernando Po / no data / known only from very few specimens

Speirops leucophoea (*Hartlaub*) PRINCIPÉ SPEIROPS Principé / forest / n tree / e 2

Speirops lugubris (*Hartlaub*) BLACK-CAPPED SPEIROPS Cameroons and São Thomé / clearings in mountain forest

Woodfordia superciliosa *North* WOODFORD'S WHITE-EYE Rennell Is / trees on small island / e 2

Woodfordia lacertosa (*Murphy and Mathews*) SANFORD'S WHITE-EYE Santa Cruz Is / no data

Megazosterops palauensis (*Reichenow*) LARGE PALAU WHITE-EYE Palau Is / forest / no other data

Rukia oleaginea (*Hartlaub and Finsch*) LARGE YAP WHITE-EYE Yap Is / swamp jungle / no other data

Rukia ruki (*Hartert*) LARGE TRUK WHITE-EYE Truk (Ruk) / no data

Rukia longirostra (*Takatsukasa and Yamashina*) LARGE PONAPÉ WHITE-EYE Ponapé / mountain forest

Tephrozosterops stalkeri (*Ogilvie-Grant*) KAROPI WHITE-EYE Mts of Ceram / scrub / n and e n/k

Madanga ruficollis *Rothschild and Hartert* BURU MOUNTAIN WHITE-EYE Mts of NW Buru / no data

Lophozosterops pinaiae (*Stresemann*) PINAIAE WHITE-EYE Mts of C Ceram / tree-fern forest / n and e n/k

Lophozosterops goodfellowi (*Hartert*) GOODFELLOW'S WHITE-EYE Mts of Mindanao / no data

Lophozosterops squamiceps (*Hartert*) CELEBES MOUNTAIN WHITE-EYE Mts of Celebes / no data

Lophozosterops javanica (*Horsfield*) JAVAN WHITE-EYE Mts of Java and Bali / forest / e 2

Lophozosterops superciliaris (*Hartert*) EYEBROWED WHITE-EYE Mts of Flores and W Sumbawa / forest / 1 empty nest found / e n/k

Lophozosterops dohertyi *Hartert* DOHERTY'S WHITE-EYE Flores and mid-mountain forest of Sumbawa / e 2

Oculocincta squamifrons (*Sharpe*) PYGMY

GREY WHITE-EYE Hills and mts of western and northern Borneo / hill forest and scrub / n and e n/k

Heleia muelleri *Hartlaub* TIMOR WHITE-EYE Lowlands of W Timor / no data

Heleia crassirostris (*Hartert*) LARGE-BILLED WHITE-EYE Flores and Sumbawa lowlands/ edges of forest ? / e 2–3

Chlorocharis emiliae *Sharpe* OLIVE BLACK-EYE Mts of Sarawak and N Borneo (Sabah)/ forests / n with young found / e n/k

Hypocryptadius cinnamomeus *Hartert* CINNAMON WHITE-EYE Mts of Mindanao / no data [NB: The position of *Hypocryptadius* remains uncertain. It has been placed as a separate sub-family within the *Zosteropidae*. Others believe that it may not belong to the family at all]

NECTARINIIDAE Sunbirds Small birds with long, thin, strongly down-curved bills. Strongly sexually dimorphic, the males usually brightly coloured with metallic feathers (though some species are dull), the females generally dull. Feed mainly on insects and nectar, the tongue being tubular for sucking up the latter. Nest, purse-shaped, hanging from a twig, eggs 1–3, incubation about 13–14 days, fledging about 17 days.

Anthreptes gabonicus (*Hartlaub*) BROWN SUNBIRD Coasts of W Africa from Gambia to River Congo mouth / forest and mangrove/n tree over water / e 1–2

Anthreptes fraseri *Jardine and Selby* SCARLET-TUFTED SUNBIRD Fernando Po, and Sierra Leone to N Angola and Uganda / forest / n and e n/k (*A. axillaris* (Reichenow) is sometimes separated)

Anthreptes reichenowi *Gunning* PLAIN-BACKED SUNBIRD Lowland forests of parts of Mozambique, Rhodesia, S Kenya and NE Tanganyika / n tree / e 2

Anthreptes anchietae (*Bocage*) ANCHIETA'S SUNBIRD C Africa from Angola to SW Tanganyika / open woodland / n tree / e 2

Anthreptes simplex (*Müller*) PLAIN SUNBIRD S Burma, Malay Peninsula, Sumatra, Nias, Borneo and N Natuna Is

Anthreptes malacensis (*Scopoli*) PLAIN-THROATED SUNBIRD Southern SE Asia and through the Greater and Lesser Sundas to Philippines / open forest, mangrove and coco-nut plantations / insects and fruit / n tree / e 2

Anthreptes rhodolaema *Shelley* RED-THROATED SUNBIRD S Burma, Malay Peninsula, Sumatra, Borneo

Anthreptes singalensis (*Gmelin*) RUBY-CHEEKED SUNBIRD E Himalayas, Burma, Thailand, Malay Peninsula, Sumatra and western islands, Java, Borneo, Banguey, Billiton and N Natuna Is / open forest, scrub jungle / insects and nectar / n tree / e 2

Anthreptes longuemarei (*Lesson*) WESTERN VIOLET-BACKED SUNBIRD Much of Africa S of Sahara, S to Angola and Rhodesia / open woodland, savannah and bush / insects / n tree / e 2

Anthreptes orientalis *Hartlaub* KENYA VIOLET-BACKED SUNBIRD E Africa from S Sudan to NE Tanganyika / open woodland and bush / n tree / e 2

Anthreptes neglectus *Neumann* ULUGURU SUNBIRD SE Kenya to N Mozambique / forest/ insects / n tree / e n/k

Anthreptes auriantium *Verreaux and Verreaux* VIOLET-TAILED SUNBIRD S Nigeria to Angola and Ituri Forest / forested rivers / n tree, often over water / e 1–2

Anthreptes pallidigaster *Sclater and Moreau* AMARI SUNBIRD E Kenya to NE Tanganyika/ lowland forest / n and e n/k

Anthreptes pujoli *Berlioz* BERLIOZ'S SUNBIRD Type only, from 8°N, 9°30′W (in former French West Africa). Mackworth-Praed and Grant express doubt as to whether this can be a true species.

Anthreptes rectirostris (*Shaw*) GREEN SUNBIRD Fernando Po and Sierra Leone to N Angola, S Sudan, W Kenya and Tanganyika/ forest and open forest / insects and fruit / n tree/ e 2

Anthreptes collaris (*Vieillot*) COLLARED SUNBIRD Fernando Po and much of Africa S of Sahara / open forest near water / insects / n tree/ e 2–3

Anthreptes platurus (*Vieillot*) PYGMY SUNBIRD S Sahara belt from Senegal to N Uganda, Ethiopia and Egypt, SW Arabia / bush/ n bush or tree / e 2–3

Hypogramma hypogrammicum *Müller* PURPLE-NAPED SUNBIRD SE Asia, Sumatra, Borneo and N Natuna Is / forest

Nectarinia seimundi (*Ogilvie-Grant*) LITTLE GREEN SUNBIRD Fernando Po and Sierra Leone to N Angola and Uganda / forest clearings and secondary forest / n ? tree / e 2

CARDINALIDAE:
(left) *Passerina amoena,*
Lazuli Bunting

CARDINALIDAE:
Passerina versicolor,
Varied Bunting

CARDINALIDAE: *Passerina ciris,* Painted Bunting

Plate 256

CARDINALIDAE:
Cardinalis cardinalis,
Common Cardinal

CARDINALIDAE:
Passerina leclancherii,
Orange-breasted Bunting

Plate 257

Nectarinia batesi (*Ogilvie-Grant*) BATES' SUNBIRD Fernando Po and S Nigeria through Gabon and Congo to NW Zambia /secondary forest and cultivation/n bush/e 2

Nectarinia olivacea (*Smith*) OLIVE SUNBIRD Fernando Po and much of Africa S of Sahara (except extreme S)/damp forest and moor/n tree/e 2

Nectarinia ursulae (*Alexander*) URSULA'S SUNBIRD Fernando Po and mts of Cameroon/forest/nectar and insects/n tree/e 1–2

Nectarinia veroxii (*Smith*) MOUSE-COLOURED SUNBIRD Zanzibar and coastal E Africa from Somalia to E Cape Province/coastal bush and forest fringes/n attached to creeper/e 2

Nectarinia balfouri (*Sclater and Hartlaub*) SOCOTRA SUNBIRD Socotra/no data

Nectarinia reichenbachii *Hartlaub* REICHENBACH'S SUNBIRD Ghana to Congo basin/forest clearings and cultivation / nectar and insects/e 1

Nectarinia hartlaubii *Hartlaub* HARTLAUB'S SUNBIRD Principé /lowland forest and cultivation/insects/n tree (1 known)/e n/k

Nectarinia newtonii (*Bocage*) NEWTON'S SUNBIRD São Thomé/ubiquitous/n tree/e 2

Nectarinia thomensis *Bocage* GIANT SUNBIRD São Thomé/forest/n tree/e 1–2

Nectarinia oritis (*Reichenow*) CAMEROON SUNBIRD Mts of Cameroon and Fernando Po

Nectarinia alinae (*Jackson*) BLUE-HEADED SUNBIRD Mts of C Africa in the vicinity of Lakes Albert, Edward, Kivu and Tanganyika/mountain forest /n hanging ferns/e 2 (1 nest known)

Nectarinia bannermani *Grant and Mackworth Praed* BANNERMAN'S SUNBIRD C Angola to NW Zambia and SW Congo/no data (*N. sororia* Ripley is the ♀)

Nectarinia verticalis (*Latham*) GREEN-HEADED SUNBIRD Upper Guinea and Cameroons to N Angola, S Sudan and NE Zambia /forest and wooded riverbanks/n bush/e 2

Nectarinia cyanolaema *Jardine and Fraser* BLUE-THROATED SUNBIRD Fernando Po and Sierra Leone to N Angola and Uganda /forest clearings/seeds/n tree/e 2

Nectarinia fuliginosa (*Shaw*) CARMELITE SUNBIRD Coastal areas from Liberia to N Angola/open country and cultivation/n tree/e 2

Nectarinia rubescens (*Vieillot*) GREEN-THROATED SUNBIRD Fernando Po and Cameroons to N Angola, S Sudan and NW Tanganyika/forest and open country /n tree/e 2

Nectarinia amethystina (*Shaw*) AMETHYST SUNBIRD E and S Africa from S Somaliland S and W to Angola and Cape / bush and open woodland/n tree/e 2

Nectarinia senegalensis (*L*) SCARLET-CHESTED SUNBIRD Much of Africa S of Sahara (except extreme S)/almost ubiquitous/n tree/e 2

Nectarinia adelberti (*Gervais*) BUFF-THROATED SUNBIRD Sierra Leone to SE Nigeria/1 nest known, containing young

Nectarinia zeylonica (*L*) PURPLE-RUMPED SUNBIRD Ceylon, peninsular India and Bangladesh /scrub and secondary jungle/insects and nectar/n tree/e 2–3/I ♀ 14–15/F 16–17

Nectarinia minima (*Sykes*) SMALL SUNBIRD Western Ghats of India (? Ceylon)/forest and plantations/nectar and insects/n tree/e 2

Nectarinia sperata (*L*) PURPLE-THROATED SUNBIRD Assam, Bangladesh, SE Asia, Greater Sunda Is and adjacent small islands, Philippines, Basilan and Sulu Archipelago / forest and cultivation, usually swampy / nectar (the Philippine races appear to be complicated, and some authorities separate *N. henkei* (Meyer))

Nectarinia sericea (*Lesson*) BLACK SUNBIRD Celebes and adjacent small islands, Moluccas, New Guinea, Bismarck Archipelago and Papuan Is/forest/insects and nectar/n tree/e 1

Nectarinia calcostetha *Jardine* MACKLOT'S SUNBIRD Southern SE Asia, through greater Sundas and adjacent small islands to Palawan/mangrove forest

Nectarinia dussumieri *Hartlaub* SEYCHELLES SUNBIRD Seychelles / forest and open country/insects and nectar/n tree/e 1

Nectarinia lotenia (*L*) MAROON-BREASTED or LONG-BILLED SUNBIRD Ceylon and peninsular India/forest and cultivation/nectar and insects/n tree/e 2/I ♀ 15

Nectarinia jugularis (*L*) OLIVE-BACKED SUNBIRD SE Asia, Hainan, and much of Indonesia (except Philippines) to New Guinea, Bismarck Archipelago and Solomons; also NE Queensland/forest, scrub and mangrove/nectar and insects/n tree or shrub/e 2

Nectarinia buettikoferi (*Hartert*) SUMBA SUNBIRD Sumba

Nectarinia solaris *Temminck* TIMOR SUNBIRD Sumbawa, Flores, Lombok, Alor, Timor, Wetar and Samau

Nectarinia asiatica (*Latham*) PURPLE SUNBIRD Oman, Iran through India and Ceylon to Thailand and Indo-Chinese peninsula/ forest, thornscrub and cultivation / nectar and insects / n tree / e 1–3 / I ♀ 14–15 / F 13–17

Nectarinia souimanga (*Gmelin*) SOUIMANGA SUNBIRD Madagascar and the Aldabra group/ forest and scrub / insects and nectar / n tree / e 2

Nectarinia humbloti (*Milne-Edwards and Oustalet*) HUMBLOT'S SUNBIRD Grand Comoro and Moheli / dry thickets / insects and nectar/ n tree / e ? 1–2

Nectarinia comorensis (*Peters*) ANJOUAN SUNBIRD Anjouan forest and scrub / insects and nectar / n tree / e 1

Nectarinia coquerellii *Hartlaub* MAYOTTE SUNBIRD Mayotte / forest and open country/ insects and nectar / n tree / e n/k / Benson, 'Birds of the Comoro Islands', *Ibis* 103b (1960), p 96 quotes this as *N. coquereli* (Verreaux)

Nectarinia venusta (*Shaw and Nodder*) VARIABLE SUNBIRD Equatorial belt of Africa/ cultivation, savannah and open woodland / n bush / e 2

Nectarinia talatala (*Smith*) WHITE-BREASTED SUNBIRD S Angola and SW Africa to S Tanganyika and Natal / acacia bush / n shrub / e 2

Nectarinia oustaleti *Bocage* ANGOLA SUNBIRD Angola to N Zambia / no data

Nectarinia fusca (*Vieillot*) DUSKY SUNBIRD Benguella to Little Namaqualand and Orange Free State

Nectarinia chalybea (*L*) SOUTHERN DOUBLE-COLLARED SUNBIRD S Africa N to S Congo and Tanganyika / hill forest / n tree or bush / e 2

Nectarinia afra (*L*) GREATER DOUBLE-COLLARED SUNBIRD Africa from Uganda to W Cape Province / n shrub / e 1

Nectarinia mediocris (*Shelley*) EASTERN DOUBLE-COLLARED SUNBIRD E Africa from Kenya to Mozambique / mountain forest and moor / n tree or shrub / e 2

Nectarinia preussi (*Reichenow*) PREUSS'S DOUBLE-COLLARED SUNBIRD Fernando Po; mts from Cameroons to S Sudan and Kenya / n tree/ e 2 [*Cinnyris reichenowi* Sharpe, preoccupied by *Nectarinia reichenowi* (Fischer) is a synonym of *Nectarinia preussi kikuyensis*]

Nectarinia neergaardi *Grant* NEERGAARD'S SUNBIRD Coastal areas of S Mozambique to Zululand / bush / n bush / e 2

Nectarinia chloropygia *Jardine* OLIVE-BELLIED SUNBIRD Fernando Po and Sierra Leone to Angola, Tanganyika and S Sudan/ scrub and forest edges / n shrub / e 2

Nectarinia minulla (*Reichenow*) TINY SUNBIRD Fernando Po and Gold Coast through Congo to Ituri Forest / scrub and forest edges/ n tree / e 2

Nectarinia regia (*Reichenow*) REGAL SUNBIRD High mountains of C Africa / forest / n attached to fern fronds / e 1

Nectarinia loveridgei (*Hartert*) LOVERIDGE'S SUNBIRD Mts of E Tanganyika / rain forest / n among moss / e n/k

Nectarinia rockefelleri (*Chapin*) ROCKEFELLER'S SUNBIRD High mountains of E Congo basin and NW of Lake Tanganyika/no data

Nectarinia violacea (*L*) ORANGE-BREASTED SUNBIRD Cape Province / hill scrub and steep open hillsides / n bush / e 1–2

Nectarinia habessinica *Ehrenberg* SHINING SUNBIRD SW and W Arabia, NE Sudan through Ethiopia to N Kenya and N Uganda / forest, savannah and coconut groves / n tree / e 1

Nectarinia bouvieri (*Shelley*) ORANGE-TUFTED SUNBIRD Scattered localities in WC and EC Africa / open bush and scrubby hillsides / n tree/ e n/k

Nectarinia osea (*Bonaparte*) PALESTINE SUNBIRD or NORTHERN ORANGE-TUFTED SUNBIRD Lake Chad to Darfur, S Sudan and N Congo: S Syria to Palestine, occurring through Arabia, but perhaps only in winter / little known/ n shrub / e 2

Nectarinia cuprea (*Shaw*) COPPER SUNBIRD Africa S of Sahara S to Rhodesia and Angola/ open woodland and forest clearings / n tree (often overhanging an anthill) / e 2

Nectarinia tacazze (*Stanley*) TACAZZE SUNBIRD Ethiopia S to W Kenya and NE Tanganyika / open country on mountains / n shrub / e 1

Nectarinia bocagii *Shelley* BOCAGE'S SUNBIRD W highlands of C and SE Angola, and Kwango district of Congo / woodland and marsh / n tree/ e 2

Nectarinia purpureiventris (*Reichenow*) PURPLE-BREASTED SUNBIRD Mts from Ruwenzori to Kivu and north end of Lake Tanganyika/ mountain valleys, feeding on flowers of *Symphonia* tree / n tree / e 1

Nectarinia shelleyi (*Alexander*) SHELLEY'S

CARDINALIDAE:
Passerina cyanea,
(=P. brissonii),
Indigo Bunting—female (left)
and male (right)

CARDINALIDAE:
Pheucticus aureoventris,
Black-bellied Grosbeak,
Black-backed Grosbeak

Plate 258

THRAUPIDAE:
Tangara cyanicollis,
Blue-necked Tanager

THRAUPIDAE:
Cyanerpes
cyaneus,
Blue
Honeycreeper,
Red-legged
Honeycreeper

Plate 259

SUNBIRD S Tanganyika to E Zambia and N Mozambique / open woodland / n tree / e 2

Nectarinia mariquensis (*Smith*) MARIQUA SUNBIRD Ethiopia to Natal and SW Africa / scrub and acacia / n shrub / e 2

Nectarinia bifasciata (*Shaw*) PURPLE-BANDED SUNBIRD Parts of Africa from Gabon and Somalia to N Angola and Mozambique / bush and mangrove / n tree / e 1–2

Nectarinia pembae (*Reichenow*) PEMBA SUNBIRD Pemba Is (? E Kenya) / n tree / e 2

Nectarinia chalcomelas (*Reichenow*) VIOLET-BREASTED SUNBIRD Juba River area of Somalia S through lowlands of E Kenya / no data

Nectarinia coccinigastra (*Latham*) SPLENDID SUNBIRD Senegal to SW Sudan, Congo and Gabon / savannah and cultivation / n tree / e 1–2

Nectarinia erythrocerca *Hartlaub* RED-CHESTED SUNBIRD S Sudan to S of Lake Victoria and N end of Lake Tanganyika / edges of lakes and rivers, and habitation / n shrub or bush / e 1–2

Nectarinia congensis *van Oort* CONGO BLACK-BELLIED SUNBIRD Parts of Upper Congo / forest / n over water (1 known) / e n/k

Nectarinia pulchella (*L*) BEAUTIFUL SUNBIRD Senegal across dry belt to Ethiopia and Nile Valley, and S to Tanganyika. Also Aïr Massif in S Sahara / cultivation (etc) / n tree / e 1–2

Nectarinia nectarinioides (*Richmond*) SMALLER BLACK-BELLIED SUNBIRD Lowlands of E Kenya to NE Tanganyika, Juba River area of Somalia / cultivation (etc) / n tree / e 1–2

Nectarinia famosa (*L*) MALACHITE SUNBIRD Highlands of E Africa from S Sudan to Cape Province / moorland and bamboo scrub / n off ground / e 1–2

Nectarinia johnstoni *Shelley* SCARLET-TUFTED MALACHITE SUNBIRD Mts from W Kenya to S Tanganyika and E Congo / alpine zone from 5,500ft (1,700m) to limit of flora / n shrub / e 1–2

Nectarinia notata (*Müller*) MADAGASCAR GREEN SUNBIRD Madagascar, Moheli and Grand Comoro / forest and scrub / insects and nectar / n and e n/k

Nectarinia johannae (*Verreaux and Verreaux*) MADAME JOANNA VERREAUX'S SUNBIRD Sierra Leone to Lower Congo, Ituri Forest, Kasai and NW Corner of Lake Tanganyika / forest / n tree / e 2

Nectarinia superba (*Shaw*) SUPERB SUNBIRD Sierra Leone to Angola, Congo and Uganda /

forest / n tree / e 1–2

Nectarinia kilimensis *Shelley* BRONZE SUNBIRD Highlands of C Africa from E Congo to W Kenya, W Tanganyika and Rhodesia; highlands of C Angola / open woodland and habitation / n bush / e 1

Nectarinia reichenowi (*Fischer*) GOLDEN-WINGED SUNBIRD Highlands of Kenya, Uganda, N Tanganyika and E Congo / open country, bush and cultivation / n bush / e 1

Aethopyga primigenius (*Hachisuka*) HACHISUKA'S SUNBIRD Mts of Mindanao

Aethopyga boltoni *Mearns* APO SUNBIRD Mts of Mindanao

Aethopyga flagrans *Oustalet* FLAMING SUNBIRD Luzon, Catanduanas, Panay, Guimaras and Negros

Aethopyga pulcherrima *Sharpe* LOVELIEST SUNBIRD Luzon, Bohol, Samar, Leyte, Dinagat, Mindanao and Basilan

Aethopyga duyvenbodei (*Schlegel*) DUYVENBODE'S SUNBIRD Sanghir Is

Aethopyga shelleyi *Sharpe* LOVELY SUNBIRD Philippines, Sulu Is, Balabac and Palawan

Aethopyga gouldiae (*Vigors*) GOULD'S SUNBIRD Himalayas, northern SE Asia and W China N to Kansu / forest / nectar and insects / n bush / e 2–3

Aethopyga nipalensis (*Hodgson*) GREEN-TAILED SUNBIRD Himalayas, northern SE Asia and Yunnan / forest and habitation / nectar / n tree or bush / e 3

Aethopyga eximia (*Horsfield*) KUHL'S SUNBIRD Mts of Java

Aethopyga christinae *Swinhoe* FORK-TAILED SUNBIRD S China, Vietnam and Hainan / forest / n tree / e 2–4

Aethopyga saturata (*Hodgson*) BLACK-THROATED SUNBIRD Himalayas, SE Asia and SE Yunnan / forest / nectar / n tree / e 2–3

Aethopyga siparaja (*Raffles*) YELLOW-BACKED SUNBIRD Himalayas and W India; SE Asia and S Yunnan, Sumatra, Borneo, Java, Celebes and adjacent small islands; C Philippines / forest and cultivation / nectar and insects / n tree / e 2–3

Aethopyga mystacalis (*Temminck*) SCARLET SUNBIRD Malay Peninsula, Sumatra, Borneo and Java / forest / nectar (? insects) / n tree

Aethopyga ignicauda (*Hodgson*) FIRETAILED SUNBIRD Himalayas, N Burma, Sikang, and S Yunnan / forest and scrub above timberline / nectar and insects / n bush / e 2–3

Arachnothera longirostra (*Latham*) LITTLE SPIDERHUNTER SW India, E Himalayas, SE Asia, Sumatra and W Sumatran Is, Java, Bali, Borneo, Natuna Is, Palawan, Basilan, Samar, Leyte, Bohol and Mindanao / forest and cultivation / nectar, insects and spiders / n attached to underside of large leaf (eg banana) / e 2

Arachnothera crassirostris (*Reichenbach*) THICK-BILLED SPIDERHUNTER Malay Peninsula, Sumatra and Borneo / lowland forest / insects/ n underside of leaf / e ?2

Arachnothera robusta *Müller and Schlegel* LONG-BILLED SPIDERHUNTER Malay Peninsula, Sumatra, Java and Borneo / forest / insects and spiders / n underside of leaf / e 2

Arachnothera flavigaster (*Eyton*) SPECTACLED SPIDERHUNTER Malay Peninsula, Sumatra, Borneo (? Indo-China) / cultivation and secondary jungle / n under leaf

Arachnothera chrysogenys (*Temminck*) YELLOW-EARED SPIDERHUNTER S Burma, Malay Peninsula, Sumatra, Java, Borneo and some adjacent small islands / lowland forest / fruit, seeds and spiders / n and e ? n/k

Arachnothera clarae *Blasius* BARE-FACED SPIDERHUNTER Samar, (? Leyte) Mindanao

Arachnothera affinis (*Horsfield*) GRAY-BREASTED SPIDERHUNTER S Burma, Malay Peninsula (? Cochin China), Sumatra, Borneo, Java, Bali / forest and garden / spiders, banana flowers and seeds / n under leaf / e 2

Arachnothera everetti (*Sharpe*) EVERETT'S SPIDERHUNTER Mts of N and C Borneo / the status of this form is uncertain and it is sometimes treated as a race of *A. affinis*

Arachnothera magna *Hodgson* STREAKED SPIDERHUNTER N India through much of SE Asia (except Malay Peninsula) and Yunnan/ forest and abandoned cultivation / nectar, insects and spiders / n under leaf / e 2–3 / I ♂♀

Arachnothera juliae *Sharpe* WHITEHEAD'S SPIDERHUNTER High mountains of northern Borneo / moss forest / insects, berries and ? nectar / n and e n/k

PROMEROPIDAE Sugarbirds The Sugarbirds are a genus of Honeyeater-like birds confined to South Africa and largely associated with bushes of the family Proteaceae. They are sometimes treated as a separate family and sometimes as a sub-family of the Meliphagidae. Three forms are known, sometimes united in one species, sometimes split between two. Feed on nectar and insects, the nest is in the fork of a bush, the eggs 2 in number.

Promerops cafer (*L*) CAPE SUGARBIRD Cape Province

Promerops gurneyi *Verreaux* GURNEY'S SUGARBIRD S Africa (except extreme S) N to Rhodesia

MELIPHAGIDAE Honeyeaters A diverse group of both brightly and dull-coloured birds with long, pointed wings and slender, pointed down-curved bills. The nest is an open cup in a tree, and most species lay 2–3 eggs. About 160 species in the Australia, New Zealand and SW Pacific areas.

Timeliopsis fulvigula (*Schlegel*) MOUNTAIN STRAIGHT-BILLED HONEYEATER Mts of New Guinea / undergrowth of mid-mountain forest/ no other data

Timeliopsis griseigula (*Schlegel*) LOWLAND STRAIGHT-BILLED HONEYEATER Lowlands of New Guinea / forest / no data

Melilestes megarhynchus (*Gray*) LONG-BILLED HONEYEATER Japen and N New Guinea/ forest

Melilestes bougainvillei (*Mayr*) BOUGAINVILLE HONEYEATER Bougainville/ mountains

Toxorhamphus novaeguinea (*Lesson*) YELLOW-BILLED LONGBILL W New Guinea, Japen, W Papuan and Aru Is / forest / nectar and insects / n and e ? n/k

Toxorhamphus poliopterus (*Sharpe*) SCALY-CHINNED LONGBILL Mts of New Guinea / forest/ nectar and insects / n shrub / e 1

Oedistoma iliolophum (*Salvadori*) GREY-BELLIED LONGBILL Waigeu, New Guinea, islands in Geelvink Bay, D'Entrecasteaux Archipelago / forest / insects and nectar / n ? tree/ e 1 [This species is placed in *Toxorhamphus* by Rand and Gilliard]

Oedistoma pygmaeum *Salvadori* PYGMY HONEYEATER Waigeu, Misol, New Guinea and D'Entrecasteaux Archipelago / forest / insects, nectar and spiders

Glycichaera fallax *Salvadori* WHITE-EYED HONEYEASTER W New Guinea, Japen, Waigeu, Batanta, Misol and Aru Is; an isolated race occurs on Claudie River, Cape York Peninsula, Australia / forest / insects / n and e n/k

Lichmera lombokia (*Mathews*) LOMBOK HONEYEATER Lombok, Flores and Sumbawa

Lichmera argentauris (*Finsch*) OLIVE

Plate 260

ICTERIDAE:
Icterus icterus,
Troupial

ICTERIDAE:
Xanthocephalus xanthocephalus,
Yellow-headed Blackbird

Opposite:
THRAUPIDAE:
Cyanerpes cyaneus,
Blue Honeycreeper,
Red-legged Honeycreeper

Plate 261

HONEYEATER Waigeu, Misol, Schildpad, Halmahera, Damar, Gebe and Lusaolate/ Ripley found it by blossoms of coconuts and papayas in the Schildpad islands/no other data

Lichmera indistincta (*Vigors and Horsfield*) AUSTRALIAN BROWN HONEYEATER Australia, Aru Is and Lesser Sunda Is/forest, mangrove, savannah and cultivation/insects and nectar/ n tree or bush/e 2

Lichmera incana (*Latham*) SILVER-EARED HONEYEATER New Caledonia, Loyalty Is and New Hebrides

Lichmera alboauricularis (*Ramsay*) WHITE-EARED HONEYEATER Lowlands of New Guinea between Idenbury River and Rama River, and islets in Bioto Creek, Hall Sound, SE New Guinea / coconut palms and tall grass / insects/ n attached to tall grass stems/e ? n/k

Lichmera squamata (*Salvadori*) BANDA SEA HONEYEATER Kuv Is, Godan Is, Tenimber Is and islands in S Banda Sea

Lichmera deningeri (*Stresemann*) BURU HONEYEATER Mts of Buru

Lichmera monticola (*Stresemann*) CERAM HONEYEATER Mts of Ceram

Lichmera flavicans (*Vieillot*) TIMOR HONEYEATER Timor

Lichmera notabilis (*Finsch*) WETAR HONEYEATER Wetar

Lichmera cockerelli (*Gould*) BRUSH-THROATED HONEYEATER Northern Cape York Peninsula/ tee-tree swamps and riverside thickets / insects and nectar/n bush or tree/e 2

Myzomela blasii (*Salvadori*) AMBOINA MYZOMELA Ceram and Amboina

Myzomela albigula *Hartert* WHITE-CHINNED MYZOMELA Louisiade Archipelago and Rossel Is/no data

Myzomela cineracea *Sclater* UMBOI MYZOMELA New Britain and Rook Is

Myzomela eques (*Lesson and Garnet*) RED-SPOT MYZOMELA New Guinea, Waigeu, Salawati and Misol/forest

Myzomela obscura *Gould* DUSKY MYZOMELA N Queensland, coastal N Territory, Melville Is, Moluccas and Biak/forest, swamp and mangrove/ insects and nectar/n tree/e 2

Myzomela cruentata *Meyer* RED MYZOMELA New Guinea, Japen and Bismark Archipelago/ mid-mountain forest

Myzomela nigrita *Gray* BLACK MYZOMELA New Guinea, and adjacent islands, including

the small, but not the main, islands of the Bismark Archipelago /forest

Myzomela pulchella *Salvadori* BEAUTIFUL MYZOMELA New Ireland

Myzomela kuehni *Rothschild* KÜHN'S MYZOMELA Wetar

Myzomela erythrocephala *Gould* RED-HEADED MYZOMELA Coasts of N Australia and S New Guinea, Aru Is, Sumba forest and mangrove/insects and nectar/n tree/e 2

Myzomela adolphinae *Salvadori* ADOLPH MYZOMELA Mts of New Guinea/mid-mountain forest

Myzomela sanguinolenta (*Latham*) SCARLET MYZOMELA Celebes, Saleyer, Djampea, Batjan, Ceram, Buru, Tenimber Is, Babber Is, Banda Is, coast of E Australia, New Caledonia/forest, savannah and mangrove / insects and nectar/ n tree/e 2

Myzomela cardinalis (*Gmelin*) CARDINAL MYZOMELA Loyalty Is, New Hebrides, Samoa, Torres and Santa Cruz Is, Solomon Is, Palau Is, Marianas and Caroline Is /open woodland and cultivation/n tree/e 1–2

Myzomela chermesina *Gray* ROTUMA MYZOMELA Rotuma Is

Myzomela sclateri *Forbes* SCLATER'S MYZOMELA Dampier and small islands of the Bismarck Archipelago

Myzomela lafargei *Pucheran* SCARLET-NAPED MYZOMELA Solomon Is: Buka, Bougainville, Shortland, Fauro, Choiseul and Santa Isabel

Myzomela melanocephala *Ramsay* GUADALCANAL MYZOMELA Guadalcanal, Savo and Florida (Solomons)

Myzomela eichhorni *Rothschild and Hartert* EICHHORN'S MYZOMELA Tetipari, Rendova, Vangunu, New Georgia, Kulambangra, Gizo, Ganongga, Vella Lavella and Baga (Solomons)

Myzomela malaitae *Mayr* MALAITA MYZOMELA Malaita (Solomons)

Myzomela tristrami *Ramsay* TRISTRAM'S MYZOMELA San Christobal, Ugi and Santa Ana (Solomons)

Myzomela jugularis *Peale* ORANGE-BREASTED MYZOMELA Fiji Is /forest clearings and cultivation /nectar and insects /n bush /e 2 /I c14

Myzomela erythromelas *Salvadori* NEW BRITAIN MYZOMELA New Britain

Myzomela vulnerata (*Müller*) TIMOR MYZOMELA Timor

Myzomela rosenbergii *Schlegel* BLACK-AND

RED HONEYEATER Mts of New Guinea and Goodenough Is / forest / n tree / e 2

Certhionyx niger (*Gould*) BLACK HONEYEATER Drier parts of Australia / highly nomadic / scrub and savannah / insects and nectar / n bush or tree / e 2

Certhionyx variegatus *Lesson* PIED HONEYEATER Arid interior of Australia / highly nomadic / scrub and savannah / insects and nectar / n tree or bush / e 2–3

Meliphaga mimikae (*Ogilvie-Grant*) LARGE SPOT-BREASTED MELIPHAGA Scattered localities in New Guinea / forest / n and e n/k

Meliphaga montana (*Salvadori*) MOUNTAIN MELIPHAGA Mts of New Guinea, Japen and Batanta / forest / n shrub / e 1

Meliphaga orientalis (*Meyer*) SMALL SPOT-BREASTED MELIPHAGA Waigeu and mts of New Guinea / forest

Meliphaga albonotata (*Salvadori*) WHITE-MARKED MELIPHAGA Parts of the lowlands of New Guinea / forest

Meliphaga aruensis (*Sharpe*) PUFF-BACKED MELIPHAGA New Guinea, Aru, W Papuan Is, D'Entrecasteaux Archipelago, Trobriand Is, islands in Geelvink Bay / forest / insects, nectar and fruit / n shrub / e 1–2

Meliphaga analoga (*Reichenbach*) MIMIC MELIPHAGA New Guinea, Aru and W Papuan Is, and islands in Geelvink Bay / forest / insects, nectar and fruit / n bush / e 2

Meliphaga vicina (*Rothschild and Hartert*) TAGULA HONEYEATER Tagula (Sudest) Is (Louisiade Archipelago)

Meliphaga gracilis (*Gould*) GRACEFUL HONEYEATER Aru Is, southern New Guinea and N Queensland / rain forest and open forest / fruit, insects and nectar / n tree / e 2

Meliphaga notata (*Gould*) LESSER LEWIN HONEYEATER Cape York Peninsula and islands in Torres Strait / forest / fruit, insects and nectar

Meliphaga flavirictus (*Salvadori*) YELLOW-GAPED MELIPHAGA New Guinea / lowland forest / insects

Meliphaga lewinii (*Swainson*) GREATER LEWIN HONEYEATER E Australia from Victoria to Cooktown / rain forest / fruit, insects and nectar / n tree or shrub / e 2

Meliphaga flava (*Gould*) YELLOW HONEYEATER Cape York Peninsula and coastal Queensland / open forest / insects and nectar / n tree or bush / e 2

Meliphaga albilineata (*White*) WHITE-STRIPED HONEYEATER Alligator and King Rivers, N Australia / deep wooded sandstone gorges / fruit and seeds / n tree / e n/k

Meliphaga virescens (*Vieillot*) SINGING HONEYEATER Australia / open forest and savannah / fruit, insects, nectar and (?) eggs / n tree / e 2–3

Meliphaga versicolor (*Gould*) VARIED HONEYEATER Coasts of New Guinea, W Papuan islands, islands in Geelvink Bay, D'Entrecasteaux Archipelago, islands in Torres Strait and E Cape York Peninsula / forest and mangrove

Meliphaga fasciogularis (*Gould*) MANGROVE HONEYEATER Mangrove belt of E Queensland and N New South Wales / mangrove / n tree / e 2–3

Meliphaga inexpectata (*Hartert*) GUADALCANAL HONEYEATER Guadalcanal Is

Meliphaga fusca *Gould* FUSCOUS HONEYEATER SE New Guinea and much of Australia / open forest / insects and nectar / n tree / e 2–3

Meliphaga plumula (*Gould*) YELLOW-FRONTED HONEYEATER Australia / dry woodland and scrub / insects and nectar / n bush / e 2

Meliphaga chrysops (*Latham*) YELLOW-FACED HONEYEATER SE Australia and coast of E Australia / forest and woodland / insects, fruit and nectar / n bush / e 2

Meliphaga cratitia (*Gould*) PURPLE-GAPED HONEYEATER S parts of Australia / mallee scrub and habitation / insects and nectar / n bush / e 2

Meliphaga keartlandi (*North*) GREY-HEADED HONEYEATER N part of interior of Australia / gullies in rocky hills of arid savannah / insects and nectar / n tree or bush / e 2

Meliphaga pencillata *Gould* WHITE-PLUMED HONEYEATER Much of E, S and W Australia / woodland / insects and nectar / n tree / e 2–3

Meliphaga ornata (*Gould*) MALLEE HONEYEATER S parts of Australia / woodland and mallee scrub / insects and nectar / n bush / e 2–3

Meliphaga reticulata *Temminck* TIMOR MELIPHAGA Timor

Meliphaga leucotis (*Latham*) WHITE-EARED MELIPHAGA S parts of Australia / open forest, mallee and heathland / insects and nectar / n tree or bush / e 2–3

Meliphaga flavicollis (*Vieillot*) YELLOW-THROATED HONEYEATER Tasmania and islands in Bass Strait / open forest and habitation /

FRINGILLIDAE:
Fringilla coelebs,
Chaffinch

FRINGILLIDAE:
Acanthis flavirostris,
Twite

Plate 262

FRINGILLIDAE:
Carduelis notata,
Neotropical Black-headed
Siskin

FRINGILLIDAE:
Serinus serinus,
Serin

Plate 263

insects and nectar/n bush/e 2–3

Meliphaga melanops (*Latham*) YELLOW-TUFTED HONEYEATER SE Australia/open forest and woodland/insects, fruit and nectar/n bush or stump/e 2

Meliphaga cassidix (*Gould*) HELMETED HONEYEATER S Victoria near Melbourne, rapidly declining, hybridises with *melanops*/ creekside trees and thickets in hill country

Meliphaga unicolor (*Gould*) WHITE-GAPED HONEYEATER N tropical Australia/mangrove and riverine forest / fruit, nectar and insects/ n tree/e 2

Meliphaga flaviventer (*Lesson and Garnot*) BUFF-BREASTED HONEYEATER W Papuan islands, New Guinea, Aru Is, Japen, D'Entrecasteaux Archipelago and Trobriand Is, N Cape York Peninsula/mangrove and forest/fruit, insects and nectar/n tree/e 2

Meliphaga polygramma (*Gray*) SPOTTED HONEYEATER New Guinea and W Papuan Is/ forest

Meliphaga macleayana (*Ramsay*) YELLOW-STREAKED HONEYEATER Cairns area of N Queensland/rain forest/fruit, nectar and insects/ n tree/e 2

Meliphaga frenata (*Ramsay*) MOUNTAIN HONEYEATER NE Queensland/rain forest/fruit, insects and nectar/n tree/e 2

Meliphaga subfrenata (*Salvadori*) BLACK-THROATED HONEYEATER Mts of New Guinea/ forest

Meliphaga obscura (*De Vis*) OBSCURE HONEYEATER Mts of New Guinea / forest/ insects and nectar/n shrub/e 2

Oreornis chrysogenys *Van Oort* ORANGE-CHEEKED HONEYEATER Upper slopes of Oranje Mts, C New Guinea/upper edge of forest and scrub in grassland above timberline / fruit, insects and seeds/n tree-ferns/e 1

Foulehaio carunculata (*Gmelin*) WATTLED HONEYEATER Samoa, Tonga and Fiji Is (except Kandavu) / forest and habitation / nectar, insects and small reptiles

Foulehaio provocator (*Layard*) KANDAVU HONEYEATER Kandavu (Fiji) feeds on honey and insects obtained from Erythrina trees (Layard)

Cleptornis marchei (*Oustalet*) GOLDEN HONEYEATER Saipan Is (Marianas)/deep forest/ n tree/e 2–3

Apalopteron familiare (*Kittlitz*) WHITE-EYED HONEYEATER Bonin Is

Melithreptus brevirostris (*Vigors and Horsfield*) BROWN-HEADED HONEYEATER S parts of Australia / open forest, scrub and habitation/ insects and nectar/n tree or bush/e 2

Melithreptus lunatus (*Vieillot*) WHITE-NAPED HONEYEATER E Australia / open forest and woodland / insects and nectar / n tree or bush/ e 2–3

Melithreptus albogularis *Gould* WHITE-THROATED HONEYEATER N and E Australia, lowlands of New Guinea / open forest and woodland/insects and nectar/n tree or bush/ e 2–3

Melithreptus affinis (*Lesson*) BLACK-HEADED HONEYEATER Tasmania and islands in Bass Strait/open forest and woodland/insects

Melithreptus gularis (*Gould*) BLACK-CHINNED HONEYEATER SE Australia/forest/insects and nectar/n tree or bush/e 2–3

Melithreptus laetior (*Gould*) GOLDEN-BACKED HONEYEATER Parts of interior of Australia/e 1–2

Melithreptus validirostris (*Gould*) STRONG-BILLED HONEYEATER Tasmania and islands in Bass Strait/forest/insects

Entomyzon cyanotis (*Latham*) BLUE-FACED HONEYEATER Parts of NW, NE and SE Australia /open forest/insects, fruit and nectar/ n tree /e 2–3

Notiomystis cincta (*Du Bus*) STITCHBIRD Little Barrier Is, New Zealand (formerly on North Is and Great Barrier Is)/forest/nectar/ n tree/e 3–5

Pycnopygius ixoides (*Salvadori*) NEW GUINEA BROWN HONEYEATER New Guinea/ lowland forest/fruit and nectar

Pycnopygius cinereus (*Sclater*) GREY HONEYEATER Mts of New Guinea/forest/fruit and nectar

Pycnopygius stictocephalus (*Salvadori*) STREAKED-CAPPED HONEYEATER Salawati, Aru Is and lowlands of New Guinea/lowland forest/ fruit and nectar

Philemon meyeri *Salvadori* MEYER'S FRIARBIRD E New Guinea/forest/insects

Philemon brassi *Rand* BRASS'S FRIARBIRD Upper Mamberano basin, NW New Guinea known only from a small area of flooded tall open cane grass and dense second-growth trees around the end of the Idenburg River/insects and fruit

Philemon citreogularis (*Gould*) LITTLE

FRIARBIRD E and N Australia, S New Guinea, Kisser, Letti and Moa Is (Banda Sea) / open forest and woodland / fruit, nectar and insects / n tree or bush / e 2–4

Philemon inornatus (*Gray*) TIMOR FRIARBIRD Timor

Philemon gilolensis (*Bonaparte*) GILOLO FRIARBIRD Batjan, Halmahera and Morotai

Philemon fuscicapillus (*Wallace*) MOROTAI FRIARBIRD Batjan, Halmahera and Morotai

Philemon subcorniculatus (*Hombron and Jacquinot*) CERAM FRIARBIRD Ceram

Philemon moluccensis (*Gmelin*) MOLUCCAN FRIARBIRD Buru, Tenimber and Kei Is

Philemon buceroides (*Swainson*) SANDSTONE FRIARBIRD Lesser Sunda Is and coastal belt of N Territory (Australia) / dense thickets in sandstone gorges

Philemon gordoni *Mathews* MELVILLE ISLAND FRIARBIRD Melville Is and mangrove belt of N Territory / no other data / see Macdonald, *Birds of Australia*, p 426 for discussion

Philemon novaeguineae (*Müller*) LEATHERHEAD New Guinea, W Papuan and Aru Is, islands in Geelvink Bay, E Papuan Is, N Queensland / forest, savannah and habitation, mainly in lowlands / fruit and insects / n tree / e 2–3

Philemon cockerelli *Sclater* BISMARCK FRIARBIRD New Britain and Rook Is

Philemon eichhorni *Rothschild and Hartert* EICHHORN'S FRIARBIRD New Ireland

Philemon albitorques *Sclater* ADMIRALTY FRIARBIRD Manus Is (Admiralty Is)

Philemon argenticeps (*Gould*) SILVER-CROWNED FRIARBIRD N Australia and Melville Is / open forest and woodland / fruit, nectar and insects / n tree / e 2

Philemon corniculatus (*Latham*) NOISY FRIARBIRD E Australia / open forest and woodland / fruit, nectar and insects / n tree / e 2–3

Philemon diemenensis (*Lesson*) NEW CALEDONIA FRIARBIRD New Caledonia, Lifu and Maré (Loyalty Is)

Ptiloprora plumbea (*Salvadori*) LEADEN HONEYEATER Mts of New Guinea / forest

Ptiloprora meekiana (*Rothschild and Hartert*) MEEK'S HONEYEATER Mts of New Guinea / forest / insects [*Meliornis schistacea*, De Vis 1897, is generally considered to be indeterminable, but may refer to this species (*meekiana*). The name

was suppressed by the International Council of Zoological Nomenclature, *Bull Zool Nomenclature* 20, pt 6 (1963), pp 418–20]

Ptiloprora erythropleura (*Salvadori*) REDSIDED HONEYEATER Mts of New Guinea / mid-mountain forest / insects and berries

Ptiloprora guisei (*De Vis*) RED-BACKED HONEYEATER Mts of New Guinea / forest / fruit and insects / n tree / e 2

Ptiloprora perstriata (*De Vis*) BLACK-HEADED HONEYEATER Mts of New Guinea / forest / insects and fruit

Melidectes fuscus (*De Vis*) SOOTY HONEYEATER Mts of New Guinea / forest / insects / n tree / e ?1 (1 nest with 1 young known)

Melidectes princeps *Mayr and Gilliard* LONG-BEARDED HONEYEATER Mts of EC New Guinea / upper forest and grassland above timberline

Melidectes nonhuysi (*Van Oort*) SHORT-BEARDED HONEYEATER Oranje Mts, WC New Guinea / upper forest and grassland above timberline / fruit, seeds and insects

Melidectes ochromelas (*Meyer*) MIDMOUNTAIN MELEDECTES Mts of New Guinea / no data

Melidectes leucostephes (*Meyer*) WHITE-FRONTED MELIDECTES Mts of Vogelkop, New Guinea / forest edge of the mid-mountain grassland / no other data

Melidectes belfordi (*De Vis*) BELFORD'S HONEYEATER Mts of New Guinea / mountain forest / insects (? nectar) / n tree / e n/k / 1 young known [*Melidectes rufocrissalis* (Reichenow) and *M. foersteri* (Rothschild and Hartert) are separated by some authors]

Melidectes torquatus *Sclater* CINNAMON-BREASTED WATTLEBIRD Mts of New Guinea / forest, secondary growth and habitation of mid-mountain levels

Melipotes gymnops *Sclater* ARFAK MELIPOTES Mts of Vogelkop / forest / berries

Melipotes fumigatus *Meyer* COMMON MELIPOTES Mts of C New Guinea / forest / berries / n tree / e 1

Melipotes ater *Rothschild and Hartert* HUON MELIPOTES New Guinea: Mts of Huon Peninsula / forest / berries

Vosea whitemanensis *Gilliard* WHITEMAN'S HONEYEATER New Britain

Myza celebensis (*Meyer and Wiglesworth*) CELEBES HONEYEATER Mts of Celebes

FRINGILLIDAE:
Serinus mozambicus,
Yellow-eyed Canary,
Yellow-fronted Canary

FRINGILLIDAE:
Acanthis hornemanni,
Hornemann's Redpoll,
Hoary Redpoll

Plate 264

FRINGILLIDAE:
Carduelis carduelis,
European Goldfinch,
Eurasian Goldfinch

FRINGILLIDAE:
Carduelis notata,
Neotropical Black-headed
Siskin

Plate 265

Myza sarasinorum *Meyer and Wiglesworth* MENGKOKA HONEYEATER Mts of Celebes

Meliarchus sclateri (*Gray*) SAN CHRISTOBAL HONEYEATER San Christobal (Solomons)

Gymnomyza viridis (*Layard*) GIANT FOREST HONEYEATER Fiji Is / forest / insects and nectar

Gymnomyza samoensis (*Hombron and Jacquinot*) MAO Samoa

Gymnomyza aubryana (*Verreaux and Des Murs*) CROW HONEYEATER New Caledonia

Moho braccatus (*Cassin*) KAUAI O-O Kauai (Hawaiian Is) / forest / insects and nectar / n tree / e n/k

Moho bishopi (*Rothschild*) BISHOP'S O-O Molokai (Hawaiian Is) probably extinct, last seen 1904 / mountain forest / insects and nectar / n and e n/k [It is probable that a fifth species of O-o (unnamed) formerly occurred on Maui; Henshaw saw an adult ♂ there (see Henshaw, *Birds of Hawaiian Islands*, 1902)]

Moho apicalis *Gould* OAHU O-O Oahu (Hawaiian Is) / extinct 1837 / 5 specimens

Moho nobilis (*Merrem*) GREAT O-O Island of Hawaii / probably extinct, last seen 1934 / forest / nectar and insects / n and e n/k

Chaetoptila angustipluma (*Peale*) KIOEA Island of Hawaii / extinct 1840 / no data

Phylidonyris pyrrhoptera (*Latham*) CRESCENT HONEYEATER Tasmania, southern Australia and islands in Bass Strait / forest and scrub / insects, nectar and fruit / n bush or grass clumps / e 2–3

Phylidonyris novaehollandiae (*Latham*) WHITE-BEARDED HONEYEATER Tasmania, S and E Australia and islands in Bass Strait / woodland and scrub / insects, nectar and fruit / n bush / e 2–3

Phylidonyris nigra (*Bechstein*) WHITE-CHEEKED HONEYEATER Coasts of E Australia and SW Australia / woodland and scrub

Phylidonyris albifrons (*Gould*) WHITE-FRONTED HONEYEATER Australia / nomadic / arid woodland and scrub / insects and nectar / n bush / e 2–3

Phylidonyris melanops (*Latham*) TAWNY-CROWNED HONEYEATER Tasmania, southern Australia and islands in Bass Strait / scrubby heath and mallee / insects and nectar / n bush / e 2

Phylidonyris undulata (*Sparrman*) BARRED HONEYEATER New Caledonia

Phylidonyris notabilis (*Sharpe*) WHITE-BREASTED HONEYEATER Northern New Hebrides

Ramsayornis fasciatus (*Gould*) BAR-BREASTED HONEYEATER Northern Australia / paperbark swamps and adjacent savannah woodland / insects and nectar / n tree, often over water / e 3–4

Ramsayornis modestus (*Gray*) MODEST HONEYEATER W Papuan Is, S coast of New Guinea, Aru Is, D'Entrecasteaux Archipelago, islands in Bass Strait and coast of N Queensland / mangrove and tee-tree swamp / insects and nectar / n tree, often over water / e 2–3

Plectorhyncha lanceolata *Gould* STRIPED HONEYEATER Local in E Australia / forest, woodland and mangrove / insects and nectar / n tree / e 3–4

Conopophila whitei (*North*) GREY HONEY-EATER Mid-western Australia / arid scrub / mistletoe berries / n tree / e 2 (1 nest known)

Conopophila albogularis (*Gould*) RUFOUS-BANDED HONEYEATER N Australia, S New Guinea and Aru Is / mangrove / insects / n tree / e 3

Conopophila rufogularis (*Gould*) RED-THROATED HONEYEATER N Australia / forest and woodland / insects, nectar and fruit / n tree / e 2–3

Conopophila picta (*Gould*) PAINTED HONEY-EATER E Australia / open forest and woodland / mistletoe berries (? insects) / n tree / e 2

Xanthomyza phrygia (*Shaw*) REGENT HONEYEATER E Australia / open forest and woodland / insects and nectar / n tree / e 2–3

Cissomela pectoralis (*Gould*) BANDED HONEYEATER N Australia / forest and woodland / insects, blossoms and nectar / n tree / e 2

Acanthorhynchus tenuirostris (*Latham*) EASTERN SPINEBILL Tasmania, E Australia and islands in Bass Strait / forest, scrub and habitation / insects and nectar / n tree or bush / e 2–3

Acanthorhynchus superciliosus *Gould* WESTERN SPINEBILL SW Australia / woodland and thickets / insects and nectar / n tree / e 2

Manorina melanophrys (*Latham*) BELL MINER SE Australia / dry forest / insects / n tree / e 2–3

Manorina melanocephala (*Latham*) NOISY MINER E Australia and Tasmania [introduced on San Christobal] woodland and habitation / insects, nectar and fruit / n tree / e 2–4

Manorina flavigula (*Gould*) WHITE-RUMPED MINER Much of Australia / dry woodland and scrub / insects, nectar and fruit / n tree / e 2–4

Manorina melanotis (*Wilson*) BLACK-EARED or DUSKY MINER Murray mallee in SE Australia/mallee/insects, nectar and fruit/n tree/e 2-4

Anthornis melanura (*Sparrman*) NEW ZEALAND BELLBIRD New Zealand and coastal islets, Auckland Is (extinct race in Chathams)/forest and scrub/insects and nectar/n tree or bush, rarely hole/e 3-4/I ♀ 13-14

Anthochaera rufogularis (*Gould*) SPINY-CHEEKED WATTLEBIRD Interior of Australia/woodland and desert scrub/insects, fruit and nectar/n tree/e 2-3

Anthochaera chrysoptera (*Latham*) LITTLE WATTLEBIRD Coasts of E and S Australia, Tasmania / open forest and coastal heath/insects, nectar and fruit/n tree/e 1-2

Anthochaera carunculata (*White*) RED WATTLEBIRD Southern Australia/open forest, woodland and habitation / fruit, nectar and insects/n tree/e 2-3

Anthochaera paradoxa (*Daudin*) YELLOW WATTLEBIRD Tasmania and islands in Bass Strait / open forest, woodland and habitation/fruit, nectar and insects/n tree/e 2-3

Prosthemadera novaeseelandiae (*Gmelin*) TUI New Zealand and coastal islets, Auckland, Kermadec and Chatham Is/forest and habitation/insects, nectar and berries/n tree/e 3-5

EMBERIZIDAE Buntings, American Sparrows, Juncos etc Small seedeaters with short, stout bills and generally drab plumage, blacks, browns and whites predominating, sometimes mottled with grey, though some species may be quite strikingly patterned.

Melophus lathami (*Gray*) CRESTED BUNTING Himalayas, mts of northern SE Asia and S China/scrub/seeds/n ground or hole in wall or bank/e 3-4/I ♀

Latoucheornis siemsseni (*Martens*) LA TOUCHE'S BUNTING Mts of SE Kansu and Szechwan/no data

Emberiza calandra *L* CORN BUNTING Europe, N to Britain and S Scandinavia; N Africa, and E to Tian Shan w S to Israel and Iran/waste ground and arable land/seeds and insects/n ground or bush/e 1-7/I ♀ 12-14/F 9-12

Emberiza citrinella *L* YELLOWHAMMER or YELLOW BUNTING Europe and W Asia to Urals w S to Tien Shan, Mongolia and N Africa/grassland and arable cultivation / seeds and insects/n ground or bush/e 2-6/I ♀ 11-14/F c16

Emberiza leucocephala *S G Gmelin* PINE BUNTING Much of Asia w S to N India and S China / pine forest and cultivation / seeds and insects/n ground/e 4-6/I ♀

Emberiza koslowi *Bianchi* KOSLOW'S BUNTING E Tibet on the Tsinghai-Szechwan border/ ? no data

Emberiza cia *L* ROCK BUNTING S Europe and N Africa across Asia to Mongolia and China/dry rocky hillsides, semi-desert and cultivation/seeds and insects /n bush or ground /e 3-6/ I ♀ 12-13/F 10-13

Emberiza cioides *Brandt* MEADOW BUNTING C and E Asia from Tien Shan to China, Japan and Amurland/scrub and open country/n bush/e 3-5

Emberiza jankowskii *Taczanowski* JANKOWSKI'S BUNTING Manchuria and N Korea/open scrub/n ? ground/e n/k (2 eggs in the British Museum (Natural History) are of very doubtful provenance)

Emberiza buchanani *Blyth* BUCHANAN'S or GREY-NECKED BUNTING E Turkey to W Mongolia w S to India/stone scrub/seeds/n ground/e 4-5/I ♀

Emberiza stewarti (*Blyth*) STEWART'S, WHITE-CAPPED or CHESTNUT-BREASTED BUNTING Mts from Kazakhstan to N Pakistan w to plains of N India/open hillsides and juniper forest/seeds/n ground/e 3-5

Emberiza cineracea *Brehm* CINEREOUS BUNTING S Turkey and S Iran w S to Yemen, Sudan and Eritrea/high rocky slopes/n n/k/e 3

Emberiza hortulana *L* ORTOLAN BUNTING Europe and Asia E to Altai and Mongolia w S to C Africa, Arabia and Iran / open country, scrub and cultivation / seeds and insects / n ground/e 4-6/I ♀ 11-14/F 10-15

Emberiza caesia *Cretzschmar* CRETZSCHMAR'S BUNTING SE Europe, Turkey and Palestine, Cyprus and Crete w Sudan/scrub and arid open areas/n ground/e 4-6

Emberiza cirlus *L* CIRL BUNTING C and S Europe, N Africa and Mediterranean islands/open woodland and scrub / seeds and insects/n ground or bush/e 2-5/I ♀ 11-13/F 11-13

Emberiza striolata (*Lichtenstein*) HOUSE BUNTING Drier parts of N Africa through SW Asia to India/scrub/seeds/n hole in wall or building, apparently on ground when away from habitation/e 2-4

FRINGILLIDAE:
Loxia curvirostra,
Red Crossbill

FRINGILLIDAE:
Serinus citrinella,
Citril Finch

Plate 266

Plate 267

Emberiza impetuani *Smith* LARK-LIKE BUNTING Dry rocky areas from Cape Province to Transvaal and Angola / seeds and insects/ n ground / e 2–4

Emberiza tahapisi *Smith* CINNAMON-BREASTED BUNTING S Arabia and much of Africa S of Sahara / scrub and rocky country/ seeds and insects / n ground / e 3

Emberiza socotrana (*Ogilvie-Grant and Forbes*) SOCOTRAN MOUNTAIN BUNTING Mts of Socotra / no data

Emberiza capensis *L* CAPE BUNTING SE and S Africa from the Cape to Angola and Malawi/ dry scrub and rocky slopes / seeds and insects/ n ground or low bush / e 2–3

Emberiza yessoensis (*Swinhoe*) SWINHOE'S BUNTING S Kuriles, Japan, Ussuriland, E Manchuria w Korea and E China / wet meadows and reedbeds / seeds and insects / n bush / e ?3

Emberiza tristrami *Swinhoe* TRISTRAM'S BUNTING Middle Amur and Ussuri Rivers w S China / taiga / seeds and insects / n bush / e ?3

Emberiza fucata *Pallas* GREY-HEADED or CHESTNUT-EARED BUNTING Himalayas E and N to China, Japan, S Kuriles, Amurland and Lake Baikal / hillscrub and swamp / seeds and insects/ n ground / e 3–4

Emberiza pusilla *Pallas* LITTLE BUNTING b tundra and northern taiga of Eurasia w N India to S China and northern SE Asia / reeds, rice-stubble and scrub (in winter) / seeds and insects / n ground / e 4–6

Emberiza chrysophrys *Pallas* YELLOW-BROWED BUNTING b Siberia from Irkutsk to Stanovai w C and SE China / taiga / n tree / e 4 (1 nest known)

Emberiza rustica *Pallas* RUSTIC BUNTING N taiga zone of Eurasia S in winter to Japan and E China / forest and marsh / seeds / n ground or bush / e 4–6 / I ♀ 12–13 / F 14

Emberiza elegans *Temminck* ELEGANT BUNTING (YELLOW-THROATED BUNTING) E Asia from Amur S to Yunnan and N Burma / forest/ seeds and insects / n ground / e 4–5

Emberiza aureola *Pallas* GOLDEN BUNTING (YELLOW-BREASTED BUNTING) b boreal zone of Eurasia, S in E to Korea and Sakhalin w India, SE Asia and S China / grassland, scrub and cultivation / seeds and insects / n ground / e 4–6/ I ♂♀ 13–14

Emberiza poliopleura (*Salvadori*) SOMALI GOLDEN-BREASTED BUNTING SE Sudan and Ethiopia to NE Tanganyika / semi-desert and dry thorn scrub / n bush / e 2–3

Emberiza flaviventris *Stephens* GOLDEN-BREASTED BUNTING E and S Africa from Uganda to Angola and the Cape / woodland, open country and cultivation / seeds and insects / n bush / e 2–3

Emberiza affinis *Heuglin* (=**E. forbesi** (*Hartlaub*)) BROWN-RUMPED BUNTING Savannah belt of Africa from Senegal to Cameroon, Uganda and Ethiopia / semi-arid country / n and e n/k

Emberiza cabanisi (*Reichenow*) CABANIS'S BUNTING Savannah belts of Africa / woodland and bushy areas / seeds and insects / n bush / e 3

Emberiza rutila *Pallas* CHESTNUT BUNTING b E Siberia from Irkutsk to N Mongolia and Sea of Okhotsk w S China and northern SE Asia / forest clearings and cultivation / seeds and insects / n ground / e 4

Emberiza melanocephala *Scopoli* BLACK-HEADED BUNTING SE Europe through Asia Minor to Iran and Palestine w India / woodland, scrub and cultivation / seeds and insects / n tree or bush / e 4–6 / I ♀ 14

Emberiza bruniceps *Brandt* (=**E. luteola** *Sparrman*, erroneously) RED-HEADED BUNTING b WC Asia from Kazakstan to Altai, Iran, W Sinkiang and Baluchistan w India / scrub and cultivation / seeds / n bush or tree / e 3–5

Emberiza sulphurata *Temminck and Schlegel* JAPANESE YELLOW BUNTING b Honshu w Kyushu, Taiwan, N Philippines and E China coast / shrubby clearings / n bush / e 3–4

Emberiza spodocephala *Pallas* MASKED BUNTING Much of E Asia from Altai to Sea of Okhotsk and S to Yunnan and northern SE Asia; Japan, Ryukyus and S Kuriles / scrub, paddyfields and habitation / seeds and insects/ n ground or bush / e 4–5

Emberiza variabilis *Temminck* GREY BUNTING b S Kamchatka, Kuriles and Sakhalin w S to Ryukyus / forest and scrub / n bush / e 5 (1 known)

Emberiza pallasi (*Cabanis*) PALLAS' BUNTING Much of N and C Asia S to Mongolia and Sinkiang / tundra, mountain steppe and steppe/ seeds and insects / n bush / e 2–5

Emberiza schoeniclus (*L*) REED BUNTING Much of Palaearctic / reedbeds, moors and cultivation / seeds and insects / n bush or reed-tussock / e 4–7 / I ♂♀ 13–14 / F 10–13

Calcarius mccowni (*Lawrence*) McCown's Longspur Great Plains of central N America/ open country / seeds and insects / n ground or bush /e 3–6/I ♀ 12/F 12

Calcarius lapponicus (*L*) Lapland Bunting Holarctic, b in the tundra zone migrating S in w open ground of tundra and cultivation / seeds and insects/n ground /e 2–7/I ♂♀ 13–14/F 8–10

Calcarius pictus (*Swainson*) Smith's Longspur b Canadian and Alaskan tundra w central N America / open country / seeds and insects/n ground /e 4–6/I 11–12

Calcarius ornatus (*Townsend*) Collared Longspur Great Plains of central N America/ open country/seeds and insects/n ground/e 3–6/ I ♀ 10–11/F 9–14

Plectrophenax nivalis (*L*) Snow Bunting Much of N Holarctic / tundra and alpine rock desert, seashores in winter / seeds and insects/ n hole in rock or among screes or stones /e 3–9/ I ♀ (?♂) 10–12/F 12–13

[Plectrophenax hyperboreus *Ridgway* McKay's Bunting Islands in Bering Sea / this form is sometimes separated, sometimes treated as a race of *P. nivalis*]

Calamospiza melanocorys *Stejneger* Lark Bunting Great Plains of N America w S to Mexico / insects and seeds / n ground /e 3–7/ I ♂♀ 12

Zonotrichia iliaca (*Merrem*) Fox Sparrow Much of N America /swampy forest and scrub/ seeds, fruit and invertebrates / n ground /e 3–5/ I ♀ ?12–14

Zonotrichia melodia (*Wilson*) Song Sparrow Much of N America and Mexico / scrub near water, and habitation /insects, seeds and fruit/ n ground, bush or tree/e 3–6/I ♀ (?♂) 10–14/F 17

Zonotrichia lincolnii (*Audubon*) Lincoln's Sparrow Irregularly through N America and S to Guatemala and El Salvador/swampy scrub or dry open forest/insects and seeds /n ground/ e 3–6/I ♀ 13

Zonotrichia georgiana (*Latham*) Swamp Sparrow Much of N America / swamp and marshes /insects and seeds /n bush /e 3–6/I ♀ 12–15/F c11

Zonotrichia capensis (*Müller*) Andean Sparrow Much of C and S America /open country, brush and garden /n ground or bush/ e 2–5/F 10–12

Zonotrichia querula (*Nuttall*) Harris's Sparrow b Canada w west, central and

southern USA /stunted timber /seeds, fruit and insects / n ground / e 3–5

Zonotrichia leucophrys (*Forster*) White-crowned Sparrow Irregularly distributed through N America / open forest and brush/ buds, seeds, fruit and insects / n ground / e 3–6/ I ♀ 11

Zonotrichia albicollis (*Gmelin*) White-throated Sparrow b Canada and northern USA w southern USA /open forest and scrub/ n ground/e 4–6/I ♀/F 10–15

Zonotrichia atricapilla (*Gmelin*) Golden-crowned Sparrow b Alaska and W Canada w western USA / bush and garden / buds, flowers and seeds /n tree or ground /e 3–5

Junco vulcani (*Boucard*) Volcano Junco Summits of high volcanos of Costa Rica and Panama

Junco hyemalis (*L*) Slate-coloured Junco Much of N America / forest edge and open woodland / seeds and insects / n ground /e 3–6/ I ♀ 12–13/F c21 (*Junco caniceps* (Woodhouse) 'Grey-headed Junco' is sometimes separated, as are various other 'species' now usually contained in this complex)

Junco phaeonotus *Wagler* Yellow-eyed Junco Mts from S Arizona through Mexico to W Guatemala /conifer forests /n ground /e 3–5/ I ♀ 15

Ammodramus sandwichensis (*Gmelin*) Savannah Sparrow Much of N America, Mexico and Guatemala / widely distributed in open habitats /seeds and insects /n ground /e 3–6/ I ♂♀ 12–14

Ammodramus maritimus (*Wilson*) Seaside Sparrow Coasts of eastern and southern USA /salt marshes /insects and marine life /n ground /e 3–6/ I ♀

Ammodramus caudacutus (*Gmelin*) Sharp-tailed Sparrow Fresh and salt marshes of S Canada and northern and eastern USA /insects/ n ground /e 4–5/I ♀

Ammodramus leconteii (*Audubon*) Le Conte's Sparrow b SC Canada and north-central USA w southern USA / grassland seeds and insects / n in grass (off ground)/ e 3–5/I ♀ 12–13

Ammodramus bairdii (*Audubon*) Baird's Sparrow Great Plains of N America /grassland/ n ground /e 3–5/I ♀ 11–12

Ammodramus baileyi (*Bangs*) Sierra Madra Sparrow Highlands of Mexico

ESTRILDIDAE:
Erythrura prasina,
Pintailed Parrot-Finch,
Long-tailed Munia

ESTRILDIDAE:
Erythrura prasina,
Pintailed Parrot-Finch,
Long-tailed Munia

Plate 268

ESTRILDIDAE: *Chloebia gouldiae,* Gouldian Finch

Plate 269

Ammodramus henslowii (*Audubon*) HENSLOW'S SPARROW Eastern USA/grasslands/ n ground/e 3–5/I ♀ 11/F 9–10

Ammodramus savannarum (*Gmelin*) GRASSHOPPER SPARROW N America (except Alaska and N Canada) S through Mexico and C America to Colombia and (?) Ecuador; Jamaica, Hispaniola, Puerto Rico, Bonaire and Curaçao/grassland/insects and seeds/n ground/ e 3–6/I ♀ ? 11–12

Ammodramus humeralis (*Bosc*) GRASSLAND SPARROW Much of S America E of Andes and S to N Argentina

Ammodramus aurifrons (*Spix*) YELLOW-BROWED SPARROW Lowlands of Colombia and Venezuela, and Amazon basin

Spizella arborea (*Wilson*) AMERICAN TREE SPARROW b Canada and Alaska w USA/scrub and forest edge/n bush/e 4–6/I 12–13

Spizella passerina (*Bechstein*) CHIPPING SPARROW N America S through Mexico to El Salvador/forest and orchard/seeds and insects/ n tree/e 3–5/I ♀ (?♂) 14

Spizella pusilla (*Wilson*) FIELD SPARROW SE Canada, eastern USA and S to Mexico (*S. wortheni* Ridgway, is sometimes separated)/ scrub and cultivation / seeds and insects / n ground or shrub/e 3–6

Spizella atrogularis (*Cabanis*) BLACK-CHINNED SPARROW Mexico and south-western USA/dry scrub/n bush/e 2–5

Spizella pallida (*Swainson*) CLAY-COLOURED SPARROW Great Plains of N America/prairie and cultivation/n low bush or almost on ground/ e 3–5/I ♂♀ 10–11

Spizella breweri *Cassin* BREWER'S SPARROW b W Canada and north western USA w south-western USA/balsam forest in N, sagebrush in S/ seeds and insects/n tree or bush/e 3–5

Pooectes gramineus (*Gmelin*) VESPER SPARROW S Canada and USA / grassland and cultivation/insects and seeds/n ground/e 3–6/ I ♂♀ 12–13/F 9–14

Chondestes grammacus (*Say*) LARK SPARROW S Canada and USA w through Mexico to Guatemala and El Salvador/plains, parks and cultivation/seeds and insects/n shrub, tree or ground/e 3–6/I ♀ 10–11

Amphispiza bilineata (*Cassin*) BLACK-THROATED SPARROW Mexico and south-western USA/open country/seeds and insects/n bush/ e 3–4

Amphispiza belli (*Cassin*) SAGE SPARROW Western USA S to Baja California/sagebrush/ seeds and insects/n bush/e 3–5

Aimophila mystacalis (*Hartlaub*) BRIDLED SPARROW Mexico

Aimophila humeralis (*Cabanis*) BLACK-CHESTED SPARROW Mexico

Aimophila ruficauda (*Bonaparte*) STRIPED-HEADED SPARROW Mexico S to Costa Rica/scrub

Aimophila sumichrasti (*Lawrence*) SUMICHRAST'S SPARROW Mexico on the arid S side of the isthmus of Tehuantepec

Aimophila stolzmanni (*Taczanowski*) TUMBES SPARROW Arid W slope of Andes of Ecuador and Peru

Aimophila strigiceps (*Gould*) STRIPED-CRESTED SPARROW Argentina / grassland

Aimophila aestivalis (*Lichtenstein*) BACHMAN'S SPARROW Eastern USA/pine forest/ seeds and insects/n ground/e 3–5

Aimophila botterii (*Sclater*) BOTTERI'S SPARROW SE Arizona and S Texas through Mexico to Costa Rica / grassland / seeds and insects/n ground/e 2–5

Aimophila cassinii (*Woodhouse*) CASSIN'S SPARROW South-central USA and Mexico/ grassland/n ground/e 3–5

Aimophila quinquestriata (*Sclater and Salvin*) FIVE-STRIPED SPARROW Mexico

Aimophila carpalis (*Coues*) RUFOUS-WINGED SPARROW SC Arizona and Mexico in Sonora and Sinaloa/variable habitat/seeds and insects/ n bush or cactus/e 2–5/I ♀/F c10

Aimophila ruficeps (*Cassin*) RUFOUS-CROWNED SPARROW South-western USA and Mexico / scrub / seeds and insects / n ground/ e 2–5/I ♀

Aimophila notosticta (*Sclater and Salvin*) OAXACA SPARROW Oaxaca highlands, Mexico

Aimophila rufescens (*Swainson*) RUSTY SPARROW Mexico, S to Costa Rica/scrub

Torreornis inexpectata *Barbour and Peters* ZAPATA SPARROW Cuba / shrubbery of Zapata swamp and arid coast of SE/n grass clump/e n/s

Oriturus superciliosus (*Swainson*) STRIPED SPARROW Mexico

Phrygilus atriceps (*Lafresnaye and d'Orbigny*) BLACK-HOODED SIERRA FINCH Andes from Peru to N Argentina/pasture and shrubbery

Phrygilus gayi (*Gervais*) GAY'S or GREY-HOODED SIERRA FINCH Chili and Argentina S to Tierra del Fuego / open country and ravines

Phrygilus patagonicus *Lowe* PATAGONIAN SIERRA FINCH Chile and Chilean islands S to Tierra del Fuego / densely vegetated ravines

Phrygilus fruticeti (*Kittlitz*) MOURNING SIERRA FINCH Andes from Peru to Argentina / bushy and rocky slopes

Phrygilus unicolor (*Lafresnaye and d'Orbigny*) PLUMBEOUS SIERRA FINCH Andes from Venezuela to Tierra del Fuego / shrubby slopes

Phrygilus dorsalis *Cabanis* RED-BACKED SIERRA FINCH Argentina in the Puna zone / rocky open slopes

Phrygilus erythronotus (*Phillipi and Landbeck*) WHITE-THROATED SIERRA FINCH Puna zone of Peru, Bolivia and N Chile / puna grassland

Phrygilus plebejus *Tschudi* ASHY-BREASTED SIERRA FINCH Andes from Ecuador to N Argentina / rocky and bushy slopes

Phrygilus carbonarius (*Lafresnaye and d'Orbigny*) CARBONATED SIERRA FINCH Pampas of Argentina / pasture and bushy ravines

Phrygilus alaudinus (*Kittlitz*) BAND-TAILED SIERRA FINCH Ecuador S to N Chile and N Argentina / rocky open slopes with scattered bushes

Melanodera melanodera (*Quoy and Gaimard*) BLACK-THROATED FINCH Llanos of Chile and Santa Cruz in Argentina, N Tierra del Fuego, Falkland Is / moist pasture and shrubbery

Melanodera xanthogramma (*Gray*) YELLOW-BRIDLED FINCH Mts of Chile and W Argentina, Tierra del Fuego, islands of Cape Horn / rocky fields and shrubbery

[**Phrygilus malvinarum** *Brooks*, based on a single specimen from W Falkland Is is thought to be an immature of one of the 2 species of *Melanodera*]

Haplospiza rustica (*Tschudi*) SLATY FINCH Highlands of Mexico and C America and Andes from Venezuela to Bolivia (apparently discontinuous) / forest edges

Haplospiza unicolor *Cabanis* UNIFORM FINCH SE Brazil to N Argentina / shrubbery near water

Acanthidops bairdii *Ridgway* PEG-BILLED FINCH Highlands of Costa Rica / rare / no data

Lophospingus pusillus (*Burmeister*) BLACK-CRESTED FINCH S Bolivia, W Paraguay and N Argentina / open shrubby plains

Lophospingus griseocristatus (*Lafresnaye and d'Orbigny*) GREY-CRESTED FINCH Bolivia and N Argentina / shrubbery

Donacospiza albifrons (*Vieillot*) LONG-TAILED REED FINCH SE Brazil S to N Argentina / sawgrass near water

Rowettia goughensis (*Clarke*) GOUGH ISLAND BUNTING Gough Is / n grass tussock / e 2

Nesospiza acunhae *Cabanis* TRISTAN FINCH Tristan da Cunha (extinct), Nightingale and Inaccessible Is / tussock grass / seeds and insects / n bush or grass tussock / e 2–5 / I ♂♀

Nesospiza wilkinsi *Lowe* BIG-BILLED BUNTING Nightingale and Inacessible Is / tussock grass with trees / seeds / n grass tuft / e 2

Diuca speculifera (*Lafresnaye and d'Orbigny*) WHITE-WINGED DIUCA Puna zone of Peru, Bolivia and N Chile / rocky slopes (sleeps in caves and glacial fissures)

Diuca diuca (*Molina*) COMMON DIUCA Chile and Argentina / hill scrub and habitation

Idiopsar brachyurus *Cassin* SHORT-TAILED FINCH Puna zone of Peru, Bolivia and N Argentina / steep mountain slopes

Puezorhina cinerea (*Lafresnaye*) CINEREOUS FINCH Arid coast of NW Peru

Xenospingus concolor (*d'Orbigny and Lafresnaye*) SLENDER-BILLED FINCH Pacific coast of Peru and N Chile / marsh-borders, campos and cultivation

Incaspiza pulchra (*Sclater*) GREAT INCA FINCH Peru / cactus scrub / cactus fruit

Incaspiza personata (*Salvin*) RUFOUS-BACKED INCA FINCH Peru

Incaspiza ortisi *Zimmer* GREY-WINGED INCA FINCH Peru

Incaspiza laeta (*Salvin*) BUFF-BRIDLED INCA FINCH Peru

Incaspiza watkinsi *Chapman* LITTLE INCA FINCH Peru

Poospiza thoracica (*Nordmann*) BAY-CHESTED WARBLING-FINCH SE Brazil

Poospiza boliviana *Sharpe* BOLIVIAN WARBLING-FINCH C Bolivia

Poospiza alticola *Salvin* PLAIN-TAILED WARBLING-FINCH N Peru

Poospiza hypochondria (*d'Orbigny and Lafresnaye*) RUFOUS-SIDED WARBLING-FINCH Andes from Bolivia to N Argentina / open scrub

Poospiza erythrophrys *Sclater* RUSTY-BROWED WARBLING-FINCH Bolivia and NW Argentina / woodland and brush

Poospiza ornata (*Leybold*) CINNAMON

ESTRILDIDAE: *Poephila bichenovii*, Double-barred Finch, Banded Finch

ESTRILDIDAE:
Poephila acuticauda,
Long-tailed Finch

Plate 270

ESTRILDIDAE:
Poephila bichenovii,
Double-barred Finch,
Banded Finch

Plate 271

WARBLING-FINCH NW Argentina / 'pastures in bushes and low trees. Feeds on ground.' (de Schaunsee 1970)

Poospiza nigrorufa (*d'Orbigny and Lafresnaye*) BLACK-AND-RUFOUS WARBLING-FINCH Bolivia and S Brazil to N Argentina / woodland, marsh and garden

Poospiza lateralis (*Nordmann*) RED-RUMPED WARBLING-FINCH SE Brazil, Paraguay, Uruguay and NE Argentina / bushy woodland

Poospiza rubecula *Salvin* RUFOUS-BREASTED WARBLING-FINCH N Peru

Poospiza garleppi (*Berlepsch*) COCHABAMBA MOUNTAIN-FINCH Puna zone of Cochabamba, Bolivia

Poospiza baeri (*Oustalet*) TUCUMAN MOUNTAIN-FINCH Tucuman in NW Argentina

Poospiza caesar *Sclater and Salvin* CHESTNUT-BREASTED MOUNTAIN-FINCH SE Peru

Poospiza hispaniolensis *Bonaparte* COLLARED WARBLING-FINCH Arid tropical zone of SW Ecuador and coast of Peru / cactus-scrub and cultivation

Poospiza torquata (*d'Orbigny and Lafresnaye*) RINGED WARBLING-FINCH Bolivia, W Paraguay and N and C Argentina / scrub and thickets

Poospiza melanoleuca (*d'Orbigny and Lafresnaye*) BLACK-CAPPED WARBLING-FINCH From E Bolivia and SW Brazil to Buenos Aires / scattered bushes and sawgrass

Poospiza cinerea *Bonaparte* CINEREOUS WARBLING-FINCH Campos of C Brazil

Sicalis citrina *Pelzeln* STRIPE-TAILED YELLOW FINCH Irregularly through parts of tropical S America / campos and open mountain slopes

Sicalis lutea (*d'Orbigny and Lafresnaye*) PUNA YELLOW FINCH Puna zone from Peru to N Argentina / scrub-pasture and mountain slopes

Sicalis uropygialis (*d'Orbigny and Lafresnaye*) BRIGHT-RUMPED YELLOW FINCH Puna zone from Peru to N Chile and N Argentina / open hillsides

Sicalis luteocephala (*d'Orbigny and Lafresnaye*) CITRON-HEADED YELLOW FINCH Highlands of Bolivia

Sicalis auriventris *Philippi and Landbeck* GREATER YELLOW FINCH Andes of Chile and N Argentina / open slopes above 6,000ft (1,800m)

Sicalis olivascens (*d'Orbigny and Lafresnaye*) GREENISH YELLOW FINCH Andes from Peru to W Argentina / open slopes

Sicalis lebruni (*Oustalet*) LE BRUN'S YELLOW FINCH Tierra del Fuego N to Río Negro, Argentina

Sicalis columbiana *Cabanis* ORANGE-FRONTED YELLOW FINCH Basins of Amazon and Orinoco / campos

Sicalis flaveola (*L*) SAFFRON FINCH Lowlands of much of tropical S America, introduced Panama and Jamaica / shrubbery, gardens, campos and palm groves

Sicalis luteola (*Sparrman*) YELLOW GRASS FINCH Widely distributed from Mexico to Argentina, introduced Lesser Antilles / grassland, cliffs and marsh borders

Sicalis raimondii *Taczanowskii* RAIMONDI'S YELLOW FINCH W slopes of Andes of Peru / rocky slopes

Sicalis taczanowskii *Sharpe* TACZANOWSKI'S YELLOW FINCH or SULPHUR-THROATED FINCH Arid coast of SW Ecuador and N Peru / grassy scrub (sometimes retained in monotypic genus *Gnathospiza*)

Emberizoides herbicola (*Vieillot*) WEDGE-TAILED GRASS FINCH Costa Rica, Panama and much of S America E of Andes and S to N Argentina / grassland (*E. duidae* Chapman is sometimes separated)

Emberizoides ypiranganus *von Ihering* (*Cat Fauna Braz*, 1 1902, p 390) LESSER GRASS FINCH S Brazil and N Argentina / no data

Embernagra platensis (*Gmelin*) GREAT PAMPA FINCH SE Brazil and Bolivia S to Argentina / marsh and sawgrass

Embernagra longicauda *Strickland* BUFF-THROATED PAMPA FINCH Known only from the type of unknown origin, and 3 specimens from NC Bahia (Brazil)

Volatinia jacarina (*L*) BLUE-BLACK GRASSQUIT Lowlands of Mexico, C America and S America S to N Chile and N Argentina / shrubs and pastures

Sporophila frontalis (*Verreaux*) BUFFY-FRONTED SEEDEATER SE Brazil to NE Argentina / shrubbery

Sporophila falcirostris (*Temminck*) TEMMINCK'S SEEDEATER Coast of SE Brazil from Bahia to São Paulo

Sporophila schistacea (*Lawrence*) SLATE-COLOURED SEEDEATER Discontinuously distributed from Mexico to S Brazil and Bolivia / forest

Sporophila intermedia *Cabanis* GREY

SEEDEATER Colombia, N Venezuela, Trinidad and Guyana / shrubbery, llanos and cultivation

Sporophila plumbea (*Wied*) PLUMBEOUS SEEDEATER Amazon basin / grassland and cerrado

Sporophila americana (*Gmelin*) VARIABLE SEEDEATER Mexico S to Peru and Amazon / grassland, forest and cultivation (sometimes considered divisible into a northern (*S. aurita* (Bonaparte)) and southern species)

Sporophila torqueola (*Bonaparte*) COLLARED SEEDEATER Rio Grande Valley through Mexico to El Salvador

Sporophila collaris (*Boddaert*) RUSTY-COLLARED SEEDEATER E and S Brazil to N Argentina / scrubland and lagoon-borders

Sporophila lineola (*L*) LINED SEEDEATER Trinidad, Tobago and much of tropical S America E of Andes and S to N Argentina / grassland and shrubbery

Sporophila luctuosa (*Lafresnaye*) BLACK-AND-WHITE SEEDEATER Andes from Venezuela to N Bolivia / grassland

Sporophila nigricollis (*Vieillot*) YELLOW-BELLIED SEEDEATER Costa Rica, Panama and much of S America S to N Argentina / shrubbery and cultivation

Sporophila ardesiaca (*Dubois*) DUBOIS'S SEEDEATER S Brazil / shrubbery

Sporophila melanops (*Pelzeln*) HOODED SEEDEATER Known only from Porto do Rio Araguaia, Goiás, Brazil

Sporophila obscura (*d'Orbigny and Lafresnaye*) DULL-COLOURED SEEDEATER Slopes of Andes from Venezuela to N Argentina, and coast of Peru / forest edge and grassland

Sporophila caerulescens (*Vieillot*) DOUBLE-COLLARED SEEDEATER C and S Brazil and Bolivia to N Argentina / shrubbery and cerrado

Sporophila albogularis (*Spix*) WHITE-THROATED SEEDEATER NE Brazil / shrubbery at forest edge

Sporophila leucoptera (*Vieillot*) WHITE-BELLIED SEEDEATER E and S Brazil and Bolivia to N Argentina / shrubbery at forest edge

Sporophila peruviana (*Lesson*) PARROT-BILLED SEEDEATER Arid coast of Ecuador and Peru / scrub, grainfields and arid scrub

Sporophila simplex (*Taczanowski*) DRAB SEEDEATER Peru

Sporophila nigrorufa (*d'Orbigny and Lafresnaye*) BLACK-AND-TAWNY SEEDEATER W Mato Grosso and E Bolivia / campos

Sporophila bouvreuil (*Müller*) CAPPED SEEDEATER E and S Brazil, E Paraguay and N Argentina / shrubbery and cerradão

Sporophila insulata *Chapman* TUMACO SEEDEATER Tumaco Is, SW Colombia

Sporophila minuta (*L*) RUDDY-BREASTED SEEDEATER Pacific lowlands of Mexico and C America, and northern S America from NW Ecuador through Colombia, Venezuela, Trinidad, Tobago and the Guianas, S to northern Amazonas and northern Pará, Brazil / tall grass and wasteland

Sporophila hypoxantha *Cabanis* TAWNY-BELLIED SEEDEATER E Bolivia and S Brazil to N Argentina

Sporophila hypochroma *Todd* RUFOUS-RUMPED SEEDEATER E Bolivia

Sporophila ruficollis *Cabanis* DARK-THROATED SEEDEATER E Bolivia and S Brazil to N Argentina / shrubby pastures

Sporophila palustris (*Barrows*) MARSH SEEDEATER S Brazil, Paraguay, Uruguay and NE Argentina / marshes

Sporophila castaneiventris *Cabanis* CHESTNUT-BELLIED SEEDEATER Amazon basin / wastelands, swampy fields and cultivation

[**Sporophila lorenzi** *Hellmayr* ? Cayenne / unique, believed to be an artifact]

Sporophila cinnamomea (*Lafresnaye*) CHESTNUT SEEDEATER Recorded from a few localities in S Brazil and E Paraguay

Sporophila melanogaster (*Pelzeln*) BLACK-BELLIED SEEDEATER SE Brazil / rare and local

Sporophila telasco (*Lesson*) CHESTNUT-THROATED SEEDEATER Arid coast from NW Ecuador to N Chile / scrub

Oryzoborus crassirostris (*Gmelin*) GREAT SEED FINCH Nicaragua to Panama and S America E of Andes S to Mato Grosso / rice-fields, marshes and forest edge (*O. maximiliani* Cabanis, is sometimes separated)

Oryzoborus angolensis (*L*) LESSER SEED FINCH Much of S America E of Andes and S to N Argentina / forest edge and shrubbery

Oryzoborus funereus *Sclater* THICK-BILLED SEED FINCH Caribbean lowlands from Mexico to Nicaragua, both slopes from Costa Rica to Panama, N and W Colombia and W Ecuador

Amaurospiza concolor *Cabanis* BLUE SEEDEATER Irregularly distributed from Mexico to Ecuador / rare and local / forest and secondary growth

ESTRILDIDAE:
Poephila cincta,
Black-throated Finch

ESTRILDIDAE:
Neochmia ruficauda,
Star Finch

Plate 272

ESTRILDIDAE:
Poephila guttata,
Zebra Finch

Plate 273

Amaurospiza moesta (*Hartlaub*) BLACKISH-BLUE SEEDEATER E Brazil to NE Argentina / rare and local / shrubbery and bamboo thickets

Melopyrrha nigra (*L*) BLACK BULLFINCH Cuba, Isle of Pines and Grand Cayman / scrub and woodland / n bush or tree / e 3–4

Dolospingus fringilloides (*Pelzeln*) WHITE-NAPED SEEDEATER Amazonas and upper Rio Negro / very rare / probably open country

Catamenia analis (*d'Orbigny and Lafresnaye*) BLACK-TAILED SEEDEATER Andes from Colombia to Bolivia / shrubbery and stony hillsides

Catamenia inornata (*Lafresnaye*) PLAIN-COLOURED SEEDEATER Andes from Venezuela to N Argentina / shrubby hillsides

Catamenia homochroa *Sclater* PARAMO SEEDEATER Andes from Venezuela to Bolivia

Catamenia oreophila *Todd* SANTA MARTA SEEDEATER Sierra Nevada de Santa Marta, Colombia / known only from 6 old female specimens (de Schaunsee (1970), p 411, believes that these are the same as the Santa Marta race of *C. homochroa*)

Tiaris canora (*Gmelin*) CUBAN GRASSQUIT Cuba and Isle of Pines / shrubbery and woodland / n bush or tree / e 2–3

Tiaris olivacea (*L*) YELLOW-FACED GRASSQUIT Atlantic slope of Mexico through C America to W Venezuela, Greater Antilles / grassland and cultivation

Tiaris bicolor (*L*) BLACK-FACED GRASSQUIT W Indies, coasts of Colombia and Venezuela and offshore islands / ricefields and thornscrub / seeds / n bush / e 2–5

Tiaris fuliginosa (*Wied*) SOOTY GRASSQUIT N, E and C Brazil, some mts of Venezuela, Trinidad / open country

Loxipasser anoxanthus (*Gosse*) YELLOW-SHOULDERED GRASSQUIT Jamaica / hill scrub / n bush or tree / e 3–4

Loxigilla portoricensis (*Daudin*) PUERTO RICAN BULLFINCH Puerto Rico; formerly also St Kitts / woodland / n bush or tree / e 3

Loxigilla violacea (*L*) GREATER ANTILLEAN BULLFINCH Hispaniola and adjacent islands, Jamaica and Bahamas / forest and scrub / n tree, shrub or ground / e 3

Loxigilla noctis (*L*) LESSER ANTILLEAN BULLFINCH Lesser Antilles / forest undergrowth / n tree or bush / e 2–3

Melanospiza richardsoni (*Cory*) ST LUCIA BLACK FINCH St Lucia / scrub and forest borders / n bush / e 2

Geospiza magnirostris *Gould* LARGE GROUND FINCH Galapagos / seeds and insects / n tree or bush / e 2–5 / I ♀ 12 / F 13–14

Geospiza fortis *Gould* MEDIUM GROUND FINCH Galapagos / seeds and insects / n tree or bush / e 2–5 / I ♀ 12 / F 13–14

Geospiza fuliginosa *Gould* SMALL GROUND FINCH Galapagos / seeds and insects / n tree or bush / e 2–5 / I ♀ 12 / F 13–14

Geospiza difficilis *Sharpe* SHARP-BEAKED FINCH Galapagos, absent from some islands / seeds, insects and flowers / n tree or bush / e 2–5 / I ♀ 12 / F 13–14

Geospiza nebulosa *Gould* Extinct, known from 2 specimens / ? Charles Is, Galapagos / status uncertain

Geospiza scandens (*Gould*) SMALL CACTUS FINCH Galapagos, except Fernandina and islands inhabited by *G. conirostris* / seeds, fruit and pulp of prickly pear cactus / n bush / e 2–5 / I ♀ 12 / F 13–14

Geospiza conirostris *Ridgway* LARGE CACTUS FINCH Wenman, Hood, Tower and Culpepper Is, Galapagos / seeds and insects / n bush / e 2–5 / I ♀ 12 / F 13–14

Camarhynchus crassirostris *Gould* VEGETARIAN FINCH Galapagos (except the drier islands) / bushes / seeds, fruit and leaves / n bush / e 2–5 / I ♀ 12 / F 13–14 (sometimes placed in the monotypic genus *Platyspiza*)

Camarhynchus psittacula *Gould* PARROT FINCH or LARGE TREE FINCH Galapagos, except Culpepper, Wenman, Tower and Hood / trees / insects / n tree / e 2–5 / I ♀ 12 / F 13–14

Camarhynchus pauper *Ridgway* MEDIUM TREE FINCH or SANTA MARIA FINCH Highlands of Charles (Santa Maria) Is, Galapagos / insects and soft seeds

[**C. conjunctus** *Swarth* and **C. aureus** *Swarth*, are believed to be hybrids *C. parvulus* × *Certhidea olivaceus*]

Camarhynchus parvulus (*Gould*) INSECTIVOROUS or SMALL TREE FINCH Galapagos, most of the main islands / trees / insects, fruit and seeds / n tree / e 2–5 / I ♀ 12 / F 13–14

Camarhynchus pallidus (*Sclater and Salvin*) WOODPECKER FINCH Higher zones of the main islands of Galapagos / large insects from decaying bark / n tree / e 2–5 / I ♀ 12 / F 13–14

[**C. giffordi** (*Swarth*), unique, is believed to be

a dwarf *C. pallidus*, or a hybrid *C. pallidus* × *Certhidea olivacea*]

Camarhynchus heliobates (*Snodgrass and Heller*) MANGROVE FINCH Fernandina and Isabella Is, Galapagos / mangrove swamps / insects, spiders and mangrove leaves / n tree / e 2–5 / I ♀ 12 / F 13–14

Certhidea olivacea *Gould* WARBLER FINCH Galapagos / insects and spiders / n tree or bush / e 2–5 / I ♀ 12 / F 13–14

Pinaroloxias inornata (*Gould*) COCOS FINCH Cocos Is

Pipilo chlorurus (*Audubon*) GREEN-TAILED TOWHEE South-western USA / scrub and bush at high altitudes / insects, seeds and fruit / n on or near ground / e 2–5

Pipilo ocai (*Lawrence*) COLLARED TOWHEE Mts of Mexico

Pipilo erythropthalmus (*L*) RUFOUS-SIDED TOWHEE SC Canada, USA and through Mexico to Guatemala / scrub insects, seeds and fruit / n ground / e 2–6 / I 12–13 (*Pipilo ocai* and *P. erythropthalmus* hybridise freely in places and may be conspecific. Some of the hybrids have been named as species)

Pipilo socorroensis *Grayson* SOCORRO TOWHEE Isla Socorro, Islas Revilla Gigedo, Mexico / possibly conspecific with *P. erythropthalmus*

Pipilo fuscus *Swainson* BROWN TOWHEE Mexico and south-western USA / scrub / seeds and insects / n tree or ground / e 3–6 / I ♀

Pipilo aberti *Baird* ABERT'S TOWHEE South-western USA / scrub and cultivation / seeds and insects / n tree / e 2–5

Pipilo albicollis *Sclater* WHITE-THROATED TOWHEE Mexico

Melozone kieneri (*Bonaparte*) RUSTY-CROWNED SPARROW Mexico

Melozone biarcuatum (*Prévost and Des Murs*) CHIAPAS SPARROW Highlands of Mexico, Guatemala, El Salvador, W Honduras and Costa Rica

Melozone leucotis *Cabanis* WHITE-EARED SPARROW Highlands from Chiapas to Costa Rica

Arremon taciturnus (*Hermann*) PECTORAL SPARROW S America E of Andes S to Bolivia and S Brazil / forest

Arremon flavirostris *Swainson* SAFFRON-BILLED SPARROW Bolivia and E and C Brazil S to N Argentina / forest

Arremon aurantiirostris *Lafresnaye* ORANGE-BILLED SPARROW Mountain slopes from Mexico to Peru / forest

Arremon schlegeli *Bonaparte* GOLDEN-WINGED SPARROW Colombia and Venezuela / semi-arid forest

Arremon abeillei *Lesson* BLACK-CAPPED SPARROW SW Ecuador and NW Peru / arid scrub

Arremonops rufivirgatus (*Lawrence*) OLIVE SPARROW S Texas through Mexico and C America to Costa Rica / scrub and undergrowth near forest edges / seeds and insects / n bush / e 3–5

Arremonops tocuyensis *Todd* TOCUYA SPARROW NE Colombia and NW Venezuela / arid scrub

Arremonops chloronotus (*Salvin*) GREEN-BACKED SPARROW Mexico, N Guatemala, Belize and N Honduras

Arremonops conirostris (*Bonaparte*) BLACK-STRIPED SPARROW E Honduras to Panama and northern S America S to Peru and N Brazil / woodland borders, plantations and cultivation

Atlapetes albinucha (*Lafresnaye and d'Orbigny*) WHITE-NAPED FINCH Mexico through C America to Colombia / forest edge and scrub / n herbage / e 2–3 / I ♀ / F 12 (*Atlapetes gutturalis* (Lafresnaye) is sometimes separated)

Atlapetes pallidinucha (*Boissonneau*) PALE-NAPED FINCH Andes of Colombia, Venezuela and Ecuador / forest and scrub

Atlapetes rufinucha (*Lafresnaye and d'Orbigny*) RUFOUS-NAPED FINCH Andes from Venezuela to Bolivia / forest and scrub

Atlapetes leucopsis (*Sclater and Salvin*) WHITE-RIMMED FINCH Local in parts of Colombia and Ecuador

Atlapetes pileatus *Wagler* RUFOUS-CAPPED FINCH Mexico

Atlapetes melanocephalus (*Salvin and Godman*) SANTA MARTA FINCH Sierra Nevada de Santa Marta, Colombia / forest and scrub

Atlapetes flaviceps *Chapman* OLIVE-HEADED FINCH E slope of C Andes, Tolima, Colombia / forest

Atlapetes fuscoolivaceus *Chapman* DUSKY-HEADED FINCH Magdalen valley, Colombia / forest

Atlapetes tricolor (*Taczanowski*) TRI-COLOURED FINCH Andes of Colombia, Ecuador and Peru / mossy forest

ESTRILDIDAE:
Emblema bella,
Fire-tailed Finch,
Beautiful Firetail

ESTRILDIDAE:
*Amandava
subflava*,
Golden-breasted
or
Zebra
Waxbill

Plate 274

ESTRILDIDAE:
Aegintha temporalis,
Red-browed Finch

ESTRILDIDAE: *Emblema oculata,* Red-eared Finch, Red-eared Firetail

Plate 275

Atlapetes albofrenatus (*Boissonneau*) MOUSTACHED FINCH Andes of Colombia and Venezuela / forest

Atlapetes schistaceus (*Boissonneau*) SLATY-BRUSH FINCH or SOOTY FINCH Andes from Venezuela to Peru / forest

Atlapetes nationi (*Sclater*) RUSTY-BELLIED FINCH Ecuador and Peru

[**Atlapetes seebohmi** (*Taczanowski*) from the Andes of NW Peru, is sometimes treated as a species, sometimes as a race of *A. nationi* and sometimes as a race of *A. schistaceus*]

Atlapetes leucopterus (*Jardine*) WHITE-WINGED FINCH Andes of Ecuador and Peru

Atlapetes albiceps (*Taczanowski*) WHITE-HEADED FINCH SE Ecuador and NW Peru

Atlapetes pallidiceps (*Sharpe*) PALE-HEADED FINCH Mts of S Ecuador / scrub

Atlapetes rufigenis (*Salvin*) RUFOUS-EARED FINCH Peru

Atlapetes semirufus (*Boissonneau*) OCHRE-BREASTED FINCH Mts of Venezuela and Colombia

Atlapetes personatus (*Cabanis*) TEPUI FINCH Venezuela / forest

Atlapetes fulviceps (*Lafresnaye and d'Orbigny*) FULVOUS-HEADED FINCH Bolivia and NW Argentina / forest

Atlapetes citrinellus (*Cabanis*) YELLOW-STRIPED FINCH Andes of Argentina / dense scrub

Atlapetes brunneinucha (*Lafresnaye*) CHESTNUT-CAPPED FINCH Mts of Mexico, and C America to Venezuela and Ecuador / forest / n tree / e 1–2 / I 14–15 (*A. apertus* Wetmore, of Sierra de Tuxtla, Veracruz, is sometimes separated)

Atlapetes torquatus (*Lafresnaye and d'Orbigny*) STRIPE-HEADED and BLACK-HEADED FINCHES Mts from Mexico to Argentina / forest (*A. atricapillus* (Lawrence), 'Black-headed Finch', is often separated, but see R. A. Paynter in Peters' *Check List*, vol xiii, p 204, footnote, for comments, and see also his comments on this genus in general)

Pezopetes capitalis *Cabanis* LARGE-FOOTED FINCH Mts of Costa Rica and W Panama / n bush / e 1–2

Oreothraupis arremonops (*Sclater*) TANAGER FINCH SW Colombia and NW Ecuador / forest

Pselliophorus tibialis (*Lawrence*) YELLOW-THIGHED FINCH Mts of Costa Rica and W Panama / insects and berries / n grass / e 2

Pselliophorus luteoviridis *Griscom* YELLOW-GREEN FINCH E Chiriqui (Panama) / unique

Lysurus castaneiceps (*Sclater*) OLIVE FINCH Costa Rica, Panama and Andes from Colombia to Peru / forest

Urothraupis stolzmanni *Taczanowski and Berlepsch* BLACK-BACKED BUSH TANAGER Mts of Colombia and Ecuador / forest (this genus is placed by some in the Thraupidae)

Charitospiza eucosma *Oberholzer* CORAL-CRESTED FINCH C and E Brazil to NE Argentina / campos and cerrado

Coryphaspiza melanotis (*Temminck*) BLACK-MASKED FINCH C and E Brazil, E Bolivia, Paraguay and NE Argentina / campos and coastal dunes

Saltatricula multicolor (*Burmeister*) MANY-COLOURED CHACO FINCH SE Bolivia, W Paraguay, W Uruguay and N Argentina / thickets bordering fields

Gubernatrix cristata (*Vieillot*) YELLOW CARDINAL SE Brazil, Uruguay, N and E Argentina / shrubbery

Coryphospingus cucullatus (*Müller*) RED-CRESTED FINCH Eastern S America from the Guianas to N Argentina / scrub and cultivation

Coryphospingus pileatus (*Wied*) PILEATED FINCH Parts of Colombia, Venezuela and Brazil / dry scrub

Rhodospingus cruentus (*Lesson*) CRIMSON FINCH Arid tropical zone of Ecuador and Peru / dry scrub (this genus is placed by some in the Thraupidae)

Paroaria coronata (*Miller*) RED-CRESTED CARDINAL SE Brazil, E Bolivia, Paraguay, Uruguay and N Argentina, introduced Hawaii / wet scrub and shrubbery

Paroaria dominicana (*L*) RED-COWLED or DOMINICAN CARDINAL NE Brazil

[**Paroaria humberti** *Angelina*, is based on a single cage bird, believed to be a melanistic example of *P. dominicana*]

Paroaria gularis (*L*) RED-CAPPED CARDINAL S America E of Andes and S to Mato Grosso / wet scrub, mangroves and river-borders

Paroaria baeri *Hellmayr* CRIMSON-FRONTED CARDINAL Goiás and Mato Grosso

Paroaria capitata (*d'Orbigny and Lafresnaye*) YELLOW-BILLED CARDINAL SE Bolivia and Mato Grosso S to N Argentina / shrubbery in humid areas

CATAMBLYRHYNCHIDAE Plush-Capped Finch The affinities of this genus are uncertain, some consider it allied to the

Emberizidae, others to the Thraupidae. It is, however, frequently placed in a separate family, and is here retained as such, for convenience. Little is known of its habits.

Catamblyrhynchus diadema *Lafresnaye* PLUSH-CAPPED FINCH Andes from Venezuela to N Argentina / insects

CARDINALIDAE Cardinal Grosbeaks Seedeaters with stocky bodies and stout, strong bills. Frequently inhabitants of woodland, they are usually sexually dimorphic.

Spiza americana (*Gmelin*) DICKCISSEL SE Canada and eastern USA w Mexico S to Colombia, Venezuela, Trinidad and the Guianas / open country / n ground / e 3–5 / I ♀ 12–13

[**Spiza townsendi** (*Audubon*) Known only from the type from Pennsylvania / status uncertain / possibly a hybrid]

Pheucticus chrysopeplus (*Vigors*) YELLOW GROSBEAK Mexico, C America and Andes from Venezuela to Peru / open woodland and cultivation (*P. tibialis* and *P. chrysogaster* are sometimes separated)

Pheucticus aureoventris *d'Orbigny and Lafresnaye* BLACK-BELLIED GROSBEAK Andes from Venezuela to Argentina / forest

Pheucticus ludovicianus (*L*) ROSE-BREASTED GROSBEAK Much of C part of N America w Mexico, C America and Venezuela to Peru / forest and cultivation / insects, seeds and fruit / n tree or bush / e 3–5 / I ♂♀ 12–13

Pheucticus melanocephalus (*Swainson*) BLACK-HEADED GROSBEAK Pacific coast and Great Plains of N America S to Mexico / forest / insects, seeds and fruit / n tree or bush / e 2–5 / I ♂♀ 12 (*P. ludovicianus* and *P. melanocephalus* hybridise where they meet and are sometimes considered conspecific)

Cardinalis cardinalis (*L*) COMMON CARDINAL C and eastern USA, Mexico and S to Guatemala / open woodland and habitation / insects, seeds and fruit / n tree or bush / e 2–5 / I ♀ (♂) 11–12

Cardinalis phoeniceus *Bonaparte* VERMILION CARDINAL Coasts of Colombia and Venezuela / thorn and cactus scrub

Cardinalis sinuatus *Bonaparte* PYRRHULOXIA or BULLFINCH CARDINAL Mexico, S Texas and S Arizona / scrub / insects, seeds and fruit / n bush / e 2–5 / I ♀ / F c10 ?

Caryothraustes canadensis (*L*) YELLOW-GREEN GROSBEAK Brazil, SE Colombia, Venezuela and the Guianas / forest

Caryothraustes poliogaster (*Du Bus*) BLACK-FACED GROSBEAK Mexico to Panama / n tree / e 3 / I ♀ 13 / F 12

Caryothraustes humeralis (*Lawrence*) YELLOW-SHOULDERED GROSBEAK Colombia (known only from 'Bogotá' trade-skins), upper Río Napo in E Ecuador, and once on Río Purús, Brazil / forest

Rhodothraupis celaeno (*Deppe*) CRIMSON-COLLARED GROSBEAK Parts of Mexico

Periporphyrus erythromelas (*Gmelin*) RED AND BLACK GROSBEAK Mt Roraima (Venezuela), Guyana, Cayenne and NE Brazil S to Para / forest

Pitylus grossus (*L*) SLATE-COLOURED GROSBEAK Nicaragua to Panama and S America E of Andes and S to Argentina (*P. fuliginosus* (*Daudin*) is sometimes separated)

Saltator atriceps (*Lesson*) BLACK-HEADED SALTATOR Mexico to Panama

Saltator maximus (*Müller*) BUFF-THROATED SALTATOR Mexico to Panama, Colombia and S America E of Andes S to Mato Grosso / forest clearings, cerradão and trees bordering streams

Saltator atripennis *Sclater* BLACK-WINGED SALTATOR Andes of Colombia and Ecuador / open woodland

Saltator similis *d'Orbigny and Lafresnaye* GREEN-WINGED SALTATOR S Brazil, E Bolivia, Paraguay, Uruguay and N Argentina / open woodland and orchards

Saltator coerulescens *Vieillot* GREY SALTATOR Mexico, C America and S America E of Andes and S to N Argentina / arid woodland, scrub, campos and edges of mangroves

Saltator orenocensis *Lafresnaye* ORINOCO SALTATOR Orinoco basin / arid thorn-scrub

Saltator maxillosus *Cabanis* THICK-BILLED SALTATOR SE Brazil, NE Argentina, E Paraguay (? Uruguay) / woodland

Saltator aurantiirostris *Vieillot* GOLDEN-BILLED SALTATOR Ecuador to N Argentina and E to S Brazil, Paraguay and Uruguay / dry scrub (*S. nigriceps* (*Chapman*) is sometimes separated)

Saltator cinctus *Zimmer* MASKED SALTATOR E Ecuador / unique

Saltator atricollis *Vieillot* BLACK-THROATED SALTATOR Campos from E Bolivia to Paraguay and S Brazil / scrub and cerrado

Saltator rufiventris *d'Orbigny and Lafresnaye* RUFOUS-BELLIED SALTATOR Bolivia

Opposite:
ESTRILDIDAE:
Pytilia melba,
Melba Finch, Green-winged
Pytilia

ESTRILDIDAE:
Pytilia melba,
Melba Finch, Green-winged
Pytilia

ESTRILDIDAE:
Pytilia afra,
Orange-winged Pytilia

Plate 276

Plate 277

Saltator albicollis *Vieillot* STREAKED SALTATOR Lesser Antilles; Costa Rica, Panama, Colombia and Venezuela to Trinidad and offshore islands; arid coasts of Ecuador and Peru/dry scrub

Passerina glaucocaerulea (*d'Orbigny and Lafresnaye*) INDIGO GROSBEAK S Brazil to N Argentina/dense thickets

Passerina cyanoides (*Lafresnaye*) BLUE-BLACK GROSBEAK SE Mexico, C America and S America S to Ecuador and Mato Grosso/forest and semi-arid scrub

Passerina brissonii (*Lichtenstein*) (=**P. cyanea** (*L* 1758) (see Paynter in Peters' *Check List*, vol XIII, p 243 footnote) ULTA-MARINE GROSBEAK Much of S America E of Andes and S to N Argentina

Passerina parellina (*Bonaparte*) BLUE BUNTING Mexico to Nicaragua

Passerina caerulea (*L*) BLUE GROSBEAK Southern USA through Mexico to Costa Rica/scrub and orchard/insects, fruit and seeds/n bush/e 2–5/I ♀ 11

Passerina cyanea (*L* 1766) (see reference in *P. brissonii*) INDIGO BUNTING b Eastern N America w Mexico, C America, Bahamas, Cuba and Jamaica (sometimes Colombia and Venezuela)/forest, scrub and swamp/insects, seeds and fruit/n bush/e 2–4/I ♀ (♂?) 12–13

Passerina amoena (*Say*) LAZULI BUNTING b Western N America w Mexico (hybridises with *cyanea* in Great Plains, sometimes the two are considered conspecific)/scrub and open forest/insects, seeds and fruit/n bush/e 3–5/I 12/F 10

Passerina versicolor (*Bonaparte*) VARIED BUNTING South-western USA, Mexico and Guatemala/arid bush and desert/seeds and insects/n bush/e 2–4

Passerina ciris (*L*) PAINTED BUNTING Southern USA through Mexico to Panama/scrub and grass/n bush/e 3–5

Passerina rositae (*Lawrence*) ROSITA BUNTING Mexico in isthmus of Tehuantepec, SE Oaxaca and W Chiapas

Passerina leclancherii *Lafresnaye* ORANGE-BREASTED BUNTING Mexico

Passerina caerulescens (*Wied*) BLUE FINCH Campos of Brazil and SE Bolivia

THRAUPIDAE Tanagers Small to medium-sized seedeaters, usually with short, rounded wings, and adapted to a basically fruit and nectar diet. Confined to the New World tropics. Most species are brightly coloured, but some are dull.

Orchesticus abeillei (*Lesson*) BROWN TANAGER SE Brazil

Schistoclamys ruficapillus (*Vieillot*) CINNAMON TANAGER E Brazil

Schistoclamys melanopis (*Latham*) BLACK-FACED TANAGER S America E of Andes and S to Mato Grosso/savannah, woodland and cerrado

Neothraupis fasciata (*Lichtenstein*) WHITE-BANDED TANAGER E and S Brazil, E Bolivia and NE Paraguay

Cypsnagra hirundinacea (*Lesson*) WHITE-RUMPED TANAGER S Brazil, N and E Bolivia and NE Paraguay/cerrado

Conothraupis speculigera (*Gould*) BLACK-AND-WHITE TANAGER Peru and S Ecuador

Conothraupis mesoleuca (*Berlioz*) CONE-BILLED TANAGER Mato Grosso/dry open woodland

Lamprospiza melanoleuca (*Vieillot*) RED-BILLED PIED TANAGER The Guianas, N Brazil and Upper Amazon basin/bushy savannah

Cissopis leveriana (*Gmelin*) MAGPIE TANAGER S America E of Andes and S to Argentina/forest edge

Chlorornis riefferii (*Boissonneau*) GRASS-GREEN TANAGER Andes from Colombia to Bolivia/forest

Compsothraupis loricata (*Lichtenstein*) SCARLET-THROATED TANAGER Interior of Brazil

Sericossypha albocristata (*Lafresnaye*) WHITE-CAPPED TANAGER Andes from Venezuela to Peru/open forest

Nesospingus speculiferus (*Lawrence*) PUERTO RICAN TANAGER Puerto Rico/forest/n tree?/e 1? (1 nest known, but identity not proven)

Chlorospingus opthalmicus (*Du Bus*) COMMON BUSH-TANAGER Mexico, C America and Andes from Venezuela to N Argentina/forest and woodland/nectar, insects and fruit/n tree or ground/e 2/I ♀ 14/F 13

Chlorospingus tacarunae *Griscom* TACARUNA BUSH-TANAGER Mt Tacaruna, Panama-Colombia border

Chlorospingus inornatus (*Nelson*) PIRRI BUSH-TANAGER Mt Pirri in E Panama

Chlorospingus punctulatus *Sclater and Salvin* DOTTED BUSH-TANAGER W Panama

Chlorospingus semifuscus *Sclater and Salvin* DUSKY-BILLED BUSH-TANAGER Andes of Colombia and W Ecuador/forest

Chlorospingus zeledoni *Ridgway* VOLCANO BUSH-TANAGER Volcanos of Turrialba and Irazú, Costa Rica

Chlorospingus pileatus *Salvin* SOOTY-CAPPED BUSH-TANAGER Mts of Costa Rica and W Panama

Chlorospingus parvirostris *Chapman* SHORT-BILLED BUSH-TANAGER Andes from Colombia to Bolivia / forest

Chlorospingus flavigularis (*Sclater*) YELLOW-THROATED BUSH TANAGER Panama and Andes from Colombia to Peru and Bolivia/ forest

Chlorospingus flavovirens (*Lawrence*) YELLOW-GREEN BUSH-TANAGER W Ecuador, known only from Santo Domingo de los Colorados and from 'Quito' trade-skins

Chlorospingus canigularis (*Lafresnaye*) ASHY-THROATED BUSH-TANAGER Costa Rica, and Andes from Venezuela to Peru / forest edge

Cnemoscopus rubrirostris (*Lafresnaye*) GREY-HOODED TANAGER Andes from Venezuela to Peru / forest

Hemispingus atropileus (*Lafresnaye*) BLACK-CAPPED HEMISPINGUS Andes from Venezuela to Bolivia / forest

Hemispingus parodii *Weiske and Terborgh* (*Wilson Bulletin* (1974), vol 86, pt 2, p 97) PARODIS TANAGER Peru in the Cordillera Vilcabamba / hill scrub / no other data

Hemispingus superciliaris (*Lafresnaye*) SUPERCILIARIED HEMISPINGUS Andes from Venezuela to Bolivia / forest

Hemispingus reyi (*Berlepsch*) GREY-CAPPED HEMISPINGUS SW Venezuela / forest

Hemispingus frontalis (*Tschudi*) OLEAGINOUS HEMISPINGUS Andes from Venezuela to Peru

Hemispingus melanotis (*Sclater*) BLACK-EARED HEMISPINGUS Andes from Venezuela to Bolivia / forest

Hemispingus goeringi (*Sclater and Salvin*) SLATY-BACKED HEMISPINGUS SW Venezuela/ forest

Hemispingus verticalis (*Lafresnaye*) BLACK-HEADED HEMISPINGUS Andes from Venezuela to Ecuador / forest

Hemispingus xanthophthalmus (*Taczanowski*) DRAB HEMISPINGUS C Peru

Hemispingus trifasciatus (*Taczanowski*) THREE-STRIPED HEMISPINGUS SE Peru and W Bolivia

Pyrrhocoma ruficeps (*Strickland*) CHESTNUT-HEADED TANAGER SE Brazil and adjoining parts of Paraguay and Argentina / forest undergrowth

Thlypopsis fulviceps *Cabanis* FULVOUS-HEADED TANAGER Venezuela and Colombia/ forest

Thlypopsis ornata (*Sclater*) RUFOUS-CHESTED TANAGER Andes from Colombia to Peru / open woodland

Thlypopsis pectoralis (*Taczanowski*) BROWN-FLANKED TANAGER C Peru / bushy mountain slopes along streams

Thlypopsis sordida (*d'Orbigny and Lafresnaye*) ORANGE-HEADED TANAGER Parts of S America E of Andes and S to N Argentina / forest edge, park and open woodland

Thlypopsis inornata (*Taczanowski*) BUFF-BELLIED TANAGER N Peru

Thlypopsis ruficeps (*d'Orbigny and Lafresnaye*) RUST AND YELLOW TANAGER SE Peru, Bolivia and NW Argentina / open woodland

Hemithraupis guira (*L*) GUIRA TANAGER S America E of Andes and S to N Argentina/ forest tree tops and parks

Hemithraupis ruficapilla (*Vieillot*) RUFOUS-HEADED TANAGER E and SE Brazil / forest edge and parkland

Hemithraupis flavicollis (*Vieillot*) YELLOW-BACKED TANAGER E Panama, Colombia and S America E of Andes S to Brazil / forest treetops, parks and cerrado

Chrysothlypis chrysomelas (*Sclater and Salvin*) BLACK AND YELLOW TANAGER Costa Rica and Panama

Chrysothlypis salmoni (*Sclater*) SCARLET AND WHITE TANAGER W Colombia and NW Ecuador / forest

Nemosia pileata (*Boddaert*) PILEATED or HOODED TANAGER S America E of Andes and S to N Argentina / forest, coffee plantations and mangroves

Nemosia rourei *Cabanis* ROURE'S TANAGER Rio de Janeiro, Brazil / unique

Phaenicophilus palmarum (*L*) BLACK-CROWNED PALM TANAGER Hispaniola and Saona/ woodland and semi-arid scrub / n bush or tree/ e 2–3

Phaenicophilus poliocephalus (*Bonaparte*) GREY-CROWNED PALM TANAGER Hispaniola, Ile à Uache and Grande Cayemite / woodland and semi-arid scrub / n bush or tree / e 2–4

Calyptophilus frugivorus (*Cory*) CHAT

ESTRILDIDAE:
Pyrenestes sanguineus,
Crimson Seed-cracker

ESTRILDIDAE:
Hypargos niveoguttatus,
Peters' Twin-spot

Plate 278

ESTRILDIDAE:
Lagonsticta senegala,
Red-billed Fire-Finch

Plate 279

TANAGER Hispaniola and Gonave / mountain thickets (Hispaniola), low arid scrub (Gonave)/ n tree? / e 1? (1 nest known, but identity not proved)

Rhodinocichla rosea (*Lesson*) ROSY THRUSH-TANAGER Mexico: Costa Rica, Panama, Venezeula and Colombia / woodland and dense secondary growth

Mitrospingus cassinii (*Lawrence*) DUSKY-FACED TANAGER Lowlands of Costa Rica and Panama, W Colombia and W Ecuador / humid forest / fruit and insects / n 'in a streamside tangle' (sic) / e ?2

Mitrospingus oleagineus (*Salvin*) OLIVE-BACKED TANAGER S Venezuela, Guyana and extreme N Brazil / humid forest

Chlorothraupis carmioli (*Lawrence*) CARMIOL'S TANAGER Nicaragua to Panama, E base of Andes from S Colombia to SE Peru

Chlorothraupis olivacea (*Cassin*) LEMON-BROWED TANAGER E Panama, W Colombia and NW Ecuador / forest

Chlorothraupis stolzmanni (*Berlepsch and Taczanowski*) OCHRE-BREASTED TANAGER SW Colombia and W Ecuador / forest

Orthogonys chloricterus (*Vieillot*) OLIVE-GREEN TANAGER SE Brazil in the coastal regions

Eucometis penicillata (*Spix*) GREY-HEADED TANAGER SE Mexico to Panama, and much of S America E of Andes and S to Paraguay / forest, woodland and swamps / army ants (which it follows)

Lanio fulvus (*Boddaert*) FULVOUS SHRIKE-TANAGER S America E of Andes and S to Amazon / forest

Lanio versicolor (*d'Orbigny and Lafresnaye*) WHITE-WINGED SHRIKE-TANAGER Upper Amazon basin and S to Mato Grosso / forest

Lanio leucothorax *Salvin* WHITE-THROATED SHRIKE-TANAGER Honduras to Panama

Lanio aurantius *Lafresnaye* BLACK-THROATED SHRIKE-TANAGER SE Mexico, Guatemala, Belize and Honduras

Creurgops verticalis *Sclater* RUFOUS-EARED TANAGER Andes from Venezuela to Peru / forest

Creurgops dentata (*Sclater and Salvin*) SLATY TANAGER SE Peru and N Bolivia

Heterospingus xanthopygius (*Sclater*) SCARLET-BROWED TANAGER Costa Rica, Panama and Pacific coast of Colombia and Ecuador forest (*H. rubrifrons* (Lawrence) is sometimes separated)

Tachyphonus cristatus (*L*) FLAME-CRESTED TANAGER S America, E of Andes and S to E Brazil / open woodland and cocoa plantations

Tachyphonus nattereri *Pelzeln* NATTERER'S TANAGER SW Brazil / known from a male and (possibly) a female (sometimes treated as conspecific with *T. cristatus*)

Tachyphonus rufiventer (*Spix*) YELLOW-CRESTED TANAGER E Peru, N Bolivia and W Brazil

Tachyphonus surinamus (*L*) FULVOUS-CRESTED TANAGER S America E of Andes S to Amazon basin / forest

Tachyphonus luctuosus *d'Orbigny and Lafresnaye* WHITE-SHOULDERED TANAGER Honduras to Panama and S America (except Andes) S to Ecuador and Mato Grosso / forest and plantation / insects and fruit / n low vegetation / e 3

Tachyphonus delatrii *Lafresnaye* TAWNY-CRESTED TANAGER Nicaragua to Panama, Colombia and W Ecuador / forest

Tachyphonus coronatus (*Vieillot*) RUBY-CROWNED TANAGER SE Brazil, E Paraguay and N Argentina / forest

Tachyphonus rufus (*Boddaert*) WHITE-LINED TANAGER Costa Rica, Panama, Colombia and S America E of Andes S to N Argentina / forest and cultivation / fruit and insects / n tree / e 2–3 / I ♀ 14–15

Tachyphonus phoenicius *Swainson* RED-SHOULDERED TANAGER C Colombia, S Venezuela, the Guianas, E Peru and Brazil S to Mato Grosso / savannah

Trichothraupis melanops (*Vieillot*) BLACK-GOGGLED TANAGER E Peru, E Bolivia, SE Brazil, Paraguay and NE Argentina / shrubbery

Habia rubrica (*Vieillot*) RED-CROWNED TANAGER Mexico to Panama and much of S America S to N Argentina / forest / arthropods and berries / n tree / e 1–3 / I ♀ 13 / F 10

Habia fuscicauda (*Cabanis*) JUNGLE TANAGER Mexico to Panama and Caribbean coast of Colombia / forest and woodland

Habia atrimaxillaris (*Dwight and Griscom*) BLACK-BILLED TANAGER SW Costa Rica (status uncertain, perhaps a race of *H. fuscicauda*)

Habia gutturalis (*Sclater*) SOOTY TANAGER NW Colombia / forest

Habia cristata (*Lawrence*) CRESTED TANAGER W Colombia / forest

Piranga bidentata (*Swainson*) FLAME-

COLOURED or STRIPED TANAGER Mexico to Panama / n tree / e ?2

Piranga flava (*Vieillot*) HEPATIC TANAGER South-western USA, Mexico, C America and S America S to N Argentina / forest and secondary growth / berries and insects / n tree / e 2–5

Piranga rubra (*L*) SUMMER TANAGER Southern USA and Mexico w S to Venezuela / forest and open woodland / insects and fruit / n tree / e 3–5 / I 12

Piranga roseogularis (*Cabot*) ROSE-THROATED TANAGER Yucatan Peninsula to Guatemala and offshore islands (? Belize)

Piranga olivacea (*Gmelin*) SCARLET TANAGER b Eastern N America w eastern S America / forest / insects and fruit / n tree / e 3–5 / I ♀ 13–14 / F 15

Piranga ludoviciana (*Wilson*) WESTERN TANAGER b western N America w Mexico to Panama / coniferous forest / insects and fruit / n tree / e 3–5 / I ♀ 13

Piranga leucoptera (*Trudeau*) WHITE-WINGED TANAGER Mexico to Panama and Andes from Venezuela to Bolivia / forest and scrub

Piranga erythrocephala (*Swainson*) RED-HEADED TANAGER Mexico

Piranga rubriceps (*Gray*) RED-HOODED TANAGER W Colombia, Ecuador and N Peru / forest

Calochetes coccineus (*Sclater*) VERMILION TANAGER S Colombia, E Ecuador and E Peru / forest

Ramphocelus sanguinolentus (*Lesson*) CRIMSON-COLLARED TANAGER Mexico to Panama

Ramphocelus nigrogularis (*Spix*) MASKED CRIMSON TANAGER Upper Amazon basin / forest

Ramphocelus dimidiatus *Lafresnaye* CRIMSON-BACKED TANAGER Panama and offshore islands, mts of Colombia and Venezuela / brushland, plantations and open woodland

Ramphocelus melanogaster (*Swainson*) BLACK-BELLIED TANAGER Peru / light woodland and cultivation

Ramphocelus carbo (*Pallas*) SILVER-BEAKED TANAGER S America E of Andes and S to Paraguay and Mato Grosso / light woodland and cultivation / fruit / n tree or bush / e 1–3 / I ♀ 11–12 [*R. uropygialis* Bonaparte, is a hybrid *R. carbo* × *R. melanogaster*]

Ramphocelus bresilius (*L*) BRAZILIAN TANAGER E Brazil / forest edge and capoeira

Ramphocelus passerinii *Bonaparte* SONG TANAGER Mexico to Panama

Ramphocelus flammigerus (*Jardine and Selby*) FLAME-RUMPED TANAGER W Colombia / secondary growth and clearings

Ramphocelus icteronotus *Bonaparte* YELLOW-RUMPED TANAGER Panama, W Colombia and W Ecuador / damp clearings

[Note: *R. flammigerus* and *R. icteronotus* are variously described as races or as full species. Apparently intergrades occur and the name *Ramphocelus chrysonotus* Lafresnaye, refers to such an one]

Spindalis zena (*L*) STRIPED-HEADED TANAGER Bahamas, Greater Antilles and Grand Cayman / forest and shrubbery / n bush or tree / e 2–3

Thraupis episcopus (*L*) BLUE TANAGER Mexico to Panama and much of S America S to Bolivia / open woodland and cultivation / fruit and insects / n tree or shrub / e 1–3 / I ♀ 14 / F 17

Thraupis sayaca (*L*) SAYACA TANAGER Bolivia, E and S Brazil, Paraguay, Uruguay and N and E Argentina / arid scrub and woodland (*T. s. glaucocolpa* Cabanis, from the Caribbean coast of Colombia and Venezuela, a well-marked isolate form is generally treated as a race of *T. sayaca*, but may possibly prove to be a species)

Thraupis cyanoptera (*Vieillot*) AZURE-SHOULDERED TANAGER SE Bolivia and E Paraguay / forest

Thraupis ornata (*Sparrman*) GOLDEN-CHEVRONED TANAGER SE Brazil / parks and capoeira

Thraupis abbas (*Deppe*) YELLOW-WINGED TANAGER Mexico to Nicaragua

Thraupis palmarum (*Wied*) PALM TANAGER Nicaragua to Panama and Pacific slope of Colombia and Ecuador, S America E of Andes S to Bolivia, Paraguay and Mato Grosso / forest and cultivation / fruit, nectar and insects / n tree / e 2–3 / I ♀ 14 / F 17–20

Thraupis cyanocephala (*d'Orbigny and Lafresnaye*) BLUE-CAPPED TANAGER Venezuela, Trinidad, Colombia and W Ecuador / forest and cultivation / berries / n tree / e 2

Thraupis bonariensis (*Gmelin*) BLUE AND YELLOW TANAGER Central belt of S America from Ecuador to Chile and from S Brazil to N Argentina / bushy pastures and parks

Opposite:
ESTRILDIDAE:
Amandava amandava,
Strawberry Finch or
Red Avadavat

ESTRILDIDAE:
Estrilda nonnula,
Black-crowned Waxbill

ESTRILDIDAE:
Estrilda erythronotos,
Black-faced Waxbill, Black-
cheeked Waxbill

ESTRILDIDAE:
Estrilda astrild, Common Waxbill

Plate 280

Plate 281

Cyanicterus cyanicterus (*Vieillot*) BLUE-BACKED TANAGER E Venezuela and the Guianas/forest and savannah

Buthraupis arcaei *Sclater and Salvin* BLUE AND GOLD TANAGER Costa Rica and Panama

Buthraupis melanochlamys *Hellmayr* BLACK AND GOLD TANAGER W Colombia/forest

Buthraupis rothschildi *Berlepsch* ROTHSCHILD'S TANAGER SW Colombia and NW Ecuador/forest

Buthraupis edwardsi *Elliot* MOSS-BACKED TANAGER SW Colombia and NW Ecuador/forest

Buthraupis aureocincta *Hellmayr* GOLD-RINGED TANAGER W Colombia/forest

Buthraupis montana (*d'Orbigny and Lafresnaye*) HOODED MOUNTAIN TANAGER Andes from Venezuela to Bolivia/forest

Buthraupis eximia (*Boissonneau*) BLACK-CHESTED MOUNTAIN TANAGER Andes from Venezuela to Ecuador/forest

Buthraupis wetmorei (*Moore*) MASKED MOUNTAIN TANAGER SW Colombia and SC Ecuador/forest

Wetmorethraupis sterrhopteron *Lowery and O'Neill* WETMORE'S TANAGER or ORANGE-THROATED TANAGER Cordillera del Condor in N Peru/forest

Anisognathus lachrymosus (*Du Bus*) LACHRYMOSE TANAGER Andes from Venezuela to Peru/forest

Anisognathus melanogenys (*Salvin and Godman*) BLACK-CHEEKED MOUNTAIN TANAGER Sierra Nevada de Santa Marta, Colombia/forest

Anisognathus igniventris (*d'Orbigny and Lafresnaye*) SCARLET-BELLIED MOUNTAIN TANAGER Andes from Venezuela to Bolivia/thickets and open woodland

Anisognathus flavinuchus (*d'Orbigny and Lafresnaye*) BLUE-WINGED MOUNTAIN TANAGER Andes from Venezuela to Bolivia/forest

Anisognathus notabilis (*Sclater*) BLACK-CHINNED MOUNTAIN TANAGER SW Colombia and NW Ecuador

Stephanophorus diadematus (*Temminck*) DIADEMED TANAGER SE Brazil, Uruguay, Paraguay and N Argentina/forest and dense shrubbery

Iridosornis porphyrocephala (*Sclater*) PURPLE-MANTLED TANAGER W Colombia and W Ecuador/forest

Iridosornis analis (*Tschudi*) YELLOW-THROATED TANAGER E Ecuador and E Peru/forest

Iridosornis jelskii (*Cabanis*) JELSKI'S TANAGER SE Peru and W Bolivia

Iridosornis rufivertex (*Lafresnaye*) SCARFED TANAGER Andes from Venezuela to Peru/forest (*I. reinhardti* (Sclater) is sometimes separated)

Dubusia taeniata (*Boissonneau*) DU BUS'S TANAGER Andes from Venezuela to Peru/forest

Delothraupis castanoventris (*Sclater*) CHESTNUT-BELLIED MOUNTAIN TANAGER E Peru and Bolivia/open woodland and cultivation

Pipraeidea melanonota (*Vieillot*) FAWN-BREASTED TANAGER Andes from Peru to N Argentina, and Mato Grosso and Bahia through Paraguay and Uruguay to NE Argentina/forest borders and clearings

Euphonia jamaica (*L*) JAMAICA EUPHONIA Jamaica/fairly ubiquitous, but commonest in open country/n tree/e 3–4

Euphonia plumbea *Du Bus* PLUMBEOUS EUPHONIA S Venezuela, Guyana, Surinam and N Brazil/forest

Euphonia affinis (*Lesson*) SCRUB EUPHONIA Mexico to Costa Rica

Euphonia luteicapilla (*Cabanis*) YELLOW-CROWNED EUPHONIA E Nicaragua, Costa Rica and Panama

Euphonia chlorotica (*L*) CHLOROTIC or PURPLE-THROATED EUPHONIA S America E of Andes and S to N Argentina/forest

Euphonia trinitatis *Strickland* TRINIDAD EUPHONIA N Colombia, N Venezuela, Trinidad and Tobago/secondary forest and cultivation/berries and insects/n tree/e 4/I ♀

Euphonia concinna *Sclater* VELVET-FRONTED EUPHONIA C Colombia

Euphonia saturata (*Cabanis*) ORANGE-CROWNED EUPHONIA W Colombia, W Ecuador and NW Peru/forest

Euphonia finschi *Sclater and Salvin* FINSCH'S EUPHONIA The Guianas/savannah and shrubbery

Euphonia violacea (*L*) VIOLET EUPHONIA E Venezuela and Guianas S through Brazil to Paraguay and NE Argentina, also Trinidad and Tobago/forest, secondary growth and plantations/fruit/n ground or stump/e 3–4/I ♀

Euphonia laniirostris *d'Orbigny and Lafresnaye* SHRIKE-BILLED EUPHONIA Costa Rica, Panama and S America on both sides of

Andes S to Peru and Bolivia / open woodland

Euphonia hirundinacea *Bonaparte* SWALLOW EUPHONIA Mexico to Panama

Euphonia chalybea (*Mikan*) GREEN-THROATED EUPHONIA SE Brazil, Paraguay and N Argentina / forest and savannah

Euphonia musica (*Gmelin*) BLUE-CROWNED EUPHONIA Mexico to Panama, S America S to N Argentina, Hispaniola, Puerto Rico and Lesser Antilles / forest and cultivation / berries / n tree / e 2–4 (*E. elegantissima* (Bonaparte) is sometimes separated)

Euphonia fulvicrissa *Sclater* FULVOUS-VENTED EUPHONIA Panama, Colombia and NW Ecuador (? Costa Rica)

Euphonia imitans (*Hellmayr*) SPOT-CROWNED EUPHONIA Pacific slope of Costa Rica and W Panama / insects and spiders / n tree / e 2–3/ I ♀ 18

Euphonia gouldi *Sclater* GOULDIAN EUPHONIA Caribbean slope from SE Mexico to Panama and Pacific slope of Costa Rica

Euphonia chrysopasta *Sclater and Salvin* GOLDEN-BELLIED EUPHONIA Amazon basin N to the Guianas and Upper Orinoco / shrubbery in open forest

Euphonia mesochrysa *Salvadori* BRONZE EUPHONIA Andes from Colombia to Bolivia / forest

Euphonia minuta *Cabanis* WHITE-VENTED EUPHONIA From S Mexico through C America to W Colombia and W Ecuador, and S America E of Andes S to Mato Grosso / insects, spiders and mistletoe berries / n tree / e 3 / I ♀ 17 / F 20

Euphonia anneae *Cassin* TAWNY-CAPPED EUPHONIA Costa Rica, Panama and NW Colombia

Euphonia xanthogaster (*Sundevall*) ORANGE-BELLIED EUPHONIA E Panama, Colombia and Ecuador W of Andes, and much of S America E of Andes S to Brazil / forest

Euphonia rufiventris (*Vieillot*) RUFOUS-BELLIED EUPHONIA Orinoco and Upper Amazon basins / forest

Euphonia pectoralis (*Latham*) CHESTNUT-BELLIED EUPHONIA SE Brazil, Paraguay and N Argentina / forest

Euphonia cayennensis (*Gmelin*) GOLDEN-SIDED EUPHONIA SE Venezuela, the Guianas and N Brazil / forest and savannah

[**Euphonia vittata** *Sclater* is probably a hybrid *E. xanthogaster* × *E. pectoralis*. *E.*

catasticta Oberholzer, is a synonym.]

Chlorophonia flavirostris *Sclater* YELLOW-COLLARED CHLOROPHONIA SW slope of Andes of W Colombia and W Ecuador / forest

Chlorophonia cyanea (*Thunberg*) BLUE CHLOROPHONIA Colombia and Venezuela, S America E of Andes and S to N Argentina / forest

Chlorophonia pyrrhophrys (*Sclater*) CHESTNUT-BREASTED CHLOROPHONIA W Venezuela, Colombia and E Ecuador / forest

Chlorophonia occipitalis (*Du Bus*) BLUE-CROWNED TANAGER SE Mexico to N Nicaragua

Chlorophonia callophrys (*Cabanis*) GOLDEN-BROWED TANAGER Costa Rica and Panama

Chlorochrysa phoenicotis (*Bonaparte*) GLISTENING GREEN TANAGER W Colombia and W Ecuador / creepers on forest trees

Chlorochrysa calliparaea (*Tschudi*) ORANGE-EARED TANAGER Andes from Colombia to Bolivia / forest (among parasitic plants)

Chlorochrysa nitidissima *Sclater* MULTI-COLOURED TANAGER W Colombia

Tangara inornata (*Gould*) PLAIN TANAGER Costa Rica, Panama and Colombia / forest

Tanagara cabanisi (*Sclater*) CABANIS'S TANAGER S Mexico and SW Guatemala

Tangara palmeri (*Hellmayr*) GREY AND GOLD TANAGER Pacific coast of E Panama, W Colombia and W Ecuador / forest

Tangara mexicana (*L*) TURQUOISE TANAGER Trinidad, Colombia, Venezuela, the Guianas and much of Brazil / forest, open woodland and cultivation / fruit and insects / n tree / e 3

Tangara chilensis (*Vigors*) PARADISE TANAGER S America E of Andes and S to Bolivia and S Brazil / forest

Tangara fastuosa (*Lesson*) SUPERB TANAGER E Brazil / forest and capoeira

Tangara seledon (*Müller*) CELADON or GREEN-HEADED TANAGER SE Brazil and adjoining parts of Paraguay and Argentina / forest

Tangara cyanocephala (*Müller*) RED-NECKED or BLUE-HEADED TANAGER E and S Brazil and adjacent parts of Paraguay and Argentina / forest

Tangara desmaresti (*Vieillot*) BRASS-BREASTED TANAGER Coast of SE Brazil

Tangara cyanoventris (*Vieillot*) GILT-EDGED TANAGER SE Brazil

[**T. gouldi** (*Sclater*) is believed to be a hybrid *T. desmaresti* × *T. cyanoventris*]

ESTRILDIDAE:
Uraeginthus cyanocephala,
Blue-capped Cordon-Bleu

ESTRILDIDAE:
Uraeginthus bengalus,
Red-cheeked Cordon-Bleu

Plate 282

A small group of Blue-capped
Cordon-Bleus, *U. cyanocephala*

Plate 283

Tangara johannae (*Dalmas*) WHISKERED TANAGER W Colombia and NW Ecuador

Tangara schrankii (*Spix*) GREEN AND GOLD TANAGER Upper Amazon basin and Pacific slope of W Andes of Colombia / forest

Tangara florida (*Sclater and Salvin*) EMERALD TANAGER Costa Rica, Panama and Pacific coast of Colombia / forest

Tangara arthus *Lesson* GOLDEN TANAGER Andes from Venezuela to Bolivia / forest

Tangara icterocephala (*Bonaparte*) SILVER-THROATED TANAGER Costa Rica, Panama, W Colombia and W Ecuador / humid forest

Tangara xanthocephala (*Tschudi*) SAFFRON-CROWNED TANAGER Andes from Venezuela to Bolivia / forest and light woodland

Tangara chrysotis (*Du Bus*) BLUE-BROWED TANAGER S Colombia, E Ecuador, E Peru and N Bolivia / forest

Tangara parzudakii (*Lafresnaye*) PARZUDAKI'S TANAGER Andes from Venezuela to Peru / forest

Tangara xanthogastra (*Sclater*) YELLOW-BELLIED TANAGER Upper Amazon basin and mts of S Colombia and Venezuela / forest

Tangara punctata (*L*) SPOTTED TANAGER Upper Amazon basin

Tangara guttata (*Cabanis*) SPECKLED TANAGER Costa Rica, Panama, Colombia, Venezuela and extreme N Brazil / forest and second growth / fruit / n ? / e 2 / I ♀ 13 / F 15

Tangara varia (*Müller*) DOTTED TANAGER S Venezuela, the Guianas and N Brazil

Tangara rufigula (*Bonaparte*) RUFOUS-THROATED TANAGER Pacific slope of Colombia and NW Ecuador / forest

Tangara gyrola (*L*) GYROLA or BAY-HEADED TANAGER Costa Rica, Panama and much of S America on both sides of Andes S to Ecuador, Bolivia and Mato Grosso / forest / fruit and insects / n tree / e 2 / I ♀ 13–14 / F 15–16

Tangara lavinia (*Cassin*) LAVINIA or RUFOUS-WINGED TANAGER Guatemala to Panama; Pacific slope of Colombia and Ecuador / forest

Tangara cayana (*L*) CAYENNE or RUFOUS-CROWNED TANAGER S America E of Andes and S to Mato Grosso / savannah, cerrado and gardens

[**Tangara arnaulti** *Berlioz* the unique type, a cage bird of uncertain origin, is believed to be a hybrid *T. cayana* × *T. preciosa*]

Tangara cucullata (*Swainson*) HOODED TANAGER Grenada and St Vincent / forest and secondary growth / n tree or bush / e 2

Tangara peruviana (*Desmarest*) BLACK-BACKED TANAGER SE Brazil / forest

Tangara preciosa (*Cabanis*) CHESTNUT-BACKED TANAGER SE Brazil, Paraguay, Uruguay and NE Argentina

Tangara vitriolina (*Cabanis*) SCRUB TANAGER W and C Colombia and W Ecuador / dry scrub

Tangara rufigenis (*Sclater*) RUFOUS-CHEEKED TANAGER Mts of N Venezuela / forest

Tangara ruficervix (*Prévost and Des Murs*) GOLDEN-NAPED TANAGER E slopes of Andes from Colombia to Bolivia

Tangara labradorides (*Boissonneau*) METALLIC-GREEN TANAGER S America W of E Andes from Colombia to Peru

Tangara cyanotis (*Sclater*) BLUE-BROWED TANAGER S Colombia, E Ecuador, E Peru and N Bolivia / forest

Tangara cyanicollis (*d'Orbigny and Lafresnaye*) BLUE-NECKED TANAGER Andes from Colombia to Bolivia and Mato Grosso; Goiás, Brazil / forest

Tangara larvata (*Du Bus*) MASKED TANAGER S Mexico to Panama and Pacific slope of Colombia and Ecuador

Tangara nigrocincta (*Bonaparte*) BLACK-TINTED TANAGER Headwaters of Amazon from Guyana, S Venezuela and S Colombia to Bolivia / forests, plantations and clearings

Tangara dowii (*Salvin*) SPANGLED TANAGER Costa Rica and Panama

Tangara nigroviridis (*Lafresnaye*) GREEN AND BLACK or BERYL-SPANGLED TANAGER Andes from Venezuela to Bolivia / open forest

Tangara vassorii (*Boissonneau*) BLUE AND BLACK TANAGER Andes from Venezuela, Colombia and E Ecuador / forest clearings

Tangara heinei (*Cabanis*) BLACK-CAPPED TANAGER Andes of NW Venezuela, Colombia and E Ecuador / forest clearings

Tangara viridicollis (*Taczanowski*) SILVER TANAGER Peru and S Ecuador / woodland and secondary growth

Tangara argyrofenges (*Sclater and Salvin*) GREEN-THROATED TANAGER N Peru: WC Bolivia

Tangara cyanoptera (*Swainson*) BLACK-HEADED TANAGER Mts of Colombia, Venezuela, Guyana and extreme N Brazil / forest

Tangara pulcherrima (*Sclater*) GOLDEN-COLLARED TANAGER Colombia and Ecuador /

orange-groves and forest (sometimes placed in the monotypic genus *Iridophanes*; de Schaunsee places *Iridophanes* next to *Chlorophanes* in the Coerebidae)

Tangara velia (*L*) OPAL TANAGER S America E of Andes and S to SE Brazil / forest

Tangara callophrys (*Cabanis*) OPAL-CROWNED TANAGER SE Colombia, E Ecuador, E Peru and W Brazil to N boundary of Bolivia / forest clearings

[NB: The remaining genera are placed by some authorities for convenience in the Coerebidae, a family not recognised here]

Dacnis albiventris (*Sclater*) WHITE-BELLIED DACNIS Upper Amazon basin / forest

Dacnis lineata (*Gmelin*) BLACK-FACED DACNIS Colombia, W Ecuador, Venezuela and Amazon basin / open forest and orange groves

Dacnis flaviventer *d'Orbigny and Lafresnaye* YELLOW-BELLIED DACNIS Upper Amazon basin / forest

Dacnis hartlaubi *Sclater* HARTLAUB'S or TURQUOISE DACNIS W Colombia (sometimes placed in the monotypic genus *Pseudodacnis*)

Dacnis nigripes *Pelzeln* BLACK-LEGGED DACNIS SE Brazil

Dacnis venusta *Lawrence* SCARLET-THIGHED DACNIS Costa Rica, Panama and Pacific slope of Colombia and Ecuador / humid forest and coffee plantations

Dacnis cayana (*L*) BLUE DACNIS E Nicaragua to Panama, and much of S America S to N Argentina / open forest and orange groves

Dacnis viguieri *Salvin and Godman* VIRIDIAN DACNIS E Panama and NW Colombia / forest and shrubbery

Dacnis berlepschi *Hartert* BERLEPSCH'S or SCARLET-BREASTED DACNIS SW Colombia and NW Ecuador / rare / forest

Chlorophanes spiza (*L*) GREEN HONEY-CREEPER S Mexico to Panama and much of S America S to Mato Grosso / forest

[**Chlorophanes purpurascens** *Sclater and Salvin* is believed to be a hybrid *C. spiza* × *Cyanerpes cyaneus*]

Cyanerpes nitidus (*Hartlaub*) SHORT-BILLED HONEYCREEPER Colombia, E Ecuador, S Venezuela, NE Peru through W Brazil to Mato Grosso / forest

Cyanerpes lucidus (*Sclater and Salvin*) SHINING HONEYCREEPER S Mexico to Panama

and extreme NW Colombia / open forest / insects nectar and fruit / n tree / e 2 / I ♀ 12–13 / F 13–14 (1 nest known)

Cyanerpes caeruleus (*L*) PURPLE HONEY-CREEPER Much of S America S to Mato Grosso and Bolivia / forest, capoeira and coffee plantations

Cyanerpes cyaneus (*L*) BLUE HONEYCREEPER Mexico to Panama, Cuba, Jamaica (once) and much of S America S to Bolivia and Mato Grosso / forest and secondary growth

Xenodacnis parina *Cabanis* TIT DACNIS Mts of Peru / 'polylepis' woodland and shrubbery

Oreomanes fraseri *Sclater* GIANT CONEBILL Highlands from SW Colombia to Bolivia / forest (this genus was formerly placed after *Conirostrum* in the family *Parulidae*)

Diglossa baritula *Wagler* SLATY HIGHLAND HONEYCREEPER Mts from Mexico to Panama and Venezuela to N Argentina / shrubby hillsides (some authorities separate *D. plumbea* Cabanis and *D. sittoides* (d'Orbigny and Lafresnaye))

Diglossa lafresnayii (*Boissonneau*) GLOSSY HONEYCREEPER Andes from Venezuela to Bolivia

Diglossa carbonaria (*d'Orbigny and Lafresnaye*) BLACK HONEYCREEPER Andes from Venezuela to N Chile (some authorities separate *D. humeralis* (Fraser))

Diglossa venezuelensis *Chapman* VENEZUELAN HONEYCREEPER NE Venezuela

Diglossa albilatera *Lafresnaye* WHITE-SIDED HONEYCREEPER Andes from Venezuela to Peru / forest edge and shrubbery

Diglossa duidae *Chapman* SCALED HONEY-CREEPER S Venezuela / shrubby hillsides

Diglossa major *Cabanis* GREAT HONEYCREEPER Mts of S Venezuela and adjacent N Brazil / shrubby hillsides

Diglossa indigotica *Sclater* INDIGO HONEY-CREEPER W slope of W Andes in SW Colombia and W Ecuador / forest

Diglossa glauca *Sclater and Salvin* DEEP-BLUE or GLAUCOUS HONEYCREEPER E slope of Andes from Colombia to Bolivia

Diglossa caerulescens (*Sclater*) BLUISH HONEYCREEPER Andes from Venezuela to Bolivia, and coastal mts of N Venezuela / forest

Diglossa cyanea (*Lafresnaye*) MASKED HONEYCREEPER Andes from Venezuela to Bolivia, and coastal mts of N Venezuela / forest

ESTRILDIDAE:
Uraeginthus granatina,
Violet-eared Waxbill

ESTRILDIDAE:
Estrilda troglodytes,
Black-rumped Waxbill

Plate 284

ESTRILDIDAE:
Uraeginthus ianthinogaster,
Purple Grenadier

ESTRILDIDAE:
Estrilda caerulescens,
Red-tailed Lavender Finch,
Bluish Waxbill

Plate 285

Euneornis campestris (*L*) ORANGEQUIT Jamaica / open woodland and clearings mainly in highlands / n tree or bush / e 2–4

TERSINIDAE Swallow Tanager This genus is sometimes treated as a family, sometimes as a subfamily within the Thraupidae.

Tersina viridis (*Illiger*) SWALLOW TANAGER E Panama and much of S America E of Andes and S to NE Argentina / forest clearings / berries and insects / n tunnel in bank or hole in wall / e 2–3 / I ♀ 13–17 / F 24

VIREONIDAE Vireos Small to medium-sized passerines, predominantly greenish in colour and warbler-like in appearance. They are believed to be most closely related to the Parulid warblers, from which they differ mainly in the thicker, heavier bill. They are insectivorous. About 40 species distributed through the Americas. The Peppershrikes and Shrike-Vireos are sometimes placed in separate families or sub-families.

Cyclarhis gujanensis (*Gmelin*) RUFOUS-NECKED PEPPERSHRIKE Mexico, C America and much of S America S to N Argentina / open woodland and cultivation / insects and spiders / n tree or bush / e 2–3 / I ♂♀

Cyclarhis nigrirostris *Lafresnaye* BLACK-BILLED PEPPERSHRIKE Colombia and Ecuador / forest edge and clearings

Vireolanius melitophrys *Bonaparte* HIGHLAND SHRIKE-VIREO Highlands from Mexico to Guatemala

Vireolanius pulchellus *Sclater and Salvin* GREEN SHRIKE-VIREO SE Mexico, C America, N Colombia and N Venezuela / forest (*V. eximius* Baird, is sometimes separated)

Vireolanius leucotis (*Swainson*) SLATY-CAPPED SHRIKE-VIREO Andes from Venezuela to N Bolivia and basin of Amazon / forest

Vireo brevipennis (*Sclater*) SLATY VIREO Mts of S Mexico

Vireo huttoni *Cassin* HUTTON'S VIREO Western N America from Vancouver to Guatemala / evergreen oak forest / insects / n oak-tree / e 3–5 / I ♂♀ c14 / F c14

Vireo atricapillus *Woodhouse* BLACK-CAPPED VIREO From S Kansas to W Mexico / forest and scrub / insects / n tree / e 3–5 / I ♂♀

Vireo griseus (*Boddaert*) WHITE-EYED VIREO Eastern and southern USA, Bermuda, E Mexico / scrub and swamp / insects / n bush or small tree / e 3–5 / I ♂♀ 12–16

Vireo pallens *Salvin* MANGROVE VIREO Coasts of Mexico and C America S to Guatemala / mangrove swamps

Vireo caribaeus *Bond and de Schaunsee* ST ANDREW VIREO St Andrew Is (Caribbean) / shrubbery and mangrove swamp / n and e n/k

Vireo bairdi *Ridgway* COZUMEL VIREO Isla Cozumel, Mexico

Vireo gundlachii *Lembeye* CUBAN VIREO Cuba and Isle of Pines / undergrowth of humid forest and semi-arid scrub / n bush / e 3

Vireo crassirostris (*Bryant*) THICK-BILLED VIREO Bahamas, Caymans, Tortue, Old Providence and Santa Catalina / shrubbery / n bush / e 2–3

Vireo bellii *Audubon* BELL'S VIREO Central-southern and south-western USA, and Mexico to Nicaragua / scrub, hedges and riverine thickets / insects / n bush / e 3–5 / I ♂♀ 14 / F 11

Vireo vicinior *Coues* GREY VIREO Southwestern USA w N Mexico / forest and scrub / insects / n tree or bush / e 3–4

Vireo nelsoni *Bond* NELSON'S VIREO S Mexico

Vireo hypochryseus *Sclater* GOLDEN VIREO Mexico and Tres Marias Is

Vireo modestus *Sclater* JAMAICAN VIREO Jamaica / humid forest to semi-arid scrub / n bush / e 2–3

Vireo nanus (*Lawrence*) FLAT-BILLED VIREO Hispaniola and Gonave Is / semi-arid scrub / n bush / e 2

Vireo latimeri *Baird* PUERTO RICAN VIREO Puerto Rico / coffee plantations and undergrowth on limestone hills / e 3

Vireo osburni (*Sclater*) BLUE MOUNTAIN VIREO Mts of Jamaica / mountain rain forest / n bush or tree / e n/s

Vireo carmioli *Baird* YELLOW-WINGED VIREO Costa Rica and Panama / n tree / e 2 / I ♂♀

Vireo solitarius (*Wilson*) BLUE-HEADED VIREO Much of N America and S through C America to Honduras and El Salvador w also to Cuba and Nicaragua / forest / insects and berries / n tree / e 3–5 / I ♂♀ 10–11 ?

Vireo flavifrons *Vieillot* YELLOW-THROATED VIREO Central belt of N America w Mexico to Venezuela / forest, scrub and cultivation / insects and berries / n tree / e 3–5 / I ♂♀ c14 / F c14

Vireo philadelphicus (*Cassin*) PHILADELPHIA VIREO S Canada and mid-USA w Yucatan to Colombia / open forest and scrub / insects / n tree / e 3–5 / I ♂♀ 14

Vireo olivaceus (*L*) RED-EYED VIREO The Americas, extreme N and S / forest / insects/ n tree or shrub/e 3–5/I ♀ 12–14/F 12 (*V. chivi* (Vieillot) and *V. flavoviridis* (Cassin) are sometimes separated)

Vireo magister (*Lawrence*) YUCATAN VIREO Yucatan, Belize and adjacent islands, Grand Cayman / low woodland and mangrove swamps/ n bush /e 2

Vireo altiloquus (*Vieillot*) (=**V. calidris** (*L*)) BLACK-WHISKERED VIREO S Florida and some Caribbean islands; some forms winter in northern S America /open forest and cultivation/ insects and berries /n tree /e 2–3

Vireo gilvus (*Vieillot*) WARBLING VIREO N America (except extreme N), Mexico, C America and Andes from Venezuela to Bolivia/ forest and habitation/insects and berries /n tree/ e 3–5/I 12

[**Vireosylvia propinqua** *Baird* 1886, is believed to be a hybrid between *Vireo flavifrons* and *Vireo solitarius*]

Hylophilus poicilotis *Temminck* RUFOUS-CROWNED VIREO E Brazil, Paraguay and extreme NE Argentina /forest

Hylophilus thoracicus *Temminck* LEMON-CHESTED VIREO E flank of Andes from Venezuela to Bolivia, SE Brazil /forest near streams

Hylophilus semicinereus *Sclater and Salvin* GREY-CHESTED VIREO S Venezuela, Cayenne and much of Brazil /forest

Hylophilus pectoralis *Sclater* ASHY-HEADED VIREO The Guianas, N and C Brazil /plantations, scrub, riparian thickets, mangroves / n tree /e 2 /I ♂♀

Hylophilus sclateri *Salvin and Godman* TEPUI VIREO S Venezuela, W Guyana and extreme NC Brazil /forest

Hylophilus muscicapinus *Sclater and Salvin* BUFF-CHESTED VIREO S Venezuela, the Guianas and N Brazil S to Mato Grosso/forest

Hylophilus brunneiceps *Sclater* BROWN-HEADED VIREO E Colombia, S Venezuela and N Brazil /forest

Hylophilus semibrunneus *Lafresnaye* RUFOUS-NAPED VIREO Colombia, NW Venezuela and E Ecuador /forest

Hylophilus aurantiifrons *Lawrence* GOLDEN-FRONTED VIREO E Panama through Colombia and Venezuela to the Orinoco and Trinidad/ forest /insects and spiders /n tree or vine /e 3

Hylophilus hypoxanthus *Pelzeln* DUSKY-CAPPED VIREO Andes from SW Venezuela to Bolivia and Brazil E to Rio Xingú /forest

Hylophilus flavipes *Lafresnaye* SCRUB VIREO Costa Rica, Panama, Colombia, Venezuela, Tobago/forest edge and savannah/insects/n tree/ e 3

Hylophilus olivaceus *Tschudi* OLIVACEOUS VIREO E Ecuador to C Peru

Hylophilus ochraceiceps *Sclater* TAWNY-HEADED VIREO S Mexico, C America and much of northern S America S to Bolivia /forest and woodland

Hylophilus minor *Berlepsch and Taczanowski* LESSER VIREO SW Colombia and W Ecuador/ woodland

Hylophilus decurtatus (*Bonaparte*) GREY-HEADED VIREO Mexico, C America, Colombia

PARULIDAE New World Warblers Small, generally brightly coloured birds believed to be related to tanagers and emberizids. Inhabit forest and scrub, feeding on insects and berries. Nest may be in trees or on the ground, one species, the Ovenbird, is so named for its curious domed nest with side entrance. Incubation, so far as known, is always by female.

Mniotilta varia (*L*) BLACK AND WHITE WARBLER Much of N America E of Rockies w S to Ecuador and Venezuela / swamp and forest /insects /n ground /e 4–5

Vermivora bachmanii (*Audubon*) BACHMANN'S WARBLER Parts of south-eastern USA w S to Caribbean / rare/heavily timbered swamp / ? insects /n bush /e 3–4

Vermivora chrysoptera (*L*) GOLDEN-WINGED WARBLER Much of eastern N America except the SE w S to C America and Venezuela [hybridises freely with *V. pinus* along S border of breeding range. These hybrids are distinctive and have been given such names as 'Brewster's Warbler' and 'Lawrence's Warbler'.]/deciduous woodland and scrub /insects /n ground /e 4–6/ I ♀ 10–11/F 10

Vermivora pinus (*L*) BLUE-WINGED WARBLER Parts of C and mid-eastern USA w to Caribbean and N Colombia /pasture, scrub, swampy woods etc/insects /n ground /e 4–6

Vermivora peregrina (*Wilson*) TENNESSEE WARBLER Canada and northern USA w S to C America and Venezuela /forest/insects/n ground/ e 4–7

Vermivora celata (*Say*) ORANGE-CROWNED WARBLER Much of N America w S to Caribbean/

ESTRILDIDAE:
Lonchura malabarica,
Silverbill or
White-throated Munia

ESTRILDIDAE:
Lonchura striata,
White-rumped Mannikin,
White-rumped Munia—
domesticated strain

Plate 286

A domesticated *L. striata* tending its young

Plate 287

forest and scrub/insects and fruit/n ground or bush/e 4–6

Vermivora ruficapilla (*Wilson*) NASHVILLE WARBLER S Canada and much of USA w S to Guatemala/bog and secondary forest/insects/n ground/e 4–5

Vermivora virginiae (*Baird*) VIRGINIA'S WARBLER Parts of central USA w Mexico/forested ravines/n ground/e 4

Vermivora crissalis (*Salvin and Godman*) COLIMA WARBLER Mexico and SW Texas/forest/n ground/e 4

Vermivora luciae (*Cooper*) LUCY'S WARBLER South-western USA w Mexico / forest and scrub/insects/n tree or shrub/e 4

Vermivora gutteralis (*Cabanis*) FLAME-THROATED WARBLER or IRAZU WARBLER High mts of Costa Rica and W Panama/mountain forests/n ground or tree/e 2/I ♀ 16/F 13

Vermivora superciliosa (*Hartlaub*) CRESCENT-CHESTED or SPOT-BREASTED WARBLER Mexico to Nicaragua/mountain forest/n ground/e 2–3

Parula americana (*L*) PARULA WARBLER Eastern and southern USA w C America and W Indies/forest/insects and spiders/n tree or Spanish moss/e 4–5

Parula pitiayumi (*Vieillot*) OLIVE-BACKED WARBLER or TROPICAL PARULA Much of C and S America S to N Argentina/forest and arid scrub/insects/n in epiphitic orchids or Spanish moss/e 2–4

Dendroica petechia (*L*) YELLOW WARBLER Widely distributed through N and C America, the Caribbean islands and northern S America/swamps and wet bush/insects and fruit/n tree or shrub / e 4–5 (*D. erithachloroides* Baird 'Mangrove Warbler' is sometimes treated as distinct)

[**Dendroica potomac** *Haller* is regarded as a hybrid between *D. dominica* and *Parula americana*]

[**Dendroica montana** (*Wilson*) (=**Sylvia montana** *Wilson*, see footnote to *Cettia fortipes*, Sylvidae) BLUE MOUNTAIN WARBLER Known only from plates of Wilson and Audubon. Never satisfactorily identified]

[**Dendroica carbonata** (*Audubon*) CARBONATED WARBLER Known only from Audubon's plate and description]

Dendroica pensylvanica (*L*) CHESTNUT-SIDED WARBLER Eastern N America w C

America and occasionally Venezuela and Colombia / forest, insects, seeds and berries/n bush/e 4–5

Dendroica cerulea (*Wilson*) CAERULEAN WARBLER Eastern N America w Colombia and Venezuela to Peru and Bolivia / forest and woodland/insects/n tree/e 3–4

Dendroica caerulescens (*Gmelin*) BLACK-THROATED BLUE WARBLER Eastern N America w Caribbean, C America and northern S America / heavy woodland / insects, seeds and berries/n tree/e 3–5/I 12/F 10

Dendroica plumbea *Lawrence* PLUMBEOUS WARBLER Dominica and Guadeloupe/mountain forest/n shrub/e 2

Dendroica pharetra (*Gosse*) ARROW-HEADED WARBLER Jamaica/mountain forest/n shrub/e 2

Dendroica pinus (*Wilson*) PINE WARBLER Eastern and southern N America, Bahamas and Hispaniola / pine forest / insects, seeds and berries/n tree/e 3–5

Dendroica graciae *Baird* GRACE'S WARBLER Central-western USA, through Mexico to Nicaragua / coniferous forest / insects / n tree/ e 3–4

Dendroica adelaidae *Baird* ADELAIDE'S WARBLER Puerto Rico, Viegues, Barbuda and St Lucia/dense thickets/n bush/e 2–3

Dendroica pityophila (*Gundlach*) OLIVE-CAPPED WARBLER Cuba and Bahamas / forest/n tree/e ? 2 (1 nest with 2 young known)

Dendroica dominica (*L*) YELLOW-THROATED WARBLER Eastern and southern USA, E Mexico, Cuba, Jamaica and .Bahamas / lagoons and cypress swamps/insects/n tree or Spanish moss/e 4–5

Dendroica nigrescens (*Townsend*) BLACK-THROATED GREY WARBLER Western N America from S British Columbia to Mexico, occasionally in Guatemala/forest and scrub/insects/n tree or bush/e 3–5

Dendroica townsendi (*Townsend*) TOWNSEND'S WARBLER S Alaska, W Canada and north-western USA w S to Nicaragua / forest and scrub/insects/n tree/e 3–5

Dendroica occidentalis (*Townsend*) HERMIT WARBLER Western USA w S to Nicaragua/forest/insects/n tree/e 3–5

Dendroica chrysoparia *Sclater and Salvin* GOLDEN-CHEEKED WARBLER b Edwards Plateau in SE Texas w parts of Mexico to Nicaragua/cedar and juniper brakes/n bush/e 4

Dendroica virens (*Gmelin*) BLACK-THROATED GREEN WARBLER S Canada and E USA w Mexico and W Indies / boreal forest / insects/ n tree / e 4–5

Dendroica discolor (*Vieillot*) PRAIRIE WARBLER E USA w W Indies / forest and scrub/ insects and spiders / n bush / e 3–5 / I ♀ 12 / F 8–10

Dendroica tigrina (*Gmelin*) CAPE MAY WARBLER S Canada and N USA w Eastern C America and W Indies / spruce forest / insects/ n tree / e 4–9

Dendroica vitellina *Cory* VITELLINE WARBLER Cayman and Swan Is / scrubby thickets / n bush/ e 2

Dendroica fusca (*Müller*) BLACKBURNIAN WARBLER SC Canada and north-eastern USA w Guatemala to Peru / coniferous forest and secondary growth / insects / n tree / e 4–5

Dendroica magnolia (*Wilson*) MAGNOLIA WARBLER Canada (except boreal regions) and northern USA w Greater Antilles and Mexico to Panama (rarely Colombia) / forest and bog/ insects / n tree / e 3–5

Dendroica coronata (*L*) MYRTLE WARBLER N and C America, southern populations sedentary, northern ones migrating S / woodland, broken forest and scrub / insects / n tree / e 3–5

Dendroica palmarum (*Gmelin*) PALM WARBLER Northern N America w Mexico, C America and southern coast of USA / open country and tundra / insects / n ground / e 4–5

Dendroica kirtlandii (*Baird*) KIRTLAND'S WARBLER Restricted area of C Michigan / young copses of jack pine / insects and berries / n ground/ e 4–5 / I ♀

Dendroica striata (*Forster*) BLACKPOLL WARBLER Canada and north-eastern USA w Panama to Chile / spruce forest / insects, seeds and berries / n tree or ground / e 4–5

Dendroica castanea (*Wilson*) BAY-BREASTED WARBLER E Canada and north-eastern USA w Panama to Venezuela / forest, swamp and orchard / insects and berries / n tree / e 3–7/ I ♀ 12

Dendroica angelae *Kepler and Parkes* (*Auk*, 89 (1972), pp 1–18) ELFIN WOODS WARBLER Puerto Rico, known only from the Sierra de Luquillo / no other data

Dendroica bishopi (*Lawrence*) WHISTLING WARBLER St Vincent / mountain forest/ n ? shrub / e ?2 (not verified)

Setophaga ruticilla (*L*) AMERICAN REDSTART Parts of N America w C America to Peru and the Guianas / woodland and scrub / insects and fruit / n tree / e 3–5 / I ♀

Seiurus aurocapillus (*L*) OVENBIRD (WARBLER) S Canada, northern and eastern USA w southern USA and C America to Venezuela / open forest / insects, worms, berries etc / n ground / e 3–6

Seiurus noveboracensis (*Gmelin*) NORTHERN WATERTHRUSH Canada, northern and north-eastern USA w southern USA and C America to Peru and the Guianas / bog and damp forest near water / insects and aquatic life / n ground/ e 4–5

Seiurus motacilla (*Vieillot*) LOUISIANA WATERTHRUSH Central and eastern USA w Caribbean and C America to Venezuela and Trinidad / bog and damp forest near water/ insects and aquatic life / n ground / e 4–6

Limnothlypis swainsonii (*Audubon*) SWAINSON'S WARBLER Central and eastern USA w Caribbean and parts of C America / forest and habitation / insects / n bush or among canes/ e 3–4 / I ♀ 14–15 / F 12

Helmitheros vermivorus (*Gmelin*) WORM-EATING WARBLER Eastern USA w C America and W Caribbean / bogs, wooded hillsides and ravines / insects / n ground / e 3–6

Protonotaria citrea (*Boddaert*) PROTONOTARY WARBLER Eastern USA w through C America to Ecuador and N Venezuela / forest, mangrove and swamp / insects / n hole / e 3–8 / I 12–13

Geothlypis trichas (*L*) COMMON YELLOW-THROAT Much of N America and Mexico w S to Colombia and Venezuela / damp woodland and scrub / insects / n ground or low herbage/ e 3–5

Geothlypis beldingi *Ridgway* BELDING'S YELLOWTHROAT C and S Baja California/ marshes / n in cat-tail clump over ground or water / e 2–4

Geothlypis flavovelata *Ridgway* YELLOW-CROWNED YELLOWTHROAT Parts of Mexico

Geothlypis rostrata *Bryant* BAHAMAN YELLOWTHROAT Bahamas / coppice and scrub/ n tree stump (1 known, containing 2 young)

Geothlypis semiflava *Sclater* OLIVE-CROWNED YELLOWTHROAT Honduras to Ecuador / tall grassland

Geothlypis speciosa *Sclater* BLACK-POLLED YELLOWTHROAT Mts of Mexico

Geothlypis nelsoni *Richmond* BRUSH

ESTRILDIDAE:
Amadina erythrocephala,
Red-headed Finch

ESTRILDIDAE:
Padda oryzivora,
Java Sparrow

Plate 288

ESTRILDIDAE:
Amadina fasciata,
Cut-throat Finch

Plate 289

YELLOWTHROAT Mts of Mexico

Geothlypis chiriquensis *Salvin* CHIRIQUI YELLOWTHROAT Slopes of Volcán de Chiriquí, W Panama / n grass / e 2 / I ♀ 15

Geothlypis aequinoctialis (*Gmelin*) MASKED YELLOWTHROAT Tropical S America S to Uruguay and NE Argentina / freshwater marshes / n off ground in grass

Geothlypis poliocephala *Baird* GROUND CHAT or MEADOW WARBLER S Texas, Mexico and C America / open scrub / insects and berries / n in grass / e 2–4

Geothlypis formosa (*Wilson*) KENTUCKY WARBLER Eastern USA w through Mexico and C America to N Colombia and W Venezuela / heavy woodland and damp thickets / insects / n ground / e 4–5

Geothlypis agilis (*Wilson*) CONNECTICUT WARBLER S Canada and north-eastern USA w Venezuela, Colombia and NE Brazil / swamps and coniferous forest / insects and spiders / n ground / e 3–5

Geothlypis philadelphia (*Wilson*) MOURNING WARBLER C and E Canada and north-eastern USA w from Nicaragua to Ecuador and W Venezuela / scrub and bog / insects and in winter 'protein bodies from the leaf bases of young Cecropia trees' / n ground or in herbage / e 3–5

Geothlypis tolmiei (*Townsend*) MACGILLIVRAY'S WARBLER Western N America w S to Panama / moist thickets / insects / n in tall weeds (off ground) / e 3–5

Microligea palustris (*Cory*) GREEN-TAILED WARBLER Hispaniola / mountain scrub / n bush / e 2

Teretistris fernandinae (*Lambeye*) YELLOW-HEADED WARBLER W Cuba and Isle of Pines / forest / n shrub / e 2–3

Teretistris fornsi *Gundlach* ORIENTE WARBLER E Cuba / forest / n shrub / e 2–3

Leucopeza semperi *Sclater* SEMPER'S WARBLER St Lucia / forest undergrowth / n ? ground

Wilsonia citrina (*Boddaert*) HOODED WARBLER SE Canada and eastern USA w Mexico to Panama / forest and cypress swamp / insects / n bush / e 3–5

Wilsonia pusilla (*Wilson*) WILSON'S WARBLER Western N America, S Canada and north-eastern USA w Mexico to Panama / bogs / insects / n ground / e 4–6

Wilsonia canadensis (*L*) CANADA WARBLER

Canada and parts of eastern USA w Honduras S to Peru and N Brazil / forest / insects and spiders / n ground or stump / e 3–5

Cardellina rubrifrons (*Giraud*) RED-FACED WARBLER C Arizona and SW New Mexico S to Durango w S to Guatemala / coniferous forest on ridges / insects / n ground / e 3–4

Ergaticus ruber (*Swainson*) RED WARBLER Mts of Mexico / ? no data

Ergaticus versicolor (*Salvin*) PINK-HEADED WARBLER Mts of C and E Chiapas and W Guatemala / mountain forest / n bank / e 2–4 / I ♀

Myioborus pictus (*Swainson*) PAINTED REDSTART Mts from Arizona to Nicaragua / forest / insects / n ground / e 3–4

Myioborus miniatus (*Swainson*) SLATE-THROATED REDSTART Mts from Mexico to Peru, the Guianas and NW Brazil / forest

Myioborus brunniceps (*Lafresnaye and d'Orbigny*) BROWN-CAPPED REDSTART Subtropical zone of E Andes from Venezuela to N Argentina / forest

Myioborus pariae *Phelps and Phelps jr* PARIA REDSTART Mts of Paria Peninsula, Venezuela / forest

Myioborus cardonai *Zimmer and Phelps* SAFFRON-BREASTED REDSTART Mt Guaiquinima, Bolivar, SE Venezuela / humid forest

Myioborus torquatus (*Baird*) COLLARED REDSTART Mountain forests of Costa Rica and W Panama / n bank / e 2–3 / I ♀ 13–15 / F 12–14

Myioborus ornatus (*Boissonneau*) GOLDEN-FRONTED REDSTART Temperate zone of Andes of Colombia and Venezuela / forest

Myioborus melanocephalus (*Tschudi*) SPECTACLED REDSTART Humid temperate zone of Andes from Colombia to Bolivia / forest

Myioborus albifrons (*Sclater and Salvin*) WHITE-FRONTED REDSTART Humid temperate zone of Andes of W Venezuela / forest

Myioborus flavivertex (*Salvin*) YELLOW-CROWNED REDSTART N Colombia (Sierra Nevada de Santa Marta) / forest treetops

Myioborus albifacies *Phelps and Phelps jr* WHITE-FACED REDSTART Mts of S Venezuela / forest

Euthlypis lachrymosa (*Bonaparte*) NEO-TROPICAL FAN-TAILED WARBLER Mexico to Nicaragua / forest undergrowth / insects / n and e n/k

Basileuterus fraseri *Sclater* FRASER'S WARBLER or SLATE AND GOLD WARBLER Ecuador and NW Peru

Basileuterus bivittatus (*Lafresnaye and d'Orbigny*) TWO-BANDED WARBLER Guyana and Venezuela, Peru to Argentina / undergrowth

Basileuterus chrysogaster (*Tschudi*) GOLDEN-BELLIED WARBLER SW Colombia, Ecuador and Peru / undergrowth

Basileuterus flaveolus (*Baird*) FLAVESCENT WARBLER From Colombia and Venezuela through Brazil to Bolivia and Paraguay / semi-arid woodland

Basileuterus luteoviridis (*Bonaparte*) CITRINE WARBLER Andes from Venezuela to Colombia and Bolivia / forest

Basileuterus signatus *Berlepsch and Stolzmann* YELLOW-GREEN WARBLER Andes from Peru to NW Argentina / thickets

Basileuterus nigrocristatus (*Lafresnaye*) BLACK-CRESTED WARBLER Andes from Venezuela to N Peru / humid mountain forest

Basileuterus griseiceps *Sclater and Salvin* GREY-HEADED WARBLER NE Venezuela / forest

Basileuterus basilicus (*Todd*) SANTA MARTA WARBLER Sierra Nevada de Santa Marta, NE Colombia / shrubbery

Basileuterus cinereicollis *Sclater* ASHY-THROATED WARBLER E Colombia / forest undergrowth

[**Basileuterus conspicillatus** *Salvin and Godman* WHITE-LORED WARBLER Sierra Nevada de Santa Marta, NE Colombia / now usually considered a race of *B. coronatus*]

Basileuterus coronatus (*Tschudi*) RUSSET-CROWNED WARBLER Andes from Venezuela and Colombia to Bolivia / thickets and fern brakes

Basileuterus culcivorus (*Deppe*) GOLDEN-CROWNED WARBLER Mexico, C America through Colombia and Venezuela, basins of Orinoco and Amazon S to Paraguay and Uruguay, Trinidad / mountain scrub, forest clearings etc / n ground / e 3 / I ♀

Basileuterus rufifrons (*Swainson*) RUFOUS-CAPPED WARBLER Mexico through C America to N Colombia and W Venezuela, Isla Coiba / secondary forest / n bank / e 2–3 / I ♀ / F 12 (*B. delattrii* Bonaparte, is sometimes separated)

Basileuterus belli (*Giraud*) BELL'S WARBLER Mexico, Guatemala, Honduras and El Salvador

Basileuterus melanogenys *Baird* BLACK-CHEEKED WARBLER Costa Rica and Panama / mountain forest / n ? rock crevice / e 2 / I ♀

Basileuterus tristriatus (*Tschudi*) THREE-STRIPED WARBLER Panama, and Andes from Venezuela to Bolivia / undergrowth of heavy forest / n and e n/k

Basileuterus trifasciatus *Taczanowski* THREE-BANDED WARBLER SW Ecuador and NW Peru / thickets

Basileuterus hypoleucus *Bonaparte* WHITE-BELLIED WARBLER Tropical zone of interior Brazil and Paraguay / forest undergrowth

Basileuterus leucoblepharus (*Vieillot*) WHITE-BROWED WARBLER S Brazil, Paraguay, Uruguay and NE Argentina / forest undergrowth

Basileuterus leucophrys *Pelzeln* WHITE-STRIPED WARBLER Mato Grosso and São Paulo

Basileuterus fulvicauda (*Spix*) BUFF-RUMPED WARBLER Honduras to Panama, Andes from Venezuela to Peru / mountain streams / n bank / e 2 / I ♀ 16–17 / F 12–15

Basileuterus rivularis (*Wied*) NEOTROPICAL RIVER WARBLER Eastern S America from Orinoco delta to Bolivia and Paraguay (*B. fulvicauda* and *B. rivularis* are often treated as conspecific)

Peucedramus taeniatus (*Du Bus*) OLIVE WARBLER C Arizona through Mexico to Nicaragua / coniferous forests / insects / n tree / e 3–4 / I ♀ [The position of *Peucedramus* is in doubt. It has been placed in the Parulidae, the Sylvidae and the Muscicapidae]

Xenoligea montana (*Chapman*) WHITE-WINGED GROUND WARBLER Mts of Hispaniola / high mountain scrub / n and e n/k (treated by some as conspecific with *Microligea*)

Granatellus venustus *Bonaparte* RED-BREASTED WARBLER Pacific Mexico and Isla María Madre / rare / forest undergrowth

Granatellus sallaei (*Bonaparte*) GREY-THROATED WARBLER Atlantic Mexico, E Guatemala and Belize

Granatellus pelzelni *Sclater* ROSE-BREASTED WARBLER SE Venezeula and Guianas S through Brazil to NE Bolivia / forest

Icteria virens (*L*) YELLOW-BREASTED CHAT S Canada and USA w Mexico and C America / scrub and overgrown pasture / insects and berries / n shrub or ground / e 3–5

Conirostrum tamaruguensis *Johnson and Millie* (*Birds of Chile* (supplement): 6, 1972) CHILEAN CONEBILL Chile

Conirostrum speciosum (*Temminck*) CHESTNUT-VENTED CONEBILL Widely but irregularly distributed in S America S to N

ESTRILDIDAE:
Lonchura castaneothorax,
Chestnut-breasted Finch,
Chestnut-breasted Mannikin

Plate 290

ESTRILDIDAE:
Lonchura pectoralis,
Pictorella Finch

ESTRILDIDAE:
Padda oryzivora,
Java Sparrow

Plate 291

Argentina / swampy forest, capoeira, campos, lake borders

Conirostrum leucogenys (*Lafresnaye*) WHITE-EARED CONEBILL E Panama, N Colombia, W and NE Venezuela / tangled woodland

Conirostrum bicolor (*Vieillot*) BICOLOURED CONEBILL Coasts of S America from Colombia to São Paulo; Upper Amazon basin / mangrove and flooded forest

Conirostrum margaritae (*Holt*) PEARLY-BREASTED CONEBILL Brazil N of Amazon and NE Peru / flooded forest

Conirostrum cinereum *Lafresnaye and d'Orbigny* CINEREOUS CONEBILL Andes from SW Colombia to Bolivia / shrubby hillsides, plantations and habitation

Conirostrum ferrugineiventre *Sclater* WHITE-BROWED CONEBILL Andes of Peru and Bolivia / open bushy slopes with stunted trees

Conirostrum rufum *Lafresnaye* RUFOUS-BROWED CONEBILL Mts of N Colombia / open slopes with low stunted trees

Conirostrum sitticolor *Lafresnaye* BLUE-BACKED CONEBILL Andes from W Venezuela to Bolivia / forest edge and shrubby slopes

Conirostrum albifrons *Lafresnaye* CAPPED CONEBILL Andes from Venezuela to Bolivia [NB: *Conirostrum fraseri* P. L. Sclater 1859 = race of *C. cinereum*, and is not the same as *Oreomanes fraseri* P. L. Sclater 1860 'Giant Conebill' formerly placed after *Conirostrum* but now transferred to the Thraupidae]

Coereba flaveola (*L*) BANANAQUIT Mexico, C America, much of S America S to N Argentina, islands of Caribbean (about 40 races are generally recognised) / gardens, parks, clearings and plantations / fruit and insects / n bush / e 3–6 / I ♀

Nephelornis oneilli *Lowery and Tallman* PARDUSCO Acomayo, Peru / cloud forest / insects etc (a genus of uncertain affinities. For all that is known of this recently discovered bird see Lowery and Tallman, *Auk*, 93 (1976), pp 415–28)

NB: All the genera from *Peucedramus* to *Nephelornis* are of uncertain affinities, and should be regarded as genera *incerta sedis*, placed here for convenience.

DREPANIDIDAE Hawaiian Honey-creepers

The birds of this family are confined to the Hawaiian group and are very variable in size and appearance. They are believed to have diverged from a common ancestor. Destruction of habitat by man has caused the extinction or near-extinction of a number of the species. Nests are open cup-like structures in bushes, eggs 2–4 white, usually spotted. Incubation is by the female, where known.

Himatione sanguinea (*Gmelin*) APAPANE Kauai, Oahu, Molokai and Hawaii / forest / insects / n tree / e 1–4 / I ♀ 13 / F 15–17

Himatione freethi *Rothschild* LAYSAN HONEYCREEPER Laysan / extinct / scrub / insects and nectar / n tree / e 1–4 (often considered a race of *H. sanguinea*)

Palmeria dolei (*Wilson*) CRESTED HONEY-CREEPER Mt forests of Maui (and formerly Molokai) / nectar and insects / n and e n/k

[**Sassius simplex** *Rothschild and Hartert* Unique / generally considered to be an artifact!]

Vestiaria coccinea (*Forster*) IIWI Mt forests of Kauai, Oahu, Molokai, Maui, Lanai and Hawaii / nectar and insects / n tree / e 1–3 / I ♀ 14 / F 21–2

Drepanis funerea *Newton* BLACK MAMO Mt forests of Molokai / extinct / undergrowth / nectar / n and e n/k

Drepanis pacifica (*Gmelin*) MAMO Mt forests of Hawaii / extinct / nectar / n and e n/k

Ciridops anna (*Dole*) ULA-AI-HAWANE Mt forests of Hawaii / extinct / no data

Viridonia virens (*Gmelin*) AMAKIHI Forests of Kauai, Oahu, Molokai, Lanai, Maui and Hawaii / insects, fruit and nectar / n tree / e 2–4 / I 14 / F 17–20

Viridonia parva (*Stejneger*) ANIANIAU Forests of Kauai / nectar and insects / n tree / e 2–4 / I ♀ 14 / F 17–19

Viridonia sagittirostris *Rothschild* GREEN SOLITAIRE Formerly in the mountain rain forest of Mauna Kea, Hawaii, which is now planted with sugar cane / extinct / no data

Hemignathus obscurus (*Gmelin*) AKIALOA Mt forests of Kauai, Oahu, Lanai, Hawaii: 4 races, all except the Kauai race are extinct / insects and nectar / n tree / e ? 1 (1 nest with 1 young known)

Hemignathus lucidus *Lichtenstein* NUKUPUU Mt forests of Kauai and Maui (extinct on Oahu) / insects / n and e n/k

Hemignathus wilsoni (*Rothschild*) AKIAPOLAAU Mt forests of Hawaii / insects / n and e n/k

Loxops coccinea (*Gmelin*) AKEPA Forests of Hawaii, Maui and Kauai (extinct on Oahu)/ insects and spiders / n tree / e 2

Paroreomyza maculata (*Cabanis*) HAWAIIAN CREEPER Forests of Kauai, Hawaii, Oahu, Maui (probably extinct on Lanai and Molokai)/ insects and nectar / n tree / e 2

[**Oreomyza perkinsi** *Rothschild* PERKINS' CREEPER Hawaii / believed to be a hybrid between *Paroreomyza maculata* and *Viridonia virens*]

Pseudonestor xanthophrys *Rothschild* PSEUDONESTOR Forests of Maui / insects / n tree / e n/k

Psittirostra psittacea (*Gmelin*) OU Forests of Kauai, Maui, Hawaii (extinct on Oahu, Molokai and Lanai) / fruit and nectar / n and e n/k

[**Dysmorodrepanis munroi** *Perkins* MUNROE'S DYSMORODREPANIS Lanai / unique/ considered to be an aberrant specimen of *Psittirostra*, but Munroe claimed to have seen similar birds on two separate occasions after collecting the type]

Loxioides cantans (*Wilson*) LAYSAN FINCH Laysan and Nihoa / habitation / almost omnivorous / n grass / e 2–4 / I c16

Loxioides palmeri (*Rothschild*) GREATER KOA FINCH Mt forests of Hawaii / probably extinct/ seeds / n tree / e n/k

Loxioides flaviceps (*Rothschild*) LESSER KOA FINCH Mt forests of Hawaii / extinct / seeds/ n and e n/k

Loxioides bailleui (*Oustalet*) PALILA Mt forests of Mauna Loa and Mauna Kea, Hawaii/ seeds and insects / n tree / e 2

Loxioides kona (*Wilson*) KONA FINCH or CHLORIDOPS Mt forests of Mauna Loa / last seen 1894 / seeds and insects / n and e n/k

Melamprosops phaeosoma *Casey and Jacobi* (*Occ Papers*, Bernice P. Bishop Mus (1974), vol 24, pt 12, p 219) PO'-O-ULI Maui

ICTERIDAE Icterids (Blackbirds, Orioles and Cowbirds and others) A family of generally fairly strikingly patterned birds, small to medium in size, but of diverse form and habit.

Psarocolius oseryi (*Deville*) CASQUED OROPENDOLA E Ecuador and E Peru / forest

Psarocolius latirostris (*Swainson*) BAND-TAILED OROPENDOLA E Ecuador, NE Peru and extreme W Brazil / forest

Psarocolius decumanus (*Pallas*) CRESTED OROPENDOLA Panama and northern S America S to Bolivia and N Argentina / forest and cultivation / insects and fruit / n tree / e 1–2/ I ♀ 15–19 / F 28–35

Psarocolius viridis (*Müller*) GREEN OROPENDOLA Amazon basin / forest

Psarocolius atrovirens (*Lafresnaye and d'Orbigny*) DUSKY-GREEN OROPENDOLA SE Peru and E Bolivia

Psarocolius angustifrons (*Spix*) RUSSET-BACKED OROPENDOLA Andes from Venezuela to Bolivia / forest

Psarocolius wagleri (*Gray*) WAGLER'S OROPENDOLA SE Mexico through C America to W Ecuador / forest

Psarocolius montezuma (*Lesson*) MONTEZUMA'S OROPENDOLA Caribbean slopes from SE Mexico to Canal Zone, Panama

Psarocolius cassini (*Richmond*) CASSIN'S OROPENDOLA NW Colombia / forest

Psarocolius bifasciatus (*Spix*) PARA OROPENDOLA Pará region of N Brazil / forest

Psarocolius guatimozinus (*Bonaparte*) BLACK OROPENDOLA E Panama and NW Colombia / forest

Psarocolius yuracares (*Lafresnaye and d'Orbigny*) OLIVE OROPENDOLA Amazon basin/ forest

Cacicus cela (*L*) YELLOW-RUMPED CACIQUE E Panama and much of northern S America S to Bolivia and Mato Grosso / open woodland and cultivation / insects, spiders etc and fruit/ n tree / e 2 / I ♀

Cacicus haemorrhous (*L*) RED-RUMPED CACIQUE Amazon basin, S to NE Argentina/ riverbank and forest edge

Cacicus uropygialis (*Lafresnaye*) SCARLET-RUMPED CACIQUE Honduras to Panama and Andes from Venezuela to Peru / forest / insects, nectar and fruit / n tree / e 2 / I ♀

Cacicus chrysopterus (*Vigors*) (=**Cassicus albirostris** *Vieillot*) GOLDEN-WINGED CACIQUE E Bolivia and Mato Grosso S to Buenos Aires/ forest

Cacicus koepckeae *Lowery and O'Neill* SELVA CACIQUE Valley of Río Curanja, SE Peru/ forest

Cacicus leucoramphus (*Bonaparte*) MOUNTAIN CACIQUE Venezuela to Peru and Bolivia / forest (*C. chrysonotus* (Lafresnaye and d'Orbigny) is sometimes separated) [*C. melanurus* (*Cassin*) is an artifact, being a typical example of *C. leucorhamphus* with yellow feathers

ESTRILDIDAE:
Lonchura punctulata,
Spice Finch or Nutmeg Man-
nikin, Spotted Munia

Plate 292

ESTRILDIDAE: *Lonchura maja,* White-headed Munia, Pale-headed Mannikin

Plate 293

glued below]
Cacicus sclateri (*Dubois*) SCLATER'S CACIQUE E Ecuador and N Peru/forest
Cacicus solitarius (*Vieillot*) SOLITARY CACIQUE Amazon basin and S to Buenos Aires/scrub, forest and woodland
Cacicus melanicterus (*Bonaparte*) MEXICAN CACIQUE W Mexico
Cacicus holosericeus (*Deppe*) YELLOW-BILLED CACIQUE SE Mexico through C America and Andes from Venezuela to Bolivia/forest
Icterus cayanensis (*L*) EPAULET ORIOLE Much of S America E of Andes and S to Buenos Aires/wet forest/insects/n tree/e 2 (*I. chrysocephalus* (L) 'Moriche Oriole' is often treated as a species, but Blake in Peters' *Check List*, vol xiv, p 150 points out that the 2 forms intergrade)
Icterus chrysater (*Lesson*) YELLOW-BACKED ORIOLE Mexico through C America to Colombia and Venezuela/forest and open woodland
Icterus nigrogularis (*Hahn*) YELLOW ORIOLE Colombia, Venezuela, the Guianas and adjacent N Brazil, also some offshore islands/open woodland, savannah and cultivation/invertebrates, berries and flowers/n tree/e 2–4
Icterus leucopteryx (*Wagler*) JAMAICAN ORIOLE Jamaica, Grand Cayman and St Andrews/rain forest and cultivation/n base of palm frond/e 3–5
Icterus auratus *Bonaparte* ORANGE ORIOLE Mexico
Icterus mesomelas (*Wagler*) YELLOW-TAILED ORIOLE SE Mexico through C America and Andes from Venezuela to Peru/forest
Icterus auricapillus *Cassin* ORANGE-CROWNED ORIOLE E Panama, coast and E lowlands of Colombia and N Venezuela S to Orinoco
Icterus graceannae *Cassin* WHITE-EDGED ORIOLE SW Ecuador and NW Peru/desert scrub
Icterus xantholaemus *Gil Lletget* LLETGET'S ORIOLE Ecuador/unique, and considered to be of questionable validity
Icterus pectoralis (*Wagler*) SPOT-BREASTED ORIOLE S Mexico to Nicaragua and NW Costa Rica, introduced SE Florida
Icterus gularis (*Wagler*) ALTAMIRA ORIOLE Rio Grande Valley through Mexico to Guatemala and El Salvador
Icterus pustulatus (*Wagler*) STREAKED-BACKED ORIOLE Mexico to Costa Rica
Icterus cucullatus *Swainson* HOODED ORIOLE South-western USA, Mexico and Belize/forest and habitation/n tree/e 3–5
Icterus icterus (*L*) TROUPIAL Much of S America E of Andes and S to Paraguay and Mato Grosso, also Puerto Rico and other small islands where probably introduced/dry woodland and mangrove / invertebrates and fruit/n tree/e n/s
Icterus galbula (*L*) BALTIMORE ORIOLE Much of N America (except the extreme N) and Mexico/forest and orchard/insects and fruit/n tree/e 3–6/I ♀ 14 (*I. bullockii* (Swainson) 'Bullock's Oriole' is sometimes separated)
Icterus spurius (*L*) ORCHARD ORIOLE Eastern N America and Mexico/cultivation/n tree/e 3–7/I ♀ 12/F 11–14 (*I. fuertesi* Chapman 'Fuerte's Oriole' is sometimes separated)
Icterus dominicensis (*L*) BLACK-COWLED ORIOLE Mexico, C America, Bahamas and Greater Antilles (not Jamaica)
Icterus wagleri *Sclater* WAGLER'S ORIOLE Mexico to Nicaragua
Icterus laudabilis *Sclater* ST LUCIA ORIOLE St Lucia/forest (lowland and mountain)/n tree/e 3
Icterus bonana (*L*) MARTINIQUE ORIOLE Martinique/semi-arid hills of south/n tree/e 2
Icterus oberi *Lawrence* MONTSERRAT ORIOLE Montserrat/mountain forest/n tree/e 2
Icterus graduacauda *Lesson* AUDUBON'S BLACK-HEADED ORIOLE Mexico and Rio Grande valley/forest/n tree/e 3–5
Icterus maculialatus *Cassin* BAR-WINGED ORIOLE Pacific slope of S Mexico, Guatemala and El Salvador
Icterus parisorum *Bonaparte* SCOTT'S ORIOLE South-western USA and Mexico / pinyon juniper scrub and semi-desert/insects/n tree/e 2–4/I ♀ 14/F 14
Nesopsar nigerrimus (*Osburn*) JAMAICAN BLACKBIRD Jamaica above 1,000ft (300m)/mountain forest/n tree/e 2
Xanthopsar flavus (*Gmelin*) SAFFRON-COWLED BLACKBIRD Paraguay, Uruguay, SE Brazil and NE Argentina
Gymnomystax mexicanus (*L*) ORIOLE BLACKBIRD Amazon and Orinoco basins/savannah and cultivation
Xanthocephalus xanthocephalus (*Bonaparte*) YELLOW-HEADED BLACKBIRD Western N America from C British Columbia S to N Mexico/swamp and marshes/n in reeds/e 3–5/I ♀

Agelaius thilius (*Molina*) YELLOW-WINGED BLACKBIRD Temperate S America from S Peru and Brazil S to Chubut / salt and freshwater marshes

Agelaius phoeniceus (*L*) RED-WINGED BLACKBIRD N and C America, Cuba and Bahamas / anywhere near water / seeds and insects / n ground, tree or herbage / e 3–5/ I ♀ 10–12

Agelaius tricolor (*Audubon*) TRICOLOURED BLACKBIRD South-western USA / scrub and marsh / seeds and insects / n tree or low herbage / e 4–6 / I 11 / F 13

Agelaius icterocephalus (*L*) YELLOW-HOODED BLACKBIRD Colombia, Venezuela, the Guianas, Orinoco basin and northern part of Amazon basin / marsh and savannah / insects and seeds / n in reeds or tree / e 3–4

Agelaius humeralis (*Vigors*) TAWNY-SHOULDERED BLACKBIRD Cuba and Haiti / cultivation and forest edge / n tree or palm / e 4

Agelaius xanthomus (*Sclater*) YELLOW-SHOULDERED BLACKBIRD Puerto Rico / open country and mangrove / n tree, palm or cactus / e 3–4

Agelaius cyanopus *Vieillot* UNICOLOURED BLACKBIRD Much of Brazil, Bolivia, Paraguay and E Argentina / marshes and cultivation

Agelaius ruficapillus *Vieillot* CHESTNUT-CAPPED BLACKBIRD Eastern S America from Cayenne to Paraguay and Buenos Aires / marshes

Agelaius xanthopthalmus *Short* (*Occ Pap Mus Zool*, Louisiana State Univ, no 36 (March 1969), p 1) PALE-EYED BLACKBIRD Huánaco in Peru / marshes

Leistes militaris (*L*) RED-BREASTED BLACKBIRD Panama and northern S America S through Orinoco and Amazon basins to Mato Grosso / savannah, grassland and marsh / insects and seeds / n long grass / e 2–4

Leistes superciliaris (*Bonaparte*) WHITE-BROWED BLACKBIRD Eastern S America from Mato Grosso S to Buenos Aires

Sturnella bellicosa *Filippi* PERUVIAN RED-BREASTED MEADOWLARK SW Ecuador to W Peru and N Chile / cultivation

Sturnella defilippi (*Bonaparte*) LESSER RED-BREASTED MEADOWLARK SE Brazil to Uruguay and Buenos Aires / grassland

Sturnella loyca (*Molina*) (=**Pezites militaris** (*L*)) LONG-TAILED MEADOWLARK Argentina and C Chile S to Tierra del Fuego and Falkland Is / cultivation

Sturnella magna (*L*) EASTERN MEADOWLARK Eastern and southern USA, Mexico, C America, Cuba, Colombia, Venezuela, the Guianas and N Brazil to lower Amazon valley / grassland and prairie / insects / n ground / e 3–7 / I ♀ (♂) 13–15 / F 11–12

Sturnella neglecta *Audubon* WESTERN MEADOWLARK S Canada and much of USA except extreme E and S / grassland and prairie / insects and seeds / n ground / e 3–7 / I ♂♀ 15

Pseudoleistes guirahuro (*Vieillot*) YELLOW-RUMPED MARSHBIRD SE Brazil, Paraguay, Uruguay and NE Argentina / cultivation, generally near water

Pseudoleistes virescens (*Vieillot*) BROWN AND YELLOW MARSHBIRD SE Brazil, Uruguay and NE Argentina / wooded pastures near water

Amblyramphus holosericeus (*Scopoli*) SCARLET-HEADED BLACKBIRD N Bolivia, S Brazil, Paraguay, Uruguay and NE Argentina / marshes and reedbeds

Hypopyrrhus pyrhoypogaster (*de Tarragon*) RED-BELLIED GRACKLE Colombia / forest and moist scrub

Curaeus curaeus (*Molina*) AUSTRAL BLACKBIRD S Chile, S Argentina and Tierra del Fuego / bushy hillsides, forest outskirts and cultivation

Curaeus forbesi (*Sclater*) FORBES'S BLACKBIRD E Brazil

Gnorimopsar chopi (*Vieillot*) CHOPI BLACKBIRD E and S Brazil, E Bolivia, Paraguay, Uruguay and N Argentina / marsh, reedbeds and cultivation

Oreopsar bolivianus *Sclater* BOLIVIAN BLACKBIRD Highlands of Bolivia / trees in dry inter-montane basins

Lampropsar tanagrinus (*Spix*) VELVET-FRONTED GRACKLE Orinoco and Amazon basins / mangrove, forest edge near water

Macroagelaius subalaris (*Boissonneau*) MOUNTAIN GRACKLE E Andes of Colombia / forest

Macroagelaius imthurni (*Sclater*) GOLDEN-TUFTED or IM THURN'S GRACKLE W Guyana, S Venezuela and adjacent Brazil / forest

Dives atroviolacea (*d'Orbigny*) CUBAN BLACKBIRD Cuba and Isle of Pines / habitation / n base of palm frond / e 3–4

Dives dives (*Deppe*) SINGING BLACKBIRD Mexico to NC Nicaragua

Dives warszewiczi (*Cabanis*) SCRUB BLACKBIRD

ESTRILDIDAE:
Chloebia gouldiae,
Gouldian Finch

ESTRILDIDAE:
Lonchura griseicapilla
(=*Odontospiza caniceps*),
Grey-headed Silverbill

Plate 294

ESTRILDIDAE:
Lonchura fringilloides,
Magpie Mannikin

ESTRILDIDAE:
Lonchura cucullata,
Bronze Mannikin

Plate 295

SW Ecuador to W Peru

Quiscalus mexicanus (*Gmelin*) GREAT-TAILED GRACKLE South-western USA, Mexico, C America to NW Peru and N Venezuela/swamp and mangrove / omnivorous / n tree or bush/ e 2–4/I ♀ 13–14/F 20–3

Quiscalus major *Vieillot* BOAT-TAILED GRACKLE Coasts of eastern and southern USA/ swamp / omnivorous / n tree or bush / e 3–5/ I ♀ 14

Quiscalus palustris (*Swainson*) SLENDER-BILLED GRACKLE Marshes of Río Lerma, Mexico/probably extinct/no data

Quiscalus nicaraguensis *Salvin and Godman* NICARAGUA GRACKLE Nicaragua on the shores of the two great lakes, Managra and Nicaragua/ no data /? endangered

Quiscalus quiscula (*L*) COMMON GRACKLE (the names 'Purple Grackle' and 'Bronzed Grackle' refer to races of this species) N America, except extreme N/almost ubiquitous/ insects, seeds and fruit/n tree or herbage/e 3–7/ I ♂♀ 14/F 18

Quiscalus niger (*Todd*) GREATER ANTILLEAN GRACKLE Cuba, Cayman Is, Jamaica, Hispaniola and Puerto Rico/ open country and habitation/ n tree/e 3–5

Quiscalus lugubris *Swainson* CARIB GRACKLE Lesser Antilles and islands off N coast of S America/open country and habitation/insects, worms, small lizards etc – omnivorous near habitation/n tree/e 2–4/I ♀ 12/F 14

Euphagus carolinus (*Müller*) RUSTY BLACK-BIRD Canada w S Canada and eastern USA/ almost ubiquitous/seeds and insects/n tree or bush/e 4–5/I ♀ 14/F 12

Euphagus cyanocephalus (*Wagler*) BREWER'S BLACKBIRD S Canada and northern USA w S to Gulf coast and S Mexico/open country and habitation/insects and seeds/n ground or tree/ e 3–7/I ♀ 12–14/F 13

Molothrus badius (*Vieillot*) BAY-WINGED COWBIRD Brazil, Bolivia, Paraguay, Uruguay and N Argentina/bushy pasture and open forest/ not a brood parasite, but often uses abandoned nests

Molothrus rufoaxillaris *Cassin* SCREAMING COWBIRD S Bolivia, Paraguay, extreme SE Brazil, Uruguay and N Argentina/marsh and bushy pasture/P on *M. badius*

Molothrus bonariensis (*Gmelin*) SHINY COWBIRD E Panama, Lesser Antilles and much of S America except extreme S / savannah/ insects, seeds and grain/P

Molothrus aeneus (*Wagler*) BRONZED, RED-EYED or BROWN COWBIRD South-western USA, Mexico and C America to C Panama / open country/insects and seeds/P

Molothrus armenti *Cabanis* BRONZE-BROWN COWBIRD Colombia at Letitia on the Amazon; formerly also occurred on the coast of Colombia, this population known from 4 specimens, of which only 2 can now be found

Molothrus ater (*Boddaert*) BROWN-HEADED COWBIRD S Canada and USA w S to Mexico/ open country / insects / P

Scapidura oryzivora (*Gmelin*) GIANT COWBIRD S Mexico through C and S America to NW Peru on the Pacific side and N Argentina on the Atlantic / savannah and cultivation/ invertebrates and grain/P

Dolichonyx oryzivorus (*L*) BOBOLINK S Canada and USA w S America S to N Argentina / prairie and cultivation / insects and seeds/n ground/e 4–7/I ♀ 10–11/F 10–14

FRINGILLIDAE Finches Seed-eating birds with conical, short, stout bills. Usually sexually dimorphic, the young resembling the female.

Fringilla coelebs *L* CHAFFINCH Europe, W Asia to Afghanistan, Near East, Mediterranean, N Africa, Azores, Canary Is/forest and habitation/seeds and insects/n tree or bush/e 4–8/ I ♀ (?♂) 11–13/F 13–14

Fringilla teydea *Webb, Berthelot and Moquin-Tandon* BLUE CHAFFINCH Pine forests of Tenerife and Gran Canaria/insects and seeds/ n tree/e 2/I ♀ 14

Fringilla montifringilla *L* BRAMBLING b in the forest belt of N Eurasia w S to Mediterranean, N India, China and Japan / forest / seeds and insects/n tree/e 4–9/I ♀

Serinus pusillus (*Pallas*) GOLD-FRONTED FINCH Mts of SC Asia from Asia Minor to Kashmir and N Baluchistan / high elevations/ seeds/n bush/e 3–5

Serinus serinus (*L*) SERIN b Continental Europe from Baltic S to Mediterranean and N Africa / open woodland and cultivation / seeds/ n tree or bush/e 3–5/I ♂♀ 13

Serinus syriacus *Bonaparte* SYRIAN SERIN Mts of Lebanon and Syria w Egypt, Palestine and Iraq/woodland/n n/k/e 4

Serinus canaria (*L*) CANARY W Canary Is, Madeira and Azores, introduced Bermuda/

almost ubiquitous / seeds / n tree or bush / e 4–5 /
I ♀ 13–14 / F 18–21

Serinus citrinella (*Pallas*) CITRIL FINCH Mts
of S Europe, Sardinia, Corsica and Balearics /
forest / seeds and insects / n tree / e 3–5 / I ♀

Serinus thibetanus (*Hume*) TIBETAN SERIN
Nepal, Sikkim, SE Tibet and SW Sikang w to
N Burma and N Yunnan / thin forest, open
hillsides and above timberline / n and e n/k

Serinus canicollis (*Swainson*) CAPE CANARY
E and S Africa from Ethiopia to Angola and
Cape / forest and cultivation / seeds / n tree or
bush / e 3–5

Serinus nigriceps *Rüppell* RÜPPELL'S SISKIN
Mts of N and C Ethiopia above 8,000ft
(2,438m) / n tree / e 2–3

Serinus citrinelloides *Rüppell* AFRICAN
CITRIL Mts of E Africa from Ethiopia to
Mozambique / bush and cultivation / seeds and
insects / n tree or shrub / e 2–3

Serinus frontalis *Reichenow* YELLOW-FRONTED
CITRIL Uganda, NW Tanganyika and NE
Zambia (formerly regarded as a race of
citrinelloides): Angola (unique type of *Serinus
frontalis martinsi* Pinto, status uncertain) / data
probably as for *citrinelloides*

Serinus capistratus (*Finsch and Hartlaub*)
BLACK-FACED CANARY Gabon and Angola to N
Zambia and N end of Lake Tanganyika / forest
edges and clearings in woodland / seeds / n tree or
bush / e 3

Serinus koliensis *Grant and Mackworth-Praed*
VAN SOMEREN'S CANARY E Congo, CE Uganda
and W Kenya / papyrus swamps / no other data

Serinus scotops (*Sundevall*) STRIPED or
FOREST CANARY Transvaal, Natal and Cape
Province / forest clearings / seeds / n tree or bush /
e 3–4

Serinus leucopygius (*Sundevall*) WHITE-
RUMPED SEEDEATER Senegal E across N Nigeria,
Chad etc, to Sudan and Ethiopia also Aïr
Massif in Sahara / open bush and cultivation /
seeds / n tree or bush / e 3–4

Serinus atrogularis (*Smith*) YELLOW-
RUMPED SEEDEATER S Arabia, E and S Africa
from Ethiopia to Angola and the Cape / bush or
woodland near water / seeds / n bush or tree / e 3
[*Serinus flavigula* Salvadori, is a yellow-throated
mutant from Ethiopia known from 3 specimens]

Serinus citrinipectus *Clancey and Lawson*
LEMON-BREASTED SEEDEATER S Mozambique to
extreme S Malawi / no data

Serinus mozambicus (*Müller*) YELLOW-EYED
CANARY Africa S of Sahara / open woodland and
cultivation / seeds / n tree / e 3–4

Serinus donaldsoni *Sharpe* GROSBEAK
CANARY S Ethiopia to NE Tanganyika / open
bush / seeds / n tree / e 3

Serinus flaviventris (*Swainson*) YELLOW
CANARY E and S Africa from Ethiopia to
Angola and the Cape / bush / n tree or bush / e 2–4

Serinus sulphuratus (*L*) BRIMSTONE CANARY
E Africa from Kenya to the Cape / open woodland and cultivation / insects and seeds / n tree /
e 3

Serinus albogularis (*Smith*) WHITE-HEADED
SEEDEATER S Africa N to SW Angola and
Orange Free State / bush and scrubby hillsides /
seeds and buds / n bush / e 3–4

Serinus gularis (*Smith*) STREAKY-HEADED
SEEDEATER Africa S of Sahara / open woodland
and cultivation / seeds and fruit / n tree / e 2–4

Serinus menelli (*Chubb*) BLACK-EARED
SEEDEATER C Africa from Angola and Malawi
to Rhodesia / highland woods and rocky hillsides / seeds and fruit / n tree / e 2–3

Serinus tristriatus *Rüppell* BROWN-RUMPED
SEEDEATER Eritrea and N Somalia to C Ethiopia /
open country / n tree or bush / e 3–4

Serinus menachensis (*Oglivie-Grant*) YEMEN
SERIN Bushy hills 6,000–7,500ft (1,800–2,300m)
from Yemen to Amiri, Arabia / no data

Serinus striolatus (*Rüppell*) STREAKY
SEEDEATER Highlands of E Africa, Ethiopia to
Tanganyika / bush and cultivation / seeds / n tree
or bush / e 3–5

Serinus burtoni (*Gray*) THICK-BILLED
SEEDEATER Mts from Cameroon and Angola to
Kenya and Tanganyika / mountain forest and
bush / seeds / n tree / e n/k

Serinus rufobrunneus (*Gray*) PRINCIPÉ
SEEDEATER Principé and São Thomé / ubiquitous /
seeds / n and e n/k

Serinus leucopterus (*Sharpe*) LAYARD'S or
WHITE-WINGED SEEDEATER Mts of SW Cape
Province / bush and scrub / seeds and buds / n
bush / e ?3

Serinus totta (*Sparrman*) CAPE SISKIN Mts of
Cape Province and Basutoland / n crevice in
rocks / e 3–5

Serinus alario (*L*) BLACKHEAD CANARY
S Africa N to Orange Free State and SW Africa /
dry and open country / seeds / n bush / e 3–5

Serinus estherae (*Finsch*) MALAY GOLDFINCH

VIDUINAE: *Vidua macroura*, Pin-tailed Whydah; female and male

Plate 296

VIDUINAE:
Vidua regia,
Queen Whydah

VIDUINAE:
Vidva macroura,
Pin-tailed Whydah

Plate 297

Mts of Sumatra, mts near Bogor (W Java), Tengger Mts (E Java) and Mt Katanglad, Mindanao (This species is sometimes placed in a monotypic genus *Chrysocorythus*, because of its isolated and relict distribution)

Neospiza concolor (*Bocage*) NEOSPIZA São Thomé / 2 specimens / ? extinct

Linurgus olivaceus (*Fraser*) ORIOLE FINCH Fernando Po and mts from Cameroons to Tanganyika and Sudan / mountain forest / seeds and caterpillars / n bush / e 2

Rhynchostruthus socotranus *Sclater and Hartlaub* GOLDEN-WINGED GROSBEAK N Somalia (British Somaliland), SW Arabia and Socotra / scrub / n and e n/k

Carduelis chloris (*L*) GREENFINCH Europe, Mediterranean, N Africa and SW Asia E to Afghanistan, absent from Malta, introduced Azores / forest and cultivation / seeds and insects / n tree or bush / e 3–8 / I ♀ 13–14 / F 13–16

Carduelis sinica (*L*) CHINESE GREENFINCH E China N to Kamchatka, Mongolia, Japan, Kuriles, Bonin and Volcano Is / forest and cultivation / seeds / n tree or bush / e 3–5 / I 12–13

Carduelis spinoides *Vigors* YELLOW-BREASTED GREENFINCH Himalayas and mts of northern SE Asia / hill forest / n tree / e 3–5 / I ♀ 13

Carduelis ambigua (*Oustalet*) BLACK-HEADED GREENFINCH SE Tibet and mts of N Burma, N Tonkin, Yunnan and S Szechwan / forest / no other data

Carduelis spinus (*L*) EURASIAN SISKIN Temperate and boreal Eurasia from Europe and N Africa to Japan and the Sea of Okhotsk / sporadic and discontinuous / forest and woodland / seeds and insects / n tree or bush / e 2–6 / I ♀ 11–12 / F 15

Carduelis pinus (*Wilson*) PINE SISKIN Much of N America and C America S to Guatemala / forest / seeds and insects / n tree / e 2–5 / I ♀ 13 / F 14–15

Carduelis atriceps (*Salvin*) BLACK-CAPPED SISKIN Mts of S Chiapas and SW Guatemala / hybridises with *C. pinus* and may be conspecific

Carduelis spinescens (*Bonaparte*) ANDEAN SISKIN Mts of Venezuela and Colombia / open country and shrubbery

Carduelis yarrellii *Audubon* YARRELL'S or YELLOW-FACED SISKIN E Brazil (arid zone) and NC Venezuela / open country and shrubbery

Carduelis cucullata *Swainson* RED SISKIN Arid tropical zone of NE Colombia and N Venezuela / dry scrub and open country

Carduelis crassirostris (*Landbeck*) THICK-BILLED SISKIN Mts from Peru to C Chile and W Argentina / bushy slopes

Carduelis magellanica (*Vieillot*) HOODED SISKIN Much of S America / woodland, savannah and swamp (*C. sanctaecrucis* (Todd) is sometimes separated)

Carduelis dominicensis (*Bryant*) ANTILLEAN SISKIN Mts of Hispaniola / mountain pine forest / n tree / e 2–3

Carduelis siemiradzkii (*Berlepsch and Taczanowski*) SAFFRON SISKIN Arid tropical zone near Guayaquil and Isla Puna, SW Ecuador / arid scrub

Carduelis olivacea (*Berlepsch and Stolzmann*) OLIVACEUS SISKIN SE Ecuador to Peru and Bolivia

Carduelis notata *Du Bus* NEOTROPICAL BLACK-HEADED SISKIN Mexico, Honduras, Belize, El Salvador and N Nicaragua

Carduelis xanthogastra (*Du Bus*) YELLOW-BELLIED SISKIN Mts from Costa Rica to Venezuela: C Bolivia / bushy slopes / n tree / e 3 / I ♀

Carduelis atrata *Lafresnaye and d'Orbigny* BLACK SISKIN Puna zone from Peru to N Chile and W Argentina / woodland and rocky places

Carduelis uropygialis (*Sclater*) YELLOW-RUMPED SISKIN Mts from S Peru to C Chile and W Argentina / ravines and scrub

Carduelis barbata (*Molina*) BLACK-CHINNED SISKIN Chile and W Argentina S to Tierra del Fuego / woodland and scrub

Carduelis tristis (*L*) AMERICAN GOLDFINCH S Canada, USA and Mexico / forest, woodland and cultivation / seeds and insects / n tree / e 4–6 / I ♀ 12 / F 16–17

Carduelis psaltria (*Say*) LESSER GOLDFINCH Western USA, Mexico and through C America to N Venezuela and NW Peru / open country and shrubbery / seeds and insects / n tree / e 3–4 / I ♀ 12

Carduelis lawrencei *Cassin* LAWRENCE'S GOLDFINCH South-western USA and Mexico / dry scrub / seeds and other vegetable matter / n tree or bush / e 3–6 / I ♀

Carduelis carduelis (*L*) EUROPEAN GOLDFINCH Europe, N Africa, Azores, Canaries and Madeira; Asia E to Lake Baikal and S to Himalayas and Baluchistan / forest, scrub and cultivation / seeds and insects / n tree / e 3–7 /

I ♀ 12–13/ F 13–14
Acanthis flammea (*L*) MEALY REDPOLL, LESSER REDPOLL Forest zone of N Holarctic, Greenland, Iceland, Alps and mts of Czechoslovakia; *A. f. cabaret* (Lesser Redpoll) has been introduced to New Zealand and Lord Howe Is / forest and scrub / seeds and insects/ n tree / e 3–8 / I ♀ 10–11/ F 11–14
Acanthis hornemanni(*Holböll*) HORNEMANN'S REDPOLL b tundra zone of Holarctic w S to Japan, Canada, north-western USA and British Isles (rarely) / seeds / n bush / e 4–6
Acanthis flavirostris (*L*) TWITE N Europe across C Asia to Kashmir, Tibet and W Kansu/ open country, moors etc / seeds / n bush / e 4–7/ I ♀ 12–13/ F 15
Acanthis cannabina (*L*) EURASIAN LINNET Europe, N Africa, Madeira, Canary Is, SW Asia E to Russian Altai and in w to NW India/ scrub and open country / seeds and insects / n bush or ground / e 4–7/ I ♀ 10–12/ F 11–13
Acanthis yemenensis (*Ogilvie-Grant*) YEMEN LINNET Mts of Yemen, Hejaz and Azir at 7–9,000ft (2,100–2,700m)
Acanthis johannis (*Clarke*) WARSANGLI LINNET Mts of extreme NE Somalia / ? unique
Leucosticte nemoricola (*Hodgson*) MOUNTAIN FINCH Mts from N Afghanistan to Tian Shan and W Sinkiang, and through Himalayas to N Burma and W China / rocky hillsides / seeds and insects / n rock crevice or rodent burrow / e 4–5
Leucosticte brandti *Bonaparte* BRANDT'S FINCH or ROSY-RUMPED FINCH Mts of C Asia from Tian Shan to Mongolia and Himalayas to W China / rocky hillsides / seeds and insects/ n hole under rock / e 3–4
Leucosticte arctoa (*Pallas*) ROSY FINCH Mts of C Asia across to NE Siberia and through much of N America S to New Mexico / rocky cliffs and above timberline / seeds / n rock crevice / e 3–5 / I ♀ 12–14 (some authorities separate the Rosy Finches into about 4 species)
Callacanthis burtoni (*Gould*) SPECTACLED or BURTON'S FINCH Himalayas from NW Pakistan to Sikkim / forest / seeds / n tree / e 3
Rhodopechys sanguinea (*Gould*) CRIMSON-WINGED FINCH Morocco and S Spain; Turkey and Caucasus to Afghanistan / rocky hillsides/ seeds / n tree (Baker) hole under stone (Ali and Ripley) / e ?1 ?4–5 / I ♀ 12 / for further details see *Oologists Record*, 43 (1969), pp 1–16
Rhodopechys githaginea (*Lichtenstein*)

TRUMPETER FINCH Canary Is; Sahara through Egypt and Arabia to Afghanistan and Pakistan/ bare hills and stony semi-desert / seeds / n rock crevice / e 4 / I 13–14 / F 14
Rhodopechys mongolica (*Swinhoe*) MONGOLIAN FINCH Transcaucasia across Asia to Mongolia / bare hills and stony plains / seeds/ n ground or bush / e 3–5
Rhodopechys obsoleta (*Lichtenstein*) DESERT FINCH Middle East to Afghanistan and Sinkiang S in w to N Pakistan / mountain scrub / seeds and flowerbuds / n tree or bush / e 4–7
Uragus sibericus (*Pallas*) LONG-TAILED ROSEFINCH S Siberia, Manchuria, China, Korea, Kuriles and Hokkaido / scrub and swamp forest / seeds / n bush / e 3–6 / I ♂♀
Urocynchramus pylzowi *Przewalski* PRZEWALSKI'S FINCH Mts of W China / no data
Carpodacus rubescens (*Blandford*) BLANDFORD'S ROSEFINCH Himalayas to mts of Yunnan and SW Sikang / open country and forest edge / n and e n/k
Carpodacus nipalensis (*Hodgson*) DARK ROSEFINCH Himalayas to N Burma and mts of W China / forest and alpine pasture [n bamboo e 3, 1 nest known, ex Baker collection, but the eggs are so unlike those of any other rosefinch that I think they must be erroneous]
Carpodacus erythrinus (*Pallas*) COMMON ROSEFINCH or SCARLET GROSBEAK Finland and much of Asia w S to N India / forest, scrub, bush and cultivation / seeds, nectar and possibly insects / n bush / e 3–6 / I ♀ 12–14 / F 11–17
Carpodacus purpureus (*Gmelin*) PURPLE FINCH N America / forest and cultivation / seeds and fruit / n tree / e 3–6 / I ♀ (?♂) 13 / F 14
Carpodacus cassinii *Baird* CASSIN'S FINCH Mts from British Columbia to Mexico / coniferous forest / seeds, buds and berries / n tree / e 3–6/ I ♀ 12
Carpodacus mexicanus (*Müller*) HOUSE FINCH Western N America and Mexico / desert, scrub and habitation / seeds, buds and fruits, almost omnivorous in cities n tree or hole in tree or building etc / e 2–6 / I ♀ 12–14 / F 11–19
Carpodacus pulcherrimus (*Moore*) BEAUTIFUL ROSEFINCH Himalayas and mts of Tibet and W China to Mongolia / forest, scrub and above timberline / n bush / e 3–5 / I ♀
Carpodacus eos (*Stresemann*) DAWN ROSEFINCH Mts of W China / no data
Carpodacus rhodochrous (*Vigors*) PINK-

Plate 298

PLOCEIDAE:
Pseudonigrita arnaudi,
Grey-headed Social Weaver

Opposite:
PLOCEIDAE:
Euplectes orix,
Red Bishop or Grenadier
Weaver

Plate 299

BROWED ROSEFINCH Himalayas from Kashmir to Sikkim (7,500–12,000ft (2,300–3,600m))/forest/seeds and berries/n tree/e 4–6

Carpodacus vinaceus *Verreaux* VINACEOUS ROSEFINCH Mts of W China and Taiwan/forest/n and e n/k

Carpodacus edwardsii *Verreaux* EDWARDS' ROSEFINCH Himalayas to mts of N Burma and W China / high elevations / bamboo jungle/seeds/n bush/e n/s (2 alleged clutches of 4 in British Museum (Natural History) collection)

Carpodacus synoicus (*Temminck*) SINAI ROSEFINCH Sinai: NE Afghanistan: SW Sinkiang: N Tsinghai and NW Kansu/rocky dry hills/n hole in rock/e 4–7

Carpodacus roseus (*Pallas*) PALLAS' ROSE-FINCH b Altai to Yakutia, Lake Baikal and Sakhalin w N China, Korea, Manchuria and Japan/forest/seeds and berries/n and e n/k

Carpodacus trifasciatus *Verreaux* THREE-BANDED ROSEFINCH Mts of W China / fruit/n and e n/k

Carpodacus rhodopeplus (*Vigors*) SPOT-WINGED ROSEFINCH Himalayas to N Burma and Yunnan/high elevations/little data/e 4–5, nest site not recorded

Carpodacus thura *Bonaparte and Schlegel* WHITE-BROWED ROSEFINCH Himalayas from Afghanistan to mts of W China/above timber-line/seeds and berries/n bush/e 3–4

Carpodacus rhodochlamys (*Brandt*) RED-MANTLED ROSEFINCH W Himalayas and mts of C Asia N to Mongolia/high elevations/seeds/n bush/e 4

Carpodacus rubicilloides *Przewalski* CRIMSON-EARED ROSEFINCH Himalayas and mts of SE Tibet and W China/arid scrub/seeds/n tree or bush/e 3–5

Carpodacus rubicilla (*Güldenstädt*) GREAT ROSEFINCH Mts from Caucasus to W Mongolia, W China, Tibet, Nepal and Kashmir / above timber-line/seeds and berries/n bush/e 3–5

Carpodacus puniceus (*Blyth*) RED-FRONTED ROSEFINCH Himalayas, mts of W China and WC Asia/high mountain scrub/seeds, flowers and buds/n bush/e 2

Carpodacus roborowskii (*Przewalski*) ROBOROWSKI'S ROSEFINCH Highest altitudes of Buckhan Boda Shan and Amne Machin Shan, in Tsinghai/no data (sometimes placed in the monotypic genus *Kozlowia*)

Chaunoproctus ferreorostris (*Vigors*) BONIN

FINCH Peel Is, Bonin Is/extinct/no data

Pinicola enucleator (*L*) PINE GROSBEAK Widely distributed through N America and N Palaearctic / forest / berries and insects / n tree/e 3–5/I ♀ 13–14

Pinicola subhimachalus (*Hodgson*) CRIMSON-BROWED FINCH Himalayas to S Sikang, N Yunnan and N Burma/forest/seeds and berries/n and e n/k

Haematospiza sipahi (*Hodgson*) SCARLET FINCH Himalayas to Burma and N Yunnan/pine forest / seeds, berries and insects / n pine tree/e 1

Loxia pytyopsittacus *Borkhausen* PARROT CROSSBILL Coniferous forests of Scandinavia/seeds/n tree/e 3–5/I ♀ 14–15?

Loxia scotica *Hartert* SCOTTISH CROSSBILL Scotland/forests of *Pinus sylvestris*/seeds and insects/n tree/e 2–5/I ♀ (?♂) 12–15/ F 17–20 (for discussion on the specific status of this form see Knox, *Bull Brit Ornith Club*, 96 (1976) pp 15–19)

Loxia curvirostra *L* RED CROSSBILL Widely distributed through the Holarctic regions S to Nicaragua and Himalayas, isolated forms in S Annam and Luzon / conifer forest / seeds of conifers/n tree/e 2–5/I ♀ 12–13/F 24+

Loxia leucoptera *Gmelin* TWO-BARRED CROSSBILL Coniferous forests of N Siberia, Canada and northern USA, isolated form in mts of Hispaniola/seeds of conifers/n tree/e 3–5

Pyrrhula nipalensis *Hodgson* BROWN BULLFINCH Himalayas, mts of northern SE Asia and S China, isolated forms in Malaya and Taiwan/mountain scrub/n bush/e 1–3

Pyrrhula leucogenys *Grant* PHILIPPINE BULLFINCH Mts of Luzon and Mindanao (Philippines)

Pyrrhula aurantiaca *Gould* ORANGE BULLFINCH NW Himalayas 6,000–13,000ft (1,830–3,963m)/high mountain scrub/n bush/e 3–4

Pyrrhula erythrocephala *Vigors* RED-HEADED BULLFINCH Himalayas and SE Tibet/forest/seeds and berries/n bush/e 3–4

Pyrrhula erythaea *Blyth* BEAVEN'S BULLFINCH Mts of W China, Hopeh, SE Tibet, Yunnan, Sikkim and Bhutan; Taiwan / forest / n tree/e n/k; a doubtful clutch in Brit Mus (Nat Hist)

Pyrrhula pyrrhula (*L*) COMMON BULLFINCH Much of C and N Palaearctic / forest and cultivation/buds, seeds and fruit/n tree or bush/

e 4–7/I ♂♀ 12–14/F 12–16

Coccothraustes coccothraustes (*L*)
HAWFINCH C belt of Palaearctic S to N Africa,
Japan and C China/forest, woodland, cultivation and scrub/seeds, kernels and insects/n tree
or bush/e 2–7/I ♀ 9–10/F 10–11

Coccothraustes migratorius (*Hartert*)
YELLOW-BILLED GROSBEAK E Asia from Amur
to China (rarely in w to Taiwan and N Indo-
China)/forest, scrub and cultivation/insects
and seeds / n tree or bush / e 3–5

Coccothraustes personatus *Temminck and
Schlegel* JAPANESE GROSBEAK Amurland to N
China; Japan / forest / seeds, nuts, fruit and
insects/n tree/e 3–4

Coccothraustes icterioides *Vigors* BLACK-
AND-YELLOW GROSBEAK NE Afghanistan and
NW Himalayas/forest/seeds and berries/n tree/
e 2–3

Coccothraustes affinis (*Blyth*) ALLIED
GROSBEAK Himalayas and mts of N Burma and
W China/forest/seeds and berries/n and e n/k

Coccothraustes melanozanthos *Hodgson*
SPOTTED-WINGED GROSBEAK Himalayas and mts
of northern SE Asia and W China/forest/n tree/
e 2–3

Coccothraustes carneipes *Hodgson* WHITE-
WINGED GROSBEAK Mts of C Asia from NE Iran
to Turkestan, Himalayas, W China and Inner
Mongolia/high mountain scrub/juniper berries/
n bush /e 2–3

Coccothraustes vespertinus (*Cooper*)
EVENING GROSBEAK S Canada, USA and
Mexico/forest /seeds and buds/n tree/e 2–5/
I ♀ 11–14/F 13–14

Coccothraustes abeillei (*Lesson*) HOODED
GROSBEAK Mexico and Guatemala

Pyrrhoplectes epauletta (*Hodgson*)
EPAULETTED or GOLD-NAPED FINCH Himalayas,
mts of SE Tibet, N Burma, Yunnan and SW
Sikang/forest/seeds and berries/n and e n/k

**ESTRILDIDAE Waxbills, Mannikins,
Munias and allies** Small seedeaters with short,
stout, pointed bills; very variable in colour, but
very uniform in anatomy and habits. Gregarious. Most build large domed nests, often in
colonies, and lay 4–10 pure white eggs.

Parmoptila woodhousei *Cassin* WOODHOUSE'S
ANTPECKER Equatorial Africa from Angola to
Ghana and Uganda/forest/n tree /e 3–4

Nigrita fusconota *Fraser* WHITE-BREASTED
NEGRO-FINCH Fernando Po and forests from

Ghana to Angola and Uganda/forest/insects/
n tree/e 1–6

Nigrita bicolor (*Hartlaub*) CHESTNUT-
BREASTED NEGRO-FINCH Principé (? introduced)
and Sierra Leone to Angola and Uganda/forest/
insects and palm-husk/n tree/e 1–5

Nigrita luteifrons *Verreaux and Verreaux*
PALE-FRONTED NEGRO-FINCH Fernando Po and
Nigeria to Angola and Uganda / secondary
forest/n tree or bush/e 4

Nigrita canicapilla (*Strickland*) GREY-
BREASTED NEGRO-FINCH Guinea to Angola,
Tanganyika and S Sudan/forest/n tree/e 4

Nesocharis shelleyi *Alexander* LITTLE OLIVE
WAXBILL Fernando Po and mts of Cameroon/
mountain forest/insects/n tree/e 3

Nesocharis ansorgei (*Hartert*) WHITE-
COLLARED OLIVEBACK E Ituri and Rwanda/
dense herbaceous scrub/n in old nests of other
birds/e ?2

Nesocharis capistrata (*Hartlaub*) GREY-
HEADED OLIVEBACK Equatorial Africa from
Gambia to Congo, W Uganda and S Sudan/
forest/insects/n tree (1 known)/e n/k

Pytilia phoenicoptera *Swainson* RED-WINGED
PYTILIA Semi-arid zone from Gambia to N
Congo, Uganda and S Sudan/local/bush and
tall grass/seeds and insects/n tree or bush/e 4

Pytilia hypogrammica *Sharpe* YELLOW-
WINGED PYTILIA Savannah woodland from
Sierra Leone to Oubangui-Shari/n shrub/e 3
(1 nest known)

Pytilia afra (*Gmelin*) ORANGE-WINGED PYTILIA
E and C Africa from Ethiopia to Angola,
Tanzania and Mozambique/bush or semi-arid
country/seeds/n bush or plant-fork/e 3–5

Pytilia melba (*L*) MELBA FINCH Much of
Africa S of Sahara / thorny thickets / seeds / n
bush/e 3–7

Mandingoa nitidula (*Hartlaub*) GREEN-
BACKED TWIN-SPOT Locally through equatorial
and S tropical Africa/forest edge/seeds/n tree/
e ?3

Cryptospiza reichenovii (*Hartlaub*) RED-
FACED CRIMSON-WING Mountain forests of C
and E Africa/forest and bamboo/seeds/n bush
or treefern/e 3

Cryptospiza salvadorii *Reichenow* ABYSSINIAN
CRIMSON-WING Mts of E Africa from C Ethiopia
to N Tanganyika/forest and scrub/seeds/n tree/
e 4–5

Cryptospiza jacksoni *Sharpe* DUSKY

PLOCEIDAE:
Euplectes orix,
Red Bishop or Grenadier
Weaver

PLOCEIDAE:
Petronia superciliaris,
Yellow-throated Petronia

Plate 300

PLOCEIDAE:
Passer griseus,
Grey-headed Sparrow

Plate 301

CRIMSON-WING Mts of E Congo, Rwanda and Uganda / forest / seeds / n tree / e 2

Cryptospiza shelleyi *Sharpe* SHELLEY'S CRIMSON-WING Ruwenzori and adjacent mountains / forest / seeds / n and e n/k

Pyrenestes sanguineus *Swainson* CRIMSON SEED-CRACKER Gambia to Ivory Coast / swampy bush / n bush / e ?3

Pyrenestes ostrinus (*Vieillot*) BLACK-BELLIED SEED-CRACKER Parts of C Africa from Ivory Coast to Angola, Uganda and Zambia / forest clearings / seeds / n tree / e 3–5 / I ♂♀

Pyrenestes minor *Shelley* LESSER SEED-CRACKER E Tanganyika to N Mozambique / forest / seeds / n tree / e 5–6

Spermophaga poliogenys (*Ogilvie-Grant*) GRANT'S BLUEBILL Parts of Congo and Bwamba forest in Uganda / forest / n and e n/k

Spermophaga haematina (*Vieillot*) BLUEBILL Gambia to Congo and Angola / swampy thickets and secondary scrub / n bush / e 3–6

Spermophaga ruficapilla (*Shelley*) RED-HEADED BLUEBILL N Angola to Uganda and Kenya / swampy forest / seeds / n ? tree / e 2–4

Clytospiza montieri (*Hartlaub*) BROWN TWIN-SPOT Savannah N and S of equatorial forest from Cameroons to Sudan and Uganda and from Gabon and Angola to Kasai / termites / n tree / e 4–6

Hypargos margaritatus (*Strickland*) PINK-THROATED TWIN-SPOT Mozambique and NE Zululand / scrub / seeds / n and e n/k

Hypargos niveoguttatus (*Peters*) PETERS' TWIN-SPOT Evergreen forest and riparian bush from Kenya to Congo, Angola and Mozambique / forest edge and bush / seeds / n tree or bush / e 3

Euschistospiza dybowskii (*Oustalet*) DYBOWSKI'S TWIN-SPOT Sierra Leone: Cameroons to Sudan / highland grasslands / n and e n/k

Euschistospiza cinereovinacea (*Souza*) DUSKY TWIN-SPOT Highlands from Angola to Lake Tanganyika and Uganda / grassland and mountain gulleys / n and e n/k

Lagonosticta rara (*Antinori*) BLACK-BELLIED WAXBILL Nigeria and Sierra Leone: highlands of N Cameroons to S Sudan and Kenya / grassland and scrub / insects and seeds / n bush or tree / e 3–4

Lagonosticta rufopicta (*Fraser*) BAR-BREASTED FIRE-FINCH Gambia to Ethiopia and S Sudan / grasslands / seeds / n bush / e 4

Lagonosticta nitidula *Hartlaub* BROWN FIRE-FINCH Angola and Bechuanaland to Katanga and Zambia / swampy thickets and reedbeds / n 'grass hut wall or similar situation' (Praed and Grant) / e 3–4

Lagonosticta senegala (*L*) RED-BILLED FIRE-FINCH Africa S of Sahara (except extreme S) / cultivation and habitation / seeds / n bush, wall or thatch / e 3–6

Lagonosticta rubricata (*Lichtenstein*) AFRICAN FIRE-FINCH Africa S of Sahara (except extreme S) / grassland / seeds and insects / n bush or grass tuft / e 3–6

Lagonosticta landanae *Sharpe* LANDANA FIRE-FINCH Cabinda and Angola / savannah and dry bush / seeds / n and e ? n/k

Lagonosticta rhodopareia (*Heuglin*) JAMESON'S FIRE-FINCH E and S Africa from S Sudan to Lower Congo, Angola and Transvaal / scrub / seeds / n shrub / e 3–4

Lagonosticta larvata (*Rüppell*) BLACK-FACED FIRE-FINCH Savannah belt from Gambia to Ethiopia and N Uganda / grass and bamboo / seeds / n bush / e 3–4

Uraeginthus angolensis (*L*) ANGOLA CORDON-BLEU Africa from Congo and Tanganyika to Natal, introduced Zanzibar and São Thomé / low herbage and cultivation / seeds and insects / n tree, bush or hut wall / e 4–6

Uraeginthus bengalus (*L*) RED-CHEEKED CORDON-BLEU From Senegal through semi-arid belt to Ethiopia and S through E Africa to Katanga and Zambia / open country and cultivation / seeds / n tree, bush or thatch / e 4–5

Uraeginthus cyanocephala (*Richmond*) BLUE-CAPPED CORDON-BLEU Arid regions from Ethiopia to Tanganyika / seeds and termites / n bush / e 4–6

Uraeginthus granatina (*L*) VIOLET-EARED WAXBILL Africa from Angola and Zambia S (but not the extreme S) / dry thorn scrub / seeds and insects / n thorn bush / e 3–5

Uraeginthus ianthinogaster *Reichenow* PURPLE GRENADIER Somalia, Kenya, Uganda and N Tanganyika / thorn scrub / seeds / n bush / e 3–5

Estrilda caerulescens (*Vieillot*) RED-TAILED LAVENDER FINCH W Africa from Senegal to N Cameroons and SW Chad / bush and cultivation / seeds / n and e n/k in wild state, but probably as *E. perreini*. Apparently has nested in captivity

Estrilda perreini (*Vieillot*) BLACK-TAILED

LAVENDER FINCH Gabon and Angola E to Tanganyika and from Tanganyika S to Natal/ open woodland/seeds/n tree or shrub/e 1–4

Estrilda thomensis *Sousa* SÃO THOMÉ WAXBILL, NEUMANN'S WAXBILL W Angola and (? São Thomé)/no data/'extremely rare and of doubtful provenance. Only one or two old specimens are known and in Angola, where an identical bird is known under the name of *E. cinderella* Neumann; it is equally rare. The possibility of human introduction arises in the case of the São Thomé birds, or even of human error' (Mackworth Praed and Grant, referring to the São Thomé bird)

Estrilda melanotis (*Temminck*) YELLOW-BELLIED WAXBILL E and S Africa from Ethiopia to Angola and the Cape/open forest/seeds/n tree or shrub/e 3–4

Estrilda paludicola *Heuglin* FAWN-BREASTED WAXBILL Africa from S Nigeria and S Sudan to Congo and Tanganyika/swampy grassland or open woodland/seeds/n ground or in grass/ e 1–10

Estrilda melopoda (*Vieillot*) ORANGE-CHEEKED WAXBILL Senegal to Congo, N Angola and Lake Chad, introduced Puerto Rico/grassland/ n ground at base of bush/e 5–6

Estrilda rhodopyga *Sundevall* CRIMSON-RUMPED WAXBILL Sudan S to N Tanganyika and N Malawi/grassland/seeds and insects/ n and e n/k

Estrilda rufibarba (*Cabanis*) ARABIAN WAXBILL SW Arabia/thornbush/n and e n/k

Estrilda troglodytes (*Lichtenstein*) BLACK-RUMPED WAXBILL Semi-arid zone from Senegal to Sudan and N Ethiopia/swamps/n ground or grass tuft/e 3–6

Estrilda astrild (*L*) COMMON WAXBILL Much of Africa S of Sahara, introduced on a number of islands, including New Caledonia/grassland and cultivation/seeds/n bush/e 4–6

Estrilda nigriloris *Chapin* KIABO WAXBILL Banks of Lualaba River and shore of Lake Upemba, Congo/grassland/n and e n/k

Estrilda nonnula *Hartlaub* BLACK-CROWNED WAXBILL Fernando Po and S Nigeria to Congo, Kenya and S Sudan/open country, cultivation and open forest/seeds/n tree or bush/e 4–6

Estrilda atricapilla *Verreaux and Verreaux* BLACK-HEADED WAXBILL S Nigeria to N Angola and Kenya/mountain forest/seeds/n shrub/ e 4–5

Estrilda erythronotos (*Vieillot*) BLACK-FACED WAXBILL E and S Africa from S Kenya S to Angola and Cape Province (but not the extreme S)/rocky scrub/seeds/n tree/e 4

Estrilda charmosyna (*Reichenow*) BLACK-CHEEKED WAXBILL Dry country from British Somaliland to Kenya and Uganda/rocky scrub/ seeds/n tree/e 4

Amandava amandava (*L*) STRAWBERRY FINCH or RED AVADAVAT India, Pakistan, S Nepal, Yunnan, SE Asia (not Malaya) Java, Bali, Lombok, Flores, Sumba and Timor, introduced Sumatra, Singapore, Mauritius, Réunion, Fiji and other places/scrub jungle and cultivation/seeds/n grass/e 5–10

Amandava formosa (*Latham*) GREEN AVADAVAT Central India/grassland and cultivation/n cane or long grass/e 5–6

Amandava subflava (*Vieillot*) GOLDEN-BREASTED or ZEBRA WAXBILL Much of Africa S of Sahara, except the extreme S/grassland and cultivation/seeds/n herbage/e 4–5

Ortygospiza atricollis (*Vieillot*) COMMON QUAIL FINCH Africa from S of Sahara to Angola and Damaraland/swamp and tussock bog/seeds/n ground/e 4–6

Ortygospiza gabonensis *Lynes* BLACK-CHINNED QUAIL FINCH C Africa from Gabon to Angola, Zambia and S Uganda/swamp and tussock bog/seeds/n and e n/k

Ortygospiza locustella (*Neave*) LOCUST FINCH Locally in parts of Congo, Angola, the Rhodesias, Tanganyika and Mozambique/bogs and wet grasslands/seeds/n ground/e 2–6

Aegintha temporalis (*Latham*) RED-BROWED FINCH Queensland, New South Wales, Victoria and eastern S Australia, introduced Tahiti/ mangrove, forest and open country/seeds and insects/n bush/e 4–6

Emblema picta *Gould* PAINTED FINCH Arid regions of interior of Australia/porcupine grass/ seeds/n grass clump/e 3–5

Emblema bella (*Latham*) FIRE-TAILED FINCH Coasts of SE Australia, Tasmania, Flinders and Kangaroo Is/scrubby heath and woodland/ seeds and insects/n tree or bush/e 5–8

Emblema oculata (*Quoy and Gaimard*) RED-EARED FINCH SW Australia/moist grassy patches in forest/seeds and insects/n tree/e 4–6

Emblema guttata (*Shaw*) DIAMOND FINCH Savannah and mallee of SE Australia/seeds and insects/n tree or bush/e 5–6

PLOCEIDAE:
Euplectes hordeaceus,
Black-winged or Red-crowned
Bishop, Black-winged Red
Bishop

Plate 302

PLOCEIDAE:
Ploceus subaureus,
Golden Weaver, Olive-headed
Golden Weaver

PLOCEIDAE:
Ploceus melanocephalus,
Black-headed Weaver, Yellow-
backed Weaver

PLOCEIDAE:
Euplectes afer,
Golden Bishop or Napoleon
Weaver, Yellow-crowned
Bishop

Plate 303

Oreostruthus fuliginosus (*De Vis*) CRIMSON-SIDED MOUNTAIN FINCH Mts of New Guinea/glades in mountain forest and grassland above timberline/seeds/n and e n/k

Neochmia phaeton (*Hombron and Jacquinot*) CRIMSON WAXBILL S New Guinea and northern Australia / grassy margins of inland waters/seeds and insects/n long grass/e 5–8

Neochmia ruficauda (*Gould*) STAR FINCH Northern and eastern Australia /grassy margins of inland waters /seeds and insects /n and e n/s

Poephila guttata (*Vieillot*) ZEBRA FINCH Australia, Lesser Sundas and South West Is/woodlands and savannah / seeds and insects/n tree or bush/e 4–6 [Domesticated and widely bred in captivity]

Poephila bichenovii (*Vigors and Horsfield*) DOUBLE-BARRED FINCH Northern and eastern Australia /savannah /seeds and insects /n grass, bush or low tree /e 4

Poephila personata *Gould* MASKED FINCH Northern Australia / grassland and savannah/seeds and insects /n grass, bush or tree /e 4–6

Poephila acuticauda (*Gould*) LONG-TAILED FINCH N Australia and parts of Queensland/forest and woodland / seeds and insects /n tree/e 5–9

Poephila cincta (*Gould*) BLACK-THROATED FINCH Queensland and N New South Wales/forest and woodland / seeds and insects/n tree/e 5–9

Erythrura hyperythra (*Reichenbach*) BAMBOO PARROT-FINCH Mts of Mindanao, N Luzon, Borneo, W Java, Lombok, Flores, Sumbawa, Celebes [and Malaya, 1 specimen]/mountain forest /n and e n/k

Erythrura prasina (*Sparrman*) PINTAILED PARROT-FINCH Thailand, Malaya, Sumatra, Java and Borneo/forest and cultivation /seeds/n and e n/k

Erythrura viridifacies *Hachisuka and Delacour* GREEN-FACED PARROT-FINCH Manila (Luzon)

Erythrura tricolor (*Vieillot*) TRICOLOURED PARROT-FINCH Timor, Tenimbar Is, Wetar, Babar, Damar and Roma

Erythrura coloria *Ripley and Rabor* MINDANAO PARROT-FINCH Mt Katanglad, Mindanao

Erythrura trichroa (*Kittlitz*) BLUE-FACED PARROT-FINCH Celebes, Moluccas, New Guinea and adjacent islands, Bismarck Archipelago, NE Australia, Palau Is, Caroline Is, Guadalcanal, Banks Is, New Hebrides and Loyalty Is /edges of mangroves and rain forest/seeds /n tree or bush /e n/k

Erythrura papuana *Hartert* PAPUAN PARROT-FINCH Mts of Vogelkop /no definite information

Erythrura psittacea (*Gmelin*) RED-THROATED PARROT-FINCH New Caledonia

Erythrura cyaneovirens (*Peale*) RED-HEADED PARROT-FINCH Samoa, Fiji and New Hebrides/ricefields, forest clearings, grasslands and gardens /seeds /n tree /e 3–4

Erythrura kleinschmidti (*Finsch*) PINK-BILLED PARROT-FINCH Viti Levu, Fiji, apparently now confined to the mountain forests of the Nadrau Plateau, about 3,000ft (900m) /no other data

Chloebia gouldiae (*Gould*) GOULDIAN FINCH Northern Australia /savannah /seeds and insects/n hole in tree or termite mound /e 4–8

Aidemosyne modesta (*Gould*) CHERRY FINCH E savannah belt of Australia / riverine scrub/seeds and thickets/n bush or grass clump/e 4–6

Lonchura malabarica (*L*) SILVERBILL or WHITE-THROATED MUNIA Dry belt of Africa just S of Sahara, S Arabia and E to Indian subcontinent / hill forest (Indian region), open country and cultivation (Africa) / seeds and insects /n tree or eaves of house /e 4–12 /I ♂♀ (some authorities separate *L. cantans* (Gmelin) the African Silverbill, from the Indian, see Harrison, *Ibis*, 1964)

Lonchura griseicapilla *Delacour* (= **Odontospiza caniceps** (*Reichenow*)) GREY-HEADED SILVERBILL Dry country from S Ethiopia to Tanganyika /thorn bush /seeds /n tree /e 4–6

Lonchura nana (*Pucheran*) MADAGASCAR MANNIKIN or NANA Madagascar /bush, grassland and cultivation /seeds /n tree or bush/e 3–7

Lonchura cucullata (*Swainson*) BRONZE MANNIKIN Africa from S of Sahara to Angola and Rhodesia; Pemba, Zanzibar, Mafia, Comoros and islands in Gulf of Guinea /open country and cultivation /seeds /n tree /e 4–8

Lonchura bicolor (*Fraser*) BLACK AND WHITE or RED-BACKED MANNIKIN Fernando Po and Africa from S of Sahara to Angola and Natal; Zanzibar, Pemba and Mafia / forest and secondary growth /seeds /n tree /e 4–6

Lonchura fringilloides (*Lafresnaye*) MAGPIE MANNIKIN Local from Senegal and Sudan S to

Congo and Natal, Zanzibar / open country and cultivation / seeds / n tree or bamboo / e 3–6

Lonchura striata (*L*) White-rumped Mannikin Indian sub-continent, SE Asia, S China, Taiwan, Sumatra, Banka, Andamans and Nicobars / jungle grassland and cultivation/ seeds and insects / n tree, bush or grass / e 3–8/ I ♂♀ 13–14

Lonchura leucogastroides (*Horsfield and Moore*) Javan Munia S Sumatra, Java, Bali and Lombok

Lonchura fuscans (*Cassin*) Dusky Munia Borneo, Natuna, Cagayan Sulu and Banguey/ grassland and cultivation / seeds / n tree / e 2–5

Lonchura molucca (*L*) Moluccan Mannikin Celebes, Sula Is, Moluccas, E Lesser Sundas and adjacent groups

Lonchura punctulata (*L*) Spice Finch or Nutmeg Mannikin India, Ceylon, SE Asia, S China, Taiwan and Hainan, through Greater and Lesser Sundas (not Borneo) to Celebes and Philippines / habitation / seeds / n tree or eaves of house / e 4–10 / I ♂♀ 16

Lonchura kelaarti (*Jerdon*) Jerdon's Mannikin Ceylon and SW coast of India / hill forest and cultivation / seeds / n tree or creeper on house / e 3–8 (6–8 in India; 3–7, usually 5, in Ceylon) / I ♂♀ 16 / F 15–17

Lonchura leucogastra (*Blyth*) White-breasted Mannikin Malay Peninsula, Sumatra, Borneo, Palawan, Sulu Archipelago and Philippines / forest and cultivation / n tree

Lonchura tristissima (*Wallace*) Streaked-headed Mannikin New Guinea / patches of mountain grassland

Lonchura leucosticta (*D'Albertis and Salvadori*) White-spotted Mannikin S New Guinea / lowland savannah

Lonchura quinticolor (*Vieillot*) Five-coloured Mannikin Lombok, Sumbawa, Flores, Alor, Sumba, Timor, Sermatta and Babar

Lonchura malacca (*L*) Black-headed or Chestnut Munia India and Ceylon through SE Asia, Sumatra, Taiwan, Philippines, Celebes, Java / grassland and cultivation / grain/ n bush or tall grass / e 4–7 / I ♂♀

Lonchura maja (*L*) White-headed Munia Malay Peninsula, Sumatra, Simalur, Nias, Java and Bali / grassland / seeds / n bush / e 4–5

Lonchura pallida (*Wallace*) Pallid Munia Celebes and Lesser Sunda Is

Lonchura grandis (*Sharpe*) Great-billed Mannikin New Guinea / marsh grassland / n low tree or bush standing in water / e 5–6

Lonchura vana (*Hartert*) Arfak Mannikin Arfak Mts, New Guinea / no data

Lonchura caniceps (*Salvadori*) Grey-headed Mannikin Lowlands of SE New Guinea/ grassland

Lonchura nevermanni *Stresemann* White-crowned Mannikin S New Guinea / savannah/ n and e n/k

Lonchura spectabilis (*Sclater*) Sclater's Mannikin New Britain and scattered localities in New Guinea / mid-mountain grassland

Lonchura forbesi (*Sclater*) Forbes' Mannikin New Ireland

Lonchura hunsteini (*Finsch*) Finsch's Mannikin N New Ireland, New Hanover and Ponapé

Lonchura flaviprymna (*Gould*) Yellow-tailed Finch Arid northern Australia / grass and reedy margins of swamps / seeds and insects/ n in grass or reeds / e 5–6

Lonchura castaneothorax (*Gould*) Chestnut-breasted Finch New Guinea, Vulcan Is, northern and eastern Australia, introduced New Caledonia, Society Is and perhaps elsewhere / grass and reedy margins of swamps / seeds and insects / n in grass or reeds / e 5–6

Lonchura stygia *Stresemann* Black Munia S New Guinea / reedbeds / n in floating grass mats on lagoons / e 4–5

Lonchura teerinki *Rand* Grand Valley Mannikin Grand Valley district in Oranje Mts, New Guinea / mid-mountain grasslands

Lonchura monticola (*De Vis*) Alpine Mannikin High Mts of New Guinea (SE)/ alpine grassland / seeds

Lonchura montana *Junge* Snow Mountain Mannikin Oranje Mts, New Guinea / alpine grassland / seeds

Lonchura melaena (*Sclater*) Brown's Mannikin New Britain

Lonchura pectoralis (*Gould*) Pictorella Finch Northern Australia / dry savannah / seeds and insects / n bush or grass tuft / e 4–6

Padda fuscata (*Vieillot*) Timor Finch Timor and Samau

Padda oryzivora (*L*) Java Sparrow Probably endemic to Java and Bali, introduced to Ceylon, S Burma, various islands of Indonesia, Zanzibar, St Helena and other places / seeds / n tree,

PLOCEIDAE:
Passer luteus,
Golden Sparrow

Plate 304

VIDUINAE:
Vidua paradisaea,
Paradise Whydah

Plate 305

wall or roof/e 1–8

Amadina erythrocephala (*L*) RED-HEADED FINCH S Africa N to Angola and Rhodesia/dry open country and thorn veldt/seeds and insects/n hole in tree or building, or deserted nest of weaver or sparrow/e 4–5

Amadina fasciata (*Gmelin*) CUT-THROAT FINCH Semi-arid country from Senegal to Sudan and S through E Africa to Orange Free State / savannah and bush / seeds and insects/n tree or hole, or deserted nest of weaver or sparrow/e 4–9

VIDUINAE Viduine Weavers, Whydahs and Indigo Birds This is a group of strongly sexually dimorphic, parasitic seedeaters, usually treated as a sub-family of the Ploceidae.

NB: The relationships of the Indigo Birds appear to be very complicated. Three species are now generally recognised, but they may be split up into a good many more. Several of these forms are apparently parasitic, others not. *chalybeata* and *funerea* interbreed extensively in some areas, but in most of the regions where they occur sympatrically they behave like good species. They inhabit open country and feed on seeds.

Vidua chalybeata (*Müller*) GREEN INDIGO BIRD, PURPLE INDIGO BIRD Widely distributed through much of Africa S of Sahara except extreme S

Vidua funerea (*Tarragon*) DUSKY INDIGO BIRD, BLACK INDIGO BIRD Widely distributed through Africa S of Sahara, except the E

[**Fringilla melanictera** *Gmelin*, may belong here in this complex, but is generally conceded to be unidentifiable]

Vidua wilsoni (*Hartert*) WILSON'S INDIGO BIRD Savannahs from Senegal to S Sudan

Vidua hypocherina *Verreaux and Verreaux* STEEL-BLUE WHYDAH Locally in dry country from Ethiopia and Somaliland to Tanganyika/dry thorn and open country/seeds/n and e n/k

Vidua fischeri (*Reichenow*) FISCHER'S WHYDAH Dry country from Ethiopia and Somaliland to Tanganyika/thorn scrub/insects and seeds/P

Vidua regia (*L*) QUEEN WHYDAH S Angola and Rhodesia S to northern Cape Province (?) Mozambique/dry thorn country/seeds/P

Vidua macroura (*Pallas*) PIN-TAILED WHYDAH Africa S of Sahara (except dense forest and deserts), Fernando Po, São Thomé, Zanzibar and Mafia/open country/seeds/P

Vidua paradisaea (*L*) PARADISE WHYDAH E and S Africa from Sudan to Angola and Natal/open country/seeds/P

Vidua orientalis *Heuglin* BROAD-TAILED WHYDAH Africa S of Sahara S to Angola and Rhodesia/open country/seeds/n and e n/k

Vidua lorenzi (*Nicolai*) (*Journal für Orn*, vol 113, pt 3 (1972), pp 236–7) LORENZ'S WHYDAH W Nigeria/P on *Lagonosticta rufopicta*

Vidua incognita (*Nicolai*) (*Journal für Orn*, vol 113, pt 3 (1972), pp 236–7) DISGUISED WHYDAH Angola/P on *Lagonosticta nitidula*

A number of hybrids of *Vidua* have been described as separate species. No attempt can be made here to list or assess these, readers should consult:

Delacour, *Ostrich*, vol 4 (1934), pp 99–102

Winterbottom, *Ostrich*, vol 36 (1965), pp 140–2

Winterbottom, *Ostrich*, vol 38 (1967), pp 54–5

Traylor in Peters', *Check List of Birds of the World*, vol XIV, p 397

PLOCEIDAE Weavers and Sparrows A family of Old World seedeaters which are distinguished by a special conformation of the horny palate. Many of the family are renowned for their large, woven nests. Not all of them, however, 'weave'.

Bubalornis albirostris (*Vieillot*) BLACK BUFFALO WEAVER Africa S of Sahara, except extreme S / scrub and cultivation / grain and insects/n tree/e 2–4

Dinemellia dinemelli (*Rüppell*) WHITE-HEADED BUFFALO WEAVER E Africa from SE Sudan to Lake Tanganyika/thorn bush/seeds, fruit and insects/n thorn tree/e 3–4

Plocepasser mahali *Smith* WHITE-BROWED SPARROW-WEAVER E and S Africa from Sudan and Angola / dry bush, semi-desert and cultivation/grain and insects/n tree/e 2–3

Plocepasser superciliosus (*Cretzschmar*) CHESTNUT-CROWNED SPARROW-WEAVER Senegal to Sudan and S to Uganda and Lake Albert/woodland and high bush/n tree/e 2

Plocepasser donaldsoni *Sharpe* DONALDSON-SMITH'S SPARROW-WEAVER Restricted area of N Kenya and Ethiopian border / rocky desert/grass seeds/n tree/e described but no data on clutch size

Plocepasser rufoscapulatus *Büttikofer* CHESTNUT-BACKED SPARROW-WEAVER S Angola,

SE Congo, NW Bechuanaland, Zambia and parts of N Malawi/savannah/n tree/e 3–4

Histurgops ruficauda *Reichenow* RUFOUS-TAILED WEAVER N Tanganyika / wooded hills/ insects and seeds/n tree/e 3

Pseudonigrita arnaudi (*Bonaparte*) GREY-HEADED SOCIAL WEAVER E Africa from S Sudan to Lake Victoria / bush / seeds / n in ant-gall acacias/e 3–5

Pseudonigrita cabanisi (*Fischer and Reichenow*) BLACK-CAPPED SOCIAL WEAVER C and S Ethiopia, E Kenya and NE Tanganyika/ thorn scrub/seeds/n tree/e 2–4

Philetairus socius (*Latham*) SOCIABLE WEAVER S Africa N to SW Africa and Transvaal / dry scrub/n tree/e 3–4

Passer ammodendri *Gould* SAXAUL SPARROW C Asia from Transcaspia to Sinkiang and Mongolia/scrub and semi-desert/seeds/n hole/ e 4–6

Passer domesticus (*L*) HOUSE SPARROW Much of Temperate Eurasia and Africa N of Sahara, introduced in a number of other parts of the world / habitation / almost omnivorous/ n hole in building, tree etc/e 3–8/I ♂♀ 12–14/ F 15/*Passer italiae* (Vieillot) may be a distinct species

Passer hispaniolensis (*Temminck*) SPANISH SPARROW Iberia, Africa N of Sahara, Canary Is, Asia to Tian Shan and Afghanistan/cultivation and habitation / grain and insects / n tree or building/e 4–8/I (?♂♀) 13

Passer pyrrhonotus *Blyth* JUNGLE SPARROW Pakistan and SE Iran/scrub jungle/seeds/n bush/e 2–4/I ♂♀

Passer castanopterus *Blyth* SOMALI SPARROW Somali area, Kenya and Ethiopian border/ habitation/no other available data

Passer rutilans (*Temminck*) CINNAMON or RUSSET SPARROW NE Afghanistan, Himalayas and SE Tibet, China, Japan, Sakhalin, Taiwan, N Burma and Tonkin/forest and cultivation/ n hole under eaves/e 5–7/I ♂♀

Passer flaveolus *Blyth* PLAIN-BACKED SPARROW Burma, Thailand, S Laos, Cambodia and Cochin China/forest and cultivation/n hole or in wall or thatch/e 2–4

Passer moabiticus *Tristram* DEAD SEA SPARROW Local in Jordan Valley, Dead Sea, Lower Tigris and parts of Iran / insects and seeds/n tree/e 4–7

Passer iagoensis (*Gould*) GREAT SPARROW E Africa from Sudan to Tanganyika, Socotra and Abd-el-Kuri: SW Africa, Benguella and Transvaal: Cape Verde Is (discontinuous)/dry savannah and cultivation / seeds and insects/ n tree or thornbush / e 3–6. The following are usually treated as races of *P. iagoensis* but sometimes as distinct:

> **P. motitensis** *Smith* RUFOUS SPARROW Sudan to the Somalilands
>
> **P. rufocinctus** *Finsch and Reichenow* KENYA RUFOUS SPARROW S Kenya and N Tanganyika
>
> **P. insularis** *Sclater and Hartlaub* SOCOTRA SPARROW Socotra and Abd-el-Kuri

Passer melanurus (*Müller*) CAPE SPARROW or MOSSIE S Africa N to Transvaal and S Angola/ dry country and habitation / seeds and insects/ n tree, bush or building/e 3–6/I 12–14/F 16–24

Passer griseus (*Vieillot*) GREY-HEADED SPARROW Africa S of Sahara / bush and habitation/omnivorous/n tree, thatch or old nest of other species/e 2–4

Passer simplex (*Lichtenstein*) DESERT SPARROW Belt of S Sahara, deserts of E Iran and E Transcaspia / habitation and scrub / seeds and insects/n bush/e 2–5

Passer montanus (*L*) TREE SPARROW Eurasia, except extreme N and NE, S to Java and Bali, introduced elsewhere/forest, cultivation etc, but outside range of *P. domesticus* also occurs round habitation/seeds and insects/n hole in tree, building, rock etc, or old nest of other species/e 4–9/I ♂♀ 12–14/F 12–14

Passer luteus (*Lichtenstein*) GOLDEN SPARROW N Nigeria to Darfur, E Sudan, Ethiopian coast, British Somaliland and SW Arabia/steppe and cultivation / seeds and insects / n tree / e 3–4 (*P. euchlorus* (Bonaparte) is sometimes separated)

Passer eminibey (*Hartlaub*) CHESTNUT SPARROW Sudan to C Tanganyika / papyrus swamps/insects and seeds/n tree/e 3–4

Petronia brachydactyla *Bonaparte* PALE ROCK SPARROW Armenia and Palestine to Iran w S to Tanganyika/rocky mountains/buds and leaves/n rock crevice/e 4–5

Petronia xanthocollis (*Burton*) (=**P. xanthosterna** (*Bonaparte*)) YELLOW-THROATED ROCK SPARROW E Africa from Sudan to Tanganyika, S Iraq to India/rocky mountains, thorn scrub and cultivation/seeds and insects/ n hole /e 3–4

Petronia petronia (*L*) ROCK SPARROW

PLOCEIDAE: *Passer luteus,* Golden Sparrow, male at right

PLOCEIDAE: *Euplectes orix,* Red Bishop or Grenadier Weaver

Plate 306

PLOCEIDAE:
Quelea quelea,
Common Quelea or Red-billed
Weaver, Red-billed Quelea

Plate 307

S Europe, N Africa, Madeira and Canaries across Near East and C Asia to Kansu and Trans-baikalia / rocky mountains and semi-desert/ insects, berries and seeds / n rock-crevice or hole in wall / e 4–7 / F 21

Petronia superciliaris (*Blyth*) YELLOW-THROATED PETRONIA S Africa N to Angola and Tanganyika / light bush and cultivation / seeds and insects / n hole / e 3–4

Petronia dentata (*Sundevall*) BUSH PETRONIA Senegal to Sudan and SW Arabia / forest and bush / seeds and insects / n stated to be in tree hole but 1 nest with 2 eggs found in a hoopoe burrow

Montifringilla nivalis (*L*) SNOW FINCH Mts from S Europe across C Asia to Mongolia and W China / high mountain steppe / insects and seeds / n rodent burrow or rock crevice / e 3–4

Montifringilla adamsi *Adams* ADAMS' FINCH N Slopes of Himalayas and Tibet to Astin Tagh and Koko Nor / rocky steppe/ n rodent burrow or rock or wall crevice / e 3–4

Montifringilla taczanowskii *Przewalski* TACZANOWSKI'S FINCH Tibet to Sikang and Koko Nor / mountain steppe / n rodent burrow/ e 4

Montifringilla davidiana (*Verreaux*) PÉRE DAVID'S FINCH Altai to Mongolia, Koko Nor and Transbaikalia / rocky mountain valleys/ seeds / n rodent burrow / e 5–6

Montifringilla ruficollis *Blanford* RUFOUS-NECKED SNOW FINCH Tibet and Tsinghai to Astin Tagh / open mountain steppes / seeds and insects / no data on n and e but these have apparently been found

Montifringilla blanfordi *Hume* BLANFORD'S FINCH Himalayas N to Astin Tagh and Zaidam/ open steppes / seeds and insects / n rodent burrows / e n/k

Montifringilla theresae *Meinertzhagen* MEINERTZHAGEN'S SNOW FINCH Afghanistan w SE Transcaspia / rocky mountain valleys / no other data

Sporopipes squamifrons (*Smith*) SCALY WEAVER S Africa (except extreme S) N to SW Africa and Rhodesia / thorn scrub / seeds / n bush/ e 3–6

Sporopipes frontalis (*Daudin*) SPECKLED WEAVER Senegal to Sudan and S to Tanganyika/ thorn scrub / seeds / n tree / e 1–4

Amblyospiza albifrons (*Vigors*) GROSBEAK WEAVER or THICK-BILLED WEAVER Africa S of

Sahara / marshes and bush country / seeds and insects / n reed beds / e 3–5

Ploceus baglafecht (*Daudin*) BAGLAFECHT WEAVER E Africa from Sudan to Zambia / bush, open forest or grassland / omnivorous / n tree/ e 2–3

Ploceus bannermanni *Chapin* BANNERMAN'S WEAVER Mts of British Cameroons / mountain forest / n and e n/k

Ploceus batesi (*Sharpe*) BATES'S WEAVER S Cameroons / forest / insects / n and e n/k

Ploceus bertrandi (*Shelley*) BERTRAND'S WEAVER Tanganyika, Malawi and Mozambique/ hillsides and streams / n tree / e 2

Ploceus nigrimentum *Reichenow* BLACK-CHINNED WEAVER Angola / no data

Ploceus pelzelni (*Hartlaub*) SLENDER-BILLED WEAVER Ghana to N Angola, Zambia and Kenya / swamps and damp woodlands / insects/ n papyrus / e 2–3

Ploceus subpersonatus (*Cabanis*) LOANGO WEAVER S Gabon to N of Congo / no data

Ploceus luteolus (*Lichtenstein*) LITTLE WEAVER Senegal to NE Congo, Ethiopia and Tanganyika / thorn scrub and cultivation / n thorn tree / e 2–3

Ploceus ocularis (*Hartlaub*) SPECTACLED WEAVER Much of Africa S of Sahara (except extreme S) / scrub and open woodland / insects, berries and flowers / n tree or palm / e 2–3/ I ♂♀ 13 / F 18–19

Ploceus nigricollis (*Vieillot*) BLACK-NECKED WEAVER Fernando Po and Senegal to S Sudan, N Angola and Tanganyika / forest / insects and vegetable matter / n tree / e 2–3

[**Ploceus anachlorus** *Reichenow* is a hybrid *P. nigricollis* × *P. brachypterus*]

Ploceus alienus (*Sharpe*) STRANGE WEAVER Mts on Congo-Uganda border / mountain forest and open country / insects and berries / n tree / e 2

Ploceus melanogaster *Shelley* BLACK-BILLED WEAVER Fernando Po: extreme E Nigeria and Cameroons: mts from Sudan to Kenya and E Congo / forest / n bush / e 2

Ploceus capensis (*Hahn*) CAPE WEAVER S Africa N to Angola and Transvaal / ubiquitous / flowers, insects and seeds / n tree / e 2–5 / I 13/ F 17

Ploceus subaureus *Smith* GOLDEN WEAVER E Africa from Kenya to E Cape Province/ insects and seeds / n tree, bush or reeds / e 2–4

Ploceus xanthops (*Hartlaub*) HOLUB'S

GOLDEN WEAVER Kenya and Congo to Transvaal and Bechuanaland / marshes / fruit and insects / n tree over water or reeds / e 2–3

Ploceus aurantius (*Vieillot*) ORANGE WEAVER Liberia to Congo, Uganda and Tanganyika / reed beds / n reeds / e 2

Ploceus atrogularis (*Heuglin*) (=**P. heuglini** *Reichenow*) HEUGLIN'S WEAVER Senegal W to Sudan, S to NE Congo and Kenya / dry country / n tree / e 2–3

Ploceus bojeri (*Cabanis*) GOLDEN PALM WEAVER Kenya and S Somalia / n tree or palm / e 2–3

Ploceus castaneiceps (*Sharpe*) TAVETA WEAVER SE Kenya and NE Tanganyika / seeds / n reeds / e 2–3

Ploceus princeps (*Bonaparte*) PRINCIPÉ WEAVER Principé Is / ubiquitous / n palm tree / e 2

Ploceus xanthopterus (*Finsch and Hartlaub*) BROWN-THROATED WEAVER SE Africa from Malawi and Zambia to Natal and Bechuanaland / n bush, tree or reeds / e ?2 ?3–4

Ploceus castanops *Shelley* NORTHERN BROWN-THROATED WEAVER Uganda, Ruanda and NW Tanganyika / scrub and reedbeds / n reeds or elephant grass / e 2–3

Ploceus galbula *Rüppell* RUPPELL'S WEAVER Sudan, Ethiopia, British Somaliland and SW Arabia / cultivation (? and scrub) / ? seeds / n tree / e 2–4

Ploceus taeniopterus *Reichenbach* NORTHERN MASKED WEAVER Sudan to Uganda and NE Congo / grassland and swamps / seeds and insects / n grass / e 2–3

Ploceus intermedius *Rüppell* LESSER MASKED WEAVER E Africa from Ethiopia S, and S Africa from Angola, but not extreme S / savannah, often near water / seeds and insects / n tree, bush or grass / e 2–3

Ploceus velatus *Vieillot* GREATER MASKED WEAVER Africa S of Sahara / bush / grain, fruit and insects / n tree / e 2–4 / I ♀

Ploceus spekei (*Heuglin*) SPEKE'S WEAVER S Ethiopia, Somaliland, Somalia, Kenya and NE Tanganyika / thorn bush / insects and seeds / n tree / e 1–4

Ploceus spekeoides *Grant and Mackworth-Praed* FOX'S WEAVER Uganda / near water / n tree standing in water / e n/k

Ploceus cucullatus (*Müller*) SPOTTED-BACKED or VILLAGE WEAVER Principé and Africa S of

Sahara, except extreme S, introduced Haiti and São Thomé / swamps, bush and habitation / grain and weed seeds / n tree / e 1–3 / I ♀

Ploceus grandis (*Gray*) GIANT WEAVER São Thomé / n tree / e 2

Ploceus nigerrimus *Vieillot* VIEILLOT'S WEAVER Liberia to N Angola, W Tanganyika and S Sudan / forest clearings and habitation / seeds and insects / n tree / e 2–3

Ploceus weynsi (*Dubois*) WEYNS'S WEAVER Congo region, S Uganda and NW Tanganyika / forest / no other data

Ploceus golandi (*Clarke*) CLARKE'S WEAVER Coastal forests of Kenya / unique

Ploceus dicrocephalus (*Salvadori*) YELLOW-BACKED WEAVER S Ethiopia, S Somalia and NE Kenya / grass seeds / n tree, grass or papyrus / e 2. The name *Ploceus capitalis* (Latham) was formerly used as a specific name for some of the forms now included in the *melanocephalus-dicrocephalus* group

Ploceus melanocephalus (*L*) BLACK-HEADED WEAVER Senegal to Sudan, Congo, Zambia and Tanganyika / riverbanks and papyrus swamps / n grass / e 2

Ploceus jacksoni *Shelley* GOLDENBACKED or JACKSON'S WEAVER Uganda (and Sudan border), W Kenya and Tanganyika / river swamps and lakesides / seeds and insects / n tree or reeds / e 2–3

Ploceus badius (*Cassin*) CINNAMON WEAVER E and S Sudan / no reliable data

Ploceus rubiginosus *Rüppell* CHESTNUT WEAVER E Africa from Ethiopia and SE Sudan to N Tanganyika, SW Angola and northern half of SW Africa / acacia bush / seeds and insects / n tree / e 3–4

Ploceus aureonucha *Sassi* GOLDEN-NAPED WEAVER NE Congo / forest / insects and fruit / n and e n/k

Ploceus tricolor (*Hartlaub*) YELLOW-MANTLED WEAVER Sierra Leone to Uganda and N Angola / forest / insects / n tree / e n/s

Ploceus albinucha (*Bocage*) BLACK WEAVER Fernando Po and Sierra Leone to NE Congo and Uganda / grassland / n tree / e n/k

Ploceus nelicourvi (*Scopoli*) NELICOURVI WEAVER Madagascar forests of E and N / n tree / e 3

Ploceus sakalava *Hartlaub* SAKALAVA WEAVER Madagascar / dry forests and plains / seeds and insects / n tree / e 1–4

Ploceus hypoxanthus (*Sparrman*) (=**P.**

Opposite:
STURNIDAE:
Sturnus vulgaris,
Common Starling

Plate 308

Plate 309

chrysaeus *Hume*) ASIATIC GOLDEN WEAVER S Burma, Thailand, Cambodia, Cochin China, Sumatra and Java / grassland and cultivation / n thorn bush or site near hornet's nest / e 2–4

Ploceus superciliosus (*Shelley*) (=**P. pachyrhynchus** *Reichenow*) COMPACT WEAVER Sierra Leone to S Ethiopia, N Angola and W Tanganyika / parkland and grassland / insects and seeds / n grass / e 3–4 [NB: Shelley's name is not preoccupied by *Ploceus superciliosus* Cretzschmar (=*Plocepasser superciliosus*) and Reichenow's name need not be utilised]

Ploceus benghalensis (*L*) BLACK-BREASTED WEAVER Pakistan, across N India to Assam and Manipur / grassland / seeds and insects / n tall grass / e 3–5

Ploceus manyar (*Horsfield*) STREAKED WEAVER Indian sub-continent, Burma, Thailand, Annam, (? Yunnan), Java, Bali and Bawean / grassland / seeds and insects / n tall grass or reeds / e 2–4

Ploceus philippinus (*L*) BAYA WEAVER Indian sub-continent, parts of SE Asia, Sumatra and Nias / light forest, orchard and cultivation / seeds / n tree or bamboo / e 2–5 / I ♀ 14–15 / F 15–17

Ploceus megarhynchus *Hume* YELLOW WEAVER or FINN'S BAYA Base of Himalayas from Kumaon to Assam and Bhutan / marshes and cultivation / seeds and insects / n tree or reeds / e 2–3 / I ♀ 14–15 / F 15

Ploceus bicolor *Vieillot* FOREST WEAVER Fernando Po and much of Africa S of Sahara except the W and extreme S / forest / insects / n tree / e 2–4

Ploceus flavipes (*Chapin*) YELLOW-LEGGED WEAVER NE Congo / forest / insects / n and e n/k / an aberrant species whose taxonomic position is uncertain. It has been placed in *Malimbus* and in a monotypic genus, *Rhinoploceus*

Ploceus preussi (*Reichenow*) GOLDEN-BACKED WEAVER Sierra Leone to Cameroons and Upper Congo / lowland forest / n tree / e n/k

Ploceus dorsomaculatus (*Reichenow*) YELLOW-CAPPED WEAVER Cameroons / known only from a few specimens / no data

Ploceus olivaceiceps (*Reichenow*) OLIVE-HEADED WEAVER Tanganyika, Malawi and Mozambique S to Zambezi / open woodland / insects / n and e n/k

[**Ploceus nicolli** (*Sclater*) USAMBARA WEAVER Usambara Mts / no data / sometimes considered

distinct, but usually as a race of *olivaceiceps*]

Ploceus insignis (*Sharpe*) BROWN-CAPPED WEAVER Fernando Po and Cameroons to S Sudan, N Angola and Tanganyika / bush and forest glade / insects / n tree / e 2

Ploceus angolensis (*Bocage*) BAR-WINGED WEAVER Angola, northern SW Africa, SE Congo and Namibia border / rare / no data

Ploceus sanctaethomae (*Hartlaub*) SÃO THOMÉ WEAVER São Thomé / forest / n tree / e n/s

Malimbus coronatus *Sharpe* RED-CROWNED MALIMBE Cameroons and NE Congo / forest / n tree / e n/k

Malimbus cassini (*Elliot*) CASSIN'S MALIMBE S Cameroons, Gabon and Congo / forest / n tree / e ?2

Malimbus scutatus (*Cassin*) RED-VENTED MALIMBE Sierra Leone to Ghana: S Nigeria / coastal forest and cultivation / n palm tree / e 2

Malimbus racheliae (*Cassin*) RACHEL'S MALIMBE E Nigeria to W Cameroons and Gabon / forest / n tree / e n/k

Malimbus ibadanensis *Elgood* IBADAN MALIMBE Ibadan (E Nigeria) / open country and cultivation / n tree (1 known) / e n/k

Malimbus nitens (*Gray*) GRAY'S MALIMBE Sierra Leone to Gabon and Congo region / swamp and streambanks / n tree over water / e 2

Malimbus rubricollis (*Swainson*) RED-HEADED MALIMBE Fernando Po and Sierra Leone to N Angola, S Sudan and S Uganda / forest / insects and berries / n tree / e 2

Malimbus erythrogaster *Reichenow* RED-BELLIED MALIMBE E Nigeria to Cameroons and Congo / forest / n tree / e n/k

Malimbus malimbicus (*Daudin*) CRESTED MALIMBE Sierra Leone to W Uganda and N Angola / forest and dense bush / insects / n undergrowth / e 2

Malimbus rubriceps (*Sundevall*) RED-HEADED WEAVER Senegal to Somaliland and S to Bechuanaland and Transvaal / open woodland, bush and cultivation, dry savannah, often near water / insects and seeds / n tree or telegraph pole / e 2–3 (*Ploceus melanotis* Lafresnaye, is a synonym)

Quelea cardinalis (*Hartlaub*) CARDINAL QUELEA E Africa from S Sudan to Tanganyika and Zambia / grassland and marsh / n grass / e 2–3

Quelea erythrops (*Hartlaub*) RED-HEADED QUELEA Senegal to Ethiopia and S to Angola and Pondoland (but absent from Kenya and forests of Congo), also islands in Gulf of Guinea / open woodland and savannah / seeds and grain / n reedbeds / e 2–3 / I ♀

Quelea quelea (*L*) COMMON QUELEA or RED-BILLED WEAVER Africa S of Sahara / savannah and cultivation (occurring in pest proportions)/ seeds and grain / n tree / e 3–5 / I 12 / F 13

Foudia madagascariensis (*L*) MADAGASCAR FODY Madagascar, introduced St Helena and also to other islands of W Indian Ocean (except Rodriguez) / forest, scrub and habitation / seeds and insects / n in long grass / e 2–5 / I 12–14 / F 11–14

Foudia eminentissima *Bonaparte* RED-HEADED FODY Forests of E Madagascar, Comoros and Aldabra / insects and some seeds / n tree, mangrove or grass / e 2–3

Foudia rubra (*Gmelin*) MAURITIUS FODY Mauritius / now very rare and confined to the last remaining piece of natural vegetation in the interior / insects / n tree / e 3

Foudia bruante (*Müller*) RÉUNION FODY Réunion / extinct / known only from travellers' accounts. There are in fact, 2 quite different *Foudias* recorded by travellers' tales from Réunion: *F. bruante* and another, 'Du Bois' Fody' which has never been named in Latin. For discussion of these, see J. H. Crook, 'Fodies of the Seychelles', *Ibis* 103a (1961), p 544 and Moreau 'Weavers of the Indian Ocean Islands' *Journal für Ornithologie*, vol 101 (1960), pp 29–49 (in English).

Foudia sechellarum *Newton* SEYCHELLES FODY Seychelles, now surviving only on Frigate, Cousin and Cousine / insects, fruit and seeds, also eggs / n bush or tree / e 2–3 / I 14 / F 13–15

Foudia flavicans *Newton* RODRIGUEZ FODY Rodriguez / forest and scrub / n tree or bush / e 2

Euplectes anomalus (*Reichenow*) BOB-TAILED WEAVER SE Cameroons and W Congo / forest clearings / n tree / e 2

Euplectes afer (*Gmelin*) GOLDEN BISHOP or NAPOLEON WEAVER Africa S of Sahara except extreme S / grassland and swamp / grass seeds / n herbage often over water / e 2–4

Euplectes diadematus *Fischer and Reichenow* FIRE-FRONTED WEAVER Lower Juba River, E Kenya and NE Tanganyika / grassland / n and e n/k

Euplectes gierowii *Cabanis* BLACK BISHOP S Sudan to Tanganyika, Congo and N Angola / open bush and grassland / grass seeds / n shrub or herbage / e 3

Euplectes nigroventris *Cassin* ZANZIBAR BISHOP Zanzibar, Kwale and coastal E Africa from Kenya to Mozambique / grassland etc / seeds and grain / n bush or reeds / e 2–3

Euplectes hordeaceus (*L*) BLACK-WINGED or RED-CROWNED BISHOP Senegal to Sudan, Angola and Rhodesia; São Thomé, Zanzibar and Pemba / grassland / seeds and grain / n grass / e 2–4

Euplectes orix (*L*) RED BISHOP or GRENADIER WEAVER Africa S of Sahara / grassland, often near water / seeds and grain / n grass / e 2–4

Euplectes aureus (*Gmelin*) GOLDEN-BACKED BISHOP São Thomé and coastal Angola / no data

Euplectes capensis (*L*) YELLOW BISHOP Africa S of Sahara except W Africa / grassland / grass seeds and insects / n herbage / e 2–4

Euplectes axillaris (*Smith*) FAN-TAILED WHYDAH Much of Africa S of Sahara except W and extreme S / swamps / seeds and insects / n herbage often over water / e 2–4

Euplectes macrourus (*Gmelin*) YELLOW-MANTLED WHYDAH Senegal to S Sudan and S to Angola and Lake Tanganyika / grassland and reed beds / n grass / e 2–4

Euplectes hartlaubi (*Bocage*) MARSH WHYDAH Cameroons to Angola, Uganda and Zambia / sedge swamps / seeds, berries and insects / n grass / e 2

Euplectes albonotatus (*Cassin*) WHITE-WINGED WHYDAH E and S Africa from Sudan and Gabon S, but not extreme S / grassland / seeds / n grass / e 2–3

Euplectes ardens (*Boddaert*) RED-COLLARED WHYDAH Africa S of Sahara except extreme S / grassland / seeds and insects / n grass / e 2–4

Euplectes progne (*Boddaert*) LONG-TAILED WHYDAH E Kenya, Angola and S Congo, Zambia S to E Cape Province / swampy grassy plains / n grass / e 3–4

Euplectes jacksoni (*Sharpe*) JACKSON'S WHYDAH C Kenya highlands and N Tanganyika / highland grassland / seeds and insects / n grass / e 2–3

Anomalospiza imberbis (*Cabanis*) CUCKOO WEAVER Sierra Leone to Ethiopia and S to Transvaal, Zanzibar and Pemba / bush and cultivation / P

STURNIDAE: *Sturnus malabaricus,* Chestnut-faced Starling, Gray-headed Starling

Plate 310

STURNIDAE:
Gracula religiosa,
Hill Myna

Plate 311

STURNIDAE Starlings Medium-sized passerines with straight or slightly down-curved bills and strong feet. Most starlings are dark-coloured with metallic sheens, but some are brightly marked. They are strong fliers, and are gregarious, most inhabiting open country, though they are believed to have originated as a group of forest birds. Basic diet is insects or fruit, but species living near man may be almost omnivorous. Nesting habits vary; most species nest in holes or cavities and lay blue or white eggs.

Aplonis zelandica (*Quoy and Gaimard*) RUSTY-WINGED STARLING New Hebrides, Banks and Santa Cruz Is/lowland forest/? no data

Aplonis santovestris *Harrisson and Marshall* WATIAMASSAU STARLING Mts of Espiritu Santo (New Hebrides)/undergrowth of cloud forest/fruit and seeds/n hole/e 2

Aplonis pelzelni *Finsch* PONAPÉ STARLING Ponapé/mountain forest/n hole/e 2

Aplonis atrifusca (*Peale*) SAMOAN STARLING Samoa/forest and habitation/fruit/n and e no data

Aplonis corvina (*Kittlitz*) KITTLITZ' STARLING Mountain forests of Kusaie (Carolines)/extinct/2 specimens

Aplonis mavornata *Buller* RAIATEA STARLING Raiatea, Society Is/extinct, type only

Aplonis cinerascens *Hartlaub and Finsch* RAROTONGA STARLING Rarotonga, Cook Is

Aplonis tabuensis (*Gmelin*) POLYNESIAN STARLING Islands of C Polynesia from Santa Cruz to Fiji, Tonga and Samoa/forest and habitation/n hole/e 2

Aplonis striata (*Gmelin*) STRIATED STARLING New Caledonia and Loyalty Is/forest fruit, insects and snails/n hole/e 2–4

Aplonis fusca *Gould* NORFOLK ISLAND STARLING Norfolk and Lord Howe Is/e 2–3

Aplonis opaca (*Kittlitz*) MICRONESIAN STARLING Caroline Is/lowland forest and cultivation/fruit/n hole in tree or cliff/e ? 2 ? 3–4

Aplonis cantoroides (*Gray*) SINGING STARLING New Guinea and outlying islands, Bismarck Archipelago, Solomons/forest edge/n hole/e 1

Aplonis crassa (*Sclater*) TIMOR-LAUT STARLING Timor-laut Is (possibly conspecific with *A. cantoroides*)

Aplonis feadensis (*Ramsay*) ATOLL STARLING Small islands of Bismarck Archipelago and Solomons: Ninigo, Matty, Hermit, Fead, Nissan, Rennell (*A. insularis* Mayr, from Rennell Is is sometimes treated as a species)/no data

Aplonis grandis (*Salvadori*) BROWN-WINGED STARLING Solomon Is (the San Christobal form, *dichroa* is sometimes treated as a species)/forest/n hole

Aplonis mysolensis (*Gray*) MOLUCCAN STARLING West Papuan islands, Moluccas, Sula Is, Peling, Banggai and E peninsula of Celebes/bushes/no other data

Aplonis magna (*Schlegel*) LONG-TAILED STARLING Biak and Numfor (islands in Geelvink Bay, New Guinea)/no data

Aplonis minor (*Bonaparte*) LESSER GLOSSY STARLING Mt Apo (Mindanao), Celebes, Lesser Sundas, South West Is, islands in Flores Sea, Java and Bali (possibly only migrant)

Aplonis panayensis (*Scopoli*) GREATER GLOSSY STARLING E India, SE Asia through Indonesia to Philippines/forest and cultivation/insects and fruit/n hole/e 2–4

Aplonis metallica (*Temminck*) METALLIC STARLING E Queensland, New Guinea, Bismarck Archipelago, Solomon Is, Moluccas and adjacent small islands/lowland forest/insects/n tree/e 2–4

Aplonis mystacea (*Ogilvie-Grant*) GRANT'S STARLING New Guinea at head of Geelvink Bay and part of S from Mimika River to Upper Fly River/forest/no other data

Aplonis brunneicapilla (*Danis*) WHITE-EYED STARLING Bougainville, Guadalcanal and Rendova (Solomons)/lowland forest/no other data

Poeoptera kenricki *Shelley* KENRICK'S STARLING Mts of Kenya and Tanganyika/forest/fruit/n hole/e n/k

Poeoptera stuhlmanni (*Reichenow*) STUHLMANN'S STARLING S Sudan to Uganda and E Congo/forest/fruit/n hole/e n/k

Poeoptera lugubris *Bonaparte* NARROW-TAILED STARLING Sierra Leone to W Uganda and S to N Angola/forest/fruit/n hole/e 3

Grafisia torquata (*Reichenow*) WHITE-COLLARED STARLING Cameroons to N Congo/savannah/fruit/n and e n/k but believed to be in hole

Onychognathus walleri (*Shelley*) WALLER'S STARLING Fernando Po and Cameroons to S

Sudan, E Congo and Malawi / forest / fruit / n hole / e n/k

Onychognathus nabouroup (*Daudin*) PALE-WINGED STARLING Angola, SW Africa, Bechuanaland and northern Cape Province / rocky hills / fruit and insects / n rock crevice / e 3–4

Onychognathus morio (*L*) RED-WINGED STARLING Senegal to Sudan and S through E Africa to Cape Province / hill country and habitation / fruit and insects / n rock crevice or hole in building / e 3–5 / I ♀ 12–23 / F 22–8

Onychognathus blythii (*Hartlaub*) SOMALI STARLING Coasts from Eritrea to British Somaliland, Socotra and Abd-el-Kuri / rocky places / fruit / n and e n/k

Onychognathus frater (*Sclater and Hartlaub*) SOCOTRA STARLING Socotra / no data

Onychognathus tristramii (*Sclater*) TRISTRAM'S STARLING W and SW Arabia from Dead Sea Valley to Yemen and W Hadramaut / ravines / fruit / n rock-crevice / e 3–5

Onychognathus fulgidus *Hartlaub* CHESTNUT-WINGED STARLING Fernando Po, São Thomé, and Sierra Leone to Uganda and N Angola / forest / fruit, seeds and insects / n hole / e n/k

Onychognathus tenuirostris (*Rüppell*) SLENDER-BILLED STARLING E Africa from Ethiopia to Malawi and Tanganyika / mountain and valley forests / insects, molluscs and fruit / n ledge of rock or cave / e 3–4

Onychognathus albirostris (*Rüppell*) WHITE-BILLED STARLING Ethiopia / cliffs and old buildings / n crevice in rock or wall / e 3–4 / I+F=35

Onychognathus salvadorii (*Sharpe*) BRISTLE-CROWNED STARLING W Somaliland, Ethiopia and N Kenya / rocky gorges / n hole in tree or cliff / e 2–3

Lamprotornis iris (*Oustalet*) EMERALD STARLING French Guinea, Sierra Leone and Ivory Coast / open savannah / insects and fruit / n and e n/k

Lamprotornis cupreocauda (*Hartlaub*) COPPER-TAILED STARLING Sierra Leone, Liberia and Ghana / forest / fruit / n and e n/k

Lamprotornis purpureiceps (*Verreaux*) PURPLE-HEADED STARLING S Nigeria to Uganda and mouth of Congo / forest / fruit / n hole / e n/k

Lamprotornis corruscus *Nordmann* BLACK-BELLIED GLOSSY STARLING Pemba, Zanzibar and coasts of E and SE Africa / forest and bush / insects and fruit / n hole / e 3–4

Lamprotornis purpureus (*Müller*) PURPLE GLOSSY STARLING Senegal to Sudan, N Congo and W Kenya / open woodland / fruit and insects / n hole / e 2

Lamprotornis nitens (*L*) RED-SHOULDERED GLOSSY STARLING S Africa N to Angola and Rhodesia / acacia thornveld / insects and fruit / n hole in tree or roof / e 3–4 / F 19–20

Lamprotornis chalcurus *Nordmann* BRONZE-TAILED GLOSSY STARLING Senegal to Sudan, N Congo and Kenya / open woodland / insects and fruit / n hole / e up to 4

Lamprotornis chalybaeus *Ehrenberg* BLUE-EARED GLOSSY STARLING Senegal to Sudan and Eritrea and S to SW Africa and Transvaal / open woodland and acacia thornveld / insects and fruit / n hole / e 3–5

Lamprotornis chloropterus *Swainson* LESSER BLUE-EARED GLOSSY STARLING Senegal to Sudan, Congo and Mozambique / open woodland / insects and fruit / n hole / e 3–5

Lamprotornis acuticaudus (*Bocage*) SHARP-TAILED GLOSSY STARLING Angola, SW Africa, Congo and Zambia / open woodland / fruit / n and e n/k

Lamprotornis splendidus (*Vieillot*) SPLENDID STARLING Principé, Fernando Po, and Senegal to Sudan, Angola and Tanganyika / woodland and secondary forest / fruit / n hole / e 2–3

Lamprotornis ornatus (*Daudin*) ORNATE STARLING Principé / forest / fruit, insects and snails / n hole / e n/k

Lamprotornis australis (*Smith*) GREATER GLOSSY STARLING or BURCHELL'S STARLING S Angola to SW Africa and E to Transvaal / dry country / insects and fruit / n hole / e 3–4

Lamprotornis mevesii (*Wahlberg*) MEVE'S STARLING Angola to SW Africa, and E to Malawi and Rhodesia / mopane veld / insects and fruit / n hole / e n/k

Lamprotornis purpuropterus *Rüppell* RÜPPELL'S STARLING E Africa from Sudan to Tanganyika and Uganda / forest and open country / omnivorous / n hole / e 2–3

Lamprotornis caudatus (*Müller*) LONG-TAILED GLOSSY STARLING Senegal to Sudan / open bush and light woodland / fruit and insects / n hole / e 2–4

Cinnyricinclus femoralis (*Richmond*) ABBOTT'S STARLING S Kenya and N Tanganyika / forest / n and e n/k

Cinnyricinclus sharpii (*Jackson*) SHARPE'S

Plate 312

DICRURIDAE:
Dicrurus hottentottus,
Spangled Drongo,
Hair-crested Drongo

ORIOLIDAE:
Oriolus sagittatus,
Olive-backed or White-bellied
Oriole

Plate 313

STARLING E Africa from S Sudan to W Congo and Tanganyika / forest / fruit / n and e n/k

Cinnyricinclus leucogaster (*Boddaert*) AMETHYST STARLING Savannah belts of Africa S of Sahara / forest / insects and fruit / n hole / e 2–4

Speculipastor bicolor *Reichenow* MAGPIE STARLING S Ethiopia and Somaliland S to NE Uganda and Kenya / apparently nomadic in varied habitats / fruit and insects / n hole in anthill / e 3–4

Neocichla gutteralis (*Bocage*) BABBLING STARLING Angola and Zambia to Congo and Tanganyika / ? forest / virtually no data

Spreo fischeri (*Reichenow*) FISCHER'S STARLING S Somaliland, Kenya and N Tanganyika / acacia scrub / insects / n thorn tree / e 1–6

Spreo bicolor (*Gmelin*) PIED STARLING Bechuanaland and Transvaal S to Cape / open veld and cultivation / insects / n hole in wall or bank / e 4–6

Spreo albicapillus *Blyth* WHITE-CROWNED STARLING British Somaliland and S Ethiopia / scrub / n thorn tree / e 1–5

Spreo superbus (*Rüppell*) SUPERB STARLING E Africa from SE Sudan to Tanganyika / scrub / insects and berries / n thorn tree / e 4

Spreo pulcher (*Müller*) CHESTNUT-BELLIED STARLING Senegal to Sudan and Ethiopia / scrub, cultivation and habitation / insects and berries / n thornbush / e 3–5

Spreo hildebranti (*Cabanis*) HILDEBRANDT'S STARLING S Kenya and N Tanganyika / thorn bush / insects and seeds (? fruit) / n hole / e 3–4

Spreo shelleyi *Sharpe* SHELLEY'S STARLING SE Sudan, S Ethiopia and British Somaliland S to E Kenya / scrub / *S. hildebrandti* and *S. shelleyi* have been variously considered to be species or races of the same species, see Amadon in Peters' *Check List*, vol xv, p 101 footnote for opinions and references. Nest and eggs of *shelleyi* first described by G. Archer *Birds of British Somaliland*, vol 4, p 1,423 – n hole, e 4–6; but there are 2 clutches apparently of 3 collected by Archer in the British Museum (Natural History) collection. These eggs are immaculate light blue, while the eggs of *hildebrandti* are white.

Cosmopsarus regius *Reichenow* REGAL STARLING S Ethiopia, S Somaliland and Kenya / dry bush / fruit and insects / n hole / e 2–4

Cosmopsarus unicolor *Shelley* ASHY

STARLING S Kenya and Tanganyika / dry-bush / insects / n and e n/k

Saroglossa aurata (*Müller*) MADAGASCAR STARLING Madagascar / forest / fruit / n and e n/k

Saroglossa spiloptera (*Vigors*) SPOT-WINGED STARLING b foothills of Himalayas w India, Burma and Thailand / forest and habitation / insects and fruit / n hole / e 3–4

Creatophora cinerea (*Meuschen*) WATTLED STARLING SW Arabia; E Africa from S Sudan to Angola and Cape / locusts / n thornbush or tree / e 2–5

Necropsar leguati *Forbes* LEGUAT'S STARLING Known from 1 specimen of doubtful origin, but believed to have come from islet of Met, off Rodriguez. May be allied to or identical with *Necropsar rodricanus* Slater, from Rodriguez (bones only) [For discussion see Hachisuka, *The Dodo and Kindred Birds* (1953)]

Fregilupus varius (*Boddaert*) DAUBENTON'S STARLING Réunion / extinct mid-nineteenth century

Sturnus senex (*Bonaparte*) WHITE-FACED STARLING Ceylon / forest / insects, fruit and nectar / n hole / e 2 (1 nest known)

Sturnus malabaricus (*Gmelin*) CHESTNUT-FACED STARLING India, SE Asia (except Malay Peninsula) and W Yunnan / thinly wooded country, secondary forest and plantations / fruit, nectar and insects / n hole / e 3–5 / I ♂♀

Sturnus erythropygius (*Blyth*) WHITE-HEADED STARLING Andaman and Nicobar Is / grassland and paddyfield / fruit, nectar and insects / n hole / e 4

Sturnus pagodarum (*Gmelin*) BRAHMINY STARLING E Afghanistan, Nepal, India and Ceylon / forest and scrub-jungle / fruit and insects / n hole / e 3–4 / I ♂♀

Sturnus sericeus *Gmelin* SILKY STARLING C and S China S in winter to N Indo-China / hills and cultivation / n hole in tree or roof / e n/s

Sturnus philippensis (*Forster*) VIOLET-BACKED STARLING S Sakhalin and N Japan w S Ryukyus, Philippines and Borneo / woodland and cultivation / insects and fruit / n hole / e 3–7 / I ♀ 13–14

Sturnus sturninus (*Pallas*) DAURIAN STARLING E Asia from Transbaikalia and Ussuriland S through Mongolia and Japan to S China w S to SE Asia and Java / forest and cultivation / insects and earthworms / n hole in tree or building / e 5–6 (?7) / I ♂♀

Sturnus roseus (*L*) ROSE-COLOURED STARLING E Europe to Russian Turkestan and S to Syria w Indian region / of widespread erratic occurrence outside normal range / cultivation, grassland and arid thorn-jungle / fruit, nectar and insects / n hole / e 3–8 / I ♀ 11–14 / F 14–19

Sturnus vulgaris *L* COMMON STARLING Much of Eurasia, introduced S Africa, Australia, New Zealand, N America and Oceania / almost ubiquitous, but particularly near habitation / omnivorous / n hole in tree or building / e 4–9 / I ♂♀ 12–13 / F 20–2

Sturnus unicolor *Temminck* SPOTLESS STARLING Iberia, Corsica, Sardinia, Sicily and Morocco to Tunisia / cliffs, woodland and habitation / n hole in tree, rock or building / e 4 / I ♀ 12–14 / F 21–3

Sturnus cineraceus *Temminck* WHITE-CHEEKED or ASHY STARLING E Asia from Transbaikalia and Ussuriland S to N China and Japan w S China, Taiwan and Hainan / cultivation / insects and fruit / n hole / e 4–9 / I ♂♀ 14–15 / F 13–15

Sturnus contra *L* ASIAN PIED STARLING India, Burma, Thailand, Laos : Sumatra, Java and Bali / cultivation and habitation / insects, fruit and grain / n tree / e 4–6

Sturnus nigricollis (*Paykull*) BLACK-COLLARED STARLING S China and SE Asia (except Malay Peninsula) / cultivation / insects, slugs, fruit etc / n hole in wall / e 4–6

Sturnus burmannicus (*Jerdon*) JERDON'S STARLING Burma, Thailand and S Indo-China / grassland, scrub and cultivation / seeds and insects / n hole in tree or building / e 2–6

Sturnus melanopterus (*Daudin*) BLACK-WINGED STARLING Java, Bali and Lombok / habitation etc / a clutch of 2 eggs in BM(NH)

Sturnus sinensis (*Gmelin*) CHINESE STARLING S China, Taiwan and N Indo-China w S through Indo-China / habitation / n hole in wall or tree / e 4

Leucopsar rothschildi *Stresemann* ROTHSCHILD'S GRACKLE Bali

Acridotheres tristis (*L*) COMMON MYNA From Afghanistan and Russian Turkestan to India and Ceylon, thence by recent extension of range or introductions to SE Asia, widely introduced in Australia, New Zealand, S Africa and islands in all oceans / forest, cultivation and habitation / omnivorous / n hole in tree, wall etc or rarely in tree / e 4–6 / I ♂♀ 17–18 / F 22–4

Acridotheres ginginianus (*Latham*) BANK MYNA Plains of N India / habitation / omnivorous / n hole in bank / e 3–5 / I ♂♀

Acridotheres fuscus (*Wagler*) JUNGLE MYNA India, Burma, Malay Peninsula, Java and S peninsula of Celebes / forest and cultivation / fruit, grain and insects / n hole / e 3–6 / I ♂♀

Acridotheres grandis *Moore* ORANGE-BILLED MYNA E India, S China, N and C Burma, Thailand and Indo-China / open country and cultivation / fruit, grain and insects / n hole in tree or bank / e 4–5

Acridotheres albocinctus *Godwin-Austen and Walden* COLLARED MYNA E India, N and C Burma and NW Yunnan / cultivation and damp jungle

Acridotheres cristatellus (*L*) CRESTED MYNA C and S China, Indo-China and Taiwan, introduced Luzon (Philippines) and Vancouver (Canada) / cultivation and habitation / insects, fruit etc / n hole in tree or wall / e 4–5

Ampeliceps coronatus *Blyth* GOLDEN-CRESTED MYNA E India and SE Asia (except Malay Peninsula) / open forest / fruit and insects / n tree / e 3

Mino anias (*Lesson*) GOLDEN-BREASTED MYNA Salawati, Japen and coasts of N, W and S New Guinea / forest / no other data

Mino dumontii *Lesson* PAPUAN or YELLOW-FACED MYNA New Guinea and some outlying islands, Bismarck Archipelago and Solomons / forest / fruit / n ? hole

Basilornis celebensis *Gray* KING STARLING or CELEBES MYNA Celebes

Basilornis galeatus *Meyer* CRESTED STARLING Banggai and Sula

Basilornis corythaix (*Wagler*) CERAM STARLING Ceram

Basilornis miranda (*Hartert*) MT APO STARLING Mindanao

Streptocitta albicollis (*Vieillot*) BUTON STARLING Celebes, Buton and Muna

Streptocitta albertinae (*Schlegel*) SULA STARLING Sula Is

Sarcops calvus (*L*) COLETO Philippines and Sulu Is

Gracula ptilogenys *Blyth* CEYLON MYNA Ceylon / forest and cultivation / fruit / n hole / e 2

Gracula religiosa *L* HILL MYNA Indian region, SE Asia and Indonesia, introduced elsewhere / forest / fruit, nectar and insects / n hole / e 2–3 / I ♂♀

ARTAMIDAE:
Artamus personatus,
Masked Wood Swallow

CRACTICIDAE:
Gymnorhina tibicen,
Bellmagpie

Plate 314

CRACTICIDAE:
Cracticus torquatus,
Grey Butcherbird

CRACTICIDAE:
Strepera versicolor,
Grey Currawong

Plate 315

Enodes erythrophris (*Temminck*) MENADO MYNA Celebes

Scissirostrum dubium (*Latham*) SCISSORBILL STARLING Celebes, Peling and Togian Is

Buphagus africanus *L* YELLOW-BILLED OXPECKER or TICKBIRD Africa S of Sahara, except extreme S / savannah / blood-sucking ticks found on large mammals / n hole / e 2–3

Buphagus erythrorhynchus (*Stanley*) RED-BILLED OXPECKER or TICKBIRD E Africa from SE Sudan to Natal / savannah / blood-sucking ticks found on large mammals / n hole in stone or wall / e 2–3 / I 11–12 / F 28–9

ORIOLIDAE Old-World Orioles Starling-sized, forest-dwelling birds. Sexually dimorphic, males being predominantly yellow and black, females duller and greener. Fly strongly, and feed on insects and fruit. Nests usually high in trees, eggs 2–5 in number. In the temperate species both sexes incubate, but in the few tropical species which have been adequately studied, the incubation is by the female only.

Oriolus szalayi (*Madarász*) BROWN ORIOLE New Guinea and W Papuan islands / forest edge / fruit / n tree / e 2

Oriolus phaeochromus *Gray* HALMAHERA ORIOLE Halmahera

Oriolus forsteni (*Bonaparte*) CERAM ORIOLE Ceram

Oriolus bouroensis (*Quoy and Gaimard*) BURU ORIOLE Buru and Tenimber Is

Oriolus viridifuscus (*Heine*) TIMOR ORIOLE Timor and Wetar

Oriolus sagittatus (*Latham*) OLIVE-BACKED or WHITE-BELLLIED ORIOLE Lowlands of S New Guinea and N and E Australia / savannah / fruit / n tree / e 2–4

Oriolus flavocinctus (*Vigors*) YELLOW ORIOLE or GREEN ORIOLE N Australia, S New Guinea, Aru, Leti, Moa and Roma Is / forest and mangrove / n tree / e 2 (Rand and Gilliard credit the name to King)

Oriolus xanthonotus *Horsfield* DARK-THROATED ORIOLE Malay Peninsula through W and N Indonesia to Philippines / forest / insects / n and e ? n/k

Oriolus albiloris *Ogilvie-Grant* WHITE-LORED ORIOLE Mts of Luzon

Oriolus isabellae *Ogilvie-Grant* ISABELLA ORIOLE Mts of Luzon

Oriolus oriolus (*L*) GOLDEN ORIOLE Europe and W Asia E to Altai and India w to E and S Africa / forest, woodland and orchard / insects and fruit / n tree / e 3–6 / I ♂♀ 14–15 / F 14–15

Oriolus auratus *Vieillot* AFRICAN GOLDEN ORIOLE Africa S of Sahara except extreme S/ thick bush / insects and berries / n tree / e 2

Oriolus chinensis *L* BLACK-NAPED ORIOLE Himalayas and N India, China, SE Asia and much of Indonesia to Moluccas / open woodland / fruit and insects / n tree / e 2–3 / I 14

Oriolus chlorocephalus *Shelley* GREEN-HEADED ORIOLE Mts from Tanganyika to Mozambique / forest / fruit / n tree / e n/k

Oriolus crassirostris *Hartlaub* GREAT-BILLED ORIOLE São Thomé / hill forest / n tree (1 known) / e n/k

Oriolus brachyrhynchus *Swainson* WESTERN BLACK-HEADED ORIOLE Sierra Leone to Congo, S Uganda and W Kenya / forest / caterpillars / n tree / e n/k

Oriolus monacha (*Gmelin*) FOREST ORIOLE Ethiopia and Eritrea / forest / data uncertain owing to confusion of this species with *O. larvatus*

Oriolus larvatus *Lichtenstein* BLACK-HEADED ORIOLE Africa from Congo and Kenya south-wards / forest and cultivation / insects and fruit / n tree / e 2

Oriolus nigripennis *Verreaux* BLACK-WINGED ORIOLE Fernando Po and Sierra Leone to N Angola and W Uganda / forest / fruit and caterpillars / n and e n/k

Oriolus xanthornus (*L*) ORIENTAL BLACK-HEADED ORIOLE India and Ceylon, parts of SE Asia, NE Sumatra, Andamans, coasts and islands of NE Borneo / open forest and culti-vation / fruit and insects / n tree / e 2–4 / I ♂♀

Oriolus hosii *Sharpe* BLACK ORIOLE Certain of the mts of Borneo / mountain forest / berries / n and e n/k

Oriolus cruentus (*Wagler*) BLACK AND CRIMSON ORIOLE Malaya, Sumatra, Java and mts of Northern Borneo / forest / insects and fruit / n and e ? n/k

Oriolus trailii (*Vigors*) MAROON ORIOLE Himalayas, mts of Yunnan and SE Asia (except Malay Peninsula) Taiwan and Hainan / forest / fruit, nectar and insects / n tree / e 2–3 / I ♂♀

Oriolus mellianus *Stresemann* SILVER ORIOLE Mts of N Kwangtung, Kwangsi and Szechwan (China); in winter has occurred in Thailand and Cambodia

Specotheres vieilloti *Vigors and Horsfield*

SOUTHERN FIGBIRD E Australia and S New Guinea / forest and savannah / fruit / n tree / e 3

[**Specotheres stalkeri** *Ingram* INGRAM'S FIGBIRD Mt Elliot, Queensland / known from 2 specimens believed possibly to be hybrids *S. vieilloti* × *S. flaviventris* (see Mathews, *Aust Av Rec*, 3 (1918), p 141)]

Specotheres flaviventris *Gould* YELLOW FIGBIRD N and NE Australia, Kei Is / savannah / fruit / n tree / e 2–3

Specotheres viridis *Vieillot* TIMOR FIGBIRD Timor

Specotheres hypoleucus *Finsch* WETAR FIGBIRD Wetar

DICRURIDAE Drongos Arboreal birds of the Old World tropics, generally black in colour with metallic reflections. Very pugnacious, particularly in defence of nest, and will attack and rout birds up to the size of an eagle. Nest high up in trees, and comparatively little is known of nesting habits. Feed largely on insects.

Chaetorhynchus papuensis *Meyer* PAPUAN MOUNTAIN DRONGO Mts of New Guinea and Yule Is / forest / no data

Dicrurus ludwigii (*Smith*) SQUARE-TAILED DRONGO Local through parts of Africa S of Sahara / forest and dense bush / insects / n tree / e 2–3

Dicrurus atripennis *Swainson* SHINING DRONGO Forests of Guinea from Sierra Leone to Gabon and Semliki valley / insects / n tree / e 2

Dicrurus adsimilis (*Bechstein*) FORK-TAILED DRONGO Principé, Fernando Po and Africa S of Sahara / open bush / insects / n tree / e 2–4 / I 16 / F 14

Dicrurus fuscipennis (*Milne-Edwards and Oustalet*) GRAND COMORO DRONGO Grand Comoro Is

Dicrurus aldabranus (*Ridgway*) ALDABRA DRONGO Aldabra

Dicrurus forficatus (*L*) CRESTED DRONGO Madagascar, Nossi Bé and Anjouan

Dicrurus waldenii *Schlegel* MAYOTTE DRONGO Mayotte

Dicrurus macrocercus (*Vieillot*) BLACK DRONGO SW Iran, through Indian sub-continent, SE Asia and China to Manchuria; Hainan, Taiwan, Java, Bali, introduced Rota Is (Marianas) / light hill forest and open woodland / insects, small animals and nectar / n tree / e 3–4 / I ♂♀

Dicrurus leucophaeus *Vieillot* ASHY DRONGO E Afghanistan, Indian sub-continent, SE Asia, China, S Manchuria and parts of Indonesia, not breeding throughout range; for more detailed ranges and migrations of the various forms see Vaurie in Peters' *Check List*, vol XV, pp 142–5 / forest and plantation / insects and nectar / n tree / e 3–4 / I ♂♀

Dicrurus caerulescens (*L*) WHITE-BELLIED DRONGO India and Ceylon / forest / insects and nectar / n tree / e 2–4 / I ♂♀

Dicrurus annectans (*Hodgson*) CROW-BILLED DRONGO Himalaya foothills, Burma and N Thailand w S to Java and N Borneo / forest / insects / n tree / e 3–4 / I ♀ ?

Dicrurus aeneus *Vieillot* BRONZE DRONGO India, SE Asia, S China, Hainan, Taiwan, Sumatra and Borneo / forest and plantation / insects and nectar / n tree / e 3–4 / I ♂♀

Dicrurus remifer (*Temminck*) LESSER RACQUET-TAILED DRONGO Himalayas, SE Asia, Java and Sumatra / forest / insects and nectar / n tree / e 3–4 / I ♂♀

Dicrurus balicassius (*L*) BALICASSIAO DRONGO Philippines

Dicrurus hottentottus (*L*) SPANGLED DRONGO India, SE Asia through Indonesia and Australasia to Solomons (apparently not New Ireland), N and E coasts of Australia / forest / insects / n tree / e 3–4 / I ♂♀

Dicrurus megarhynchus (*Quoy and Gaimard*) RIBBON-TAILED DRONGO New Ireland

Dicrurus montanus (*Riley*) MOUNTAIN DRONGO Mts of Celebes

Dicrurus andamanensis *Beavan* ANDAMAN DRONGO Andaman, Great Coco and Table Is / forest / insects / n tree / e 2–3

Dicrurus paradiseus (*L*) GREATER RACQUET-TAILED DRONGO Kashmir, Ceylon, India, SE Asia, Hainan, Sumatra, Java, Borneo and adjacent small islands / forest / insects and nectar / n tree / e 3–4 / I ♂♀

CALLAEIDAE Wattlebirds New Zealand forest birds with weak wings, large, strong legs and feet and fleshy, coloured wattles at the corners of the jaws.

Callaeus cinerea (*Gmelin*) KOKAKO or WATTLED CROW New Zealand / now very restricted in range / forest / leaves, fruit and berries / n tree / e 2–3

Creadion carunculatus (*Gmelin*) SADDLEBACK New Zealand / now confined to Hen Is and 3 islets off SW coast of Stewart Is / insects and

PTILONORHYNCHIDAE:
Ailuroedus melanotus,
Spotted Catbird,
Green Catbird

PTILONORHYNCHIDAE:
Chlamydera maculata,
Spotted Bowerbird

Plate 316

PTILONORHYNCHIDAE:
Prionodura newtoniana,
Golden Bowerbird

Plate 317

fruit / n hole / e 3

Heteralocha acutirostris (*Gould*) HUIA N Island, New Zealand / believed extinct since 1907 / forest / insects and fruit / n hole / e – no authentic description

GRALLINIDAE Mudnest Builders An Australasian family of weak-flying birds which build beep bowl-shaped mud nests, usually on high horizontal branches. Generally gregarious except for the Torrent Lark.

Grallina cyanoleuca (*Latham*) MAGPIE LARK Australia / open forest and parkland / insects/ n tree / e 3–5

Grallina bruijni *Salvadori* TORRENT LARK Mts of New Guinea / swiftly flowing mountain streams / insects / n beside streams / e 1

Corcorax melanorhamphos (*Vieillot*) WHITE-WINGED CHOUGH S Queensland to S Australia / forest / insects, vertebrates and seeds/ n tree / e 3–5

Struthidea cinerea *Gould* APOSTLEBIRD Interior of Victoria, New South Wales and S Queensland / open woodland, scrub and cultivation / insects and seeds / n tree / e 4–5

ARTAMIDAE Wood Swallows Plain-coloured, aerial birds with long, pointed wings, plump bodies and soft fluffy plumage. They are the only passerines possessing powder-downs. Feed mainly on insects, caught in the air, and are expert gliders. Nests are frail saucer-shaped structures, usually on a branch. Eggs 2–4 and, so far as is known, nesting duties are shared by both sexes.

Artamus fuscus *Vieillot* ASHY WOOD SWALLOW Ceylon, E India, Burma, Thailand, Indo-China, Hainan and S China / savannah/ insects / n tree / e 2–3 / I ♂♀

Artamus leucorhynchus (*L*) WHITE-BREASTED WOOD SWALLOW From Andamans through Indonesia to Palau Is, Fiji and N Australia / open woodland / insects / n tree / e 3/ I ♂♀

Artamus monachus *Bonaparte* HOODED WOOD SWALLOW Celebes, Banggai and Sula Is

Artamus maximus *Meyer* PAPUAN WOOD SWALLOW Mts of New Guinea / mid-mountain grasslands and clearings / n tree / e 3

Artamus insignis *Sclater* INSIGNIA WOOD SWALLOW New Britain and New Ireland

Artamus personatus (*Gould*) MASKED WOOD SWALLOW Savannah woodlands of Australia/ n tree or bush

Artamus superciliosus (*Gould*) WHITE-BROWED WOOD SWALLOW Wooded areas of E Australia

Artamus cinereus *Vieillot* BLACK-FACED WOOD SWALLOW Timor, Letti, Sermatta, S New Guinea and interior of E Australia/ savannah / n tree / e 3–4

Artamus cyanopterus (*Latham*) DUSKY WOOD SWALLOW Tasmania, E and S Australia/ forest and woodland

Artamus minor *Vieillot* LITTLE WOOD SWALLOW N and C Australia / forest and savannah / n tree, ledge or rock crevice

CRACTICIDAE Butcherbirds and Currawongs A group of Australian and Papuan crow and jay-like birds building large nests generally in trees. Butcherbirds have a long incubation period for passerines – 23 days, with a fledging period of 25–6 days.

Cracticus mentalis *Salvadori and D'Albertis* WHITE-THROATED or BLACK-BACKED BUTCHER-BIRD SW New Guinea and Cape York Peninsula / savannah / insects / n tree / e 3 / I ♀

Cracticus torquatus (*Latham*) GREY BUTCHERBIRD Australia and Tasmania / forest and woodland / n tree

Cracticus nigrogularis (*Gould*) PIED BUTCHERBIRD Australia / woodland and parkland/ insects and small vertebrates / n tree / e 3–4

Cracticus cassicus (*Boddaert*) BLACK-HEADED BUTCHERBIRD New Guinea and adjacent islands/ lowland forest / fruit and insects / n tree / e 2–3

Cracticus louisiadensis *Tristram* LOUISIADE BUTCHERBIRD Tagula (Louisiade Archipelago)/ no data

Cracticus quoyi (*Lesson*) BLACK BUTCHERBIRD New Guinea, Japen, W Paupan Is, Aru Is, N Queensland and coast of N Territory / forest/ insects and fruit / n tree / e 4

Gymnorhina tibicen (*Latham*) BELLMAGPIE S New Guinea, Australia and Tasmania/ savannah / insects / n tree / e 3–5 / has territorial relationships unknown in any other bird, living and breeding promiscuously in clans

Strepera graculina (*White*) PIED CURRAWONG E Australia and Lord Howe Is / forest / omnivorous / n tree / e 3–4

Strepera fuliginosa (*Gould*) BLACK CURRAWONG Tasmania and King Is / forest/ omnivorous / n tree / e 3–4

Strepera versicolor (*Latham*) GREY CURRAWONG Tasmania and southern Australia/

forest and woodland / omnivorous
PTILONORHYNCHIDAE Bower Birds
Generally brightly coloured crow-like birds closely related to Birds of Paradise, and remarkable for their intricately constructed display areas called 'bowers' which the males make and decorate with bright objects. Nest-building, incubation and care of young is carried out solely by the ♀. Nest a shallow cup.
Ailuroedus buccoides (*Temminck*) WHITE-EARED CATBIRD New Guinea, Japen and W Papuan islands / fruit / n tree / e 1
Ailuroedus melanotis (*Gray*) SPOTTED CATBIRD Parts of New Guinea, Misol, Aru Is and NE Australia / fruit / n tree / e 2 / I ? ♂♀ – ♂ is said to help feed young
Ailuroedus crassirostris (*Paykull*) GREEN CATBIRD SE Australia / fruit / n tree / e 2–3
Scenopoeetes dentirostris (*Ramsay*) TOOTH-BILLED BOWERBIRD or STAGEMAKER N Queensland / fruit and insects / n 'in thick vegetation' / e 2
Archboldia papuensis *Rand* ARCHBOLD'S BOWERBIRD Scattered localities in mts of New Guinea / n and e n/k
Amblyornis inornatus (*Schlegel*) GARDENER BOWERBIRD Mts of NW New Guinea / n and e n/k
Amblyornis macgregoriae *De Vis* MACGREGOR'S BOWERBIRD Mts of New Guinea (not the NW) / n tree / e 1
Amblyornis subalaris *Sharpe* STRIPED BOWERBIRD Mts of SE New Guinea / n ? tree / e 1
Amblyornis flavifrons *Rothschild* YELLOW-FRONTED BOWERBIRD Known only from the type series of unknown origin, but believed to have come from NW New Guinea
Prionodura newtoniana *De Vis* GOLDEN BOWERBIRD Forests of Cairns District, Queensland / fruit / n tree / e 2
Sericulus aureus (*L*) BLACK-FACED GOLDEN BOWERBIRD W and S New Guinea / n and e n/k
Sericulus bakeri (*Chapin*) ADELBERT BOWERBIRD Adelbert Mts of N New Guinea / fruit and insects / n and e n/k
Sericulus chrysocephalus (*Lewin*) REGENT BOWERBIRD S Queensland and New South Wales / fruit / n tree / e 2–3
Ptilonorhynchus violaceus (*Vieillot*) SATIN BOWERBIRD E Australia / fruit and insects / n tree / e 1–3
Chlamydera maculata (*Gould*) SPOTTED

BOWERBIRD Interior of Australia / fruit and insects / n tree / e 2–3
Chlamydera nuchalis (*Jardine and Selby*) GREAT GREY BOWERBIRD N Australia and Melville Is / fruit and insects / n tree / e 1–2
Chlamydera lauterbachi *Reichenow* LAUTERBACH'S BOWERBIRD River valleys of N and S New Guinea / fruit and insects / n tree / e 1
Chlamydera cerviniventris *Gould* FAWN-BREASTED BOWERBIRD Cape York Peninsula, islands in Torres Strait, E New Guinea and Kebar Valley of Vogelkop, supposedly also Sudest Is (De Vis, *Ann Queensland Mus*, no 2 (1892), p 9) / fruit and insects / n tree / e 1–2
PARADISAEIDAE Birds of Paradise
Birds related to crows and Bowerbirds. Strikingly sexually dimorphic, females generally dull, males brightly coloured with remarkably highly developed, bizarre plumes and decorative feathers used in highly complex courtship displays. Inhabit forests. Nesting little known, but males not known to take part in breeding biology, which is carried out by female in species where this is known. Nest (where known) generally in tree, eggs usually 1 or 2.
[Birds of Paradise produce a number of hybrids many of which have been described as species. It is beyond the scope of this book to discuss these, but a list can be found in Peters' *Check List of the Birds of the World*, vol XV, pp 202–4, together with references for further reading.]
Loria loriae *Salvadori* LORIA'S BIRD OF PARADISE Mts of New Guinea / no data
Loboparadisea sericea *Rothschild* WATTLE-BILLED BIRD OF PARADISE Mts of New Guinea / fruit / n tree / e 1
Cnemophilus macgregorii *De Vis* SICKLE-CRESTED BIRD OF PARADISE Mts of C and SE New Guinea / fruit / n tree / e ?1
Macgregoria pulchra *De Vis* MACGREGOR'S BIRD OF PARADISE Mts of C and SE New Guinea
Lycocorax pyrrhopterus (*Bonaparte*) PARADISE CROW Moluccas / fruit / n tree / e 1
Manucodia ater (*Lesson*) GLOSSY-MANTLED MANUCODE New Guinea, Aru and W Papuan Is, Tagula / n tree / e 1 / I ♀ 15–17
Manucodia jobiensis *Salvadori* JOBI MANUCODE Japen and N Coast of New Guinea / fruit / n tree / e 2
Manucodia chalybatus (*Pennant*) CRINKLE-

PTILONORHYNCHIDAE:
Chlamydera nuchalis,
Great Grey Bowerbird

PTILONORHYNCHIDAE:
Ptilonorhynchus violaceus,
Satin Bowerbird

Plate 318

PARADISAEIDAE:
Paradisea apoda,
Greater Bird of Paradise

PARADISAEIDAE:
Cicinnurus regius,
King Bird of Paradise

Young *C. regius* peering from
nest.

Plate 319

COLLARED MANUCODE New Guinea and Misol/ n tree, no data on clutch size, 3 eggs known/ I – a ♂ was shot at nest

Manucodia comrii *Sclater* CURL-CRESTED MANUCODE D'Entrecasteaux and Trobriand Is/ n tree/e 2

Phonygammus keraudrenii (*Lesson and Garnot*) TRUMPET BIRD New Guinea, Aru and D'Entrecasteaux Is, N Queensland/no definite information on nesting but believed to be at least partially nest-parasitic, though probably not brood parasitic/e 2

Ptiloris paradiseus *Swainson* PARADISE RIFLEBIRD New South Wales and S Queensland/ insects and fruit/n tree/e 2

Ptiloris victoriae *Gould* VICTORIA RIFLEBIRD N Queensland/invertebrates and fruit/n tree/ e 2

Ptiloris magnificus (*Vieillot*) MAGNIFICENT RIFLEBIRD New Guinea and N Queensland/ n tree/e 2

Semioptera wallacei *Gould* WALLACE'S STANDARD-WING Halmahera and Batjan/fruit and insects/n and e n/k

Seleucidis melanoleuca (*Daudin*) TWELVE-WIRED BIRD OF PARADISE New Guinea and Salawati/lowland forest/n tree/e 1

Paradigalla carunculata *Lesson* LONG-TAILED PARADIGALLA Arfak Mts of NW New Guinea/ mountain forest/no data

Paradigalla brevicauda *Rothschild and Hartert* SHORT-TAILED PARADIGALLA Mts of C New Guinea/fruit/n bush (? or tree)/e 1

Drepanornis albertisi (*Sclater*) D'ALBERTIS'S BIRD OF PARADISE Mts of New Guinea/insects/ n tree/e 1

Drepanornis bruijnii *Oustalet* BRUIJN'S BIRD OR PARADISE N New Guinea/lowlands/local/ ? no data

Epimachus fastuosus (*Hermann*) BLACK SICKLEBILL Mts of New Guinea/fruit/n and e n/k

Epimachus meyeri *Finsch* BROWN SICKLEBILL Mts of New Guinea/fruit and insects/n tree/e 1

[In areas where *E. fastuosus* and *E. meyeri* occur together they displace each other altitudinally, *E. meyeri* occurring at higher altitudes]

Astrapia nigra (*Gmelin*) ARFAK ASTRAPIA Arfak Mts of NW New Guinea/only in the highest mountain forests/no data

Astrapia splendidissima *Rothschild*

SPLENDID ASTRAPIA Mts of W and C New Guinea/fruit and insects/n and e n/k

Astrapia mayeri *Stonor* SHAW-MAYER'S RIBBON-TAILED BIRD OF PARADISE Mts of C New Guinea/fruit/n tree/e ? n/k

Astrapia stephaniae (*Finsch*) PRINCESS STEPHANIE'S BIRD OF PARADISE Mts of New Guinea/insects and fruit/n tree/e 1

[In the Yanka region of Mt Hagen range *A. mayeri* and *A. stephaniae* hybridise freely, the persistent hybrid being described as a species *Astrapia barnesi* Iredale; yet in Mt Giluwe they live side by side, apparently without hybridisation]

Astrapia rothschildi *Foerster* LORD ROTHSCHILD'S BIRD OF PARADISE OR HUON ASTRAPIA Mts of Huon Peninsula, NE New Guinea/no data/1 egg known

Lophorina superba (*Pennant*) SUPERB BIRD OF PARADISE Mts of New Guinea/n ? tree/e 2 (1 nest with eggs known)

Parotia sefilata (*Pennant*) ARFAK SIX-PLUMED BIRD OF PARADISE Mts of W New Guinea/fruit/ n and e n/k

Parotia carolae *Meyer* QUEEN CAROLA OF SAXONY'S SIX-PLUMED BIRD OF PARADISE Mts of New Guinea/fruit/n and e n/k

Parotia lawesii *Ramsay* LAWES'S SIX-PLUMED BIRD OF PARADISE Mts of New Guinea/fruit/ n in creepers (1 known)/e 1

Parotia wahnesi *Rothschild* WAHNES'S SIX-PLUMED BIRD OF PARADISE Mts of Huon Peninsula, New Guinea/no data

Pteridophora alberti *Meyer* KING OF SAXONY'S BIRD OF PARADISE Mts of New Guinea/ n and e n/k

Cicinnurus regius (*L*) KING BIRD OF PARADISE New Guinea, Japen, Misol, Salawati, Batanta and Aru Is/lowland forest/fruit/n tree/ e 2/I 17/F 14

Diphyllodes magnificus (*Pennant*) MAGNIFICENT BIRD OF PARADISE New Guinea, Misol, Salawati and Japen/fruit/n tree/e 2

Diphyllodes respublica (*Bonaparte*) WILSON'S BIRD OF PARADISE Batanta and Waigeu/n and e n/k

Paradisea apoda *L* GREATER BIRD OF PARADISE Lowlands of New Guinea and Aru Is, introduced Tobago/fruit and ? insects/n n/k (sic)/e 2

Paradisea raggiana *Sclater* COUNT RAGGI'S

BIRD OF PARADISE Extreme SE New Guinea/ fruit/n tree/e 2/I 13–15 (sometimes treated as a race of *P. apoda*)

Paradisea minor *Shaw* LESSER BIRD OF PARADISE N and W New Guinea, Japen, Misol/ lowland forest/fruit and insects/n tree/e ? 1 [*P. mixta* is a persistent hybrid *P. apoda × minor* occurring in the upper Ramu River]

Paradisea decora *Salvin and Godman* GOLDIE'S BIRD OF PARADISE Fergusson and Normanby Is, D'Entrecasteaux Archipelago/ mountain forests/no other data

Paradisea rubra *Daudin* RED BIRD OF PARADISE Waigeu, Batanta and ? Ghemien/ lowland forests / fruit and insects / eggs have been collected, but apparently no description of n or e

Paradisea guilielmi *Cabanis* EMPEROR OF GERMANY'S BIRD OF PARADISE Mts of Huon Peninsula/fruit/n ?/e ?1, ?2

Paradisea rudolphi (*Finsch*) ARCHDUKE RUDOLPH'S BLUE BIRD OF PARADISE Mts of SE New Guinea/fruit /n and e doubtful, but there are 3 eggs in British Museum (Natural History) ascribed to this species

CORVIDAE Crows and Jays Large and fairly powerful passerines, crows have fairly long, pointed wings and short tails; jays have shorter, rounded wings and longer tails; they are also more brightly coloured. Much of the data for this family is based on Goodwin *Crows of the World* (1976).

Platylophus galericulatus (*Cuvier*) CRESTED JAY Malay Peninsula, Sumatra, Java, Borneo/ lowland forest / insects and millipedes / n and e ? n/k

Platysmurus leucopterus (*Temminck*) BLACK MAGPIE or BLACK JAY Malay Peninsula, Sumatra and Borneo / lowland forest / fruit, beetles and small mammals / n tree / e 2–3

Gymnorhinus cyanocephala *Wied* PIÑON JAY Western USA, S to Baja California / hill forest/insects, coniferous nuts and seeds/n tree/ e 3–6/I ♂♀ 16/F c21

Cyanocitta cristata (*L*) BLUE JAY S Canada and USA, E of Rockies / forest and habitation/ omnivorous /n tree or bush/e 3–7/I ♂♀ 17–18/ F 17–21

Cyanocitta stelleri (*Gmelin*) STELLER'S JAY Western N America from S Alaska to Nicaragua/ forest and cultivation/insects, grain and fruit/ n tree/e 2–6/I ♂♀ 16

Aphelocoma coerulescens (*Bosc*) SCRUB JAY Western USA, Mexico and peninsular Florida/ scrub/omnivorous/n bush/e 3–5/I ♂♀ 16/F 18

Aphelocoma ultamarina (*Bonaparte*) MEXICAN or ULTAMARINE JAY Arizona, Texas and Mexico/hill forest and scrub/insects, seeds and fruit/n tree/e 4–7/I 16

Aphelocoma unicolor (*Cassin*) UNICOLOURED JAY Mts of Mexico, Guatemala, El Salvador and Honduras/forest/no other data

Cyanolyca viridicyana (*Lafresnaye and d'Orbigny*) COLLARED JAY Andes from Venezeula to Bolivia/forest (*C. turcosa* (Bonaparte) 'Turquoise Jay' is often separated)

Cyanolyca pulchra (*Lawrence*) BEAUTIFUL JAY Andes of Ecuador and SW Colombia/forest/no other data

Cyanolyca cucullata (*Ridgway*) AZURE-HOODED JAY Mts from Mexico to Panama/ mountain forest/insects/n and e n/k

Cyanolyca pumilo (*Strickland*) BLACK-THROATED JAY Mts of SE Mexico, Guatemala, El Salvador and W Honduras/insects/etc/n and e n/k

Cyanolyca nana (*Du Bus*) DWARF JAY S Mexico/forest/insects and invertebrates/n tree/ e 1–3/I ♀ c20

Cyanolyca mirabilis *Nelson* WHITE-THROATED JAY SW Mexico/forest

Cyanolyca argentigula (*Lawrence*) SILVER-THROATED JAY Mts of Costa Rica and W Panama/mountain forest/no other data

Cissilopha melanocyanea (*Hartlaub*) HARTLAUB'S JAY Mts of Guatemala, El Salvador, Honduras and N Nicaragua/woodland, scrub and plantation/insects and fruit/n bush or tree/ e 3–4

Cissilopha sanblasiana (*Lafresnaye*) SAN BLAS JAY SW Mexico / scrub and mangrove/ insects, lizards and palm-nut pericarp/n tree or shrub/e n/s/I ♀

Cissilopha yucatanica (*Dubois*) YUCATAN JAY E Mexico, N Guatemala and Belize (sometimes treated as conspecific with *C. sanblasiana*)/ forest and scrub

Cissilopha beecheii (*Vigors*) BEECHEY'S JAY NW Mexico / scrubby forest / e 3 / I ♀ 15 / F 12–14 (based on captive data, nest n/k in wild)

Cyanocorax caeruleus (*Vieillot*) AZURE JAY SE Brazil, Paraguay and NE Argentina / forest/ e ? 2

Cyanocorax cyanomelas (*Vieillot*) PURPLISH

CORVIDAE:
Cyanocitta cristata,
Blue Jay

CORVIDAE:
Corvus orru,
Australian Crow

Plate 320

PARADISAEIDAE
Superb Bird of Paradise,
Lophorina superba

JAY SE Peru, E Bolivia, SW Brazil, Paraguay, N Argentina / groves of trees and tall trees in stream beds / fruit and insects / n tree or shrub / e 2–6

Cyanocorax violaceus *Du Bus* VIOLACEUS JAY E Colombia, Ecuador, Peru, Venezuela, SW Guyana and NW Brazil / forests and clearings / omnivorous / n tree / e 5 / n and e no data

Cyanocorax cristatellus (*Temminck*) CURL-CRESTED JAY Tableland of E and C Brazil / cerrado

Cyanocorax heilprini *Gentry* AZURE-NAPED JAY S Venezuela and adjacent Brazil and Colombia / forest and savannah

Cyanocorax cayanus (*L*) CAYENNE JAY SE Venezuela, the Guianas and Rio Negro and Rio Branco regions of N Brazil / forest, savannah and cultivation / insects and fruit / n and e n/k

Cyanocorax affinis *Pelzeln* BLACK-CHESTED JAY SE Costa Rica, Panama, N and NE Colombia and NW Venezuela / woodland and plantation / n tree / e 3–5

Cyanocorax chrysops (*Vieillot*) PLUSH-CRESTED JAY Brazil S of Amazon, E Bolivia, Paraguay, Uruguay and N Argentina / forest, groves and cerrado [*C. cyanopogon* (Wied) 'White-naped Jay' is sometimes separated, but apparently a perfect intermediate exists in the form of the unique type of the form *C. chrysops interpositus* Pinto, from Mangabeira] / n tree / e 2–4 (? 6–7)

Cyanocorax mystacalis (*St Hilaire*) WHITE-TAILED JAY Arid zone of SW Ecuador and NW Peru / dry scrub, forest and woodland / insects and seeds / n n/k?/e/n/s (Goodwin describes 1 egg)

Cyanocorax dickeyi *Moore* TUFTED JAY Mts of W Mexico / forest / fruit and insects / n tree / e 3–5 / I ♀ 18 / F 24

Cyanocorax yncas (*Boddaert*) GREEN JAY From Rio Grande Valley of Texas through Mexico and C America, Andes from Venezuela to Bolivia / forest / seeds and insects / n tree or bush / e 3–5 / I ♀

Psilorhinus morio (*Wagler*) BROWN JAY Mexico to Panama open country and cultivation / omnivorous / n tree or shrub / e 3–6 / I ♀ 18–20

Calocitta formosa (*Swainson*) MAGPIE JAY Mexico to Costa Rica / forest, woodland and scrub / omnivorous / n tree / e 3–4 / I ♀ (*C. colliei* (Vigors) is sometimes separated)

Garrulus glandarius (*L*) COMMON JAY Much of Palaearctic; S on E to Himalayas, Burma, China and Taiwan, and on W to N Africa / forest and orchard / omnivorous / n tree / e 3–10 / I ♀ (?♂) 16–17 / F 19–20

Garrulus lanceolatus *Vigors* LANCEOLATED JAY E Afghanistan and Himalayas to Nepal / hill forest / n tree / e 3–5 / I ♂♀ 16

Garrulus lidthi *Bonaparte* LIDTH'S or RYUKYU JAY Amami Oshimi and Toku-no-Shima in N Ryukyu Is / oak forests / acorns / n hole / e 4–5

Perisoreus canadensis (*L*) GREY JAY N America (except eastern and southern USA) / forest, chiefly coniferous / almost omnivorous / n tree / e 2–5 / I ♀ 16–18 / F 15

Perisoreus infaustus (*L*) SIBERIAN JAY N Europe and across N and C Asia to Amur and Manchuria / coniferous forest belt / insects, small animals and seeds / n tree / e 3–5 / I (? 16–17) (? 19) / F 21–5

Perisoreus internigrans (*Thayer and Bangs*) SZECHWAN JAY N and NW Szechwan to E Sikang / forest / no other data

Urocissa ornata (*Wagler*) CEYLON MAGPIE Ceylon / forest and tea gardens / insects and tree frogs / n tree / e 3–5 (see reference given in *Dendrocitta vagabunda*)

Urocissa caerulea *Gould* TAIWAN MAGPIE Taiwan / forest / berries, crabs, fish and small birds / n tree / e 7–8

Urocissa flavirostris (*Blyth*) GOLDEN-BILLED MAGPIE Himalayas and mts of W Burma and NW Tonkin / forest / insects, vertebrates and fruit / n tree / e 3–4 (?5) / I ♂♀

Urocissa erythrorhyncha (*Boddaert*) RED-BILLED MAGPIE Himalayas, SE Asia (except Malay Peninsula) China and SW Manchuria / forest / insects, vertebrates and fruit / n tree / e 3–6 / I ♂♀

Urocissa whiteheadi *Ogilvie-Grant* WHITEHEAD'S MAGPIE Hainan, C Laos and N Vietnam / forest / berries and insects / n tree / e 6

Cissa chinensis (*Boddaert*) GREEN MAGPIE Lower Himalayas, parts of SE Asia, Sumatra, NW Borneo / forest / insects and vertebrates / n tree / e 3–7

Cissa thalassina (*Temminck*) SHORT-TAILED MAGPIE Yaoshan (Kwangsi), Hainan, Vietnam, S Laos and E Thailand, Java and mts of N Borneo (discontinuous) / forest / insects / n ? tree / e ? 2 (*C. hypoleuca* Salvadori and Giglioli, is sometimes separated)

Cyanopica cyana (*Pallas*) AZURE-WINGED MAGPIE E Asia from Transbaikalia and Ussuriland S to China and Japan, an isolated race occurs in the Iberian Peninsula / scrub and woodland often near water / fruit and insects / n tree / e 5–9 / I ♀ 15

Dendrocitta vagabunda (*Latham*) RUFOUS TREEPIE Himalayas, India and SE Asia (except Malay Peninsula) / forest, plantation and habitation / omnivorous / n tree / e 2–6 (see Goodwin, *Crows of the World*, for reasons for merging *Urocissa* in *Cissa* and *Dendrocitta* in *Crypsirina*)

Dendrocitta cinerascens *Sharpe* BORNEAN TREEPIE Borneo / forest, scrub and cultivation / seeds, berries and insects / n tree / e 2

Dendrocitta occipitalis (*Müller*) SUMATRAN TREEPIE Sumatra / no data

Dendrocitta formosae *Swinhoe* GREY TREEPIE Himalayas, E India, northern SE Asia, Yunnan, S and E China, Hainan and Taiwan / forest and cultivation / fruit, nectar, insects and vertebrates / n bush or tree / e 3–5 / I ♂♀

Dendrocitta leucogastra *Gould* WHITE-BELLIED TREEPIE S India / forest / fruit, nectar, insects and vertebrates / n shrub or tree / e 3–4

Dendrocitta frontalis *Horsfield* COLLARED or BLACKBROWED TREEPIE Himalayas across hills of N Burma to N Tonkin / forest / fruit, nectar, insects and vertebrates / n tree or shrub / e 3–4

Dendrocitta baileyi *Blyth* ANDAMAN TREEPIE Andaman Is / forest / n sapling / e 3 (2 nests known)

Crypsirina temia (*Daudin*) RACQUET-TAILED TREEPIE S Burma, Thailand, Indo-China, Sumatra, Java and Bali / open forest and bamboo scrub / fruit and insects / n shrub or bamboo / e 2–4

Crypsirina cucullata *Jerdon* HOODED TREEPIE N and C Burma / dry forest, scrub and cultivation / n tree or shrub / e 2–4

Temnurus temnurus (*Temminck*) TEMNURUS MAGPIE or NOTCH-TAILED TREEPIE Tonkin, N and C Annam, Hainan / open forest / ? insectivorous / n and e n/k

Pica pica (*L*) BLACK-BILLED MAGPIE Widely distributed through Palaearctic, S to Himalayas and northern SE Asia, also western N America / open woodland, thickets and grasslands / omnivorous / n tree or bush / e 5–10 / I ♀ 17–18 / F 22–7

Pica nuttalli (*Audubon*) YELLOW-BILLED MAGPIE California / tall trees bordering streams, orchards and cultivation / n tree / e 5–8 / I ? 18

Zavattariornis stresemanni *Moltoni* STRESEMANN'S BUSH CROW S Ethiopia / acacia thorn scrub / n thorn tree / e up to 6

Podoces hendersoni *Hume* HENDERSON'S GROUND-JAY Deserts of C Asia from Mongolia to Kansu and through Tsinghai to Sinkiang and N Tibet / insects / n ground / e n/k

Podoces biddulphi *Hume* BIDDULPH'S GROUND-JAY W Sinkiang and Tian Shan foothills / n tree / e 1–3

Podoces panderi *Fischer* PANDER'S GROUND-JAY or SAXAUL JAY Deserts of Russian Turkestan / seeds and invertebrates / n bush / e 4–5 / I ♀ 16–19

Podoces pleskei *Zarudny* PLESKE'S GROUND-JAY E Iran / no data

Pseudopodoces humilis (*Hume*) HUME'S GROUND CHOUGH S Kansu and NW Szechwan to S Sinkiang, Tibet and N Sikkim / open sandy and stony country / insects / n hole in bank / e 4–6

Nucifraga columbiana (*Wilson*) CLARK'S NUTCRACKER Mts of western N America / coniferous forest / omnivorous / n tree / e 2–6 / I ♂♀ 16–17 / F 22

Nucifraga caryocatactes (*L*) NUTCRACKER Taiga belt of Eurasia, and S through mountain ranges to Himalayas and Pyrenees / forest / insects, seeds of conifers, young birds etc / n tree / e 2–5 / I ♀ 18 / F 18–21 approx

Testudophaga bicolor *Hachisuka* BI-COLOURED CHOUGH Rodriguez / extinct / contemporary accounts only

Pyrrhocorax pyrrhocorax (*L*) RED-BILLED CHOUGH Locally distributed from Europe across Asia to China and Transbaikalia and S to Mediterranean and Himalayas / sea cliffs and mountains / chiefly invertebrates / n crevice in cliff / e 2–7 / I ♀ 17–18 / F 38

Pyrrhocorax graculus (*L*) ALPINE or YELLOW-BILLED CHOUGH Mts from S Europe across C Asia to Tibet and Sikang / mountain pasture, cultivation and cliffs / insects and fruit / n hole in cliff / e 3–4 / I 17–21

Ptilostomus afer (*L*) PIAPIAC Africa from Senegal to Ethiopia and S to Lake Albert and Lake Edward / palm groves / insects / n palm tree / e 3–7

Corvus monedula *L* JACKDAW Europe, N Africa and across Asia to the Yenisei and NW

India, frequently wanders outside normal range/ forest, grassland and cliffs/omnivorous/n hole in tree, building or cliff, sometimes tree nest/ e 2–9/I ♀ 17–18/F 30–5

Corvus dauuricus *Pallas* DAURIAN JACKDAW Siberia from Kansk to Amurland w S to Russian Turkestan, China and Japan/forest and rocky places/insects/n hole in tree or rock/e 6 [**Corvus neglectus** *Schlegel* is believed to be a colour phase of *C. dauuricus*]

Corvus splendens *Vieillot* HOUSE CROW Indian sub-continent, Burma, SW Thailand, Maldives and Laccadives, introduced Muscat, Port Sudan and Zanzibar/habitation/omnivorous/n tree/e 4–5/I ♀ (?♂) 16–17

Corvus moneduloides *Lesson* NEW CALEDONIAN CROW New Caledonia and Loyalty Is/omnivorous/n tree/e 2

Corvus enca (*Horsfield*) SLENDER-BILLED CROW Malaya, Sumatra, W Sumatran islands, Borneo, Java, Bali, Banggai, Mentawei Is, Sula Archipelago, Philippines, Ceram (? Buru)/forest and mangrove/lizards and insects/n tree/e 4 (2 nests known) [**Corvus fallax** *Brüggemann* is apparently indeterminable and based on a skin of unknown origin ?=a form of *C. enca*]

Corvus typicus (*Bonaparte*) CELEBES CROW C and S Celebes and Butang/forest edge and woodland/no other data

Corvus unicolor *Rothschild and Hartert* BANGGAI CROW Banggai and Sula Is/no data

Corvus florensis *Büttikofer* FLORES CROW Flores/no data

Corvus kubaryi *Reichenow* GUAM CROW Guam and Rota/forest and coconut plantations/ omnivorous/n tree/e n/k

Corvus validus *Bonaparte* MOLUCCAN CROW Morotai, Halmahera, Kajoa, Batjan and Obi/ no data

Corvus woodfordi (*Ogilvie-Grant*) WHITE-BILLED CROW Solomon Is/forest (*C. meeki* Rothschild, 'Bougainville Crow' is sometimes separated)/beetles and fruits/n and e n/k

Corvus fuscicapillus *Gray* BROWN-HEADED CROW NW New Guinea, Aru Is, Waigeu and Gam/forest/fruit/n and e n/k

Corvus tristis *Lesson and Garnot* GREY CROW or BARE-FACED CROW New Guinea, Japen, Ron, Batanta, Salwati, and D'Entrecasteaux Archipelago/forest/fruit/n n/k/e 2 (1 clutch known)

Corvus capensis *Lichtenstein* CAPE CROW E and S Africa from Sudan to Angola and the Cape/open country/omnivorous/n tree/e 3–5/ I ♂♀ 18–19/F 38–9

Corvus frugilegus *L* ROOK Europe, N Africa and across Asia to Amurland and China, wanders outside normal range/open country/ omnivorous/n tree/e 3–9/I ♀ 16–18/F 29–30

Corvus brachyrhynchos *Brehm* COMMON CROW N America/almost ubiquitous/omnivorous/n tree/e 3–9/I ♂♀ 18/F c35

Corvus caurinus *Baird* NORTHWESTERN CROW Coasts and offshore islands from Alaska to Washington / beaches and coastal forests/ omnivorous/n tree/e 4–5

Corvus imparatus *Peters* MEXICAN CROW N Mexico/semi-desert scrub and bush/n and e n/k [**Corvus sinaloae** *Davis* SINALOA CROW Sinaloa, Mexico / this species is based on the distinctive voice, but this is not accepted by all authorities as a valid character for specific recognition]

Corvus ossifragus *Wilson* FISH CROW Eastern and southern USA/rivers, marshes and seashores/omnivorous/n tree/e 4–5/I ♂♀ 16–18

Corvus palmarum *Württemburg* PALM CROW Cuba and Hispaniola/forest/fruit, grain and insects/n tree/e 3–4

Corvus jamaicensis *Gmelin* JAMAICAN CROW Jamaica/woodland and open park/fruit, grain and insects/n tree/e 3–4

Corvus nasicus *Temminck* CUBAN CROW Cuba, Isle of Pines and Grand Caicos/forest and habitation/fruit, grain and insects/n tree/ e 3–4

Corvus leucognaphalus *Daudin* WHITE-NECKED CROW Hispaniola and Puerto Rico/ forest/fruit, grain and insects/n tree/e 3–4

Corvus corone *L* CARRION CROW Europe and across much of temperate Asia to Japan and Kamchatka, S to Egypt and (in winter), India, wanders far outside normal range/open forest, grassland and cultivation/omnivorous/n tree or cliff ledge/e 4–7/I ♀ 18–21/F 26–35 [*Corvus cornix* L 'Hooded Crow', formerly considered distinct, is now treated as conspecific with *C. corone*]

Corvus macrorhynchos *Wagler* JUNGLE CROW (LARGE-BILLED CROW) [Some authorities separate *C. levaillanti* but the evidence seems to indicate that it intergrades with the nominate and other forms of *macrorhynchos*. If separated, *macrorhynchos* is usually called 'Large-billed Crow', and *levaillanti* 'Jungle Crow', otherwise the latter name covers the whole species]. From Ussuriland through Manchuria, China, the Japanese islands (and Kuriles) to Transcaspia, Indian sub-continent, SE Asia, Greater and Lesser Sunda Is and Philippines / forest/ omnivorous / n tree / e 3–5 / I ♂♀ 17–19 / F c21–8

Corvus orru *Bonaparte* AUSTRALIAN CROW Australia, New Guinea, W and E Papuan islands, Bismarck Archipelago, islands in Geelvink Bay and Moluccas / mangrove and savannah/omnivorous / n tree /e 2–4 [*Corvus annectens* Brüggemann is apparently based on a specimen of *C. orru* erroneously stated to have come from Celebes]

Corvus bennetti *North* LITTLE CROW Australia / dry scrub / omnivorous / n tree or shrub /e 3–6

Corvus coronoides *Vigors and Horsfield* AUSTRALIAN RAVEN Eastern and southern Australia /woodland, rocky outcrops and dunes/ omnivorous /n tree /e 3–5 /I ♀ 20/F 45

Corvus mellori *Mathews* LITTLE RAVEN SE Australia/scrub and woodland/omnivorous/ n tree or shrub /e 3–5/ F 36

Corvus tasmanicus *Mathews* FOREST RAVEN Tasmania; south-east Australia on Wilson's Promontory and in the Otway Ranges. An isolated population in and near the forested areas of the northern tablelands of the north-eastern New South Wales /forest, but also open country in areas where it is the only crow/ ? omnivorous / n and e said to be similar to *C. coronoides* [NB: The specific distinctness of *mellori* and *tasmanicus* was only recently recognised (see Rowley: 1970 The genus *Corvus* in Australia CSIRO Wildlife Research vol 15, pp 27–71]

[**Corvus difficilis** *Stresemann* from N Queens-land is based on a single specimen which Vaurie believed to be either an aberrant specimen of *coronoides* or a hybrid *coronoides* × *bennetti*]

Corvus torquatus *Lesson* COLLARED CROW SW Manchuria through China to Hainan, Tonkin and N Annam /cultivation/omnivorous/ n tree/e 3–7 (2–6) authorities differ

Corvus albus *Müller* PIED CROW Africa S of Sahara / ubiquitous / omnivorous /n tree, telegraph pole etc /e 3–5/I ♀ 18–19/F 43

Corvus tropicus *Kerr* HAWAIIAN CROW Island of Hawaii, now restricted to the western slopes /scrub / ? mainly fruit /n tree /e 4–5 /I♂♀

Corvus cryptoleucus *Couch* WHITE-NECKED RAVEN Western USA and Mexico /deserts and open plains /omnivorous /n tree /e 3–8

Corvus ruficollis *Lesson* BROWN-NECKED RAVEN Cape Verde Is, Sahara and across deserts of Arabia and Middle East to Baluchistan, Afghanistan and Transcaspia; British and Italian Somaliland / desert and semi-desert/ n cliff ledge /e 1–6 /I 20–2 /F 42–5

Corvus corax *L* GREAT RAVEN Widely but irregularly distributed through the Holarctic almost ubiquitous /omnivorous /n tree or cliff ledge / e 3–7/ I ♀ 20–1 / F 35–42

Corvus rhipidurus *Hartert* FAN-TAILED RAVEN S Syria and Arabia, S to Kenya and W to Aïr in Sahara /cliffs /omnivorous /n hole in cliff /e 2–4

Corvus albicollis *Latham* CAPE or WHITE-NAPED RAVEN E Africa from Uganda and Kenya to the Cape / mountainous country/ insects, fruit and carrion /n cliff ledge /e 3–6

Corvus crassirostris *Rüppell* THICK-BILLED RAVEN Eritrea and Ethiopia / mountainous country /omnivorous /n on rock or in tree /e ?

Corvus moriorum *Forbes* CHATHAM CROW Chatham Is /extinct /bones only

Corvus antipodum *Forbes* ANTIPODAL CROW N Island, New Zealand /extinct /bones only

Bibliography

Ali S. and Ripley S. D. *Handbook of the Birds of India and Pakistan*, 10 vols (Oxford University Press, 1968–74)

Austin O. L. and Kuroda N. 'The Birds of Japan, Their Status and Distribution' *Bulletin of the Museum of Comparative Zoology at Harvard College* (Cambridge, Mass, USA, 1953)

Baker E. C. Stuart *Fauna of British India: Birds*, 8 vols (Taylor & Francis, 1922–30)

Baker R. H. *Avifauna of Micronesia*, vol 3 (University of Kansas Publications: Museum of Natural History, 1951)

Bannerman D. A. and W. M. *Birds of the Atlantic Islands*, 4 vols (Oliver & Boyd, 1963–8)

Benson C. W. 'The Birds of the Comoro Islands', *Ibis*, vol 103b (1960) pp 1–106

Benson C. W. 'The Birds of Aldabra and their Status', *Atoll Research Bulletin*, vol 118 (1967) pp 63–111

Bent A. C. *Life Histories of North American Birds*, various volumes (New York: Dover Publications Inc, 1962–5)

Berger A. J. *Hawaiian Birdlife* (Honolulu: University Press of Hawaii, 1972)

Bond J. *Check List of Birds of the West Indies* (Academy of Natural Sciences of Philadelphia, 3rd and 4th eds, 1950 and 1956)

Bond J. *Birds of the West Indies* (Collins, 1960)

Brown L. and Amadon D. *Eagles, Hawks and Falcons of the World*, 2 vols (*Country Life*, 1968)

Burton J. A. (editor) *Owls of the World* (Eurobooks, Peter Lowe, 1973)

Caldwell and Caldwell *South China Birds* (Shanghai: H. M. Vanderburgh, 1931)

Cory, Hellmayr and Conover *Catalogue of the Birds of the Americas*, 15 vols (Chicago: Field Museum of Natural History Publications, 1918–49)

Delacour J. *Birds of Malaysia* (New York: Macmillan, 1947)

Delacour J. *Pheasants of the World* (*Country Life*, 1951)

Delacour J. *The Waterfowl of the World*, 4 vols (*Country Life*, 1954)

Delacour J. and Amadon D. *Curassows and Related Birds* (New York: American Museum of Natural History, 1973)

Dementiev G. P. and Gladkov N. A. (editors) *Ptitsy Sovetskogo Soyusa*, 6 vols (Moscow: Sovetskaya Nauka, 1951–4); *Birds of the Soviet Union*,

English translation (Jerusalem: Israel Program for Scientific Translations, 1966–70)

DuPont J. E. *Philippine Birds* (Greenville: Delaware Museum of Natural History, 1971)

Edwards E. P. *A Coded List of the Birds of the World* (the author: at Sweetbriar, Virginia, 1974)

ffrench R. *A Guide to the Birds of Trinidad and Tobago* (Wynnewood, USA: Livingstone Publishing Co, 1973)

Forshaw J. M. *Parrots of the World* (Melbourne: Lansdowne Press)

Gilliard E. T. *Birds of Paradise and Bower Birds* (London: Weidenfeld & Nicolson, 1969)

Goodwin D. *Pigeons and Doves of the World*, revised edition (British Museum, Natural History, 1970)

Goodwin D. *Crows of the World* (British Museum, Natural History, 1977)

Greenway J. C. *Extinct and Vanishing Birds of the World*, second revised edition (New York: Dover Publications Inc, 1967)

Griscom L. and Sprunt A. *The Warblers of America* (New York: Devin-Adair, 1957)

Hachisuka M. *Birds of the Philippines*, first 2 vols only, complete (Witherby, 1931–5)

Hachisuka M. *The Dodo and Kindred Birds* (Witherby, 1953)

Hagen Y. 'Birds of Tristan da Cunha', *Results Norwegian Scientific Expedition, Tristan da Cunha*, vol 20 (1952) pp 1–248

Hall and Moreau *An Atlas of Speciation in African Passerine Birds* (British Museum, Natural History, 1970)

Harrison C. J. O. *A Field Guide to the Nests, Eggs and Nestlings of British and European Birds* (Collins, 1975)

Haverschmidt F. *Birds of Surinam* (Oliver & Boyd, 1968)

Johnsgaard P. A. *Grouse and Quails of North America* (Lincoln, USA: University of Nebraska Press, 1973)

Johnson A. W. and Goodall J. D. *The Birds of Chile*, 2 vols (Buenos Aires: Platt Establicimentos Gráficos)

Kuroda N. *Birds of the Island of Java*, 2 vols (Tokyo: published by author, 1953)

La Touche J. D. D. *A Handbook of the Birds of Eastern China*, 2 vols (Taylor & Francis, 1925–34)

Land H. C. *Birds of Guatemala* (Wynnewood, USA: Livingstone Publishing Co, 1970)

Macdonald J. D. *Birds of Australia* (Sydney, Wellington and London: A. H. & A. W. Reed, 1973)

Mackworth-Praed C. W. and Grant C. H. B. *African Handbook of Birds*, 6 vols (Longmans, 1952–73)

Mathews G. M. *Systema Avium Australasianarum*, 2 vols (British Ornithologists' Union, 1927–30)

Matthews, L. H. 'Birds of South Georgia', *Discovery Reports*, vol 1 (Cambridge University Press, 1929) pp 561–92

Mayr E. *Birds of the Southwest Pacific* (New York: Macmillan, 1945)

Mayer de Schaunsee R. *The Species of Birds of South America* (Narberth, USA: Livingstone Publishing Co, 1966)

Meyer de Schaunsee R. *A Guide to the Birds of South America* (Wynnewood, USA: Livingstone Publishing Co, 1970)

Monroe B. L. *A Distributional Survey of the Birds of Honduras* (American Ornithologists' Union, 1968)

Morony J. L., Bock W. J. and Farrand J. *Reference Lists of the Birds of the World* (The Department of Ornithology, American Museum of Natural History, 1975) not commercially available

Murphy R. C. *Oceanic Birds of South America*, 2 vols (New York: American Museum of Natural History, 1936)

Olsen S. L. 'Paleornithology of St Helena Island, South Atlantic Ocean', *Smithsonian Contributions to Paleobiology* No 23 (Washington: Smithsonian Institution Press, 1975)

Oliver W. R. B. *New Zealand Birds*, second edition (Wellington: A. H. & A. W. Reed, 1955)

Palmer R. S. *Handbook of North American Birds*, 3 vols so far published (New Haven, Conn: Yale University Press, 1962–   )

Penny M. *The Birds of the Seychelles and Outlying Islands* (Collins, 1974)

Peters J. L. *Checklist of Birds of the World*, vols 1–6 (Cambridge, Mass: Harvard University Press) vols 7–15 (Museum of Comparative Zoology), 1930 vols 8 and 11 still unpublished

Rand A. L. 'Distribution and Habits of Madagascar Birds', *Bulletin of the American Museum of Natural History*, vol 72 (1936) pp 143–499

Rand A. L. and Gilliard E. T. *Handbook of New Guinea Birds* (Weidenfeld & Nicolson, 1967)

Ripley S. D. *Rails of the World* (Toronto: M. F. Feheley, 1977)

Sclater W. L. *Systema Avium Ethiopicarum*, 2 vols (British Ornithologists' Union, 1924–30)

Sharpe R. B. et al *Catalogue of the Birds of the British Museum*, 27 vols (British Museum, Natural History, 1874–95)

Slud P. 'Birds of Costa Rica', *Bulletin of the American Museum of Natural History* (1964)

Smythies B. E. *Birds of Burma*, revised edition (Oliver & Boyd, 1953)

Smythies B. E. *Birds of Borneo* (Oliver & Boyd, 1960)

Wetmore A. *Birds of the Republic of Panama*, 3 vols, continuing (Smithsonian Miscellaneous Collections, 1965)

White C. M. N. *Check List of African Birds*, 3 vols (publication sponsored by the Department of Game and Fisheries, 1960–65)

Witherby H. F. et al *Handbook of British Birds*, 5 vols, various reprintings (Witherby, 1938–43)

Addenda

STRIGIDAE

Add:

p 87 (following *Otus clarkii*)

[**Otus psilopoda** (*Vieillot*) VIEILLOT'S OWL ?Santo Domingo and Puerto Rico/ ?extinct. Based on the unique type (destroyed). Originally named *Bubo nudipes* Vieillot, pre-occupied by *Otus nudipes* (Daudin). Not identified with any known owl and name (*nudipes*) formerly used erroneously for *Otus clarkii*. See Peters' Check List vol 4 p 107 footnote, and Kelso and Kelso, Biological Leaflet no 5, 1935.]

p 88 (following *Glaucidium cuculoides*)

[**Strix lathami Bonaparte,** based on the Rufous Owl of Latham's *General History of Birds* (1821–4) vol 1 (1821) p 375, is usually considered to be unidentifiable, but very like a south-east Asian *Glaucidium*. It may, however, be a species awaiting rediscovery.]

p 89 (following *Strix varia*)

[**Strix fasciata** *Vieillot, Nouv Dict Hist Nat* vol 7 (1817) p 21, from Martinique, has never been identified, and no owl appears now to occur on that island.]

p 90 (following *Aegolius ridgwayi*)

Aegolius rostratus (*Griscom*) GRISCOM'S OWL Costa Rica/ unique (*A. ridgwayi* and *A. rostratus* are probably conspecific and possibly conspecific with *A. acadicus*)

Indexes

Index of Latin Family Names

INDEX OF LATIN FAMILY NAMES
OF BIRDS ILLUSTRATED

Following is an index of the various families of birds illustrated in this book. The number following each name refers to the plate number on which each bird is shown.

INDEX OF GENERIC NAMES OF
BIRDS DISCUSSED IN TEXT

This is an index to the genera of birds discussed in the text; all numbers listed here refer to page numbers, not plate numbers.

A separate index listing the scientific names of birds shown on the color plates throughout this book appears immediately following this index.

338

Enodes, 316
Ensifera, 106
Entomodestes, 200
Entomyzon, 264
Entotriccus, 159
Eolophus, 72
Eopsaltria, 241
Eos, 70
Ephippiorhynchus, 14
Ephthianura, 233
Epimachus, 320
Eremiornis, 233
Eremobius, 137
Eremomela, 230
Eremophila, 174
Eremopterix, 172
Ergaticus, 290
Eriocnemis, 107
Erithacus, 197
Erythrocercus, 242
Erythrogonys, 51
Erythropygia, 196
Erythrotriorchis, 25
Erythrura, 304
Esacus, 55
Estrilda, 302
Eubucco, 121
Eucephala, 102
Euchlornis, 154
Eucometis, 280
Eudocimus, 15
Eudromia, 3
Eudromias, 51
Eudynamis, 82
Eudyptes, 3
Eudyptula, 3
Eugenes, 105
Eugralla, 153
Eulabeornis, 46
Eulacestoma, 245
Eulampis, 100
Eulidia, 109
Eumomota, 115
Euneornis, 286
Eunymphicus, 79
Eupetes, 208
Eupetomena, 100
Euphagus, 296
Eupherusa, 104
Euphonia, 282
Euplectes, 311
Eupoda, 51
Eupodotis, 48
Euptilotis, 110
Eurocephalus, 187
Eurostopodus, 91

Euryanas, 17
Euryceros, 190
Eurylaimus, 134
Eurynorhynchus, 54
Euryptila, 230
Eurypyga, 48
Eurystomus, 117
Euscarthmus, 167
Euschistospiza, 302
Euthlypis, 290
Eutoxeres, 99
Eutrichomyias, 245
Eutriorchis, 24
Euxenura, 14
Excalfactoria, 38

F
Falcipennis, 35
Falco, 22 31
Falculea, 190
Falcunculus, 245
Ferminia, 192
Finschia, 220
Florisuga, 100
Fluvicola, 159
Formicarius, 149
Formicivora, 147
Forpus, 74
Foudia, 311
Foulehaio, 264
Francolinus, 36
Fraseria, 240
Fratercula, 60
Frederickena, 144
Fregata, 11
Fregetta, 8
Fregilupus, 314
Fringilla, 296
Fulica, 47
Fulmaris, 5
Fulmarus, 5
Furnarius, 138

G
Galbalcyrhynchus, 120
Galbula, 100, 120
Galerida, 174
Gallicolumba, 66
Gallicrex, 46
Gallinago, 53
Gallinula, 46
Gallirallus, 43
Gallirex, 80
Galloperdix, 39
Gallus, 39
Gampsonyx, 22

Gampsorhynchus, 215
Garritornis, 209
Garrodia, 8
Garrulax, 213
Garrulus, 322
Gavia, 4
Gecinulus, 130
Geobates, 136
Geococcyx, 84
Geocolaptes, 127
Geoffroyus, 77
Geomalia, 203
Geopelia, 64
Geopsittacus, 80
Geositta, 136
Geospiza, 274
Geothlypis, 289
Geotrygon, 65
Geranoaetus, 27
Geranospiza, 24
Geronticus, 15
Gerygone, 233
Glareola, 55
Glaucidium, 88
Glaucis, 98
Glossopsitta, 71
Glycichaera, 261
Glyphorhynchus, 135
Gnorimopsar, 295
Goethalsia, 103
Goldmania, 103
Gorsachius, 13
Goura, 66
Gracula, 315
Grafisia, 312
Grallaria, 150
Grallaricula, 150
Grallina, 318
Graminicola, 223
Granatellus, 291
Grandala, 199
Graueria, 231
Graydidascalus, 75
Grus, 41
Gubernatrix, 276
Gubernetes, 159
Guira, 83
Guttera, 40
Gyalophylax, 139
Gygis, 59
Gymnobucco, 122
Gymnocichla, 148
Gymnocrex, 45
Gymnoderus, 155
Gymnogyps, 21
Gymnomystax, 294

344

346

INDEX OF SCIENTIFIC NAMES OF
BIRDS ILLUSTRATED

This is an index to the scientific names of birds illustrated on the color plates in this book. All numbers listed refer to plate numbers, not page numbers. (For a listing of the generic names of birds discussed in the text, refer to the index immediately preceding this one.)

INDEX OF COMMON NAMES OF
BIRDS DISCUSSED IN TEXT

This is an index to the common names of birds discussed in the text. All numbers listed here refer to page numbers, not plate numbers. A separate index listing the common names of birds shown on the color plates appears immediately following this index.

356

Bustards, 48
Butcherbirds, 318
Buttonquail, 41
Buzzard, Honey, 22
Buzzards, 27-8

C
Cachalotes, 142
Cahow, 7
Caiques, 75 (Psittacidae),
  293-4 (Icteriadae)
Calfbird, 155
Camaropteras, 230
Cameroons, 124
Canaries, 296-7
Canasteros, 140-1
Canvasback, 19
Capercaillies, 34
Capuchinbird, 155
Caracaras, 30
Cardinals, 276 (Emberizidae),
  277 (Cardinalidae)
Caribs, 100
Casiornis, 162
Cassowaries, 1
Castlebuilders, 139
Catbirds, 193-4 (Mimidae), 216
  (Timaliidae), 319
  (Ptilonorhynchidae)
Cettias, 219
Chachalacas, 33-4
Chaffinches, 296
Chat, Palm, 191
Chat, Robin, 202
Chats, 195-207 (Turdidae), 233
  (Ephthianuridae),
  290-1 (Parulidae)
Chats, Australian, 233
Chats, Black, 201
Chats, Cliff, 201
Chats, Robin, 198
Chats, Rock, 200-1
Chatterers, 212
Chickadees, 248
Chicken, Prairie, 34
Chiffchaff, 224
Chilia, 137
Chimango, 30
Chloridops, 293
Chlorophonias, 283
Chough, Ground, 323
Chough, 318 (Grallinidae),
  323 (Corvidae)
Chucao, 152
Chururo, 16
Cinclodes, 137-8

Cisticolas, 226-7
Citrils, 297
Cochoas, 200
Cockatiel, 72
Cockatoos, 71-2
Cocks-of-the-Rock, 153
Coleto, 315
Colies, See Mousebirds
Colin, 36
Comets, 107-8
Condors, 21
Conebill, 285 (Thraupidae),
  291-2 (Parulidae)
Conures, 73-4
Coots, 47
Coppersmith, 122
Coquettes, 100-1
Cordon-Bleus, 302
Corellas, 72
Cormorants, 10-11
Corncrake, 44
Coronets, 106
Cotingas, 153-5
Couas, 84
Coucal, 83-5
Courol, 116
Coursers, 55
Cowbirds, 296
Crakes, 42-6
Cranes, 41-2
Creeper, Red-fronted, 250
Creepers, 134-6,
  (Dendrocolaptidae),
  220 (Sylviidae),
  251 (Rhabdornithidae),
  293 (Drepanididae)
Creepers, Philippine, 251
Creeper, Spotted, 251
Crescentchests, 152
Crested-Flycatchers, 243
Crimson-wings, 301-2
Crombecs, 230-1
Crossbills, 300
Crow, Bush, 323
Crows, 317 (Callaeidae),
  319 (Paradisaeidae),
  321-5 (Corvidae)
Crows, Bald, See Picathartes
Cuckoo-roller, 116
Cuckoos, 63 (Columbidae),
  81-5 (Cuculidae)
Cuckoos, Ground, 84
Cuckoos, Hawk, 81
Cuckoos, Lizard, 83
Curassows, 34
Curlews, 51-2, 55

Currawongs, 318-9
Cutia, 215

D
Dabchick, 4
Dacnis, 285
Darters, See Anhingas
Diamondbirds, 253-4
Dickcissel, 277
Dikkop, 55
Dippers, 191
Diucas, 271
Diucon, 158
Divers, 4
Dodos, 61
Dollar Bird, 117
Doraditos, 167
Dotterels, 50-1
Doves, 61-8
Doves, Cuckoo, 63
Doves, Fruit, 66-8
Doves, Ground, 64-6
Doves, Quail, 65-6
Dowitcher, 53
Drongos, 317
Drongos, Mountain, 317
Drongos, Racquet-tailed, 317
Ducks, 16-21
Duiker, Reed, 11
Dunlin, 54
Dunnock, 195
Dysmorodrepanis, 293

E
Eagle-Buzzard, 27
Eagle, Harrier, 24
Eagles, 23-30
Eagles, Buzzard, 27
Eagles, Fish, 23
Eagles, Fishing, 23
Eagles, Hawk, 29-30
Eagles, Serpent, 24
Eagles, Snake, 24
Eagles, Solitary, 27
Eagles, Spotted, 28
Eared-Pheasant, 39
Egrets, 12-3
Eiders, 19
Elaenias, 168-9
Elepaio, 237
Elephant Birds, 1
Elminias, 243
Emeralds, 101-4
Emus, 1
Emu-Tails, 231

Swifts, 96-8
Swifts, Crested, 98
Swift, Tree, 98
Sylphs, 108

T

Tachuris, 167
Tailorbirds, 222
Takahe, 46
Tanager, Bush, 276
Tanager, Green, 283
Tanagers, 279-85
Tanagers, Mountain, 282
Tanagers, Palm, 279, 281
Tanager, Swallow, 286
Tapaculos, 152, 153
Tattlers, 52
Teals, 18-20
Ternlet, 59
Terns, 58-9
Tesias, 231
Tetrakas, 185
Thick-heads, See Whistlers
Thick-knees, 55
Thistletails, 138-9
Thornbill, Loddiges', 108
Thornbills, 107-8
   (Trochilidae), 234
   (Acanthizidae)
Thornbirds, 141
Thorntail, 101
Thrashers, 193-5
Thrushers, 195-6, 200, 203-7
Thrushes, Ground, 203-4
Thrushes, Laughing, 213-4
Thrushes, Mountain, 204-5
Thrushes, Quail, 207
Thrushes, Rock, 202-3
Thrushes, Whistling, 203
Thrush-Flycatchers, 247
Thrush, New Zealand, 247
Thrush-Tanager, 280
Tickbirds, 316
Tinamous, 2-3
Tinkerbirds, 123
Tit-Babblers, 211
Tit-Flycatcher, 240
Titmice, 248-9
Titmice, Long-tailed, 247
Tits, 217 (Paradoxornithidae),
   247-50 (Aegithalidae)
Tits, Black, 249
Tit, Scrub, 235
Tits, Grey, 249
Tits, Penduline, 247-8
Tit-Spinetail, 138

Tit-tyrants, 167
Tit-Warblers, 231-2
   (Regulidae), 248 (Remizidae)
Tityras, 155
Tococo, 16
Todies, 115
Tody-tyrant, 165
Tomtit, 241
Topaz, 100, 105
Toucanets, 125-6
Toucans, 125-6
Towhees, 275
Tragopan, 39
Trainbearers, 107
Treecreepers, 251-2
Treecreepers, Australian, 251-2
Treehunters, 143
Treepies, 323
Treerunners, 142, 144
   (Furnariidae), See also
   Sitellas
Tremblers, 194
Trillers, 181
Trogons, 110-11
Tropic Birds, 9
Troupial, 294
Trumpet Bird, 320
Trumpeters, 42
Tsikirities, 229
Tucuchillo, 92
Tuftedcheeks, 142
Tui, 267
Turacos, 80
Turka, 152
Turkey, 40
Turkey, Brush, 33
Turnstones, 52
Twin-spots, 301-2
Twite, 299
Tyrannulets, 166-9
Tyrant, Rush, 167
Tyrants, 158-9, 161, 166-8
Tyrants, Black, 159
Tyrants, Bristle, 166
Tyrants, Bush, 158
Tyrants, Chat, 158-9
Tyrants, Ground, 158
Tyrants, Pygmy, 165-7
Tyrants, Shrike, 157
Tyrants, Water, 159-60
Tyrant, Wood, 166
Tystie, 60

U

Ula-ai-Hawane, 292
Umbrellabird, 155

V

Vangas, 190
Veery, 205
Velvet Breast, 106
Verdin, 248
Violet ears, 100
Vireos, 286-7
Visorbearer, 108
Vultures, New World, 21
Vultures, Old World, 23-4
Vulture, Turkey, 21

W

Wading Birds, 51-5
Wagtails, 177 (Motacillidae),
   237 (Pachycephalinae)
Wagtail-tyrants, 167
Waldrapp, 15
Wallcreeper, 250
Warbler, 196 (Turdidae)
Warbler, Blue, 288
Warbler, Cane, 221, 231
Warbler, Fairy, 231
Warbler, Fan-tailed, 290
Warbler, Green, 289
Warbler, Mountain, 220
Warbler, River, 291
Warbler, Rock, 235
Warbler, Rush, 220
Warblers, Australian, 233-5
Warblers, Brush, 230
Warblers, Bush, 219-20
Warblers, Crowned, 224
Warbler, Sedge, 220-1
Warblers, Forest, 220, 229
Warblers, Grass, 218, 220,
   222-3, 227
Warblers, Grasshopper, 220-1
Warblers, Grey, 229-30
   (Sylviidae), 288 (Parulidae)
Warblers, Ground, 219
   (Sylviidae), 291 (Parulidae)
Warblers, Leaf, 224-5
Warblers, Marsh, 221, 223
Warblers, Morning, 198
Warblers, Mouse, 235
Warblers, New World, 287-91
Warblers, Old World, 218-31
Warblers, Reed, 221-2
Warblers, Swamp, 220, 222,
   231
Warblers, Thicket, 218-9
Warblers, Yellow, 222
Warbling-Finches, 271-2
Watercock, 46
Waterhens, 45

363

INDEX OF COMMON NAMES OF
BIRDS ILLUSTRATED

This is an index to the common names of the birds illustrated on the color plates. All numbers listed refer to plate numbers, not page numbers. (For a listing of the common names of the birds discussed in the text, refer to the index immediately preceding this one.)

364